BATMAN

THE GOLDEN AGE VOL. 4

BILL FINGER
with DON CAMERON, JOSEPH GREENE
JOE SAMACHSON and JACK SCHIFF
WRITERS

BOB KANE
with JACK BURNLEY, RAY BURNLEY
JERRY ROBINSON and GEORGE ROUSSOS
ARTISTS

EVAN "DOC" SHANER
COVER ARTIST

BATMAN created by BOB KANE with BILL FINGER
SUPERMAN created by JERRY SIEGEL and JOE SHUSTER
By special arrangement with the JERRY SIEGEL family

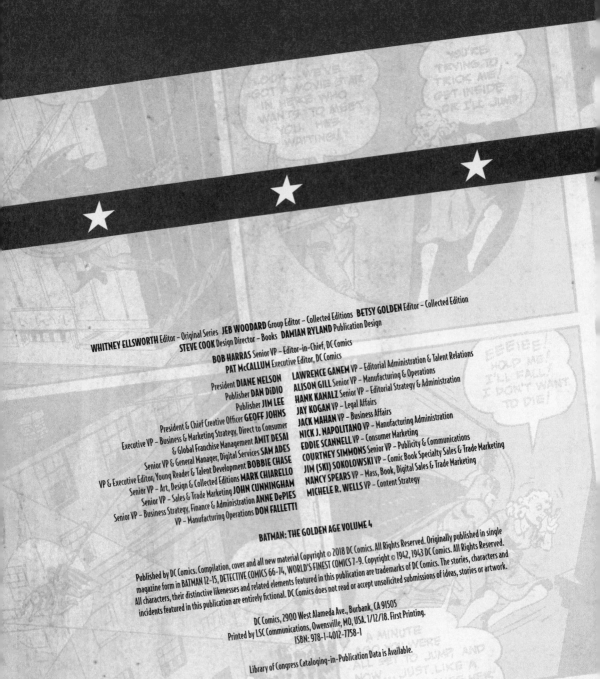

WHITNEY ELLSWORTH Editor – Original Series   JEB WOODARD Group Editor – Collected Editions   BETSY GOLDEN Editor – Collected Edition
STEVE COOK Design Director – Books   DAMIAN RYLAND Publication Design

BOB HARRAS Senior VP – Editor-in-Chief, DC Comics
PAT McCALLUM Executive Editor, DC Comics

President DIANE NELSON
Publisher DAN DiDIO
Publisher JIM LEE
President & Chief Creative Officer GEOFF JOHNS
Executive VP – Business & Marketing Strategy, Direct to Consumer
& Global Franchise Management AMIT DESAI
Senior VP & General Manager, Digital Services SAM ADES
VP & Executive Editor, Young Reader & Talent Development BOBBIE CHASE
Senior VP – Art, Design & Collected Editions MARK CHIARELLO
Senior VP – Sales & Trade Marketing JOHN CUNNINGHAM
Senior VP – Business Strategy, Finance & Administration ANNE DePIES
VP – Manufacturing Operations DON FALLETTI

LAWRENCE GANEM VP – Editorial Administration & Talent Relations
ALISON GILL Senior VP – Manufacturing & Operations
HANK KANALZ Senior VP – Editorial Strategy & Administration
JAY KOGAN VP – Legal Affairs
JACK MAHAN VP – Business Affairs
NICK J. NAPOLITANO VP – Manufacturing Administration
EDDIE SCANNELL VP – Consumer Marketing
COURTNEY SIMMONS Senior VP – Publicity & Communications
JIM (SKI) SOKOLOWSKI VP – Comic Book Specialty Sales & Trade Marketing
NANCY SPEARS VP – Mass, Book, Digital Sales & Trade Marketing
MICHELE R. WELLS VP – Content Strategy

BATMAN: THE GOLDEN AGE VOLUME 4

Published by DC Comics. Compilation, cover and all new material Copyright © 2018 DC Comics. All Rights Reserved. Originally published in single magazine form in BATMAN 12-15, DETECTIVE COMICS 66-74, WORLD'S FINEST COMICS 7-9. Copyright © 1942, 1943 DC Comics. All Rights Reserved. All characters, their distinctive likenesses and related elements featured in this publication are trademarks of DC Comics. The stories, characters and incidents featured in this publication are entirely fictional. DC Comics does not read or accept unsolicited submissions of ideas, stories or artwork.

DC Comics, 2900 West Alameda Ave., Burbank, CA 91505
Printed by LSC Communications, Owensville, MO, USA. 1/12/18. First Printing.
ISBN: 978-1-4012-7758-1

Library of Congress Cataloging-in-Publication Data is Available.

All stories by **BILL FINGER**, except where noted. All covers and stories pencilled by **BOB KANE** and inked by **JERRY ROBINSON**, except where noted.

*These stories were originally untitled and are titled here for reader convenience. In the preparation of this collection, we have used our best efforts to review any surviving records and consult any available databases and knowledgeable parties. We regret the innate limitations of this process and any missing or misassigned attributions that may occur.

Until the 1970s, it was not common practice in the comic book industry to credit all stories.

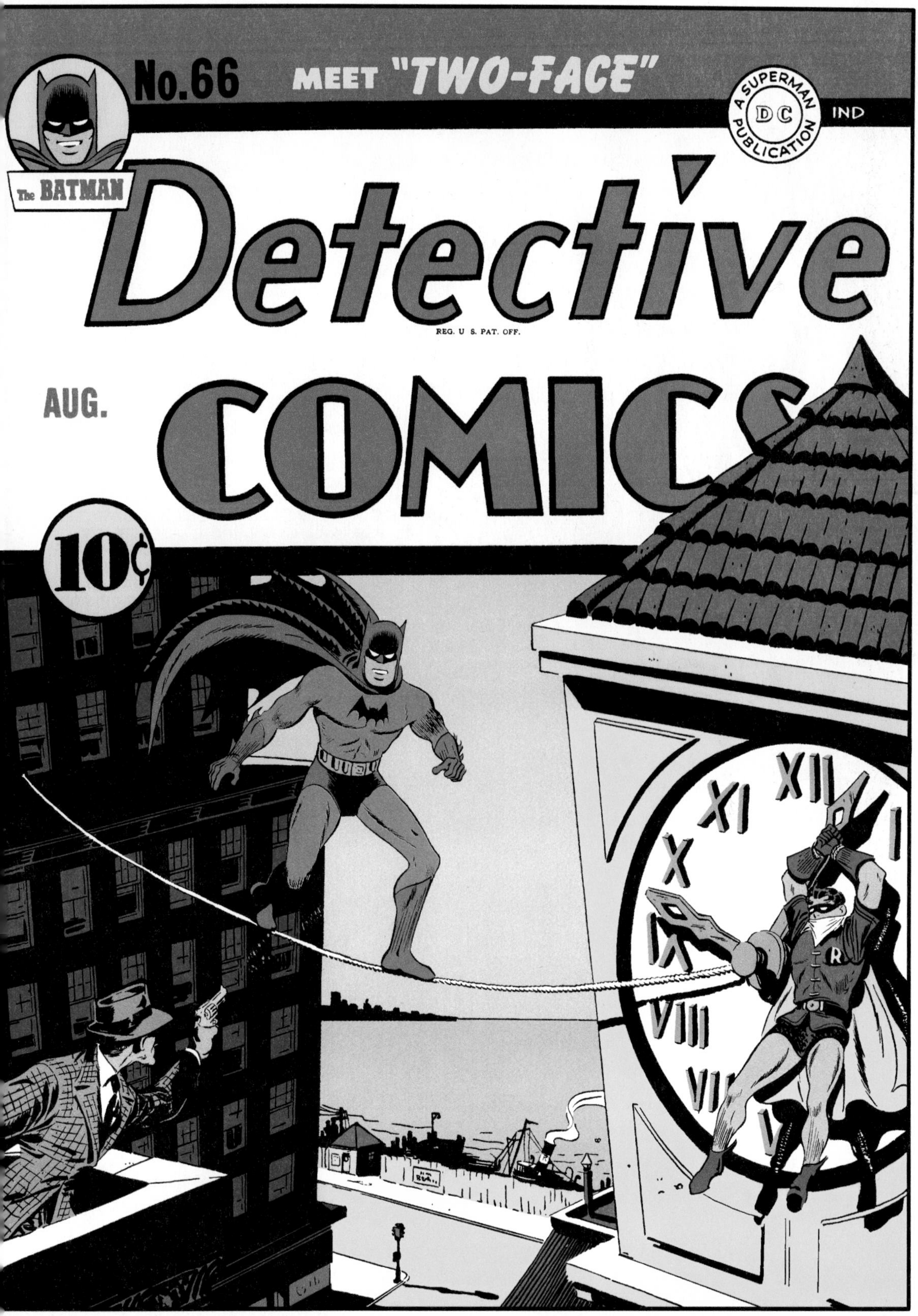
No. 66
MEET "TWO-FACE"
A SUPERMAN PUBLICATION
DC
IND
The BATMAN
Detective
REG. U. S. PAT. OFF.
AUG.
COMICS
10¢

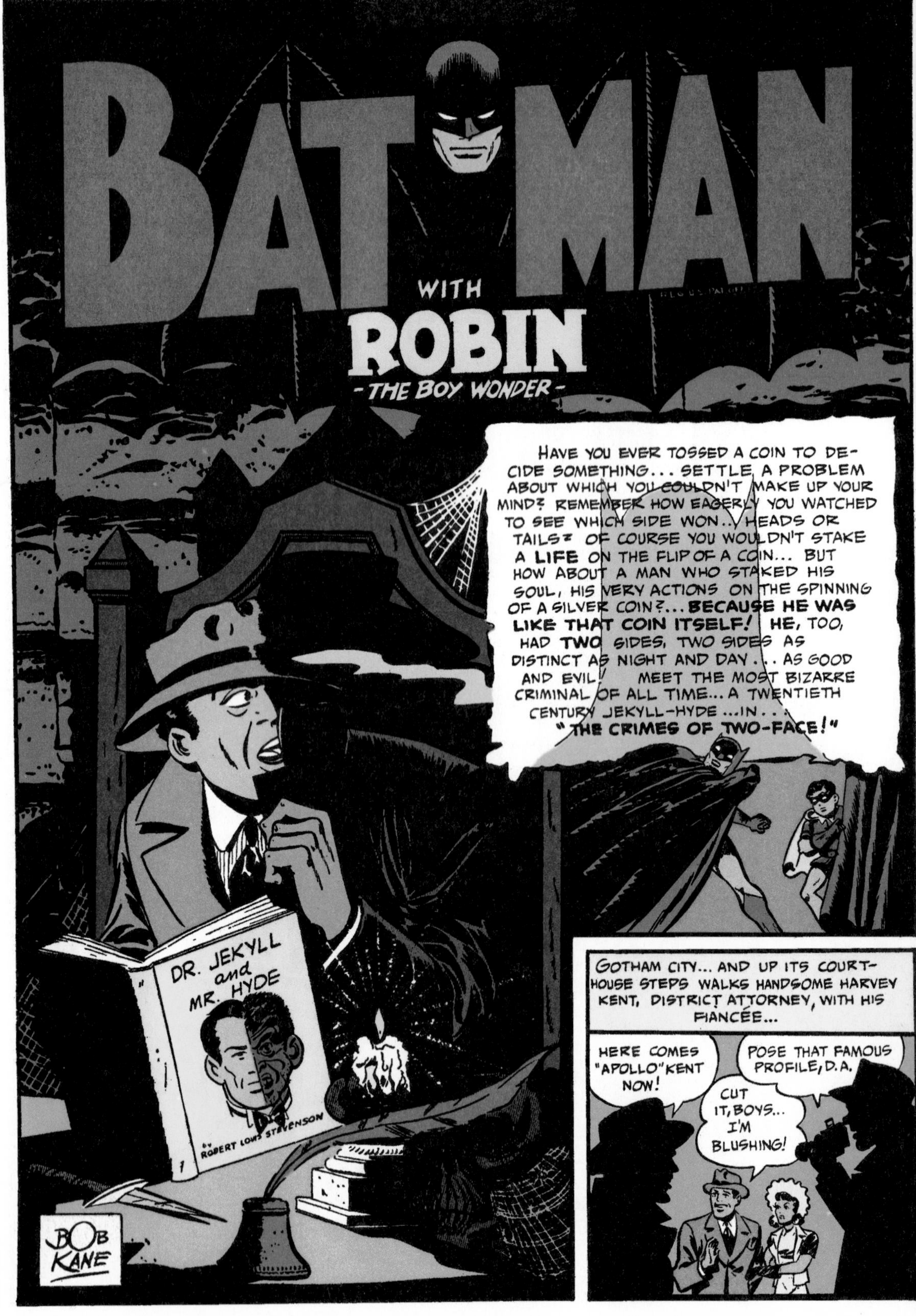
BATMAN
WITH
ROBIN
-THE BOY WONDER-
HAVE YOU EVER TOSSED A COIN TO DECIDE SOMETHING... SETTLE A PROBLEM ABOUT WHICH YOU COULDN'T MAKE UP YOUR MIND? REMEMBER HOW EAGERLY YOU WATCHED TO SEE WHICH SIDE WON... HEADS OR TAILS? OF COURSE YOU WOULDN'T STAKE A LIFE ON THE FLIP OF A COIN... BUT HOW ABOUT A MAN WHO STAKED HIS SOUL, HIS VERY ACTIONS ON THE SPINNING OF A SILVER COIN?... BECAUSE HE WAS LIKE THAT COIN ITSELF! HE, TOO, HAD TWO SIDES, TWO SIDES AS DISTINCT AS NIGHT AND DAY... AS GOOD AND EVIL! MEET THE MOST BIZARRE CRIMINAL OF ALL TIME... A TWENTIETH CENTURY JEKYLL-HYDE ...IN... "THE CRIMES OF TWO-FACE!"
DR. JEKYLL and MR. HYDE
by ROBERT LOUIS STEVENSON
BOB KANE
GOTHAM CITY... AND UP ITS COURTHOUSE STEPS WALKS HANDSOME HARVEY KENT, DISTRICT ATTORNEY, WITH HIS FIANCÉE...
HERE COMES "APOLLO" KENT NOW!
POSE THAT FAMOUS PROFILE, D.A.
CUT IT, BOYS... I'M BLUSHING!

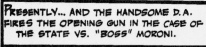

PRESENTLY... AND THE HANDSOME D.A. FIRES THE OPENING GUN IN THE CASE OF THE STATE VS. "BOSS" MORONI.

YOUR HONOR, I CALL THE STATE'S FIRST WITNESS ...THE BATMAN!

KENT SURE ISN'T WASTING ANY TIME ON MORONI, IS HE?

AS THE RICH, STRONG VOICE OF THE CRIME-FIGHTER RECOUNTS A TALE OF MURDER...

...WE HAD A FIGHT AND MORONI GOT AWAY ...BUT HE IS THE MAN WHO SHOT "BOOKIE" BENSON!

HE'S LYIN'!/... HE'S LYIN', I TELL YA!

HERE'S THE PROOF... FOUND ON THE SCENE OF THE CRIME. MORONI'S LUCKY PIECE... A TWO-HEADED SILVER DOLLAR... WITH HIS FINGERPRINTS ON IT!

OKAY, PRETTY BOY, I'LL FIX YOU!

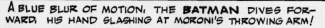

A BLUE BLUR OF MOTION, THE BATMAN DIVES FORWARD, HIS HAND SLASHING AT MORONI'S THROWING ARM!

LOOK OUT, D.A! HE'S THROWING ACID!

UGH! MY FACE!

PANDEMONIUM BREAKS LOOSE! A DOCTOR HURRIES TO THE STRICKEN D.A....

IT WAS VITRIOL, WASN'T IT, DOCTOR?

YES...A CONCENTRATED SOLUTION, TOO! LUCKY FOR KENT YOUR HAND DEFLECTED IT SO IT ONLY STRUCK ONE SIDE OF HIS FACE!

MY POOR DARLING!

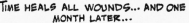

TIME HEALS ALL WOUNDS... AND ONE MONTH LATER...

WELL, TODAY WE TAKE THE BANDAGES OFF!

HAND ME A MIRROR, BATMAN! GOSH! I'M WORRIED STIFF, WONDERING WHAT MY FACE WILL LOOK LIKE!

THE BANDAGES REMOVED, KENT SEES HIS FACE FOR THE FIRST TIME... AND WITH HORROR-STRICKEN EYES!

MY FACE! THE ACID HAS LEFT ONE SIDE SCARRED AND HIDEOUS!

YOU'RE THINKING OF PLASTIC SURGERY, I KNOW... BUT I'M AFRAID ONLY A MIRACLE COULD...

I KNOW ONE MAN WHO CAN PERFORM THAT MIRACLE...DR. EKHART, THE EUROPEAN SPECIALIST!

I HOPE SO... OH, MY FACE... MY FACE!

2

7

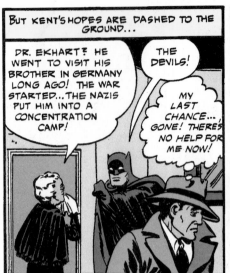

BUT KENT'S HOPES ARE DASHED TO THE GROUND...

DR. EKHART? HE WENT TO VISIT HIS BROTHER IN GERMANY LONG AGO! THE WAR STARTED...THE NAZIS PUT HIM INTO A CONCENTRATION CAMP!

THE DEVILS!

MY LAST CHANCE... GONE! THERE'S NO HELP FOR ME NOW!

BACK IN KENT'S APARTMENT...

BATMAN, MY FIANCÉE IS A SCULPTRESS! SHE WORSHIPS BEAUTY! SHE'D HATE ME NOW... UGLY... HORRIBLE! WHAT AM I TO DO?

FACE HER! SHE'S BOUND TO FIND IT OUT SOONER OR LATER! GOOD-BYE, KENT...AND GOOD LUCK!

MINUTES LATER, TAUT AND GRIM, HARVEY KENT STALKS PURPOSE-FULLY THROUGH THE STREETS.

UGH! WHAT A HORRIBLE-LOOKING MAN!

SHHH! HE'LL HEAR YOU!

MOMMY! THAT MAN FRIGHTENS ME! BOO-HOO!

NOW, DARLING, HE WON'T HURT YOU!

A FACE LIKE THAT WOULD FRIGHTEN ANY-BODY!

SOON, HE REACHES HIS FIANCÉE'S APARTMENT...

HARVEY DARLING! THE BANDAGE IS GONE FROM YOUR FACE! WHAT A LOVELY SURPRISE! LET ME SEE!

YES, GILDA... SURPRISE! NOW...

LOOK! LOOK AGAIN! A FACE DIVIDED INTO BEAUTY AND UGLINESS! QUEER... FRIGHTENING, ISN'T IT?

SO, MY FACE IS REPULSIVE EVEN TO YOU WHO I THOUGHT LOVED ME! LOOK AGAIN! LOOK AT THE MAN WHO WAS ONCE CALLED "APOLLO"...LOOK!

NO! NO! I CAN'T BEAR IT! PLEASE DON'T!

HARVEY KENT D.A.

FOR AN INSTANT, SOMETHING SNAPS IN KENT'S ANGUISH-TORN BRAIN...

MY FACE YOU'VE SO OFTEN CHISELED IN STONE AND PLASTER...BUT NOT MY TRUE FACE... MY NEW FACE! I MUST MAKE THEM AS I REALLY AM....UGLY.. UGLY!...HEE... HEE!

HARVEY KENT D.A.

8

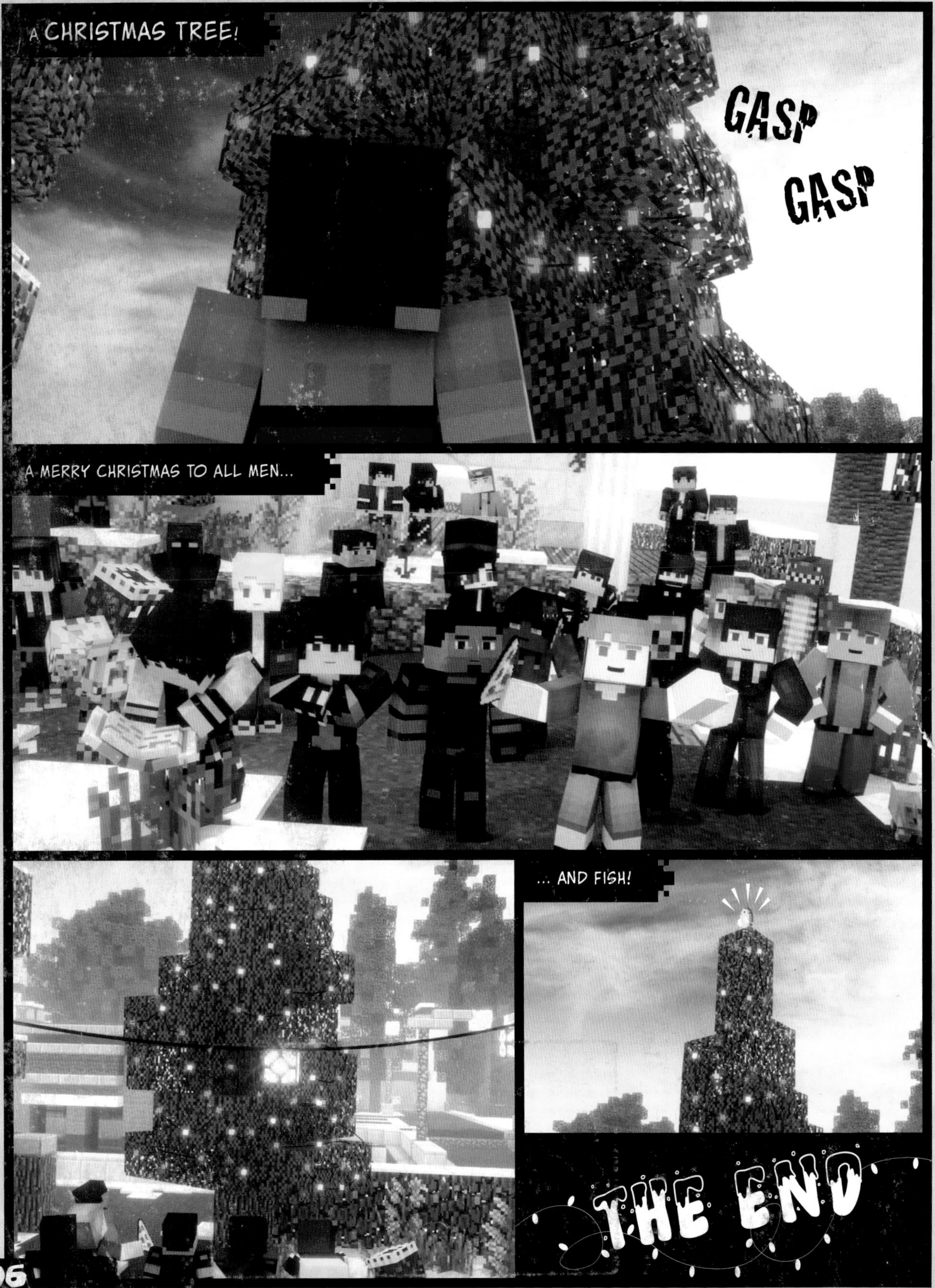
A CHRISTMAS TREE!
GASP
GASP
A MERRY CHRISTMAS TO ALL MEN...
... AND FISH!
THE END

IT'S CHRISTMAS AT **BLACK PLASMA STUDIOS**.

BLACK PLASMA
S T U D I O S

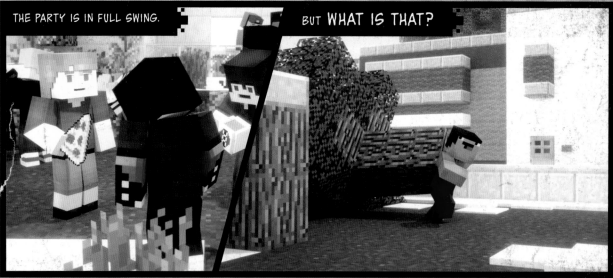

THE PARTY IS IN FULL SWING.

BUT **WHAT IS THAT?**

DERP HAS BROUGHT A TREE.

CLICK

NOT JUST ANY TREE.

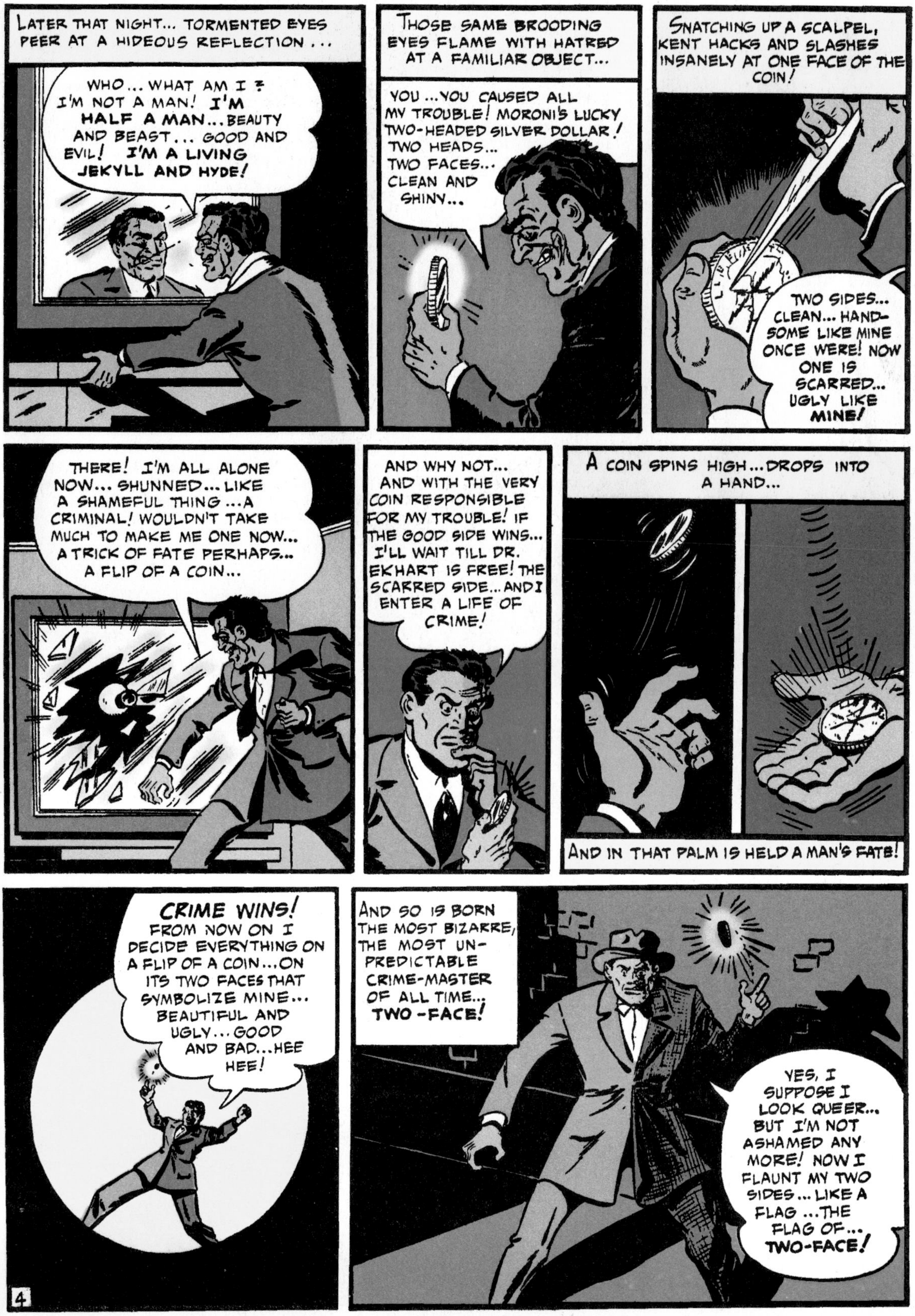

LATER THAT NIGHT... TORMENTED EYES PEER AT A HIDEOUS REFLECTION ...
WHO... WHAT AM I ? I'M NOT A MAN! I'M HALF A MAN... BEAUTY AND BEAST... GOOD AND EVIL! I'M A LIVING JEKYLL AND HYDE!
THOSE SAME BROODING EYES FLAME WITH HATRED AT A FAMILIAR OBJECT...
YOU ...YOU CAUSED ALL MY TROUBLE! MORONI'S LUCKY TWO-HEADED SILVER DOLLAR! TWO HEADS... TWO FACES... CLEAN AND SHINY...
SNATCHING UP A SCALPEL, KENT HACKS AND SLASHES INSANELY AT ONE FACE OF THE COIN!
TWO SIDES... CLEAN... HANDSOME LIKE MINE ONCE WERE! NOW ONE IS SCARRED... UGLY LIKE MINE!
THERE! I'M ALL ALONE NOW... SHUNNED... LIKE A SHAMEFUL THING ...A CRIMINAL! WOULDN'T TAKE MUCH TO MAKE ME ONE NOW... A TRICK OF FATE PERHAPS... A FLIP OF A COIN...
AND WHY NOT... AND WITH THE VERY COIN RESPONSIBLE FOR MY TROUBLE! IF THE GOOD SIDE WINS... I'LL WAIT TILL DR. EKHART IS FREE! THE SCARRED SIDE... AND I ENTER A LIFE OF CRIME!
A COIN SPINS HIGH...DROPS INTO A HAND...
AND IN THAT PALM IS HELD A MAN'S FATE!
CRIME WINS! FROM NOW ON I DECIDE EVERYTHING ON A FLIP OF A COIN...ON ITS TWO FACES THAT SYMBOLIZE MINE... BEAUTIFUL AND UGLY... GOOD AND BAD...HEE HEE!
AND SO IS BORN THE MOST BIZARRE, THE MOST UNPREDICTABLE CRIME-MASTER OF ALL TIME... TWO-FACE!
YES, I SUPPOSE I LOOK QUEER... BUT I'M NOT ASHAMED ANY MORE! NOW I FLAUNT MY TWO SIDES ... LIKE A FLAG ...THE FLAG OF... TWO-FACE!
4

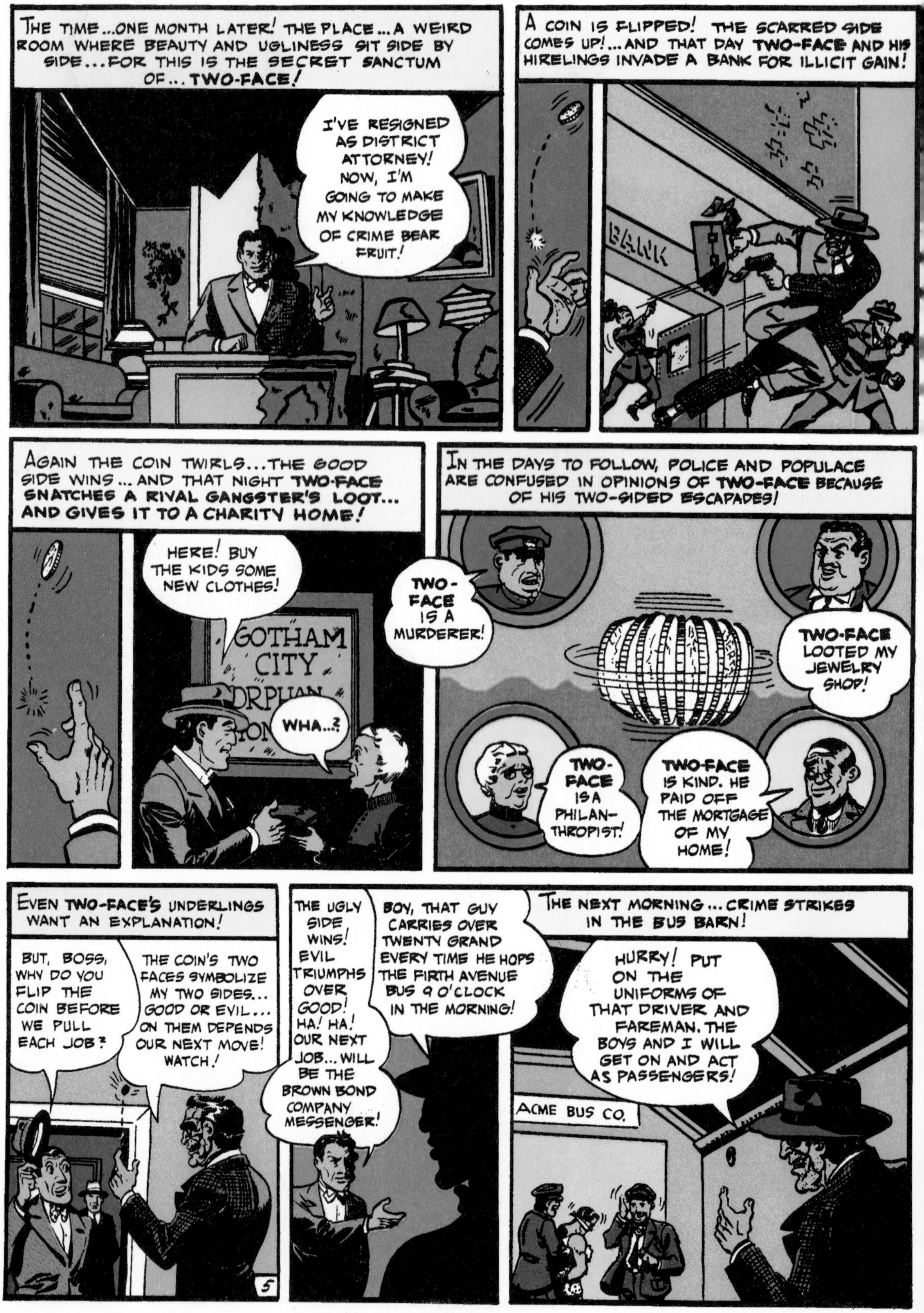

THE TIME...ONE MONTH LATER! THE PLACE...A WEIRD ROOM WHERE BEAUTY AND UGLINESS SIT SIDE BY SIDE...FOR THIS IS THE SECRET SANCTUM OF...TWO-FACE!
I'VE RESIGNED AS DISTRICT ATTORNEY! NOW, I'M GOING TO MAKE MY KNOWLEDGE OF CRIME BEAR FRUIT!
A COIN IS FLIPPED! THE SCARRED SIDE COMES UP!...AND THAT DAY TWO-FACE AND HIS HIRELINGS INVADE A BANK FOR ILLICIT GAIN!
BANK
AGAIN THE COIN TWIRLS...THE GOOD SIDE WINS...AND THAT NIGHT TWO-FACE SNATCHES A RIVAL GANGSTER'S LOOT...AND GIVES IT TO A CHARITY HOME!
HERE! BUY THE KIDS SOME NEW CLOTHES!
GOTHAM CITY
WHA...?
IN THE DAYS TO FOLLOW, POLICE AND POPULACE ARE CONFUSED IN OPINIONS OF TWO-FACE BECAUSE OF HIS TWO-SIDED ESCAPADES!
TWO-FACE IS A MURDERER!
TWO-FACE LOOTED MY JEWELRY SHOP!
TWO-FACE IS A PHILANTHROPIST!
TWO-FACE IS KIND. HE PAID OFF THE MORTGAGE OF MY HOME!
EVEN TWO-FACE'S UNDERLINGS WANT AN EXPLANATION!
BUT, BOSS, WHY DO YOU FLIP THE COIN BEFORE WE PULL EACH JOB?
THE COIN'S TWO FACES SYMBOLIZE MY TWO SIDES...GOOD OR EVIL...ON THEM DEPENDS OUR NEXT MOVE! WATCH!
5
THE UGLY SIDE WINS! EVIL TRIUMPHS OVER GOOD! HA! HA! OUR NEXT JOB...WILL BE THE BROWN BOND COMPANY MESSENGER!
BOY, THAT GUY CARRIES OVER TWENTY GRAND EVERY TIME HE HOPS THE FIRTH AVENUE BUS 9 O'CLOCK IN THE MORNING!
THE NEXT MORNING...CRIME STRIKES IN THE BUS BARN!
HURRY! PUT ON THE UNIFORMS OF THAT DRIVER AND FAREMAN. THE BOYS AND I WILL GET ON AND ACT AS PASSENGERS!
ACME BUS CO.

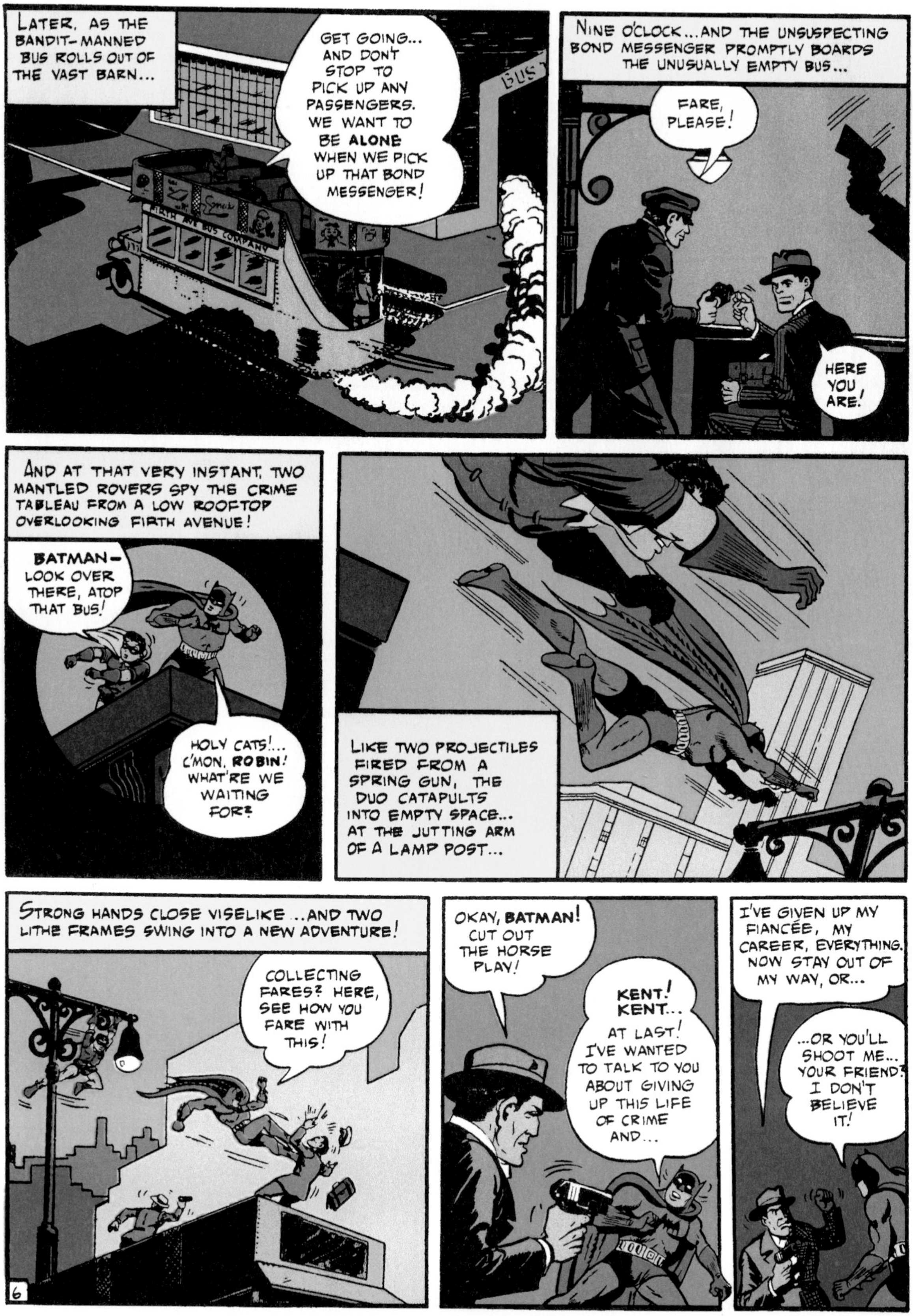
LATER, AS THE BANDIT-MANNED BUS ROLLS OUT OF THE VAST BARN...
GET GOING... AND DON'T STOP TO PICK UP ANY PASSENGERS. WE WANT TO BE ALONE WHEN WE PICK UP THAT BOND MESSENGER!
BUS
FIFTH AVE BUS COMPANY
NINE O'CLOCK... AND THE UNSUSPECTING BOND MESSENGER PROMPTLY BOARDS THE UNUSUALLY EMPTY BUS...
FARE, PLEASE!
HERE YOU ARE!
AND AT THAT VERY INSTANT, TWO MANTLED ROVERS SPY THE CRIME TABLEAU FROM A LOW ROOFTOP OVERLOOKING FIFTH AVENUE!
BATMAN— LOOK OVER THERE, ATOP THAT BUS!
HOLY CATS!... C'MON, ROBIN! WHAT'RE WE WAITING FOR?
LIKE TWO PROJECTILES FIRED FROM A SPRING GUN, THE DUO CATAPULTS INTO EMPTY SPACE... AT THE JUTTING ARM OF A LAMP POST...
STRONG HANDS CLOSE VISELIKE ...AND TWO LITHE FRAMES SWING INTO A NEW ADVENTURE!
COLLECTING FARES? HERE, SEE HOW YOU FARE WITH THIS!
6
OKAY, BATMAN! CUT OUT THE HORSE PLAY!
KENT! KENT... AT LAST! I'VE WANTED TO TALK TO YOU ABOUT GIVING UP THIS LIFE OF CRIME AND...
I'VE GIVEN UP MY FIANCÉE, MY CAREER, EVERYTHING. NOW STAY OUT OF MY WAY, OR...
...OR YOU'LL SHOOT ME... YOUR FRIEND? I DON'T BELIEVE IT!

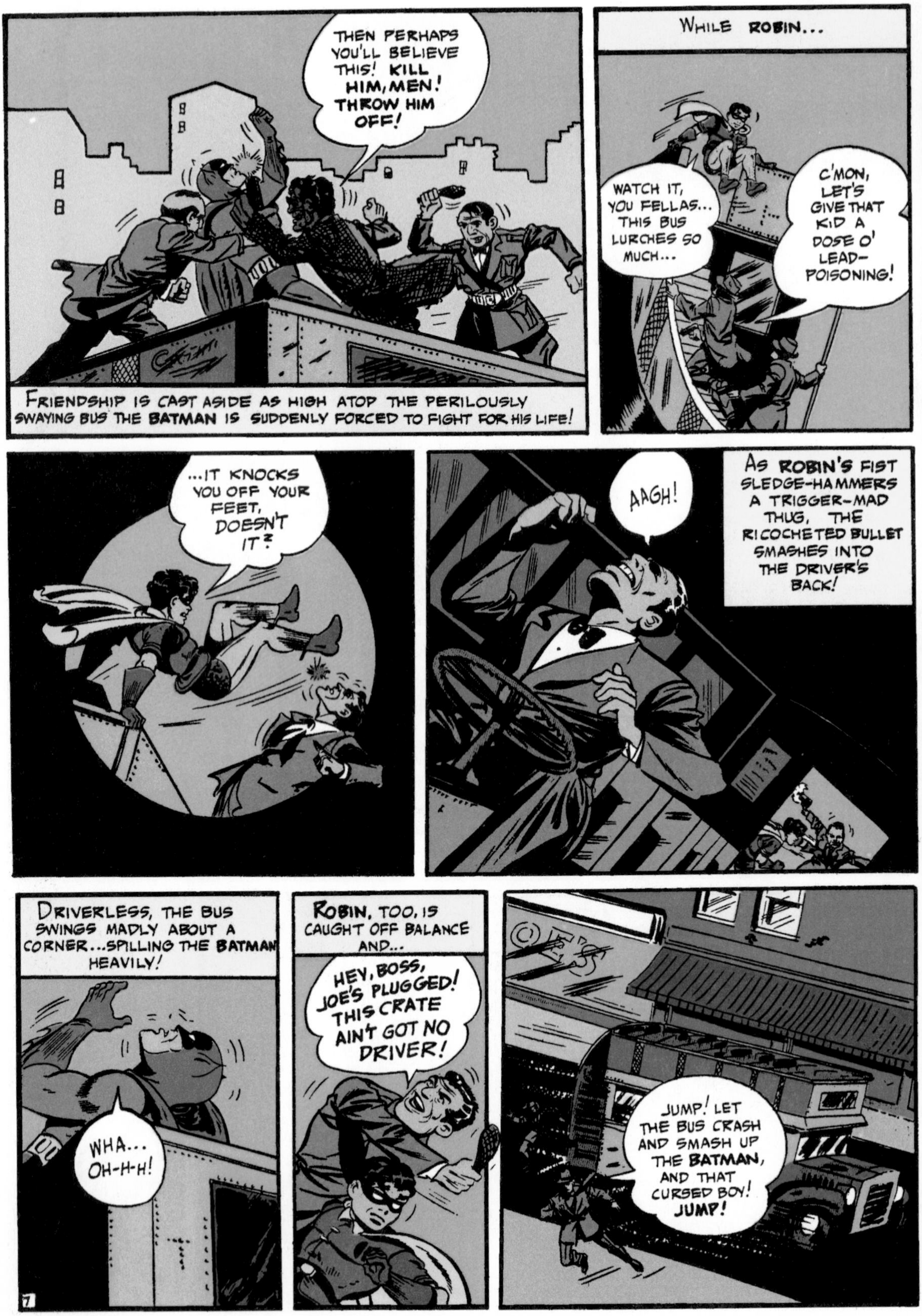
THEN PERHAPS YOU'LL BELIEVE THIS! KILL HIM, MEN! THROW HIM OFF!
FRIENDSHIP IS CAST ASIDE AS HIGH ATOP THE PERILOUSLY SWAYING BUS THE BATMAN IS SUDDENLY FORCED TO FIGHT FOR HIS LIFE!
WHILE ROBIN...
WATCH IT, YOU FELLAS... THIS BUS LURCHES SO MUCH...
C'MON, LET'S GIVE THAT KID A DOSE O' LEAD-POISONING!
...IT KNOCKS YOU OFF YOUR FEET, DOESN'T IT?
AAGH!
AS ROBIN'S FIST SLEDGE-HAMMERS A TRIGGER-MAD THUG, THE RICOCHETED BULLET SMASHES INTO THE DRIVER'S BACK!
DRIVERLESS, THE BUS SWINGS MADLY ABOUT A CORNER...SPILLING THE BATMAN HEAVILY!
WHA... OH-H-H!
ROBIN, TOO, IS CAUGHT OFF BALANCE AND...
HEY, BOSS, JOE'S PLUGGED! THIS CRATE AIN'T GOT NO DRIVER!
JUMP! LET THE BUS CRASH AND SMASH UP THE BATMAN, AND THAT CURSED BOY! JUMP!
7

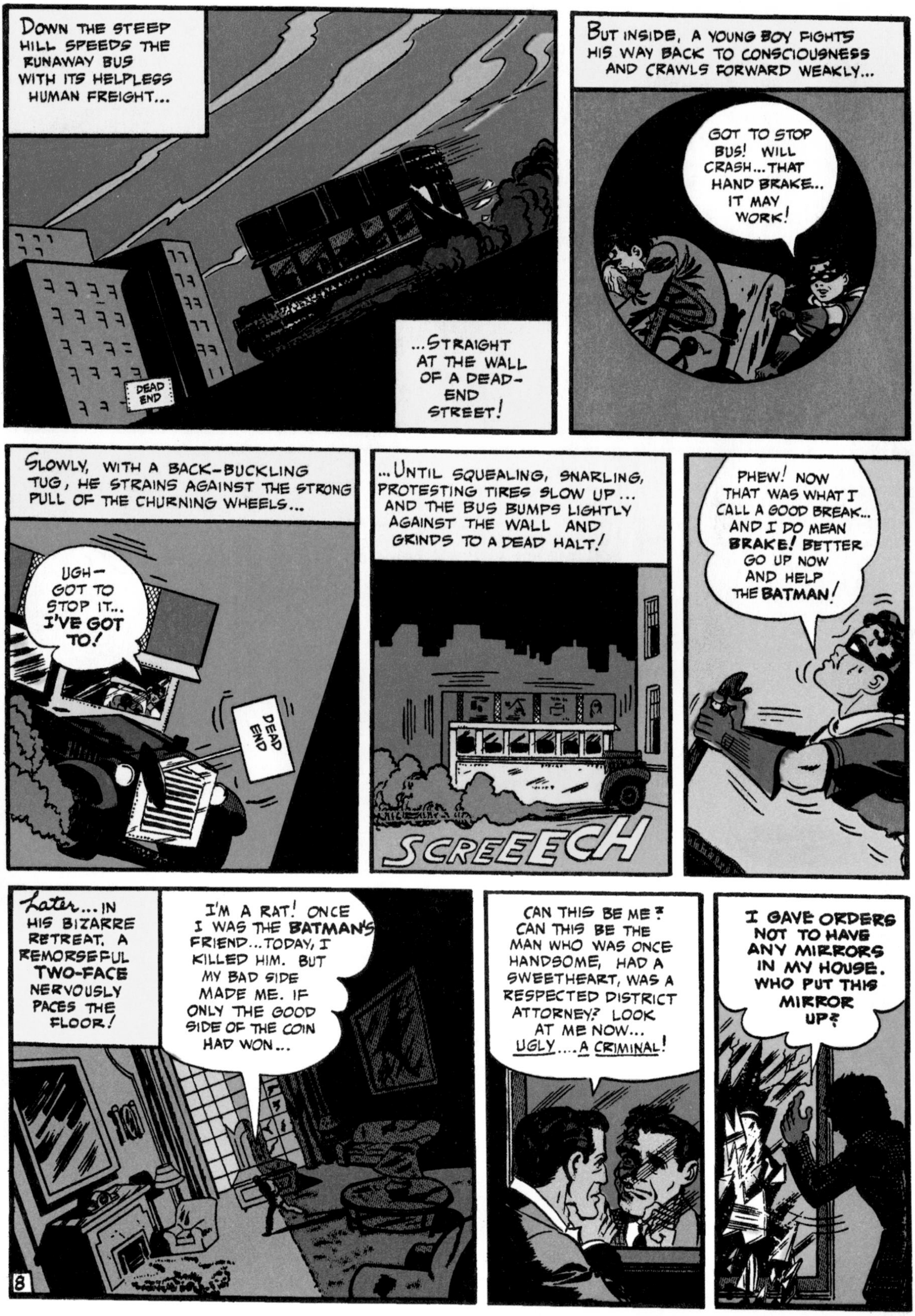
DOWN THE STEEP HILL SPEEDS THE RUNAWAY BUS WITH ITS HELPLESS HUMAN FREIGHT...
DEAD END
...STRAIGHT AT THE WALL OF A DEAD-END STREET!
BUT INSIDE, A YOUNG BOY FIGHTS HIS WAY BACK TO CONSCIOUSNESS AND CRAWLS FORWARD WEAKLY...
GOT TO STOP BUS! WILL CRASH...THAT HAND BRAKE.. IT MAY WORK!
SLOWLY, WITH A BACK-BUCKLING TUG, HE STRAINS AGAINST THE STRONG PULL OF THE CHURNING WHEELS...
UGH— GOT TO STOP IT... I'VE GOT TO!
DEAD END
...UNTIL SQUEALING, SNARLING, PROTESTING TIRES SLOW UP... AND THE BUS BUMPS LIGHTLY AGAINST THE WALL AND GRINDS TO A DEAD HALT!
SCREEECH
PHEW! NOW THAT WAS WHAT I CALL A GOOD BREAK... AND I DO MEAN BRAKE! BETTER GO UP NOW AND HELP THE BATMAN!
Later... IN HIS BIZARRE RETREAT, A REMORSEFUL TWO-FACE NERVOUSLY PACES THE FLOOR!
I'M A RAT! ONCE I WAS THE BATMAN'S FRIEND...TODAY, I KILLED HIM. BUT MY BAD SIDE MADE ME. IF ONLY THE GOOD SIDE OF THE COIN HAD WON...
8
CAN THIS BE ME? CAN THIS BE THE MAN WHO WAS ONCE HANDSOME, HAD A SWEETHEART, WAS A RESPECTED DISTRICT ATTORNEY? LOOK AT ME NOW... UGLY....A CRIMINAL!
I GAVE ORDERS NOT TO HAVE ANY MIRRORS IN MY HOUSE. WHO PUT THIS MIRROR UP?

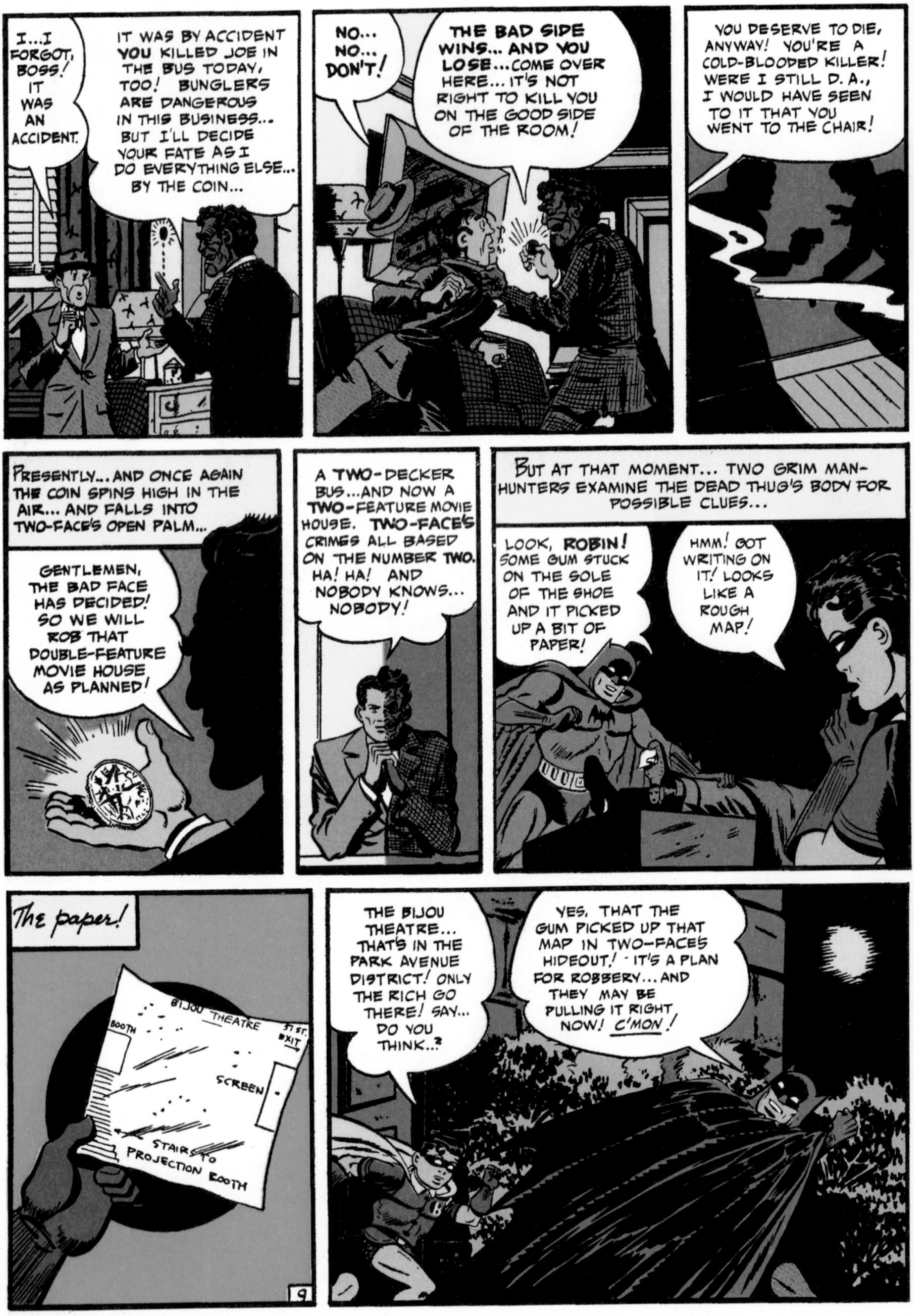
I...I FORGOT, BOSS! IT WAS AN ACCIDENT.
IT WAS BY ACCIDENT YOU KILLED JOE IN THE BUS TODAY, TOO! BUNGLERS ARE DANGEROUS IN THIS BUSINESS... BUT I'LL DECIDE YOUR FATE AS I DO EVERYTHING ELSE... BY THE COIN...
NO... NO... DON'T!
THE BAD SIDE WINS... AND YOU LOSE...COME OVER HERE... IT'S NOT RIGHT TO KILL YOU ON THE GOOD SIDE OF THE ROOM!
YOU DESERVE TO DIE, ANYWAY! YOU'RE A COLD-BLOODED KILLER! WERE I STILL D. A., I WOULD HAVE SEEN TO IT THAT YOU WENT TO THE CHAIR!
PRESENTLY... AND ONCE AGAIN THE COIN SPINS HIGH IN THE AIR... AND FALLS INTO TWO-FACE'S OPEN PALM...
GENTLEMEN, THE BAD FACE HAS DECIDED! SO WE WILL ROB THAT DOUBLE-FEATURE MOVIE HOUSE AS PLANNED!
A TWO-DECKER BUS...AND NOW A TWO-FEATURE MOVIE HOUSE. TWO-FACE'S CRIMES ALL BASED ON THE NUMBER TWO. HA! HA! AND NOBODY KNOWS... NOBODY!
BUT AT THAT MOMENT... TWO GRIM MAN-HUNTERS EXAMINE THE DEAD THUG'S BODY FOR POSSIBLE CLUES...
LOOK, ROBIN! SOME GUM STUCK ON THE SOLE OF THE SHOE AND IT PICKED UP A BIT OF PAPER!
HMM! GOT WRITING ON IT! LOOKS LIKE A ROUGH MAP!
The paper!
BIJOU THEATRE
BOOTH
51 ST. EXIT
SCREEN
STAIRS TO PROJECTION BOOTH
9
THE BIJOU THEATRE... THAT'S IN THE PARK AVENUE DISTRICT! ONLY THE RICH GO THERE! SAY... DO YOU THINK..?
YES, THAT THE GUM PICKED UP THAT MAP IN TWO-FACE'S HIDEOUT! IT'S A PLAN FOR ROBBERY... AND THEY MAY BE PULLING IT RIGHT NOW! C'MON!

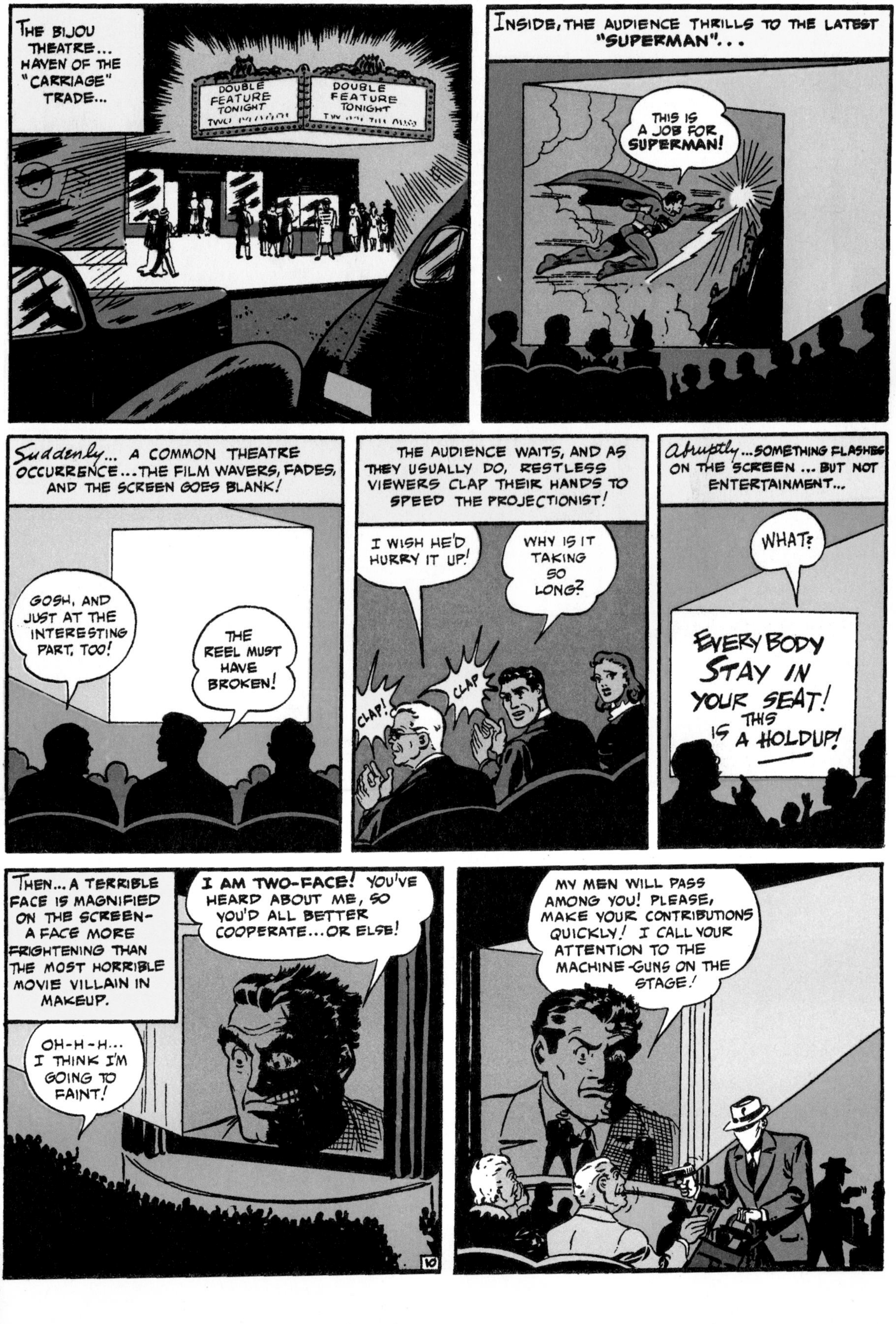
THE BIJOU THEATRE... HAVEN OF THE "CARRIAGE" TRADE...
DOUBLE FEATURE TONIGHT
DOUBLE FEATURE TONIGHT
INSIDE, THE AUDIENCE THRILLS TO THE LATEST "SUPERMAN"...
THIS IS A JOB FOR SUPERMAN!
Suddenly... A COMMON THEATRE OCCURRENCE...THE FILM WAVERS, FADES, AND THE SCREEN GOES BLANK!
GOSH, AND JUST AT THE INTERESTING PART, TOO!
THE REEL MUST HAVE BROKEN!
THE AUDIENCE WAITS, AND AS THEY USUALLY DO, RESTLESS VIEWERS CLAP THEIR HANDS TO SPEED THE PROJECTIONIST!
I WISH HE'D HURRY IT UP!
WHY IS IT TAKING SO LONG?
CLAP!
CLAP
abruptly...SOMETHING FLASHES ON THE SCREEN ... BUT NOT ENTERTAINMENT...
WHAT?
EVERYBODY STAY IN YOUR SEAT! THIS IS A HOLDUP!
THEN... A TERRIBLE FACE IS MAGNIFIED ON THE SCREEN- A FACE MORE FRIGHTENING THAN THE MOST HORRIBLE MOVIE VILLAIN IN MAKEUP.
I AM TWO-FACE! YOU'VE HEARD ABOUT ME, SO YOU'D ALL BETTER COOPERATE...OR ELSE!
OH-H-H... I THINK I'M GOING TO FAINT!
10
MY MEN WILL PASS AMONG YOU! PLEASE, MAKE YOUR CONTRIBUTIONS QUICKLY! I CALL YOUR ATTENTION TO THE MACHINE-GUNS ON THE STAGE!

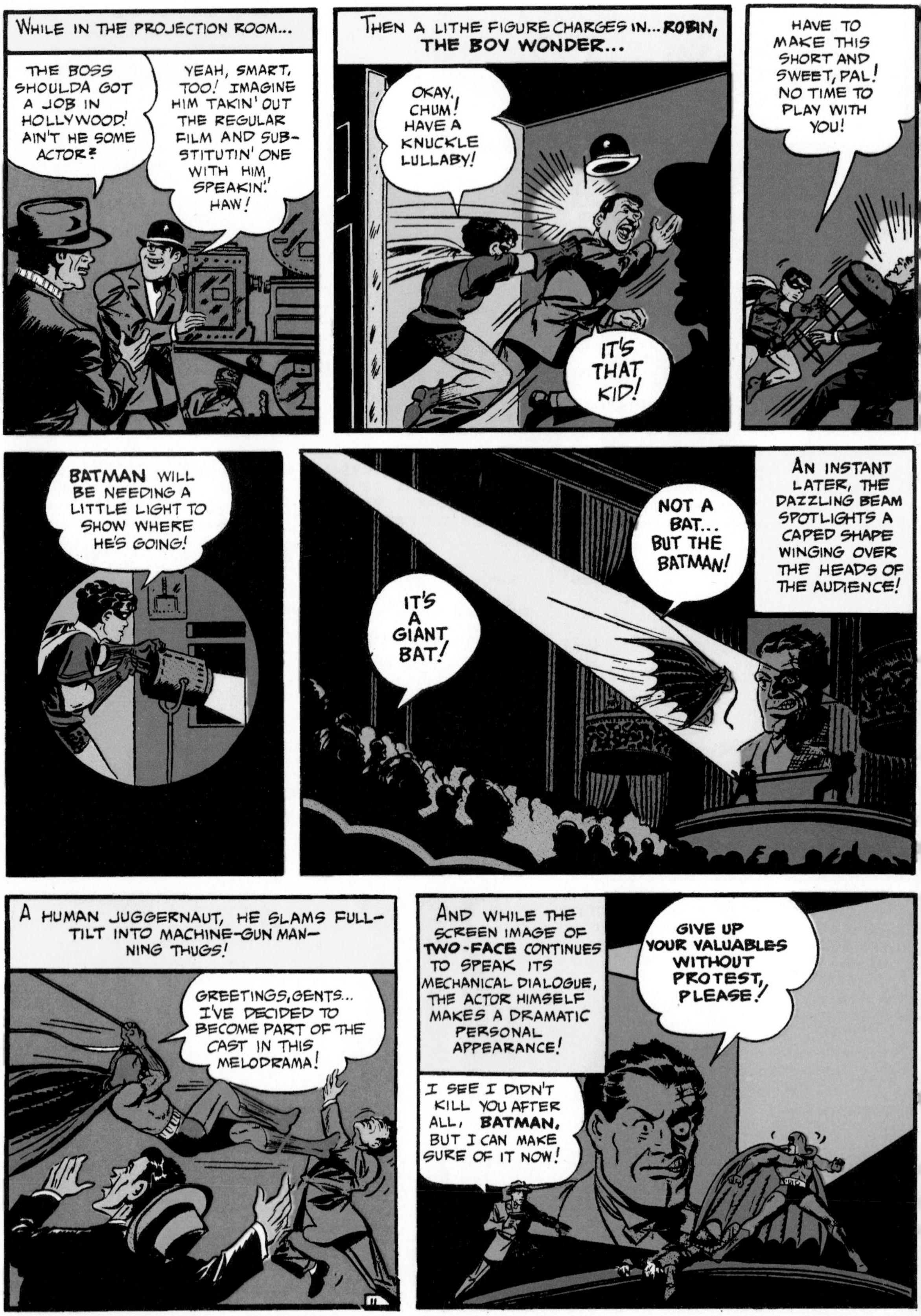
WHILE IN THE PROJECTION ROOM...
THE BOSS SHOULDA GOT A JOB IN HOLLYWOOD! AIN'T HE SOME ACTOR?
YEAH, SMART, TOO! IMAGINE HIM TAKIN' OUT THE REGULAR FILM AND SUBSTITUTIN' ONE WITH HIM SPEAKIN'! HAW!
THEN A LITHE FIGURE CHARGES IN... ROBIN, THE BOY WONDER...
OKAY, CHUM! HAVE A KNUCKLE LULLABY!
IT'S THAT KID!
HAVE TO MAKE THIS SHORT AND SWEET, PAL! NO TIME TO PLAY WITH YOU!
BATMAN WILL BE NEEDING A LITTLE LIGHT TO SHOW WHERE HE'S GOING!
AN INSTANT LATER, THE DAZZLING BEAM SPOTLIGHTS A CAPED SHAPE WINGING OVER THE HEADS OF THE AUDIENCE!
IT'S A GIANT BAT!
NOT A BAT... BUT THE BATMAN!
A HUMAN JUGGERNAUT, HE SLAMS FULL-TILT INTO MACHINE-GUN MANNING THUGS!
GREETINGS, GENTS... I'VE DECIDED TO BECOME PART OF THE CAST IN THIS MELODRAMA!
AND WHILE THE SCREEN IMAGE OF TWO-FACE CONTINUES TO SPEAK ITS MECHANICAL DIALOGUE, THE ACTOR HIMSELF MAKES A DRAMATIC PERSONAL APPEARANCE!
GIVE UP YOUR VALUABLES WITHOUT PROTEST, PLEASE!
I SEE I DIDN'T KILL YOU AFTER ALL, BATMAN. BUT I CAN MAKE SURE OF IT NOW!

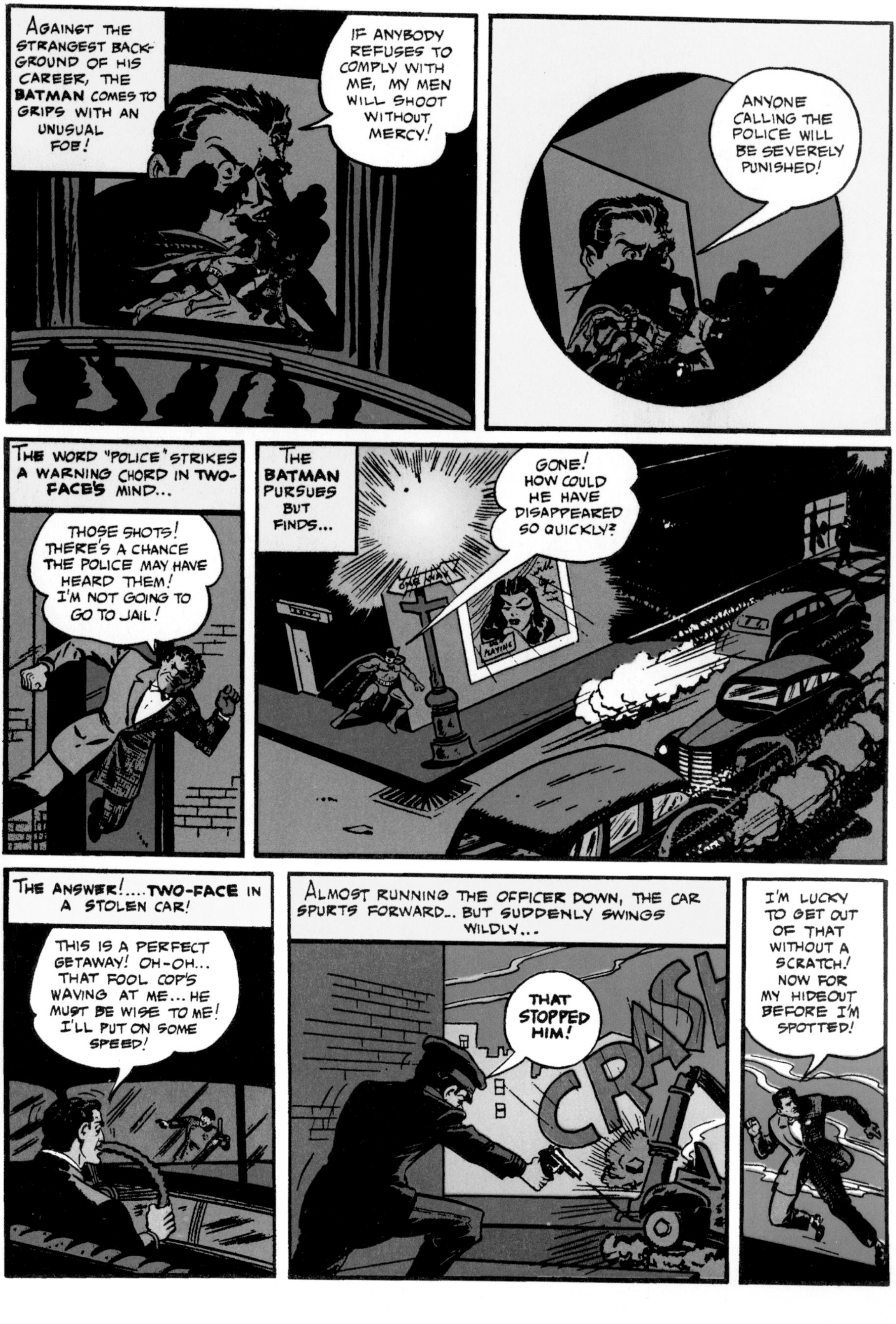

AGAINST THE STRANGEST BACKGROUND OF HIS CAREER, THE BATMAN COMES TO GRIPS WITH AN UNUSUAL FOE!
IF ANYBODY REFUSES TO COMPLY WITH ME, MY MEN WILL SHOOT WITHOUT MERCY!
ANYONE CALLING THE POLICE WILL BE SEVERELY PUNISHED!
THE WORD "POLICE" STRIKES A WARNING CHORD IN TWO-FACE'S MIND...
THOSE SHOTS! THERE'S A CHANCE THE POLICE MAY HAVE HEARD THEM! I'M NOT GOING TO GO TO JAIL!
THE BATMAN PURSUES BUT FINDS...
GONE! HOW COULD HE HAVE DISAPPEARED SO QUICKLY?
THE ANSWER!....TWO-FACE IN A STOLEN CAR!
THIS IS A PERFECT GETAWAY! OH-OH... THAT FOOL COP'S WAVING AT ME... HE MUST BE WISE TO ME! I'LL PUT ON SOME SPEED!
ALMOST RUNNING THE OFFICER DOWN, THE CAR SPURTS FORWARD.. BUT SUDDENLY SWINGS WILDLY...
THAT STOPPED HIM!
CRASH
I'M LUCKY TO GET OUT OF THAT WITHOUT A SCRATCH! NOW FOR MY HIDEOUT BEFORE I'M SPOTTED!

SOME TIME LATER, AS TWO-FACE STEPS CONFIDENTLY INTO HIS LAIR...

AT LAST! SAFE AT HOME!

NOT QUITE!

BATMAN! HOW...?

VERY SIMPLE! WHEN THE POLICE-MAN HIT YOUR TIRE, I WAS ATTRACTED BY THE SHOT...SPOTTED YOU, AND TRAILED YOU HERE!

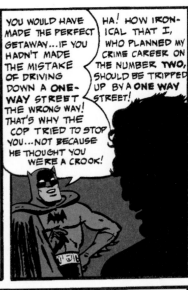

YOU WOULD HAVE MADE THE PERFECT GETAWAY...IF YOU HADN'T MADE THE MISTAKE OF DRIVING DOWN A ONE-WAY STREET THE WRONG WAY! THAT'S WHY THE COP TRIED TO STOP YOU...NOT BECAUSE HE THOUGHT YOU WERE A CROOK!

HA! HOW IRON-ICAL THAT I, WHO PLANNED MY CRIME CAREER ON THE NUMBER TWO, SHOULD BE TRIPPED UP BY A ONE WAY STREET!

WAIT! YOU'RE NOT TAKING ME IN! I'LL KILL YOU FIRST!

GO AHEAD! SHOOT...YOU FOOL! KENT, BE SMART! GIVE YOURSELF UP! THE COURT REMEMBERS YOUR FINE RECORD AS A D.A.! THEY'LL KNOW THIS IS ONLY TEMPORARY INSANITY INDUCED BY YOUR TERRIBLE MISFORTUNE!

I'LL EVEN SPEAK FOR YOU! YOU'LL GET A LIGHT SENTENCE! BY THE TIME YOUR TERM IS UP, PERHAPS DR. EKHART WILL BE FREE. YOU'LL GET YOUR FACE FIXED! YOU CAN START YOUR LIFE ALL OVER AGAIN. WHAT DO YOU SAY?

IT'S WHAT THE COIN SAYS! IT DECIDES EVERYTHING FOR ME! IF THE SCARRED SIDE COMES UP... I KILL YOU AND CONTINUE A CAREER OF CRIME, AND IF THE GOOD SIDE COMES... I GO WITH YOU!

A QUICK FLIP... AND THE COIN SPINS HIGH INTO THE AIR!

DOWN IT DROPS LIKE A SHINING SUN... HITS THE FLOOR!...

...ROLLS OVER THE FLOOR-BOARDS... HITS A CRACK, AND...

... AND STANDS ON ITS EDGE!

THE BATMAN WAITS ON THE GOOD SIDE OF THE ROOM...TWO-FACE ON THE BAD...

WELL...STANDING UP. LOOKS LIKE YOU'LL HAVE TO FLIP OVER AGAIN!

NO, BATMAN!...I TOSS ONCE AGAINST CHANCE! AND SINCE I CAN'T DE-CIDE FOR MYSELF, IT'S UP TO FATE TO DECIDE WHAT TO DO WITH MY LIFE NOW!

A MAN'S WHOLE BEING AND FUTURE RESTS IN FATE'S HAND! WHICH WAY WILL SHE TOSS HIM... TO GOOD...OR TO EVIL? THE ANSWER TO THIS AMAZING RIDDLE OF TWO-FACE WILL BE FOUND IN THE OCTOBER ISSUE OF --- DETECTIVE COMICS.

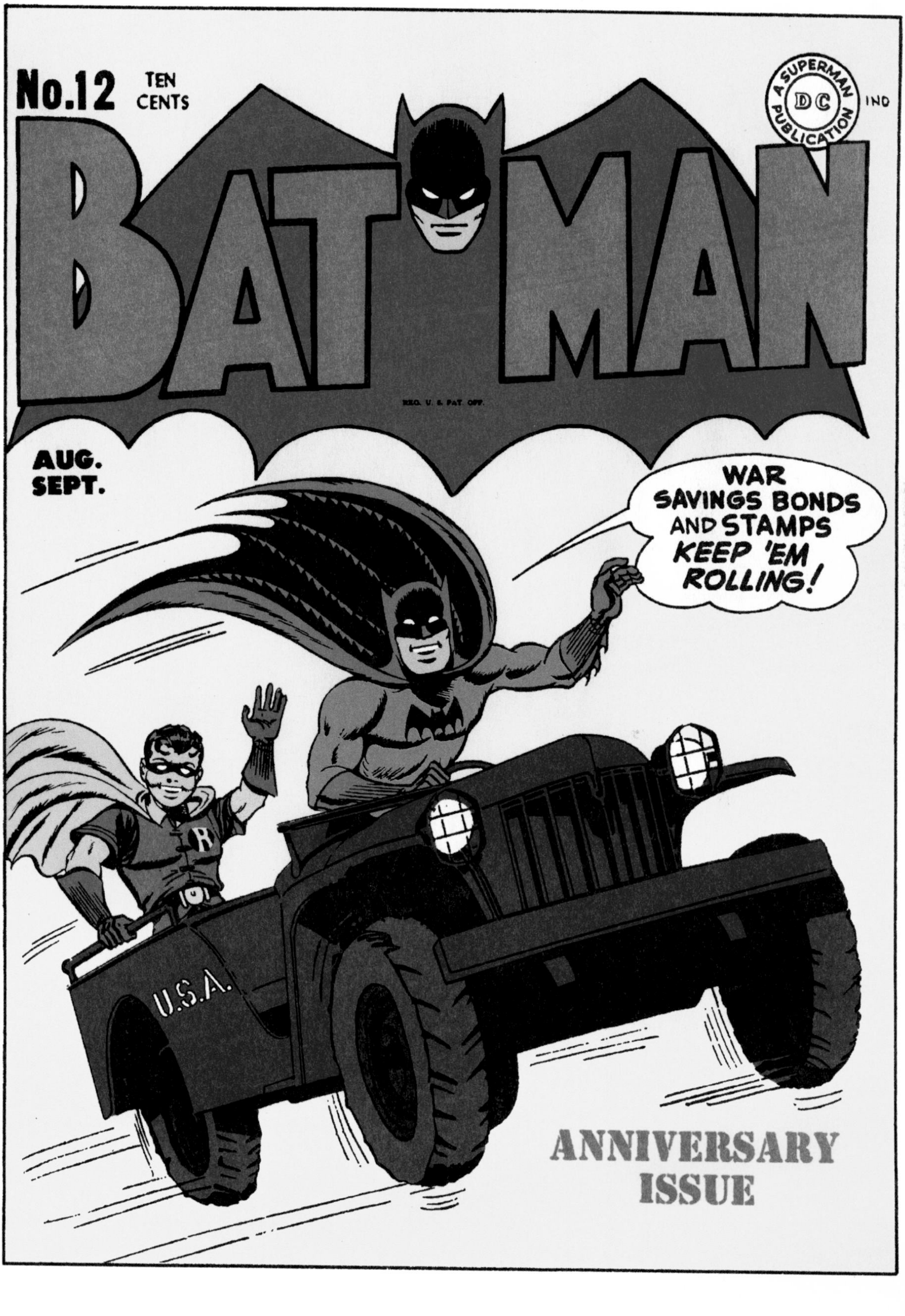
No.12
TEN CENTS
A SUPERMAN DC PUBLICATION
INC
BATMAN
AUG. SEPT.
WAR SAVINGS BONDS AND STAMPS KEEP 'EM ROLLING!
U.S.A.
ANNIVERSARY ISSUE

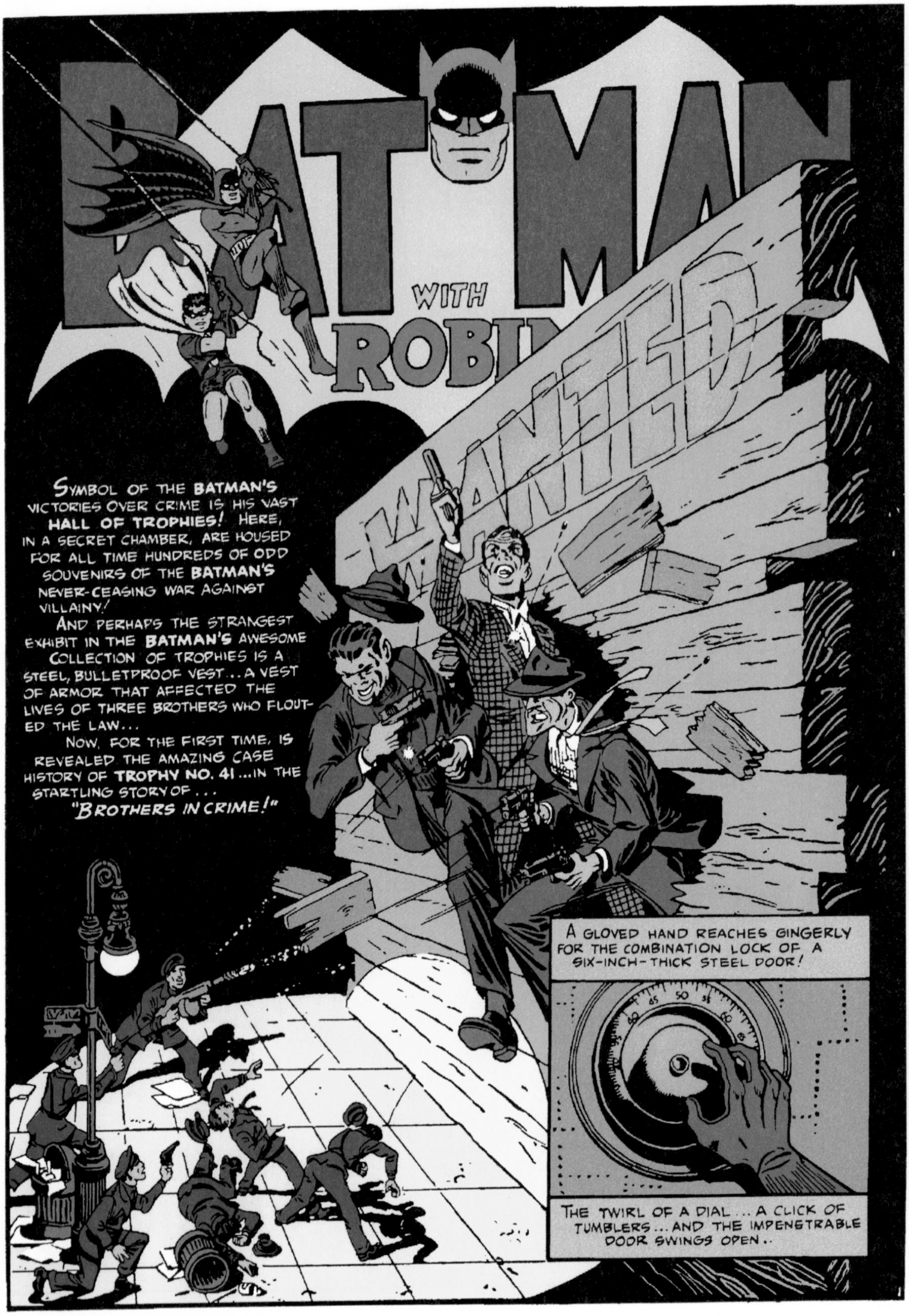
BATMAN
WITH
ROBIN
WANTED
SYMBOL OF THE BATMAN'S VICTORIES OVER CRIME IS HIS VAST HALL OF TROPHIES! HERE, IN A SECRET CHAMBER, ARE HOUSED FOR ALL TIME HUNDREDS OF ODD SOUVENIRS OF THE BATMAN'S NEVER-CEASING WAR AGAINST VILLAINY!
AND PERHAPS THE STRANGEST EXHIBIT IN THE BATMAN'S AWESOME COLLECTION OF TROPHIES IS A STEEL, BULLETPROOF VEST... A VEST OF ARMOR THAT AFFECTED THE LIVES OF THREE BROTHERS WHO FLOUTED THE LAW...
NOW, FOR THE FIRST TIME, IS REVEALED THE AMAZING CASE HISTORY OF TROPHY NO. 41 ...IN THE STARTLING STORY OF ...
"BROTHERS IN CRIME!"
A GLOVED HAND REACHES GINGERLY FOR THE COMBINATION LOCK OF A SIX-INCH-THICK STEEL DOOR!
THE TWIRL OF A DIAL ... A CLICK OF TUMBLERS ... AND THE IMPENETRABLE DOOR SWINGS OPEN ..

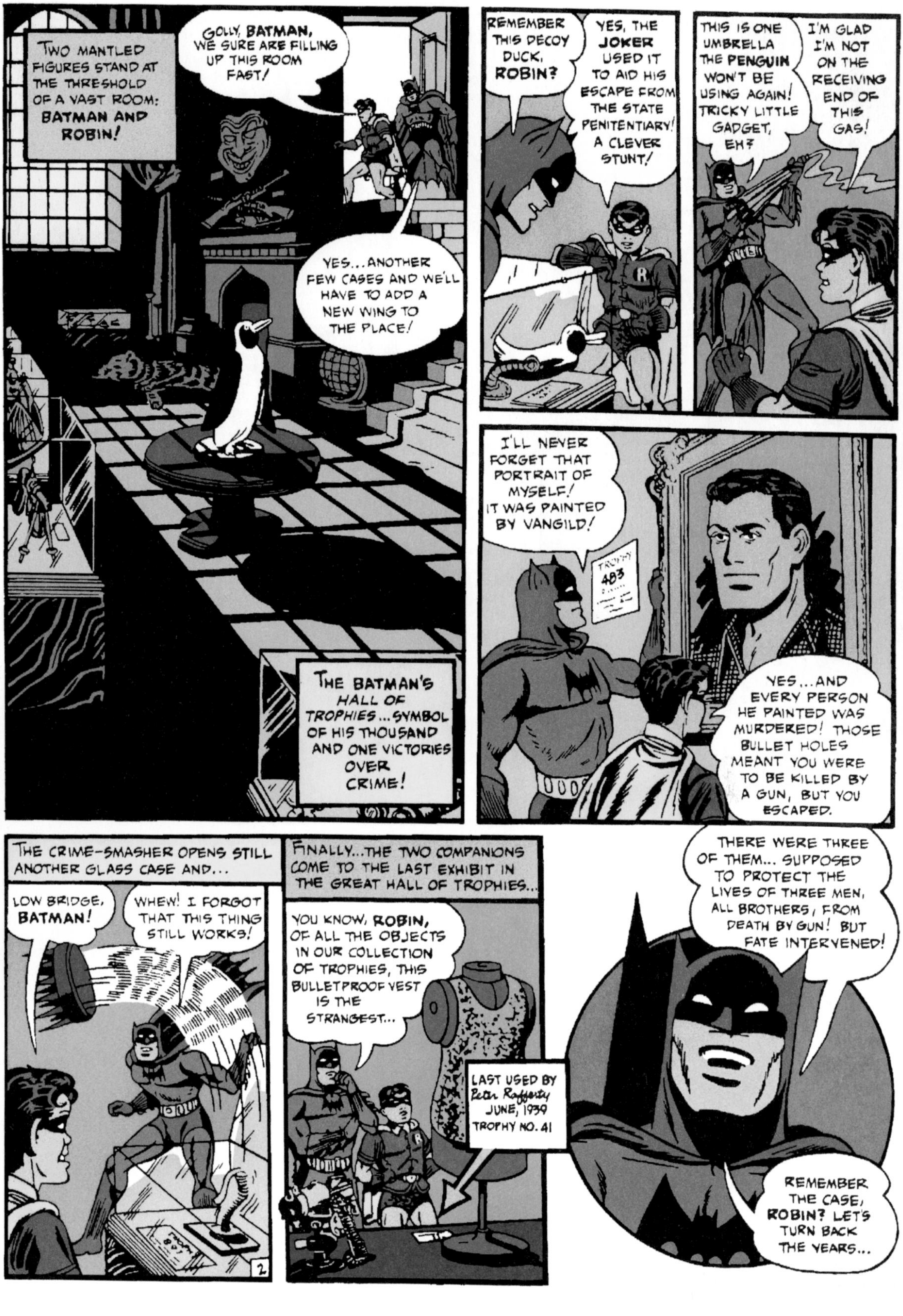
TWO MANTLED FIGURES STAND AT THE THRESHOLD OF A VAST ROOM: BATMAN AND ROBIN!
GOLLY, BATMAN, WE SURE ARE FILLING UP THIS ROOM FAST!
YES... ANOTHER FEW CASES AND WE'LL HAVE TO ADD A NEW WING TO THE PLACE!
THE BATMAN'S HALL OF TROPHIES... SYMBOL OF HIS THOUSAND AND ONE VICTORIES OVER CRIME!
REMEMBER THIS DECOY DUCK, ROBIN?
YES, THE JOKER USED IT TO AID HIS ESCAPE FROM THE STATE PENITENTIARY! A CLEVER STUNT!
THIS IS ONE UMBRELLA THE PENGUIN WON'T BE USING AGAIN! TRICKY LITTLE GADGET, EH?
I'M GLAD I'M NOT ON THE RECEIVING END OF THIS GAS!
I'LL NEVER FORGET THAT PORTRAIT OF MYSELF! IT WAS PAINTED BY VANGILD!
TROPHY 483
YES,...AND EVERY PERSON HE PAINTED WAS MURDERED! THOSE BULLET HOLES MEANT YOU WERE TO BE KILLED BY A GUN, BUT YOU ESCAPED.
THE CRIME-SMASHER OPENS STILL ANOTHER GLASS CASE AND...
LOW BRIDGE, BATMAN!
WHEW! I FORGOT THAT THIS THING STILL WORKS!
2
FINALLY...THE TWO COMPANIONS COME TO THE LAST EXHIBIT IN THE GREAT HALL OF TROPHIES...
YOU KNOW, ROBIN, OF ALL THE OBJECTS IN OUR COLLECTION OF TROPHIES, THIS BULLETPROOF VEST IS THE STRANGEST...
LAST USED BY Peter Rafferty JUNE, 1939 TROPHY NO. 41
THERE WERE THREE OF THEM... SUPPOSED TO PROTECT THE LIVES OF THREE MEN, ALL BROTHERS, FROM DEATH BY GUN! BUT FATE INTERVENED!
REMEMBER THE CASE, ROBIN? LET'S TURN BACK THE YEARS...

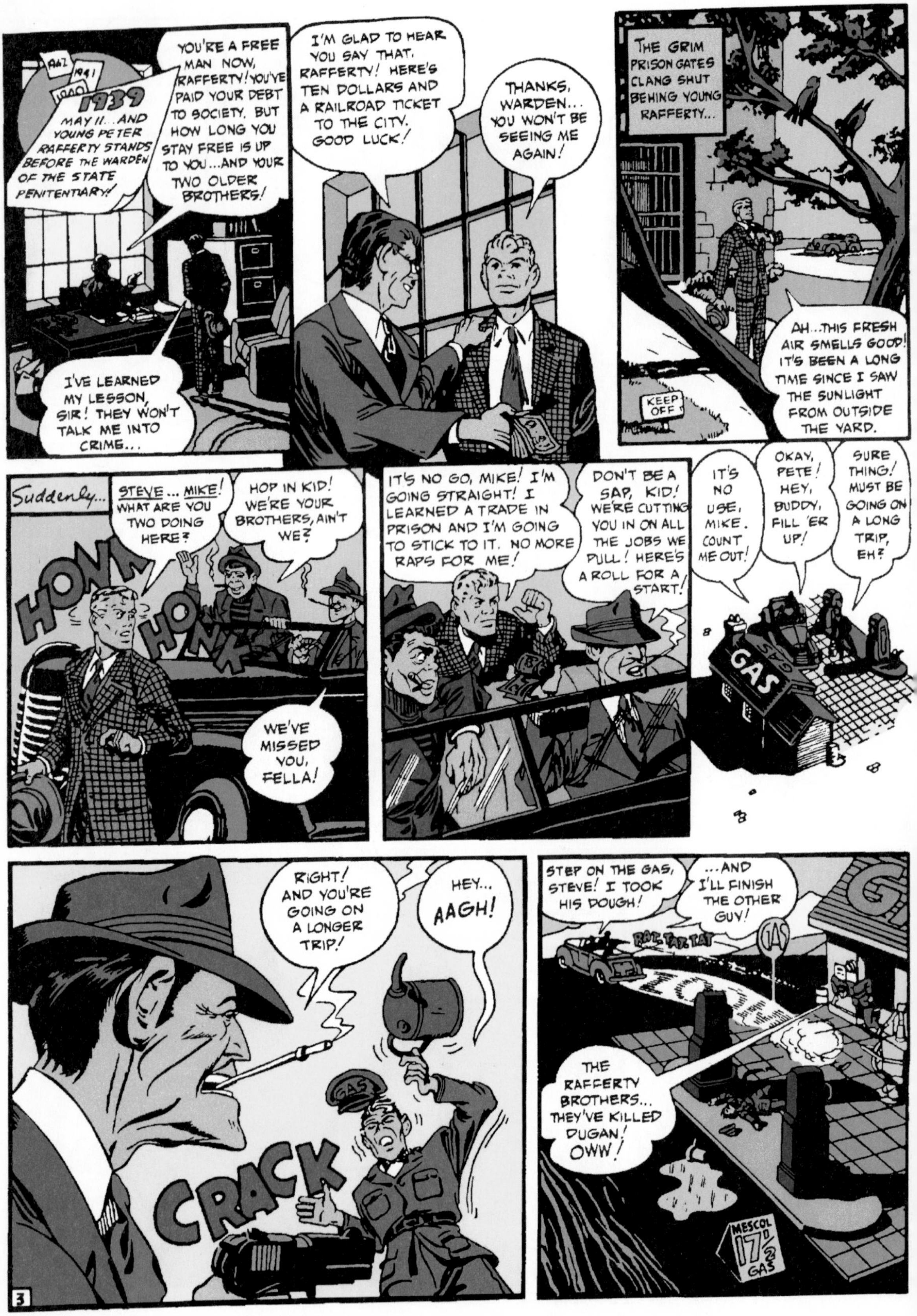
1942
1941
1940
1939 MAY 11... AND YOUNG PETER RAFFERTY STANDS BEFORE THE WARDEN OF THE STATE PENITENTIARY!
YOU'RE A FREE MAN NOW, RAFFERTY! YOU'VE PAID YOUR DEBT TO SOCIETY. BUT HOW LONG YOU STAY FREE IS UP TO YOU... AND YOUR TWO OLDER BROTHERS!
I'VE LEARNED MY LESSON, SIR! THEY WON'T TALK ME INTO CRIME...
I'M GLAD TO HEAR YOU SAY THAT, RAFFERTY! HERE'S TEN DOLLARS AND A RAILROAD TICKET TO THE CITY. GOOD LUCK!
THANKS, WARDEN... YOU WON'T BE SEEING ME AGAIN!
THE GRIM PRISON GATES CLANG SHUT BEHING YOUNG RAFFERTY...
AH... THIS FRESH AIR SMELLS GOOD! IT'S BEEN A LONG TIME SINCE I SAW THE SUNLIGHT FROM OUTSIDE THE YARD.
KEEP OFF
Suddenly...
STEVE ... MIKE! WHAT ARE YOU TWO DOING HERE?
HOP IN KID! WE'RE YOUR BROTHERS, AIN'T WE?
HONK
HONK
WE'VE MISSED YOU, FELLA!
IT'S NO GO, MIKE! I'M GOING STRAIGHT! I LEARNED A TRADE IN PRISON AND I'M GOING TO STICK TO IT. NO MORE RAPS FOR ME!
DON'T BE A SAP, KID! WE'RE CUTTING YOU IN ON ALL THE JOBS WE PULL! HERE'S A ROLL FOR A START!
IT'S NO USE, MIKE. COUNT ME OUT!
OKAY, PETE! HEY, BUDDY, FILL 'ER UP!
SURE THING! MUST BE GOING ON A LONG TRIP, EH?
GAS
RIGHT! AND YOU'RE GOING ON A LONGER TRIP!
HEY... AAGH!
CRACK
GAS
3
STEP ON THE GAS, STEVE! I TOOK HIS DOUGH!
...AND I'LL FINISH THE OTHER GUY!
RAT-TAT-TAT
GAS
THE RAFFERTY BROTHERS... THEY'VE KILLED DUGAN! OWW!
MESCOL 17 2/10 GAS

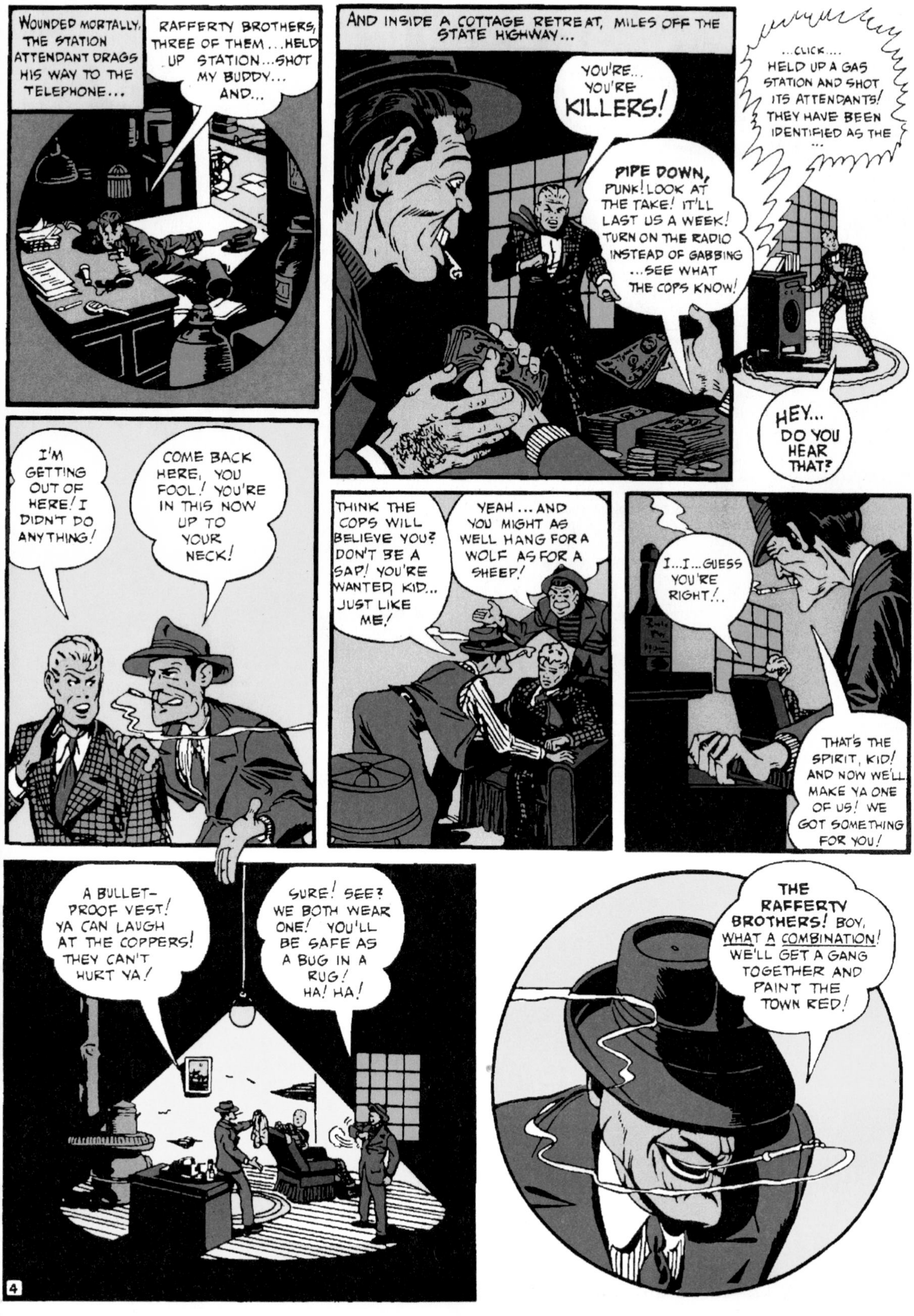

WOUNDED MORTALLY, THE STATION ATTENDANT DRAGS HIS WAY TO THE TELEPHONE...
RAFFERTY BROTHERS, THREE OF THEM...HELD UP STATION...SHOT MY BUDDY... AND...
AND INSIDE A COTTAGE RETREAT, MILES OFF THE STATE HIGHWAY...
YOU'RE.. YOU'RE KILLERS!
PIPE DOWN, PUNK! LOOK AT THE TAKE! IT'LL LAST US A WEEK! TURN ON THE RADIO INSTEAD OF GABBING ...SEE WHAT THE COPS KNOW!
...CLICK.... HELD UP A GAS STATION AND SHOT ITS ATTENDANTS! THEY HAVE BEEN IDENTIFIED AS THE ...
HEY... DO YOU HEAR THAT?
I'M GETTING OUT OF HERE! I DIDN'T DO ANYTHING!
COME BACK HERE, YOU FOOL! YOU'RE IN THIS NOW UP TO YOUR NECK!
THINK THE COPS WILL BELIEVE YOU? DON'T BE A SAP! YOU'RE WANTED, KID... JUST LIKE ME!
YEAH ... AND YOU MIGHT AS WELL HANG FOR A WOLF AS FOR A SHEEP!
I...I...GUESS YOU'RE RIGHT!..
THAT'S THE SPIRIT, KID! AND NOW WE'LL MAKE YA ONE OF US! WE GOT SOMETHING FOR YOU!
A BULLET-PROOF VEST! YA CAN LAUGH AT THE COPPERS! THEY CAN'T HURT YA!
SURE! SEE? WE BOTH WEAR ONE! YOU'LL BE SAFE AS A BUG IN A RUG! HA! HA!
4
THE RAFFERTY BROTHERS! BOY, WHAT A COMBINATION! WE'LL GET A GANG TOGETHER AND PAINT THE TOWN RED!

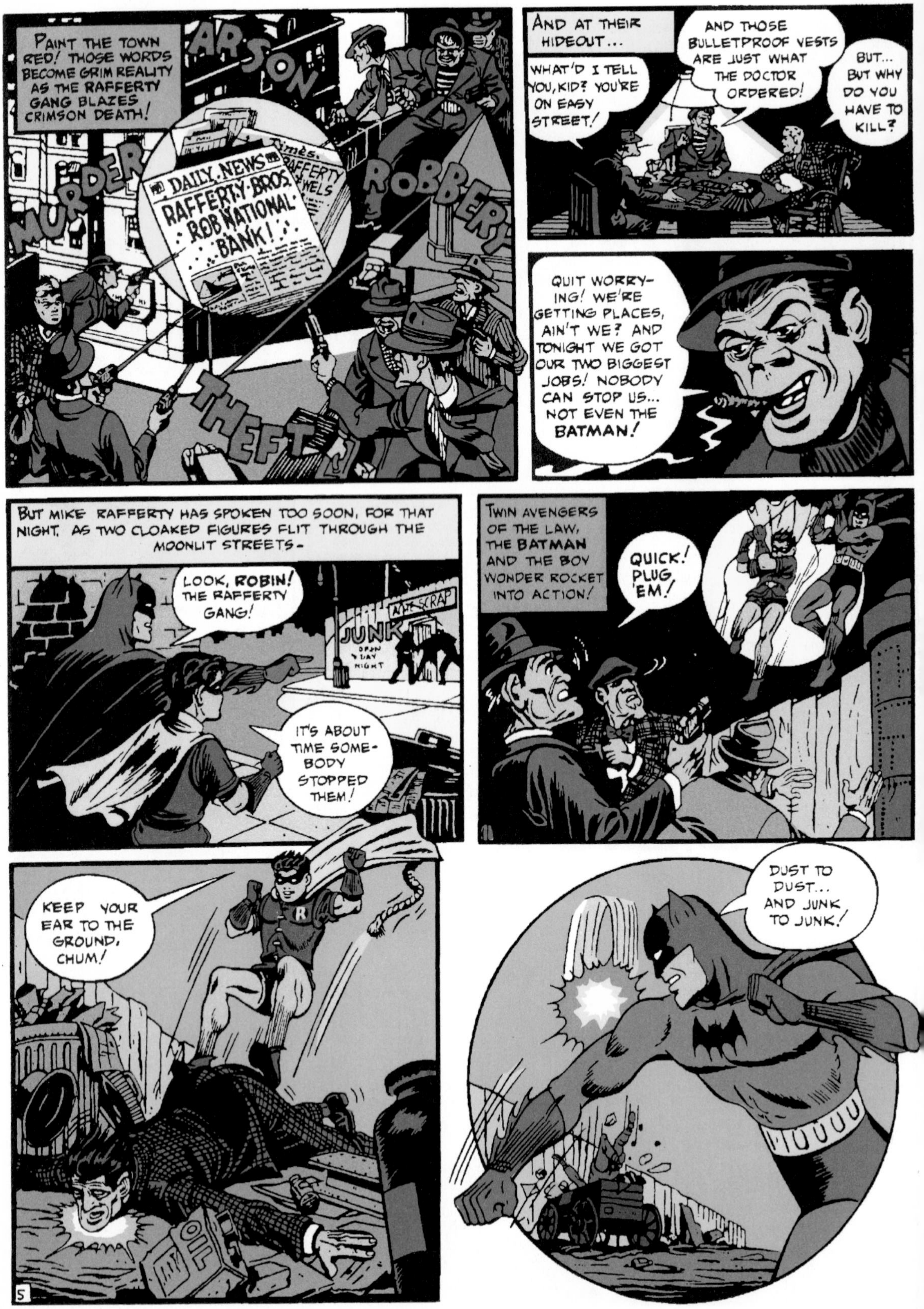
PAINT THE TOWN RED! THOSE WORDS BECOME GRIM REALITY AS THE RAFFERTY GANG BLAZES CRIMSON DEATH!
ARSON
DAILY NEWS
RAFFERTY BROS. ROB NATIONAL BANK!
MURDER
ROBBERY
THEFT
AND AT THEIR HIDEOUT...
WHAT'D I TELL YOU, KID? YOU'RE ON EASY STREET!
AND THOSE BULLETPROOF VESTS ARE JUST WHAT THE DOCTOR ORDERED!
BUT... BUT WHY DO YOU HAVE TO KILL?
QUIT WORRYING! WE'RE GETTING PLACES, AIN'T WE? AND TONIGHT WE GOT OUR TWO BIGGEST JOBS! NOBODY CAN STOP US... NOT EVEN THE BATMAN!
BUT MIKE RAFFERTY HAS SPOKEN TOO SOON, FOR THAT NIGHT, AS TWO CLOAKED FIGURES FLIT THROUGH THE MOONLIT STREETS-
LOOK, ROBIN! THE RAFFERTY GANG!
JUNK
OPEN DAY NIGHT
SCRAP
IT'S ABOUT TIME SOMEBODY STOPPED THEM!
TWIN AVENGERS OF THE LAW, THE BATMAN AND THE BOY WONDER ROCKET INTO ACTION!
QUICK! PLUG 'EM!
KEEP YOUR EAR TO THE GROUND, CHUM!
OIL
5
DUST TO DUST... AND JUNK TO JUNK!

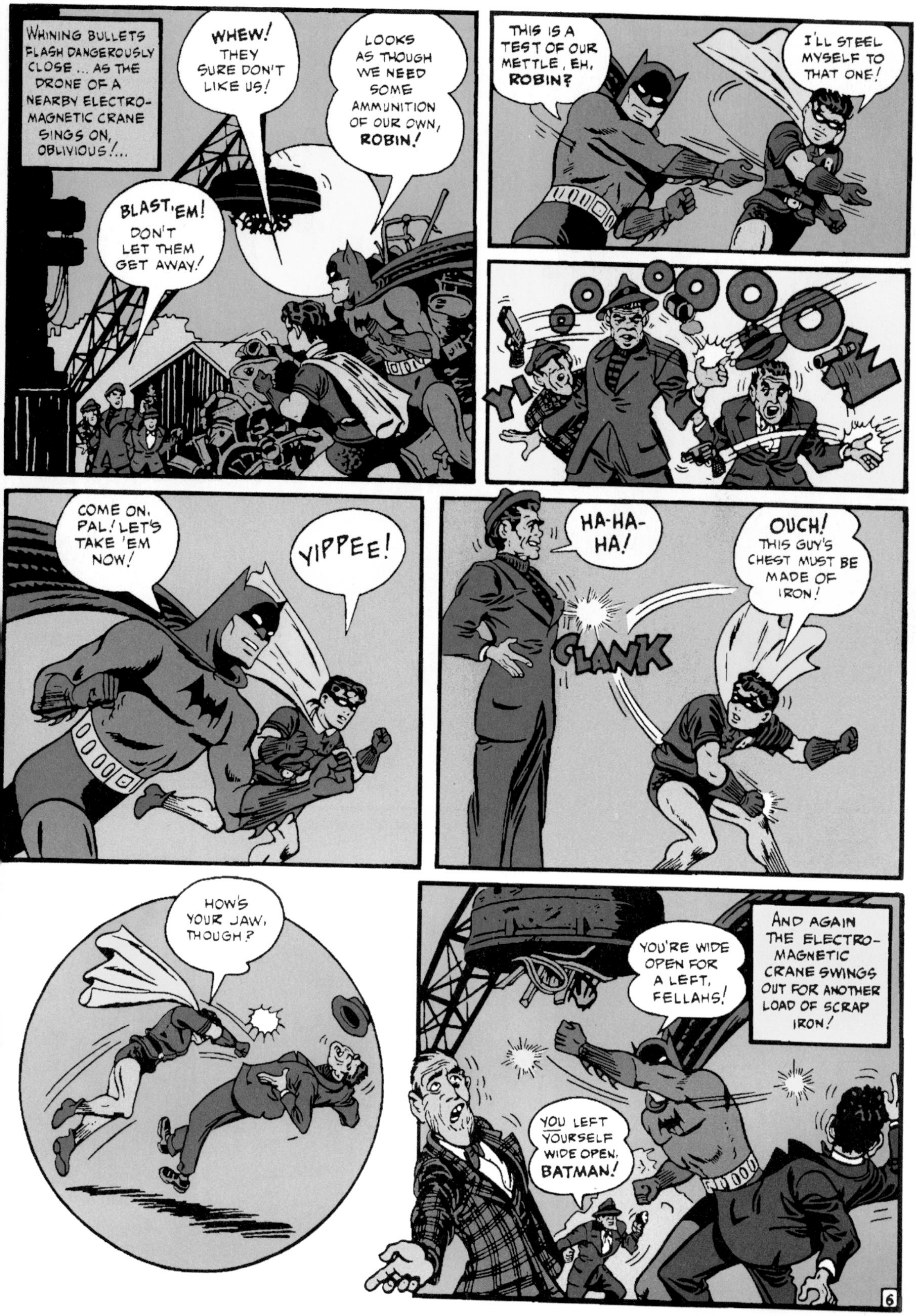
WHINING BULLETS FLASH DANGEROUSLY CLOSE ... AS THE DRONE OF A NEARBY ELECTRO-MAGNETIC CRANE SINGS ON, OBLIVIOUS!...
WHEW! THEY SURE DON'T LIKE US!
LOOKS AS THOUGH WE NEED SOME AMMUNITION OF OUR OWN, ROBIN!
BLAST 'EM! DON'T LET THEM GET AWAY!
THIS IS A TEST OF OUR METTLE, EH, ROBIN?
I'LL STEEL MYSELF TO THAT ONE!
OOOOOOOW
COME ON, PAL! LET'S TAKE 'EM NOW!
YIPPEE!
HA-HA-HA!
OUCH! THIS GUY'S CHEST MUST BE MADE OF IRON!
CLANK
HOW'S YOUR JAW, THOUGH?
AND AGAIN THE ELECTRO-MAGNETIC CRANE SWINGS OUT FOR ANOTHER LOAD OF SCRAP IRON!
YOU'RE WIDE OPEN FOR A LEFT, FELLAHS!
YOU LEFT YOURSELF WIDE OPEN, BATMAN!
6

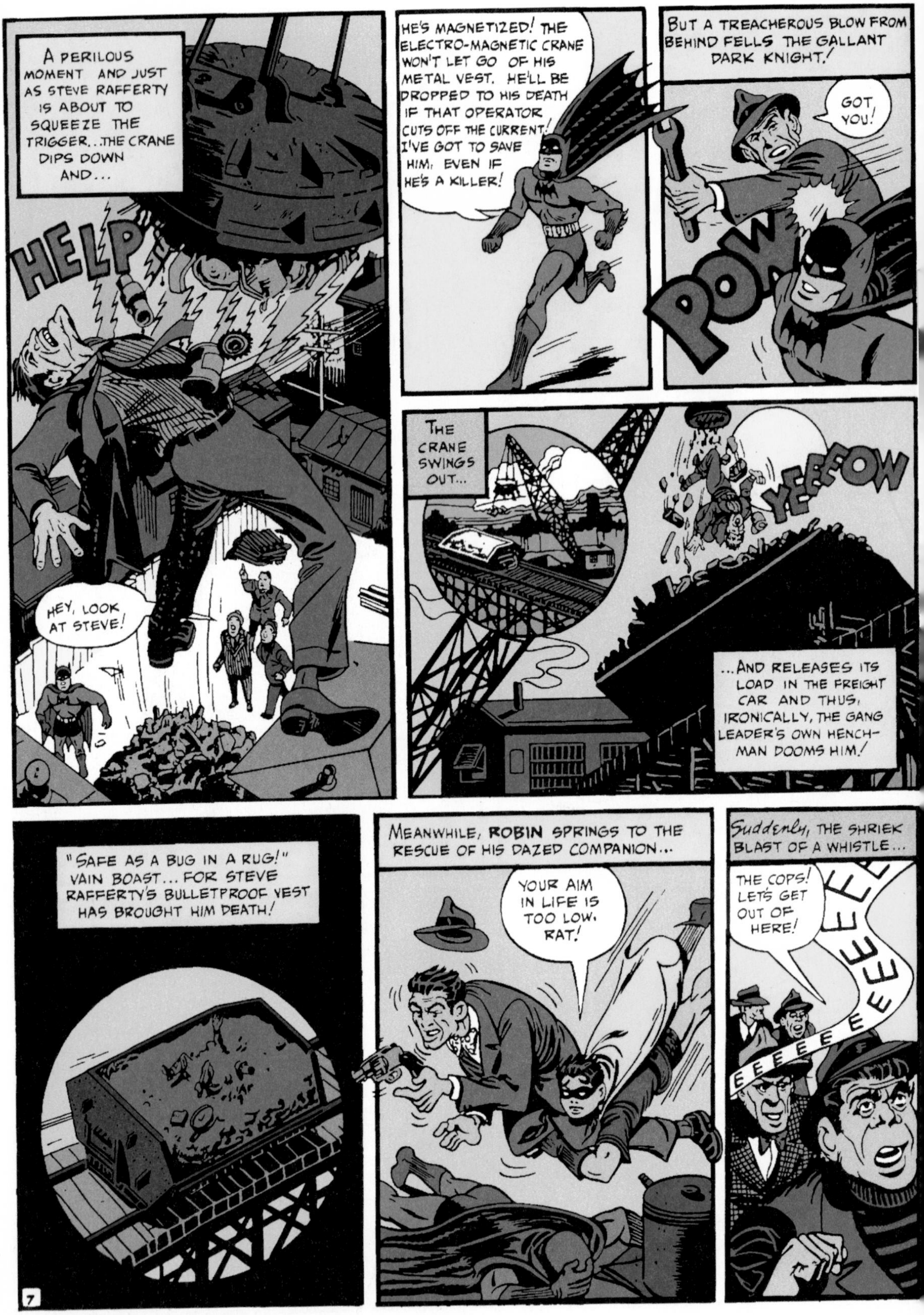
A PERILOUS MOMENT AND JUST AS STEVE RAFFERTY IS ABOUT TO SQUEEZE THE TRIGGER...THE CRANE DIPS DOWN AND...
HELP
HEY, LOOK AT STEVE!
HE'S MAGNETIZED! THE ELECTRO-MAGNETIC CRANE WON'T LET GO OF HIS METAL VEST. HE'LL BE DROPPED TO HIS DEATH IF THAT OPERATOR CUTS OFF THE CURRENT! I'VE GOT TO SAVE HIM, EVEN IF HE'S A KILLER!
BUT A TREACHEROUS BLOW FROM BEHIND FELLS THE GALLANT DARK KNIGHT!
GOT YOU!
POW
THE CRANE SWINGS OUT...
YEEOW
...AND RELEASES ITS LOAD IN THE FREIGHT CAR AND THUS, IRONICALLY, THE GANG LEADER'S OWN HENCHMAN DOOMS HIM!
"SAFE AS A BUG IN A RUG!" VAIN BOAST... FOR STEVE RAFFERTY'S BULLETPROOF VEST HAS BROUGHT HIM DEATH!
7
MEANWHILE, ROBIN SPRINGS TO THE RESCUE OF HIS DAZED COMPANION...
YOUR AIM IN LIFE IS TOO LOW, RAT!
Suddenly, THE SHRIEK BLAST OF A WHISTLE...
THE COPS! LET'S GET OUT OF HERE!
EEEEEEEEEEEE

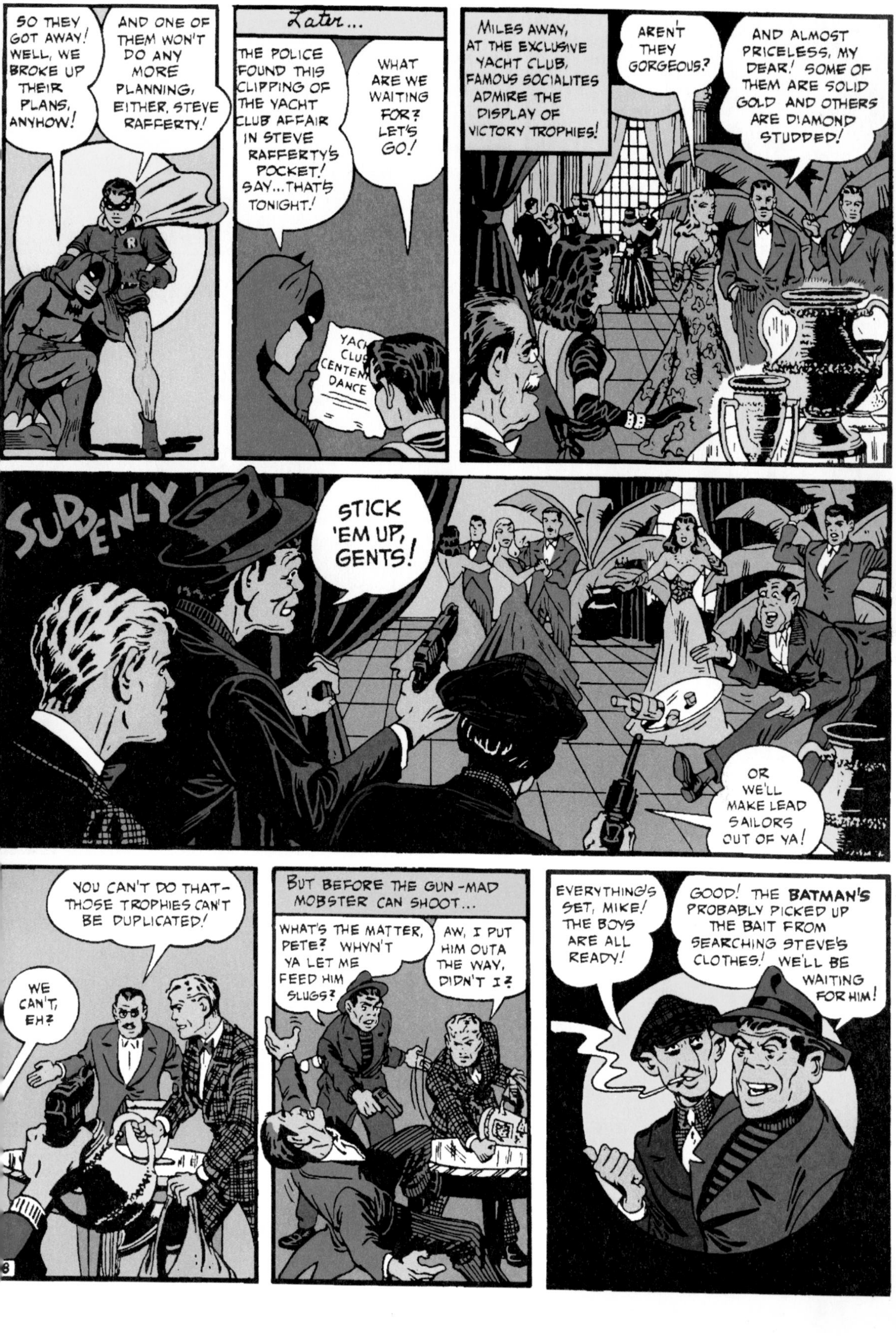
SO THEY GOT AWAY! WELL, WE BROKE UP THEIR PLANS, ANYHOW!
AND ONE OF THEM WON'T DO ANY MORE PLANNING, EITHER, STEVE RAFFERTY!
Later...
THE POLICE FOUND THIS CLIPPING OF THE YACHT CLUB AFFAIR IN STEVE RAFFERTY'S POCKET! SAY...THAT'S TONIGHT!
WHAT ARE WE WAITING FOR? LET'S GO!
MILES AWAY, AT THE EXCLUSIVE YACHT CLUB, FAMOUS SOCIALITES ADMIRE THE DISPLAY OF VICTORY TROPHIES!
AREN'T THEY GORGEOUS?
AND ALMOST PRICELESS, MY DEAR! SOME OF THEM ARE SOLID GOLD AND OTHERS ARE DIAMOND STUDDED!
SUDDENLY
STICK 'EM UP, GENTS!
OR WE'LL MAKE LEAD SAILORS OUT OF YA!
YOU CAN'T DO THAT-THOSE TROPHIES CAN'T BE DUPLICATED!
WE CAN'T, EH?
BUT BEFORE THE GUN-MAD MOBSTER CAN SHOOT...
WHAT'S THE MATTER, PETE? WHYN'T YA LET ME FEED HIM SLUGS?
AW, I PUT HIM OUTA THE WAY, DIDN'T I?
EVERYTHING'S SET, MIKE! THE BOYS ARE ALL READY!
GOOD! THE **BATMAN'S** PROBABLY PICKED UP THE BAIT FROM SEARCHING STEVE'S CLOTHES! WE'LL BE WAITING FOR HIM!
8

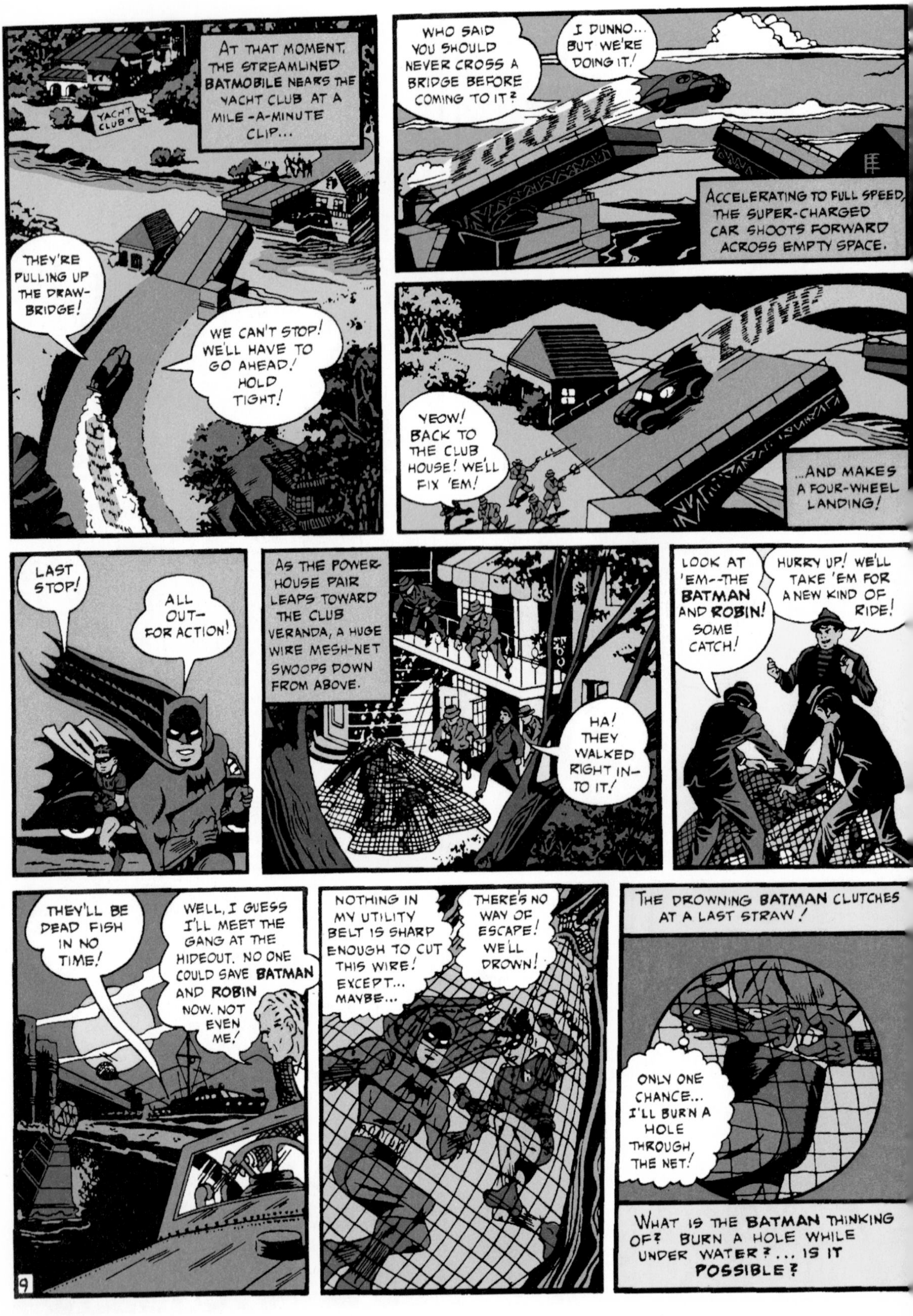
AT THAT MOMENT, THE STREAMLINED BATMOBILE NEARS THE YACHT CLUB AT A MILE-A-MINUTE CLIP...
YACHT CLUB
THEY'RE PULLING UP THE DRAW-BRIDGE!
WE CAN'T STOP! WE'LL HAVE TO GO AHEAD! HOLD TIGHT!
WHO SAID YOU SHOULD NEVER CROSS A BRIDGE BEFORE COMING TO IT?
I DUNNO... BUT WE'RE DOING IT!
ZOOM
ACCELERATING TO FULL SPEED, THE SUPER-CHARGED CAR SHOOTS FORWARD ACROSS EMPTY SPACE.
ZUMP
YEOW! BACK TO THE CLUB HOUSE! WE'LL FIX 'EM!
...AND MAKES A FOUR-WHEEL LANDING!
LAST STOP!
ALL OUT-FOR ACTION!
AS THE POWER-HOUSE PAIR LEAPS TOWARD THE CLUB VERANDA, A HUGE WIRE MESH-NET SWOOPS DOWN FROM ABOVE.
HA! THEY WALKED RIGHT IN-TO IT!
LOOK AT 'EM--THE BATMAN AND ROBIN! SOME CATCH!
HURRY UP! WE'LL TAKE 'EM FOR A NEW KIND OF RIDE!
THEY'LL BE DEAD FISH IN NO TIME!
WELL, I GUESS I'LL MEET THE GANG AT THE HIDEOUT. NO ONE COULD SAVE BATMAN AND ROBIN NOW. NOT EVEN ME!
9
NOTHING IN MY UTILITY BELT IS SHARP ENOUGH TO CUT THIS WIRE! EXCEPT... MAYBE...
THERE'S NO WAY OF ESCAPE! WE'LL DROWN!
THE DROWNING BATMAN CLUTCHES AT A LAST STRAW!
ONLY ONE CHANCE... I'LL BURN A HOLE THROUGH THE NET!
WHAT IS THE BATMAN THINKING OF? BURN A HOLE WHILE UNDER WATER?... IS IT POSSIBLE?

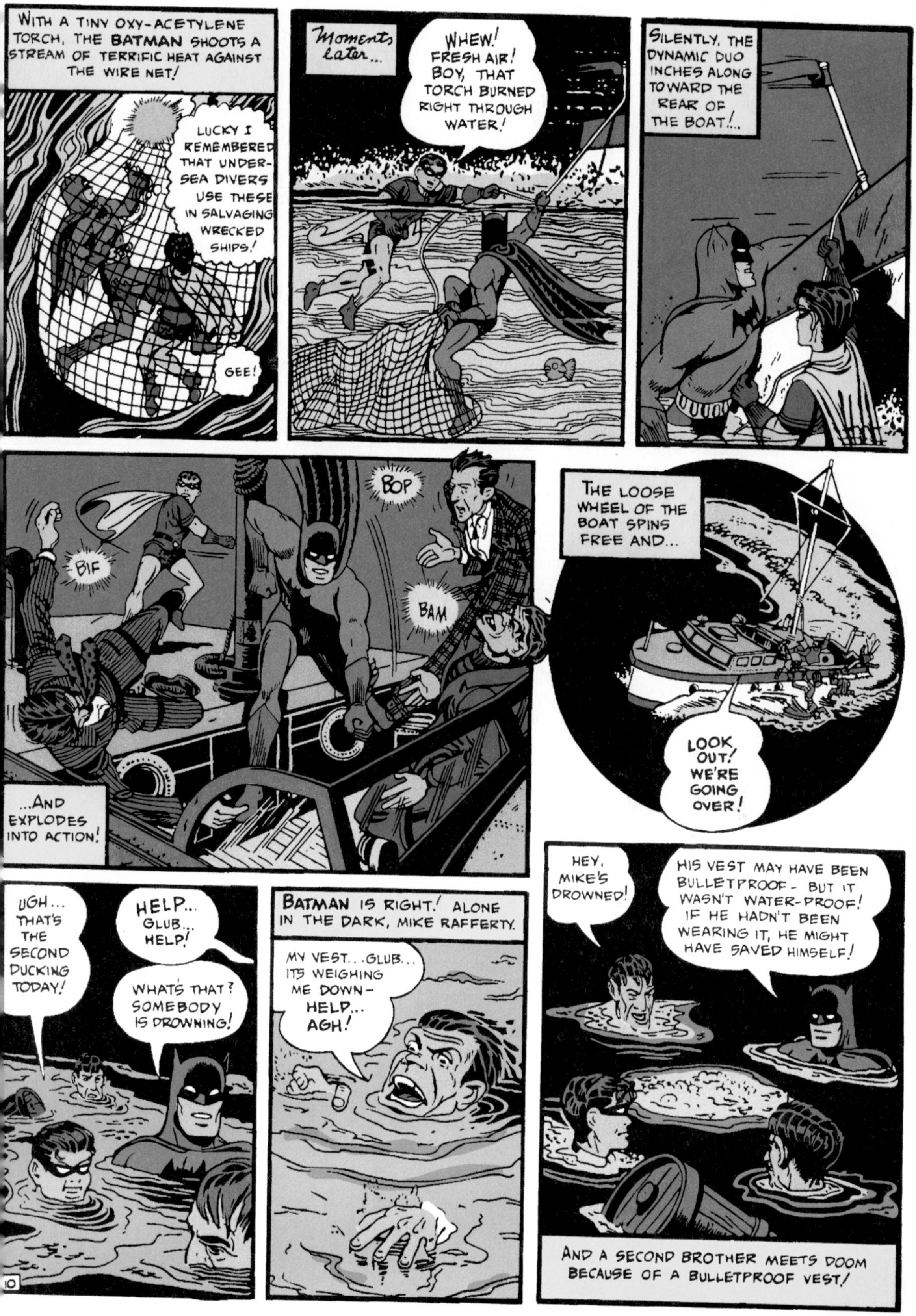

WITH A TINY OXY-ACETYLENE TORCH, THE BATMAN SHOOTS A STREAM OF TERRIFIC HEAT AGAINST THE WIRE NET!
LUCKY I REMEMBERED THAT UNDER-SEA DIVERS USE THESE IN SALVAGING WRECKED SHIPS!
GEE!
Moments later...
WHEW! FRESH AIR! BOY, THAT TORCH BURNED RIGHT THROUGH WATER!
SILENTLY, THE DYNAMIC DUO INCHES ALONG TOWARD THE REAR OF THE BOAT!...
BOP
BIF
BAM
...AND EXPLODES INTO ACTION!
THE LOOSE WHEEL OF THE BOAT SPINS FREE AND...
LOOK OUT! WE'RE GOING OVER!
UGH... THAT'S THE SECOND DUCKING TODAY!
HELP... GLUB... HELP!
WHAT'S THAT? SOMEBODY IS DROWNING!
BATMAN IS RIGHT! ALONE IN THE DARK, MIKE RAFFERTY.
MY VEST... GLUB... ITS WEIGHING ME DOWN- HELP... AGH!
HEY, MIKE'S DROWNED!
HIS VEST MAY HAVE BEEN BULLETPROOF - BUT IT WASN'T WATER-PROOF! IF HE HADN'T BEEN WEARING IT, HE MIGHT HAVE SAVED HIMSELF!
AND A SECOND BROTHER MEETS DOOM BECAUSE OF A BULLETPROOF VEST!
10

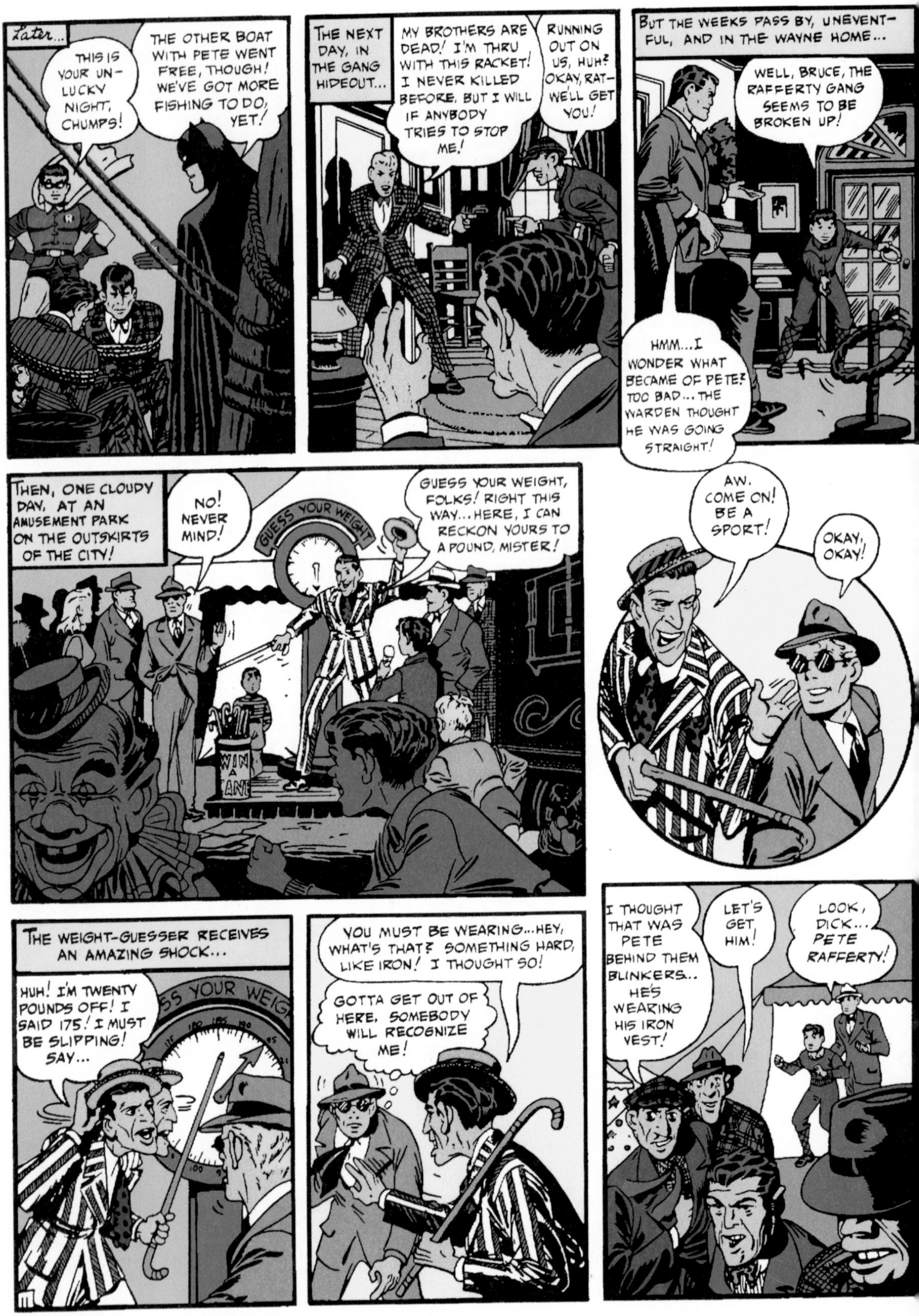
Later...
THIS IS YOUR UN-LUCKY NIGHT, CHUMPS!
THE OTHER BOAT WITH PETE WENT FREE, THOUGH! WE'VE GOT MORE FISHING TO DO, YET!
THE NEXT DAY, IN THE GANG HIDEOUT...
MY BROTHERS ARE DEAD! I'M THRU WITH THIS RACKET! I NEVER KILLED BEFORE, BUT I WILL IF ANYBODY TRIES TO STOP ME!
RUNNING OUT ON US, HUH? OKAY, RAT-WE'LL GET YOU!
BUT THE WEEKS PASS BY, UNEVENTFUL, AND IN THE WAYNE HOME...
WELL, BRUCE, THE RAFFERTY GANG SEEMS TO BE BROKEN UP!
HMM...I WONDER WHAT BECAME OF PETE? TOO BAD...THE WARDEN THOUGHT HE WAS GOING STRAIGHT!
THEN, ONE CLOUDY DAY, AT AN AMUSEMENT PARK ON THE OUTSKIRTS OF THE CITY!
NO! NEVER MIND!
GUESS YOUR WEIGHT, FOLKS! RIGHT THIS WAY...HERE, I CAN RECKON YOURS TO A POUND, MISTER!
GUESS YOUR WEIGHT
WIN A CANE
AW. COME ON! BE A SPORT!
OKAY, OKAY!
THE WEIGHT-GUESSER RECEIVES AN AMAZING SHOCK...
HUH! I'M TWENTY POUNDS OFF! I SAID 175! I MUST BE SLIPPING! SAY...
YOU MUST BE WEARING...HEY, WHAT'S THAT? SOMETHING HARD, LIKE IRON! I THOUGHT SO!
GOTTA GET OUT OF HERE. SOMEBODY WILL RECOGNIZE ME!
I THOUGHT THAT WAS PETE BEHIND THEM BLINKERS.. HE'S WEARING HIS IRON VEST!
LET'S GET HIM!
LOOK, DICK... PETE RAFFERTY!

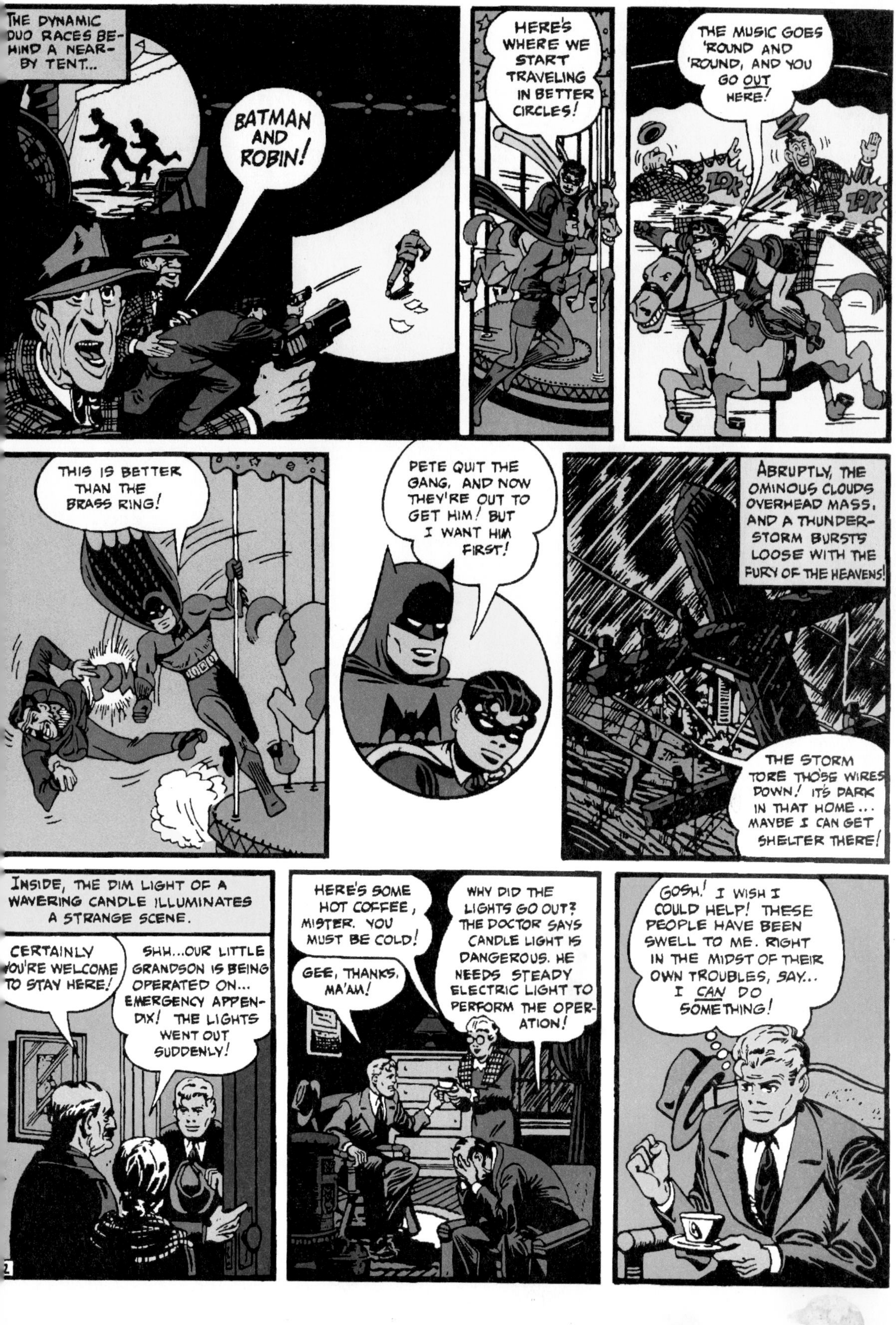
THE DYNAMIC DUO RACES BE-HIND A NEAR-BY TENT...
BATMAN AND ROBIN!
HERE'S WHERE WE START TRAVELING IN BETTER CIRCLES!
THE MUSIC GOES 'ROUND AND 'ROUND, AND YOU GO OUT HERE!
ZOK
ZOK
THIS IS BETTER THAN THE BRASS RING!
PETE QUIT THE GANG, AND NOW THEY'RE OUT TO GET HIM! BUT I WANT HIM FIRST!
ABRUPTLY, THE OMINOUS CLOUDS OVERHEAD MASS, AND A THUNDER-STORM BURSTS LOOSE WITH THE FURY OF THE HEAVENS!
THE STORM TORE THOSE WIRES DOWN! IT'S DARK IN THAT HOME... MAYBE I CAN GET SHELTER THERE!
INSIDE, THE DIM LIGHT OF A WAVERING CANDLE ILLUMINATES A STRANGE SCENE.
CERTAINLY YOU'RE WELCOME TO STAY HERE!
SHH...OUR LITTLE GRANDSON IS BEING OPERATED ON... EMERGENCY APPEN-DIX! THE LIGHTS WENT OUT SUDDENLY!
HERE'S SOME HOT COFFEE, MISTER. YOU MUST BE COLD!
GEE, THANKS, MA'AM!
WHY DID THE LIGHTS GO OUT? THE DOCTOR SAYS CANDLE LIGHT IS DANGEROUS. HE NEEDS STEADY ELECTRIC LIGHT TO PERFORM THE OPER-ATION!
GOSH! I WISH I COULD HELP! THESE PEOPLE HAVE BEEN SWELL TO ME. RIGHT IN THE MIDST OF THEIR OWN TROUBLES, SAY... I CAN DO SOMETHING!

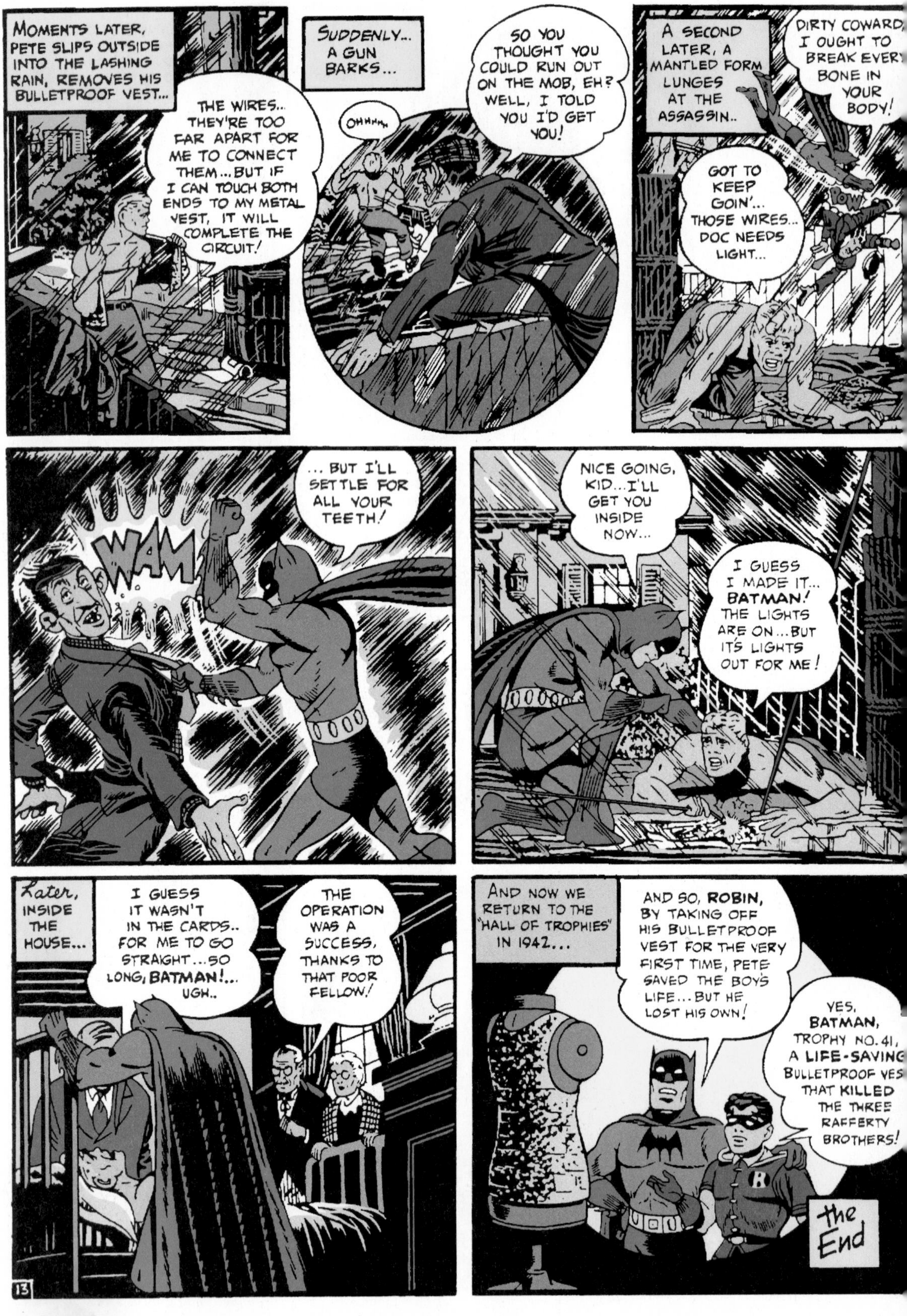

MOMENTS LATER, PETE SLIPS OUTSIDE INTO THE LASHING RAIN, REMOVES HIS BULLETPROOF VEST...
THE WIRES... THEY'RE TOO FAR APART FOR ME TO CONNECT THEM... BUT IF I CAN TOUCH BOTH ENDS TO MY METAL VEST, IT WILL COMPLETE THE CIRCUIT!
SUDDENLY... A GUN BARKS...
OHHHH...
SO YOU THOUGHT YOU COULD RUN OUT ON THE MOB, EH? WELL, I TOLD YOU I'D GET YOU!
A SECOND LATER, A MANTLED FORM LUNGES AT THE ASSASSIN..
DIRTY COWARD, I OUGHT TO BREAK EVERY BONE IN YOUR BODY!
POW
GOT TO KEEP GOIN'... THOSE WIRES... DOC NEEDS LIGHT...
WAM
... BUT I'LL SETTLE FOR ALL YOUR TEETH!
NICE GOING, KID... I'LL GET YOU INSIDE NOW...
I GUESS I MADE IT... BATMAN! THE LIGHTS ARE ON... BUT IT'S LIGHTS OUT FOR ME!
Later, INSIDE THE HOUSE...
I GUESS IT WASN'T IN THE CARDS.. FOR ME TO GO STRAIGHT... SO LONG, BATMAN!... UGH..
THE OPERATION WAS A SUCCESS, THANKS TO THAT POOR FELLOW!
13
AND NOW WE RETURN TO THE "HALL OF TROPHIES" IN 1942...
AND SO, ROBIN, BY TAKING OFF HIS BULLETPROOF VEST FOR THE VERY FIRST TIME, PETE SAVED THE BOY'S LIFE... BUT HE LOST HIS OWN!
YES, BATMAN, TROPHY NO. 41, A LIFE-SAVING BULLETPROOF VEST THAT KILLED THE THREE RAFFERTY BROTHERS!
the End

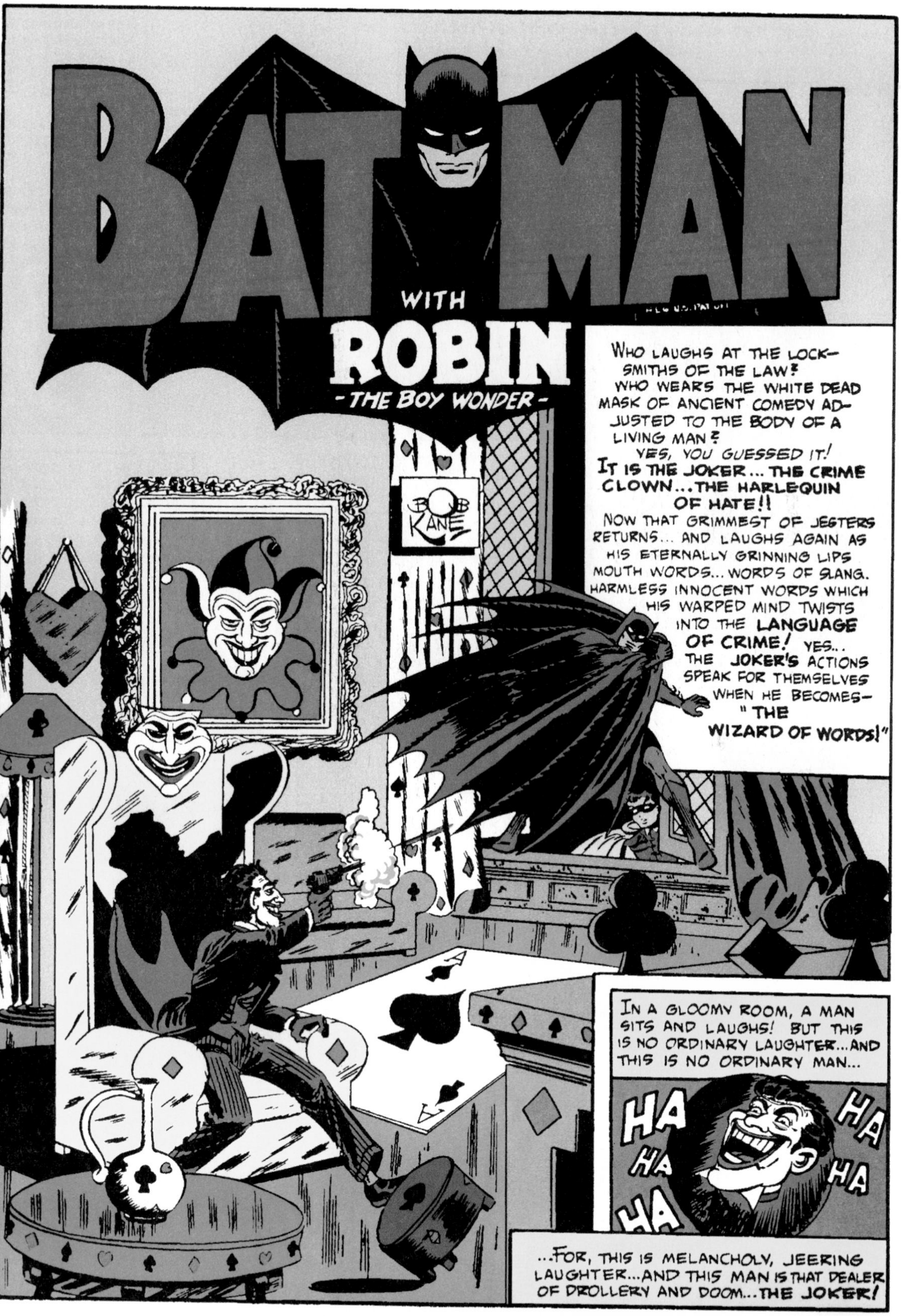
BATMAN
WITH ROBIN
-THE BOY WONDER-
BOB KANE
WHO LAUGHS AT THE LOCKSMITHS OF THE LAW? WHO WEARS THE WHITE DEAD MASK OF ANCIENT COMEDY ADJUSTED TO THE BODY OF A LIVING MAN? YES, YOU GUESSED IT! IT IS THE JOKER... THE CRIME CLOWN... THE HARLEQUIN OF HATE!! NOW THAT GRIMMEST OF JESTERS RETURNS... AND LAUGHS AGAIN AS HIS ETERNALLY GRINNING LIPS MOUTH WORDS... WORDS OF SLANG. HARMLESS INNOCENT WORDS WHICH HIS WARPED MIND TWISTS INTO THE LANGUAGE OF CRIME! YES... THE JOKER'S ACTIONS SPEAK FOR THEMSELVES WHEN HE BECOMES- "THE WIZARD OF WORDS!"
IN A GLOOMY ROOM, A MAN SITS AND LAUGHS! BUT THIS IS NO ORDINARY LAUGHTER... AND THIS IS NO ORDINARY MAN...
HA HA HA HA HA HA
...FOR, THIS IS MELANCHOLY, JEERING LAUGHTER... AND THIS MAN IS THAT DEALER OF DROLLERY AND DOOM... THE JOKER!

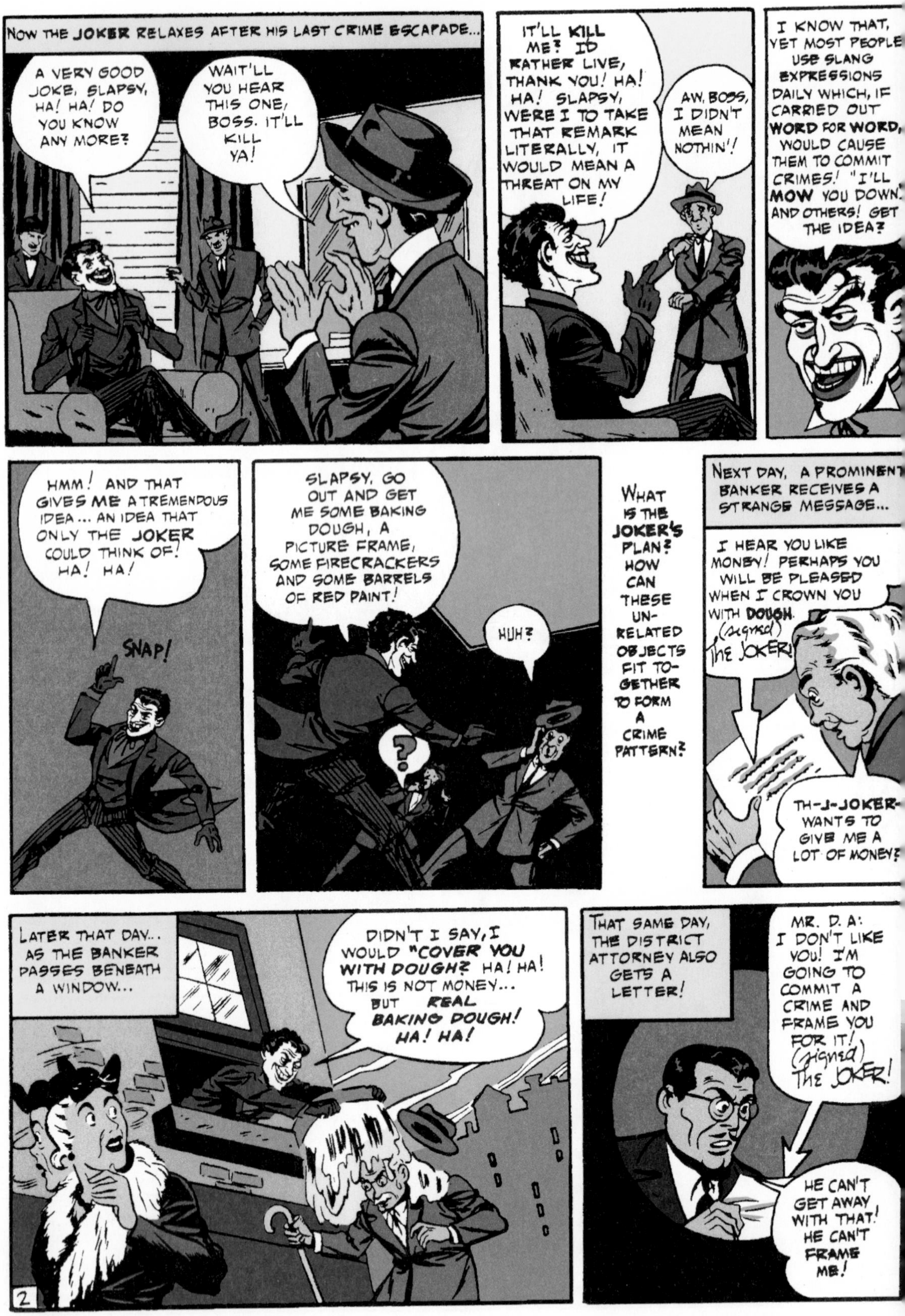
NOW THE JOKER RELAXES AFTER HIS LAST CRIME ESCAPADE...
A VERY GOOD JOKE, SLAPSY, HA! HA! DO YOU KNOW ANY MORE?
WAIT'LL YOU HEAR THIS ONE, BOSS. IT'LL KILL YA!
IT'LL KILL ME? ID RATHER LIVE, THANK YOU! HA! HA! SLAPSY, WERE I TO TAKE THAT REMARK LITERALLY, IT WOULD MEAN A THREAT ON MY LIFE!
AW, BOSS, I DIDN'T MEAN NOTHIN'!
I KNOW THAT, YET MOST PEOPLE USE SLANG EXPRESSIONS DAILY WHICH, IF CARRIED OUT WORD FOR WORD, WOULD CAUSE THEM TO COMMIT CRIMES! "I'LL MOW YOU DOWN" AND OTHERS! GET THE IDEA?
HMM! AND THAT GIVES ME A TREMENDOUS IDEA... AN IDEA THAT ONLY THE JOKER COULD THINK OF! HA! HA!
SNAP!
SLAPSY, GO OUT AND GET ME SOME BAKING DOUGH, A PICTURE FRAME, SOME FIRECRACKERS AND SOME BARRELS OF RED PAINT!
HUH?
WHAT IS THE JOKER'S PLAN? HOW CAN THESE UN-RELATED OBJECTS FIT TO-GETHER TO FORM A CRIME PATTERN?
NEXT DAY, A PROMINENT BANKER RECEIVES A STRANGE MESSAGE...
I HEAR YOU LIKE MONEY! PERHAPS YOU WILL BE PLEASED WHEN I CROWN YOU WITH DOUGH. (signed) THE JOKER!
TH-J-JOKER WANTS TO GIVE ME A LOT OF MONEY?
LATER THAT DAY... AS THE BANKER PASSES BENEATH A WINDOW...
DIDN'T I SAY, I WOULD "COVER YOU WITH DOUGH"? HA! HA! THIS IS NOT MONEY... BUT REAL BAKING DOUGH! HA! HA!
THAT SAME DAY, THE DISTRICT ATTORNEY ALSO GETS A LETTER!
MR. D. A: I DON'T LIKE YOU! I'M GOING TO COMMIT A CRIME AND FRAME YOU FOR IT! (signed) THE JOKER!
HE CAN'T GET AWAY WITH THAT! HE CAN'T FRAME ME!
2

BUT THE D.A. IS WRONG... ALL THE WAY! FOR, THE NEXT DAY...

WH... WHAT'S HAPPENED?

THE JOKER FRAMED ME... BUT NOT IN THE WAY I EXPECTED!

THEN, THE MAYOR RECEIVES A MESSAGE!

"You'll see fireworks in your office when I start with you, The JOKER"

OH-H-H... FIREWORKS! THAT MEANS HE'S GOING TO MAKE SOME SORT OF TROUBLE FOR ME!

BUT WHEN THE MAYOR ENTERS HIS OFFICE THE NEXT DAY, HE IS GREETED BY...

FIREWORKS! THE JOKER ACTUALLY DID MAKE FIREWORKS IN MY OFFICE!

THE PLAGUE OF MAD PRANKS MAKES HEAD-LINE NEWS, AND THE PUBLIC WONDERS... AS DO BRUCE WAYNE AND DICK GRAYSON.

FIREWORKS! PICTURE FRAMES! THE JOKER'S GONE CRAZY AT LAST!

GOLLY, BRUCE, IT CERTAINLY LOOKS LIKE IT!

DON'T KID YOUR-SELF! ANY TIME THAT BABY STARTS CLOWNING... HE ENDS UP WITH A CRIME!

IS BRUCE RIGHT? IS THERE A CALCULAT-ING THREAD OF EVIL WINDING THROUGH THIS PATTERN OF MAD MIRTH? LET'S SEE...

THE NEXT DAY... COMMISSIONER GORDON GETS A NOTE.

SO... HE EXPECTS TO HAVE A RIP-ROARING TIME MAKING WHOOPEE, EH? I'LL HAVE THE BOYS PATROL THE NIGHT CLUB!

Gordon: Your police force had better watch out, for my men and I are going to PAINT THE TOWN RED! Sincerely, The JOKER

SOME TIME LATER, A POLICE-MAN STARES IN WIDE-EYED ASTONISHMENT...

WHA... WHAT'S GOING ON AROUND HERE?

NOTHIN' MUCH! I'M JUST PAINTIN' THE SIDEWALK RED! HA!

AND SO IT GOES, AS AT VARIOUS SPOTS IN THE CITY FUGITIVE HOODLUMS LEAVE BEHIND A WAKE OF RED PAINT...

HEY, YOU! COME BACK HERE!

HAW! HAW!

WHILE HIGH IN THE SKY, THE JOKER RELEASES A FLOOD OF SCARLET OVER THE ROOF-TOPS...

HA... HA! I WARNED THEM I WOULD PAINT THE TOWN RED... AND I AM! HA... HA!

BANK

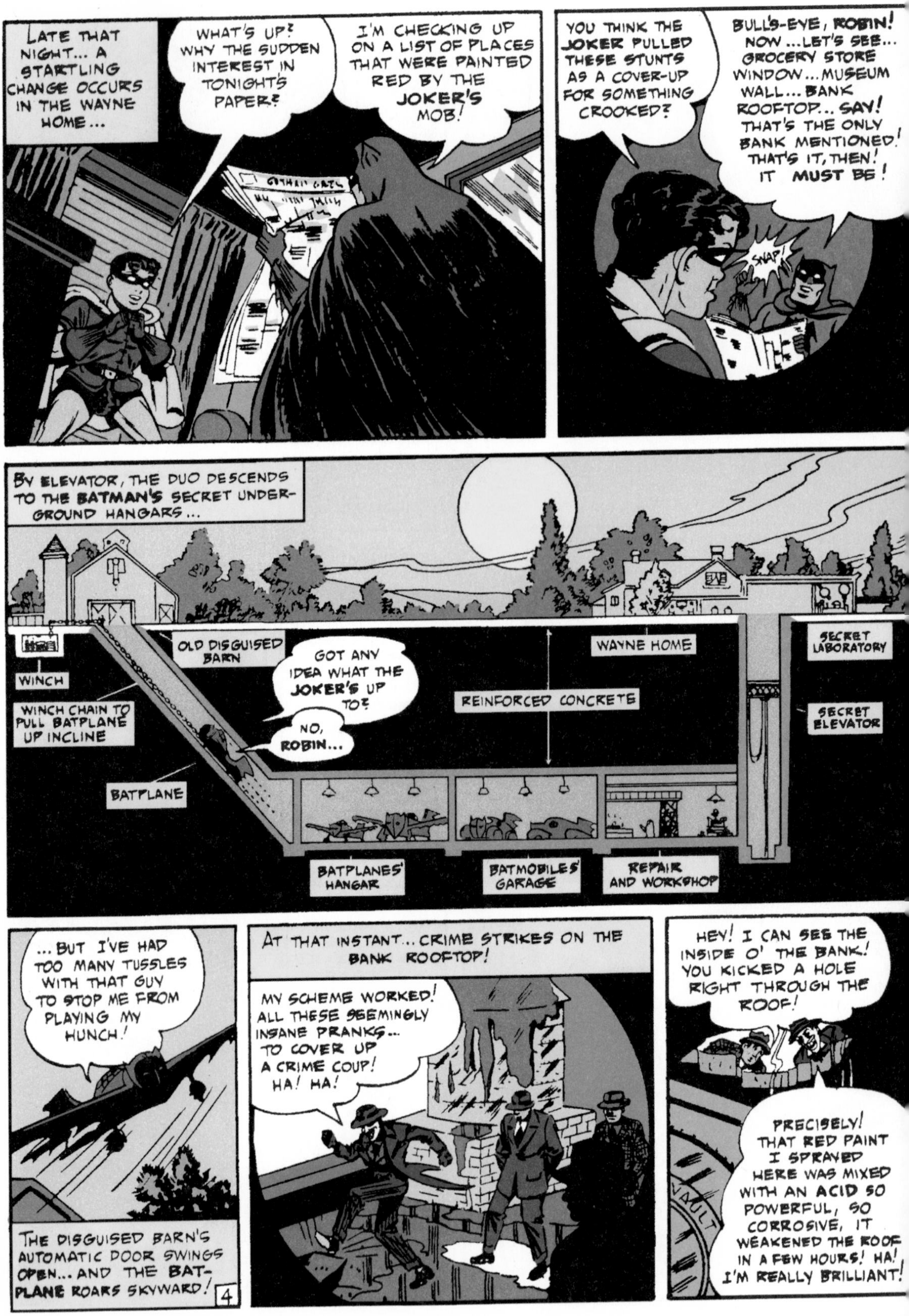

LATE THAT NIGHT... A STARTLING CHANGE OCCURS IN THE WAYNE HOME...
WHAT'S UP? WHY THE SUDDEN INTEREST IN TONIGHT'S PAPER?
I'M CHECKING UP ON A LIST OF PLACES THAT WERE PAINTED RED BY THE JOKER'S MOB!
YOU THINK THE JOKER PULLED THESE STUNTS AS A COVER-UP FOR SOMETHING CROOKED?
BULL'S-EYE, ROBIN! NOW ...LET'S SEE... GROCERY STORE WINDOW... MUSEUM WALL... BANK ROOFTOP... SAY! THAT'S THE ONLY BANK MENTIONED! THAT'S IT, THEN! IT MUST BE!
SNAP!
BY ELEVATOR, THE DUO DESCENDS TO THE BATMAN'S SECRET UNDER-GROUND HANGARS...
OLD DISGUISED BARN
WAYNE HOME
SECRET LABORATORY
WINCH
GOT ANY IDEA WHAT THE JOKER'S UP TO?
NO, ROBIN...
WINCH CHAIN TO PULL BATPLANE UP INCLINE
REINFORCED CONCRETE
SECRET ELEVATOR
BATPLANE
BATPLANES' HANGAR
BATMOBILES' GARAGE
REPAIR AND WORKSHOP
...BUT I'VE HAD TOO MANY TUSSLES WITH THAT GUY TO STOP ME FROM PLAYING MY HUNCH!
THE DISGUISED BARN'S AUTOMATIC DOOR SWINGS OPEN... AND THE BAT-PLANE ROARS SKYWARD!
4
AT THAT INSTANT... CRIME STRIKES ON THE BANK ROOFTOP!
MY SCHEME WORKED! ALL THESE SEEMINGLY INSANE PRANKS... TO COVER UP A CRIME COUP! HA! HA!
HEY! I CAN SEE THE INSIDE O' THE BANK! YOU KICKED A HOLE RIGHT THROUGH THE ROOF!
PRECISELY! THAT RED PAINT I SPRAYED HERE WAS MIXED WITH AN ACID SO POWERFUL, SO CORROSIVE, IT WEAKENED THE ROOF IN A FEW HOURS! HA! I'M REALLY BRILLIANT!
VAULT

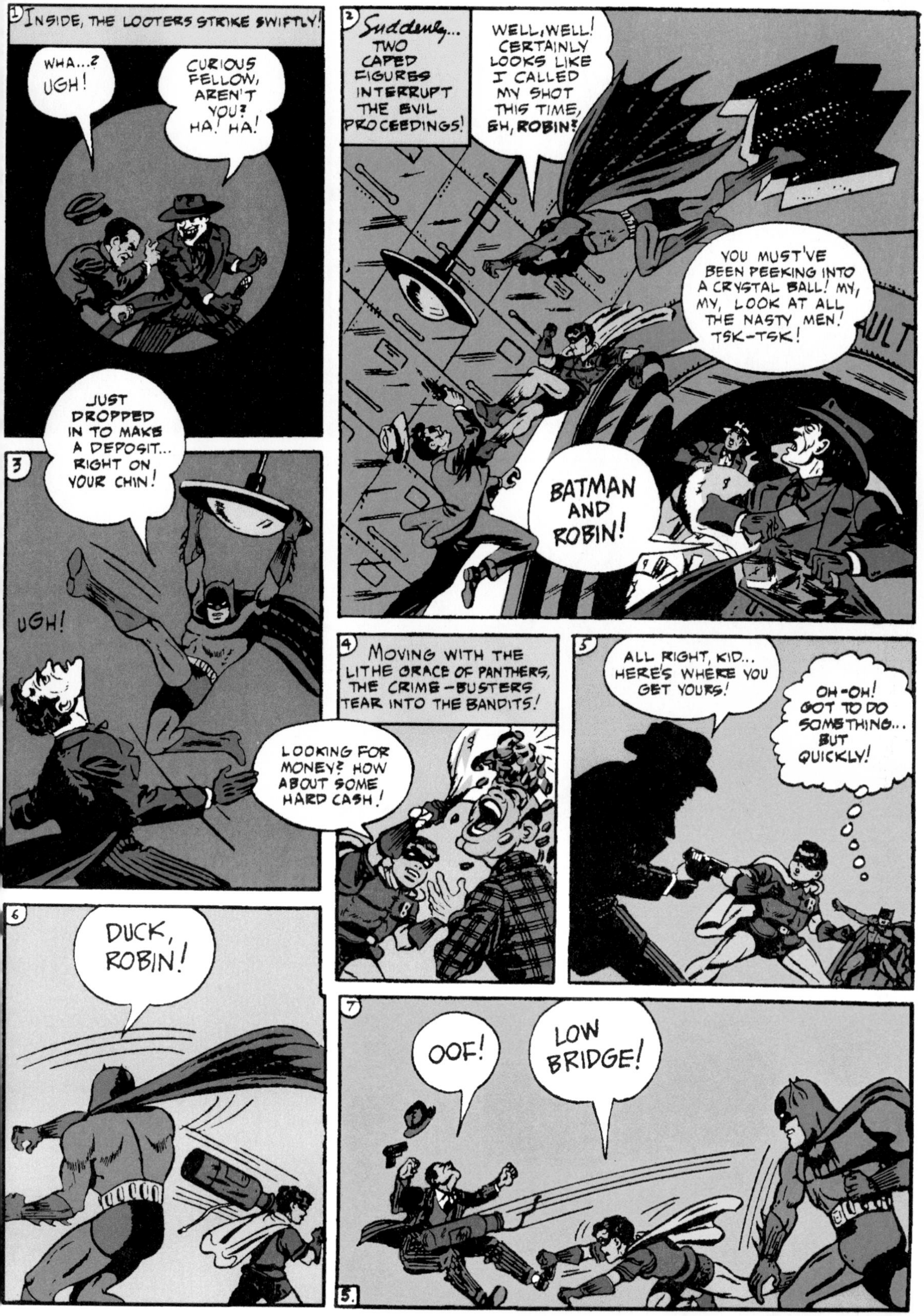
1
INSIDE, THE LOOTERS STRIKE SWIFTLY!
WHA...? UGH!
CURIOUS FELLOW, AREN'T YOU? HA! HA!
2
Suddenly... TWO CAPED FIGURES INTERRUPT THE EVIL PROCEEDINGS!
WELL, WELL! CERTAINLY LOOKS LIKE I CALLED MY SHOT THIS TIME, EH, ROBIN?
YOU MUST'VE BEEN PEEKING INTO A CRYSTAL BALL! MY, MY, LOOK AT ALL THE NASTY MEN! TSK-TSK!
BATMAN AND ROBIN!
3
JUST DROPPED IN TO MAKE A DEPOSIT... RIGHT ON YOUR CHIN!
UGH!
4
MOVING WITH THE LITHE GRACE OF PANTHERS, THE CRIME-BUSTERS TEAR INTO THE BANDITS!
LOOKING FOR MONEY? HOW ABOUT SOME HARD CASH!
5
ALL RIGHT, KID... HERE'S WHERE YOU GET YOURS!
OH-OH! GOT TO DO SOMETHING... BUT QUICKLY!
6
DUCK, ROBIN!
7
OOF!
LOW BRIDGE!
5.

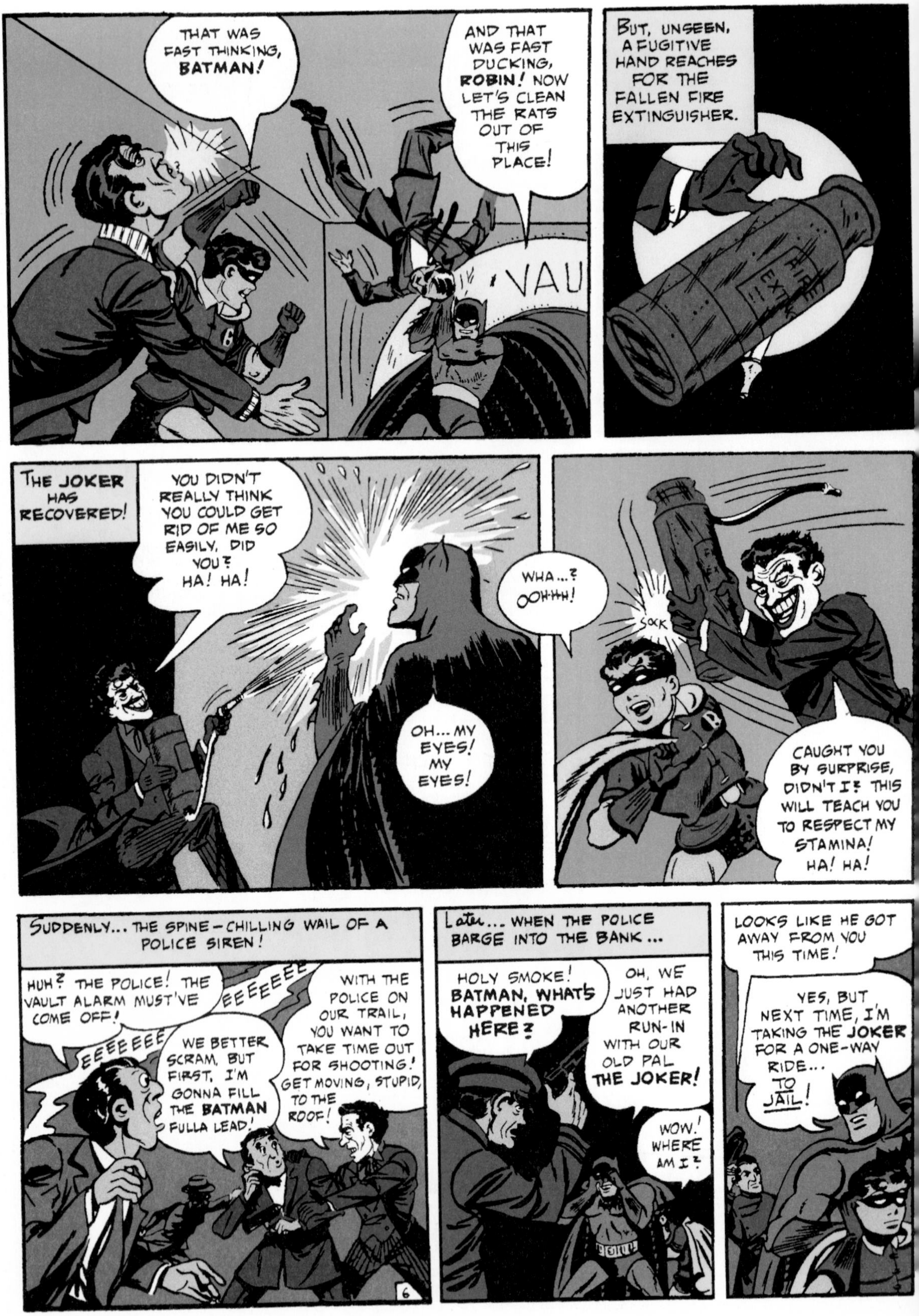
THAT WAS FAST THINKING, BATMAN!
AND THAT WAS FAST DUCKING, ROBIN! NOW LET'S CLEAN THE RATS OUT OF THIS PLACE!
VAU
BUT, UNSEEN, A FUGITIVE HAND REACHES FOR THE FALLEN FIRE EXTINGUISHER.
THE JOKER HAS RECOVERED!
YOU DIDN'T REALLY THINK YOU COULD GET RID OF ME SO EASILY, DID YOU? HA! HA!
OH... MY EYES! MY EYES!
WHA...? OOHHHH!
SOCK
CAUGHT YOU BY SURPRISE, DIDN'T I? THIS WILL TEACH YOU TO RESPECT MY STAMINA! HA! HA!
SUDDENLY... THE SPINE-CHILLING WAIL OF A POLICE SIREN!
HUH? THE POLICE! THE VAULT ALARM MUST'VE COME OFF!
EEEEEEE
EEEEEEE
WE BETTER SCRAM, BUT FIRST, I'M GONNA FILL THE BATMAN FULLA LEAD!
WITH THE POLICE ON OUR TRAIL, YOU WANT TO TAKE TIME OUT FOR SHOOTING! GET MOVING, STUPID, TO THE ROOF!
6
LATER... WHEN THE POLICE BARGE INTO THE BANK...
HOLY SMOKE! BATMAN, WHAT'S HAPPENED HERE?
OH, WE JUST HAD ANOTHER RUN-IN WITH OUR OLD PAL THE JOKER!
WOW! WHERE AM I?
LOOKS LIKE HE GOT AWAY FROM YOU THIS TIME!
YES, BUT NEXT TIME, I'M TAKING THE JOKER FOR A ONE-WAY RIDE... TO JAIL!

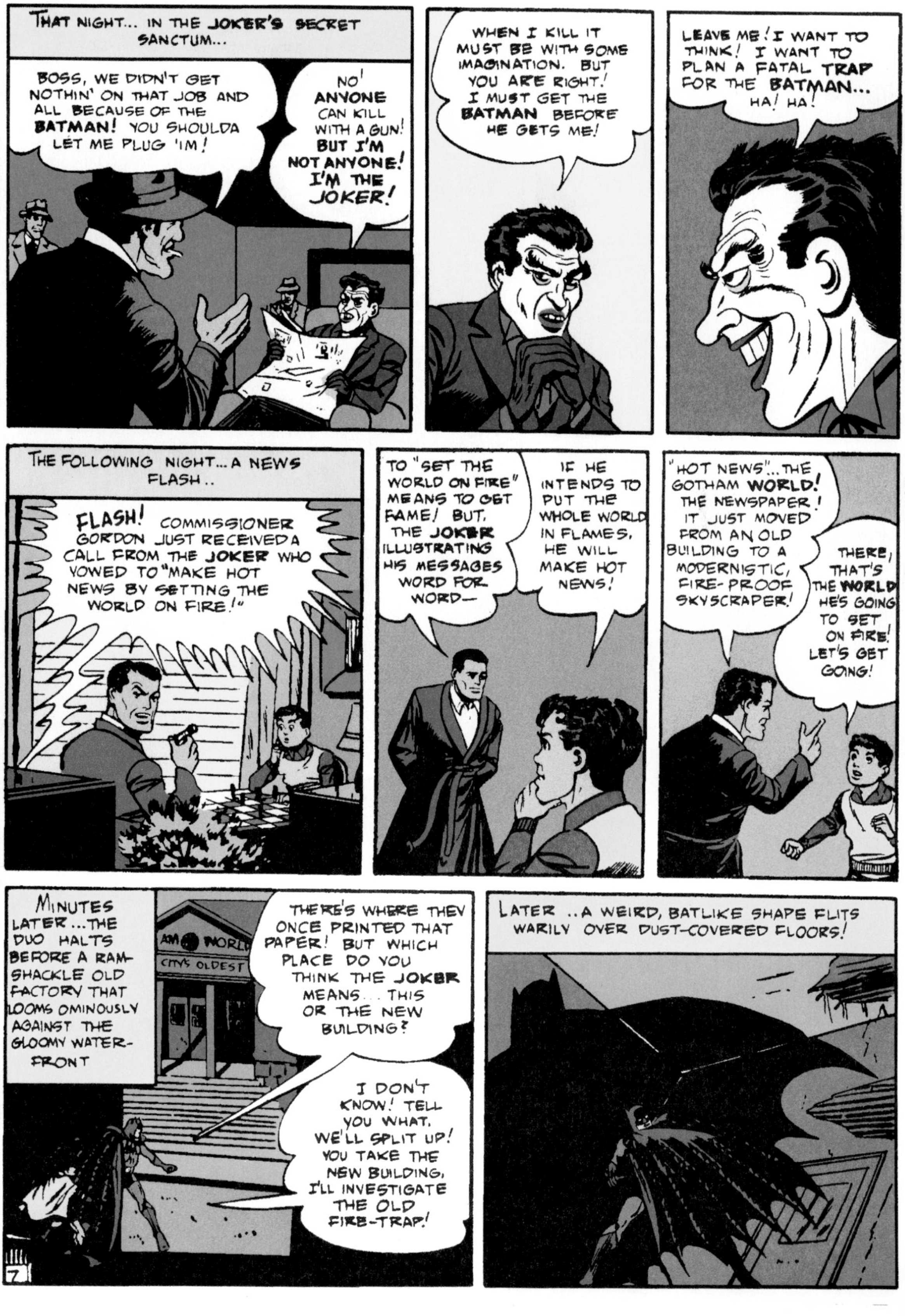
THAT NIGHT... IN THE JOKER'S SECRET SANCTUM...
BOSS, WE DIDN'T GET NOTHIN' ON THAT JOB AND ALL BECAUSE OF THE BATMAN! YOU SHOULDA LET ME PLUG 'IM!
NO! ANYONE CAN KILL WITH A GUN! BUT I'M NOT ANYONE! I'M THE JOKER!
WHEN I KILL IT MUST BE WITH SOME IMAGINATION. BUT YOU ARE RIGHT! I MUST GET THE BATMAN BEFORE HE GETS ME!
LEAVE ME! I WANT TO THINK! I WANT TO PLAN A FATAL TRAP FOR THE BATMAN... HA! HA!
THE FOLLOWING NIGHT... A NEWS FLASH..
FLASH! COMMISSIONER GORDON JUST RECEIVED A CALL FROM THE JOKER WHO VOWED TO "MAKE HOT NEWS BY SETTING THE WORLD ON FIRE!"
TO "SET THE WORLD ON FIRE" MEANS TO GET FAME! BUT, THE JOKER ILLUSTRATING HIS MESSAGES WORD FOR WORD—
IF HE INTENDS TO PUT THE WHOLE WORLD IN FLAMES, HE WILL MAKE HOT NEWS!
"HOT NEWS"... THE GOTHAM WORLD! THE NEWSPAPER! IT JUST MOVED FROM AN OLD BUILDING TO A MODERNISTIC, FIRE-PROOF SKYSCRAPER!
THERE, THAT'S THE WORLD HE'S GOING TO SET ON FIRE! LET'S GET GOING!
MINUTES LATER... THE DUO HALTS BEFORE A RAM-SHACKLE OLD FACTORY THAT LOOMS OMINOUSLY AGAINST THE GLOOMY WATER-FRONT
CITY'S OLDEST
THERE'S WHERE THEY ONCE PRINTED THAT PAPER! BUT WHICH PLACE DO YOU THINK THE JOKER MEANS... THIS OR THE NEW BUILDING?
I DON'T KNOW! TELL YOU WHAT. WE'LL SPLIT UP! YOU TAKE THE NEW BUILDING, I'LL INVESTIGATE THE OLD FIRE-TRAP!
7
LATER .. A WEIRD, BATLIKE SHAPE FLITS WARILY OVER DUST-COVERED FLOORS!

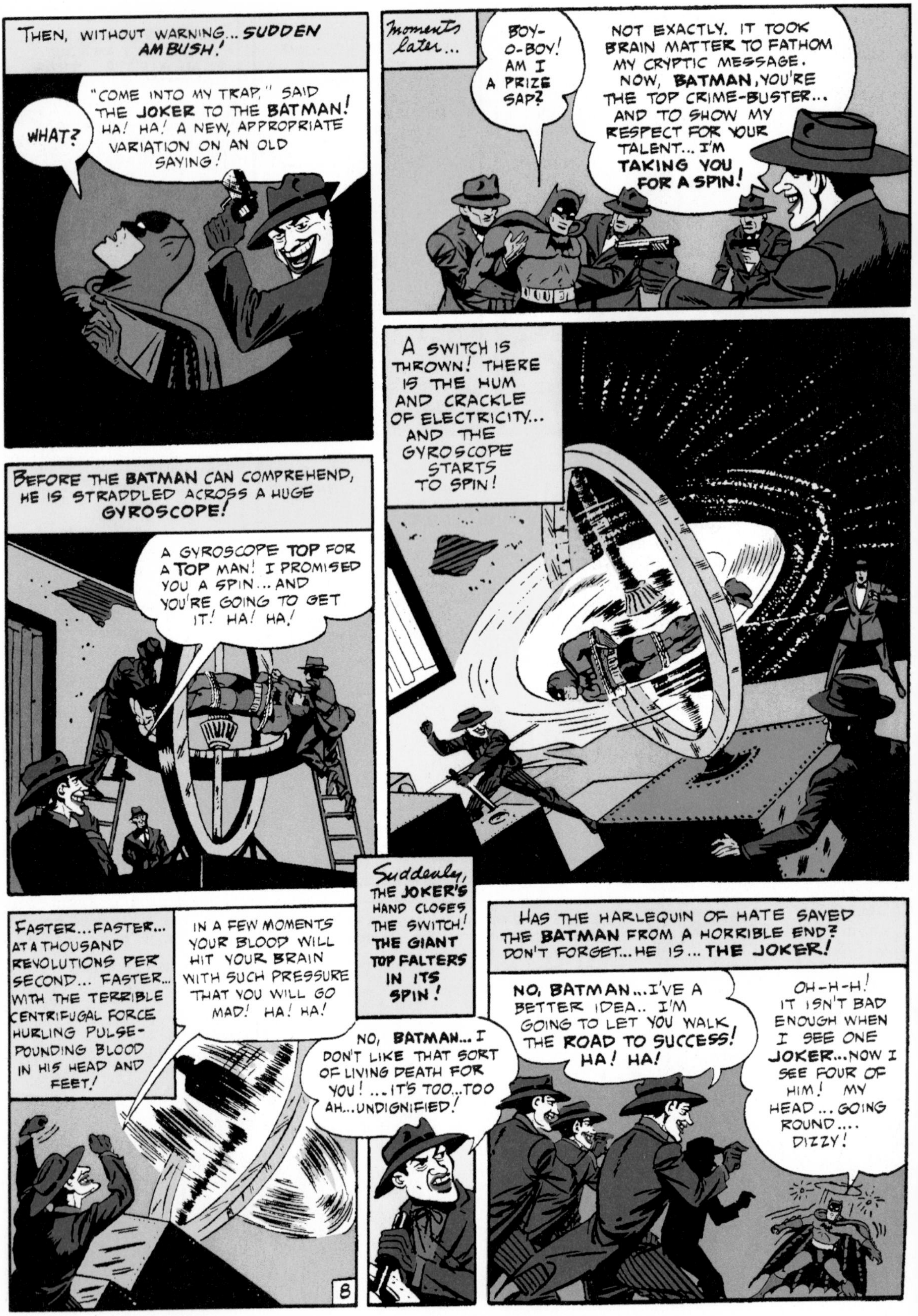

THEN, WITHOUT WARNING... SUDDEN AMBUSH!
WHAT?
"COME INTO MY TRAP," SAID THE JOKER TO THE BATMAN! HA! HA! A NEW, APPROPRIATE VARIATION ON AN OLD SAYING!
Moments later...
BOY-O-BOY! AM I A PRIZE SAP?
NOT EXACTLY. IT TOOK BRAIN MATTER TO FATHOM MY CRYPTIC MESSAGE. NOW, BATMAN, YOU'RE THE TOP CRIME-BUSTER... AND TO SHOW MY RESPECT FOR YOUR TALENT... I'M TAKING YOU FOR A SPIN!
BEFORE THE BATMAN CAN COMPREHEND, HE IS STRADDLED ACROSS A HUGE GYROSCOPE!
A GYROSCOPE TOP FOR A TOP MAN! I PROMISED YOU A SPIN... AND YOU'RE GOING TO GET IT! HA! HA!
A SWITCH IS THROWN! THERE IS THE HUM AND CRACKLE OF ELECTRICITY... AND THE GYROSCOPE STARTS TO SPIN!
FASTER... FASTER... AT A THOUSAND REVOLUTIONS PER SECOND... FASTER... WITH THE TERRIBLE CENTRIFUGAL FORCE HURLING PULSE-POUNDING BLOOD IN HIS HEAD AND FEET!
IN A FEW MOMENTS YOUR BLOOD WILL HIT YOUR BRAIN WITH SUCH PRESSURE THAT YOU WILL GO MAD! HA! HA!
8
Suddenly, THE JOKER'S HAND CLOSES THE SWITCH! THE GIANT TOP FALTERS IN ITS SPIN!
NO, BATMAN... I DON'T LIKE THAT SORT OF LIVING DEATH FOR YOU! ...IT'S TOO...TOO AH...UNDIGNIFIED!
HAS THE HARLEQUIN OF HATE SAVED THE BATMAN FROM A HORRIBLE END? DON'T FORGET... HE IS... THE JOKER!
NO, BATMAN...I'VE A BETTER IDEA.. I'M GOING TO LET YOU WALK THE ROAD TO SUCCESS! HA! HA!
OH-H-H! IT ISN'T BAD ENOUGH WHEN I SEE ONE JOKER...NOW I SEE FOUR OF HIM! MY HEAD... GOING ROUND.... DIZZY!

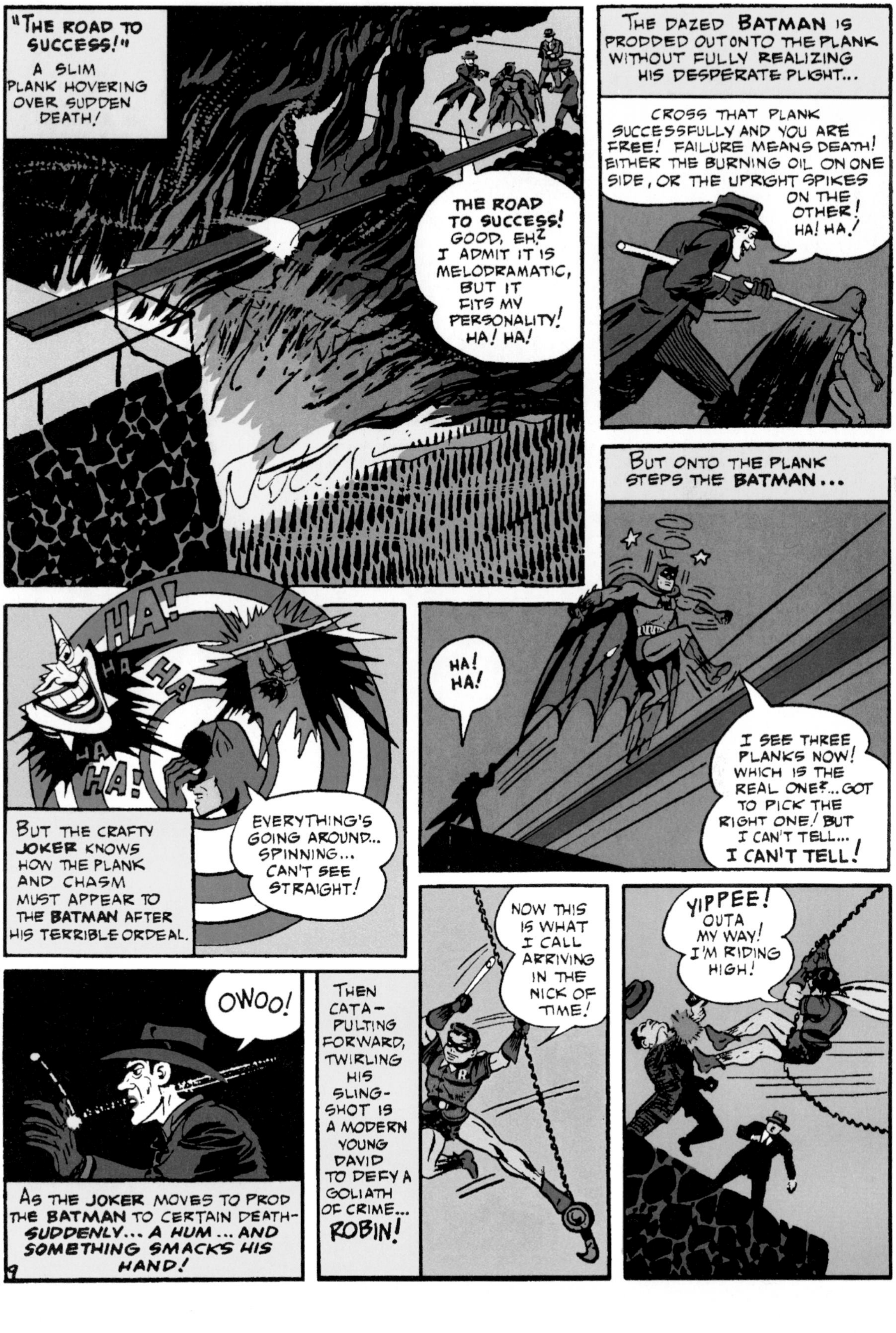
"THE ROAD TO SUCCESS!" A SLIM PLANK HOVERING OVER SUDDEN DEATH!
THE ROAD TO SUCCESS! GOOD, EH? I ADMIT IT IS MELODRAMATIC, BUT IT FITS MY PERSONALITY! HA! HA!
THE DAZED BATMAN IS PRODDED OUT ONTO THE PLANK WITHOUT FULLY REALIZING HIS DESPERATE PLIGHT...
CROSS THAT PLANK SUCCESSFULLY AND YOU ARE FREE! FAILURE MEANS DEATH! EITHER THE BURNING OIL ON ONE SIDE, OR THE UPRIGHT SPIKES ON THE OTHER! HA! HA!
HA! HA HA HA HA!
BUT THE CRAFTY JOKER KNOWS HOW THE PLANK AND CHASM MUST APPEAR TO THE BATMAN AFTER HIS TERRIBLE ORDEAL.
EVERYTHING'S GOING AROUND... SPINNING... CAN'T SEE STRAIGHT!
BUT ONTO THE PLANK STEPS THE BATMAN...
HA! HA!
I SEE THREE PLANKS NOW! WHICH IS THE REAL ONE?...GOT TO PICK THE RIGHT ONE! BUT I CAN'T TELL... I CAN'T TELL!
OWOO!
AS THE JOKER MOVES TO PROD THE BATMAN TO CERTAIN DEATH- SUDDENLY... A HUM... AND SOMETHING SMACKS HIS HAND!
9
THEN CATA-PULTING FORWARD, TWIRLING HIS SLING-SHOT IS A MODERN YOUNG DAVID TO DEFY A GOLIATH OF CRIME... ROBIN!
NOW THIS IS WHAT I CALL ARRIVING IN THE NICK OF TIME!
YIPPEE! OUTA MY WAY! I'M RIDING HIGH!

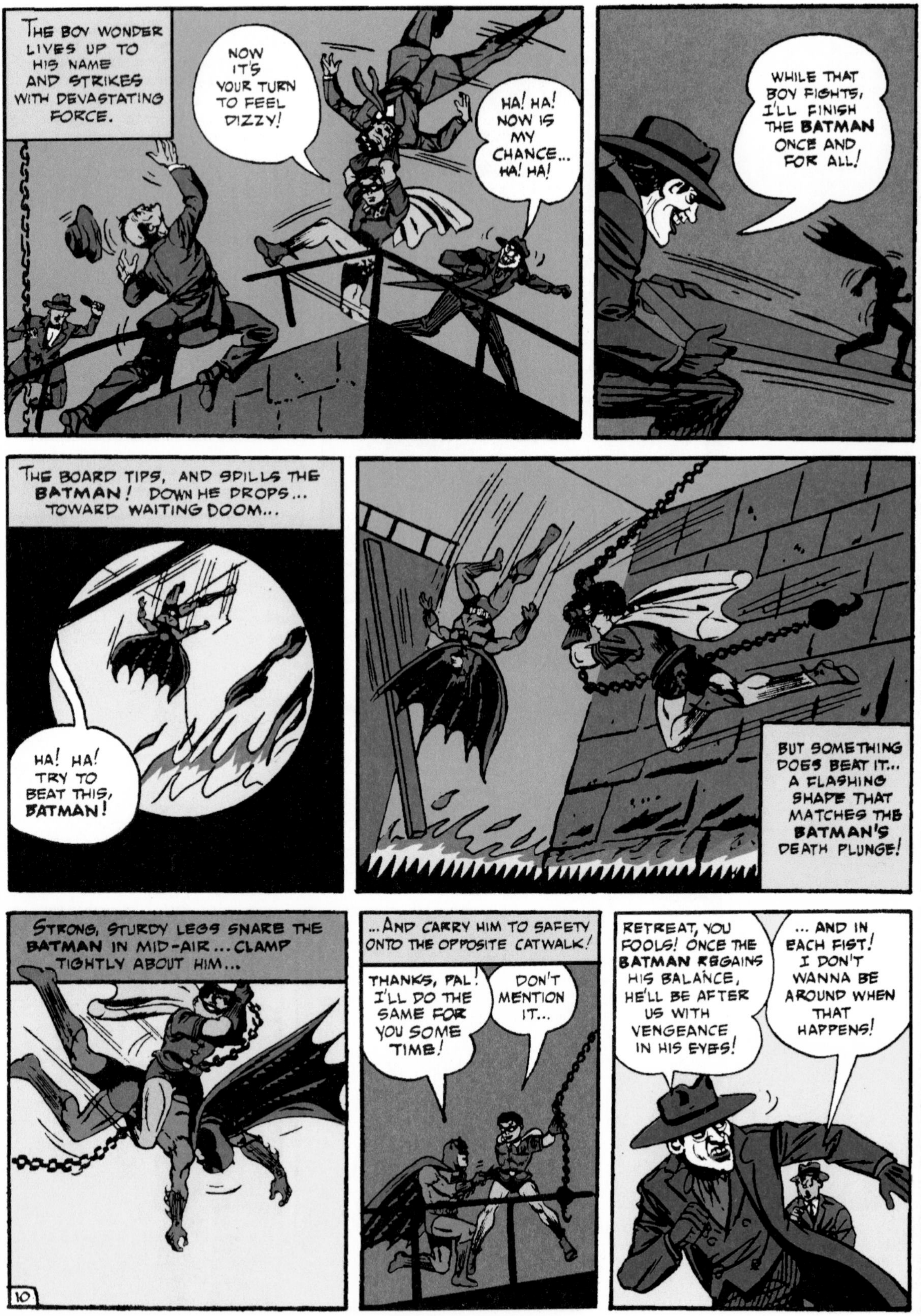

THE BOY WONDER LIVES UP TO HIS NAME AND STRIKES WITH DEVASTATING FORCE.
NOW IT'S YOUR TURN TO FEEL DIZZY!
HA! HA! NOW IS MY CHANCE... HA! HA!
WHILE THAT BOY FIGHTS, I'LL FINISH THE BATMAN ONCE AND FOR ALL!
THE BOARD TIPS, AND SPILLS THE BATMAN! DOWN HE DROPS... TOWARD WAITING DOOM...
HA! HA! TRY TO BEAT THIS, BATMAN!
BUT SOMETHING DOES BEAT IT... A FLASHING SHAPE THAT MATCHES THE BATMAN'S DEATH PLUNGE!
STRONG, STURDY LEGS SNARE THE BATMAN IN MID-AIR... CLAMP TIGHTLY ABOUT HIM...
10
...AND CARRY HIM TO SAFETY ONTO THE OPPOSITE CATWALK!
THANKS, PAL! I'LL DO THE SAME FOR YOU SOME TIME!
DON'T MENTION IT...
RETREAT, YOU FOOLS! ONCE THE BATMAN REGAINS HIS BALANCE, HE'LL BE AFTER US WITH VENGEANCE IN HIS EYES!
... AND IN EACH FIST! I DON'T WANNA BE AROUND WHEN THAT HAPPENS!

YOU HURT?

ONLY 'CAUSE THE JOKER GOT AWAY! I'D GIVE A PRETTY PENNY TO KNOW WHAT HE INTENDS TO DO NEXT!

THE NEXT DAY... AN ASSAY OFFICE IN THE FINANCIAL DISTRICT...

THE PAPERS HAVE THE STORY OF OUR CLIENT DISCOVERING GOLD! I'M WORRIED. SOMEONE MAY ATTEMPT TO STEAL THE SAMPLES HE'S BRINGING ME!

DON'T WORRY! NOBODY KNOWS WHAT HE LOOKS LIKE... AND HE'LL BE CARRYING THE GOLD IN A PLAIN SATCHEL!

BUT IN THE NEXT OFFICE... AN EAVESDROPPER ON A DICTAPHONE...THE JOKER!

HMM! I'D HAVE A HARD JOB PICKING THE RIGHT SATCHEL OUT OF ALL THOSE ON A TRAIN! HMM! UNLESS... YES... I'VE ANOTHER OF MY USUALLY BRILLIANT IDEAS!

THE NEXT DAY... A MESSAGE FROM THE CRIME-CLOWN!

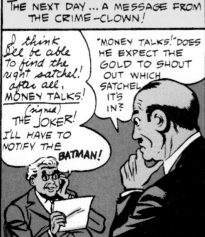

I think I'll be able to find the right satchel! after all, MONEY TALKS! (signed) THE JOKER! I'LL HAVE TO NOTIFY THE BATMAN!

"MONEY TALKS!" DOES HE EXPECT THE GOLD TO SHOUT OUT WHICH SATCHEL IT'S IN?

AS A TRAIN STOPS OUTSIDE GOTHAM CITY, A MAN BOARDS IT AND, HOLDING UP A STRANGE APPARATUS, STROLLS THROUGH THE CARS!

Suddenly, THE INSTRUMENT EMITS A SHRILL WHISTLE!

EEEEEEEE

MAKEUP IS QUICKLY REMOVED... AND THE STROLLER IS REVEALED. ... THE GRIM JESTER!

FOOLS! AS SOON AS THIS INSTRUMENT PASSED THE GOLD IN THAT SATCHEL, IT CAUSED A CHEMICAL FREQUENCY AND SIGNALED A LOUD WHISTLE! MONEY DOES TALK AFTER ALL, EH?

BEFORE THE PASSENGERS CAN RECOVER THEIR WITS, THE JOKER RACES TO THE REAR CAR...WHERE...

HAH! CLEVER OF ME TO HAVE ATTACHED THIS HAND CAR. NOW THE PERFECT GETAWAY! HA! HA!

11

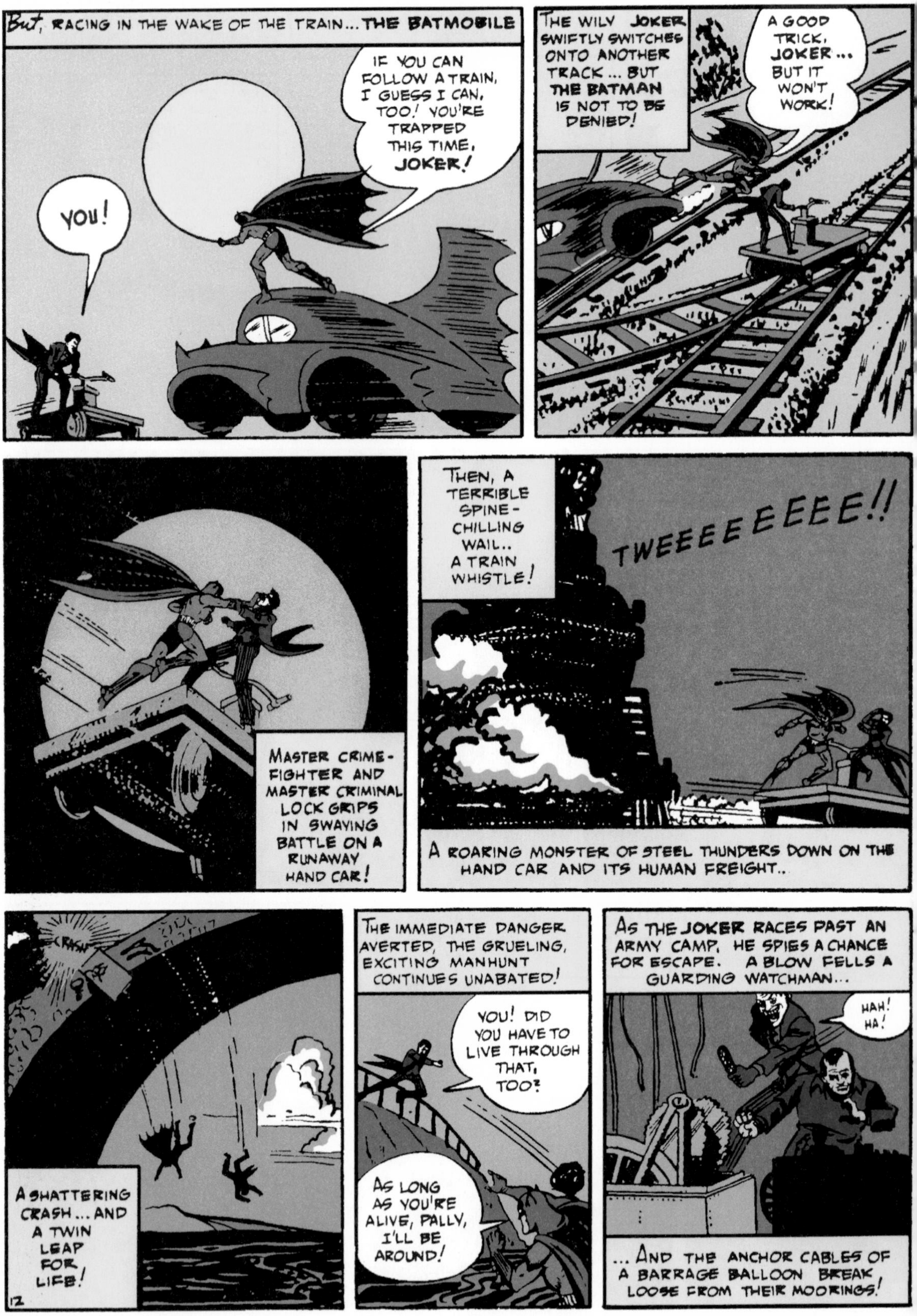
But, racing in the wake of the train... THE BATMOBILE
If you can follow a train, I guess I can, too! You're trapped this time, Joker!
You!
The wily Joker swiftly switches onto another track... but the Batman is not to be denied!
A good trick, Joker... but it won't work!
Master crime-fighter and master criminal lock grips in swaying battle on a runaway hand car!
Then, a terrible spine-chilling wail.. a train whistle!
TWEEEEEEEE!!
A roaring monster of steel thunders down on the hand car and its human freight..
CRASH
A shattering crash... and a twin leap for life!
12
The immediate danger averted, the grueling, exciting manhunt continues unabated!
You! Did you have to live through that, too?
As long as you're alive, pally, I'll be around!
As the Joker races past an army camp, he spies a chance for escape. A blow fells a guarding watchman...
Hah! Ha!
...And the anchor cables of a barrage balloon break loose from their moorings!

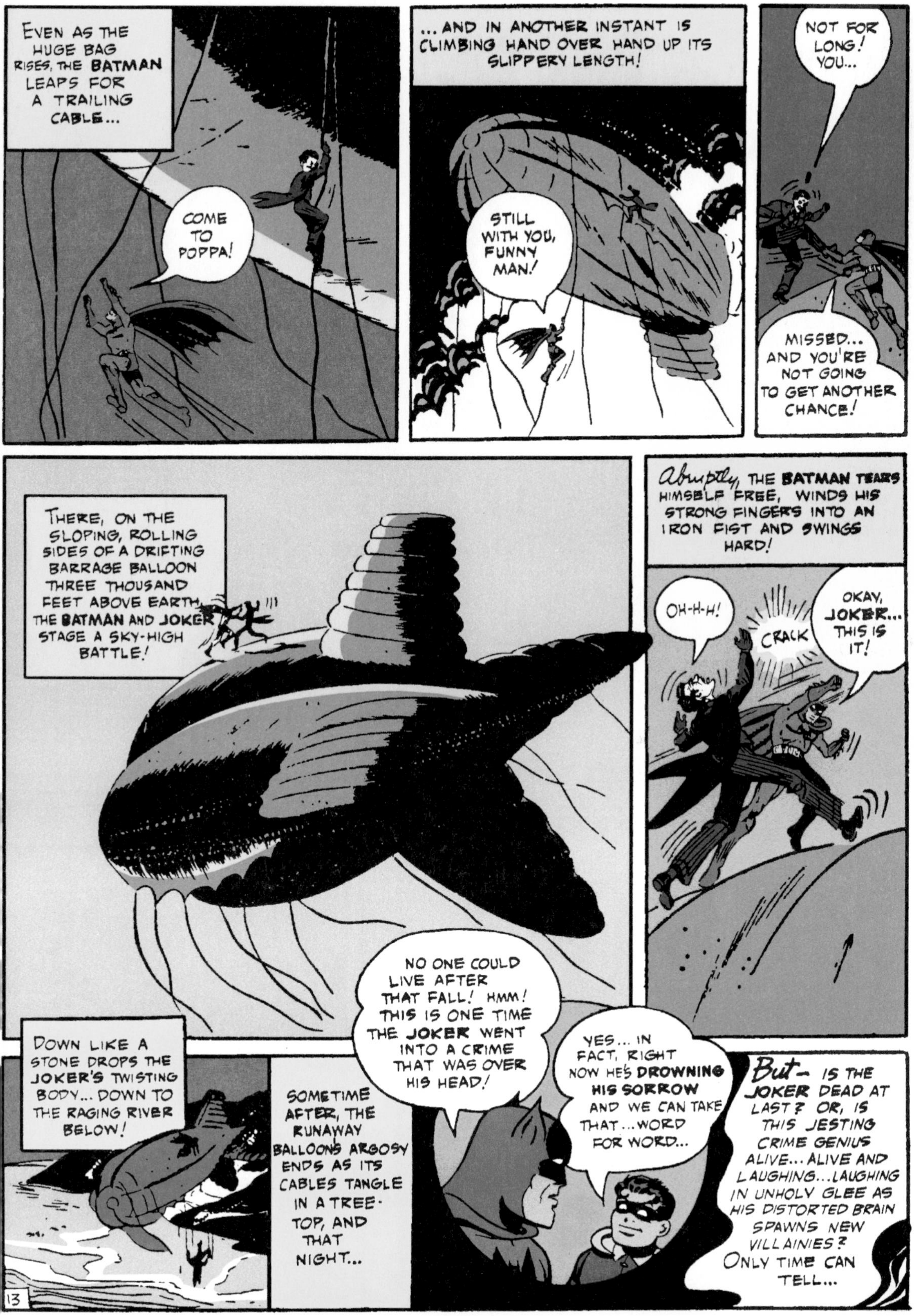
EVEN AS THE HUGE BAG RISES, THE BATMAN LEAPS FOR A TRAILING CABLE...
COME TO POPPA!
...AND IN ANOTHER INSTANT IS CLIMBING HAND OVER HAND UP ITS SLIPPERY LENGTH!
STILL WITH YOU, FUNNY MAN!
NOT FOR LONG! YOU...
MISSED... AND YOU'RE NOT GOING TO GET ANOTHER CHANCE!
THERE, ON THE SLOPING, ROLLING SIDES OF A DRIFTING BARRAGE BALLOON THREE THOUSAND FEET ABOVE EARTH, THE BATMAN AND JOKER STAGE A SKY-HIGH BATTLE!
Abruptly, THE BATMAN TEARS HIMSELF FREE, WINDS HIS STRONG FINGERS INTO AN IRON FIST AND SWINGS HARD!
OH-H-H!
CRACK
OKAY, JOKER... THIS IS IT!
DOWN LIKE A STONE DROPS THE JOKER'S TWISTING BODY... DOWN TO THE RAGING RIVER BELOW!
13
SOMETIME AFTER, THE RUNAWAY BALLOON'S ARGOSY ENDS AS ITS CABLES TANGLE IN A TREE-TOP, AND THAT NIGHT...
NO ONE COULD LIVE AFTER THAT FALL! HMM! THIS IS ONE TIME THE JOKER WENT INTO A CRIME THAT WAS OVER HIS HEAD!
YES... IN FACT, RIGHT NOW HE'S DROWNING HIS SORROW AND WE CAN TAKE THAT...WORD FOR WORD...
But- IS THE JOKER DEAD AT LAST? OR, IS THIS JESTING CRIME GENIUS ALIVE... ALIVE AND LAUGHING...LAUGHING IN UNHOLY GLEE AS HIS DISTORTED BRAIN SPAWNS NEW VILLAINIES? ONLY TIME CAN TELL...

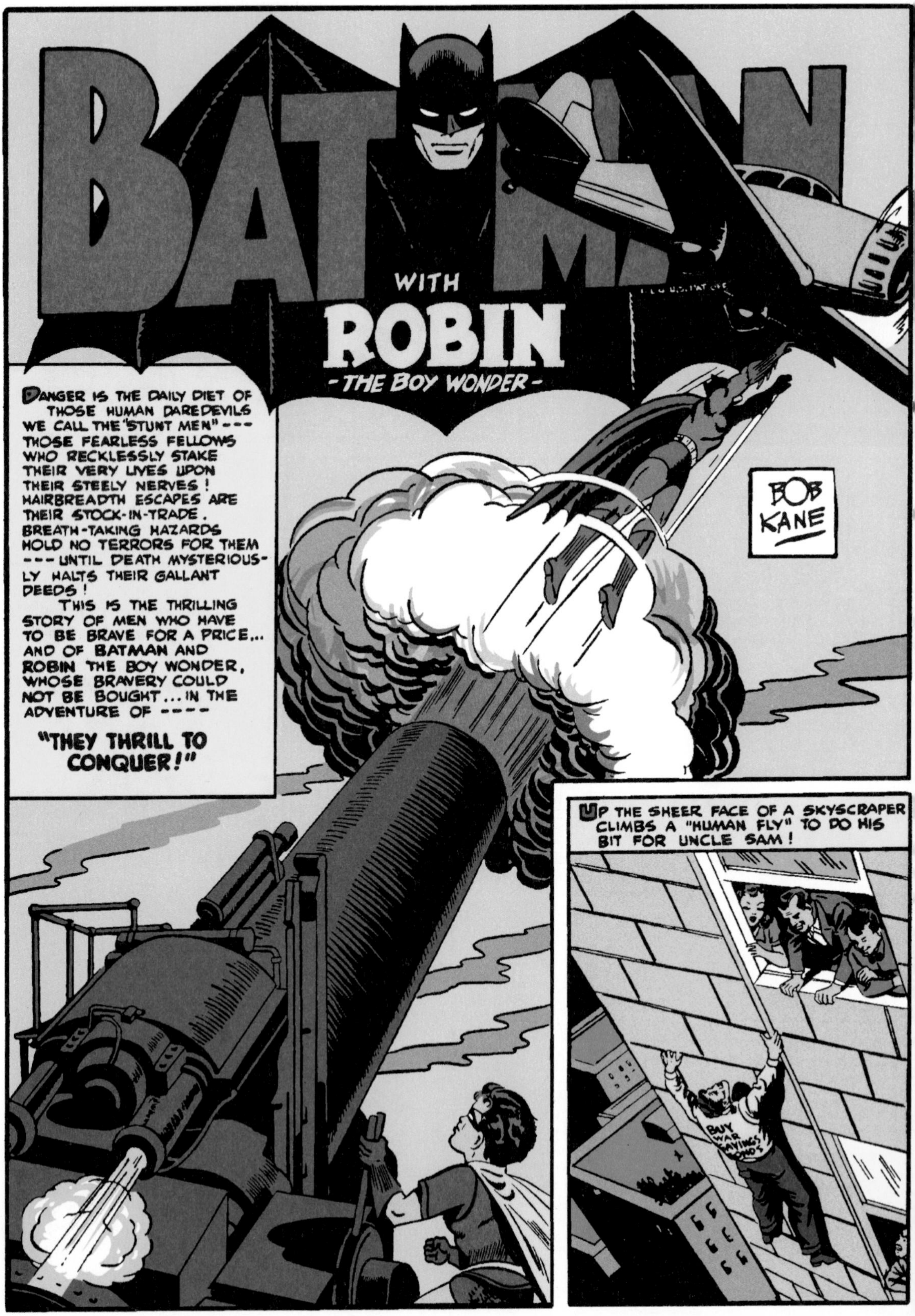

BATMAN
WITH
ROBIN
-THE BOY WONDER-
DANGER IS THE DAILY DIET OF THOSE HUMAN DAREDEVILS WE CALL THE "STUNT MEN" --- THOSE FEARLESS FELLOWS WHO RECKLESSLY STAKE THEIR VERY LIVES UPON THEIR STEELY NERVES! HAIRBREADTH ESCAPES ARE THEIR STOCK-IN-TRADE. BREATH-TAKING HAZARDS HOLD NO TERRORS FOR THEM --- UNTIL DEATH MYSTERIOUSLY HALTS THEIR GALLANT DEEDS!
THIS IS THE THRILLING STORY OF MEN WHO HAVE TO BE BRAVE FOR A PRICE... AND OF BATMAN AND ROBIN THE BOY WONDER, WHOSE BRAVERY COULD NOT BE BOUGHT... IN THE ADVENTURE OF ----
"THEY THRILL TO CONQUER!"
BOB KANE
UP THE SHEER FACE OF A SKYSCRAPER CLIMBS A "HUMAN FLY" TO DO HIS BIT FOR UNCLE SAM!
BUY WAR SAVINGS BONDS

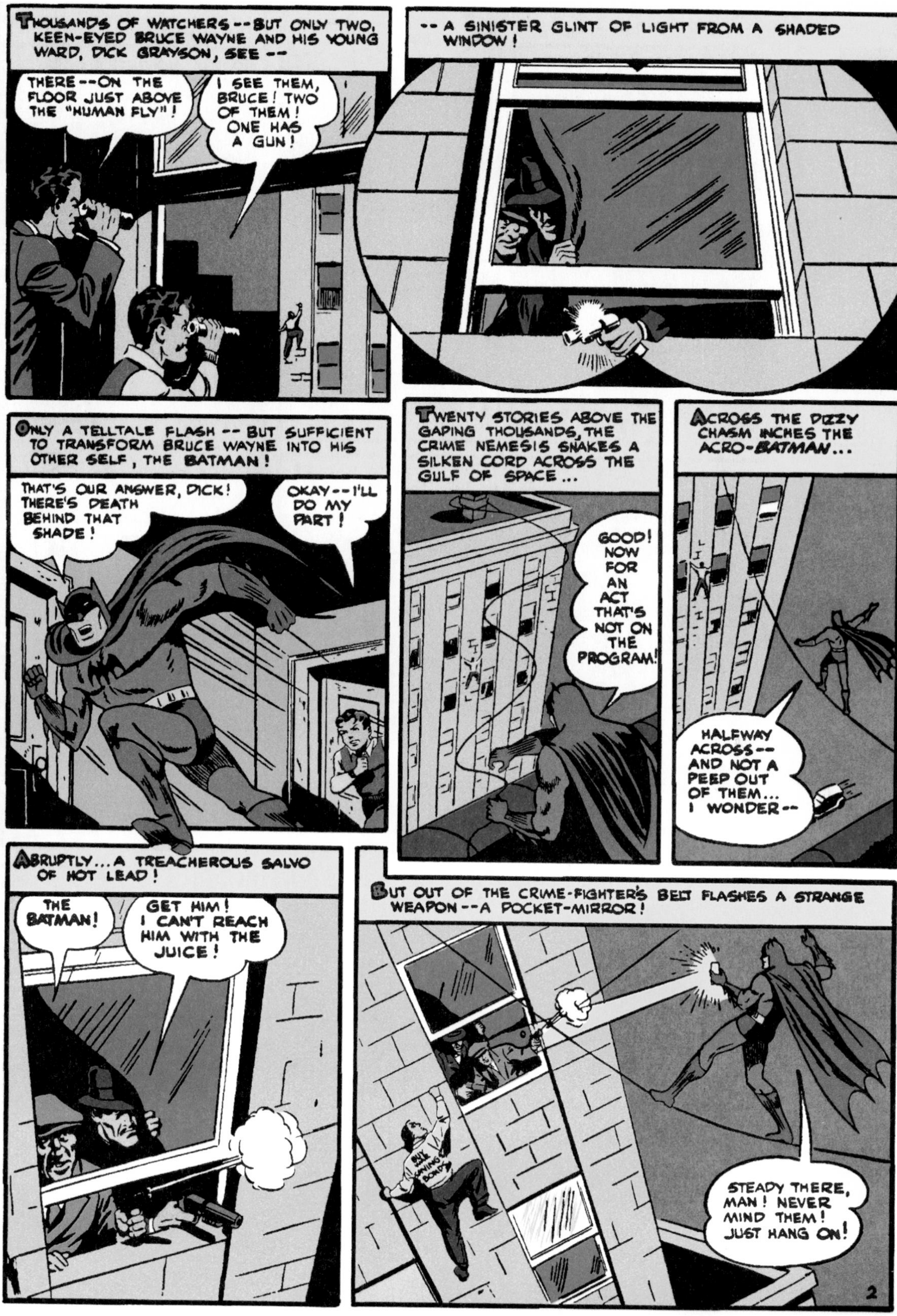
THOUSANDS OF WATCHERS--BUT ONLY TWO, KEEN-EYED BRUCE WAYNE AND HIS YOUNG WARD, DICK GRAYSON, SEE--
THERE--ON THE FLOOR JUST ABOVE THE "HUMAN FLY"!
I SEE THEM, BRUCE! TWO OF THEM! ONE HAS A GUN!
--A SINISTER GLINT OF LIGHT FROM A SHADED WINDOW!
ONLY A TELLTALE FLASH--BUT SUFFICIENT TO TRANSFORM BRUCE WAYNE INTO HIS OTHER SELF, THE BATMAN!
THAT'S OUR ANSWER, DICK! THERE'S DEATH BEHIND THAT SHADE!
OKAY--I'LL DO MY PART!
TWENTY STORIES ABOVE THE GAPING THOUSANDS, THE CRIME NEMESIS SNAKES A SILKEN CORD ACROSS THE GULF OF SPACE...
GOOD! NOW FOR AN ACT THAT'S NOT ON THE PROGRAM!
ACROSS THE DIZZY CHASM INCHES THE ACRO-BATMAN...
HALFWAY ACROSS--AND NOT A PEEP OUT OF THEM... I WONDER--
ABRUPTLY... A TREACHEROUS SALVO OF HOT LEAD!
THE BATMAN!
GET HIM! I CAN'T REACH HIM WITH THE JUICE!
BUT OUT OF THE CRIME-FIGHTER'S BELT FLASHES A STRANGE WEAPON--A POCKET-MIRROR!
STEADY THERE, MAN! NEVER MIND THEM! JUST HANG ON!
2

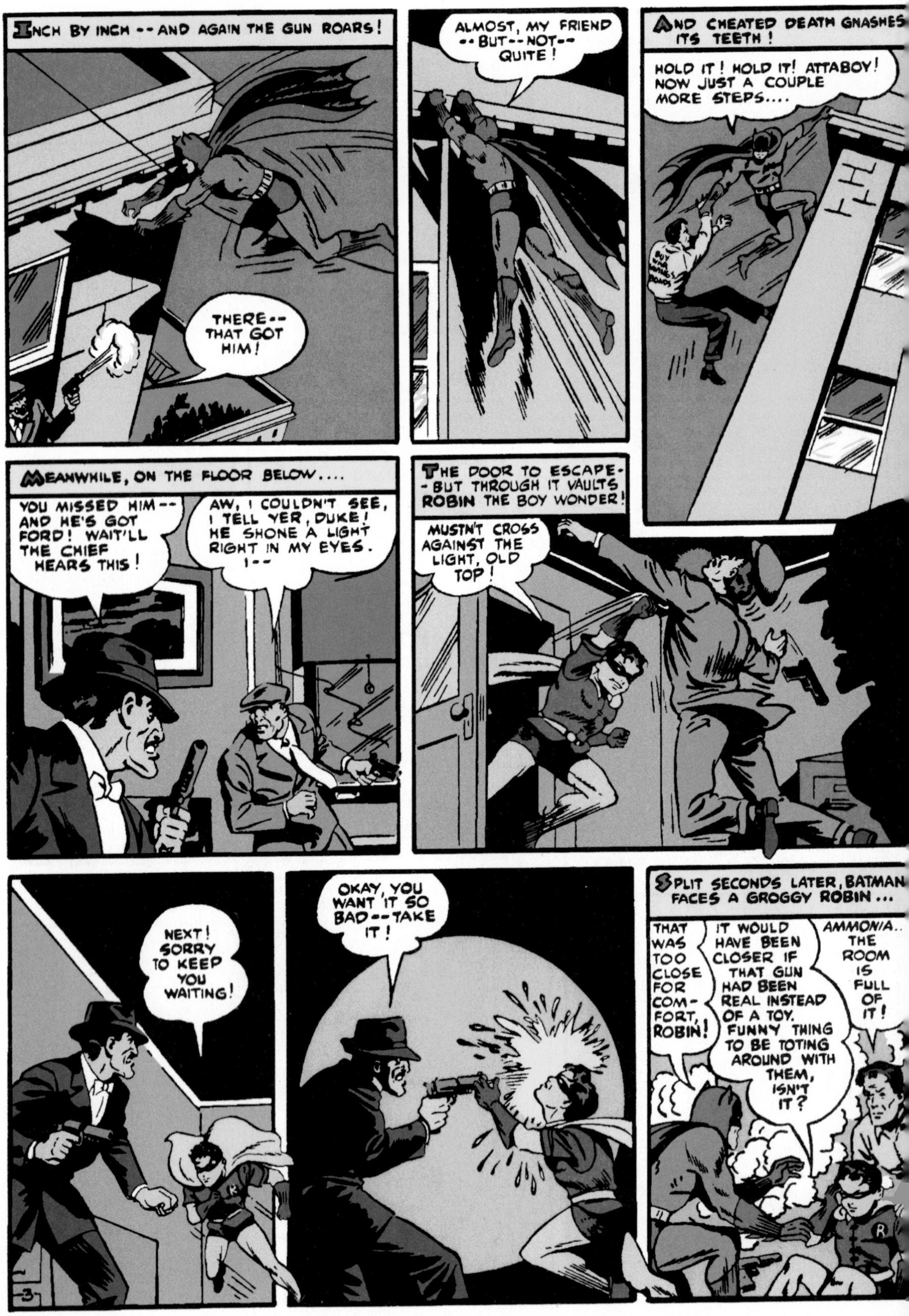
INCH BY INCH -- AND AGAIN THE GUN ROARS!
THERE-- THAT GOT HIM!
ALMOST, MY FRIEND -- BUT -- NOT -- QUITE!
AND CHEATED DEATH GNASHES ITS TEETH!
HOLD IT! HOLD IT! ATTABOY! NOW JUST A COUPLE MORE STEPS....
MEANWHILE, ON THE FLOOR BELOW....
YOU MISSED HIM -- AND HE'S GOT FORD! WAIT'LL THE CHIEF HEARS THIS!
AW, I COULDN'T SEE, I TELL YER, DUKE! HE SHONE A LIGHT RIGHT IN MY EYES. I--
THE DOOR TO ESCAPE -- BUT THROUGH IT VAULTS ROBIN THE BOY WONDER!
MUSTN'T CROSS AGAINST THE LIGHT, OLD TOP!
NEXT! SORRY TO KEEP YOU WAITING!
OKAY, YOU WANT IT SO BAD -- TAKE IT!
SPLIT SECONDS LATER, BATMAN FACES A GROGGY ROBIN...
THAT WAS TOO CLOSE FOR COM-FORT, ROBIN!
IT WOULD HAVE BEEN CLOSER IF THAT GUN HAD BEEN REAL INSTEAD OF A TOY. FUNNY THING TO BE TOTING AROUND WITH THEM, ISN'T IT?
AMMONIA... THE ROOM IS FULL OF IT!
3

THIS DEVILISH GUN IS NO TOY! ALL THEY HAD TO DO WAS SHOOT ITS LOAD OF AMMONIA GAS IN MY FACE AND I'D PITCH DOWN TO THE STREET! EVERYONE WOULD CONSIDER IT ANOTHER ACCIDENTAL DEATH -- LIKE THESE....

OUT OF FORD'S POCKET COME THREE NEWSPAPER CLIPPINGS....

MOVIE STUNT MAN TAKES LAST RIDE

ED SOMMERS PLU... TO DEATH IN AC...

DAREDEVIL DALY DIES IN PARACHUTE JUMP!

NOTED AERIAL CLOWN MAKES FATAL LEAP.

MOTOR MATT MEETS DEATH IN RACE!

MATT NORHEIM ME... CRASH...

THOSE WEREN'T ACCIDENTS, BATMAN. THEY WERE MURDERS! SOMEONE IS FORCING US STUNT MEN TO BUY PROTECTION. THOSE THREE WOULDN'T PAY -- SO THEY DIED! I'M NEXT!

BUT WHY DIDN'T YOU PAY -- RATHER THAN BE KILLED?

I CAN'T AFFORD TO PAY! I'M ONE OF THE FLYING FORDS, REMEMBER US? THERE WERE THREE OF US -- ME AND NAN AND YOUNG TOM. HE'S JUST ABOUT ROBIN'S AGE...

"LITTLE TOMMY WAS A GREAT PERFORMER, BUT WE DIDN'T LET HIM DO ANYTHING DANGEROUS -- JUST GOING UP WITH US AND TAKING EASY SWINGS."

"UNTIL THAT DAY WHEN MY GEAR BROKE, I WAS FALLING STRAIGHT FOR A BIG ANIMAL WAGON. TOM SAW WHAT WAS COMING AND DIVED AT THE ROPE."

I'VE GOT IT, DAD!

"THAT CHECKED ME SO THAT I MISSED THE WAGON -- BUT TOM LANDED IN THE ARENA IN A HEAP. HE CRUSHED HIS SPINE -- AND HE'S NEVER WALKED SINCE!

TOMMY! OH, TOMMY! DARLING!

TOMMY NEEDS AN OPERATION THAT WILL COST THOUSANDS OF DOLLARS. THAT'S WHY I TAKE THESE DANGEROUS JOBS AND WHY I WON'T PAY THOSE CROOKS!

DON'T WORRY, YOU WON'T NEED TO!

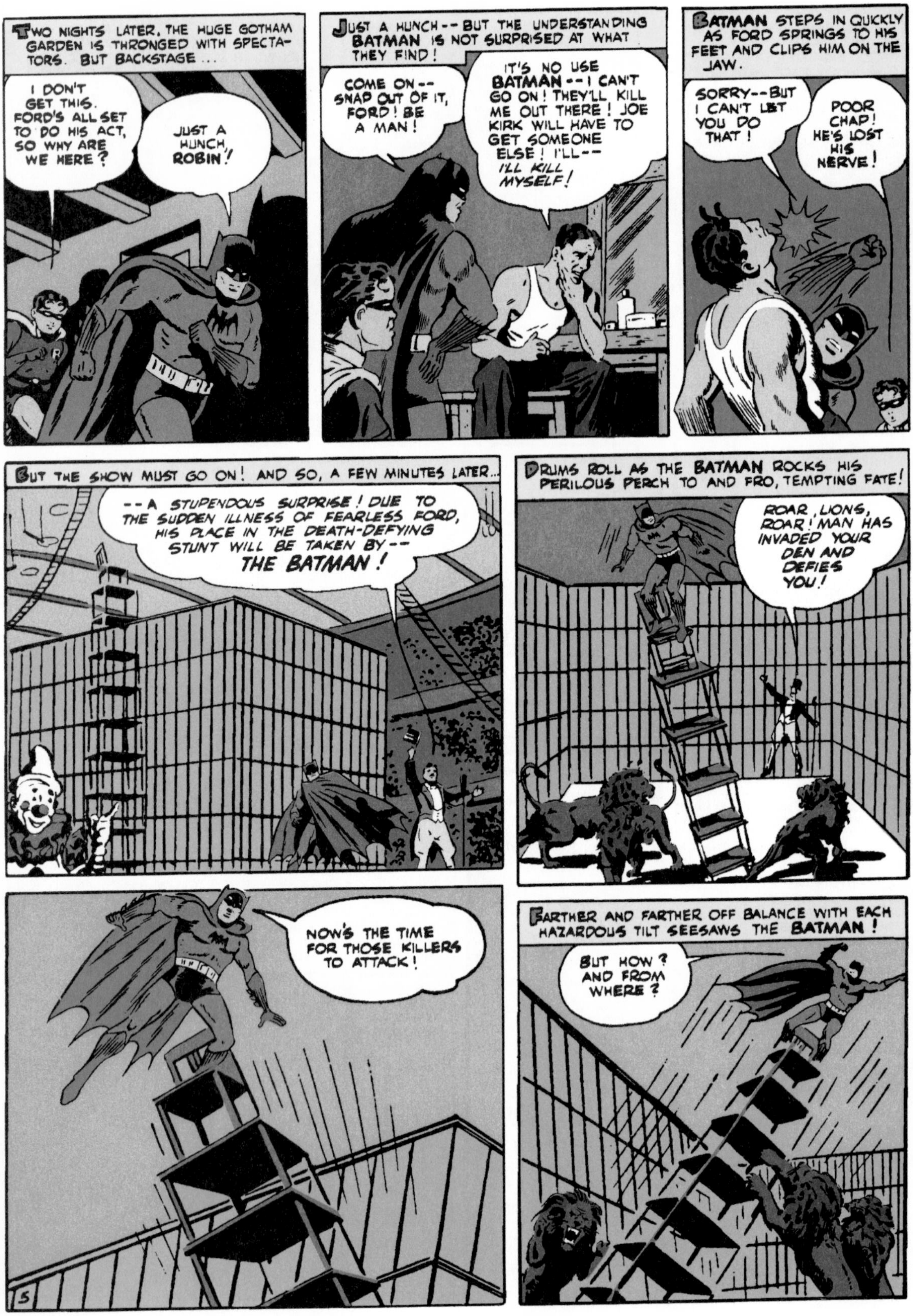
TWO NIGHTS LATER, THE HUGE GOTHAM GARDEN IS THRONGED WITH SPECTATORS. BUT BACKSTAGE ...
I DON'T GET THIS. FORD'S ALL SET TO DO HIS ACT, SO WHY ARE WE HERE?
JUST A HUNCH, ROBIN!
JUST A HUNCH -- BUT THE UNDERSTANDING BATMAN IS NOT SURPRISED AT WHAT THEY FIND!
COME ON -- SNAP OUT OF IT, FORD! BE A MAN!
IT'S NO USE BATMAN -- I CAN'T GO ON! THEY'LL KILL ME OUT THERE! JOE KIRK WILL HAVE TO GET SOMEONE ELSE! I'LL -- I'LL KILL MYSELF!
BATMAN STEPS IN QUICKLY AS FORD SPRINGS TO HIS FEET AND CLIPS HIM ON THE JAW.
SORRY -- BUT I CAN'T LET YOU DO THAT!
POOR CHAP! HE'S LOST HIS NERVE!
BUT THE SHOW MUST GO ON! AND SO, A FEW MINUTES LATER...
-- A STUPENDOUS SURPRISE! DUE TO THE SUDDEN ILLNESS OF FEARLESS FORD, HIS PLACE IN THE DEATH-DEFYING STUNT WILL BE TAKEN BY -- THE BATMAN!
DRUMS ROLL AS THE BATMAN ROCKS HIS PERILOUS PERCH TO AND FRO, TEMPTING FATE!
ROAR, LIONS, ROAR! MAN HAS INVADED YOUR DEN AND DEFIES YOU!
NOW'S THE TIME FOR THOSE KILLERS TO ATTACK!
5
FARTHER AND FARTHER OFF BALANCE WITH EACH HAZARDOUS TILT SEESAWS THE BATMAN!
BUT HOW? AND FROM WHERE?

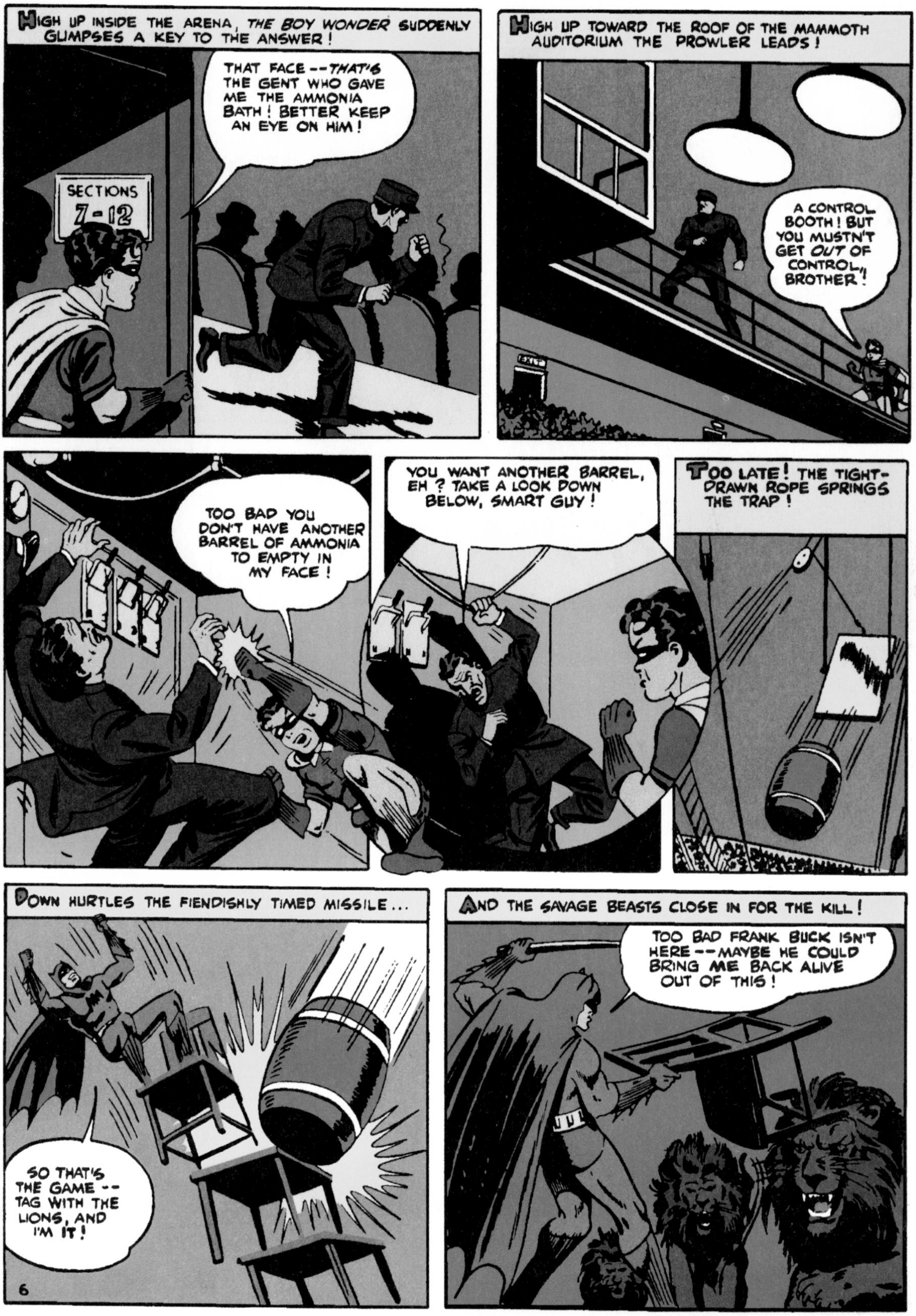
HIGH UP INSIDE THE ARENA, *THE BOY WONDER* SUDDENLY GLIMPSES A KEY TO THE ANSWER!
THAT FACE -- *THAT'S* THE GENT WHO GAVE ME THE AMMONIA BATH! BETTER KEEP AN EYE ON HIM!
SECTIONS 7-12
HIGH UP TOWARD THE ROOF OF THE MAMMOTH AUDITORIUM THE PROWLER LEADS!
A CONTROL BOOTH! BUT YOU MUSTN'T GET *OUT* OF CONTROL, BROTHER!
TOO BAD YOU DON'T HAVE ANOTHER BARREL OF AMMONIA TO EMPTY IN MY FACE!
YOU WANT ANOTHER BARREL, EH? TAKE A LOOK DOWN BELOW, SMART GUY!
TOO LATE! THE TIGHT-DRAWN ROPE SPRINGS THE TRAP!
DOWN HURTLES THE FIENDISHLY TIMED MISSILE...
SO THAT'S THE GAME -- TAG WITH THE LIONS, AND I'M **IT**!
6
AND THE SAVAGE BEASTS CLOSE IN FOR THE KILL!
TOO BAD FRANK BUCK ISN'T HERE -- MAYBE HE COULD BRING ME BACK ALIVE OUT OF THIS!

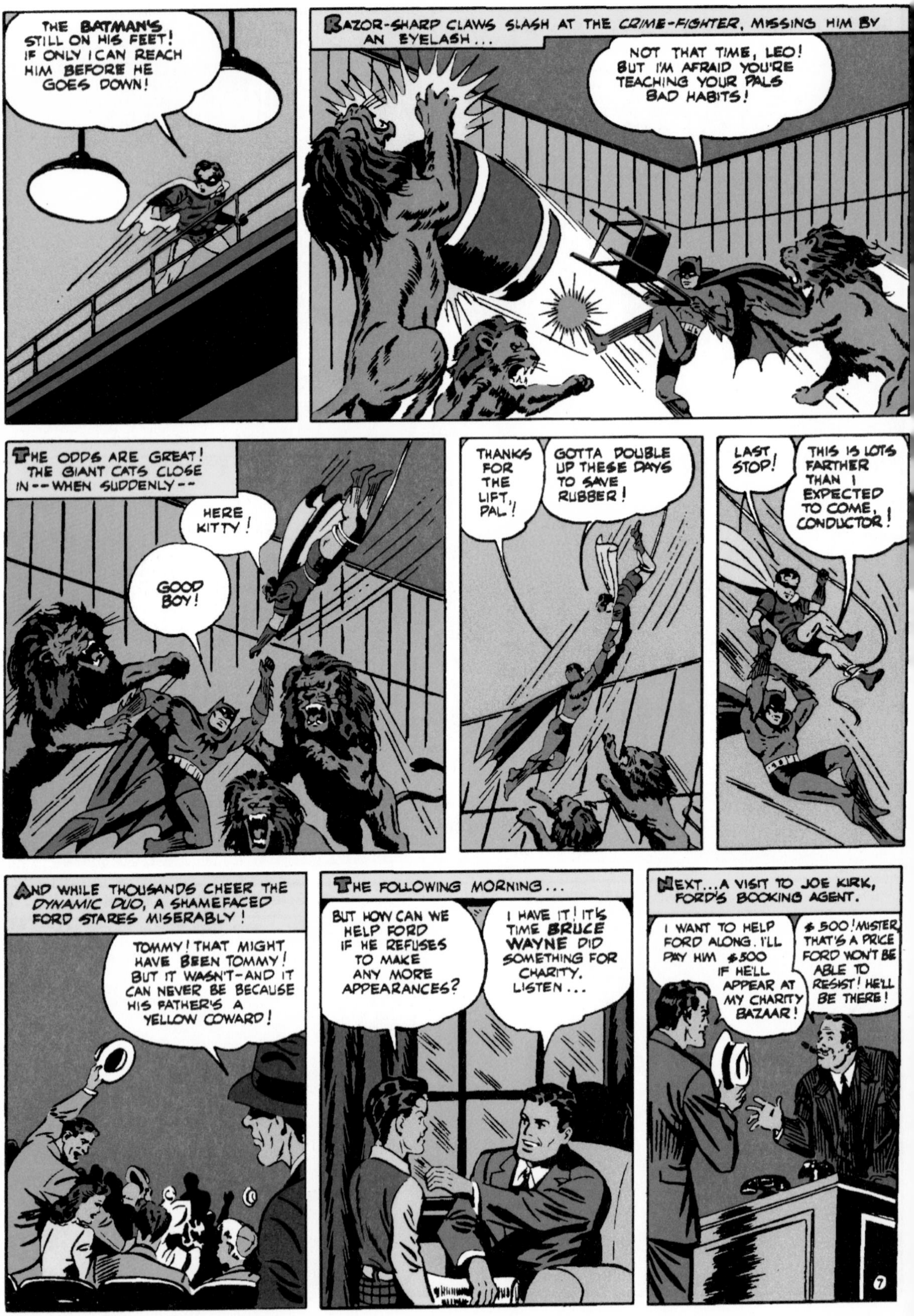
THE BATMAN'S STILL ON HIS FEET! IF ONLY I CAN REACH HIM BEFORE HE GOES DOWN!
RAZOR-SHARP CLAWS SLASH AT THE CRIME-FIGHTER, MISSING HIM BY AN EYELASH...
NOT THAT TIME, LEO! BUT I'M AFRAID YOU'RE TEACHING YOUR PALS BAD HABITS!
THE ODDS ARE GREAT! THE GIANT CATS CLOSE IN--WHEN SUDDENLY--
HERE KITTY!
GOOD BOY!
THANKS FOR THE LIFT, PAL!
GOTTA DOUBLE UP THESE DAYS TO SAVE RUBBER!
LAST STOP!
THIS IS LOTS FARTHER THAN I EXPECTED TO COME, CONDUCTOR!
AND WHILE THOUSANDS CHEER THE DYNAMIC DUO, A SHAMEFACED FORD STARES MISERABLY!
TOMMY! THAT MIGHT HAVE BEEN TOMMY! BUT IT WASN'T-AND IT CAN NEVER BE BECAUSE HIS FATHER'S A YELLOW COWARD!
THE FOLLOWING MORNING...
BUT HOW CAN WE HELP FORD IF HE REFUSES TO MAKE ANY MORE APPEARANCES?
I HAVE IT! IT'S TIME BRUCE WAYNE DID SOMETHING FOR CHARITY. LISTEN...
NEXT...A VISIT TO JOE KIRK, FORD'S BOOKING AGENT.
I WANT TO HELP FORD ALONG. I'LL PAY HIM $500 IF HE'LL APPEAR AT MY CHARITY BAZAAR!
$500! MISTER THAT'S A PRICE FORD WON'T BE ABLE TO RESIST! HE'LL BE THERE!
7

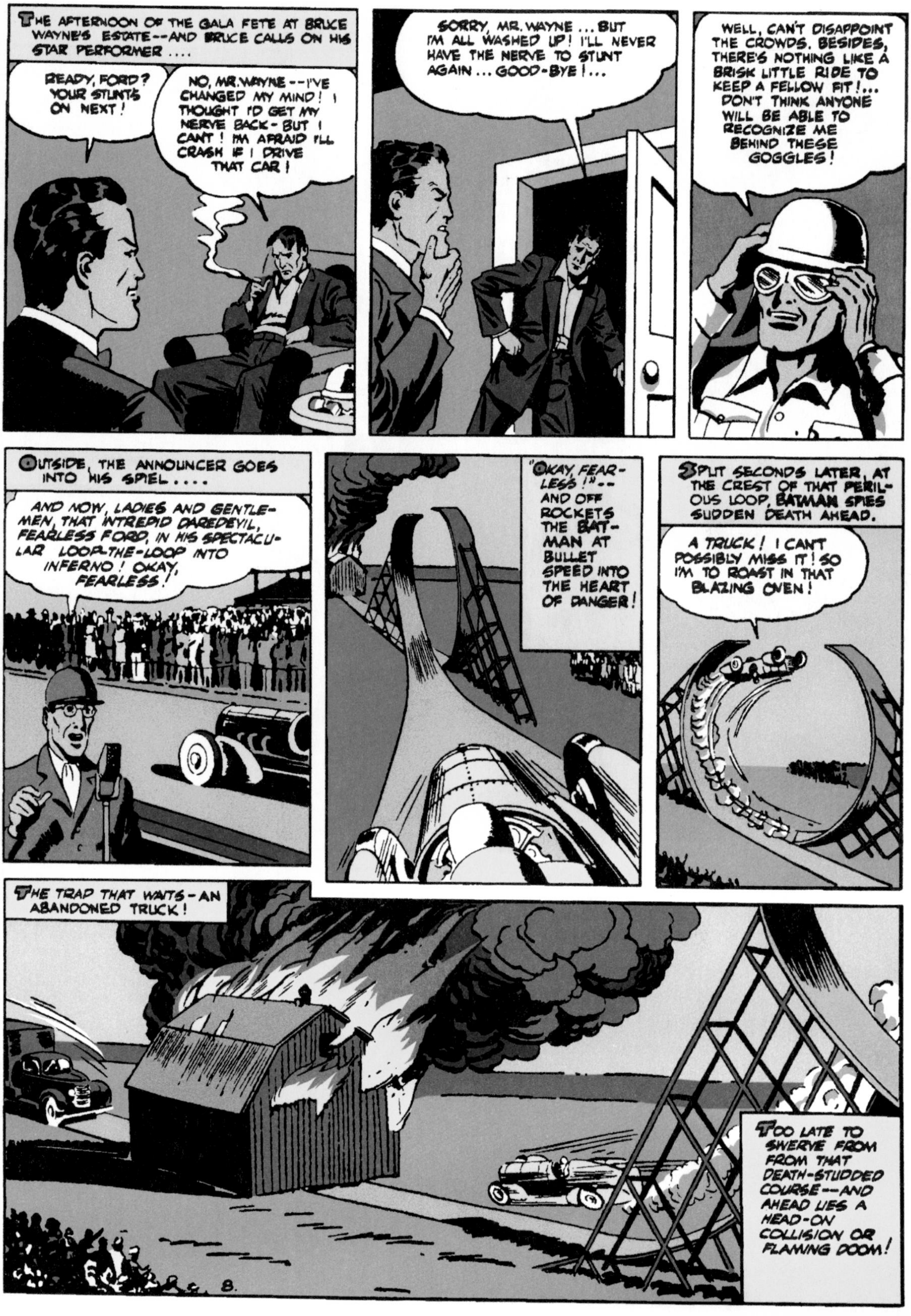
THE AFTERNOON OF THE GALA FETE AT BRUCE WAYNE'S ESTATE--AND BRUCE CALLS ON HIS STAR PERFORMER ....
READY, FORD? YOUR STUNT'S ON NEXT!
NO, MR. WAYNE--I'VE CHANGED MY MIND! I THOUGHT I'D GET MY NERVE BACK-BUT I CAN'T! I'M AFRAID I'LL CRASH IF I DRIVE THAT CAR!
SORRY, MR. WAYNE ... BUT I'M ALL WASHED UP! I'LL NEVER HAVE THE NERVE TO STUNT AGAIN ... GOOD-BYE! ...
WELL, CAN'T DISAPPOINT THE CROWDS. BESIDES, THERE'S NOTHING LIKE A BRISK LITTLE RIDE TO KEEP A FELLOW FIT! ... DON'T THINK ANYONE WILL BE ABLE TO RECOGNIZE ME BEHIND THESE GOGGLES!
OUTSIDE, THE ANNOUNCER GOES INTO HIS SPIEL ....
AND NOW, LADIES AND GENTLEMEN, THAT INTREPID DAREDEVIL, FEARLESS FORD, IN HIS SPECTACULAR LOOP-THE-LOOP INTO INFERNO! OKAY, FEARLESS!
"OKAY, FEARLESS!"--AND OFF ROCKETS THE BATMAN AT BULLET SPEED INTO THE HEART OF DANGER!
SPLIT SECONDS LATER, AT THE CREST OF THAT PERILOUS LOOP, BATMAN SPIES SUDDEN DEATH AHEAD.
A TRUCK! I CAN'T POSSIBLY MISS IT! SO I'M TO ROAST IN THAT BLAZING OVEN!
THE TRAP THAT WAITS-AN ABANDONED TRUCK!
TOO LATE TO SWERVE FROM FROM THAT DEATH-STUDDED COURSE--AND AHEAD LIES A HEAD-ON COLLISION OR FLAMING DOOM!
8.

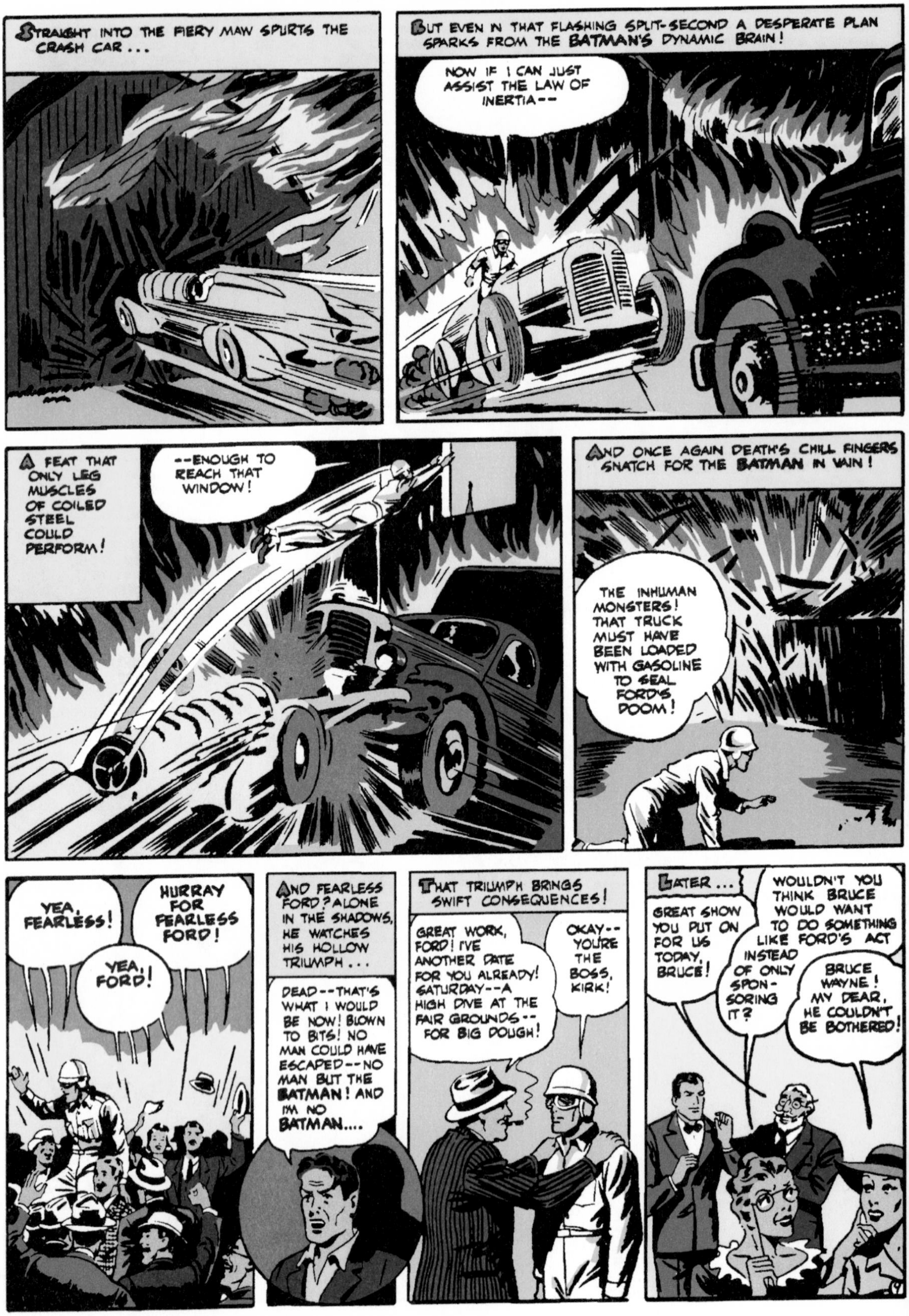
STRAIGHT INTO THE FIERY MAW SPURTS THE CRASH CAR ...
BUT EVEN IN THAT FLASHING SPLIT-SECOND A DESPERATE PLAN SPARKS FROM THE BATMAN'S DYNAMIC BRAIN!
NOW IF I CAN JUST ASSIST THE LAW OF INERTIA--
A FEAT THAT ONLY LEG MUSCLES OF COILED STEEL COULD PERFORM!
--ENOUGH TO REACH THAT WINDOW!
AND ONCE AGAIN DEATH'S CHILL FINGERS SNATCH FOR THE BATMAN IN VAIN!
THE INHUMAN MONSTERS! THAT TRUCK MUST HAVE BEEN LOADED WITH GASOLINE TO SEAL FORD'S DOOM!
YEA, FEARLESS!
HURRAY FOR FEARLESS FORD!
YEA, FORD!
AND FEARLESS FORD? ALONE IN THE SHADOWS, HE WATCHES HIS HOLLOW TRIUMPH ...
DEAD--THAT'S WHAT I WOULD BE NOW! BLOWN TO BITS! NO MAN COULD HAVE ESCAPED--NO MAN BUT THE BATMAN! AND I'M NO BATMAN....
THAT TRIUMPH BRINGS SWIFT CONSEQUENCES!
GREAT WORK, FORD! I'VE ANOTHER DATE FOR YOU ALREADY! SATURDAY--A HIGH DIVE AT THE FAIR GROUNDS--FOR BIG DOUGH!
OKAY--YOU'RE THE BOSS, KIRK!
LATER ...
GREAT SHOW YOU PUT ON FOR US TODAY, BRUCE!
WOULDN'T YOU THINK BRUCE WOULD WANT TO DO SOMETHING LIKE FORD'S ACT INSTEAD OF ONLY SPON-SORING IT?
BRUCE WAYNE! MY DEAR, HE COULDN'T BE BOTHERED!

THE NIGHT BEFORE THE FAIR--TWO CLOAKED FIGURES GLIDE SOFTLY OVER THE GROUNDS!

TWO ATTEMPTS ON FORD'S LIFE HAVE FAILED...TOMORROW THE KILLERS WILL HAVE A FINE CHANCE AT HIM!

AND AS USUAL, WHILE HE'S AT WORK-- TO MAKE HIS DEATH SEEM ACCIDENTAL!

LOOK AT THAT FURROW! SOMEONE'S BEEN DIGGING HERE!

JUST AS I EXPECTED... CLEVER JOB-- THE GROUND IS HARDLY DISTURBED-- BUT LET'S SEE WHERE THAT FAINT TRAIL LEADS US....

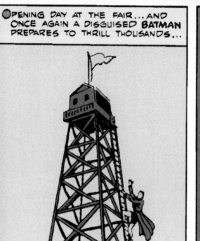

OPENING DAY AT THE FAIR...AND ONCE AGAIN A DISGUISED BATMAN PREPARES TO THRILL THOUSANDS...

HE'LL NEVER DO IT...I DON'T WANT TO WATCH HIM!...HE'LL KILL HIMSELF!

AND "FEARLESS FORD" PLUNGES-- JUST AS A MIGHTY EXPLOSION ROCKS THE FAIRGROUNDS!

BOOM!

AND NOW... THE GREAT FEARLESS FORD WILL PLUNGE 150 FEET INTO LESS THAN THREE FEET OF WATER!

STUNNED SILENCE--UNTIL SUDDENLY A SHRILL SHRIEK SOUNDS "FORD'S" REQUIEM!

BEN! OH, BEN!

DADDY!

BUT THE REAL FEARLESS FORD IS FAR FROM DEATH!

NAN! TOMMY! THEY THINK I'M DEAD! BUT IT'S THE BATMAN WHO TOOK MY PLACE! HE'S DEAD!!!

10

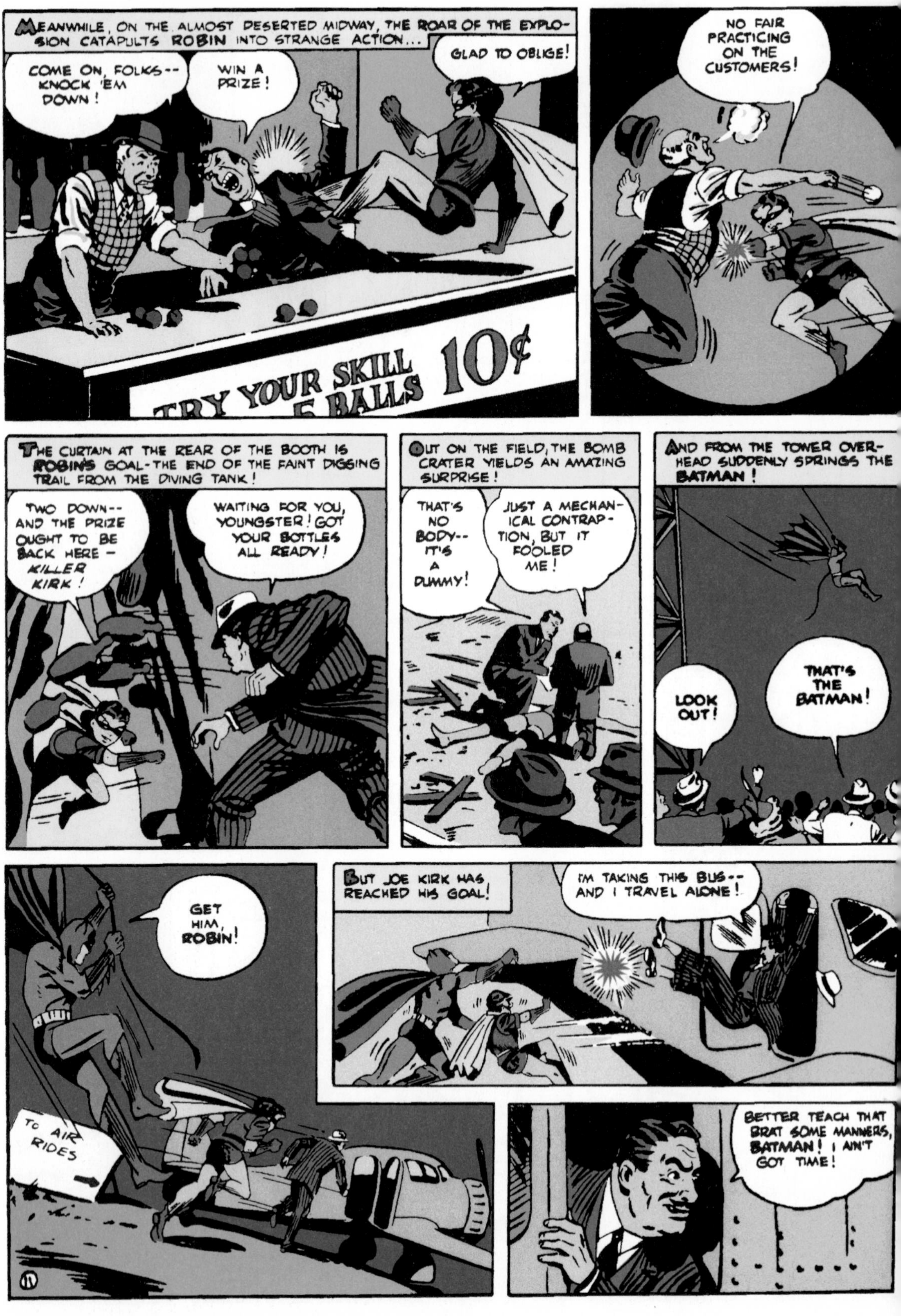
MEANWHILE, ON THE ALMOST DESERTED MIDWAY, THE ROAR OF THE EXPLOSION CATAPULTS ROBIN INTO STRANGE ACTION...
COME ON, FOLKS-- KNOCK 'EM DOWN!
WIN A PRIZE!
GLAD TO OBLIGE!
TRY YOUR SKILL 5 BALLS 10¢
NO FAIR PRACTICING ON THE CUSTOMERS!
THE CURTAIN AT THE REAR OF THE BOOTH IS ROBIN'S GOAL-THE END OF THE FAINT DIGGING TRAIL FROM THE DIVING TANK!
TWO DOWN-- AND THE PRIZE OUGHT TO BE BACK HERE- KILLER KIRK!
WAITING FOR YOU, YOUNGSTER! GOT YOUR BOTTLES ALL READY!
OUT ON THE FIELD, THE BOMB CRATER YIELDS AN AMAZING SURPRISE!
THAT'S NO BODY-- IT'S A DUMMY!
JUST A MECHANICAL CONTRAPTION, BUT IT FOOLED ME!
AND FROM THE TOWER OVERHEAD SUDDENLY SPRINGS THE BATMAN!
LOOK OUT!
THAT'S THE BATMAN!
GET HIM, ROBIN!
TO AIR RIDES
11
BUT JOE KIRK HAS REACHED HIS GOAL!
I'M TAKING THIS BUS-- AND I TRAVEL ALONE!
BETTER TEACH THAT BRAT SOME MANNERS, BATMAN! I AIN'T GOT TIME!

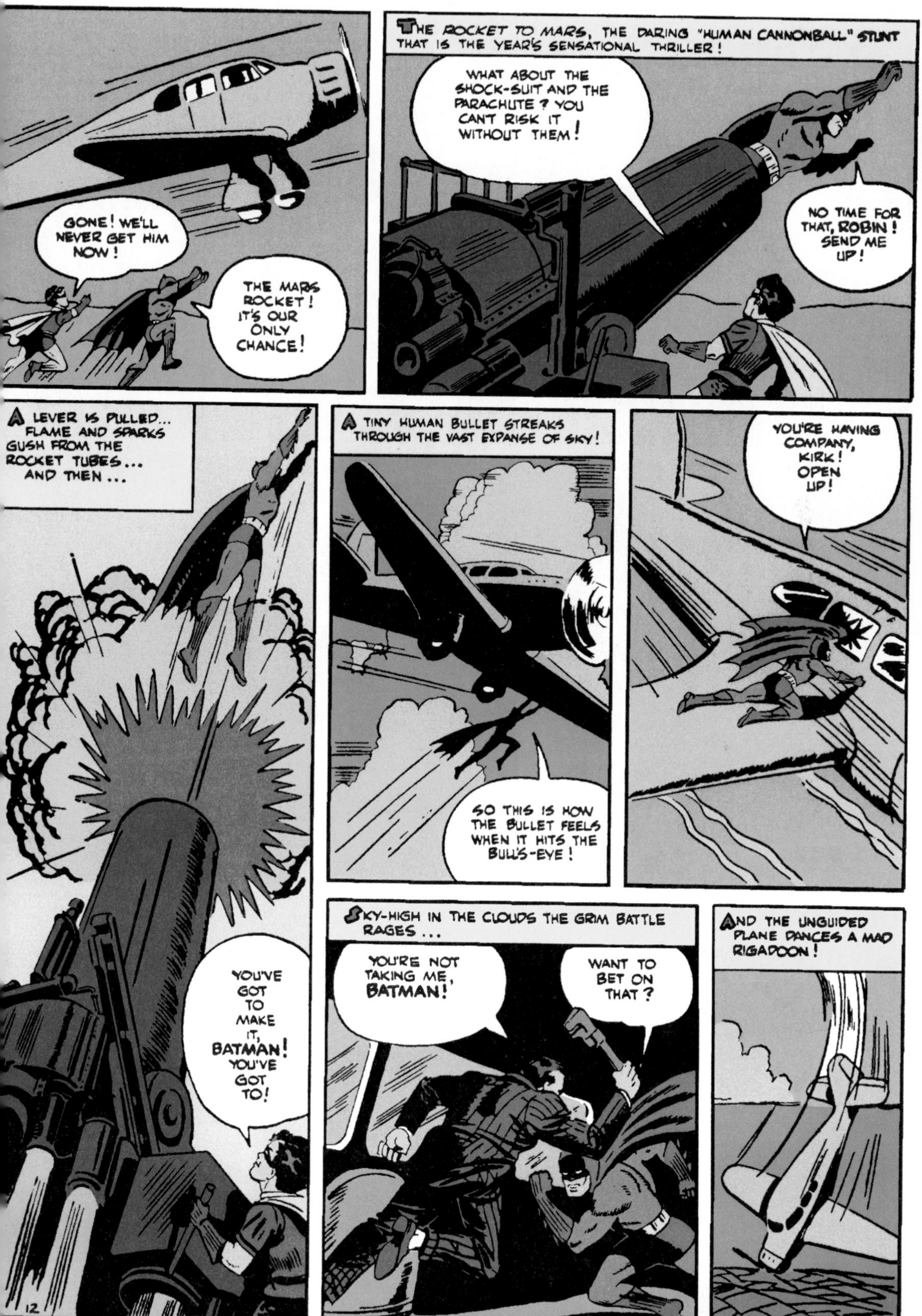
GONE! WE'LL NEVER GET HIM NOW!
THE MARS ROCKET! IT'S OUR ONLY CHANCE!
THE ROCKET TO MARS, THE DARING "HUMAN CANNONBALL" STUNT THAT IS THE YEAR'S SENSATIONAL THRILLER!
WHAT ABOUT THE SHOCK-SUIT AND THE PARACHUTE? YOU CAN'T RISK IT WITHOUT THEM!
NO TIME FOR THAT, ROBIN! SEND ME UP!
A LEVER IS PULLED... FLAME AND SPARKS GUSH FROM THE ROCKET TUBES... AND THEN...
YOU'VE GOT TO MAKE IT, BATMAN! YOU'VE GOT TO!
12
A TINY HUMAN BULLET STREAKS THROUGH THE VAST EXPANSE OF SKY!
SO THIS IS HOW THE BULLET FEELS WHEN IT HITS THE BULL'S-EYE!
YOU'RE HAVING COMPANY, KIRK! OPEN UP!
SKY-HIGH IN THE CLOUDS THE GRIM BATTLE RAGES...
YOU'RE NOT TAKING ME, BATMAN!
WANT TO BET ON THAT?
AND THE UNGUIDED PLANE DANCES A MAD RIGADOON!

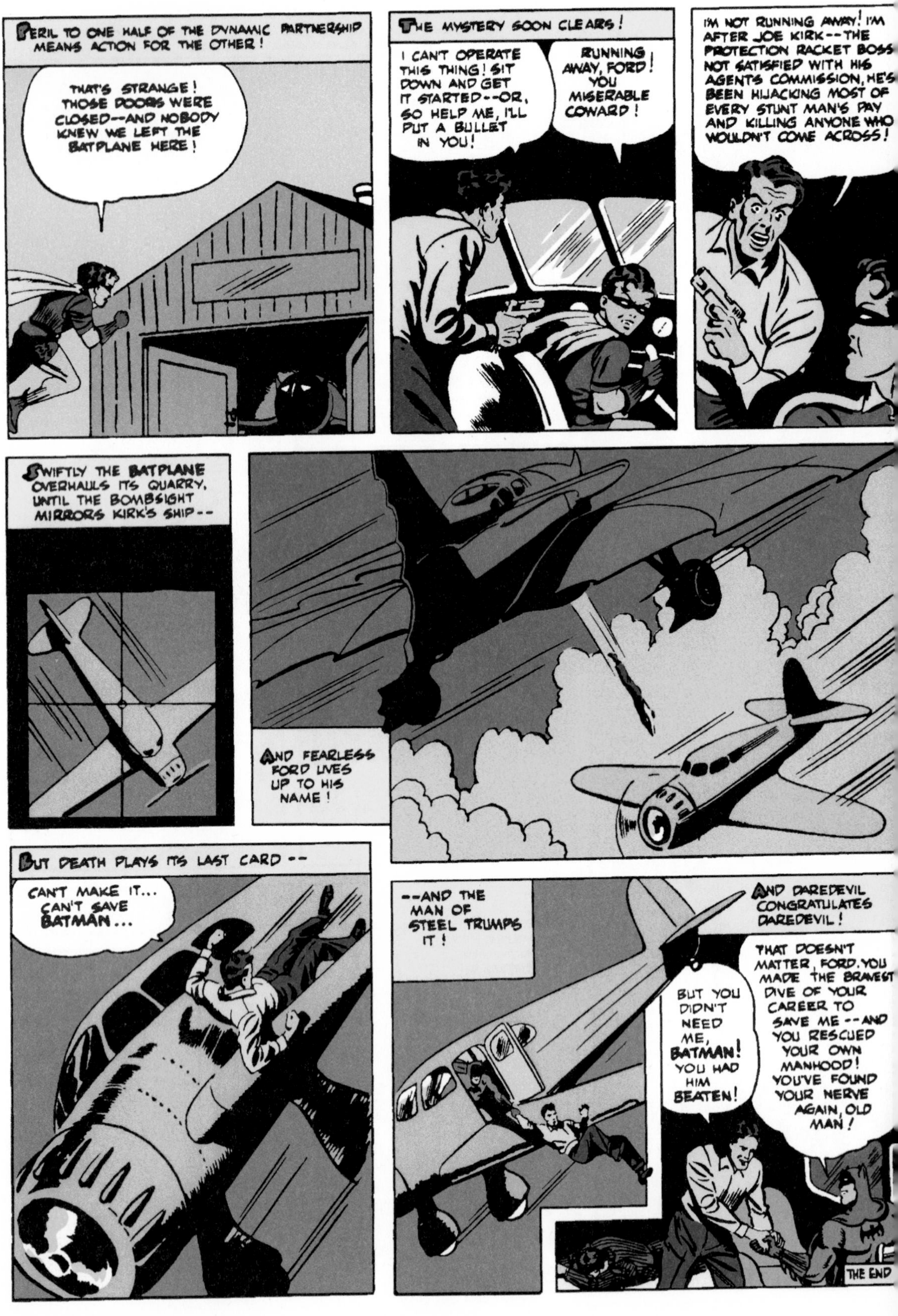
PERIL TO ONE HALF OF THE DYNAMIC PARTNERSHIP MEANS ACTION FOR THE OTHER!
THAT'S STRANGE! THOSE DOORS WERE CLOSED--AND NOBODY KNEW WE LEFT THE BATPLANE HERE!
THE MYSTERY SOON CLEARS!
I CAN'T OPERATE THIS THING! SIT DOWN AND GET IT STARTED--OR, SO HELP ME, I'LL PUT A BULLET IN YOU!
RUNNING AWAY, FORD! YOU MISERABLE COWARD!
I'M NOT RUNNING AWAY! I'M AFTER JOE KIRK--THE PROTECTION RACKET BOSS! NOT SATISFIED WITH HIS AGENTS COMMISSION, HE'S BEEN HIJACKING MOST OF EVERY STUNT MAN'S PAY AND KILLING ANYONE WHO WOULDN'T COME ACROSS!
SWIFTLY THE BATPLANE OVERHAULS ITS QUARRY, UNTIL THE BOMBSIGHT MIRRORS KIRK'S SHIP--
AND FEARLESS FORD LIVES UP TO HIS NAME!
BUT DEATH PLAYS ITS LAST CARD--
CAN'T MAKE IT... CAN'T SAVE BATMAN...
--AND THE MAN OF STEEL TRUMPS IT!
AND DAREDEVIL CONGRATULATES DAREDEVIL!
BUT YOU DIDN'T NEED ME, BATMAN! YOU HAD HIM BEATEN!
THAT DOESN'T MATTER, FORD. YOU MADE THE BRAVEST DIVE OF YOUR CAREER TO SAVE ME--AND YOU RESCUED YOUR OWN MANHOOD! YOU'VE FOUND YOUR NERVE AGAIN, OLD MAN!
THE END

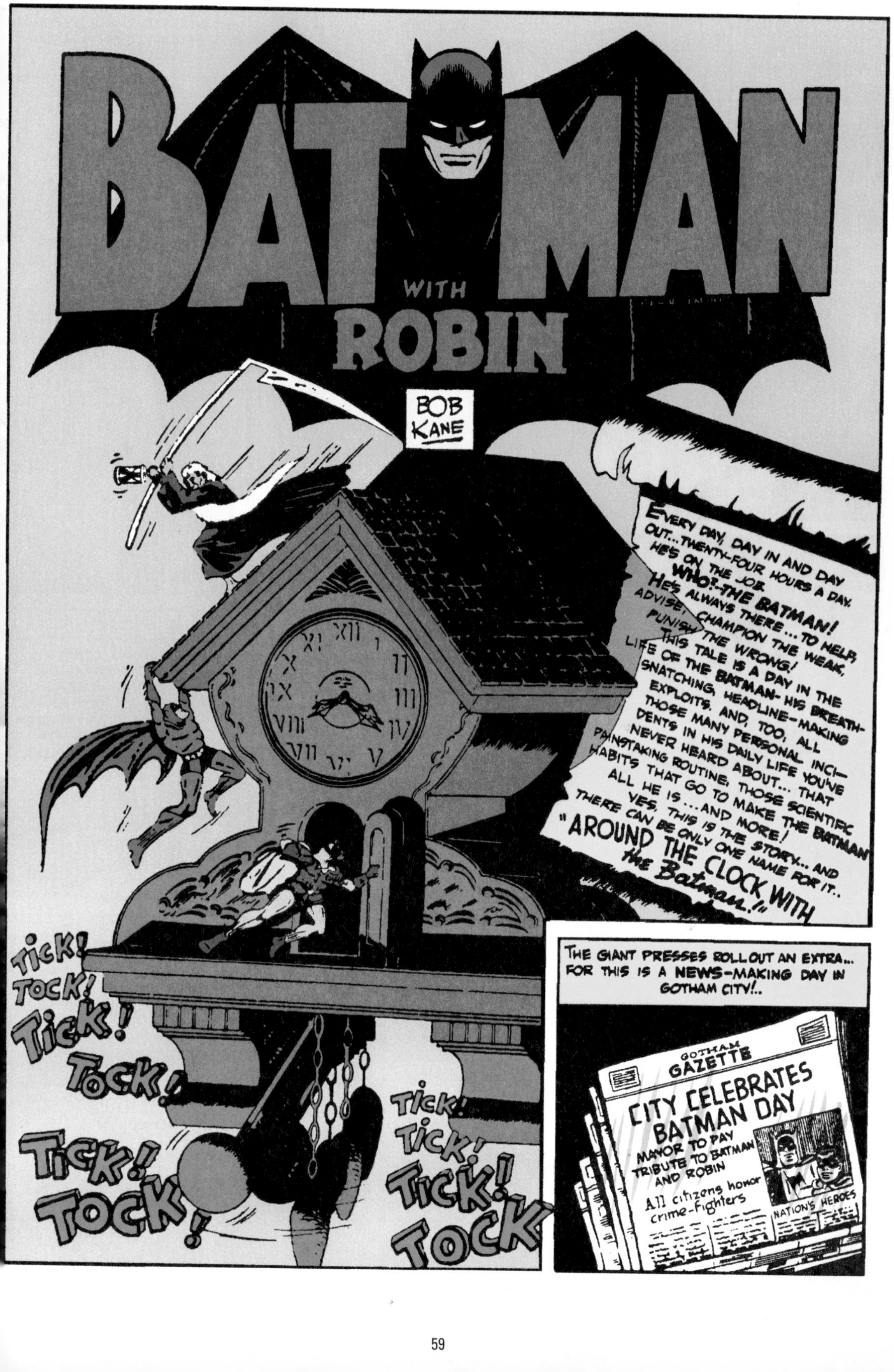
BATMAN
WITH
ROBIN
BOB KANE
EVERY DAY, DAY IN AND DAY OUT...TWENTY-FOUR HOURS A DAY. HE'S ON THE JOB. WHO?-THE BATMAN! HE'S ALWAYS THERE...TO HELP, ADVISE, CHAMPION THE WEAK, PUNISH THE WRONG! THIS TALE IS A DAY IN THE LIFE OF THE BATMAN- HIS BREATH-SNATCHING, HEADLINE-MAKING EXPLOITS. AND, TOO, ALL THOSE MANY PERSONAL INCI-DENTS IN HIS DAILY LIFE YOU'VE NEVER HEARD ABOUT... THAT PAINSTAKING ROUTINE, THOSE SCIENTIFIC HABITS THAT GO TO MAKE THE BATMAN ALL HE IS...AND MORE! YES, THIS IS THE STORY... AND THERE CAN BE ONLY ONE NAME FOR IT.. "AROUND THE CLOCK WITH the Batman!"
TICK! TOCK! TICK! TOCK!
TICK! TOCK!
TICK! TICK! TICK! TOCK
THE GIANT PRESSES ROLL OUT AN EXTRA... FOR THIS IS A NEWS-MAKING DAY IN GOTHAM CITY!..
GOTHAM GAZETTE
CITY CELEBRATES BATMAN DAY
MAYOR TO PAY TRIBUTE TO BATMAN AND ROBIN
All citizens honor crime-fighters
NATION'S HEROES

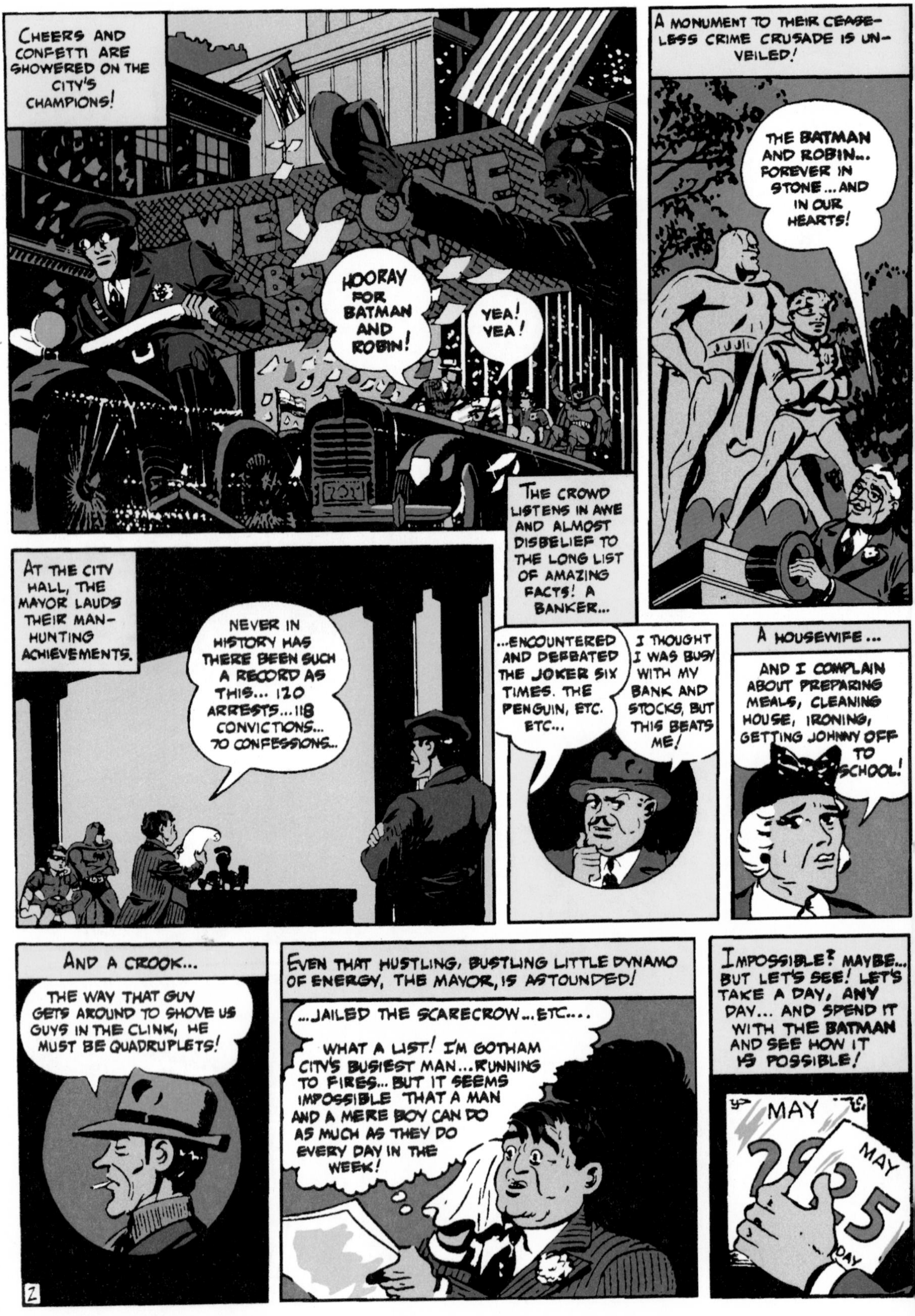
CHEERS AND CONFETTI ARE SHOWERED ON THE CITY'S CHAMPIONS!
HOORAY FOR BATMAN AND ROBIN!
YEA! YEA!
A MONUMENT TO THEIR CEASELESS CRIME CRUSADE IS UNVEILED!
THE BATMAN AND ROBIN... FOREVER IN STONE ... AND IN OUR HEARTS!
AT THE CITY HALL, THE MAYOR LAUDS THEIR MAN-HUNTING ACHIEVEMENTS.
NEVER IN HISTORY HAS THERE BEEN SUCH A RECORD AS THIS... 120 ARRESTS...118 CONVICTIONS... 70 CONFESSIONS...
THE CROWD LISTENS IN AWE AND ALMOST DISBELIEF TO THE LONG LIST OF AMAZING FACTS! A BANKER...
...ENCOUNTERED AND DEFEATED THE JOKER SIX TIMES. THE PENGUIN, ETC. ETC...
I THOUGHT I WAS BUSY WITH MY BANK AND STOCKS, BUT THIS BEATS ME!
A HOUSEWIFE ...
AND I COMPLAIN ABOUT PREPARING MEALS, CLEANING HOUSE, IRONING, GETTING JOHNNY OFF TO SCHOOL!
AND A CROOK...
THE WAY THAT GUY GETS AROUND TO SHOVE US GUYS IN THE CLINK, HE MUST BE QUADRUPLETS!
EVEN THAT HUSTLING, BUSTLING LITTLE DYNAMO OF ENERGY, THE MAYOR, IS ASTOUNDED!
...JAILED THE SCARECROW...ETC....
WHAT A LIST! I'M GOTHAM CITY'S BUSIEST MAN...RUNNING TO FIRES... BUT IT SEEMS IMPOSSIBLE THAT A MAN AND A MERE BOY CAN DO AS MUCH AS THEY DO EVERY DAY IN THE WEEK!
IMPOSSIBLE? MAYBE... BUT LET'S SEE! LET'S TAKE A DAY, ANY DAY... AND SPEND IT WITH THE BATMAN AND SEE HOW IT IS POSSIBLE!
MAY
MAY
25
DAY
2

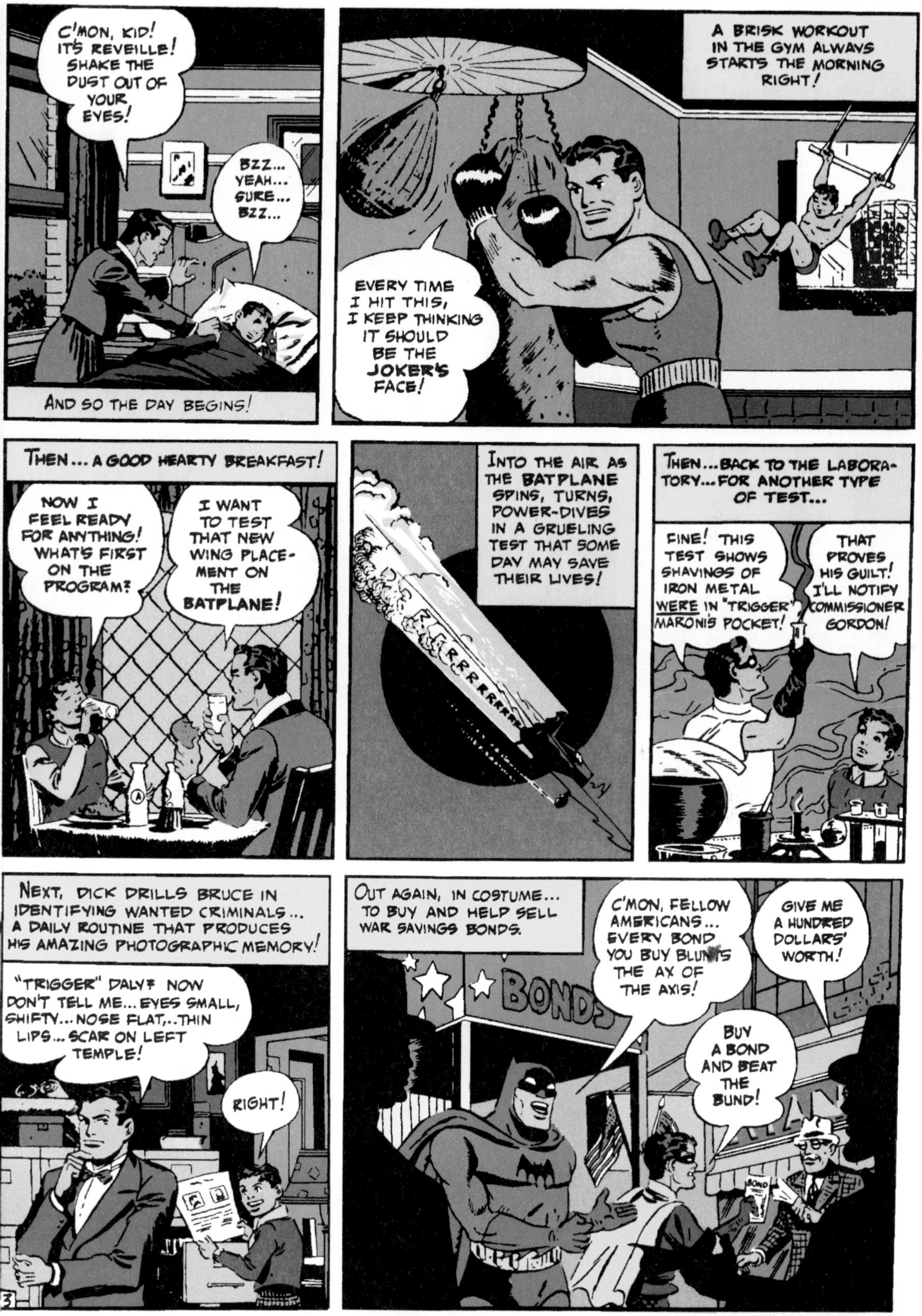
C'MON, KID! IT'S REVEILLE! SHAKE THE DUST OUT OF YOUR EYES!
BZZ... YEAH... SURE... BZZ...
AND SO THE DAY BEGINS!
A BRISK WORKOUT IN THE GYM ALWAYS STARTS THE MORNING RIGHT!
EVERY TIME I HIT THIS, I KEEP THINKING IT SHOULD BE THE JOKER'S FACE!
THEN... A GOOD HEARTY BREAKFAST!
NOW I FEEL READY FOR ANYTHING! WHAT'S FIRST ON THE PROGRAM?
I WANT TO TEST THAT NEW WING PLACEMENT ON THE BATPLANE!
INTO THE AIR AS THE BATPLANE SPINS, TURNS, POWER-DIVES IN A GRUELING TEST THAT SOME DAY MAY SAVE THEIR LIVES!
RRRRRRRRR
THEN... BACK TO THE LABORATORY... FOR ANOTHER TYPE OF TEST...
FINE! THIS TEST SHOWS SHAVINGS OF IRON METAL WERE IN "TRIGGER" MARONI'S POCKET!
THAT PROVES HIS GUILT! I'LL NOTIFY COMMISSIONER GORDON!
NEXT, DICK DRILLS BRUCE IN IDENTIFYING WANTED CRIMINALS... A DAILY ROUTINE THAT PRODUCES HIS AMAZING PHOTOGRAPHIC MEMORY!
"TRIGGER" DALY? NOW DON'T TELL ME... EYES SMALL, SHIFTY... NOSE FLAT... THIN LIPS... SCAR ON LEFT TEMPLE!
RIGHT!
3
OUT AGAIN, IN COSTUME... TO BUY AND HELP SELL WAR SAVINGS BONDS.
BONDS
C'MON, FELLOW AMERICANS... EVERY BOND YOU BUY BLUNTS THE AX OF THE AXIS!
GIVE ME A HUNDRED DOLLARS' WORTH!
BUY A BOND AND BEAT THE BUND!
BOND

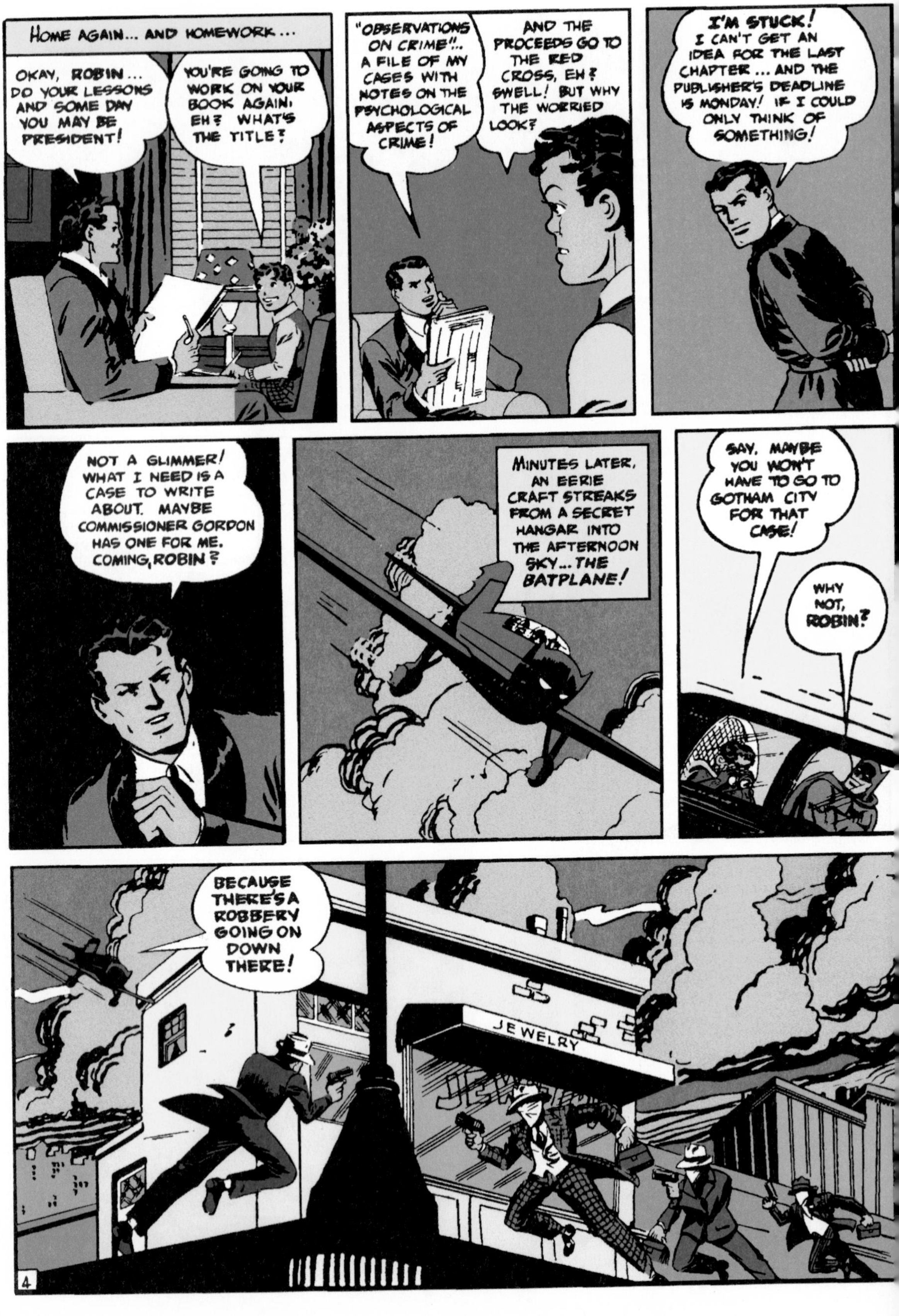
HOME AGAIN... AND HOMEWORK...
OKAY, ROBIN... DO YOUR LESSONS AND SOME DAY YOU MAY BE PRESIDENT!
YOU'RE GOING TO WORK ON YOUR BOOK AGAIN, EH? WHAT'S THE TITLE?
"OBSERVATIONS ON CRIME"... A FILE OF MY CASES WITH NOTES ON THE PSYCHOLOGICAL ASPECTS OF CRIME!
AND THE PROCEEDS GO TO THE RED CROSS, EH? SWELL! BUT WHY THE WORRIED LOOK?
I'M STUCK! I CAN'T GET AN IDEA FOR THE LAST CHAPTER ... AND THE PUBLISHER'S DEADLINE IS MONDAY! IF I COULD ONLY THINK OF SOMETHING!
NOT A GLIMMER! WHAT I NEED IS A CASE TO WRITE ABOUT. MAYBE COMMISSIONER GORDON HAS ONE FOR ME. COMING, ROBIN?
MINUTES LATER, AN EERIE CRAFT STREAKS FROM A SECRET HANGAR INTO THE AFTERNOON SKY... THE BATPLANE!
SAY, MAYBE YOU WON'T HAVE TO GO TO GOTHAM CITY FOR THAT CASE!
WHY NOT, ROBIN?
BECAUSE THERE'S A ROBBERY GOING ON DOWN THERE!
JEWELRY
4

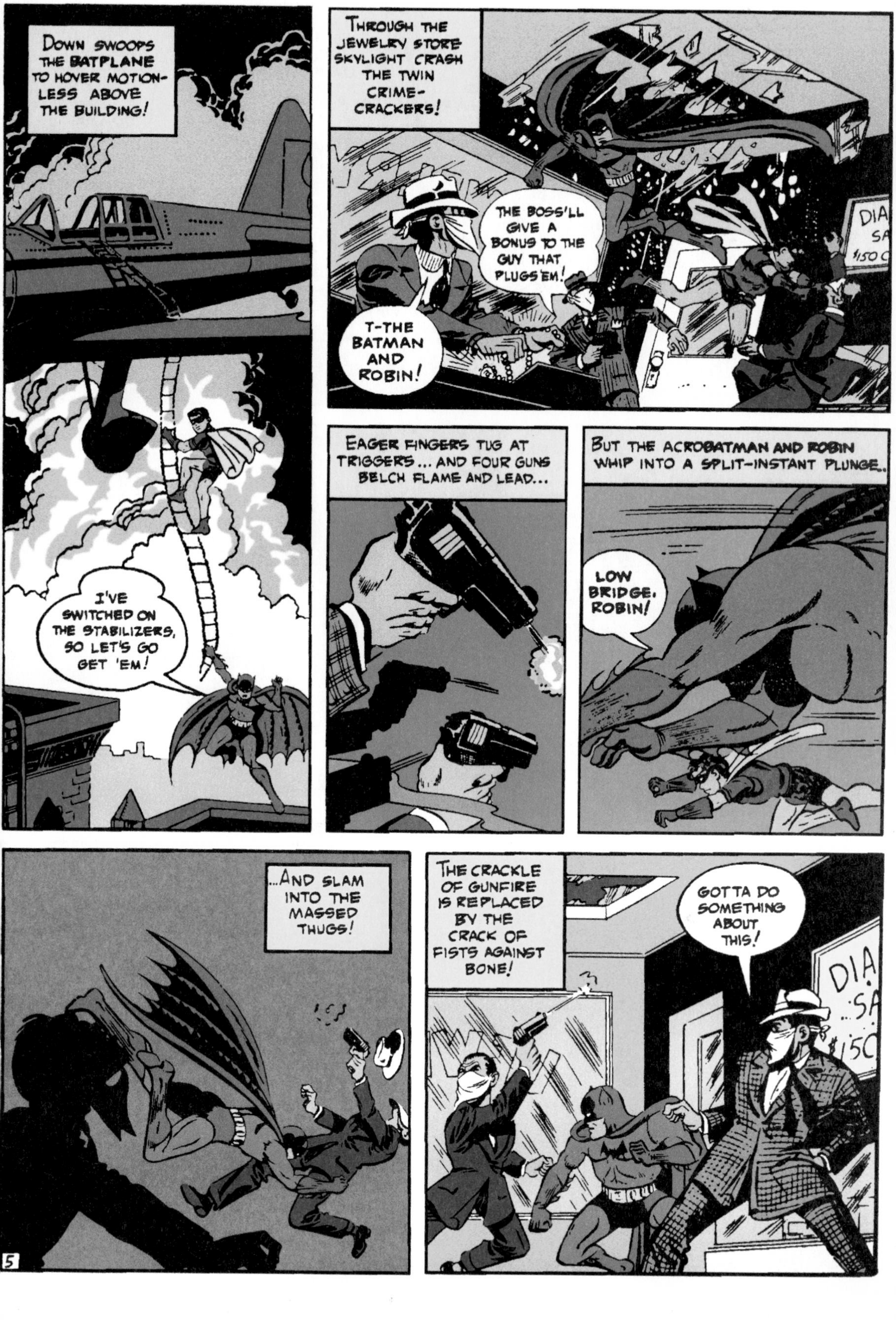
DOWN SWOOPS THE BATPLANE TO HOVER MOTIONLESS ABOVE THE BUILDING!
I'VE SWITCHED ON THE STABILIZERS, SO LET'S GO GET 'EM!
THROUGH THE JEWELRY STORE SKYLIGHT CRASH THE TWIN CRIME-CRACKERS!
T-THE BATMAN AND ROBIN!
THE BOSS'LL GIVE A BONUS TO THE GUY THAT PLUGS 'EM!
EAGER FINGERS TUG AT TRIGGERS ... AND FOUR GUNS BELCH FLAME AND LEAD...
BUT THE ACROBATMAN AND ROBIN WHIP INTO A SPLIT-INSTANT PLUNGE..
LOW BRIDGE, ROBIN!
...AND SLAM INTO THE MASSED THUGS!
5
THE CRACKLE OF GUNFIRE IS REPLACED BY THE CRACK OF FISTS AGAINST BONE!
GOTTA DO SOMETHING ABOUT THIS!

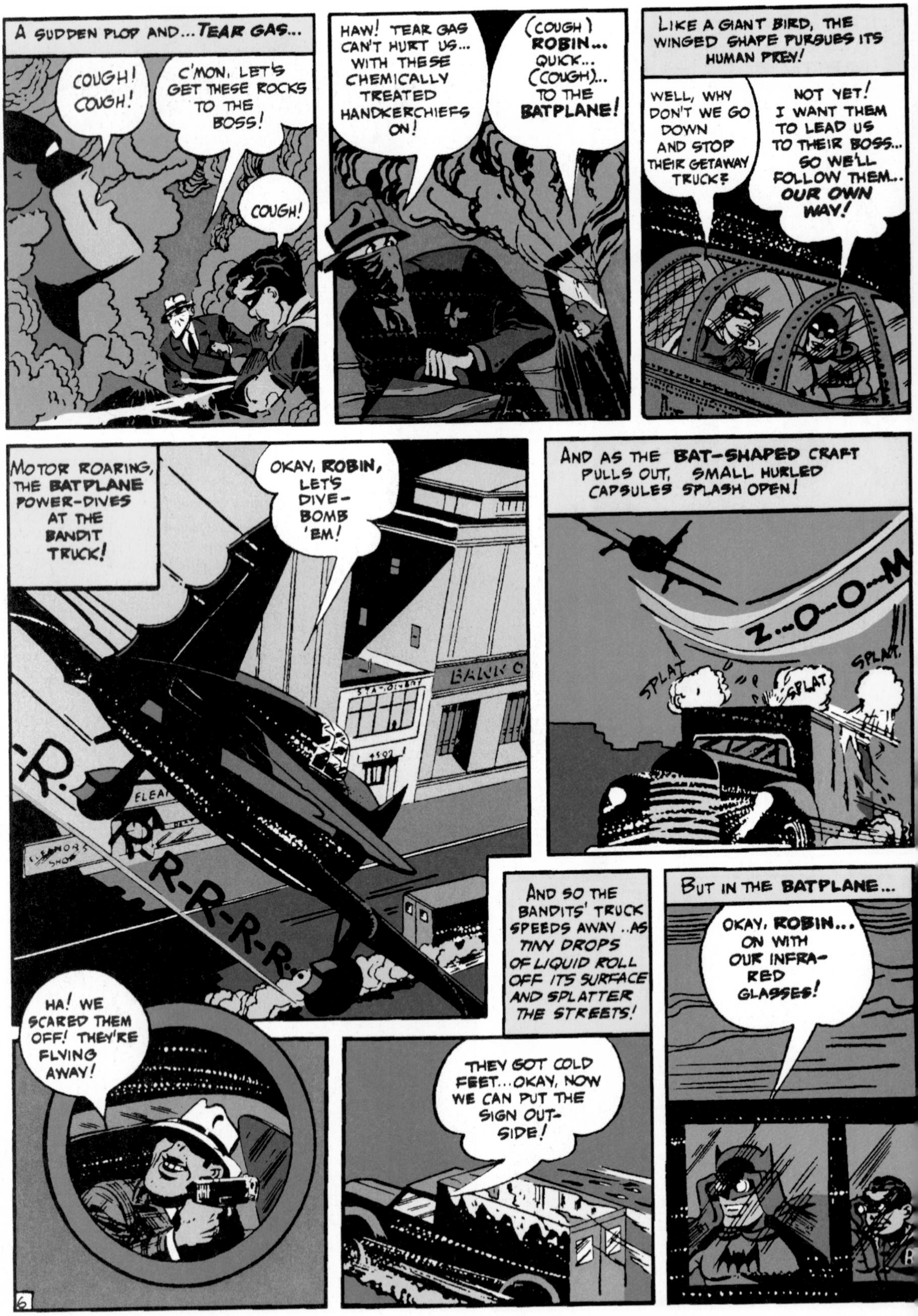

A SUDDEN PLOP AND... TEAR GAS...
COUGH! COUGH!
C'MON, LET'S GET THESE ROCKS TO THE BOSS!
COUGH!
HAW! TEAR GAS CAN'T HURT US... WITH THESE CHEMICALLY TREATED HANDKERCHIEFS ON!
(COUGH) ROBIN... QUICK... (COUGH)... TO THE BATPLANE!
LIKE A GIANT BIRD, THE WINGED SHAPE PURSUES ITS HUMAN PREY!
WELL, WHY DON'T WE GO DOWN AND STOP THEIR GETAWAY TRUCK?
NOT YET! I WANT THEM TO LEAD US TO THEIR BOSS... SO WE'LL FOLLOW THEM... OUR OWN WAY!
MOTOR ROARING, THE BATPLANE POWER-DIVES AT THE BANDIT TRUCK!
OKAY, ROBIN, LET'S DIVE-BOMB 'EM!
-R-R-R-R-R-R-R-
BANK O
STATIONERY
AND AS THE BAT-SHAPED CRAFT PULLS OUT, SMALL HURLED CAPSULES SPLASH OPEN!
Z-O-O-O-M
SPLAT SPLAT SPLAT
HA! WE SCARED THEM OFF! THEY'RE FLYING AWAY!
AND SO THE BANDITS' TRUCK SPEEDS AWAY.. AS TINY DROPS OF LIQUID ROLL OFF ITS SURFACE AND SPLATTER THE STREETS!
THEY GOT COLD FEET... OKAY, NOW WE CAN PUT THE SIGN OUT-SIDE!
BUT IN THE BATPLANE...
OKAY, ROBIN... ON WITH OUR INFRA-RED GLASSES!
6

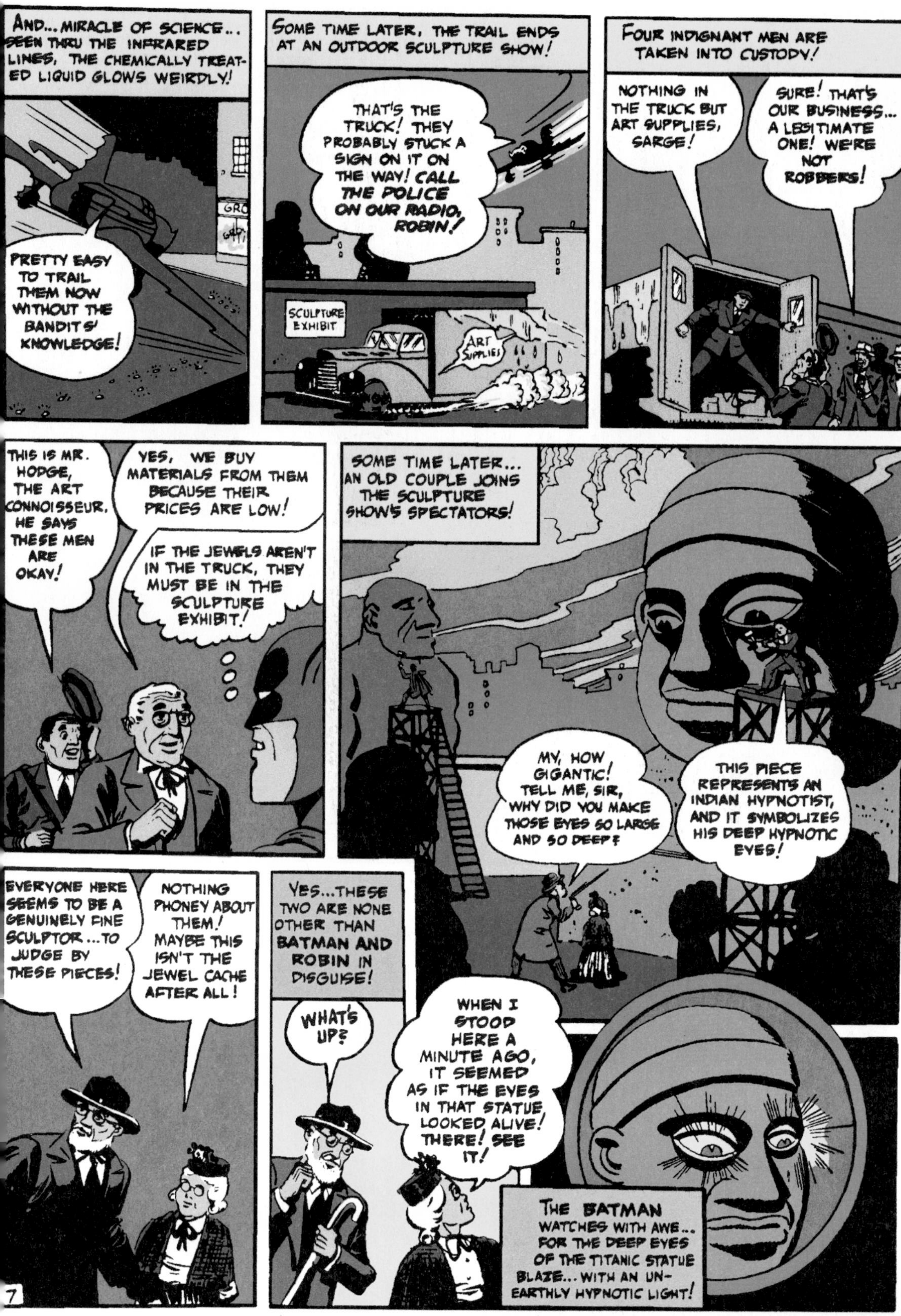
AND... MIRACLE OF SCIENCE... SEEN THRU THE INFRARED LINES, THE CHEMICALLY TREATED LIQUID GLOWS WEIRDLY!
PRETTY EASY TO TRAIL THEM NOW WITHOUT THE BANDITS' KNOWLEDGE!
SOME TIME LATER, THE TRAIL ENDS AT AN OUTDOOR SCULPTURE SHOW!
THAT'S THE TRUCK! THEY PROBABLY STUCK A SIGN ON IT ON THE WAY! CALL THE POLICE ON OUR RADIO, ROBIN!
SCULPTURE EXHIBIT
ART SUPPLIES
FOUR INDIGNANT MEN ARE TAKEN INTO CUSTODY!
NOTHING IN THE TRUCK BUT ART SUPPLIES, SARGE!
SURE! THAT'S OUR BUSINESS... A LEGITIMATE ONE! WE'RE NOT ROBBERS!
THIS IS MR. HODGE, THE ART CONNOISSEUR. HE SAYS THESE MEN ARE OKAY!
YES, WE BUY MATERIALS FROM THEM BECAUSE THEIR PRICES ARE LOW!
IF THE JEWELS AREN'T IN THE TRUCK, THEY MUST BE IN THE SCULPTURE EXHIBIT!
SOME TIME LATER... AN OLD COUPLE JOINS THE SCULPTURE SHOW'S SPECTATORS!
MY, HOW GIGANTIC! TELL ME, SIR, WHY DID YOU MAKE THOSE EYES SO LARGE AND SO DEEP?
THIS PIECE REPRESENTS AN INDIAN HYPNOTIST, AND IT SYMBOLIZES HIS DEEP HYPNOTIC EYES!
EVERYONE HERE SEEMS TO BE A GENUINELY FINE SCULPTOR... TO JUDGE BY THESE PIECES!
NOTHING PHONEY ABOUT THEM! MAYBE THIS ISN'T THE JEWEL CACHE AFTER ALL!
7
YES... THESE TWO ARE NONE OTHER THAN BATMAN AND ROBIN IN DISGUISE!
WHAT'S UP?
WHEN I STOOD HERE A MINUTE AGO, IT SEEMED AS IF THE EYES IN THAT STATUE LOOKED ALIVE! THERE! SEE IT!
THE BATMAN WATCHES WITH AWE... FOR THE DEEP EYES OF THE TITANIC STATUE BLAZE... WITH AN UNEARTHLY HYPNOTIC LIGHT!

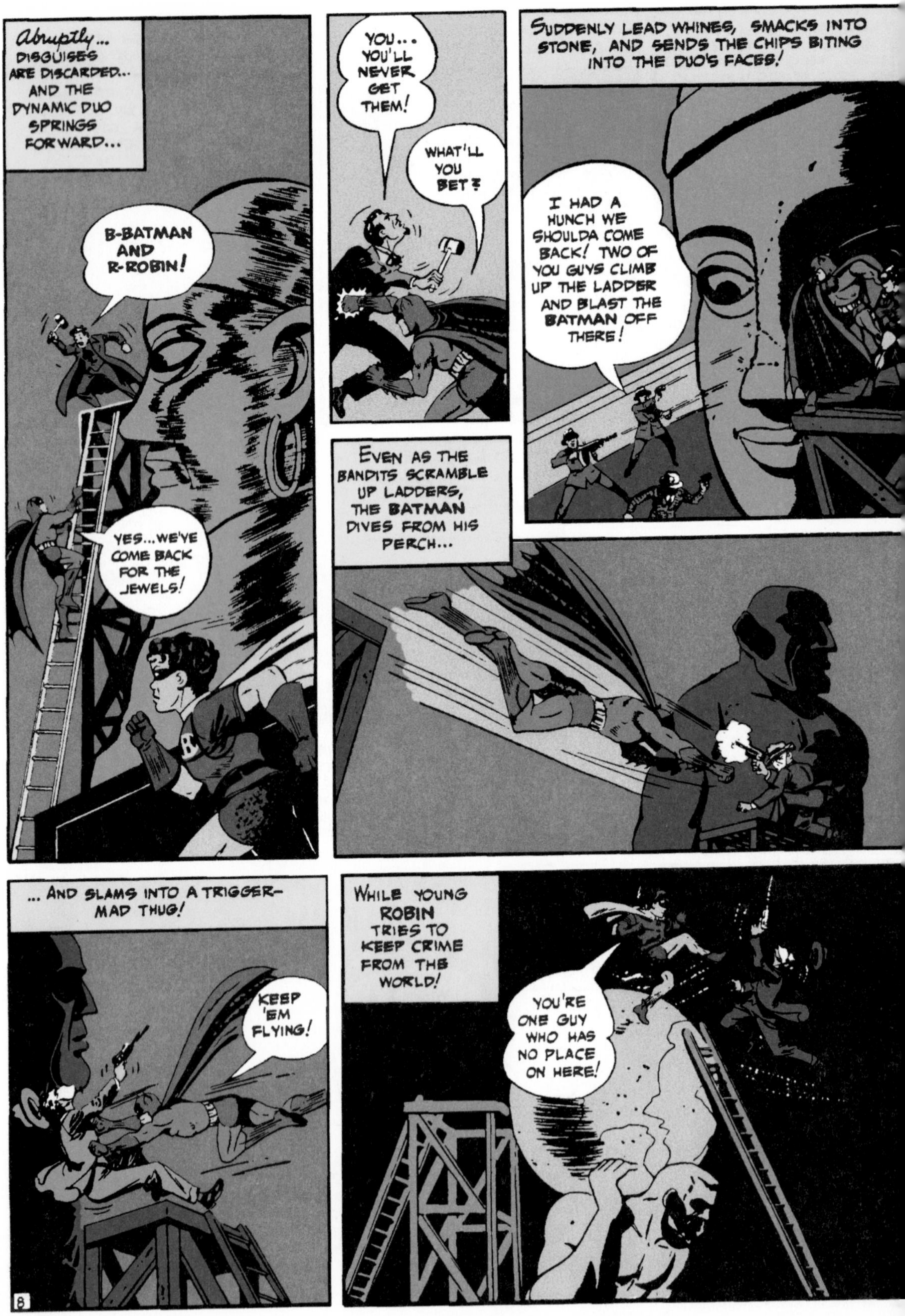
Abruptly... DISGUISES ARE DISCARDED... AND THE DYNAMIC DUO SPRINGS FORWARD...
B-BATMAN AND R-ROBIN!
YES...WE'VE COME BACK FOR THE JEWELS!
YOU... YOU'LL NEVER GET THEM!
WHAT'LL YOU BET?
SUDDENLY LEAD WHINES, SMACKS INTO STONE, AND SENDS THE CHIPS BITING INTO THE DUO'S FACES!
I HAD A HUNCH WE SHOULDA COME BACK! TWO OF YOU GUYS CLIMB UP THE LADDER AND BLAST THE BATMAN OFF THERE!
EVEN AS THE BANDITS SCRAMBLE UP LADDERS, THE BATMAN DIVES FROM HIS PERCH...
... AND SLAMS INTO A TRIGGER-MAD THUG!
KEEP 'EM FLYING!
8
WHILE YOUNG ROBIN TRIES TO KEEP CRIME FROM THE WORLD!
YOU'RE ONE GUY WHO HAS NO PLACE ON HERE!

THEN...THE WAIL OF A POLICE SIREN!

WHEEEEEEE

COPS! THIS IS NO PLACE FER US! C'MON, LET'S BEAT IT!

BUT ALREADY ROBIN RIDES A SCAFFOLD LADDER THAT ARCS DOWN...

...AND SNARES THE HOODLUMS WHILE HE BREAKS HIS FALL WITH AN OLD CIRCUS STUNT!

THE POLICE TAKE OVER...

OUR SCULPTOR FRIEND WAS USING THIS SHOW AS A HIDEOUT FOR STOLEN GEMS. HIS MEN POSED AS ART SUPPLY DEALERS!

BUT WHERE ARE THE GEMS?

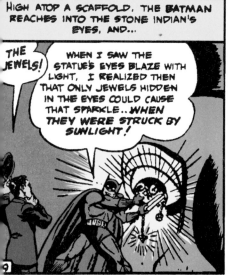

HIGH ATOP A SCAFFOLD, THE BATMAN REACHES INTO THE STONE INDIAN'S EYES, AND...

THE JEWELS!

WHEN I SAW THE STATUE'S EYES BLAZE WITH LIGHT, I REALIZED THEN THAT ONLY JEWELS HIDDEN IN THE EYES COULD CAUSE THAT SPARKLE...WHEN THEY WERE STRUCK BY SUNLIGHT!

GENTLEMEN, THE SCULPTURE SHOW IS SPONSORED BY A CONSERVATIVE PATRON. THIS UNFAVORABLE PUBLICITY WOULD PUT US IN A BAD LIGHT... HE MIGHT WITHDRAW HIS SUPPORT!

DON'T WORRY, I'LL SEE THAT THIS IS KEPT OUT OF THE PAPERS!

LATER, IN THE BATMOBILE...

WELL, NOW YOU CAN WRITE THIS STORY UP FOR THE LAST CHAPTER OF YOUR BOOK!

NO, ROBIN... IT WOULD HURT THE HONEST SCULPTORS AND THE SHOW! THEIR ART MUST BE PROTECTED! BUT... NOW WE'VE A DATE AT A HOSPITAL!

DON'T THINK THE DAY IS OVER YET... THIS IS ONLY THE BEGINNING, FOLKS... ONLY THE BEGINNING!

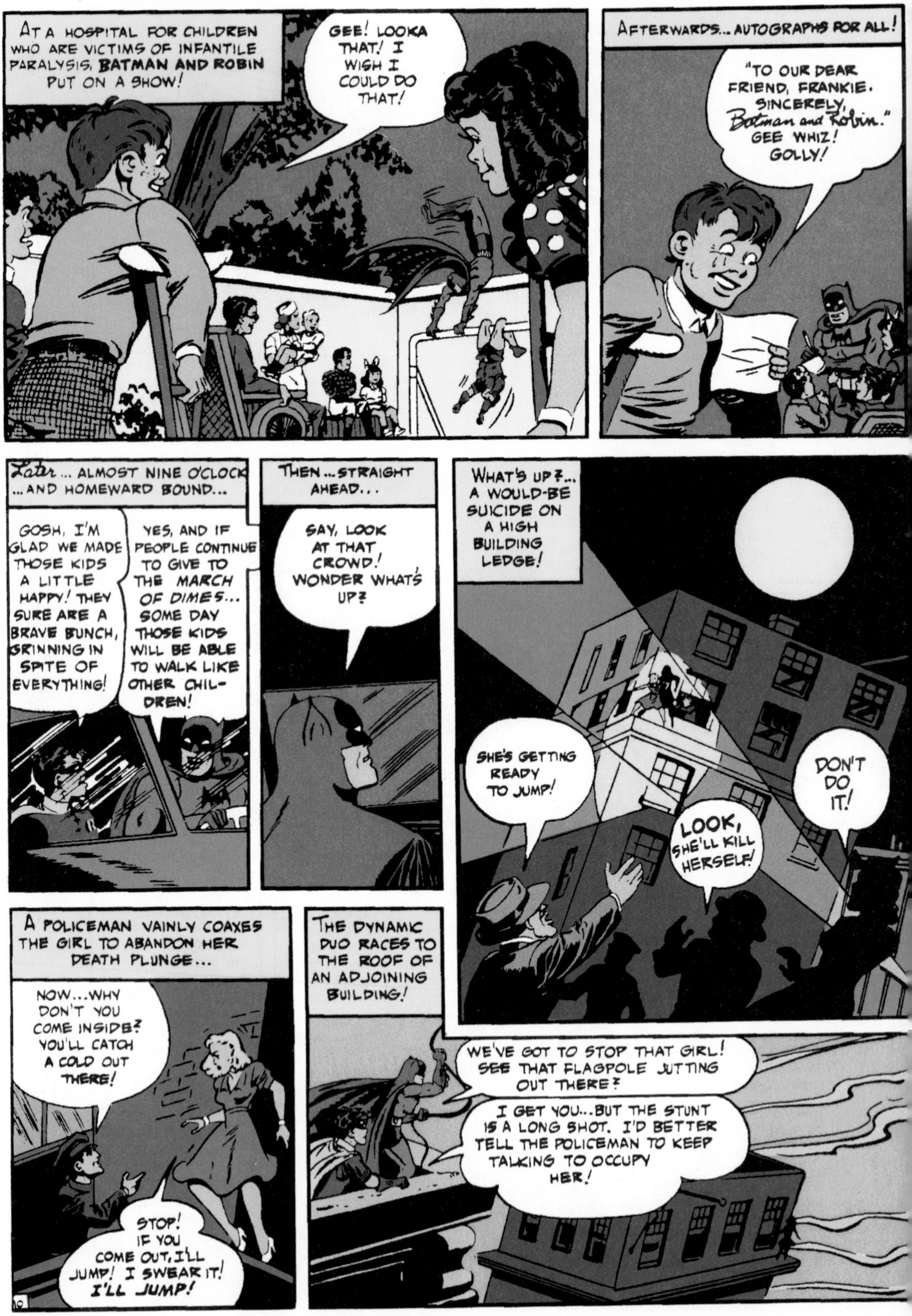
AT A HOSPITAL FOR CHILDREN WHO ARE VICTIMS OF INFANTILE PARALYSIS, BATMAN AND ROBIN PUT ON A SHOW!
GEE! LOOKA THAT! I WISH I COULD DO THAT!
AFTERWARDS... AUTOGRAPHS FOR ALL!
"TO OUR DEAR FRIEND, FRANKIE. SINCERELY, Batman and Robin." GEE WHIZ! GOLLY!
Later ... ALMOST NINE O'CLOCK ...AND HOMEWARD BOUND...
GOSH, I'M GLAD WE MADE THOSE KIDS A LITTLE HAPPY! THEY SURE ARE A BRAVE BUNCH, GRINNING IN SPITE OF EVERYTHING!
YES, AND IF PEOPLE CONTINUE TO GIVE TO THE MARCH OF DIMES... SOME DAY THOSE KIDS WILL BE ABLE TO WALK LIKE OTHER CHILDREN!
THEN ... STRAIGHT AHEAD...
SAY, LOOK AT THAT CROWD! WONDER WHAT'S UP?
WHAT'S UP?... A WOULD-BE SUICIDE ON A HIGH BUILDING LEDGE!
SHE'S GETTING READY TO JUMP!
DON'T DO IT!
LOOK, SHE'LL KILL HERSELF!
A POLICEMAN VAINLY COAXES THE GIRL TO ABANDON HER DEATH PLUNGE...
NOW...WHY DON'T YOU COME INSIDE? YOU'LL CATCH A COLD OUT THERE!
STOP! IF YOU COME OUT, I'LL JUMP! I SWEAR IT! I'LL JUMP!
THE DYNAMIC DUO RACES TO THE ROOF OF AN ADJOINING BUILDING!
WE'VE GOT TO STOP THAT GIRL! SEE THAT FLAGPOLE JUTTING OUT THERE?
I GET YOU...BUT THE STUNT IS A LONG SHOT. I'D BETTER TELL THE POLICEMAN TO KEEP TALKING TO OCCUPY HER!

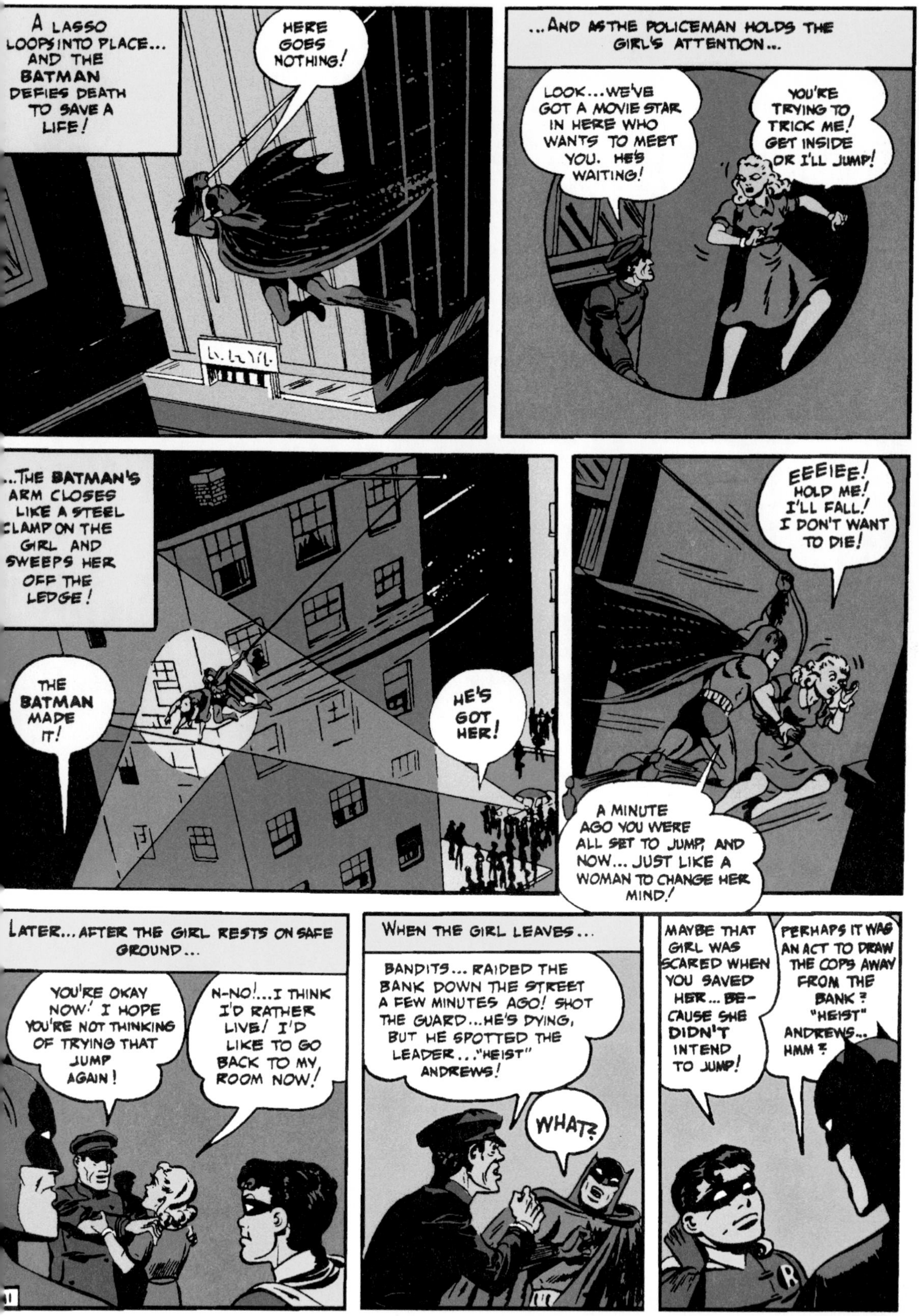

A LASSO LOOPS INTO PLACE... AND THE BATMAN DEFIES DEATH TO SAVE A LIFE!
HERE GOES NOTHING!
...AND AS THE POLICEMAN HOLDS THE GIRL'S ATTENTION...
LOOK...WE'VE GOT A MOVIE STAR IN HERE WHO WANTS TO MEET YOU. HE'S WAITING!
YOU'RE TRYING TO TRICK ME! GET INSIDE OR I'LL JUMP!
...THE BATMAN'S ARM CLOSES LIKE A STEEL CLAMP ON THE GIRL AND SWEEPS HER OFF THE LEDGE!
THE BATMAN MADE IT!
HE'S GOT HER!
EEEIEE! HOLD ME! I'LL FALL! I DON'T WANT TO DIE!
A MINUTE AGO YOU WERE ALL SET TO JUMP, AND NOW... JUST LIKE A WOMAN TO CHANGE HER MIND!
LATER... AFTER THE GIRL RESTS ON SAFE GROUND...
YOU'RE OKAY NOW! I HOPE YOU'RE NOT THINKING OF TRYING THAT JUMP AGAIN!
N-NO!...I THINK I'D RATHER LIVE! I'D LIKE TO GO BACK TO MY ROOM NOW!
WHEN THE GIRL LEAVES...
BANDITS... RAIDED THE BANK DOWN THE STREET A FEW MINUTES AGO! SHOT THE GUARD...HE'S DYING, BUT HE SPOTTED THE LEADER..."HEIST" ANDREWS!
WHAT?
MAYBE THAT GIRL WAS SCARED WHEN YOU SAVED HER... BE-CAUSE SHE DIDN'T INTEND TO JUMP!
PERHAPS IT WAS AN ACT TO DRAW THE COPS AWAY FROM THE BANK? "HEIST" ANDREWS... HMM?

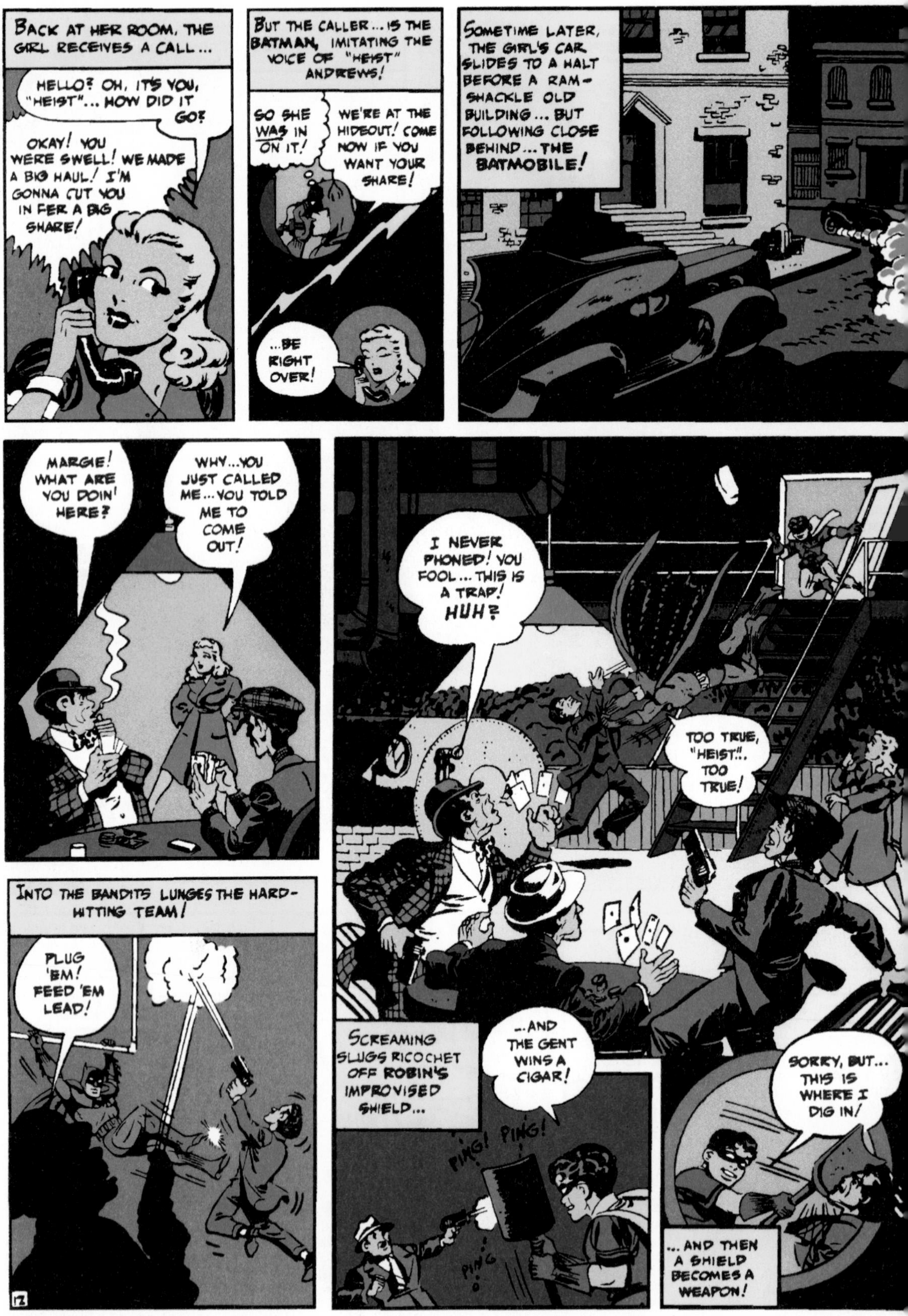
BACK AT HER ROOM, THE GIRL RECEIVES A CALL...
HELLO? OH, IT'S YOU, "HEIST"... HOW DID IT GO?
OKAY! YOU WERE SWELL! WE MADE A BIG HAUL! I'M GONNA CUT YOU IN FER A BIG SHARE!
BUT THE CALLER... IS THE BATMAN, IMITATING THE VOICE OF "HEIST" ANDREWS!
SO SHE WAS IN ON IT!
WE'RE AT THE HIDEOUT! COME NOW IF YOU WANT YOUR SHARE!
...BE RIGHT OVER!
SOMETIME LATER, THE GIRL'S CAR SLIDES TO A HALT BEFORE A RAM-SHACKLE OLD BUILDING... BUT FOLLOWING CLOSE BEHIND... THE BATMOBILE!
MARGIE! WHAT ARE YOU DOIN' HERE?
WHY...YOU JUST CALLED ME...YOU TOLD ME TO COME OUT!
I NEVER PHONED! YOU FOOL... THIS IS A TRAP! HUH?
TOO TRUE, "HEIST"!.. TOO TRUE!
INTO THE BANDITS LUNGES THE HARD-HITTING TEAM!
PLUG 'EM! FEED 'EM LEAD!
12
SCREAMING SLUGS RICOCHET OFF ROBIN'S IMPROVISED SHIELD...
..AND THE GENT WINS A CIGAR!
PING! PING!
PING
SORRY, BUT... THIS IS WHERE I DIG IN!
...AND THEN A SHIELD BECOMES A WEAPON!

THE HURRICANE ACTION OF THE TYPHOON TEAM PANICS THE HOODLUMS AND...

MAKE WAY FER A GUY WHAT'S IN A HURRY!

ONE SIDE!

BUT THE WORD "ESCAPE" IS KNOCKED RIGHT OUT OF THE THUG'S VOCABULARY!

ASHES TO ASHES...

RIGHT BEHIND YOU, PAL!

FROM NOW ON, "HEIST"— YOU'RE GOING TO BE SINGING THE "PRISONER'S SONG".. AND IT WON'T BE A SOLO, EITHER!

LATER... AT THE JAIL, A THUG MAKES A SHAMEFUL PLEA ...

LOOK! MY MOM'S PRETTY SICK... SHE AIN'T WISE I'M A CROOK... IF SHE READS ABOUT IT, THE SHOCK WILL KILL HER!

ALL RIGHT... FOR YOUR MOTHER'S SAKE, WE'LL KEEP THIS OUT OF THE PAPERS.

OH-H-H! THERE GOES MY LAST CHAPTER AGAIN!

STILL LATER...HOME AGAIN FOR THE CRIME-FIGHTERS...

TOO BAD YOU CAN'T WRITE THAT STORY UP! WHAT ABOUT YOUR LAST CHAPTER NOW?

YOU TELL ME! I'VE GOT TO WRITE ABOUT SOMETHING... BUT WHAT? ..WHAT?

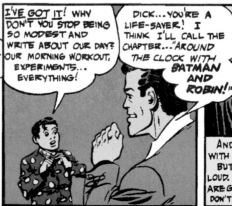

I'VE GOT IT! WHY DON'T YOU STOP BEING SO MODEST AND WRITE ABOUT OUR DAY? OUR MORNING WORKOUT, EXPERIMENTS... EVERYTHING!

DICK...YOU'RE A LIFE-SAVER! I THINK I'LL CALL THE CHAPTER..."AROUND THE CLOCK WITH BATMAN AND ROBIN!"

AND SO TO BED!

AND SO ENDS A TYPICAL DAY WITH BATMAN AND ROBIN!... BUT...SHH! LET'S NOT TALK SO LOUD. WE MIGHT WAKE THEM! THEY ARE GETTING A GOOD SLEEP! DON'T YOU THINK THEY DESERVE IT?

13

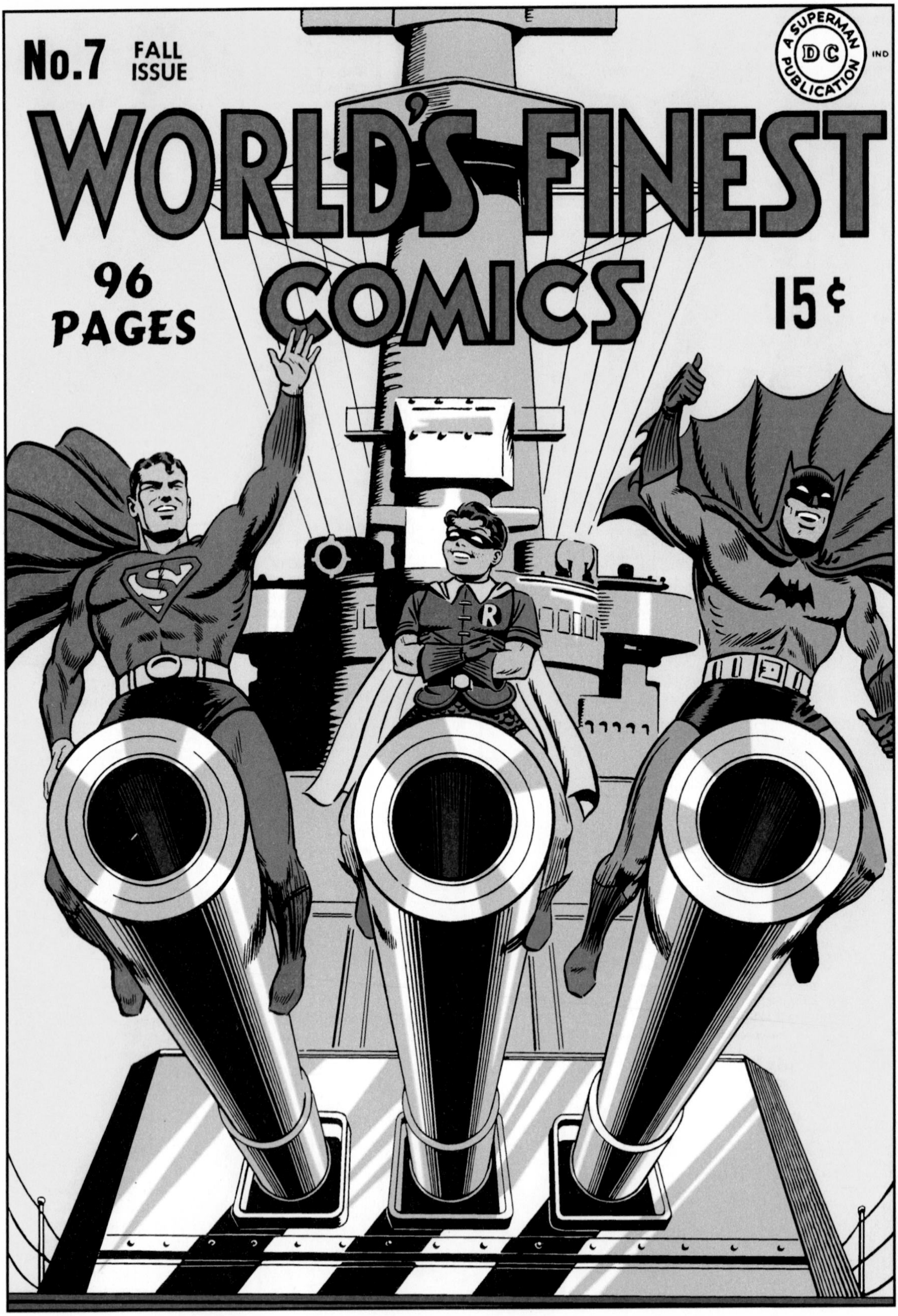
No.7 FALL ISSUE
A SUPERMAN DC PUBLICATION
IND
WORLD'S FINEST COMICS
96 PAGES
15¢
S
R

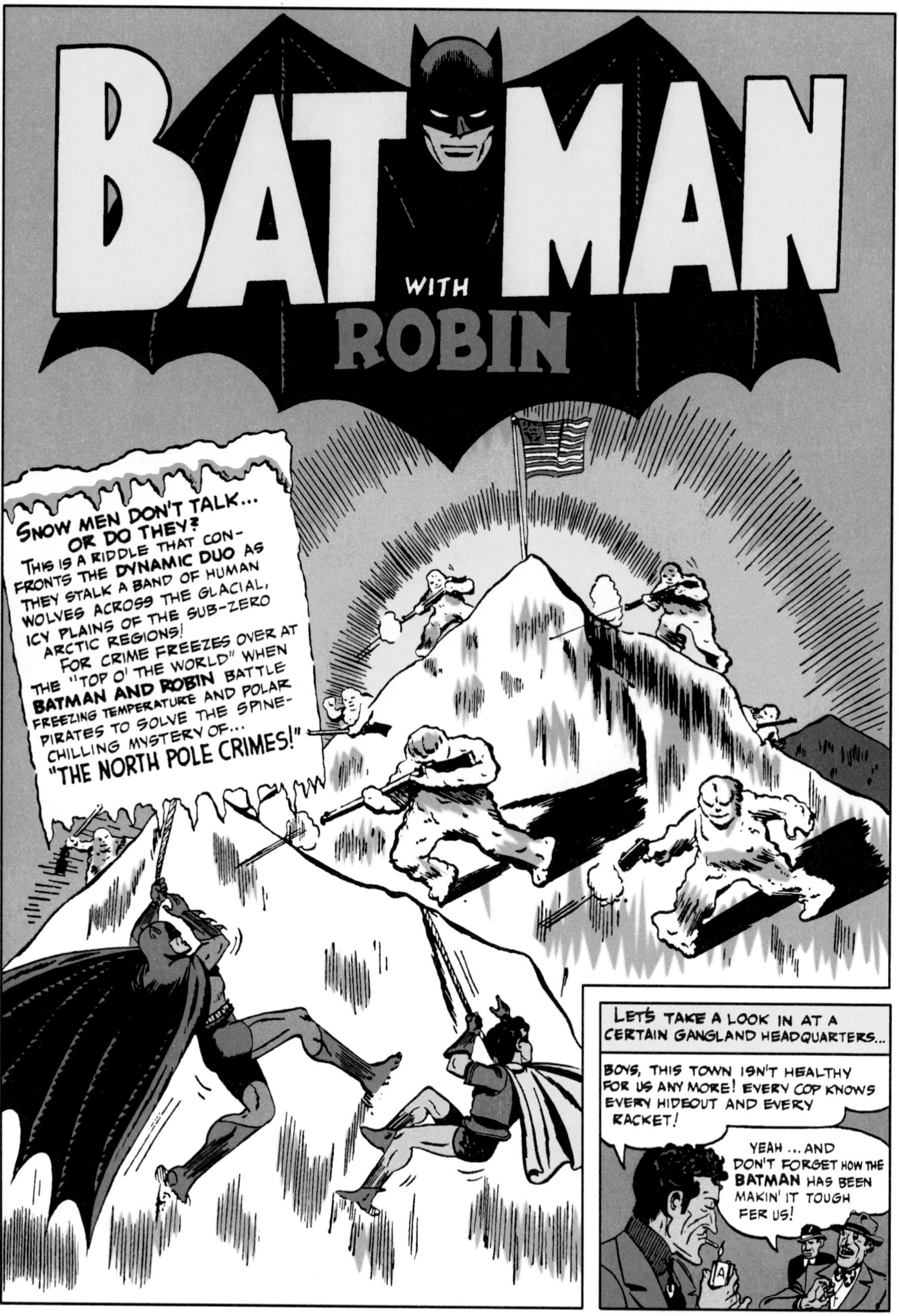
BATMAN
WITH
ROBIN
SNOW MEN DON'T TALK... OR DO THEY?
THIS IS A RIDDLE THAT CONFRONTS THE DYNAMIC DUO AS THEY STALK A BAND OF HUMAN WOLVES ACROSS THE GLACIAL, ICY PLAINS OF THE SUB-ZERO ARCTIC REGIONS!
FOR CRIME FREEZES OVER AT THE "TOP O' THE WORLD" WHEN BATMAN AND ROBIN BATTLE FREEZING TEMPERATURE AND POLAR PIRATES TO SOLVE THE SPINE-CHILLING MYSTERY OF...
"THE NORTH POLE CRIMES!"
LET'S TAKE A LOOK IN AT A CERTAIN GANGLAND HEADQUARTERS...
BOYS, THIS TOWN ISN'T HEALTHY FOR US ANY MORE! EVERY COP KNOWS EVERY HIDEOUT AND EVERY RACKET!
YEAH ... AND DON'T FORGET HOW THE BATMAN HAS BEEN MAKIN' IT TOUGH FER US!

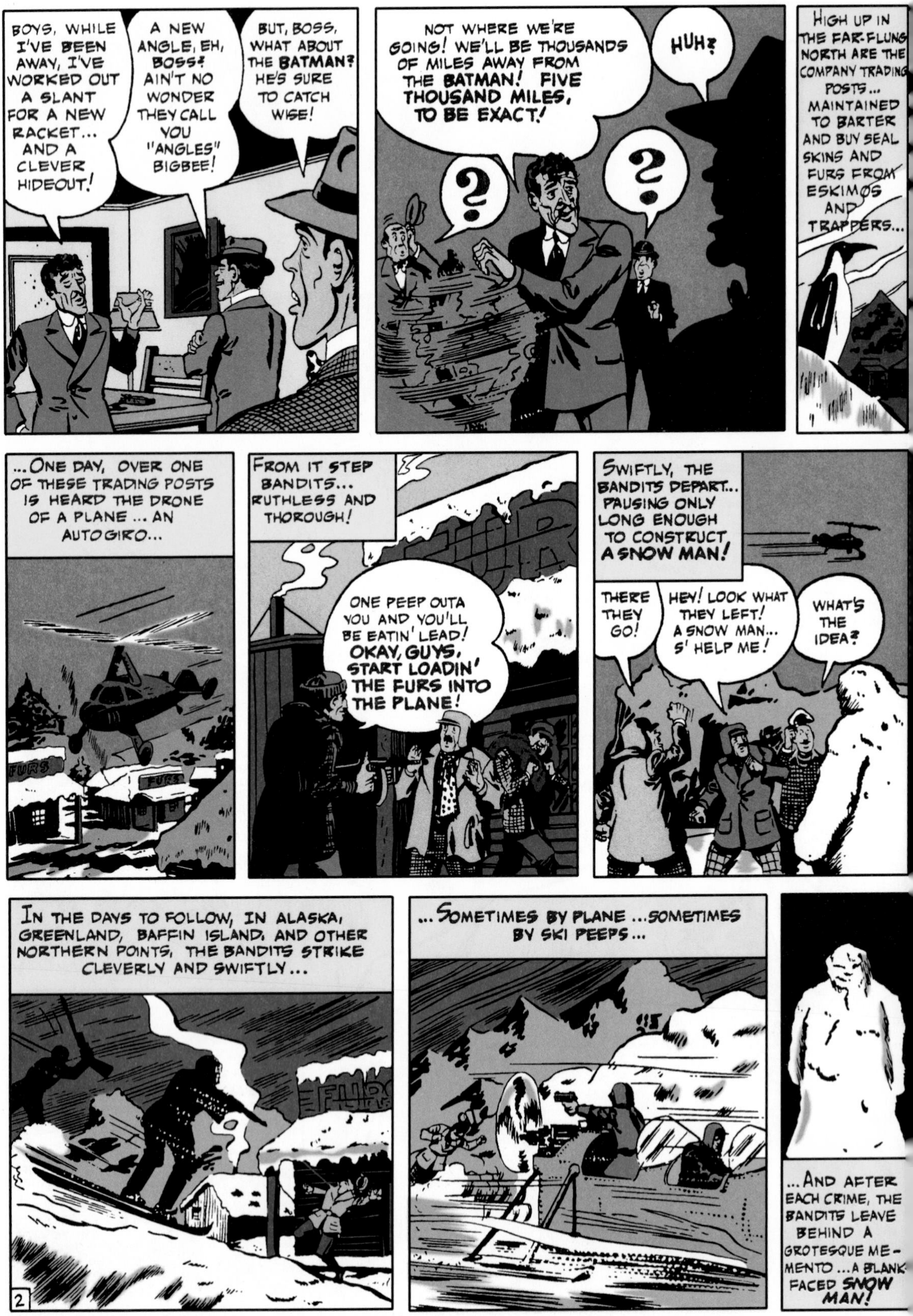
BOYS, WHILE I'VE BEEN AWAY, I'VE WORKED OUT A SLANT FOR A NEW RACKET... AND A CLEVER HIDEOUT!
A NEW ANGLE, EH, BOSS? AIN'T NO WONDER THEY CALL YOU "ANGLES" BIGBEE!
BUT, BOSS, WHAT ABOUT THE BATMAN? HE'S SURE TO CATCH WISE!
NOT WHERE WE'RE GOING! WE'LL BE THOUSANDS OF MILES AWAY FROM THE BATMAN! FIVE THOUSAND MILES, TO BE EXACT!
HUH?
?
?
HIGH UP IN THE FAR-FLUNG NORTH ARE THE COMPANY TRADING POSTS... MAINTAINED TO BARTER AND BUY SEAL SKINS AND FURS FROM ESKIMOS AND TRAPPERS...
...ONE DAY, OVER ONE OF THESE TRADING POSTS IS HEARD THE DRONE OF A PLANE ... AN AUTOGIRO...
FURS
FURS
FROM IT STEP BANDITS... RUTHLESS AND THOROUGH!
ONE PEEP OUTA YOU AND YOU'LL BE EATIN' LEAD! OKAY, GUYS, START LOADIN' THE FURS INTO THE PLANE!
SWIFTLY, THE BANDITS DEPART... PAUSING ONLY LONG ENOUGH TO CONSTRUCT A SNOW MAN!
THERE THEY GO!
HEY! LOOK WHAT THEY LEFT! A SNOW MAN... S' HELP ME!
WHAT'S THE IDEA?
IN THE DAYS TO FOLLOW, IN ALASKA, GREENLAND, BAFFIN ISLAND, AND OTHER NORTHERN POINTS, THE BANDITS STRIKE CLEVERLY AND SWIFTLY...
FURS
2
...SOMETIMES BY PLANE ...SOMETIMES BY SKI PEEPS...
...AND AFTER EACH CRIME, THE BANDITS LEAVE BEHIND A GROTESQUE MEMENTO ...A BLANK-FACED SNOW MAN!

FARTHER TO THE NORTH, A MAN SITS IN A ROOM AND LAUGHS!

A NICE HAUL, BOYS! YESSIR, WE'RE DOING ALL RIGHT FOR OURSELVES UP HERE! HA! HA!

YEAH ... AN' WHAT A HIDEOUT! I NEVER SEEN NOTHIN' LIKE IT BEFORE!

THE HIDEOUT? LOOK AT THIS GLACIER THAT SEEMS SO MUCH A PART OF THE LANDSCAPE ABOUT IT...

BUT, THE SECRET OF THAT GLACIER LIES INSIDE!

FOR THAT GLACIER IS IN REALITY THE FORTRESS AND LAIR OF..."THE "SNOW MAN BANDITS!"

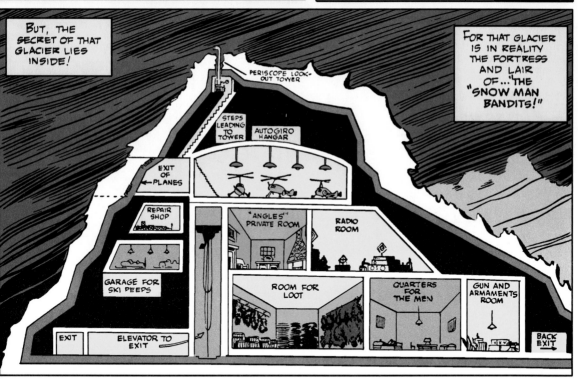

PERISCOPE LOOK-OUT TOWER

STEPS LEADING TO TOWER

AUTOGIRO HANGAR

EXIT OF ←PLANES

REPAIR SHOP

"ANGLES" PRIVATE ROOM

RADIO ROOM

GARAGE FOR SKI PEEPS

ROOM FOR LOOT

QUARTERS FOR THE MEN

GUN AND ARMAMENTS ROOM

EXIT

ELEVATOR TO EXIT

BACK EXIT

AT THAT MOMENT...OVER ANOTHER MOUNTAIN OF ICE!

BUT THIS IS A MOUNTAIN OF ICE CREAM, SET BEFORE DICK GRAYSON IN SUMMERY GOTHAM CITY!

BOY, AM I GOING TO ENJOY THIS! MMM!

BETTER ENJOY IT FAST, DICK... WE'VE GOT TO GO A-CALLING!

SOME TIME LATER, TWO COSTUMED ROVERS RACE OVER ROOFTOPS IN ANSWER TO A SUMMONS FROM THE SKY...THE SYMBOL OF A GIANT BAT!

POLICE WANT US, ROBIN!

3

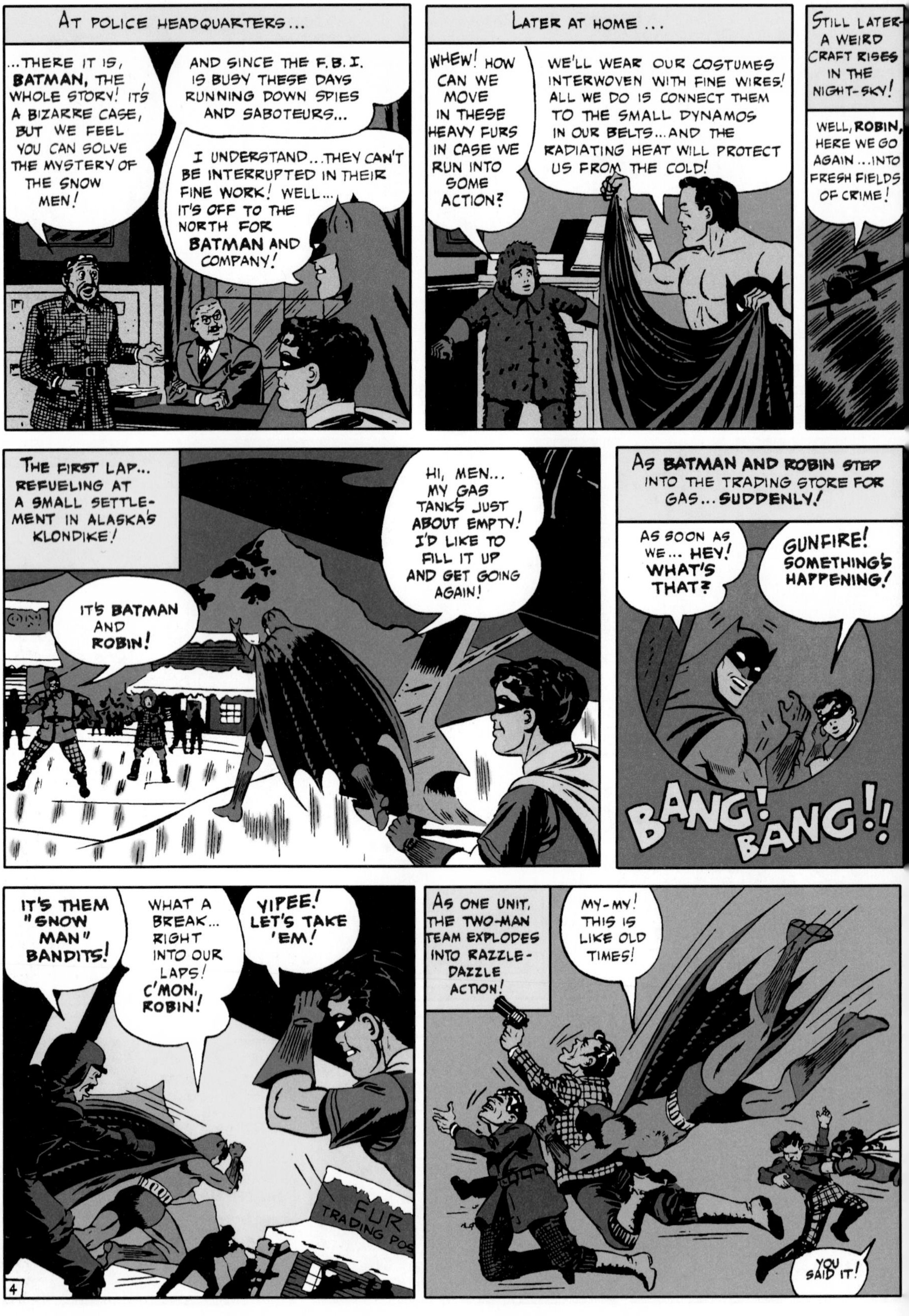
AT POLICE HEADQUARTERS...
...THERE IT IS, BATMAN, THE WHOLE STORY! IT'S A BIZARRE CASE, BUT WE FEEL YOU CAN SOLVE THE MYSTERY OF THE SNOW MEN!
AND SINCE THE F.B.I. IS BUSY THESE DAYS RUNNING DOWN SPIES AND SABOTEURS...
I UNDERSTAND...THEY CAN'T BE INTERRUPTED IN THEIR FINE WORK! WELL... IT'S OFF TO THE NORTH FOR BATMAN AND COMPANY!
LATER AT HOME ...
WHEW! HOW CAN WE MOVE IN THESE HEAVY FURS IN CASE WE RUN INTO SOME ACTION?
WE'LL WEAR OUR COSTUMES INTERWOVEN WITH FINE WIRES! ALL WE DO IS CONNECT THEM TO THE SMALL DYNAMOS IN OUR BELTS...AND THE RADIATING HEAT WILL PROTECT US FROM THE COLD!
STILL LATER-A WEIRD CRAFT RISES IN THE NIGHT-SKY!
WELL, ROBIN, HERE WE GO AGAIN ...INTO FRESH FIELDS OF CRIME!
THE FIRST LAP... REFUELING AT A SMALL SETTLEMENT IN ALASKA'S KLONDIKE!
HI, MEN... MY GAS TANK'S JUST ABOUT EMPTY! I'D LIKE TO FILL IT UP AND GET GOING AGAIN!
IT'S BATMAN AND ROBIN!
AS BATMAN AND ROBIN STEP INTO THE TRADING STORE FOR GAS... SUDDENLY!
AS SOON AS WE... HEY! WHAT'S THAT?
GUNFIRE! SOMETHING'S HAPPENING!
BANG! BANG!!
IT'S THEM "SNOW MAN" BANDITS!
WHAT A BREAK... RIGHT INTO OUR LAPS! C'MON, ROBIN!
YIPEE! LET'S TAKE 'EM!
FUR TRADING POS
4
AS ONE UNIT, THE TWO-MAN TEAM EXPLODES INTO RAZZLE-DAZZLE ACTION!
MY-MY! THIS IS LIKE OLD TIMES!
YOU SAID IT!

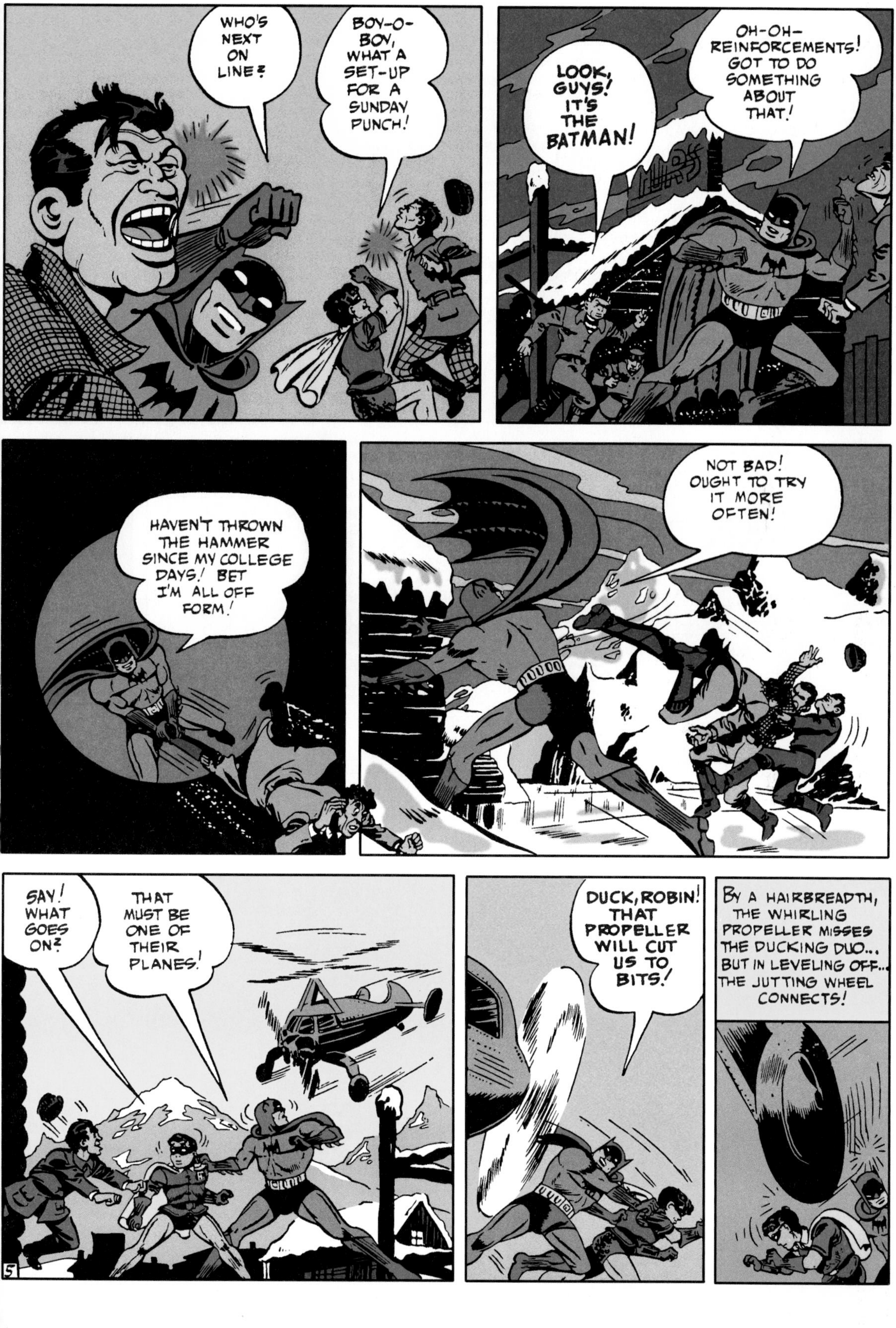
WHO'S NEXT ON LINE?
BOY-O-BOY, WHAT A SET-UP FOR A SUNDAY PUNCH!
LOOK, GUYS! IT'S THE BATMAN!
OH-OH- REINFORCEMENTS! GOT TO DO SOMETHING ABOUT THAT!
HAVEN'T THROWN THE HAMMER SINCE MY COLLEGE DAYS! BET I'M ALL OFF FORM!
NOT BAD! OUGHT TO TRY IT MORE OFTEN!
SAY! WHAT GOES ON?
THAT MUST BE ONE OF THEIR PLANES!
5
DUCK, ROBIN! THAT PROPELLER WILL CUT US TO BITS!
BY A HAIRBREADTH, THE WHIRLING PROPELLER MISSES THE DUCKING DUO... BUT IN LEVELING OFF... THE JUTTING WHEEL CONNECTS!

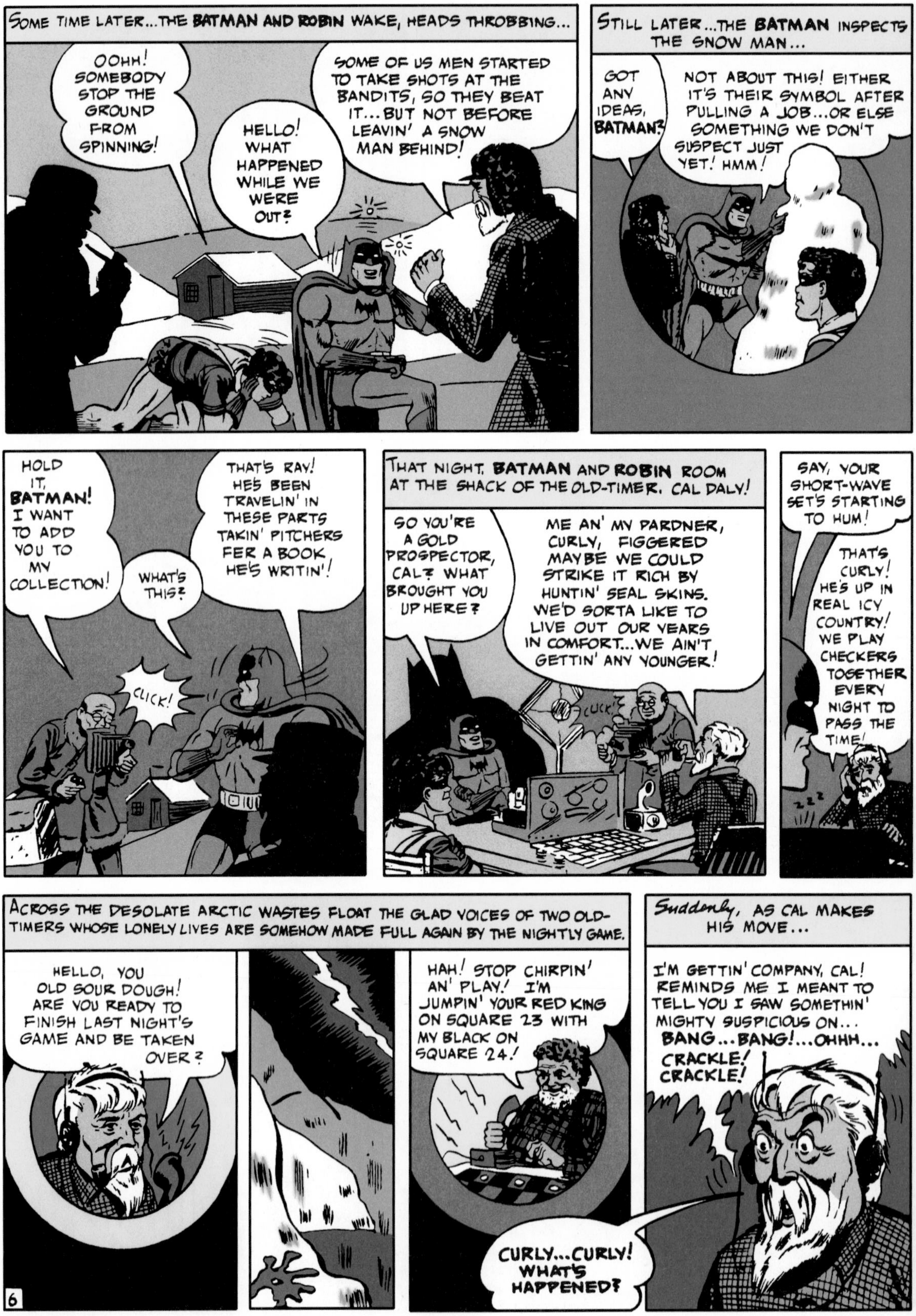
SOME TIME LATER...THE BATMAN AND ROBIN WAKE, HEADS THROBBING...
OOHH! SOMEBODY STOP THE GROUND FROM SPINNING!
HELLO! WHAT HAPPENED WHILE WE WERE OUT?
SOME OF US MEN STARTED TO TAKE SHOTS AT THE BANDITS, SO THEY BEAT IT...BUT NOT BEFORE LEAVIN' A SNOW MAN BEHIND!
STILL LATER...THE BATMAN INSPECTS THE SNOW MAN...
GOT ANY IDEAS, BATMAN?
NOT ABOUT THIS! EITHER IT'S THEIR SYMBOL AFTER PULLING A JOB...OR ELSE SOMETHING WE DON'T SUSPECT JUST YET! HMM!
HOLD IT, BATMAN! I WANT TO ADD YOU TO MY COLLECTION!
WHAT'S THIS?
THAT'S RAY! HE'S BEEN TRAVELIN' IN THESE PARTS TAKIN' PITCHERS FER A BOOK HE'S WRITIN'!
CLICK!
THAT NIGHT, BATMAN AND ROBIN ROOM AT THE SHACK OF THE OLD-TIMER, CAL DALY!
SO YOU'RE A GOLD PROSPECTOR, CAL? WHAT BROUGHT YOU UP HERE?
ME AN' MY PARDNER, CURLY, FIGGERED MAYBE WE COULD STRIKE IT RICH BY HUNTIN' SEAL SKINS. WE'D SORTA LIKE TO LIVE OUT OUR YEARS IN COMFORT...WE AIN'T GETTIN' ANY YOUNGER!
CLICK!
SAY, YOUR SHORT-WAVE SET'S STARTING TO HUM!
THAT'S CURLY! HE'S UP IN REAL ICY COUNTRY! WE PLAY CHECKERS TOGETHER EVERY NIGHT TO PASS THE TIME!
ACROSS THE DESOLATE ARCTIC WASTES FLOAT THE GLAD VOICES OF TWO OLD-TIMERS WHOSE LONELY LIVES ARE SOMEHOW MADE FULL AGAIN BY THE NIGHTLY GAME.
HELLO, YOU OLD SOUR DOUGH! ARE YOU READY TO FINISH LAST NIGHT'S GAME AND BE TAKEN OVER?
HAH! STOP CHIRPIN' AN' PLAY! I'M JUMPIN' YOUR RED KING ON SQUARE 23 WITH MY BLACK ON SQUARE 24!
Suddenly, AS CAL MAKES HIS MOVE...
I'M GETTIN' COMPANY, CAL! REMINDS ME I MEANT TO TELL YOU I SAW SOMETHIN' MIGHTY SUSPICIOUS ON...
BANG...BANG!...OHHH...
CRACKLE! CRACKLE!
CURLY...CURLY! WHAT'S HAPPENED?
6

HIS...HIS RADIO IS DEAD! SOMETHIN'S POWERFUL WRONG!

I'M GOING, TOO!

ROBIN, WHEEL OUT THE BATPLANE! WE'RE GOING TO SEE WHAT HAPPENED TO CURLY!

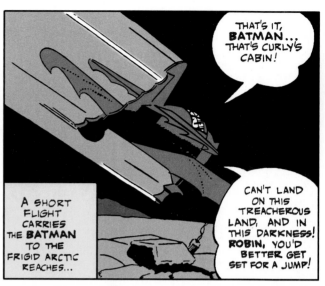

THAT'S IT, BATMAN... THAT'S CURLY'S CABIN!

A SHORT FLIGHT CARRIES THE BATMAN TO THE FRIGID ARCTIC REACHES...

CAN'T LAND ON THIS TREACHEROUS LAND, AND IN THIS DARKNESS! ROBIN, YOU'D BETTER GET SET FOR A JUMP!

AN INSTANT LATER, A SMALL FIGURE PLUNGES EARTHWARD...THEN STRAIGHTENS WITH A SNAP AS A PARACHUTE PUFFS OPEN!

LIGHTED FLARES CAST EERIE DANCING SHADOWS ON THE SNOW AS ROBIN GUIDES THE BATMAN VIA THEIR TWO-WAY RADIO!

OKAY...WATCH OUT FOR DRIFT ON RIGHT... COME IN EASY!

CHECK!

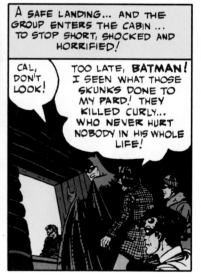

A SAFE LANDING... AND THE GROUP ENTERS THE CABIN ... TO STOP SHORT, SHOCKED AND HORRIFIED!

CAL, DON'T LOOK!

TOO LATE, BATMAN! I SEEN WHAT THOSE SKUNKS DONE TO MY PARD! THEY KILLED CURLY... WHO NEVER HURT NOBODY IN HIS WHOLE LIFE!

BATMAN, SOMETHING'S WRONG HERE! THE WAY THESE CHECKERS IS ON THAT BOARD DON'T MAKE SENSE!

HMM ... CAL, I THINK CURLY SET THE BOARD LIKE THAT TO SEND US A MESSAGE BEFORE HE DIED!

HE RECOGNIZED HIS MURDERERS! HE HAD NO PENCIL, BUT WANTED TO GIVE US A CLUE! CAL, WHY DOES EACH SQUARE HAVE A NUMBER ON IT?

SO WE COULD TELL EACH OTHER'S MOVES! CURLY AN' ME SET EACH OTHER'S BOARD BY THEM!

EXACTLY! NOTICE THE CHECKERS ARE ON SQUARES 2-9-11-15 -AND 21! IF WE SUBSTITUTE THE CORRESPONDING LETTERS OF THE ALPHABET WE GET... BIKOU!

7

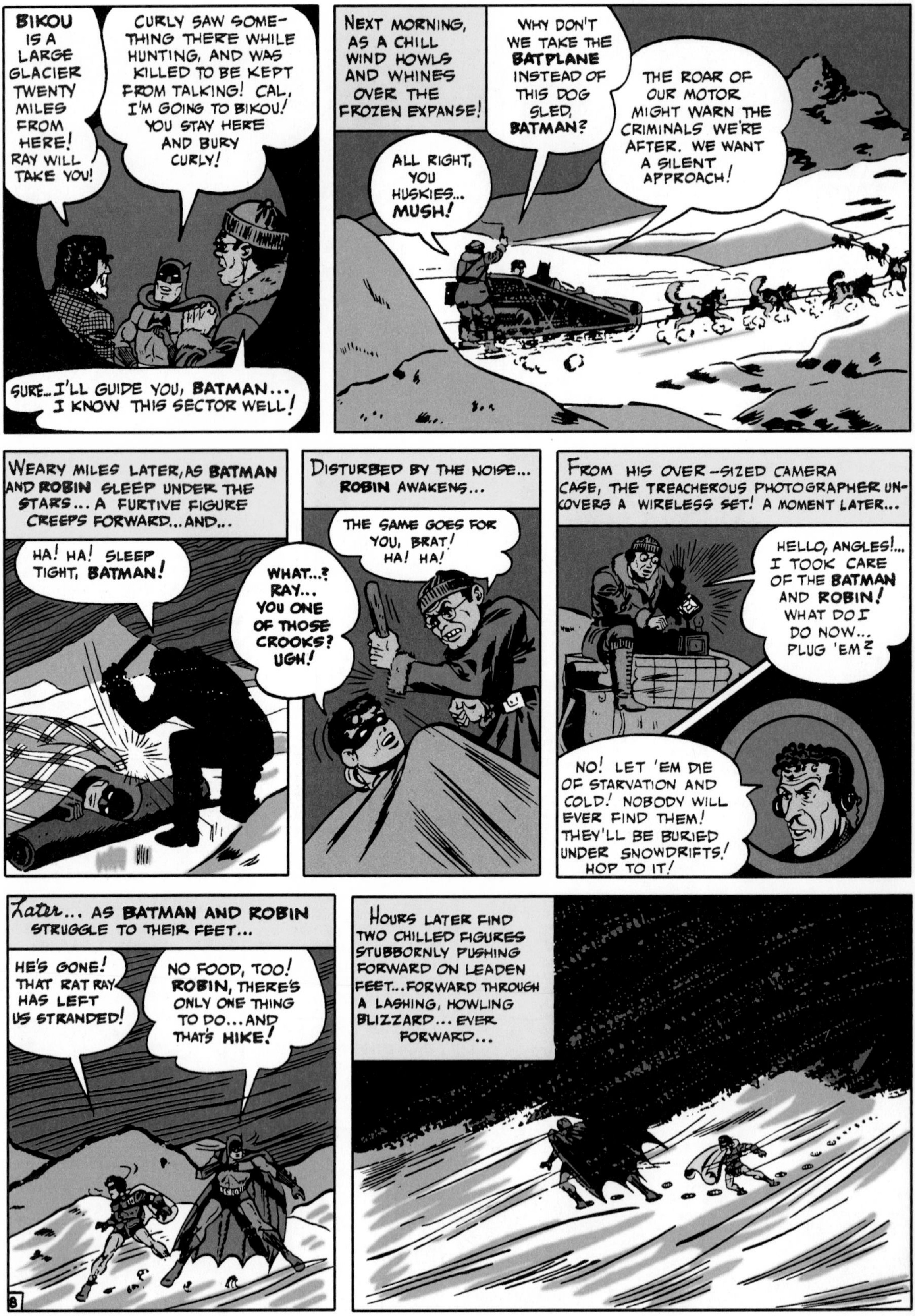
BIKOU IS A LARGE GLACIER TWENTY MILES FROM HERE! RAY WILL TAKE YOU!
CURLY SAW SOMETHING THERE WHILE HUNTING, AND WAS KILLED TO BE KEPT FROM TALKING! CAL, I'M GOING TO BIKOU! YOU STAY HERE AND BURY CURLY!
SURE...I'LL GUIDE YOU, BATMAN... I KNOW THIS SECTOR WELL!
NEXT MORNING, AS A CHILL WIND HOWLS AND WHINES OVER THE FROZEN EXPANSE!
WHY DON'T WE TAKE THE BATPLANE INSTEAD OF THIS DOG SLED, BATMAN?
THE ROAR OF OUR MOTOR MIGHT WARN THE CRIMINALS WE'RE AFTER. WE WANT A SILENT APPROACH!
ALL RIGHT, YOU HUSKIES... MUSH!
WEARY MILES LATER, AS BATMAN AND ROBIN SLEEP UNDER THE STARS... A FURTIVE FIGURE CREEPS FORWARD... AND...
HA! HA! SLEEP TIGHT, BATMAN!
DISTURBED BY THE NOISE... ROBIN AWAKENS...
THE SAME GOES FOR YOU, BRAT! HA! HA!
WHAT...? RAY... YOU ONE OF THOSE CROOKS? UGH!
FROM HIS OVER-SIZED CAMERA CASE, THE TREACHEROUS PHOTOGRAPHER UNCOVERS A WIRELESS SET! A MOMENT LATER...
HELLO, ANGLES!... I TOOK CARE OF THE BATMAN AND ROBIN! WHAT DO I DO NOW... PLUG 'EM?
NO! LET 'EM DIE OF STARVATION AND COLD! NOBODY WILL EVER FIND THEM! THEY'LL BE BURIED UNDER SNOWDRIFTS! HOP TO IT!
Later... AS BATMAN AND ROBIN STRUGGLE TO THEIR FEET...
HE'S GONE! THAT RAT RAY HAS LEFT US STRANDED!
NO FOOD, TOO! ROBIN, THERE'S ONLY ONE THING TO DO... AND THAT'S HIKE!
8
HOURS LATER FIND TWO CHILLED FIGURES STUBBORNLY PUSHING FORWARD ON LEADEN FEET... FORWARD THROUGH A LASHING, HOWLING BLIZZARD... EVER FORWARD...

THE TERRIBLE COLD CUTS LIKE AN ICY KNIFE AND CHILLS TO THE BONE!

SO COLD... CAN'T GO ON... I CAN'T!

YOU'VE GOT TO, ROBIN! IF WE STOP NOW, WE'RE GONERS!

ONE MILE LATER!....

S'FUNNY... I FEEL WARM NOW ...AND I'M GETTING SO SLEEPY... SO SLEEPY!

NO, ROBIN, NO! THAT'S THE FIRST SIGN THAT A PERSON'S FREEZING TO DEATH. FIGHT IT, KID...PRETEND YOU'RE HITTING THE JOKER! SWING... FIGHT... PUNCH!

WITHOUT WARNING, BATMAN SLAPS ROBIN SHARPLY!

SLEEPY! WANT TO SL.... UH!

QUITTING, EH? YOU HAVEN'T GOT WHAT IT TAKES TO KEEP FIGHTING! YOU'RE YELLOW... CLEAR THROUGH!

I SHOULD HAVE KNOWN BETTER THAN TO TEAM UP WITH A YELLOW LITTLE BRAT LIKE YOU!

YELLOW? ME, YELLOW!? AND AFTER ALL THE TIME I'VE HELPED YOU OUT OF SCRAPES!

I'M NOT YELLOW! YOU HEAR... I'M NOT YELLOW... I'M N--

HA! HA! TAKE IT EASY, CHUMP! I ONLY DID THAT TO GET YOU HOT UNDER THE COLLAR SO YOU'D FIGHT OFF THE COLD! IT WORKED, TOO!

UNITED AGAIN, THE TWO PALS TRUDGE ONWARD...AND THE BLIZZARD GIVES WAY TO A BLAZING SUN THAT REFLECTS DAZZLING RAYS OFF THE WHITE SNOW...

THAT SNOW... SO WHITE... IT HURTS MY EYES...

DON'T THINK ABOUT IT, ROBIN.., KEEP MOVING... GOT TO GO ON...

THEN... LATE UNDER THE AFTERNOON SUN... CATASTROPHE!

ME, TOO, ROBIN! IT'S THE SNOW... THE WHITE SNOW! WE'RE BLIND! SNOW BLIND!

BATMAN... MY EYES... I CAN'T SEE!

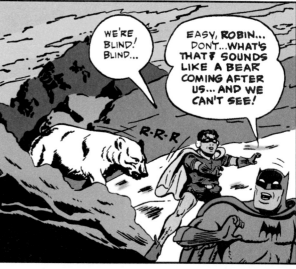

WE'RE BLIND! BLIND...

EASY, ROBIN... DON'T...WHAT'S THAT? SOUNDS LIKE A BEAR COMING AFTER US... AND WE CAN'T SEE!

R-R-R

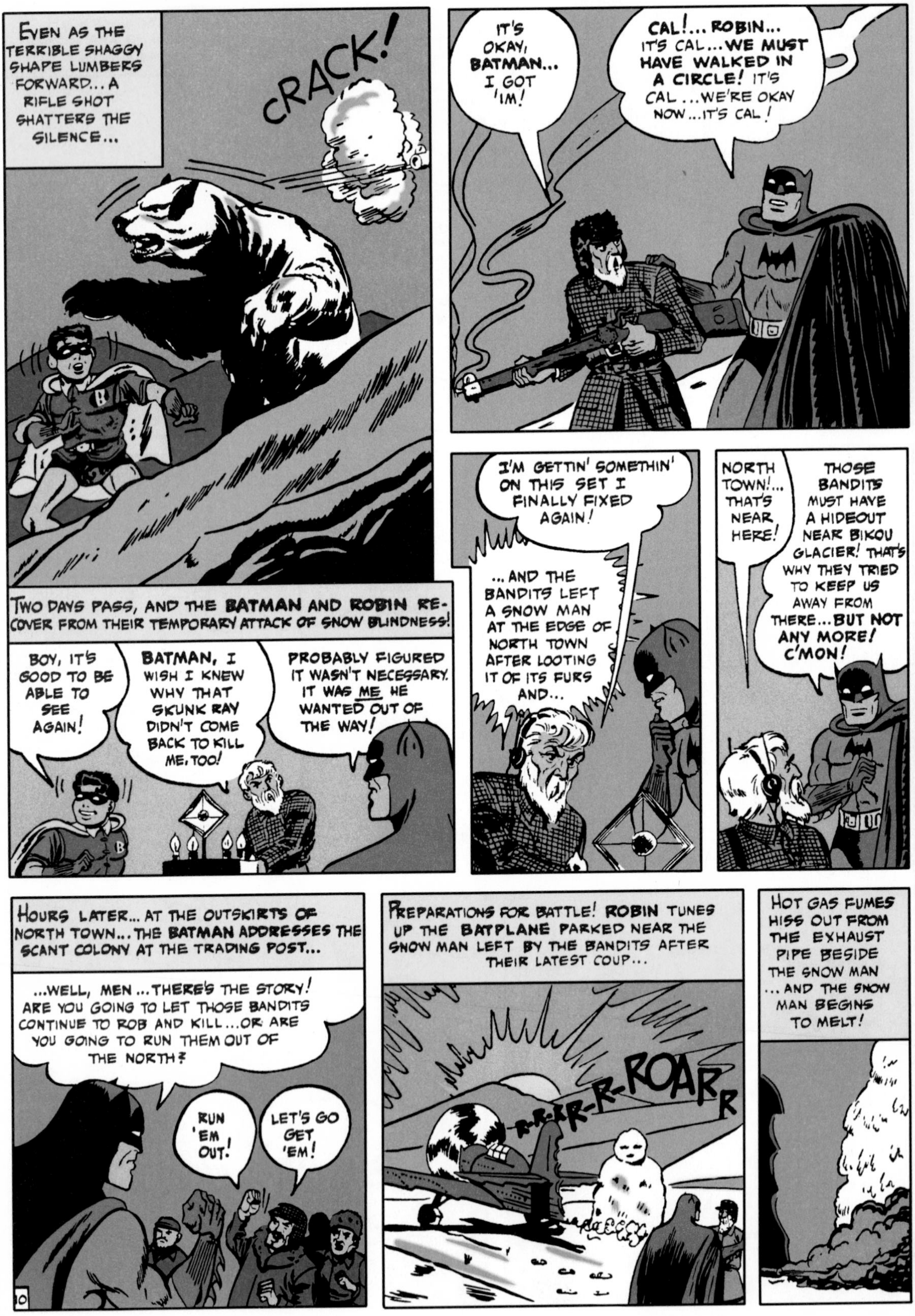

EVEN AS THE TERRIBLE SHAGGY SHAPE LUMBERS FORWARD... A RIFLE SHOT SHATTERS THE SILENCE...
CRACK!
IT'S OKAY, BATMAN... I GOT 'IM!
CAL!... ROBIN... IT'S CAL... WE MUST HAVE WALKED IN A CIRCLE! IT'S CAL... WE'RE OKAY NOW... IT'S CAL!
TWO DAYS PASS, AND THE BATMAN AND ROBIN RECOVER FROM THEIR TEMPORARY ATTACK OF SNOW BLINDNESS!
BOY, IT'S GOOD TO BE ABLE TO SEE AGAIN!
BATMAN, I WISH I KNEW WHY THAT SKUNK RAY DIDN'T COME BACK TO KILL ME, TOO!
PROBABLY FIGURED IT WASN'T NECESSARY. IT WAS ME HE WANTED OUT OF THE WAY!
I'M GETTIN' SOMETHIN' ON THIS SET I FINALLY FIXED AGAIN!
... AND THE BANDITS LEFT A SNOW MAN AT THE EDGE OF NORTH TOWN AFTER LOOTING IT OF ITS FURS AND...
NORTH TOWN!... THAT'S NEAR HERE!
THOSE BANDITS MUST HAVE A HIDEOUT NEAR BIKOU GLACIER! THAT'S WHY THEY TRIED TO KEEP US AWAY FROM THERE... BUT NOT ANY MORE! C'MON!
HOURS LATER... AT THE OUTSKIRTS OF NORTH TOWN... THE BATMAN ADDRESSES THE SCANT COLONY AT THE TRADING POST...
...WELL, MEN... THERE'S THE STORY! ARE YOU GOING TO LET THOSE BANDITS CONTINUE TO ROB AND KILL... OR ARE YOU GOING TO RUN THEM OUT OF THE NORTH?
RUN 'EM OUT!
LET'S GO GET 'EM!
10
PREPARATIONS FOR BATTLE! ROBIN TUNES UP THE BATPLANE PARKED NEAR THE SNOW MAN LEFT BY THE BANDITS AFTER THEIR LATEST COUP...
R-R-R-R-R-ROARRR
HOT GAS FUMES HISS OUT FROM THE EXHAUST PIPE BESIDE THE SNOW MAN ... AND THE SNOW MAN BEGINS TO MELT!

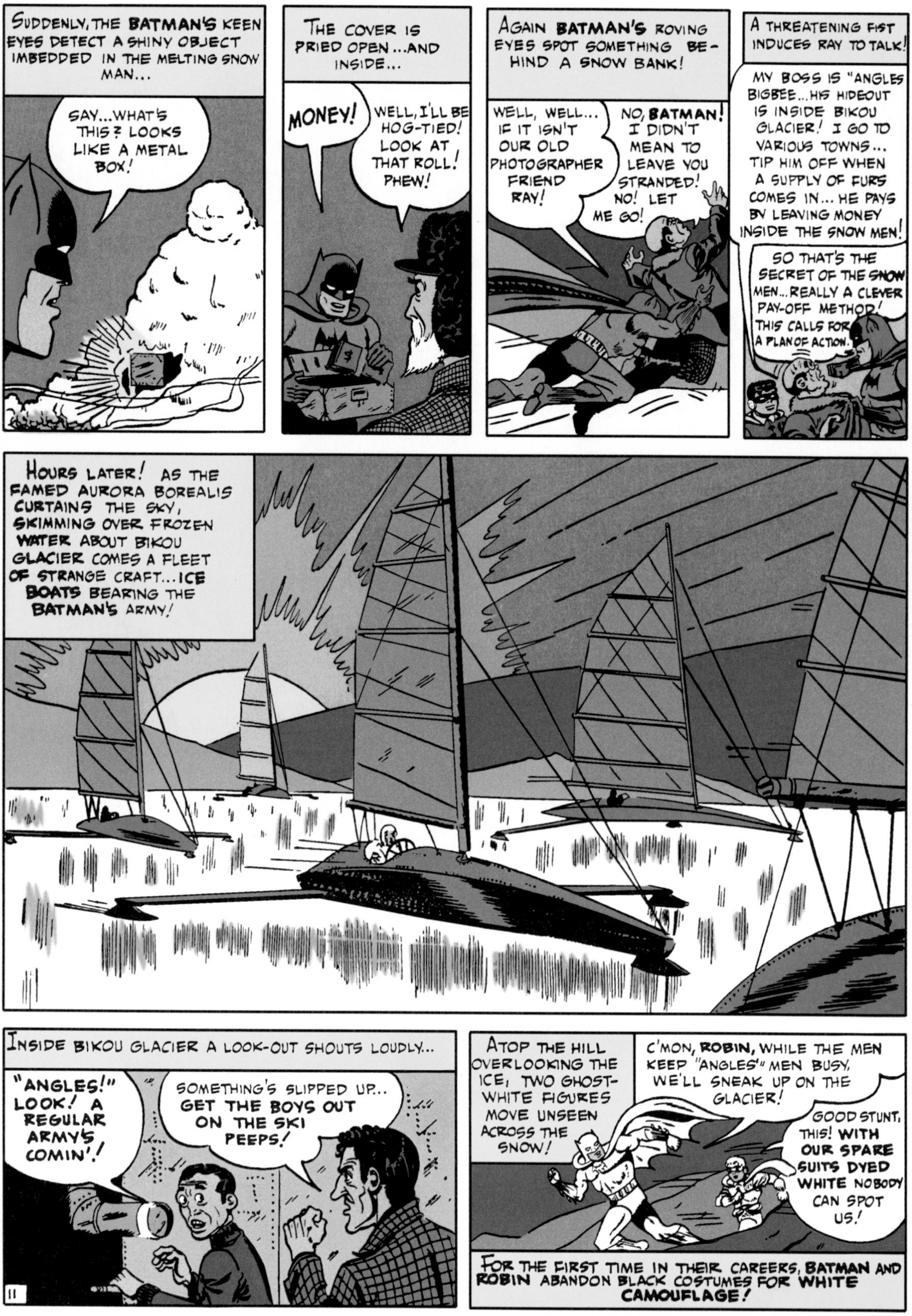

SUDDENLY, THE BATMAN'S KEEN EYES DETECT A SHINY OBJECT IMBEDDED IN THE MELTING SNOW MAN...
SAY...WHAT'S THIS? LOOKS LIKE A METAL BOX!
THE COVER IS PRIED OPEN...AND INSIDE...
MONEY!
WELL, I'LL BE HOG-TIED! LOOK AT THAT ROLL! PHEW!
AGAIN BATMAN'S ROVING EYES SPOT SOMETHING BEHIND A SNOW BANK!
WELL, WELL... IF IT ISN'T OUR OLD PHOTOGRAPHER FRIEND RAY!
NO, BATMAN! I DIDN'T MEAN TO LEAVE YOU STRANDED! NO! LET ME GO!
A THREATENING FIST INDUCES RAY TO TALK!
MY BOSS IS "ANGLES BIGBEE...HIS HIDEOUT IS INSIDE BIKOU GLACIER! I GO TO VARIOUS TOWNS... TIP HIM OFF WHEN A SUPPLY OF FURS COMES IN... HE PAYS BY LEAVING MONEY INSIDE THE SNOW MEN!
SO THAT'S THE SECRET OF THE SNOW MEN...REALLY A CLEVER PAY-OFF METHOD! THIS CALLS FOR A PLAN OF ACTION.
HOURS LATER! AS THE FAMED AURORA BOREALIS CURTAINS THE SKY, SKIMMING OVER FROZEN WATER ABOUT BIKOU GLACIER COMES A FLEET OF STRANGE CRAFT...ICE BOATS BEARING THE BATMAN'S ARMY!
INSIDE BIKOU GLACIER A LOOK-OUT SHOUTS LOUDLY...
"ANGLES!" LOOK! A REGULAR ARMY'S COMIN'!
SOMETHING'S SLIPPED UP.. GET THE BOYS OUT ON THE SKI PEEPS!
11
ATOP THE HILL OVERLOOKING THE ICE, TWO GHOST-WHITE FIGURES MOVE UNSEEN ACROSS THE SNOW!
C'MON, ROBIN, WHILE THE MEN KEEP "ANGLES'" MEN BUSY, WE'LL SNEAK UP ON THE GLACIER!
GOOD STUNT, THIS! WITH OUR SPARE SUITS DYED WHITE NOBODY CAN SPOT US!
FOR THE FIRST TIME IN THEIR CAREERS, BATMAN AND ROBIN ABANDON BLACK COSTUMES FOR WHITE CAMOUFLAGE!

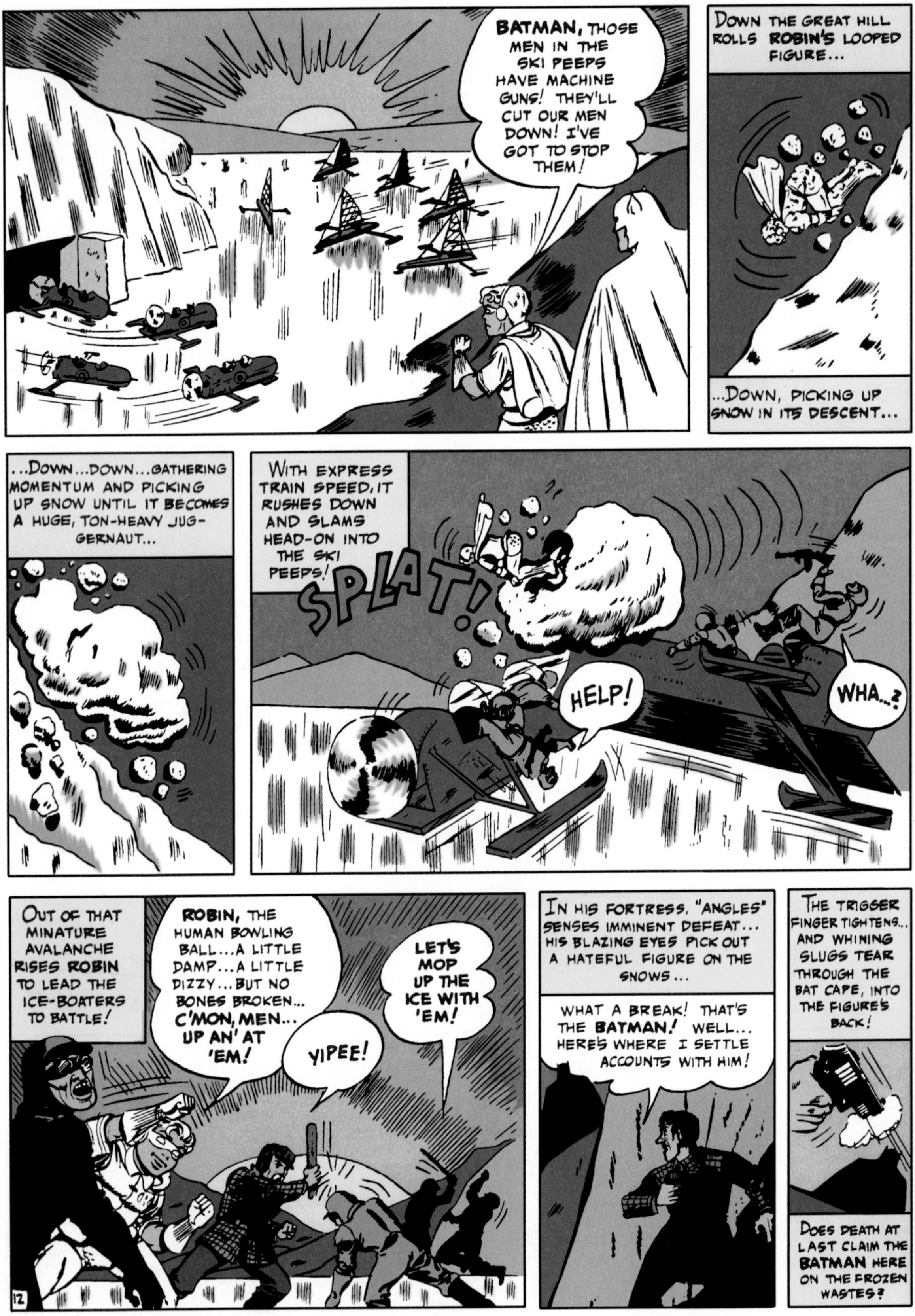

BATMAN, THOSE MEN IN THE SKI PEEPS HAVE MACHINE GUNS! THEY'LL CUT OUR MEN DOWN! I'VE GOT TO STOP THEM!
DOWN THE GREAT HILL ROLLS ROBIN'S LOOPED FIGURE...
...DOWN, PICKING UP SNOW IN ITS DESCENT...
...DOWN...DOWN...GATHERING MOMENTUM AND PICKING UP SNOW UNTIL IT BECOMES A HUGE, TON-HEAVY JUG-GERNAUT...
WITH EXPRESS TRAIN SPEED, IT RUSHES DOWN AND SLAMS HEAD-ON INTO THE SKI PEEPS!
SPLAT!
HELP!
WHA..?
OUT OF THAT MINATURE AVALANCHE RISES ROBIN TO LEAD THE ICE-BOATERS TO BATTLE!
ROBIN, THE HUMAN BOWLING BALL...A LITTLE DAMP...A LITTLE DIZZY...BUT NO BONES BROKEN... C'MON, MEN... UP AN' AT 'EM!
YIPEE!
LET'S MOP UP THE ICE WITH 'EM!
12
IN HIS FORTRESS, "ANGLES" SENSES IMMINENT DEFEAT... HIS BLAZING EYES PICK OUT A HATEFUL FIGURE ON THE SNOWS...
WHAT A BREAK! THAT'S THE BATMAN! WELL... HERE'S WHERE I SETTLE ACCOUNTS WITH HIM!
THE TRIGGER FINGER TIGHTENS... AND WHINING SLUGS TEAR THROUGH THE BAT CAPE, INTO THE FIGURE'S BACK!
DOES DEATH AT LAST CLAIM THE BATMAN HERE ON THE FROZEN WASTES?

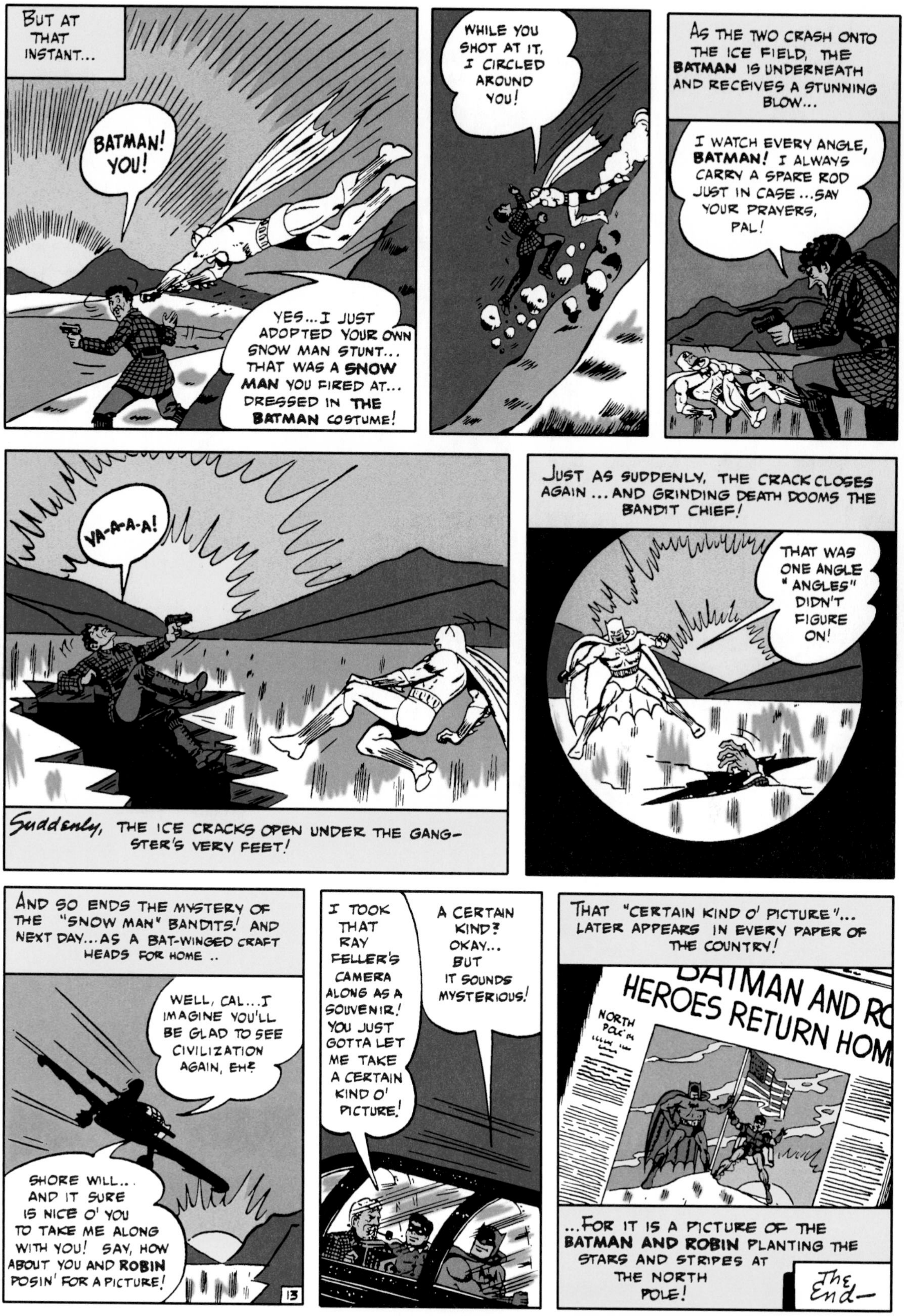

BUT AT THAT INSTANT...
BATMAN! YOU!
YES...I JUST ADOPTED YOUR OWN SNOW MAN STUNT... THAT WAS A SNOW MAN YOU FIRED AT... DRESSED IN THE BATMAN COSTUME!
WHILE YOU SHOT AT IT, I CIRCLED AROUND YOU!
AS THE TWO CRASH ONTO THE ICE FIELD, THE BATMAN IS UNDERNEATH AND RECEIVES A STUNNING BLOW...
I WATCH EVERY ANGLE, BATMAN! I ALWAYS CARRY A SPARE ROD JUST IN CASE...SAY YOUR PRAYERS, PAL!
YA-A-A-A!
Suddenly, THE ICE CRACKS OPEN UNDER THE GANGSTER'S VERY FEET!
JUST AS SUDDENLY, THE CRACK CLOSES AGAIN...AND GRINDING DEATH DOOMS THE BANDIT CHIEF!
THAT WAS ONE ANGLE "ANGLES" DIDN'T FIGURE ON!
AND SO ENDS THE MYSTERY OF THE "SNOW MAN" BANDITS! AND NEXT DAY...AS A BAT-WINGED CRAFT HEADS FOR HOME ..
WELL, CAL...I IMAGINE YOU'LL BE GLAD TO SEE CIVILIZATION AGAIN, EH?
SHORE WILL... AND IT SURE IS NICE O' YOU TO TAKE ME ALONG WITH YOU! SAY, HOW ABOUT YOU AND ROBIN POSIN' FOR A PICTURE!
13
I TOOK THAT RAY FELLER'S CAMERA ALONG AS A SOUVENIR! YOU JUST GOTTA LET ME TAKE A CERTAIN KIND O' PICTURE!
A CERTAIN KIND? OKAY... BUT IT SOUNDS MYSTERIOUS!
THAT "CERTAIN KIND O' PICTURE"... LATER APPEARS IN EVERY PAPER OF THE COUNTRY!
BATMAN AND RO
HEROES RETURN HOM
NORTH POLE
...FOR IT IS A PICTURE OF THE BATMAN AND ROBIN PLANTING THE STARS AND STRIPES AT THE NORTH POLE!
The End—

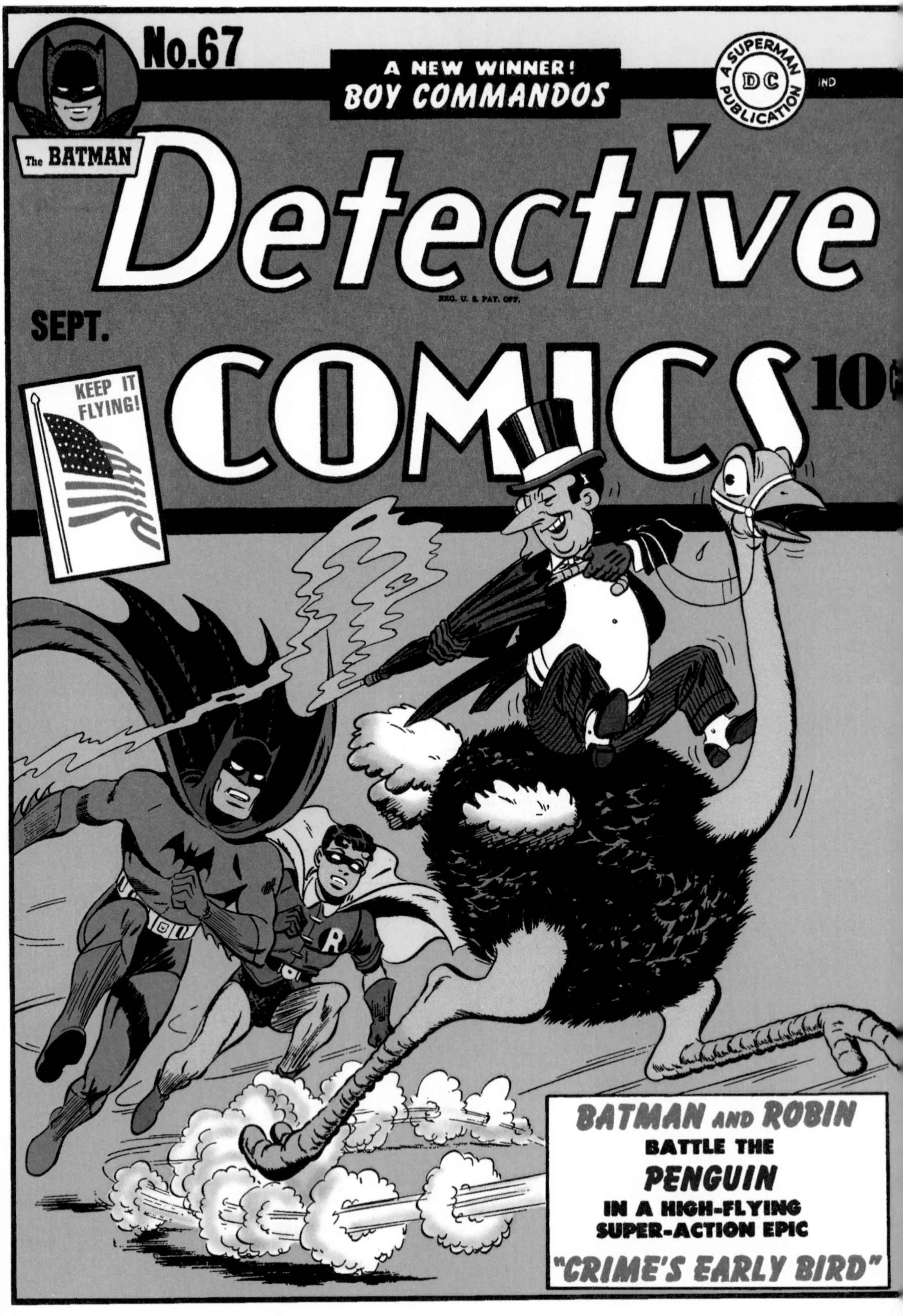

No.67
A NEW WINNER!
BOY COMMANDOS
A SUPERMAN DC PUBLICATION
IND
The BATMAN
Detective
REG. U. S. PAT. OFF.
SEPT.
COMICS
10¢
KEEP IT FLYING!
BATMAN AND ROBIN
BATTLE THE
PENGUIN
IN A HIGH-FLYING
SUPER-ACTION EPIC
"CRIME'S EARLY BIRD"

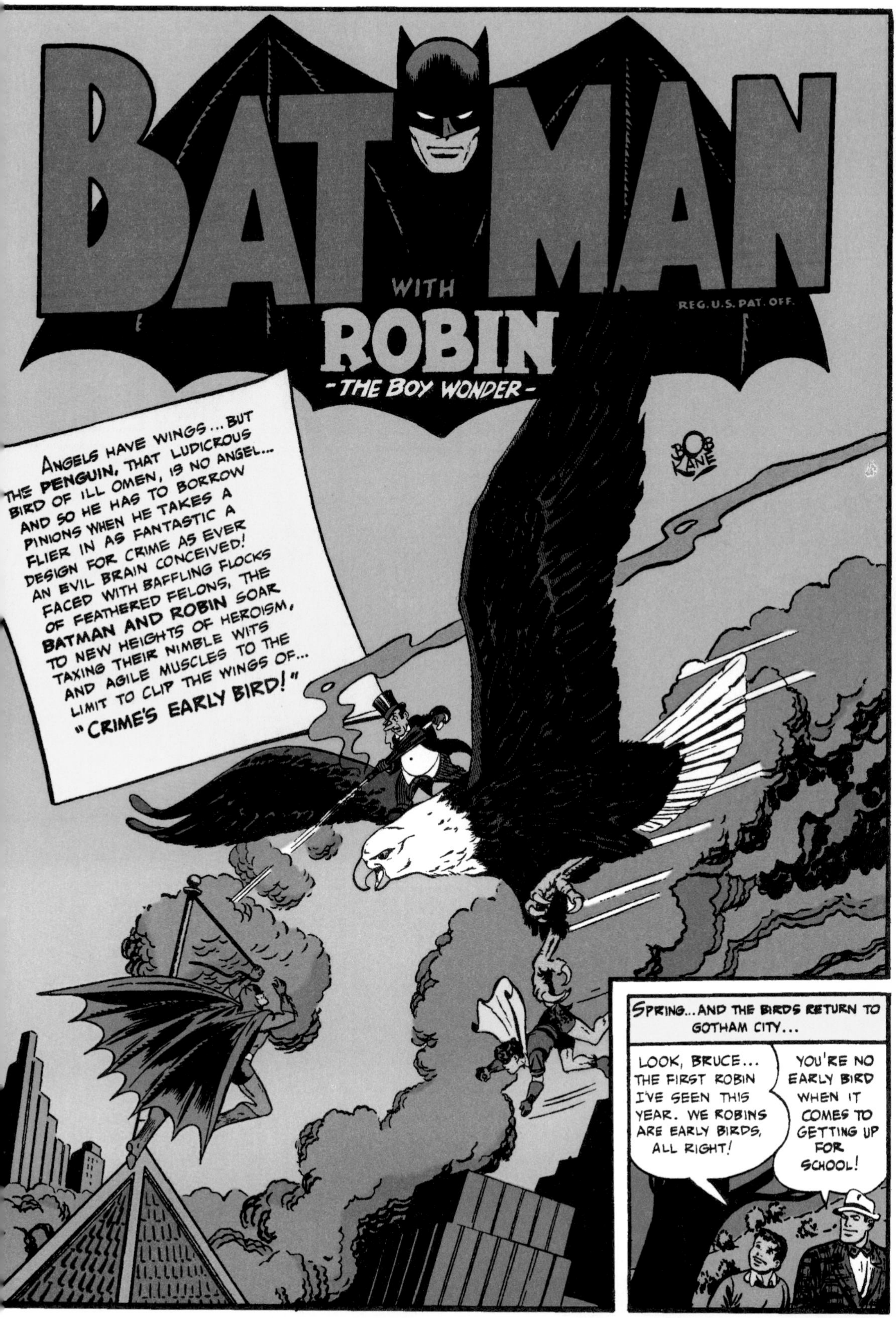
BATMAN
WITH
ROBIN
-THE BOY WONDER-
REG. U.S. PAT. OFF.
BOB KANE
ANGELS HAVE WINGS... BUT THE PENGUIN, THAT LUDICROUS BIRD OF ILL OMEN, IS NO ANGEL... AND SO HE HAS TO BORROW PINIONS WHEN HE TAKES A FLIER IN AS FANTASTIC A DESIGN FOR CRIME AS EVER AN EVIL BRAIN CONCEIVED! FACED WITH BAFFLING FLOCKS OF FEATHERED FELONS, THE BATMAN AND ROBIN SOAR TO NEW HEIGHTS OF HEROISM, TAXING THEIR NIMBLE WITS AND AGILE MUSCLES TO THE LIMIT TO CLIP THE WINGS OF...
"CRIME'S EARLY BIRD!"
SPRING...AND THE BIRDS RETURN TO GOTHAM CITY...
LOOK, BRUCE... THE FIRST ROBIN I'VE SEEN THIS YEAR. WE ROBINS ARE EARLY BIRDS, ALL RIGHT!
YOU'RE NO EARLY BIRD WHEN IT COMES TO GETTING UP FOR SCHOOL!

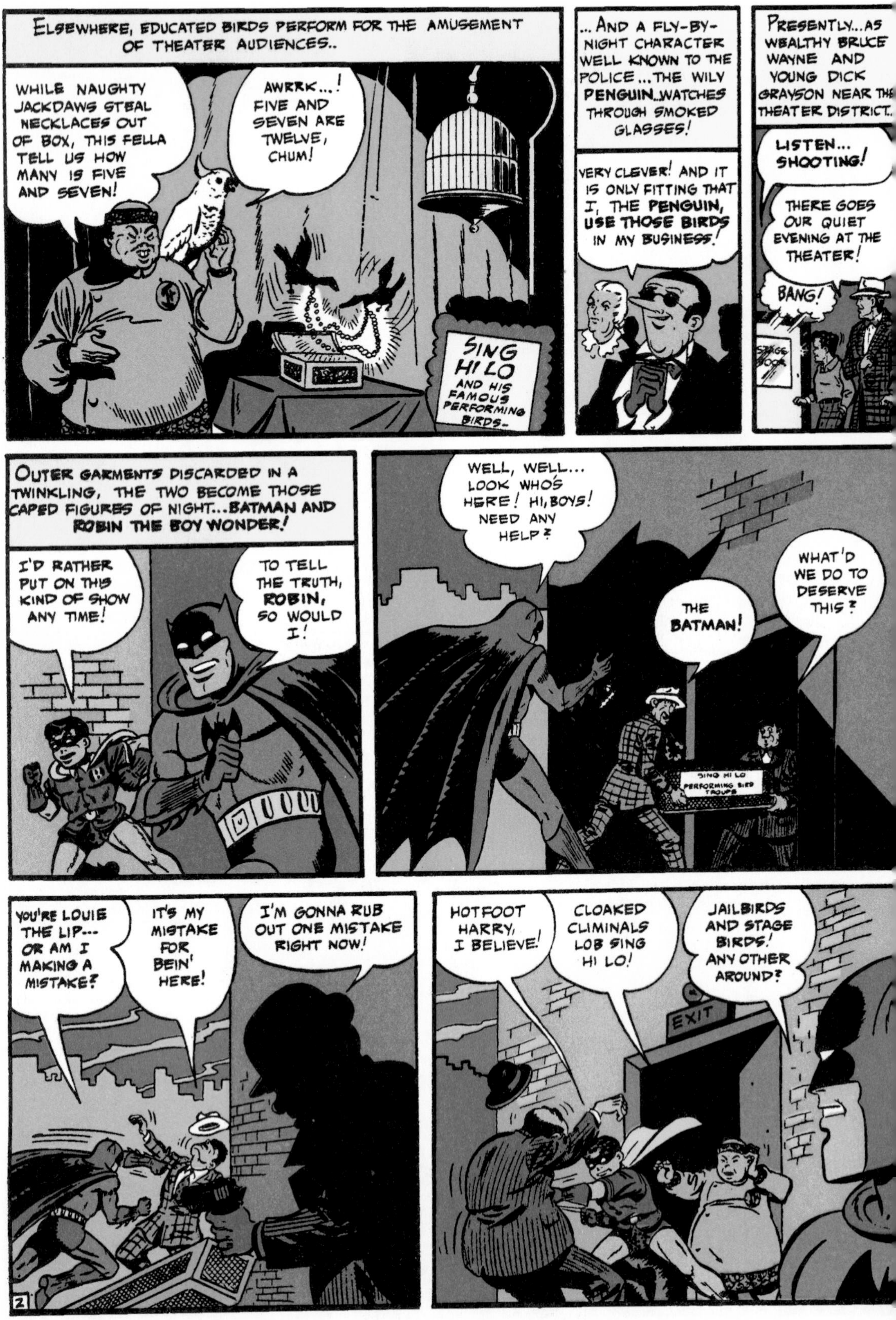

ELSEWHERE, EDUCATED BIRDS PERFORM FOR THE AMUSEMENT OF THEATER AUDIENCES..
WHILE NAUGHTY JACKDAWS STEAL NECKLACES OUT OF BOX, THIS FELLA TELL US HOW MANY IS FIVE AND SEVEN!
AWRRK...! FIVE AND SEVEN ARE TWELVE, CHUM!
SING HI LO AND HIS FAMOUS PERFORMING BIRDS.
...AND A FLY-BY-NIGHT CHARACTER WELL KNOWN TO THE POLICE...THE WILY PENGUIN...WATCHES THROUGH SMOKED GLASSES!
VERY CLEVER! AND IT IS ONLY FITTING THAT I, THE PENGUIN, USE THOSE BIRDS IN MY BUSINESS!
PRESENTLY...AS WEALTHY BRUCE WAYNE AND YOUNG DICK GRAYSON NEAR THE THEATER DISTRICT..
LISTEN... SHOOTING!
THERE GOES OUR QUIET EVENING AT THE THEATER!
BANG!
STAGE DOOR
OUTER GARMENTS DISCARDED IN A TWINKLING, THE TWO BECOME THOSE CAPED FIGURES OF NIGHT...BATMAN AND ROBIN THE BOY WONDER!
I'D RATHER PUT ON THIS KIND OF SHOW ANY TIME!
TO TELL THE TRUTH, ROBIN, SO WOULD I!
WELL, WELL... LOOK WHO'S HERE! HI, BOYS! NEED ANY HELP?
THE BATMAN!
WHAT'D WE DO TO DESERVE THIS?
SING HI LO PERFORMING BIRD TROUPE
YOU'RE LOUIE THE LIP--- OR AM I MAKING A MISTAKE?
IT'S MY MISTAKE FOR BEIN' HERE!
I'M GONNA RUB OUT ONE MISTAKE RIGHT NOW!
2
HOTFOOT HARRY, I BELIEVE!
CLOAKED CLIMINALS LOB SING HI LO!
JAILBIRDS AND STAGE BIRDS! ANY OTHER AROUND?
EXIT

ENTER THE MAN OF A THOUSAND UMBRELLAS!

THE OTHER... BATMAN...THE SMARTEST BIRD OF ALL!

THE PENGUIN!

YI-I-I-!

THE PENGUIN'S INSEPARABLE UMBRELLA, SOURCE OF COUNTLESS SUR- PRISES, EXPLODES A SMOKE CARTRIDGE!

A PLEASANT MEETING, INDEED! TOO BAD IT HAD TO BE A SHORT ONE!

HE'S BLACKING HIMSELF OUT!

WATCH THAT UMBRELLA, ROBIN!

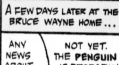

I'VE GOT ONE OF THEM!

HANG ON, TIGHT!

BUT WHEN THE SMOKE CLEARS...

WE'LL TAKE HIM TO JAIL AND... HUH? IT'S SING HI LO!

FINE STUFF! YOU GLAB SING WHILE CLIMINAL LOBBERS ESCAPE!

THEY ESCAPED, ALL RIGHT... BUT WE'LL REMEMBER THEM!

A FEW DAYS LATER AT THE BRUCE WAYNE HOME...

ANY NEWS ABOUT TRAINED BIRDS BEING USED IN CRIMES?

NOT YET. THE PENGUIN IS PROBABLY LAYING HIS PLANS...BUT EVENTUALLY HE'LL CROSS OUR PATH, AS HE ALWAYS DOES!

SOON A NEW BUSINESS ESTAB- LISHMENT OPENS ITS DOORS IN A FASHIONABLE NEIGHBORHOOD!

STRANGE, HOW I MISS MY PARROT SINCE HE DIED... PERHAPS, IF I GOT ANOTHER!

GILDED CAGE BIRD SHOPPE

AH, MR. GEMLY, THE FAMOUS JEWEL COLLECTOR! IT IS AN HONOR INDEED TO WELCOME YOU TO MY HUMBLE SHOP!

HAVE YOU A WELL- BEHAVED, REFINED PARROT?

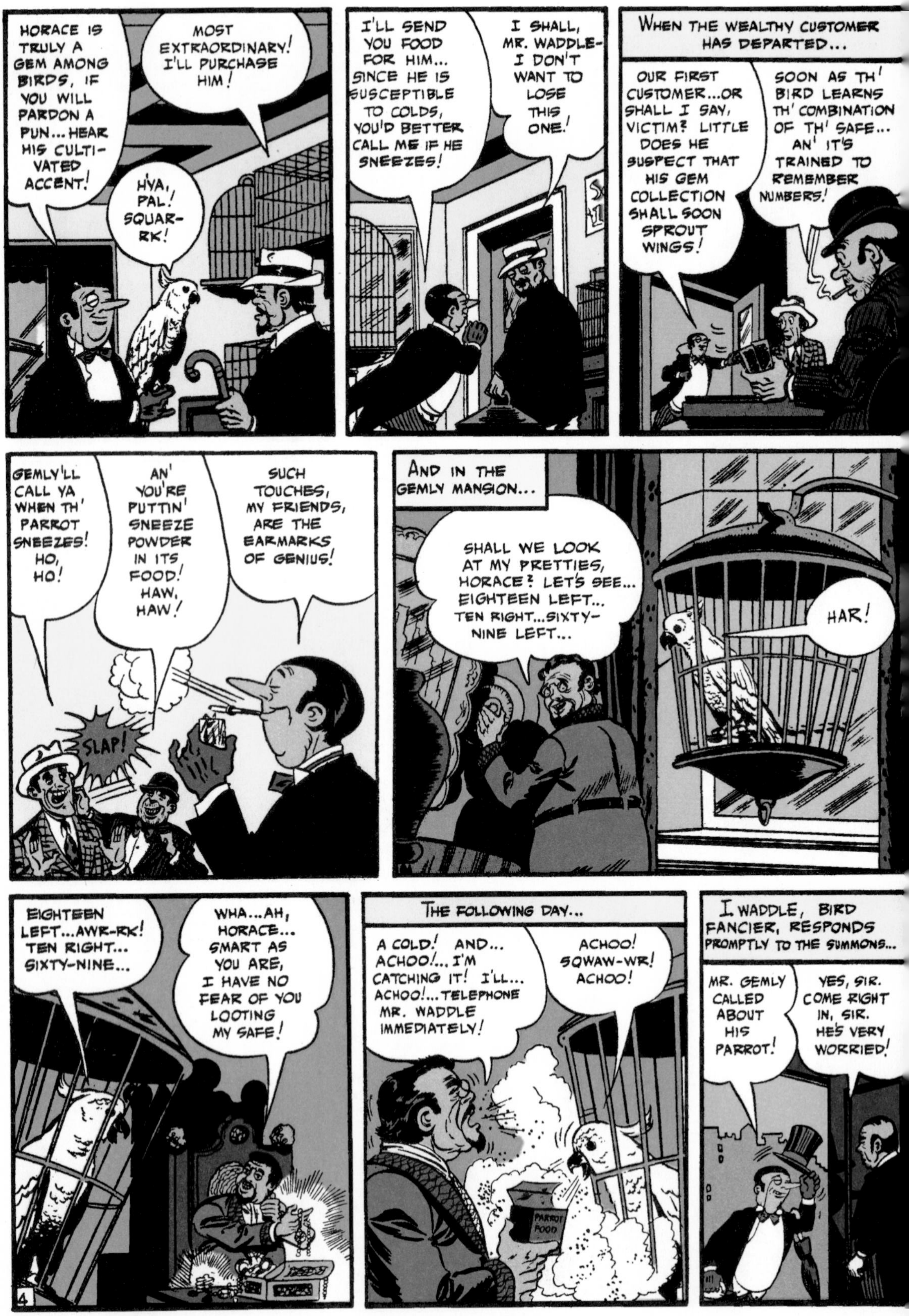
HORACE IS TRULY A GEM AMONG BIRDS, IF YOU WILL PARDON A PUN... HEAR HIS CULTIVATED ACCENT!
MOST EXTRAORDINARY! I'LL PURCHASE HIM!
H'YA, PAL! SQUAR-RK!
I'LL SEND YOU FOOD FOR HIM... SINCE HE IS SUSCEPTIBLE TO COLDS, YOU'D BETTER CALL ME IF HE SNEEZES!
I SHALL, MR. WADDLE- I DON'T WANT TO LOSE THIS ONE!
WHEN THE WEALTHY CUSTOMER HAS DEPARTED...
OUR FIRST CUSTOMER...OR SHALL I SAY, VICTIM? LITTLE DOES HE SUSPECT THAT HIS GEM COLLECTION SHALL SOON SPROUT WINGS!
SOON AS TH' BIRD LEARNS TH' COMBINATION OF TH' SAFE... AN' IT'S TRAINED TO REMEMBER NUMBERS!
GEMLY'LL CALL YA WHEN TH' PARROT SNEEZES! HO, HO!
AN' YOU'RE PUTTIN' SNEEZE POWDER IN ITS FOOD! HAW, HAW!
SUCH TOUCHES, MY FRIENDS, ARE THE EARMARKS OF GENIUS!
SLAP!
AND IN THE GEMLY MANSION...
SHALL WE LOOK AT MY PRETTIES, HORACE? LET'S SEE... EIGHTEEN LEFT... TEN RIGHT...SIXTY-NINE LEFT...
HAR!
EIGHTEEN LEFT...AWR-RK! TEN RIGHT... SIXTY-NINE...
WHA...AH, HORACE... SMART AS YOU ARE, I HAVE NO FEAR OF YOU LOOTING MY SAFE!
4
THE FOLLOWING DAY...
A COLD! AND... ACHOO!... I'M CATCHING IT! I'LL... ACHOO!...TELEPHONE MR. WADDLE IMMEDIATELY!
ACHOO! SQWAW-WR! ACHOO!
PARROT FOOD
I. WADDLE, BIRD FANCIER, RESPONDS PROMPTLY TO THE SUMMONS...
MR. GEMLY CALLED ABOUT HIS PARROT!
YES, SIR. COME RIGHT IN, SIR. HE'S VERY WORRIED!

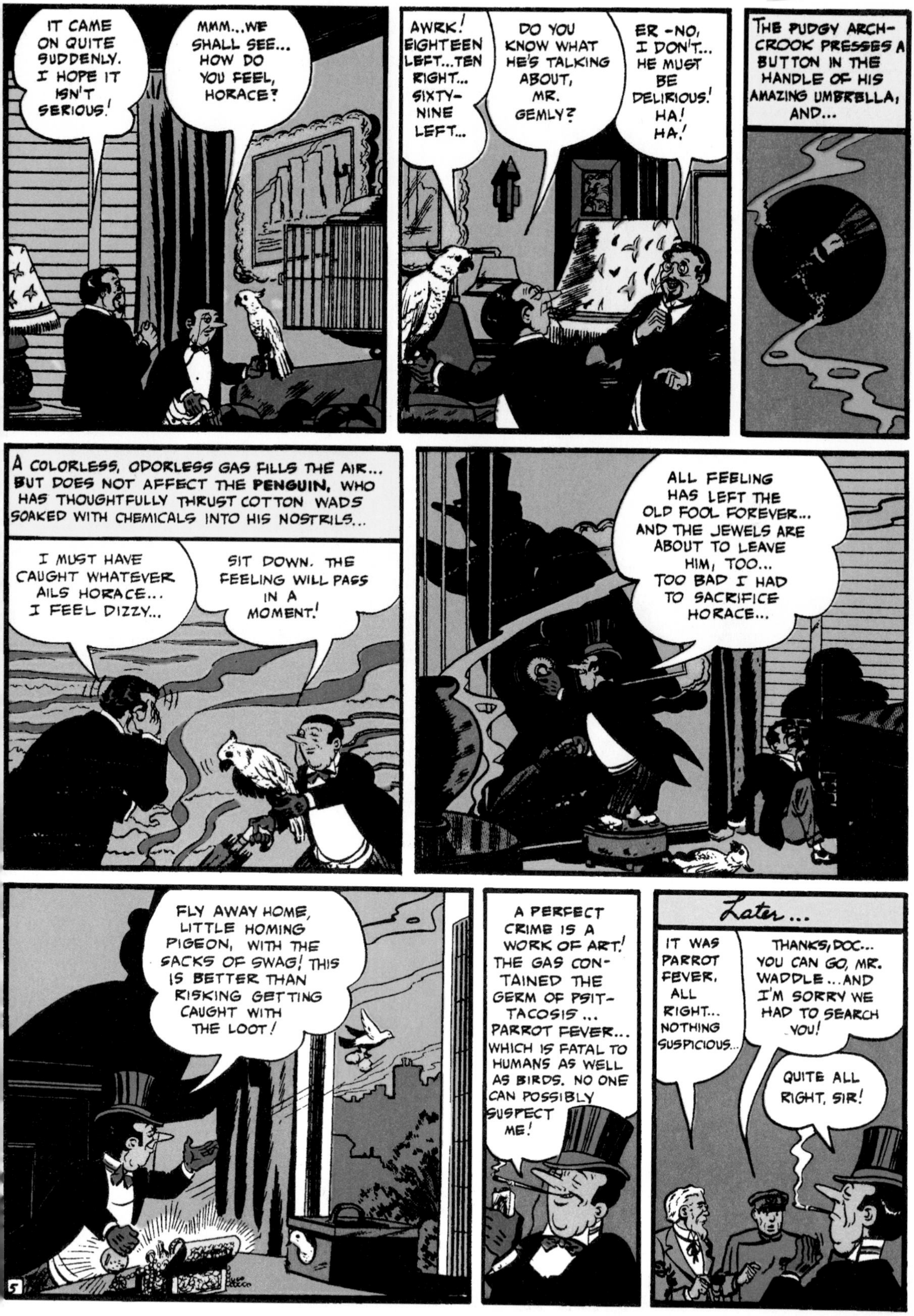
IT CAME ON QUITE SUDDENLY. I HOPE IT ISN'T SERIOUS!
MMM...WE SHALL SEE... HOW DO YOU FEEL, HORACE?
AWRK! EIGHTEEN LEFT...TEN RIGHT... SIXTY-NINE LEFT...
DO YOU KNOW WHAT HE'S TALKING ABOUT, MR. GEMLY?
ER-NO, I DON'T... HE MUST BE DELIRIOUS! HA! HA!
THE PUDGY ARCH-CROOK PRESSES A BUTTON IN THE HANDLE OF HIS AMAZING UMBRELLA, AND...
A COLORLESS, ODORLESS GAS FILLS THE AIR... BUT DOES NOT AFFECT THE PENGUIN, WHO HAS THOUGHTFULLY THRUST COTTON WADS SOAKED WITH CHEMICALS INTO HIS NOSTRILS...
I MUST HAVE CAUGHT WHATEVER AILS HORACE... I FEEL DIZZY...
SIT DOWN. THE FEELING WILL PASS IN A MOMENT!
ALL FEELING HAS LEFT THE OLD FOOL FOREVER... AND THE JEWELS ARE ABOUT TO LEAVE HIM, TOO... TOO BAD I HAD TO SACRIFICE HORACE...
FLY AWAY HOME, LITTLE HOMING PIGEON, WITH THE SACKS OF SWAG! THIS IS BETTER THAN RISKING GETTING CAUGHT WITH THE LOOT!
5
A PERFECT CRIME IS A WORK OF ART! THE GAS CONTAINED THE GERM OF PSITTACOSIS... PARROT FEVER... WHICH IS FATAL TO HUMANS AS WELL AS BIRDS. NO ONE CAN POSSIBLY SUSPECT ME!
Later...
IT WAS PARROT FEVER, ALL RIGHT... NOTHING SUSPICIOUS...
THANKS, DOC... YOU CAN GO, MR. WADDLE...AND I'M SORRY WE HAD TO SEARCH YOU!
QUITE ALL RIGHT, SIR!

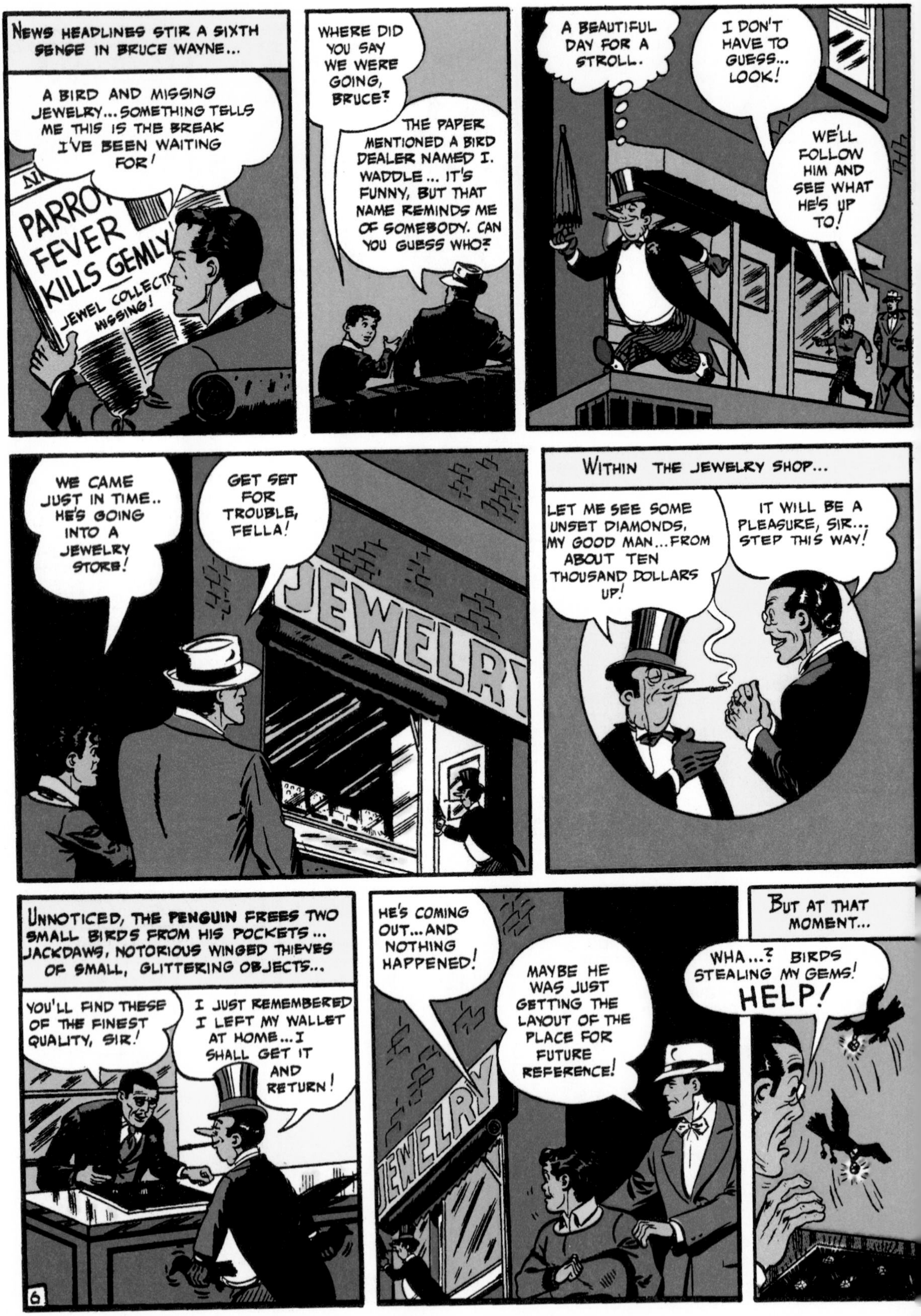

NEWS HEADLINES STIR A SIXTH SENSE IN BRUCE WAYNE...
A BIRD AND MISSING JEWELRY... SOMETHING TELLS ME THIS IS THE BREAK I'VE BEEN WAITING FOR!
PARROT FEVER KILLS GEMLY
JEWEL COLLECT MISSING!
WHERE DID YOU SAY WE WERE GOING, BRUCE?
THE PAPER MENTIONED A BIRD DEALER NAMED I. WADDLE... IT'S FUNNY, BUT THAT NAME REMINDS ME OF SOMEBODY. CAN YOU GUESS WHO?
A BEAUTIFUL DAY FOR A STROLL.
I DON'T HAVE TO GUESS... LOOK!
WE'LL FOLLOW HIM AND SEE WHAT HE'S UP TO!
WE CAME JUST IN TIME.. HE'S GOING INTO A JEWELRY STORE!
GET SET FOR TROUBLE, FELLA!
JEWELRY
WITHIN THE JEWELRY SHOP...
LET ME SEE SOME UNSET DIAMONDS, MY GOOD MAN... FROM ABOUT TEN THOUSAND DOLLARS UP!
IT WILL BE A PLEASURE, SIR... STEP THIS WAY!
UNNOTICED, THE PENGUIN FREES TWO SMALL BIRDS FROM HIS POCKETS... JACKDAWS, NOTORIOUS WINGED THIEVES OF SMALL, GLITTERING OBJECTS...
YOU'LL FIND THESE OF THE FINEST QUALITY, SIR!
I JUST REMEMBERED I LEFT MY WALLET AT HOME... I SHALL GET IT AND RETURN!
6
HE'S COMING OUT... AND NOTHING HAPPENED!
MAYBE HE WAS JUST GETTING THE LAYOUT OF THE PLACE FOR FUTURE REFERENCE!
JEWELRY
BUT AT THAT MOMENT...
WHA...? BIRDS STEALING MY GEMS! HELP!

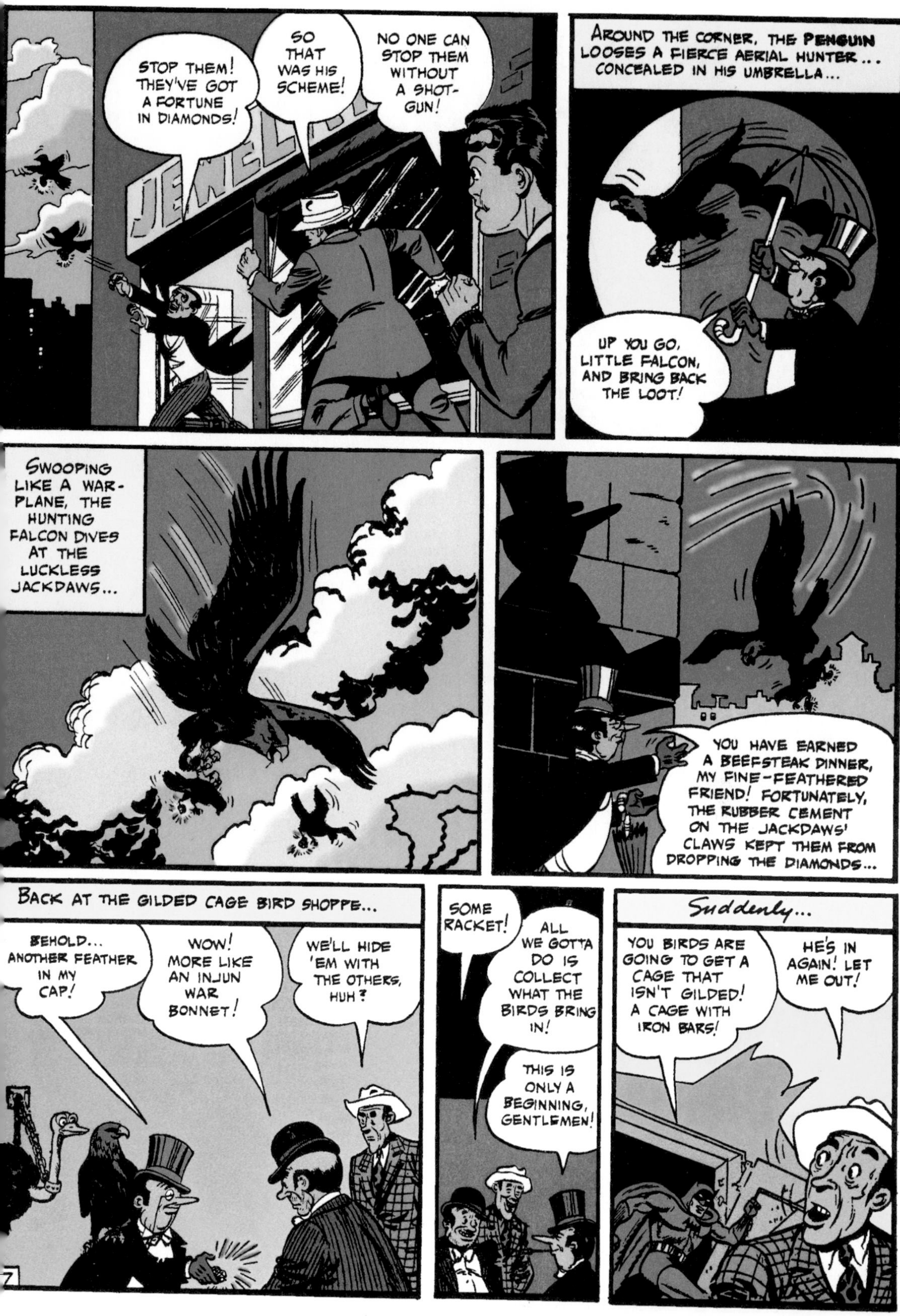
STOP THEM! THEY'VE GOT A FORTUNE IN DIAMONDS!
SO THAT WAS HIS SCHEME!
NO ONE CAN STOP THEM WITHOUT A SHOT-GUN!
AROUND THE CORNER, THE PENGUIN LOOSES A FIERCE AERIAL HUNTER... CONCEALED IN HIS UMBRELLA...
UP YOU GO, LITTLE FALCON, AND BRING BACK THE LOOT!
SWOOPING LIKE A WAR-PLANE, THE HUNTING FALCON DIVES AT THE LUCKLESS JACKDAWS...
YOU HAVE EARNED A BEEFSTEAK DINNER, MY FINE-FEATHERED FRIEND! FORTUNATELY, THE RUBBER CEMENT ON THE JACKDAWS' CLAWS KEPT THEM FROM DROPPING THE DIAMONDS...
BACK AT THE GILDED CAGE BIRD SHOPPE...
BEHOLD... ANOTHER FEATHER IN MY CAP!
WOW! MORE LIKE AN INJUN WAR BONNET!
WE'LL HIDE 'EM WITH THE OTHERS, HUH?
SOME RACKET!
ALL WE GOTTA DO IS COLLECT WHAT THE BIRDS BRING IN!
THIS IS ONLY A BEGINNING, GENTLEMEN!
Suddenly...
YOU BIRDS ARE GOING TO GET A CAGE THAT ISN'T GILDED! A CAGE WITH IRON BARS!
HE'S IN AGAIN! LET ME OUT!

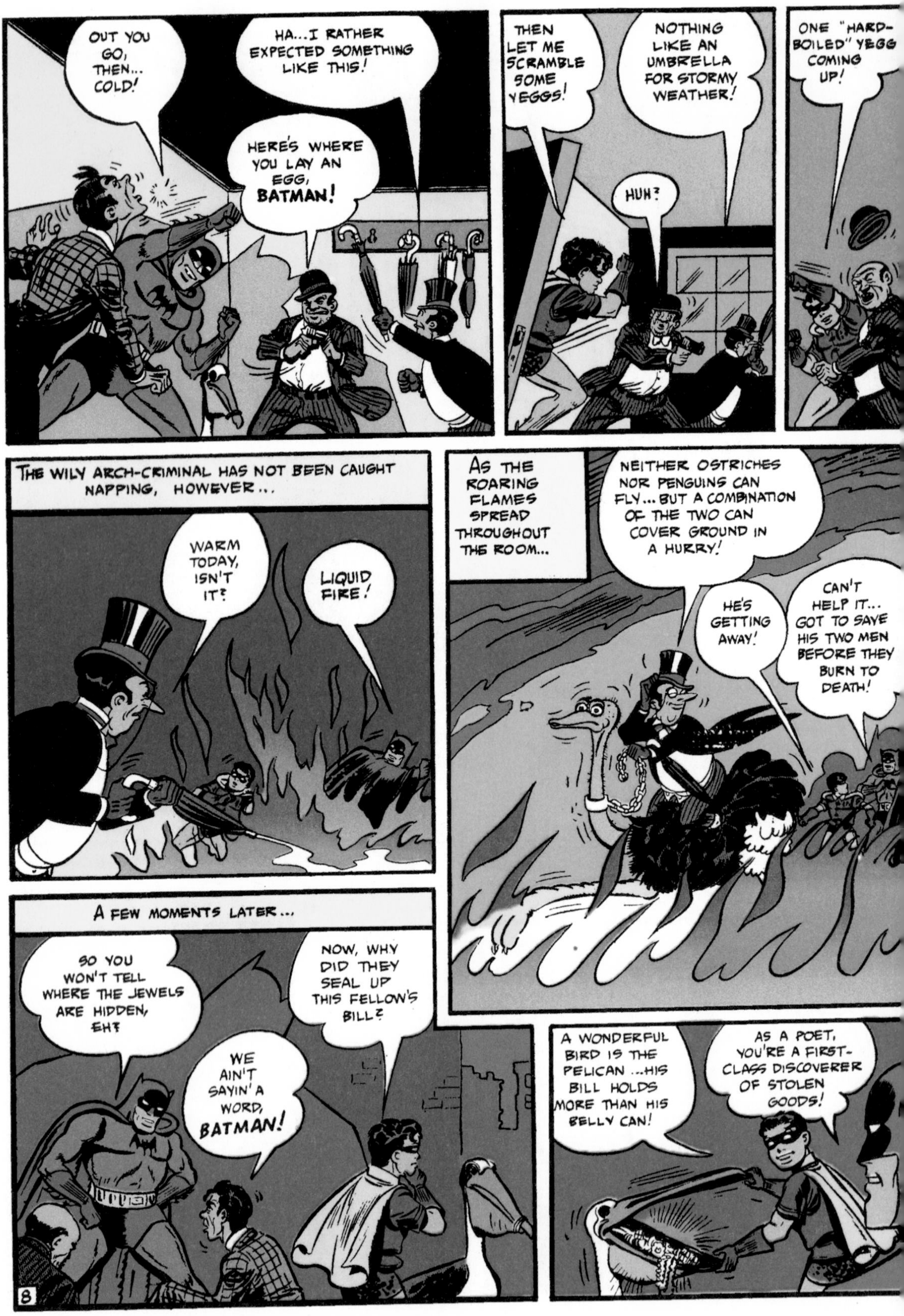

OUT YOU GO, THEN... COLD!
HA...I RATHER EXPECTED SOMETHING LIKE THIS!
HERE'S WHERE YOU LAY AN EGG, BATMAN!
THEN LET ME SCRAMBLE SOME YEGGS!
NOTHING LIKE AN UMBRELLA FOR STORMY WEATHER!
HUH?
ONE "HARD-BOILED" YEGG COMING UP!
THE WILY ARCH-CRIMINAL HAS NOT BEEN CAUGHT NAPPING, HOWEVER...
WARM TODAY, ISN'T IT?
LIQUID FIRE!
AS THE ROARING FLAMES SPREAD THROUGHOUT THE ROOM...
NEITHER OSTRICHES NOR PENGUINS CAN FLY... BUT A COMBINATION OF THE TWO CAN COVER GROUND IN A HURRY!
HE'S GETTING AWAY!
CAN'T HELP IT... GOT TO SAVE HIS TWO MEN BEFORE THEY BURN TO DEATH!
A FEW MOMENTS LATER...
SO YOU WON'T TELL WHERE THE JEWELS ARE HIDDEN, EH?
NOW, WHY DID THEY SEAL UP THIS FELLOW'S BILL?
WE AIN'T SAYIN' A WORD, BATMAN!
8
A WONDERFUL BIRD IS THE PELICAN ...HIS BILL HOLDS MORE THAN HIS BELLY CAN!
AS A POET, YOU'RE A FIRST-CLASS DISCOVERER OF STOLEN GOODS!

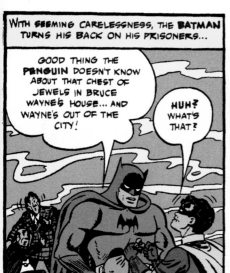 WITH SEEMING CARELESSNESS, THE **BATMAN** TURNS HIS BACK ON HIS PRISONERS...

GOOD THING THE **PENGUIN** DOESN'T KNOW ABOUT THAT CHEST OF JEWELS IN BRUCE WAYNE'S HOUSE... AND WAYNE'S OUT OF THE CITY!

HUH? WHAT'S THAT?

 THEY'RE GETTING AWAY!

LET THEM! THE POLICE CAN PICK THEM UP ANY TIME... AND MEANWHILE, I'VE GOT A SCHEME FOR DOSING THE **PENGUIN** WITH SOME OF HIS OWN MEDICINE!

 THAT AFTERNOON, A WEIRD CRAFT STREAKS FROM A SECRET UNDERGROUND HANGAR INTO THE BLUE SKY... THE **BATPLANE**...

 YOU THINK THESE HOMING PIGEONS WE RESCUED FROM THE FIRE WILL LEAD US TO THE **PENGUIN'S** HIDEOUT?

ALL WE CAN DO IS KEEP 'EM FLYING AND SEE!

GUIDED BY AN INSTINCT THAT HAS BAFFLED SCIENTISTS, THE PIGEONS SET A STRAIGHT COURSE FOR THEIR HOME LOFT...

UNLESS I'M MAKING A BIG MISTAKE, THAT PENTHOUSE IS WHERE WE ATTEND A PARTY TONIGHT!

A SURPRISE PARTY! I CAN HARDLY WAIT!

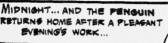

 MIDNIGHT... AND THE **PENGUIN** RETURNS HOME AFTER A PLEASANT EVENING'S WORK...

THE JEWELS OF PLAYBOY BRUCE WAYNE! HA! THE **BATMAN** HIMSELF TIPPED ME OFF TO THEM, THROUGH LOUIE THE LIP AND HARRY!

I EVEN USED BIRDS ON THIS JOB... FOR AREN'T HARRY AND LOUIE <u>STOOL</u> PIGEONS? NOW LET US SEE HOW MUCH RICHER THE EVENING HAS MADE ME!

 BATS! I'VE BEEN TRICKED! THIS IS THE **BATMAN'S** IDEA OF A JOKE!

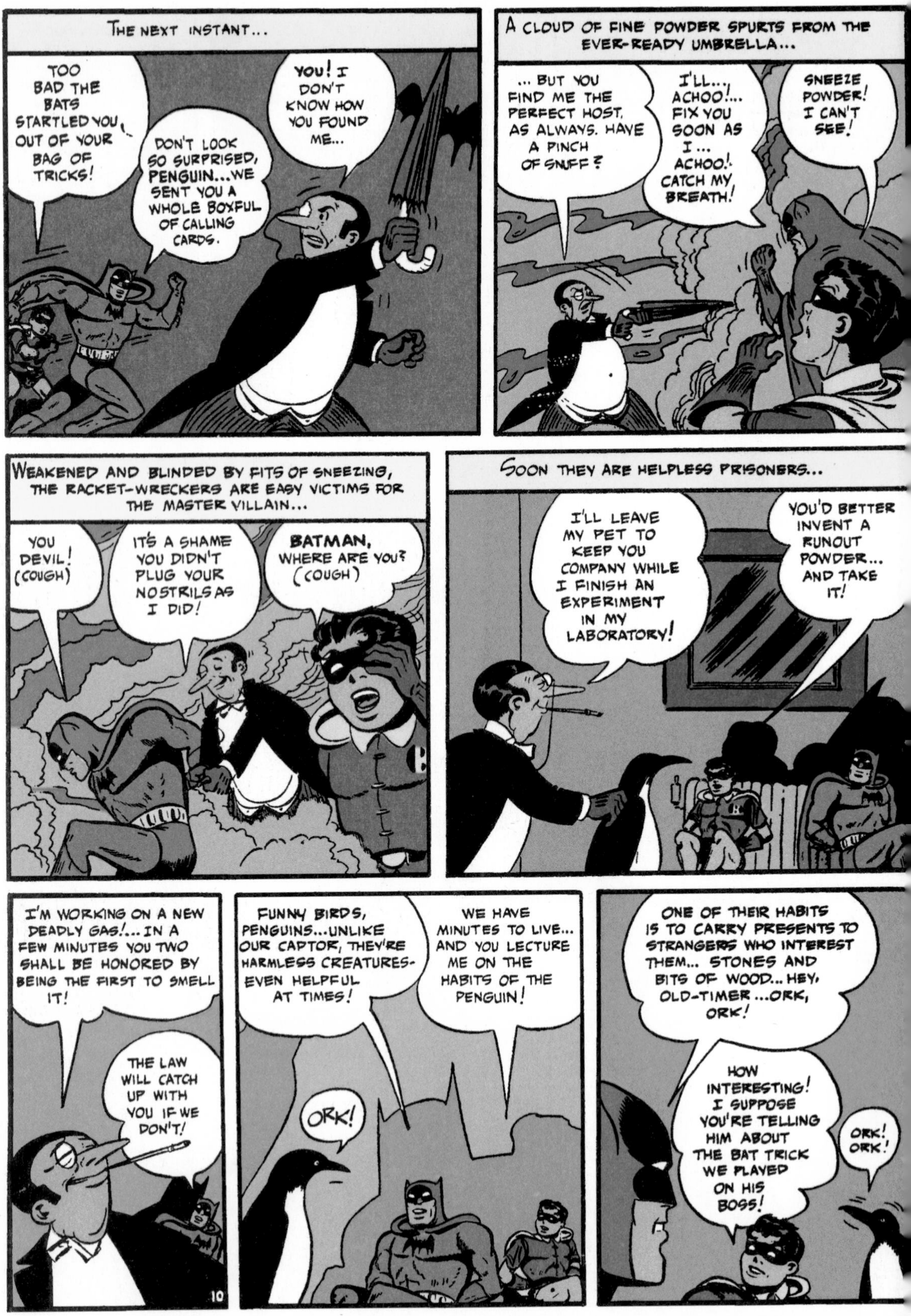

THE NEXT INSTANT...
TOO BAD THE BATS STARTLED YOU OUT OF YOUR BAG OF TRICKS!
DON'T LOOK SO SURPRISED, PENGUIN...WE SENT YOU A WHOLE BOXFUL OF CALLING CARDS.
YOU! I DON'T KNOW HOW YOU FOUND ME...
A CLOUD OF FINE POWDER SPURTS FROM THE EVER-READY UMBRELLA...
... BUT YOU FIND ME THE PERFECT HOST, AS ALWAYS. HAVE A PINCH OF SNUFF?
I'LL... ACHOO!... FIX YOU SOON AS I... ACHOO! CATCH MY BREATH!
SNEEZE POWDER! I CAN'T SEE!
WEAKENED AND BLINDED BY FITS OF SNEEZING, THE RACKET-WRECKERS ARE EASY VICTIMS FOR THE MASTER VILLAIN...
YOU DEVIL! (COUGH)
IT'S A SHAME YOU DIDN'T PLUG YOUR NOSTRILS AS I DID!
BATMAN, WHERE ARE YOU? (COUGH)
SOON THEY ARE HELPLESS PRISONERS...
I'LL LEAVE MY PET TO KEEP YOU COMPANY WHILE I FINISH AN EXPERIMENT IN MY LABORATORY!
YOU'D BETTER INVENT A RUNOUT POWDER... AND TAKE IT!
I'M WORKING ON A NEW DEADLY GAS!... IN A FEW MINUTES YOU TWO SHALL BE HONORED BY BEING THE FIRST TO SMELL IT!
THE LAW WILL CATCH UP WITH YOU IF WE DON'T!
10
FUNNY BIRDS, PENGUINS...UNLIKE OUR CAPTOR, THEY'RE HARMLESS CREATURES- EVEN HELPFUL AT TIMES!
WE HAVE MINUTES TO LIVE... AND YOU LECTURE ME ON THE HABITS OF THE PENGUIN!
ORK!
ONE OF THEIR HABITS IS TO CARRY PRESENTS TO STRANGERS WHO INTEREST THEM... STONES AND BITS OF WOOD... HEY, OLD-TIMER ...ORK, ORK!
HOW INTERESTING! I SUPPOSE YOU'RE TELLING HIM ABOUT THE BAT TRICK WE PLAYED ON HIS BOSS!
ORK! ORK!

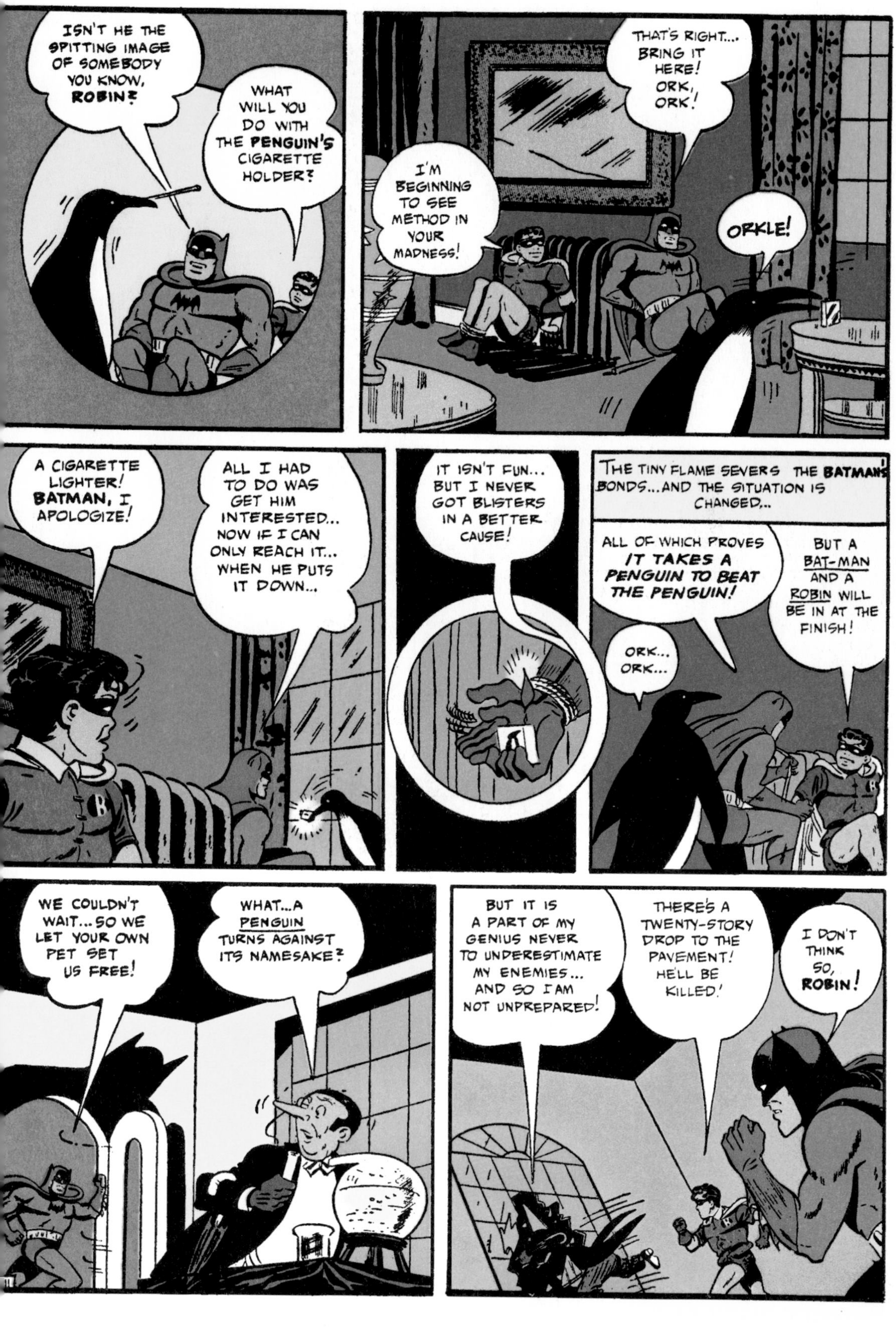
ISN'T HE THE SPITTING IMAGE OF SOMEBODY YOU KNOW, ROBIN?
WHAT WILL YOU DO WITH THE PENGUIN'S CIGARETTE HOLDER?
THAT'S RIGHT... BRING IT HERE! ORK, ORK!
I'M BEGINNING TO SEE METHOD IN YOUR MADNESS!
ORKLE!
A CIGARETTE LIGHTER! BATMAN, I APOLOGIZE!
ALL I HAD TO DO WAS GET HIM INTERESTED... NOW IF I CAN ONLY REACH IT... WHEN HE PUTS IT DOWN...
IT ISN'T FUN... BUT I NEVER GOT BLISTERS IN A BETTER CAUSE!
THE TINY FLAME SEVERS THE BATMAN'S BONDS... AND THE SITUATION IS CHANGED...
ALL OF WHICH PROVES IT TAKES A PENGUIN TO BEAT THE PENGUIN!
BUT A BAT-MAN AND A ROBIN WILL BE IN AT THE FINISH!
ORK... ORK...
WE COULDN'T WAIT... SO WE LET YOUR OWN PET SET US FREE!
WHAT...A PENGUIN TURNS AGAINST ITS NAMESAKE?
BUT IT IS A PART OF MY GENIUS NEVER TO UNDERESTIMATE MY ENEMIES... AND SO I AM NOT UNPREPARED!
THERE'S A TWENTY-STORY DROP TO THE PAVEMENT! HE'LL BE KILLED!
I DON'T THINK SO, ROBIN!

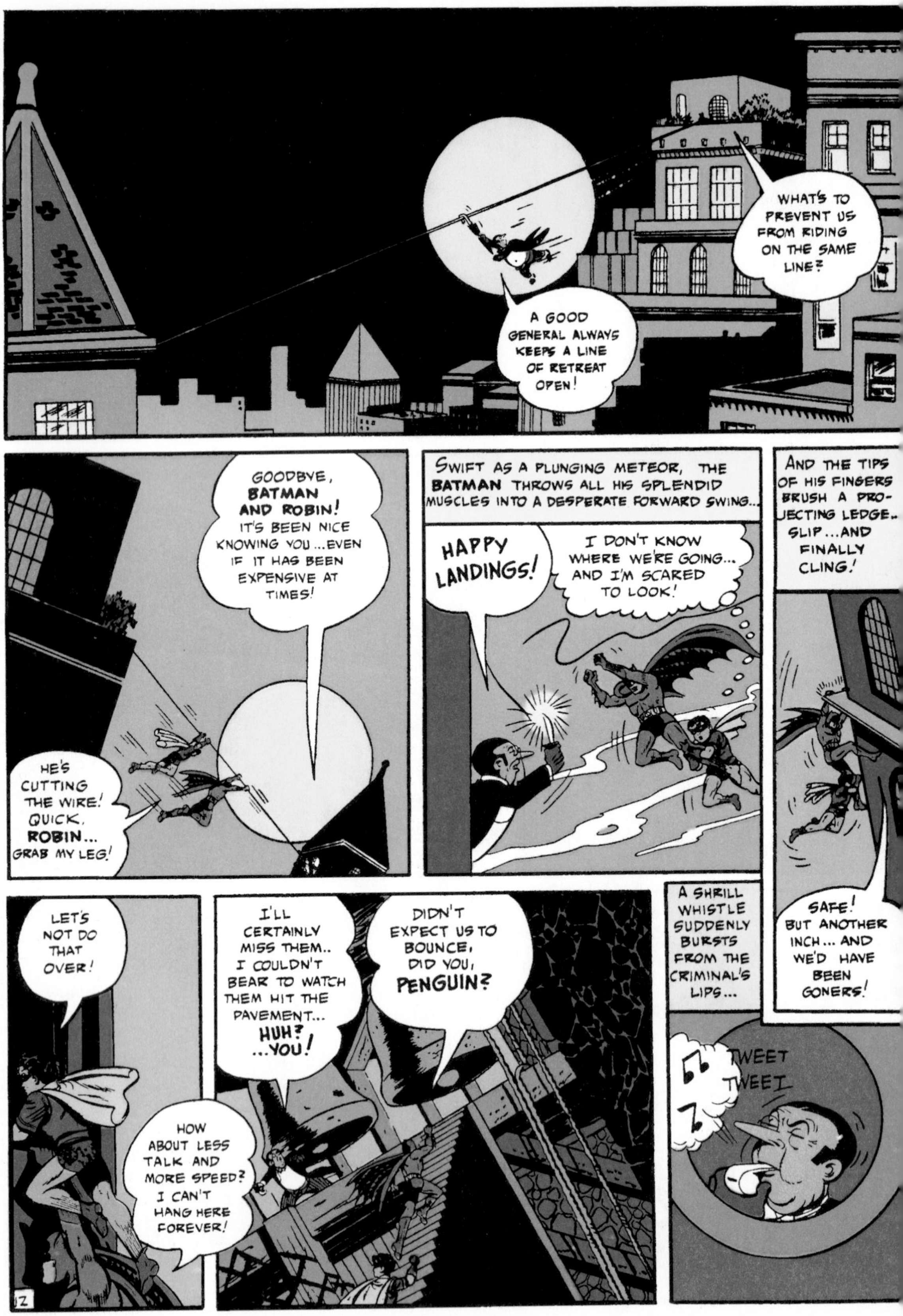
WHAT'S TO PREVENT US FROM RIDING ON THE SAME LINE?
A GOOD GENERAL ALWAYS KEEPS A LINE OF RETREAT OPEN!
GOODBYE, BATMAN AND ROBIN! IT'S BEEN NICE KNOWING YOU ...EVEN IF IT HAS BEEN EXPENSIVE AT TIMES!
HE'S CUTTING THE WIRE! QUICK, ROBIN... GRAB MY LEG!
SWIFT AS A PLUNGING METEOR, THE BATMAN THROWS ALL HIS SPLENDID MUSCLES INTO A DESPERATE FORWARD SWING...
HAPPY LANDINGS!
I DON'T KNOW WHERE WE'RE GOING... AND I'M SCARED TO LOOK!
AND THE TIPS OF HIS FINGERS BRUSH A PROJECTING LEDGE.. SLIP...AND FINALLY CLING!
SAFE! BUT ANOTHER INCH... AND WE'D HAVE BEEN GONERS!
LET'S NOT DO THAT OVER!
HOW ABOUT LESS TALK AND MORE SPEED? I CAN'T HANG HERE FOREVER!
I'LL CERTAINLY MISS THEM.. I COULDN'T BEAR TO WATCH THEM HIT THE PAVEMENT... HUH? ...YOU!
DIDN'T EXPECT US TO BOUNCE, DID YOU, PENGUIN?
A SHRILL WHISTLE SUDDENLY BURSTS FROM THE CRIMINAL'S LIPS...
TWEET TWEET
12

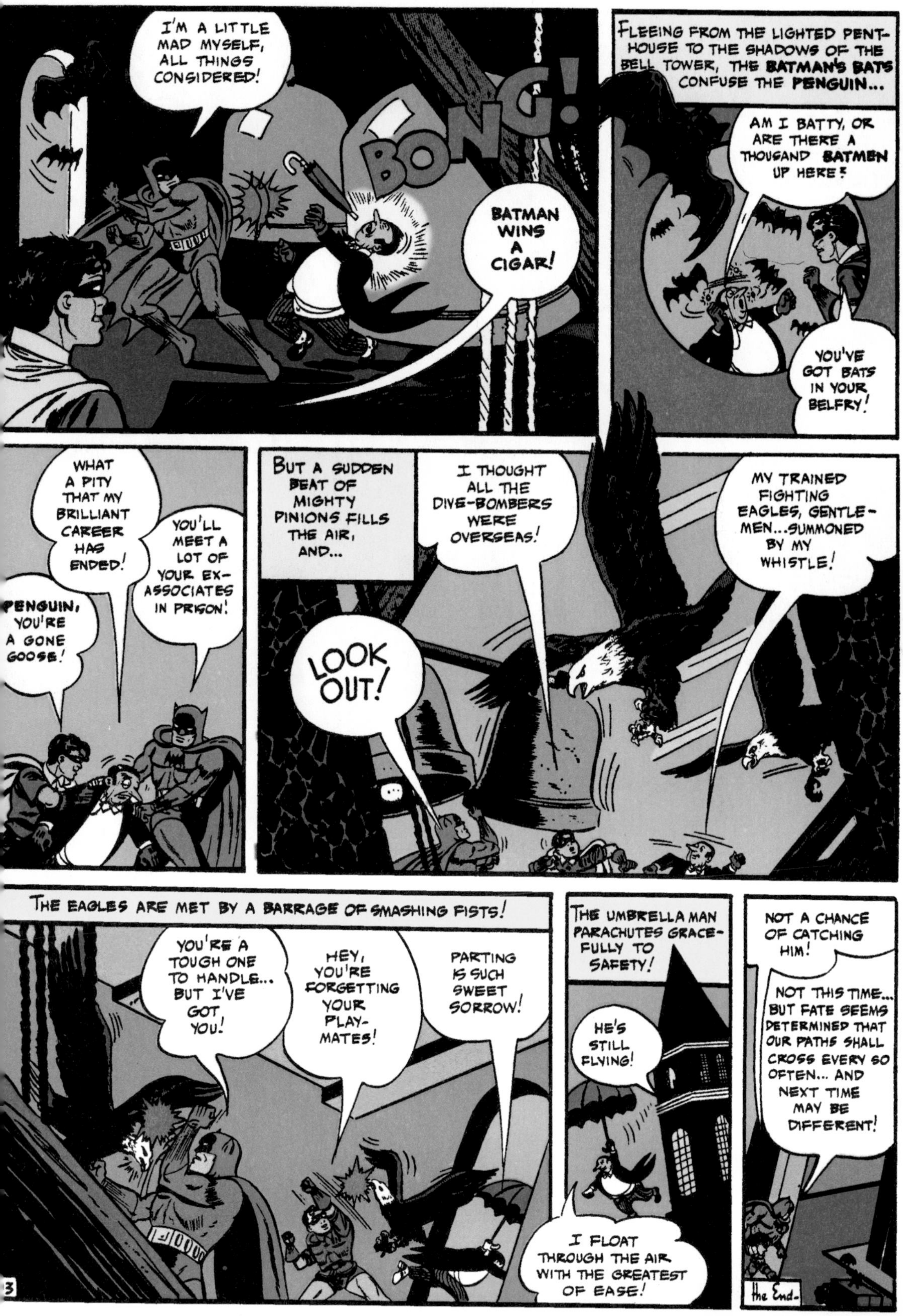
I'M A LITTLE MAD MYSELF, ALL THINGS CONSIDERED!
BONG!
BATMAN WINS A CIGAR!
FLEEING FROM THE LIGHTED PENT-HOUSE TO THE SHADOWS OF THE BELL TOWER, THE BATMAN'S BATS CONFUSE THE PENGUIN...
AM I BATTY, OR ARE THERE A THOUSAND BATMEN UP HERE?
YOU'VE GOT BATS IN YOUR BELFRY!
PENGUIN, YOU'RE A GONE GOOSE!
WHAT A PITY THAT MY BRILLIANT CAREER HAS ENDED!
YOU'LL MEET A LOT OF YOUR EX-ASSOCIATES IN PRISON!
BUT A SUDDEN BEAT OF MIGHTY PINIONS FILLS THE AIR, AND...
I THOUGHT ALL THE DIVE-BOMBERS WERE OVERSEAS!
MY TRAINED FIGHTING EAGLES, GENTLE-MEN...SUMMONED BY MY WHISTLE!
LOOK OUT!
THE EAGLES ARE MET BY A BARRAGE OF SMASHING FISTS!
YOU'RE A TOUGH ONE TO HANDLE... BUT I'VE GOT YOU!
HEY, YOU'RE FORGETTING YOUR PLAY-MATES!
PARTING IS SUCH SWEET SORROW!
13
THE UMBRELLA MAN PARACHUTES GRACE-FULLY TO SAFETY!
HE'S STILL FLYING!
I FLOAT THROUGH THE AIR WITH THE GREATEST OF EASE!
NOT A CHANCE OF CATCHING HIM!
NOT THIS TIME... BUT FATE SEEMS DETERMINED THAT OUR PATHS SHALL CROSS EVERY SO OFTEN... AND NEXT TIME MAY BE DIFFERENT!
The End.

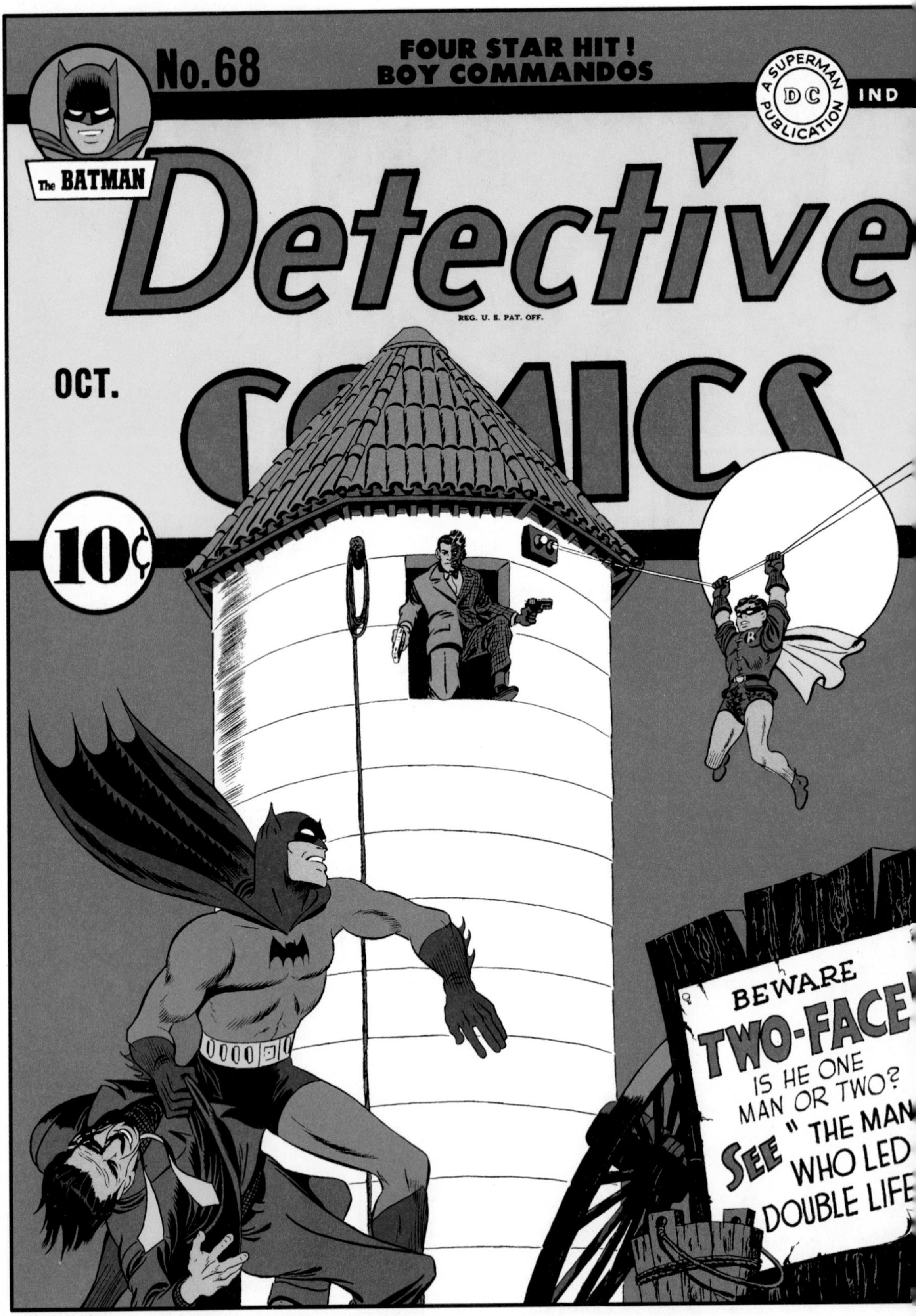
No. 68
FOUR STAR HIT!
BOY COMMANDOS
A SUPERMAN DC PUBLICATION
IND
The BATMAN
Detective
REG. U. S. PAT. OFF.
OCT.
COMICS
10¢
BEWARE
TWO-FACE
IS HE ONE
MAN OR TWO?
SEE "THE MAN
WHO LED
DOUBLE LIFE

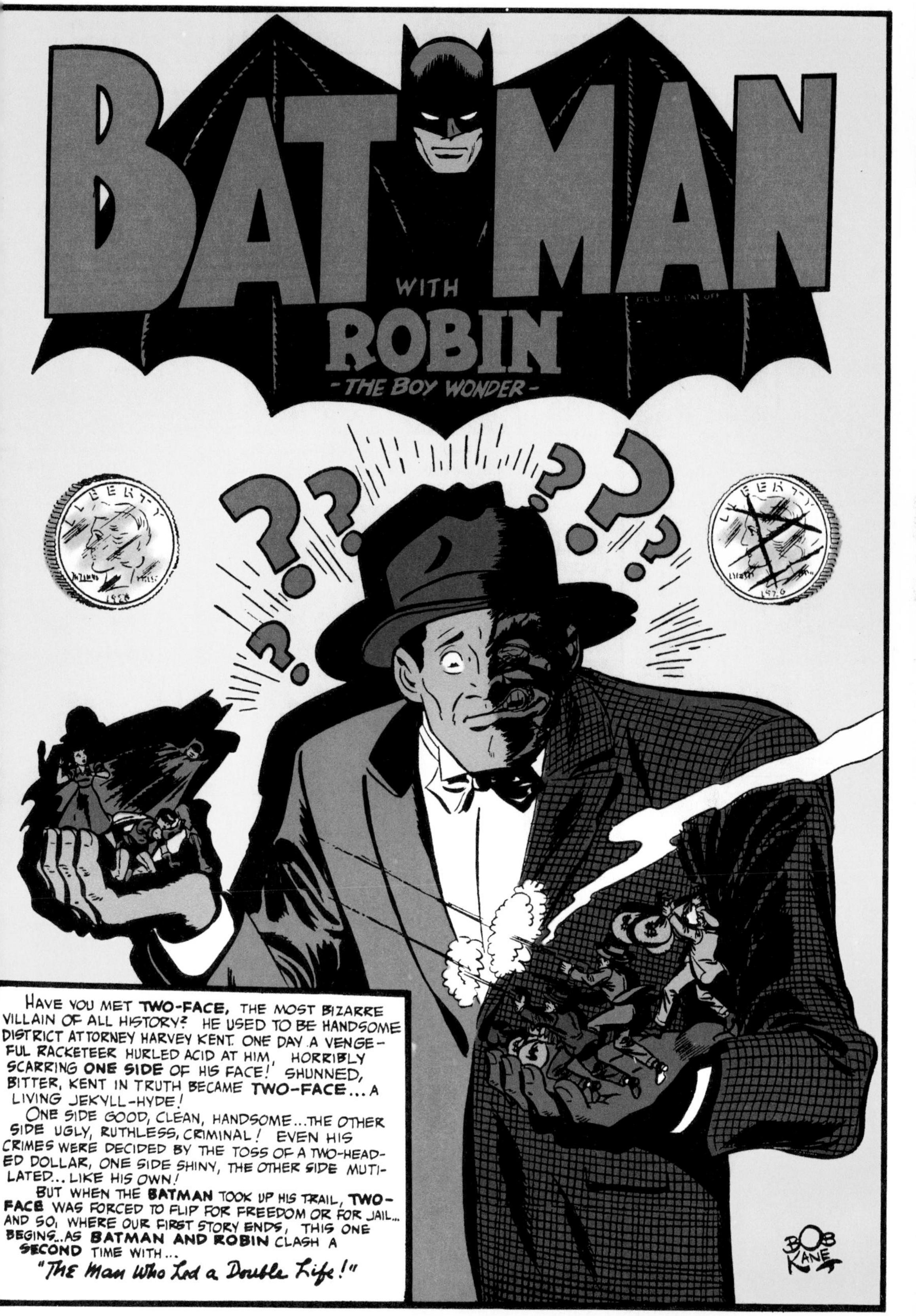
BATMAN
WITH
ROBIN
-THE BOY WONDER-
HAVE YOU MET TWO-FACE, THE MOST BIZARRE VILLAIN OF ALL HISTORY? HE USED TO BE HANDSOME DISTRICT ATTORNEY HARVEY KENT. ONE DAY A VENGEFUL RACKETEER HURLED ACID AT HIM, HORRIBLY SCARRING ONE SIDE OF HIS FACE! SHUNNED, BITTER, KENT IN TRUTH BECAME TWO-FACE... A LIVING JEKYLL-HYDE!
ONE SIDE GOOD, CLEAN, HANDSOME... THE OTHER SIDE UGLY, RUTHLESS, CRIMINAL! EVEN HIS CRIMES WERE DECIDED BY THE TOSS OF A TWO-HEADED DOLLAR, ONE SIDE SHINY, THE OTHER SIDE MUTILATED... LIKE HIS OWN!
BUT WHEN THE BATMAN TOOK UP HIS TRAIL, TWO-FACE WAS FORCED TO FLIP FOR FREEDOM OR FOR JAIL... AND SO, WHERE OUR FIRST STORY ENDS, THIS ONE BEGINS... AS BATMAN AND ROBIN CLASH A SECOND TIME WITH...
"THE Man Who Led a Double Life!"
BOB KANE

A FLIPPED SILVER DOLLAR IRONICALLY STANDS ON ITS EDGE IN A CRACK BETWEEN THE ROOM'S FLOOR BOARDS AS TWO MEN PEER AT IT!

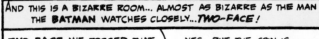
AND THIS IS A BIZARRE ROOM... ALMOST AS BIZARRE AS THE MAN THE **BATMAN** WATCHES CLOSELY... **TWO-FACE!**

TWO-FACE, WE TOSSED THAT COIN TO DECIDE SOMETHING! IF THE GOOD SIDE WON... YOU WERE TO GIVE YOURSELF UP! IF THE SCARRED SIDE WON... YOU WOULD CONTINUE A LIFE OF CRIME!

YES... BUT THE COIN IS STANDING ON ITS EDGE, SO IT CAN'T DECIDE ONE WAY OR ANOTHER!

TWO-FACE SCOOPS UP THE COIN... AND DROPS IT INTO THE BREAST POCKET OF HIS VEST...

WHY PUT THE COIN AWAY? WHY NOT FLIP OVER AGAIN?

I REPEAT, **BATMAN.** I ONLY TOSS ONCE AGAINST CHANCE! SINCE I CAN'T DECIDE FOR MYSELF, NOW IT'S UP TO FATE TO DECIDE WHAT TO DO WITH MY LIFE!

AND FATE COMES BANGING IN... AS A BULLET SPEEDS UNERRINGLY AT **TWO-FACE'S** BREAST!

IT'S OKAY, **BATMAN...** I WON'T GIVE HIM A CHANCE TO FIRE THAT GUN!

NO, DON'T!

UGH!

YOU SHOULDN'T HAVE DONE IT! I MIGHT HAVE REFORMED HIM YET!

SORRY, BUT I THOUGHT YOU WERE IN DANGER! I GUESS I ACTED TOO FAST TO THINK!

MAYBE YOU DON'T, BUT WHEN I ACT... I THINK... FAST!

A HEADLONG CRASH CARRIES **TWO-FACE** AWAY FROM THE GROGGY PURSUERS...

HA! GOT AWAY! THE ONLY THING THAT SAVED MY LIFE WAS THE COIN... BECAUSE THAT'S WHAT THE BULLET HIT! MY BREAST POCKET!

THE BULLET... IT HIT THE SCARRED SIDE! FATE'S GIVEN ME MY ANSWER! THE SCARRED SIDE SAVED MY LIFE... FOR **A LIFE OF CRIME!**

THIS IS THE PATH DESTINY'S CHOSEN FOR ME... GOOD-BYE FOREVER TO HARVEY KENT, D.A.... IT'S **TWO-FACE,** CRIME KING, FROM NOW ON!

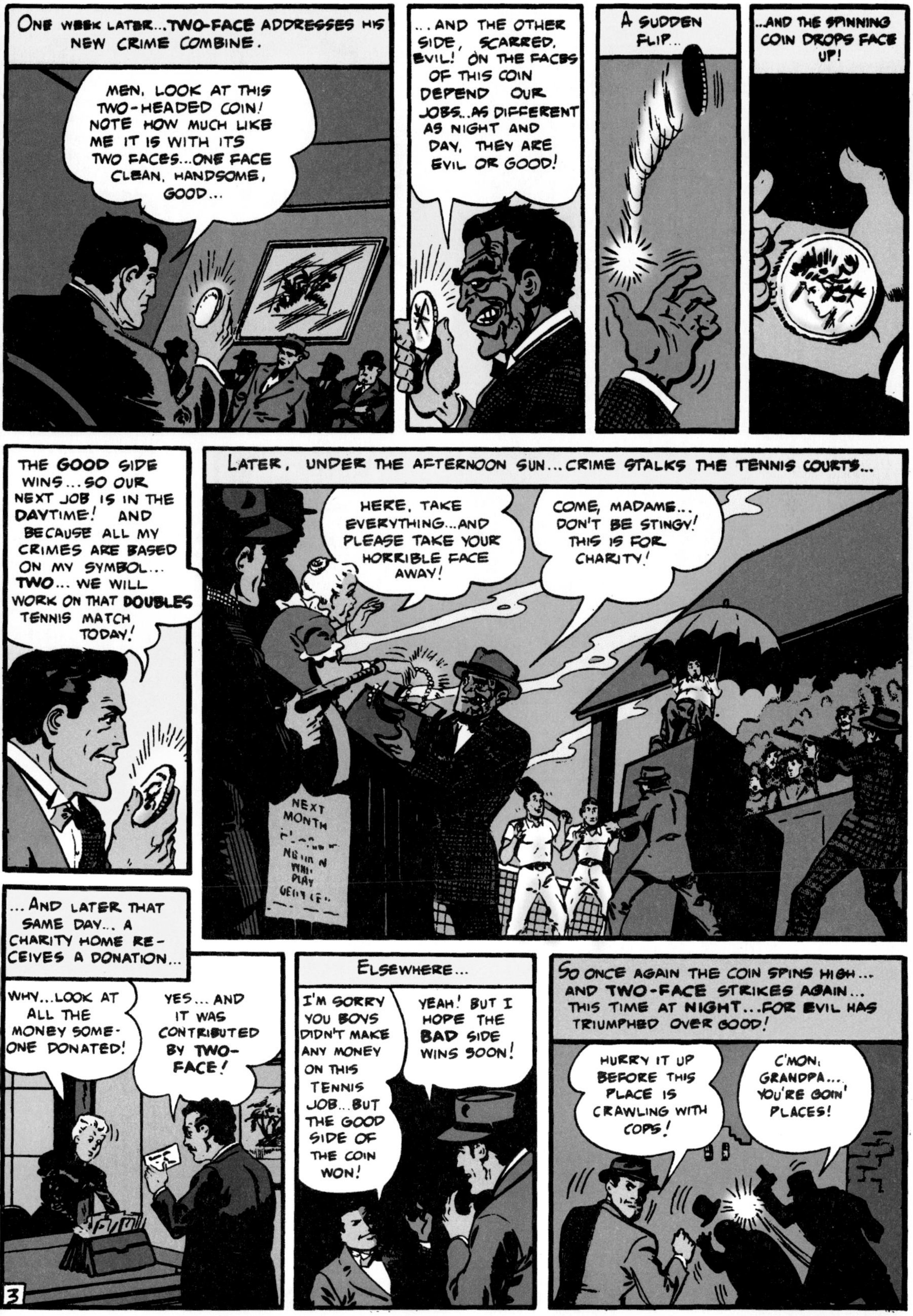
One week later... Two-Face addresses his new crime combine.
Men, look at this two-headed coin! Note how much like me it is with its two faces...one face clean, handsome, good...
...and the other side, scarred, evil! On the faces of this coin depend our jobs...as different as night and day, they are evil or good!
A sudden flip...
...and the spinning coin drops face up!
The good side wins...so our next job is in the daytime! And because all my crimes are based on my symbol... two... we will work on that doubles tennis match today!
Later, under the afternoon sun...crime stalks the tennis courts...
Here, take everything...and please take your horrible face away!
Come, madame... don't be stingy! This is for charity!
Next month
...and later that same day... a charity home receives a donation...
Why...look at all the money someone donated!
Yes...and it was contributed by Two-Face!
Elsewhere...
I'm sorry you boys didn't make any money on this tennis job...but the good side of the coin won!
Yeah! But I hope the bad side wins soon!
So once again the coin spins high... and Two-Face strikes again... this time at night...for evil has triumphed over good!
Hurry it up before this place is crawling with cops!
C'mon, grandpa... you're goin' places!
3

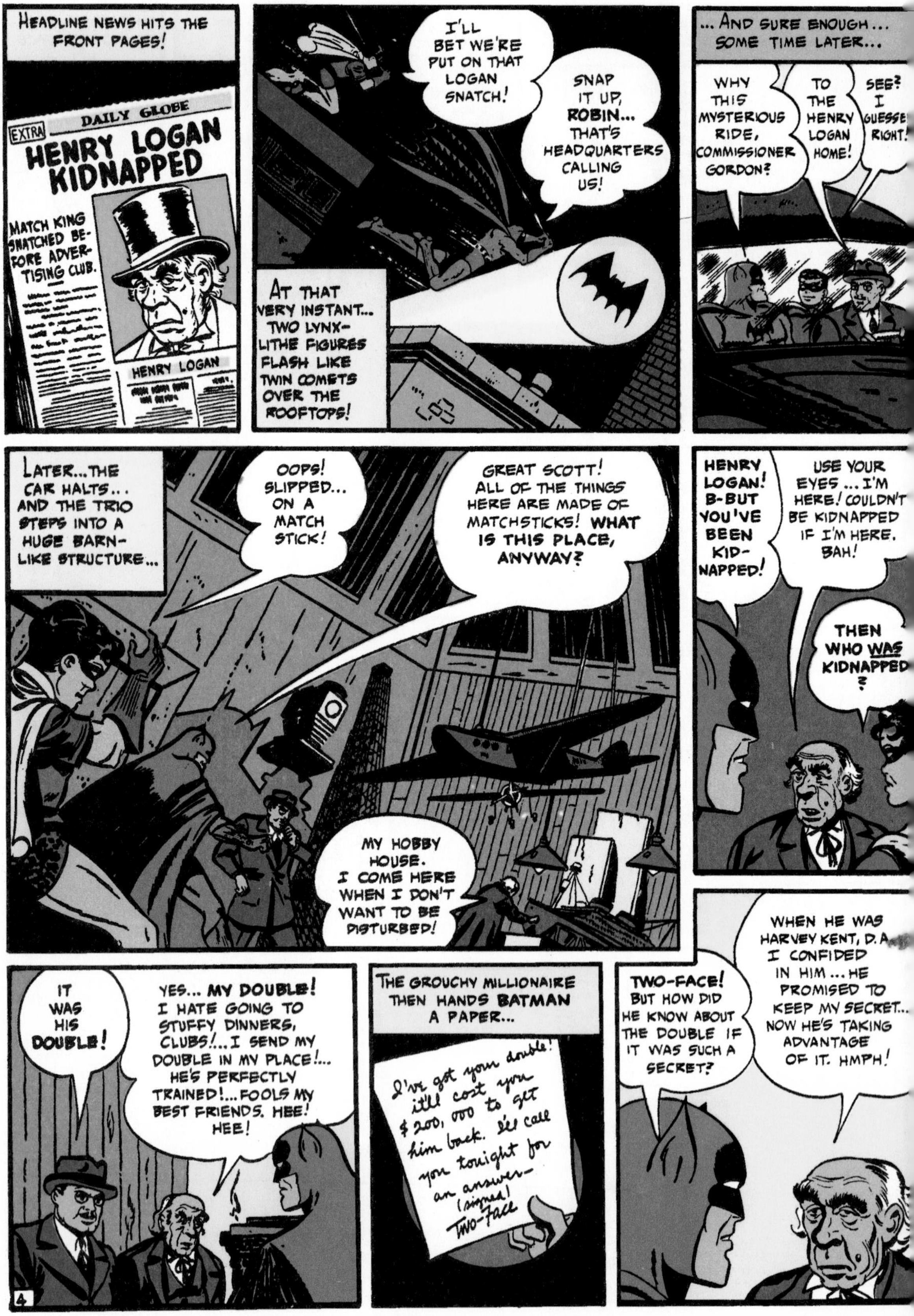
HEADLINE NEWS HITS THE FRONT PAGES!
DAILY GLOBE
EXTRA
HENRY LOGAN KIDNAPPED
MATCH KING SNATCHED BEFORE ADVERTISING CLUB.
HENRY LOGAN
I'LL BET WE'RE PUT ON THAT LOGAN SNATCH!
SNAP IT UP, ROBIN... THAT'S HEADQUARTERS CALLING US!
AT THAT VERY INSTANT... TWO LYNX-LITHE FIGURES FLASH LIKE TWIN COMETS OVER THE ROOFTOPS!
... AND SURE ENOUGH... SOME TIME LATER...
WHY THIS MYSTERIOUS RIDE, COMMISSIONER GORDON?
TO THE HENRY LOGAN HOME!
SEE? I GUESSED RIGHT!
LATER... THE CAR HALTS... AND THE TRIO STEPS INTO A HUGE BARN-LIKE STRUCTURE...
OOPS! SLIPPED... ON A MATCH STICK!
GREAT SCOTT! ALL OF THE THINGS HERE ARE MADE OF MATCHSTICKS! WHAT IS THIS PLACE, ANYWAY?
MY HOBBY HOUSE. I COME HERE WHEN I DON'T WANT TO BE DISTURBED!
HENRY LOGAN! B-BUT YOU'VE BEEN KID-NAPPED!
USE YOUR EYES... I'M HERE! COULDN'T BE KIDNAPPED IF I'M HERE. BAH!
THEN WHO WAS KIDNAPPED?
IT WAS HIS DOUBLE!
YES... MY DOUBLE! I HATE GOING TO STUFFY DINNERS, CLUBS!... I SEND MY DOUBLE IN MY PLACE!... HE'S PERFECTLY TRAINED!... FOOLS MY BEST FRIENDS. HEE! HEE!
THE GROUCHY MILLIONAIRE THEN HANDS BATMAN A PAPER...
I've got your double! It'll cost you $200,000 to get him back. I'll call you tonight for an answer— (signed) Two-Face
TWO-FACE! BUT HOW DID HE KNOW ABOUT THE DOUBLE IF IT WAS SUCH A SECRET?
WHEN HE WAS HARVEY KENT, D.A. I CONFIDED IN HIM... HE PROMISED TO KEEP MY SECRET... NOW HE'S TAKING ADVANTAGE OF IT. HMPH!
4

I'M TAKING A CHANCE TELLING YOU AND GORDON! BUT I WANT MY DOUBLE... I'VE GOT TO BE FREE TO CONTINUE MY HOBBY! GET HIM BACK FOR ME!

YOU SELFISH OLD FOSSIL! YOU'RE ONLY THINKING OF YOURSELF, NOT OF THAT POOR MAN!

ALL RIGHT... BUT YOU DO AS I SAY! LISTEN...

TIME DRAGS ON IN THE ECCENTRIC MATCH-KING'S HOBBY HOUSE...

WHY, YOU INGRATE, IT WOULD ONLY TAKE ONE FIST TO MAKE YOU MORE POLITE!

CAREFUL, YOU BLUNDERING IDIOT! YOU ALMOST PUSHED OVER MY EIFFEL TOWER! IT TOOK 25,000 MATCHSTICKS TO MAKE THAT!

THEN, AT LONG LAST...THE PHONE CALL FROM TWO-FACE.

ALL RIGHT...I'LL PAY... BUT ONLY WHEN I MYSELF SEE THAT MY DOUBLE IS UNHARMED!

FINE! I'LL HAVE ONE OF MY BOYS CALL FOR YOU AND THE DOUGH... BUT NO TRICKS!

WORKIN' THIS JOB ON YOUR FORMULA IS OKAY! TWO LOGANS... AND WE GET TWO HUNDRED GRAND!

HA! HA! YOU'RE LEARNING FAST! OKAY, JOE...GO PICK UP LOGAN! MEET US AT THE BARN!

SOME TIME AFTER... LOGAN AND A COMPANION ARE BROUGHT BEFORE AN OLD RAM-SHACKLE BARN...

INSIDE!

YOU DON'T HAVE TO PUSH ME, YOU RUFFIAN!

DID THEY HURT YOU?

THAT'S THE DOUBLE GUY'S WIFE! SHE WAS WORRIED ABOUT HIM!

WIFE! HE'S A BACHELOR! IT'S A TRICK!

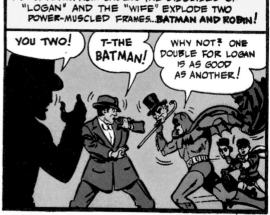

ABRUPTLY...FROM UNDER THE DISGUISES OF "LOGAN" AND THE "WIFE" EXPLODE TWO POWER-MUSCLED FRAMES...BATMAN AND ROBIN!

YOU TWO!

T-THE BATMAN!

WHY NOT? ONE DOUBLE FOR LOGAN IS AS GOOD AS ANOTHER!

5

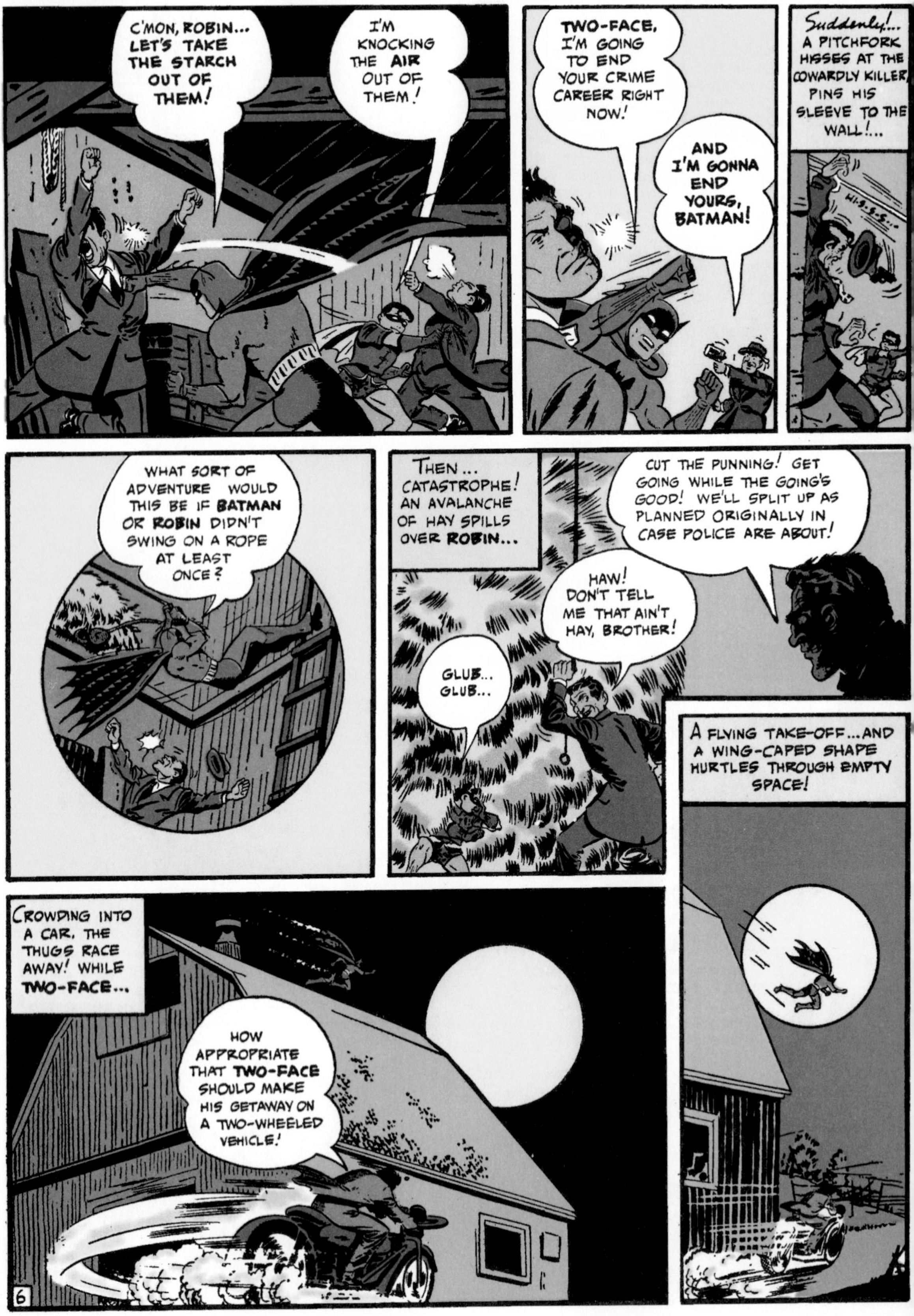
C'MON, ROBIN... LET'S TAKE THE STARCH OUT OF THEM!
I'M KNOCKING THE AIR OUT OF THEM!
TWO-FACE, I'M GOING TO END YOUR CRIME CAREER RIGHT NOW!
AND I'M GONNA END YOURS, BATMAN!
Suddenly!... A PITCHFORK HISSES AT THE COWARDLY KILLER, PINS HIS SLEEVE TO THE WALL!...
WHAT SORT OF ADVENTURE WOULD THIS BE IF BATMAN OR ROBIN DIDN'T SWING ON A ROPE AT LEAST ONCE?
THEN... CATASTROPHE! AN AVALANCHE OF HAY SPILLS OVER ROBIN...
CUT THE PUNNING! GET GOING WHILE THE GOING'S GOOD! WE'LL SPLIT UP AS PLANNED ORIGINALLY IN CASE POLICE ARE ABOUT!
HAW! DON'T TELL ME THAT AIN'T HAY, BROTHER!
GLUB... GLUB...
A FLYING TAKE-OFF... AND A WING-CAPED SHAPE HURTLES THROUGH EMPTY SPACE!
CROWDING INTO A CAR, THE THUGS RACE AWAY! WHILE TWO-FACE...
HOW APPROPRIATE THAT TWO-FACE SHOULD MAKE HIS GETAWAY ON A TWO-WHEELED VEHICLE!
6

OH... YOU AGAIN!

IT ISN'T MY TWIN BROTHER!

TWO-FISTED BATMAN VS. TWO-FACE!

WHO KNOWS? MAYBE I CAN STILL KNOCK SOME SENSE INTO YOU!

BUT THE OVER-EAGER BATMAN DOES NOT SPY A FUGITIVE DIPPING INTO A VEST POCKET!

SOMETHING STREAKS THROUGH THE AIR LIKE A SILVER COMET... AND THUDS HEAVILY AGAINST THE BATMAN'S TEMPLE!

THIS HEAVY SILVER DOLLAR OF MINE CAME IN HANDY AGAIN! I COULD KILL THE BATMAN... BUT I'M NOT A KILLER YET... BESIDES, HE WAS MY FRIEND! WELL...I'LL GET GOING BEFORE I GIVE IN TO TEMPTATION!

SOME TIME LATER...THE RECOVERED BATMAN AND ROBIN RETURN TO THE MATCH-KING'S HOBBY HOUSE ...

WELL, LOGAN... I'VE COME BACK WITH YOUR DOUBLE!

UH?...OH YES... DON'T ANNOY ME NOW...CAN'T YOU SEE I'M BUSY! GET OUT... GET OUT!

WHY, YOU COLD, SELFISH, MEAN OLD CRAB! I'M RUNNING OUT OF ADJECTIVES. HE DIDN'T EVEN ASK HOW HIS DOUBLE FELT OR ANY-THING!

HUMPH... PEOPLE ALWAYS BOTHERING ME... WISH THEY'D LEAVE ME ALONE! HMM...NOW ANOTHER MATCH HERE...

ROBIN! YOU NAUGHTY BOY! TCH-TCH - YOU SHOULDN'T HAVE GIVEN LOGAN A "HOT FOOT"...EVEN THOUGH HE DID DESERVE IT!

OWOOO!

HE LIKES TO PLAY AROUND WITH MATCHES SO MUCH...LET HIM TRY PLAYING AROUND WITH THAT!

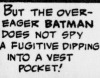

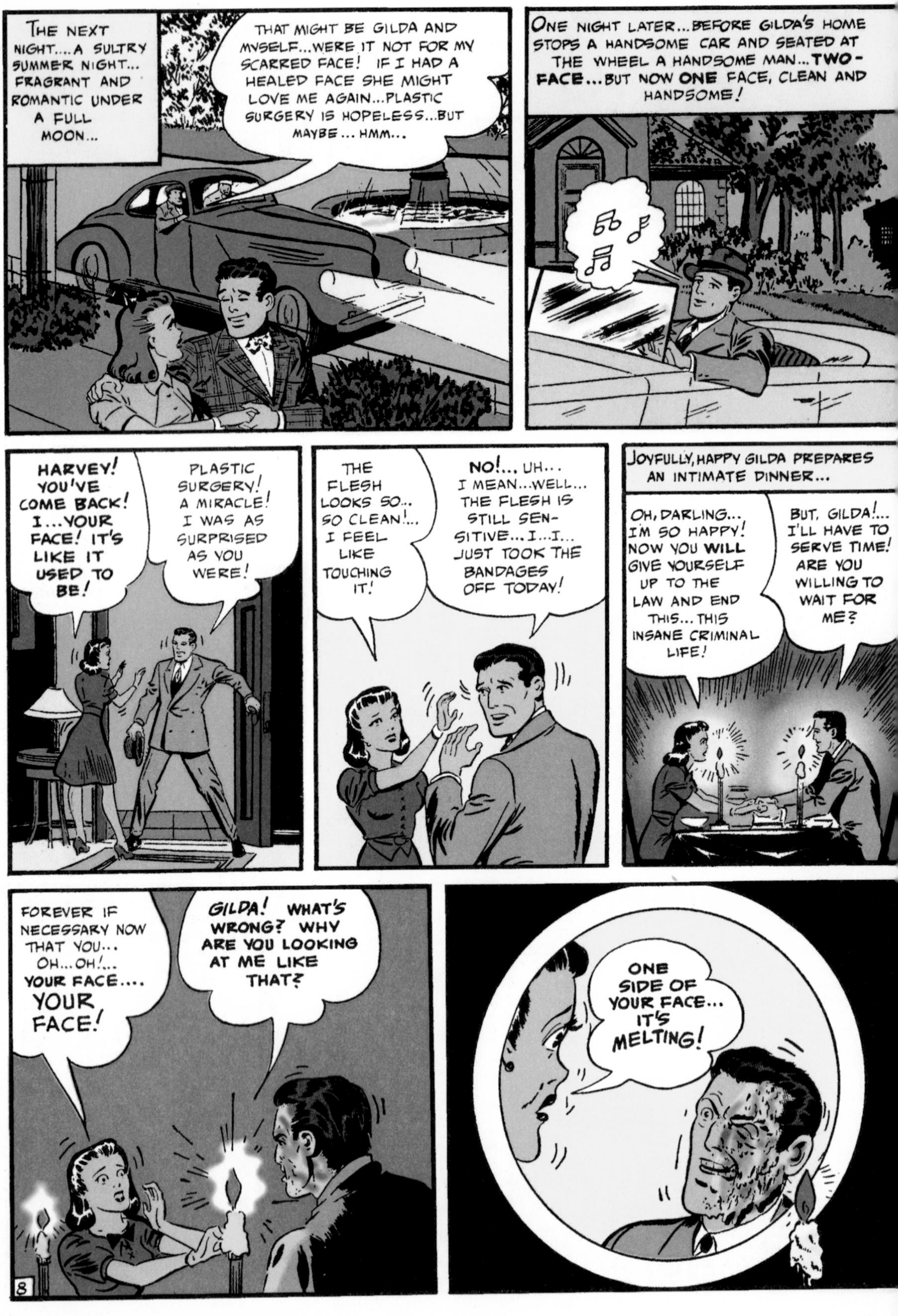

THE NEXT NIGHT....A SULTRY SUMMER NIGHT... FRAGRANT AND ROMANTIC UNDER A FULL MOON...
THAT MIGHT BE GILDA AND MYSELF...WERE IT NOT FOR MY SCARRED FACE! IF I HAD A HEALED FACE SHE MIGHT LOVE ME AGAIN...PLASTIC SURGERY IS HOPELESS...BUT MAYBE... HMM...
ONE NIGHT LATER...BEFORE GILDA'S HOME STOPS A HANDSOME CAR AND SEATED AT THE WHEEL A HANDSOME MAN...TWO-FACE...BUT NOW ONE FACE, CLEAN AND HANDSOME!
HARVEY! YOU'VE COME BACK! I...YOUR FACE! IT'S LIKE IT USED TO BE!
PLASTIC SURGERY! A MIRACLE! I WAS AS SURPRISED AS YOU WERE!
THE FLESH LOOKS SO... SO CLEAN!... I FEEL LIKE TOUCHING IT!
NO!... UH... I MEAN...WELL... THE FLESH IS STILL SEN-SITIVE... I...I... JUST TOOK THE BANDAGES OFF TODAY!
JOYFULLY, HAPPY GILDA PREPARES AN INTIMATE DINNER...
OH, DARLING... I'M SO HAPPY! NOW YOU WILL GIVE YOURSELF UP TO THE LAW AND END THIS... THIS INSANE CRIMINAL LIFE!
BUT, GILDA!... I'LL HAVE TO SERVE TIME! ARE YOU WILLING TO WAIT FOR ME?
FOREVER IF NECESSARY NOW THAT YOU... OH...OH!... YOUR FACE.... YOUR FACE!
GILDA! WHAT'S WRONG? WHY ARE YOU LOOKING AT ME LIKE THAT?
8
ONE SIDE OF YOUR FACE... IT'S MELTING!

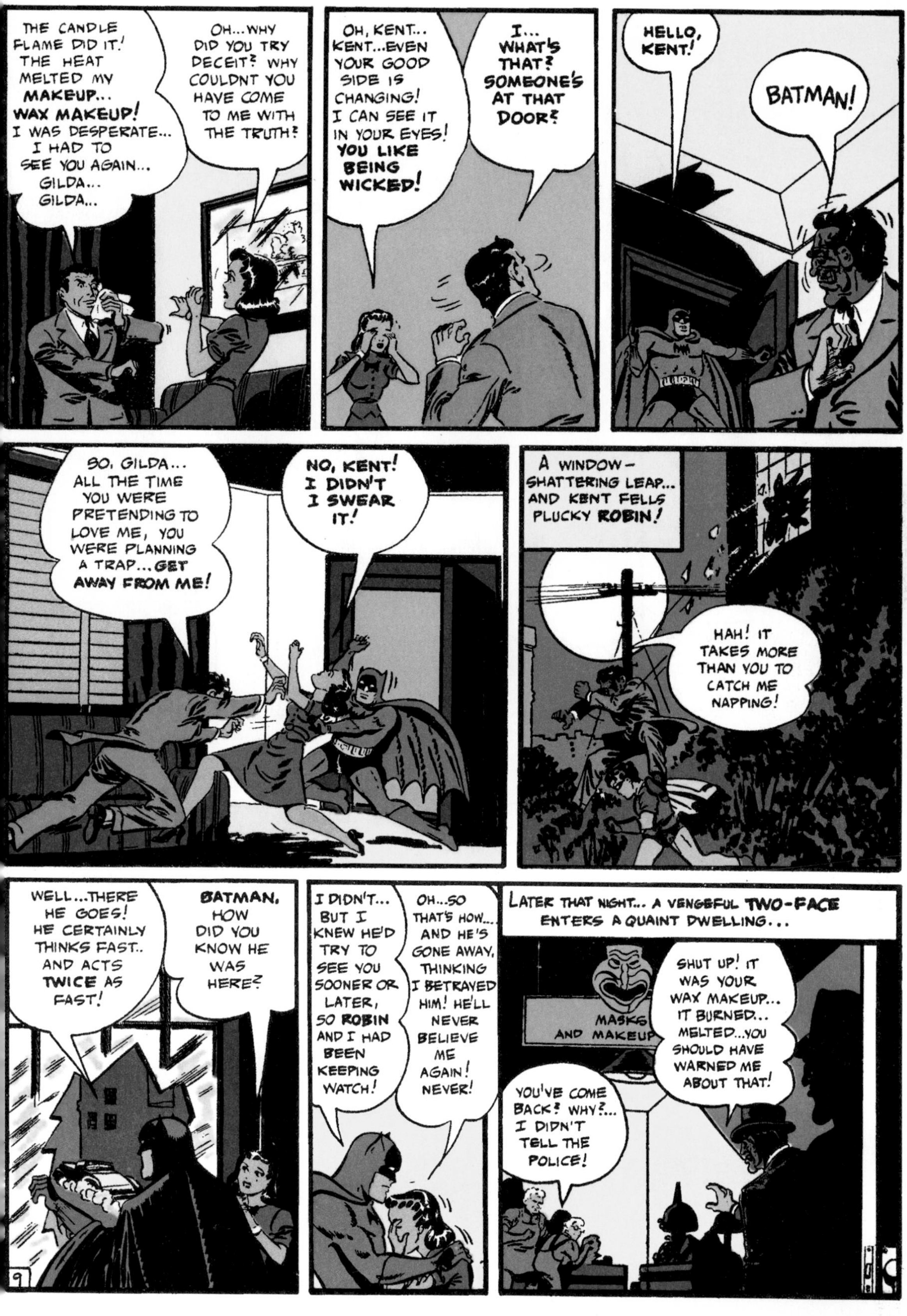
THE CANDLE FLAME DID IT! THE HEAT MELTED MY MAKEUP... WAX MAKEUP! I WAS DESPERATE... I HAD TO SEE YOU AGAIN... GILDA... GILDA...
OH...WHY DID YOU TRY DECEIT? WHY COULDNT YOU HAVE COME TO ME WITH THE TRUTH?
OH, KENT... KENT...EVEN YOUR GOOD SIDE IS CHANGING! I CAN SEE IT IN YOUR EYES! YOU LIKE BEING WICKED!
I... WHAT'S THAT? SOMEONE'S AT THAT DOOR?
HELLO, KENT!
BATMAN!
SO, GILDA... ALL THE TIME YOU WERE PRETENDING TO LOVE ME, YOU WERE PLANNING A TRAP... GET AWAY FROM ME!
NO, KENT! I DIDN'T I SWEAR IT!
A WINDOW-SHATTERING LEAP... AND KENT FELLS PLUCKY ROBIN!
HAH! IT TAKES MORE THAN YOU TO CATCH ME NAPPING!
WELL...THERE HE GOES! HE CERTAINLY THINKS FAST.. AND ACTS TWICE AS FAST!
BATMAN, HOW DID YOU KNOW HE WAS HERE?
I DIDN'T... BUT I KNEW HE'D TRY TO SEE YOU SOONER OR LATER, SO ROBIN AND I HAD BEEN KEEPING WATCH!
OH...SO THAT'S HOW... AND HE'S GONE AWAY, THINKING I BETRAYED HIM! HE'LL NEVER BELIEVE ME AGAIN! NEVER!
LATER THAT NIGHT... A VENGEFUL TWO-FACE ENTERS A QUAINT DWELLING...
MASKS AND MAKEUP
SHUT UP! IT WAS YOUR WAX MAKEUP... IT BURNED... MELTED...YOU SHOULD HAVE WARNED ME ABOUT THAT!
YOU'VE COME BACK? WHY?... I DIDN'T TELL THE POLICE!
9

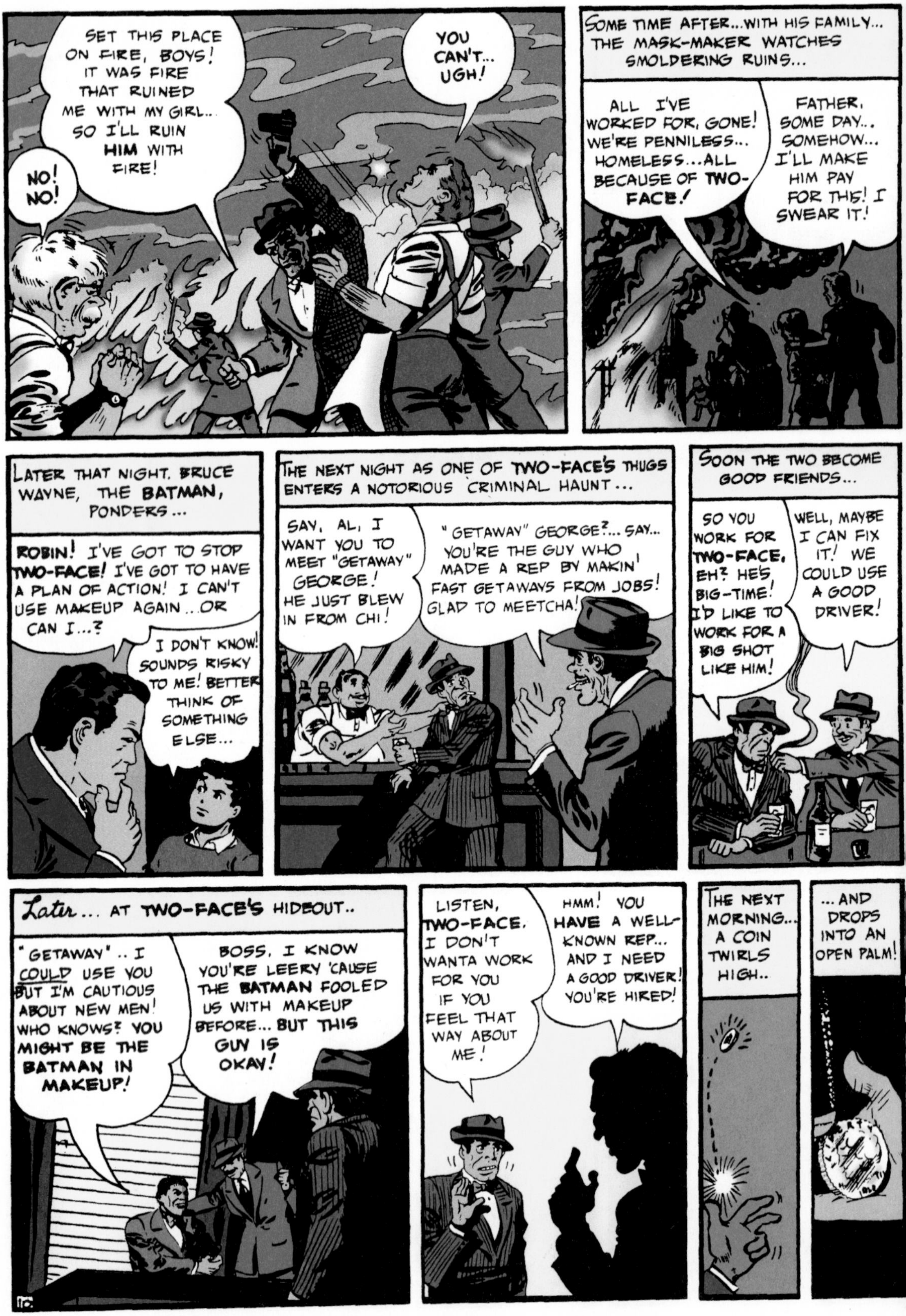
SET THIS PLACE ON FIRE, BOYS! IT WAS FIRE THAT RUINED ME WITH MY GIRL.. SO I'LL RUIN HIM WITH FIRE!
NO! NO!
YOU CAN'T.. UGH!
SOME TIME AFTER...WITH HIS FAMILY... THE MASK-MAKER WATCHES SMOLDERING RUINS...
ALL I'VE WORKED FOR, GONE! WE'RE PENNILESS... HOMELESS...ALL BECAUSE OF TWO-FACE!
FATHER, SOME DAY... SOMEHOW... I'LL MAKE HIM PAY FOR THIS! I SWEAR IT!
LATER THAT NIGHT, BRUCE WAYNE, THE BATMAN, PONDERS...
ROBIN! I'VE GOT TO STOP TWO-FACE! I'VE GOT TO HAVE A PLAN OF ACTION! I CAN'T USE MAKEUP AGAIN...OR CAN I...?
I DON'T KNOW! SOUNDS RISKY TO ME! BETTER THINK OF SOMETHING ELSE...
THE NEXT NIGHT AS ONE OF TWO-FACE'S THUGS ENTERS A NOTORIOUS CRIMINAL HAUNT...
SAY, AL, I WANT YOU TO MEET "GETAWAY" GEORGE! HE JUST BLEW IN FROM CHI!
"GETAWAY" GEORGE?... SAY... YOU'RE THE GUY WHO MADE A REP BY MAKIN' FAST GETAWAYS FROM JOBS! GLAD TO MEETCHA!
SOON THE TWO BECOME GOOD FRIENDS...
SO YOU WORK FOR TWO-FACE, EH? HE'S BIG-TIME! I'D LIKE TO WORK FOR A BIG SHOT LIKE HIM!
WELL, MAYBE I CAN FIX IT! WE COULD USE A GOOD DRIVER!
Later... AT TWO-FACE'S HIDEOUT..
"GETAWAY".. I COULD USE YOU BUT I'M CAUTIOUS ABOUT NEW MEN! WHO KNOWS? YOU MIGHT BE THE BATMAN IN MAKEUP!
BOSS, I KNOW YOU'RE LEERY 'CAUSE THE BATMAN FOOLED US WITH MAKEUP BEFORE... BUT THIS GUY IS OKAY!
LISTEN, TWO-FACE, I DON'T WANTA WORK FOR YOU IF YOU FEEL THAT WAY ABOUT ME!
HMM! YOU HAVE A WELL-KNOWN REP... AND I NEED A GOOD DRIVER! YOU'RE HIRED!
THE NEXT MORNING... A COIN TWIRLS HIGH..
...AND DROPS INTO AN OPEN PALM!

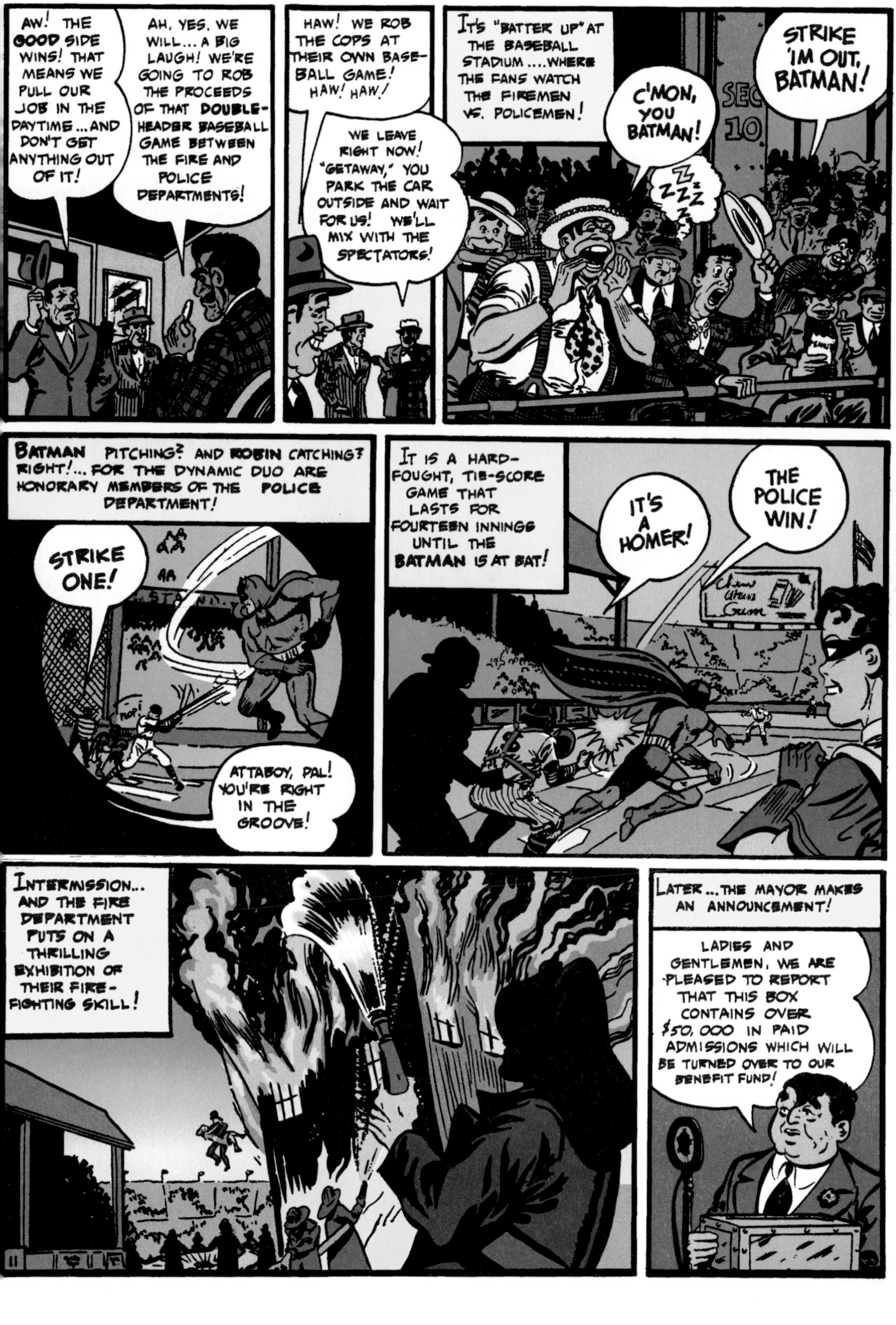
AW! THE GOOD SIDE WINS! THAT MEANS WE PULL OUR JOB IN THE DAYTIME...AND DON'T GET ANYTHING OUT OF IT!
AH, YES, WE WILL...A BIG LAUGH! WE'RE GOING TO ROB THE PROCEEDS OF THAT DOUBLE-HEADER BASEBALL GAME BETWEEN THE FIRE AND POLICE DEPARTMENTS!
HAW! WE ROB THE COPS AT THEIR OWN BASE-BALL GAME! HAW! HAW!
WE LEAVE RIGHT NOW! "GETAWAY," YOU PARK THE CAR OUTSIDE AND WAIT FOR US! WE'LL MIX WITH THE SPECTATORS!
IT'S "BATTER UP" AT THE BASEBALL STADIUM....WHERE THE FANS WATCH THE FIREMEN VS. POLICEMEN!
C'MON, YOU BATMAN!
ZZZZ
STRIKE 'IM OUT, BATMAN!
BATMAN PITCHING? AND ROBIN CATCHING? RIGHT!...FOR THE DYNAMIC DUO ARE HONORARY MEMBERS OF THE POLICE DEPARTMENT!
STRIKE ONE!
ATTABOY, PAL! YOU'RE RIGHT IN THE GROOVE!
IT IS A HARD-FOUGHT, TIE-SCORE GAME THAT LASTS FOR FOURTEEN INNINGS UNTIL THE BATMAN IS AT BAT!
IT'S A HOMER!
THE POLICE WIN!
INTERMISSION...AND THE FIRE DEPARTMENT PUTS ON A THRILLING EXHIBITION OF THEIR FIRE-FIGHTING SKILL!
LATER...THE MAYOR MAKES AN ANNOUNCEMENT!
LADIES AND GENTLEMEN, WE ARE PLEASED TO REPORT THAT THIS BOX CONTAINS OVER $50,000 IN PAID ADMISSIONS WHICH WILL BE TURNED OVER TO OUR BENEFIT FUND!

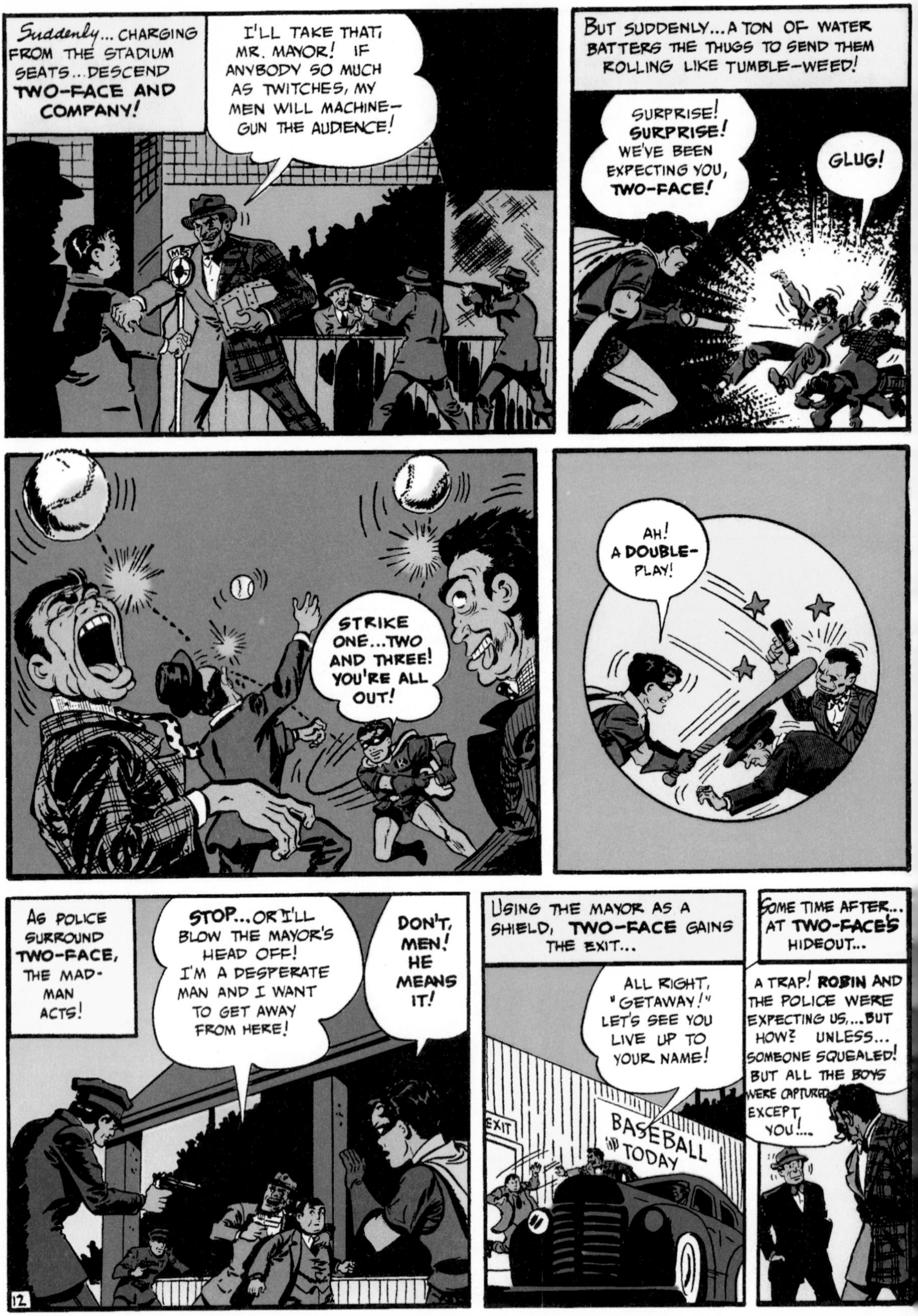
Suddenly... CHARGING FROM THE STADIUM SEATS...DESCEND TWO-FACE AND COMPANY!
I'LL TAKE THAT, MR. MAYOR! IF ANYBODY SO MUCH AS TWITCHES, MY MEN WILL MACHINE-GUN THE AUDIENCE!
BUT SUDDENLY...A TON OF WATER BATTERS THE THUGS TO SEND THEM ROLLING LIKE TUMBLE-WEED!
SURPRISE! SURPRISE! WE'VE BEEN EXPECTING YOU, TWO-FACE!
GLUG!
STRIKE ONE...TWO AND THREE! YOU'RE ALL OUT!
AH! A DOUBLE-PLAY!
AS POLICE SURROUND TWO-FACE, THE MAD-MAN ACTS!
STOP...OR I'LL BLOW THE MAYOR'S HEAD OFF! I'M A DESPERATE MAN AND I WANT TO GET AWAY FROM HERE!
DON'T, MEN! HE MEANS IT!
12
USING THE MAYOR AS A SHIELD, TWO-FACE GAINS THE EXIT...
ALL RIGHT, "GETAWAY!" LET'S SEE YOU LIVE UP TO YOUR NAME!
EXIT
BASEBALL TODAY
SOME TIME AFTER... AT TWO-FACE'S HIDEOUT...
A TRAP! ROBIN AND THE POLICE WERE EXPECTING US,...BUT HOW? UNLESS... SOMEONE SQUEALED! BUT ALL THE BOYS WERE CAPTURED EXCEPT YOU!...

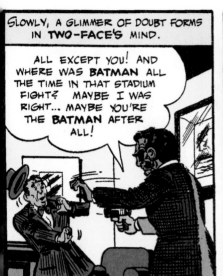

SLOWLY, A GLIMMER OF DOUBT FORMS IN **TWO-FACE'S** MIND.

ALL EXCEPT YOU! AND WHERE WAS **BATMAN** ALL THE TIME IN THAT STADIUM FIGHT? MAYBE I WAS RIGHT... MAYBE YOU'RE THE **BATMAN** AFTER ALL!

PUTTY! A FALSE NOSE! YOU ARE WEARING MAKEUP! DON'T MOVE, BATMAN ...I'M GOING TO SEE WHAT YOUR **REAL** FACE LOOKS LIKE!

MAKEUP AND WIG PEEL OFF ... AND A FACE UN-COVERED... THE FACE OF...

THE **MASK-MAKER'S SON!** THEN, YOU'RE NOT THE **BATMAN**, AFTER ALL!

OBVIOUSLY I'M NOT!

BUT... I **AM!**

THIS TIME YOU DON'T GET AWAY, **KENT!**

A THOROUGHLY SUBDUED **TWO-FACE** LISTENS IN SURPRISE ...

I WANTED TO GET EVEN WITH YOU FOR RUINING MY FATHER, SO I MADE UP AS "GETAWAY" TO GET INTO YOUR MOB AND GET INSIDE INFORMATION!

AT THE BALL GAME, HE MANAGED TO SLIP AWAY AND TOLD ME YOUR PLANS! I TIPPED OFF **ROBIN!**

BUT TO CHECK-MATE YOU, I HID IN THE TRUNK OF YOUR CAR! SO HERE I AM... AND YOU'RE GOING TO JAIL!

HA! WHAT IRONY! I BASED ALL MY CRIMES ON THE NUMBER **TWO** AND END UP FINALLY BEING **DOUBLE-**CROSSED BY ONE OF MY OWN MOB!

AND SO, AT LONG LAST, **TWO-FACE** GOES TO JAIL ...

TWO-FACE... YOUR **DOUBLE-**LIFE IS OVER! FROM NOW ON, YOU'LL LEAD ONLY **ONE** EXISTENCE... AS HARVEY KENT, PRISONER!

THAT'S ONLY YOUR SIDE OF THE STORY! BUT THERE ARE ALWAYS **TWO** SIDES TO A STORY. I'LL ESCAPE, BAT-MAN... AND I'LL BET YOU ON THAT, **DOU-**BLE OR NOTHING!

The End

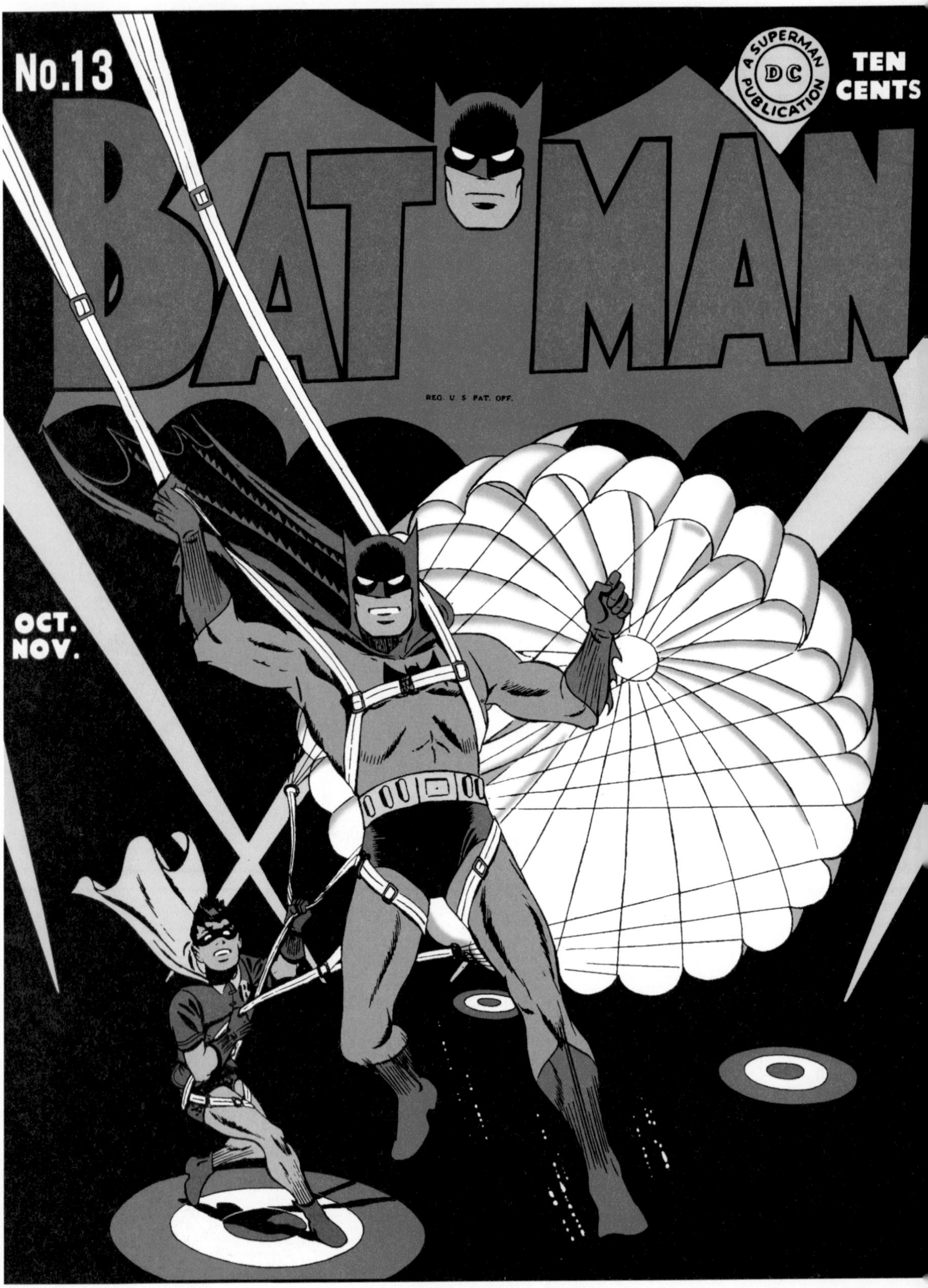
No.13
A SUPERMAN DC PUBLICATION
TEN CENTS
BATMAN
REG. U. S. PAT. OFF.
OCT. NOV.

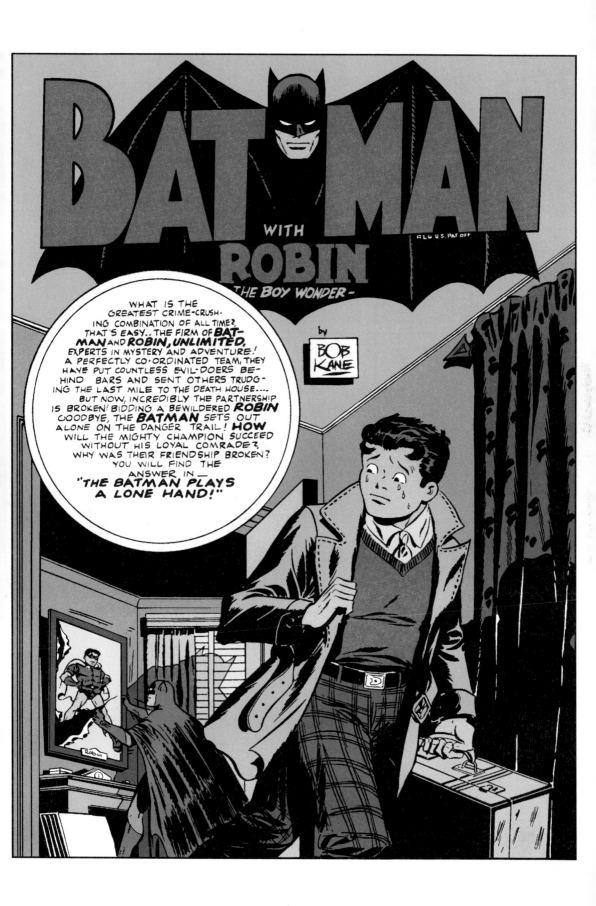

BAT MAN

REG. U.S. PAT OFF

WITH

ROBIN

THE BOY WONDER –

by
BOB
KANE

WHAT IS THE GREATEST CRIME-CRUSH-ING COMBINATION OF ALL TIME? THAT'S EASY.. THE FIRM OF *BAT-MAN* AND *ROBIN, UNLIMITED,* EXPERTS IN MYSTERY AND ADVENTURE! A PERFECTLY CO-ORDINATED TEAM, THEY HAVE PUT COUNTLESS EVIL-DOERS BE-HIND BARS AND SENT OTHERS TRUDG-ING THE LAST MILE TO THE DEATH HOUSE.... BUT NOW, INCREDIBLY THE PARTNERSHIP IS BROKEN! BIDDING A BEWILDERED *ROBIN* GOODBYE, THE *BATMAN* SETS OUT ALONE ON THE DANGER TRAIL! *HOW* WILL THE MIGHTY CHAMPION SUCCEED WITHOUT HIS LOYAL COMRADE? WHY WAS THEIR FRIENDSHIP BROKEN? YOU WILL FIND THE ANSWER IN — *"THE BATMAN PLAYS A LONE HAND!"*

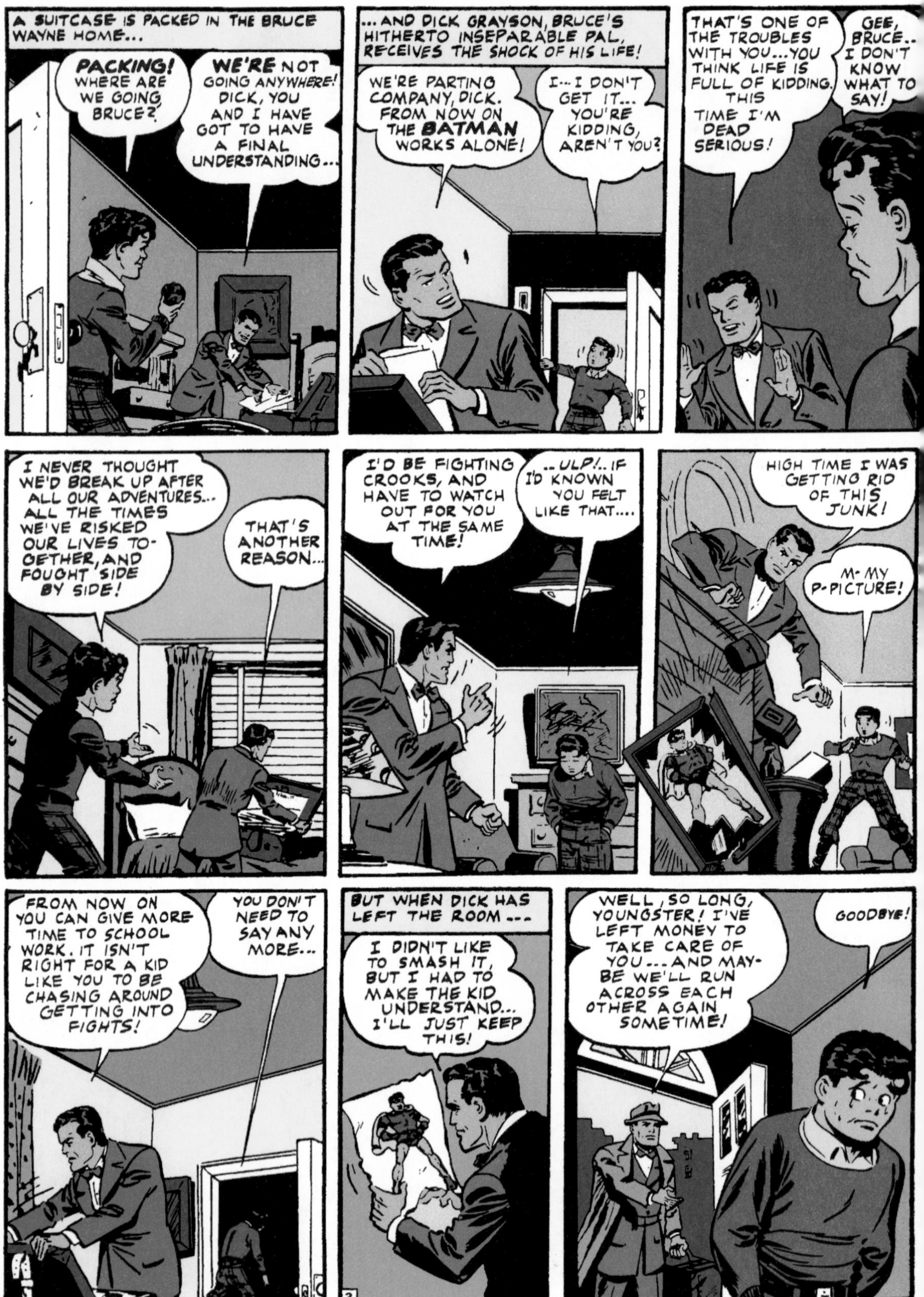
A SUITCASE IS PACKED IN THE BRUCE WAYNE HOME...
PACKING! WHERE ARE WE GOING BRUCE?
WE'RE NOT GOING ANYWHERE! DICK, YOU AND I HAVE GOT TO HAVE A FINAL UNDERSTANDING...
...AND DICK GRAYSON, BRUCE'S HITHERTO INSEPARABLE PAL, RECEIVES THE SHOCK OF HIS LIFE!
WE'RE PARTING COMPANY, DICK. FROM NOW ON THE BATMAN WORKS ALONE!
I--I DON'T GET IT... YOU'RE KIDDING, AREN'T YOU?
THAT'S ONE OF THE TROUBLES WITH YOU...YOU THINK LIFE IS FULL OF KIDDING. THIS TIME I'M DEAD SERIOUS!
GEE, BRUCE.. I DON'T KNOW WHAT TO SAY!
I NEVER THOUGHT WE'D BREAK UP AFTER ALL OUR ADVENTURES... ALL THE TIMES WE'VE RISKED OUR LIVES TOGETHER, AND FOUGHT SIDE BY SIDE!
THAT'S ANOTHER REASON...
I'D BE FIGHTING CROOKS, AND HAVE TO WATCH OUT FOR YOU AT THE SAME TIME!
..ULP!.. IF I'D KNOWN YOU FELT LIKE THAT....
HIGH TIME I WAS GETTING RID OF THIS JUNK!
M-MY P-PICTURE!
FROM NOW ON YOU CAN GIVE MORE TIME TO SCHOOL WORK. IT ISN'T RIGHT FOR A KID LIKE YOU TO BE CHASING AROUND GETTING INTO FIGHTS!
YOU DON'T NEED TO SAY ANY MORE...
BUT WHEN DICK HAS LEFT THE ROOM ---
I DIDN'T LIKE TO SMASH IT, BUT I HAD TO MAKE THE KID UNDERSTAND... I'LL JUST KEEP THIS!
2
WELL, SO LONG, YOUNGSTER! I'VE LEFT MONEY TO TAKE CARE OF YOU --- AND MAYBE WE'LL RUN ACROSS EACH OTHER AGAIN SOMETIME!
GOODBYE!

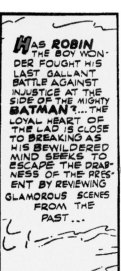

Has **ROBIN** the Boy Wonder fought his last gallant battle against injustice at the side of the mighty **BATMAN**?... The loyal heart of the lad is close to breaking as his bewildered mind seeks to escape the drabness of the present by reviewing glamorous scenes from the past...

He called me a nuisance, after all the times I've stood by him when things looked hopeless...

...When the Joker thought he had us trapped and was going to get rid of us for good...

...When the **PENGUIN** pulled surprises out of that deadly umbrella of his...

...And more times than I can count, if it hadn't been for me, there wouldn't have been any more **BATMAN**!

It isn't true (sob) I wasn't ever in his way! He just (sob) he just doesn't like me any more!

Suspicion rears its ugly head as the boy's grief wears itself out...

Or maybe he wants all the glory for himself! Maybe he thought Robin was getting too popular!

And inevitably comes blind, unreasoning anger...

I don't want his money and I won't live in his house! I'll run away and show him I can take care of myself!

SLAM!

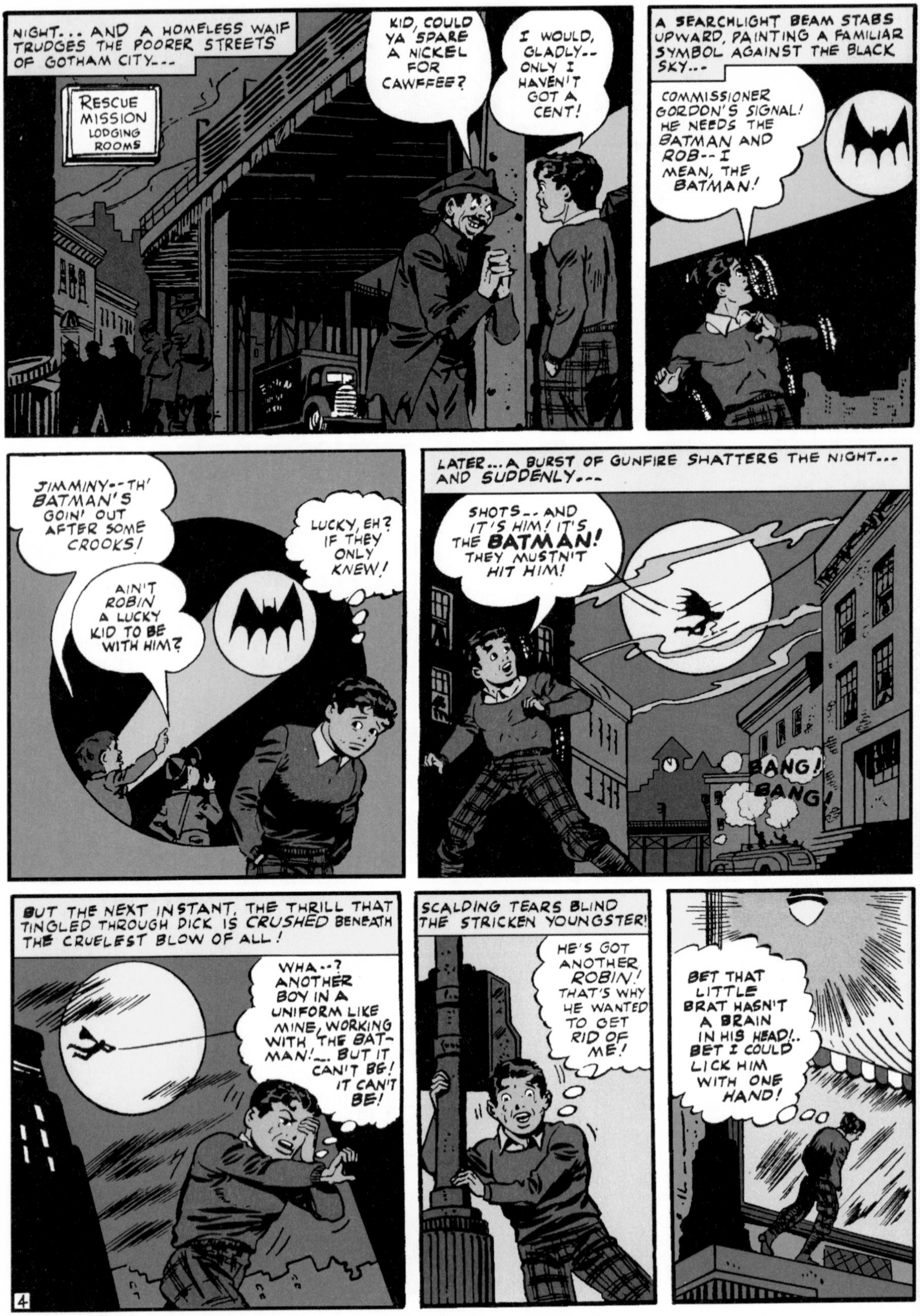
NIGHT... AND A HOMELESS WAIF TRUDGES THE POORER STREETS OF GOTHAM CITY---
RESCUE MISSION LODGING ROOMS
KID, COULD YA SPARE A NICKEL FOR CAWFFEE?
I WOULD, GLADLY-- ONLY I HAVEN'T GOT A CENT!
A SEARCHLIGHT BEAM STABS UPWARD, PAINTING A FAMILIAR SYMBOL AGAINST THE BLACK SKY...
COMMISSIONER GORDON'S SIGNAL! HE NEEDS THE BATMAN AND ROB-- I MEAN, THE BATMAN!
JIMMINY--TH' BATMAN'S GOIN' OUT AFTER SOME CROOKS!
AIN'T ROBIN A LUCKY KID TO BE WITH HIM?
LUCKY, EH? IF THEY ONLY KNEW!
LATER... A BURST OF GUNFIRE SHATTERS THE NIGHT... AND SUDDENLY...
SHOTS-- AND IT'S HIM! IT'S THE BATMAN! THEY MUSTN'T HIT HIM!
BANG! BANG!
BUT THE NEXT INSTANT, THE THRILL THAT TINGLED THROUGH DICK IS CRUSHED BENEATH THE CRUELEST BLOW OF ALL!
WHA--? ANOTHER BOY IN A UNIFORM LIKE MINE, WORKING WITH THE BAT-MAN!... BUT IT CAN'T BE! IT CAN'T BE!
4
SCALDING TEARS BLIND THE STRICKEN YOUNGSTER!
HE'S GOT ANOTHER ROBIN! THAT'S WHY HE WANTED TO GET RID OF ME!
BET THAT LITTLE BRAT HASN'T A BRAIN IN HIS HEAD!.. BET I COULD LICK HIM WITH ONE HAND!

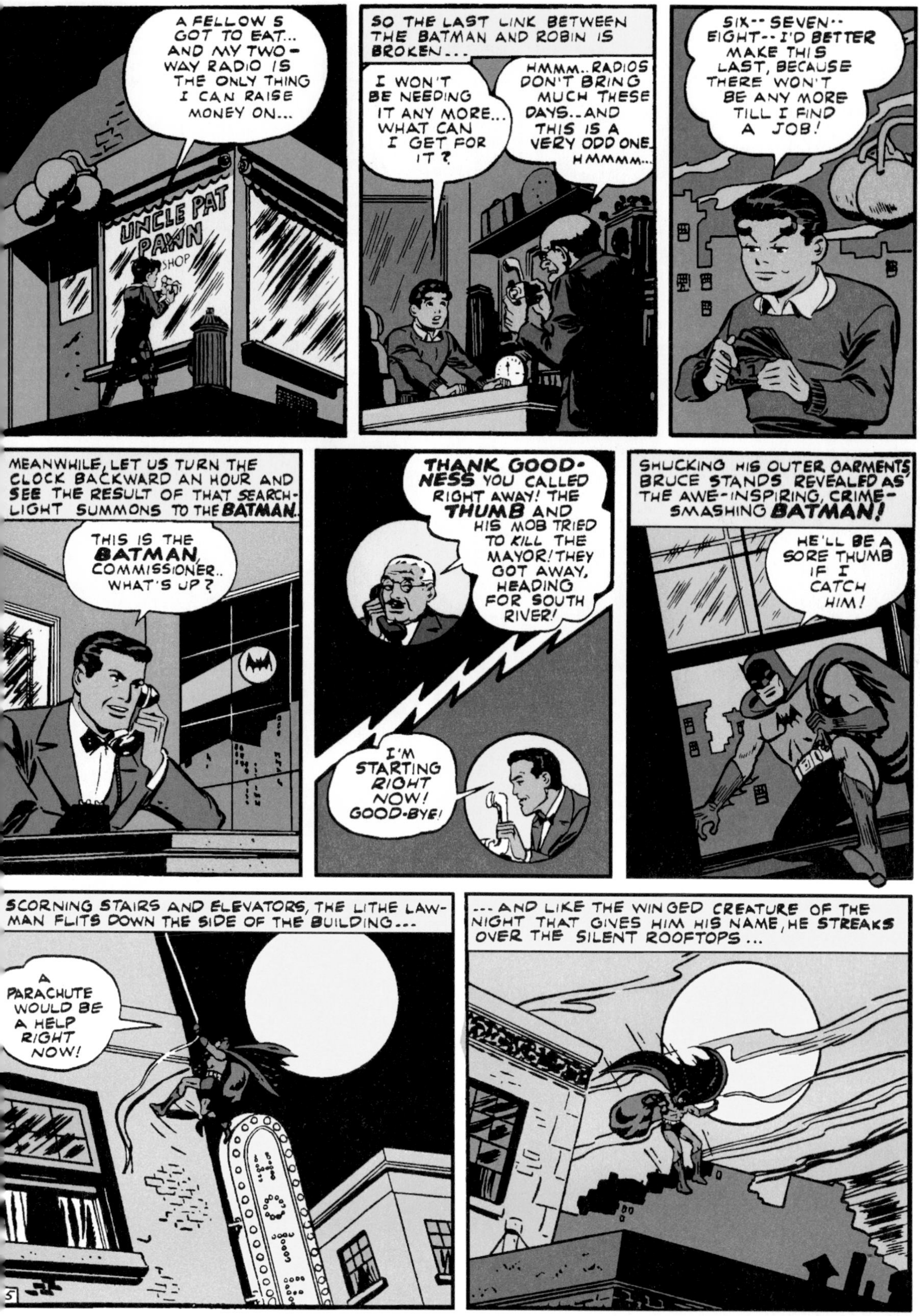

A FELLOW S GOT TO EAT... AND MY TWO-WAY RADIO IS THE ONLY THING I CAN RAISE MONEY ON...
UNCLE PAT PAWN SHOP
SO THE LAST LINK BETWEEN THE BATMAN AND ROBIN IS BROKEN...
I WON'T BE NEEDING IT ANY MORE... WHAT CAN I GET FOR IT?
HMMM.. RADIOS DON'T BRING MUCH THESE DAYS.. AND THIS IS A VERY ODD ONE. HMMMM...
SIX-- SEVEN-- EIGHT-- I'D BETTER MAKE THIS LAST, BECAUSE THERE WON'T BE ANY MORE TILL I FIND A JOB!
MEANWHILE, LET US TURN THE CLOCK BACKWARD AN HOUR AND SEE THE RESULT OF THAT SEARCHLIGHT SUMMONS TO THE BATMAN..
THIS IS THE BATMAN, COMMISSIONER.. WHAT'S UP?
THANK GOODNESS YOU CALLED RIGHT AWAY! THE THUMB AND HIS MOB TRIED TO KILL THE MAYOR! THEY GOT AWAY, HEADING FOR SOUTH RIVER!
I'M STARTING RIGHT NOW! GOOD-BYE!
SHUCKING HIS OUTER GARMENTS, BRUCE STANDS REVEALED AS THE AWE-INSPIRING, CRIME-SMASHING BATMAN!
HE'LL BE A SORE THUMB IF I CATCH HIM!
SCORNING STAIRS AND ELEVATORS, THE LITHE LAWMAN FLITS DOWN THE SIDE OF THE BUILDING...
A PARACHUTE WOULD BE A HELP RIGHT NOW!
5
...AND LIKE THE WINGED CREATURE OF THE NIGHT THAT GIVES HIM HIS NAME, HE STREAKS OVER THE SILENT ROOFTOPS...

FROM A PRECARIOUS PERCH, HIS KEEN EYES SIGHT A SPEEDING VEHICLE....

BUT THERE'S TRAFFIC DOWN THERE... A CAR LOADED WITH MEN, DOING FIFTY AT LEAST! THIS IS WHERE THE FUN STARTS!

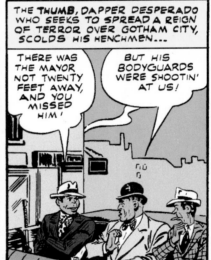

THE **THUMB**, DAPPER DESPERADO WHO SEEKS TO SPREAD A REIGN OF TERROR OVER GOTHAM CITY, SCOLDS HIS HENCHMEN...

THERE WAS THE MAYOR NOT TWENTY FEET AWAY, AND YOU MISSED HIM!

BUT HIS BODYGUARDS WERE SHOOTIN' AT US!

NO ALIBIS! I'LL SHOW YOU HOW YOU SHOULD HAVE DONE IT!

DON'T, **THUMB!** WE'LL DO BETTER NEXT TIME!

AT THAT INSTANT...

TH' **BAT-MAN!**

HUH? IF YOU GUYS WANT TO LIVE.. GET HIM FOR ME!

IF HE'D ONLY STAY STILL FOR A MINUTE!

STOP THE CAR! THE KID IS THE ONE I REALLY WANT!

WITH TH' KID GONE, TH' **BATMAN** WILL GO CRAZY!

AS THE MACHINE GUN CHATTERS, THE SMALL FIGURE SHUDDERS, THEN DROPS SICKENINGLY!

GOT HIM! NOW THE BATMAN WILL KNOW I MEAN BUSINESS!

RAT-TAT-TAT-TAT...

I'D FEEL BETTER IF YOU'D GOT TH' **BATMAN** TOO!

6

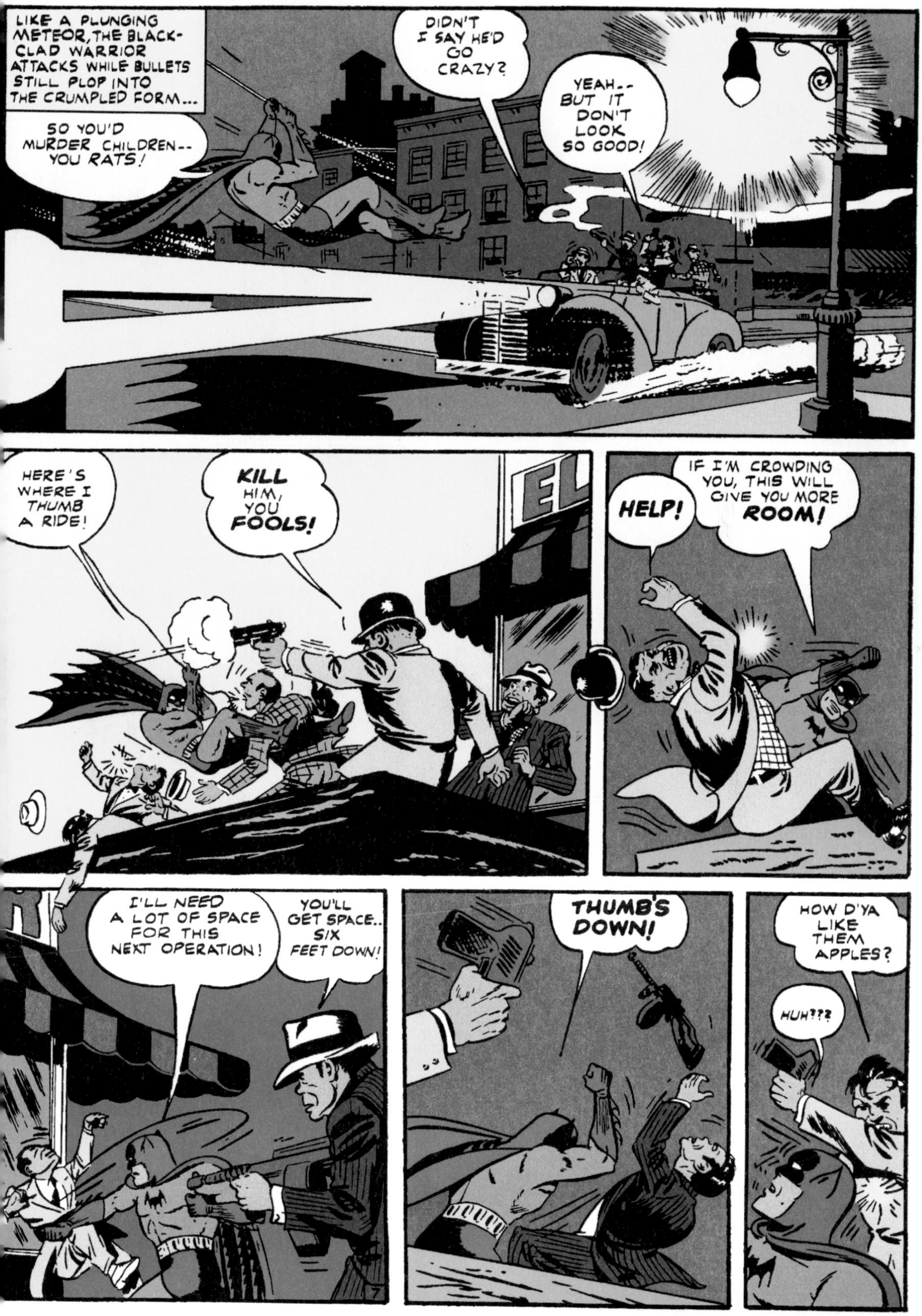
LIKE A PLUNGING METEOR, THE BLACK-CLAD WARRIOR ATTACKS WHILE BULLETS STILL PLOP INTO THE CRUMPLED FORM...
SO YOU'D MURDER CHILDREN-- YOU RATS!
DIDN'T I SAY HE'D GO CRAZY?
YEAH.- BUT IT DON'T LOOK SO GOOD!
HERE'S WHERE I THUMB A RIDE!
KILL HIM, YOU FOOLS!
HELP!
IF I'M CROWDING YOU, THIS WILL GIVE YOU MORE ROOM!
I'LL NEED A LOT OF SPACE FOR THIS NEXT OPERATION!
YOU'LL GET SPACE.. SIX FEET DOWN!
THUMB'S DOWN!
HOW D'YA LIKE THEM APPLES?
HUH???

BEFORE THE STUNNED CHAMPION CAN RECOVER, THE THUMB AND HIS HIRELINGS HAVE FLED...

NO CHANCE OF CATCHING THEM--BUT I'LL FIND THEIR HIDEOUT IF IT TAKES A LIFETIME!

THAT SHOOTING WILL BRING THE COPS! STEP ON IT!

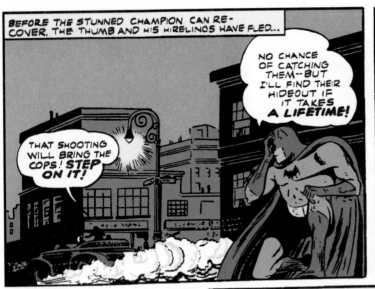

SLOWLY, THE BATMAN APPROACHES THE BULLET-RIDDLED FIGURE ON THE SIDEWALK...

KILLERS WHO WOULD DELIBERATELY MURDER A BOY DON'T DESERVE THE SLIGHTEST CONSIDERATION!

HIS MUSCULAR SHOULDERS SHAKE AS HE CRADLES THE STILL FORM IN HIS ARMS...BUT WHAT'S THIS? HE'S LAUGHING!!

TOWING THIS DUMMY BEHIND ME WITH A WIRE CERTAINLY FOOLED THEM! WHILE THEY BLASTED AT IT, I HAD A CHANCE TO TACKLE THEM BY SURPRISE!

THERE IS NO LAUGHTER IN THE SECRET STRONGHOLD OF THE THUMB, HOWEVER...

THE BATMAN WON'T GIVE US A MINUTE'S PEACE FROM NOW ON! I'LL NEVER GET THIS TOWN UNDER MY THUMB WHILE HE'S ALIVE!

YEAH--WE GOTTA POLISH HIM OFF-- BUT HOW?

WE DON'T WANT ANOTHER FIGHT-- HE CAN MOVE LIKE LIGHTNING AND HIT LIKE A THUNDERBOLT!

YA DON'T HAVE TO WISE US UP TO WHAT WE ALREADY KNOW!

I'VE GOT IT! WE'LL HAVE HIM PAY US A SOCIAL CALL!

HAVE YA GONE BATTY?

SNAP!

NEXT MORNING...

HMMM! A TRAP, OF COURSE... BUT IT'S MY ONLY CHANCE TO LOCATE THE THUMB BEFORE HE CARRIES OUT ANY MORE OF HIS MURDEROUS SCHEMES!

ADVERTISEMENT: BATMAN: INTERESTING INFORMATION AWAITS YOU AT 44 ARDLEE ST. ...A FRIEND.

MEANWHILE, AT THE THUMB'S HIDEOUT, PREPARATIONS ARE MADE TO RECEIVE THE DISTINGUISHED VISITOR ...

TH' THUMB'S WATCHIN' THE BACK DOOR AN' MONK TH' FRONT, AN' I'M UP HERE IN CASE HE TRIES ANY AERIAL TRICKS-- TH' POOR SAP AIN'T GOT A CHANCE!

8

A PEDDLER AT THE KITCHEN DOOR FINDS AN UNPROMISING PROSPECT...

I'M THE FILLER BRUSH MAN!

NO SALE! SWEEP YOUR-SELF ON YOUR WAY!

YOU CAN'T BRUSH ME OFF THAT SIMPLY!

SAY--- ARE YOU TIRED OF LIVING?

I INSIST ON DEMONSTRATING THE NEWEST WRINKLES IN HOUSECLEANING!

MONK! SLASHER! HE'S HERE!

FLINGING ASIDE HIS DISGUISE, THE BATMAN GIRDS FOR BATTLE---

I'LL MOP UP THE WHOLE GANG OF YOU!

MAKE IT A GOOD JOB... HERE'S SOME SOAP!

SOAP!

NO SOAP!

THEN PERHAPS YOU'D LIKE TO START WITH THE CELLAR!

SOAP

HOW'D HE GET IN?

WHA...?

DOWN-STAIRS! AFTER HIM, YOU GUYS!

FILLER BRUSHES

THE FORCE OF THE FALL STUNS THE BATMAN...

GRAB HIM BE-FORE HE COMES TO!

9

AND WHEN CONSCIOUS-NESS RETURNS...

WHERE AM I?

IN OUR GUEST ROOM, NICE AND COZY WITH ALL YOUR PRETTY BRUSHES!

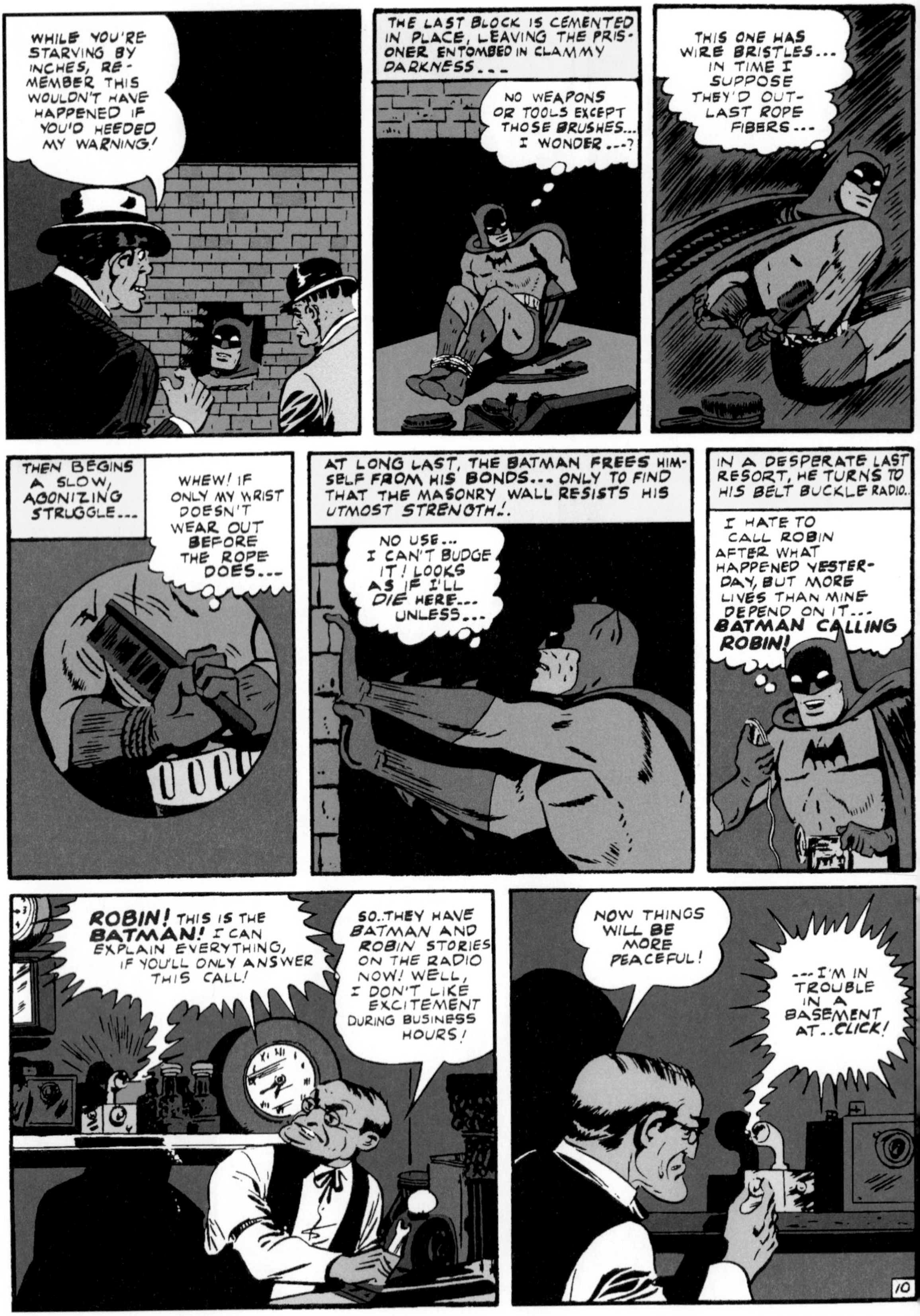
WHILE YOU'RE STARVING BY INCHES, RE-MEMBER THIS WOULDN'T HAVE HAPPENED IF YOU'D HEEDED MY WARNING!
THE LAST BLOCK IS CEMENTED IN PLACE, LEAVING THE PRISONER ENTOMBED IN CLAMMY DARKNESS...
NO WEAPONS OR TOOLS EXCEPT THOSE BRUSHES... I WONDER...?
THIS ONE HAS WIRE BRISTLES... IN TIME I SUPPOSE THEY'D OUT-LAST ROPE FIBERS...
THEN BEGINS A SLOW, AGONIZING STRUGGLE...
WHEW! IF ONLY MY WRIST DOESN'T WEAR OUT BEFORE THE ROPE DOES...
AT LONG LAST, THE BATMAN FREES HIMSELF FROM HIS BONDS... ONLY TO FIND THAT THE MASONRY WALL RESISTS HIS UTMOST STRENGTH!.
NO USE... I CAN'T BUDGE IT! LOOKS AS IF I'LL DIE HERE... UNLESS...
IN A DESPERATE LAST RESORT, HE TURNS TO HIS BELT BUCKLE RADIO..
I HATE TO CALL ROBIN AFTER WHAT HAPPENED YESTERDAY, BUT MORE LIVES THAN MINE DEPEND ON IT... BATMAN CALLING ROBIN!
ROBIN! THIS IS THE BATMAN! I CAN EXPLAIN EVERYTHING, IF YOU'LL ONLY ANSWER THIS CALL!
SO..THEY HAVE BATMAN AND ROBIN STORIES ON THE RADIO NOW! WELL, I DON'T LIKE EXCITEMENT DURING BUSINESS HOURS!
NOW THINGS WILL BE MORE PEACEFUL!
---I'M IN TROUBLE IN A BASEMENT AT..CLICK!
10

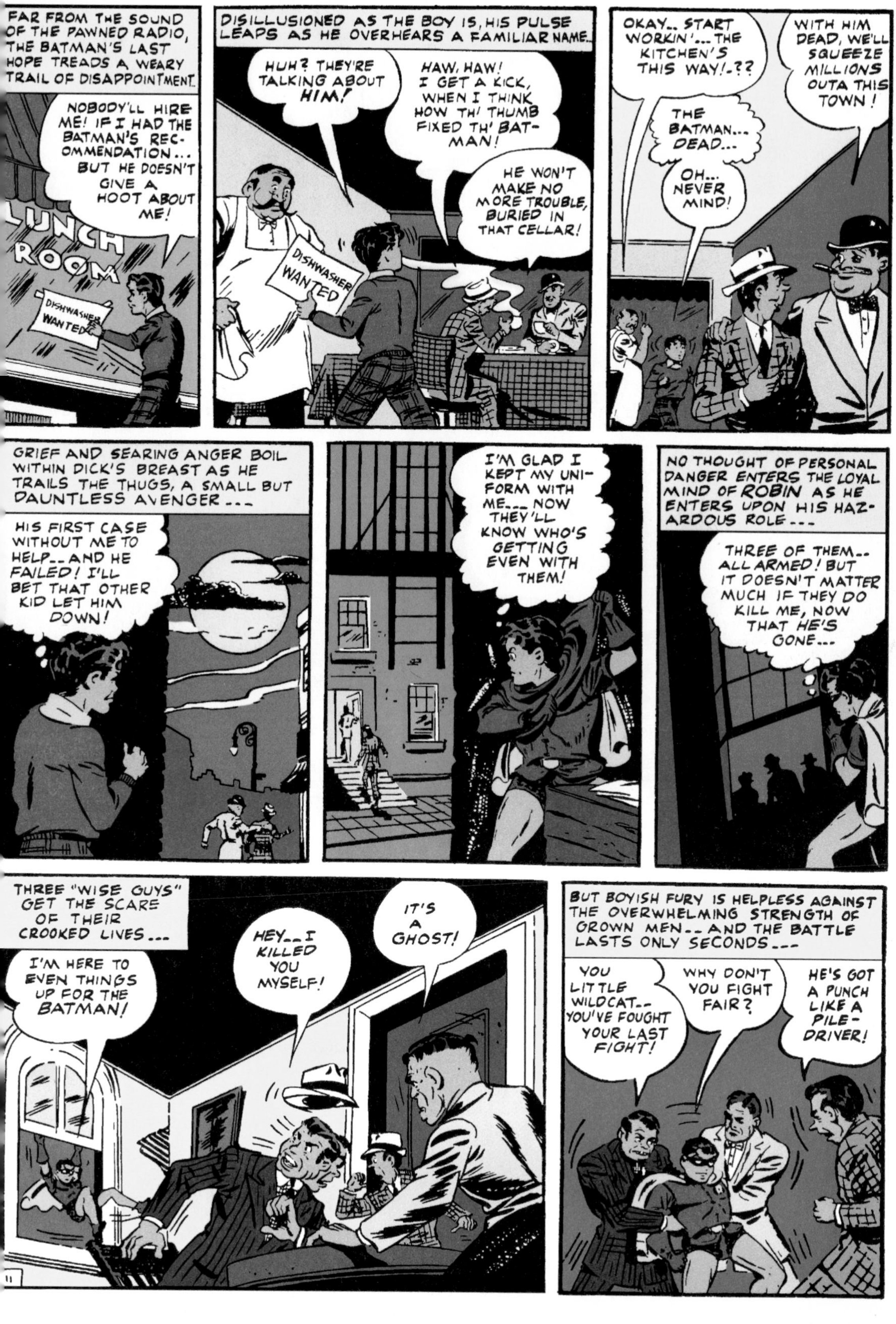

FAR FROM THE SOUND OF THE PAWNED RADIO, THE BATMAN'S LAST HOPE TREADS A WEARY TRAIL OF DISAPPOINTMENT...
NOBODY'LL HIRE ME! IF I HAD THE BATMAN'S RECOMMENDATION... BUT HE DOESN'T GIVE A HOOT ABOUT ME!
LUNCH ROOM
DISHWASHER WANTED
DISILLUSIONED AS THE BOY IS, HIS PULSE LEAPS AS HE OVERHEARS A FAMILIAR NAME...
HUH? THEY'RE TALKING ABOUT HIM!
HAW, HAW! I GET A KICK, WHEN I THINK HOW TH' THUMB FIXED TH' BATMAN!
HE WON'T MAKE NO MORE TROUBLE, BURIED IN THAT CELLAR!
DISHWASHER WANTED
OKAY.. START WORKIN'... THE KITCHEN'S THIS WAY!-??
WITH HIM DEAD, WE'LL SQUEEZE MILLIONS OUTA THIS TOWN!
THE BATMAN... DEAD...
OH... NEVER MIND!
GRIEF AND SEARING ANGER BOIL WITHIN DICK'S BREAST AS HE TRAILS THE THUGS, A SMALL BUT DAUNTLESS AVENGER ---
HIS FIRST CASE WITHOUT ME TO HELP-- AND HE FAILED! I'LL BET THAT OTHER KID LET HIM DOWN!
I'M GLAD I KEPT MY UNIFORM WITH ME--- NOW THEY'LL KNOW WHO'S GETTING EVEN WITH THEM!
NO THOUGHT OF PERSONAL DANGER ENTERS THE LOYAL MIND OF ROBIN AS HE ENTERS UPON HIS HAZARDOUS ROLE ---
THREE OF THEM-- ALL ARMED! BUT IT DOESN'T MATTER MUCH IF THEY DO KILL ME, NOW THAT HE'S GONE---
THREE "WISE GUYS" GET THE SCARE OF THEIR CROOKED LIVES ---
I'M HERE TO EVEN THINGS UP FOR THE BATMAN!
HEY-- I KILLED YOU MYSELF!
IT'S A GHOST!
11
BUT BOYISH FURY IS HELPLESS AGAINST THE OVERWHELMING STRENGTH OF GROWN MEN-- AND THE BATTLE LASTS ONLY SECONDS ---
YOU LITTLE WILDCAT-- YOU'VE FOUGHT YOUR LAST FIGHT!
WHY DON'T YOU FIGHT FAIR?
HE'S GOT A PUNCH LIKE A PILE-DRIVER!

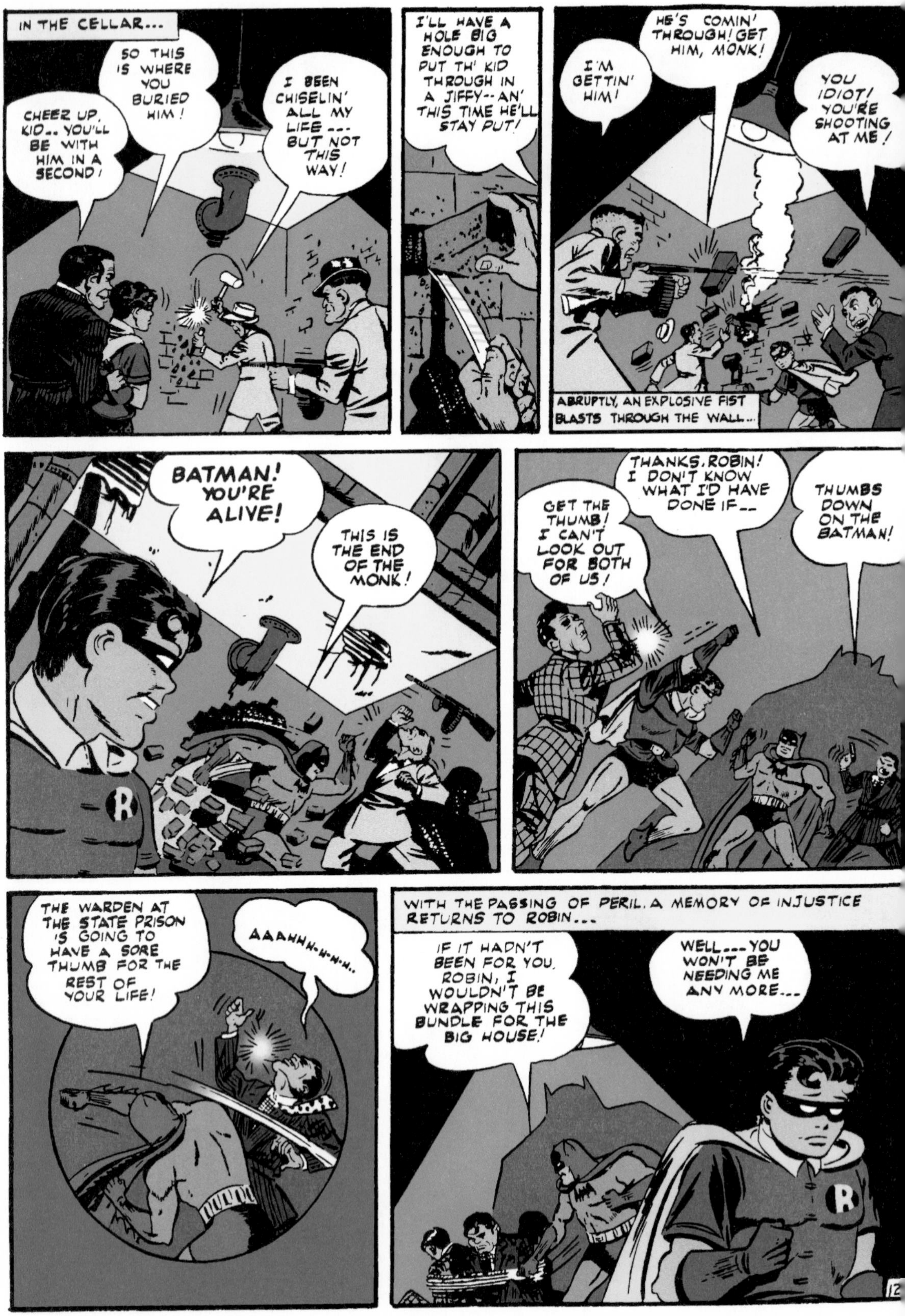
IN THE CELLAR...
SO THIS IS WHERE YOU BURIED HIM!
CHEER UP, KID.. YOU'LL BE WITH HIM IN A SECOND!
I BEEN CHISELIN' ALL MY LIFE --- BUT NOT THIS WAY!
I'LL HAVE A HOLE BIG ENOUGH TO PUT TH' KID THROUGH IN A JIFFY-- AN' THIS TIME HE'LL STAY PUT!
HE'S COMIN' THROUGH! GET HIM, MONK!
I'M GETTIN' HIM!
YOU IDIOT! YOU'RE SHOOTING AT ME!
ABRUPTLY, AN EXPLOSIVE FIST BLASTS THROUGH THE WALL...
BATMAN! YOU'RE ALIVE!
THIS IS THE END OF THE MONK!
THANKS, ROBIN! I DON'T KNOW WHAT I'D HAVE DONE IF--
GET THE THUMB! I CAN'T LOOK OUT FOR BOTH OF US!
THUMBS DOWN ON THE BATMAN!
THE WARDEN AT THE STATE PRISON IS GOING TO HAVE A SORE THUMB FOR THE REST OF YOUR LIFE!
AAAHHH-H-H-H..
WITH THE PASSING OF PERIL, A MEMORY OF INJUSTICE RETURNS TO ROBIN...
IF IT HADN'T BEEN FOR YOU, ROBIN, I WOULDN'T BE WRAPPING THIS BUNDLE FOR THE BIG HOUSE!
WELL--- YOU WON'T BE NEEDING ME ANY MORE...
12

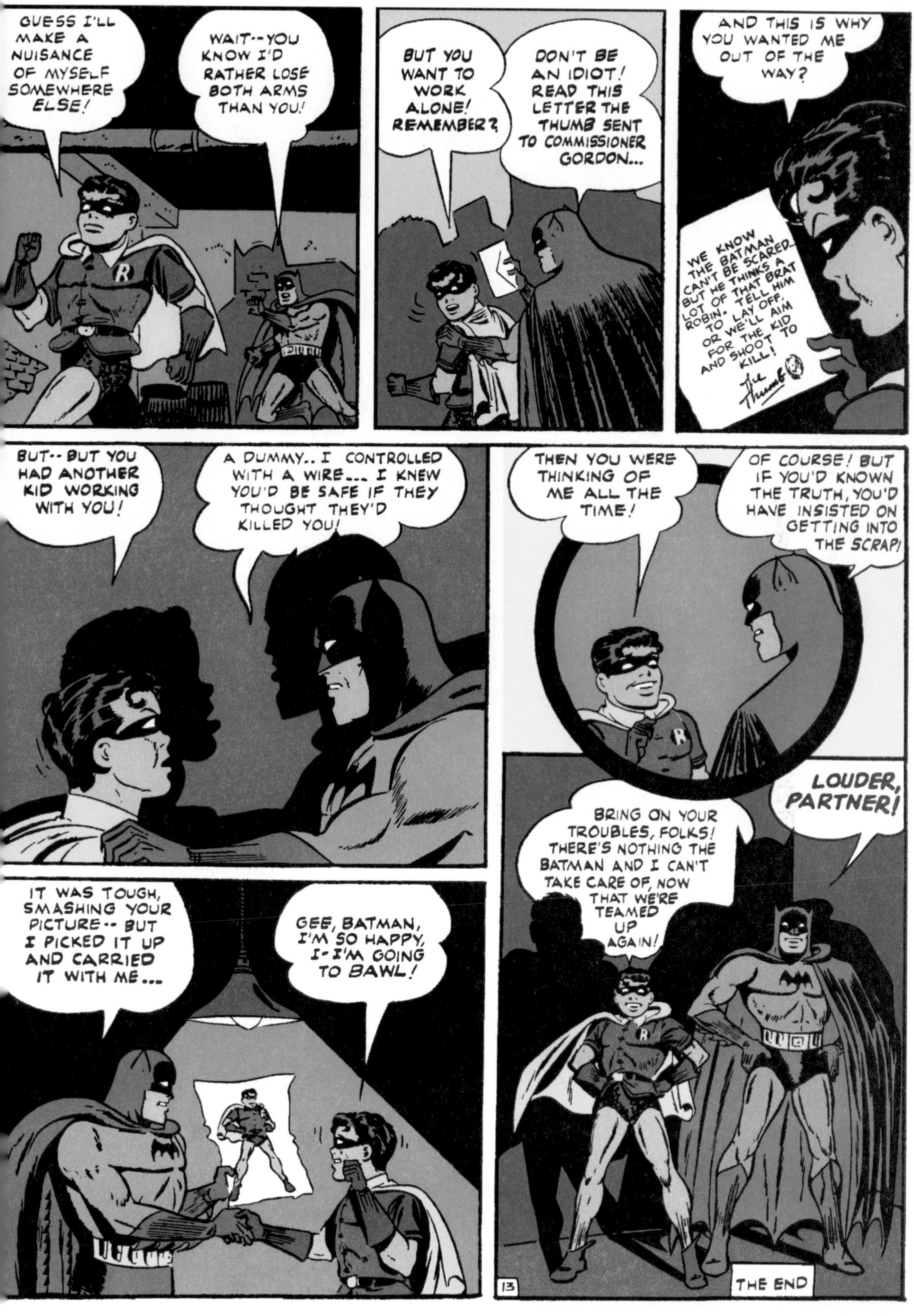
GUESS I'LL MAKE A NUISANCE OF MYSELF SOMEWHERE ELSE!
WAIT--YOU KNOW I'D RATHER LOSE BOTH ARMS THAN YOU!
BUT YOU WANT TO WORK ALONE! REMEMBER?
DON'T BE AN IDIOT! READ THIS LETTER THE THUMB SENT TO COMMISSIONER GORDON...
AND THIS IS WHY YOU WANTED ME OUT OF THE WAY?
WE KNOW THE BATMAN CAN'T BE SCARED-- BUT HE THINKS A LOT OF THAT BRAT ROBIN. TELL HIM TO LAY OFF, OR WE'LL AIM FOR THE KID AND SHOOT TO KILL!
BUT--BUT YOU HAD ANOTHER KID WORKING WITH YOU!
A DUMMY.. I CONTROLLED WITH A WIRE... I KNEW YOU'D BE SAFE IF THEY THOUGHT THEY'D KILLED YOU!
THEN YOU WERE THINKING OF ME ALL THE TIME!
OF COURSE! BUT IF YOU'D KNOWN THE TRUTH, YOU'D HAVE INSISTED ON GETTING INTO THE SCRAP!
IT WAS TOUGH, SMASHING YOUR PICTURE-- BUT I PICKED IT UP AND CARRIED IT WITH ME...
GEE, BATMAN, I'M SO HAPPY, I-I'M GOING TO BAWL!
LOUDER, PARTNER!
BRING ON YOUR TROUBLES, FOLKS! THERE'S NOTHING THE BATMAN AND I CAN'T TAKE CARE OF, NOW THAT WE'RE TEAMED UP AGAIN!
13
THE END

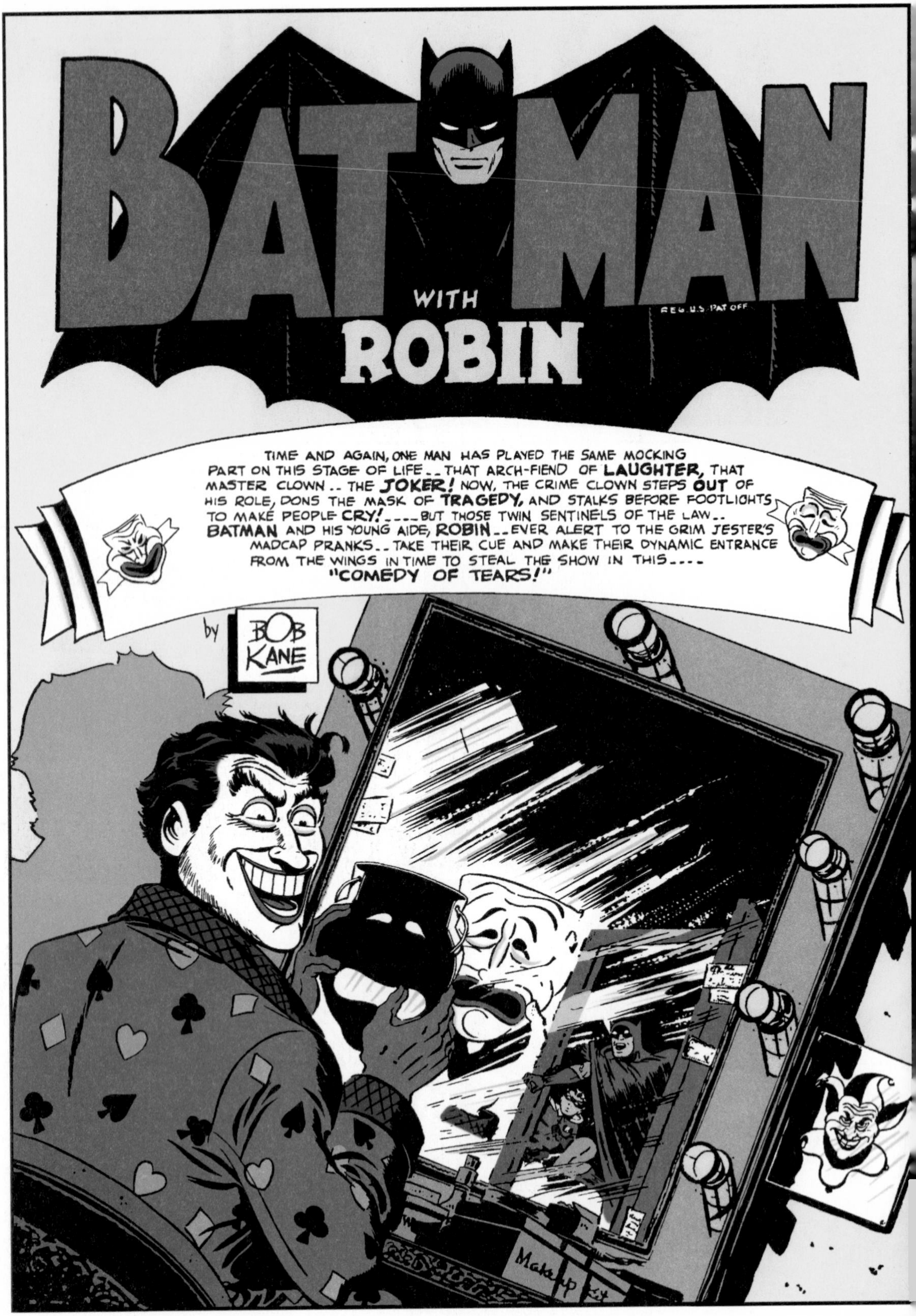
BATMAN
WITH
ROBIN
REG. U.S. PAT. OFF.
TIME AND AGAIN, ONE MAN HAS PLAYED THE SAME MOCKING PART ON THIS STAGE OF LIFE -- THAT ARCH-FIEND OF LAUGHTER, THAT MASTER CLOWN -- THE JOKER! NOW, THE CRIME CLOWN STEPS OUT OF HIS ROLE, DONS THE MASK OF TRAGEDY, AND STALKS BEFORE FOOTLIGHTS TO MAKE PEOPLE CRY! ---- BUT THOSE TWIN SENTINELS OF THE LAW -- BATMAN AND HIS YOUNG AIDE, ROBIN -- EVER ALERT TO THE GRIM JESTER'S MADCAP PRANKS -- TAKE THEIR CUE AND MAKE THEIR DYNAMIC ENTRANCE FROM THE WINGS IN TIME TO STEAL THE SHOW IN THIS ---- "COMEDY OF TEARS!"
by BOB KANE
Makeup Kit

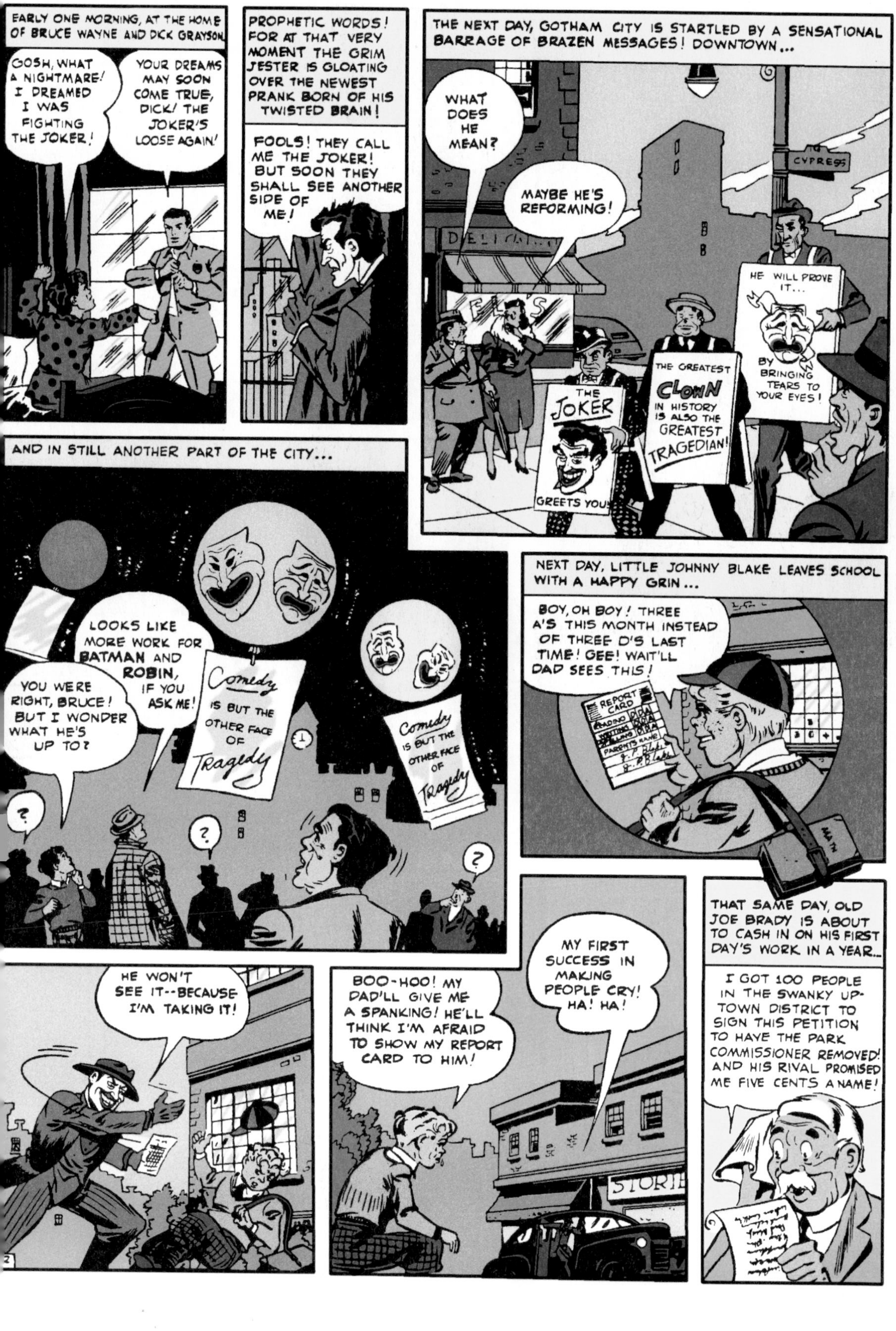
EARLY ONE MORNING, AT THE HOME OF BRUCE WAYNE AND DICK GRAYSON...
GOSH, WHAT A NIGHTMARE! I DREAMED I WAS FIGHTING THE JOKER!
YOUR DREAMS MAY SOON COME TRUE, DICK! THE JOKER'S LOOSE AGAIN!
PROPHETIC WORDS! FOR AT THAT VERY MOMENT THE GRIM JESTER IS GLOATING OVER THE NEWEST PRANK BORN OF HIS TWISTED BRAIN!
FOOLS! THEY CALL ME THE JOKER! BUT SOON THEY SHALL SEE ANOTHER SIDE OF ME!
THE NEXT DAY, GOTHAM CITY IS STARTLED BY A SENSATIONAL BARRAGE OF BRAZEN MESSAGES! DOWNTOWN...
WHAT DOES HE MEAN?
MAYBE HE'S REFORMING!
CYPRESS
THE JOKER GREETS YOU!
THE GREATEST CLOWN IN HISTORY IS ALSO THE GREATEST TRAGEDIAN!
HE WILL PROVE IT... BY BRINGING TEARS TO YOUR EYES!
AND IN STILL ANOTHER PART OF THE CITY...
LOOKS LIKE MORE WORK FOR BATMAN AND ROBIN, IF YOU ASK ME!
YOU WERE RIGHT, BRUCE! BUT I WONDER WHAT HE'S UP TO?
Comedy IS BUT THE OTHER FACE OF Tragedy
Comedy IS BUT THE OTHER FACE OF Tragedy
?
?
?
NEXT DAY, LITTLE JOHNNY BLAKE LEAVES SCHOOL WITH A HAPPY GRIN...
BOY, OH BOY! THREE A'S THIS MONTH INSTEAD OF THREE D'S LAST TIME! GEE! WAIT'LL DAD SEES THIS!
REPORT CARD
HE WON'T SEE IT--BECAUSE I'M TAKING IT!
BOO-HOO! MY DAD'LL GIVE ME A SPANKING! HE'LL THINK I'M AFRAID TO SHOW MY REPORT CARD TO HIM!
MY FIRST SUCCESS IN MAKING PEOPLE CRY! HA! HA!
STORE
THAT SAME DAY, OLD JOE BRADY IS ABOUT TO CASH IN ON HIS FIRST DAY'S WORK IN A YEAR...
I GOT 100 PEOPLE IN THE SWANKY UPTOWN DISTRICT TO SIGN THIS PETITION TO HAVE THE PARK COMMISSIONER REMOVED! AND HIS RIVAL PROMISED ME FIVE CENTS A NAME!

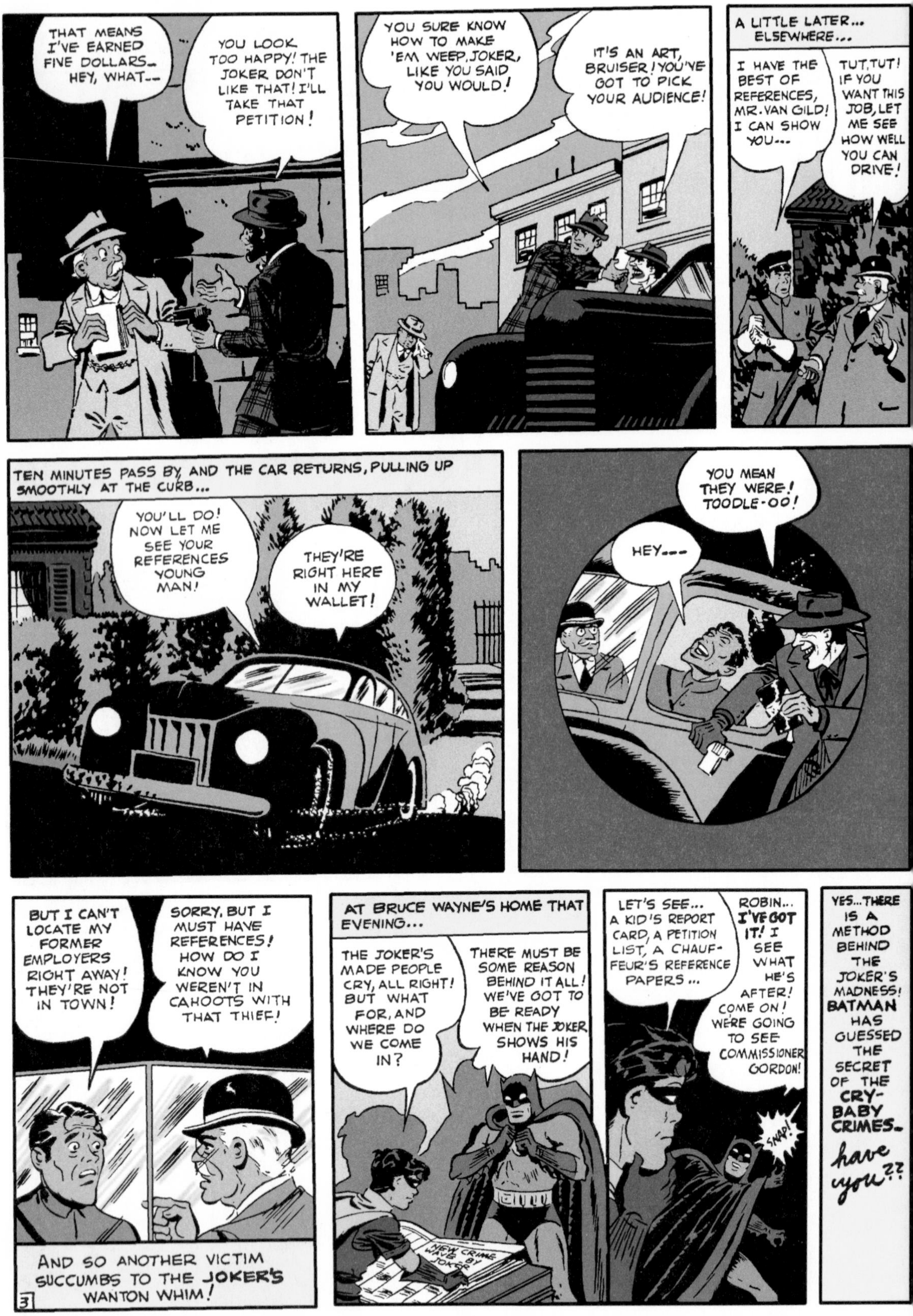
THAT MEANS I'VE EARNED FIVE DOLLARS-- HEY, WHAT--
YOU LOOK TOO HAPPY! THE JOKER DON'T LIKE THAT! I'LL TAKE THAT PETITION!
YOU SURE KNOW HOW TO MAKE 'EM WEEP, JOKER, LIKE YOU SAID YOU WOULD!
IT'S AN ART, BRUISER! YOU'VE GOT TO PICK YOUR AUDIENCE!
A LITTLE LATER... ELSEWHERE...
I HAVE THE BEST OF REFERENCES, MR. VAN GILD! I CAN SHOW YOU...
TUT, TUT! IF YOU WANT THIS JOB, LET ME SEE HOW WELL YOU CAN DRIVE!
TEN MINUTES PASS BY, AND THE CAR RETURNS, PULLING UP SMOOTHLY AT THE CURB...
YOU'LL DO! NOW LET ME SEE YOUR REFERENCES YOUNG MAN!
THEY'RE RIGHT HERE IN MY WALLET!
HEY---
YOU MEAN THEY WERE! TOODLE-OO!
BUT I CAN'T LOCATE MY FORMER EMPLOYERS RIGHT AWAY! THEY'RE NOT IN TOWN!
SORRY, BUT I MUST HAVE REFERENCES! HOW DO I KNOW YOU WEREN'T IN CAHOOTS WITH THAT THIEF!
AND SO ANOTHER VICTIM SUCCUMBS TO THE JOKER'S WANTON WHIM!
3
AT BRUCE WAYNE'S HOME THAT EVENING...
THE JOKER'S MADE PEOPLE CRY, ALL RIGHT! BUT WHAT FOR, AND WHERE DO WE COME IN?
THERE MUST BE SOME REASON BEHIND IT ALL! WE'VE GOT TO BE READY WHEN THE JOKER SHOWS HIS HAND!
NEW CRIME WAVE BY JOKER
LET'S SEE... A KID'S REPORT CARD, A PETITION LIST, A CHAUFFEUR'S REFERENCE PAPERS...
ROBIN... I'VE GOT IT! I SEE WHAT HE'S AFTER! COME ON! WE'RE GOING TO SEE COMMISSIONER GORDON!
SNAP!
YES... THERE IS A METHOD BEHIND THE JOKER'S MADNESS! BATMAN HAS GUESSED THE SECRET OF THE CRY-BABY CRIMES-- have you??

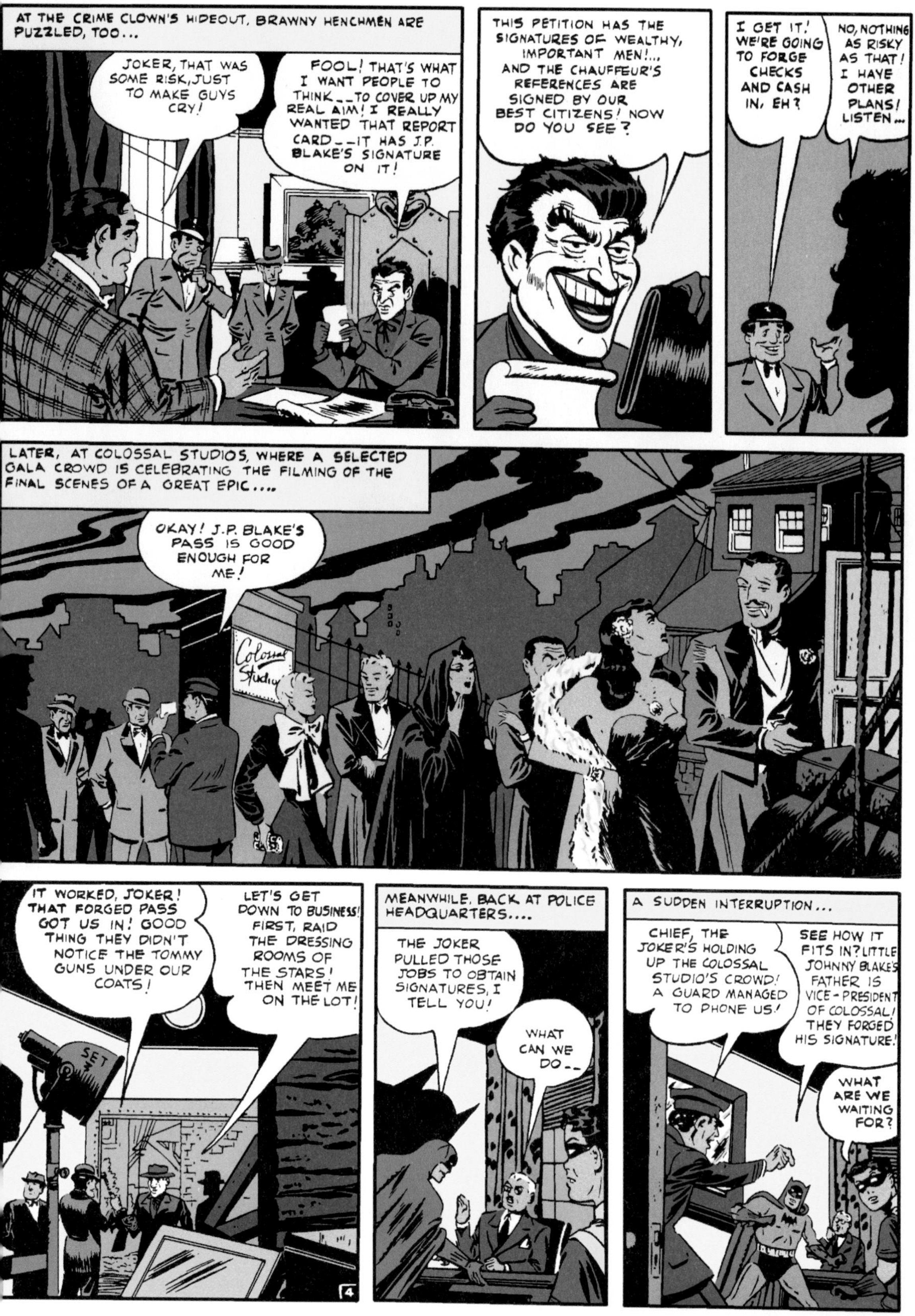
AT THE CRIME CLOWN'S HIDEOUT, BRAWNY HENCHMEN ARE PUZZLED, TOO...
JOKER, THAT WAS SOME RISK, JUST TO MAKE GUYS CRY!
FOOL! THAT'S WHAT I WANT PEOPLE TO THINK--TO COVER UP MY REAL AIM! I REALLY WANTED THAT REPORT CARD--IT HAS J.P. BLAKE'S SIGNATURE ON IT!
THIS PETITION HAS THE SIGNATURES OF WEALTHY, IMPORTANT MEN!... AND THE CHAUFFEUR'S REFERENCES ARE SIGNED BY OUR BEST CITIZENS! NOW DO YOU SEE?
I GET IT! WE'RE GOING TO FORGE CHECKS AND CASH IN, EH?
NO, NOTHING AS RISKY AS THAT! I HAVE OTHER PLANS! LISTEN...
LATER, AT COLOSSAL STUDIOS, WHERE A SELECTED GALA CROWD IS CELEBRATING THE FILMING OF THE FINAL SCENES OF A GREAT EPIC....
OKAY! J.P. BLAKE'S PASS IS GOOD ENOUGH FOR ME!
Colossal Studios
IT WORKED, JOKER! THAT FORGED PASS GOT US IN! GOOD THING THEY DIDN'T NOTICE THE TOMMY GUNS UNDER OUR COATS!
LET'S GET DOWN TO BUSINESS! FIRST, RAID THE DRESSING ROOMS OF THE STARS! THEN MEET ME ON THE LOT!
SET
4
MEANWHILE, BACK AT POLICE HEADQUARTERS....
THE JOKER PULLED THOSE JOBS TO OBTAIN SIGNATURES, I TELL YOU!
WHAT CAN WE DO--
A SUDDEN INTERRUPTION...
CHIEF, THE JOKER'S HOLDING UP THE COLOSSAL STUDIO'S CROWD! A GUARD MANAGED TO PHONE US!
SEE HOW IT FITS IN? LITTLE JOHNNY BLAKE'S FATHER IS VICE-PRESIDENT OF COLOSSAL! THEY FORGED HIS SIGNATURE!
WHAT ARE WE WAITING FOR?

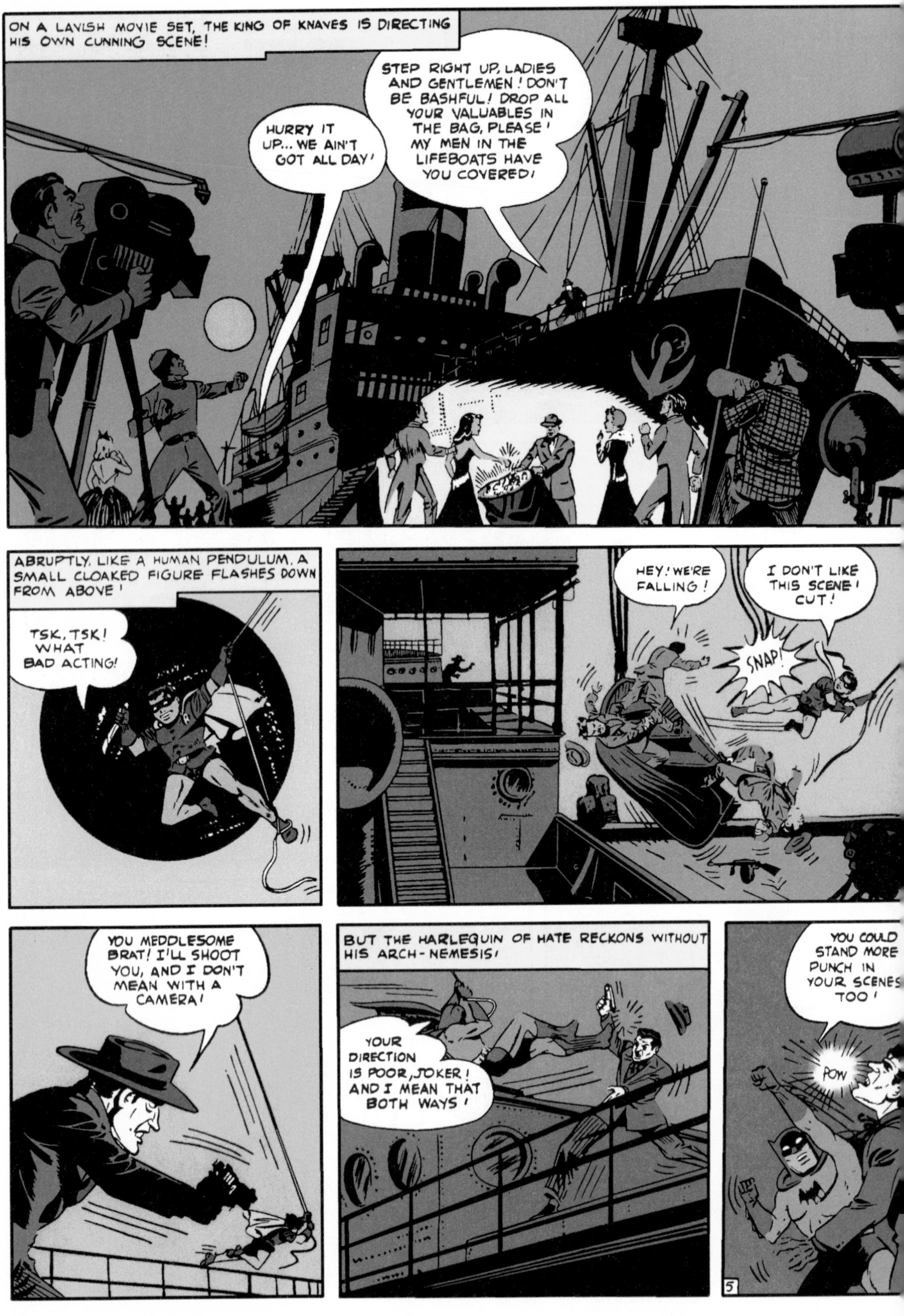

ON A LAVISH MOVIE SET, THE KING OF KNAVES IS DIRECTING HIS OWN CUNNING SCENE!
HURRY IT UP... WE AIN'T GOT ALL DAY!
STEP RIGHT UP, LADIES AND GENTLEMEN! DON'T BE BASHFUL! DROP ALL YOUR VALUABLES IN THE BAG, PLEASE! MY MEN IN THE LIFEBOATS HAVE YOU COVERED!
ABRUPTLY, LIKE A HUMAN PENDULUM, A SMALL CLOAKED FIGURE FLASHES DOWN FROM ABOVE!
TSK, TSK! WHAT BAD ACTING!
HEY! WE'RE FALLING!
I DON'T LIKE THIS SCENE! CUT!
SNAP!
YOU MEDDLESOME BRAT! I'LL SHOOT YOU, AND I DON'T MEAN WITH A CAMERA!
BUT THE HARLEQUIN OF HATE RECKONS WITHOUT HIS ARCH-NEMESIS!
YOUR DIRECTION IS POOR, JOKER! AND I MEAN THAT BOTH WAYS!
YOU COULD STAND MORE PUNCH IN YOUR SCENES TOO!
POW
5

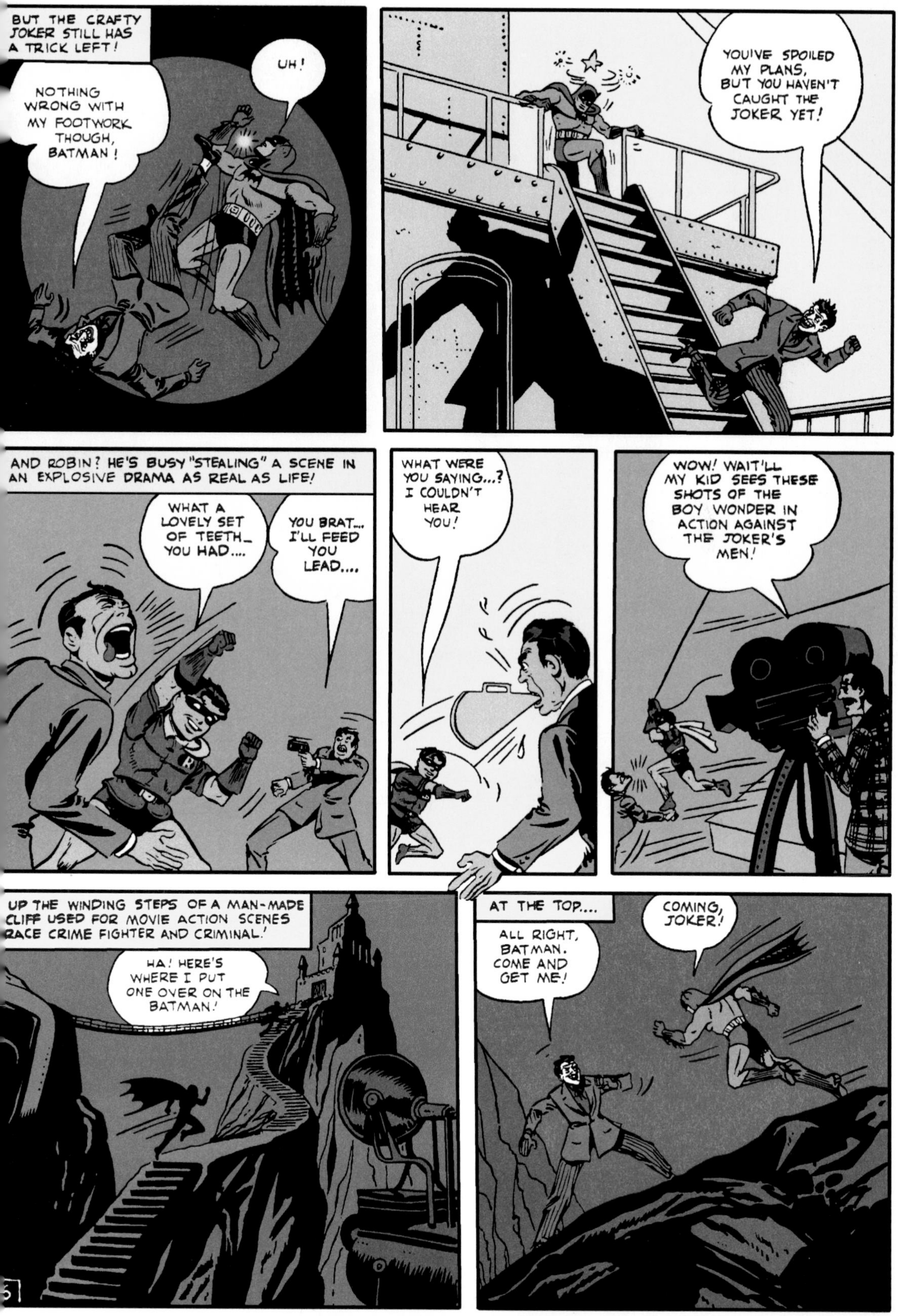
BUT THE CRAFTY JOKER STILL HAS A TRICK LEFT!
NOTHING WRONG WITH MY FOOTWORK THOUGH, BATMAN!
UH!
YOU'VE SPOILED MY PLANS, BUT YOU HAVEN'T CAUGHT THE JOKER YET!
AND ROBIN? HE'S BUSY "STEALING" A SCENE IN AN EXPLOSIVE DRAMA AS REAL AS LIFE!
WHAT A LOVELY SET OF TEETH_ YOU HAD....
YOU BRAT... I'LL FEED YOU LEAD....
WHAT WERE YOU SAYING...? I COULDN'T HEAR YOU!
WOW! WAIT'LL MY KID SEES THESE SHOTS OF THE BOY WONDER IN ACTION AGAINST THE JOKER'S MEN!
UP THE WINDING STEPS OF A MAN-MADE CLIFF USED FOR MOVIE ACTION SCENES RACE CRIME FIGHTER AND CRIMINAL!
HA! HERE'S WHERE I PUT ONE OVER ON THE BATMAN!
AT THE TOP....
ALL RIGHT, BATMAN. COME AND GET ME!
COMING, JOKER!

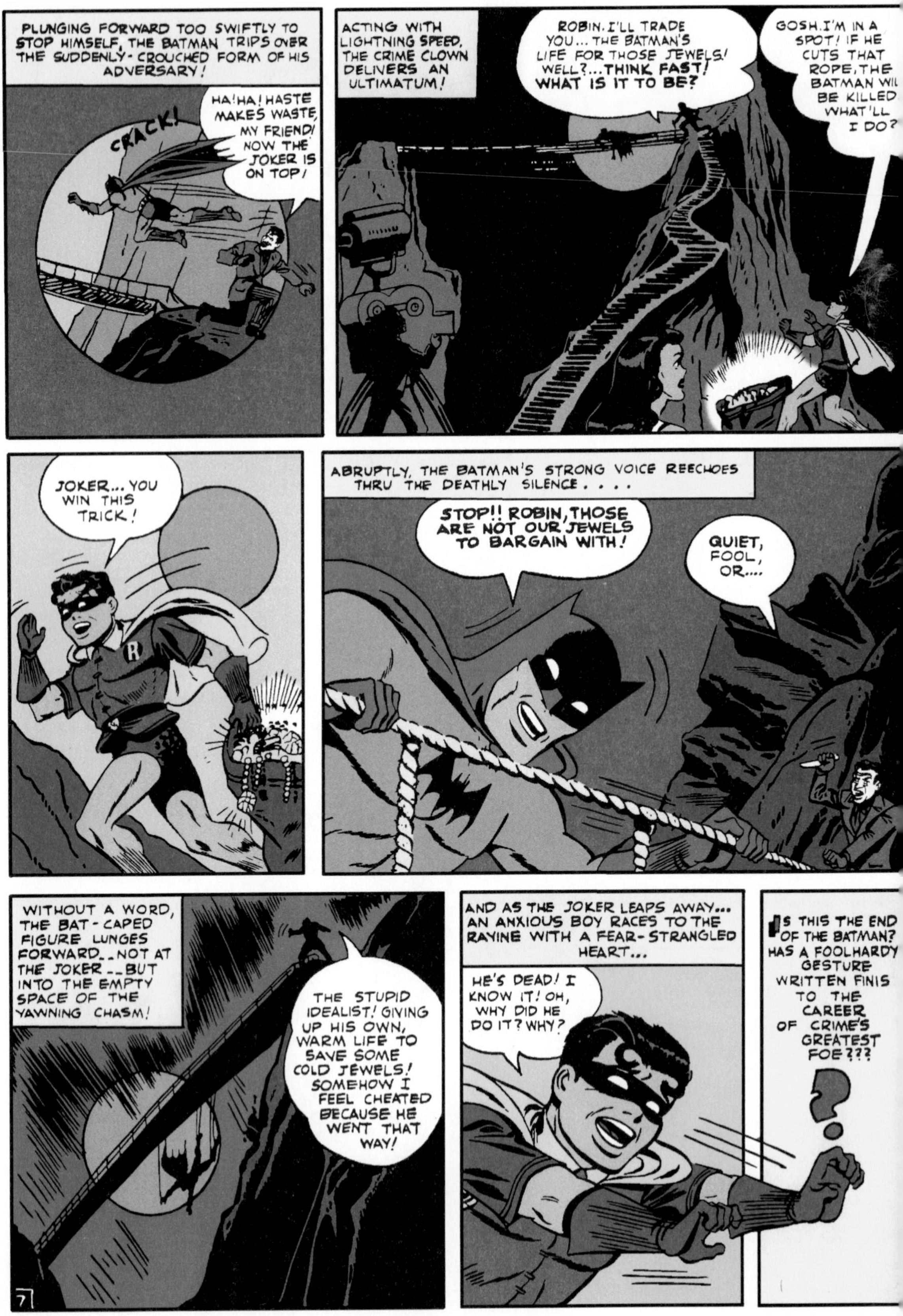
PLUNGING FORWARD TOO SWIFTLY TO STOP HIMSELF, THE BATMAN TRIPS OVER THE SUDDENLY-CROUCHED FORM OF HIS ADVERSARY!
CRACK!
HA! HA! HASTE MAKES WASTE, MY FRIEND! NOW THE JOKER IS ON TOP!
ACTING WITH LIGHTNING SPEED, THE CRIME CLOWN DELIVERS AN ULTIMATUM!
ROBIN, I'LL TRADE YOU... THE BATMAN'S LIFE FOR THOSE JEWELS! WELL?... THINK FAST! WHAT IS IT TO BE?
GOSH, I'M IN A SPOT! IF HE CUTS THAT ROPE, THE BATMAN WIL BE KILLED WHAT'LL I DO?
JOKER... YOU WIN THIS TRICK!
ABRUPTLY, THE BATMAN'S STRONG VOICE REECHOES THRU THE DEATHLY SILENCE....
STOP!! ROBIN, THOSE ARE NOT OUR JEWELS TO BARGAIN WITH!
QUIET, FOOL, OR....
WITHOUT A WORD, THE BAT-CAPED FIGURE LUNGES FORWARD--NOT AT THE JOKER--BUT INTO THE EMPTY SPACE OF THE YAWNING CHASM!
THE STUPID IDEALIST! GIVING UP HIS OWN, WARM LIFE TO SAVE SOME COLD JEWELS! SOMEHOW I FEEL CHEATED BECAUSE HE WENT THAT WAY!
7
AND AS THE JOKER LEAPS AWAY... AN ANXIOUS BOY RACES TO THE RAVINE WITH A FEAR-STRANGLED HEART...
HE'S DEAD! I KNOW IT! OH, WHY DID HE DO IT? WHY?
IS THIS THE END OF THE BATMAN? HAS A FOOLHARDY GESTURE WRITTEN FINIS TO THE CAREER OF CRIME'S GREATEST FOE???

A STRANGE SIGHT GREETS ROBIN'S EYES!

I CAUGHT A GLIMPSE OF THIS SAFETY NET THEY OFTEN USE ON SETS IN CASE OF ACCIDENTS! GUESS I FOOLED THE JOKER, EH?

WHEW! YOU HAD **ME** FOOLED, TOO!

BUT WE'VE GOT TO GET AFTER HIM!

HE'S GONE BY NOW, AND SO ARE HIS MEN! BUT LOOK AT WHAT ONE OF THOSE MUGGS DROPPED!

"PRETTY BOY" DUGAN WHO WILL BE ELECTROCUTED AT 11:15 TONIGHT UNLESS THE GOVERNOR GIVES HIM A LAST-MINUTE REPRIEVE!

HMM! THE JOKER MUST BE PLANNING SOME DIRTY WORK AT THE PRISON! ROBIN, THIS LOOKS LIKE OUR BUSY NIGHT!

Colossal Studio

LATER... A POWERFUL OFFICIAL SEDAN, FILLED WITH STATE TROOPERS, SCREECHES TO A HALT BEFORE THE GRIM WALLS OF STATE PRISON!

I MUST SPEAK TO THE WARDEN.. IMMEDIATELY! I'M FROM THE GOVERNOR'S OFFICE!

I'LL GET HIM RIGHT AWAY, CAPTAIN!

MOMENTS LATER...

THE GOVERNOR HAS REPRIEVED DUGAN AND WANTS US TO BRING HIM TO HIS OFFICE AT ONCE FOR AN INTERVIEW! HERE ARE HIS ORDERS!

VERY WELL, I'LL PLACE HIM IN YOUR CUSTODY, CAPTAIN!

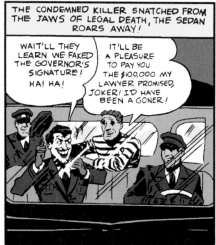

THE CONDEMNED KILLER SNATCHED FROM THE JAWS OF LEGAL DEATH, THE SEDAN ROARS AWAY!

WAIT'LL THEY LEARN WE FAKED THE GOVERNOR'S SIGNATURE! HA! HA!

IT'LL BE A PLEASURE TO PAY YOU THE $100,000 MY LAWYER PROMISED, JOKER! I'D HAVE BEEN A GONER!

THE GRIM JESTER AND HIS MEN CHANGE BACK TO THEIR CIVILIAN CLOTHES!

HEY JOKER, LOOK-- THE BATMOBILE!

WHAT! THE BATMAN ALIVE! STEP ON IT, BRUISER!

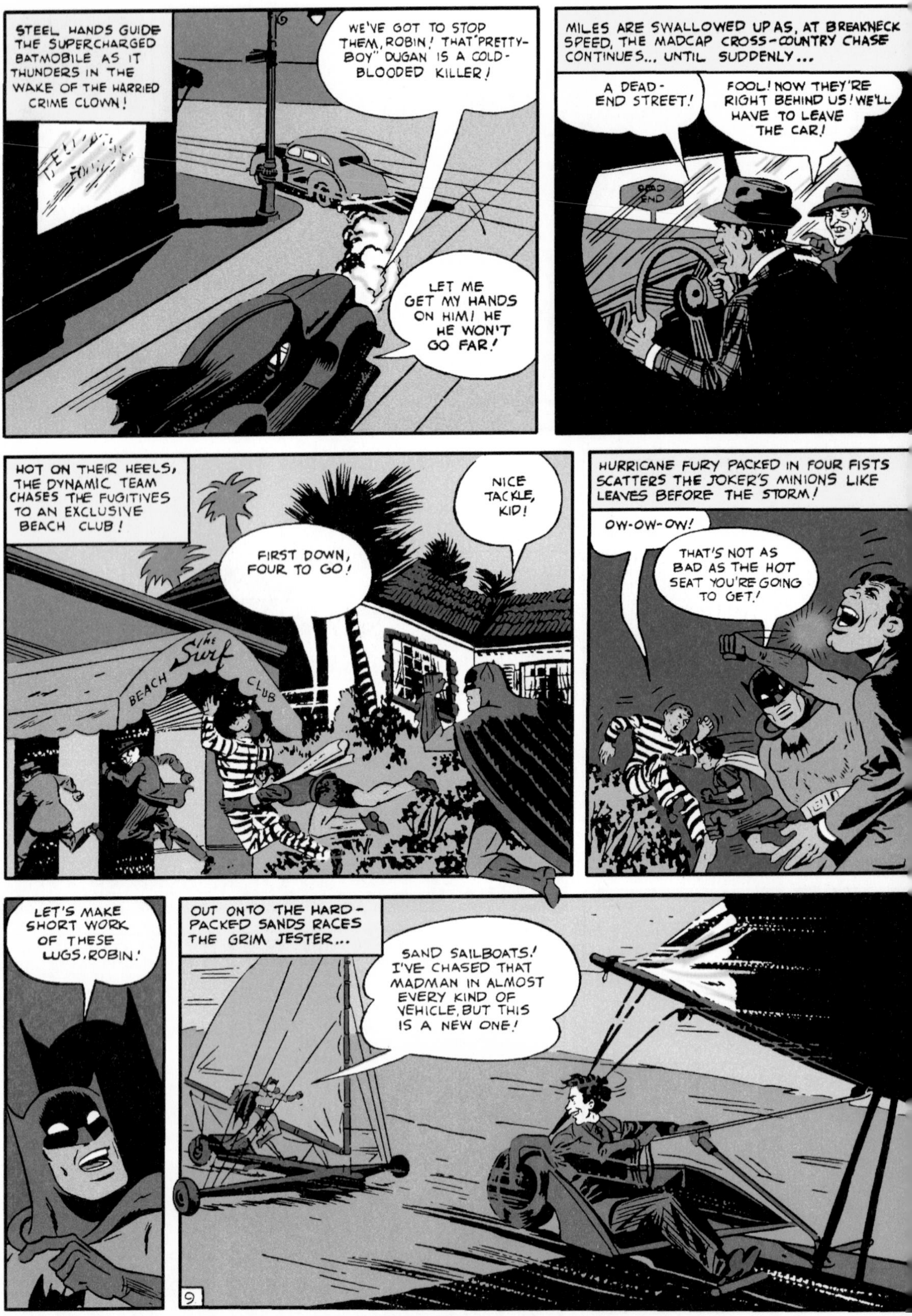
STEEL HANDS GUIDE THE SUPERCHARGED BATMOBILE AS IT THUNDERS IN THE WAKE OF THE HARRIED CRIME CLOWN!
WE'VE GOT TO STOP THEM, ROBIN! THAT "PRETTY-BOY" DUGAN IS A COLD-BLOODED KILLER!
LET ME GET MY HANDS ON HIM! HE HE WON'T GO FAR!
MILES ARE SWALLOWED UP AS, AT BREAKNECK SPEED, THE MADCAP CROSS-COUNTRY CHASE CONTINUES... UNTIL SUDDENLY...
A DEAD-END STREET!
FOOL! NOW THEY'RE RIGHT BEHIND US! WE'LL HAVE TO LEAVE THE CAR!
DEAD END
HOT ON THEIR HEELS, THE DYNAMIC TEAM CHASES THE FUGITIVES TO AN EXCLUSIVE BEACH CLUB!
FIRST DOWN, FOUR TO GO!
NICE TACKLE, KID!
The Surf BEACH CLUB
HURRICANE FURY PACKED IN FOUR FISTS SCATTERS THE JOKER'S MINIONS LIKE LEAVES BEFORE THE STORM!
OW-OW-OW!
THAT'S NOT AS BAD AS THE HOT SEAT YOU'RE GOING TO GET!
LET'S MAKE SHORT WORK OF THESE LUGS, ROBIN!
OUT ONTO THE HARD-PACKED SANDS RACES THE GRIM JESTER...
SAND SAILBOATS! I'VE CHASED THAT MADMAN IN ALMOST EVERY KIND OF VEHICLE, BUT THIS IS A NEW ONE!
9

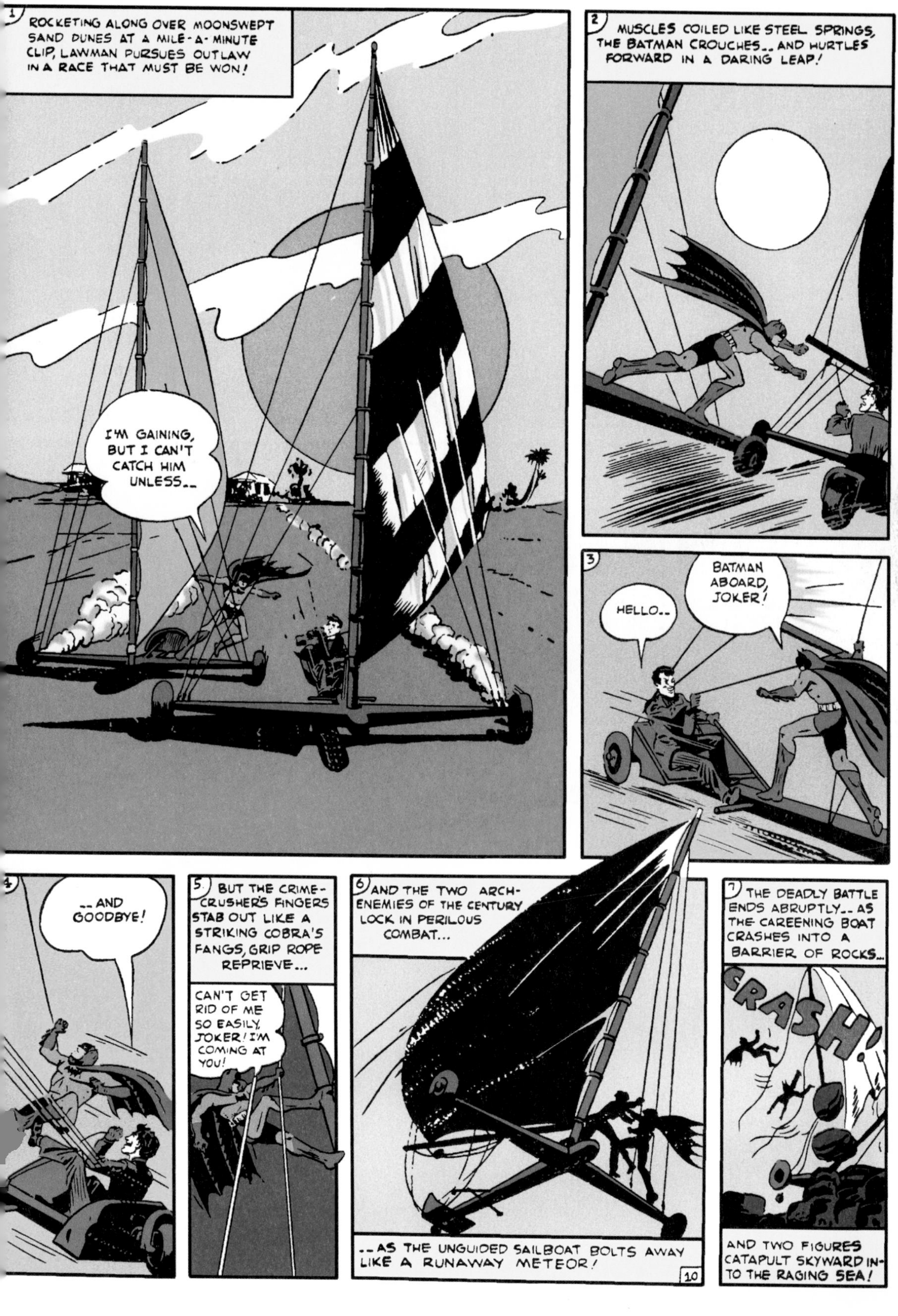
1
ROCKETING ALONG OVER MOONSWEPT SAND DUNES AT A MILE-A-MINUTE CLIP, LAWMAN PURSUES OUTLAW IN A RACE THAT MUST BE WON!
I'M GAINING, BUT I CAN'T CATCH HIM UNLESS--
2
MUSCLES COILED LIKE STEEL SPRINGS, THE BATMAN CROUCHES-- AND HURTLES FORWARD IN A DARING LEAP!
3
HELLO--
BATMAN ABOARD, JOKER!
4
--AND GOODBYE!
5
BUT THE CRIME-CRUSHER'S FINGERS STAB OUT LIKE A STRIKING COBRA'S FANGS, GRIP ROPE REPRIEVE...
CAN'T GET RID OF ME SO EASILY, JOKER! I'M COMING AT YOU!
6
AND THE TWO ARCH-ENEMIES OF THE CENTURY LOCK IN PERILOUS COMBAT...
--AS THE UNGUIDED SAILBOAT BOLTS AWAY LIKE A RUNAWAY METEOR!
10
7
THE DEADLY BATTLE ENDS ABRUPTLY-- AS THE CAREENING BOAT CRASHES INTO A BARRIER OF ROCKS...
CRASH!
AND TWO FIGURES CATAPULT SKYWARD INTO THE RAGING SEA!

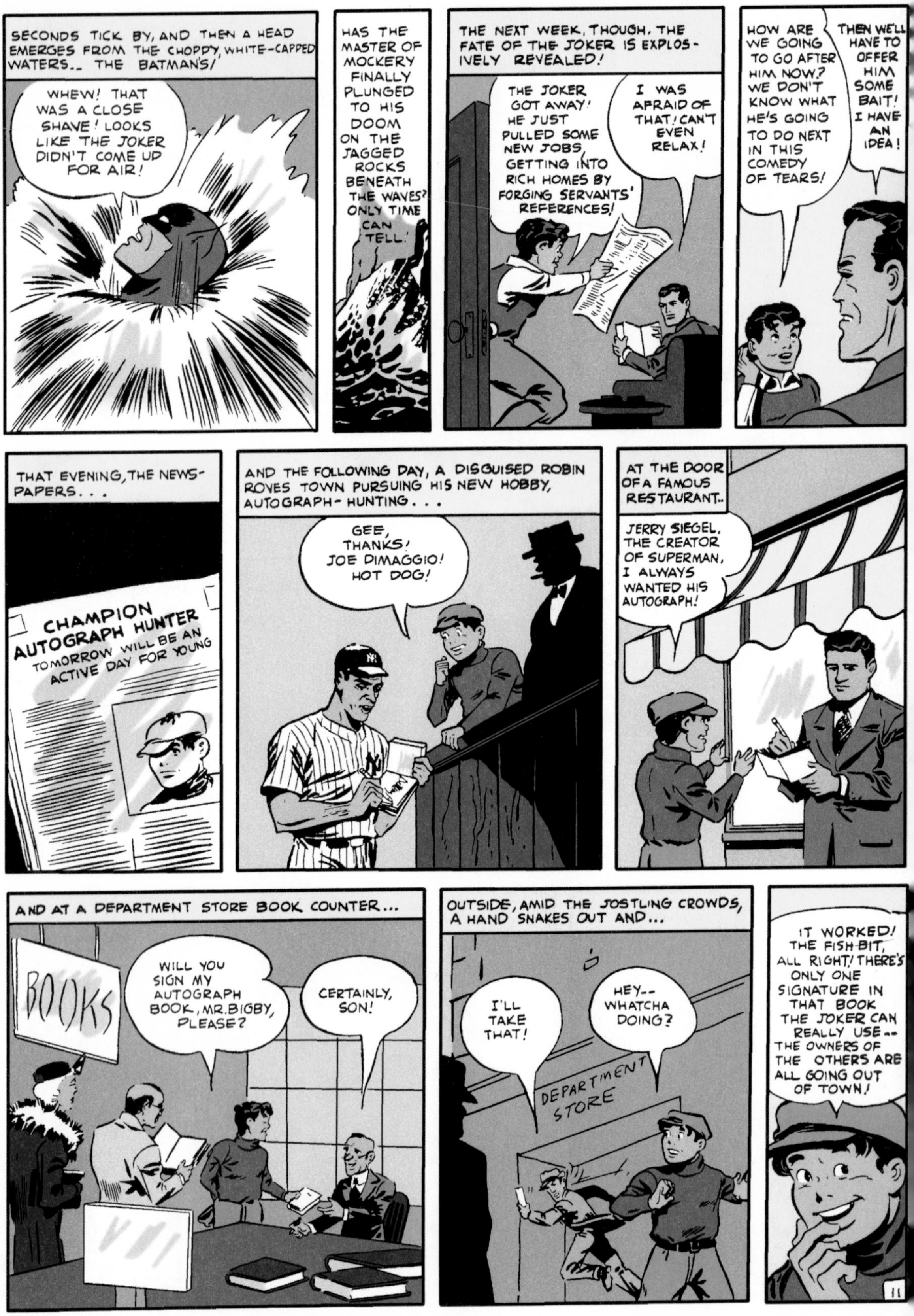
SECONDS TICK BY, AND THEN A HEAD EMERGES FROM THE CHOPPY, WHITE-CAPPED WATERS.. THE BATMAN'S!
WHEW! THAT WAS A CLOSE SHAVE! LOOKS LIKE THE JOKER DIDN'T COME UP FOR AIR!
HAS THE MASTER OF MOCKERY FINALLY PLUNGED TO HIS DOOM ON THE JAGGED ROCKS BENEATH THE WAVES? ONLY TIME CAN TELL!
THE NEXT WEEK, THOUGH, THE FATE OF THE JOKER IS EXPLOSIVELY REVEALED!
THE JOKER GOT AWAY! HE JUST PULLED SOME NEW JOBS, GETTING INTO RICH HOMES BY FORGING SERVANTS' REFERENCES!
I WAS AFRAID OF THAT! CAN'T EVEN RELAX!
HOW ARE WE GOING TO GO AFTER HIM NOW? WE DON'T KNOW WHAT HE'S GOING TO DO NEXT IN THIS COMEDY OF TEARS!
THEN WE'LL HAVE TO OFFER HIM SOME BAIT! I HAVE AN IDEA!
THAT EVENING, THE NEWSPAPERS . . .
CHAMPION AUTOGRAPH HUNTER
TOMORROW WILL BE AN ACTIVE DAY FOR YOUNG
AND THE FOLLOWING DAY, A DISGUISED ROBIN ROVES TOWN PURSUING HIS NEW HOBBY, AUTOGRAPH-HUNTING . . .
GEE, THANKS! JOE DIMAGGIO! HOT DOG!
AT THE DOOR OF A FAMOUS RESTAURANT..
JERRY SIEGEL, THE CREATOR OF SUPERMAN, I ALWAYS WANTED HIS AUTOGRAPH!
AND AT A DEPARTMENT STORE BOOK COUNTER...
BOOKS
WILL YOU SIGN MY AUTOGRAPH BOOK, MR. BIGBY, PLEASE?
CERTAINLY, SON!
OUTSIDE, AMID THE JOSTLING CROWDS, A HAND SNAKES OUT AND...
I'LL TAKE THAT!
HEY-- WHATCHA DOING?
DEPARTMENT STORE
IT WORKED! THE FISH BIT, ALL RIGHT! THERE'S ONLY ONE SIGNATURE IN THAT BOOK THE JOKER CAN REALLY USE-- THE OWNERS OF THE OTHERS ARE ALL GOING OUT OF TOWN!
11

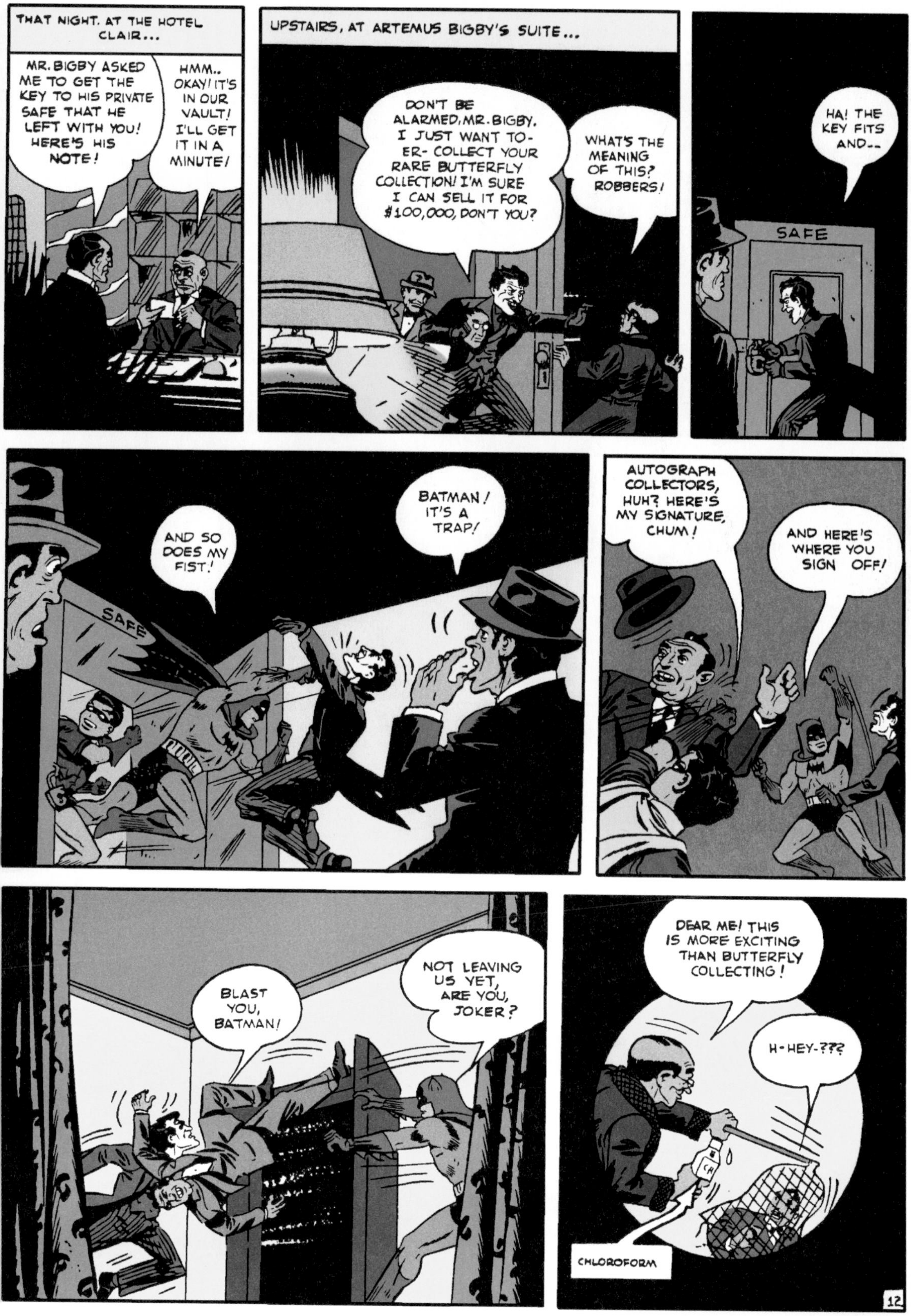
THAT NIGHT, AT THE HOTEL CLAIR...
MR. BIGBY ASKED ME TO GET THE KEY TO HIS PRIVATE SAFE THAT HE LEFT WITH YOU! HERE'S HIS NOTE!
HMM.. OKAY! IT'S IN OUR VAULT! I'LL GET IT IN A MINUTE!
UPSTAIRS, AT ARTEMUS BIGBY'S SUITE...
DON'T BE ALARMED, MR. BIGBY. I JUST WANT TO- ER- COLLECT YOUR RARE BUTTERFLY COLLECTION! I'M SURE I CAN SELL IT FOR $100,000, DON'T YOU?
WHAT'S THE MEANING OF THIS? ROBBERS!
HA! THE KEY FITS AND--
SAFE
AND SO DOES MY FIST!
BATMAN! IT'S A TRAP!
SAFE
AUTOGRAPH COLLECTORS, HUH? HERE'S MY SIGNATURE, CHUM!
AND HERE'S WHERE YOU SIGN OFF!
BLAST YOU, BATMAN!
NOT LEAVING US YET, ARE YOU, JOKER?
DEAR ME! THIS IS MORE EXCITING THAN BUTTERFLY COLLECTING!
H-HEY-???
CHLOROFORM
12

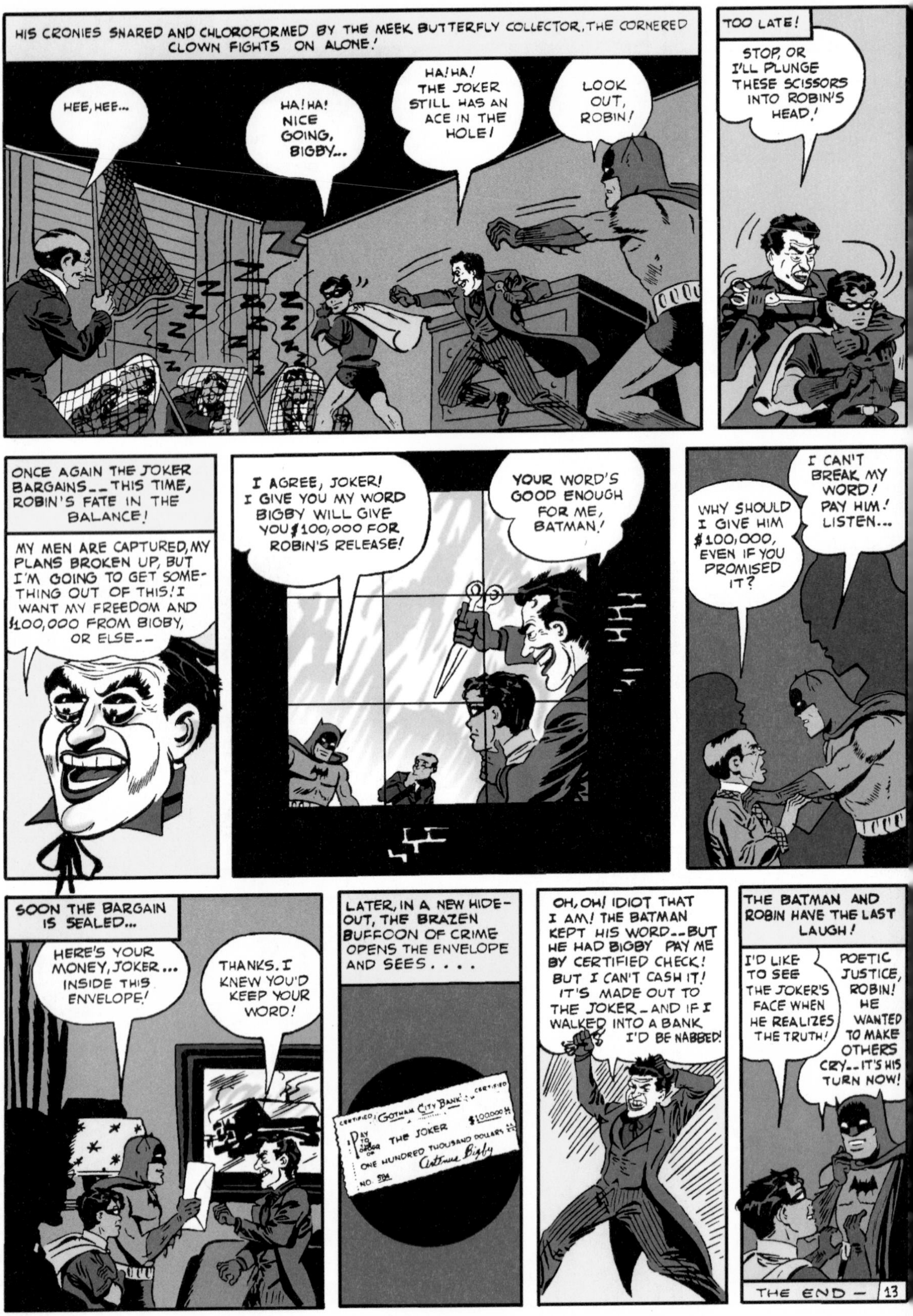
HIS CRONIES SNARED AND CHLOROFORMED BY THE MEEK BUTTERFLY COLLECTOR, THE CORNERED CLOWN FIGHTS ON ALONE!
HEE, HEE...
HA! HA! NICE GOING, BIGBY...
HA! HA! THE JOKER STILL HAS AN ACE IN THE HOLE!
LOOK OUT, ROBIN!
TOO LATE!
STOP, OR I'LL PLUNGE THESE SCISSORS INTO ROBIN'S HEAD!
ONCE AGAIN THE JOKER BARGAINS -- THIS TIME, ROBIN'S FATE IN THE BALANCE!
MY MEN ARE CAPTURED, MY PLANS BROKEN UP, BUT I'M GOING TO GET SOMETHING OUT OF THIS! I WANT MY FREEDOM AND $100,000 FROM BIGBY, OR ELSE--
I AGREE, JOKER! I GIVE YOU MY WORD BIGBY WILL GIVE YOU $100,000 FOR ROBIN'S RELEASE!
YOUR WORD'S GOOD ENOUGH FOR ME, BATMAN!
WHY SHOULD I GIVE HIM $100,000, EVEN IF YOU PROMISED IT?
I CAN'T BREAK MY WORD! PAY HIM! LISTEN...
SOON THE BARGAIN IS SEALED...
HERE'S YOUR MONEY, JOKER... INSIDE THIS ENVELOPE!
THANKS. I KNEW YOU'D KEEP YOUR WORD!
LATER, IN A NEW HIDE-OUT, THE BRAZEN BUFFOON OF CRIME OPENS THE ENVELOPE AND SEES . . . .
CERTIFIED GOTHAM CITY BANK CERTIFIED
PAY TO THE ORDER OF THE JOKER $100,000
ONE HUNDRED THOUSAND DOLLARS
Arthur Bigby
NO. 984
OH, OH! IDIOT THAT I AM! THE BATMAN KEPT HIS WORD--BUT HE HAD BIGBY PAY ME BY CERTIFIED CHECK! BUT I CAN'T CASH IT! IT'S MADE OUT TO THE JOKER - AND IF I WALKED INTO A BANK I'D BE NABBED!
THE BATMAN AND ROBIN HAVE THE LAST LAUGH!
I'D LIKE TO SEE THE JOKER'S FACE WHEN HE REALIZES THE TRUTH!
POETIC JUSTICE, ROBIN! HE WANTED TO MAKE OTHERS CRY-- IT'S HIS TURN NOW!
THE END —
13

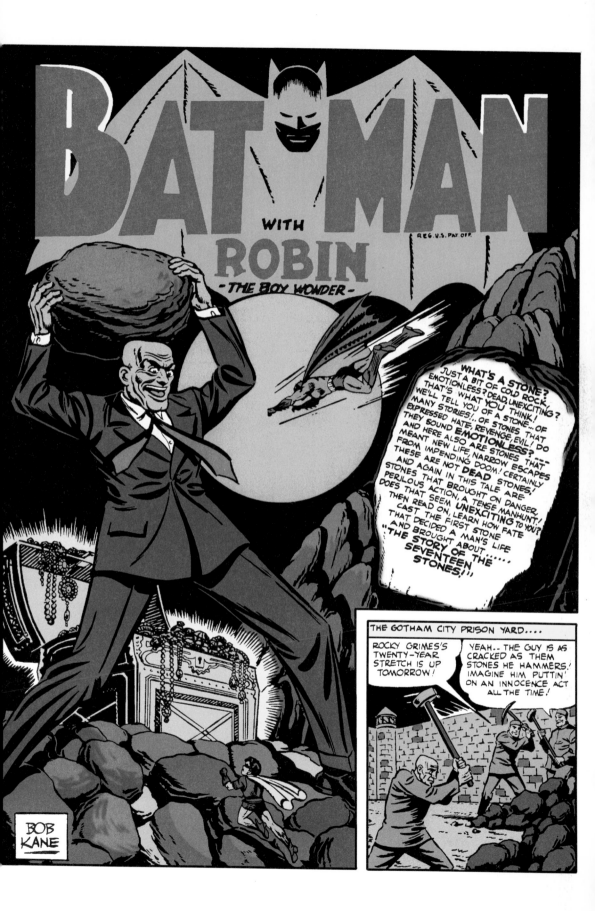

BAT MAN

WITH ROBIN
— THE BOY WONDER —

REG. U.S. PAT. OFF.

WHAT'S A STONE? JUST A BIT OF COLD ROCK? EMOTIONLESS? DEAD, UNEXCITING? THAT'S WHAT YOU THINK! WE'LL TELL YOU OF A STONE -- OF MANY STORIES!... OF STONES THAT EXPRESSED HATE, REVENGE, EVIL! DO THEY SOUND EMOTIONLESS? AND HERE ALSO ARE STONES THAT MEANT NEW LIFE, NARROW ESCAPES FROM IMPENDING DOOM! CERTAINLY THESE ARE NOT DEAD STONES! AND AGAIN IN THIS TALE ARE STONES THAT BROUGHT ON DANGER, PERILOUS ACTION, A TENSE MANHUNT! DOES THAT SEEM UNEXCITING TO YOU? THEN READ ON, LEARN HOW FATE CAST THE FIRST STONE THAT DECIDED A MAN'S LIFE AND BROUGHT ABOUT...... "THE STORY OF THE SEVENTEEN STONES!"

THE GOTHAM CITY PRISON YARD....

ROCKY GRIMES'S TWENTY-YEAR STRETCH IS UP TOMORROW!

YEAH.. THE GUY IS AS CRACKED AS THEM STONES HE HAMMERS! IMAGINE HIM PUTTIN' ON AN INNOCENCE ACT ALL THE TIME!

BOB KANE

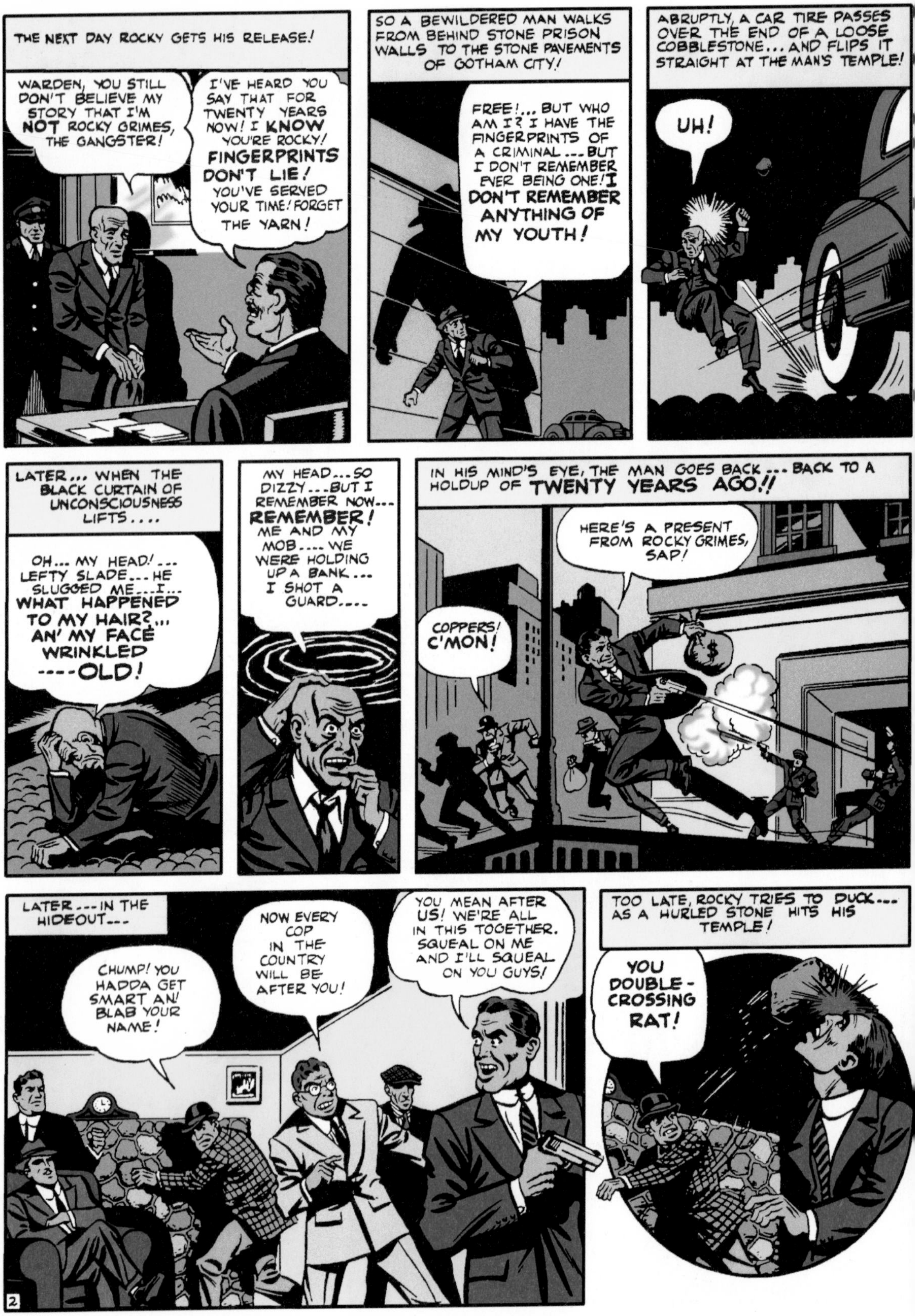
THE NEXT DAY ROCKY GETS HIS RELEASE!
WARDEN, YOU STILL DON'T BELIEVE MY STORY THAT I'M NOT ROCKY GRIMES, THE GANGSTER!
I'VE HEARD YOU SAY THAT FOR TWENTY YEARS NOW! I KNOW YOU'RE ROCKY! FINGERPRINTS DON'T LIE! YOU'VE SERVED YOUR TIME! FORGET THE YARN!
SO A BEWILDERED MAN WALKS FROM BEHIND STONE PRISON WALLS TO THE STONE PAVEMENTS OF GOTHAM CITY!
FREE!... BUT WHO AM I? I HAVE THE FINGERPRINTS OF A CRIMINAL ... BUT I DON'T REMEMBER EVER BEING ONE! I DON'T REMEMBER ANYTHING OF MY YOUTH!
ABRUPTLY, A CAR TIRE PASSES OVER THE END OF A LOOSE COBBLESTONE... AND FLIPS IT STRAIGHT AT THE MAN'S TEMPLE!
UH!
LATER... WHEN THE BLACK CURTAIN OF UNCONSCIOUSNESS LIFTS....
OH... MY HEAD! ... LEFTY SLADE... HE SLUGGED ME...I... WHAT HAPPENED TO MY HAIR?... AN' MY FACE WRINKLED ----OLD!
MY HEAD...SO DIZZY...BUT I REMEMBER NOW... REMEMBER! ME AND MY MOB.... WE WERE HOLDING UP A BANK... I SHOT A GUARD....
IN HIS MIND'S EYE, THE MAN GOES BACK ... BACK TO A HOLDUP OF TWENTY YEARS AGO!!
HERE'S A PRESENT FROM ROCKY GRIMES, SAP!
COPPERS! C'MON!
LATER ... IN THE HIDEOUT...
CHUMP! YOU HADDA GET SMART AN' BLAB YOUR NAME!
NOW EVERY COP IN THE COUNTRY WILL BE AFTER YOU!
YOU MEAN AFTER US! WE'RE ALL IN THIS TOGETHER. SQUEAL ON ME AND I'LL SQUEAL ON YOU GUYS!
TOO LATE, ROCKY TRIES TO DUCK... AS A HURLED STONE HITS HIS TEMPLE!
YOU DOUBLE-CROSSING RAT!
2

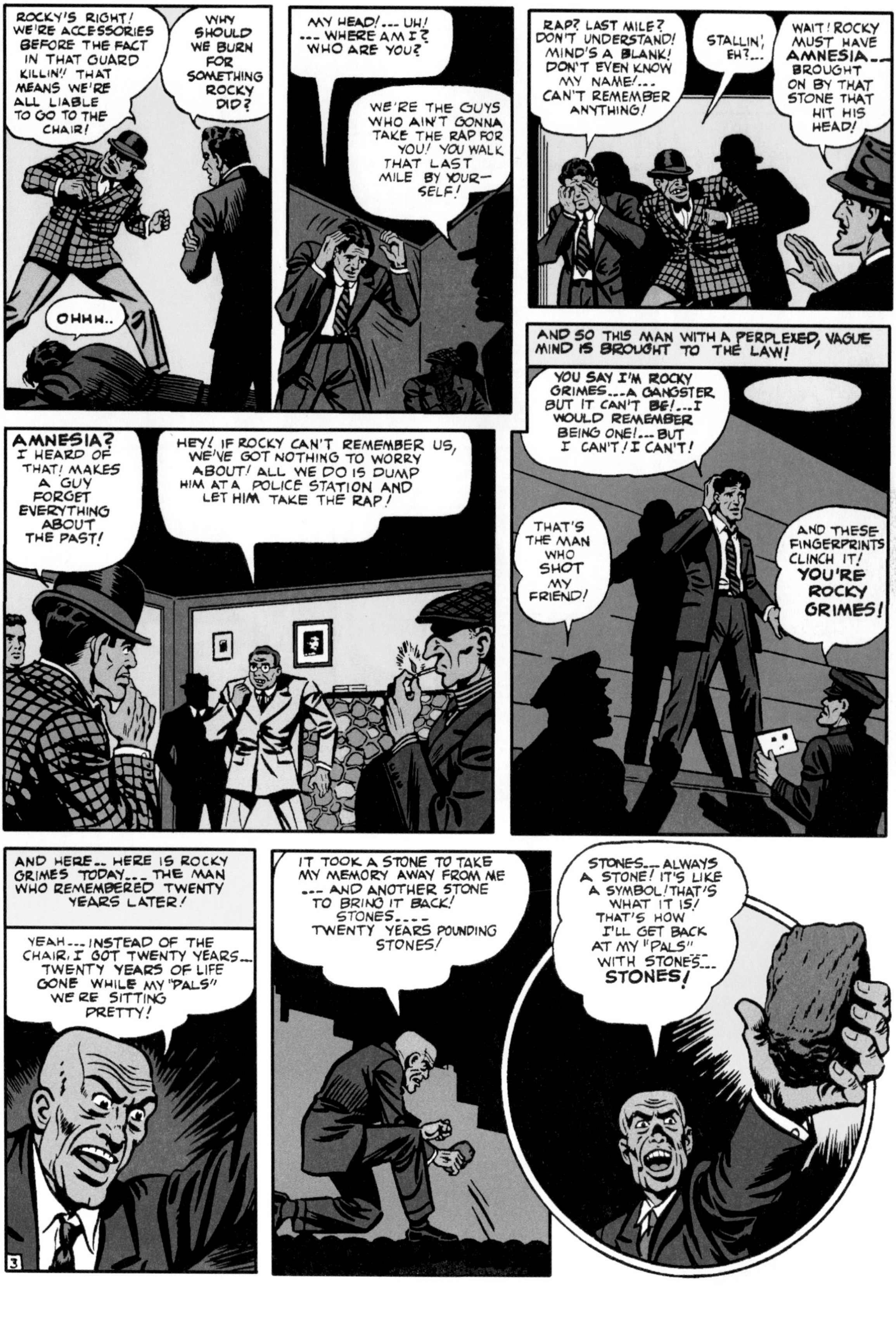

ROCKY'S RIGHT! WE'RE ACCESSORIES BEFORE THE FACT IN THAT GUARD KILLIN'! THAT MEANS WE'RE ALL LIABLE TO GO TO THE CHAIR!
WHY SHOULD WE BURN FOR SOMETHING ROCKY DID?
OHHH..
MY HEAD! --- UH! --- WHERE AM I? WHO ARE YOU?
WE'RE THE GUYS WHO AIN'T GONNA TAKE THE RAP FOR YOU! YOU WALK THAT LAST MILE BY YOURSELF!
RAP? LAST MILE? DON'T UNDERSTAND! MIND'S A BLANK! DON'T EVEN KNOW MY NAME!... CAN'T REMEMBER ANYTHING!
STALLIN', EH?...
WAIT! ROCKY MUST HAVE AMNESIA... BROUGHT ON BY THAT STONE THAT HIT HIS HEAD!
AMNESIA? I HEARD OF THAT! MAKES A GUY FORGET EVERYTHING ABOUT THE PAST!
HEY! IF ROCKY CAN'T REMEMBER US, WE'VE GOT NOTHING TO WORRY ABOUT! ALL WE DO IS DUMP HIM AT A POLICE STATION AND LET HIM TAKE THE RAP!
AND SO THIS MAN WITH A PERPLEXED, VAGUE MIND IS BROUGHT TO THE LAW!
YOU SAY I'M ROCKY GRIMES...A GANGSTER BUT IT CAN'T BE!...I WOULD REMEMBER BEING ONE!... BUT I CAN'T! I CAN'T!
THAT'S THE MAN WHO SHOT MY FRIEND!
AND THESE FINGERPRINTS CLINCH IT! YOU'RE ROCKY GRIMES!
AND HERE.. HERE IS ROCKY GRIMES TODAY... THE MAN WHO REMEMBERED TWENTY YEARS LATER!
YEAH... INSTEAD OF THE CHAIR, I GOT TWENTY YEARS... TWENTY YEARS OF LIFE GONE WHILE MY "PALS" WERE SITTING PRETTY!
3
IT TOOK A STONE TO TAKE MY MEMORY AWAY FROM ME --- AND ANOTHER STONE TO BRING IT BACK! STONES.... TWENTY YEARS POUNDING STONES!
STONES... ALWAYS A STONE! IT'S LIKE A SYMBOL! THAT'S WHAT IT IS! THAT'S HOW I'LL GET BACK AT MY "PALS" WITH STONES... STONES!

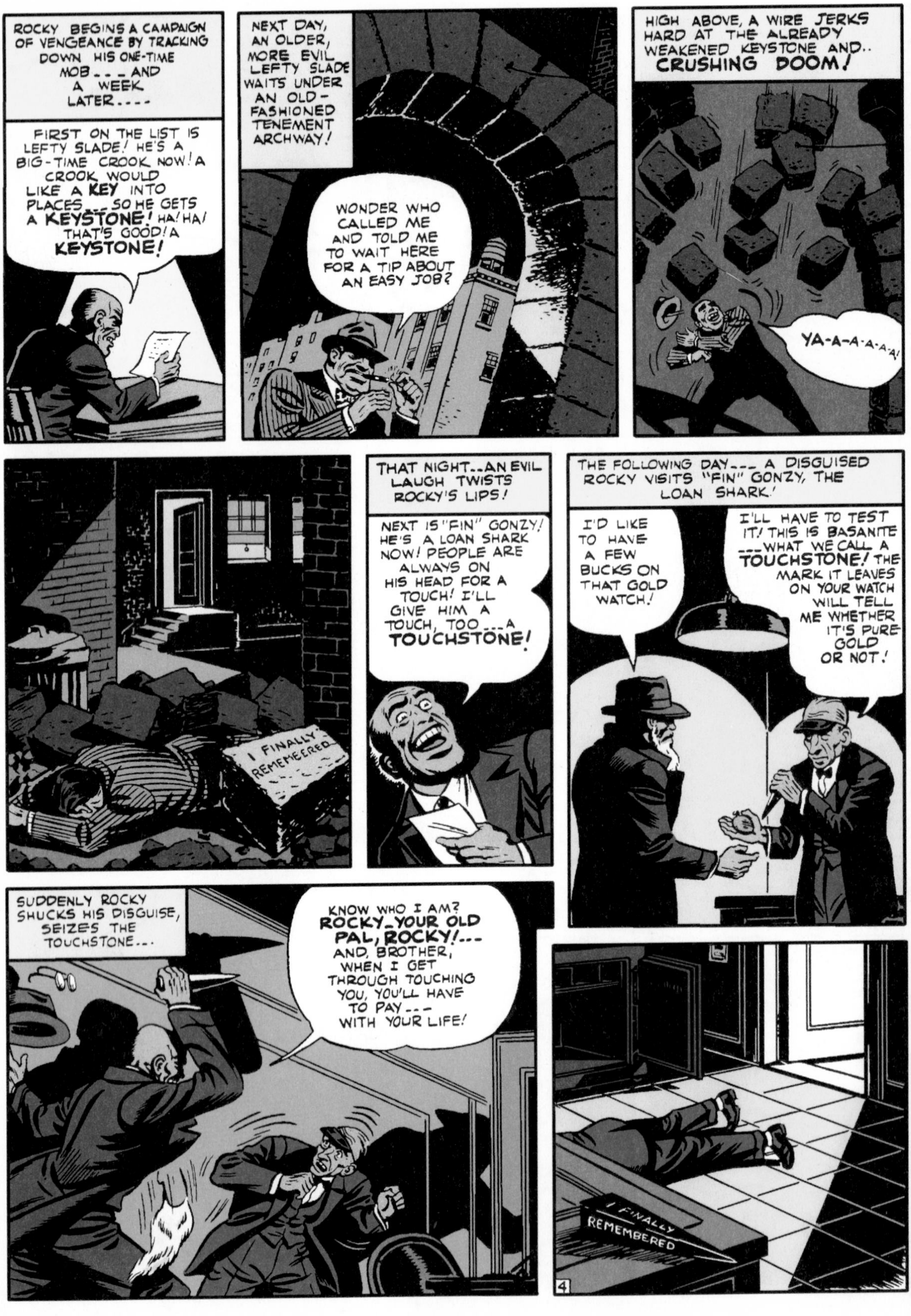
ROCKY BEGINS A CAMPAIGN OF VENGEANCE BY TRACKING DOWN HIS ONE-TIME MOB --- AND A WEEK LATER----
FIRST ON THE LIST IS LEFTY SLADE! HE'S A BIG-TIME CROOK NOW! A CROOK WOULD LIKE A KEY INTO PLACES... SO HE GETS A KEYSTONE! HA! HA! THAT'S GOOD! A KEYSTONE!
NEXT DAY, AN OLDER, MORE EVIL LEFTY SLADE WAITS UNDER AN OLD-FASHIONED TENEMENT ARCHWAY!
WONDER WHO CALLED ME AND TOLD ME TO WAIT HERE FOR A TIP ABOUT AN EASY JOB?
HIGH ABOVE, A WIRE JERKS HARD AT THE ALREADY WEAKENED KEYSTONE AND.. CRUSHING DOOM!
YA-A-A-A-A-A!
I FINALLY REMEMBERED
THAT NIGHT--AN EVIL LAUGH TWISTS ROCKY'S LIPS!
NEXT IS "FIN" GONZY! HE'S A LOAN SHARK NOW! PEOPLE ARE ALWAYS ON HIS HEAD FOR A TOUCH! I'LL GIVE HIM A TOUCH, TOO ... A TOUCHSTONE!
THE FOLLOWING DAY--- A DISGUISED ROCKY VISITS "FIN" GONZY, THE LOAN SHARK!
I'D LIKE TO HAVE A FEW BUCKS ON THAT GOLD WATCH!
I'LL HAVE TO TEST IT! THIS IS BASANITE ---WHAT WE CALL A TOUCHSTONE! THE MARK IT LEAVES ON YOUR WATCH WILL TELL ME WHETHER IT'S PURE GOLD OR NOT!
SUDDENLY ROCKY SHUCKS HIS DISGUISE, SEIZES THE TOUCHSTONE...
KNOW WHO I AM? ROCKY-YOUR OLD PAL, ROCKY!--- AND, BROTHER, WHEN I GET THROUGH TOUCHING YOU, YOU'LL HAVE TO PAY--- WITH YOUR LIFE!
I FINALLY REMEMBERED
4

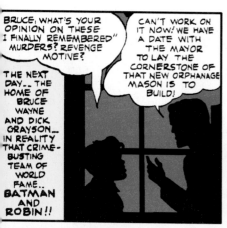

BRUCE, WHAT'S YOUR OPINION ON THESE "I FINALLY REMEMBERED" MURDERS? REVENGE MOTIVE?

CAN'T WORK ON IT NOW! WE HAVE A DATE WITH THE MAYOR TO LAY THE CORNERSTONE OF THAT NEW ORPHANAGE MASON IS TO BUILD!

THE NEXT DAY... THE HOME OF BRUCE WAYNE AND DICK GRAYSON... IN REALITY THAT CRIME-BUSTING TEAM OF WORLD FAME.. BATMAN AND ROBIN!!

LATER... AT THE BUILDING SITE...

YOU KNOW MASON, THE ARCHITECT?

HELLO, MASON!

HELLO, BATMAN! (WHAT A STRONG FACE HE HAS! I'M GLAD I WENT STRAIGHT! I WOULDN'T WANT HIM AFTER ME!)

THERE'S THE CORNERSTONE THAT IS TO SERVE AS THE FIRST STEP IN BUILDING THE NEW ORPHANAGE!

WITHOUT WARNING, THE CABLE HOLDING THE HUGE CORNERSTONE GOES SLACK!

MASON! LOOK OUT!

WRITING ON THE CORNERSTONE'S SURFACE CATCHES THE BATMAN'S EYE!

"I FINALLY REMEM..." THE STONE MURDERS! THAT MAN WORKING THE CRANE TRIED TO KILL MASON!!

I FINALLY REMEMBERED

CRASH!

OH, MAN! THAT WAS CLOSE!

HE'S TRYING TO ESCAPE! C'MON, ROBIN--- WE'RE WORKING ON THAT CASE NOW!

HOT DOG!

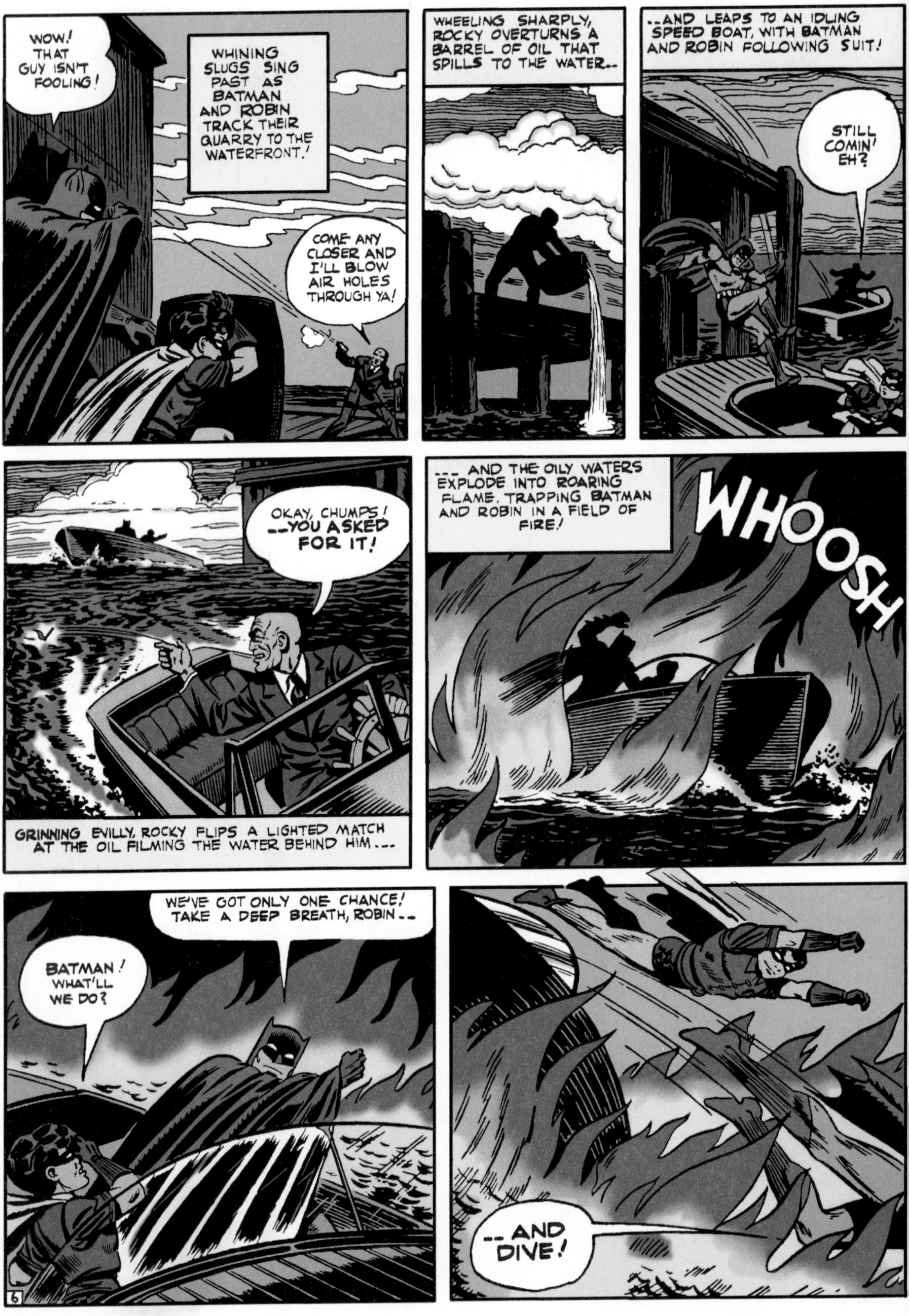
WOW! THAT GUY ISN'T FOOLING!
WHINING SLUGS SING PAST AS BATMAN AND ROBIN TRACK THEIR QUARRY TO THE WATERFRONT!
COME ANY CLOSER AND I'LL BLOW AIR HOLES THROUGH YA!
WHEELING SHARPLY, ROCKY OVERTURNS A BARREL OF OIL THAT SPILLS TO THE WATER..
..AND LEAPS TO AN IDLING SPEED BOAT, WITH BATMAN AND ROBIN FOLLOWING SUIT!
STILL COMIN' EH?
OKAY, CHUMPS! --YOU ASKED FOR IT!
GRINNING EVILLY, ROCKY FLIPS A LIGHTED MATCH AT THE OIL FILMING THE WATER BEHIND HIM...
... AND THE OILY WATERS EXPLODE INTO ROARING FLAME, TRAPPING BATMAN AND ROBIN IN A FIELD OF FIRE!
WHOOSH
WE'VE GOT ONLY ONE CHANCE! TAKE A DEEP BREATH, ROBIN..
BATMAN! WHAT'LL WE DO?
6
--AND DIVE!

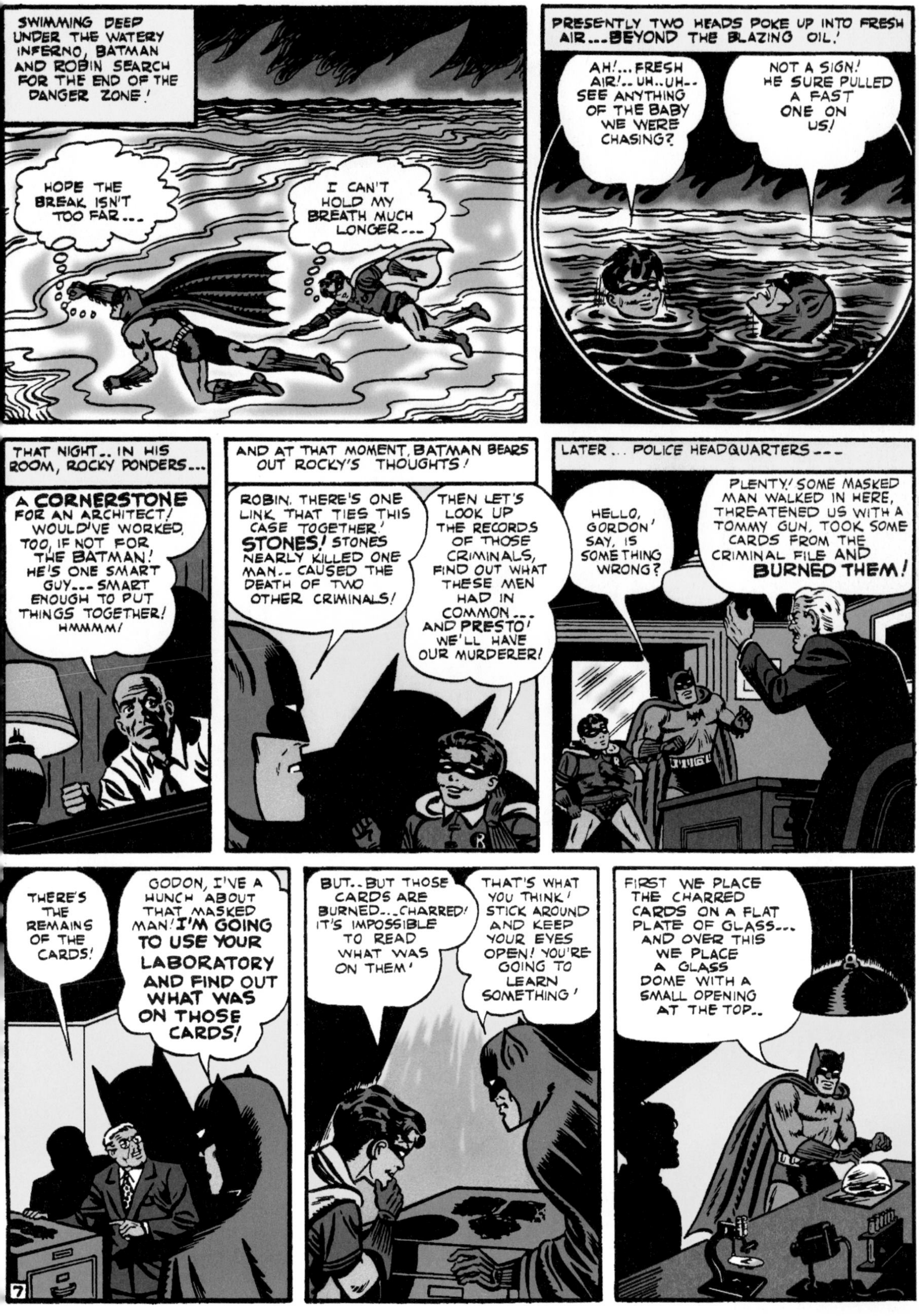
SWIMMING DEEP UNDER THE WATERY INFERNO, BATMAN AND ROBIN SEARCH FOR THE END OF THE DANGER ZONE!
HOPE THE BREAK ISN'T TOO FAR...
I CAN'T HOLD MY BREATH MUCH LONGER...
PRESENTLY TWO HEADS POKE UP INTO FRESH AIR...BEYOND THE BLAZING OIL!
AH!...FRESH AIR!..UH..UH..SEE ANYTHING OF THE BABY WE WERE CHASING?
NOT A SIGN! HE SURE PULLED A FAST ONE ON US!
THAT NIGHT.. IN HIS ROOM, ROCKY PONDERS...
A CORNERSTONE FOR AN ARCHITECT! WOULD'VE WORKED, TOO, IF NOT FOR THE BATMAN! HE'S ONE SMART GUY... SMART ENOUGH TO PUT THINGS TOGETHER! HMMMM!
AND AT THAT MOMENT, BATMAN BEARS OUT ROCKY'S THOUGHTS!
ROBIN, THERE'S ONE LINK THAT TIES THIS CASE TOGETHER! STONES! STONES NEARLY KILLED ONE MAN.. CAUSED THE DEATH OF TWO OTHER CRIMINALS!
THEN LET'S LOOK UP THE RECORDS OF THOSE CRIMINALS, FIND OUT WHAT THESE MEN HAD IN COMMON... AND PRESTO! WE'LL HAVE OUR MURDERER!
LATER... POLICE HEADQUARTERS...
HELLO, GORDON! SAY, IS SOMETHING WRONG?
PLENTY! SOME MASKED MAN WALKED IN HERE, THREATENED US WITH A TOMMY GUN, TOOK SOME CARDS FROM THE CRIMINAL FILE AND BURNED THEM!
THERE'S THE REMAINS OF THE CARDS!
GODON, I'VE A HUNCH ABOUT THAT MASKED MAN! I'M GOING TO USE YOUR LABORATORY AND FIND OUT WHAT WAS ON THOSE CARDS!
7
BUT..BUT THOSE CARDS ARE BURNED...CHARRED! IT'S IMPOSSIBLE TO READ WHAT WAS ON THEM!
THAT'S WHAT YOU THINK! STICK AROUND AND KEEP YOUR EYES OPEN! YOU'RE GOING TO LEARN SOMETHING!
FIRST WE PLACE THE CHARRED CARDS ON A FLAT PLATE OF GLASS... AND OVER THIS WE PLACE A GLASS DOME WITH A SMALL OPENING AT THE TOP..

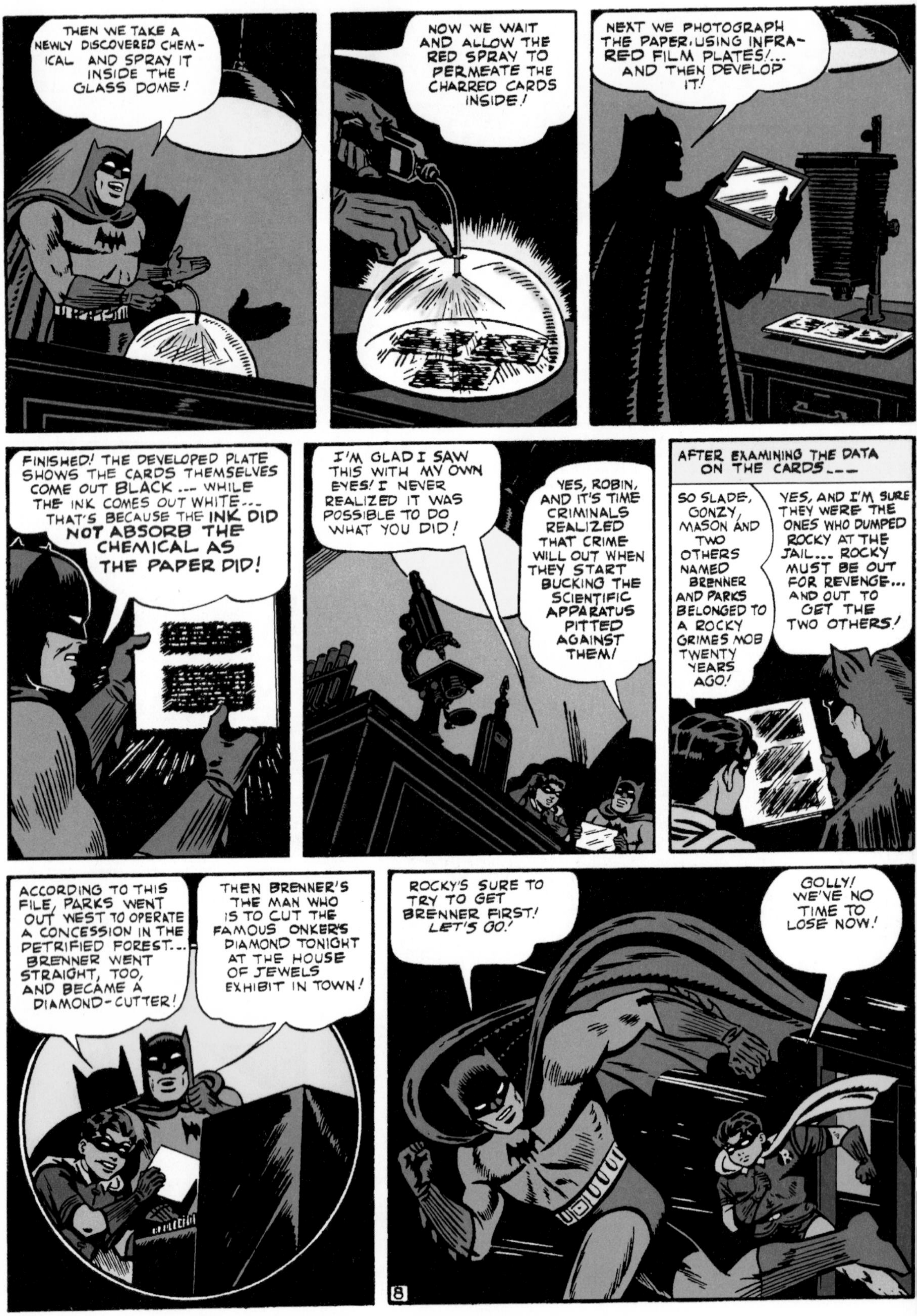
THEN WE TAKE A NEWLY DISCOVERED CHEM-ICAL AND SPRAY IT INSIDE THE GLASS DOME!
NOW WE WAIT AND ALLOW THE RED SPRAY TO PERMEATE THE CHARRED CARDS INSIDE!
NEXT WE PHOTOGRAPH THE PAPER, USING INFRA-RED FILM PLATES!... AND THEN DEVELOP IT!
FINISHED! THE DEVELOPED PLATE SHOWS THE CARDS THEMSELVES COME OUT BLACK--- WHILE THE INK COMES OUT WHITE--- THAT'S BECAUSE THE INK DID NOT ABSORB THE CHEMICAL AS THE PAPER DID!
I'M GLAD I SAW THIS WITH MY OWN EYES! I NEVER REALIZED IT WAS POSSIBLE TO DO WHAT YOU DID!
YES, ROBIN, AND IT'S TIME CRIMINALS REALIZED THAT CRIME WILL OUT WHEN THEY START BUCKING THE SCIENTIFIC APPARATUS PITTED AGAINST THEM!
AFTER EXAMINING THE DATA ON THE CARDS---
SO SLADE, GONZY, MASON AND TWO OTHERS NAMED BRENNER AND PARKS BELONGED TO A ROCKY GRIMES MOB TWENTY YEARS AGO!
YES, AND I'M SURE THEY WERE THE ONES WHO DUMPED ROCKY AT THE JAIL... ROCKY MUST BE OUT FOR REVENGE... AND OUT TO GET THE TWO OTHERS!
ACCORDING TO THIS FILE, PARKS WENT OUT WEST TO OPERATE A CONCESSION IN THE PETRIFIED FOREST... BRENNER WENT STRAIGHT, TOO, AND BECAME A DIAMOND-CUTTER!
THEN BRENNER'S THE MAN WHO IS TO CUT THE FAMOUS ONKER'S DIAMOND TONIGHT AT THE HOUSE OF JEWELS EXHIBIT IN TOWN!
ROCKY'S SURE TO TRY TO GET BRENNER FIRST! LET'S GO!
GOLLY! WE'VE NO TIME TO LOSE NOW!
8

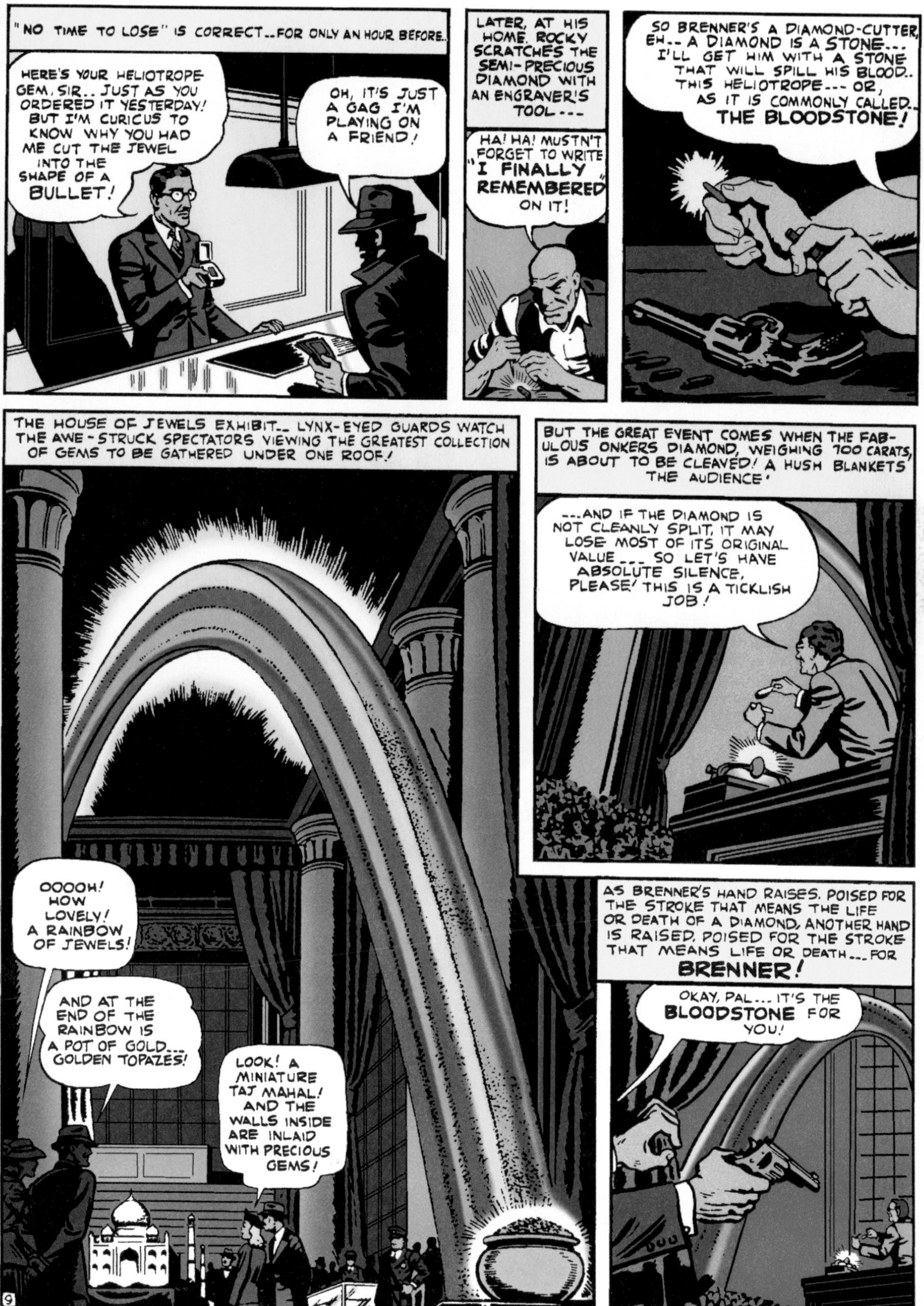
"NO TIME TO LOSE" IS CORRECT..FOR ONLY AN HOUR BEFORE..
HERE'S YOUR HELIOTROPE GEM, SIR.. JUST AS YOU ORDERED IT YESTERDAY! BUT I'M CURIOUS TO KNOW WHY YOU HAD ME CUT THE JEWEL INTO THE SHAPE OF A BULLET!
OH, IT'S JUST A GAG I'M PLAYING ON A FRIEND!
LATER, AT HIS HOME, ROCKY SCRATCHES THE SEMI-PRECIOUS DIAMOND WITH AN ENGRAVER'S TOOL---
HA! HA! MUSTN'T FORGET TO WRITE "I FINALLY REMEMBERED" ON IT!
SO BRENNER'S A DIAMOND-CUTTER, EH.. A DIAMOND IS A STONE... I'LL GET HIM WITH A STONE THAT WILL SPILL HIS BLOOD.. THIS HELIOTROPE--- OR, AS IT IS COMMONLY CALLED.. THE BLOODSTONE!
THE HOUSE OF JEWELS EXHIBIT.. LYNX-EYED GUARDS WATCH THE AWE-STRUCK SPECTATORS VIEWING THE GREATEST COLLECTION OF GEMS TO BE GATHERED UNDER ONE ROOF!
OOOOH! HOW LOVELY! A RAINBOW OF JEWELS!
AND AT THE END OF THE RAINBOW IS A POT OF GOLD... GOLDEN TOPAZES!
LOOK! A MINIATURE TAJ MAHAL! AND THE WALLS INSIDE ARE INLAID WITH PRECIOUS GEMS!
9
BUT THE GREAT EVENT COMES WHEN THE FABULOUS ONKERS DIAMOND, WEIGHING 700 CARATS, IS ABOUT TO BE CLEAVED! A HUSH BLANKETS THE AUDIENCE!
---AND IF THE DIAMOND IS NOT CLEANLY SPLIT, IT MAY LOSE MOST OF ITS ORIGINAL VALUE --- SO LET'S HAVE ABSOLUTE SILENCE, PLEASE! THIS IS A TICKLISH JOB!
AS BRENNER'S HAND RAISES, POISED FOR THE STROKE THAT MEANS THE LIFE OR DEATH OF A DIAMOND, ANOTHER HAND IS RAISED, POISED FOR THE STROKE THAT MEANS LIFE OR DEATH --- FOR BRENNER!
OKAY, PAL... IT'S THE BLOODSTONE FOR YOU!

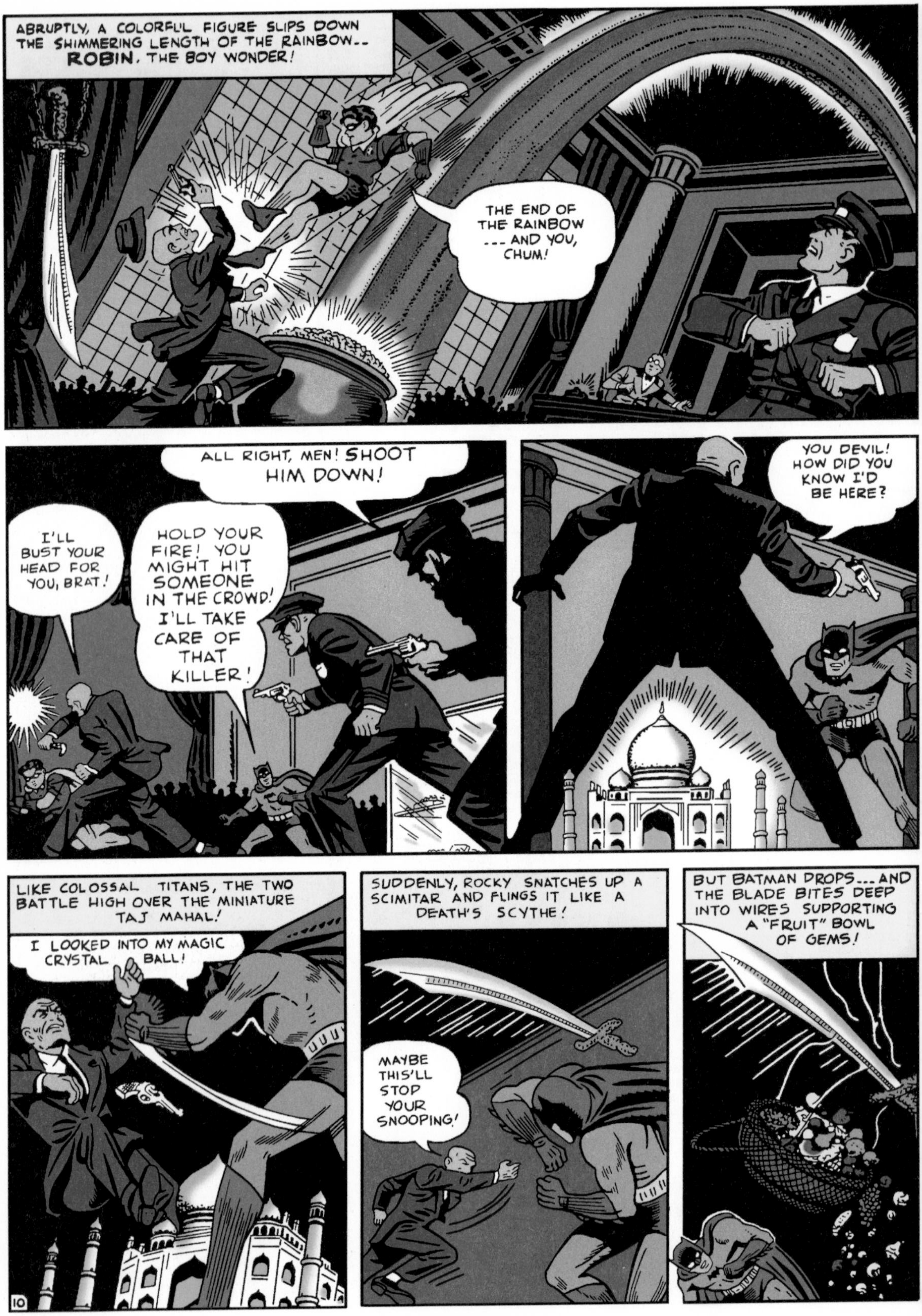

ABRUPTLY, A COLORFUL FIGURE SLIPS DOWN THE SHIMMERING LENGTH OF THE RAINBOW-- **ROBIN**, THE BOY WONDER!
THE END OF THE RAINBOW --- AND YOU, CHUM!
ALL RIGHT, MEN! SHOOT HIM DOWN!
I'LL BUST YOUR HEAD FOR YOU, BRAT!
HOLD YOUR FIRE! YOU MIGHT HIT SOMEONE IN THE CROWD! I'LL TAKE CARE OF THAT KILLER!
YOU DEVIL! HOW DID YOU KNOW I'D BE HERE?
LIKE COLOSSAL TITANS, THE TWO BATTLE HIGH OVER THE MINIATURE TAJ MAHAL!
I LOOKED INTO MY MAGIC CRYSTAL BALL!
10
SUDDENLY, ROCKY SNATCHES UP A SCIMITAR AND FLINGS IT LIKE A DEATH'S SCYTHE!
MAYBE THIS'LL STOP YOUR SNOOPING!
BUT BATMAN DROPS ... AND THE BLADE BITES DEEP INTO WIRES SUPPORTING A "FRUIT" BOWL OF GEMS!

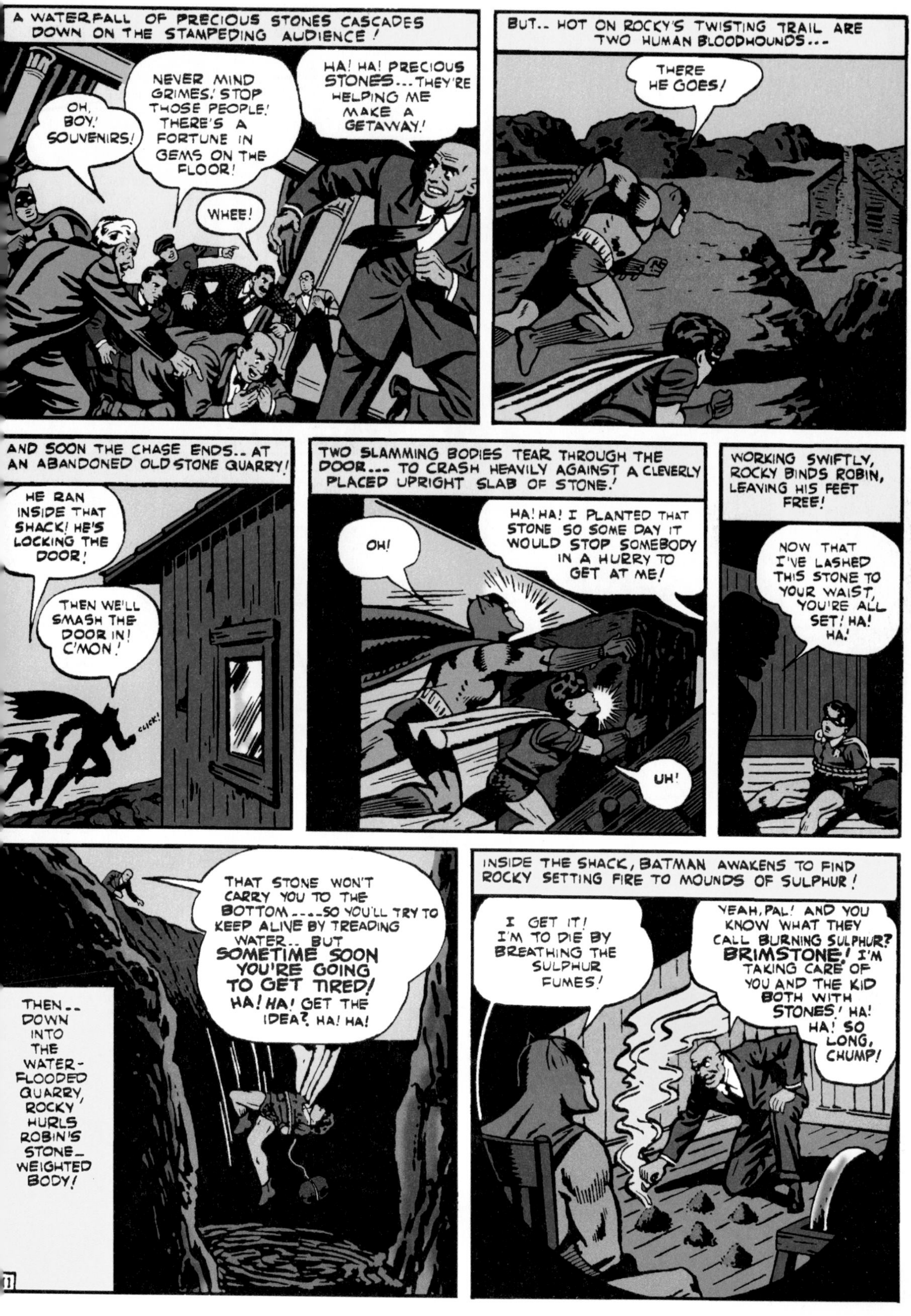
A WATERFALL OF PRECIOUS STONES CASCADES DOWN ON THE STAMPEDING AUDIENCE!
OH, BOY! SOUVENIRS!
NEVER MIND GRIMES! STOP THOSE PEOPLE! THERE'S A FORTUNE IN GEMS ON THE FLOOR!
WHEE!
HA! HA! PRECIOUS STONES... THEY'RE HELPING ME MAKE A GETAWAY!
BUT.. HOT ON ROCKY'S TWISTING TRAIL ARE TWO HUMAN BLOODHOUNDS...
THERE HE GOES!
AND SOON THE CHASE ENDS.. AT AN ABANDONED OLD STONE QUARRY!
HE RAN INSIDE THAT SHACK! HE'S LOCKING THE DOOR!
THEN WE'LL SMASH THE DOOR IN! C'MON!
CLICK!
TWO SLAMMING BODIES TEAR THROUGH THE DOOR... TO CRASH HEAVILY AGAINST A CLEVERLY PLACED UPRIGHT SLAB OF STONE!
OH!
HA! HA! I PLANTED THAT STONE SO SOME DAY IT WOULD STOP SOMEBODY IN A HURRY TO GET AT ME!
UH!
WORKING SWIFTLY, ROCKY BINDS ROBIN, LEAVING HIS FEET FREE!
NOW THAT I'VE LASHED THIS STONE TO YOUR WAIST, YOU'RE ALL SET! HA! HA!
THEN.. DOWN INTO THE WATER-FLOODED QUARRY, ROCKY HURLS ROBIN'S STONE-WEIGHTED BODY!
THAT STONE WON'T CARRY YOU TO THE BOTTOM ----SO YOU'LL TRY TO KEEP ALIVE BY TREADING WATER.. BUT SOMETIME SOON YOU'RE GOING TO GET TIRED! HA! HA! GET THE IDEA? HA! HA!
INSIDE THE SHACK, BATMAN AWAKENS TO FIND ROCKY SETTING FIRE TO MOUNDS OF SULPHUR!
I GET IT! I'M TO DIE BY BREATHING THE SULPHUR FUMES!
YEAH, PAL! AND YOU KNOW WHAT THEY CALL BURNING SULPHUR? BRIMSTONE! I'M TAKING CARE OF YOU AND THE KID BOTH WITH STONES! HA! HA! SO LONG, CHUMP!

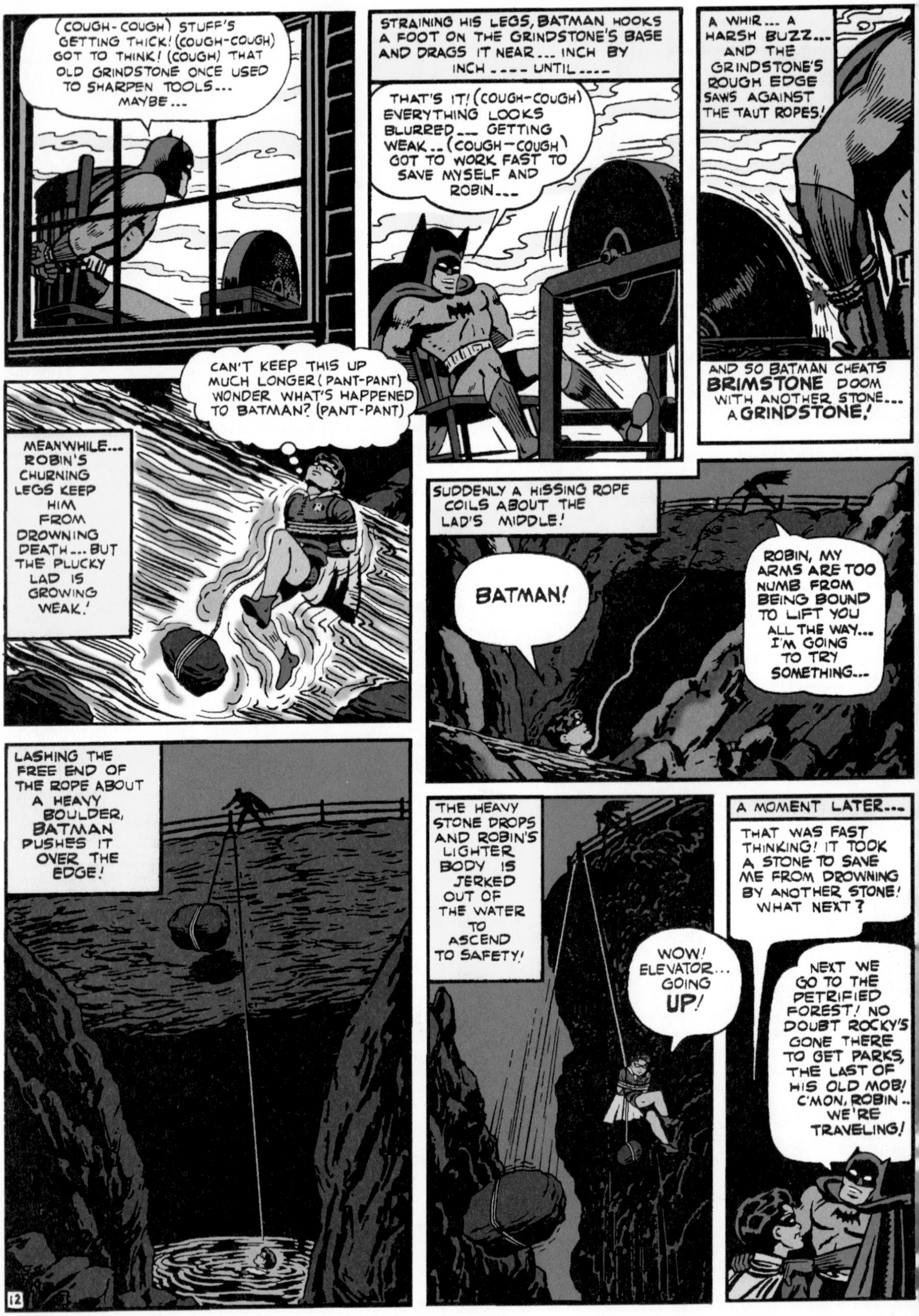

(COUGH-COUGH) STUFF'S GETTING THICK! (COUGH-COUGH) GOT TO THINK! (COUGH) THAT OLD GRINDSTONE ONCE USED TO SHARPEN TOOLS... MAYBE...
STRAINING HIS LEGS, BATMAN HOOKS A FOOT ON THE GRINDSTONE'S BASE AND DRAGS IT NEAR... INCH BY INCH ---- UNTIL ----
THAT'S IT! (COUGH-COUGH) EVERYTHING LOOKS BLURRED... GETTING WEAK.. (COUGH-COUGH) GOT TO WORK FAST TO SAVE MYSELF AND ROBIN...
A WHIR... A HARSH BUZZ... AND THE GRINDSTONE'S ROUGH EDGE SAWS AGAINST THE TAUT ROPES!
AND SO BATMAN CHEATS BRIMSTONE DOOM WITH ANOTHER STONE... A GRINDSTONE!
MEANWHILE... ROBIN'S CHURNING LEGS KEEP HIM FROM DROWNING DEATH... BUT THE PLUCKY LAD IS GROWING WEAK!
CAN'T KEEP THIS UP MUCH LONGER (PANT-PANT) WONDER WHAT'S HAPPENED TO BATMAN? (PANT-PANT)
SUDDENLY A HISSING ROPE COILS ABOUT THE LAD'S MIDDLE!
BATMAN!
ROBIN, MY ARMS ARE TOO NUMB FROM BEING BOUND TO LIFT YOU ALL THE WAY... I'M GOING TO TRY SOMETHING...
LASHING THE FREE END OF THE ROPE ABOUT A HEAVY BOULDER, BATMAN PUSHES IT OVER THE EDGE!
12
THE HEAVY STONE DROPS AND ROBIN'S LIGHTER BODY IS JERKED OUT OF THE WATER TO ASCEND TO SAFETY!
WOW! ELEVATOR... GOING UP!
A MOMENT LATER...
THAT WAS FAST THINKING! IT TOOK A STONE TO SAVE ME FROM DROWNING BY ANOTHER STONE! WHAT NEXT?
NEXT WE GO TO THE PETRIFIED FOREST! NO DOUBT ROCKY'S GONE THERE TO GET PARKS, THE LAST OF HIS OLD MOB! C'MON, ROBIN.. WE'RE TRAVELING!

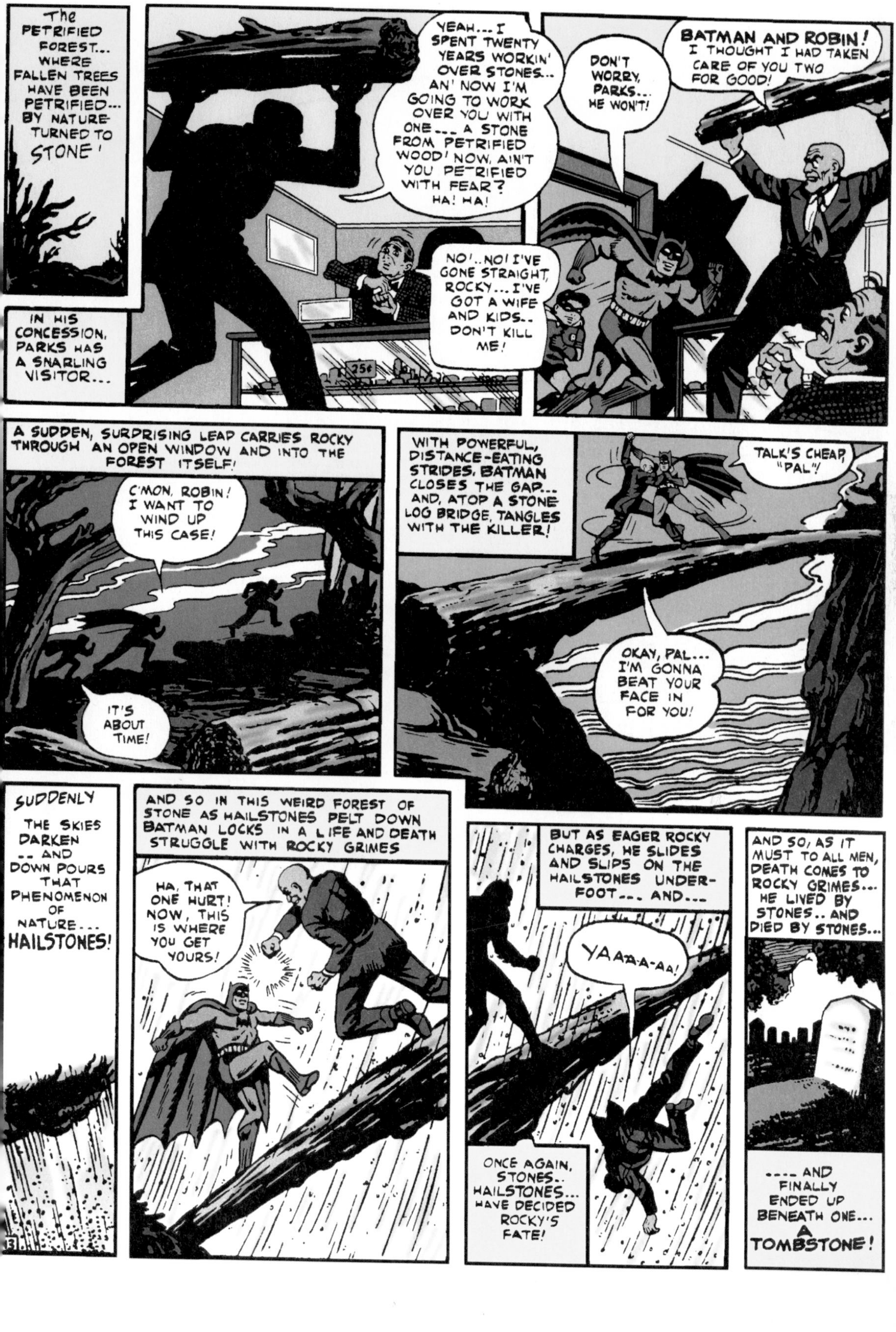

The PETRIFIED FOREST... WHERE FALLEN TREES HAVE BEEN PETRIFIED... BY NATURE TURNED TO STONE!
IN HIS CONCESSION, PARKS HAS A SNARLING VISITOR...
YEAH... I SPENT TWENTY YEARS WORKIN' OVER STONES... AN' NOW I'M GOING TO WORK OVER YOU WITH ONE... A STONE FROM PETRIFIED WOOD! NOW, AIN'T YOU PE-RIFIED WITH FEAR? HA! HA!
NO!..NO! I'VE GONE STRAIGHT, ROCKY... I'VE GOT A WIFE AND KIDS.. DON'T KILL ME!
25¢
BATMAN AND ROBIN! I THOUGHT I HAD TAKEN CARE OF YOU TWO FOR GOOD!
DON'T WORRY, PARKS... HE WON'T!
A SUDDEN, SURPRISING LEAP CARRIES ROCKY THROUGH AN OPEN WINDOW AND INTO THE FOREST ITSELF!
C'MON, ROBIN! I WANT TO WIND UP THIS CASE!
IT'S ABOUT TIME!
WITH POWERFUL, DISTANCE-EATING STRIDES, BATMAN CLOSES THE GAP... AND, ATOP A STONE LOG BRIDGE, TANGLES WITH THE KILLER!
TALK'S CHEAP, "PAL"!
OKAY, PAL... I'M GONNA BEAT YOUR FACE IN FOR YOU!
SUDDENLY THE SKIES DARKEN -- AND DOWN POURS THAT PHENOMENON OF NATURE... HAILSTONES!
AND SO IN THIS WEIRD FOREST OF STONE AS HAILSTONES PELT DOWN BATMAN LOCKS IN A LIFE AND DEATH STRUGGLE WITH ROCKY GRIMES
HA, THAT ONE HURT! NOW, THIS IS WHERE YOU GET YOURS!
BUT AS EAGER ROCKY CHARGES, HE SLIDES AND SLIPS ON THE HAILSTONES UNDER-FOOT... AND...
YAAA-A-AA!
ONCE AGAIN, STONES.. HAILSTONES... HAVE DECIDED ROCKY'S FATE!
AND SO, AS IT MUST TO ALL MEN, DEATH COMES TO ROCKY GRIMES... HE LIVED BY STONES.. AND DIED BY STONES...
.... AND FINALLY ENDED UP BENEATH ONE... A TOMBSTONE!

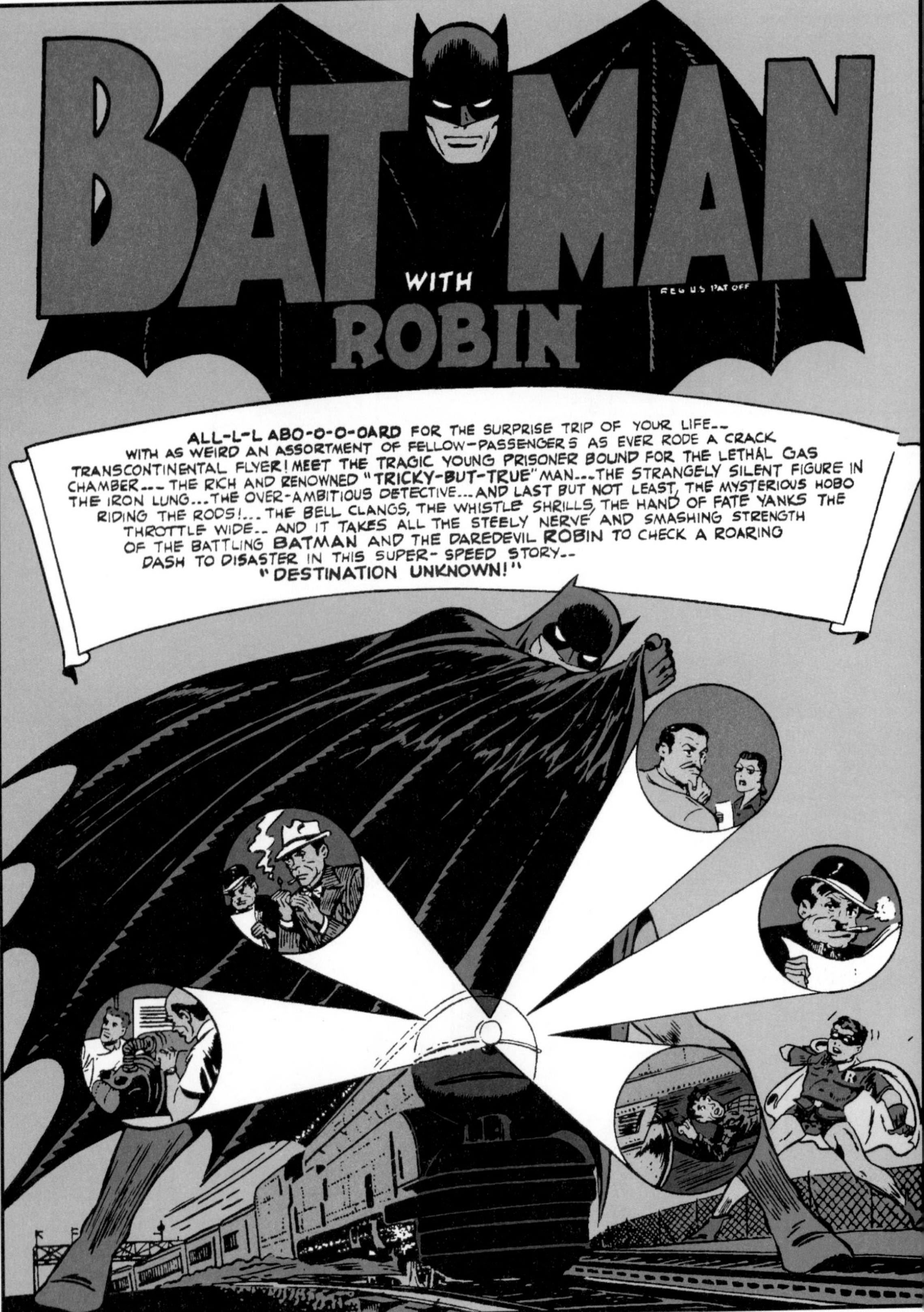
BATMAN
WITH
ROBIN
REG U.S. PAT OFF
ALL-L-L ABO-O-O-OARD FOR THE SURPRISE TRIP OF YOUR LIFE-- WITH AS WEIRD AN ASSORTMENT OF FELLOW-PASSENGERS AS EVER RODE A CRACK TRANSCONTINENTAL FLYER! MEET THE TRAGIC YOUNG PRISONER BOUND FOR THE LETHAL GAS CHAMBER--- THE RICH AND RENOWNED "TRICKY-BUT-TRUE" MAN---THE STRANGELY SILENT FIGURE IN THE IRON LUNG...THE OVER-AMBITIOUS DETECTIVE...AND LAST BUT NOT LEAST, THE MYSTERIOUS HOBO RIDING THE RODS!... THE BELL CLANGS, THE WHISTLE SHRILLS, THE HAND OF FATE YANKS THE THROTTLE WIDE.. AND IT TAKES ALL THE STEELY NERVE AND SMASHING STRENGTH OF THE BATTLING BATMAN AND THE DAREDEVIL ROBIN TO CHECK A ROARING DASH TO DISASTER IN THIS SUPER-SPEED STORY--
"DESTINATION UNKNOWN!"

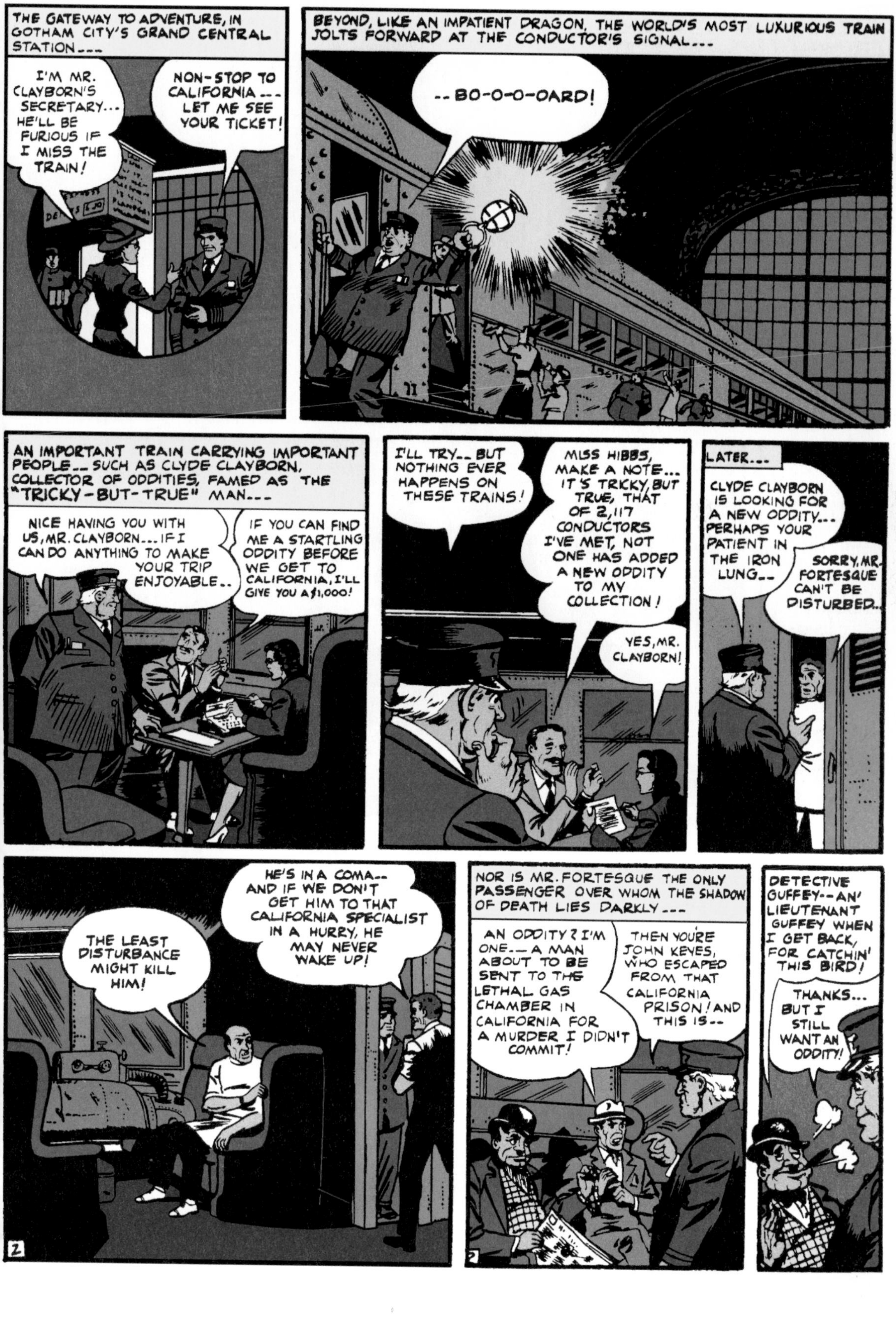
THE GATEWAY TO ADVENTURE, IN GOTHAM CITY'S GRAND CENTRAL STATION ---
I'M MR. CLAYBORN'S SECRETARY... HE'LL BE FURIOUS IF I MISS THE TRAIN!
NON-STOP TO CALIFORNIA --- LET ME SEE YOUR TICKET!
BEYOND, LIKE AN IMPATIENT DRAGON, THE WORLD'S MOST LUXURIOUS TRAIN JOLTS FORWARD AT THE CONDUCTOR'S SIGNAL ---
-- BO-O-O-OARD!
AN IMPORTANT TRAIN CARRYING IMPORTANT PEOPLE -- SUCH AS CLYDE CLAYBORN, COLLECTOR OF ODDITIES, FAMED AS THE "TRICKY-BUT-TRUE" MAN ---
NICE HAVING YOU WITH US, MR. CLAYBORN --- IF I CAN DO ANYTHING TO MAKE YOUR TRIP ENJOYABLE ..
IF YOU CAN FIND ME A STARTLING ODDITY BEFORE WE GET TO CALIFORNIA, I'LL GIVE YOU A $1,000!
I'LL TRY -- BUT NOTHING EVER HAPPENS ON THESE TRAINS!
MISS HIBBS, MAKE A NOTE... IT'S TRICKY, BUT TRUE, THAT OF 2,117 CONDUCTORS I'VE MET, NOT ONE HAS ADDED A NEW ODDITY TO MY COLLECTION!
YES, MR. CLAYBORN!
LATER ---
CLYDE CLAYBORN IS LOOKING FOR A NEW ODDITY --- PERHAPS YOUR PATIENT IN THE IRON LUNG --
SORRY, MR. FORTESQUE CAN'T BE DISTURBED..
THE LEAST DISTURBANCE MIGHT KILL HIM!
HE'S IN A COMA -- AND IF WE DON'T GET HIM TO THAT CALIFORNIA SPECIALIST IN A HURRY, HE MAY NEVER WAKE UP!
NOR IS MR. FORTESQUE THE ONLY PASSENGER OVER WHOM THE SHADOW OF DEATH LIES DARKLY ---
AN ODDITY? I'M ONE -- A MAN ABOUT TO BE SENT TO THE LETHAL GAS CHAMBER IN CALIFORNIA FOR A MURDER I DIDN'T COMMIT!
THEN YOU'RE JOHN KEYES, WHO ESCAPED FROM THAT CALIFORNIA PRISON! AND THIS IS --
DETECTIVE GUFFEY -- AN' LIEUTENANT GUFFEY WHEN I GET BACK, FOR CATCHIN' THIS BIRD!
THANKS... BUT I STILL WANT AN ODDITY!

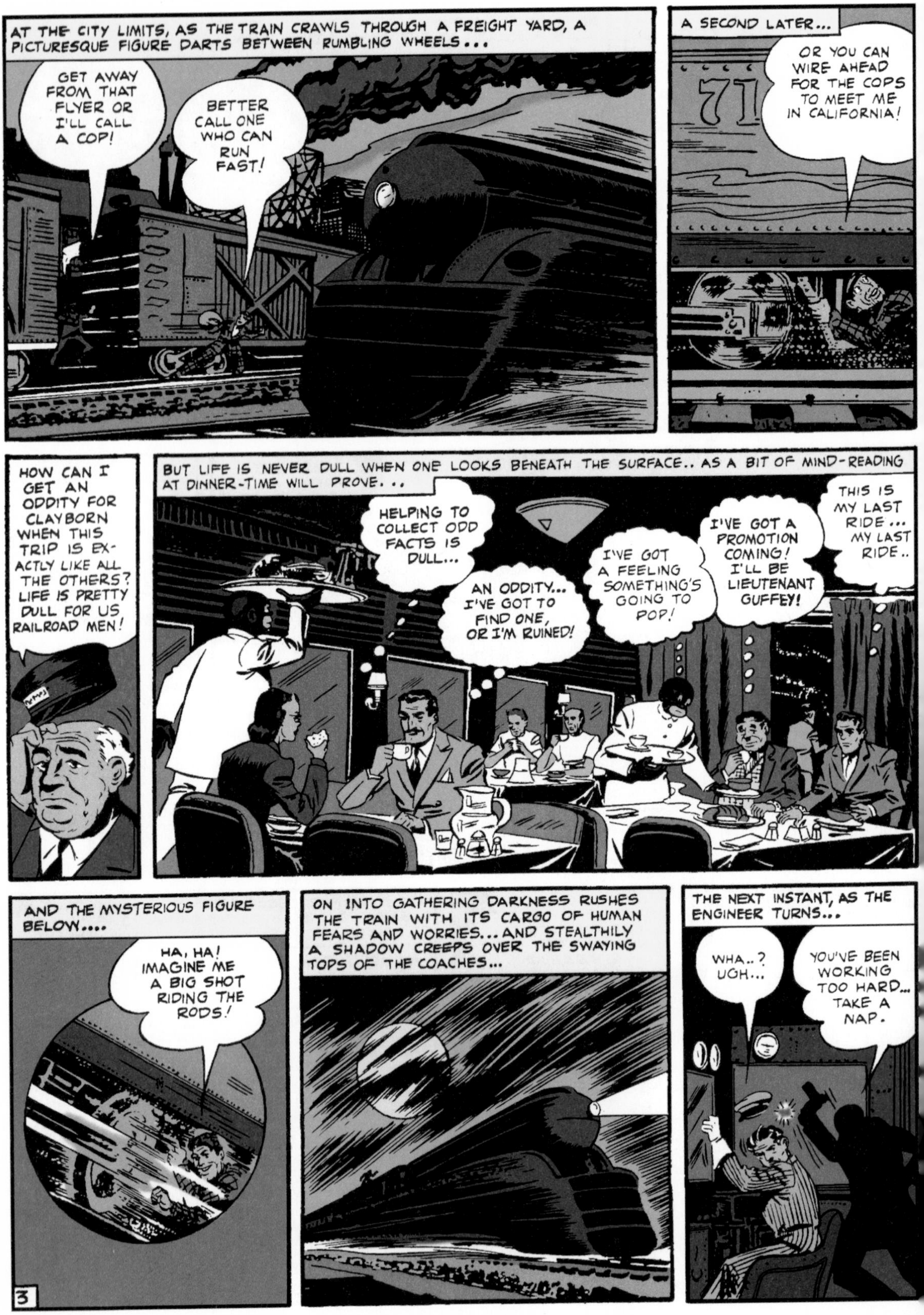
AT THE CITY LIMITS, AS THE TRAIN CRAWLS THROUGH A FREIGHT YARD, A PICTURESQUE FIGURE DARTS BETWEEN RUMBLING WHEELS...
GET AWAY FROM THAT FLYER OR I'LL CALL A COP!
BETTER CALL ONE WHO CAN RUN FAST!
A SECOND LATER...
OR YOU CAN WIRE AHEAD FOR THE COPS TO MEET ME IN CALIFORNIA!
HOW CAN I GET AN ODDITY FOR CLAYBORN WHEN THIS TRIP IS EXACTLY LIKE ALL THE OTHERS? LIFE IS PRETTY DULL FOR US RAILROAD MEN!
BUT LIFE IS NEVER DULL WHEN ONE LOOKS BENEATH THE SURFACE.. AS A BIT OF MIND-READING AT DINNER-TIME WILL PROVE...
HELPING TO COLLECT ODD FACTS IS DULL...
AN ODDITY... I'VE GOT TO FIND ONE, OR I'M RUINED!
I'VE GOT A FEELING SOMETHING'S GOING TO POP!
I'VE GOT A PROMOTION COMING! I'LL BE LIEUTENANT GUFFEY!
THIS IS MY LAST RIDE... MY LAST RIDE..
AND THE MYSTERIOUS FIGURE BELOW....
HA, HA! IMAGINE ME A BIG SHOT RIDING THE RODS!
3
ON INTO GATHERING DARKNESS RUSHES THE TRAIN WITH ITS CARGO OF HUMAN FEARS AND WORRIES... AND STEALTHILY A SHADOW CREEPS OVER THE SWAYING TOPS OF THE COACHES...
THE NEXT INSTANT, AS THE ENGINEER TURNS...
WHA..? UGH...
YOU'VE BEEN WORKING TOO HARD... TAKE A NAP.

A PURPOSEFUL HAND PULLS AT THE THROTTLE, AND THE HUGE ENGINE CANNONBALLS AHEAD IN A SURGE OF POWER...

SOMEBODY'S LIABLE TO GET KILLED.. BUT IT WON'T BE ME!

HEY! SHE'S SUPPOSED TO SLOW DOWN TO FORTY PAST HERE. BUT SHE'S DOIN' MORE LIKE EIGHTY!

HAS THE ENGINEER GONE CRAZY? SHE'LL LEAVE THE TRACKS AT THIS SPEED!

LURCHING AND SWAYING, THE RUNAWAY TRAIN STREAKS LIKE THE COMET FOR WHICH IT IS NAMED THROUGH VILLAGE AND COUNTRYSIDE...

SHE PASSED THROUGH JAMESTOWN DOING NINETY, AND THERE WASN'T ANYBODY IN SIGHT IN THE ENGINE!

SHE'LL NEVER MAKE THAT CURVE ON TRAVERS TRESTLE!

IN GOTHAM CITY, THE TELETYPE BRINGS STARTLING NEWS TO GORDON...

THE COMET RUNNING WILD? HOW COULD ANYONE STOP IT, UNLESS-- THE BATMAN!

STABBING UPWARD THROUGH THE NIGHT, A DAZZLING FINGER OF LIGHT OUTLINES A WEIRD BLACK SHAPE AGAINST THE CLOUDS...

IT LOOKS LIKE A BAT!

OF COURSE! THAT'S THE SIGNAL FOR THE BATMAN!

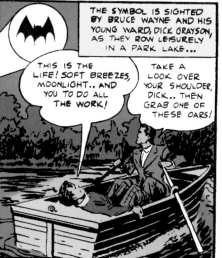

THE SYMBOL IS SIGHTED BY BRUCE WAYNE AND HIS YOUNG WARD, DICK GRAYSON, AS THEY ROW LEISURELY IN A PARK LAKE...

THIS IS THE LIFE! SOFT BREEZES, MOONLIGHT.. AND YOU TO DO ALL THE WORK!

TAKE A LOOK OVER YOUR SHOULDER, DICK.. THEN GRAB ONE OF THESE OARS!

OH, BOY... ACTION AGAIN!

WHO DO THEY THINK THEY ARE.. THE YALE CREW?

STOW THE GAB, SAILOR! LESS TALK AND MORE SPEED!

4

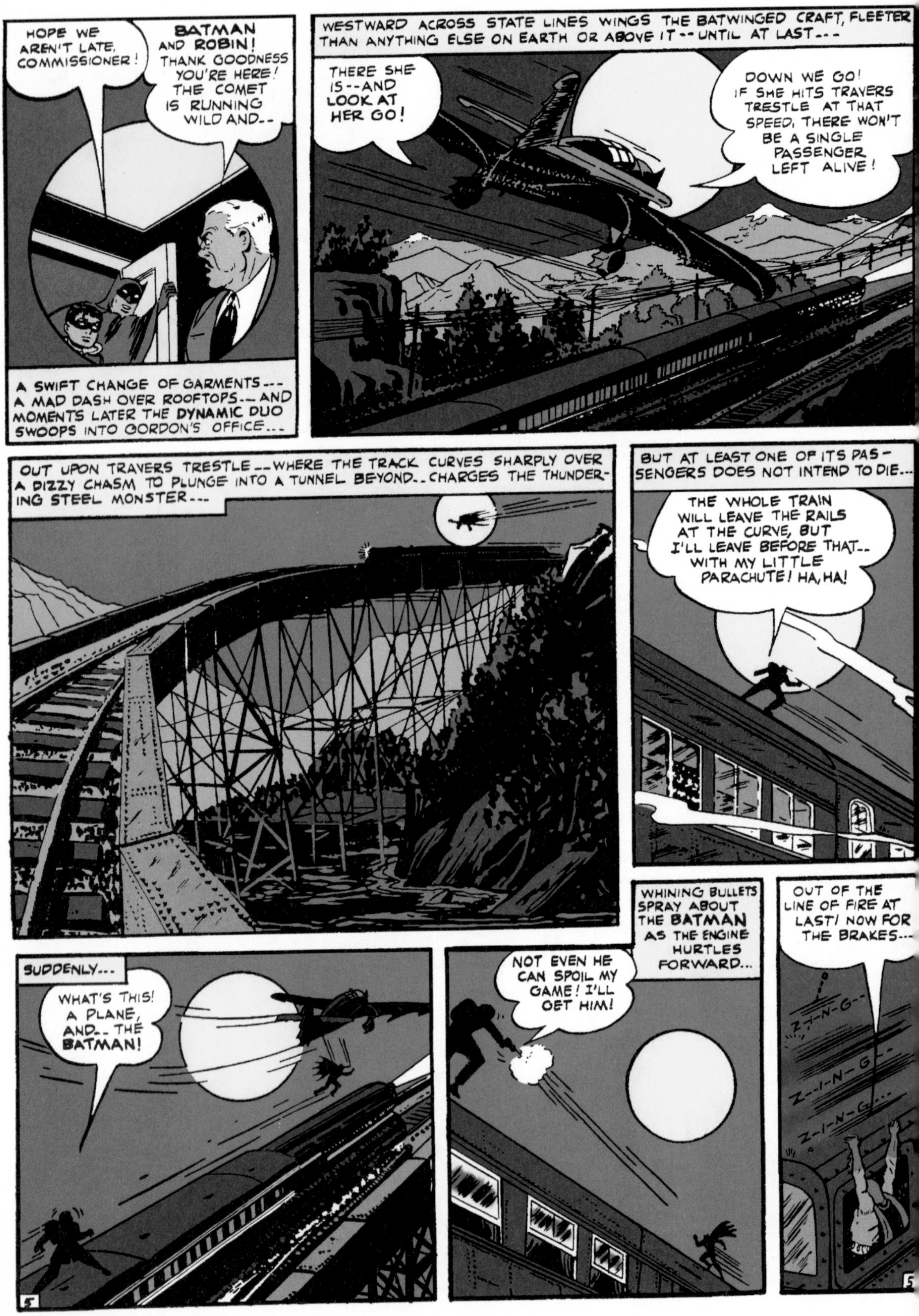
HOPE WE AREN'T LATE, COMMISSIONER!
BATMAN AND ROBIN! THANK GOODNESS YOU'RE HERE! THE COMET IS RUNNING WILD AND--
A SWIFT CHANGE OF GARMENTS--- A MAD DASH OVER ROOFTOPS--- AND MOMENTS LATER THE DYNAMIC DUO SWOOPS INTO GORDON'S OFFICE---
WESTWARD ACROSS STATE LINES WINGS THE BATWINGED CRAFT, FLEETER THAN ANYTHING ELSE ON EARTH OR ABOVE IT -- UNTIL AT LAST---
THERE SHE IS--AND LOOK AT HER GO!
DOWN WE GO! IF SHE HITS TRAVERS TRESTLE AT THAT SPEED, THERE WON'T BE A SINGLE PASSENGER LEFT ALIVE!
OUT UPON TRAVERS TRESTLE -- WHERE THE TRACK CURVES SHARPLY OVER A DIZZY CHASM TO PLUNGE INTO A TUNNEL BEYOND -- CHARGES THE THUNDERING STEEL MONSTER---
BUT AT LEAST ONE OF ITS PASSENGERS DOES NOT INTEND TO DIE---
THE WHOLE TRAIN WILL LEAVE THE RAILS AT THE CURVE, BUT I'LL LEAVE BEFORE THAT-- WITH MY LITTLE PARACHUTE! HA, HA!
SUDDENLY---
WHAT'S THIS! A PLANE, AND-- THE BATMAN!
WHINING BULLETS SPRAY ABOUT THE BATMAN AS THE ENGINE HURTLES FORWARD...
NOT EVEN HE CAN SPOIL MY GAME! I'LL GET HIM!
OUT OF THE LINE OF FIRE AT LAST! NOW FOR THE BRAKES---
Z-I-N-G--
Z-I-N-G--
Z-I-N-G--
Z-I-N-G--

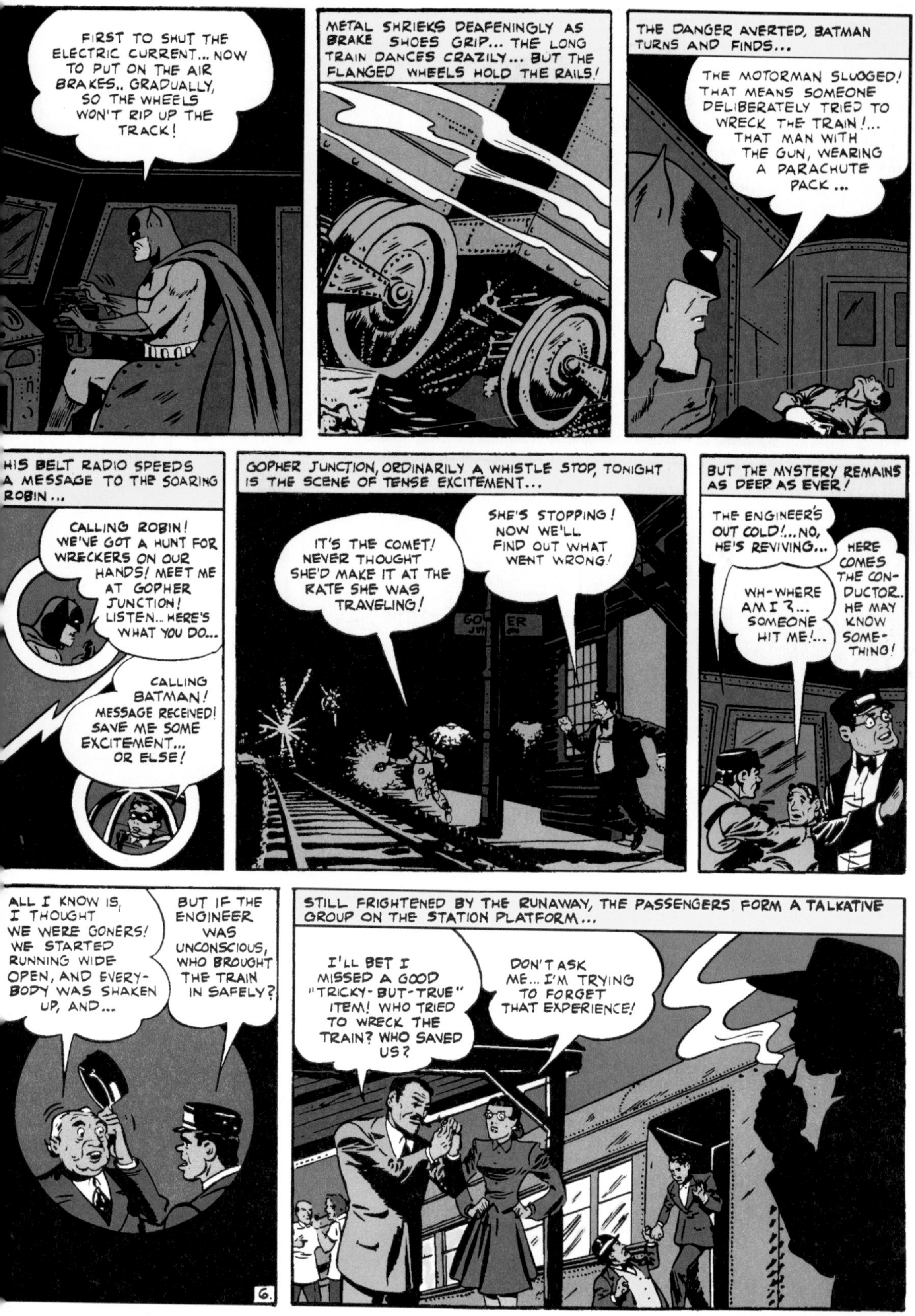

FIRST TO SHUT THE ELECTRIC CURRENT... NOW TO PUT ON THE AIR BRAKES.. GRADUALLY, SO THE WHEELS WON'T RIP UP THE TRACK!
METAL SHRIEKS DEAFENINGLY AS BRAKE SHOES GRIP... THE LONG TRAIN DANCES CRAZILY... BUT THE FLANGED WHEELS HOLD THE RAILS!
THE DANGER AVERTED, BATMAN TURNS AND FINDS...
THE MOTORMAN SLUGGED! THAT MEANS SOMEONE DELIBERATELY TRIED TO WRECK THE TRAIN!... THAT MAN WITH THE GUN, WEARING A PARACHUTE PACK ...
HIS BELT RADIO SPEEDS A MESSAGE TO THE SOARING ROBIN ...
CALLING ROBIN! WE'VE GOT A HUNT FOR WRECKERS ON OUR HANDS! MEET ME AT GOPHER JUNCTION! LISTEN... HERE'S WHAT YOU DO...
CALLING BATMAN! MESSAGE RECEIVED! SAVE ME SOME EXCITEMENT... OR ELSE!
GOPHER JUNCTION, ORDINARILY A WHISTLE STOP, TONIGHT IS THE SCENE OF TENSE EXCITEMENT...
IT'S THE COMET! NEVER THOUGHT SHE'D MAKE IT AT THE RATE SHE WAS TRAVELING!
SHE'S STOPPING! NOW WE'LL FIND OUT WHAT WENT WRONG!
BUT THE MYSTERY REMAINS AS DEEP AS EVER!
THE ENGINEER'S OUT COLD!... NO, HE'S REVIVING...
WH-WHERE AM I?... SOMEONE HIT ME!...
HERE COMES THE CONDUCTOR.. HE MAY KNOW SOMETHING!
ALL I KNOW IS, I THOUGHT WE WERE GONERS! WE STARTED RUNNING WIDE OPEN, AND EVERYBODY WAS SHAKEN UP, AND...
BUT IF THE ENGINEER WAS UNCONSCIOUS, WHO BROUGHT THE TRAIN IN SAFELY?
6.
STILL FRIGHTENED BY THE RUNAWAY, THE PASSENGERS FORM A TALKATIVE GROUP ON THE STATION PLATFORM...
I'LL BET I MISSED A GOOD "TRICKY-BUT-TRUE" ITEM! WHO TRIED TO WRECK THE TRAIN? WHO SAVED US?
DON'T ASK ME... I'M TRYING TO FORGET THAT EXPERIENCE!

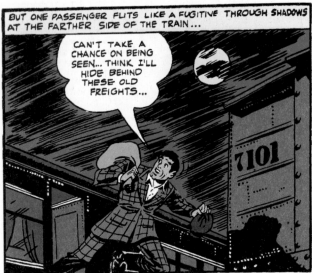

BUT ONE PASSENGER FLITS LIKE A FUGITIVE THROUGH SHADOWS AT THE FARTHER SIDE OF THE TRAIN...

CAN'T TAKE A CHANCE ON BEING SEEN... THINK I'LL HIDE BEHIND THESE OLD FREIGHTS...

7101

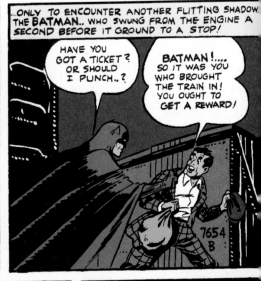

...ONLY TO ENCOUNTER ANOTHER FLITTING SHADOW... THE BATMAN.. WHO SWUNG FROM THE ENGINE A SECOND BEFORE IT GROUND TO A STOP!

HAVE YOU GOT A TICKET? OR SHOULD I PUNCH..?

BATMAN!.... SO IT WAS YOU WHO BROUGHT THE TRAIN IN! YOU OUGHT TO GET A REWARD!

7654 B

I DON'T TAKE REWARDS... BUT IF I DID, I MIGHT COLLECT ONE FOR TURNING YOU OVER TO THE AUTHORITIES!

NOT GUILTY, BATMAN! I WAS HANGING ONTO THE RODS, SCARED TO DEATH, WHEN WE HIT THE TRESTLE!

I HOPE HE BELIEVES ME!

WHEN A FELLOW'S DOWN AND OUT, I NEVER KICK HIM! I'LL TAKE YOUR WORD.. TILL I DO A LITTLE INVESTIGATING!

THEN WHY ARE YOU TYING ME UP?

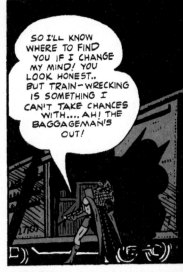

SO I'LL KNOW WHERE TO FIND YOU IF I CHANGE MY MIND! YOU LOOK HONEST.. BUT TRAIN-WRECKING IS SOMETHING I CAN'T TAKE CHANCES WITH.... AH! THE BAGGAGEMAN'S OUT!

SHUCKING HIS FIGHTING GARB, THE BATMAN DISAPPEARS..AND A MOMENT LATER BRUCE WAYNE STANDS AT THE TICKET WINDOW AT THE STATION...

LUCKY FOR ME THIS TRAIN STOPPED HERE... I'LL TAKE A TICKET THROUGH TO THE END OF THE RUN!

HERE Y'ARE!

MEANWHILE, AT A MAGAZINE STAND, A YOUNG MAN SEEMS TO BE STOCKING UP FOR A LONG LITERARY SESSION...

I'LL TAKE THESE COMIC BOOKS!

GOLLY, KID.. AREN'T YOU GOIN' TO DO NOTHIN' BUT READ FROM HERE ON?

7

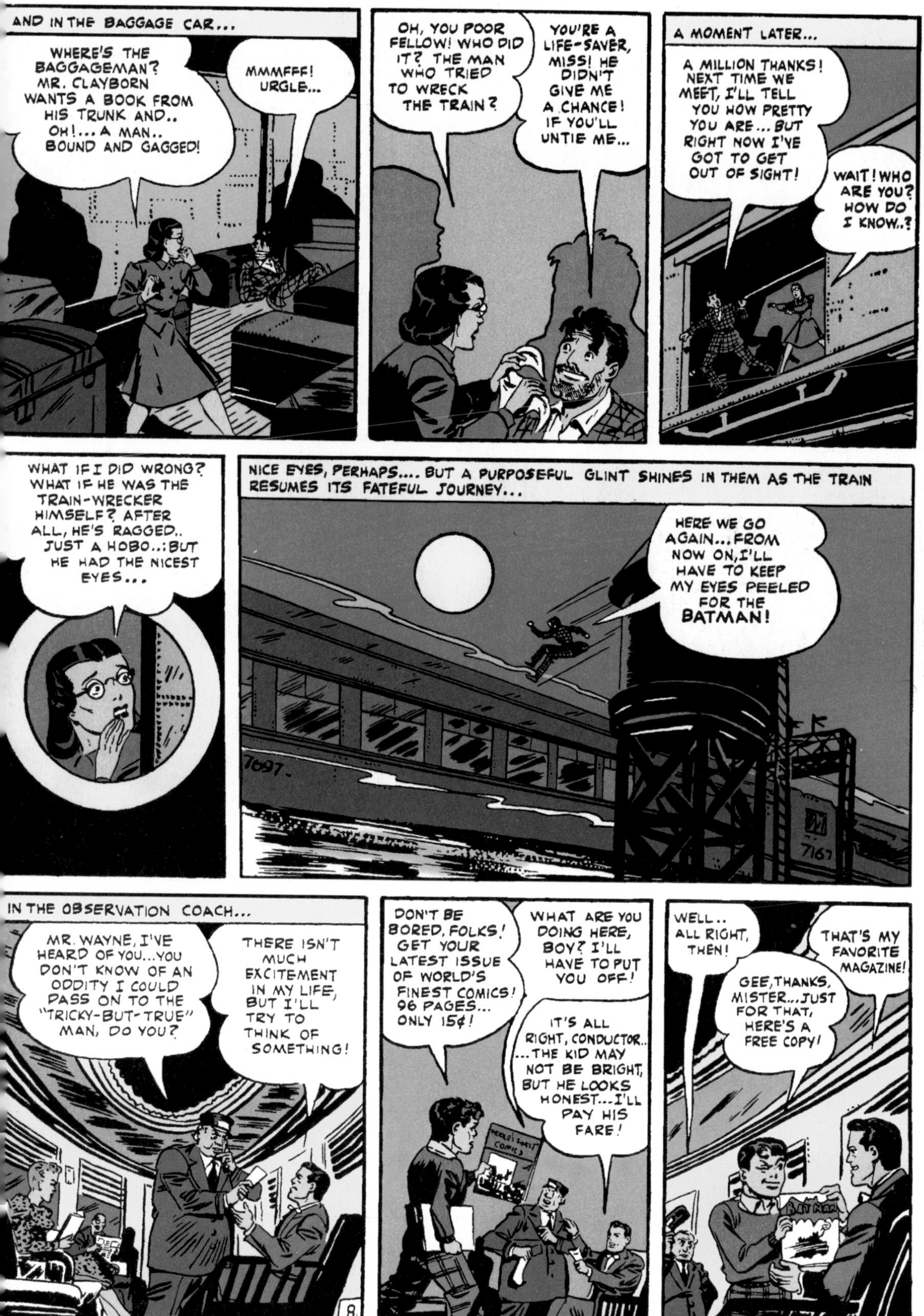
AND IN THE BAGGAGE CAR...
WHERE'S THE BAGGAGEMAN? MR. CLAYBORN WANTS A BOOK FROM HIS TRUNK AND.. OH!... A MAN.. BOUND AND GAGGED!
MMMFFF! URGLE...
OH, YOU POOR FELLOW! WHO DID IT? THE MAN WHO TRIED TO WRECK THE TRAIN?
YOU'RE A LIFE-SAVER, MISS! HE DIDN'T GIVE ME A CHANCE! IF YOU'LL UNTIE ME...
A MOMENT LATER...
A MILLION THANKS! NEXT TIME WE MEET, I'LL TELL YOU HOW PRETTY YOU ARE... BUT RIGHT NOW I'VE GOT TO GET OUT OF SIGHT!
WAIT! WHO ARE YOU? HOW DO I KNOW..?
WHAT IF I DID WRONG? WHAT IF HE WAS THE TRAIN-WRECKER HIMSELF? AFTER ALL, HE'S RAGGED.. JUST A HOBO..: BUT HE HAD THE NICEST EYES...
NICE EYES, PERHAPS.... BUT A PURPOSEFUL GLINT SHINES IN THEM AS THE TRAIN RESUMES ITS FATEFUL JOURNEY...
HERE WE GO AGAIN... FROM NOW ON, I'LL HAVE TO KEEP MY EYES PEELED FOR THE BATMAN!
7697
7167
IN THE OBSERVATION COACH...
MR. WAYNE, I'VE HEARD OF YOU... YOU DON'T KNOW OF AN ODDITY I COULD PASS ON TO THE "TRICKY-BUT-TRUE" MAN, DO YOU?
THERE ISN'T MUCH EXCITEMENT IN MY LIFE, BUT I'LL TRY TO THINK OF SOMETHING!
8
DON'T BE BORED, FOLKS! GET YOUR LATEST ISSUE OF WORLD'S FINEST COMICS! 96 PAGES... ONLY 15¢!
WHAT ARE YOU DOING HERE, BOY? I'LL HAVE TO PUT YOU OFF!
IT'S ALL RIGHT, CONDUCTOR.. ...THE KID MAY NOT BE BRIGHT, BUT HE LOOKS HONEST... I'LL PAY HIS FARE!
WELL.. ALL RIGHT, THEN!
THAT'S MY FAVORITE MAGAZINE!
GEE, THANKS, MISTER... JUST FOR THAT, HERE'S A FREE COPY!

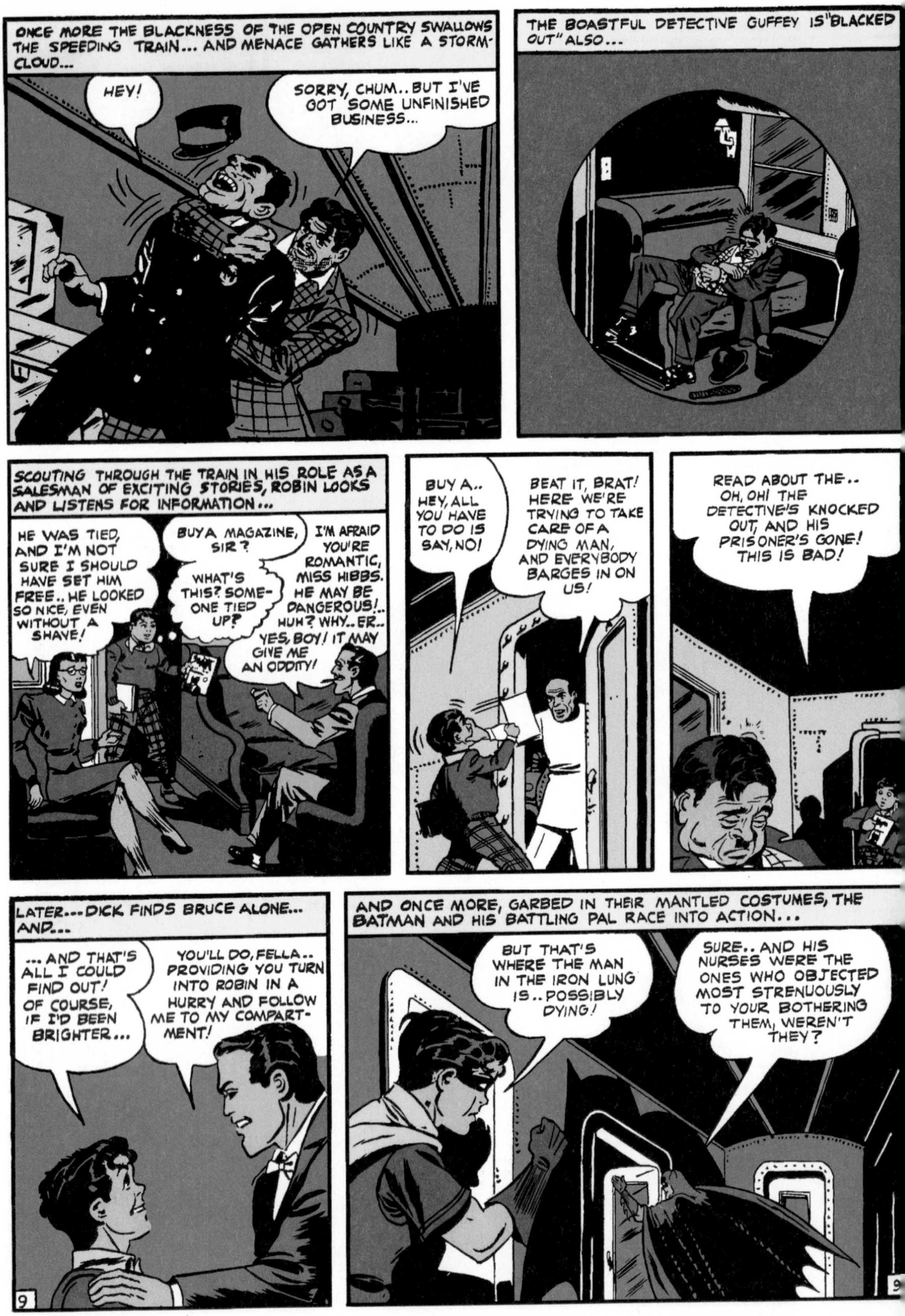
ONCE MORE THE BLACKNESS OF THE OPEN COUNTRY SWALLOWS THE SPEEDING TRAIN... AND MENACE GATHERS LIKE A STORM-CLOUD...
HEY!
SORRY, CHUM.. BUT I'VE GOT SOME UNFINISHED BUSINESS...
THE BOASTFUL DETECTIVE GUFFEY IS "BLACKED OUT" ALSO...
SCOUTING THROUGH THE TRAIN IN HIS ROLE AS A SALESMAN OF EXCITING STORIES, ROBIN LOOKS AND LISTENS FOR INFORMATION...
HE WAS TIED, AND I'M NOT SURE I SHOULD HAVE SET HIM FREE.. HE LOOKED SO NICE, EVEN WITHOUT A SHAVE!
BUY A MAGAZINE, SIR?
WHAT'S THIS? SOMEONE TIED UP?
I'M AFRAID YOU'RE ROMANTIC, MISS HIBBS. HE MAY BE DANGEROUS!.. HUH? WHY..ER.. YES, BOY! IT MAY GIVE ME AN ODDITY!
BUY A.. HEY, ALL YOU HAVE TO DO IS SAY, NO!
BEAT IT, BRAT! HERE WE'RE TRYING TO TAKE CARE OF A DYING MAN, AND EVERYBODY BARGES IN ON US!
READ ABOUT THE.. OH, OH! THE DETECTIVE'S KNOCKED OUT, AND HIS PRISONER'S GONE! THIS IS BAD!
LATER... DICK FINDS BRUCE ALONE... AND...
... AND THAT'S ALL I COULD FIND OUT! OF COURSE, IF I'D BEEN BRIGHTER...
YOU'LL DO, FELLA.. PROVIDING YOU TURN INTO ROBIN IN A HURRY AND FOLLOW ME TO MY COMPARTMENT!
9
AND ONCE MORE, GARBED IN THEIR MANTLED COSTUMES, THE BATMAN AND HIS BATTLING PAL RACE INTO ACTION...
BUT THAT'S WHERE THE MAN IN THE IRON LUNG IS.. POSSIBLY DYING!
SURE.. AND HIS NURSES WERE THE ONES WHO OBJECTED MOST STRENUOUSLY TO YOUR BOTHERING THEM, WEREN'T THEY?

DEATH HAS INDEED COME CLOSE TO THE MAN IN THE IRON LUNG...FOR THE NEXT INSTANT...

NOT OXYGEN.. POISON GAS! IN ANOTHER MINUTE, HE'D HAVE BEEN DEAD!

THE NURSES.. THEY'VE GONE! AND THE WINDOWS ARE OPEN!

THAT FELLOW WILL LIVE, AND THE NURSES COULDN'T HAVE JUMPED OFF AT THIS SPEED! I'M GOING UP ON TOP! YOU GO FORWARD AND SEE WHAT YOU CAN DO!

RIGHT!

CLAMBERING PRECARIOUSLY OVER THE SWAYING TOP OF THE COACH, THE BATMAN SIGHTS.. AND IS SIGHTED BY.. HIS QUARRY!

THE BATMAN AGAIN! I MISSED HIM BEFORE.. BUT THIS TIME I WON'T!

BETTER SHOOT FAST, THEN, RAT!

A PANTHER-SWIFT LUNGE OF A TRAINED, POWERFUL FRAME, AND...

HANG ON WHEN YOU'RE HIT, OR THE JAIL AT THE END OF THE LINE WILL BE OUT A CUSTOMER!

SHUT YOUR EYES, BATMAN...

I'D RATHER FALL OFF THAN GET HIT AGAIN!

BUT NOT EVEN THE BATMAN'S LIGHTNING SPEED CAN OUTMATCH BLASTING LEAD.. AND THE CRIMINAL'S BULLET STRIKES WITH PILE-DRIVER FORCE!

...I GOT A SURPRISE FOR YOU!

CRACK!

OOHHH-H-H... HE'S GOT ME...

FAR TOWARD THE FRONT OF THE TRAIN, ROBIN HEARS THE BARK OF THE SHOT...

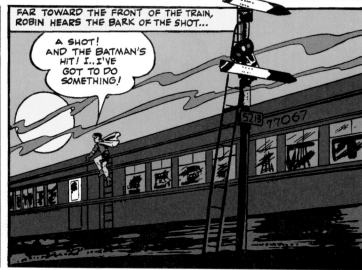

A SHOT! AND THE BATMAN'S HIT! I.. I'VE GOT TO DO SOMETHING!

10

TURNING SHARPLY AND SNATCHING THE EXTENDED ARM OF A SEMAPHORE SIGNAL, THE BOY LETS THE TRAIN THUNDER BENEATH HIM...

PLEASE DON'T LET ME BE TOO LATE....

TOUGH, EH? WELL, A SLUG IN THE HEAD WILL TAKE CARE OF THAT!

LOW BRIDGE.. BUT NOT LOWER THAN YOU!

Y-111!

ROBIN! SAVED... MY... LIFE...

SUDDENLY, A SICKENING LURCH OF THE TRAIN WARNS OF FRESH DANGER...

WHA..? THE TRAIN'S SWINGING TO THE EAST-BOUND TRACK!

DON'T WORRY ABOUT THE TRAIN... WATCH YOURSELF! YOU'RE WOUNDED!

THAT SEMAPHORE MUST HAVE OPERATED A SWITCH AHEAD OF THE ENGINE... AND AN EASTBOUND TRAIN IS COMING TOWARD US!

WON'T THE ENGINEER KNOW ENOUGH TO STOP?

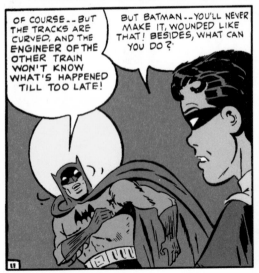

OF COURSE--BUT THE TRACKS ARE CURVED, AND THE ENGINEER OF THE OTHER TRAIN WON'T KNOW WHAT'S HAPPENED TILL TOO LATE!

BUT BATMAN--YOU'LL NEVER MAKE IT, WOUNDED LIKE THAT! BESIDES, WHAT CAN YOU DO?

WITHOUT A WAY OF SIGNALING THE ON-RUSHING TRAIN, HOW CAN BATMAN PREVENT A HEAD-ON CRASH? YET DOGGEDLY HE STRUGGLES FORWARD...

GOT TO MAKE IT... GOT TO...

THE ENGINEER, HELPLESSLY AWARE OF THE PERIL, KNOWS NOTHING OF THE WOUNDED MAN FIGHTING A VALIANT BATTLE OVERHEAD...

GOT TO.. KEEP GOING...

I'VE CUT THE ELECTRIC AND SET THE BRAKES... WHAT ELSE CAN I DO?

NOW HE LOWERS HIMSELF TO THE COWCATCHER!... BUT WHAT DOES THAT MEAN, EXCEPT THAT BATMAN WILL BE THE FIRST TO DIE WHEN STEEL MEETS STEEL IN THUNDERING CHAOS?...

AT LAST... IF ONLY I'M IN TIME...

ABOARD THE EASTBOUND EXPRESS, THE ENGINEER BLINKS AT A STRANGE SIGHT...

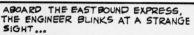

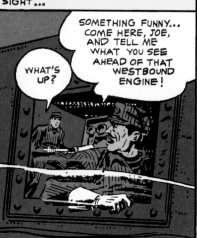

SOMETHING FUNNY... COME HERE, JOE, AND TELL ME WHAT YOU SEE AHEAD OF THAT WESTBOUND ENGINE!

WHAT'S UP?

WHY, IT'S A BAT! WHAT'S A BAT DOING OUT HERE ON THE PRAIRIE?

MAKES ME THINK OF.. LET'S SEE.. THE BATMAN, WHO SHOWS UP WHEN THERE'S TROUBLE... TROUBLE??? QUICK, JOE—THE BRAKES'!!

A BAT!....BUT BENEATH THE WEIRD SYMBOL, A MAN'S GRIM DETERMINATION KEEPS IT FLYING!

THE BAT EMBLEM... RIPPED FROM THE FRONT OF MY UNIFORM ... MAYBE IT WILL WARN THEM!

TWO THUNDERING DRAGONS SHUDDER AND SCREECH UNDER THE SQUEEZE OF AIR BRAKES... SHUDDER AND SLACKEN THEIR TERRIFIC SPEED...

BATMAN! YOU -- YOU SAVED US!

EXCUSE ME.. TIRED—GOT TO SIT DOWN SOMEWHERE...

ANOTHER SECOND WOULD HAVE SEEN THE WORST WRECK IN TEN YEARS!

12

"DESTINATION UNKNOWN," WE HAVE CALLED THIS STORY OF A GROUP OF VERY HUMAN BEINGS, ALL IN SEARCH OF SOMETHING.....AND NOW, AS REPORTERS FLOCK AROUND, LET US SEE WHETHER THEIR QUESTS WERE SUCCESSFUL...

JOHN KEYES, NO LONGER A MURDER SUSPECT, IS INTERVIEWED...

I TOLD THEM I WAS INNOCENT! I ESCAPED, WENT EAST--AND FOUND CERTAIN EVIDENCE WHICH I HOPED WOULD WIN ME A NEW TRIAL...

TODAY THE WHOLE WORLD WILL KNOW YOU WERE INNOCENT!

DETECTIVE GUFFEY, THE AMBITIOUS SLEUTH...

I CAUGHT KEYES, AND THOUGHT I'D GET PROMOTED FOR THAT--BUT IT LOOKED BAD WHEN THOSE CROOKS SLUGGED ME, TOOK MY PRISONER! BUT ALL'S WELL NOW, SINCE I NABBED THEM!

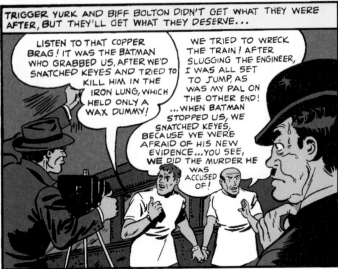

TRIGGER YURK AND BIFF BOLTON DIDN'T GET WHAT THEY WERE AFTER, BUT THEY'LL GET WHAT THEY DESERVE...

LISTEN TO THAT COPPER BRAG! IT WAS THE BATMAN WHO GRABBED US, AFTER WE'D SNATCHED KEYES AND TRIED TO KILL HIM IN THE IRON LUNG, WHICH HELD ONLY A WAX DUMMY!

WE TRIED TO WRECK THE TRAIN! AFTER SLUGGING THE ENGINEER, I WAS ALL SET TO JUMP, AS WAS MY PAL ON THE OTHER END! ...WHEN BATMAN STOPPED US, WE SNATCHED KEYES, BECAUSE WE WERE AFRAID OF HIS NEW EVIDENCE...YOU SEE, WE DID THE MURDER HE WAS ACCUSED OF!

AND LOOK WHAT WE HAVE HERE!

MISS HIBBS, IS IT TRUE THAT YOU'RE GOING TO MARRY THIS --ER-- HOBO?

HOBO? HE'S KEN THORNE, PRESIDENT OF THIS RAILROAD! HE GOT SICK OF HIS JOB AND DECIDED TO LOOK FOR ADVENTURE-- JUST AS I DID-- AND WE MET IN THE BAGGAGE COACH!

THE "TRICKY-BUT-TRUE" MAN'S WORRIES ARE OVER...

I'VE LOST A SECRETARY-- BUT LOOK AT THE ODDITIES I'VE GOT! MILLIONAIRE TURNS HOBO, WINS WORKING GIRL! BATMAN SAVES TRAIN SINGLE-HANDED! CROOKS PLAN TO USE LIFE-SAVING IRON LUNG AS INSTRUMENT OF MURDER!

YOUR NEW RADIO PROGRAM SHOULD BE A WOW!

CLICK!

BOB KANE

AS FOR THE BORED CONDUCTOR...

HO-HUM! WHAT A LIFE! FORTY YEARS OF CARTING FOLKS BACK AND FORTH-- AND NOTHING EVER HAPPENS!

The End—

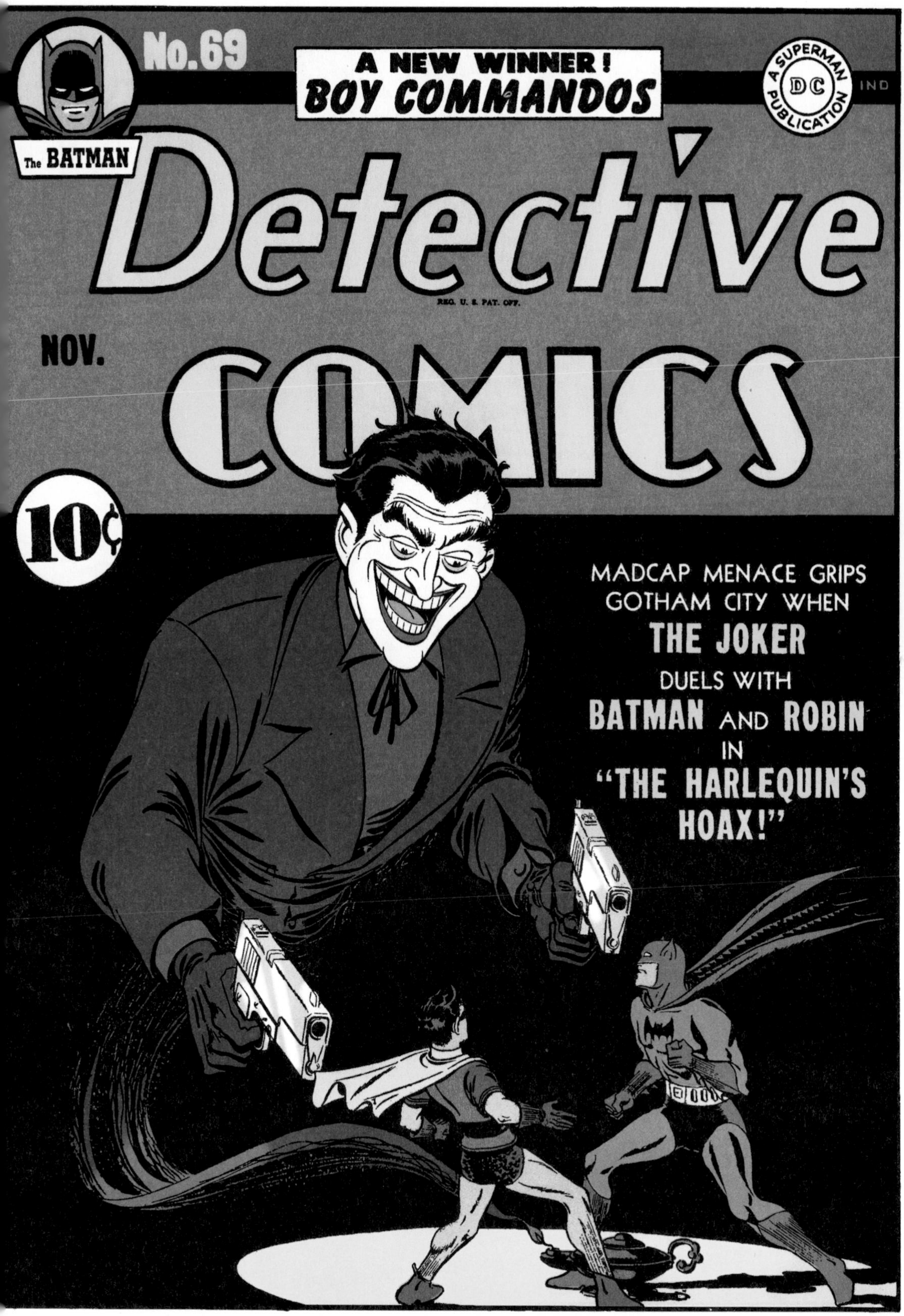
No. 69
A NEW WINNER!
BOY COMMANDOS
A SUPERMAN DC PUBLICATION
IND
The BATMAN
Detective
REG. U. S. PAT. OFF.
NOV.
COMICS
10¢
MADCAP MENACE GRIPS
GOTHAM CITY WHEN
THE JOKER
DUELS WITH
BATMAN AND ROBIN
IN
"THE HARLEQUIN'S
HOAX!"

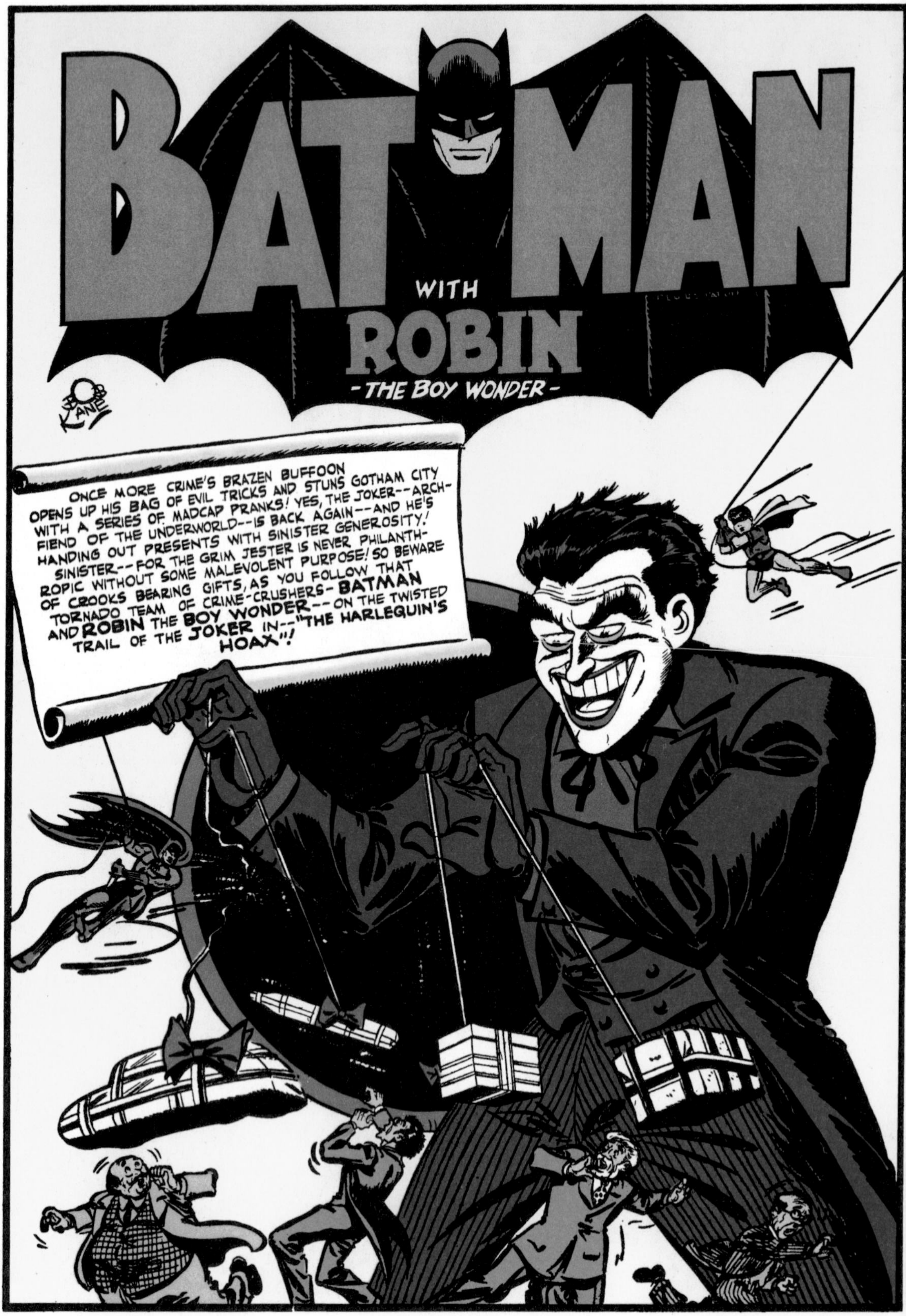
BATMAN
WITH
ROBIN
-THE BOY WONDER-
BOB KANE
ONCE MORE CRIME'S BRAZEN BUFFOON OPENS UP HIS BAG OF EVIL TRICKS AND STUNS GOTHAM CITY WITH A SERIES OF MADCAP PRANKS! YES, THE JOKER--ARCH-FIEND OF THE UNDERWORLD--IS BACK AGAIN--AND HE'S HANDING OUT PRESENTS WITH SINISTER GENEROSITY! SINISTER--FOR THE GRIM JESTER IS NEVER PHILANTHROPIC WITHOUT SOME MALEVOLENT PURPOSE! SO BEWARE OF CROOKS BEARING GIFTS, AS YOU FOLLOW THAT TORNADO TEAM OF CRIME-CRUSHERS- BATMAN AND ROBIN THE BOY WONDER--ON THE TWISTED TRAIL OF THE JOKER IN--"THE HARLEQUIN'S HOAX"!

IN THE HEART OF PEACEFUL GOTHAM CITY, A MELANCHOLY MAN WITH LAUGHING FACE PLOTS AN EVIL GAME!

HA! HA! THIS SHALL BE MY GREATEST COUP!

THAT SAME MORNING, AT THE HOME OF CHARLES SAUNDERS...

PACKAGE FOR YOU, MR. SAUNDERS!

HMM-- WONDER WHAT IT CAN BE? BRING IT IN, WILL YOU, BILL?

A RADIO WITHOUT A LOUDSPEAKER! WHAT KIND OF GAG IS THAT?

THERE'S A CARD ENCLOSED!

A gift from the Joker! Quite valuable to you, eh, Saunders?

VALUABLE? THIS IS ANOTHER OF THE JOKER'S CRAZY TRICKS!

I--I DON'T THINK SO! YOU SEE.... THIS IS VALUABLE TO ME!

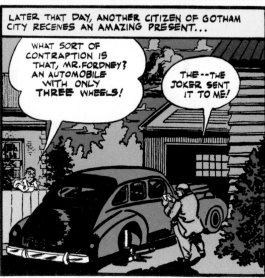

LATER THAT DAY, ANOTHER CITIZEN OF GOTHAM CITY RECEIVES AN AMAZING PRESENT...

WHAT SORT OF CONTRAPTION IS THAT, MR. FORDNEY? AN AUTOMOBILE WITH ONLY THREE WHEELS!

THE--THE JOKER SENT IT TO ME!

IN ANOTHER PART OF THE CITY..

A TELESCOPE WITHOUT A LENS! WONDER WHAT CRAZY FOOL SENT IT TO ME?

TO RICHARD MORSE-- WITH THE JOKER'S COMPLIMENTS!

OH--OH --THE JOKER

ELSEWHERE....

JIM BROWN, WHO WOULD GIVE YOU SUCH A FOOLISH THING AS A CLOCK WITHOUT AN HOUR HAND?

THE JOKER! AND-- AND I'M AFRAID I DON'T LIKE THIS GENEROSITY!

THE JOKER'S OFF AGAIN! CAN YOU MATCH WITS WITH THIS MASTER OF CRIME? CAN YOU GUESS, BEFORE THE BATMAN DOES, THE MOTIVE FOR THESE QUEER GIFTS? WHAT'S THE JOKER'S GAME THIS TIME?

MEANWHILE OTHER PERSONS PLAY A GAME -- A GAME OF CHANCE! BRUCE WAYNE AND LINDA PAGE MAKE MERRY AT THE FUN PARK!

MISSED AGAIN, BUD! HOW ABOUT TRYIN' SOME MORE?

OH, BRUCE, COME ON! I WANT TO GO ON THE PARACHUTE JUMP!

MINUTES LATER... BRUCE AND LINDA ARE BEING PULLED UP 200 FEET INTO THE SKY!

SAY, I HADN'T REALIZED THESE THINGS GO UP SO HIGH!

SISSY! DON'T TELL ME YOU'RE SCARED, BRUCE?

THE 'CHUTE REACHES THE TOP! CONTACT -- AND THE DUO BEGINS A THRILLING PLUNGE THRU SPACE!

WHEEEE!

BETTER HOLD TIGHT, LINDA!

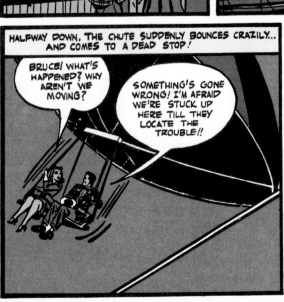

HALFWAY DOWN, THE CHUTE SUDDENLY BOUNCES CRAZILY... AND COMES TO A DEAD STOP!

BRUCE! WHAT'S HAPPENED? WHY AREN'T WE MOVING?

SOMETHING'S GONE WRONG! I'M AFRAID WE'RE STUCK UP HERE TILL THEY LOCATE THE TROUBLE!!

THE NEWS SPREADS LIKE WILDFIRE! SHOUTING, EXCITED HUMANS PUSH FORWARD, EYES TURNED UP TO THE HELPLESS COUPLE!

THAT'S THEM! THEY'RE HANGING 100 FEET UP!

THAT'S LINDA PAGE AND PLAYBOY BRUCE WAYNE! WOW! I'VE GOT A STORY!

ONE INSANE HOUR LATER! SANDWICHES AND A MIKE ARE HAULED UP TO THE PAIR ...

IF ANY OF MY FAMILY ARE LISTENING IN, I DON'T WANT THEM TO WORRY IF I'M LATE FOR SUPPER!

AND IF MY WARD, DICK, IS LISTENING TO MY VOICE, DON'T WORRY IF I'M LATE FOR SUPPER!

ANOTHER HOUR PASSES... SLOWLY! THEN A MILE-LONG FLOOD OF LIGHT BLAZONS A WEIRD SYMBOL AGAINST THE SKY!

LOOK! A BAT!

THAT'S FROM POLICE HEADQUARTERS! THEY'RE CALLING M..THE BATMAN!

JUST THINK, BRUCE! SOMEWHERE THE BATMAN IS GOING INTO ACTION NOW!

LIKE FUN! HE'S STUCK HERE IN A PARACHUTE!

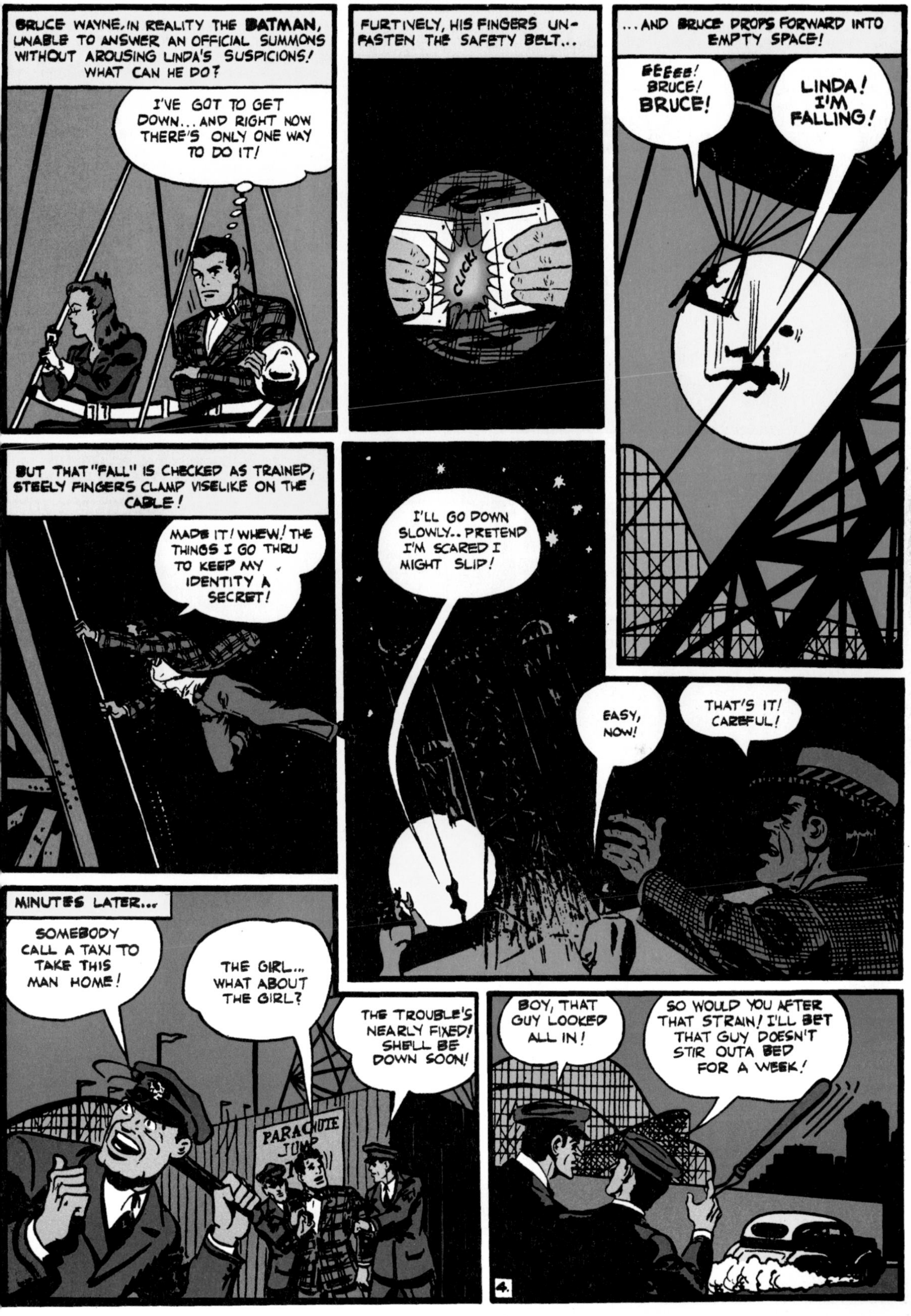

BRUCE WAYNE, IN REALITY THE BATMAN, UNABLE TO ANSWER AN OFFICIAL SUMMONS WITHOUT AROUSING LINDA'S SUSPICIONS! WHAT CAN HE DO?
I'VE GOT TO GET DOWN... AND RIGHT NOW THERE'S ONLY ONE WAY TO DO IT!
FURTIVELY, HIS FINGERS UNFASTEN THE SAFETY BELT...
CLICK!
...AND BRUCE DROPS FORWARD INTO EMPTY SPACE!
EEEee! BRUCE! BRUCE!
LINDA! I'M FALLING!
BUT THAT "FALL" IS CHECKED AS TRAINED, STEELY FINGERS CLAMP VISELIKE ON THE CABLE!
MADE IT! WHEW! THE THINGS I GO THRU TO KEEP MY IDENTITY A SECRET!
I'LL GO DOWN SLOWLY.. PRETEND I'M SCARED I MIGHT SLIP!
EASY, NOW!
THAT'S IT! CAREFUL!
MINUTES LATER...
SOMEBODY CALL A TAXI TO TAKE THIS MAN HOME!
THE GIRL... WHAT ABOUT THE GIRL?
THE TROUBLE'S NEARLY FIXED! SHE'LL BE DOWN SOON!
PARACHUTE JUMP
BOY, THAT GUY LOOKED ALL IN!
SO WOULD YOU AFTER THAT STRAIN! I'LL BET THAT GUY DOESN'T STIR OUTA BED FOR A WEEK!
4.

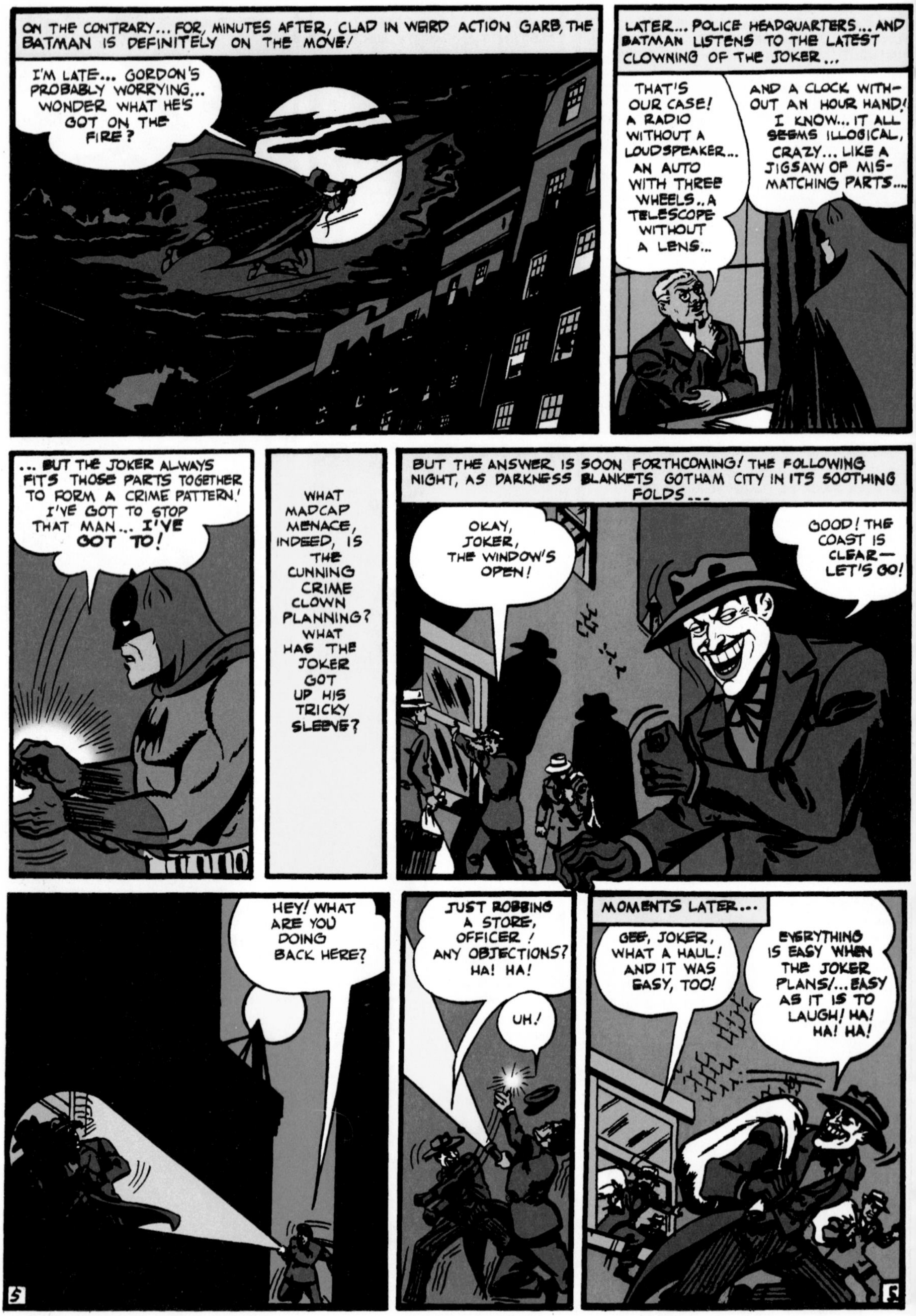
ON THE CONTRARY... FOR, MINUTES AFTER, CLAD IN WEIRD ACTION GARB, THE BATMAN IS DEFINITELY ON THE MOVE!
I'M LATE... GORDON'S PROBABLY WORRYING... WONDER WHAT HE'S GOT ON THE FIRE?
LATER... POLICE HEADQUARTERS... AND BATMAN LISTENS TO THE LATEST CLOWNING OF THE JOKER...
THAT'S OUR CASE! A RADIO WITHOUT A LOUDSPEAKER... AN AUTO WITH THREE WHEELS.. A TELESCOPE WITHOUT A LENS...
AND A CLOCK WITHOUT AN HOUR HAND! I KNOW... IT ALL SEEMS ILLOGICAL, CRAZY... LIKE A JIGSAW OF MISMATCHING PARTS...
... BUT THE JOKER ALWAYS FITS THOSE PARTS TOGETHER TO FORM A CRIME PATTERN! I'VE GOT TO STOP THAT MAN... I'VE GOT TO!
WHAT MADCAP MENACE, INDEED, IS THE CUNNING CRIME CLOWN PLANNING? WHAT HAS THE JOKER GOT UP HIS TRICKY SLEEVE?
BUT THE ANSWER IS SOON FORTHCOMING! THE FOLLOWING NIGHT, AS DARKNESS BLANKETS GOTHAM CITY IN ITS SOOTHING FOLDS...
OKAY, JOKER, THE WINDOW'S OPEN!
GOOD! THE COAST IS CLEAR— LET'S GO!
HEY! WHAT ARE YOU DOING BACK HERE?
JUST ROBBING A STORE, OFFICER! ANY OBJECTIONS? HA! HA!
UH!
MOMENTS LATER...
GEE, JOKER, WHAT A HAUL! AND IT WAS EASY, TOO!
EVERYTHING IS EASY WHEN THE JOKER PLANS!... EASY AS IT IS TO LAUGH! HA! HA! HA!
5
5

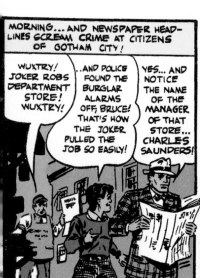

MORNING... AND NEWSPAPER HEADLINES SCREAM CRIME AT CITIZENS OF GOTHAM CITY!

WUXTRY! JOKER ROBS DEPARTMENT STORE! WUXTRY!

..AND POLICE FOUND THE BURGLAR ALARMS OFF, BRUCE! THAT'S HOW THE JOKER PULLED THE JOB SO EASILY!

YES... AND NOTICE THE NAME OF THE MANAGER OF THAT STORE... CHARLES SAUNDERS!

WHY... HE'S THE FELLOW WHO RECEIVED THAT RADIO WITHOUT A LOUDSPEAKER FROM THE JOKER! SAY, THINK IT WAS AN INSIDE JOB?

MIGHTY QUEER, DICK! BATMAN AND ROBIN ARE GOING TO DO SOME DETECTIVE WORK TONIGHT!

SNAP!

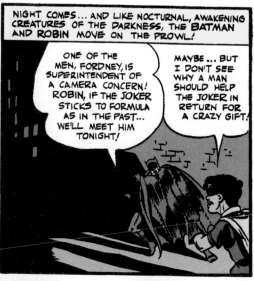

NIGHT COMES... AND LIKE NOCTURNAL, AWAKENING CREATURES OF THE DARKNESS, THE BATMAN AND ROBIN MOVE ON THE PROWL!

ONE OF THE MEN, FORDNEY, IS SUPERINTENDENT OF A CAMERA CONCERN! ROBIN, IF THE JOKER STICKS TO FORMULA AS IN THE PAST... WE'LL MEET HIM TONIGHT!

MAYBE... BUT I DON'T SEE WHY A MAN SHOULD HELP THE JOKER IN RETURN FOR A CRAZY GIFT!

THE STORAGE WAREHOUSE OF THE SHUTTER CAMERA CO...

THESE BARRELS WERE STORED HERE TONIGHT, AND FORDNEY SAID NOT TO TOUCH 'EM! WONDER WHAT'S IN 'EM?

YOU WON'T HAVE TO WONDER LONG! HA! HA!

OWW-HH-HH...

HAW! HAW! THAT WAS A SWELL STUNT, JOKER, SNEAKING US IN INSIDE THE BARRELS!

YES.. FORDNEY WAS VERY OBLIGING, WASN'T HE? NOW LET'S GET AT THOSE EXPENSIVE CAMERAS STORED IN HERE!

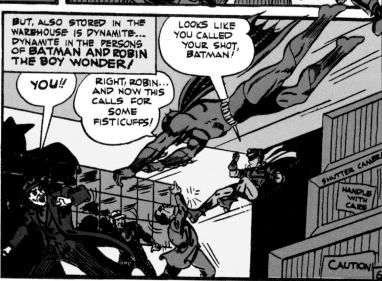

BUT, ALSO STORED IN THE WAREHOUSE IS DYNAMITE... DYNAMITE IN THE PERSONS OF BATMAN AND ROBIN THE BOY WONDER!

YOU!!

RIGHT, ROBIN... AND NOW THIS CALLS FOR SOME FISTICUFFS!

LOOKS LIKE YOU CALLED YOUR SHOT, BATMAN!

SHUTTER CAMER

HANDLE WITH CARE

CAUTION!

6

173

GET HIM! G... UH!

MY-MY! SUCH SHORT DIALOGUE!

OKAY, JOKER! I'LL... OOH!

THEN! .45 CALIBER DANGER MENACES THE BATMAN!

THE GREAT BATMAN, EH? LET'S SEE HOW GREAT YA ARE WITH A SLUG IN YER BACK!

AND I'M NOT GOING TO PULL THAT PUN ABOUT "ROLLING OUT THE BARREL", ... RAT!

BANG!

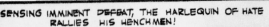

SENSING IMMINENT DEFEAT, THE HARLEQUIN OF HATE RALLIES HIS HENCHMEN!

AT THEM, FOOLS! ALL TOGETHER NOW! THEN THEY CAN'T STOP US!

OH-OH! ROBIN, THIS CALLS FOR STRATEGY!

AN IRRESISTIBLE FORCE, ROBIN BLASTS THRU THE BREAKING RANKS!

MOVE IT OVER THERE, BATMAN! I MISSED THE JOKER!

A JOLTING RIGHT, AND THE JOKER ROCKS BACK ON HIS HEELS!

SORRY, ROBIN, THE JOKER'S MY PERSONAL DISH!

ROBIN, EVERY TIME WE WENT AFTER THE JOKER IN THE PAST, HE CLOUTED US AND GOT AWAY!

YES... BUT NOT THIS TIME! THIS TIME WE'VE GOT HIM FOR KEEPS!

IS THIS CASE OVER ALREADY?? IS THE JOKER STOPPED BE- FORE HE CAN GET STARTED? OR DOES THE CUNNING CRIME CLOWN STILL HOLD AN ACE UP HIS SLEEVE ?

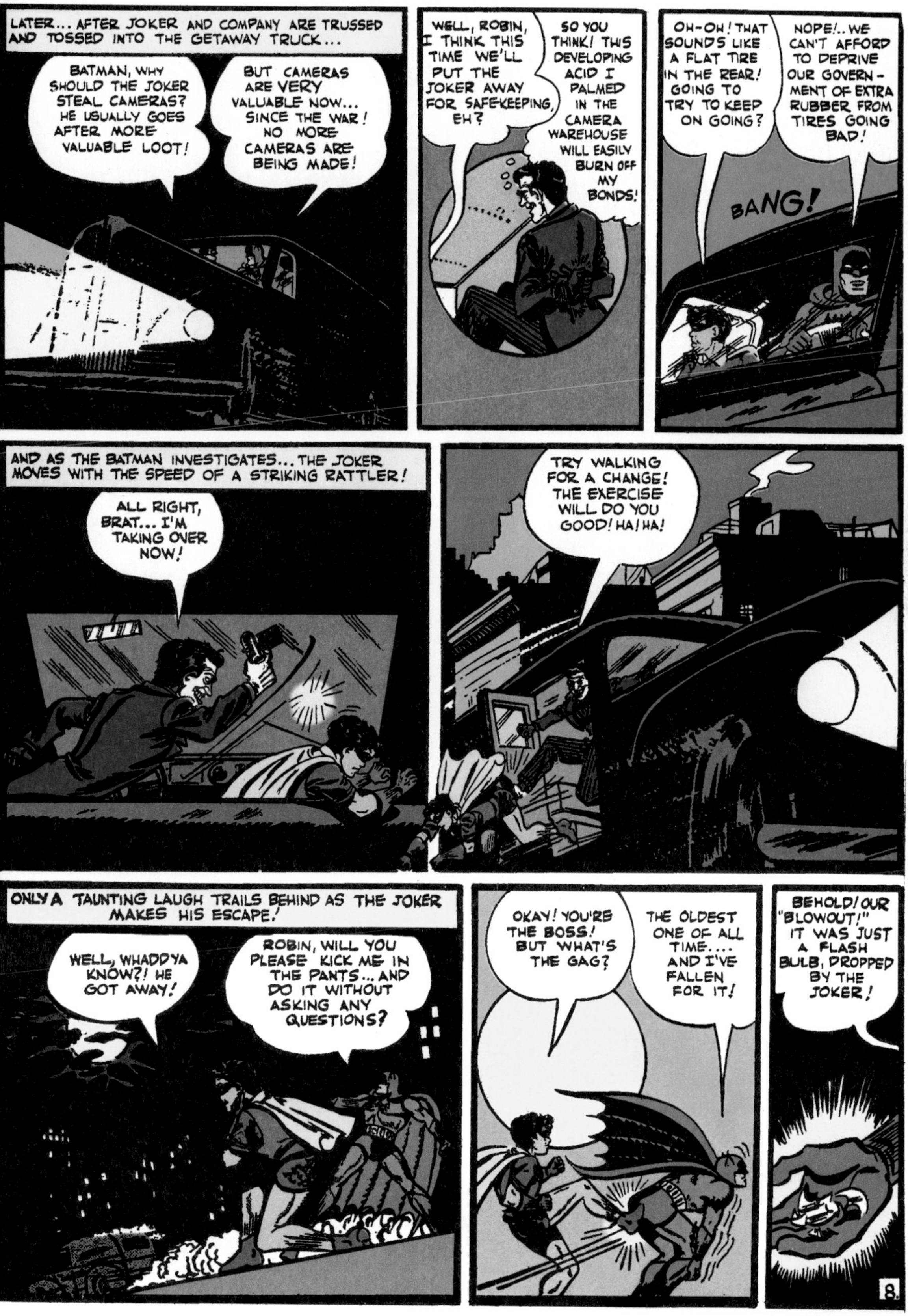
LATER... AFTER JOKER AND COMPANY ARE TRUSSED AND TOSSED INTO THE GETAWAY TRUCK...
BATMAN, WHY SHOULD THE JOKER STEAL CAMERAS? HE USUALLY GOES AFTER MORE VALUABLE LOOT!
BUT CAMERAS ARE VERY VALUABLE NOW... SINCE THE WAR! NO MORE CAMERAS ARE BEING MADE!
WELL, ROBIN, I THINK THIS TIME WE'LL PUT THE JOKER AWAY FOR SAFE-KEEPING, EH?
SO YOU THINK! THIS DEVELOPING ACID I PALMED IN THE CAMERA WAREHOUSE WILL EASILY BURN OFF MY BONDS!
OH-OH! THAT SOUNDS LIKE A FLAT TIRE IN THE REAR! GOING TO TRY TO KEEP ON GOING?
NOPE!.. WE CAN'T AFFORD TO DEPRIVE OUR GOVERN-MENT OF EXTRA RUBBER FROM TIRES GOING BAD!
BANG!
AND AS THE BATMAN INVESTIGATES... THE JOKER MOVES WITH THE SPEED OF A STRIKING RATTLER!
ALL RIGHT, BRAT... I'M TAKING OVER NOW!
TRY WALKING FOR A CHANGE! THE EXERCISE WILL DO YOU GOOD! HA! HA!
ONLY A TAUNTING LAUGH TRAILS BEHIND AS THE JOKER MAKES HIS ESCAPE!
WELL, WHADDYA KNOW?! HE GOT AWAY!
ROBIN, WILL YOU PLEASE KICK ME IN THE PANTS... AND DO IT WITHOUT ASKING ANY QUESTIONS?
OKAY! YOU'RE THE BOSS! BUT WHAT'S THE GAG?
THE OLDEST ONE OF ALL TIME.... AND I'VE FALLEN FOR IT!
BEHOLD! OUR "BLOWOUT!" IT WAS JUST A FLASH BULB, DROPPED BY THE JOKER!
8.

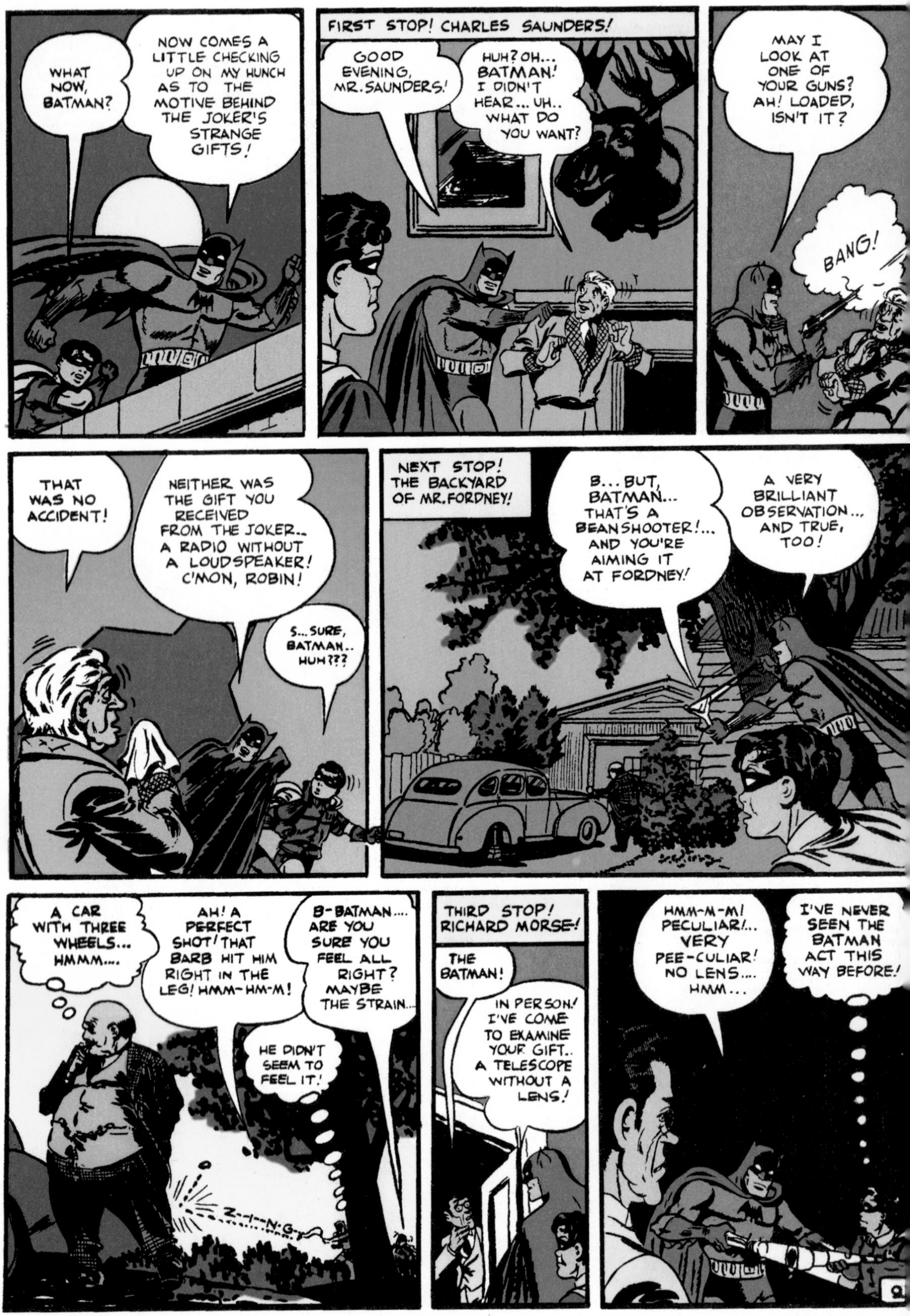

WHAT NOW, BATMAN?
NOW COMES A LITTLE CHECKING UP ON MY HUNCH AS TO THE MOTIVE BEHIND THE JOKER'S STRANGE GIFTS!
FIRST STOP! CHARLES SAUNDERS!
GOOD EVENING, MR. SAUNDERS!
HUH? OH... BATMAN! I DIDN'T HEAR... UH.. WHAT DO YOU WANT?
MAY I LOOK AT ONE OF YOUR GUNS? AH! LOADED, ISN'T IT?
BANG!
THAT WAS NO ACCIDENT!
NEITHER WAS THE GIFT YOU RECEIVED FROM THE JOKER.. A RADIO WITHOUT A LOUDSPEAKER! C'MON, ROBIN!
S...SURE, BATMAN.. HUH???
NEXT STOP! THE BACKYARD OF MR. FORDNEY!
B... BUT, BATMAN... THAT'S A BEANSHOOTER!... AND YOU'RE AIMING IT AT FORDNEY!
A VERY BRILLIANT OBSERVATION... AND TRUE, TOO!
A CAR WITH THREE WHEELS... HMMM....
AH! A PERFECT SHOT! THAT BARB HIT HIM RIGHT IN THE LEG! HMM-HM-M!
B-BATMAN.... ARE YOU SURE YOU FEEL ALL RIGHT? MAYBE THE STRAIN...
HE DIDN'T SEEM TO FEEL IT!
Z-I-I-N-G
THIRD STOP! RICHARD MORSE!
THE BATMAN!
IN PERSON! I'VE COME TO EXAMINE YOUR GIFT.. A TELESCOPE WITHOUT A LENS!
HMM-M-M! PECULIAR!... VERY PEE-CULIAR! NO LENS.... HMM...
I'VE NEVER SEEN THE BATMAN ACT THIS WAY BEFORE!
9

SUDDENLY, BATMAN SHINES THE BEAM DIRECTLY INTO MORSE'S LEFT EYE...

GIVES A BRIGHT LIGHT, DOESN'T IT? YES, INDEEDY!

BATMAN! WHAT'S WRONG WITH YOU? YOU'RE ACTING...

... CRAZY, IS THE WORD, ROBIN! TUM-DE-DUM! C'MON, WATSON..... SHERLOCK HOLMES HAS ONE MORE STOP TO MAKE!

?

LAST STOP! JIM BROWN!

SO THIS IS THE CLOCK WITHOUT AN HOUR HAND! WELL, WELL! MUST BE AWKWARD IF YOU WANT THE RIGHT TIME, EH?

YES, IT IS AW. HUH?!!

OOPS! SORRY! BUTTERFINGERS, THAT'S ME!

THAT'S ALL RIGHT! IT DIDN'T HURT MY HAND!

I DON'T IMAGINE IT COULD... SINCE THAT'S AN ARTIFICIAL ARM!

WHA...?

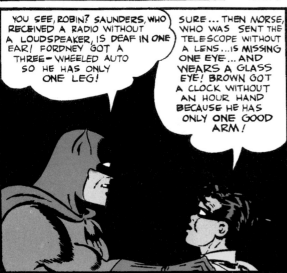

YOU SEE, ROBIN? SAUNDERS, WHO RECEIVED A RADIO WITHOUT A LOUDSPEAKER, IS DEAF IN ONE EAR! FORDNEY GOT A THREE-WHEELED AUTO SO HE HAS ONLY ONE LEG!

SURE... THEN MORSE, WHO WAS SENT THE TELESCOPE WITHOUT A LENS...IS MISSING ONE EYE... AND WEARS A GLASS EYE! BROWN GOT A CLOCK WITHOUT AN HOUR HAND BECAUSE HE HAS ONLY ONE GOOD ARM!

THE JOKER HAD A HOLD ON YOU MEN AND TOOK THAT CRAZY WAY OF TELLING YOU TO DO WHAT HE WANTED, EH?

YES, BATMAN! YEARS AGO WE FOUR WERE TOGETHER IN ANOTHER CITY WHEN AN EXPLOSION TOOK PLACE! THAT'S HOW WE ALL RE-CEIVED OUR INJURIES!

10

BUT TWO OTHER MEN WERE KILLED! WE WERE BLAMED FOR IT ALL! WE WERE FINALLY CLEARED, BUT THE STIGMA FORCED US TO LEAVE!

THEN THE JOKER FOUND YOU, BLACK-MAILED YOU INTO LETTING HIM ROB YOUR EMPLOYERS! YOU CONSENTED—FOR IF THE NEWS LEAKED OUT YOU'D BE RUINED HERE, TOO!

SUDDENLY!

MORSE WORKS THERE! HE MUST HAVE AGREED TO THE JOKER'S DEMANDS!

FLASH! THE JOKER HAS JUST LOOTED THE J. I. WOLF FUR COMPANY AND....

NOT ME! I'LL TELL THE POLICE FIRST!

I WOULDN'T! WELL... GOOD THING I CAME BACK TO CHECK UP ON YOU!

DON'T NOBODY MOVE... OR THE KID GETS IT!

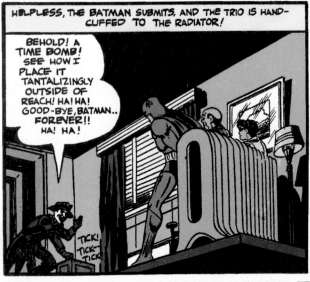

HELPLESS, THE BATMAN SUBMITS, AND THE TRIO IS HAND-CUFFED TO THE RADIATOR!

BEHOLD! A TIME BOMB! SEE HOW I PLACE IT TANTALIZINGLY OUTSIDE OF REACH! HA! HA! GOOD-BYE, BATMAN.. FOREVER!! HA! HA!

TICK! TICK! TICK!

THE DOOR SLAMS SHUT...AND THE MEN ARE LEFT ALONE WITH TICKING DEATH!

ONLY ONE INCH MORE... BUT I CAN'T MAKE IT!

PERHAPS I CAN!

TICK TICK

TICK!! TICK-

TICK-TICK

A SUDDEN WRENCH... A RIP OF CLOTH... AND BROWN'S ARM DANGLES LOOSE FROM HIS BODY!!

DON'T BE ALARMED! IT'S MY ARTIFICIAL ARM! THE JOKER FORGOT THAT WHEN HE HANDCUFFED ME!

HUH!?!

HUH!?!

R-R-IP!

AND THAT'S WHERE HE SLIPPED.. BECAUSE NOW I'M ABLE TO REACH OUT-- AND KICK THE TIME-BOMB THRU THAT WINDOW!

A MOMENT LATER...

BOOM!

11

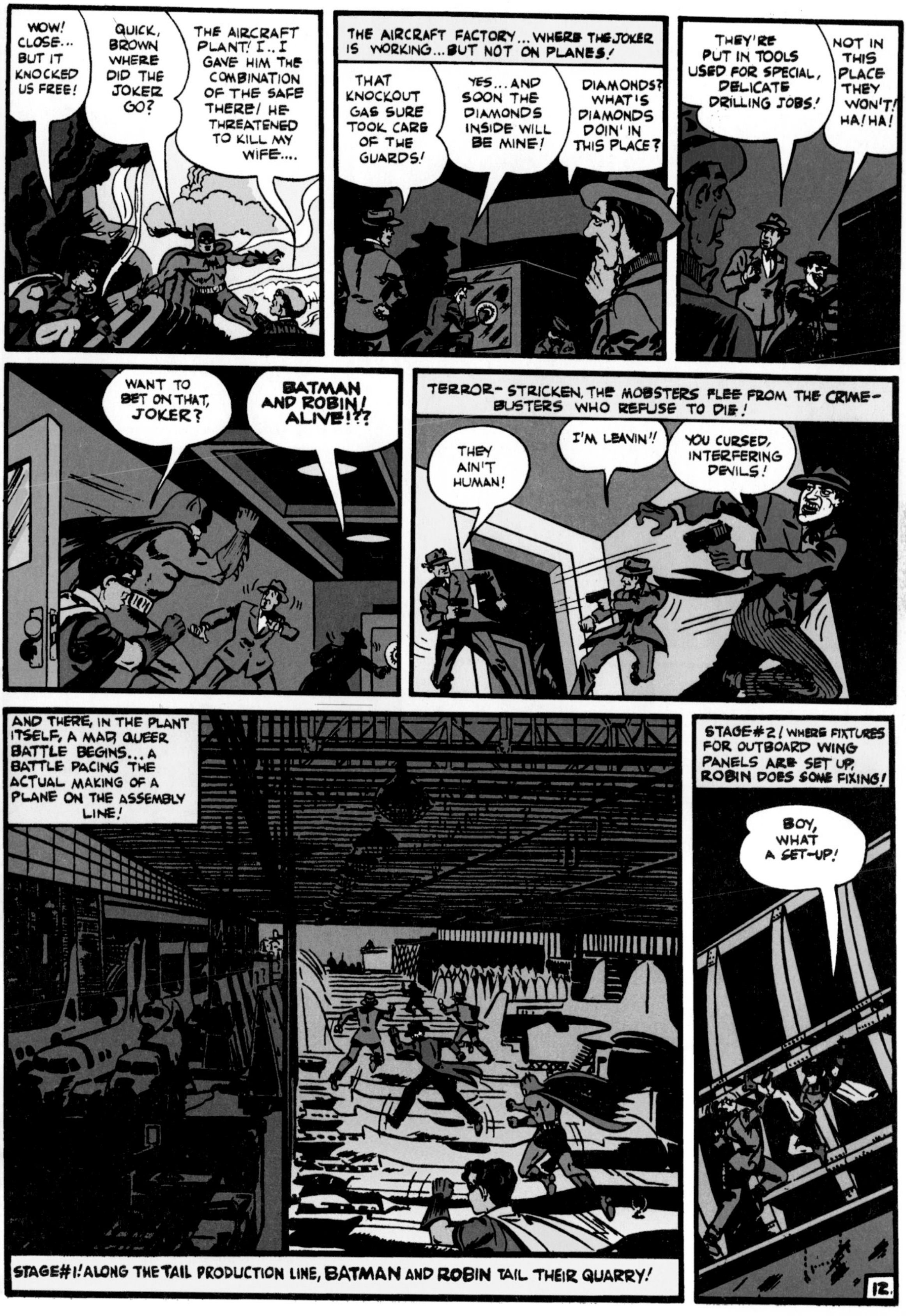
WOW! CLOSE... BUT IT KNOCKED US FREE!
QUICK, BROWN WHERE DID THE JOKER GO?
THE AIRCRAFT PLANT! I.. I GAVE HIM THE COMBINATION OF THE SAFE THERE! HE THREATENED TO KILL MY WIFE....
THE AIRCRAFT FACTORY... WHERE THE JOKER IS WORKING... BUT NOT ON PLANES!
THAT KNOCKOUT GAS SURE TOOK CARE OF THE GUARDS!
YES... AND SOON THE DIAMONDS INSIDE WILL BE MINE!
DIAMONDS? WHAT'S DIAMONDS DOIN' IN THIS PLACE?
THEY'RE PUT IN TOOLS USED FOR SPECIAL, DELICATE DRILLING JOBS!
NOT IN THIS PLACE THEY WON'T! HA! HA!
WANT TO BET ON THAT, JOKER?
BATMAN AND ROBIN! ALIVE!??
TERROR-STRICKEN, THE MOBSTERS FLEE FROM THE CRIME-BUSTERS WHO REFUSE TO DIE!
THEY AIN'T HUMAN!
I'M LEAVIN'!
YOU CURSED, INTERFERING DEVILS!
AND THERE, IN THE PLANT ITSELF, A MAD QUEER BATTLE BEGINS... A BATTLE PACING THE ACTUAL MAKING OF A PLANE ON THE ASSEMBLY LINE!
STAGE#1! ALONG THE TAIL PRODUCTION LINE, BATMAN AND ROBIN TAIL THEIR QUARRY!
STAGE #2! WHERE FIXTURES FOR OUTBOARD WING PANELS ARE SET UP, ROBIN DOES SOME FIXING!
BOY, WHAT A SET-UP!
12.

STAGE #3! HIGH ON THE SLANT OF A WING ALREADY PLACED, BATMAN WINGS A WELL-PLACED BLOW TO A THUGGISH JAW!

STAGE #4! AND ON THE BOMBER'S TIRE, ROBIN RETIRES THE OTHER GUNMEN!

A PERFECT STRIKE!

THE MAD CHASE LEADS OUTSIDE INTO THE YARD OF THE HUGE PLANT. AS THE JOKER CLAMBERS TO A PROPELLERLESS BOMBER, THE BATMAN PROPELS HIMSELF THRU THE AIR!

NOT SO FAST, JOKER!

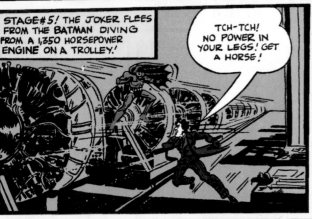

STAGE #5! THE JOKER FLEES FROM THE BATMAN DIVING FROM A 1,350 HORSEPOWER ENGINE ON A TROLLEY!

TCH-TCH! NO POWER IN YOUR LEGS! GET A HORSE!

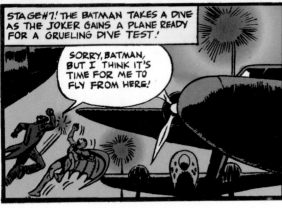

STAGE #7! THE BATMAN TAKES A DIVE AS THE JOKER GAINS A PLANE READY FOR A GRUELING DIVE TEST!

SORRY, BATMAN, BUT I THINK IT'S TIME FOR ME TO FLY FROM HERE!

STAGE #8! IN A COMPLETED PLANE, THE JOKER COMPLETES HIS ESCAPE!

ADIEU, BATMAN! I'LL SEND THE BOMBER BACK SO IT CAN DROP A FEW "EGGS" ON THE JAPS! HA! HA!

AND SO THE BOMBER DWINDLES TO A MERE SPECK ON THE HORIZON...

WELL, THERE HE GOES!

HE'LL BE BACK! AND WHEN HE DOES, WE'LL MEET HIM... AND BOY, WILL THAT BE A SCRAP!

THE END

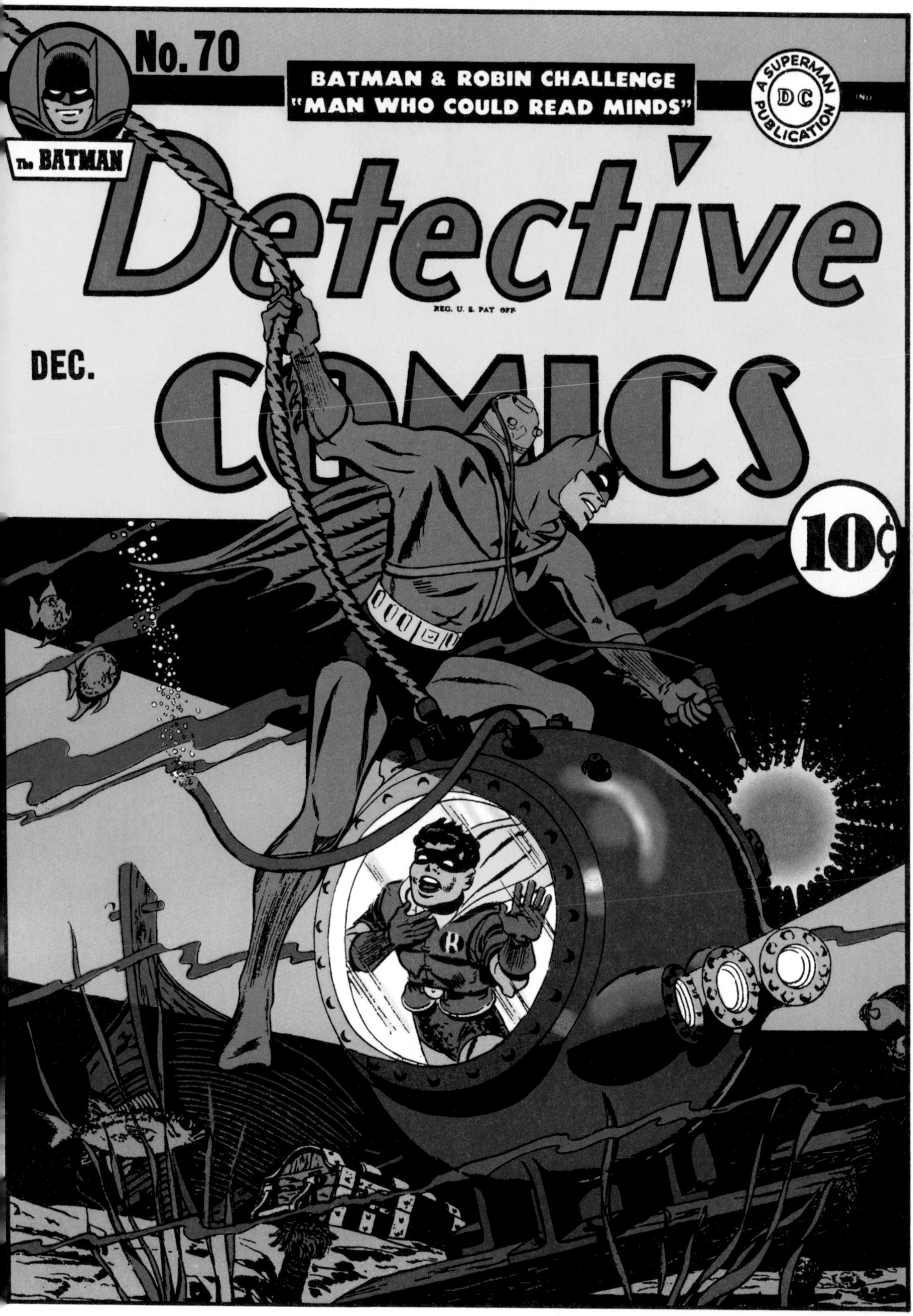
No. 70
BATMAN & ROBIN CHALLENGE
"MAN WHO COULD READ MINDS"
A SUPERMAN DC PUBLICATION
The BATMAN
Detective
REG. U. S. PAT. OFF.
DEC.
COMICS
10¢

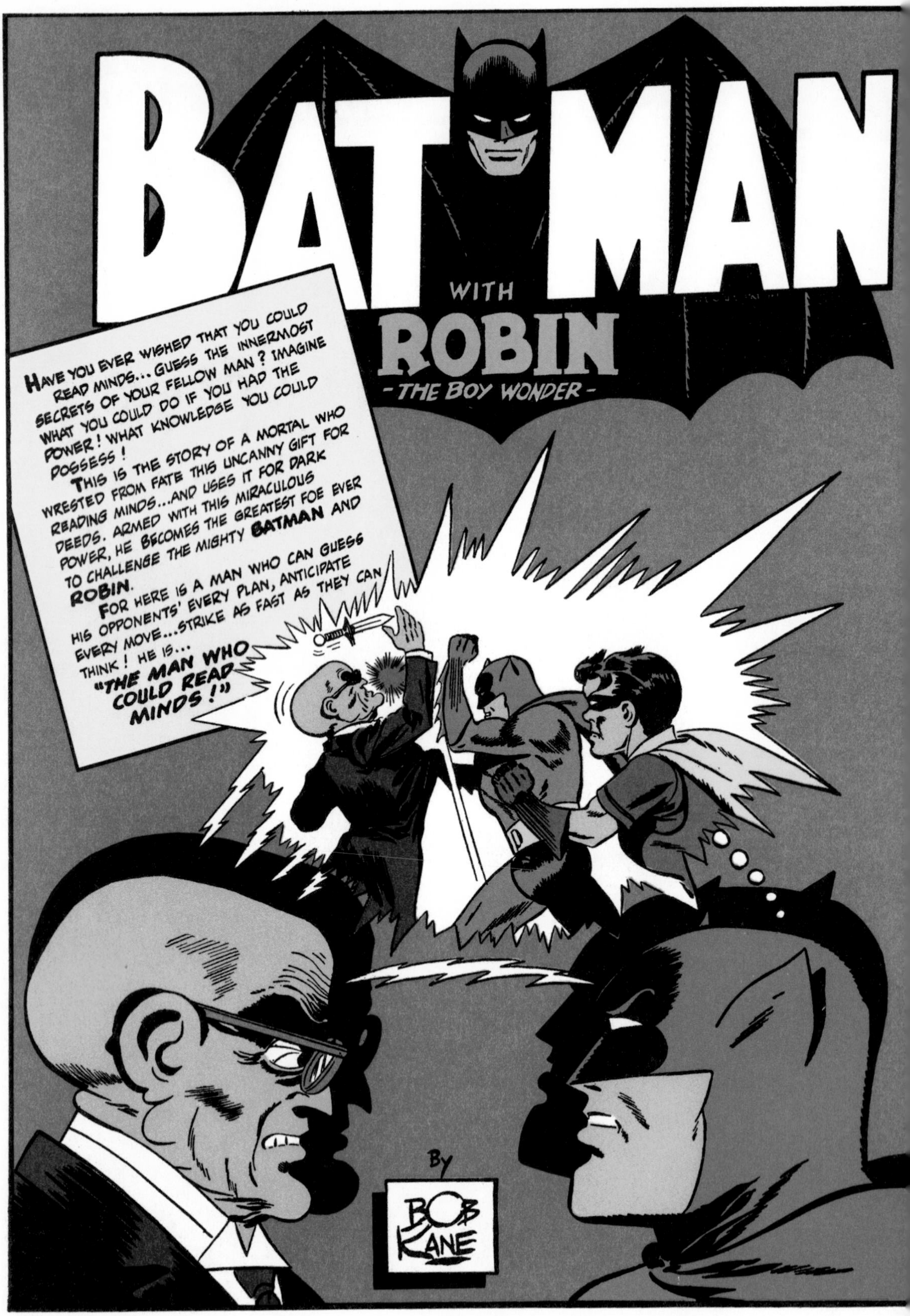
BATMAN
WITH
ROBIN
-THE BOY WONDER-
HAVE YOU EVER WISHED THAT YOU COULD READ MINDS... GUESS THE INNERMOST SECRETS OF YOUR FELLOW MAN? IMAGINE WHAT YOU COULD DO IF YOU HAD THE POWER! WHAT KNOWLEDGE YOU COULD POSSESS!
THIS IS THE STORY OF A MORTAL WHO WRESTED FROM FATE THIS UNCANNY GIFT FOR READING MINDS...AND USES IT FOR DARK DEEDS. ARMED WITH THIS MIRACULOUS POWER, HE BECOMES THE GREATEST FOE EVER TO CHALLENGE THE MIGHTY BATMAN AND ROBIN.
FOR HERE IS A MAN WHO CAN GUESS HIS OPPONENTS' EVERY PLAN, ANTICIPATE EVERY MOVE...STRIKE AS FAST AS THEY CAN THINK! HE IS...
"THE MAN WHO COULD READ MINDS!"
By
BOB KANE

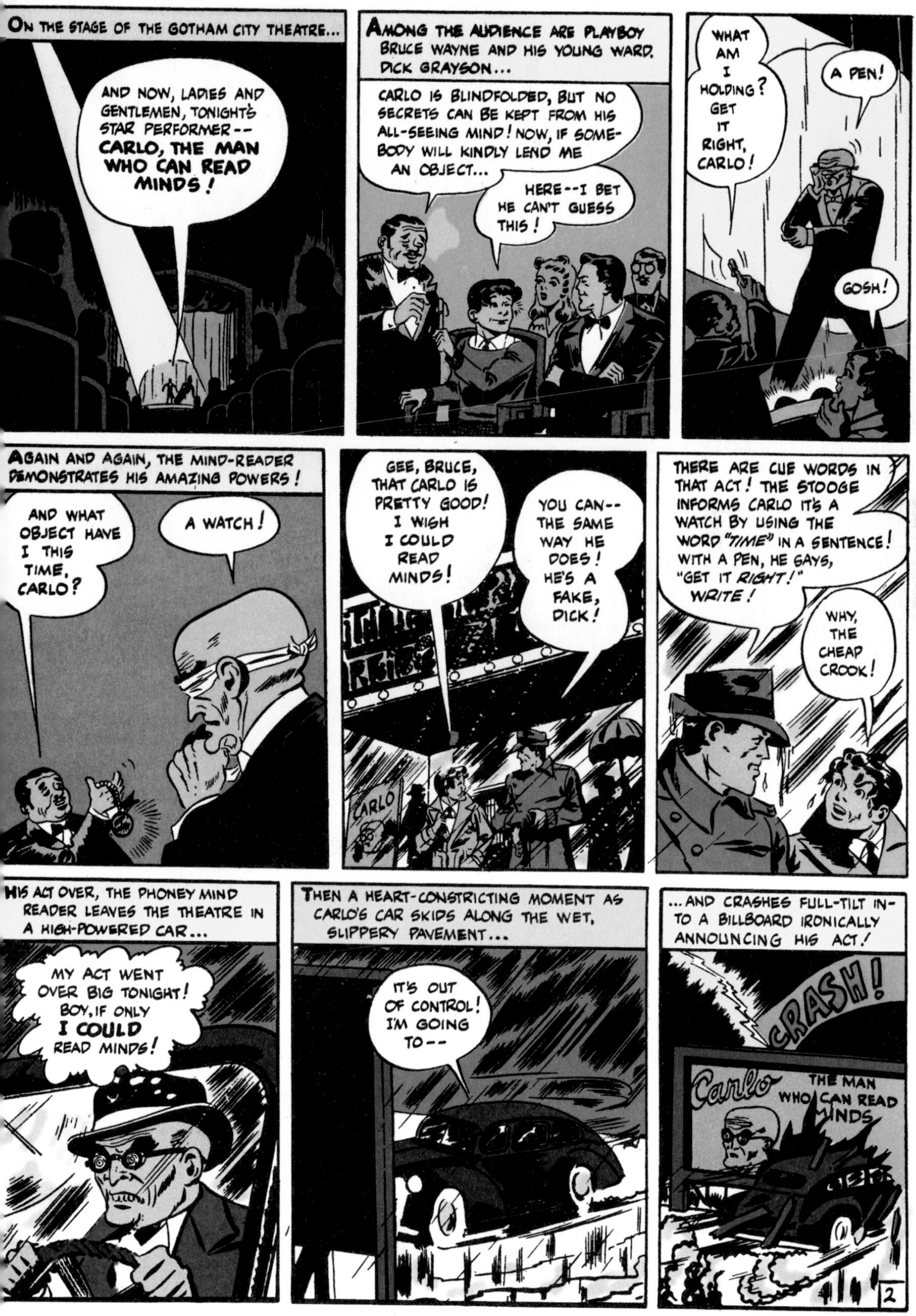

ON THE STAGE OF THE GOTHAM CITY THEATRE...
AND NOW, LADIES AND GENTLEMEN, TONIGHT'S STAR PERFORMER -- CARLO, THE MAN WHO CAN READ MINDS!
AMONG THE AUDIENCE ARE PLAYBOY BRUCE WAYNE AND HIS YOUNG WARD, DICK GRAYSON...
CARLO IS BLINDFOLDED, BUT NO SECRETS CAN BE KEPT FROM HIS ALL-SEEING MIND! NOW, IF SOMEBODY WILL KINDLY LEND ME AN OBJECT...
HERE--I BET HE CAN'T GUESS THIS!
WHAT AM I HOLDING? GET IT RIGHT, CARLO!
A PEN!
GOSH!
AGAIN AND AGAIN, THE MIND-READER DEMONSTRATES HIS AMAZING POWERS!
AND WHAT OBJECT HAVE I THIS TIME, CARLO?
A WATCH!
GEE, BRUCE, THAT CARLO IS PRETTY GOOD! I WISH I COULD READ MINDS!
YOU CAN-- THE SAME WAY HE DOES! HE'S A FAKE, DICK!
CARLO
THERE ARE CUE WORDS IN THAT ACT! THE STOOGE INFORMS CARLO IT'S A WATCH BY USING THE WORD "TIME" IN A SENTENCE! WITH A PEN, HE SAYS, "GET IT RIGHT!" WRITE!
WHY, THE CHEAP CROOK!
HIS ACT OVER, THE PHONEY MIND READER LEAVES THE THEATRE IN A HIGH-POWERED CAR...
MY ACT WENT OVER BIG TONIGHT! BOY, IF ONLY I COULD READ MINDS!
THEN A HEART-CONSTRICTING MOMENT AS CARLO'S CAR SKIDS ALONG THE WET, SLIPPERY PAVEMENT...
IT'S OUT OF CONTROL! I'M GOING TO--
...AND CRASHES FULL-TILT INTO A BILLBOARD IRONICALLY ANNOUNCING HIS ACT!
CRASH!
Carlo THE MAN WHO CAN READ MINDS
2

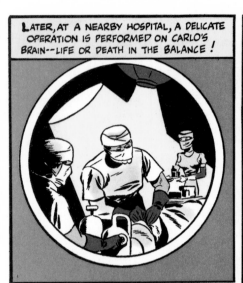

LATER, AT A NEARBY HOSPITAL, A DELICATE OPERATION IS PERFORMED ON CARLO'S BRAIN--LIFE OR DEATH IN THE BALANCE!

SUDDENLY, A JAGGED STREAK OF LIGHTNING LANCES DOWN...A GREAT FLARE ILLUMINATES THE ROOM...

CRACK

...AND THE LIGHTS ABRUPTLY GO OUT!

LIGHTNING HIT THE MAIN ELECTRIC WIRE!

GET THE EMERGENCY LIGHTS ON! FAST!

MOMENTS LATER...

I HOPE MY SCALPEL DIDN'T SLIP WHEN THOSE LIGHTS WENT OUT!

CRACK!

HE'LL BE GOOD AS NEW!

CONGRATULATIONS, DOCTOR-- A GREAT OPER- ATION!

CARLO WILL BE JUST THE SAME AS BEFORE!

BUT WILL HE? FOR FATE'S TRICKY FINGERS HAVE SLYLY GUIDED THE SURGEON'S SCALPEL DURING THAT MOMEN- TARY BLACKOUT!

A WEEK LATER...

GREAT GUNS! I KNOW WHAT THEY'RE THINKING

SOME PRETTY NURSE!

I HATE THAT OLD SAW- BONES!

THE FOOD IS TERRIBLE

WHAT A FUNNY FACE THIS FELLOW NEXT TO ME HAS!

DID YOU EVER LOOK AT YOURSELF IN THE MIRROR, SMART GUY?

I CAN REALLY READ MINDS! MY BRAIN IS LIKE A RECEIV- ING SET! THAT OPERATION MUST HAVE DONE IT!

HOW'D HE KNOW WHAT I WAS THINKIN'?

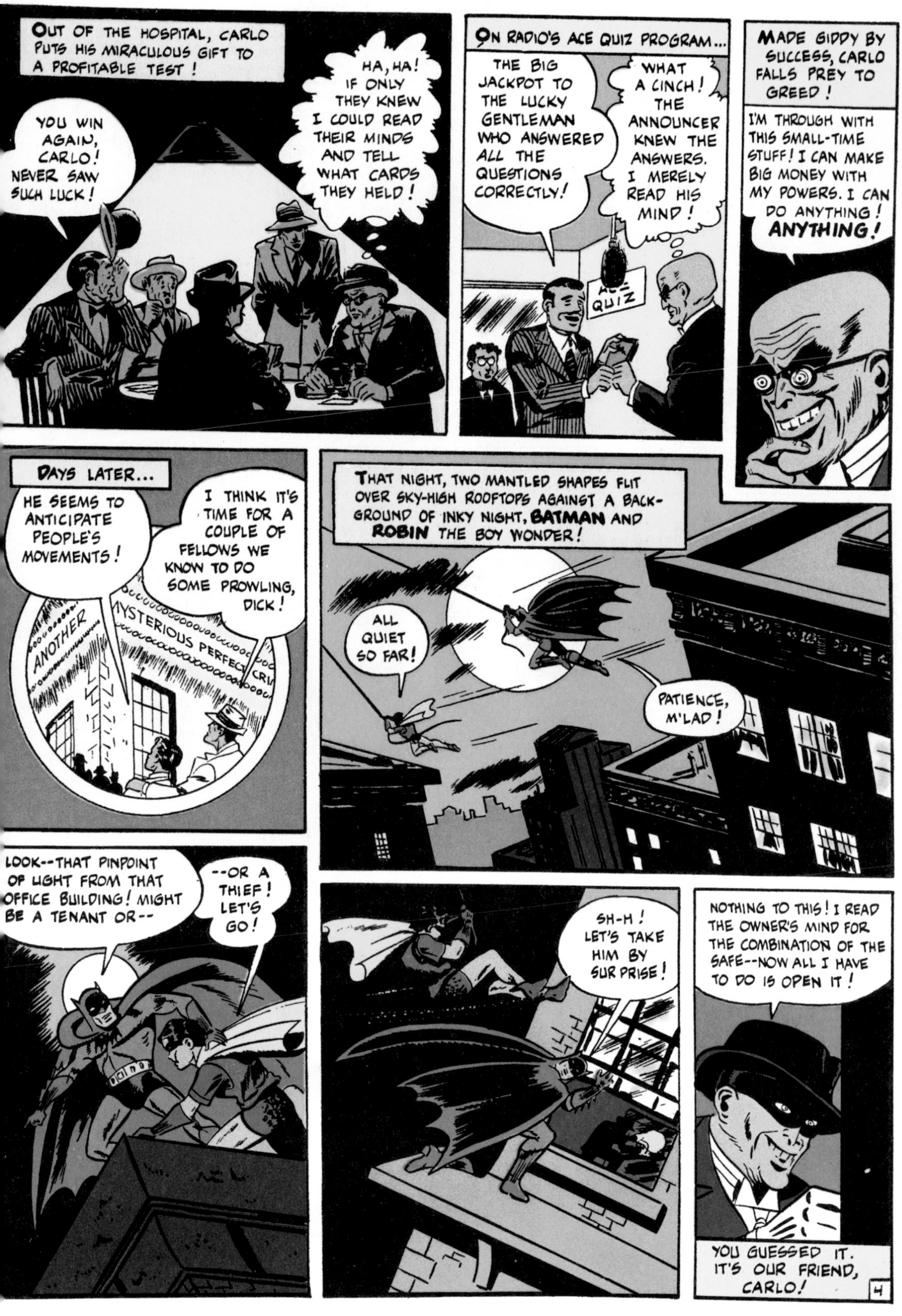
OUT OF THE HOSPITAL, CARLO PUTS HIS MIRACULOUS GIFT TO A PROFITABLE TEST!
YOU WIN AGAIN, CARLO! NEVER SAW SUCH LUCK!
HA, HA! IF ONLY THEY KNEW I COULD READ THEIR MINDS AND TELL WHAT CARDS THEY HELD!
ON RADIO'S ACE QUIZ PROGRAM...
THE BIG JACKPOT TO THE LUCKY GENTLEMAN WHO ANSWERED ALL THE QUESTIONS CORRECTLY!
WHAT A CINCH! THE ANNOUNCER KNEW THE ANSWERS. I MERELY READ HIS MIND!
QUIZ
MADE GIDDY BY SUCCESS, CARLO FALLS PREY TO GREED!
I'M THROUGH WITH THIS SMALL-TIME STUFF! I CAN MAKE BIG MONEY WITH MY POWERS. I CAN DO ANYTHING! ANYTHING!
DAYS LATER...
HE SEEMS TO ANTICIPATE PEOPLE'S MOVEMENTS!
I THINK IT'S TIME FOR A COUPLE OF FELLOWS WE KNOW TO DO SOME PROWLING, DICK!
ANOTHER
MYSTERIOUS PERFECT CRI
THAT NIGHT, TWO MANTLED SHAPES FLIT OVER SKY-HIGH ROOFTOPS AGAINST A BACKGROUND OF INKY NIGHT, BATMAN AND ROBIN THE BOY WONDER!
ALL QUIET SO FAR!
PATIENCE, M'LAD!
LOOK--THAT PINPOINT OF LIGHT FROM THAT OFFICE BUILDING! MIGHT BE A TENANT OR--
--OR A THIEF! LET'S GO!
SH-H! LET'S TAKE HIM BY SURPRISE!
NOTHING TO THIS! I READ THE OWNER'S MIND FOR THE COMBINATION OF THE SAFE--NOW ALL I HAVE TO DO IS OPEN IT!
YOU GUESSED IT. IT'S OUR FRIEND, CARLO!
4

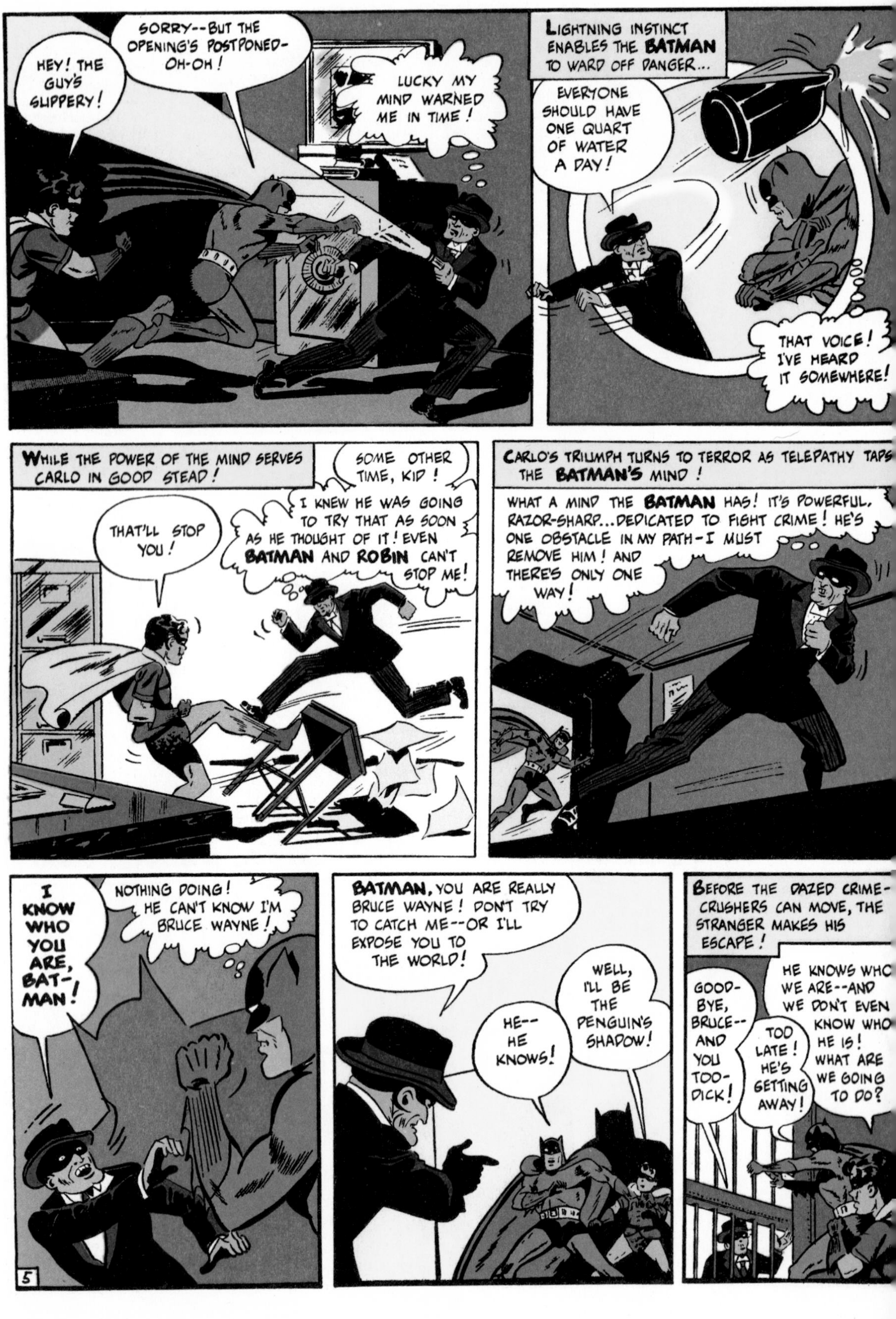
SORRY--BUT THE OPENING'S POSTPONED-OH-OH!
HEY! THE GUY'S SLIPPERY!
LUCKY MY MIND WARNED ME IN TIME!
LIGHTNING INSTINCT ENABLES THE BATMAN TO WARD OFF DANGER...
EVERYONE SHOULD HAVE ONE QUART OF WATER A DAY!
THAT VOICE! I'VE HEARD IT SOMEWHERE!
WHILE THE POWER OF THE MIND SERVES CARLO IN GOOD STEAD!
SOME OTHER TIME, KID!
I KNEW HE WAS GOING TO TRY THAT AS SOON AS HE THOUGHT OF IT! EVEN BATMAN AND ROBIN CAN'T STOP ME!
THAT'LL STOP YOU!
CARLO'S TRIUMPH TURNS TO TERROR AS TELEPATHY TAPS THE BATMAN'S MIND!
WHAT A MIND THE BATMAN HAS! IT'S POWERFUL, RAZOR-SHARP...DEDICATED TO FIGHT CRIME! HE'S ONE OBSTACLE IN MY PATH - I MUST REMOVE HIM! AND THERE'S ONLY ONE WAY!
I KNOW WHO YOU ARE, BAT-MAN!
NOTHING DOING! HE CAN'T KNOW I'M BRUCE WAYNE!
5
BATMAN, YOU ARE REALLY BRUCE WAYNE! DON'T TRY TO CATCH ME--OR I'LL EXPOSE YOU TO THE WORLD!
HE--HE KNOWS!
WELL, I'LL BE THE PENGUIN'S SHADOW!
BEFORE THE DAZED CRIME-CRUSHERS CAN MOVE, THE STRANGER MAKES HIS ESCAPE!
GOOD-BYE, BRUCE--AND YOU TOO-DICK!
TOO LATE! HE'S GETTING AWAY!
HE KNOWS WHO WE ARE--AND WE DON'T EVEN KNOW WHO HE IS! WHAT ARE WE GOING TO DO?

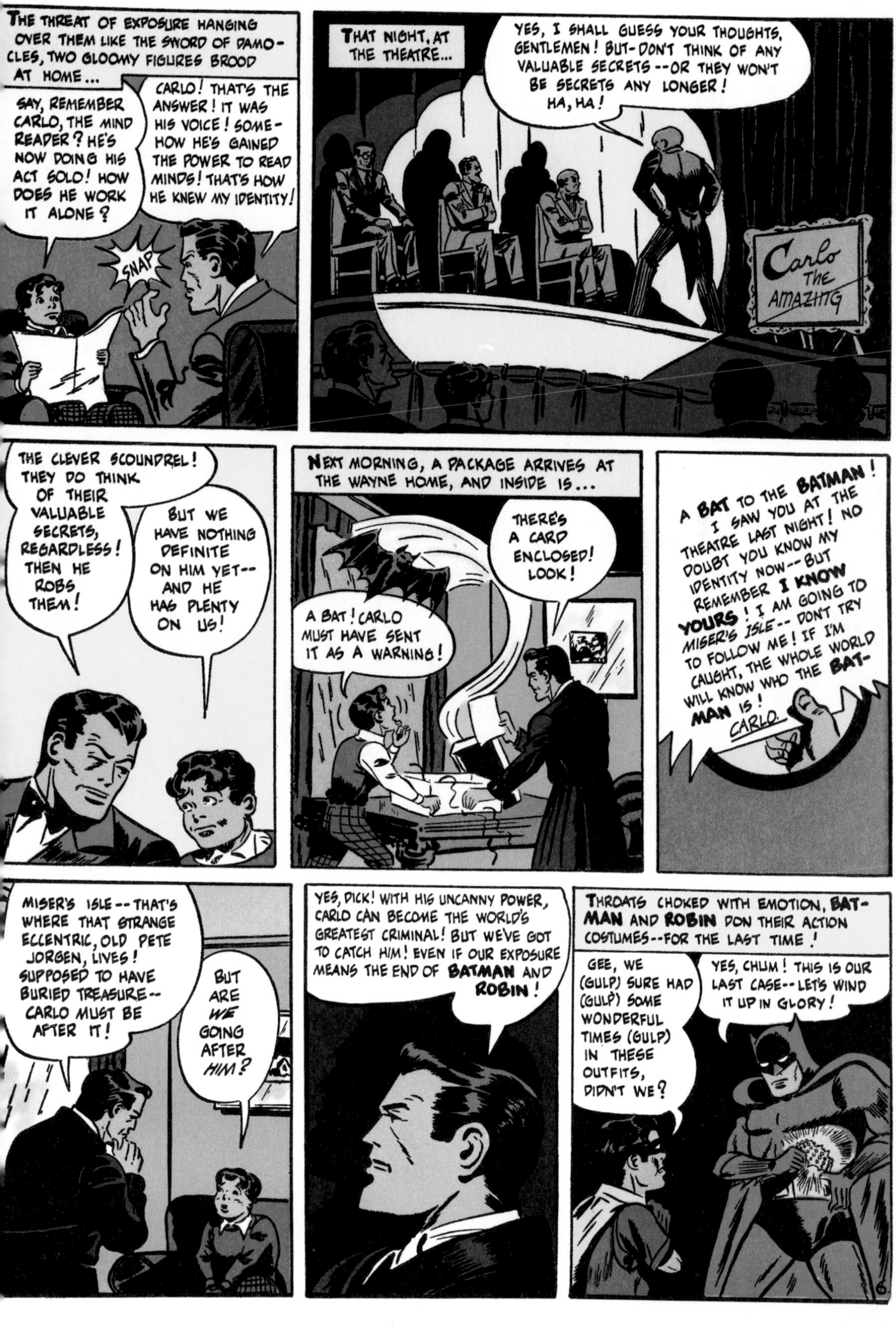
THE THREAT OF EXPOSURE HANGING OVER THEM LIKE THE SWORD OF DAMOCLES, TWO GLOOMY FIGURES BROOD AT HOME...
SAY, REMEMBER CARLO, THE MIND READER? HE'S NOW DOING HIS ACT SOLO! HOW DOES HE WORK IT ALONE?
CARLO! THAT'S THE ANSWER! IT WAS HIS VOICE! SOMEHOW HE'S GAINED THE POWER TO READ MINDS! THAT'S HOW HE KNEW MY IDENTITY!
SNAP
THAT NIGHT, AT THE THEATRE...
YES, I SHALL GUESS YOUR THOUGHTS, GENTLEMEN! BUT-DON'T THINK OF ANY VALUABLE SECRETS --OR THEY WON'T BE SECRETS ANY LONGER! HA, HA!
Carlo THE AMAZING
THE CLEVER SCOUNDREL! THEY DO THINK OF THEIR VALUABLE SECRETS, REGARDLESS! THEN HE ROBS THEM!
BUT WE HAVE NOTHING DEFINITE ON HIM YET-- AND HE HAS PLENTY ON US!
NEXT MORNING, A PACKAGE ARRIVES AT THE WAYNE HOME, AND INSIDE IS...
THERE'S A CARD ENCLOSED! LOOK!
A BAT! CARLO MUST HAVE SENT IT AS A WARNING!
A BAT TO THE BATMAN! I SAW YOU AT THE THEATRE LAST NIGHT! NO DOUBT YOU KNOW MY IDENTITY NOW--BUT REMEMBER I KNOW YOURS! I AM GOING TO MISER'S ISLE-- DON'T TRY TO FOLLOW ME! IF I'M CAUGHT, THE WHOLE WORLD WILL KNOW WHO THE BATMAN IS!
CARLO.
MISER'S ISLE--THAT'S WHERE THAT STRANGE ECCENTRIC, OLD PETE JORGEN, LIVES! SUPPOSED TO HAVE BURIED TREASURE-- CARLO MUST BE AFTER IT!
BUT ARE WE GOING AFTER HIM?
YES, DICK! WITH HIS UNCANNY POWER, CARLO CAN BECOME THE WORLD'S GREATEST CRIMINAL! BUT WE'VE GOT TO CATCH HIM! EVEN IF OUR EXPOSURE MEANS THE END OF BATMAN AND ROBIN!
THROATS CHOKED WITH EMOTION, BATMAN AND ROBIN DON THEIR ACTION COSTUMES--FOR THE LAST TIME!
GEE, WE (GULP) SURE HAD (GULP) SOME WONDERFUL TIMES (GULP) IN THESE OUTFITS, DIDN'T WE?
YES, CHUM! THIS IS OUR LAST CASE--LET'S WIND IT UP IN GLORY!
6

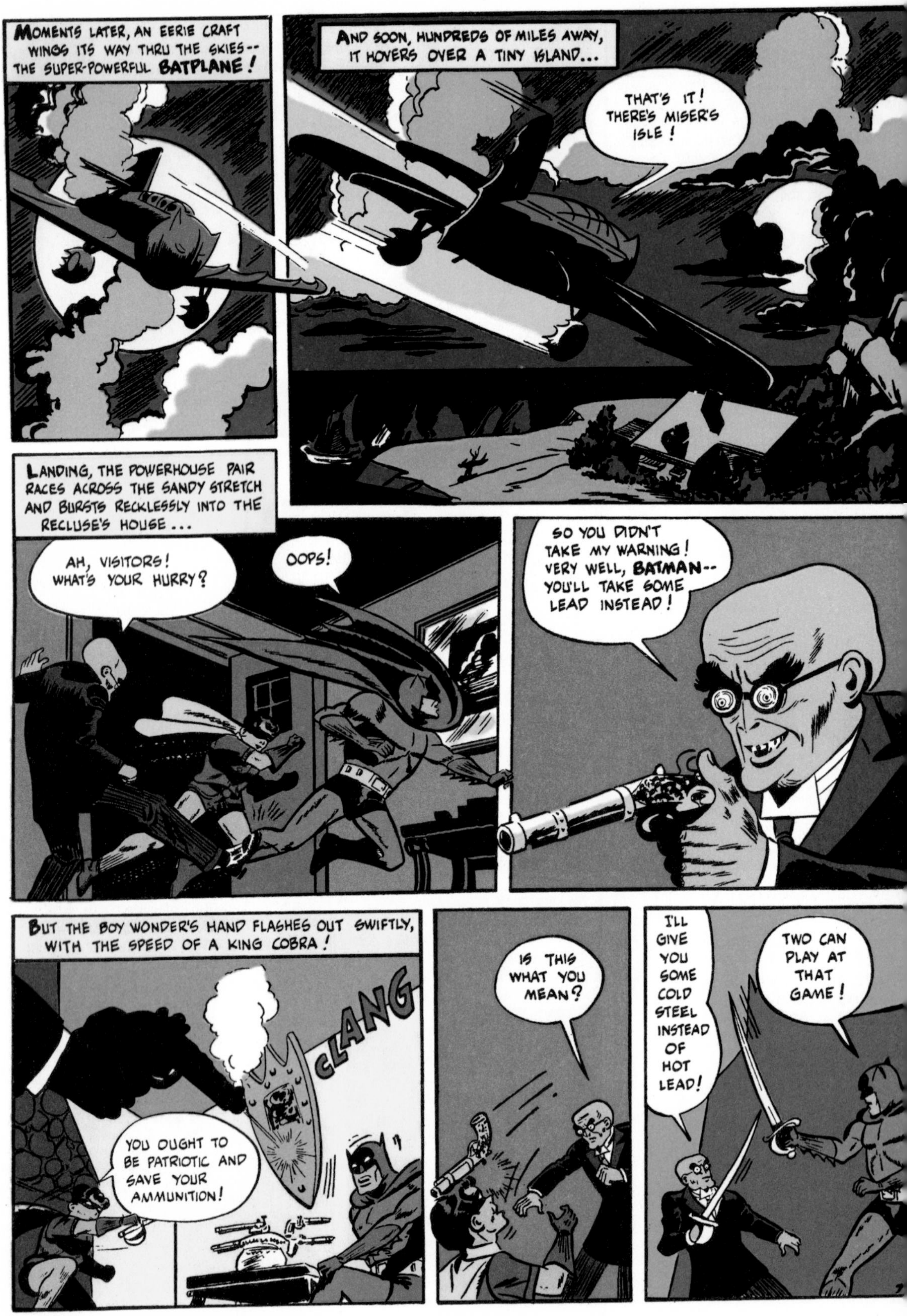
MOMENTS LATER, AN EERIE CRAFT WINGS ITS WAY THRU THE SKIES-- THE SUPER-POWERFUL BATPLANE!
AND SOON, HUNDREDS OF MILES AWAY, IT HOVERS OVER A TINY ISLAND...
THAT'S IT! THERE'S MISER'S ISLE!
LANDING, THE POWERHOUSE PAIR RACES ACROSS THE SANDY STRETCH AND BURSTS RECKLESSLY INTO THE RECLUSE'S HOUSE...
AH, VISITORS! WHAT'S YOUR HURRY?
OOPS!
SO YOU DIDN'T TAKE MY WARNING! VERY WELL, BATMAN-- YOU'LL TAKE SOME LEAD INSTEAD!
BUT THE BOY WONDER'S HAND FLASHES OUT SWIFTLY, WITH THE SPEED OF A KING COBRA!
CLANG
YOU OUGHT TO BE PATRIOTIC AND SAVE YOUR AMMUNITION!
IS THIS WHAT YOU MEAN?
I'LL GIVE YOU SOME COLD STEEL INSTEAD OF HOT LEAD!
TWO CAN PLAY AT THAT GAME!

AND NOW...THE RASP OF STEEL AGAINST STEEL AS MASTER SWORDSMEN CROSS WEAPONS IN A DEADLY DUEL!

HA! YOU'VE MET YOUR MASTER! THE MIND IS QUICKER THAN THE HAND!

THIS FELLOW PARRIES EVERY THRUST I MAKE!

NOW--THIS SURPRISE STROKE SHOULD DISARM HIM!

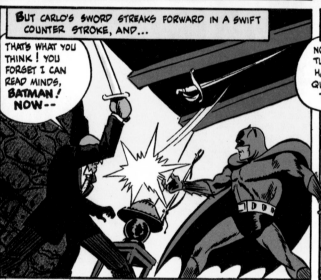

BUT CARLO'S SWORD STREAKS FORWARD IN A SWIFT COUNTER STROKE, AND...

THAT'S WHAT YOU THINK! YOU FORGET I CAN READ MINDS, BATMAN! NOW--

SNATCHING A WHIP FROM THE WALL, THE CAPED MANHUNTER MOVES WITH ELECTRIC SPEED!

NOW IT'S MY TURN! THE HAND IS QUICKER THAN THE EYE!

LET'S SEE WHAT YOU CAN DO WITHOUT WEAPONS!

NOT A CHANCE, BATMAN! YOU'RE MUCH TOO DANGEROUS!

SNAP!

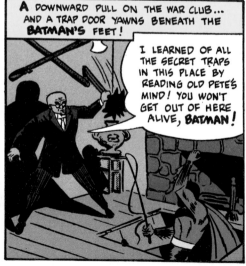

A DOWNWARD PULL ON THE WAR CLUB... AND A TRAP DOOR YAWNS BENEATH THE BATMAN'S FEET!

I LEARNED OF ALL THE SECRET TRAPS IN THIS PLACE BY READING OLD PETE'S MIND! YOU WON'T GET OUT OF HERE ALIVE, BATMAN!

I WON'T PUT THE TWO OF YOU TO-GETHER--YOU MIGHT HELP EACH OTHER ESCAPE! I'VE A NICE RESTING PLACE FOR YOU, BRAT!

189

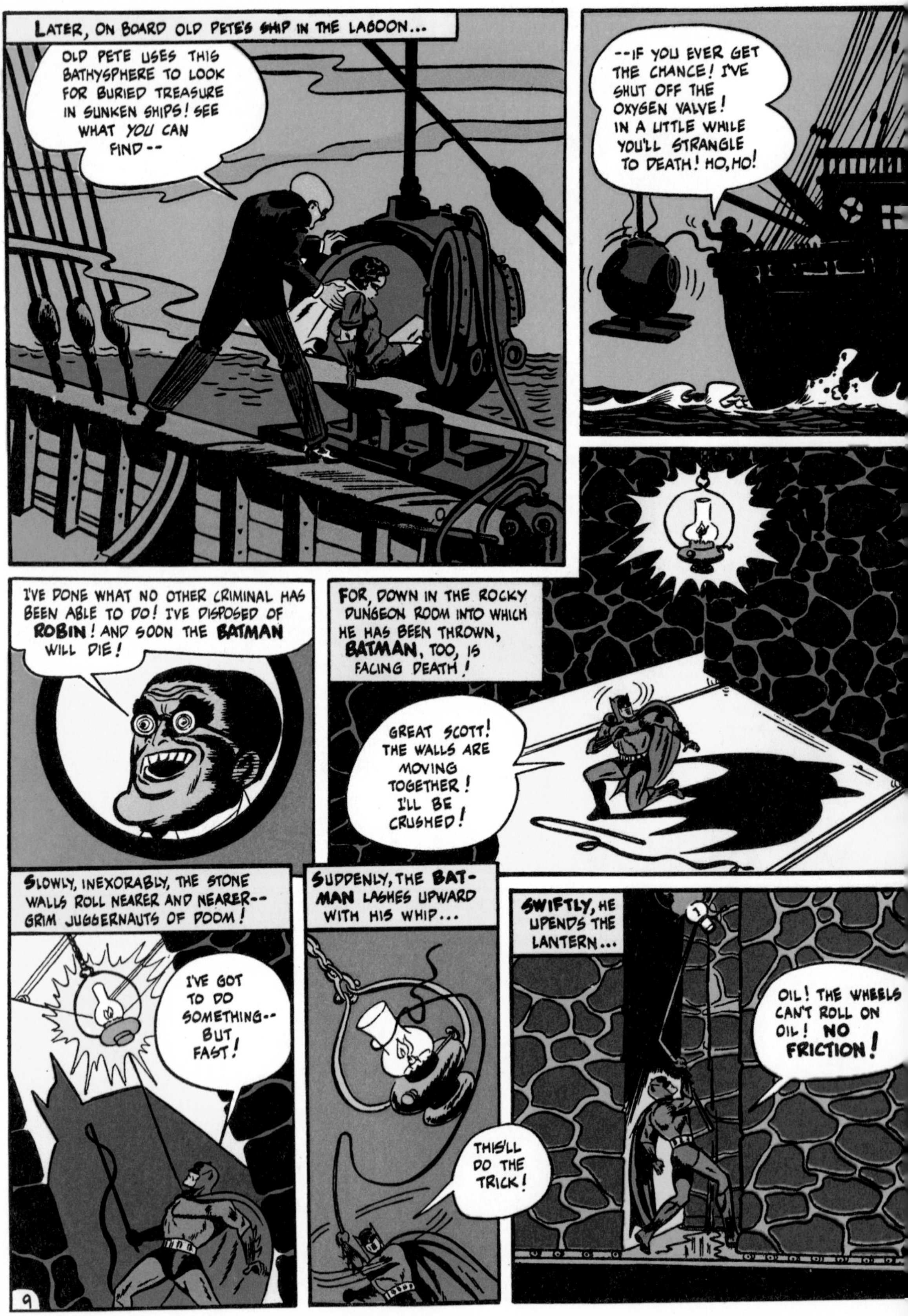

LATER, ON BOARD OLD PETE'S SHIP IN THE LAGOON...
OLD PETE USES THIS BATHYSPHERE TO LOOK FOR BURIED TREASURE IN SUNKEN SHIPS! SEE WHAT YOU CAN FIND--
--IF YOU EVER GET THE CHANCE! I'VE SHUT OFF THE OXYGEN VALVE! IN A LITTLE WHILE YOU'LL STRANGLE TO DEATH! HO, HO!
I'VE DONE WHAT NO OTHER CRIMINAL HAS BEEN ABLE TO DO! I'VE DISPOSED OF ROBIN! AND SOON THE BATMAN WILL DIE!
FOR, DOWN IN THE ROCKY DUNGEON ROOM INTO WHICH HE HAS BEEN THROWN, BATMAN, TOO, IS FACING DEATH!
GREAT SCOTT! THE WALLS ARE MOVING TOGETHER! I'LL BE CRUSHED!
SLOWLY, INEXORABLY, THE STONE WALLS ROLL NEARER AND NEARER-- GRIM JUGGERNAUTS OF DOOM!
I'VE GOT TO DO SOMETHING-- BUT FAST!
9
SUDDENLY, THE BATMAN LASHES UPWARD WITH HIS WHIP...
THIS'LL DO THE TRICK!
SWIFTLY, HE UPENDS THE LANTERN...
OIL! THE WHEELS CAN'T ROLL ON OIL! NO FRICTION!

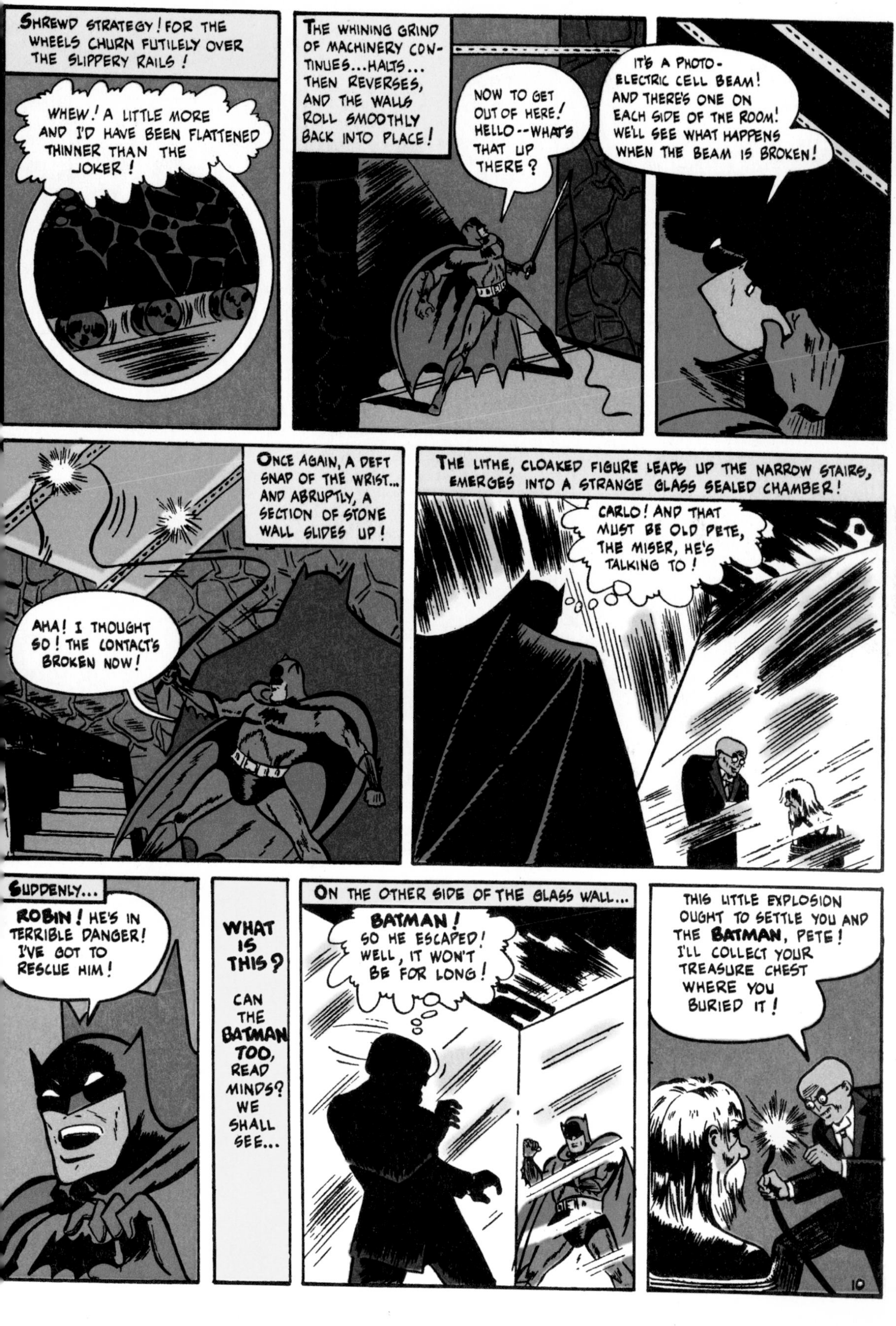

SHREWD STRATEGY! FOR THE WHEELS CHURN FUTILELY OVER THE SLIPPERY RAILS!
WHEW! A LITTLE MORE AND I'D HAVE BEEN FLATTENED THINNER THAN THE JOKER!
THE WHINING GRIND OF MACHINERY CONTINUES...HALTS... THEN REVERSES, AND THE WALLS ROLL SMOOTHLY BACK INTO PLACE!
NOW TO GET OUT OF HERE! HELLO--WHAT'S THAT UP THERE?
IT'S A PHOTO-ELECTRIC CELL BEAM! AND THERE'S ONE ON EACH SIDE OF THE ROOM! WE'LL SEE WHAT HAPPENS WHEN THE BEAM IS BROKEN!
ONCE AGAIN, A DEFT SNAP OF THE WRIST... AND ABRUPTLY, A SECTION OF STONE WALL SLIDES UP!
AHA! I THOUGHT SO! THE CONTACT'S BROKEN NOW!
THE LITHE, CLOAKED FIGURE LEAPS UP THE NARROW STAIRS, EMERGES INTO A STRANGE GLASS SEALED CHAMBER!
CARLO! AND THAT MUST BE OLD PETE, THE MISER, HE'S TALKING TO!
SUDDENLY...
ROBIN! HE'S IN TERRIBLE DANGER! I'VE GOT TO RESCUE HIM!
WHAT IS THIS? CAN THE BATMAN TOO, READ MINDS? WE SHALL SEE...
ON THE OTHER SIDE OF THE GLASS WALL...
BATMAN! SO HE ESCAPED! WELL, IT WON'T BE FOR LONG!
THIS LITTLE EXPLOSION OUGHT TO SETTLE YOU AND THE BATMAN, PETE! I'LL COLLECT YOUR TREASURE CHEST WHERE YOU BURIED IT!
10

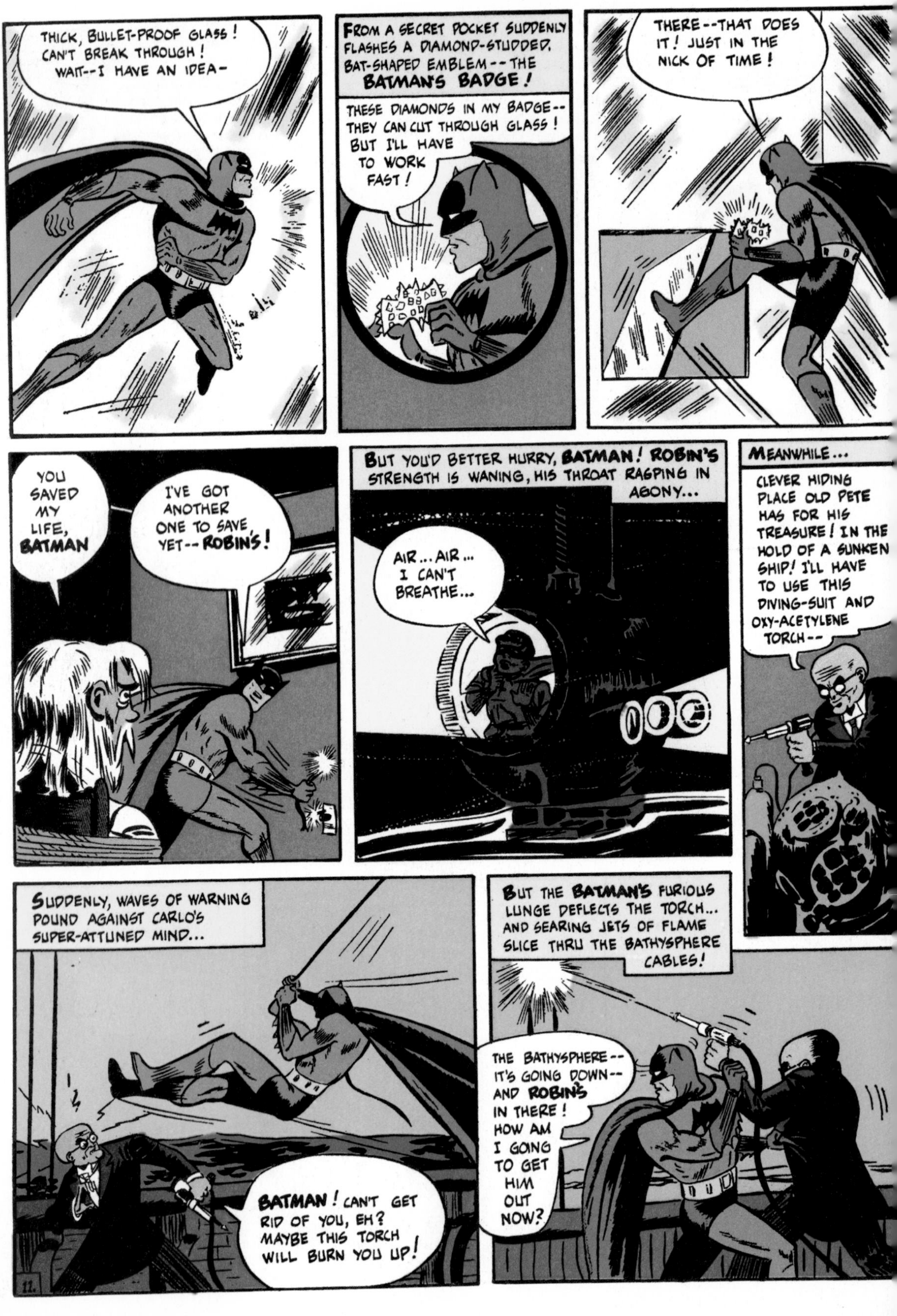
THICK, BULLET-PROOF GLASS! CAN'T BREAK THROUGH! WAIT--I HAVE AN IDEA-
FROM A SECRET POCKET SUDDENLY FLASHES A DIAMOND-STUDDED, BAT-SHAPED EMBLEM--THE BATMAN'S BADGE!
THESE DIAMONDS IN MY BADGE--THEY CAN CUT THROUGH GLASS! BUT I'LL HAVE TO WORK FAST!
THERE--THAT DOES IT! JUST IN THE NICK OF TIME!
YOU SAVED MY LIFE, BATMAN
I'VE GOT ANOTHER ONE TO SAVE YET--ROBIN'S!
BUT YOU'D BETTER HURRY, BATMAN! ROBIN'S STRENGTH IS WANING, HIS THROAT RASPING IN AGONY...
AIR... AIR... I CAN'T BREATHE...
MEANWHILE...
CLEVER HIDING PLACE OLD PETE HAS FOR HIS TREASURE! IN THE HOLD OF A SUNKEN SHIP! I'LL HAVE TO USE THIS DIVING-SUIT AND OXY-ACETYLENE TORCH--
SUDDENLY, WAVES OF WARNING POUND AGAINST CARLO'S SUPER-ATTUNED MIND...
BATMAN! CAN'T GET RID OF YOU, EH? MAYBE THIS TORCH WILL BURN YOU UP!
11.
BUT THE BATMAN'S FURIOUS LUNGE DEFLECTS THE TORCH... AND SEARING JETS OF FLAME SLICE THRU THE BATHYSPHERE CABLES!
THE BATHYSPHERE--IT'S GOING DOWN--AND ROBIN'S IN THERE! HOW AM I GOING TO GET HIM OUT NOW?

A FURY-PACKED FIST EXPLODES AGAINST CARLO'S CHIN!

OUT OF MY WAY!

THIS IS MY ONLY CHANCE! DIVERS USE THEM FOR UNDERSEA SALVAGING!

DRAWING A DEEP BREATH, THE BATMAN DIVES OVER THE RAIL, TORCH IN HAND!

A LIVID BOLT OF HEAT BLASTS AGAINST THE STEEL SIDES OF THE BATHYSPHERE.

HOLD ON, ROBIN! JUST A LITTLE WHILE, KID--JUST A LITTLE WHILE!

LUNGS YEARNING FOR PRECIOUS OXYGEN, BATMAN STICKS TO HIS TASK UNTIL FINALLY....

PRESSURE TOUGH... GOT TO GET TO THE SURFACE!

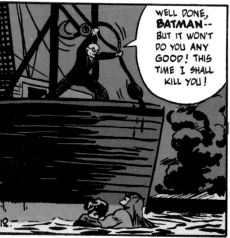

WELL DONE, BATMAN-- BUT IT WON'T DO YOU ANY GOOD! THIS TIME I SHALL KILL YOU!

18.

SUDDENLY, A SHOT RINGS OUT...

BANG!

UGH-- SHOT....

AND ON SHORE...

TRY TO TAKE MY FORTUNE, HUH? SNEAKING THIEF! WELL, THAT SQUARES ME WITH THE BATMAN NOW!

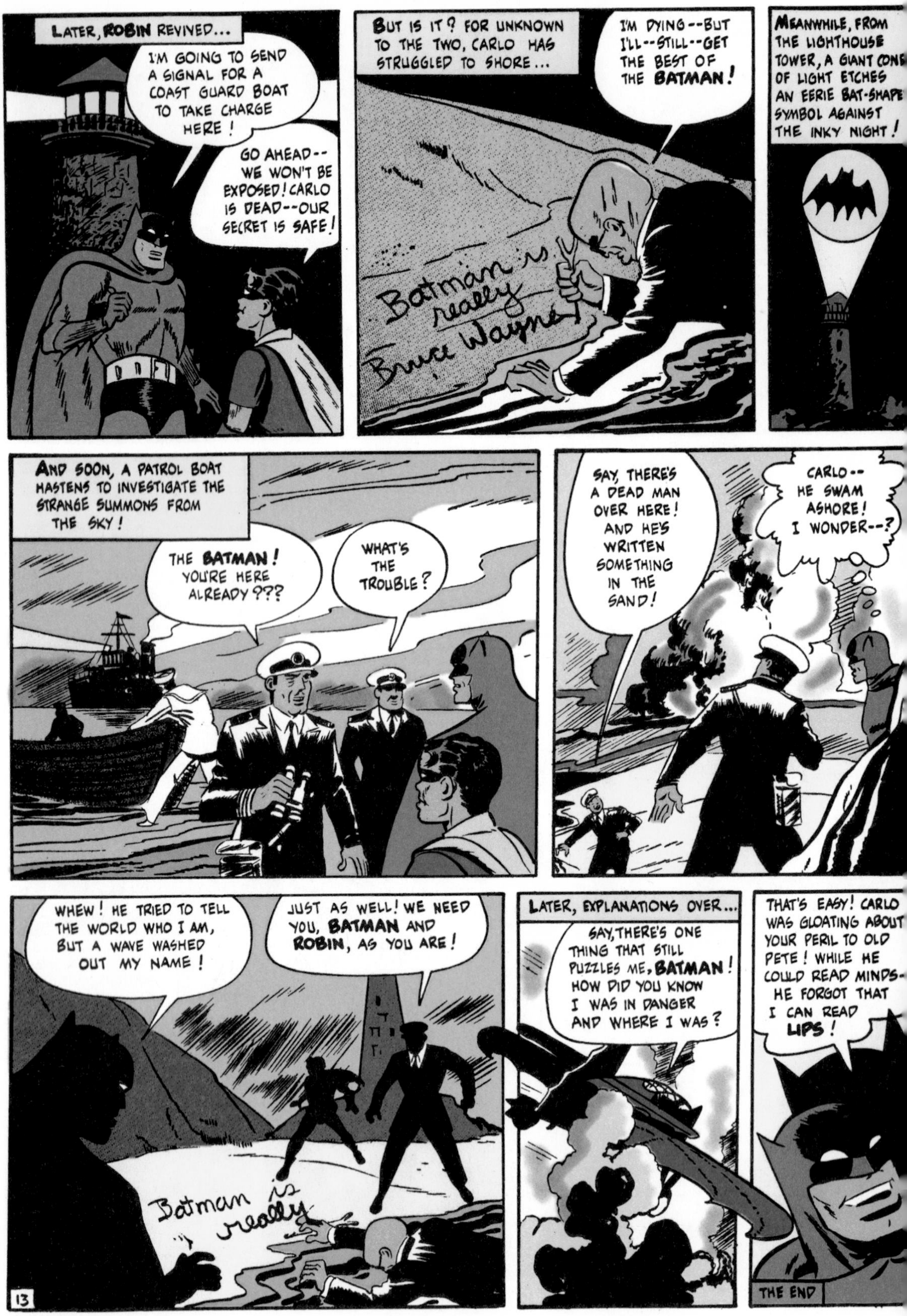
LATER, ROBIN REVIVED...
I'M GOING TO SEND A SIGNAL FOR A COAST GUARD BOAT TO TAKE CHARGE HERE!
GO AHEAD-- WE WON'T BE EXPOSED! CARLO IS DEAD--OUR SECRET IS SAFE!
BUT IS IT? FOR UNKNOWN TO THE TWO, CARLO HAS STRUGGLED TO SHORE...
I'M DYING--BUT I'LL--STILL--GET THE BEST OF THE BATMAN!
Batman is really Bruce Wayne
MEANWHILE, FROM THE LIGHTHOUSE TOWER, A GIANT CONE OF LIGHT ETCHES AN EERIE BAT-SHAPE SYMBOL AGAINST THE INKY NIGHT!
AND SOON, A PATROL BOAT HASTENS TO INVESTIGATE THE STRANGE SUMMONS FROM THE SKY!
THE BATMAN! YOU'RE HERE ALREADY???
WHAT'S THE TROUBLE?
SAY, THERE'S A DEAD MAN OVER HERE! AND HE'S WRITTEN SOMETHING IN THE SAND!
CARLO-- HE SWAM ASHORE! I WONDER--?
WHEW! HE TRIED TO TELL THE WORLD WHO I AM, BUT A WAVE WASHED OUT MY NAME!
JUST AS WELL! WE NEED YOU, BATMAN AND ROBIN, AS YOU ARE!
Batman is really
13
LATER, EXPLANATIONS OVER...
SAY, THERE'S ONE THING THAT STILL PUZZLES ME, BATMAN! HOW DID YOU KNOW I WAS IN DANGER AND WHERE I WAS?
THAT'S EASY! CARLO WAS GLOATING ABOUT YOUR PERIL TO OLD PETE! WHILE HE COULD READ MINDS-HE FORGOT THAT I CAN READ LIPS!
THE END

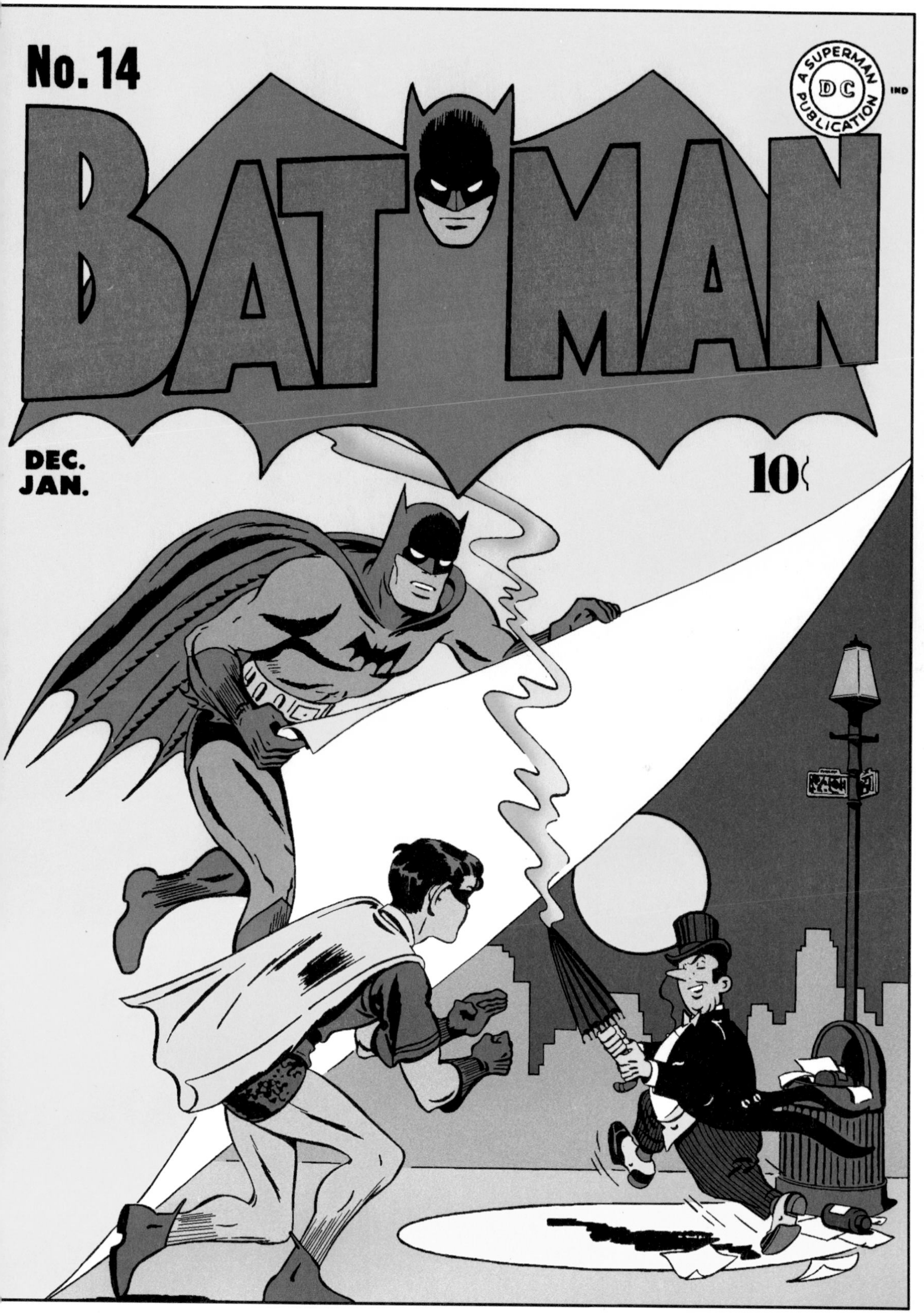
No. 14
A SUPERMAN DC PUBLICATION
IND
BATMAN
DEC.
JAN.
10¢

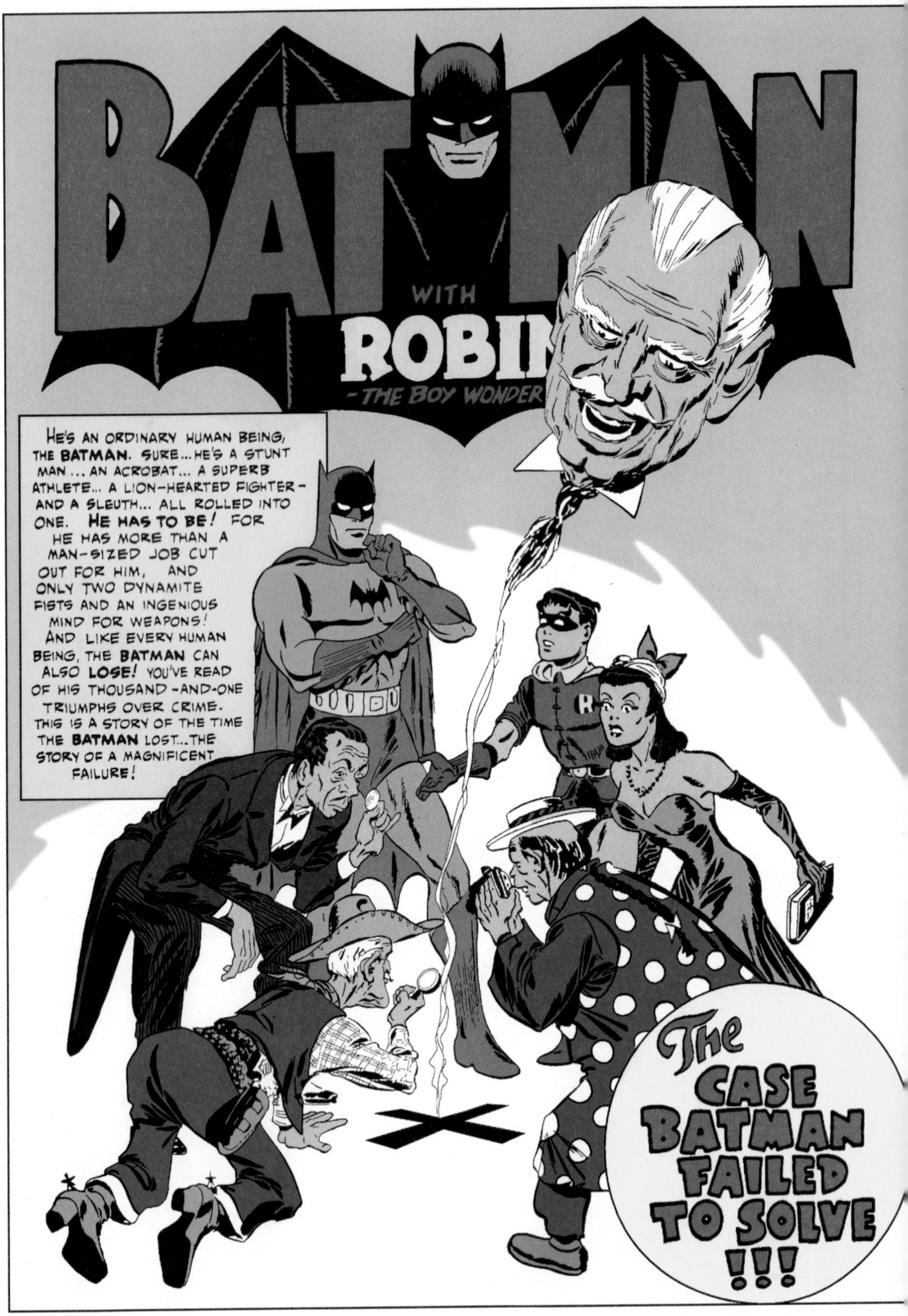
BATMAN
WITH ROBIN -THE BOY WONDER
HE'S AN ORDINARY HUMAN BEING, THE BATMAN. SURE... HE'S A STUNT MAN ... AN ACROBAT... A SUPERB ATHLETE... A LION-HEARTED FIGHTER - AND A SLEUTH... ALL ROLLED INTO ONE. HE HAS TO BE! FOR HE HAS MORE THAN A MAN-SIZED JOB CUT OUT FOR HIM, AND ONLY TWO DYNAMITE FISTS AND AN INGENIOUS MIND FOR WEAPONS! AND LIKE EVERY HUMAN BEING, THE BATMAN CAN ALSO LOSE! YOU'VE READ OF HIS THOUSAND-AND-ONE TRIUMPHS OVER CRIME. THIS IS A STORY OF THE TIME THE BATMAN LOST...THE STORY OF A MAGNIFICENT FAILURE!
The CASE BATMAN FAILED TO SOLVE !!!

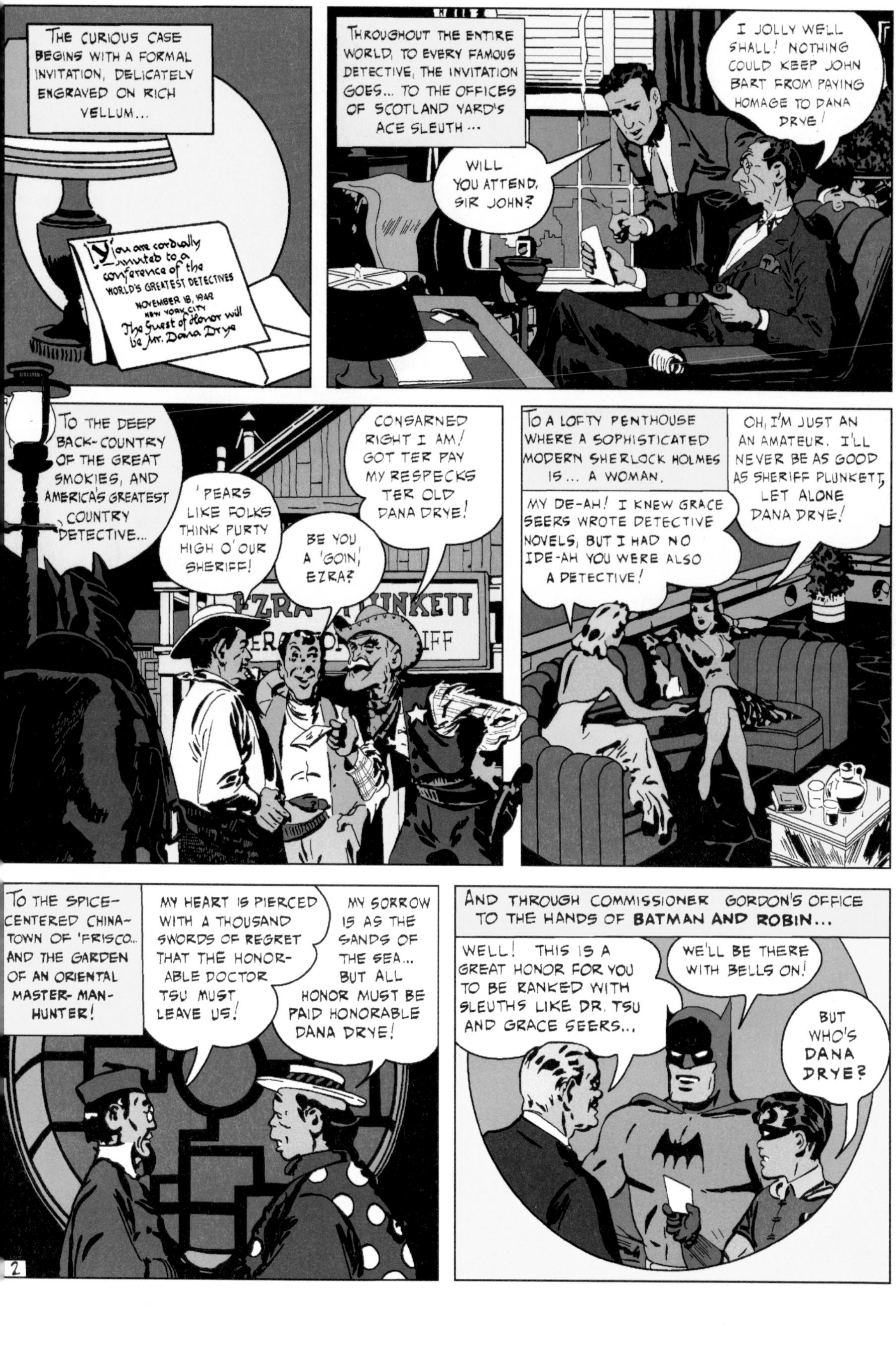
THE CURIOUS CASE BEGINS WITH A FORMAL INVITATION, DELICATELY ENGRAVED ON RICH VELLUM...
You are cordially invited to a conference of the WORLD'S GREATEST DETECTIVES NOVEMBER 18, 1942 NEW YORK CITY The Guest of Honor will be Mr. Dana Drye
THROUGHOUT THE ENTIRE WORLD, TO EVERY FAMOUS DETECTIVE, THE INVITATION GOES... TO THE OFFICES OF SCOTLAND YARD'S ACE SLEUTH ...
WILL YOU ATTEND, SIR JOHN?
I JOLLY WELL SHALL! NOTHING COULD KEEP JOHN BART FROM PAYING HOMAGE TO DANA DRYE!
TO THE DEEP BACK-COUNTRY OF THE GREAT SMOKIES, AND AMERICA'S GREATEST COUNTRY DETECTIVE...
'PEARS LIKE FOLKS THINK PURTY HIGH O' OUR SHERIFF!
BE YOU A 'GOIN', EZRA?
CONSARNED RIGHT I AM! GOT TER PAY MY RESPECKS TER OLD DANA DRYE!
TO A LOFTY PENTHOUSE WHERE A SOPHISTICATED MODERN SHERLOCK HOLMES IS... A WOMAN.
MY DE-AH! I KNEW GRACE SEERS WROTE DETECTIVE NOVELS, BUT I HAD NO IDE-AH YOU WERE ALSO A DETECTIVE!
OH, I'M JUST AN AN AMATEUR. I'LL NEVER BE AS GOOD AS SHERIFF PLUNKETT, LET ALONE DANA DRYE!
TO THE SPICE-CENTERED CHINA-TOWN OF 'FRISCO... AND THE GARDEN OF AN ORIENTAL MASTER-MAN-HUNTER!
MY HEART IS PIERCED WITH A THOUSAND SWORDS OF REGRET THAT THE HONOR-ABLE DOCTOR TSU MUST LEAVE US!
MY SORROW IS AS THE SANDS OF THE SEA... BUT ALL HONOR MUST BE PAID HONORABLE DANA DRYE!
AND THROUGH COMMISSIONER GORDON'S OFFICE TO THE HANDS OF BATMAN AND ROBIN...
WELL! THIS IS A GREAT HONOR FOR YOU TO BE RANKED WITH SLEUTHS LIKE DR. TSU AND GRACE SEERS...
WE'LL BE THERE WITH BELLS ON!
BUT WHO'S DANA DRYE?
2

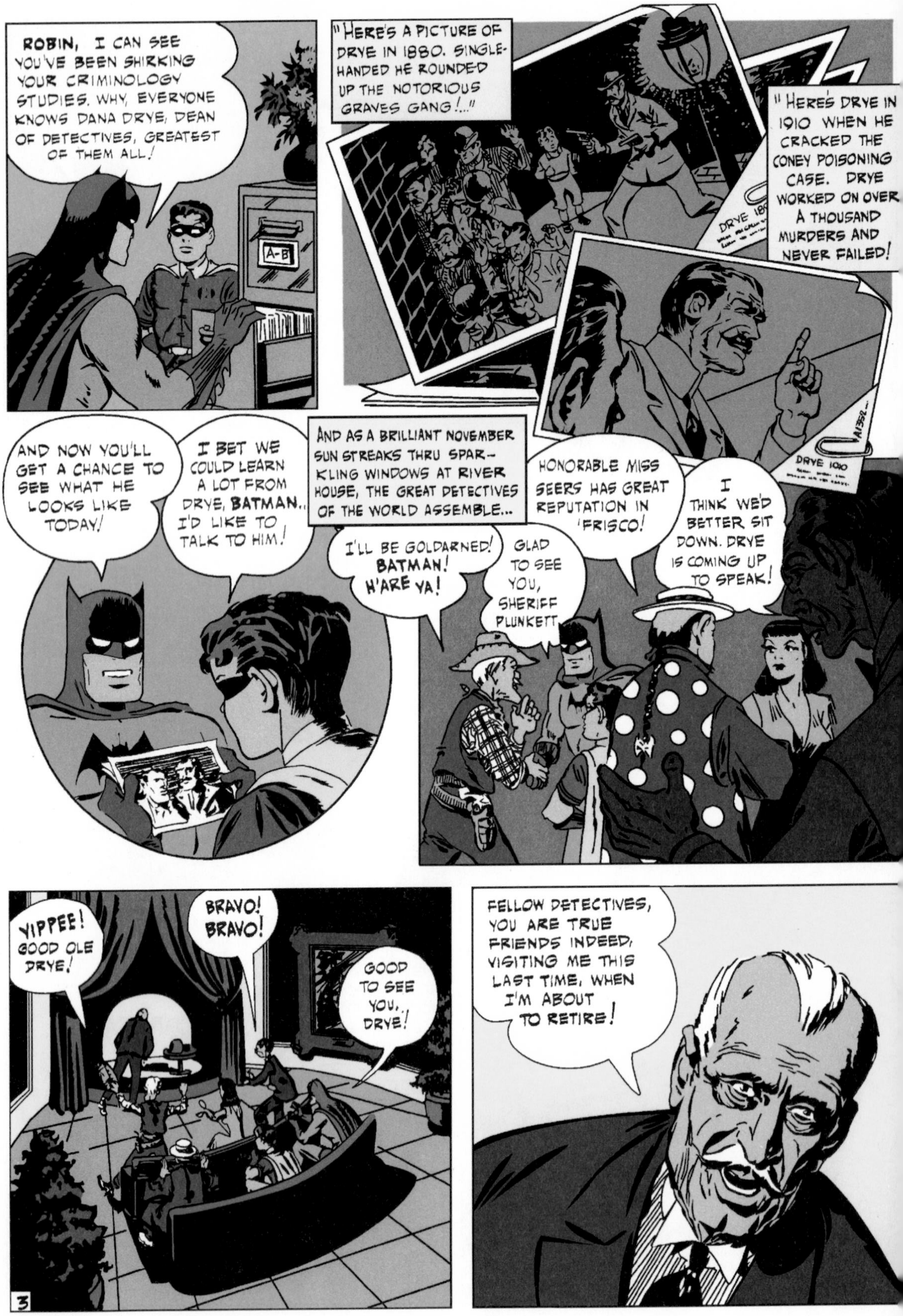
ROBIN, I CAN SEE YOU'VE BEEN SHIRKING YOUR CRIMINOLOGY STUDIES. WHY, EVERYONE KNOWS DANA DRYE, DEAN OF DETECTIVES, GREATEST OF THEM ALL!
A-B
"HERE'S A PICTURE OF DRYE IN 1880. SINGLE-HANDED HE ROUNDED UP THE NOTORIOUS GRAVES GANG!..."
"HERE'S DRYE IN 1910 WHEN HE CRACKED THE CONEY POISONING CASE. DRYE WORKED ON OVER A THOUSAND MURDERS AND NEVER FAILED!
DRYE 1910
AND NOW YOU'LL GET A CHANCE TO SEE WHAT HE LOOKS LIKE TODAY!
I BET WE COULD LEARN A LOT FROM DRYE, BATMAN.. I'D LIKE TO TALK TO HIM!
AND AS A BRILLIANT NOVEMBER SUN STREAKS THRU SPAR-KLING WINDOWS AT RIVER HOUSE, THE GREAT DETECTIVES OF THE WORLD ASSEMBLE...
I'LL BE GOLDARNED! BATMAN! H'ARE YA!
GLAD TO SEE YOU, SHERIFF PLUNKETT
HONORABLE MISS SEERS HAS GREAT REPUTATION IN 'FRISCO!
I THINK WE'D BETTER SIT DOWN. DRYE IS COMING UP TO SPEAK!
YIPPEE! GOOD OLE DRYE!
BRAVO! BRAVO!
GOOD TO SEE YOU, DRYE!
3
FELLOW DETECTIVES, YOU ARE TRUE FRIENDS INDEED, VISITING ME THIS LAST TIME, WHEN I'M ABOUT TO RETIRE!

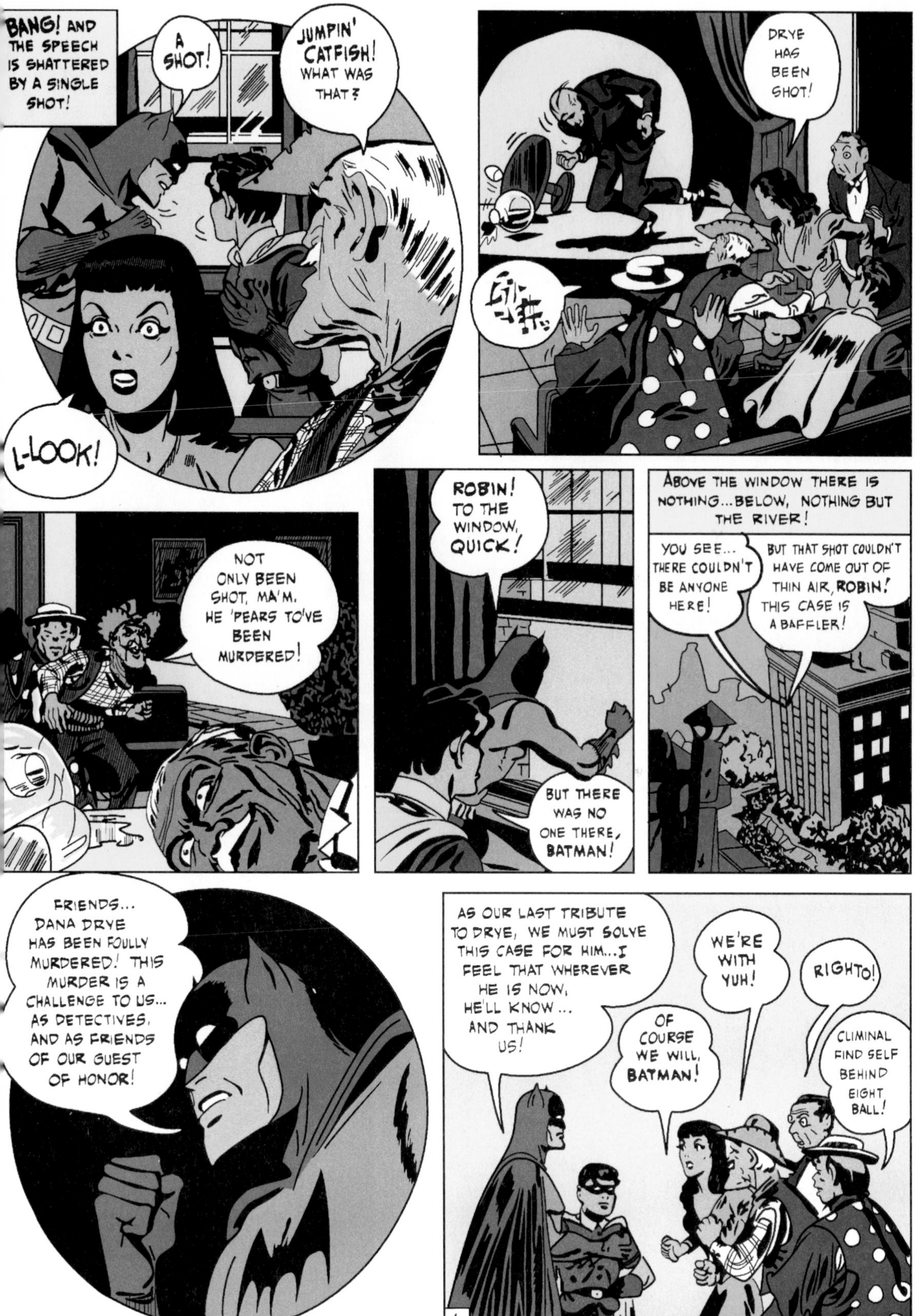
BANG! AND THE SPEECH IS SHATTERED BY A SINGLE SHOT!
A SHOT!
JUMPIN' CATFISH! WHAT WAS THAT?
L-LOOK!
DRYE HAS BEEN SHOT!
NOT ONLY BEEN SHOT, MA'M. HE 'PEARS TO'VE BEEN MURDERED!
ROBIN! TO THE WINDOW, QUICK!
BUT THERE WAS NO ONE THERE, BATMAN!
ABOVE THE WINDOW THERE IS NOTHING...BELOW, NOTHING BUT THE RIVER!
YOU SEE... THERE COULDN'T BE ANYONE HERE!
BUT THAT SHOT COULDN'T HAVE COME OUT OF THIN AIR, ROBIN! THIS CASE IS A BAFFLER!
FRIENDS... DANA DRYE HAS BEEN FOULLY MURDERED! THIS MURDER IS A CHALLENGE TO US... AS DETECTIVES, AND AS FRIENDS OF OUR GUEST OF HONOR!
AS OUR LAST TRIBUTE TO DRYE, WE MUST SOLVE THIS CASE FOR HIM...I FEEL THAT WHEREVER HE IS NOW, HE'LL KNOW... AND THANK US!
OF COURSE WE WILL, BATMAN!
WE'RE WITH YUH!
RIGHTO!
CLIMINAL FIND SELF BEHIND EIGHT BALL!
4

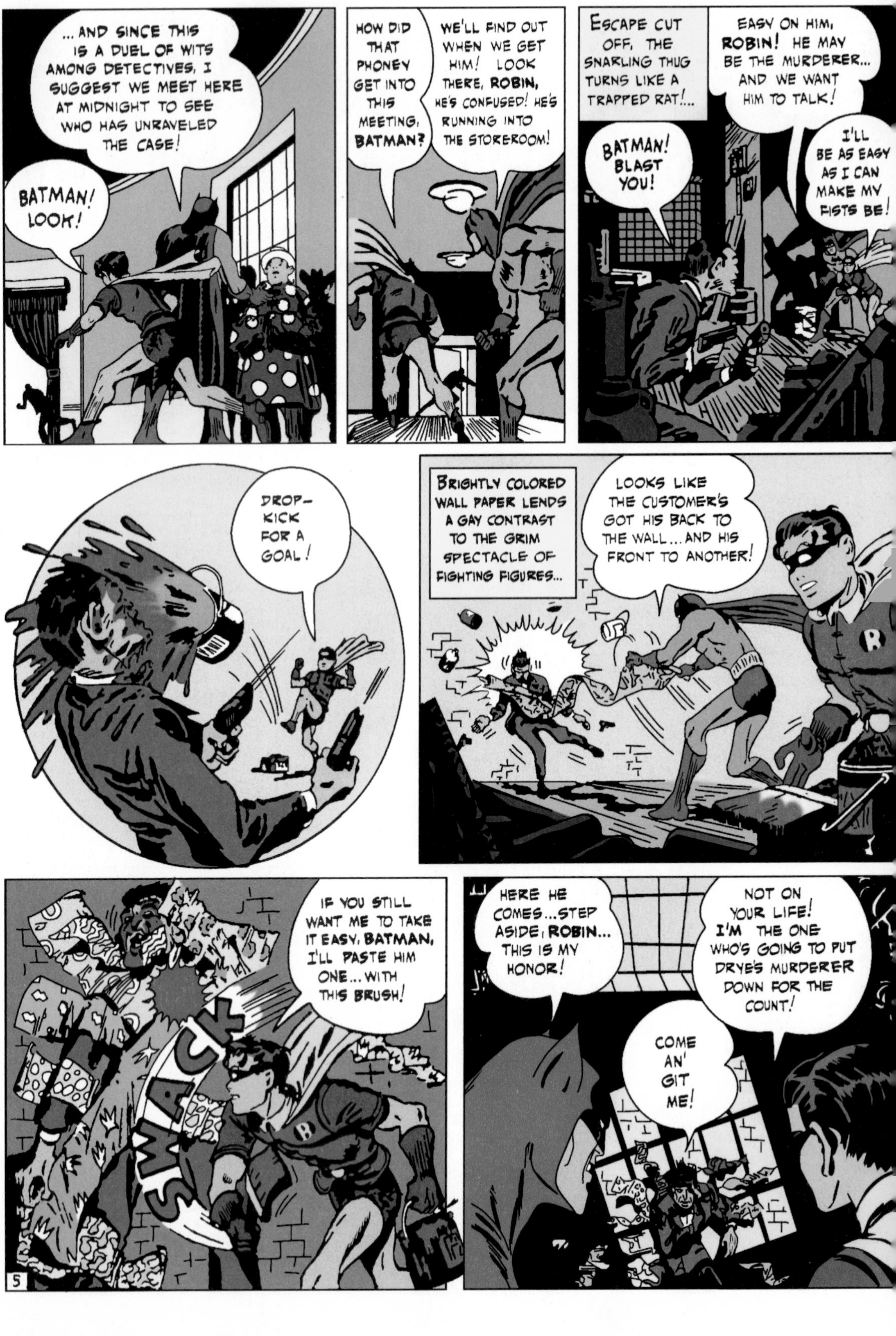
... AND SINCE THIS IS A DUEL OF WITS AMONG DETECTIVES, I SUGGEST WE MEET HERE AT MIDNIGHT TO SEE WHO HAS UNRAVELED THE CASE!
BATMAN! LOOK!
HOW DID THAT PHONEY GET INTO THIS MEETING, BATMAN?
WE'LL FIND OUT WHEN WE GET HIM! LOOK THERE, ROBIN, HE'S CONFUSED! HE'S RUNNING INTO THE STOREROOM!
ESCAPE CUT OFF, THE SNARLING THUG TURNS LIKE A TRAPPED RAT!...
EASY ON HIM, ROBIN! HE MAY BE THE MURDERER... AND WE WANT HIM TO TALK!
BATMAN! BLAST YOU!
I'LL BE AS EASY AS I CAN MAKE MY FISTS BE!
DROP-KICK FOR A GOAL!
BRIGHTLY COLORED WALL PAPER LENDS A GAY CONTRAST TO THE GRIM SPECTACLE OF FIGHTING FIGURES...
LOOKS LIKE THE CUSTOMER'S GOT HIS BACK TO THE WALL... AND HIS FRONT TO ANOTHER!
IF YOU STILL WANT ME TO TAKE IT EASY, BATMAN, I'LL PASTE HIM ONE... WITH THIS BRUSH!
SMACK
5
HERE HE COMES...STEP ASIDE, ROBIN... THIS IS MY HONOR!
NOT ON YOUR LIFE! I'M THE ONE WHO'S GOING TO PUT DRYE'S MURDERER DOWN FOR THE COUNT!
COME AN' GIT ME!

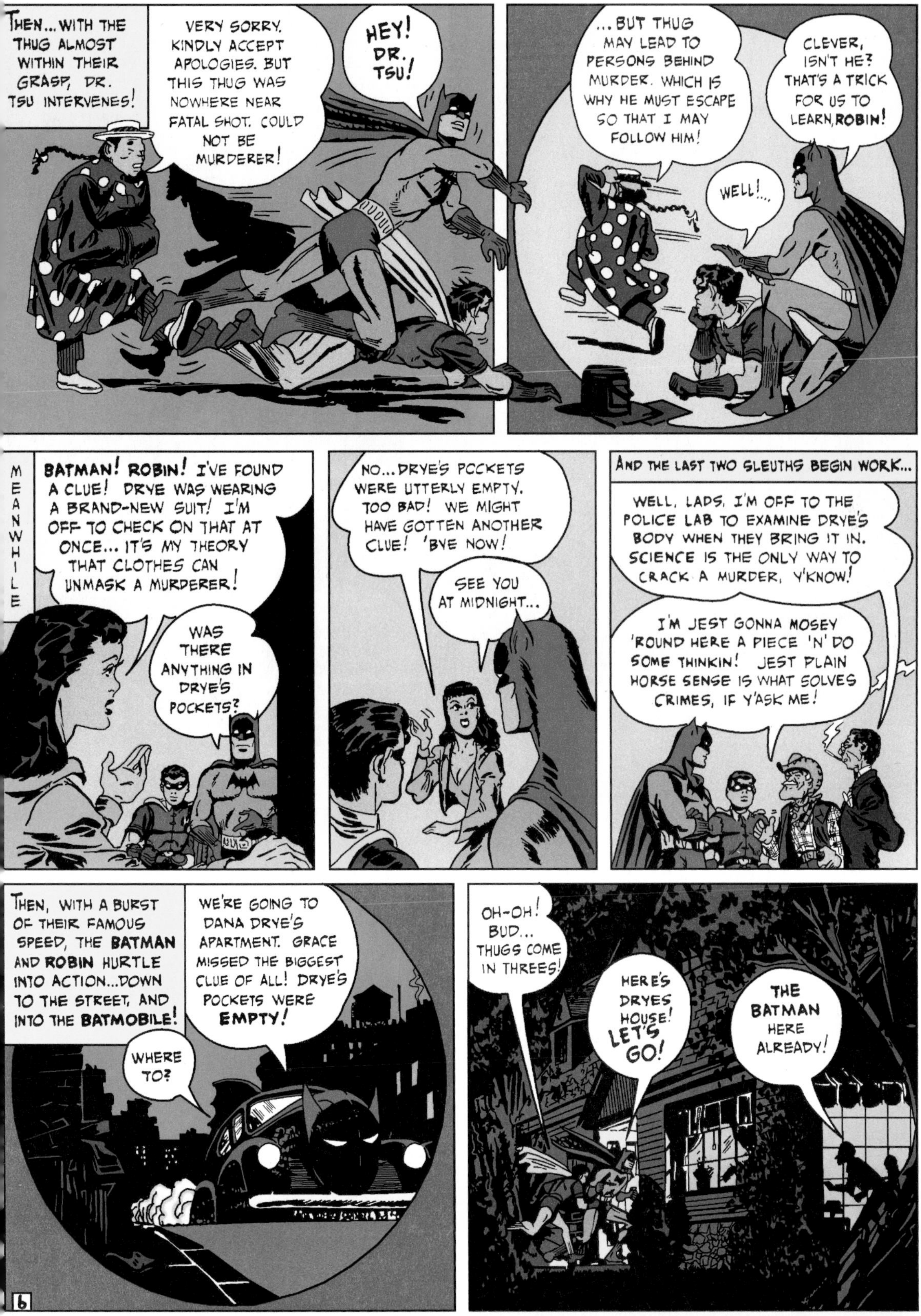
THEN... WITH THE THUG ALMOST WITHIN THEIR GRASP, DR. TSU INTERVENES!
VERY SORRY. KINDLY ACCEPT APOLOGIES. BUT THIS THUG WAS NOWHERE NEAR FATAL SHOT. COULD NOT BE MURDERER!
HEY! DR. TSU!
...BUT THUG MAY LEAD TO PERSONS BEHIND MURDER. WHICH IS WHY HE MUST ESCAPE SO THAT I MAY FOLLOW HIM!
CLEVER, ISN'T HE? THAT'S A TRICK FOR US TO LEARN, ROBIN!
WELL!...
MEANWHILE
BATMAN! ROBIN! I'VE FOUND A CLUE! DRYE WAS WEARING A BRAND-NEW SUIT! I'M OFF TO CHECK ON THAT AT ONCE... IT'S MY THEORY THAT CLOTHES CAN UNMASK A MURDERER!
WAS THERE ANYTHING IN DRYE'S POCKETS?
NO... DRYE'S POCKETS WERE UTTERLY EMPTY. TOO BAD! WE MIGHT HAVE GOTTEN ANOTHER CLUE! 'BYE NOW!
SEE YOU AT MIDNIGHT...
AND THE LAST TWO SLEUTHS BEGIN WORK...
WELL, LADS, I'M OFF TO THE POLICE LAB TO EXAMINE DRYE'S BODY WHEN THEY BRING IT IN. SCIENCE IS THE ONLY WAY TO CRACK A MURDER, Y'KNOW!
I'M JEST GONNA MOSEY 'ROUND HERE A PIECE 'N' DO SOME THINKIN! JEST PLAIN HORSE SENSE IS WHAT SOLVES CRIMES, IF Y'ASK ME!
THEN, WITH A BURST OF THEIR FAMOUS SPEED, THE BATMAN AND ROBIN HURTLE INTO ACTION...DOWN TO THE STREET, AND INTO THE BATMOBILE!
WE'RE GOING TO DANA DRYE'S APARTMENT. GRACE MISSED THE BIGGEST CLUE OF ALL! DRYE'S POCKETS WERE EMPTY!
WHERE TO?
6
OH-OH! BUD... THUGS COME IN THREES!
HERE'S DRYES HOUSE! LET'S GO!
THE BATMAN HERE ALREADY!

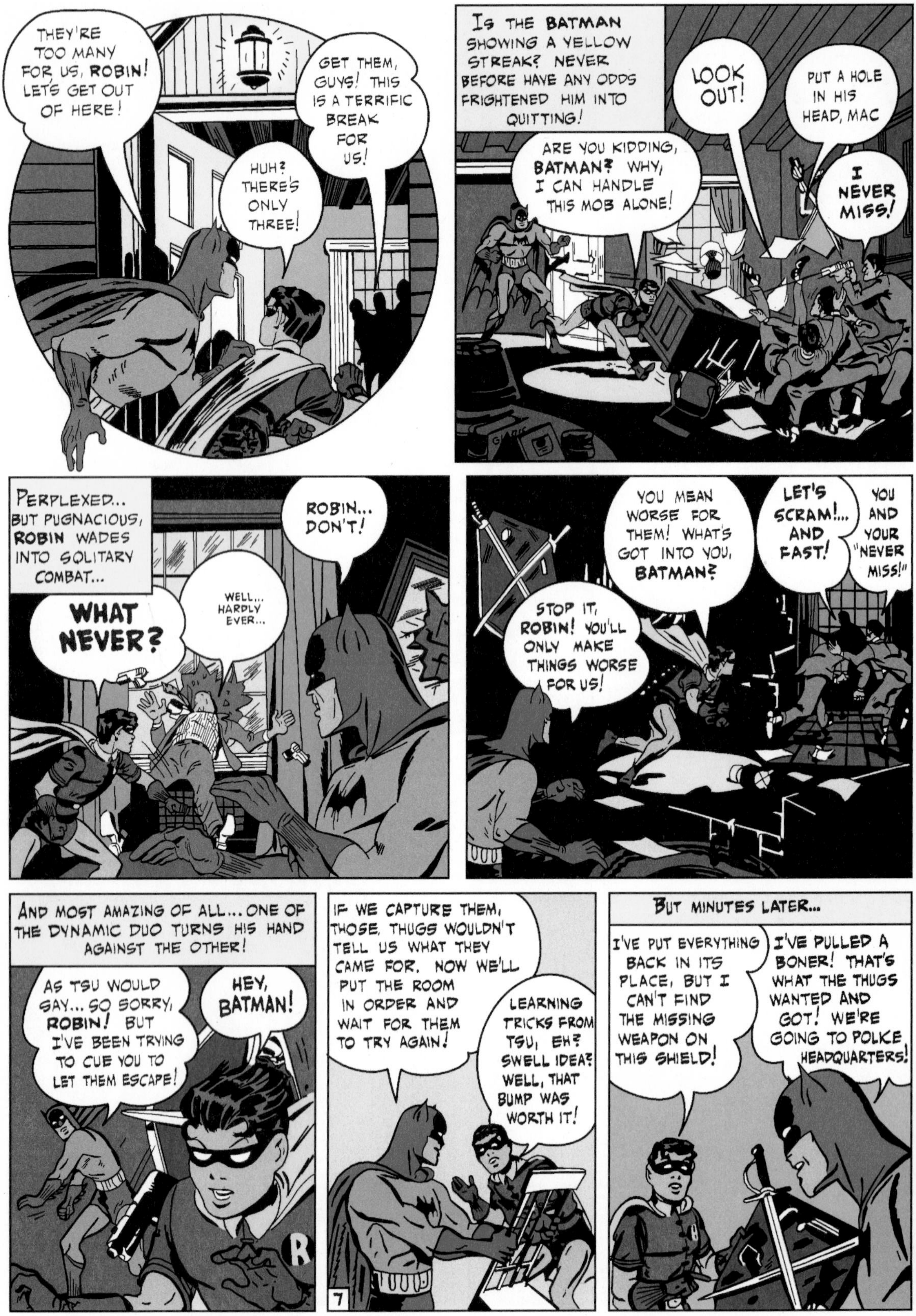
THEY'RE TOO MANY FOR US, ROBIN! LET'S GET OUT OF HERE!
GET THEM, GUYS! THIS IS A TERRIFIC BREAK FOR US!
HUH? THERE'S ONLY THREE!
IS THE BATMAN SHOWING A YELLOW STREAK? NEVER BEFORE HAVE ANY ODDS FRIGHTENED HIM INTO QUITTING!
LOOK OUT!
PUT A HOLE IN HIS HEAD, MAC
ARE YOU KIDDING, BATMAN? WHY, I CAN HANDLE THIS MOB ALONE!
I NEVER MISS!
PERPLEXED... BUT PUGNACIOUS, ROBIN WADES INTO SOLITARY COMBAT...
ROBIN... DON'T!
WHAT NEVER?
WELL... HARDLY EVER...
YOU MEAN WORSE FOR THEM! WHAT'S GOT INTO YOU, BATMAN?
LET'S SCRAM!... AND FAST!
YOU AND YOUR "NEVER MISS!"
STOP IT, ROBIN! YOU'LL ONLY MAKE THINGS WORSE FOR US!
AND MOST AMAZING OF ALL... ONE OF THE DYNAMIC DUO TURNS HIS HAND AGAINST THE OTHER!
AS TSU WOULD SAY... SO SORRY, ROBIN! BUT I'VE BEEN TRYING TO CUE YOU TO LET THEM ESCAPE!
HEY, BATMAN!
IF WE CAPTURE THEM, THOSE THUGS WOULDN'T TELL US WHAT THEY CAME FOR. NOW WE'LL PUT THE ROOM IN ORDER AND WAIT FOR THEM TO TRY AGAIN!
LEARNING TRICKS FROM TSU, EH? SWELL IDEA? WELL, THAT BUMP WAS WORTH IT!
7
BUT MINUTES LATER...
I'VE PUT EVERYTHING BACK IN ITS PLACE, BUT I CAN'T FIND THE MISSING WEAPON ON THIS SHIELD!
I'VE PULLED A BONER! THAT'S WHAT THE THUGS WANTED AND GOT! WE'RE GOING TO POLKE HEADQUARTERS!

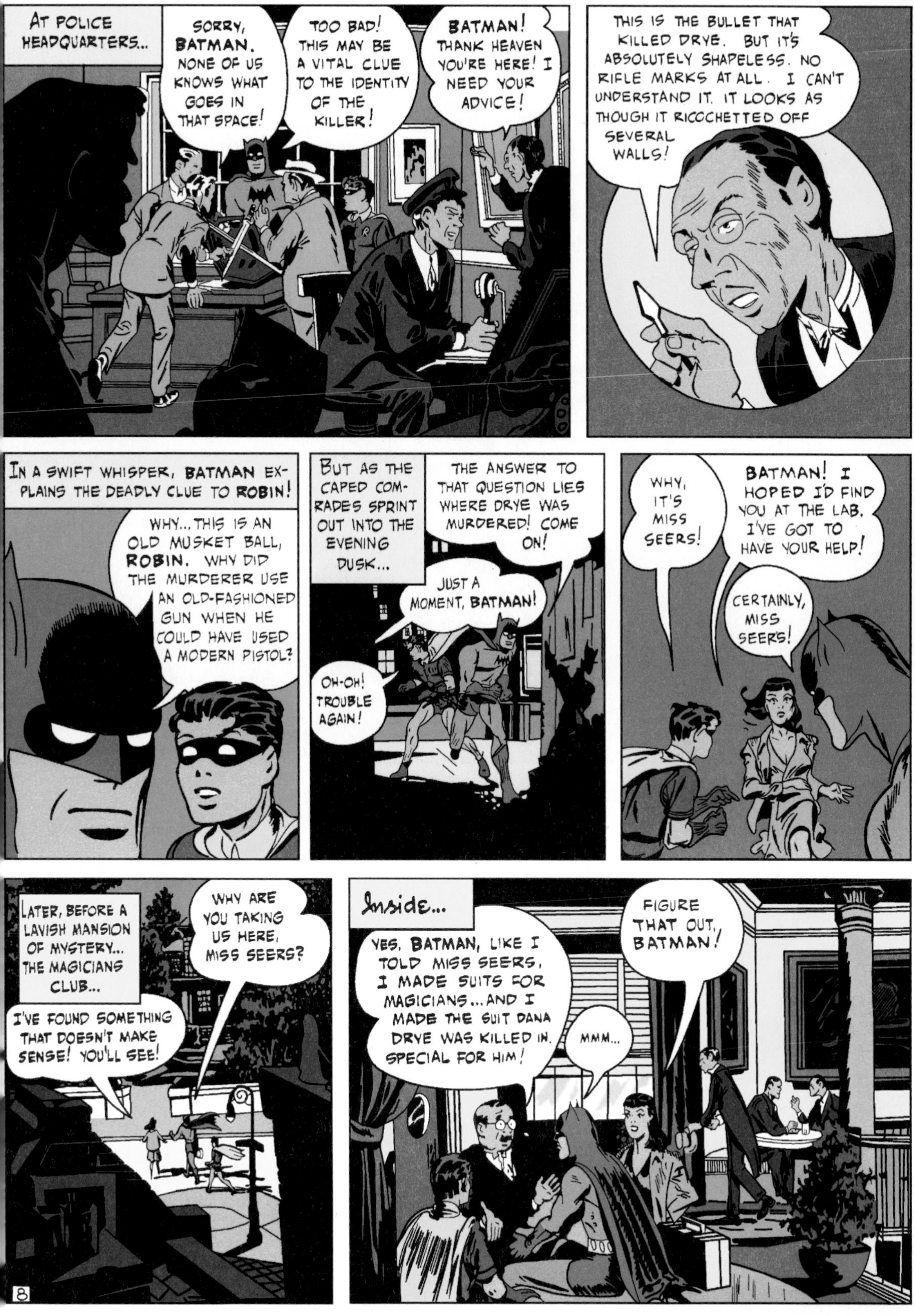
AT POLICE HEADQUARTERS...
SORRY, BATMAN. NONE OF US KNOWS WHAT GOES IN THAT SPACE!
TOO BAD! THIS MAY BE A VITAL CLUE TO THE IDENTITY OF THE KILLER!
BATMAN! THANK HEAVEN YOU'RE HERE! I NEED YOUR ADVICE!
THIS IS THE BULLET THAT KILLED DRYE. BUT IT'S ABSOLUTELY SHAPELESS. NO RIFLE MARKS AT ALL. I CAN'T UNDERSTAND IT. IT LOOKS AS THOUGH IT RICOCHETTED OFF SEVERAL WALLS!
IN A SWIFT WHISPER, BATMAN EXPLAINS THE DEADLY CLUE TO ROBIN!
WHY... THIS IS AN OLD MUSKET BALL, ROBIN. WHY DID THE MURDERER USE AN OLD-FASHIONED GUN WHEN HE COULD HAVE USED A MODERN PISTOL?
BUT AS THE CAPED COMRADES SPRINT OUT INTO THE EVENING DUSK...
THE ANSWER TO THAT QUESTION LIES WHERE DRYE WAS MURDERED! COME ON!
JUST A MOMENT, BATMAN!
OH-OH! TROUBLE AGAIN!
WHY, IT'S MISS SEERS!
BATMAN! I HOPED I'D FIND YOU AT THE LAB. I'VE GOT TO HAVE YOUR HELP!
CERTAINLY, MISS SEERS!
LATER, BEFORE A LAVISH MANSION OF MYSTERY... THE MAGICIANS CLUB...
WHY ARE YOU TAKING US HERE, MISS SEERS?
I'VE FOUND SOMETHING THAT DOESN'T MAKE SENSE! YOU'LL SEE!
8
Inside...
YES, BATMAN, LIKE I TOLD MISS SEERS, I MADE SUITS FOR MAGICIANS... AND I MADE THE SUIT DANA DRYE WAS KILLED IN. SPECIAL FOR HIM!
MMM...
FIGURE THAT OUT, BATMAN!

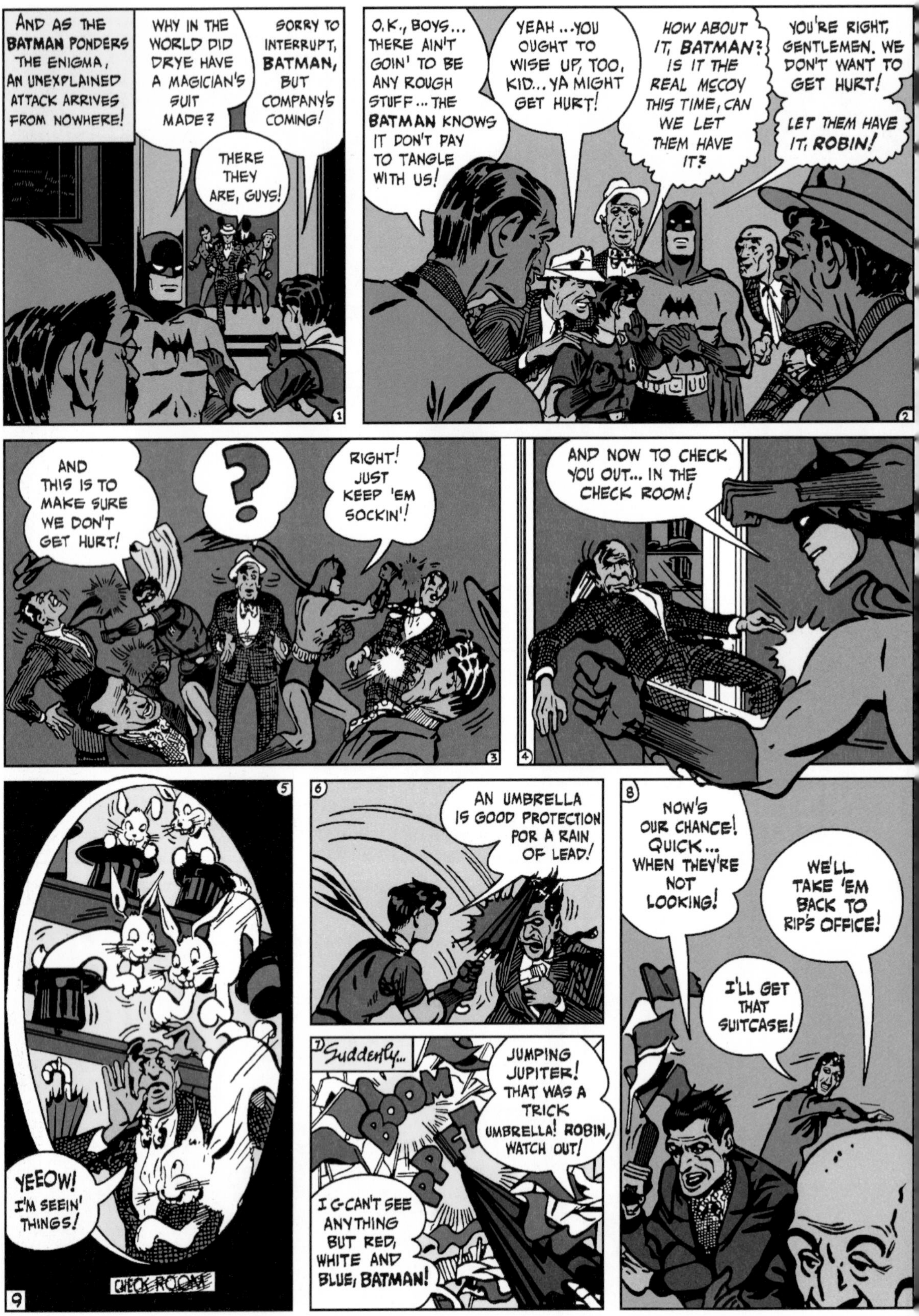

AND AS THE BATMAN PONDERS THE ENIGMA, AN UNEXPLAINED ATTACK ARRIVES FROM NOWHERE!
WHY IN THE WORLD DID DRYE HAVE A MAGICIAN'S SUIT MADE?
SORRY TO INTERRUPT, BATMAN, BUT COMPANY'S COMING!
THERE THEY ARE, GUYS!
O.K., BOYS... THERE AIN'T GOIN' TO BE ANY ROUGH STUFF... THE BATMAN KNOWS IT DON'T PAY TO TANGLE WITH US!
YEAH ...YOU OUGHT TO WISE UP, TOO, KID... YA MIGHT GET HURT!
HOW ABOUT IT, BATMAN? IS IT THE REAL McCOY THIS TIME, CAN WE LET THEM HAVE IT?
YOU'RE RIGHT, GENTLEMEN. WE DON'T WANT TO GET HURT!
LET THEM HAVE IT, ROBIN!
AND THIS IS TO MAKE SURE WE DON'T GET HURT!
?
RIGHT! JUST KEEP 'EM SOCKIN'!
AND NOW TO CHECK YOU OUT... IN THE CHECK ROOM!
AN UMBRELLA IS GOOD PROTECTION FOR A RAIN OF LEAD!
Suddenly...
BOOM
JUMPING JUPITER! THAT WAS A TRICK UMBRELLA! ROBIN, WATCH OUT!
I C-CAN'T SEE ANYTHING BUT RED, WHITE AND BLUE, BATMAN!
NOW'S OUR CHANCE! QUICK... WHEN THEY'RE NOT LOOKING!
WE'LL TAKE 'EM BACK TO RIP'S OFFICE!
I'LL GET THAT SUITCASE!
YEEOW! I'M SEEIN' THINGS!
CHECK ROOM

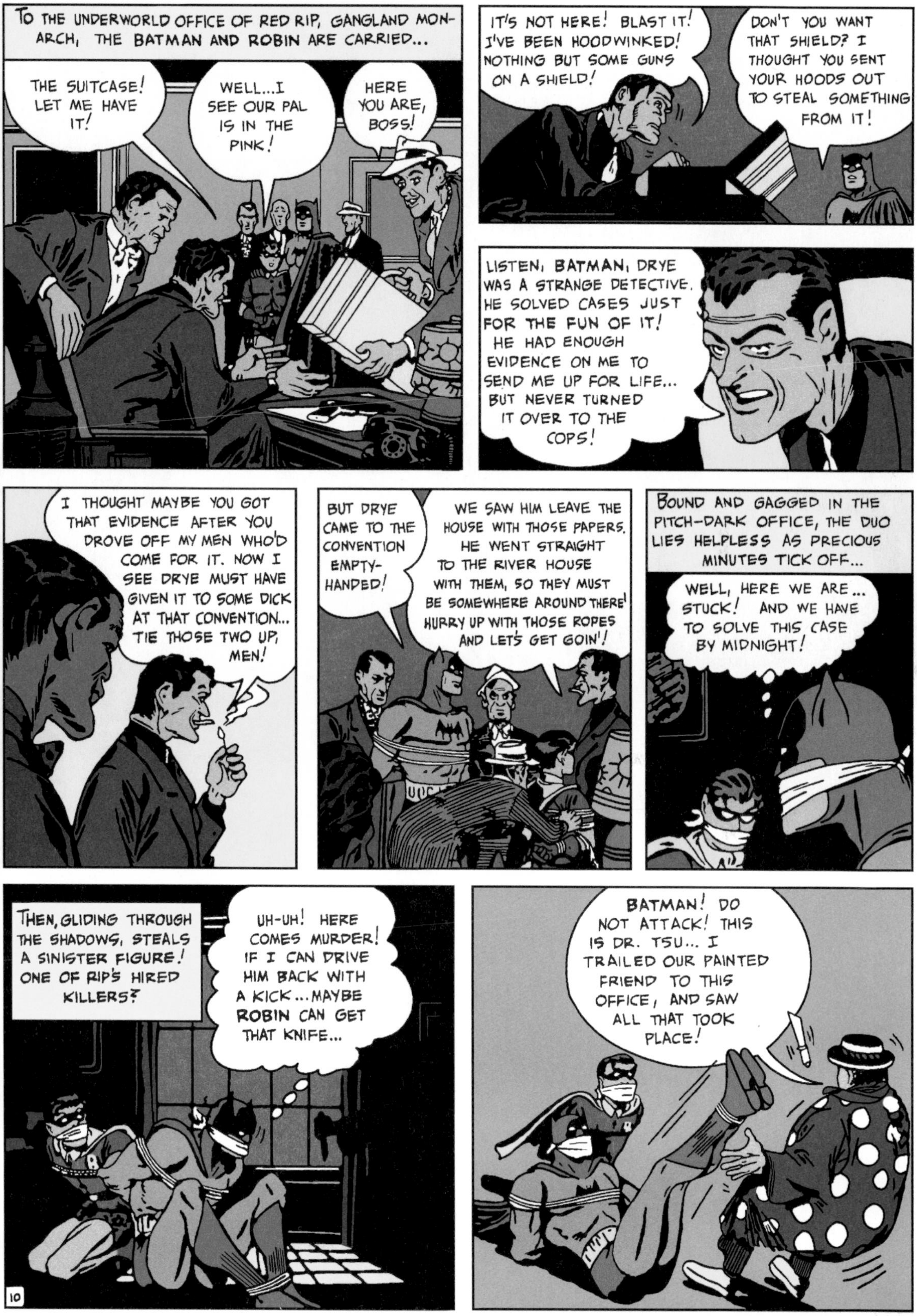

TO THE UNDERWORLD OFFICE OF RED RIP, GANGLAND MONARCH, THE BATMAN AND ROBIN ARE CARRIED...
THE SUITCASE! LET ME HAVE IT!
WELL...I SEE OUR PAL IS IN THE PINK!
HERE YOU ARE, BOSS!
IT'S NOT HERE! BLAST IT! I'VE BEEN HOODWINKED! NOTHING BUT SOME GUNS ON A SHIELD!
DON'T YOU WANT THAT SHIELD? I THOUGHT YOU SENT YOUR HOODS OUT TO STEAL SOMETHING FROM IT!
LISTEN, BATMAN, DRYE WAS A STRANGE DETECTIVE. HE SOLVED CASES JUST FOR THE FUN OF IT! HE HAD ENOUGH EVIDENCE ON ME TO SEND ME UP FOR LIFE... BUT NEVER TURNED IT OVER TO THE COPS!
I THOUGHT MAYBE YOU GOT THAT EVIDENCE AFTER YOU DROVE OFF MY MEN WHO'D COME FOR IT. NOW I SEE DRYE MUST HAVE GIVEN IT TO SOME DICK AT THAT CONVENTION... TIE THOSE TWO UP, MEN!
BUT DRYE CAME TO THE CONVENTION EMPTY-HANDED!
WE SAW HIM LEAVE THE HOUSE WITH THOSE PAPERS. HE WENT STRAIGHT TO THE RIVER HOUSE WITH THEM, SO THEY MUST BE SOMEWHERE AROUND THERE! HURRY UP WITH THOSE ROPES AND LET'S GET GOIN'!
BOUND AND GAGGED IN THE PITCH-DARK OFFICE, THE DUO LIES HELPLESS AS PRECIOUS MINUTES TICK OFF...
WELL, HERE WE ARE... STUCK! AND WE HAVE TO SOLVE THIS CASE BY MIDNIGHT!
THEN, GLIDING THROUGH THE SHADOWS, STEALS A SINISTER FIGURE! ONE OF RIP'S HIRED KILLERS?
UH-UH! HERE COMES MURDER! IF I CAN DRIVE HIM BACK WITH A KICK...MAYBE ROBIN CAN GET THAT KNIFE...
10
BATMAN! DO NOT ATTACK! THIS IS DR. TSU... I TRAILED OUR PAINTED FRIEND TO THIS OFFICE, AND SAW ALL THAT TOOK PLACE!

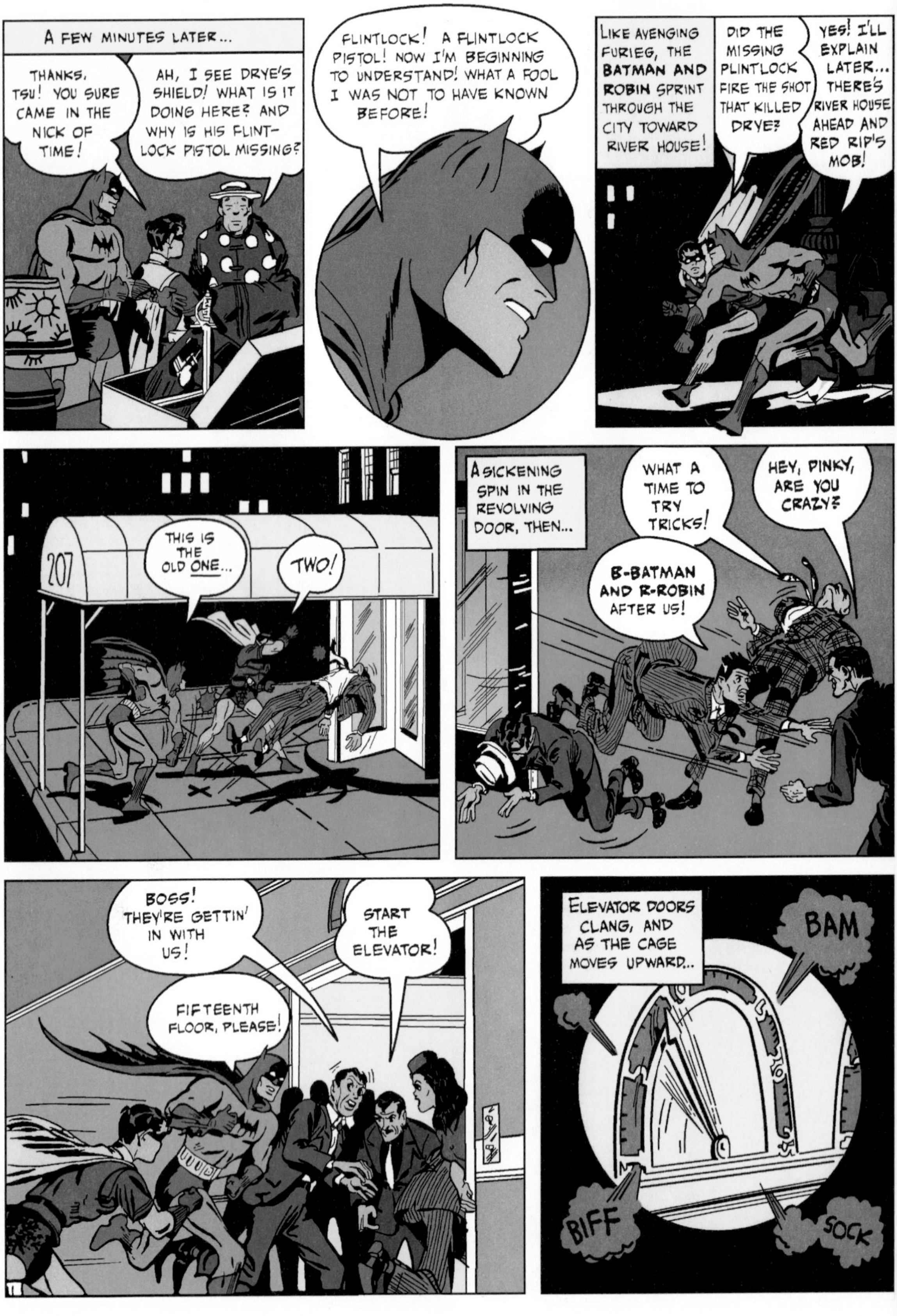
A FEW MINUTES LATER...
THANKS, TSU! YOU SURE CAME IN THE NICK OF TIME!
AH, I SEE DRYE'S SHIELD! WHAT IS IT DOING HERE? AND WHY IS HIS FLINT-LOCK PISTOL MISSING?
FLINTLOCK! A FLINTLOCK PISTOL! NOW I'M BEGINNING TO UNDERSTAND! WHAT A FOOL I WAS NOT TO HAVE KNOWN BEFORE!
LIKE AVENGING FURIES, THE BATMAN AND ROBIN SPRINT THROUGH THE CITY TOWARD RIVER HOUSE!
DID THE MISSING FLINTLOCK FIRE THE SHOT THAT KILLED DRYE?
YES! I'LL EXPLAIN LATER... THERE'S RIVER HOUSE AHEAD AND RED RIP'S MOB!
207
THIS IS THE OLD ONE...
TWO!
A SICKENING SPIN IN THE REVOLVING DOOR, THEN...
WHAT A TIME TO TRY TRICKS!
HEY, PINKY, ARE YOU CRAZY?
B-BATMAN AND R-ROBIN AFTER US!
BOSS! THEY'RE GETTIN' IN WITH US!
START THE ELEVATOR!
FIFTEENTH FLOOR, PLEASE!
ELEVATOR DOORS CLANG, AND AS THE CAGE MOVES UPWARD...
BAM
BIFF
SOCK

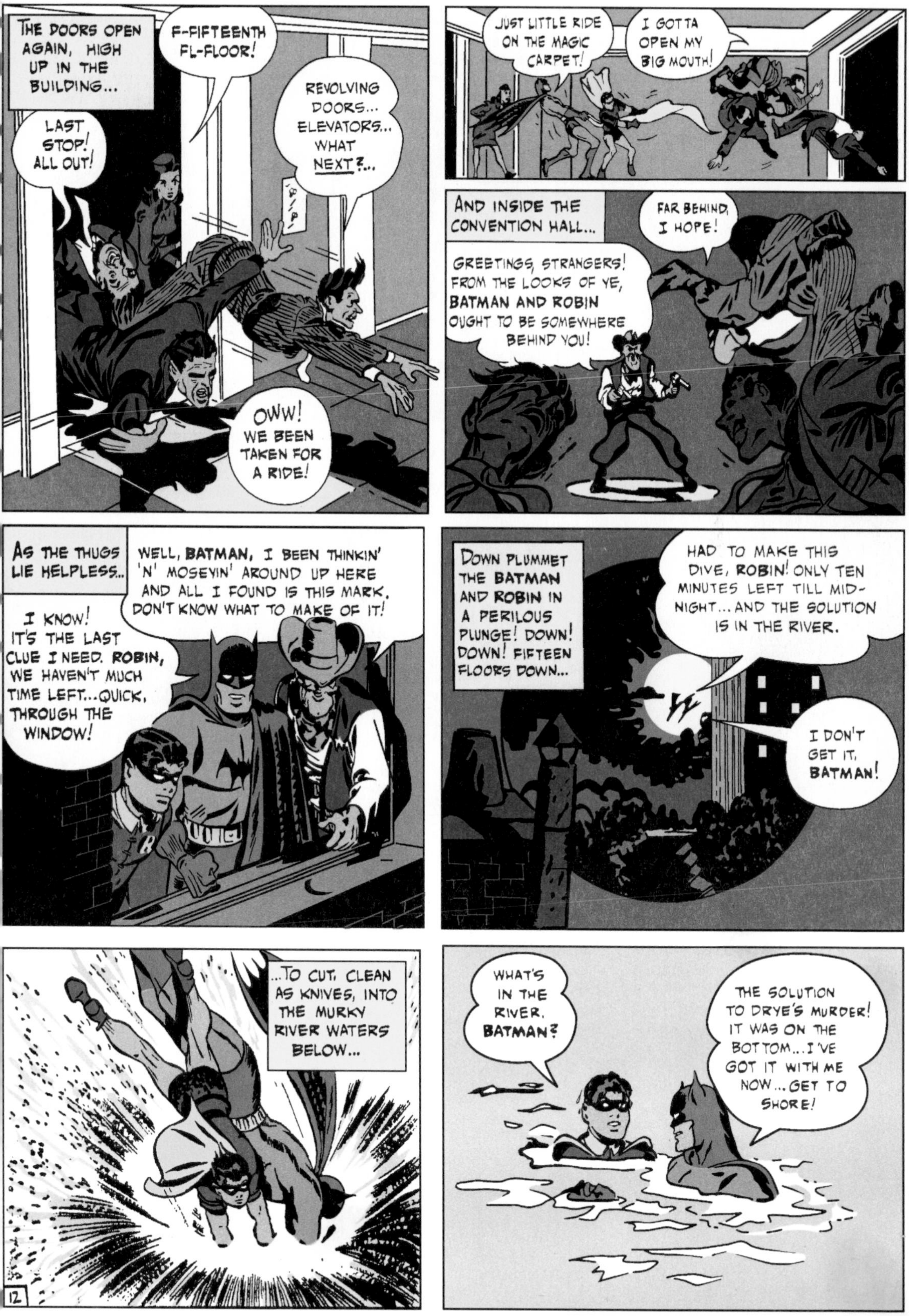
THE DOORS OPEN AGAIN, HIGH UP IN THE BUILDING...
F-FIFTEENTH FL-FLOOR!
LAST STOP! ALL OUT!
REVOLVING DOORS... ELEVATORS... WHAT NEXT?...
OWW! WE BEEN TAKEN FOR A RIDE!
JUST LITTLE RIDE ON THE MAGIC CARPET!
I GOTTA OPEN MY BIG MOUTH!
AND INSIDE THE CONVENTION HALL...
FAR BEHIND, I HOPE!
GREETINGS, STRANGERS! FROM THE LOOKS OF YE, BATMAN AND ROBIN OUGHT TO BE SOMEWHERE BEHIND YOU!
AS THE THUGS LIE HELPLESS...
WELL, BATMAN, I BEEN THINKIN' 'N' MOSEYIN' AROUND UP HERE AND ALL I FOUND IS THIS MARK. DON'T KNOW WHAT TO MAKE OF IT!
I KNOW! IT'S THE LAST CLUE I NEED. ROBIN, WE HAVEN'T MUCH TIME LEFT...QUICK, THROUGH THE WINDOW!
DOWN PLUMMET THE BATMAN AND ROBIN IN A PERILOUS PLUNGE! DOWN! DOWN! FIFTEEN FLOORS DOWN...
HAD TO MAKE THIS DIVE, ROBIN! ONLY TEN MINUTES LEFT TILL MIDNIGHT... AND THE SOLUTION IS IN THE RIVER.
I DON'T GET IT, BATMAN!
...TO CUT, CLEAN AS KNIVES, INTO THE MURKY RIVER WATERS BELOW...
12
WHAT'S IN THE RIVER, BATMAN?
THE SOLUTION TO DRYE'S MURDER! IT WAS ON THE BOTTOM...I'VE GOT IT WITH ME NOW...GET TO SHORE!

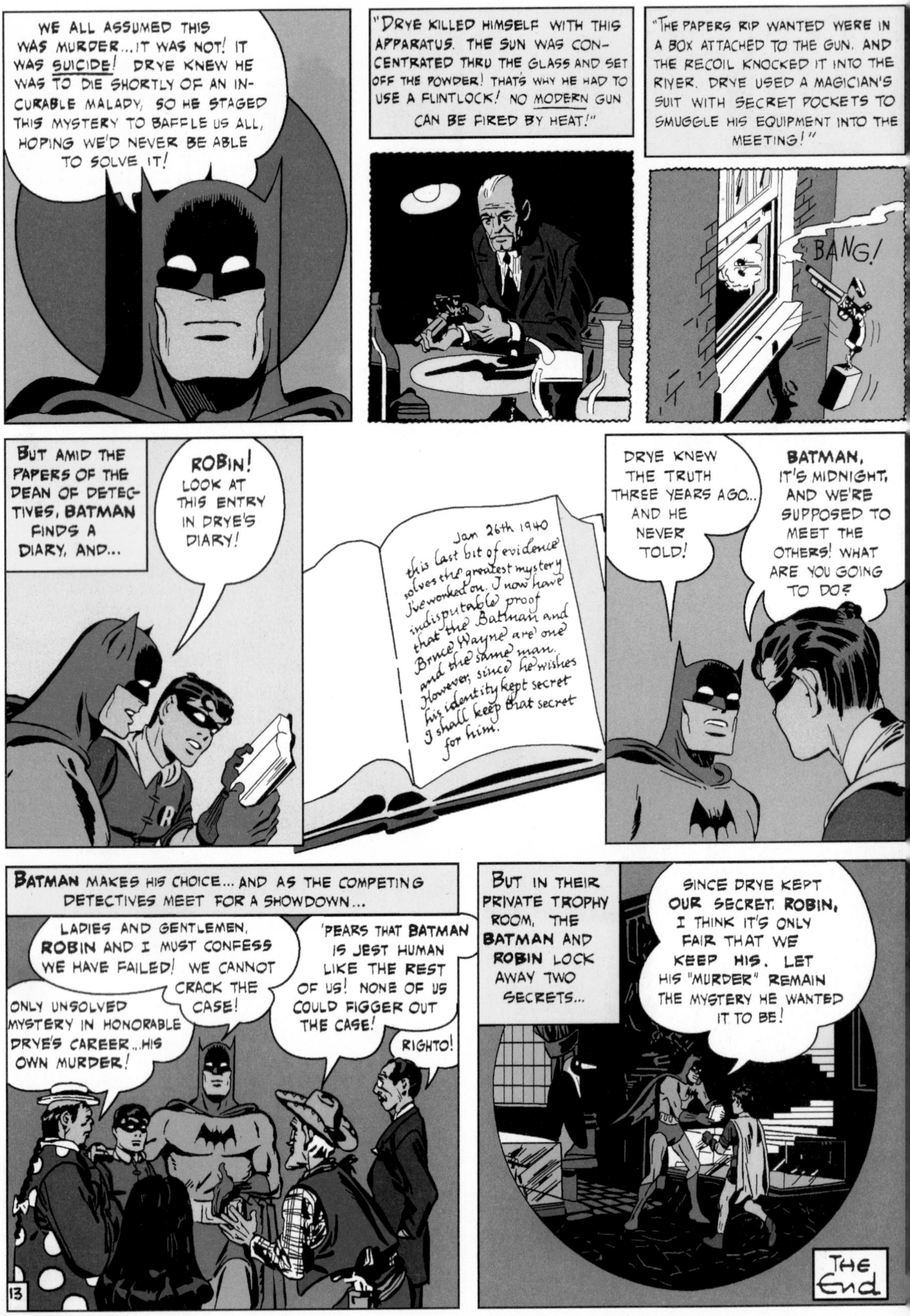

WE ALL ASSUMED THIS WAS MURDER...IT WAS NOT! IT WAS SUICIDE! DRYE KNEW HE WAS TO DIE SHORTLY OF AN INCURABLE MALADY, SO HE STAGED THIS MYSTERY TO BAFFLE US ALL, HOPING WE'D NEVER BE ABLE TO SOLVE IT!
"DRYE KILLED HIMSELF WITH THIS APPARATUS. THE SUN WAS CONCENTRATED THRU THE GLASS AND SET OFF THE POWDER! THAT'S WHY HE HAD TO USE A FLINTLOCK! NO MODERN GUN CAN BE FIRED BY HEAT!"
"THE PAPERS RIP WANTED WERE IN A BOX ATTACHED TO THE GUN. AND THE RECOIL KNOCKED IT INTO THE RIVER. DRYE USED A MAGICIAN'S SUIT WITH SECRET POCKETS TO SMUGGLE HIS EQUIPMENT INTO THE MEETING!"
BANG!
BUT AMID THE PAPERS OF THE DEAN OF DETECTIVES, BATMAN FINDS A DIARY, AND...
ROBIN! LOOK AT THIS ENTRY IN DRYE'S DIARY!
Jan 26th 1940 this last bit of evidence solves the greatest mystery I've worked on. I now have indisputable proof that the Batman and Bruce Wayne are one and the same man. However, since he wishes his identity kept secret I shall keep that secret for him.
DRYE KNEW THE TRUTH THREE YEARS AGO... AND HE NEVER TOLD!
BATMAN, IT'S MIDNIGHT, AND WE'RE SUPPOSED TO MEET THE OTHERS! WHAT ARE YOU GOING TO DO?
BATMAN MAKES HIS CHOICE... AND AS THE COMPETING DETECTIVES MEET FOR A SHOWDOWN...
LADIES AND GENTLEMEN, ROBIN AND I MUST CONFESS WE HAVE FAILED! WE CANNOT CRACK THE CASE!
'PEARS THAT BATMAN IS JEST HUMAN LIKE THE REST OF US! NONE OF US COULD FIGGER OUT THE CASE!
ONLY UNSOLVED MYSTERY IN HONORABLE DRYE'S CAREER...HIS OWN MURDER!
RIGHTO!
13
BUT IN THEIR PRIVATE TROPHY ROOM, THE BATMAN AND ROBIN LOCK AWAY TWO SECRETS...
SINCE DRYE KEPT OUR SECRET, ROBIN, I THINK IT'S ONLY FAIR THAT WE KEEP HIS. LET HIS "MURDER" REMAIN THE MYSTERY HE WANTED IT TO BE!
THE End

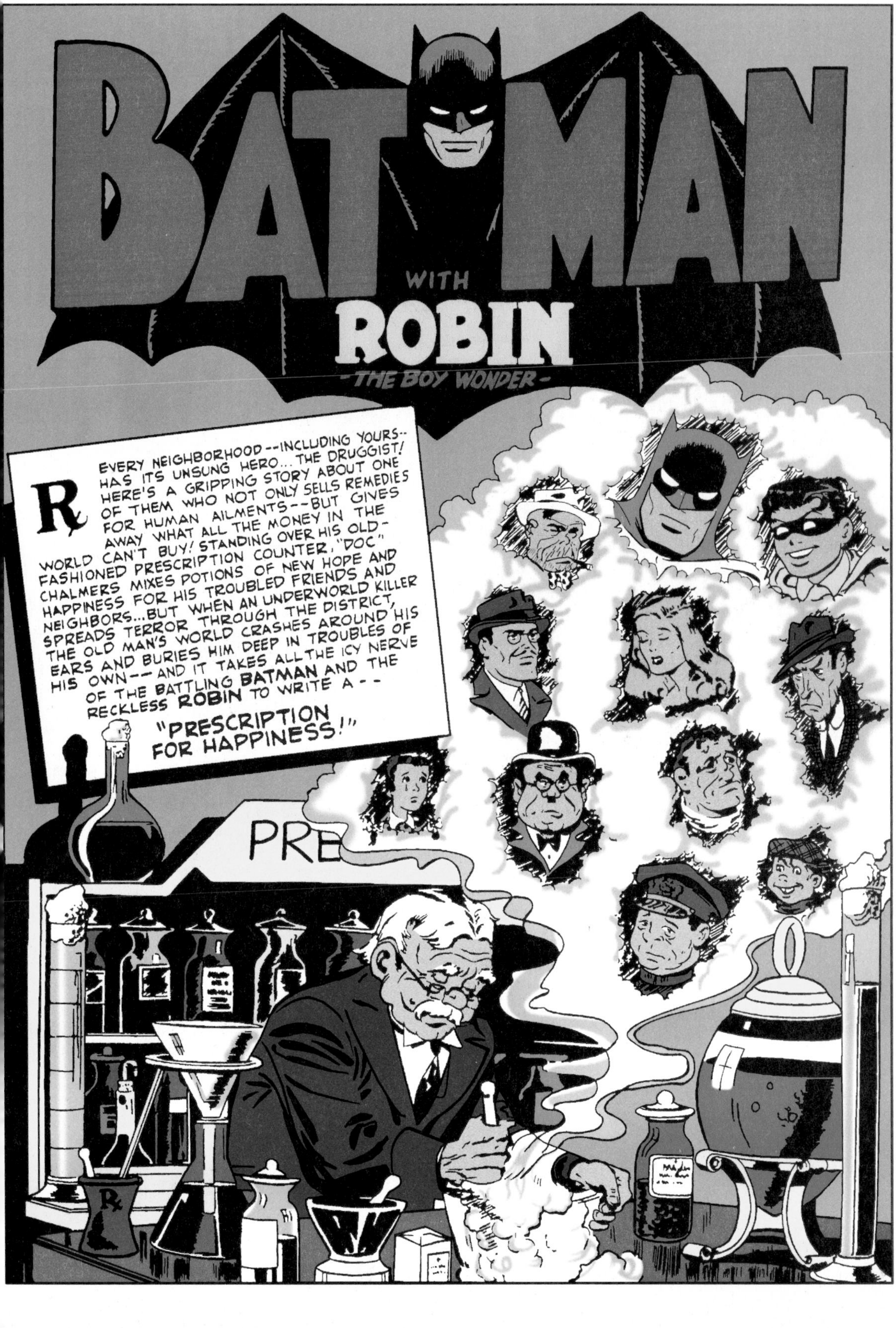

BATMAN
WITH
ROBIN
-THE BOY WONDER-
R EVERY NEIGHBORHOOD--INCLUDING YOURS--HAS ITS UNSUNG HERO... THE DRUGGIST! HERE'S A GRIPPING STORY ABOUT ONE OF THEM WHO NOT ONLY SELLS REMEDIES FOR HUMAN AILMENTS--BUT GIVES AWAY WHAT ALL THE MONEY IN THE WORLD CAN'T BUY! STANDING OVER HIS OLD-FASHIONED PRESCRIPTION COUNTER, "DOC" CHALMERS MIXES POTIONS OF NEW HOPE AND HAPPINESS FOR HIS TROUBLED FRIENDS AND NEIGHBORS...BUT WHEN AN UNDERWORLD KILLER SPREADS TERROR THROUGH THE DISTRICT, THE OLD MAN'S WORLD CRASHES AROUND HIS EARS AND BURIES HIM DEEP IN TROUBLES OF HIS OWN-- AND IT TAKES ALL THE ICY NERVE OF THE BATTLING BATMAN AND THE RECKLESS ROBIN TO WRITE A --
"PRESCRIPTION FOR HAPPINESS!"
PRE

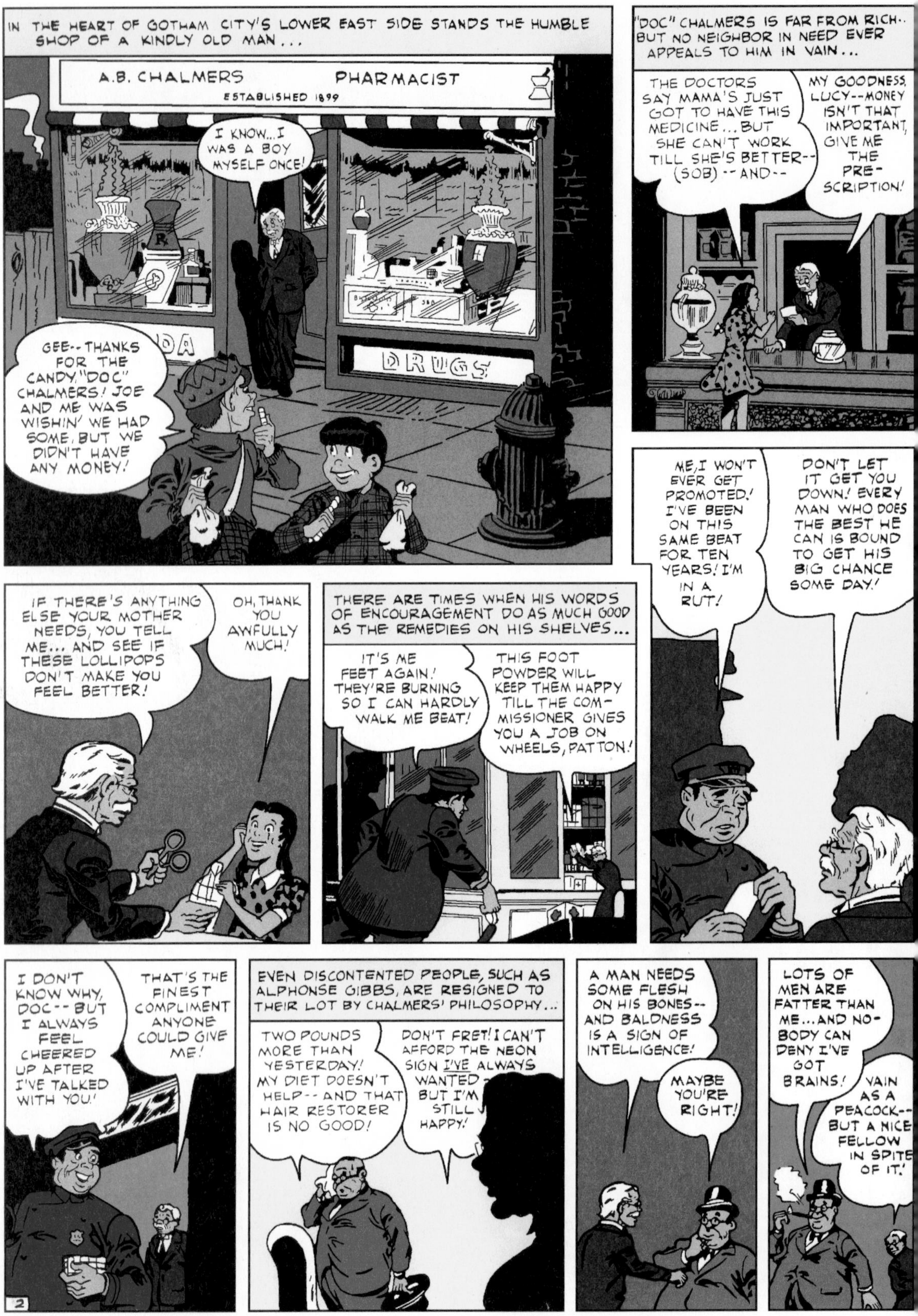
IN THE HEART OF GOTHAM CITY'S LOWER EAST SIDE STANDS THE HUMBLE SHOP OF A KINDLY OLD MAN...
A.B. CHALMERS PHARMACIST
ESTABLISHED 1899
I KNOW...I WAS A BOY MYSELF ONCE!
GEE--THANKS FOR THE CANDY, "DOC" CHALMERS! JOE AND ME WAS WISHIN' WE HAD SOME, BUT WE DIDN'T HAVE ANY MONEY!
DRUGS
"DOC" CHALMERS IS FAR FROM RICH.. BUT NO NEIGHBOR IN NEED EVER APPEALS TO HIM IN VAIN...
THE DOCTORS SAY MAMA'S JUST GOT TO HAVE THIS MEDICINE... BUT SHE CAN'T WORK TILL SHE'S BETTER--(SOB)--AND--
MY GOODNESS, LUCY--MONEY ISN'T THAT IMPORTANT, GIVE ME THE PRE-SCRIPTION!
IF THERE'S ANYTHING ELSE YOUR MOTHER NEEDS, YOU TELL ME... AND SEE IF THESE LOLLIPOPS DON'T MAKE YOU FEEL BETTER!
OH, THANK YOU AWFULLY MUCH!
THERE ARE TIMES WHEN HIS WORDS OF ENCOURAGEMENT DO AS MUCH GOOD AS THE REMEDIES ON HIS SHELVES...
IT'S ME FEET AGAIN! THEY'RE BURNING SO I CAN HARDLY WALK ME BEAT!
THIS FOOT POWDER WILL KEEP THEM HAPPY TILL THE COM-MISSIONER GIVES YOU A JOB ON WHEELS, PATTON!
ME, I WON'T EVER GET PROMOTED! I'VE BEEN ON THIS SAME BEAT FOR TEN YEARS! I'M IN A RUT!
DON'T LET IT GET YOU DOWN! EVERY MAN WHO DOES THE BEST HE CAN IS BOUND TO GET HIS BIG CHANCE SOME DAY!
I DON'T KNOW WHY, DOC--BUT I ALWAYS FEEL CHEERED UP AFTER I'VE TALKED WITH YOU!
THAT'S THE FINEST COMPLIMENT ANYONE COULD GIVE ME!
2
EVEN DISCONTENTED PEOPLE, SUCH AS ALPHONSE GIBBS, ARE RESIGNED TO THEIR LOT BY CHALMERS' PHILOSOPHY...
TWO POUNDS MORE THAN YESTERDAY! MY DIET DOESN'T HELP--AND THAT HAIR RESTORER IS NO GOOD!
DON'T FRET! I CAN'T AFFORD THE NEON SIGN I'VE ALWAYS WANTED--BUT I'M STILL HAPPY!
A MAN NEEDS SOME FLESH ON HIS BONES--AND BALDNESS IS A SIGN OF INTELLIGENCE!
MAYBE YOU'RE RIGHT!
LOTS OF MEN ARE FATTER THAN ME...AND NO-BODY CAN DENY I'VE GOT BRAINS!
VAIN AS A PEACOCK--BUT A NICE FELLOW IN SPITE OF IT!

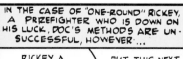

IN THE CASE OF "ONE-ROUND" RICKEY, A PRIZEFIGHTER WHO IS DOWN ON HIS LUCK, DOC'S METHODS ARE UNSUCCESSFUL, HOWEVER...

RICKEY, A TONIC TO MAKE YOU SUPER-STRONG FOR ONE NIGHT WON'T HELP YOU YOU NEED SELF-CONFIDENCE!

BUT THIS NEXT FIGHT IS MY LAST CHANCE, DOC! IF I LOSE, THEY'LL NEVER LET ME IN THE RING AGAIN!

OH, WELL-- MAYBE I'D BETTER QUIT TRYING AND ADMIT I'M A HAS-BEEN!

POOR FELLOW. IF ONLY I KNEW OF SOME WAY TO RESTORE HIS FAITH IN HIMSELF...

ROY AINSLEE, A STRUGGLING YOUNG PHYSICIAN, IS A PARTICULAR FRIEND OF THE DRUGGIST...

I WAS HOPING YOU'D COME IN, ROY! COME BACK IN THE PRE-SCRIPTION ROOM AND TELL ME HOW YOU'RE GETTING ALONG!

WELL, I'M STILL LOOKING FOR MY FIRST PATIENT!

TO TELL THE TRUTH, I'M A LITTLE DISCOURAGED! MAYBE I PICKED THE WRONG PART OF TOWN TO PRACTICE IN!

NONSENSE! SOON AS THE PEOPLE GET USED TO YOU-- HUH? A CUSTOMER! EXCUSE ME ...

PRESCRIPTION
PHARMACIST SINCE 1899

BIOLOGICALS   SERUMS

A STRANGELY TENSE YOUNG WOMAN ASKS FOR ONE OF THE MOST DANGEROUS OF CHEMICALS...

PRUSSIC ACID? WHY, THAT'S A DEADLY POISON! WHAT DO YOU WANT IT FOR?

WHAT DO YOU CARE? I HAVE ENOUGH MONEY TO PAY FOR IT!

YOU'RE UPSET, MISS...PERHAPS YOU AND I HAD BETTER HAVE A LITTLE CHAT...

NO! I DON'T WANT TO TALK TO ANYBODY-- NOT EVER! (SOB)

I WANT TO DIE! DO YOU UNDERSTAND? I'M TIRED OF BEING OUT OF WORK--HALF-STARVED-- LONELY-- HOPELESS!

YOU POOR CHILD --COME BACK HERE WITH ME!

HERE'S YOUR FIRST PATIENT! A CASE OF HYSTERIA, UNDER-NOURISHMENT-- AND I DON'T KNOW WHAT ELSE!

HUH?

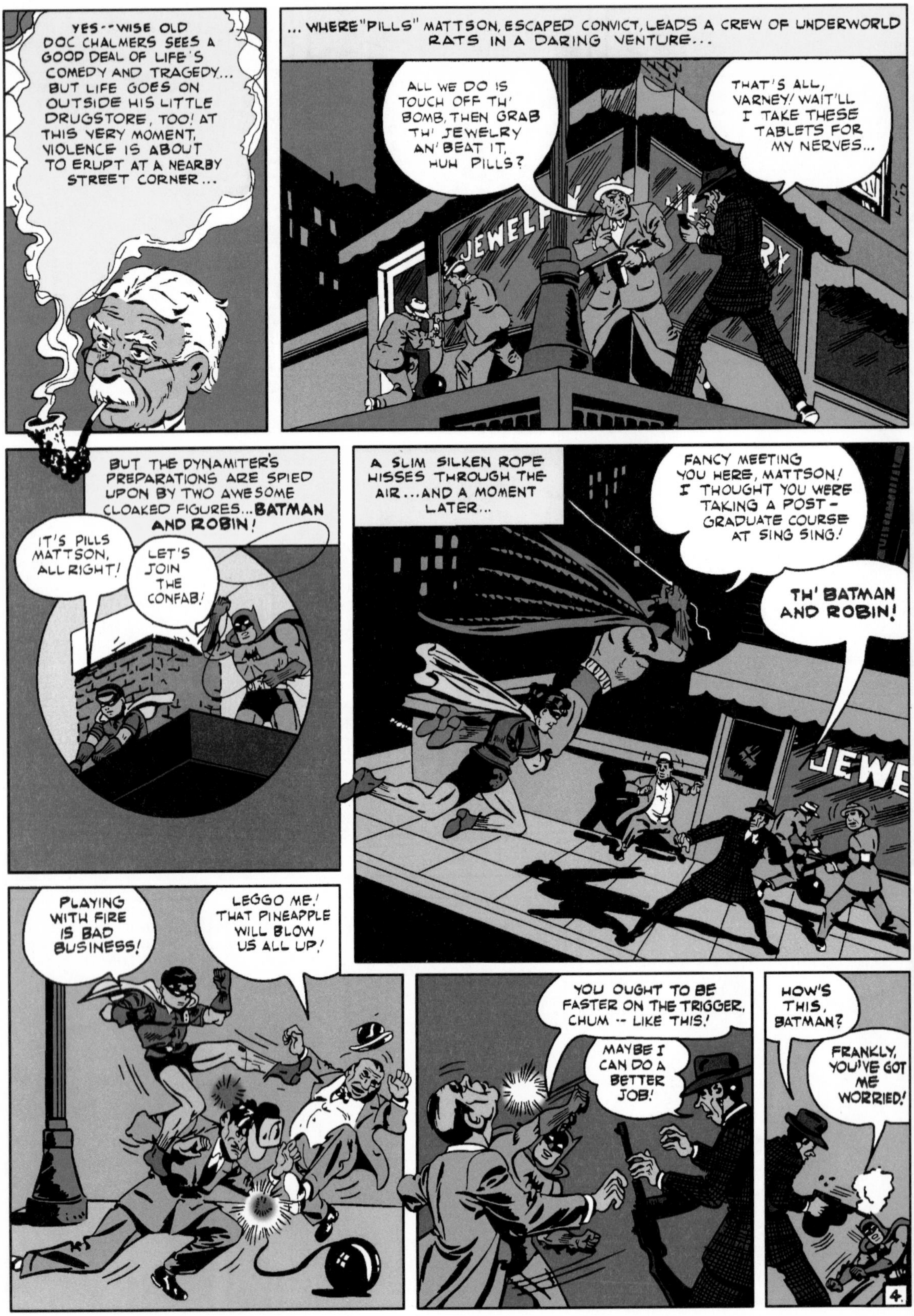
YES--WISE OLD DOC CHALMERS SEES A GOOD DEAL OF LIFE'S COMEDY AND TRAGEDY... BUT LIFE GOES ON OUTSIDE HIS LITTLE DRUGSTORE, TOO! AT THIS VERY MOMENT, VIOLENCE IS ABOUT TO ERUPT AT A NEARBY STREET CORNER...
... WHERE "PILLS" MATTSON, ESCAPED CONVICT, LEADS A CREW OF UNDERWORLD RATS IN A DARING VENTURE...
ALL WE DO IS TOUCH OFF TH' BOMB, THEN GRAB TH' JEWELRY AN' BEAT IT, HUH PILLS?
THAT'S ALL, VARNEY! WAIT'LL I TAKE THESE TABLETS FOR MY NERVES...
JEWELRY
BUT THE DYNAMITER'S PREPARATIONS ARE SPIED UPON BY TWO AWESOME CLOAKED FIGURES... BATMAN AND ROBIN!
IT'S PILLS MATTSON, ALL RIGHT!
LET'S JOIN THE CONFAB!
A SLIM SILKEN ROPE HISSES THROUGH THE AIR... AND A MOMENT LATER...
FANCY MEETING YOU HERE, MATTSON! I THOUGHT YOU WERE TAKING A POST-GRADUATE COURSE AT SING SING!
TH' BATMAN AND ROBIN!
JEWE
PLAYING WITH FIRE IS BAD BUSINESS!
LEGGO ME! THAT PINEAPPLE WILL BLOW US ALL UP!
YOU OUGHT TO BE FASTER ON THE TRIGGER, CHUM -- LIKE THIS!
MAYBE I CAN DO A BETTER JOB!
HOW'S THIS, BATMAN?
FRANKLY, YOU'VE GOT ME WORRIED!
4.

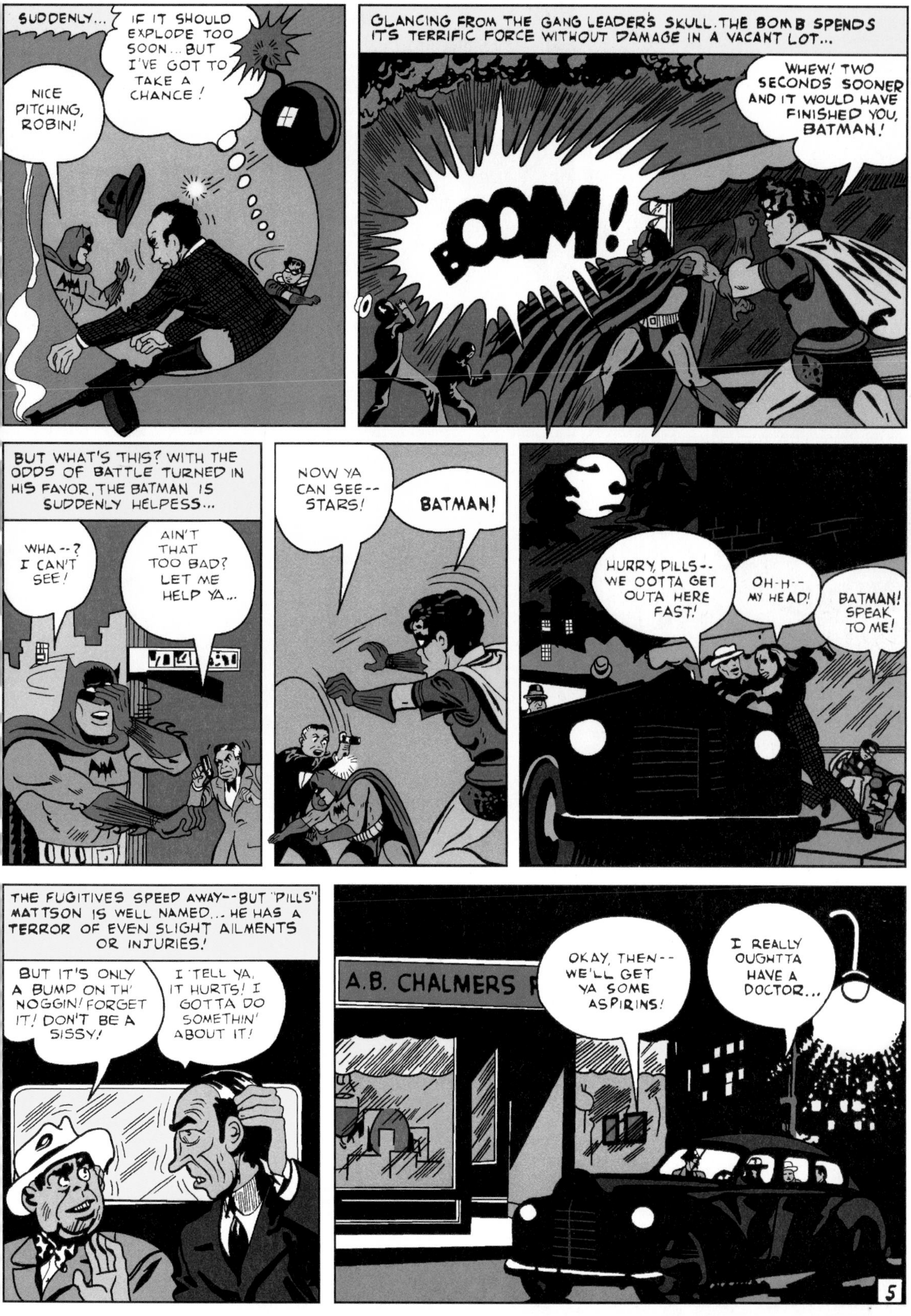
SUDDENLY...
IF IT SHOULD EXPLODE TOO SOON... BUT I'VE GOT TO TAKE A CHANCE!
NICE PITCHING, ROBIN!
GLANCING FROM THE GANG LEADER'S SKULL, THE BOMB SPENDS ITS TERRIFIC FORCE WITHOUT DAMAGE IN A VACANT LOT...
WHEW! TWO SECONDS SOONER AND IT WOULD HAVE FINISHED YOU, BATMAN!
BOOM!
BUT WHAT'S THIS? WITH THE ODDS OF BATTLE TURNED IN HIS FAVOR, THE BATMAN IS SUDDENLY HELPESS...
WHA--? I CAN'T SEE!
AIN'T THAT TOO BAD? LET ME HELP YA...
NOW YA CAN SEE-- STARS!
BATMAN!
HURRY, PILLS-- WE OOTTA GET OUTA HERE FAST!
OH-H-- MY HEAD!
BATMAN! SPEAK TO ME!
THE FUGITIVES SPEED AWAY--BUT "PILLS" MATTSON IS WELL NAMED... HE HAS A TERROR OF EVEN SLIGHT AILMENTS OR INJURIES!
BUT IT'S ONLY A BUMP ON TH' NOGGIN! FORGET IT! DON'T BE A SISSY!
I TELL YA, IT HURTS! I GOTTA DO SOMETHIN' ABOUT IT!
A.B. CHALMERS
OKAY, THEN-- WE'LL GET YA SOME ASPIRINS!
I REALLY OUGHTTA HAVE A DOCTOR...
5

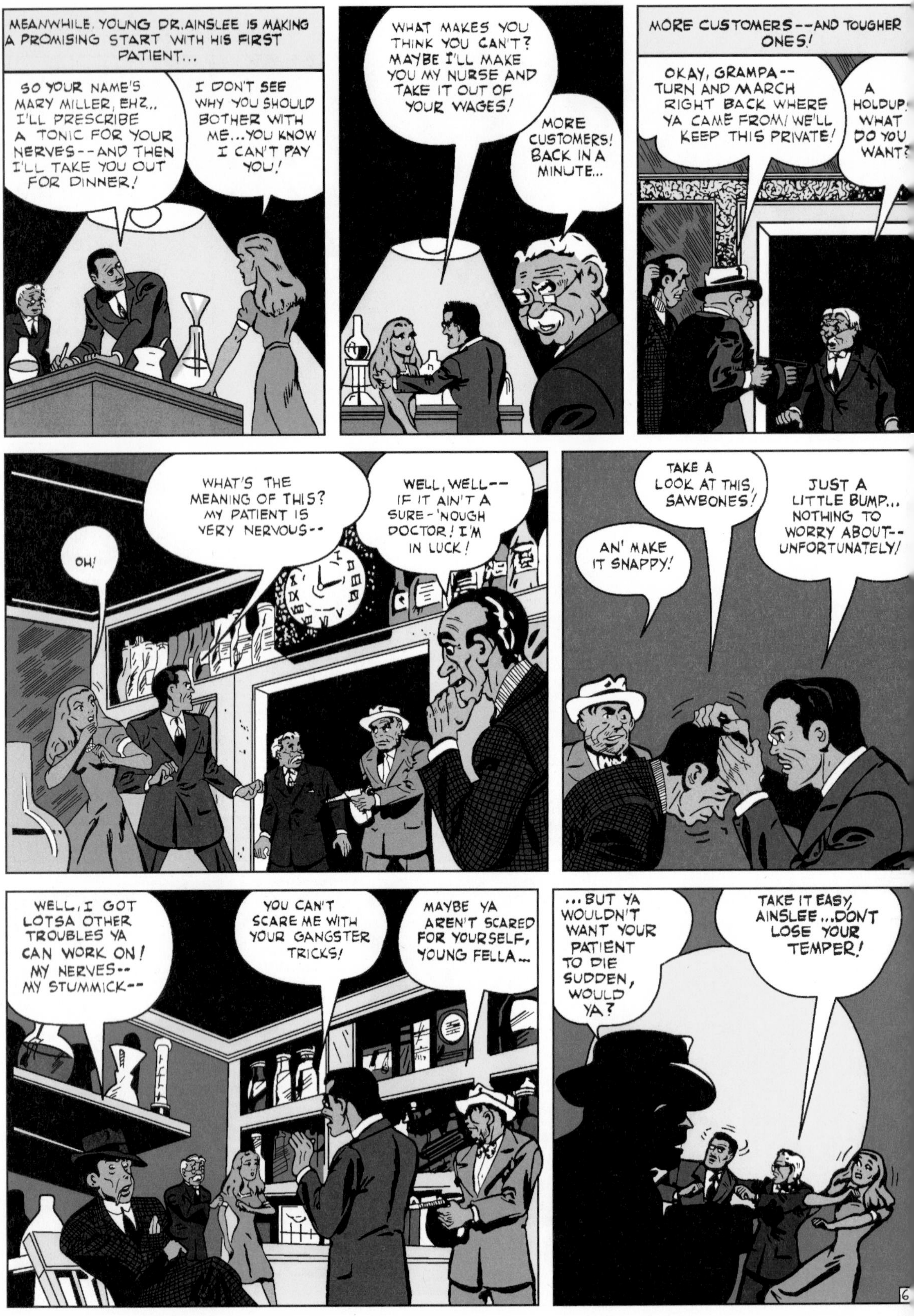
MEANWHILE, YOUNG DR. AINSLEE IS MAKING A PROMISING START WITH HIS FIRST PATIENT...
SO YOUR NAME'S MARY MILLER, EH?.. I'LL PRESCRIBE A TONIC FOR YOUR NERVES--AND THEN I'LL TAKE YOU OUT FOR DINNER!
I DON'T SEE WHY YOU SHOULD BOTHER WITH ME...YOU KNOW I CAN'T PAY YOU!
WHAT MAKES YOU THINK YOU CAN'T? MAYBE I'LL MAKE YOU MY NURSE AND TAKE IT OUT OF YOUR WAGES!
MORE CUSTOMERS! BACK IN A MINUTE...
MORE CUSTOMERS--AND TOUGHER ONES!
OKAY, GRAMPA-- TURN AND MARCH RIGHT BACK WHERE YA CAME FROM! WE'LL KEEP THIS PRIVATE!
A HOLDUP! WHAT DO YOU WANT?
OH!
WHAT'S THE MEANING OF THIS? MY PATIENT IS VERY NERVOUS--
WELL, WELL-- IF IT AIN'T A SURE-'NOUGH DOCTOR! I'M IN LUCK!
TAKE A LOOK AT THIS, SAWBONES!
AN' MAKE IT SNAPPY!
JUST A LITTLE BUMP... NOTHING TO WORRY ABOUT-- UNFORTUNATELY!
WELL, I GOT LOTSA OTHER TROUBLES YA CAN WORK ON! MY NERVES-- MY STUMMICK--
YOU CAN'T SCARE ME WITH YOUR GANGSTER TRICKS!
MAYBE YA AREN'T SCARED FOR YOURSELF, YOUNG FELLA...
...BUT YA WOULDN'T WANT YOUR PATIENT TO DIE SUDDEN, WOULD YA?
TAKE IT EASY, AINSLEE...DON'T LOSE YOUR TEMPER!
6

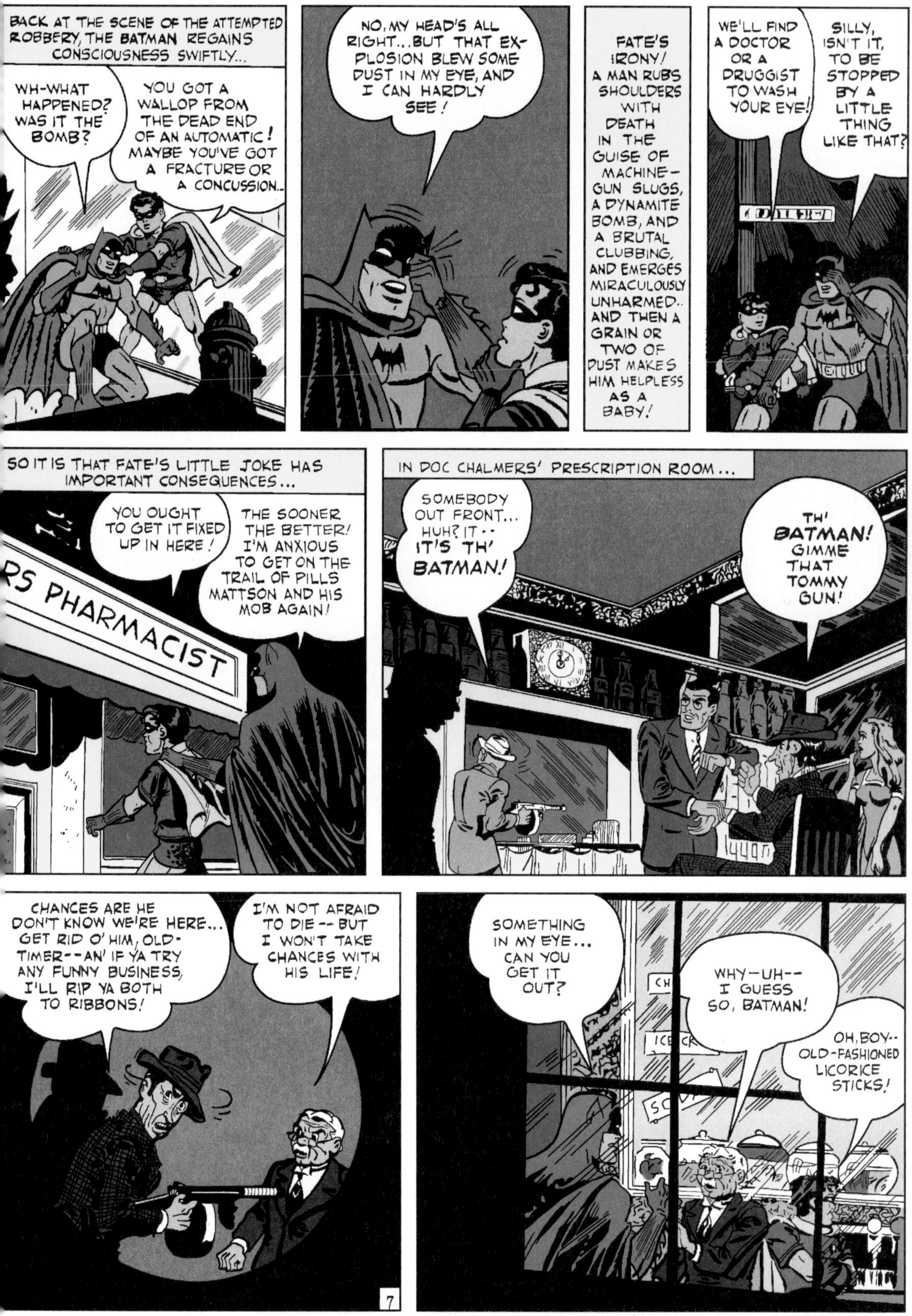
BACK AT THE SCENE OF THE ATTEMPTED ROBBERY, THE BATMAN REGAINS CONSCIOUSNESS SWIFTLY...
WH-WHAT HAPPENED? WAS IT THE BOMB?
YOU GOT A WALLOP FROM THE DEAD END OF AN AUTOMATIC! MAYBE YOU'VE GOT A FRACTURE OR A CONCUSSION...
NO, MY HEAD'S ALL RIGHT...BUT THAT EXPLOSION BLEW SOME DUST IN MY EYE, AND I CAN HARDLY SEE!
FATE'S IRONY! A MAN RUBS SHOULDERS WITH DEATH IN THE GUISE OF MACHINE-GUN SLUGS, A DYNAMITE BOMB, AND A BRUTAL CLUBBING, AND EMERGES MIRACULOUSLY UNHARMED.. AND THEN A GRAIN OR TWO OF DUST MAKES HIM HELPLESS AS A BABY!
WE'LL FIND A DOCTOR OR A DRUGGIST TO WASH YOUR EYE!
SILLY, ISN'T IT, TO BE STOPPED BY A LITTLE THING LIKE THAT?
SO IT IS THAT FATE'S LITTLE JOKE HAS IMPORTANT CONSEQUENCES...
YOU OUGHT TO GET IT FIXED UP IN HERE!
THE SOONER THE BETTER! I'M ANXIOUS TO GET ON THE TRAIL OF PILLS MATTSON AND HIS MOB AGAIN!
RS PHARMACIST
IN DOC CHALMERS' PRESCRIPTION ROOM...
SOMEBODY OUT FRONT... HUH? IT-- IT'S TH' BATMAN!
TH' BATMAN! GIMME THAT TOMMY GUN!
CHANCES ARE HE DON'T KNOW WE'RE HERE... GET RID O' HIM, OLD-TIMER--AN' IF YA TRY ANY FUNNY BUSINESS, I'LL RIP YA BOTH TO RIBBONS!
I'M NOT AFRAID TO DIE -- BUT I WON'T TAKE CHANCES WITH HIS LIFE!
7
SOMETHING IN MY EYE... CAN YOU GET IT OUT?
WHY-UH-- I GUESS SO, BATMAN!
OH, BOY-- OLD-FASHIONED LICORICE STICKS!

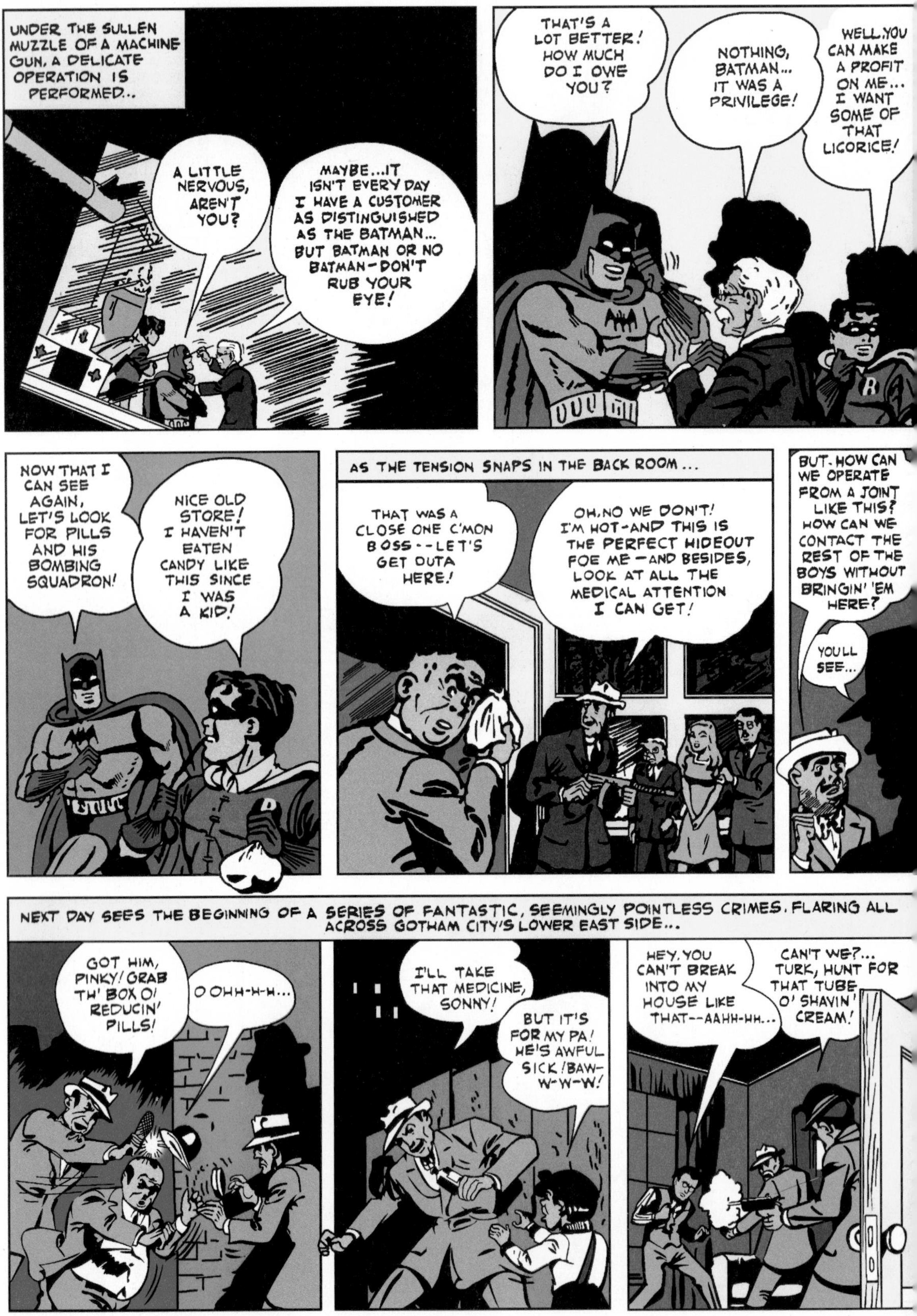

UNDER THE SULLEN MUZZLE OF A MACHINE GUN, A DELICATE OPERATION IS PERFORMED..
A LITTLE NERVOUS, AREN'T YOU?
MAYBE...IT ISN'T EVERY DAY I HAVE A CUSTOMER AS DISTINGUISHED AS THE BATMAN... BUT BATMAN OR NO BATMAN-DON'T RUB YOUR EYE!
THAT'S A LOT BETTER! HOW MUCH DO I OWE YOU?
NOTHING, BATMAN... IT WAS A PRIVILEGE!
WELL,YOU CAN MAKE A PROFIT ON ME... I WANT SOME OF THAT LICORICE!
NOW THAT I CAN SEE AGAIN, LET'S LOOK FOR PILLS AND HIS BOMBING SQUADRON!
NICE OLD STORE! I HAVEN'T EATEN CANDY LIKE THIS SINCE I WAS A KID!
AS THE TENSION SNAPS IN THE BACK ROOM ...
THAT WAS A CLOSE ONE C'MON BOSS--LET'S GET OUTA HERE!
OH,NO WE DON'T! I'M HOT-AND THIS IS THE PERFECT HIDEOUT FOE ME-AND BESIDES, LOOK AT ALL THE MEDICAL ATTENTION I CAN GET!
BUT-HOW CAN WE OPERATE FROM A JOINT LIKE THIS? HOW CAN WE CONTACT THE REST OF THE BOYS WITHOUT BRINGIN' 'EM HERE?
YOU'LL SEE...
NEXT DAY SEES THE BEGINNING OF A SERIES OF FANTASTIC, SEEMINGLY POINTLESS CRIMES, FLARING ALL ACROSS GOTHAM CITY'S LOWER EAST SIDE...
GOT HIM, PINKY! GRAB TH' BOX O' REDUCIN' PILLS!
OOHH-H-H...
I'LL TAKE THAT MEDICINE, SONNY!
BUT IT'S FOR MY PA! HE'S AWFUL SICK! BAW-W-W-W!
HEY, YOU CAN'T BREAK INTO MY HOUSE LIKE THAT--AAHH-HH...
CAN'T WE?... TURK, HUNT FOR THAT TUBE O' SHAVIN' CREAM!

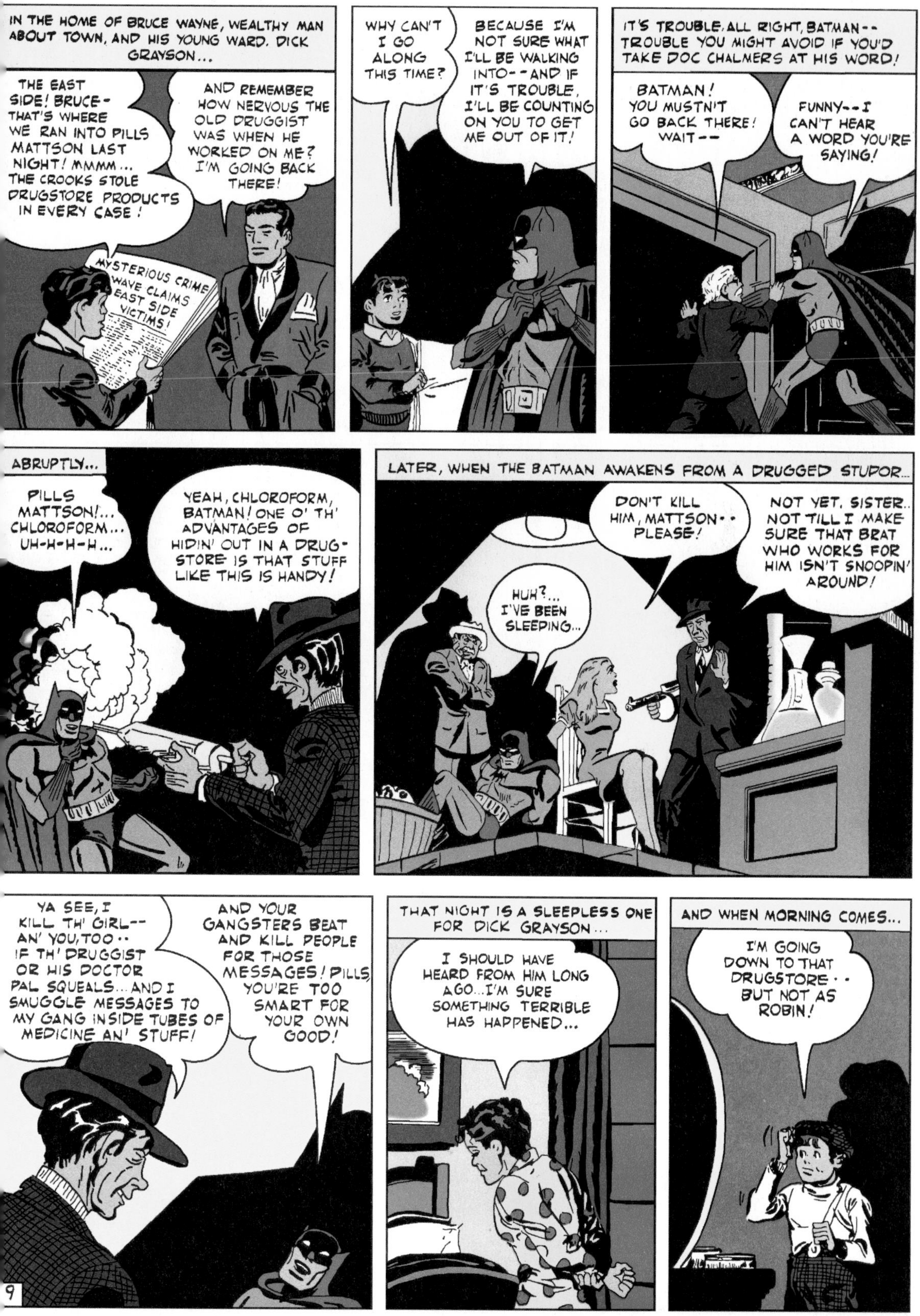

IN THE HOME OF BRUCE WAYNE, WEALTHY MAN ABOUT TOWN, AND HIS YOUNG WARD, DICK GRAYSON...
THE EAST SIDE! BRUCE-THAT'S WHERE WE RAN INTO PILLS MATTSON LAST NIGHT! MMMM... THE CROOKS STOLE DRUGSTORE PRODUCTS IN EVERY CASE!
AND REMEMBER HOW NERVOUS THE OLD DRUGGIST WAS WHEN HE WORKED ON ME? I'M GOING BACK THERE!
MYSTERIOUS CRIME WAVE CLAIMS EAST SIDE VICTIMS!
WHY CAN'T I GO ALONG THIS TIME?
BECAUSE I'M NOT SURE WHAT I'LL BE WALKING INTO--AND IF IT'S TROUBLE, I'LL BE COUNTING ON YOU TO GET ME OUT OF IT!
IT'S TROUBLE, ALL RIGHT, BATMAN--TROUBLE YOU MIGHT AVOID IF YOU'D TAKE DOC CHALMERS AT HIS WORD!
BATMAN! YOU MUSTN'T GO BACK THERE! WAIT--
FUNNY--I CAN'T HEAR A WORD YOU'RE SAYING!
ABRUPTLY...
PILLS MATTSON!... CHLOROFORM... UH-H-H-H...
YEAH, CHLOROFORM, BATMAN! ONE O' TH' ADVANTAGES OF HIDIN' OUT IN A DRUG-STORE IS THAT STUFF LIKE THIS IS HANDY!
LATER, WHEN THE BATMAN AWAKENS FROM A DRUGGED STUPOR...
DON'T KILL HIM, MATTSON--PLEASE!
NOT YET, SISTER.. NOT TILL I MAKE SURE THAT BRAT WHO WORKS FOR HIM ISN'T SNOOPIN' AROUND!
HUH?... I'VE BEEN SLEEPING...
YA SEE, I KILL TH' GIRL--AN' YOU, TOO--IF TH' DRUGGIST OR HIS DOCTOR PAL SQUEALS... AND I SMUGGLE MESSAGES TO MY GANG INSIDE TUBES OF MEDICINE AN' STUFF!
AND YOUR GANGSTERS BEAT AND KILL PEOPLE FOR THOSE MESSAGES! PILLS, YOU'RE TOO SMART FOR YOUR OWN GOOD!
9
THAT NIGHT IS A SLEEPLESS ONE FOR DICK GRAYSON...
I SHOULD HAVE HEARD FROM HIM LONG AGO... I'M SURE SOMETHING TERRIBLE HAS HAPPENED...
AND WHEN MORNING COMES...
I'M GOING DOWN TO THAT DRUGSTORE--BUT NOT AS ROBIN!

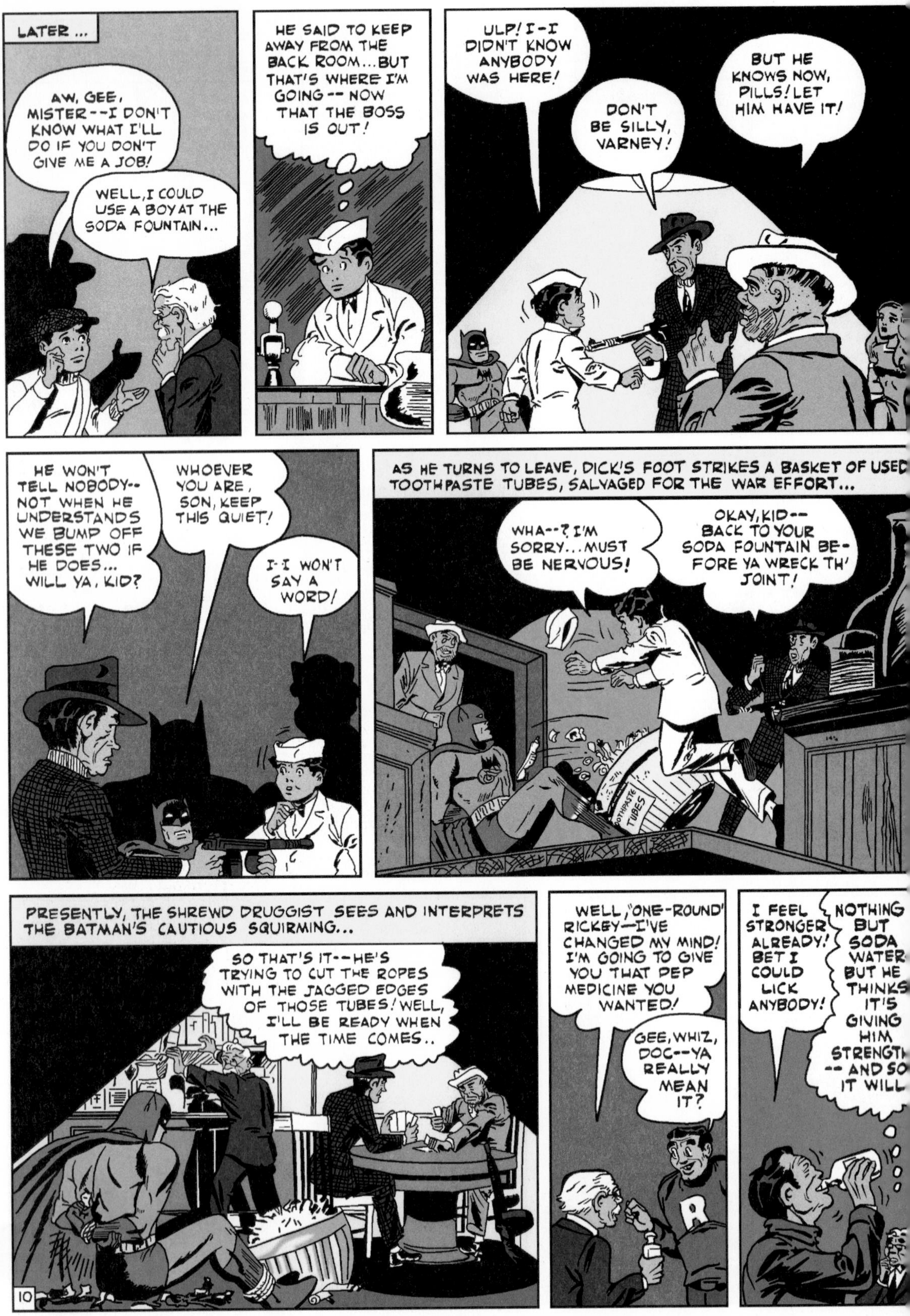
LATER ...
AW, GEE, MISTER--I DON'T KNOW WHAT I'LL DO IF YOU DON'T GIVE ME A JOB!
WELL, I COULD USE A BOY AT THE SODA FOUNTAIN...
HE SAID TO KEEP AWAY FROM THE BACK ROOM...BUT THAT'S WHERE I'M GOING -- NOW THAT THE BOSS IS OUT!
ULP! I-I DIDN'T KNOW ANYBODY WAS HERE!
DON'T BE SILLY, VARNEY!
BUT HE KNOWS NOW, PILLS! LET HIM HAVE IT!
HE WON'T TELL NOBODY--NOT WHEN HE UNDERSTANDS WE BUMP OFF THESE TWO IF HE DOES... WILL YA, KID?
WHOEVER YOU ARE, SON, KEEP THIS QUIET!
I-I WON'T SAY A WORD!
AS HE TURNS TO LEAVE, DICK'S FOOT STRIKES A BASKET OF USED TOOTHPASTE TUBES, SALVAGED FOR THE WAR EFFORT...
WHA--? I'M SORRY...MUST BE NERVOUS!
OKAY, KID-- BACK TO YOUR SODA FOUNTAIN BEFORE YA WRECK TH' JOINT!
TOOTHPASTE TUBES
PRESENTLY, THE SHREWD DRUGGIST SEES AND INTERPRETS THE BATMAN'S CAUTIOUS SQUIRMING...
SO THAT'S IT--HE'S TRYING TO CUT THE ROPES WITH THE JAGGED EDGES OF THOSE TUBES! WELL, I'LL BE READY WHEN THE TIME COMES..
10
WELL, 'ONE-ROUND' RICKEY--I'VE CHANGED MY MIND! I'M GOING TO GIVE YOU THAT PEP MEDICINE YOU WANTED!
GEE, WHIZ, DOC--YA REALLY MEAN IT?
I FEEL STRONGER ALREADY! BET I COULD LICK ANYBODY!
NOTHING BUT SODA WATER BUT HE THINKS IT'S GIVING HIM STRENGTH -- AND SO IT WILL

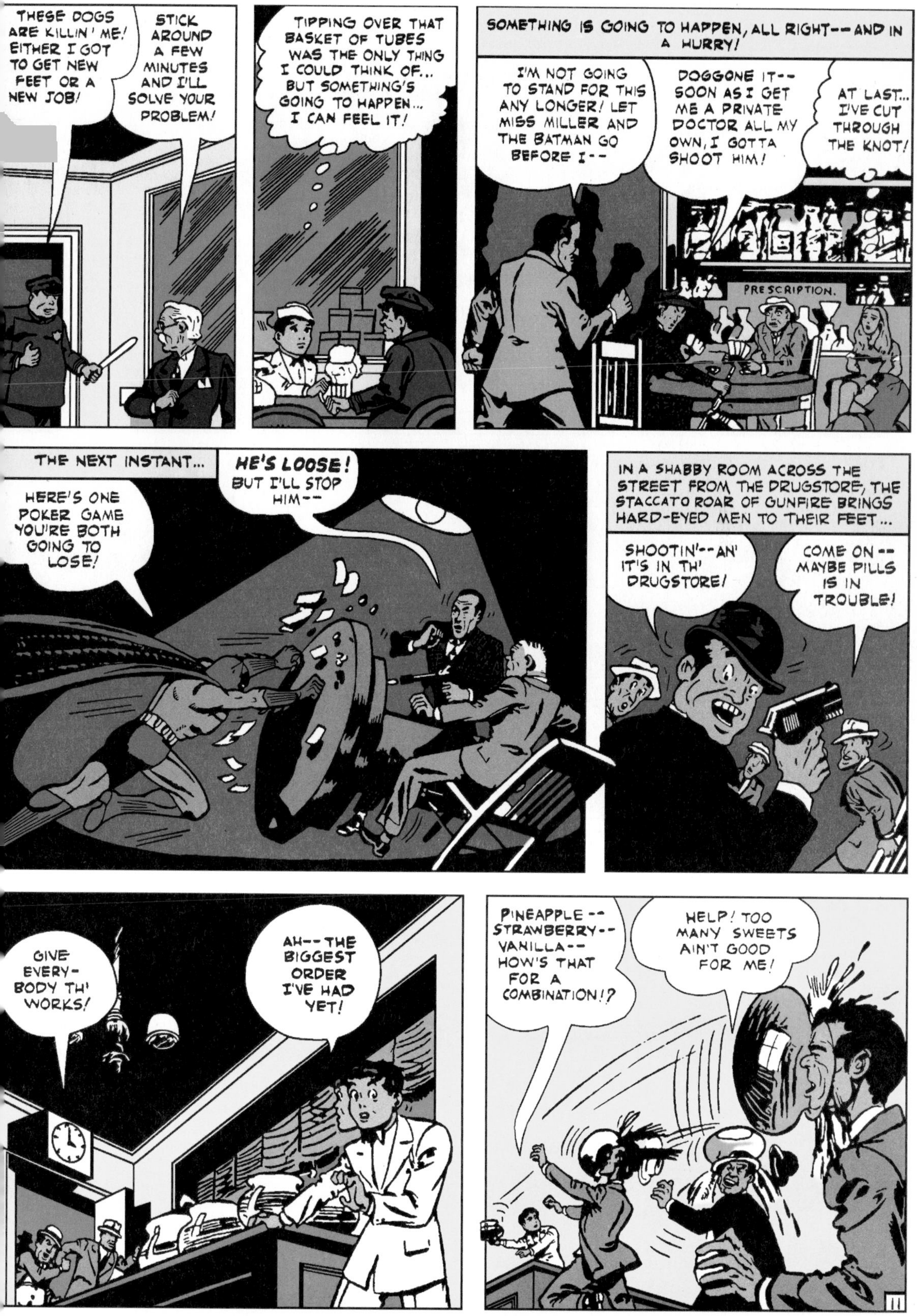
THESE DOGS ARE KILLIN' ME! EITHER I GOT TO GET NEW FEET OR A NEW JOB!
STICK AROUND A FEW MINUTES AND I'LL SOLVE YOUR PROBLEM!
TIPPING OVER THAT BASKET OF TUBES WAS THE ONLY THING I COULD THINK OF... BUT SOMETHING'S GOING TO HAPPEN... I CAN FEEL IT!
SOMETHING IS GOING TO HAPPEN, ALL RIGHT-- AND IN A HURRY!
I'M NOT GOING TO STAND FOR THIS ANY LONGER! LET MISS MILLER AND THE BATMAN GO BEFORE I--
DOGGONE IT-- SOON AS I GET ME A PRIVATE DOCTOR ALL MY OWN, I GOTTA SHOOT HIM!
AT LAST... I'VE CUT THROUGH THE KNOT!
PRESCRIPTION.
THE NEXT INSTANT...
HERE'S ONE POKER GAME YOU'RE BOTH GOING TO LOSE!
HE'S LOOSE! BUT I'LL STOP HIM--
IN A SHABBY ROOM ACROSS THE STREET FROM THE DRUGSTORE, THE STACCATO ROAR OF GUNFIRE BRINGS HARD-EYED MEN TO THEIR FEET...
SHOOTIN'-- AN' IT'S IN TH' DRUGSTORE!
COME ON -- MAYBE PILLS IS IN TROUBLE!
GIVE EVERY-BODY TH' WORKS!
AH-- THE BIGGEST ORDER I'VE HAD YET!
PINEAPPLE -- STRAWBERRY-- VANILLA-- HOW'S THAT FOR A COMBINATION!?
HELP! TOO MANY SWEETS AIN'T GOOD FOR ME!
11

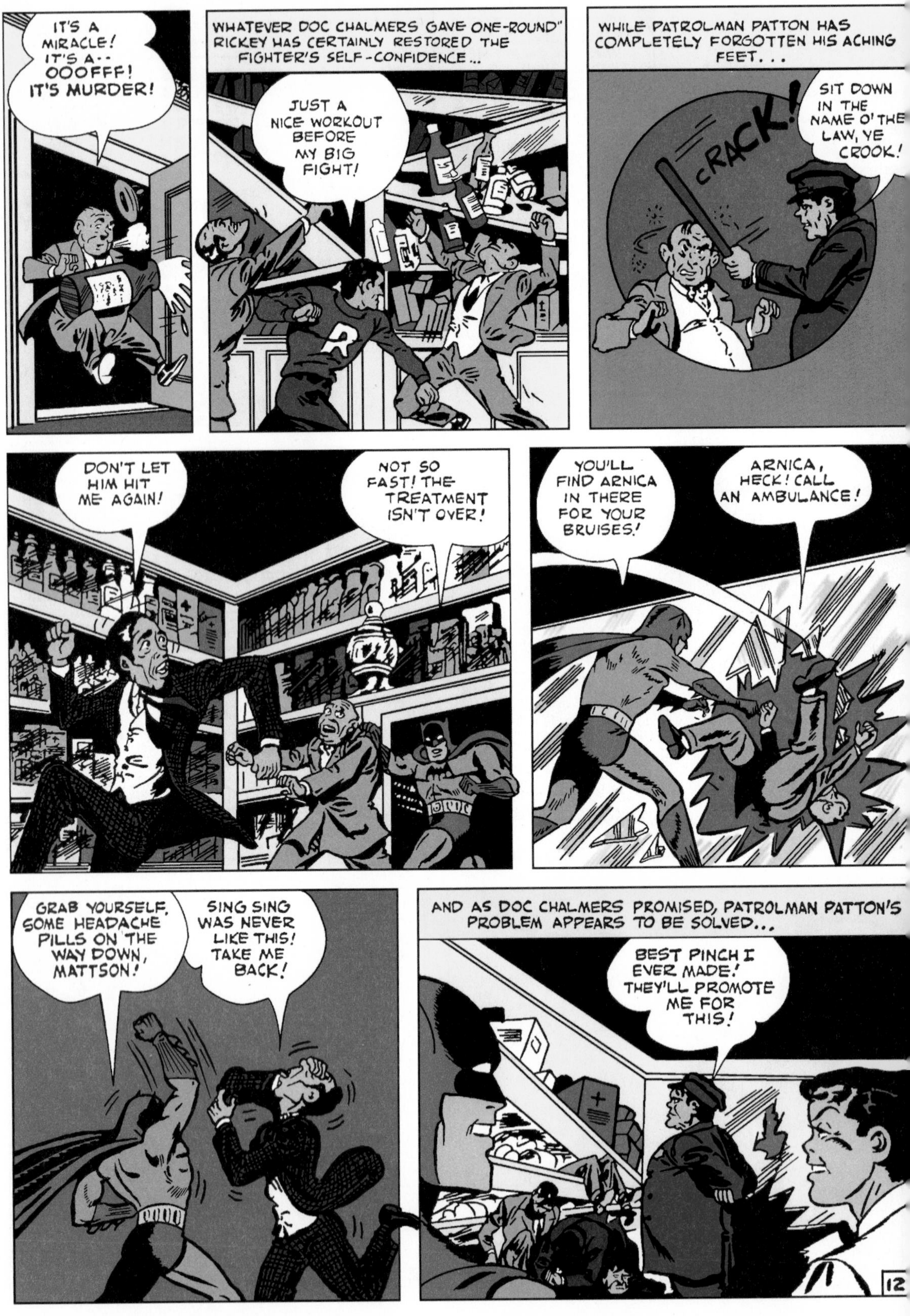
IT'S A MIRACLE! IT'S A-- OOOFFF! IT'S MURDER!
WHATEVER DOC CHALMERS GAVE ONE-ROUND" RICKEY HAS CERTAINLY RESTORED THE FIGHTER'S SELF-CONFIDENCE...
JUST A NICE WORKOUT BEFORE MY BIG FIGHT!
WHILE PATROLMAN PATTON HAS COMPLETELY FORGOTTEN HIS ACHING FEET...
CRACK!
SIT DOWN IN THE NAME O' THE LAW, YE CROOK!
DON'T LET HIM HIT ME AGAIN!
NOT SO FAST! THE TREATMENT ISN'T OVER!
YOU'LL FIND ARNICA IN THERE FOR YOUR BRUISES!
ARNICA, HECK! CALL AN AMBULANCE!
GRAB YOURSELF SOME HEADACHE PILLS ON THE WAY DOWN, MATTSON!
SING SING WAS NEVER LIKE THIS! TAKE ME BACK!
AND AS DOC CHALMERS PROMISED, PATROLMAN PATTON'S PROBLEM APPEARS TO BE SOLVED...
BEST PINCH I EVER MADE! THEY'LL PROMOTE ME FOR THIS!
12

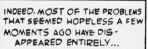

INDEED, MOST OF THE PROBLEMS THAT SEEMED HOPELESS A FEW MOMENTS AGO HAVE DISAPPEARED ENTIRELY...
LOOK! MY HAIR STARTED TO SPROUT WHEN I GOT SLUGGED-- AND I TOOK OFF SEVEN OUNCES IN THIS FIGHT!
LEMME WEIGH IN! I'M SO STRONG, I'M GONNA CHALLENGE TH' CHAMP!
WEIGHT
HOW ABOUT IT MARY-- WILL YOU TAKE THAT JOB IN MY OFFICE? I'VE GOT A COUPLE OF PATIENTS ALREADY!
OH, ROY-- OF COURSE I WILL!
BUT IN THEIR PLACE A NEW PROBLEM HAS ARISEN TO FACE THE GENTLE OLD MAN WHO WAS NEVER TOO BUSY TO HELP OTHERS...
I HAVEN'T ENOUGH MONEY TO FIX IT UP.. IT LOOKS LIKE MY FINISH--BUT IT WAS WORTH IT, TO SEND THOSE RATS BACK TO PRISON!
DOC, SOMETHING TELLS ME YOU'RE GOING TO GET A SURPRISE!
THAT NIGHT, THE BATMAN ADDRESSES A HASTILY-CALLED MASS MEETING...
FOLKS, YOU KNOW DOC CHALMERS NEVER REFUSED TO HELP A NEIGHBOR! NOW HE'S IN TROUBLE BECAUSE HE RISKED EVERYTHING TO MAKE THIS COMMUNITY SAFE FOR YOU AND YOUR CHILDREN...
SOME TIME LATER, A SPECTACULAR PARADE WINDS ITS NOISY WAY THROUGH THE DISTRICT...
HOORAY FOR DOC CHALMERS!
SILLY OF ME -- BUT I FEEL LIKE BAWLING!
'RAY FOR DOC!
"DOC" MADE ME CHAMP!
LOOK WHAT "DOC" DID FOR ME- Folks!
THANKS TO DOC FOR PUTTING ME ON WHEELS!
POLIC
P.D.
AND HALTS WHERE A GLITTERING NEW BUSINESS IS READY FOR ITS GRAND OPENING...
NOTHING COULD BE GRANDER THAN THIS, COULD IT, CHILDREN? (SNIFF-SNIFF)
DOC
THE FRIENDLY DRUGGIST
OPENING TO
WELCOME
OPENING TODA
GRAND OPENING
YES, OUR WEDDING! AND DON'T FORGET YOU'RE GIVING THE BRIDE AWAY!
FAR INTO THE EVENING...
DOC CHALMERS
YESSIR, ALL MY LIFE I WANTED A SIGN LIKE THAT! BUT I HAD TO WAIT FOR THE BATMAN AND ROBIN!
GEE.. DO YOU KNOW THEM, TOO?
THE END
13

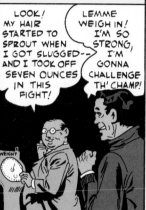

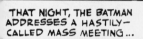

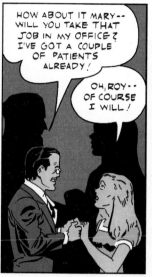

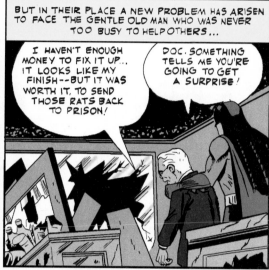

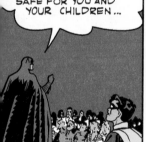

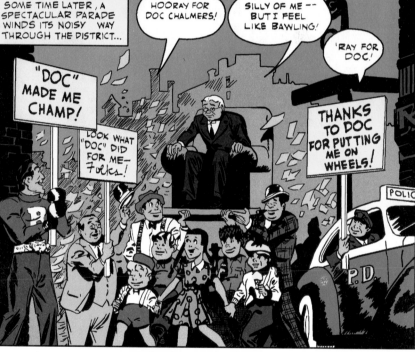

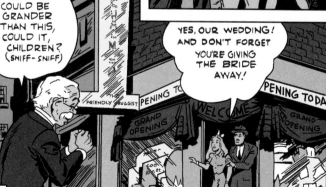

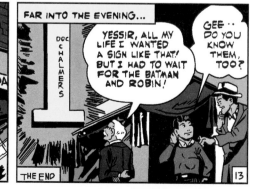

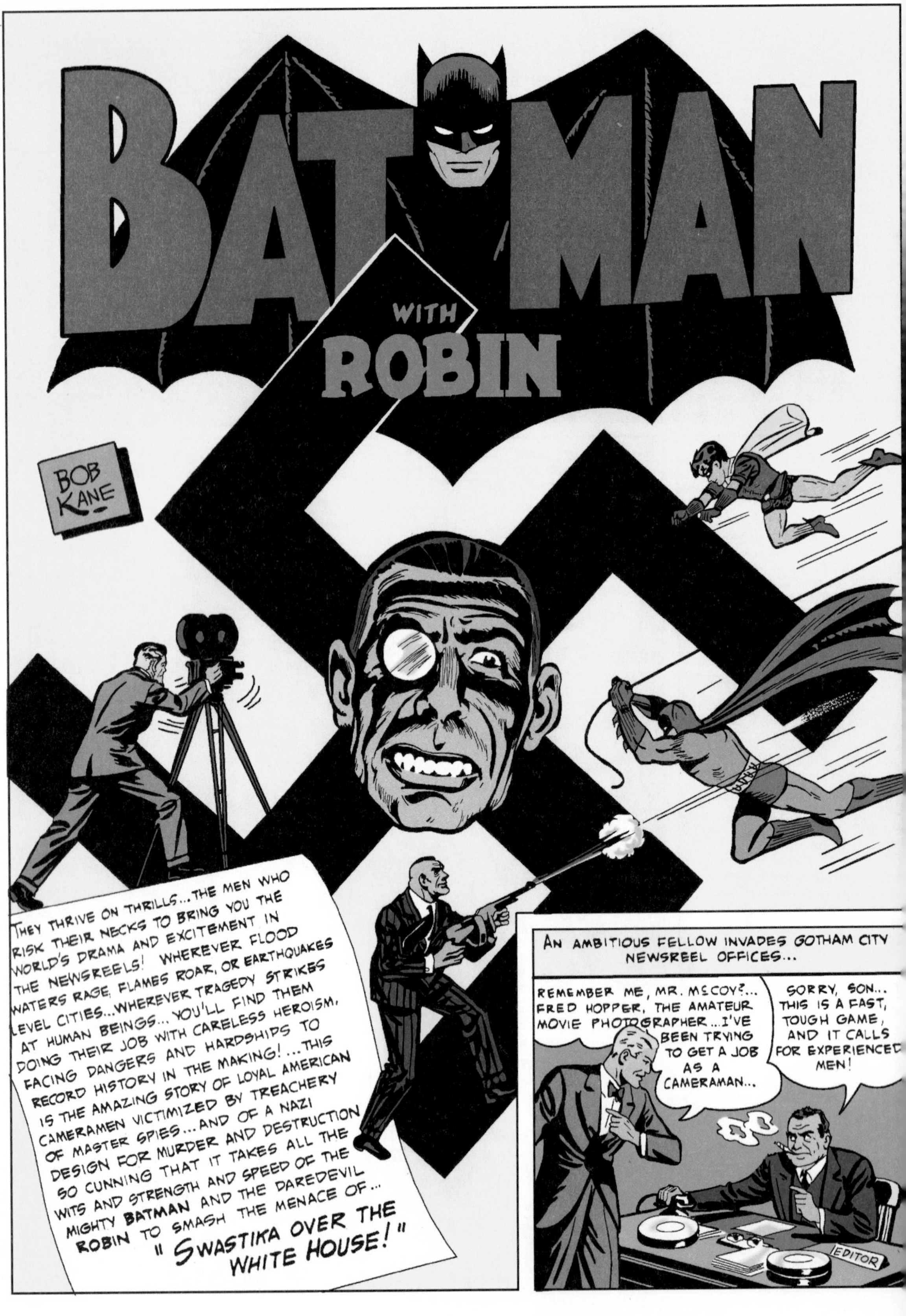
BATMAN
WITH ROBIN
BOB KANE
THEY THRIVE ON THRILLS...THE MEN WHO RISK THEIR NECKS TO BRING YOU THE WORLD'S DRAMA AND EXCITEMENT IN THE NEWSREELS! WHEREVER FLOOD WATERS RAGE, FLAMES ROAR, OR EARTHQUAKES LEVEL CITIES...WHEREVER TRAGEDY STRIKES AT HUMAN BEINGS... YOU'LL FIND THEM DOING THEIR JOB WITH CARELESS HEROISM, FACING DANGERS AND HARDSHIPS TO RECORD HISTORY IN THE MAKING! ...THIS IS THE AMAZING STORY OF LOYAL AMERICAN CAMERAMEN VICTIMIZED BY TREACHERY OF MASTER SPIES... AND OF A NAZI DESIGN FOR MURDER AND DESTRUCTION SO CUNNING THAT IT TAKES ALL THE WITS AND STRENGTH AND SPEED OF THE MIGHTY BATMAN AND THE DAREDEVIL ROBIN TO SMASH THE MENACE OF... "SWASTIKA OVER THE WHITE HOUSE!"
AN AMBITIOUS FELLOW INVADES GOTHAM CITY NEWSREEL OFFICES...
REMEMBER ME, MR. McCOY?... FRED HOPPER, THE AMATEUR MOVIE PHOTOGRAPHER...I'VE BEEN TRYING TO GET A JOB AS A CAMERAMAN...
SORRY, SON... THIS IS A FAST, TOUGH GAME, AND IT CALLS FOR EXPERIENCED MEN!
EDITOR

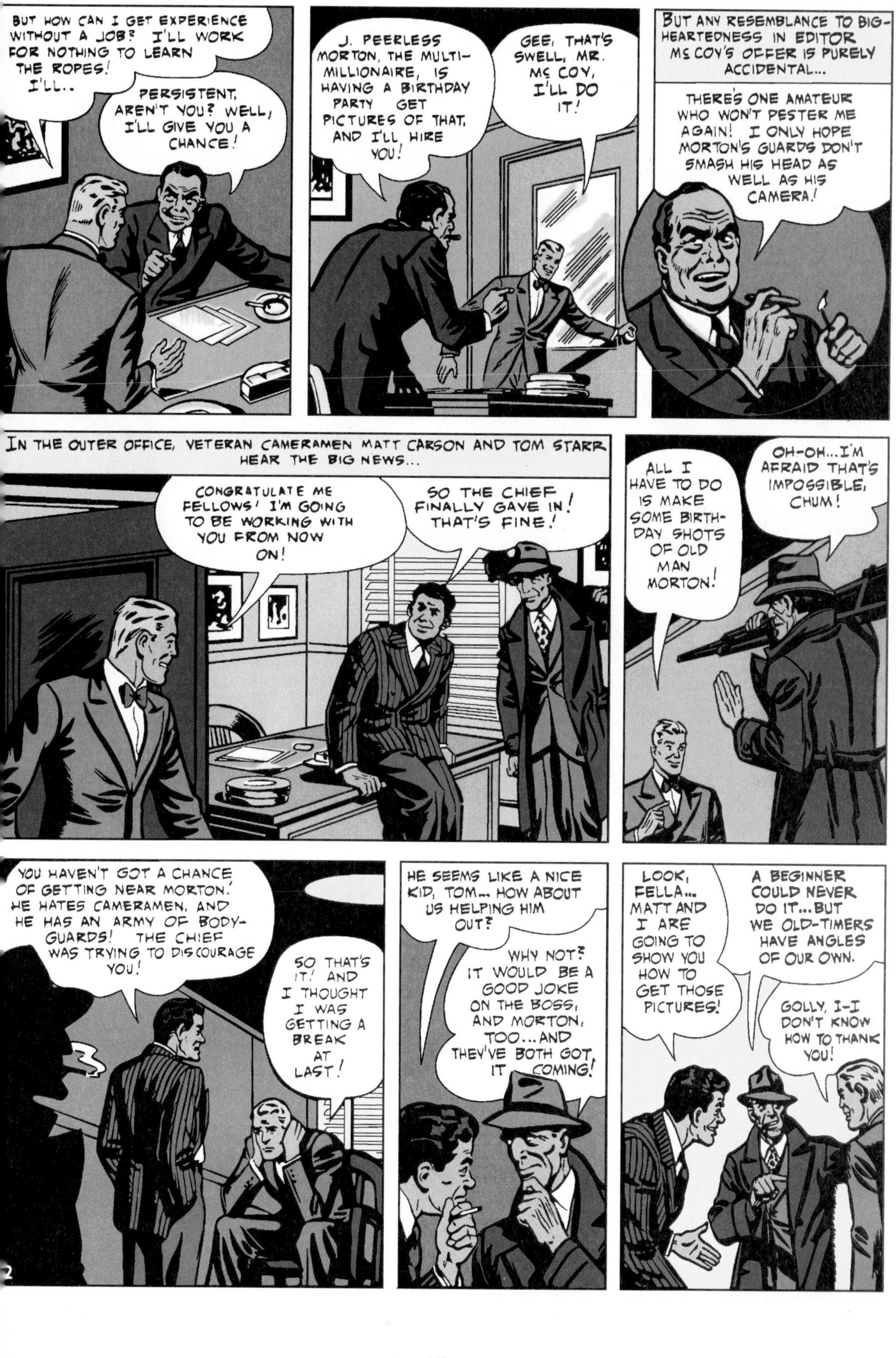
BUT HOW CAN I GET EXPERIENCE WITHOUT A JOB? I'LL WORK FOR NOTHING TO LEARN THE ROPES! I'LL..
PERSISTENT, AREN'T YOU? WELL, I'LL GIVE YOU A CHANCE!
J. PEERLESS MORTON, THE MULTI-MILLIONAIRE, IS HAVING A BIRTHDAY PARTY GET PICTURES OF THAT, AND I'LL HIRE YOU!
GEE, THAT'S SWELL, MR. McCOY, I'LL DO IT!
BUT ANY RESEMBLANCE TO BIG-HEARTEDNESS IN EDITOR McCOY'S OFFER IS PURELY ACCIDENTAL...
THERE'S ONE AMATEUR WHO WON'T PESTER ME AGAIN! I ONLY HOPE MORTON'S GUARDS DON'T SMASH HIS HEAD AS WELL AS HIS CAMERA!
IN THE OUTER OFFICE, VETERAN CAMERAMEN MATT CARSON AND TOM STARR HEAR THE BIG NEWS...
CONGRATULATE ME FELLOWS! I'M GOING TO BE WORKING WITH YOU FROM NOW ON!
SO THE CHIEF FINALLY GAVE IN! THAT'S FINE!
ALL I HAVE TO DO IS MAKE SOME BIRTHDAY SHOTS OF OLD MAN MORTON!
OH-OH...I'M AFRAID THAT'S IMPOSSIBLE, CHUM!
YOU HAVEN'T GOT A CHANCE OF GETTING NEAR MORTON! HE HATES CAMERAMEN, AND HE HAS AN ARMY OF BODY-GUARDS! THE CHIEF WAS TRYING TO DISCOURAGE YOU!
SO THAT'S IT! AND I THOUGHT I WAS GETTING A BREAK AT LAST!
HE SEEMS LIKE A NICE KID, TOM... HOW ABOUT US HELPING HIM OUT?
WHY NOT? IT WOULD BE A GOOD JOKE ON THE BOSS, AND MORTON, TOO...AND THEY'VE BOTH GOT IT COMING!
LOOK, FELLA... MATT AND I ARE GOING TO SHOW YOU HOW TO GET THOSE PICTURES!
A BEGINNER COULD NEVER DO IT...BUT WE OLD-TIMERS HAVE ANGLES OF OUR OWN.
GOLLY, I-I DON'T KNOW HOW TO THANK YOU!
2

LATER...WEARING EXPRESSMAN'S CAPS BY WAY OF DISGUISE, THE RESOURCEFUL CAMERAMEN DELIVER A BULKY PACKAGE AT THE HOME OF J. PEERLESS MORTON...

BIRTHDAY PRESENT FOR MR. MORTON... AND IT WEIGHS PLENTY!

A STATUE FOR HIS ART COLLECTION... NO DOUBT... BRING IT IN, MY GOOD MEN!

A PACKAGE FOR YOU MR. MORTON!

WELL, BRING IT IN... AND IF I DON'T LIKE IT, YOU CAN TAKE IT BACK WHERE IT CAME FROM!

MAKE IT SNAPPY!

HOW ABOUT A LITTLE SMILE, MR. MORTON!

PHOTOGRAPHERS! DON'T YOU DARE TAKE PICTURES! I FORBID IT!

GUARDS! THROW THIS MAN OUT! SMASH HIS CAMERA!

OKAY, HOPPER... TIME FOR US TO LEAVE!

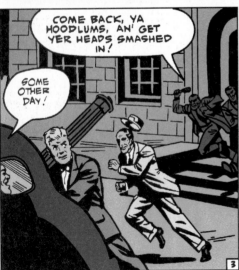

COME BACK, YA HOODLUMS, AN' GET YER HEADS SMASHED IN!

SOME OTHER DAY!

3

WHEW! THAT WAS CLOSE! McCOY WAS RIGHT WHEN HE SAID IT WAS A TOUGH GAME!

YOU'LL LIKE IT WHEN YOU LEARN THE ROPES... AND WE'LL TEACH 'EM TO YOU!

AND SO, AS IS OFTEN THE CASE, A JEST BACKFIRES ON ITS MAKER...

HERE'S THE MORTON FILMS, MR. McCOY... I GUESS I'M A MEMBER ON THE STAFF NOW, EH?

WHAT! YOU ACTUALLY GOT IT! WHY...ER, CONGRATULATION I GUESS I'LL HAVE TO HIRE YOU NOW!

WITH THE EASY-GOING COMRADESHIP OF THEIR CALLING, THE NEWS-REEL VETERANS "ADOPT" YOUNG FRED HOPPER... GUIDE HIM THROUGH HIS FIRST ASSIGNMENTS... EVEN INVITE HIM TO SHARE THEIR APARTMENT...

WE'RE GOING TO MAKE WAR INDUSTRY PICTURES NEXT...AND THE CHIEF SAYS THE THREE OF US CAN WORK TOGETHER!

YOU'RE REAL PALS! I'D HAVE BEEN SUNK WITHOUT YOU...

HA! I'VE DONE IT! I'M IN! I'VE TRICKED THOSE AMERICANS! THE LEADER WILL EE PLEASED!

WHAT'S THIS ABOUT "THE LEADER?" PERHAPS WE'D BETTER KEEP AN EYE ON THIS YOUNG STRANGER AS HE WALKS ALONE, LATE AT NIGHT...

AH, MY YOUNG FRIEND... CAN I SHOW YOU SOMETHING VERY OLD, OUT OF THE PAST?

NO, BUT YOU MAY SHOW ME SOMETHING NEW, HAVING TO DO WITH THE FUTURE!

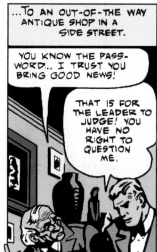

...TO AN OUT-OF-THE WAY ANTIQUE SHOP IN A SIDE STREET.

YOU KNOW THE PASS-WORD... I TRUST YOU BRING GOOD NEWS!

THAT IS FOR THE LEADER TO JUDGE! YOU HAVE NO RIGHT TO QUESTION ME.

A HIDDEN BUTTON SLIDES BACK A SECRET PANEL IN THE REAR WALL...

YOU WILL FIND THE COUNT IN THE CONFERENCE ROOM...

I KNOW... I HAVE BEEN HERE BEFORE!

COUNT FELIX... OUR PLAN HAS SUCCEEDED! I AM A NEWSREEL CAMERAMAN ASSIGNED TO PHOTOGRAPH WAR INDUSTRIES!

AH! FRITZ HOFFNER! THE FUEHRER HIMSELF SHALL HEAR OF THIS!

4

HEINRICH, OUR FRITZ HAS GOT THE JOB HE WAS AFTER!

EXCELLENT! THE AUTHORITIES WILL CENSOR THE REGULAR FILM... BUT INSIDE THE BIG CAMERA WILL BE THE LITTLE SECRET CAMERA, NEIN?

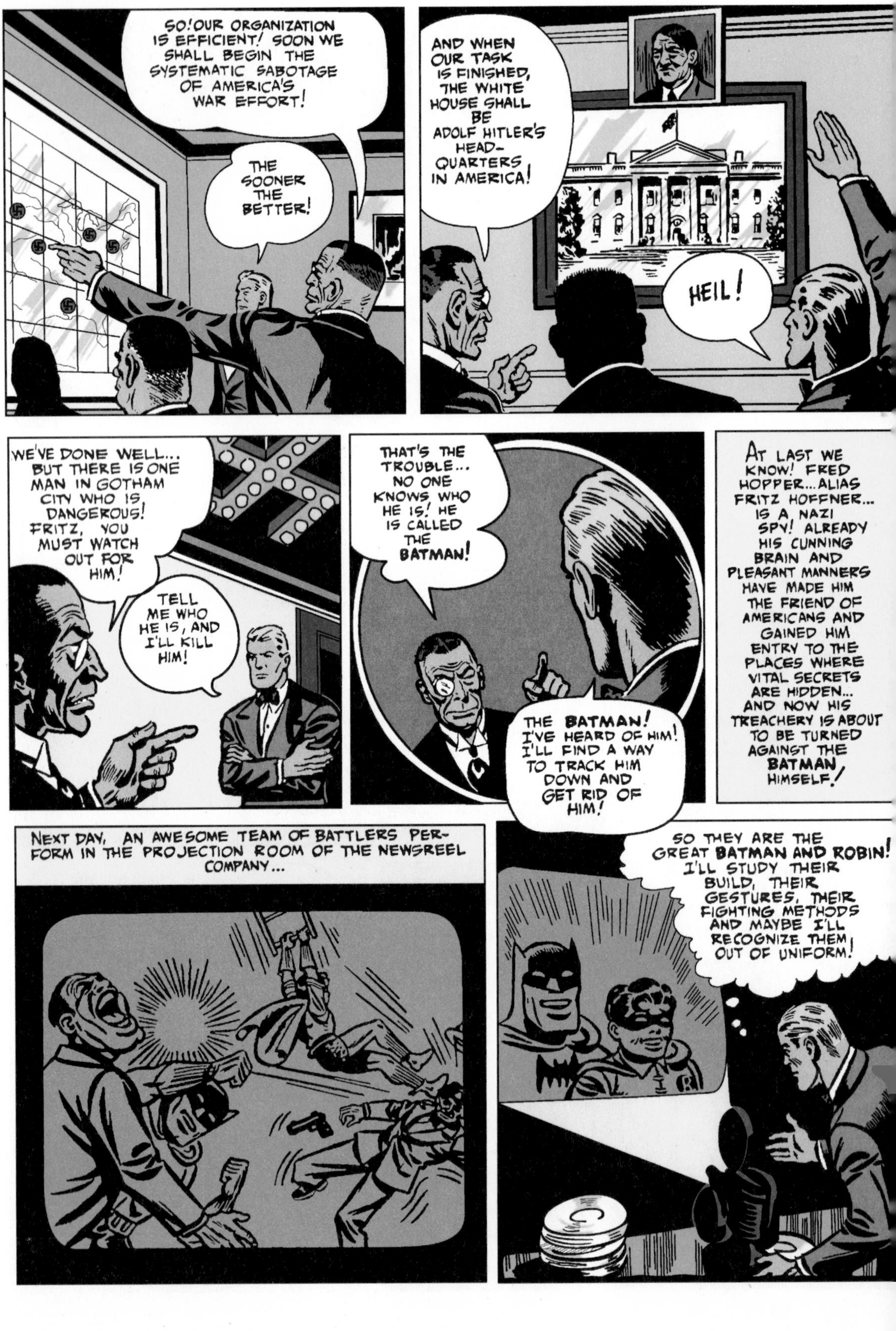
SO! OUR ORGANIZATION IS EFFICIENT! SOON WE SHALL BEGIN THE SYSTEMATIC SABOTAGE OF AMERICA'S WAR EFFORT!
THE SOONER THE BETTER!
AND WHEN OUR TASK IS FINISHED, THE WHITE HOUSE SHALL BE ADOLF HITLER'S HEAD-QUARTERS IN AMERICA!
HEIL!
WE'VE DONE WELL... BUT THERE IS ONE MAN IN GOTHAM CITY WHO IS DANGEROUS! FRITZ, YOU MUST WATCH OUT FOR HIM!
TELL ME WHO HE IS, AND I'LL KILL HIM!
THAT'S THE TROUBLE... NO ONE KNOWS WHO HE IS! HE IS CALLED THE BATMAN!
THE BATMAN! I'VE HEARD OF HIM! I'LL FIND A WAY TO TRACK HIM DOWN AND GET RID OF HIM!
AT LAST WE KNOW! FRED HOPPER...ALIAS FRITZ HOFFNER... IS A NAZI SPY! ALREADY HIS CUNNING BRAIN AND PLEASANT MANNERS HAVE MADE HIM THE FRIEND OF AMERICANS AND GAINED HIM ENTRY TO THE PLACES WHERE VITAL SECRETS ARE HIDDEN... AND NOW HIS TREACHERY IS ABOUT TO BE TURNED AGAINST THE BATMAN HIMSELF!
NEXT DAY, AN AWESOME TEAM OF BATTLERS PER-FORM IN THE PROJECTION ROOM OF THE NEWSREEL COMPANY...
SO THEY ARE THE GREAT BATMAN AND ROBIN! I'LL STUDY THEIR BUILD, THEIR GESTURES, THEIR FIGHTING METHODS AND MAYBE I'LL RECOGNIZE THEM OUT OF UNIFORM!

LOOKING OVER THE OLD FILMS IN THE FILES, EH, FRED?

MATT AND I MADE THOSE PICTURES OF THE BATMAN MONTHS AGO!

WHY...UH...ER... THE BATMAN IS MY FAVORITE HERO! THAT'S WHY I RAN OFF THESE PICTURES!

HE IS A GREAT FIGHTER...BUT BULLETS HAVE STOPPED TOUGHER MEN THAN THAT!

THEN THIS IS YOUR LUCKY DAY! THE BATMAN IS COMING HERE THIS AFTERNOON TO LET US TAKE SOME PICTURES FOR THE WAR BOND CAMPAIGN!

HERE? I'LL SAY IT'S MY LUCKY DAY!

MINUTES LATER, THE NAZI SPYMASTER RECEIVES A PHONE CALL IN HIS SECRET OFFICE...

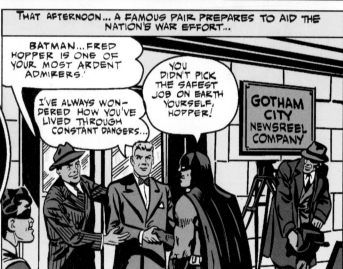

THE BATMAN? AH, FRITZ...YOU SHOULD RECEIVE THE IRON CROSS FOR THIS! I SHALL SEND OUR MOST DEPENDABLE ASSASSIN IMMEDIATELY!

THAT AFTERNOON...A FAMOUS PAIR PREPARES TO AID THE NATION'S WAR EFFORT...

BATMAN...FRED HOPPER IS ONE OF YOUR MOST ARDENT ADMIRERS!

I'VE ALWAYS WONDERED HOW YOU'VE LIVED THROUGH CONSTANT DANGERS...

YOU DIDN'T PICK THE SAFEST JOB ON EARTH YOURSELF, HOPPER!

GOTHAM CITY NEWSREEL COMPANY

UNNOTICED, A BLACK SEDAN CREEPS NEAR THE LITTLE GROUP...

ROBIN AND I DO THIS EVERY MORNING TO KEEP IN TRIM!

GREAT STUFF! THE PUBLIC WILL LOVE IT!

Suddenly...

WHA...? SOMEBODY DOESN'T LIKE OUR ACT!

WE'LL TRY ANOTHER ONE, THEN...GRAB FOR THOSE PHONE WIRES ABOVE YOU!

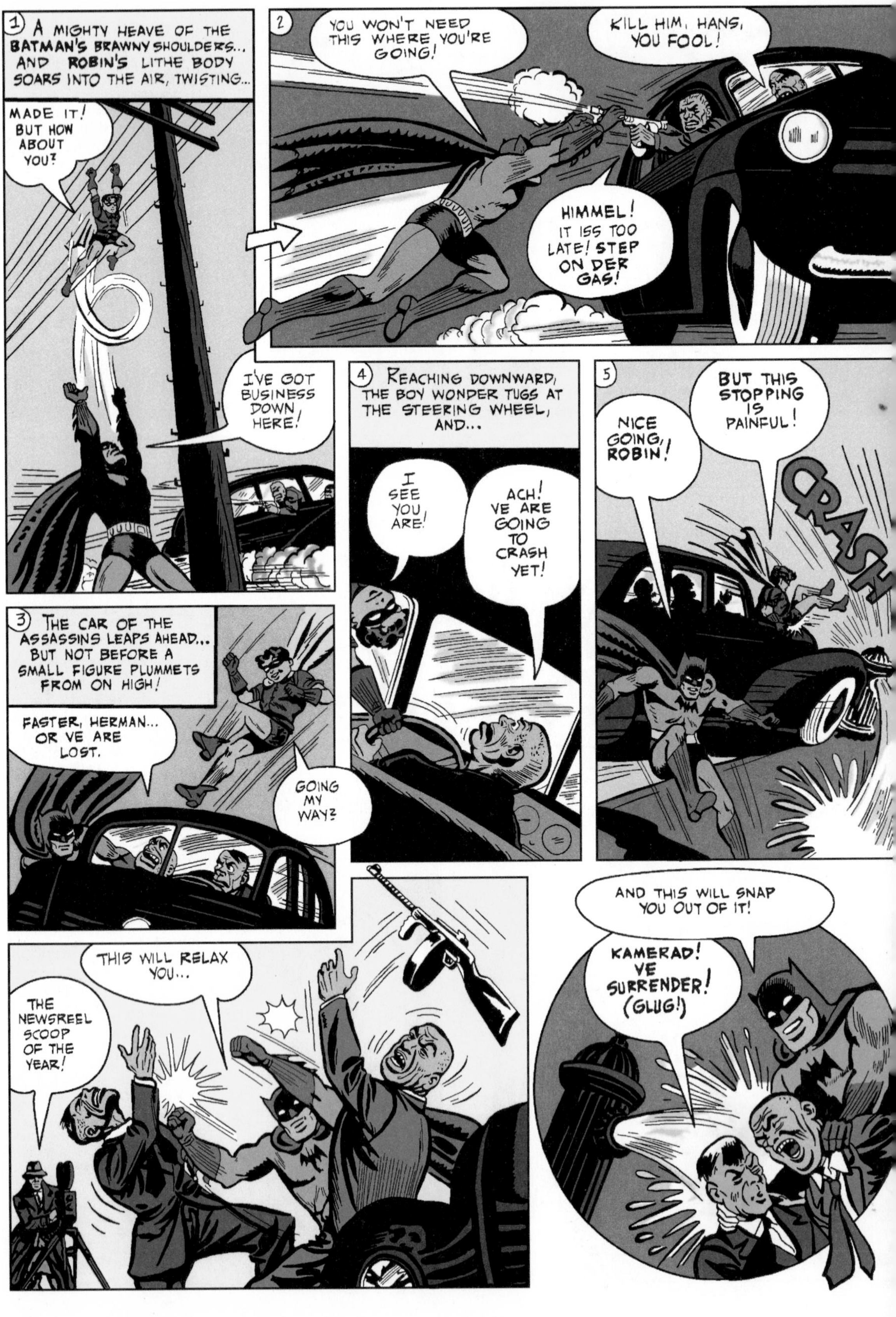

1 A MIGHTY HEAVE OF THE BATMAN'S BRAWNY SHOULDERS... AND ROBIN'S LITHE BODY SOARS INTO THE AIR, TWISTING...
MADE IT! BUT HOW ABOUT YOU?
I'VE GOT BUSINESS DOWN HERE!
2
YOU WON'T NEED THIS WHERE YOU'RE GOING!
KILL HIM, HANS, YOU FOOL!
HIMMEL! IT ISS TOO LATE! STEP ON DER GAS!
3 THE CAR OF THE ASSASSINS LEAPS AHEAD... BUT NOT BEFORE A SMALL FIGURE PLUMMETS FROM ON HIGH!
FASTER, HERMAN... OR VE ARE LOST.
GOING MY WAY?
4 REACHING DOWNWARD, THE BOY WONDER TUGS AT THE STEERING WHEEL, AND...
I SEE YOU ARE!
ACH! VE ARE GOING TO CRASH YET!
5
NICE GOING, ROBIN!
BUT THIS STOPPING IS PAINFUL!
CRASH
THE NEWSREEL SCOOP OF THE YEAR!
THIS WILL RELAX YOU...
AND THIS WILL SNAP YOU OUT OF IT!
KAMERAD! VE SURRENDER! (GLUG!)

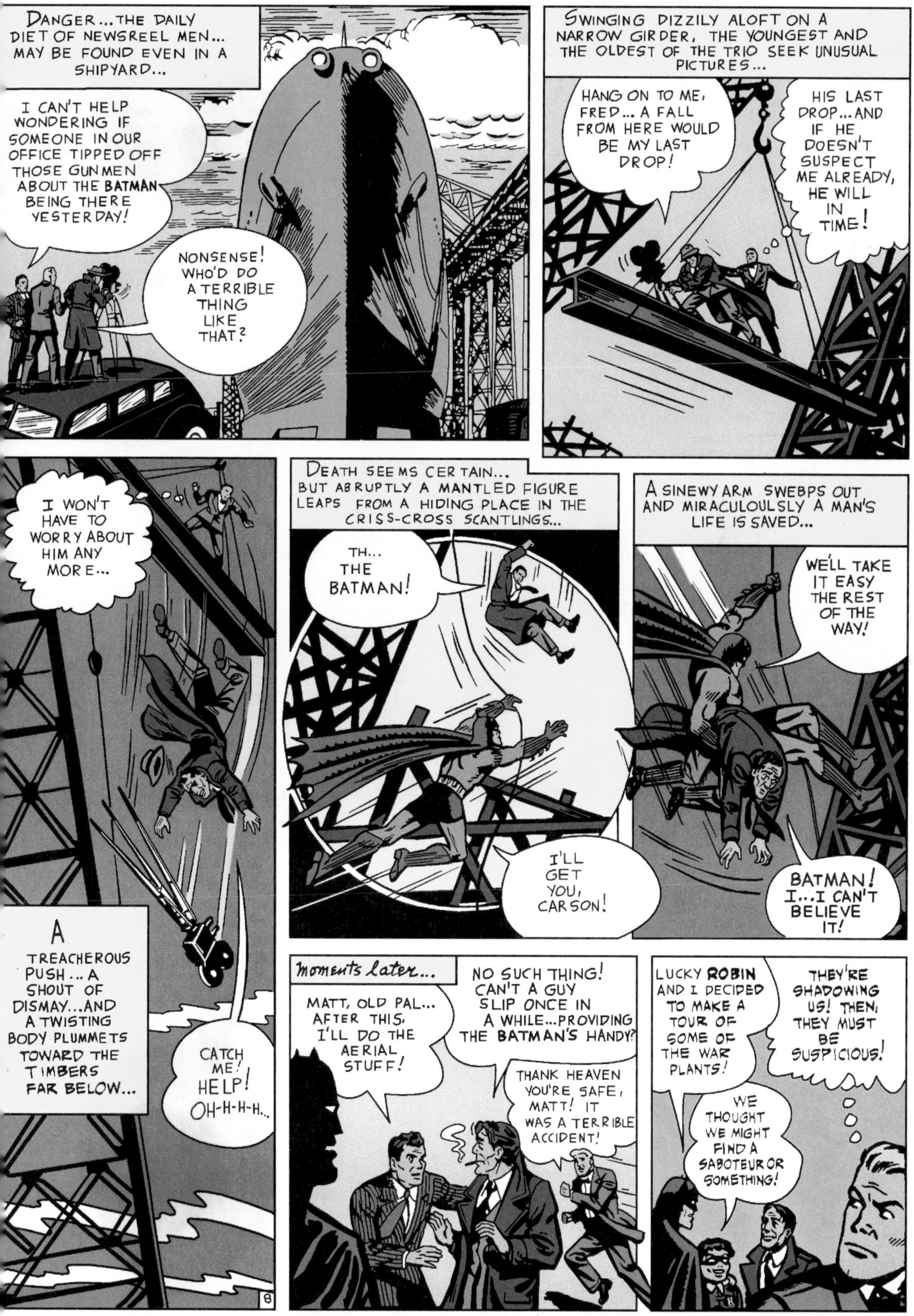
DANGER... THE DAILY DIET OF NEWSREEL MEN... MAY BE FOUND EVEN IN A SHIPYARD...
I CAN'T HELP WONDERING IF SOMEONE IN OUR OFFICE TIPPED OFF THOSE GUNMEN ABOUT THE BATMAN BEING THERE YESTERDAY!
NONSENSE! WHO'D DO A TERRIBLE THING LIKE THAT?
SWINGING DIZZILY ALOFT ON A NARROW GIRDER, THE YOUNGEST AND THE OLDEST OF THE TRIO SEEK UNUSUAL PICTURES...
HANG ON TO ME, FRED... A FALL FROM HERE WOULD BE MY LAST DROP!
HIS LAST DROP... AND IF HE DOESN'T SUSPECT ME ALREADY, HE WILL IN TIME!
I WON'T HAVE TO WORRY ABOUT HIM ANY MORE...
A TREACHEROUS PUSH... A SHOUT OF DISMAY... AND A TWISTING BODY PLUMMETS TOWARD THE TIMBERS FAR BELOW...
CATCH ME! HELP! OH-H-H-H...
8
DEATH SEEMS CERTAIN... BUT ABRUPTLY A MANTLED FIGURE LEAPS FROM A HIDING PLACE IN THE CRISS-CROSS SCANTLINGS...
TH... THE BATMAN!
I'LL GET YOU, CARSON!
A SINEWY ARM SWEBPS OUT AND MIRACULOULSLY A MAN'S LIFE IS SAVED...
WE'LL TAKE IT EASY THE REST OF THE WAY!
BATMAN! I...I CAN'T BELIEVE IT!
moments later...
MATT, OLD PAL... AFTER THIS, I'LL DO THE AERIAL STUFF!
NO SUCH THING! CAN'T A GUY SLIP ONCE IN A WHILE... PROVIDING THE BATMAN'S HANDY?
THANK HEAVEN YOU'RE SAFE, MATT! IT WAS A TERRIBLE ACCIDENT!
LUCKY ROBIN AND I DECIDED TO MAKE A TOUR OF SOME OF THE WAR PLANTS!
WE THOUGHT WE MIGHT FIND A SABOTEUR OR SOMETHING!
THEY'RE SHADOWING US! THEN, THEY MUST BE SUSPICIOUS!

REGULATIONS REQUIRE THAT ALL FILMS OF WAR PRODUCTION BE CENSORED BEFORE SHOWING...

HERE'S EVERYTHING MY CAMERA GOT, CAPTAIN!

WE'LL DEVELOP AND CHECK THEM, AND SEND THEM TO YOUR OFFICE... EXCEPT FOR THE PARTS WE CUT OUT!

BUT AS SOON AS THE YOUNG NAZI AGENT IS ALONE...

HOW EASY IT IS TO TRICK PEOPLE OF THESE TRUSTING DEMOCRACIES! IN THIS MINIATURE CAMERA ARE ALL THE PICTURES THE LARGER ONE TOOK... BUT UNCENSORED!

IN THE HEART OF THE ENEMY SPY WEB, A VERY PRIVATE SHOW TAKES PLACE...

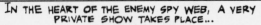

ONE OF THE BIG BOMBER PLANTS... I HAVE MADE NOTES ABOUT THE MANNER IN WHICH IT IS GUARDED!

WHEN IT IS BLOWN UP BY OUR AGENTS, IT WILL MAKE A PRETTIER PICTURE! HA! HA! HA!

STORAGE TANKS FOR THE SPECIAL HIGH-TEST GASOLINE THAT TAKES AMERICAN BOMBERS ACROSS THE OCEAN...

STOP THE FILM! THESE WILL MAKE A SPECTACULAR BEGINNING FOR ONE CAMPAIGN OF SABOTAGE!

MEANWHILE, IN THE HOME OF BRUCE WAYNE AND HIS YOUNG WARD DICK GRAYSON, WHO IN REALITY ARE THE BATMAN AND ROBIN...

THOSE FELLOWS WHO TRIED TO KILL US WON'T TALK TO THE POLICE... BUT THERE'S NO DOUBT THEY'RE MEMBERS OF A NAZI SPY GROUP!

AND YOU STILL THINK SOMEONE IN THAT NEWSREEL OFFICE PUT US ON THE SPOT?

NO ONE ELSE KNEW WE WERE GOING TO BE THERE... THAT'S WHY WE'RE KEEPING AN EYE EVERY NIGHT ON THE PLACES THOSE CAMERAMEN HAVE VISITED!

ALL THE NEWSREEL FELLOWS I'VE MET HAVE BEEN SWELL... I'D HATE TO THINK OF ANY OF THEM MIXED UP IN A SABOTAGE!

NIGHT... AND A SWIFT BLACK SHAPE STREAKS THROUGH THE INDUSTRIAL SUBURBS OF GOTHAM CITY... THE BATMOBILE...

EVERYTHING'S UNDER CONTROL AT THE PLANE FACTORY AND SHIPYARDS. WHERE DO WE GO FROM HERE?

YOU'LL SEE!

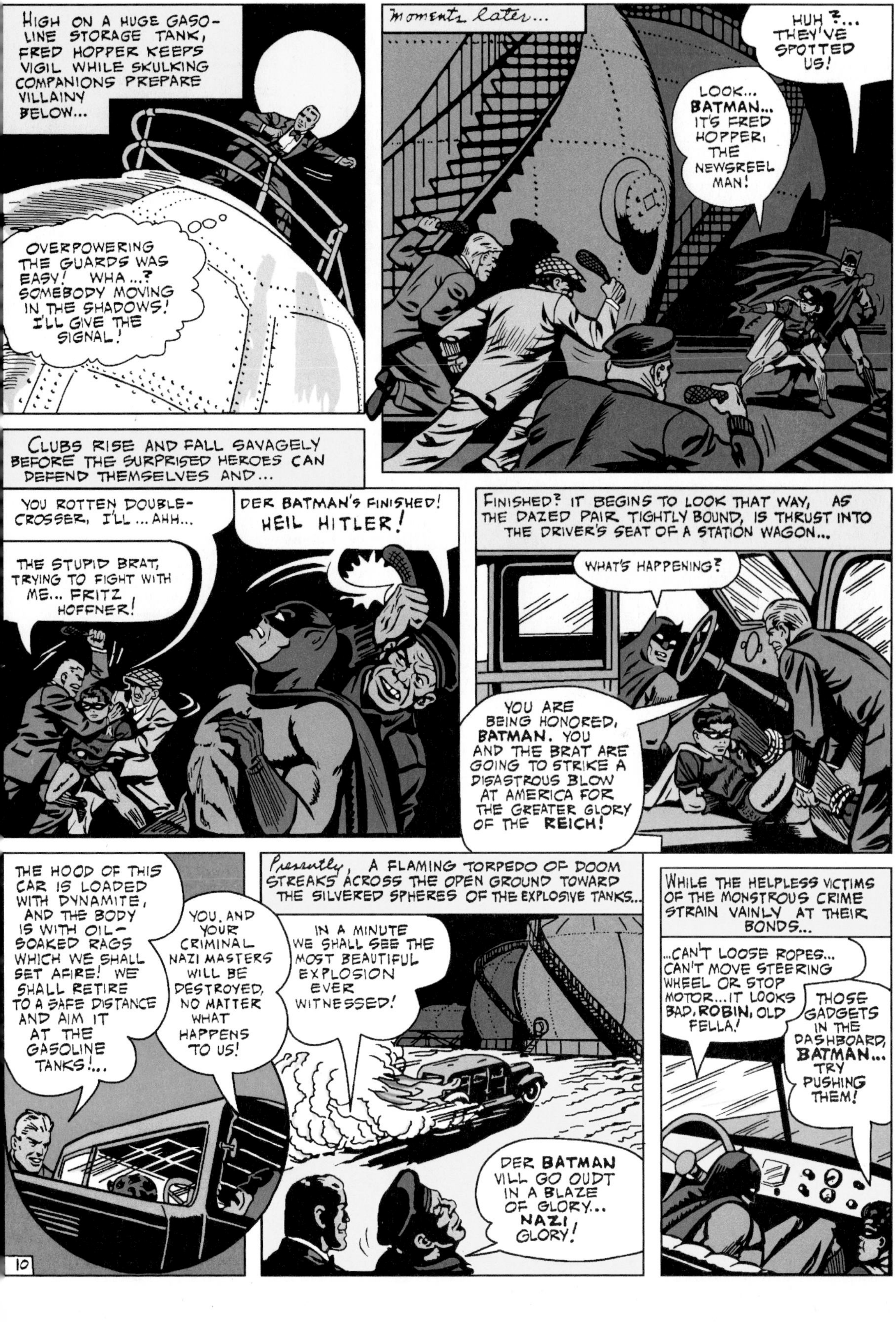
HIGH ON A HUGE GASOLINE STORAGE TANK, FRED HOPPER KEEPS VIGIL WHILE SKULKING COMPANIONS PREPARE VILLAINY BELOW...
OVERPOWERING THE GUARDS WAS EASY! WHA...? SOMEBODY MOVING IN THE SHADOWS! I'LL GIVE THE SIGNAL!
Moments later...
HUH?... THEY'VE SPOTTED US!
LOOK... BATMAN... IT'S FRED HOPPER, THE NEWSREEL MAN!
CLUBS RISE AND FALL SAVAGELY BEFORE THE SURPRISED HEROES CAN DEFEND THEMSELVES AND...
YOU ROTTEN DOUBLE-CROSSER, I'LL ... AHH...
DER BATMAN'S FINISHED! HEIL HITLER!
THE STUPID BRAT, TRYING TO FIGHT WITH ME... FRITZ HOFFNER!
FINISHED? IT BEGINS TO LOOK THAT WAY, AS THE DAZED PAIR, TIGHTLY BOUND, IS THRUST INTO THE DRIVER'S SEAT OF A STATION WAGON...
WHAT'S HAPPENING?
YOU ARE BEING HONORED, BATMAN. YOU AND THE BRAT ARE GOING TO STRIKE A DISASTROUS BLOW AT AMERICA FOR THE GREATER GLORY OF THE REICH!
THE HOOD OF THIS CAR IS LOADED WITH DYNAMITE, AND THE BODY IS WITH OIL-SOAKED RAGS WHICH WE SHALL SET AFIRE! WE SHALL RETIRE TO A SAFE DISTANCE AND AIM IT AT THE GASOLINE TANKS!...
YOU, AND YOUR CRIMINAL NAZI MASTERS WILL BE DESTROYED, NO MATTER WHAT HAPPENS TO US!
10
Presently, A FLAMING TORPEDO OF DOOM STREAKS ACROSS THE OPEN GROUND TOWARD THE SILVERED SPHERES OF THE EXPLOSIVE TANKS...
IN A MINUTE WE SHALL SEE THE MOST BEAUTIFUL EXPLOSION EVER WITNESSED!
DER BATMAN VILL GO OUDT IN A BLAZE OF GLORY... NAZI GLORY!
WHILE THE HELPLESS VICTIMS OF THE MONSTROUS CRIME STRAIN VAINLY AT THEIR BONDS...
...CAN'T LOOSE ROPES... CAN'T MOVE STEERING WHEEL OR STOP MOTOR...IT LOOKS BAD, ROBIN, OLD FELLA!
THOSE GADGETS IN THE DASHBOARD, BATMAN... TRY PUSHING THEM!

HURRY! WE'RE GOING TO CRASH IN A FEW SECONDS!

THIS MUST BE THE RIGHT ONE!

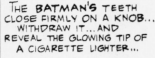

THE BATMAN'S TEETH CLOSE FIRMLY ON A KNOB... WITHDRAW IT... AND REVEAL THE GLOWING TIP OF A CIGARETTE LIGHTER...

IF ONLY THERE'S TIME TO BURN THROUGH MY ROPES BEFORE WE HIT!

A STRETCH OF ROUGH GROUND JOLTS AND SWERVES THE FLAMING COFFIN...

THE NEXT SECOND...

BOOM!

AS THE THUNDEROUS ECHOES OF THE BLAST DIE AWAY, THE SABOTEURS DEPART IN HASTE...

ACH...TOO BAD DER MACHINE TURNED UND EGGSPLODED ONLY A PILE OF RAILROAD TIES!

AT LEAST, WE'VE GOT RID OF THE BATMAN! FROM NOW ON WE CAN EXPECT COMPLETE SUCCESS WHENEVER WE STRIKE!

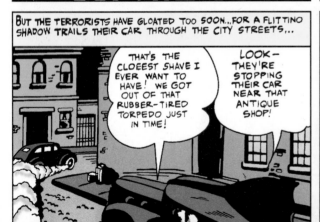

BUT THE TERRORISTS HAVE GLOATED TOO SOON...FOR A FLITTING SHADOW TRAILS THEIR CAR THROUGH THE CITY STREETS...

THAT'S THE CLOSEST SHAVE I EVER WANT TO HAVE! WE GOT OUT OF THAT RUBBER-TIRED TORPEDO JUST IN TIME!

LOOK— THEY'RE STOPPING THEIR CAR NEAR THAT ANTIQUE SHOP!

I CAN TELL BY YOUR FACE THAT IT IS GOOD NEWS THIS TIME, HERR HOFFNER!

THE BEST! FROM NOW ON WE HAVE NOTHING TO FEAR! THE BATMAN AND ROBIN ARE...

ANTIQUE SHOP

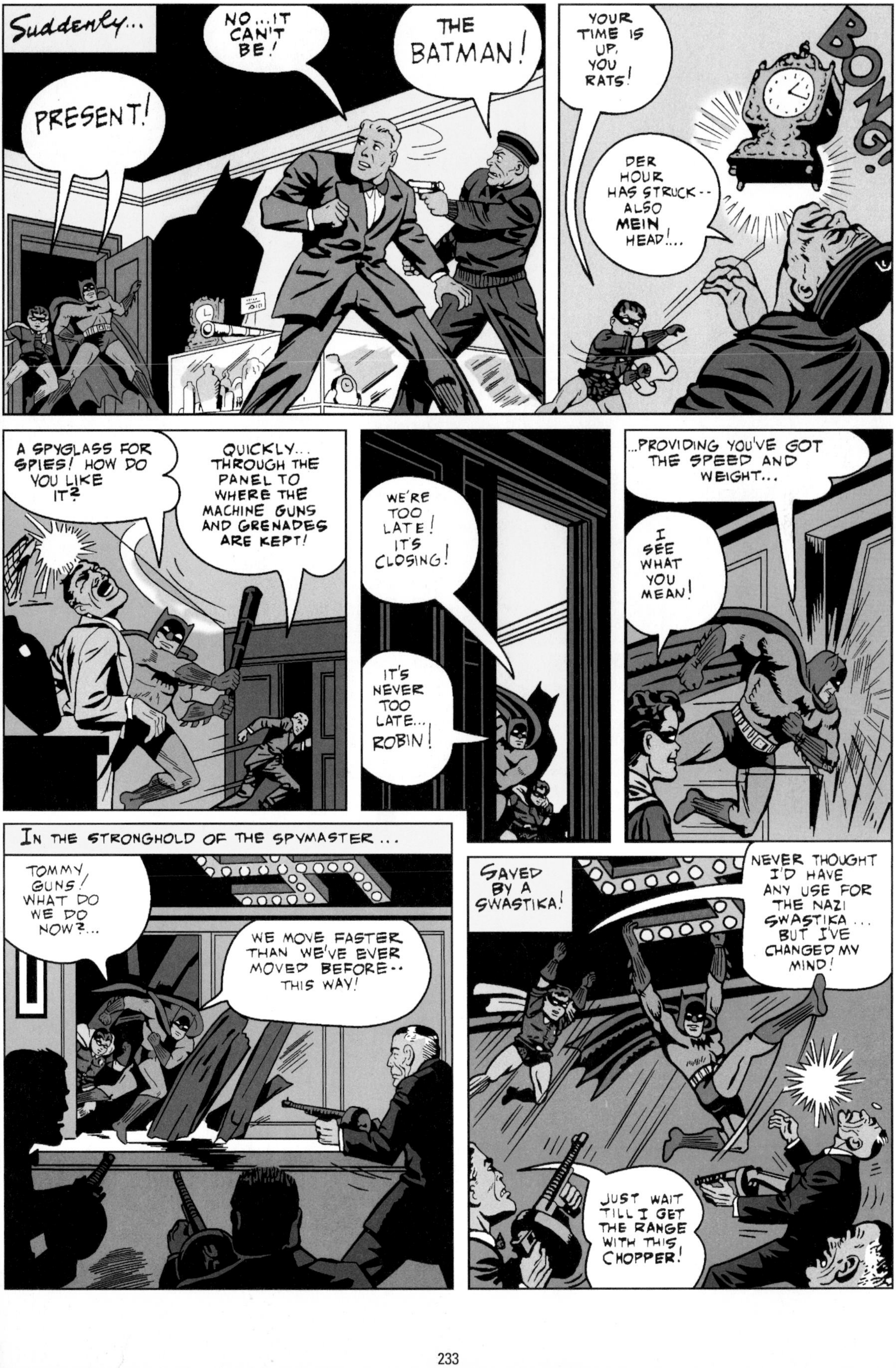
Suddenly...
PRESENT!
NO...IT CAN'T BE!
THE BATMAN!
YOUR TIME IS UP, YOU RATS!
BONG!
DER HOUR HAS STRUCK-- ALSO MEIN HEAD!...
A SPYGLASS FOR SPIES! HOW DO YOU LIKE IT?
QUICKLY... THROUGH THE PANEL TO WHERE THE MACHINE GUNS AND GRENADES ARE KEPT!
WE'RE TOO LATE! IT'S CLOSING!
IT'S NEVER TOO LATE... ROBIN!
...PROVIDING YOU'VE GOT THE SPEED AND WEIGHT...
I SEE WHAT YOU MEAN!
IN THE STRONGHOLD OF THE SPYMASTER...
TOMMY GUNS! WHAT DO WE DO NOW?...
WE MOVE FASTER THAN WE'VE EVER MOVED BEFORE-- THIS WAY!
SAVED BY A SWASTIKA!
NEVER THOUGHT I'D HAVE ANY USE FOR THE NAZI SWASTIKA... BUT I'VE CHANGED MY MIND!
JUST WAIT TILL I GET THE RANGE WITH THIS CHOPPER!

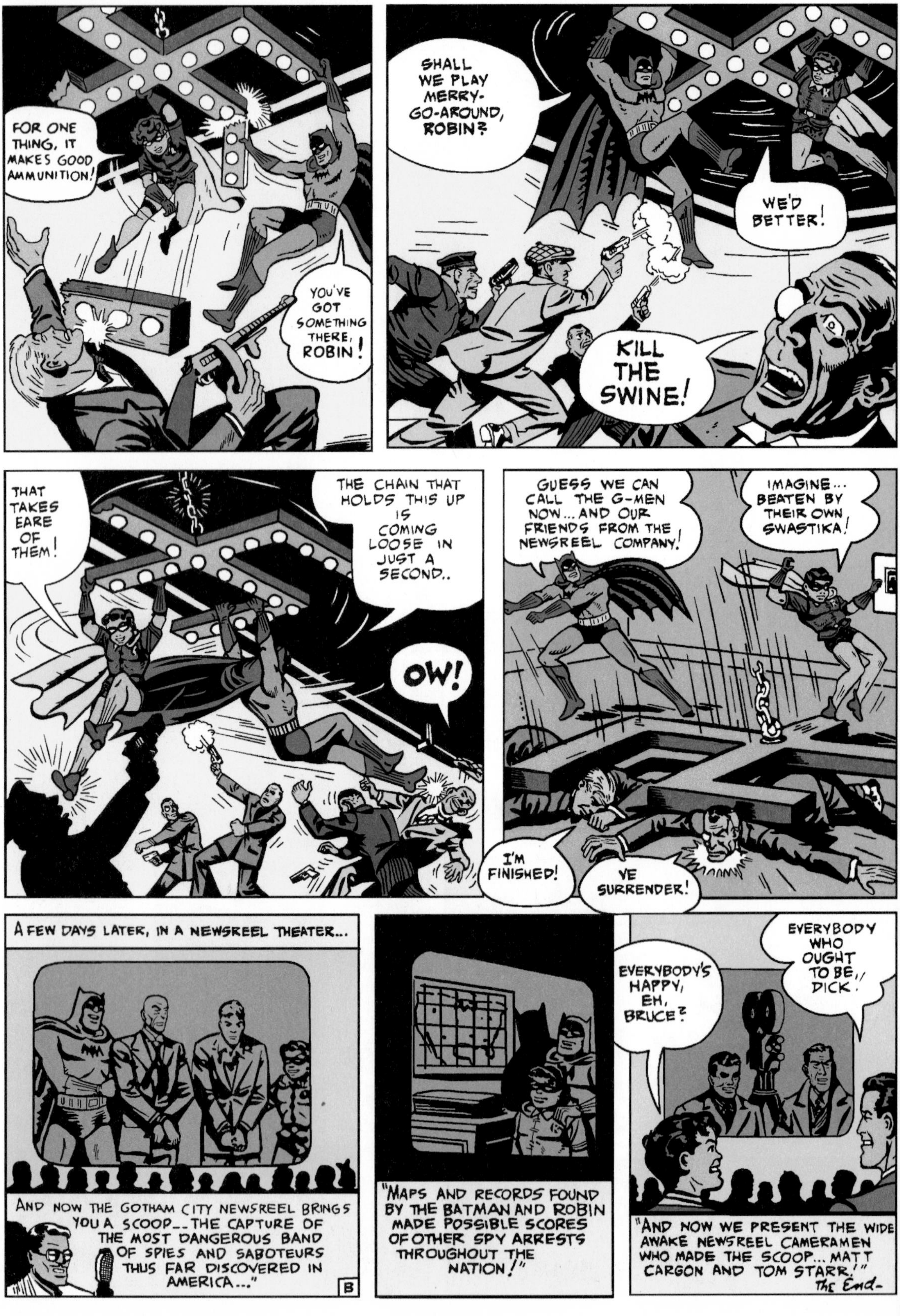
FOR ONE THING, IT MAKES GOOD AMMUNITION!
YOU'VE GOT SOMETHING THERE, ROBIN!
SHALL WE PLAY MERRY-GO-AROUND, ROBIN?
WE'D BETTER!
KILL THE SWINE!
THAT TAKES EARE OF THEM!
THE CHAIN THAT HOLDS THIS UP IS COMING LOOSE IN JUST A SECOND..
OW!
GUESS WE CAN CALL THE G-MEN NOW... AND OUR FRIENDS FROM THE NEWSREEL COMPANY!
IMAGINE... BEATEN BY THEIR OWN SWASTIKA!
I'M FINISHED!
VE SURRENDER!
A FEW DAYS LATER, IN A NEWSREEL THEATER...
AND NOW THE GOTHAM CITY NEWSREEL BRINGS YOU A SCOOP--THE CAPTURE OF THE MOST DANGEROUS BAND OF SPIES AND SABOTEURS THUS FAR DISCOVERED IN AMERICA..."
B
"MAPS AND RECORDS FOUND BY THE BATMAN AND ROBIN MADE POSSIBLE SCORES OF OTHER SPY ARRESTS THROUGHOUT THE NATION!"
EVERYBODY'S HAPPY, EH, BRUCE?
EVERYBODY WHO OUGHT TO BE, DICK!
"AND NOW WE PRESENT THE WIDE AWAKE NEWSREEL CAMERAMEN WHO MADE THE SCOOP... MATT CARGON AND TOM STARR!"
The End-

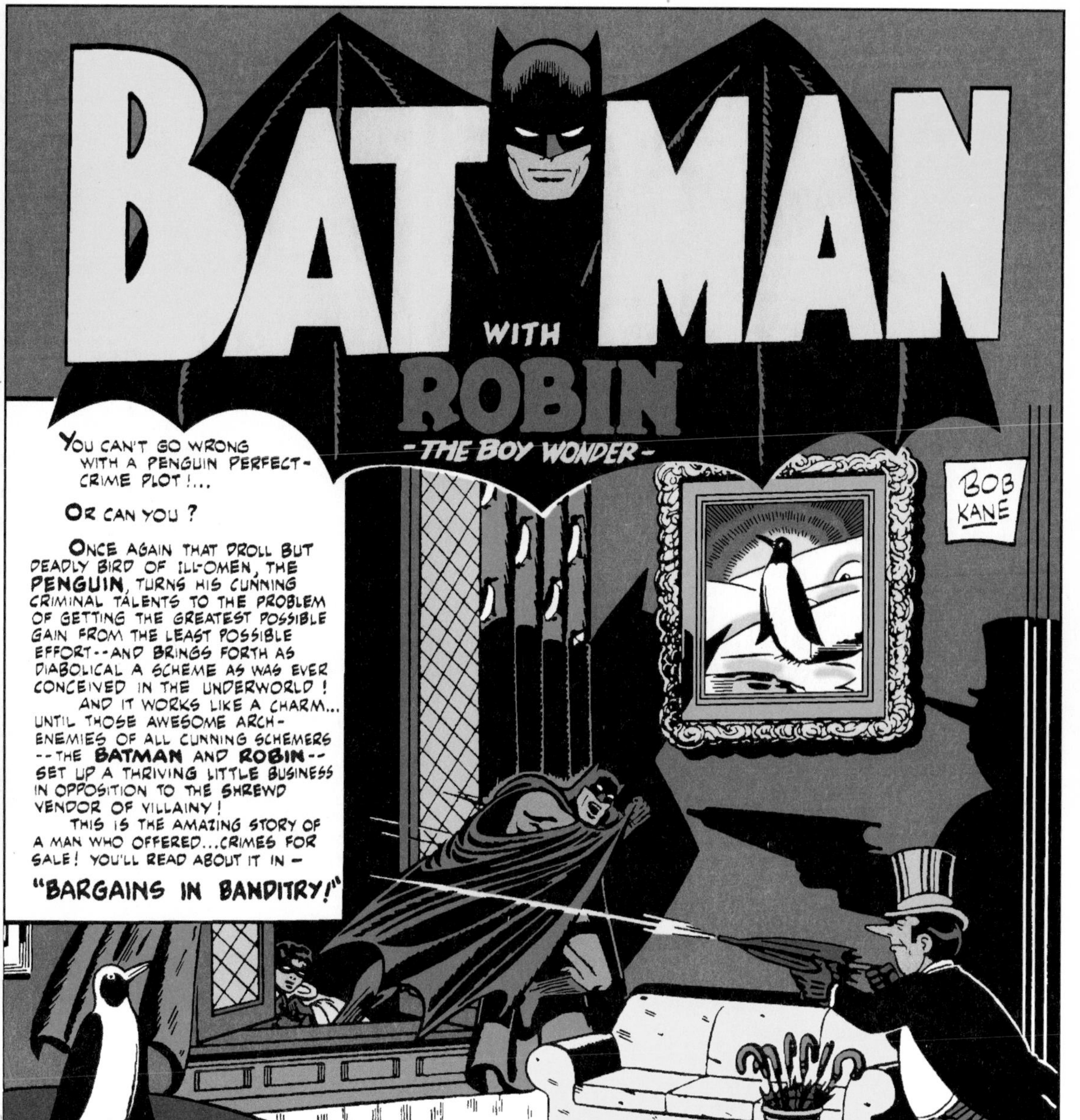
BATMAN
WITH
ROBIN
-THE BOY WONDER-
BOB KANE
YOU CAN'T GO WRONG WITH A PENGUIN PERFECT-CRIME PLOT!...
OR CAN YOU?
ONCE AGAIN THAT DROLL BUT DEADLY BIRD OF ILL-OMEN, THE PENGUIN, TURNS HIS CUNNING CRIMINAL TALENTS TO THE PROBLEM OF GETTING THE GREATEST POSSIBLE GAIN FROM THE LEAST POSSIBLE EFFORT--AND BRINGS FORTH AS DIABOLICAL A SCHEME AS WAS EVER CONCEIVED IN THE UNDERWORLD!
AND IT WORKS LIKE A CHARM... UNTIL THOSE AWESOME ARCH-ENEMIES OF ALL CUNNING SCHEMERS --THE BATMAN AND ROBIN-- SET UP A THRIVING LITTLE BUSINESS IN OPPOSITION TO THE SHREWD VENDOR OF VILLAINY!
THIS IS THE AMAZING STORY OF A MAN WHO OFFERED...CRIMES FOR SALE! YOU'LL READ ABOUT IT IN -
"BARGAINS IN BANDITRY!"

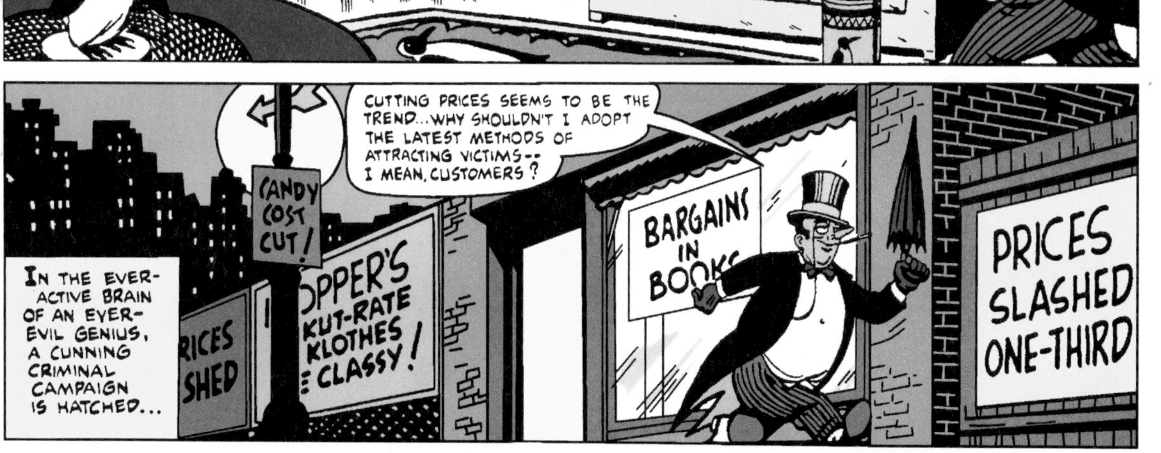
IN THE EVER-ACTIVE BRAIN OF AN EVER-EVIL GENIUS, A CUNNING CRIMINAL CAMPAIGN IS HATCHED...
CUTTING PRICES SEEMS TO BE THE TREND...WHY SHOULDN'T I ADOPT THE LATEST METHODS OF ATTRACTING VICTIMS-- I MEAN, CUSTOMERS?
CANDY COST CUT!
RICES SHED
OPPER'S KUT-RATE KLOTHES CLASSY!
BARGAINS IN BOOKS
PRICES SLASHED ONE-THIRD

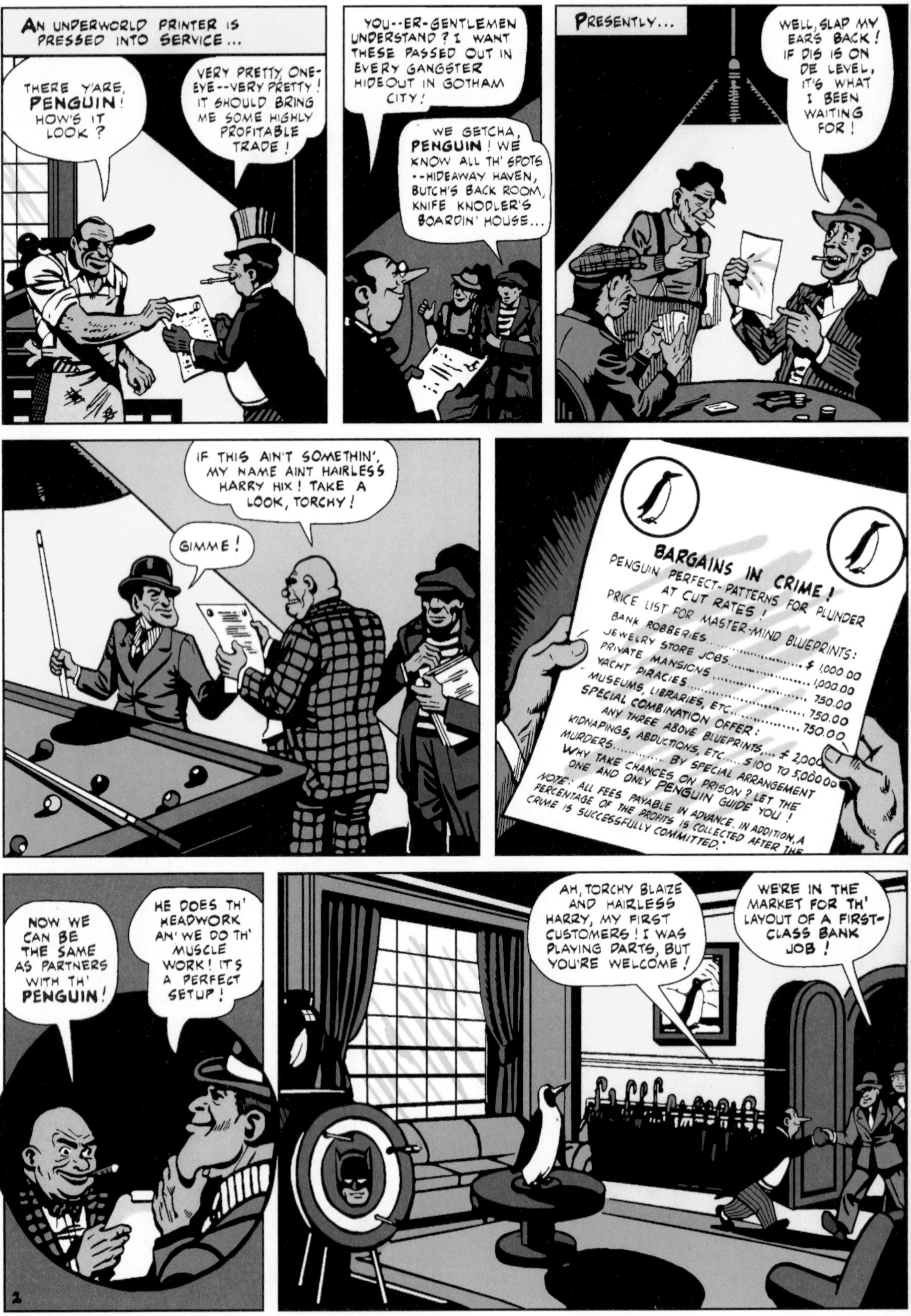

AN UNDERWORLD PRINTER IS PRESSED INTO SERVICE...
THERE Y'ARE, PENGUIN! HOW'S IT LOOK?
VERY PRETTY, ONE-EYE--VERY PRETTY! IT SHOULD BRING ME SOME HIGHLY PROFITABLE TRADE!
YOU--ER-GENTLEMEN UNDERSTAND? I WANT THESE PASSED OUT IN EVERY GANGSTER HIDEOUT IN GOTHAM CITY!
WE GETCHA, PENGUIN! WE KNOW ALL TH' SPOTS --HIDEAWAY HAVEN, BUTCH'S BACK ROOM, KNIFE KNODLER'S BOARDIN' HOUSE...
PRESENTLY...
WELL, SLAP MY EARS BACK! IF DIS IS ON DE LEVEL, IT'S WHAT I BEEN WAITING FOR!
IF THIS AIN'T SOMETHIN', MY NAME AINT HAIRLESS HARRY HIX! TAKE A LOOK, TORCHY!
GIMME!
BARGAINS IN CRIME!
PENGUIN PERFECT-PATTERNS FOR PLUNDER AT CUT RATES!
PRICE LIST FOR MASTER-MIND BLUEPRINTS:
BANK ROBBERIES......$ 1,000.00
JEWELRY STORE JOBS......1,000.00
PRIVATE MANSIONS......750.00
YACHT PIRACIES......750.00
MUSEUMS, LIBRARIES, ETC......750.00
SPECIAL COMBINATION OFFER: ANY THREE ABOVE BLUEPRINTS,... $ 2,000
KIDNAPINGS, ABDUCTIONS, ETC.....$100 TO 5,000.00
MURDERS......BY SPECIAL ARRANGEMENT
WHY TAKE CHANCES ON PRISON? LET THE ONE AND ONLY PENGUIN GUIDE YOU!
NOTE: ALL FEES PAYABLE IN ADVANCE. IN ADDITION, A PERCENTAGE OF THE PROFITS IS COLLECTED AFTER THE CRIME IS SUCCESSFULLY COMMITTED.
NOW WE CAN BE THE SAME AS PARTNERS WITH TH' PENGUIN!
HE DOES TH' HEADWORK AN' WE DO TH' MUSCLE WORK! IT'S A PERFECT SETUP!
2
AH, TORCHY BLAIZE AND HAIRLESS HARRY, MY FIRST CUSTOMERS! I WAS PLAYING DARTS, BUT YOU'RE WELCOME!
WE'RE IN THE MARKET FOR TH' LAYOUT OF A FIRST-CLASS BANK JOB!

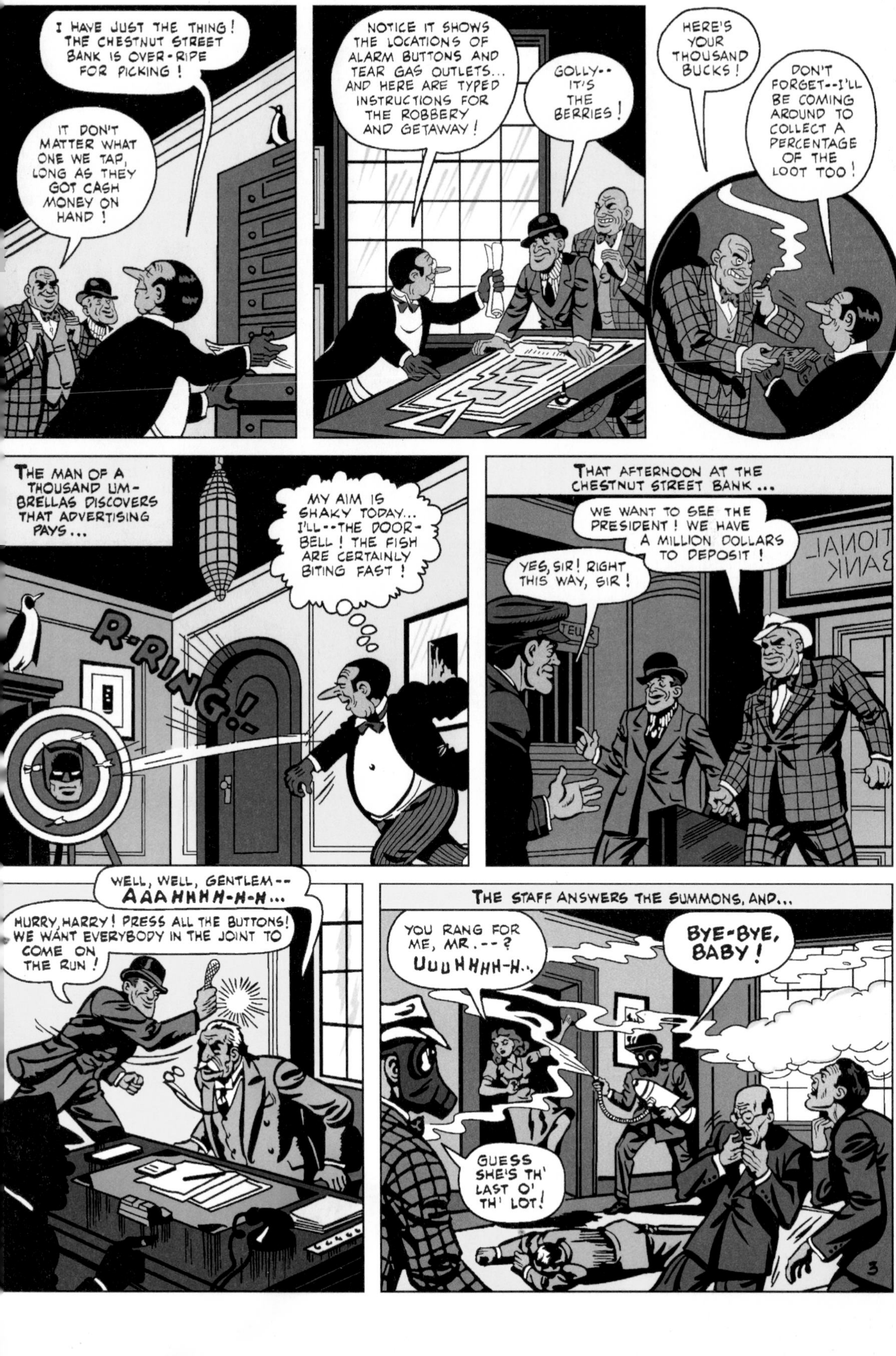
I HAVE JUST THE THING! THE CHESTNUT STREET BANK IS OVER-RIPE FOR PICKING!
IT DON'T MATTER WHAT ONE WE TAP, LONG AS THEY GOT CASH MONEY ON HAND!
NOTICE IT SHOWS THE LOCATIONS OF ALARM BUTTONS AND TEAR GAS OUTLETS... AND HERE ARE TYPED INSTRUCTIONS FOR THE ROBBERY AND GETAWAY!
GOLLY-- IT'S THE BERRIES!
HERE'S YOUR THOUSAND BUCKS!
DON'T FORGET--I'LL BE COMING AROUND TO COLLECT A PERCENTAGE OF THE LOOT TOO!
THE MAN OF A THOUSAND UMBRELLAS DISCOVERS THAT ADVERTISING PAYS...
MY AIM IS SHAKY TODAY... I'LL--THE DOORBELL! THE FISH ARE CERTAINLY BITING FAST!
R-RING!
THAT AFTERNOON AT THE CHESTNUT STREET BANK...
WE WANT TO SEE THE PRESIDENT! WE HAVE A MILLION DOLLARS TO DEPOSIT!
YES, SIR! RIGHT THIS WAY, SIR!
WELL, WELL, GENTLEM-- AAAHHHH-H-H...
HURRY, HARRY! PRESS ALL THE BUTTONS! WE WANT EVERYBODY IN THE JOINT TO COME ON THE RUN!
THE STAFF ANSWERS THE SUMMONS, AND...
YOU RANG FOR ME, MR.--? UUUHHHH-H..
BYE-BYE, BABY!
GUESS SHE'S TH' LAST O' TH' LOT!
3

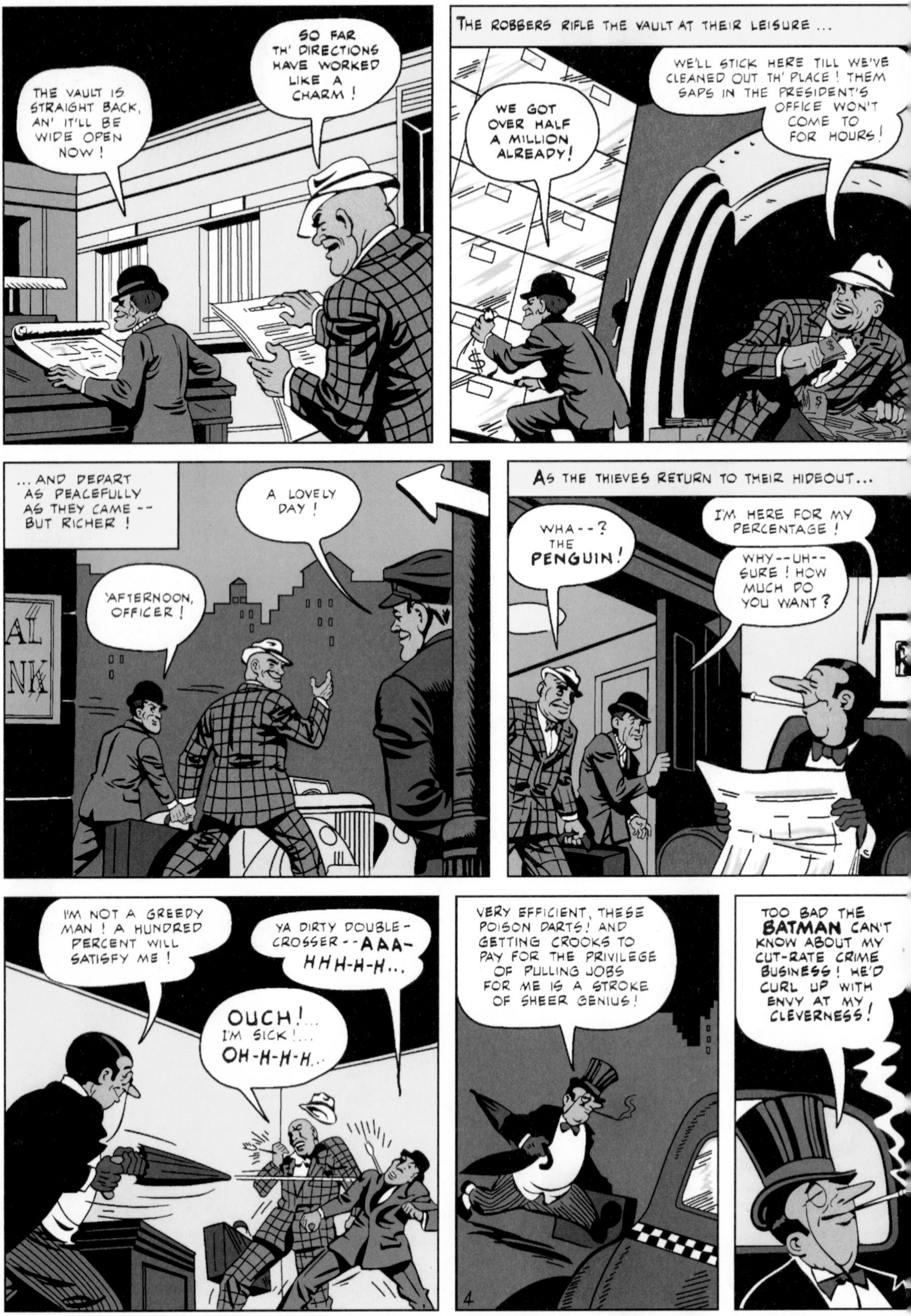
SO FAR TH' DIRECTIONS HAVE WORKED LIKE A CHARM !
THE VAULT IS STRAIGHT BACK, AN' IT'LL BE WIDE OPEN NOW !
THE ROBBERS RIFLE THE VAULT AT THEIR LEISURE ...
WE GOT OVER HALF A MILLION ALREADY !
WE'LL STICK HERE TILL WE'VE CLEANED OUT TH' PLACE ! THEM SAPS IN THE PRESIDENT'S OFFICE WON'T COME TO FOR HOURS !
... AND DEPART AS PEACEFULLY AS THEY CAME -- BUT RICHER !
A LOVELY DAY !
'AFTERNOON, OFFICER !
AS THE THIEVES RETURN TO THEIR HIDEOUT ...
WHA--? THE PENGUIN !
I'M HERE FOR MY PERCENTAGE !
WHY--UH-- SURE ! HOW MUCH DO YOU WANT ?
I'M NOT A GREEDY MAN ! A HUNDRED PERCENT WILL SATISFY ME !
YA DIRTY DOUBLE-CROSSER--AAA-HHH-H-H...
OUCH !... I'M SICK !... OH-H-H-H..
VERY EFFICIENT, THESE POISON DARTS ! AND GETTING CROOKS TO PAY FOR THE PRIVILEGE OF PULLING JOBS FOR ME IS A STROKE OF SHEER GENIUS !
4
TOO BAD THE BATMAN CAN'T KNOW ABOUT MY CUT-RATE CRIME BUSINESS ! HE'D CURL UP WITH ENVY AT MY CLEVERNESS !

BUT THE **BATMAN** IS NEARER THE FANTASTIC TRUTH THAN THE **PENGUIN** SUSPECTS, FOR AT THAT VERY MOMENT TWO FAMILIAR FIGURES ENTER THE LOOTED BANK...

...BRUCE WAYNE, SOCIETY PLAYBOY, AND HIS YOUNG WARD, DICK GRAYSON!

I'LL PUT A FEW MORE THOUSANDS IN **WAR BONDS**, AND--WHA-! NO ONE IN SIGHT!

DO I SMELL GAS?

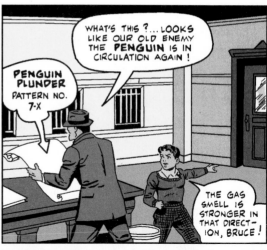

WHAT'S THIS?...LOOKS LIKE OUR OLD ENEMY THE **PENGUIN** IS IN CIRCULATION AGAIN!

PENGUIN PLUNDER PATTERN NO. 7-X

THE GAS SMELL IS STRONGER IN THAT DIRECTION, BRUCE!

WH-WHERE AM I?...WHY, MR. WAYNE!...NOW I REMEMBER-- TWO MEN WITH A SUITCASE! ONE OF THEM SLUGGED ME...

DESCRIBE THEM!

FRESH AIR WILL BRING THE OTHERS AROUND!

THAT EVENING IN THE WAYNE MANSION...

THE **PENGUIN** IS UP TO HIS OLD TRICKS! THESE MURDERED GANGSTERS, HAIRLESS HARRY HIX AND TORCHY BLAIZE, ANSWER THE DESCRIPTION OF THE BANK ROBBERS!

WHAT ARE WE WAITING FOR?

DAILY PL POISON DARTS KILL THUGS

WHAT DO YOU MEAN, **WAITING**?

I'VE BEEN HOPING FOR ANOTHER CHANCE AT THE **PENGUIN** EVER SINCE HE GOT AWAY WHILE WE WERE FIGHTING HIS TRAINED EAGLES!

A WEIRD CRAFT WINGS SWIFTLY THROUGH THE NIGHT-- **THE BATPLANE!**

WHERE TO, BATMAN?

WE'LL HAVE A LOOK ALONG GRAND BOULEVARD, WHERE THE BIG JEWELRY STORES ARE LOCATED... THE **PENGUIN'S** DUPES ARE BOUND TO SHOW UP THERE!

ONCE AGAIN THE HOODED CRIME-FIGHTER'S SIXTH SENSE HAS CALLED THE PLAY-- FOR MINUTES LATER...

SLIPPERY ELMER AND HIS GANG! WE'RE IN THE NICK OF TIME!

WE **WILL** BE IN THE NICK OF TIME IF WE GET DOWN THERE FAST!

JEWELERS

JEWEL

5

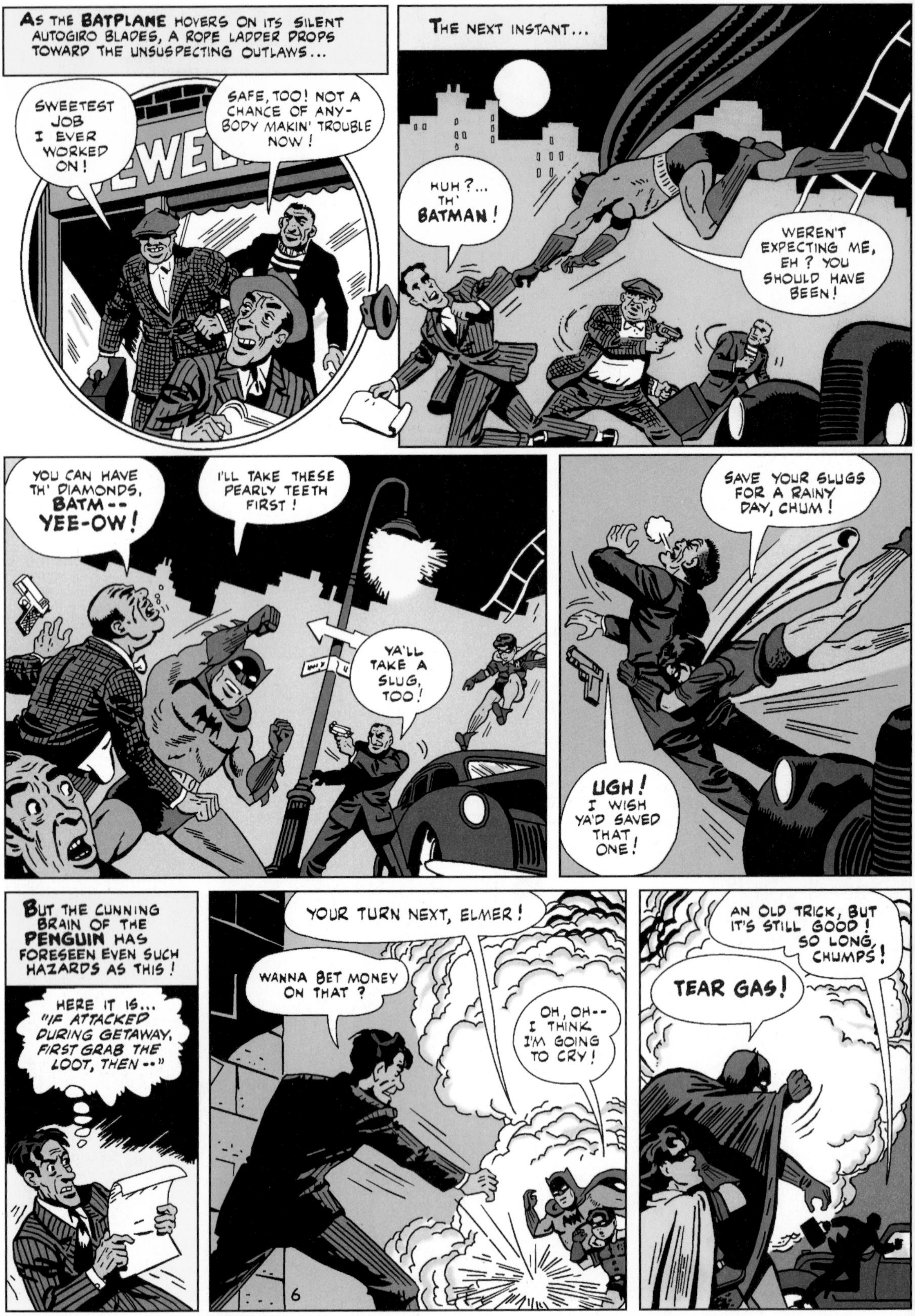
AS THE BATPLANE HOVERS ON ITS SILENT AUTOGIRO BLADES, A ROPE LADDER DROPS TOWARD THE UNSUSPECTING OUTLAWS...
SWEETEST JOB I EVER WORKED ON!
SAFE, TOO! NOT A CHANCE OF ANY-BODY MAKIN' TROUBLE NOW!
THE NEXT INSTANT...
HUH?... TH' BATMAN!
WEREN'T EXPECTING ME, EH? YOU SHOULD HAVE BEEN!
YOU CAN HAVE TH' DIAMONDS, BATM-- YEE-OW!
I'LL TAKE THESE PEARLY TEETH FIRST!
YA'LL TAKE A SLUG, TOO!
SAVE YOUR SLUGS FOR A RAINY DAY, CHUM!
UGH! I WISH YA'D SAVED THAT ONE!
BUT THE CUNNING BRAIN OF THE PENGUIN HAS FORESEEN EVEN SUCH HAZARDS AS THIS!
HERE IT IS... "IF ATTACKED DURING GETAWAY, FIRST GRAB THE LOOT, THEN--"
YOUR TURN NEXT, ELMER!
WANNA BET MONEY ON THAT?
OH, OH-- I THINK I'M GOING TO CRY!
AN OLD TRICK, BUT IT'S STILL GOOD! SO LONG, CHUMPS!
TEAR GAS!
6

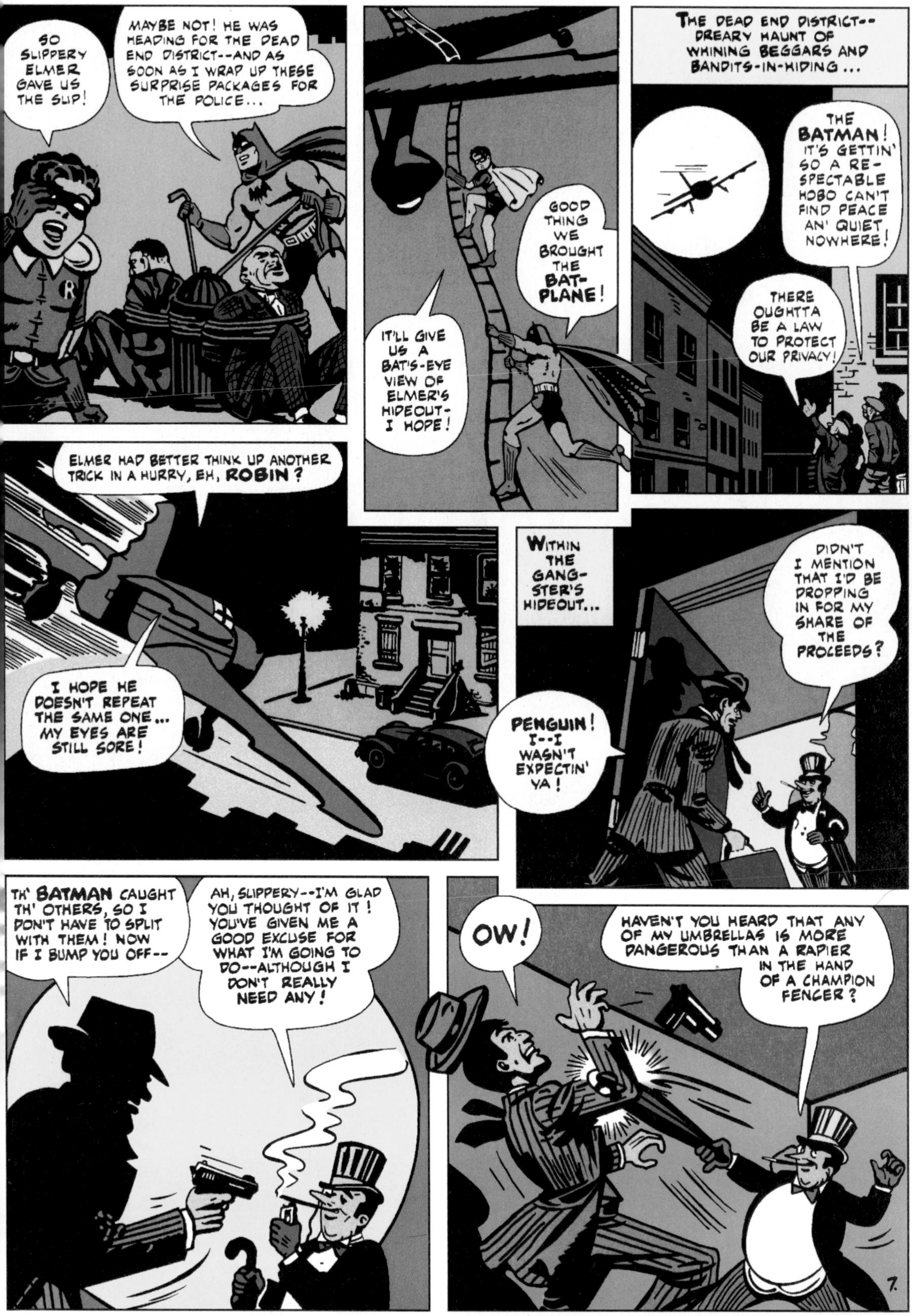
SO SLIPPERY ELMER GAVE US THE SLIP!
MAYBE NOT! HE WAS HEADING FOR THE DEAD END DISTRICT--AND AS SOON AS I WRAP UP THESE SURPRISE PACKAGES FOR THE POLICE...
GOOD THING WE BROUGHT THE BAT-PLANE!
IT'LL GIVE US A BAT'S-EYE VIEW OF ELMER'S HIDEOUT-I HOPE!
THE DEAD END DISTRICT--DREARY HAUNT OF WHINING BEGGARS AND BANDITS-IN-HIDING...
THE BATMAN! IT'S GETTIN' SO A RE-SPECTABLE HOBO CAN'T FIND PEACE AN' QUIET NOWHERE!
THERE OUGHTTA BE A LAW TO PROTECT OUR PRIVACY!
ELMER HAD BETTER THINK UP ANOTHER TRICK IN A HURRY, EH, ROBIN?
I HOPE HE DOESN'T REPEAT THE SAME ONE... MY EYES ARE STILL SORE!
WITHIN THE GANG-STER'S HIDEOUT...
DIDN'T I MENTION THAT I'D BE DROPPING IN FOR MY SHARE OF THE PROCEEDS?
PENGUIN! I--I WASN'T EXPECTIN' YA!
TH' BATMAN CAUGHT TH' OTHERS, SO I DON'T HAVE TO SPLIT WITH THEM! NOW IF I BUMP YOU OFF--
AH, SLIPPERY--I'M GLAD YOU THOUGHT OF IT! YOU'VE GIVEN ME A GOOD EXCUSE FOR WHAT I'M GOING TO DO--ALTHOUGH I DON'T REALLY NEED ANY!
OW!
HAVEN'T YOU HEARD THAT ANY OF MY UMBRELLAS IS MORE DANGEROUS THAN A RAPIER IN THE HAND OF A CHAMPION FENCER?
7.

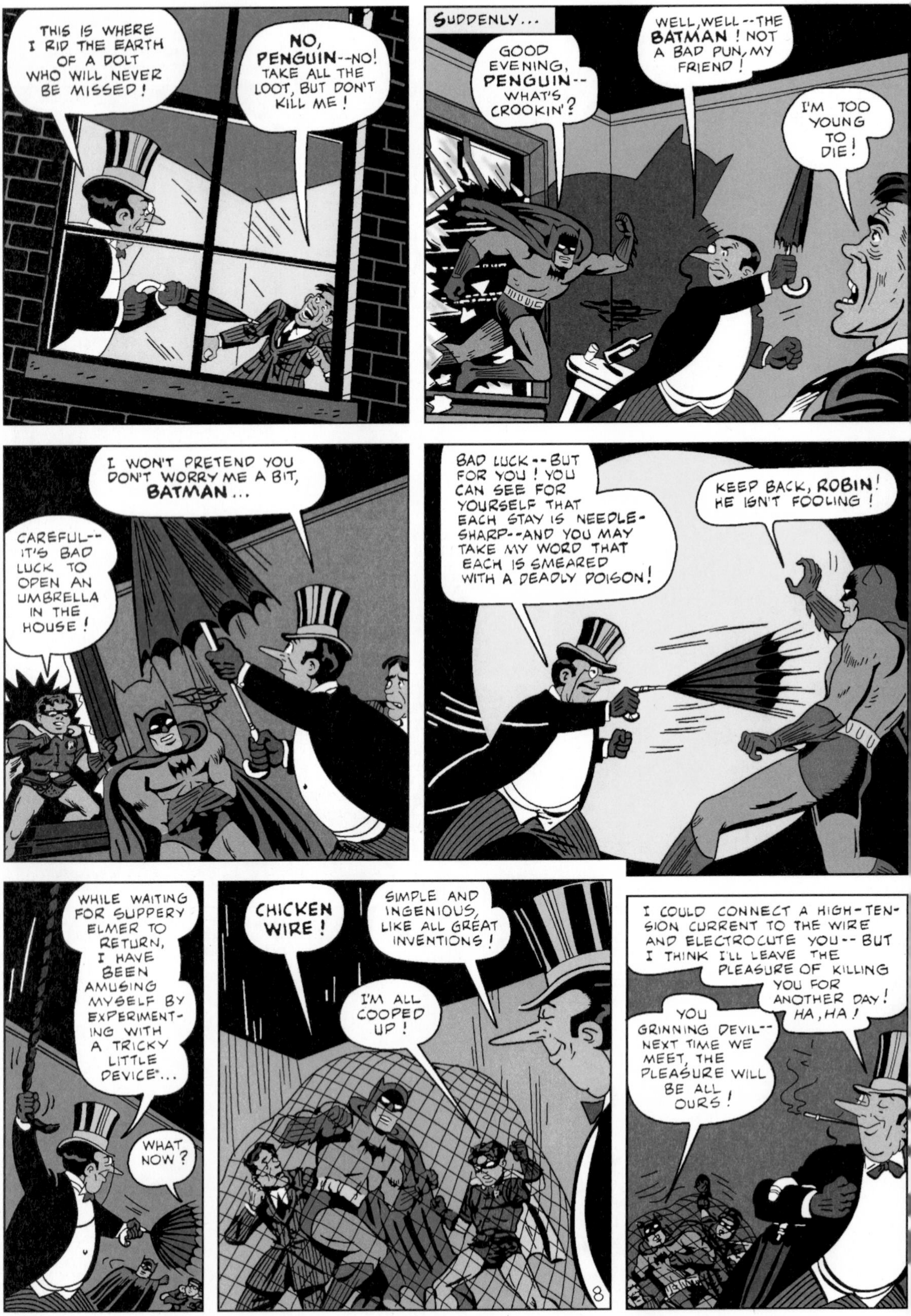
THIS IS WHERE I RID THE EARTH OF A DOLT WHO WILL NEVER BE MISSED!
NO, PENGUIN--NO! TAKE ALL THE LOOT, BUT DON'T KILL ME!
SUDDENLY...
GOOD EVENING, PENGUIN--WHAT'S CROOKIN'?
WELL, WELL--THE BATMAN! NOT A BAD PUN, MY FRIEND!
I'M TOO YOUNG TO DIE!
I WON'T PRETEND YOU DON'T WORRY ME A BIT, BATMAN...
CAREFUL--IT'S BAD LUCK TO OPEN AN UMBRELLA IN THE HOUSE!
BAD LUCK--BUT FOR YOU! YOU CAN SEE FOR YOURSELF THAT EACH STAY IS NEEDLE-SHARP--AND YOU MAY TAKE MY WORD THAT EACH IS SMEARED WITH A DEADLY POISON!
KEEP BACK, ROBIN! HE ISN'T FOOLING!
WHILE WAITING FOR SLIPPERY ELMER TO RETURN, I HAVE BEEN AMUSING MYSELF BY EXPERIMENTING WITH A TRICKY LITTLE DEVICE*...
WHAT NOW?
CHICKEN WIRE!
SIMPLE AND INGENIOUS, LIKE ALL GREAT INVENTIONS!
I'M ALL COOPED UP!
8
I COULD CONNECT A HIGH-TENSION CURRENT TO THE WIRE AND ELECTROCUTE YOU--BUT I THINK I'LL LEAVE THE PLEASURE OF KILLING YOU FOR ANOTHER DAY! HA, HA!
YOU GRINNING DEVIL--NEXT TIME WE MEET, THE PLEASURE WILL BE ALL OURS!

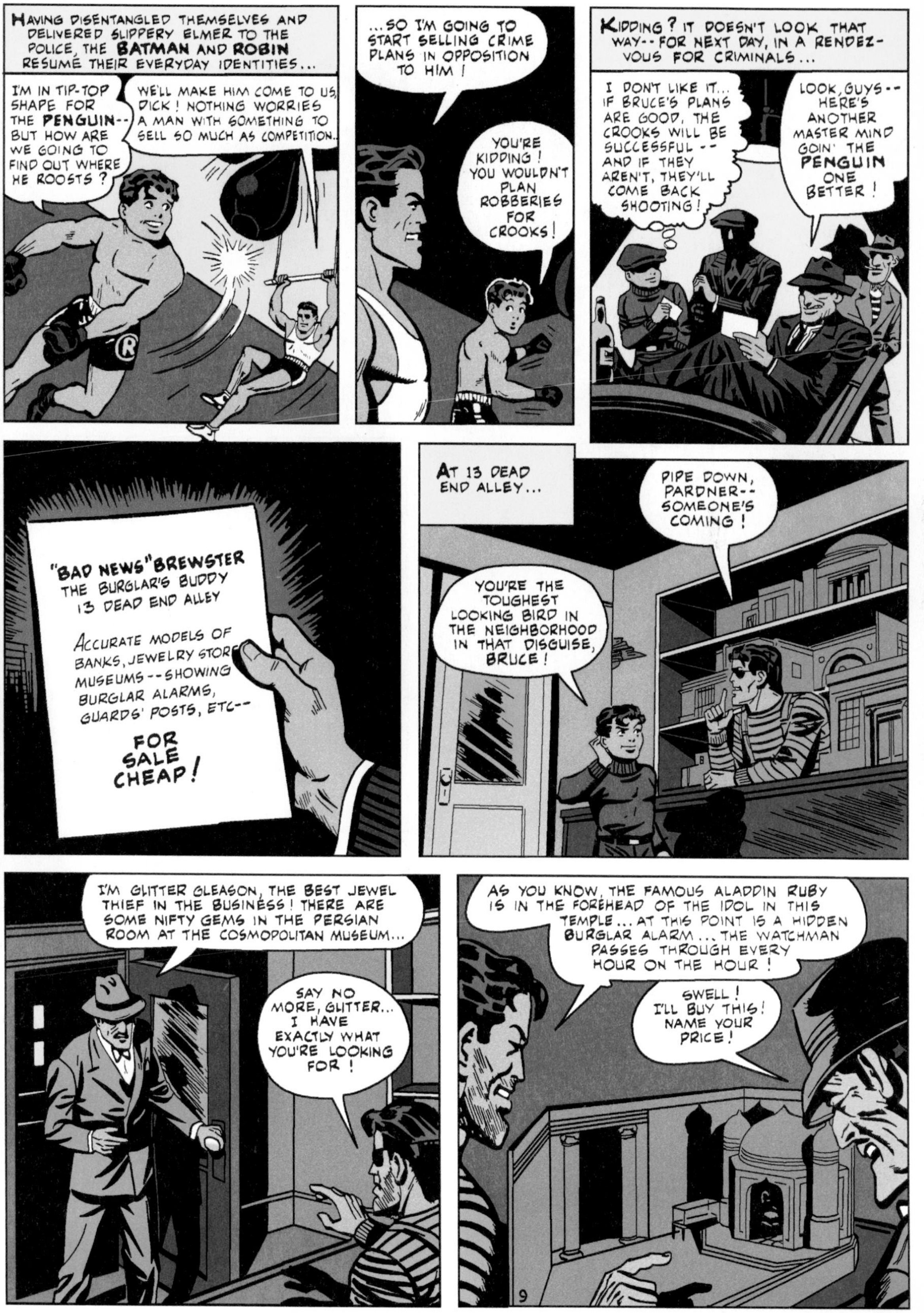
HAVING DISENTANGLED THEMSELVES AND DELIVERED SLIPPERY ELMER TO THE POLICE, THE BATMAN AND ROBIN RESUME THEIR EVERYDAY IDENTITIES...
I'M IN TIP-TOP SHAPE FOR THE PENGUIN-- BUT HOW ARE WE GOING TO FIND OUT WHERE HE ROOSTS ?
WE'LL MAKE HIM COME TO US, DICK ! NOTHING WORRIES A MAN WITH SOMETHING TO SELL SO MUCH AS COMPETITION...
...SO I'M GOING TO START SELLING CRIME PLANS IN OPPOSITION TO HIM !
YOU'RE KIDDING ! YOU WOULDN'T PLAN ROBBERIES FOR CROOKS !
KIDDING ? IT DOESN'T LOOK THAT WAY-- FOR NEXT DAY, IN A RENDEZ-VOUS FOR CRIMINALS...
I DON'T LIKE IT... IF BRUCE'S PLANS ARE GOOD, THE CROOKS WILL BE SUCCESSFUL -- AND IF THEY AREN'T, THEY'LL COME BACK SHOOTING !
LOOK, GUYS -- HERE'S ANOTHER MASTER MIND GOIN' THE PENGUIN ONE BETTER !
"BAD NEWS" BREWSTER
THE BURGLAR'S BUDDY
13 DEAD END ALLEY
ACCURATE MODELS OF BANKS, JEWELRY STORE MUSEUMS -- SHOWING BURGLAR ALARMS, GUARDS' POSTS, ETC--
FOR SALE CHEAP !
AT 13 DEAD END ALLEY...
PIPE DOWN, PARDNER-- SOMEONE'S COMING !
YOU'RE THE TOUGHEST LOOKING BIRD IN THE NEIGHBORHOOD IN THAT DISGUISE, BRUCE !
I'M GLITTER GLEASON, THE BEST JEWEL THIEF IN THE BUSINESS ! THERE ARE SOME NIFTY GEMS IN THE PERSIAN ROOM AT THE COSMOPOLITAN MUSEUM...
SAY NO MORE, GLITTER... I HAVE EXACTLY WHAT YOU'RE LOOKING FOR !
AS YOU KNOW, THE FAMOUS ALADDIN RUBY IS IN THE FOREHEAD OF THE IDOL IN THIS TEMPLE... AT THIS POINT IS A HIDDEN BURGLAR ALARM... THE WATCHMAN PASSES THROUGH EVERY HOUR ON THE HOUR !
SWELL ! I'LL BUY THIS ! NAME YOUR PRICE !
9

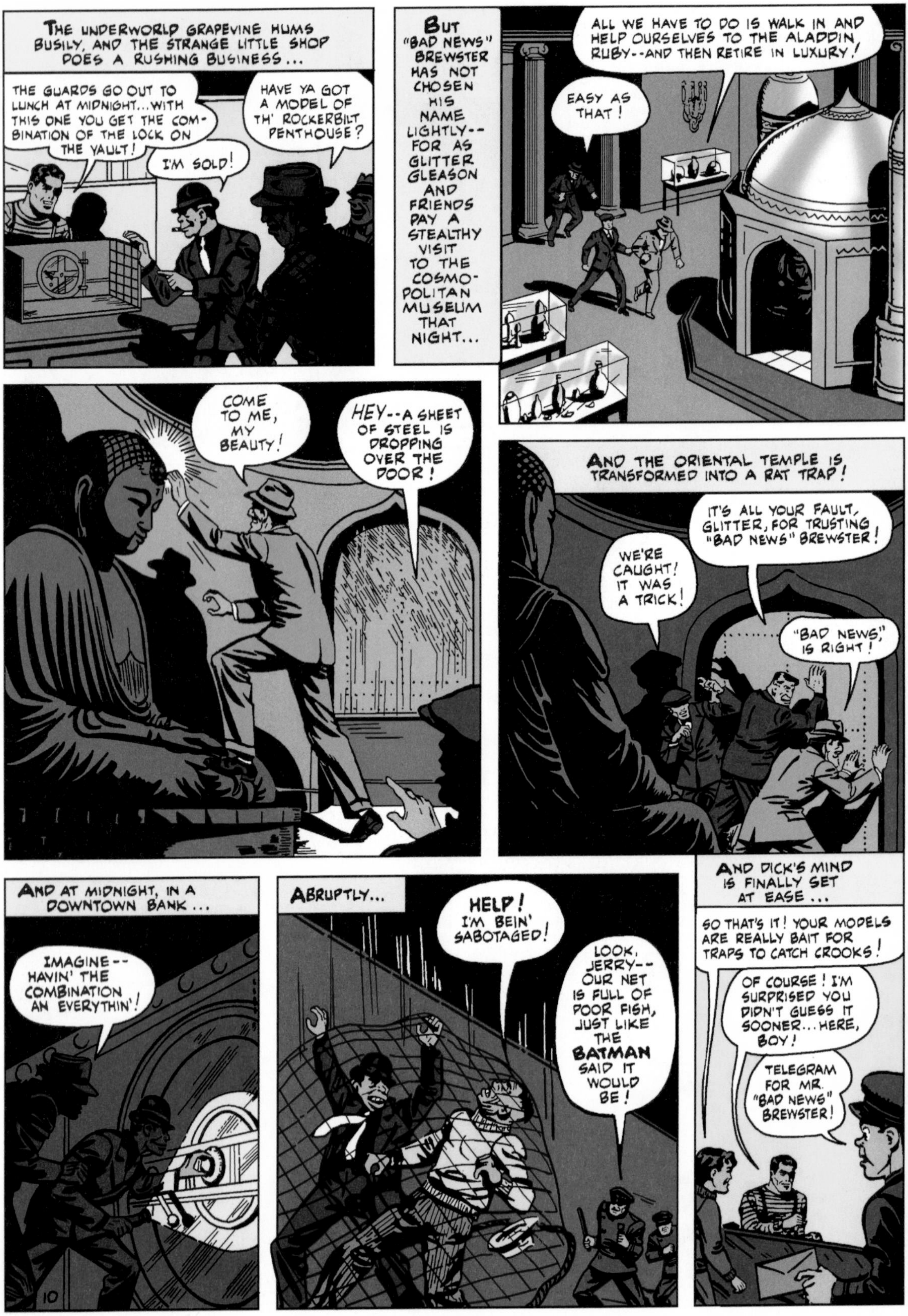

THE UNDERWORLD GRAPEVINE HUMS BUSILY, AND THE STRANGE LITTLE SHOP DOES A RUSHING BUSINESS...
THE GUARDS GO OUT TO LUNCH AT MIDNIGHT...WITH THIS ONE YOU GET THE COMBINATION OF THE LOCK ON THE VAULT!
HAVE YA GOT A MODEL OF TH' ROCKERBILT PENTHOUSE?
I'M SOLD!
BUT "BAD NEWS" BREWSTER HAS NOT CHOSEN HIS NAME LIGHTLY--FOR AS GLITTER GLEASON AND FRIENDS PAY A STEALTHY VISIT TO THE COSMOPOLITAN MUSEUM THAT NIGHT...
ALL WE HAVE TO DO IS WALK IN AND HELP OURSELVES TO THE ALADDIN RUBY--AND THEN RETIRE IN LUXURY!
EASY AS THAT!
COME TO ME, MY BEAUTY!
HEY--A SHEET OF STEEL IS DROPPING OVER THE DOOR!
AND THE ORIENTAL TEMPLE IS TRANSFORMED INTO A RAT TRAP!
IT'S ALL YOUR FAULT, GLITTER, FOR TRUSTING "BAD NEWS" BREWSTER!
WE'RE CAUGHT! IT WAS A TRICK!
"BAD NEWS," IS RIGHT!
AND AT MIDNIGHT, IN A DOWNTOWN BANK...
IMAGINE--HAVIN' THE COMBINATION AN EVERYTHIN'!
10
ABRUPTLY...
HELP! I'M BEIN' SABOTAGED!
LOOK, JERRY--OUR NET IS FULL OF POOR FISH, JUST LIKE THE BATMAN SAID IT WOULD BE!
AND DICK'S MIND IS FINALLY SET AT EASE...
SO THAT'S IT! YOUR MODELS ARE REALLY BAIT FOR TRAPS TO CATCH CROOKS!
OF COURSE! I'M SURPRISED YOU DIDN'T GUESS IT SOONER...HERE, BOY!
TELEGRAM FOR MR. "BAD NEWS" BREWSTER!

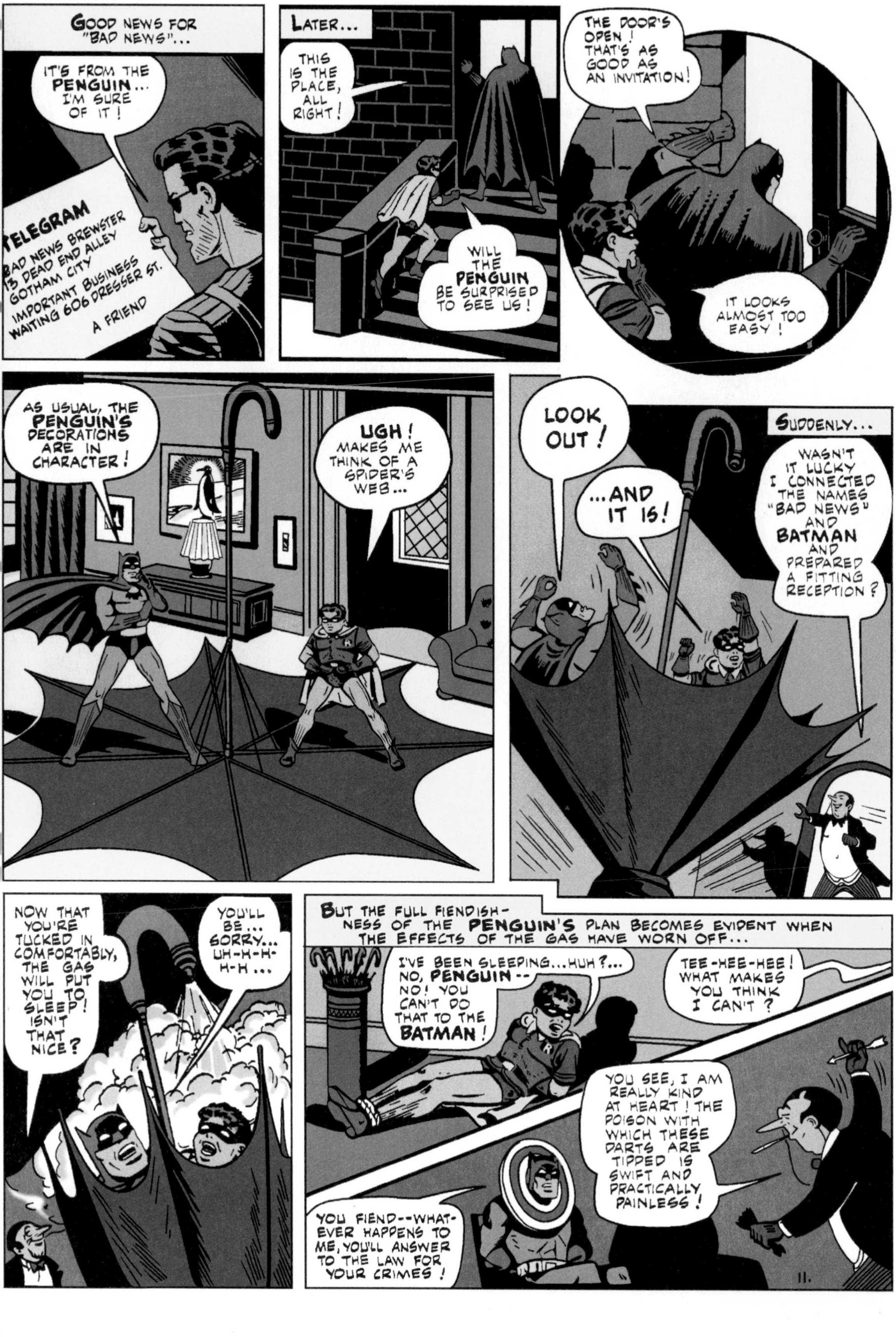
GOOD NEWS FOR "BAD NEWS"...
IT'S FROM THE PENGUIN... I'M SURE OF IT!
TELEGRAM
BAD NEWS BREWSTER
13 DEAD END ALLEY
GOTHAM CITY
IMPORTANT BUSINESS
WAITING 606 DRESSER ST.
A FRIEND
LATER...
THIS IS THE PLACE, ALL RIGHT!
WILL THE PENGUIN BE SURPRISED TO SEE US!
THE DOOR'S OPEN! THAT'S AS GOOD AS AN INVITATION!
IT LOOKS ALMOST TOO EASY!
AS USUAL, THE PENGUIN'S DECORATIONS ARE IN CHARACTER!
UGH! MAKES ME THINK OF A SPIDER'S WEB...
SUDDENLY...
LOOK OUT!
...AND IT IS!
WASN'T IT LUCKY I CONNECTED THE NAMES "BAD NEWS" AND BATMAN AND PREPARED A FITTING RECEPTION?
NOW THAT YOU'RE TUCKED IN COMFORTABLY, THE GAS WILL PUT YOU TO SLEEP! ISN'T THAT NICE?
YOU'LL BE... SORRY... UH-H-H-H-H...
BUT THE FULL FIENDISHNESS OF THE PENGUIN'S PLAN BECOMES EVIDENT WHEN THE EFFECTS OF THE GAS HAVE WORN OFF...
I'VE BEEN SLEEPING...HUH?... NO, PENGUIN-- NO! YOU CAN'T DO THAT TO THE BATMAN!
TEE-HEE-HEE! WHAT MAKES YOU THINK I CAN'T?
YOU SEE, I AM REALLY KIND AT HEART! THE POISON WITH WHICH THESE DARTS ARE TIPPED IS SWIFT AND PRACTICALLY PAINLESS!
YOU FIEND--WHATEVER HAPPENS TO ME, YOU'LL ANSWER TO THE LAW FOR YOUR CRIMES!
11.

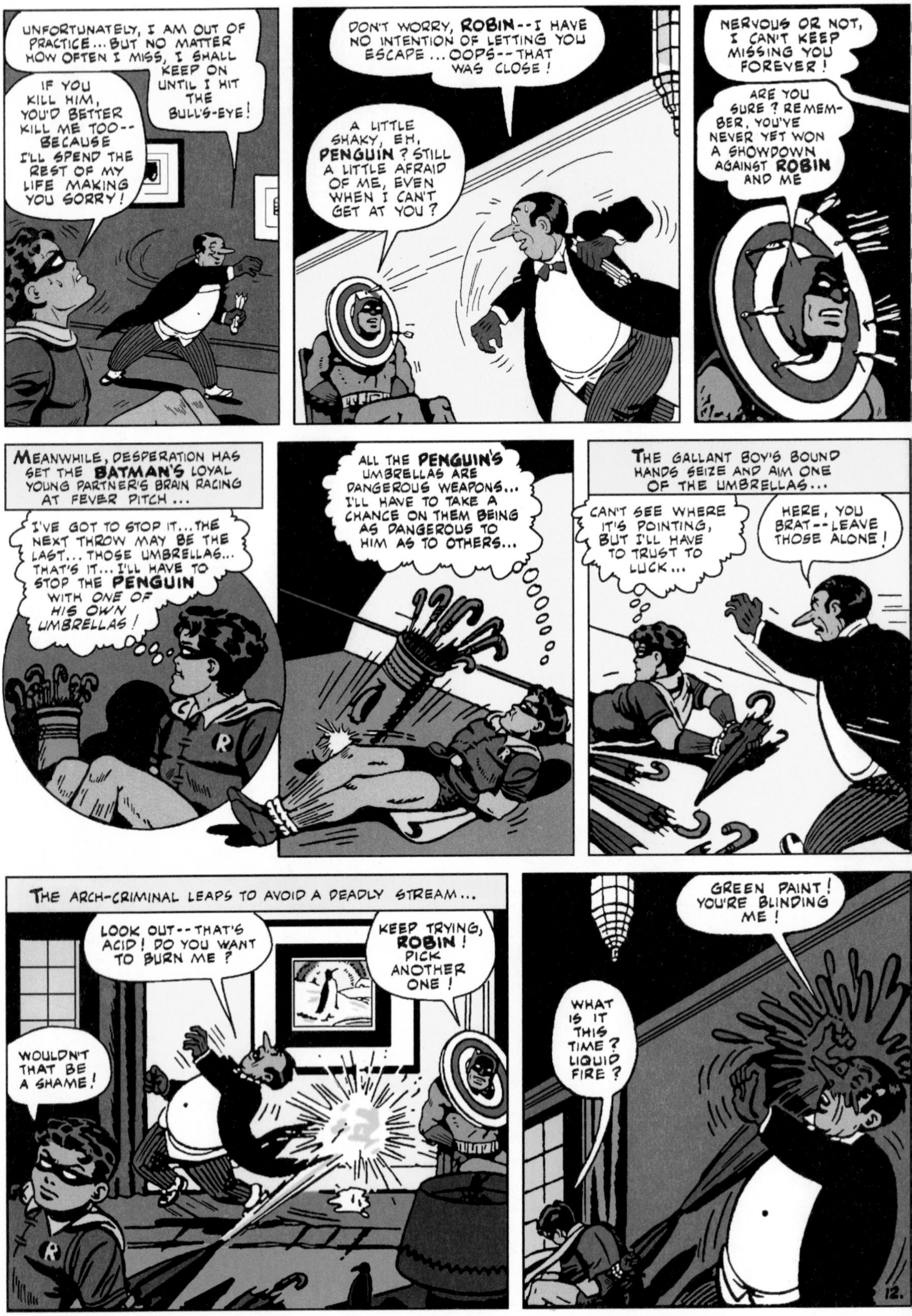
UNFORTUNATELY, I AM OUT OF PRACTICE... BUT NO MATTER HOW OFTEN I MISS, I SHALL KEEP ON UNTIL I HIT THE BULL'S-EYE!
IF YOU KILL HIM, YOU'D BETTER KILL ME TOO-- BECAUSE I'LL SPEND THE REST OF MY LIFE MAKING YOU SORRY!
DON'T WORRY, ROBIN--I HAVE NO INTENTION OF LETTING YOU ESCAPE... OOPS--THAT WAS CLOSE!
A LITTLE SHAKY, EH, PENGUIN? STILL A LITTLE AFRAID OF ME, EVEN WHEN I CAN'T GET AT YOU?
NERVOUS OR NOT, I CAN'T KEEP MISSING YOU FOREVER!
ARE YOU SURE? REMEMBER, YOU'VE NEVER YET WON A SHOWDOWN AGAINST ROBIN AND ME
MEANWHILE, DESPERATION HAS SET THE BATMAN'S LOYAL YOUNG PARTNER'S BRAIN RACING AT FEVER PITCH...
I'VE GOT TO STOP IT... THE NEXT THROW MAY BE THE LAST... THOSE UMBRELLAS... THAT'S IT... I'LL HAVE TO STOP THE PENGUIN WITH ONE OF HIS OWN UMBRELLAS!
ALL THE PENGUIN'S UMBRELLAS ARE DANGEROUS WEAPONS... I'LL HAVE TO TAKE A CHANCE ON THEM BEING AS DANGEROUS TO HIM AS TO OTHERS...
THE GALLANT BOY'S BOUND HANDS SEIZE AND AIM ONE OF THE UMBRELLAS...
CAN'T SEE WHERE IT'S POINTING, BUT I'LL HAVE TO TRUST TO LUCK...
HERE, YOU BRAT--LEAVE THOSE ALONE!
THE ARCH-CRIMINAL LEAPS TO AVOID A DEADLY STREAM...
LOOK OUT--THAT'S ACID! DO YOU WANT TO BURN ME?
KEEP TRYING, ROBIN! PICK ANOTHER ONE!
WOULDN'T THAT BE A SHAME!
GREEN PAINT! YOU'RE BLINDING ME!
WHAT IS IT THIS TIME? LIQUID FIRE?
12.

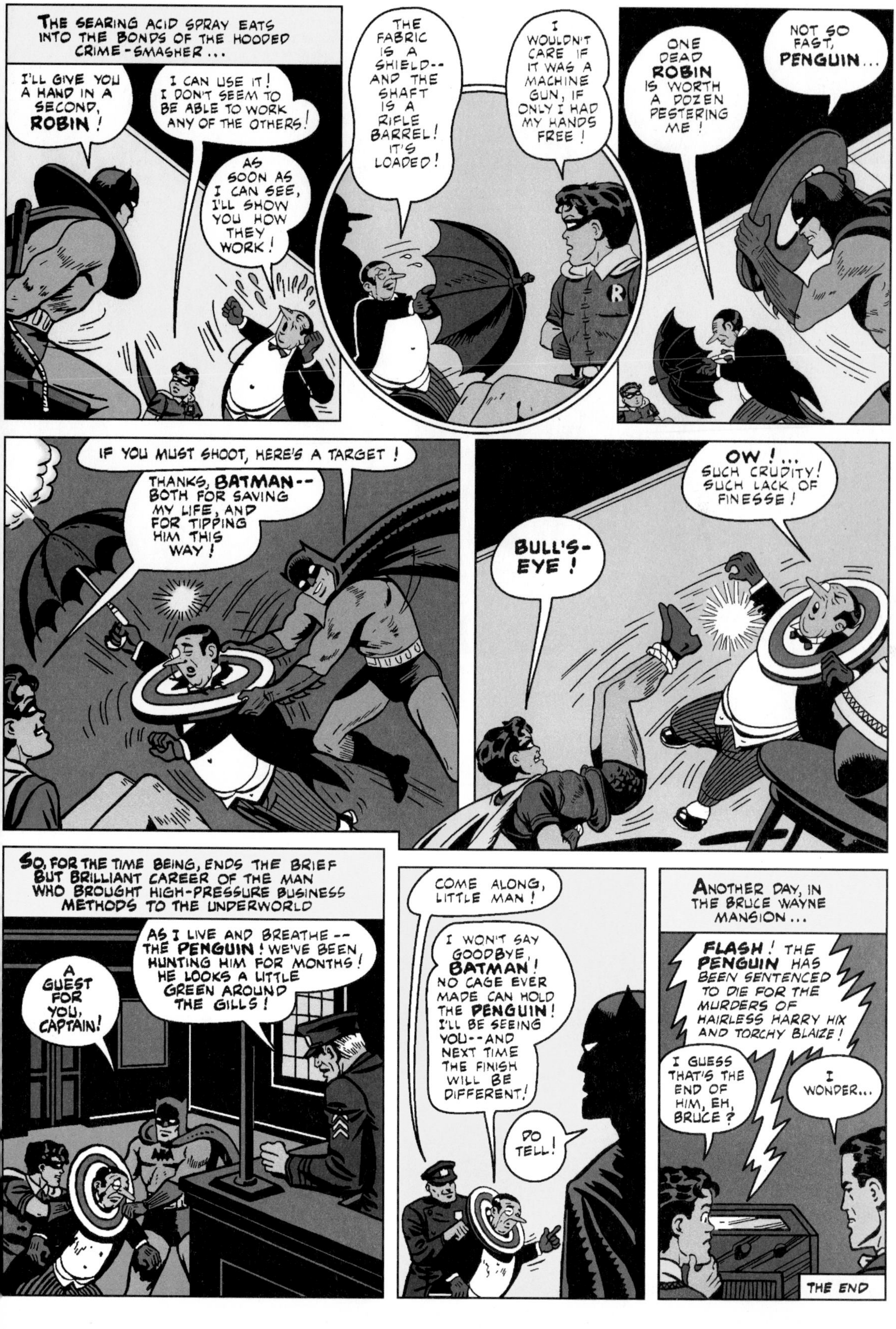
THE SEARING ACID SPRAY EATS INTO THE BONDS OF THE HOODED CRIME-SMASHER ...
I'LL GIVE YOU A HAND IN A SECOND, ROBIN!
I CAN USE IT! I DON'T SEEM TO BE ABLE TO WORK ANY OF THE OTHERS!
AS SOON AS I CAN SEE, I'LL SHOW YOU HOW THEY WORK!
THE FABRIC IS A SHIELD-- AND THE SHAFT IS A RIFLE BARREL! IT'S LOADED!
I WOULDN'T CARE IF IT WAS A MACHINE GUN, IF ONLY I HAD MY HANDS FREE!
ONE DEAD ROBIN IS WORTH A DOZEN PESTERING ME!
NOT SO FAST, PENGUIN...
IF YOU MUST SHOOT, HERE'S A TARGET!
THANKS, BATMAN-- BOTH FOR SAVING MY LIFE, AND FOR TIPPING HIM THIS WAY!
OW!... SUCH CRUDITY! SUCH LACK OF FINESSE!
BULL'S-EYE!
SO, FOR THE TIME BEING, ENDS THE BRIEF BUT BRILLIANT CAREER OF THE MAN WHO BROUGHT HIGH-PRESSURE BUSINESS METHODS TO THE UNDERWORLD
A GUEST FOR YOU, CAPTAIN!
AS I LIVE AND BREATHE -- THE PENGUIN! WE'VE BEEN HUNTING HIM FOR MONTHS! HE LOOKS A LITTLE GREEN AROUND THE GILLS!
COME ALONG, LITTLE MAN!
I WON'T SAY GOODBYE, BATMAN! NO CAGE EVER MADE CAN HOLD THE PENGUIN! I'LL BE SEEING YOU--AND NEXT TIME THE FINISH WILL BE DIFFERENT!
DO TELL!
ANOTHER DAY, IN THE BRUCE WAYNE MANSION ...
FLASH! THE PENGUIN HAS BEEN SENTENCED TO DIE FOR THE MURDERS OF HAIRLESS HARRY HIX AND TORCHY BLAIZE!
I GUESS THAT'S THE END OF HIM, EH, BRUCE?
I WONDER...
THE END

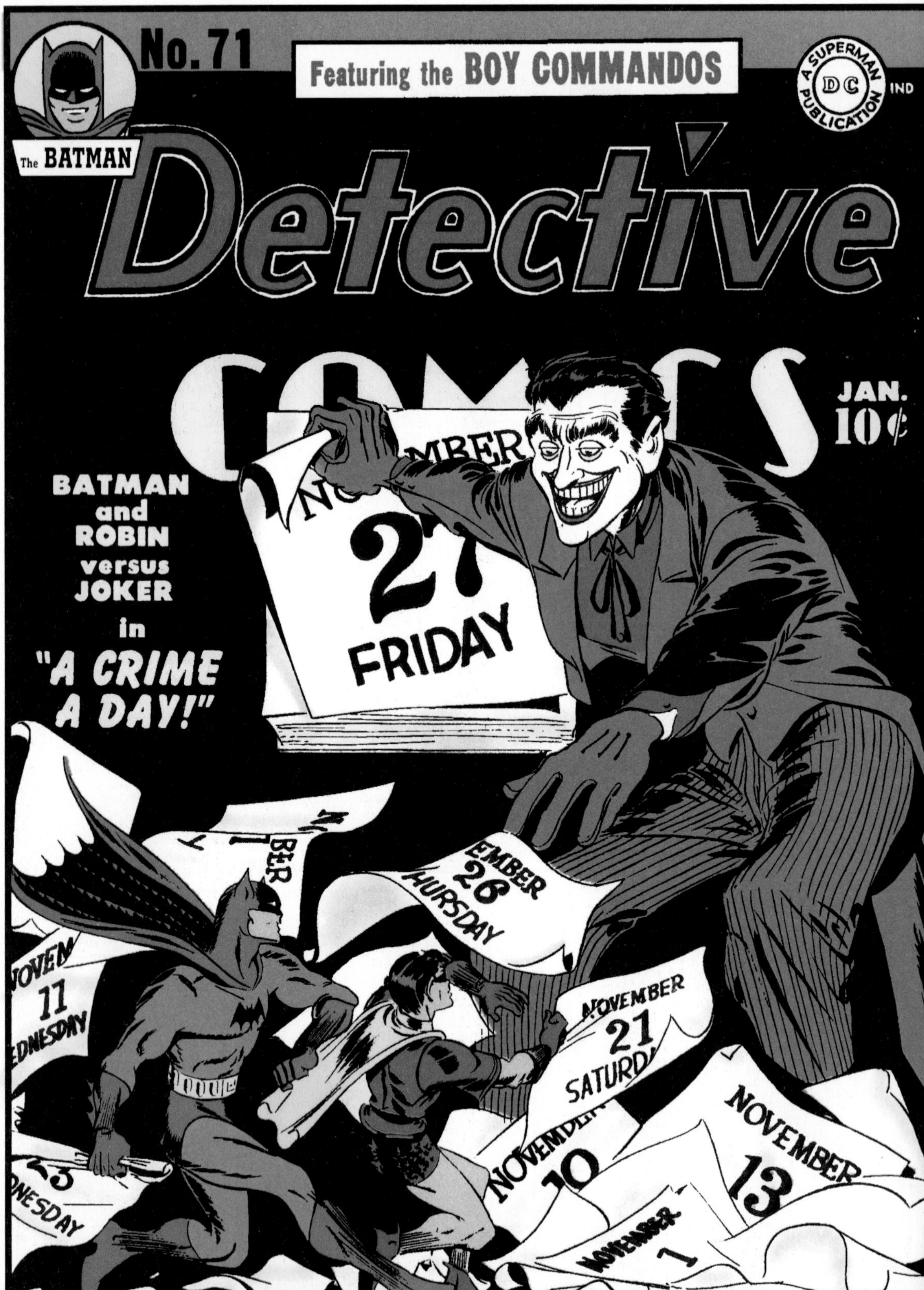
No. 71
Featuring the BOY COMMANDOS
A SUPERMAN DC PUBLICATION
IND
The BATMAN
Detective
JAN.
10¢
BATMAN and ROBIN versus JOKER in "A CRIME A DAY!"
27
FRIDAY
26
NOVEMBER
21
NOVEMBER
13
10

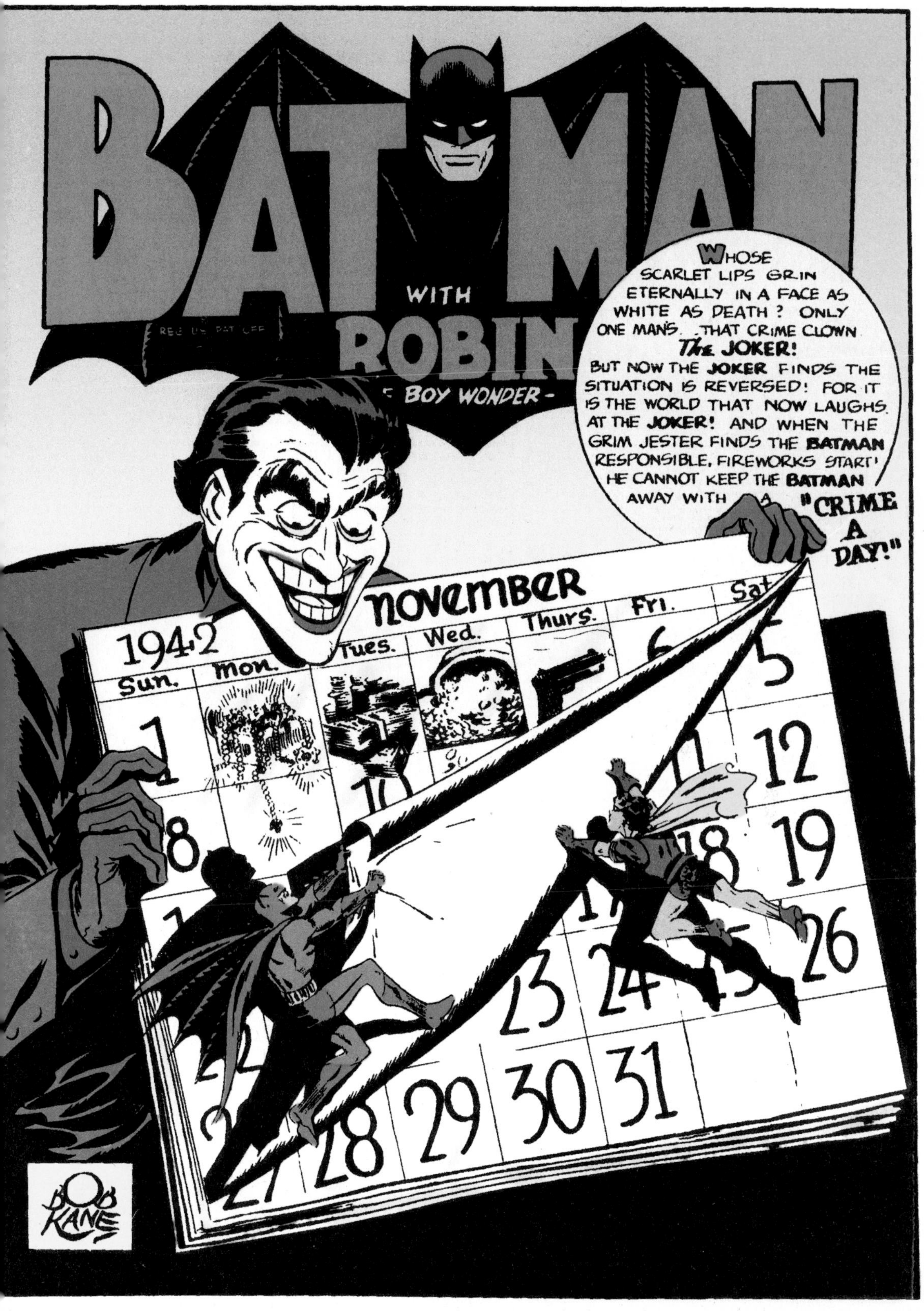
BATMAN
WITH
ROBIN
BOY WONDER -
WHOSE SCARLET LIPS GRIN ETERNALLY IN A FACE AS WHITE AS DEATH ? ONLY ONE MAN'S...THAT CRIME CLOWN The JOKER! BUT NOW THE JOKER FINDS THE SITUATION IS REVERSED! FOR IT IS THE WORLD THAT NOW LAUGHS AT THE JOKER! AND WHEN THE GRIM JESTER FINDS THE BATMAN RESPONSIBLE, FIREWORKS START! HE CANNOT KEEP THE BATMAN AWAY WITH A "CRIME A DAY!"
november
1942
Sun. Mon. Tues. Wed. Thurs. Fri. Sat
BOB KANE

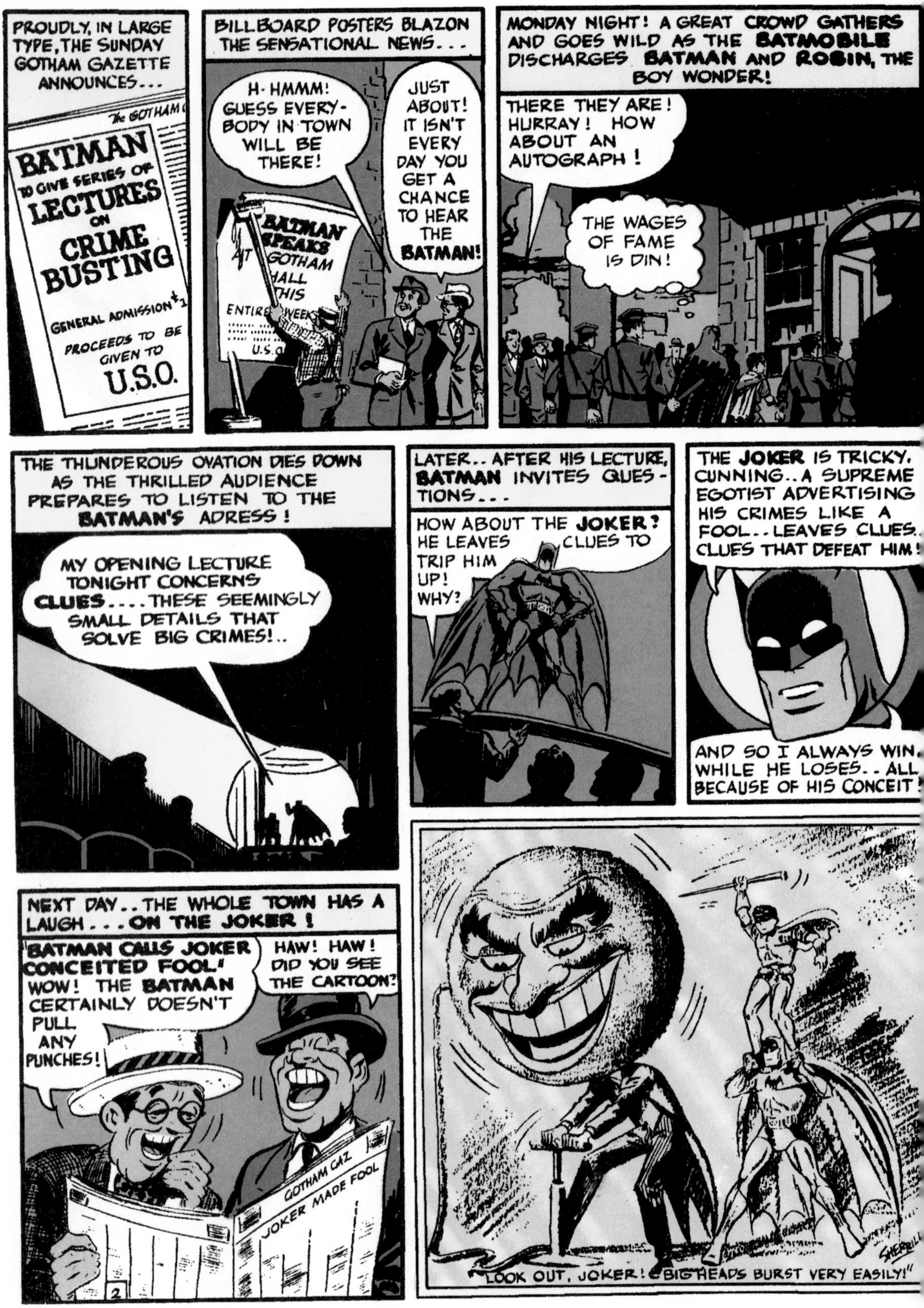
PROUDLY, IN LARGE TYPE, THE SUNDAY GOTHAM GAZETTE ANNOUNCES...
The GOTHAM
BATMAN TO GIVE SERIES OF LECTURES ON CRIME BUSTING
GENERAL ADMISSION $1
PROCEEDS TO BE GIVEN TO U.S.O.
BILLBOARD POSTERS BLAZON THE SENSATIONAL NEWS...
H-HMMM! GUESS EVERY-BODY IN TOWN WILL BE THERE!
JUST ABOUT! IT ISN'T EVERY DAY YOU GET A CHANCE TO HEAR THE BATMAN!
BATMAN SPEAKS AT GOTHAM HALL THIS ENTIRE WEEK
MONDAY NIGHT! A GREAT CROWD GATHERS AND GOES WILD AS THE BATMOBILE DISCHARGES BATMAN AND ROBIN, THE BOY WONDER!
THERE THEY ARE! HURRAY! HOW ABOUT AN AUTOGRAPH!
THE WAGES OF FAME IS DIN!
THE THUNDEROUS OVATION DIES DOWN AS THE THRILLED AUDIENCE PREPARES TO LISTEN TO THE BATMAN'S ADRESS!
MY OPENING LECTURE TONIGHT CONCERNS CLUES.... THESE SEEMINGLY SMALL DETAILS THAT SOLVE BIG CRIMES!..
LATER.. AFTER HIS LECTURE, BATMAN INVITES QUES-TIONS...
HOW ABOUT THE JOKER? HE LEAVES CLUES TO TRIP HIM UP! WHY?
THE JOKER IS TRICKY. CUNNING.. A SUPREME EGOTIST ADVERTISING HIS CRIMES LIKE A FOOL.. LEAVES CLUES. CLUES THAT DEFEAT HIM!
AND SO I ALWAYS WIN. WHILE HE LOSES.. ALL BECAUSE OF HIS CONCEIT!
NEXT DAY.. THE WHOLE TOWN HAS A LAUGH... ON THE JOKER!
'BATMAN CALLS JOKER CONCEITED FOOL.' WOW! THE BATMAN CERTAINLY DOESN'T PULL ANY PUNCHES!
HAW! HAW! DID YOU SEE THE CARTOON?
GOTHAM GAZ
JOKER MADE FOOL
SHERRILL
LOOK OUT, JOKER! BIG HEADS BURST VERY EASILY!"

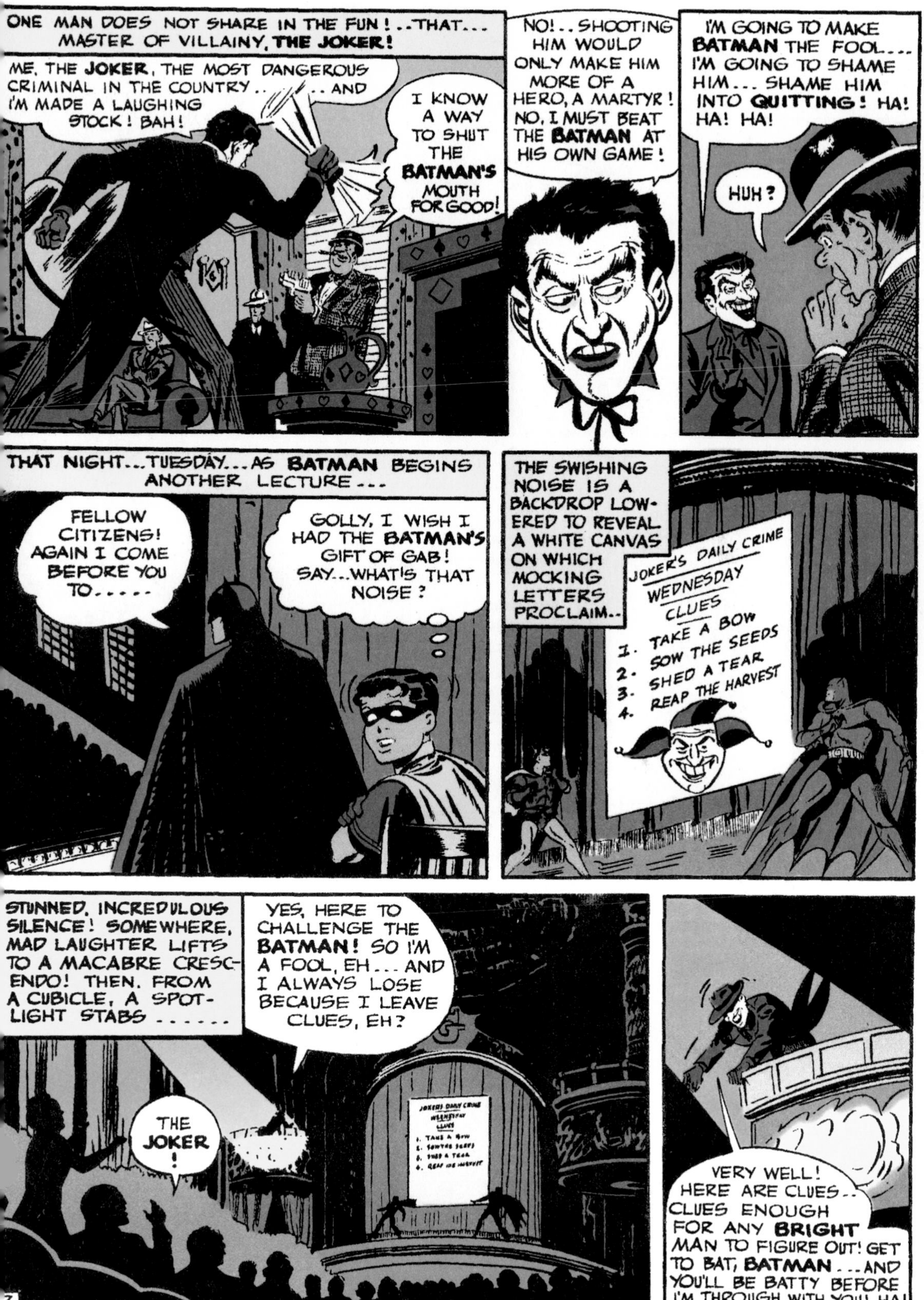
ONE MAN DOES NOT SHARE IN THE FUN! ..THAT... MASTER OF VILLAINY, THE JOKER!
ME, THE JOKER, THE MOST DANGEROUS CRIMINAL IN THE COUNTRY ... AND I'M MADE A LAUGHING STOCK! BAH!
I KNOW A WAY TO SHUT THE BATMAN'S MOUTH FOR GOOD!
NO!.. SHOOTING HIM WOULD ONLY MAKE HIM MORE OF A HERO, A MARTYR! NO, I MUST BEAT THE BATMAN AT HIS OWN GAME!
I'M GOING TO MAKE BATMAN THE FOOL... I'M GOING TO SHAME HIM... SHAME HIM INTO QUITTING! HA! HA! HA!
HUH?
THAT NIGHT...TUESDAY...AS BATMAN BEGINS ANOTHER LECTURE...
FELLOW CITIZENS! AGAIN I COME BEFORE YOU TO.....
GOLLY, I WISH I HAD THE BATMAN'S GIFT OF GAB! SAY...WHAT'S THAT NOISE?
THE SWISHING NOISE IS A BACKDROP LOWERED TO REVEAL A WHITE CANVAS ON WHICH MOCKING LETTERS PROCLAIM..
JOKER'S DAILY CRIME
WEDNESDAY
CLUES
1. TAKE A BOW
2. SOW THE SEEDS
3. SHED A TEAR
4. REAP THE HARVEST
STUNNED, INCREDULOUS SILENCE! SOMEWHERE, MAD LAUGHTER LIFTS TO A MACABRE CRESCENDO! THEN, FROM A CUBICLE, A SPOTLIGHT STABS ......
YES, HERE TO CHALLENGE THE BATMAN! SO I'M A FOOL, EH... AND I ALWAYS LOSE BECAUSE I LEAVE CLUES, EH?
THE JOKER!
VERY WELL! HERE ARE CLUES.. CLUES ENOUGH FOR ANY BRIGHT MAN TO FIGURE OUT! GET TO BAT, BATMAN...AND YOU'LL BE BATTY BEFORE I'M THROUGH WITH YOU! HA!
3

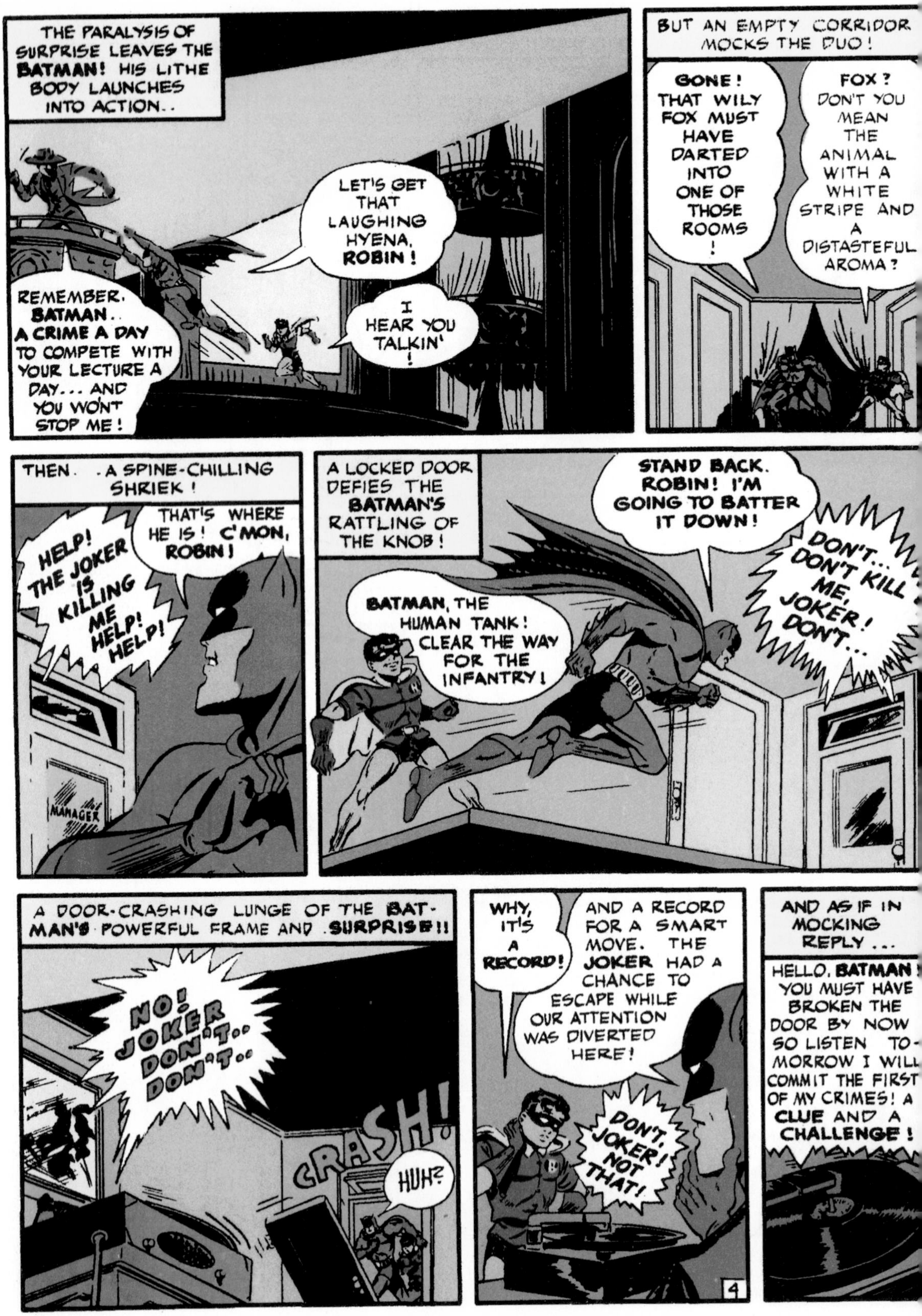
THE PARALYSIS OF SURPRISE LEAVES THE BATMAN! HIS LITHE BODY LAUNCHES INTO ACTION..
REMEMBER, BATMAN.. A CRIME A DAY TO COMPETE WITH YOUR LECTURE A DAY... AND YOU WON'T STOP ME!
LET'S GET THAT LAUGHING HYENA, ROBIN!
I HEAR YOU TALKIN'!
BUT AN EMPTY CORRIDOR MOCKS THE DUO!
GONE! THAT WILY FOX MUST HAVE DARTED INTO ONE OF THOSE ROOMS!
FOX? DON'T YOU MEAN THE ANIMAL WITH A WHITE STRIPE AND A DISTASTEFUL AROMA?
THEN. .A SPINE-CHILLING SHRIEK!
HELP! THE JOKER IS KILLING ME HELP! HELP!
THAT'S WHERE HE IS! C'MON, ROBIN!
MANAGER
A LOCKED DOOR DEFIES THE BATMAN'S RATTLING OF THE KNOB!
STAND BACK, ROBIN! I'M GOING TO BATTER IT DOWN!
DON'T... DON'T KILL ME, JOKER! DON'T...
BATMAN, THE HUMAN TANK! CLEAR THE WAY FOR THE INFANTRY!
A DOOR-CRASHING LUNGE OF THE BATMAN'S POWERFUL FRAME AND SURPRISE!!
NO! JOKER DON'T.. DON'T..
CRASH!
HUH?
WHY, IT'S A RECORD!
AND A RECORD FOR A SMART MOVE. THE JOKER HAD A CHANCE TO ESCAPE WHILE OUR ATTENTION WAS DIVERTED HERE!
DON'T, JOKER! NOT THAT!
4
AND AS IF IN MOCKING REPLY...
HELLO, BATMAN! YOU MUST HAVE BROKEN THE DOOR BY NOW SO LISTEN TO-MORROW I WILL COMMIT THE FIRST OF MY CRIMES! A CLUE AND A CHALLENGE!

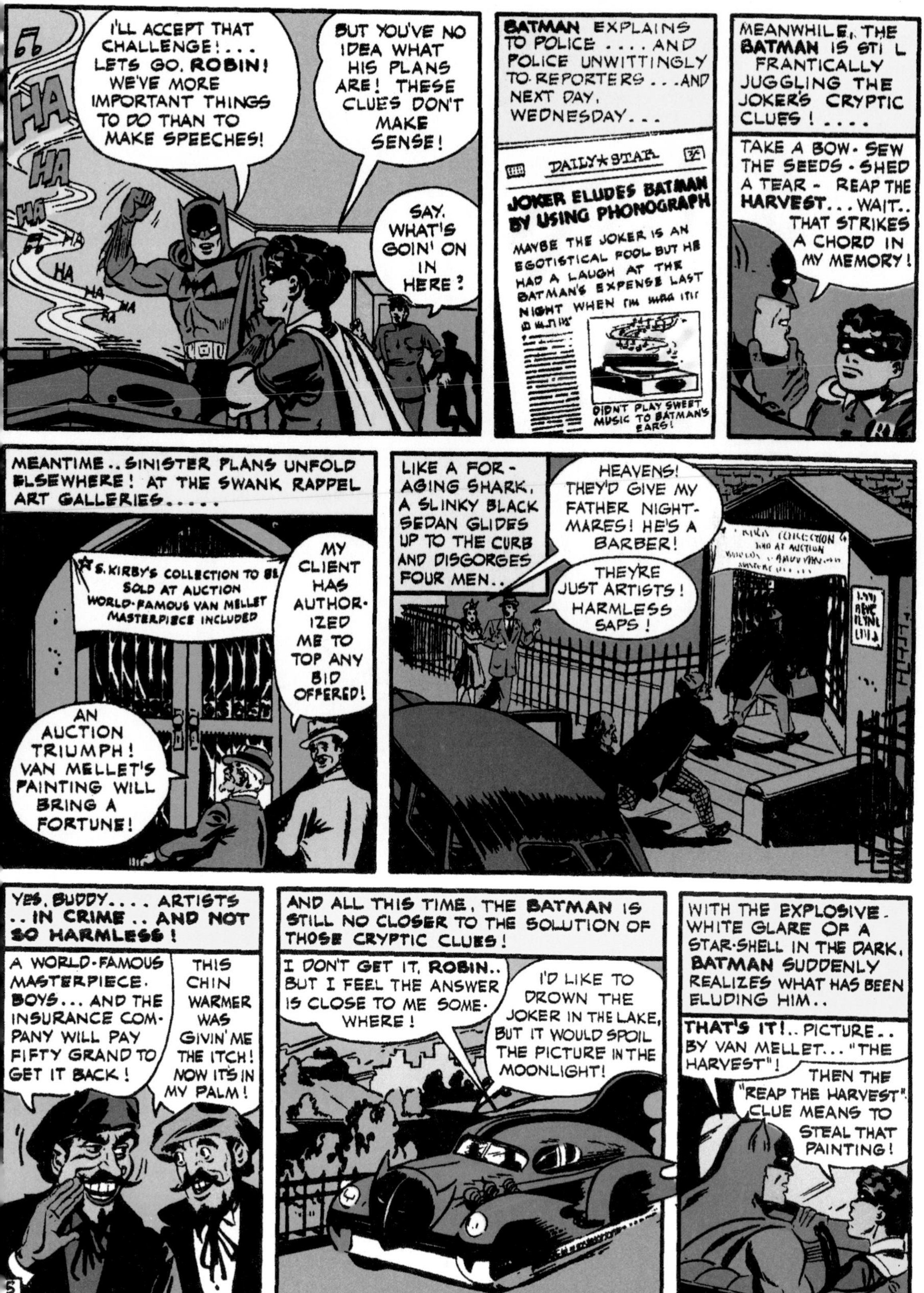
I'LL ACCEPT THAT CHALLENGE! . . . LETS GO, ROBIN! WE'VE MORE IMPORTANT THINGS TO DO THAN TO MAKE SPEECHES!
BUT YOU'VE NO IDEA WHAT HIS PLANS ARE! THESE CLUES DON'T MAKE SENSE!
HA HA HA HA HA HA HA
SAY, WHAT'S GOIN' ON IN HERE?
BATMAN EXPLAINS TO POLICE . . . . AND POLICE UNWITTINGLY TO REPORTERS . . . AND NEXT DAY, WEDNESDAY . . .
DAILY★STAR
JOKER ELUDES BATMAN BY USING PHONOGRAPH
MAYBE THE JOKER IS AN EGOTISTICAL FOOL BUT HE HAD A LAUGH AT THE BATMAN'S EXPENSE LAST NIGHT
DIDN'T PLAY SWEET MUSIC TO BATMAN'S EARS!
MEANWHILE, THE BATMAN IS STILL FRANTICALLY JUGGLING THE JOKER'S CRYPTIC CLUES! . . . .
TAKE A BOW - SEW THE SEEDS - SHED A TEAR - REAP THE HARVEST . . . WAIT . . THAT STRIKES A CHORD IN MY MEMORY!
MEANTIME . . SINISTER PLANS UNFOLD ELSEWHERE! AT THE SWANK RAPPEL ART GALLERIES . . . . .
S. KIRBY'S COLLECTION TO BE SOLD AT AUCTION WORLD-FAMOUS VAN MELLET MASTERPIECE INCLUDED
MY CLIENT HAS AUTHORIZED ME TO TOP ANY BID OFFERED!
AN AUCTION TRIUMPH! VAN MELLET'S PAINTING WILL BRING A FORTUNE!
LIKE A FORAGING SHARK, A SLINKY BLACK SEDAN GLIDES UP TO THE CURB AND DISGORGES FOUR MEN . .
HEAVENS! THEY'D GIVE MY FATHER NIGHTMARES! HE'S A BARBER!
THEY'RE JUST ARTISTS! HARMLESS SAPS!
YES, BUDDY . . . . ARTISTS . . IN CRIME . . AND NOT SO HARMLESS!
A WORLD-FAMOUS MASTERPIECE, BOYS . . . AND THE INSURANCE COMPANY WILL PAY FIFTY GRAND TO GET IT BACK!
THIS CHIN WARMER WAS GIVIN' ME THE ITCH! NOW IT'S IN MY PALM!
AND ALL THIS TIME, THE BATMAN IS STILL NO CLOSER TO THE SOLUTION OF THOSE CRYPTIC CLUES!
I DON'T GET IT, ROBIN . . BUT I FEEL THE ANSWER IS CLOSE TO ME SOMEWHERE!
I'D LIKE TO DROWN THE JOKER IN THE LAKE, BUT IT WOULD SPOIL THE PICTURE IN THE MOONLIGHT!
WITH THE EXPLOSIVE WHITE GLARE OF A STAR-SHELL IN THE DARK, BATMAN SUDDENLY REALIZES WHAT HAS BEEN ELUDING HIM . .
THAT'S IT! . . PICTURE . . BY VAN MELLET . . . "THE HARVEST"!
THEN THE "REAP THE HARVEST" CLUE MEANS TO STEAL THAT PAINTING!
5

AND IN THE MAIN EXHIBITION ROOM, WHILE ALL EYES ARE ON THE FAMOUS PAINTING...

ALL RIGHT, MEN, LET'S GO! YOU HAVE YOUR INSTRUCTIONS!

DONNING GOGGLES, THE OMINOUS QUARTET DISPERSES ABOUT THE ROOM....

THE JOKER!

PLEASE INFORM THE BATMAN THAT THE JOKER FIRST TOOK A BOW-SO!

RELAX, FOLKS. WE'RE JUST THE EXTERMINATORS HAW!

NOW MY MEN WILL SOW THE SEEDS! TOO BAD YOU HAVEN'T THE GOGGLES AND CHEMICALLY TREATED BEARDS WE WEAR! SOW THE SEEDS, BOYS!

GROUND SEEDS OF RED PEPPER! IT OUGHT TO SPICE UP THE PARTY!

DEVILISH CLOUDS OF GROUND RED PEPPER INSTANTLY SMART EYES AND SEAR LUNGS! A CHOKING PANDEMONIUM BREAKS LOOSE!

I CAN'T BREATHE!

OW, MY EYES!

ATCH-OO!

AND AS THE JOKER'S VOICE SHRILLY LIFTS ITSELF ABOVE THE CRIES AND SCREAMS!

SHED A TEAR, FOLKS.. WHILE I REAP THE HARVEST! WON'T THIS BE A LAUGH ON BATMAN!

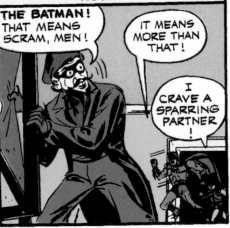

BUT AT THAT INSTANT, TWO GRIM AVENGERS CHARGE INTO THE ROOM...

THE BATMAN! THAT MEANS SCRAM, MEN!

IT MEANS MORE THAN THAT!

I CRAVE A SPARRING PARTNER!

6

LIKE SCURRYING RATS, THE QUARTET FLEES... BUT RELENTLESS PURSUIT IS BEHIND THEM...

REMEMBER, ROBIN... THE JOKER'S MY MEAT!

AW! YOU HAVE ALL THE FUN!

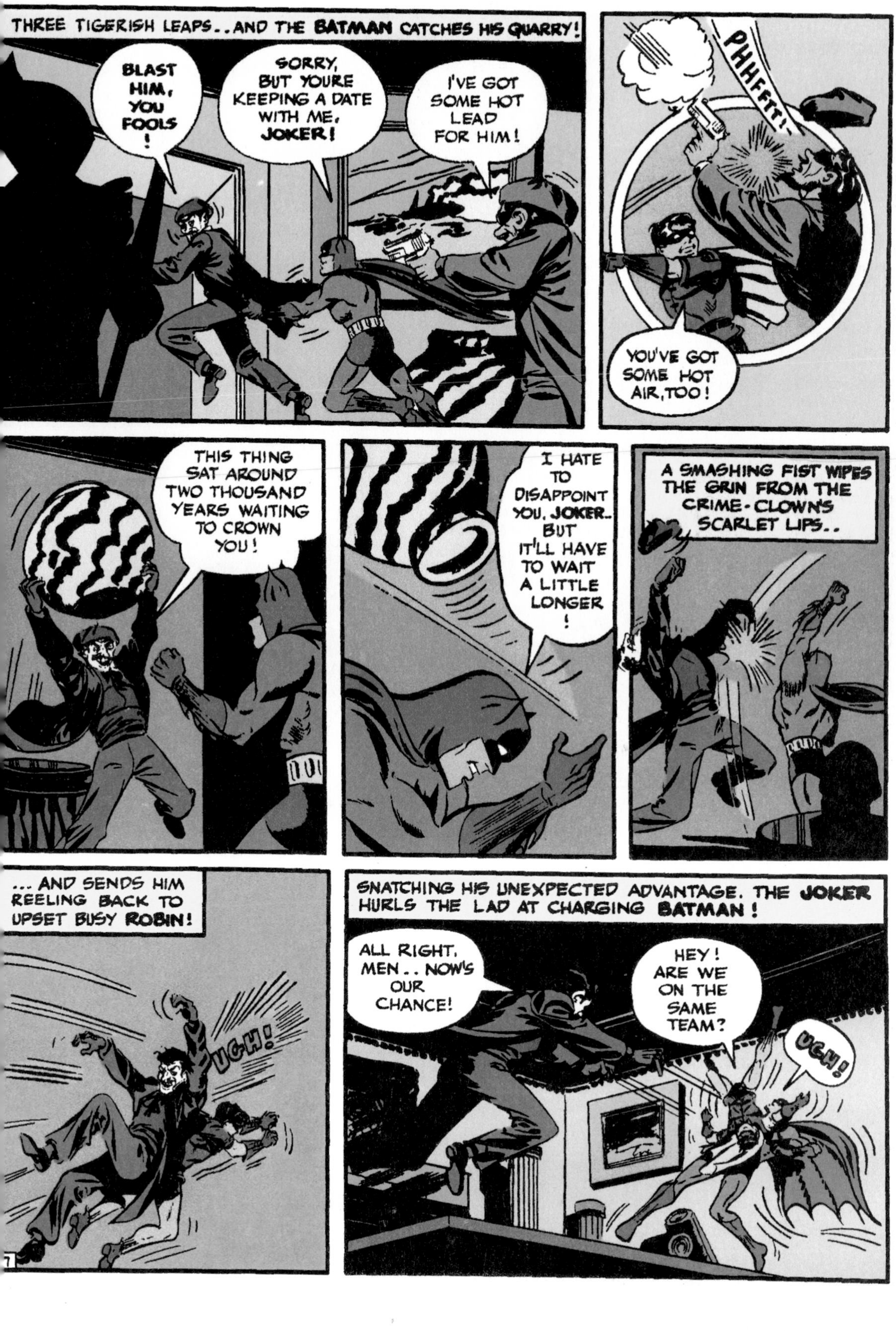
THREE TIGERISH LEAPS..AND THE BATMAN CATCHES HIS QUARRY!
BLAST HIM, YOU FOOLS!
SORRY, BUT YOURE KEEPING A DATE WITH ME, JOKER!
I'VE GOT SOME HOT LEAD FOR HIM!
PHHFFTT!
YOU'VE GOT SOME HOT AIR, TOO!
THIS THING SAT AROUND TWO THOUSAND YEARS WAITING TO CROWN YOU!
I HATE TO DISAPPOINT YOU, JOKER.. BUT IT'LL HAVE TO WAIT A LITTLE LONGER!
A SMASHING FIST WIPES THE GRIN FROM THE CRIME-CLOWN'S SCARLET LIPS..
... AND SENDS HIM REELING BACK TO UPSET BUSY ROBIN!
UGH!
SNATCHING HIS UNEXPECTED ADVANTAGE, THE JOKER HURLS THE LAD AT CHARGING BATMAN!
ALL RIGHT, MEN.. NOW'S OUR CHANCE!
HEY! ARE WE ON THE SAME TEAM?
UGH!

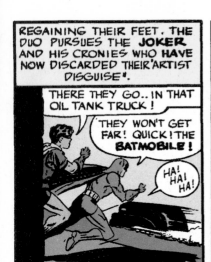

REGAINING THEIR FEET, THE DUO PURSUES THE **JOKER** AND HIS CRONIES WHO **HAVE** NOW DISCARDED THEIR "ARTIST DISGUISE".

THERE THEY GO.. IN THAT OIL TANK TRUCK!

THEY WON'T GET FAR! QUICK! THE **BATMOBILE**!

HA! HA! HA!

AS THE **BATMOBILE** ROARS FORWARD..

GOOD! THEY'RE FOLLOWING US AS WE FIGURED! NOW **OPEN UP THE ESCAPE VALVES!**

LESSO OIL CO.

OIL FLOWS.. AND IN THE WAKE OF THE TRUCK, THE SPEEDING **BATMOBILE** SKIDS AND SLIDES CRAZILY!

WOW! THIS IS LIKE RIDING ON GLASS! HOLD ONTO YOUR HAT, KID!

LOOK OUT!

THE RELENTLESS **BATMOBILE** CLOSES UP THE GAP... AND IS HOSED WITH A TORRENT OF BLACK OIL!

TAKE IT, CHUMP!

TRAPPED IN A FLAMING COFFIN!

THIS THING'S AN OVEN! WE'LL BE HAMBURGERS IF WE DON'T GET OUT!

LIKE A FIERY METEOR, THE BLAZING **BAT-MOBILE** FLASHES... TOWARD WHAT ??

GET SET, ROBIN! HERE WE GO!

HERE.. HAVE A LIGHT!

WHOOSH!

WE DAREN'T OPEN UP THE DOORS AND RUN FOR IT! WE'RE TRAPPED!... WE'VE GOT A CHANCE... A LONG CHANCE!

WHAT IS THE BAT-MAN'S PLAN? CAN YOU GUESS ??

8

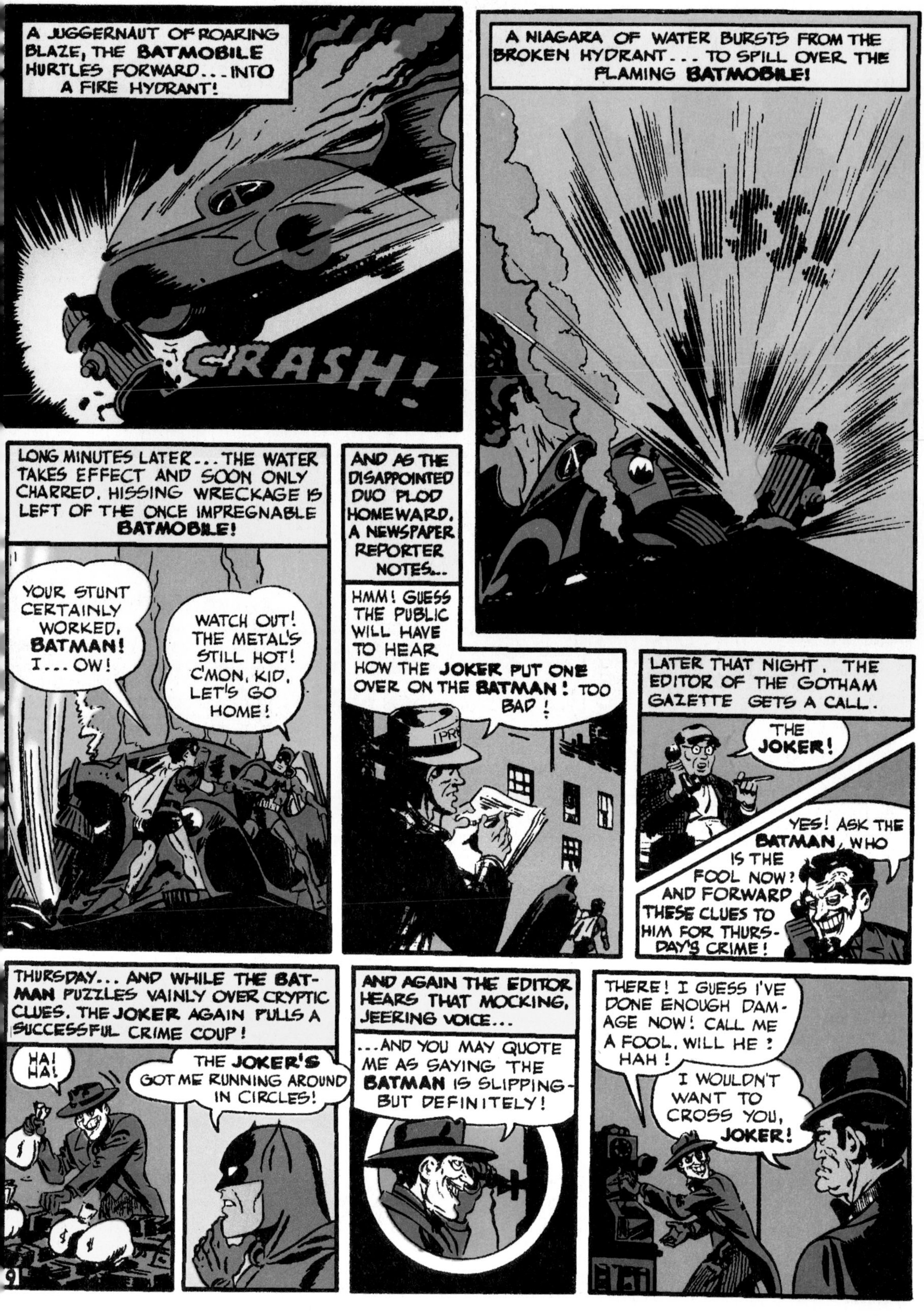

A JUGGERNAUT OF ROARING BLAZE, THE BATMOBILE HURTLES FORWARD... INTO A FIRE HYDRANT!
CRASH!
A NIAGARA OF WATER BURSTS FROM THE BROKEN HYDRANT... TO SPILL OVER THE FLAMING BATMOBILE!
HISS!
LONG MINUTES LATER... THE WATER TAKES EFFECT AND SOON ONLY CHARRED, HISSING WRECKAGE IS LEFT OF THE ONCE IMPREGNABLE BATMOBILE!
YOUR STUNT CERTAINLY WORKED, BATMAN! I... OW!
WATCH OUT! THE METAL'S STILL HOT! C'MON, KID, LET'S GO HOME!
AND AS THE DISAPPOINTED DUO PLOD HOMEWARD, A NEWSPAPER REPORTER NOTES...
HMM! GUESS THE PUBLIC WILL HAVE TO HEAR HOW THE JOKER PUT ONE OVER ON THE BATMAN! TOO BAD!
LATER THAT NIGHT, THE EDITOR OF THE GOTHAM GAZETTE GETS A CALL.
THE JOKER!
YES! ASK THE BATMAN WHO IS THE FOOL NOW? AND FORWARD THESE CLUES TO HIM FOR THURSDAY'S CRIME!
THURSDAY... AND WHILE THE BATMAN PUZZLES VAINLY OVER CRYPTIC CLUES, THE JOKER AGAIN PULLS A SUCCESSFUL CRIME COUP!
HA! HA!
THE JOKER'S GOT ME RUNNING AROUND IN CIRCLES!
AND AGAIN THE EDITOR HEARS THAT MOCKING, JEERING VOICE...
...AND YOU MAY QUOTE ME AS SAYING THE BATMAN IS SLIPPING - BUT DEFINITELY!
THERE! I GUESS I'VE DONE ENOUGH DAMAGE NOW! CALL ME A FOOL, WILL HE? HAH!
I WOULDN'T WANT TO CROSS YOU, JOKER!
9

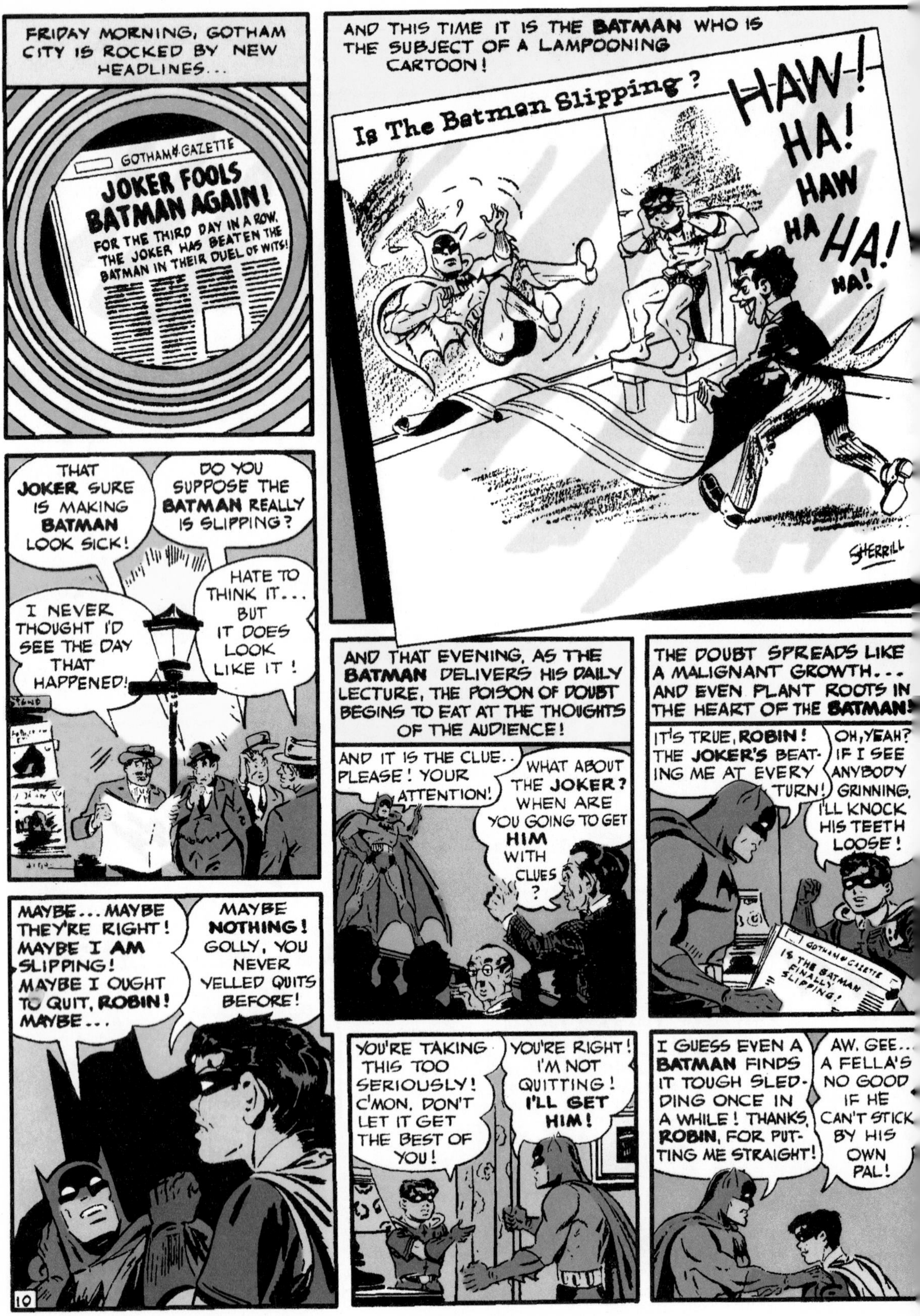
FRIDAY MORNING, GOTHAM CITY IS ROCKED BY NEW HEADLINES...
GOTHAM GAZETTE
JOKER FOOLS BATMAN AGAIN!
FOR THE THIRD DAY IN A ROW, THE JOKER HAS BEATEN THE BATMAN IN THEIR DUEL OF WITS!
AND THIS TIME IT IS THE BATMAN WHO IS THE SUBJECT OF A LAMPOONING CARTOON!
Is The Batman Slipping?
HAW! HA! HAW HA HA! HA!
SHERRILL
THAT JOKER SURE IS MAKING BATMAN LOOK SICK!
DO YOU SUPPOSE THE BATMAN REALLY IS SLIPPING?
I NEVER THOUGHT I'D SEE THE DAY THAT HAPPENED!
HATE TO THINK IT... BUT IT DOES LOOK LIKE IT!
AND THAT EVENING, AS THE BATMAN DELIVERS HIS DAILY LECTURE, THE POISON OF DOUBT BEGINS TO EAT AT THE THOUGHTS OF THE AUDIENCE!
AND IT IS THE CLUE.. PLEASE! YOUR ATTENTION!
WHAT ABOUT THE JOKER? WHEN ARE YOU GOING TO GET HIM WITH CLUES?
THE DOUBT SPREADS LIKE A MALIGNANT GROWTH... AND EVEN PLANT ROOTS IN THE HEART OF THE BATMAN!
IT'S TRUE, ROBIN! THE JOKER'S BEATING ME AT EVERY TURN!
OH, YEAH? IF I SEE ANYBODY GRINNING, I'LL KNOCK HIS TEETH LOOSE!
GOTHAM GAZETTE
IS THE BATMAN FINALLY SLIPPING?
MAYBE... MAYBE THEY'RE RIGHT! MAYBE I AM SLIPPING! MAYBE I OUGHT TO QUIT, ROBIN! MAYBE...
MAYBE NOTHING! GOLLY, YOU NEVER YELLED QUITS BEFORE!
10
YOU'RE TAKING THIS TOO SERIOUSLY! C'MON, DON'T LET IT GET THE BEST OF YOU!
YOU'RE RIGHT! I'M NOT QUITTING! I'LL GET HIM!
I GUESS EVEN A BATMAN FINDS IT TOUGH SLEDDING ONCE IN A WHILE! THANKS, ROBIN, FOR PUTTING ME STRAIGHT!
AW, GEE... A FELLA'S NO GOOD IF HE CAN'T STICK BY HIS OWN PAL!

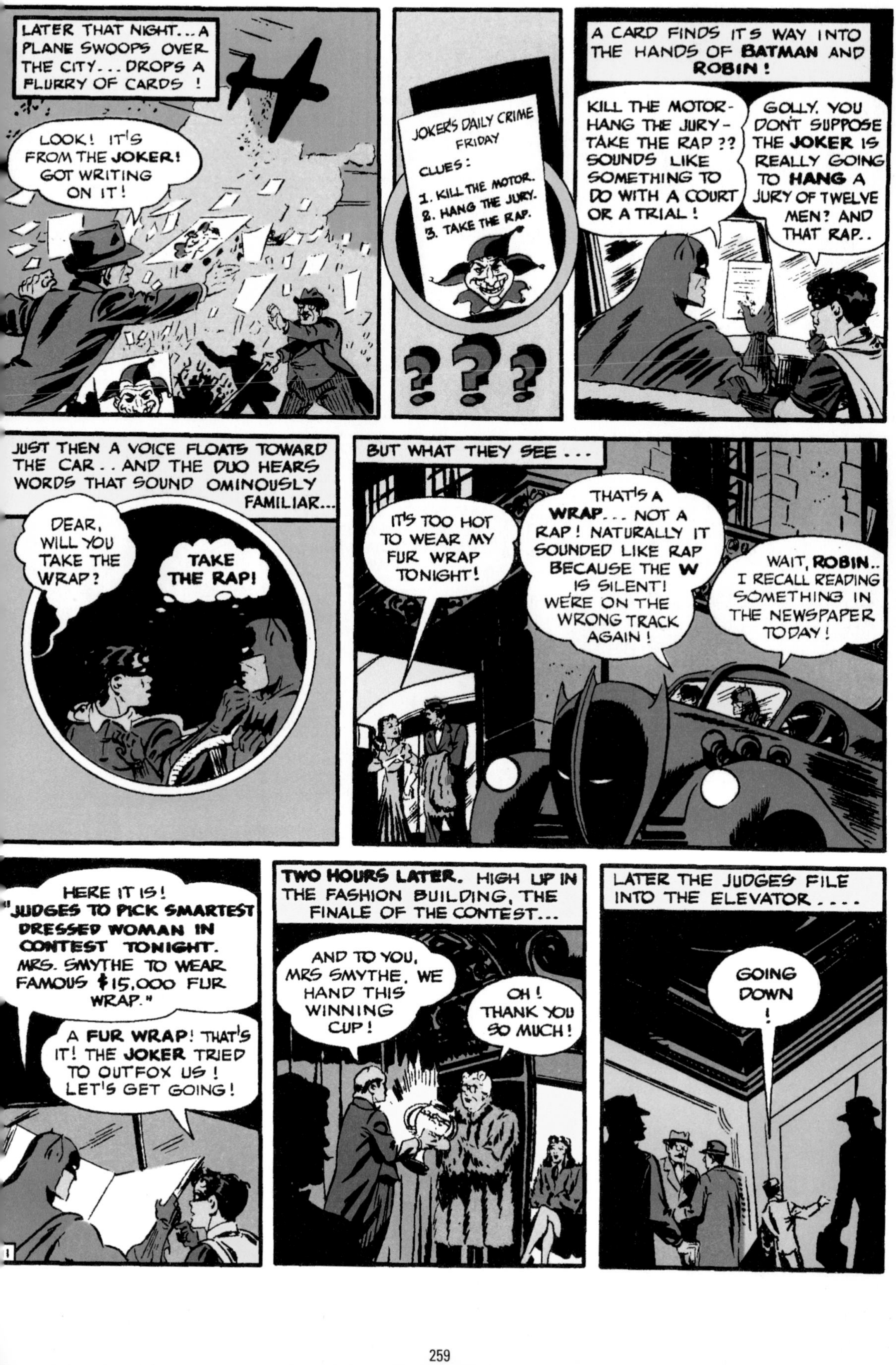
LATER THAT NIGHT... A PLANE SWOOPS OVER THE CITY... DROPS A FLURRY OF CARDS !
LOOK! IT'S FROM THE JOKER! GOT WRITING ON IT!
JOKER'S DAILY CRIME FRIDAY CLUES: 1. KILL THE MOTOR. 2. HANG THE JURY. 3. TAKE THE RAP.
???
A CARD FINDS ITS WAY INTO THE HANDS OF BATMAN AND ROBIN!
KILL THE MOTOR- HANG THE JURY- TAKE THE RAP?? SOUNDS LIKE SOMETHING TO DO WITH A COURT OR A TRIAL!
GOLLY, YOU DON'T SUPPOSE THE JOKER IS REALLY GOING TO HANG A JURY OF TWELVE MEN? AND THAT RAP..
JUST THEN A VOICE FLOATS TOWARD THE CAR.. AND THE DUO HEARS WORDS THAT SOUND OMINOUSLY FAMILIAR...
DEAR, WILL YOU TAKE THE WRAP?
TAKE THE RAP!
BUT WHAT THEY SEE...
IT'S TOO HOT TO WEAR MY FUR WRAP TONIGHT!
THAT'S A WRAP... NOT A RAP! NATURALLY IT SOUNDED LIKE RAP BECAUSE THE W IS SILENT! WE'RE ON THE WRONG TRACK AGAIN!
WAIT, ROBIN.. I RECALL READING SOMETHING IN THE NEWSPAPER TODAY!
HERE IT IS! "JUDGES TO PICK SMARTEST DRESSED WOMAN IN CONTEST TONIGHT. MRS. SMYTHE TO WEAR FAMOUS $15,000 FUR WRAP."
A FUR WRAP! THAT'S IT! THE JOKER TRIED TO OUTFOX US! LET'S GET GOING!
TWO HOURS LATER. HIGH UP IN THE FASHION BUILDING, THE FINALE OF THE CONTEST...
AND TO YOU, MRS SMYTHE, WE HAND THIS WINNING CUP!
OH! THANK YOU SO MUCH!
LATER THE JUDGES FILE INTO THE ELEVATOR....
GOING DOWN!

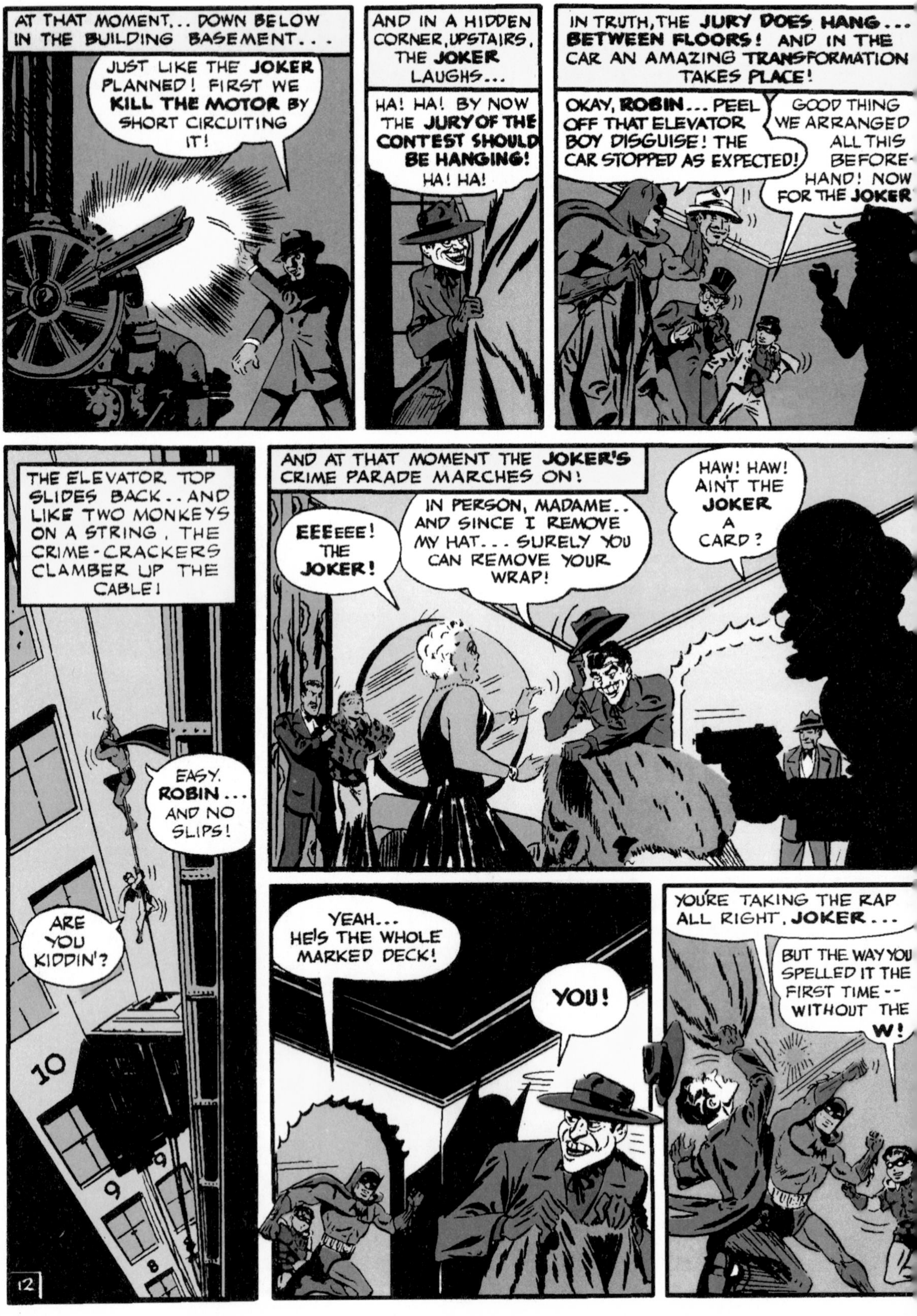

AT THAT MOMENT... DOWN BELOW IN THE BUILDING BASEMENT...
JUST LIKE THE JOKER PLANNED! FIRST WE KILL THE MOTOR BY SHORT CIRCUITING IT!
AND IN A HIDDEN CORNER, UPSTAIRS, THE JOKER LAUGHS...
HA! HA! BY NOW THE JURY OF THE CONTEST SHOULD BE HANGING! HA! HA!
IN TRUTH, THE JURY DOES HANG... BETWEEN FLOORS! AND IN THE CAR AN AMAZING TRANSFORMATION TAKES PLACE!
OKAY, ROBIN... PEEL OFF THAT ELEVATOR BOY DISGUISE! THE CAR STOPPED AS EXPECTED!
GOOD THING WE ARRANGED ALL THIS BEFORE-HAND! NOW FOR THE JOKER
THE ELEVATOR TOP SLIDES BACK.. AND LIKE TWO MONKEYS ON A STRING, THE CRIME-CRACKERS CLAMBER UP THE CABLE!
EASY, ROBIN... AND NO SLIPS!
ARE YOU KIDDIN'?
10
9
9
8
12
AND AT THAT MOMENT THE JOKER'S CRIME PARADE MARCHES ON!
EEEeee! THE JOKER!
IN PERSON, MADAME.. AND SINCE I REMOVE MY HAT... SURELY YOU CAN REMOVE YOUR WRAP!
HAW! HAW! AIN'T THE JOKER A CARD?
YEAH... HE'S THE WHOLE MARKED DECK!
YOU!
YOU'RE TAKING THE RAP ALL RIGHT, JOKER...
BUT THE WAY YOU SPELLED IT THE FIRST TIME -- WITHOUT THE W!

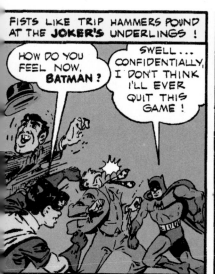

FISTS LIKE TRIP HAMMERS POUND AT THE **JOKER'S** UNDERLINGS!

HOW DO YOU FEEL NOW, **BATMAN**?

SWELL... CONFIDENTIALLY, I DON'T THINK I'LL EVER QUIT THIS GAME!

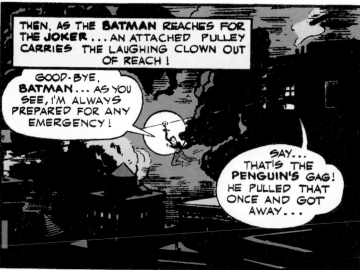

THEN, AS THE **BATMAN** REACHES FOR THE **JOKER**...AN ATTACHED PULLEY CARRIES THE LAUGHING CLOWN OUT OF REACH!

GOOD-BYE, **BATMAN**... AS YOU SEE, I'M ALWAYS PREPARED FOR ANY EMERGENCY!

SAY... THAT'S THE **PENGUIN'S** GAG! HE PULLED THAT ONCE AND GOT AWAY...

A HISSING SOUND... AND A LASSO WHIPS UP ABOUT THE **JOKER'S** MIDDLE!

...BUT YOU WON'T !

BETTER NOT LET GO IN ORDER TO KILL ME, **JOKER**... 'CAUSE YOU'LL ONLY BE CUTTING OFF YOUR NOSE TO SPITE YOUR FACE!

AND AS THEY REACH THE OTHER ROOF, A JAW-CRACKING SMASH WRITES "FINIS" TO THE **JOKER'S** ESCAPE!

NOW IT'S TIME YOU HOLLERED "UNCLE"!

C-R-A-C-K

AND SO, THAT NIGHT **BATMAN** DELIVERS HIS LECTURE.... BUT THIS TIME WITH A FLESH AND BLOOD EXHIBIT!

THE **JOKER** IS AN EGOTISTICAL FOOL WHO LEAVES HIS CLUES BEHIND AND...

BAH!

AND SO THE CASE ENDED BUT FOR THE GAZETTE'S CARTOON!

Rap... "Not only did The Joker take the Rap --- He also got the LUMPS!"

3

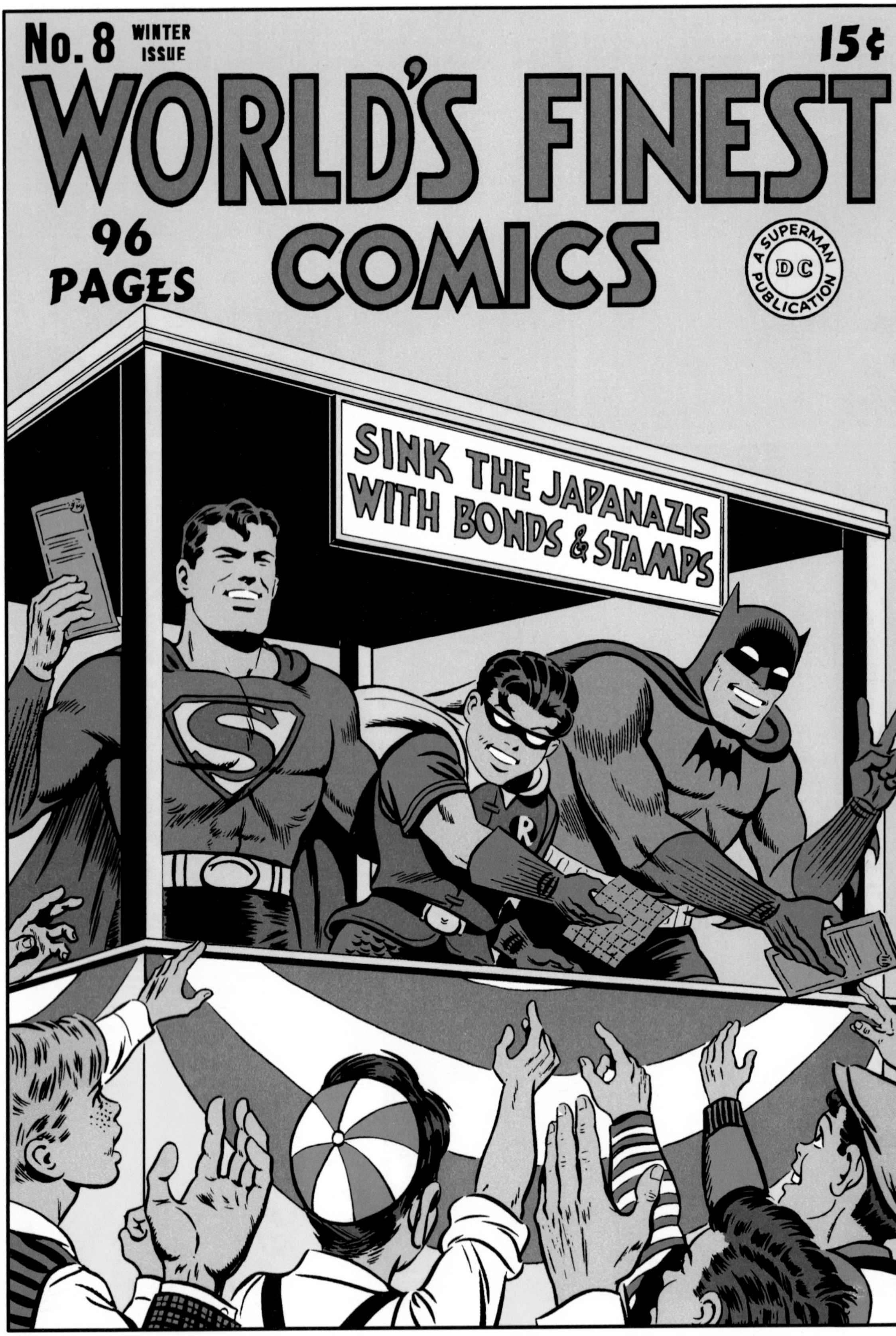

No. 8 WINTER ISSUE
15¢
WORLD'S FINEST COMICS
96 PAGES
A SUPERMAN DC PUBLICATION
SINK THE JAPANAZIS WITH BONDS & STAMPS

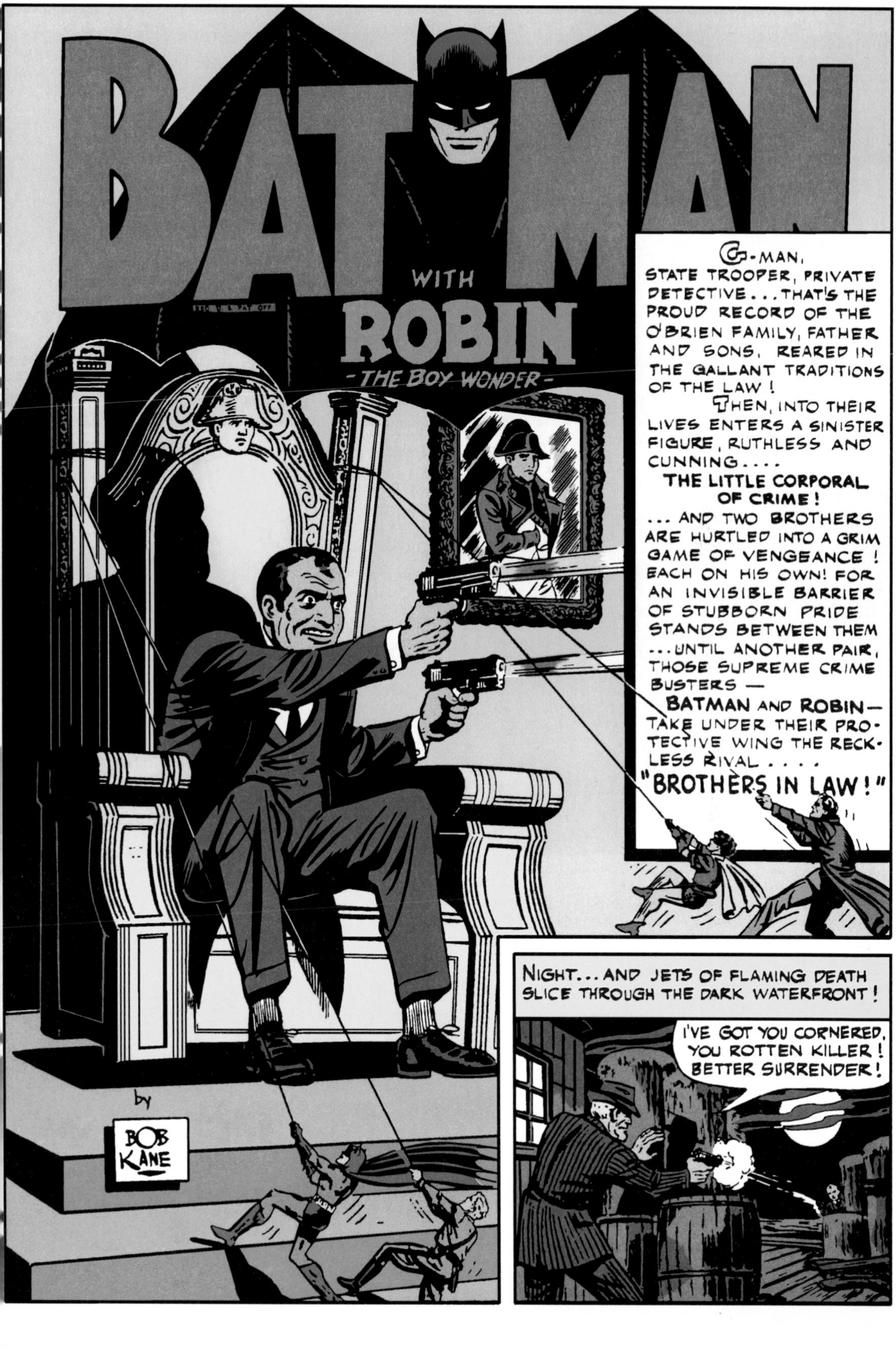
BATMAN
WITH
ROBIN
-THE BOY WONDER-
G-MAN, STATE TROOPER, PRIVATE DETECTIVE... THAT'S THE PROUD RECORD OF THE O'BRIEN FAMILY, FATHER AND SONS, REARED IN THE GALLANT TRADITIONS OF THE LAW! THEN, INTO THEIR LIVES ENTERS A SINISTER FIGURE, RUTHLESS AND CUNNING.... THE LITTLE CORPORAL OF CRIME! ... AND TWO BROTHERS ARE HURTLED INTO A GRIM GAME OF VENGEANCE! EACH ON HIS OWN! FOR AN INVISIBLE BARRIER OF STUBBORN PRIDE STANDS BETWEEN THEM ...UNTIL ANOTHER PAIR, THOSE SUPREME CRIME BUSTERS — BATMAN AND ROBIN — TAKE UNDER THEIR PROTECTIVE WING THE RECKLESS RIVAL....
"BROTHERS IN LAW!"
by
BOB KANE
NIGHT... AND JETS OF FLAMING DEATH SLICE THROUGH THE DARK WATERFRONT!
I'VE GOT YOU CORNERED, YOU ROTTEN KILLER! BETTER SURRENDER!

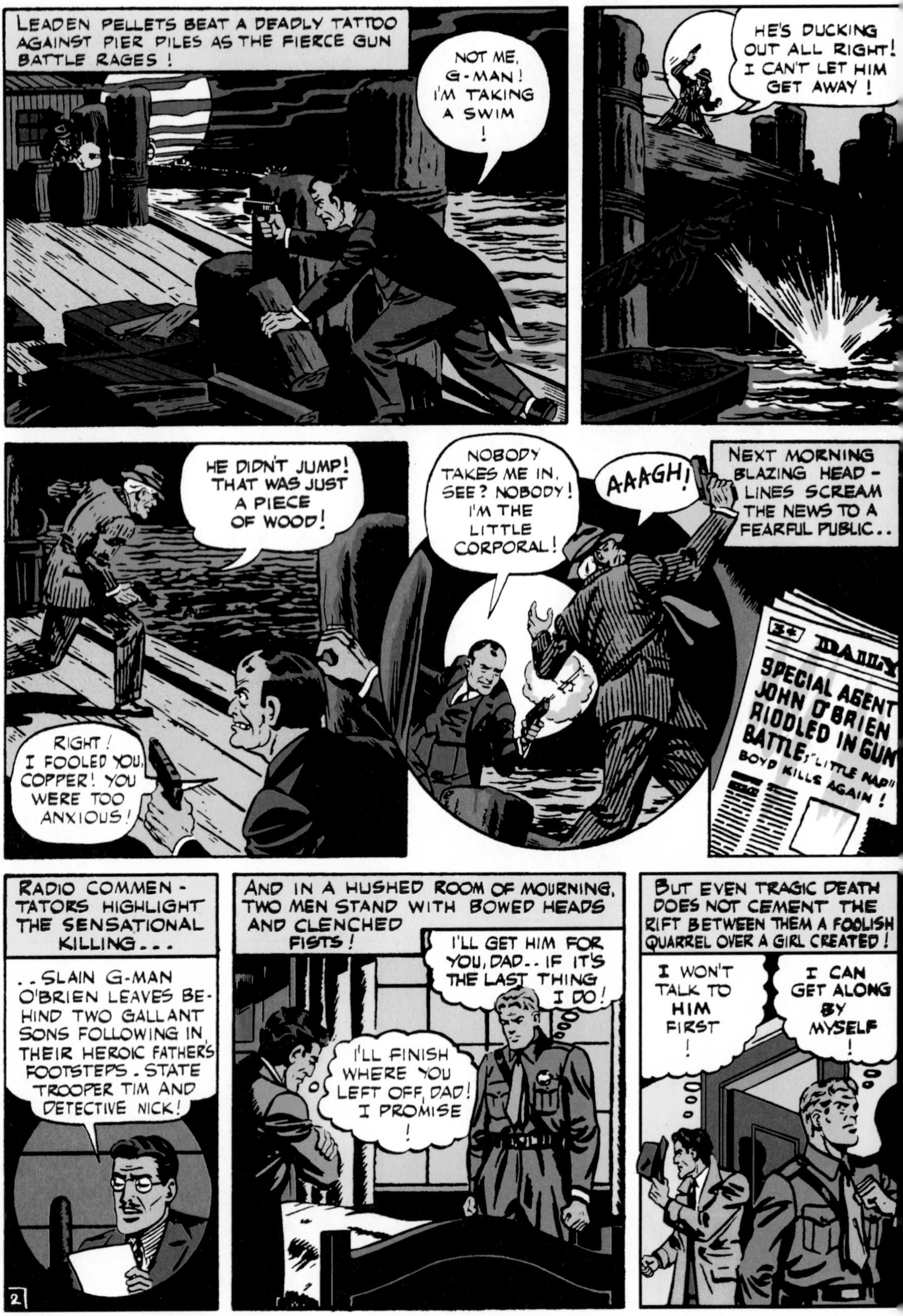
LEADEN PELLETS BEAT A DEADLY TATTOO AGAINST PIER PILES AS THE FIERCE GUN BATTLE RAGES !
NOT ME, G-MAN ! I'M TAKING A SWIM !
HE'S DUCKING OUT ALL RIGHT! I CAN'T LET HIM GET AWAY !
HE DIDN'T JUMP! THAT WAS JUST A PIECE OF WOOD!
RIGHT ! I FOOLED YOU, COPPER! YOU WERE TOO ANXIOUS!
NOBODY TAKES ME IN. SEE? NOBODY! I'M THE LITTLE CORPORAL!
AAAGH!
NEXT MORNING BLAZING HEAD-LINES SCREAM THE NEWS TO A FEARFUL PUBLIC..
DAILY
SPECIAL AGENT JOHN O'BRIEN RIDDLED IN GUN BATTLE; "LITTLE NAP" BOYD KILLS AGAIN !
RADIO COMMEN-TATORS HIGHLIGHT THE SENSATIONAL KILLING...
..SLAIN G-MAN O'BRIEN LEAVES BE-HIND TWO GALLANT SONS FOLLOWING IN THEIR HEROIC FATHER'S FOOTSTEPS. STATE TROOPER TIM AND DETECTIVE NICK!
2
AND IN A HUSHED ROOM OF MOURNING, TWO MEN STAND WITH BOWED HEADS AND CLENCHED FISTS!
I'LL GET HIM FOR YOU, DAD.. IF IT'S THE LAST THING I DO!
I'LL FINISH WHERE YOU LEFT OFF, DAD! I PROMISE !
BUT EVEN TRAGIC DEATH DOES NOT CEMENT THE RIFT BETWEEN THEM A FOOLISH QUARREL OVER A GIRL CREATED!
I WON'T TALK TO HIM FIRST !
I CAN GET ALONG BY MYSELF !

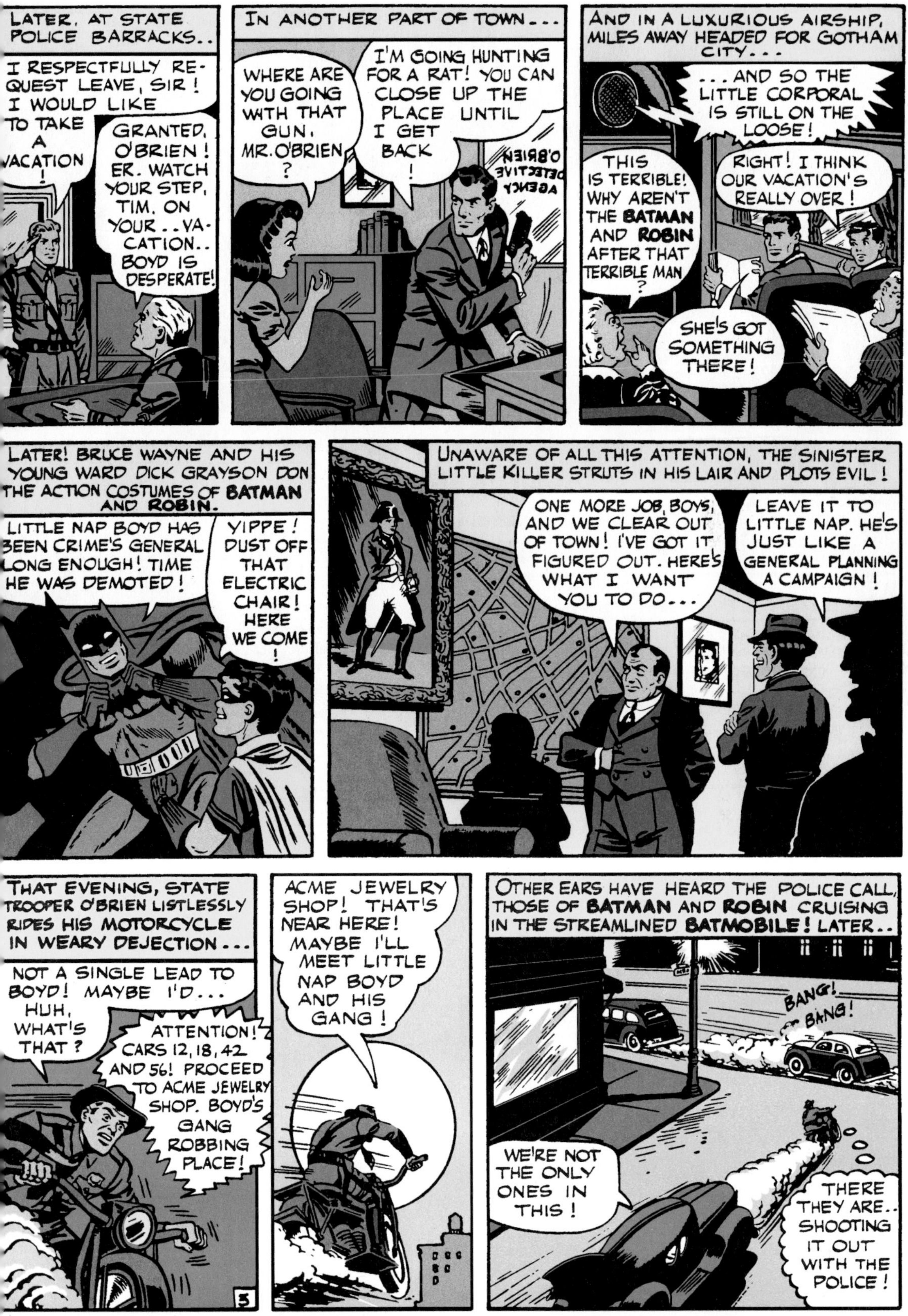
LATER, AT STATE POLICE BARRACKS..
I RESPECTFULLY REQUEST LEAVE, SIR! I WOULD LIKE TO TAKE A VACATION!
GRANTED, O'BRIEN! ER, WATCH YOUR STEP, TIM, ON YOUR.. VACATION.. BOYD IS DESPERATE!
IN ANOTHER PART OF TOWN...
WHERE ARE YOU GOING WITH THAT GUN, MR. O'BRIEN?
I'M GOING HUNTING FOR A RAT! YOU CAN CLOSE UP THE PLACE UNTIL I GET BACK!
AND IN A LUXURIOUS AIRSHIP, MILES AWAY HEADED FOR GOTHAM CITY...
...AND SO THE LITTLE CORPORAL IS STILL ON THE LOOSE!
THIS IS TERRIBLE! WHY AREN'T THE BATMAN AND ROBIN AFTER THAT TERRIBLE MAN?
RIGHT! I THINK OUR VACATION'S REALLY OVER!
SHE'S GOT SOMETHING THERE!
LATER! BRUCE WAYNE AND HIS YOUNG WARD DICK GRAYSON DON THE ACTION COSTUMES OF BATMAN AND ROBIN.
LITTLE NAP BOYD HAS BEEN CRIME'S GENERAL LONG ENOUGH! TIME HE WAS DEMOTED!
YIPPE! DUST OFF THAT ELECTRIC CHAIR! HERE WE COME!
UNAWARE OF ALL THIS ATTENTION, THE SINISTER LITTLE KILLER STRUTS IN HIS LAIR AND PLOTS EVIL!
ONE MORE JOB, BOYS, AND WE CLEAR OUT OF TOWN! I'VE GOT IT FIGURED OUT. HERE'S WHAT I WANT YOU TO DO...
LEAVE IT TO LITTLE NAP. HE'S JUST LIKE A GENERAL PLANNING A CAMPAIGN!
THAT EVENING, STATE TROOPER O'BRIEN LISTLESSLY RIDES HIS MOTORCYCLE IN WEARY DEJECTION...
NOT A SINGLE LEAD TO BOYD! MAYBE I'D... HUH, WHAT'S THAT?
ATTENTION! CARS 12, 18, 42 AND 56! PROCEED TO ACME JEWELRY SHOP. BOYD'S GANG ROBBING PLACE!
5
ACME JEWELRY SHOP! THAT'S NEAR HERE! MAYBE I'LL MEET LITTLE NAP BOYD AND HIS GANG!
OTHER EARS HAVE HEARD THE POLICE CALL, THOSE OF BATMAN AND ROBIN CRUISING IN THE STREAMLINED BATMOBILE! LATER..
BANG! BANG!
WE'RE NOT THE ONLY ONES IN THIS!
THERE THEY ARE.. SHOOTING IT OUT WITH THE POLICE!

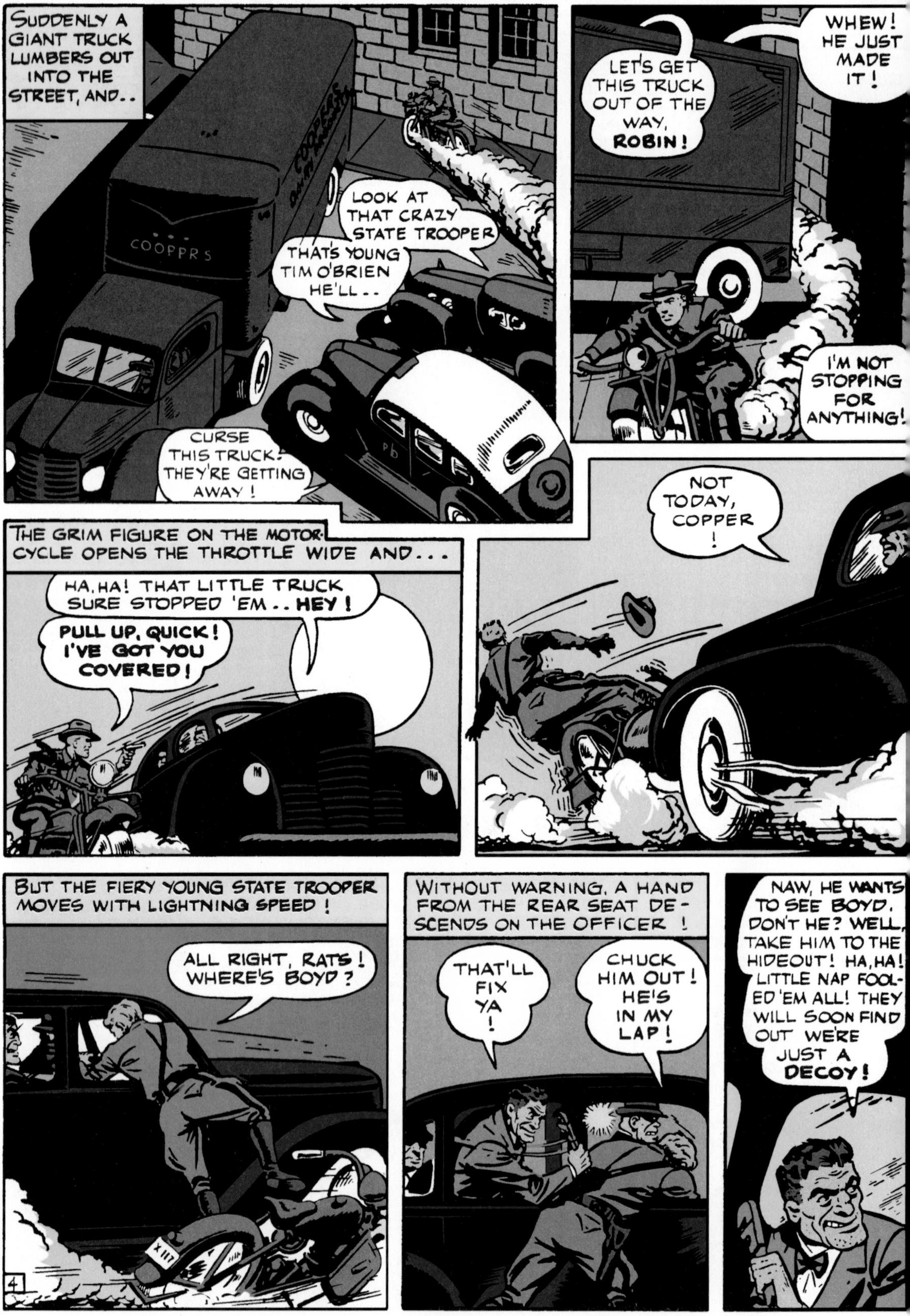
SUDDENLY A GIANT TRUCK LUMBERS OUT INTO THE STREET, AND..
COOPPRS
LOOK AT THAT CRAZY STATE TROOPER
THAT'S YOUNG TIM O'BRIEN HE'LL..
CURSE THIS TRUCK! THEY'RE GETTING AWAY!
LET'S GET THIS TRUCK OUT OF THE WAY, ROBIN!
WHEW! HE JUST MADE IT!
I'M NOT STOPPING FOR ANYTHING!
THE GRIM FIGURE ON THE MOTOR-CYCLE OPENS THE THROTTLE WIDE AND...
HA, HA! THAT LITTLE TRUCK SURE STOPPED 'EM.. HEY!
PULL UP, QUICK! I'VE GOT YOU COVERED!
NOT TODAY, COPPER!
BUT THE FIERY YOUNG STATE TROOPER MOVES WITH LIGHTNING SPEED!
ALL RIGHT, RATS! WHERE'S BOYD?
4
WITHOUT WARNING, A HAND FROM THE REAR SEAT DE-SCENDS ON THE OFFICER!
THAT'LL FIX YA!
CHUCK HIM OUT! HE'S IN MY LAP!
NAW, HE WANTS TO SEE BOYD, DON'T HE? WELL, TAKE HIM TO THE HIDEOUT! HA, HA! LITTLE NAP FOOL-ED 'EM ALL! THEY WILL SOON FIND OUT WE'RE JUST A DECOY!

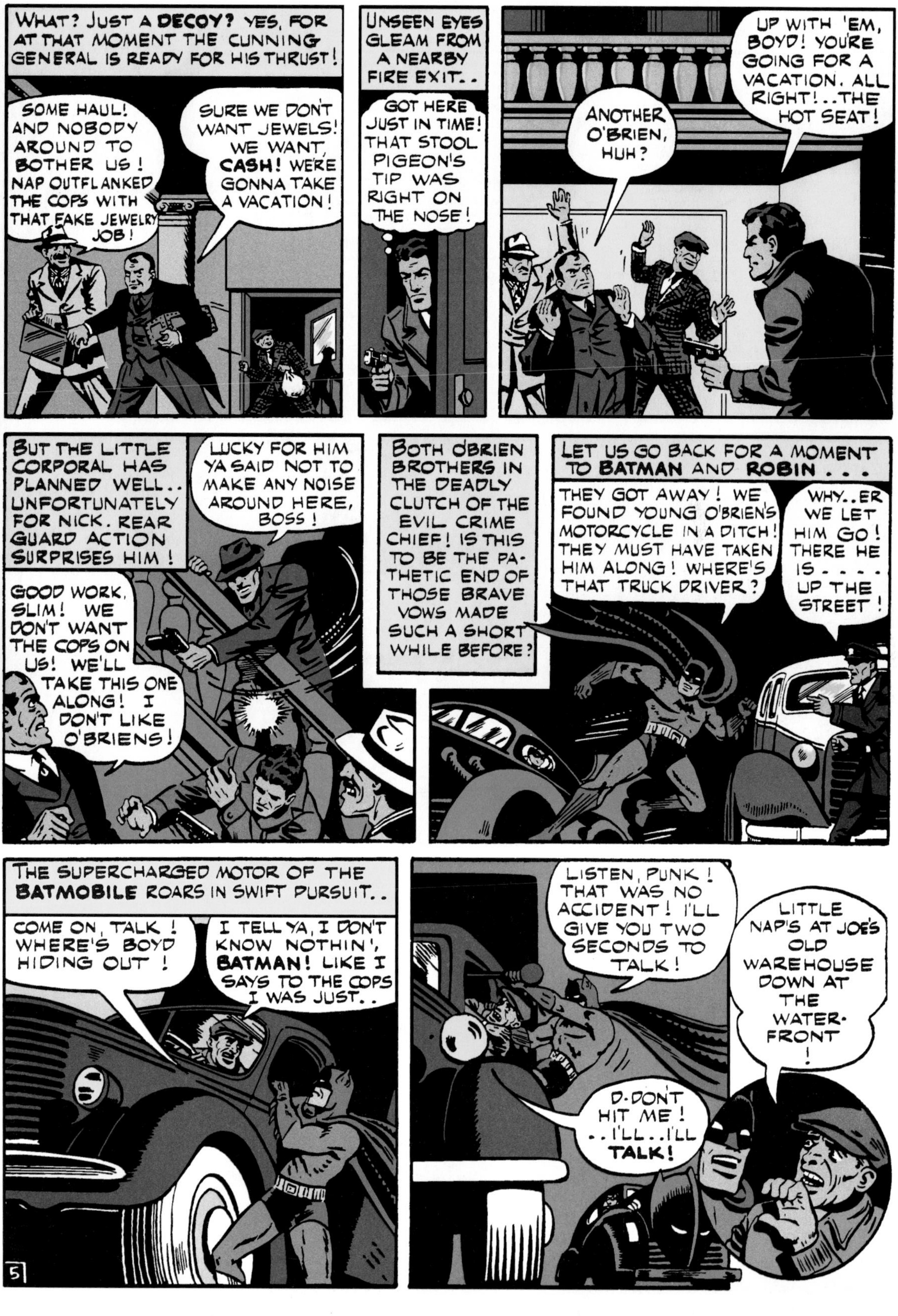
WHAT? JUST A DECOY? YES, FOR AT THAT MOMENT THE CUNNING GENERAL IS READY FOR HIS THRUST!
SOME HAUL! AND NOBODY AROUND TO BOTHER US! NAP OUTFLANKED THE COPS WITH THAT FAKE JEWELRY JOB!
SURE WE DON'T WANT JEWELS! WE WANT, CASH! WE'RE GONNA TAKE A VACATION!
UNSEEN EYES GLEAM FROM A NEARBY FIRE EXIT..
GOT HERE JUST IN TIME! THAT STOOL PIGEON'S TIP WAS RIGHT ON THE NOSE!
UP WITH 'EM, BOYD! YOU'RE GOING FOR A VACATION. ALL RIGHT!..THE HOT SEAT!
ANOTHER O'BRIEN, HUH?
BUT THE LITTLE CORPORAL HAS PLANNED WELL.. UNFORTUNATELY FOR NICK. REAR GUARD ACTION SURPRISES HIM!
LUCKY FOR HIM YA SAID NOT TO MAKE ANY NOISE AROUND HERE, BOSS!
GOOD WORK, SLIM! WE DON'T WANT THE COPS ON US! WE'LL TAKE THIS ONE ALONG! I DON'T LIKE O'BRIENS!
BOTH O'BRIEN BROTHERS IN THE DEADLY CLUTCH OF THE EVIL CRIME CHIEF! IS THIS TO BE THE PATHETIC END OF THOSE BRAVE VOWS MADE SUCH A SHORT WHILE BEFORE?
LET US GO BACK FOR A MOMENT TO BATMAN AND ROBIN . . .
THEY GOT AWAY! WE FOUND YOUNG O'BRIEN'S MOTORCYCLE IN A DITCH! THEY MUST HAVE TAKEN HIM ALONG! WHERE'S THAT TRUCK DRIVER?
WHY..ER WE LET HIM GO! THERE HE IS - - - - UP THE STREET!
THE SUPERCHARGED MOTOR OF THE BATMOBILE ROARS IN SWIFT PURSUIT..
COME ON, TALK! WHERE'S BOYD HIDING OUT!
I TELL YA, I DON'T KNOW NOTHIN', BATMAN! LIKE I SAYS TO THE COPS I WAS JUST..
5
LISTEN, PUNK! THAT WAS NO ACCIDENT! I'LL GIVE YOU TWO SECONDS TO TALK!
LITTLE NAP'S AT JOE'S OLD WAREHOUSE DOWN AT THE WATER-FRONT!
D-DON'T HIT ME! ..I'LL..I'LL TALK!

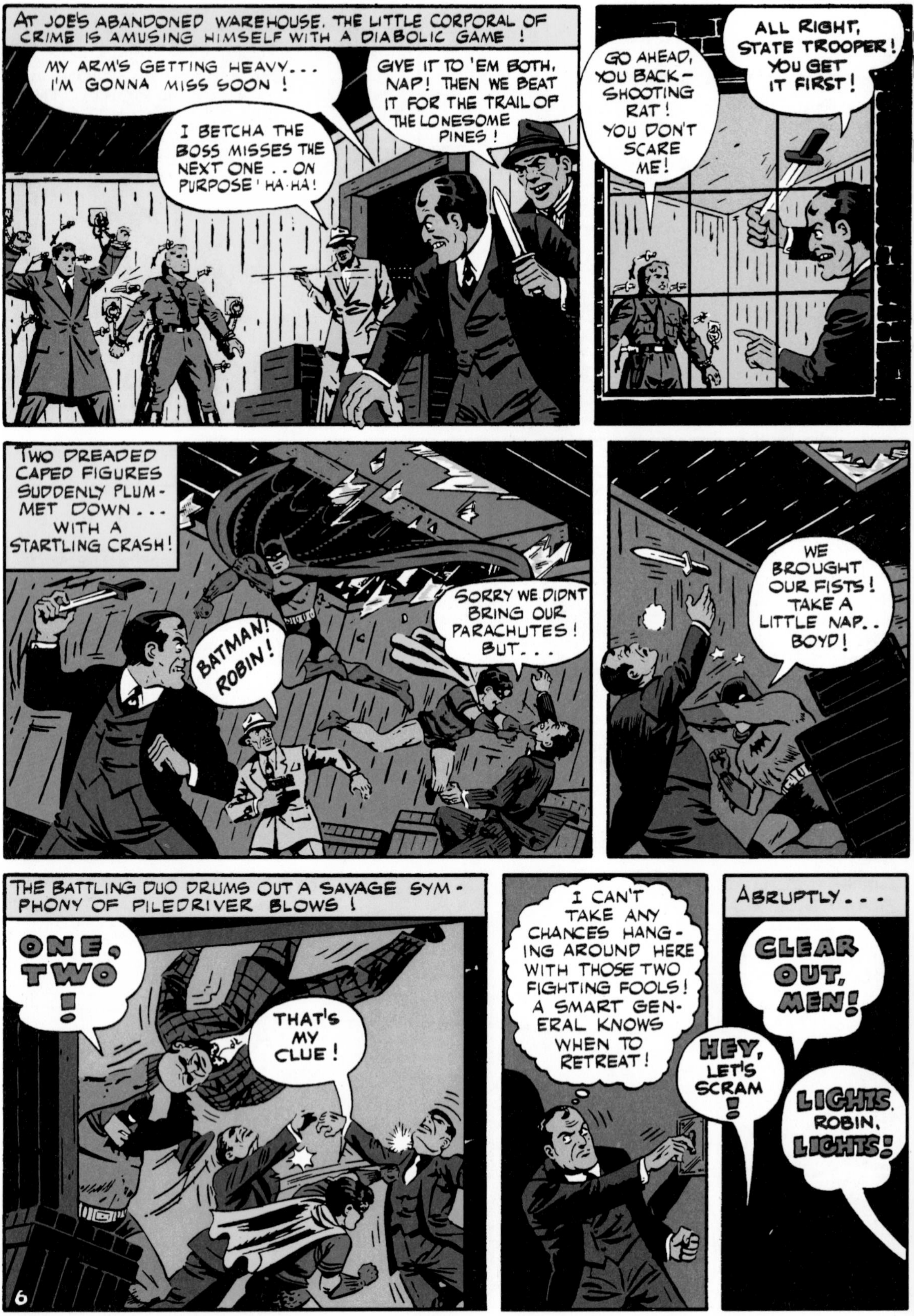

AT JOE'S ABANDONED WAREHOUSE, THE LITTLE CORPORAL OF CRIME IS AMUSING HIMSELF WITH A DIABOLIC GAME!
MY ARM'S GETTING HEAVY... I'M GONNA MISS SOON!
I BETCHA THE BOSS MISSES THE NEXT ONE.. ON PURPOSE! HA-HA!
GIVE IT TO 'EM BOTH, NAP! THEN WE BEAT IT FOR THE TRAIL OF THE LONESOME PINES!
GO AHEAD, YOU BACK-SHOOTING RAT! YOU DON'T SCARE ME!
ALL RIGHT, STATE TROOPER! YOU GET IT FIRST!
TWO DREADED CAPED FIGURES SUDDENLY PLUMMET DOWN... WITH A STARTLING CRASH!
BATMAN! ROBIN!
SORRY WE DIDNT BRING OUR PARACHUTES! BUT...
WE BROUGHT OUR FISTS! TAKE A LITTLE NAP.. BOYD!
THE BATTLING DUO DRUMS OUT A SAVAGE SYMPHONY OF PILEDRIVER BLOWS!
ONE, TWO!
THAT'S MY CLUE!
6
I CAN'T TAKE ANY CHANCES HANGING AROUND HERE WITH THOSE TWO FIGHTING FOOLS! A SMART GENERAL KNOWS WHEN TO RETREAT!
ABRUPTLY...
CLEAR OUT, MEN!
HEY, LET'S SCRAM!
LIGHTS, ROBIN, LIGHTS!

MOMENTS LATER...

THEY'RE GONE!

LOOK.. A TRAP DOOR!

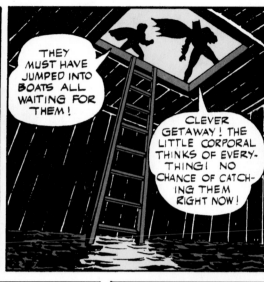

THEY MUST HAVE JUMPED INTO BOATS ALL WAITING FOR THEM!

CLEVER GETAWAY! THE LITTLE CORPORAL THINKS OF EVERYTHING! NO CHANCE OF CATCHING THEM RIGHT NOW!

AS BATMAN FREES THE O'BRIEN BROTHERS—

THANKS! YOU SAVED OUR LIVES!

YES, AND I STILL WANT TO LIVE TO GET THAT KILLER!

THESE O'BRIENS ARE TOO ANXIOUS TO AVENGE THEIR FATHER'S DEATH! BOYD'S BOUND TO GET THEM! I'LL DO SOMETHING!

LISTEN, WE ALL WANT TO GET THE LITTLE CORPORAL! HOW ABOUT YOU TWO JOINING FORCES WITH US?

I'LL BE GLAD TO WORK WITH THE BATMAN AND ROBIN BUT NOT WITH HIM!

THAT GOES FOR ME, TOO!

BATMAN SWIFTLY SENSES THE VEILED ANTAGONISM · · · · · ·

WELL, IT WOULD BE AWKWARD ANYHOW FOR ALL FOUR OF US TOGETHER! WE'LL SPLIT—TIM AND I, ROBIN AND NICK!

I SEE WHAT HE'S TRYING TO DO!

OKAY, PAL! WE'LL SEE WHICH TEAM BRINGS HIM IN!

BATMAN AND TIM HOLD A COUNCIL OF WAR TO MAKE PLANS!

ONE OF BOYD'S MEN MENTIONED "THE TRAIL OF THE LONE-SOME PINES". THERE'S A TRAILER CAMP BY THAT NAME UP-STATE ON MY OLD BEAT.

GOOD! BOYD WOULD USE A SLICK HIDE-OUT LIKE THAT!

WHILE ROBIN AND NICK PREPARE TO OPEN A SECOND FRONT!

MY UNDERWORLD CON-NECTIONS SHOULD GIVE US A LEAD TO BOYD! THERE'S ONE CROOK, "GABBY" IKE, WHO KNOWS ALL THE INSIDE TIPS!

GREAT! WE'LL SCOOP BATMAN AND TIM!

BACK IN TOWN....

WELL, SO LONG, BATMAN! WE'LL USE NICK'S CAR!

HA, HA! HE DOESN'T KNOW WE'LL SOON BE AFTER BOYD!

SO LONG, ROBIN!

WE'LL ROUND UP LITTLE NAP BEFORE THEY EVEN GET STARTED!

7

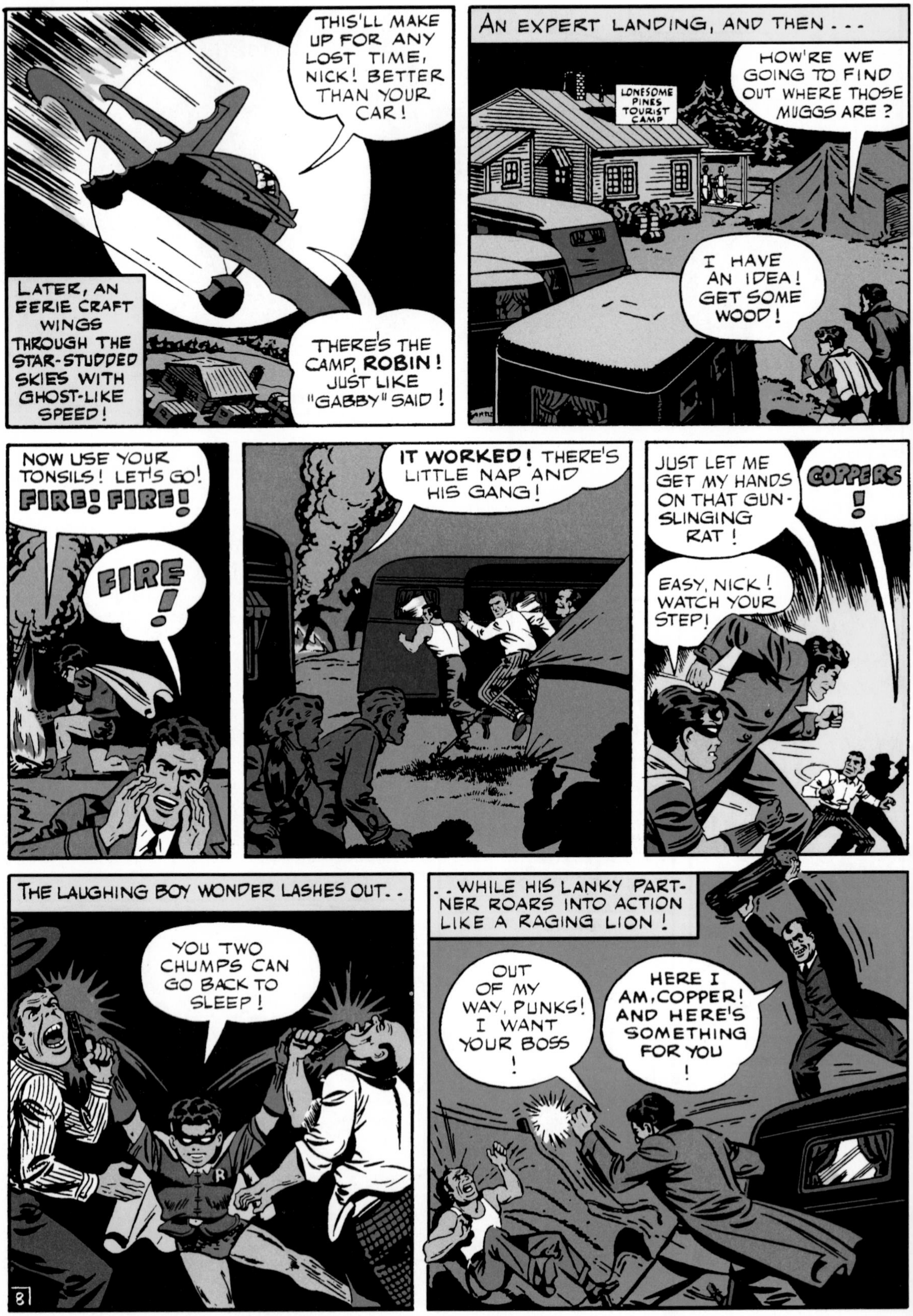
THIS'LL MAKE UP FOR ANY LOST TIME, NICK! BETTER THAN YOUR CAR!
LATER, AN EERIE CRAFT WINGS THROUGH THE STAR-STUDDED SKIES WITH GHOST-LIKE SPEED!
THERE'S THE CAMP, ROBIN! JUST LIKE "GABBY" SAID!
AN EXPERT LANDING, AND THEN . . .
LONESOME PINES TOURIST CAMP
HOW'RE WE GOING TO FIND OUT WHERE THOSE MUGGS ARE?
I HAVE AN IDEA! GET SOME WOOD!
NOW USE YOUR TONSILS! LET'S GO! FIRE! FIRE!
FIRE!
IT WORKED! THERE'S LITTLE NAP AND HIS GANG!
JUST LET ME GET MY HANDS ON THAT GUN-SLINGING RAT!
COPPERS!
EASY, NICK! WATCH YOUR STEP!
THE LAUGHING BOY WONDER LASHES OUT. .
YOU TWO CHUMPS CAN GO BACK TO SLEEP!
8
. . WHILE HIS LANKY PARTNER ROARS INTO ACTION LIKE A RAGING LION!
OUT OF MY WAY, PUNKS! I WANT YOUR BOSS!
HERE I AM, COPPER! AND HERE'S SOMETHING FOR YOU!

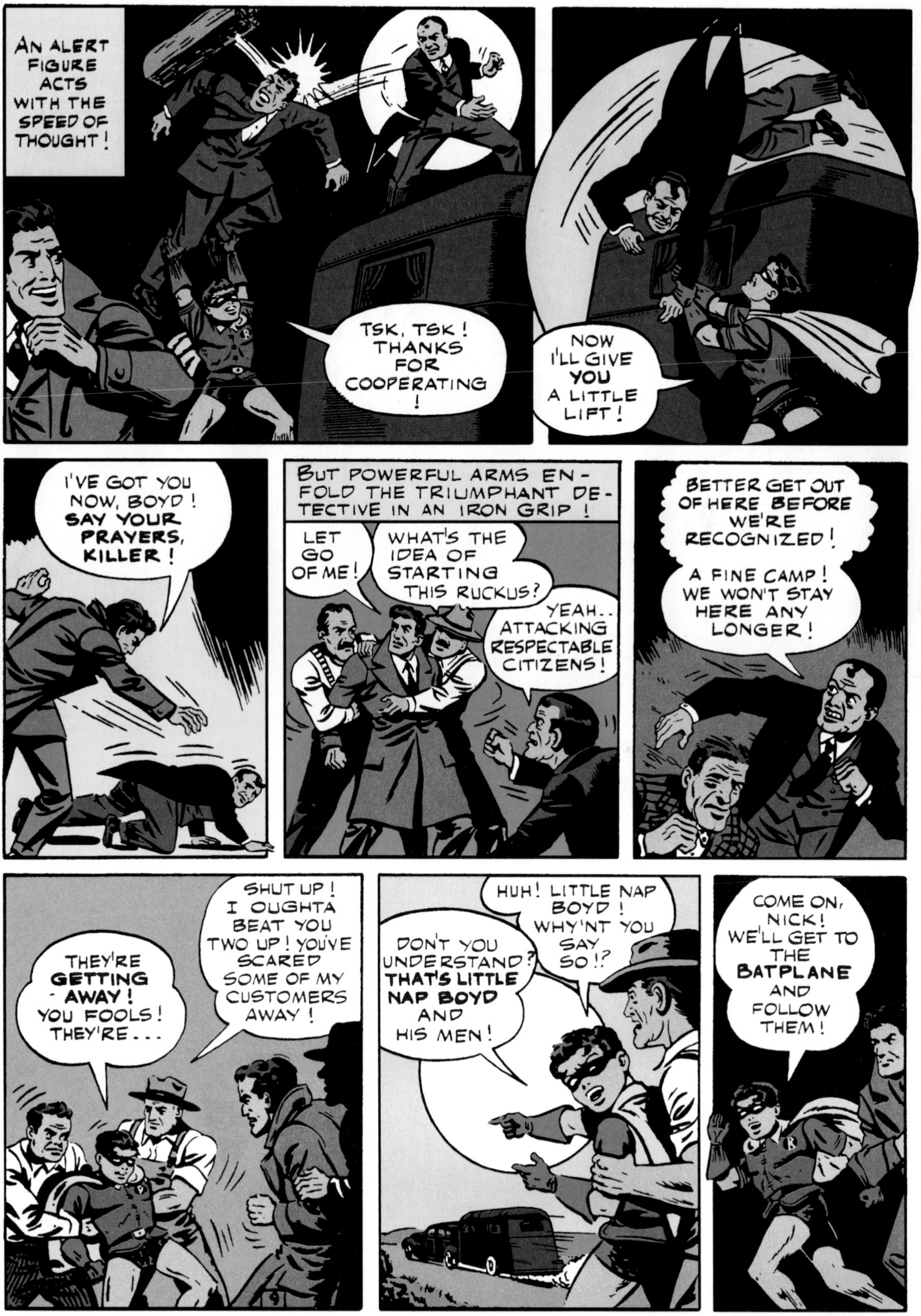

AN ALERT FIGURE ACTS WITH THE SPEED OF THOUGHT!
TSK, TSK! THANKS FOR COOPERATING!
NOW I'LL GIVE **YOU** A LITTLE LIFT!
I'VE GOT YOU NOW, BOYD! **SAY YOUR PRAYERS, KILLER!**
BUT POWERFUL ARMS ENFOLD THE TRIUMPHANT DETECTIVE IN AN IRON GRIP!
LET GO OF ME!
WHAT'S THE IDEA OF STARTING THIS RUCKUS?
YEAH.. ATTACKING RESPECTABLE CITIZENS!
BETTER GET OUT OF HERE **BEFORE** WE'RE RECOGNIZED!
A FINE CAMP! WE WON'T STAY HERE ANY LONGER!
THEY'RE **GETTING AWAY!** YOU FOOLS! THEY'RE...
SHUT UP! I OUGHTA BEAT YOU TWO UP! YOU'VE SCARED SOME OF MY CUSTOMERS AWAY!
DON'T YOU UNDERSTAND? **THAT'S LITTLE NAP BOYD** AND HIS MEN!
HUH! LITTLE NAP BOYD! WHY'NT YOU SAY SO!?
COME ON, NICK! WE'LL GET TO THE **BATPLANE** AND FOLLOW THEM!

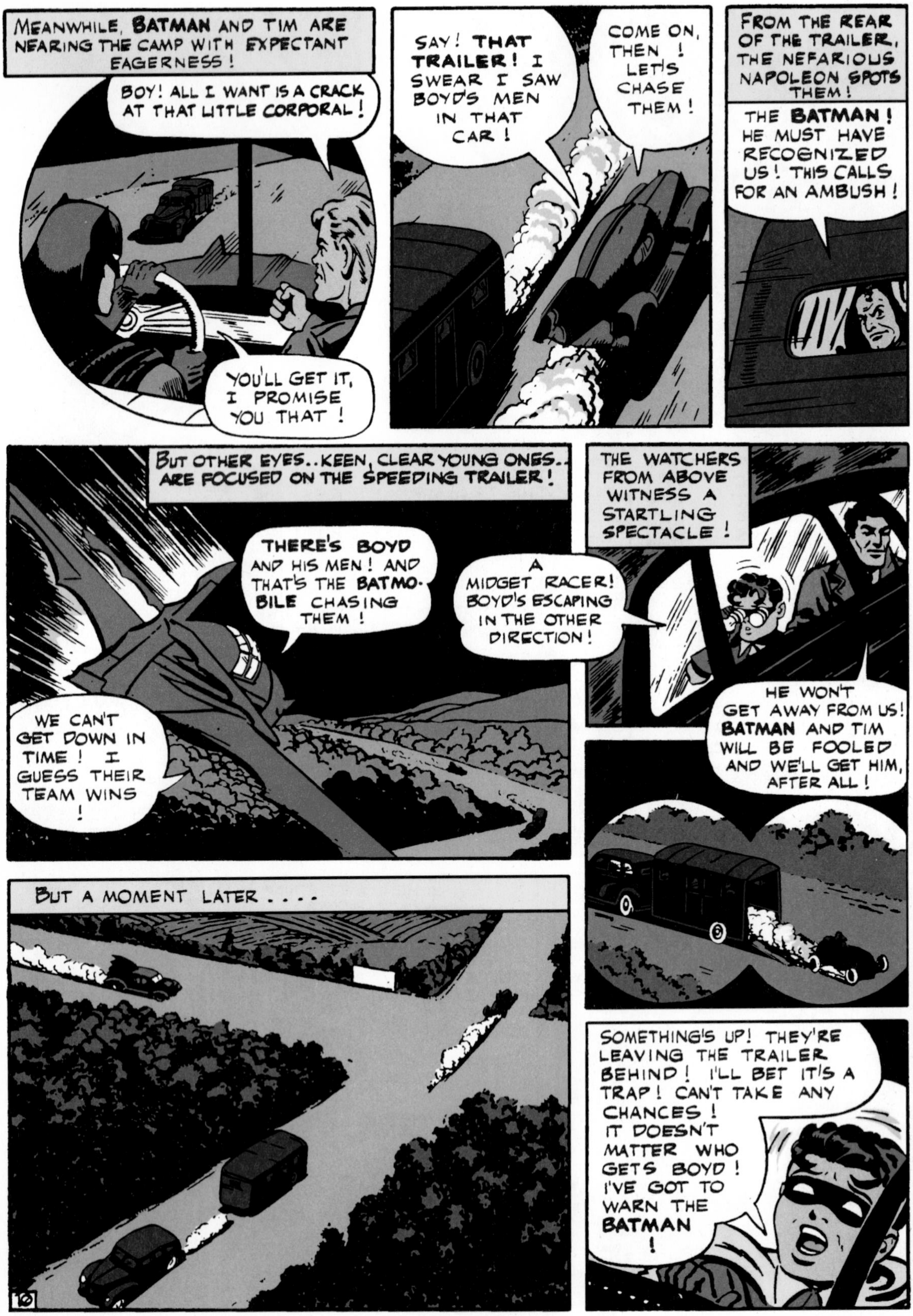
MEANWHILE, BATMAN AND TIM ARE NEARING THE CAMP WITH EXPECTANT EAGERNESS!
BOY! ALL I WANT IS A CRACK AT THAT LITTLE CORPORAL!
YOU'LL GET IT, I PROMISE YOU THAT!
SAY! THAT TRAILER! I SWEAR I SAW BOYD'S MEN IN THAT CAR!
COME ON, THEN! LET'S CHASE THEM!
FROM THE REAR OF THE TRAILER, THE NEFARIOUS NAPOLEON SPOTS THEM!
THE BATMAN! HE MUST HAVE RECOGNIZED US! THIS CALLS FOR AN AMBUSH!
BUT OTHER EYES..KEEN, CLEAR YOUNG ONES.. ARE FOCUSED ON THE SPEEDING TRAILER!
THERE'S BOYD AND HIS MEN! AND THAT'S THE BATMOBILE CHASING THEM!
WE CAN'T GET DOWN IN TIME! I GUESS THEIR TEAM WINS!
THE WATCHERS FROM ABOVE WITNESS A STARTLING SPECTACLE!
A MIDGET RACER! BOYD'S ESCAPING IN THE OTHER DIRECTION!
HE WON'T GET AWAY FROM US! BATMAN AND TIM WILL BE FOOLED AND WE'LL GET HIM, AFTER ALL!
BUT A MOMENT LATER....
10
SOMETHING'S UP! THEY'RE LEAVING THE TRAILER BEHIND! I'LL BET IT'S A TRAP! CAN'T TAKE ANY CHANCES! IT DOESN'T MATTER WHO GETS BOYD! I'VE GOT TO WARN THE BATMAN!

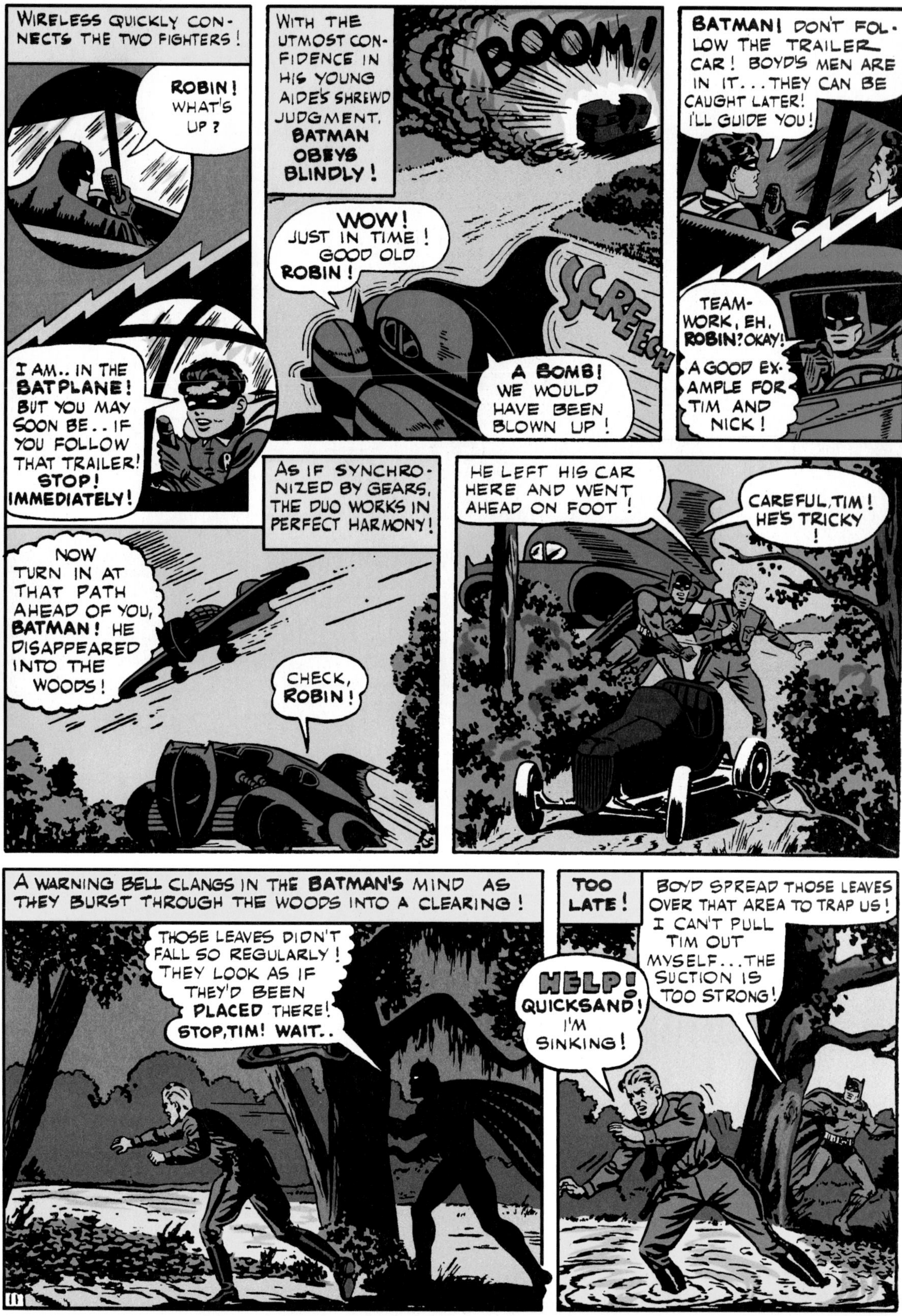
WIRELESS QUICKLY CONNECTS THE TWO FIGHTERS!
ROBIN! WHAT'S UP?
I AM.. IN THE BATPLANE! BUT YOU MAY SOON BE.. IF YOU FOLLOW THAT TRAILER! STOP! IMMEDIATELY!
WITH THE UTMOST CONFIDENCE IN HIS YOUNG AIDE'S SHREWD JUDGMENT, BATMAN OBEYS BLINDLY!
BOOM!
WOW! JUST IN TIME! GOOD OLD ROBIN!
SCREEECH
A BOMB! WE WOULD HAVE BEEN BLOWN UP!
BATMAN! DON'T FOLLOW THE TRAILER CAR! BOYD'S MEN ARE IN IT...THEY CAN BE CAUGHT LATER! I'LL GUIDE YOU!
TEAMWORK, EH, ROBIN? OKAY! A GOOD EXAMPLE FOR TIM AND NICK!
AS IF SYNCHRONIZED BY GEARS, THE DUO WORKS IN PERFECT HARMONY!
NOW TURN IN AT THAT PATH AHEAD OF YOU, BATMAN! HE DISAPPEARED INTO THE WOODS!
CHECK, ROBIN!
HE LEFT HIS CAR HERE AND WENT AHEAD ON FOOT!
CAREFUL, TIM! HE'S TRICKY!
A WARNING BELL CLANGS IN THE BATMAN'S MIND AS THEY BURST THROUGH THE WOODS INTO A CLEARING!
THOSE LEAVES DIDN'T FALL SO REGULARLY! THEY LOOK AS IF THEY'D BEEN PLACED THERE! STOP, TIM! WAIT..
11
TOO LATE!
HELP! QUICKSAND! I'M SINKING!
BOYD SPREAD THOSE LEAVES OVER THAT AREA TO TRAP US! I CAN'T PULL TIM OUT MYSELF...THE SUCTION IS TOO STRONG!

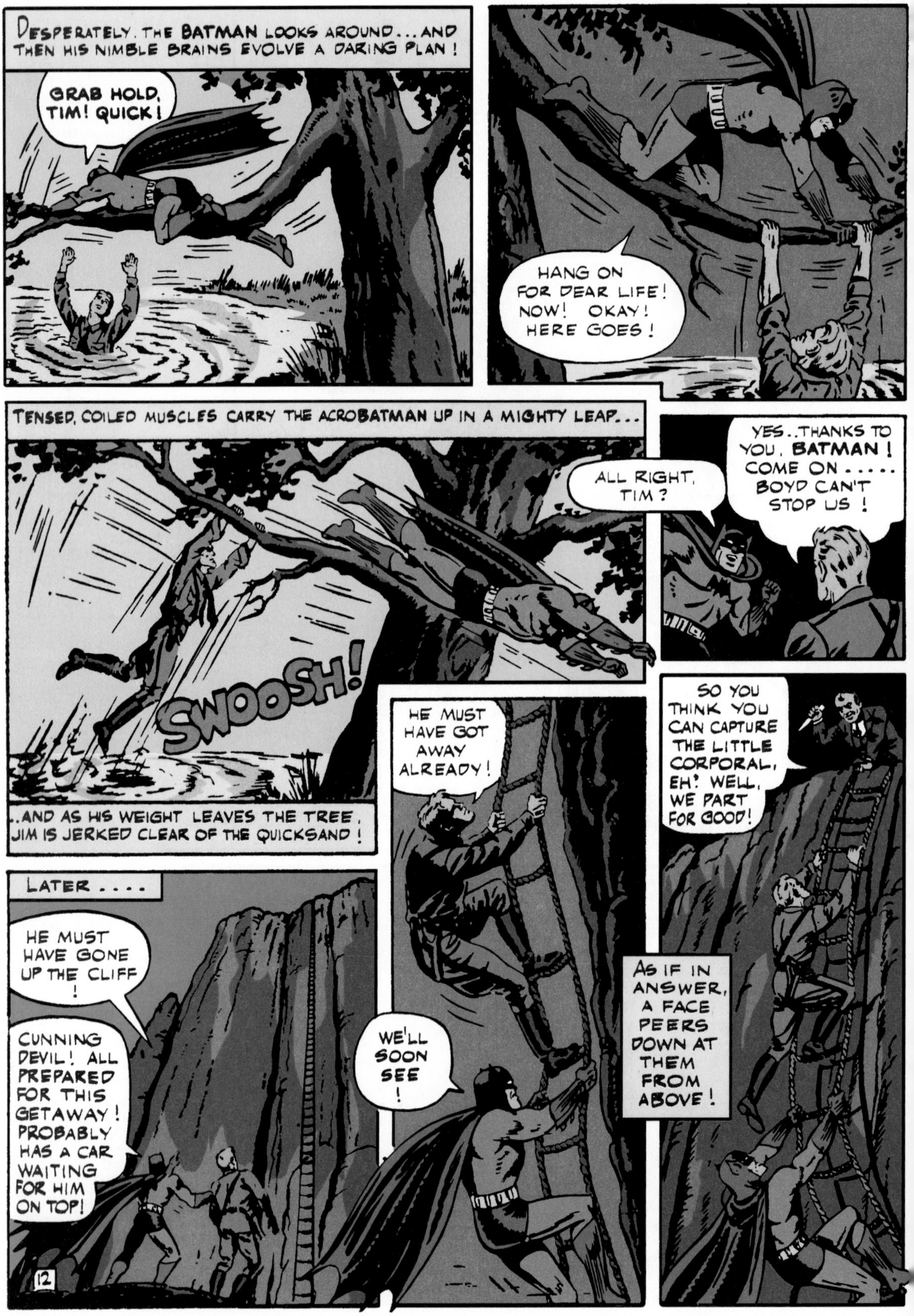
DESPERATELY, THE BATMAN LOOKS AROUND... AND THEN HIS NIMBLE BRAINS EVOLVE A DARING PLAN!
GRAB HOLD, TIM! QUICK!
HANG ON FOR DEAR LIFE! NOW! OKAY! HERE GOES!
TENSED, COILED MUSCLES CARRY THE ACROBATMAN UP IN A MIGHTY LEAP...
SWOOSH!
..AND AS HIS WEIGHT LEAVES THE TREE, JIM IS JERKED CLEAR OF THE QUICKSAND!
ALL RIGHT, TIM?
YES..THANKS TO YOU, BATMAN! COME ON..... BOYD CAN'T STOP US!
LATER....
HE MUST HAVE GONE UP THE CLIFF!
CUNNING DEVIL! ALL PREPARED FOR THIS GETAWAY! PROBABLY HAS A CAR WAITING FOR HIM ON TOP!
12
HE MUST HAVE GOT AWAY ALREADY!
WE'LL SOON SEE!
SO YOU THINK YOU CAN CAPTURE THE LITTLE CORPORAL, EH? WELL, WE PART FOR GOOD!
AS IF IN ANSWER, A FACE PEERS DOWN AT THEM FROM ABOVE!

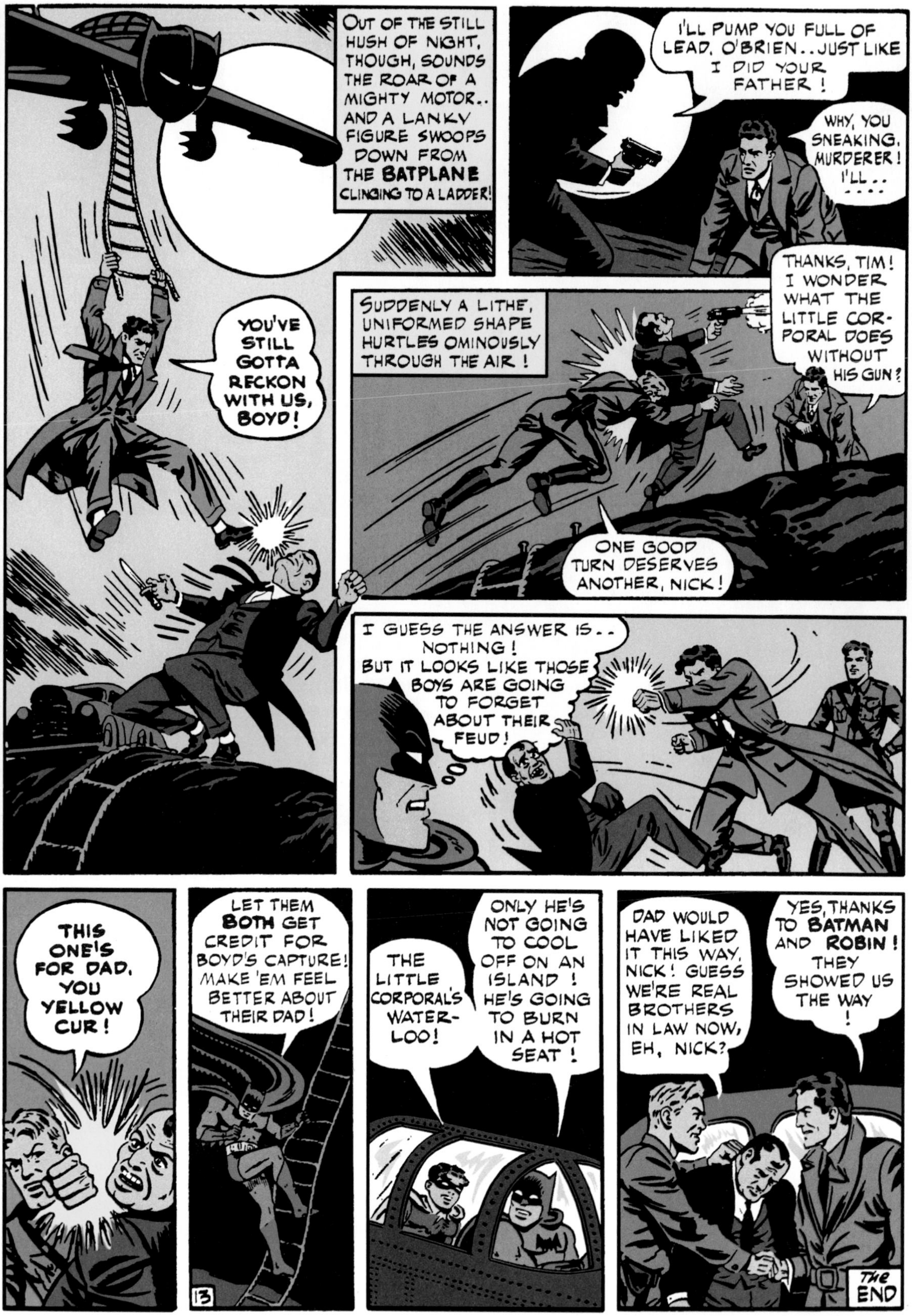
OUT OF THE STILL HUSH OF NIGHT, THOUGH, SOUNDS THE ROAR OF A MIGHTY MOTOR.. AND A LANKY FIGURE SWOOPS DOWN FROM THE BATPLANE CLINGING TO A LADDER!
YOU'VE STILL GOTTA RECKON WITH US, BOYD!
I'LL PUMP YOU FULL OF LEAD, O'BRIEN.. JUST LIKE I DID YOUR FATHER!
WHY, YOU SNEAKING, MURDERER! I'LL.. ....
SUDDENLY A LITHE, UNIFORMED SHAPE HURTLES OMINOUSLY THROUGH THE AIR!
THANKS, TIM! I WONDER WHAT THE LITTLE CORPORAL DOES WITHOUT HIS GUN?
ONE GOOD TURN DESERVES ANOTHER, NICK!
I GUESS THE ANSWER IS.. NOTHING! BUT IT LOOKS LIKE THOSE BOYS ARE GOING TO FORGET ABOUT THEIR FEUD!
THIS ONE'S FOR DAD, YOU YELLOW CUR!
LET THEM BOTH GET CREDIT FOR BOYD'S CAPTURE! MAKE 'EM FEEL BETTER ABOUT THEIR DAD!
13
THE LITTLE CORPORAL'S WATER-LOO!
ONLY HE'S NOT GOING TO COOL OFF ON AN ISLAND! HE'S GOING TO BURN IN A HOT SEAT!
DAD WOULD HAVE LIKED IT THIS WAY, NICK! GUESS WE'RE REAL BROTHERS IN LAW NOW, EH, NICK?
YES, THANKS TO BATMAN AND ROBIN! THEY SHOWED US THE WAY!
THE END

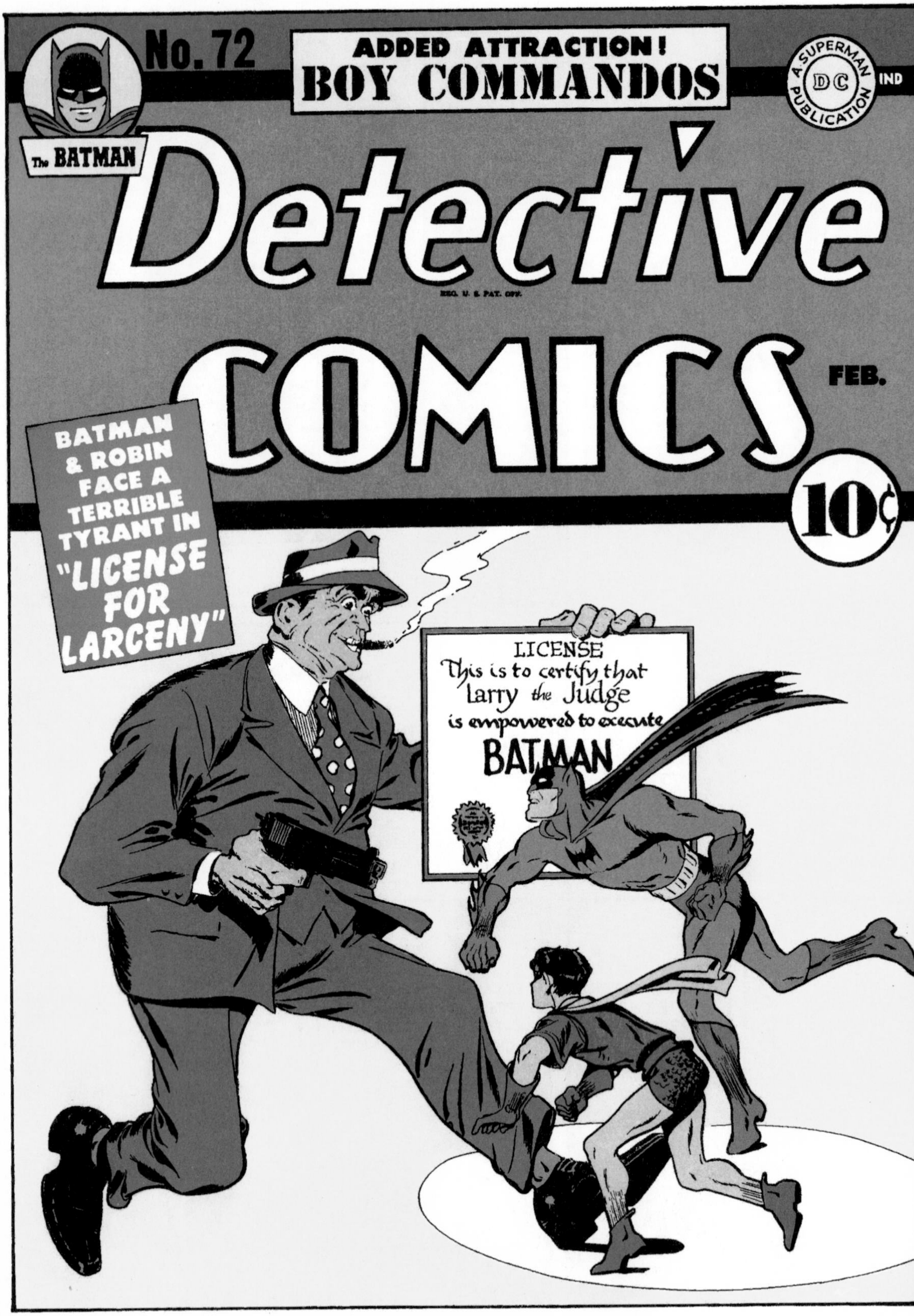
No. 72
ADDED ATTRACTION!
BOY COMMANDOS
A SUPERMAN DC PUBLICATION
IND
The BATMAN
Detective
REG. U. S. PAT. OFF.
COMICS
FEB.
10¢
BATMAN & ROBIN FACE A TERRIBLE TYRANT IN "LICENSE FOR LARCENY"
LICENSE
This is to certify that
larry the Judge
is empowered to execute
BATMAN

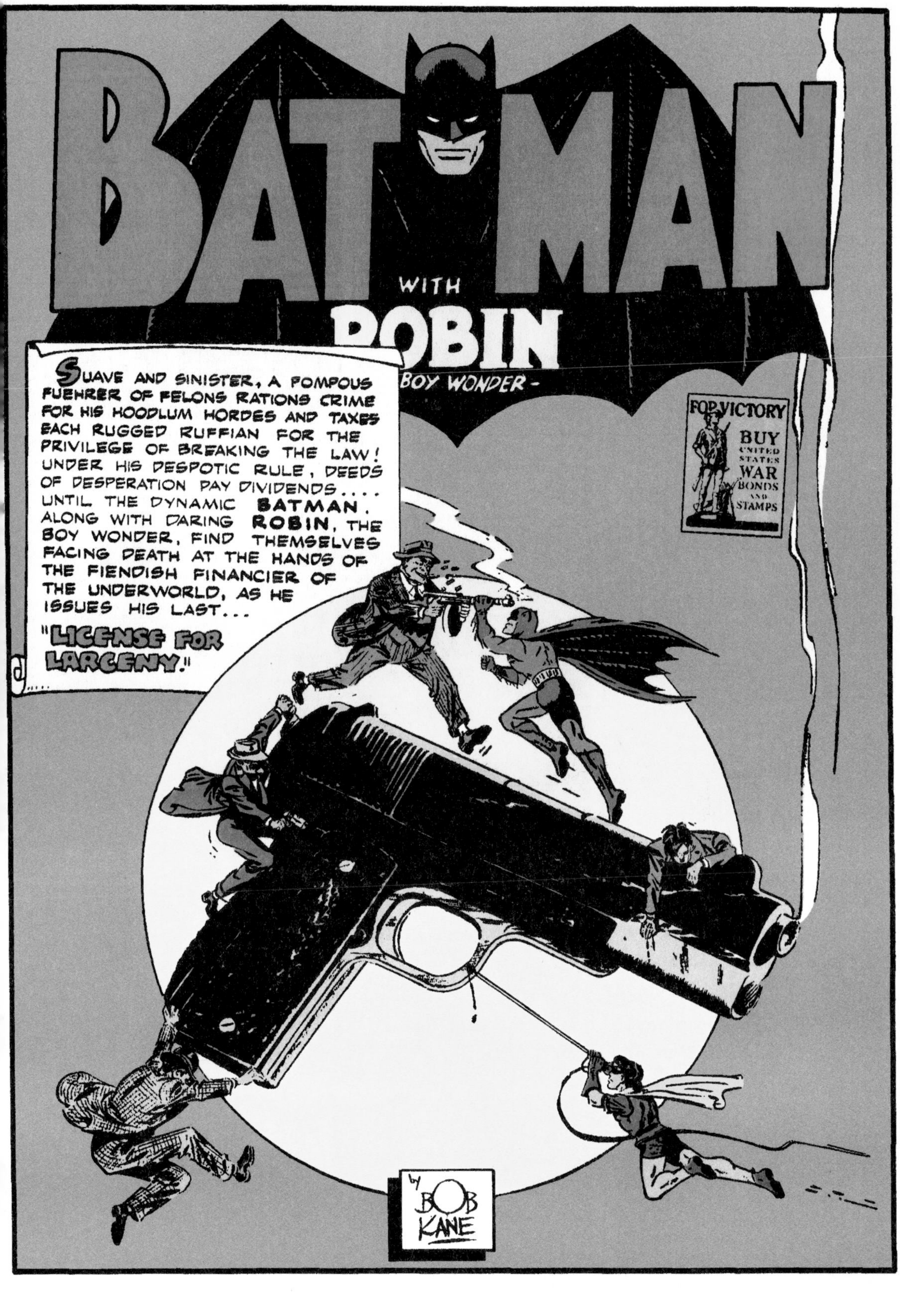
BATMAN
WITH
ROBIN
THE BOY WONDER-
SUAVE AND SINISTER, A POMPOUS FUEHRER OF FELONS RATIONS CRIME FOR HIS HOODLUM HORDES AND TAXES EACH RUGGED RUFFIAN FOR THE PRIVILEGE OF BREAKING THE LAW! UNDER HIS DESPOTIC RULE, DEEDS OF DESPERATION PAY DIVIDENDS.... UNTIL THE DYNAMIC BATMAN, ALONG WITH DARING ROBIN, THE BOY WONDER, FIND THEMSELVES FACING DEATH AT THE HANDS OF THE FIENDISH FINANCIER OF THE UNDERWORLD, AS HE ISSUES HIS LAST...
"LICENSE FOR LARCENY!"
FOR VICTORY
BUY
UNITED STATES
WAR
BONDS
AND
STAMPS
by BOB KANE

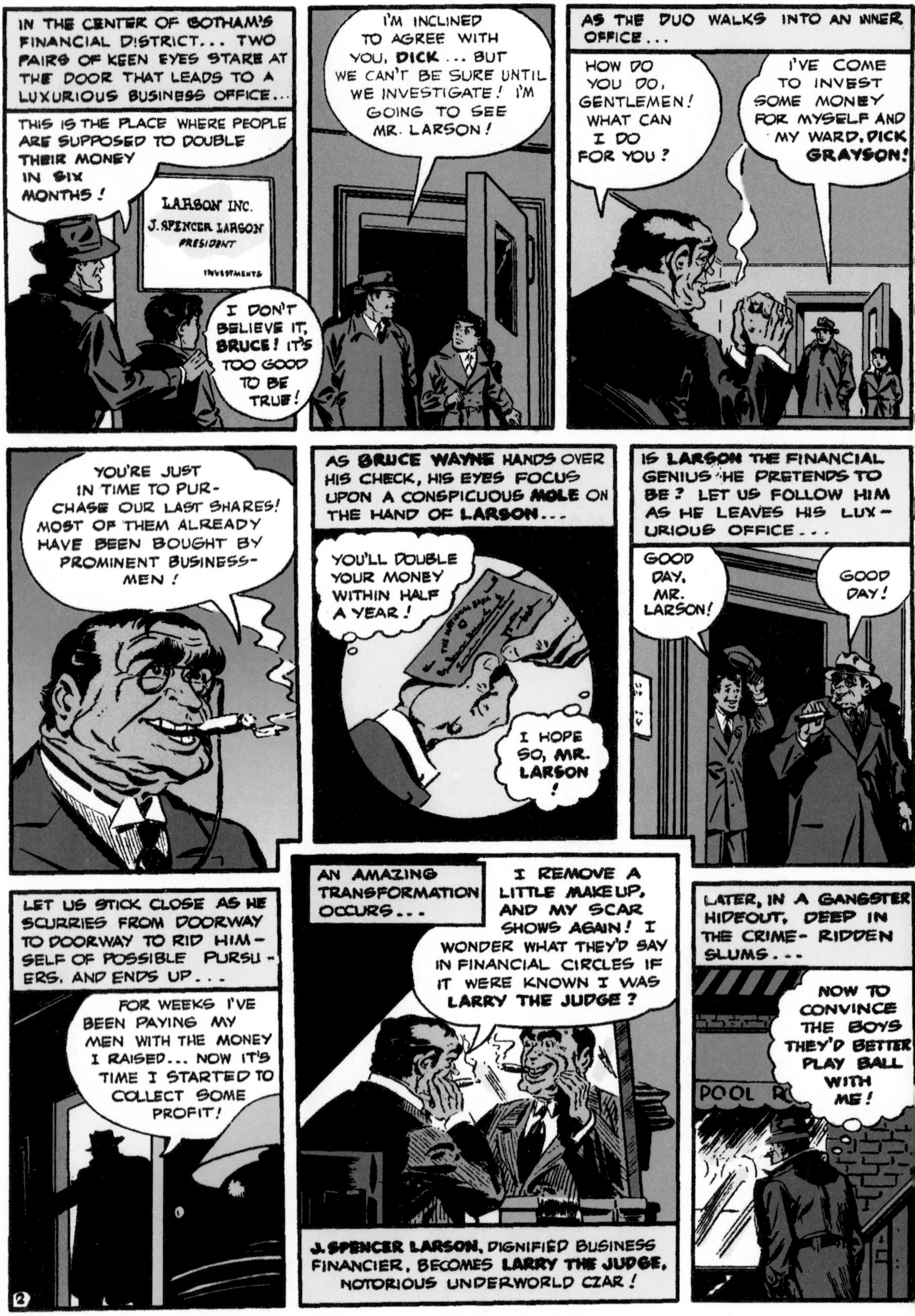
IN THE CENTER OF GOTHAM'S FINANCIAL DISTRICT... TWO PAIRS OF KEEN EYES STARE AT THE DOOR THAT LEADS TO A LUXURIOUS BUSINESS OFFICE...
THIS IS THE PLACE WHERE PEOPLE ARE SUPPOSED TO DOUBLE THEIR MONEY IN SIX MONTHS!
LARSON INC.
J. SPENCER LARSON
PRESIDENT
INVESTMENTS
I DON'T BELIEVE IT, BRUCE! IT'S TOO GOOD TO BE TRUE!
I'M INCLINED TO AGREE WITH YOU, DICK... BUT WE CAN'T BE SURE UNTIL WE INVESTIGATE! I'M GOING TO SEE MR. LARSON!
AS THE DUO WALKS INTO AN INNER OFFICE...
HOW DO YOU DO, GENTLEMEN! WHAT CAN I DO FOR YOU?
I'VE COME TO INVEST SOME MONEY FOR MYSELF AND MY WARD, DICK GRAYSON!
YOU'RE JUST IN TIME TO PURCHASE OUR LAST SHARES! MOST OF THEM ALREADY HAVE BEEN BOUGHT BY PROMINENT BUSINESSMEN!
AS BRUCE WAYNE HANDS OVER HIS CHECK, HIS EYES FOCUS UPON A CONSPICUOUS MOLE ON THE HAND OF LARSON...
YOU'LL DOUBLE YOUR MONEY WITHIN HALF A YEAR!
I HOPE SO, MR. LARSON!
IS LARSON THE FINANCIAL GENIUS HE PRETENDS TO BE? LET US FOLLOW HIM AS HE LEAVES HIS LUXURIOUS OFFICE...
GOOD DAY, MR. LARSON!
GOOD DAY!
LET US STICK CLOSE AS HE SCURRIES FROM DOORWAY TO DOORWAY TO RID HIMSELF OF POSSIBLE PURSUERS, AND ENDS UP...
FOR WEEKS I'VE BEEN PAYING MY MEN WITH THE MONEY I RAISED... NOW IT'S TIME I STARTED TO COLLECT SOME PROFIT!
2
AN AMAZING TRANSFORMATION OCCURS...
I REMOVE A LITTLE MAKEUP, AND MY SCAR SHOWS AGAIN! I WONDER WHAT THEY'D SAY IN FINANCIAL CIRCLES IF IT WERE KNOWN I WAS LARRY THE JUDGE?
J. SPENCER LARSON, DIGNIFIED BUSINESS FINANCIER, BECOMES LARRY THE JUDGE, NOTORIOUS UNDERWORLD CZAR!
LATER, IN A GANGSTER HIDEOUT, DEEP IN THE CRIME-RIDDEN SLUMS...
POOL R
NOW TO CONVINCE THE BOYS THEY'D BETTER PLAY BALL WITH ME!

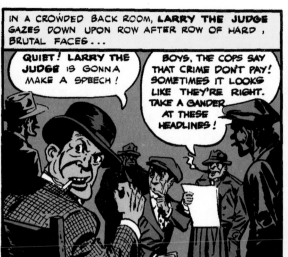

IN A CROWDED BACK ROOM, **LARRY THE JUDGE** GAZES DOWN UPON ROW AFTER ROW OF HARD, BRUTAL FACES...

QUIET! LARRY THE JUDGE IS GONNA MAKE A SPEECH!

BOYS, THE COPS SAY THAT CRIME DON'T PAY! SOMETIMES IT LOOKS LIKE THEY'RE RIGHT. TAKE A GANDER AT THESE HEADLINES!

YOU WORK HARD AND WHAT DO YOU GET? NOTHIN'!

THIEVES ROB FILLING STATION - SAFE EMPTY

HOLD-UP MAN GETS FEW COINS FROM WEALTHY VICTIM

BANK ROBBERS GET THOUSANDS IN CHECKS THEY CANNOT CASH

SAN FRANCISCO & CHRONICLE

COMPETITION IS KILLIN' BUSINESS! IT'S GOTTA STOP! SO... FROM NOW ON **NOBODY** PULLS A JOB UNLESS I GIVE HIM A LICENSE TO DO IT!

SUDDENLY...

YEAH? WHO'S GONNA STOP US FROM CHOOSIN' OUR OWN JOBS?

THAT'S A GOOD QUESTION, SECOND-STORY SAM!

THE ANSWER IS... MY MEN! I PAY THEM TO TAKE MY ORDERS! ANY MORE QUESTIONS?

A CHILL SILENCE FILLS THE ROOM... AND THEN...

IT'S FOR YOUR OWN GOOD, BOYS! YOU'LL MAKE MORE DOUGH! NO PETTY CRIMES THAT DON'T PAY! ONLY HIGH-CLASS LARCENIES!

OKAY! WE'RE WITH YOU, BOSS!

AND IN THE DAYS THAT FOLLOW...

I WANTA LICENSE TO HOLD UP A CANDY STORE BY AN OLD GUY! I CAN KNOCK OFF THE PLACE EASY!

NO, PAL, THERE'S NO DOUGH IN CANDY STORES. YOU'LL ROB A THEATRE BOX OFFICE TOMORROW NIGHT! THERE'LL BE TEN GRAND IN THE HOUSE... BUT, REMEMBER, I GET MY CUT!

JUDGE, I'M A DIP! I WANTA FRISK THE CROWD IN A SUBWAY TRAIN!

THERE AIN'T NO DOUGH IN THAT! BUT HERE'S SOMETHING TO SUIT YOUR TOUCH - A LICENSE TO ROB A BANKER! HE'S GONNA HAVE FIVE GRAND ON HIM! BUT DON'T FORGET I GET MY SHARE!

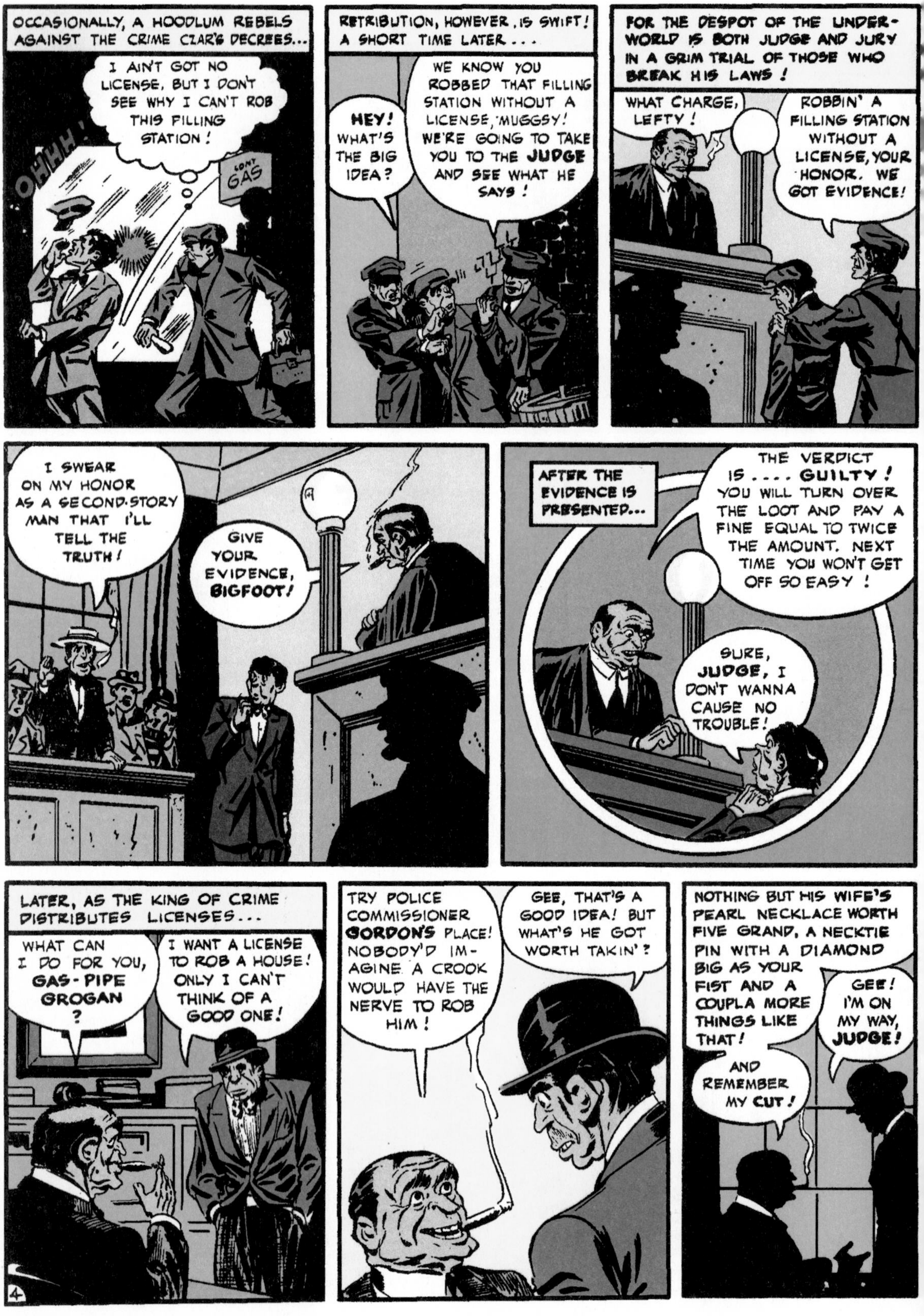
OCCASIONALLY, A HOODLUM REBELS AGAINST THE CRIME CZAR'S DECREES...
I AIN'T GOT NO LICENSE, BUT I DON'T SEE WHY I CAN'T ROB THIS FILLING STATION!
OHHH!
GAS
RETRIBUTION, HOWEVER, IS SWIFT! A SHORT TIME LATER...
HEY! WHAT'S THE BIG IDEA?
WE KNOW YOU ROBBED THAT FILLING STATION WITHOUT A LICENSE, MUGGSY! WE'RE GOING TO TAKE YOU TO THE JUDGE AND SEE WHAT HE SAYS!
FOR THE DESPOT OF THE UNDERWORLD IS BOTH JUDGE AND JURY IN A GRIM TRIAL OF THOSE WHO BREAK HIS LAWS!
WHAT CHARGE, LEFTY!
ROBBIN' A FILLING STATION WITHOUT A LICENSE, YOUR HONOR. WE GOT EVIDENCE!
I SWEAR ON MY HONOR AS A SECOND-STORY MAN THAT I'LL TELL THE TRUTH!
GIVE YOUR EVIDENCE, BIGFOOT!
AFTER THE EVIDENCE IS PRESENTED...
THE VERDICT IS.... GUILTY! YOU WILL TURN OVER THE LOOT AND PAY A FINE EQUAL TO TWICE THE AMOUNT. NEXT TIME YOU WON'T GET OFF SO EASY!
SURE, JUDGE, I DON'T WANNA CAUSE NO TROUBLE!
LATER, AS THE KING OF CRIME DISTRIBUTES LICENSES...
WHAT CAN I DO FOR YOU, GAS-PIPE GROGAN?
I WANT A LICENSE TO ROB A HOUSE! ONLY I CAN'T THINK OF A GOOD ONE!
TRY POLICE COMMISSIONER GORDON'S PLACE! NOBODY'D IMAGINE A CROOK WOULD HAVE THE NERVE TO ROB HIM!
GEE, THAT'S A GOOD IDEA! BUT WHAT'S HE GOT WORTH TAKIN'?
NOTHING BUT HIS WIFE'S PEARL NECKLACE WORTH FIVE GRAND, A NECKTIE PIN WITH A DIAMOND BIG AS YOUR FIST AND A COUPLA MORE THINGS LIKE THAT!
GEE! I'M ON MY WAY, JUDGE!
AND REMEMBER MY CUT!
4

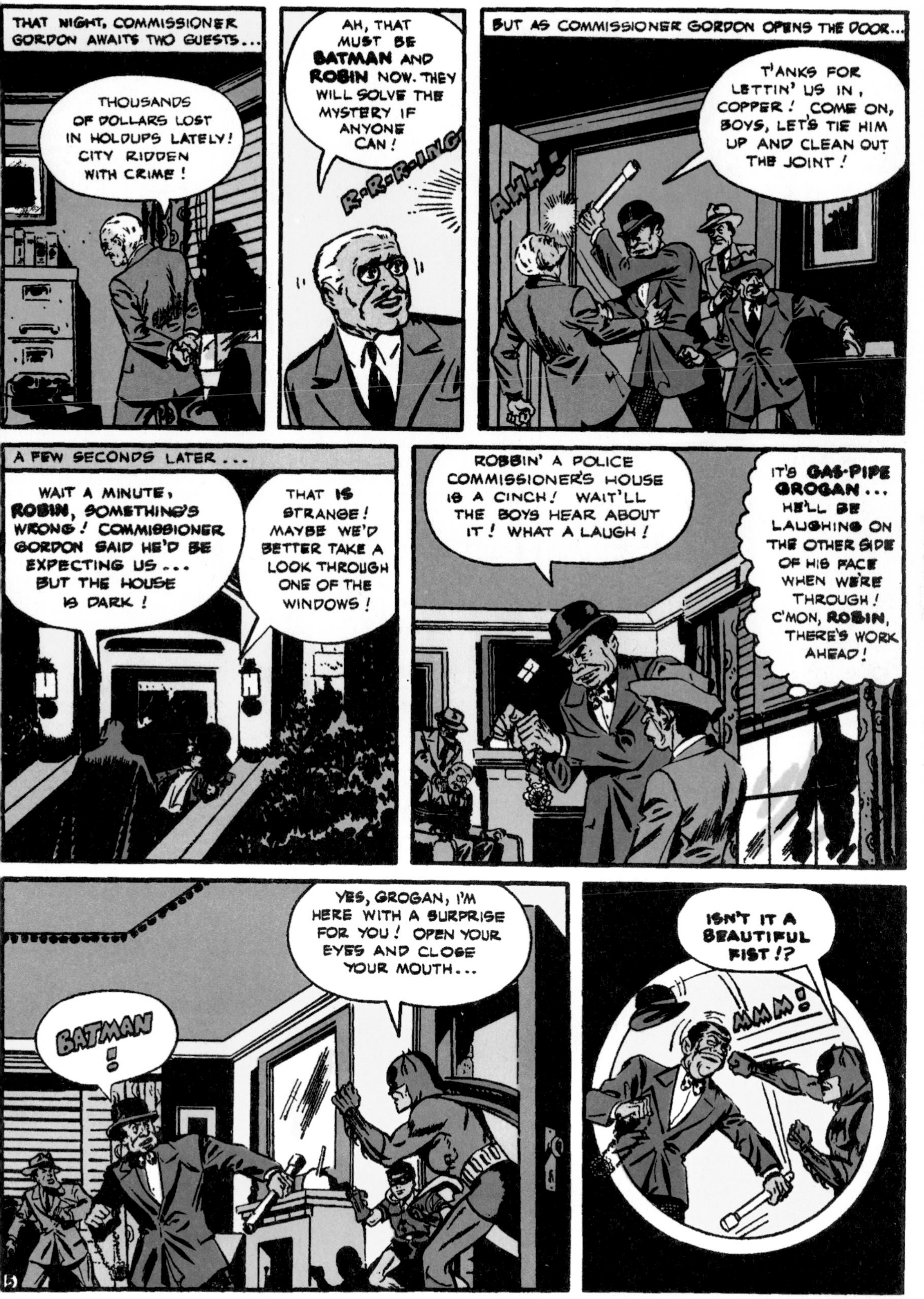
THAT NIGHT, COMMISSIONER GORDON AWAITS TWO GUESTS...
THOUSANDS OF DOLLARS LOST IN HOLDUPS LATELY! CITY RIDDEN WITH CRIME!
AH, THAT MUST BE BATMAN AND ROBIN NOW. THEY WILL SOLVE THE MYSTERY IF ANYONE CAN!
R-R-R-I-N-G!
BUT AS COMMISSIONER GORDON OPENS THE DOOR...
T'ANKS FOR LETTIN' US IN, COPPER! COME ON, BOYS, LET'S TIE HIM UP AND CLEAN OUT THE JOINT!
AHH!
A FEW SECONDS LATER...
WAIT A MINUTE, ROBIN, SOMETHING'S WRONG! COMMISSIONER GORDON SAID HE'D BE EXPECTING US... BUT THE HOUSE IS DARK!
THAT IS STRANGE! MAYBE WE'D BETTER TAKE A LOOK THROUGH ONE OF THE WINDOWS!
ROBBIN' A POLICE COMMISSIONER'S HOUSE IS A CINCH! WAIT'LL THE BOYS HEAR ABOUT IT! WHAT A LAUGH!
IT'S GAS-PIPE GROGAN... HE'LL BE LAUGHING ON THE OTHER SIDE OF HIS FACE WHEN WE'RE THROUGH! C'MON, ROBIN, THERE'S WORK AHEAD!
YES, GROGAN, I'M HERE WITH A SURPRISE FOR YOU! OPEN YOUR EYES AND CLOSE YOUR MOUTH...
BATMAN!
5
ISN'T IT A BEAUTIFUL FIST!?
MMM!

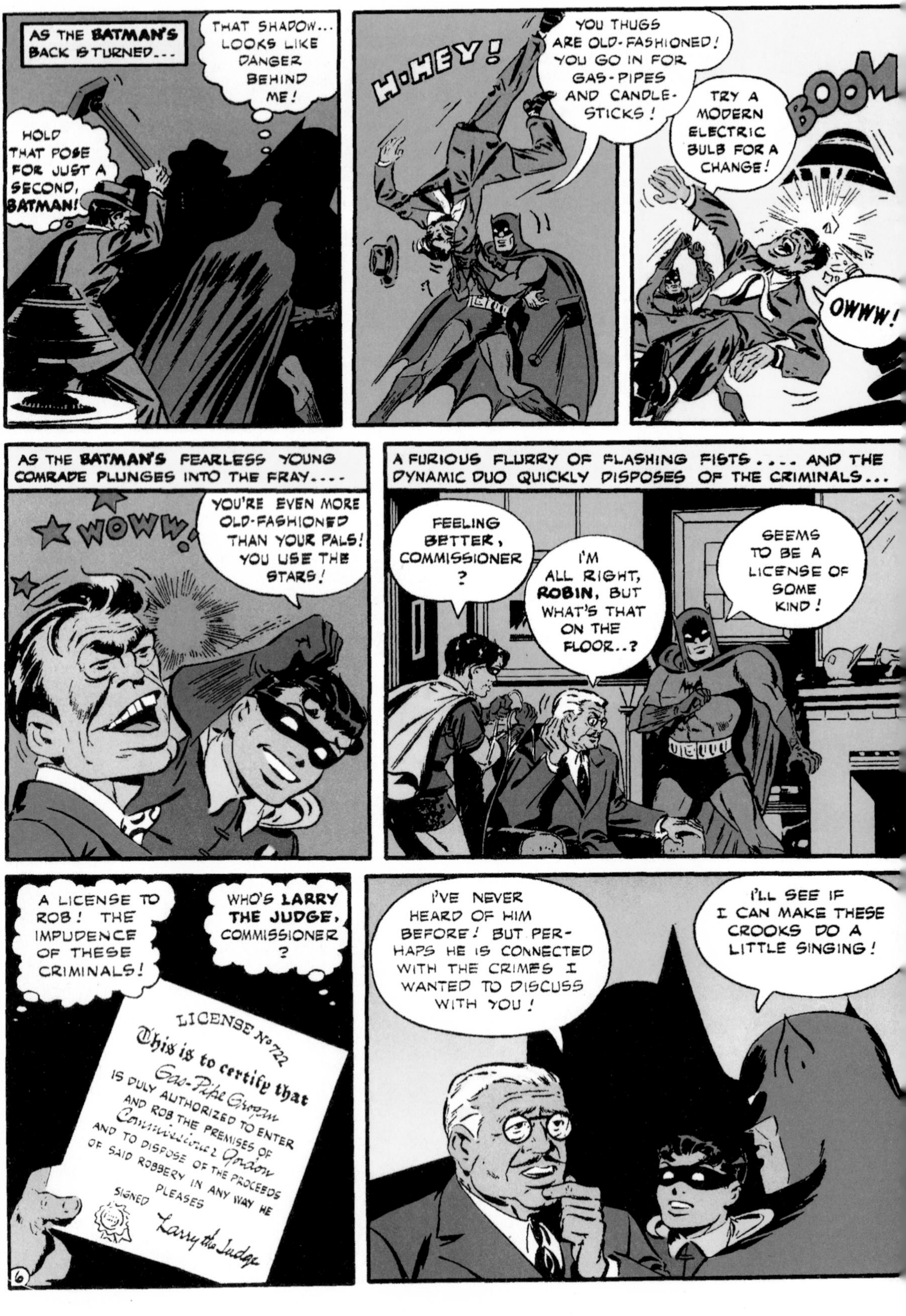
AS THE BATMAN'S BACK IS TURNED...
THAT SHADOW... LOOKS LIKE DANGER BEHIND ME!
HOLD THAT POSE FOR JUST A SECOND, BATMAN!
H-HEY!
YOU THUGS ARE OLD-FASHIONED! YOU GO IN FOR GAS-PIPES AND CANDLE-STICKS!
TRY A MODERN ELECTRIC BULB FOR A CHANGE!
BOOM
OWWW!
AS THE BATMAN'S FEARLESS YOUNG COMRADE PLUNGES INTO THE FRAY....
WOWW!
YOU'RE EVEN MORE OLD-FASHIONED THAN YOUR PALS! YOU USE THE STARS!
A FURIOUS FLURRY OF FLASHING FISTS.... AND THE DYNAMIC DUO QUICKLY DISPOSES OF THE CRIMINALS...
FEELING BETTER, COMMISSIONER ?
I'M ALL RIGHT, ROBIN, BUT WHAT'S THAT ON THE FLOOR..?
SEEMS TO BE A LICENSE OF SOME KIND!
A LICENSE TO ROB! THE IMPUDENCE OF THESE CRIMINALS!
WHO'S LARRY THE JUDGE, COMMISSIONER ?
LICENSE No 722
This is to certify that
Gas-Pipe Gropin
IS DULY AUTHORIZED TO ENTER AND ROB THE PREMISES OF
Commissioner Gordon
AND TO DISPOSE OF THE PROCEEDS OF SAID ROBBERY IN ANY WAY HE PLEASES
SIGNED
Larry the Judge
6
I'VE NEVER HEARD OF HIM BEFORE! BUT PERHAPS HE IS CONNECTED WITH THE CRIMES I WANTED TO DISCUSS WITH YOU!
I'LL SEE IF I CAN MAKE THESE CROOKS DO A LITTLE SINGING!

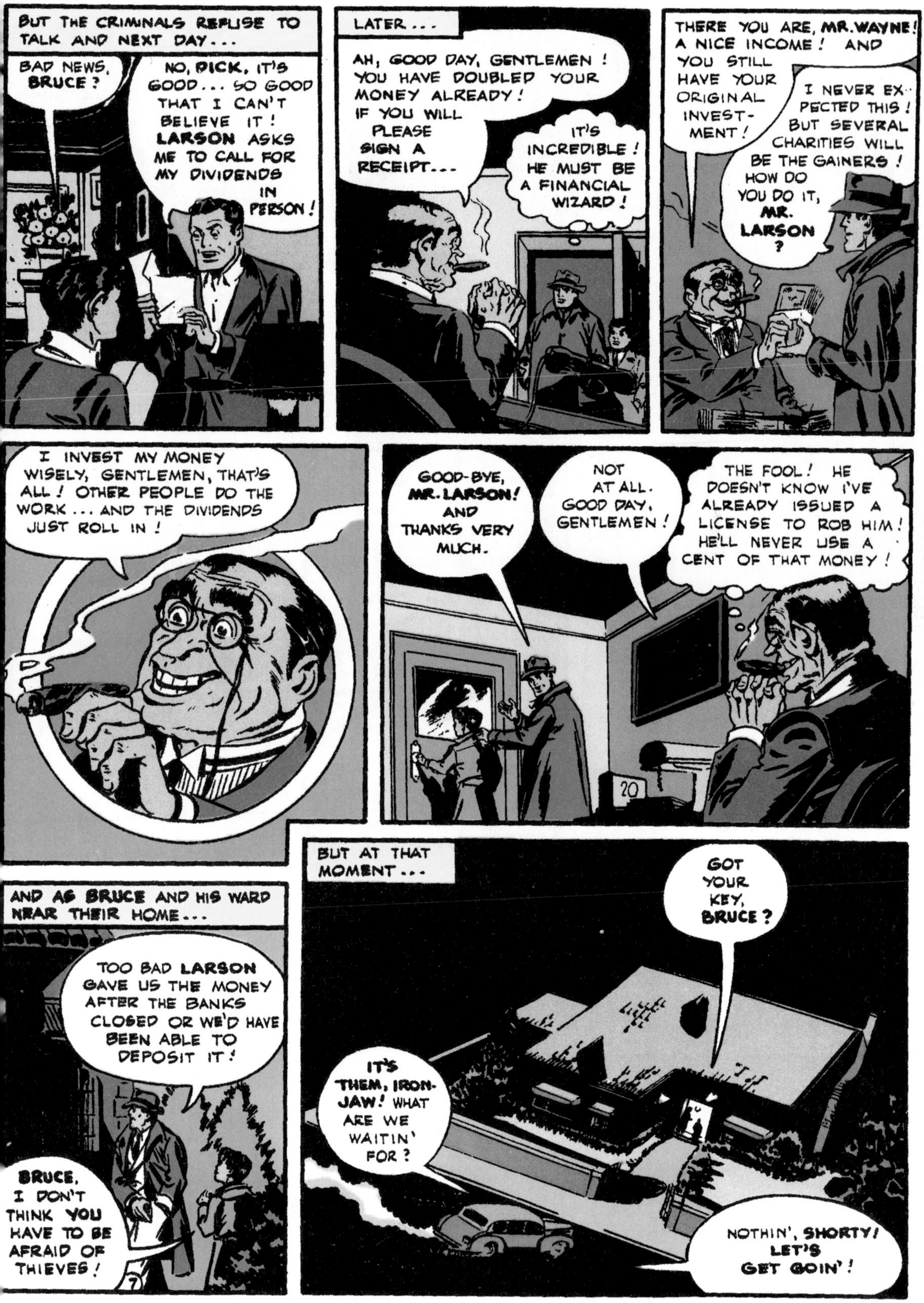
BUT THE CRIMINALS REFUSE TO TALK AND NEXT DAY...
BAD NEWS, BRUCE?
NO, DICK, IT'S GOOD... SO GOOD THAT I CAN'T BELIEVE IT! LARSON ASKS ME TO CALL FOR MY DIVIDENDS IN PERSON!
LATER...
AH, GOOD DAY, GENTLEMEN! YOU HAVE DOUBLED YOUR MONEY ALREADY! IF YOU WILL PLEASE SIGN A RECEIPT...
IT'S INCREDIBLE! HE MUST BE A FINANCIAL WIZARD!
THERE YOU ARE, MR. WAYNE! A NICE INCOME! AND YOU STILL HAVE YOUR ORIGINAL INVEST-MENT!
I NEVER EX-PECTED THIS! BUT SEVERAL CHARITIES WILL BE THE GAINERS! HOW DO YOU DO IT, MR. LARSON?
I INVEST MY MONEY WISELY, GENTLEMEN, THAT'S ALL! OTHER PEOPLE DO THE WORK... AND THE DIVIDENDS JUST ROLL IN!
GOOD-BYE, MR. LARSON! AND THANKS VERY MUCH.
NOT AT ALL. GOOD DAY, GENTLEMEN!
THE FOOL! HE DOESN'T KNOW I'VE ALREADY ISSUED A LICENSE TO ROB HIM! HE'LL NEVER USE A CENT OF THAT MONEY!
20
AND AS BRUCE AND HIS WARD NEAR THEIR HOME...
TOO BAD LARSON GAVE US THE MONEY AFTER THE BANKS CLOSED OR WE'D HAVE BEEN ABLE TO DEPOSIT IT!
BRUCE, I DON'T THINK YOU HAVE TO BE AFRAID OF THIEVES!
BUT AT THAT MOMENT...
GOT YOUR KEY, BRUCE?
IT'S THEM, IRON-JAW! WHAT ARE WE WAITIN' FOR?
NOTHIN', SHORTY! LET'S GET GOIN'!

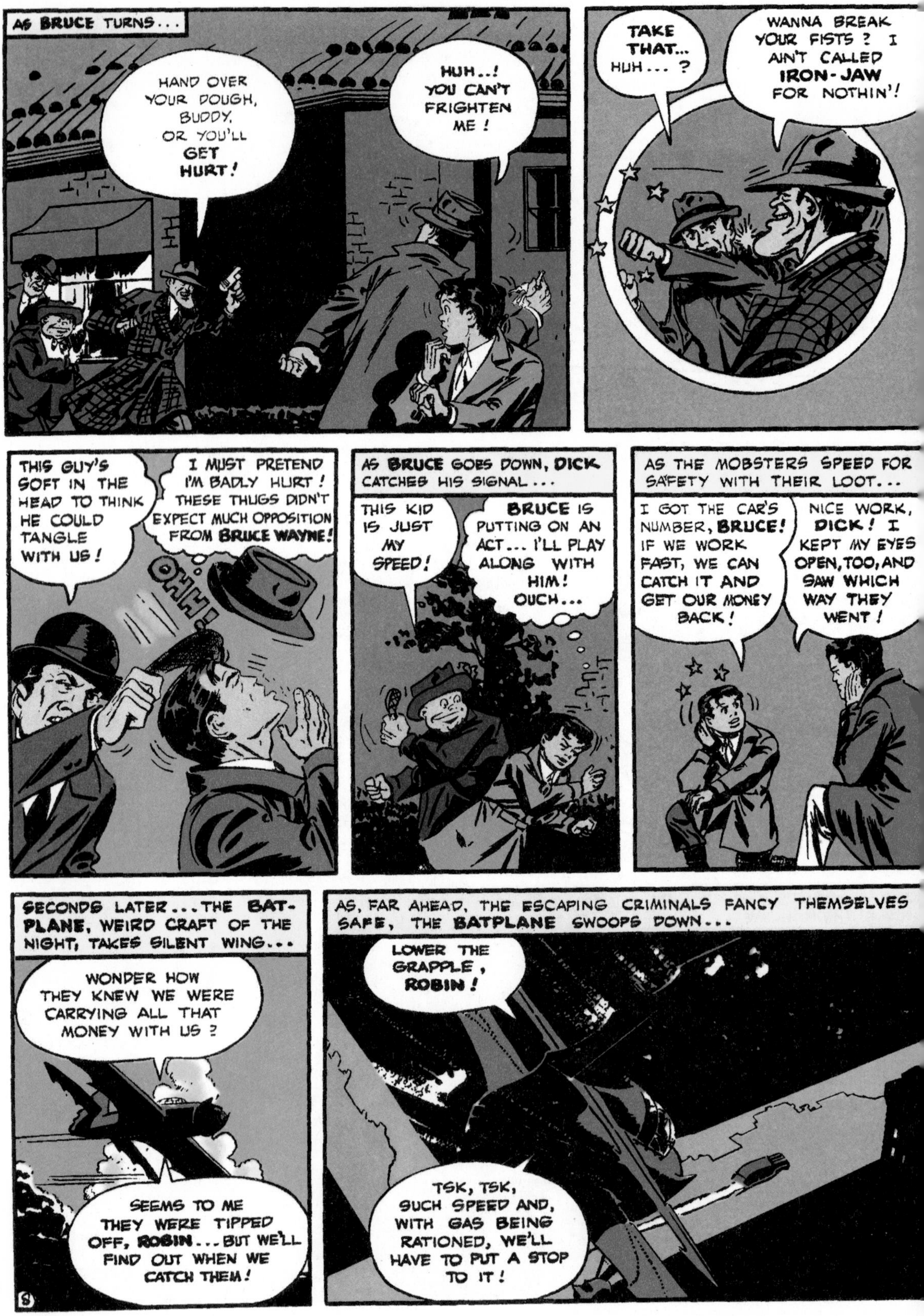
AS BRUCE TURNS...
HAND OVER YOUR DOUGH, BUDDY, OR YOU'LL GET HURT!
HUH..! YOU CAN'T FRIGHTEN ME!
TAKE THAT... HUH... ?
WANNA BREAK YOUR FISTS ? I AIN'T CALLED IRON-JAW FOR NOTHIN'!
THIS GUY'S SOFT IN THE HEAD TO THINK HE COULD TANGLE WITH US!
I MUST PRETEND I'M BADLY HURT! THESE THUGS DIDN'T EXPECT MUCH OPPOSITION FROM BRUCE WAYNE!
OHH!
AS BRUCE GOES DOWN, DICK CATCHES HIS SIGNAL...
THIS KID IS JUST MY SPEED!
BRUCE IS PUTTING ON AN ACT... I'LL PLAY ALONG WITH HIM! OUCH...
AS THE MOBSTERS SPEED FOR SAFETY WITH THEIR LOOT...
I GOT THE CAR'S NUMBER, BRUCE! IF WE WORK FAST, WE CAN CATCH IT AND GET OUR MONEY BACK!
NICE WORK, DICK! I KEPT MY EYES OPEN, TOO, AND SAW WHICH WAY THEY WENT!
SECONDS LATER... THE BAT-PLANE, WEIRD CRAFT OF THE NIGHT, TAKES SILENT WING...
WONDER HOW THEY KNEW WE WERE CARRYING ALL THAT MONEY WITH US ?
SEEMS TO ME THEY WERE TIPPED OFF, ROBIN... BUT WE'LL FIND OUT WHEN WE CATCH THEM!
8
AS, FAR AHEAD, THE ESCAPING CRIMINALS FANCY THEMSELVES SAFE, THE BATPLANE SWOOPS DOWN...
LOWER THE GRAPPLE, ROBIN!
TSK, TSK, SUCH SPEED AND, WITH GAS BEING RATIONED, WE'LL HAVE TO PUT A STOP TO IT!

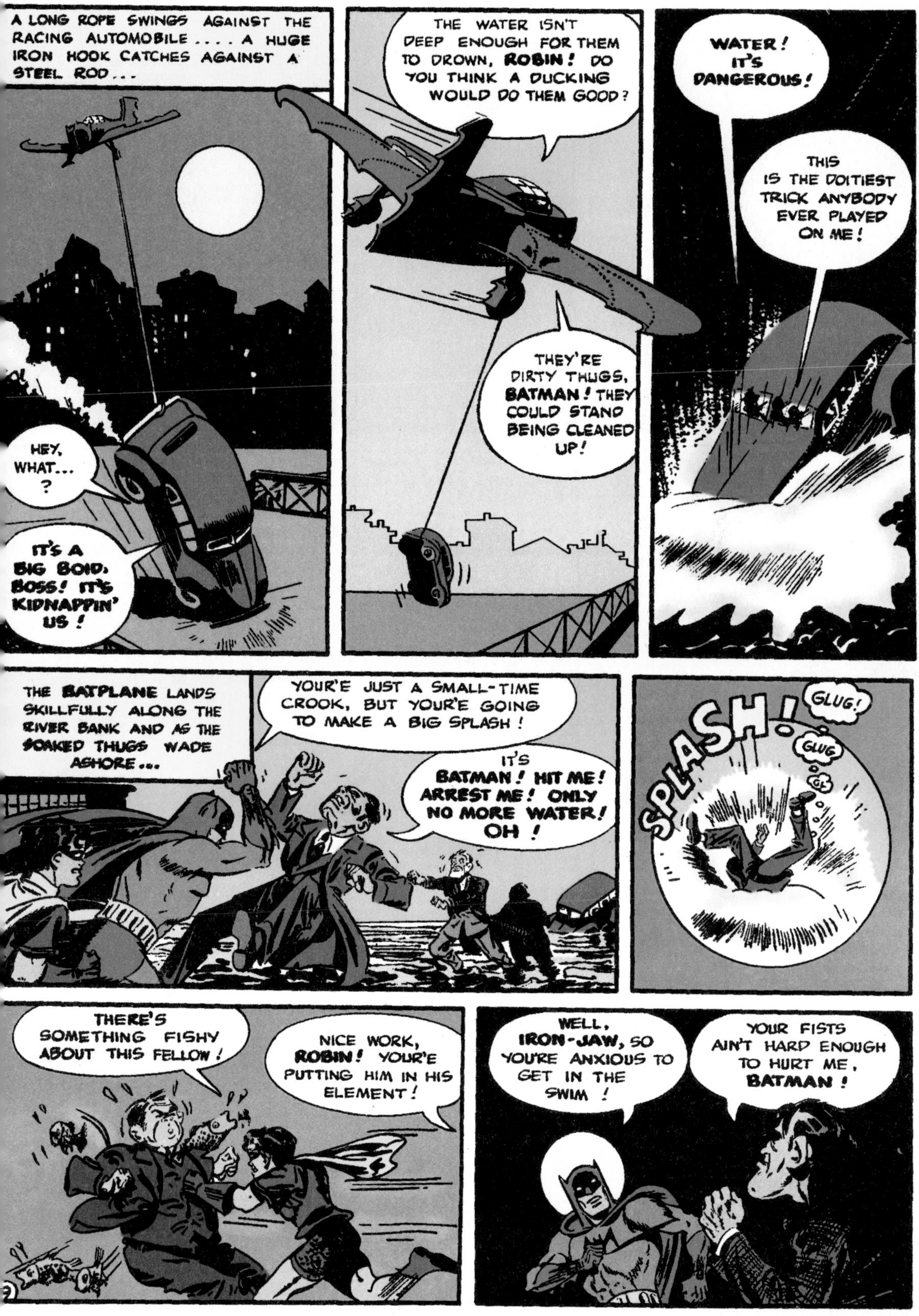
A LONG ROPE SWINGS AGAINST THE RACING AUTOMOBILE .... A HUGE IRON HOOK CATCHES AGAINST A STEEL ROD...
HEY, WHAT... ?
IT'S A BIG BOID, BOSS! IT'S KIDNAPPIN' US!
THE WATER ISN'T DEEP ENOUGH FOR THEM TO DROWN, ROBIN! DO YOU THINK A DUCKING WOULD DO THEM GOOD?
THEY'RE DIRTY THUGS, BATMAN! THEY COULD STAND BEING CLEANED UP!
WATER! IT'S DANGEROUS!
THIS IS THE DOITIEST TRICK ANYBODY EVER PLAYED ON ME!
THE BATPLANE LANDS SKILLFULLY ALONG THE RIVER BANK AND AS THE SOAKED THUGS WADE ASHORE...
YOUR'E JUST A SMALL-TIME CROOK, BUT YOUR'E GOING TO MAKE A BIG SPLASH!
IT'S BATMAN! HIT ME! ARREST ME! ONLY NO MORE WATER! OH!
SPLASH!
GLUG!
GLUG
THERE'S SOMETHING FISHY ABOUT THIS FELLOW!
NICE WORK, ROBIN! YOUR'E PUTTING HIM IN HIS ELEMENT!
WELL, IRON-JAW, SO YOU'RE ANXIOUS TO GET IN THE SWIM!
YOUR FISTS AIN'T HARD ENOUGH TO HURT ME, BATMAN!

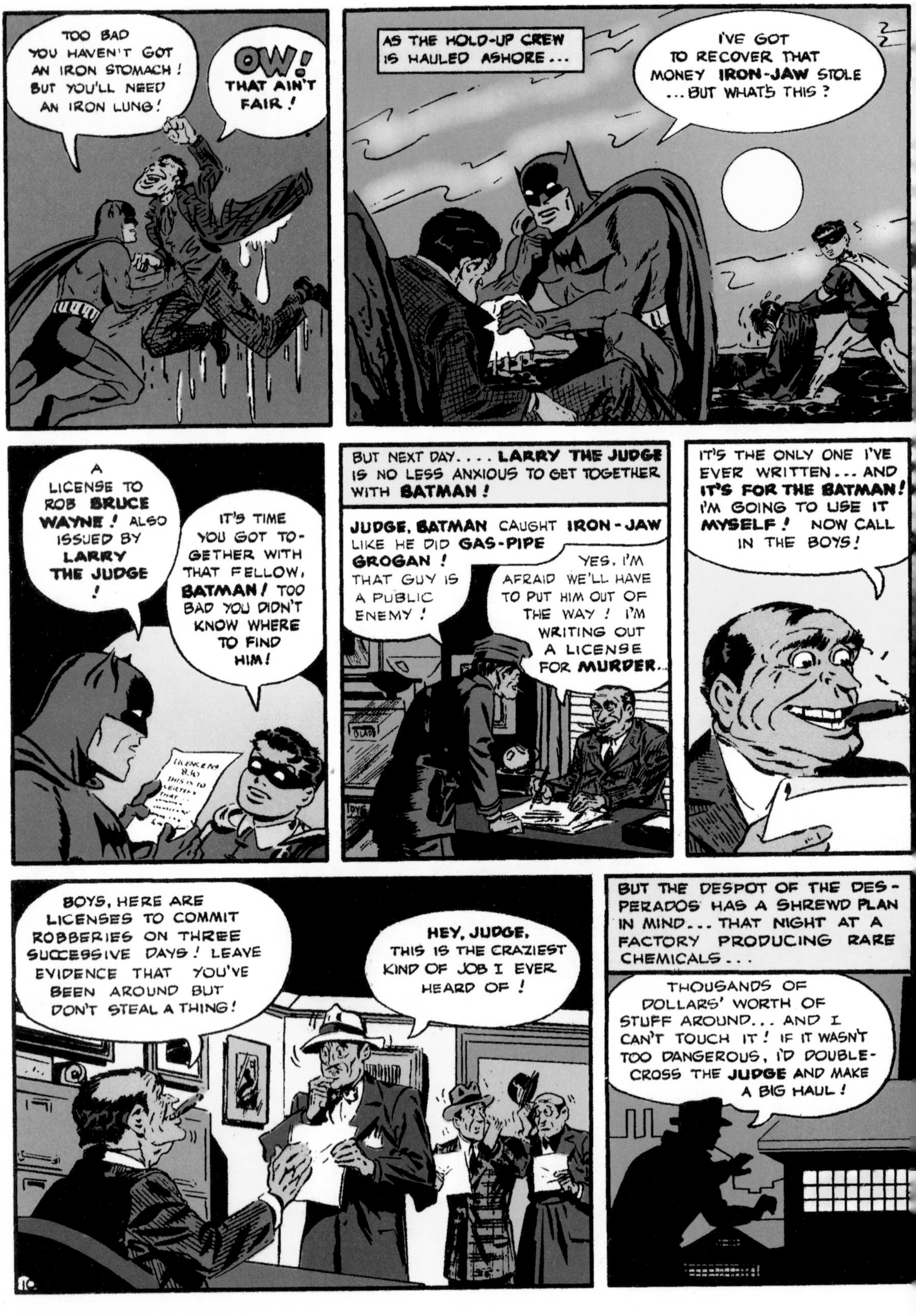
TOO BAD YOU HAVEN'T GOT AN IRON STOMACH! BUT YOU'LL NEED AN IRON LUNG!
OW! THAT AIN'T FAIR!
AS THE HOLD-UP CREW IS HAULED ASHORE...
I'VE GOT TO RECOVER THAT MONEY IRON-JAW STOLE ...BUT WHAT'S THIS?
A LICENSE TO ROB BRUCE WAYNE! ALSO ISSUED BY LARRY THE JUDGE!
IT'S TIME YOU GOT TOGETHER WITH THAT FELLOW, BATMAN! TOO BAD YOU DIDN'T KNOW WHERE TO FIND HIM!
BUT NEXT DAY.... LARRY THE JUDGE IS NO LESS ANXIOUS TO GET TOGETHER WITH BATMAN!
JUDGE, BATMAN CAUGHT IRON-JAW LIKE HE DID GAS-PIPE GROGAN! THAT GUY IS A PUBLIC ENEMY!
YES, I'M AFRAID WE'LL HAVE TO PUT HIM OUT OF THE WAY! I'M WRITING OUT A LICENSE FOR MURDER...
IT'S THE ONLY ONE I'VE EVER WRITTEN... AND IT'S FOR THE BATMAN! I'M GOING TO USE IT MYSELF! NOW CALL IN THE BOYS!
BOYS, HERE ARE LICENSES TO COMMIT ROBBERIES ON THREE SUCCESSIVE DAYS! LEAVE EVIDENCE THAT YOU'VE BEEN AROUND BUT DON'T STEAL A THING!
HEY, JUDGE, THIS IS THE CRAZIEST KIND OF JOB I EVER HEARD OF!
BUT THE DESPOT OF THE DESPERADOS HAS A SHREWD PLAN IN MIND... THAT NIGHT AT A FACTORY PRODUCING RARE CHEMICALS...
THOUSANDS OF DOLLARS' WORTH OF STUFF AROUND... AND I CAN'T TOUCH IT! IF IT WASN'T TOO DANGEROUS, I'D DOUBLE-CROSS THE JUDGE AND MAKE A BIG HAUL!
10

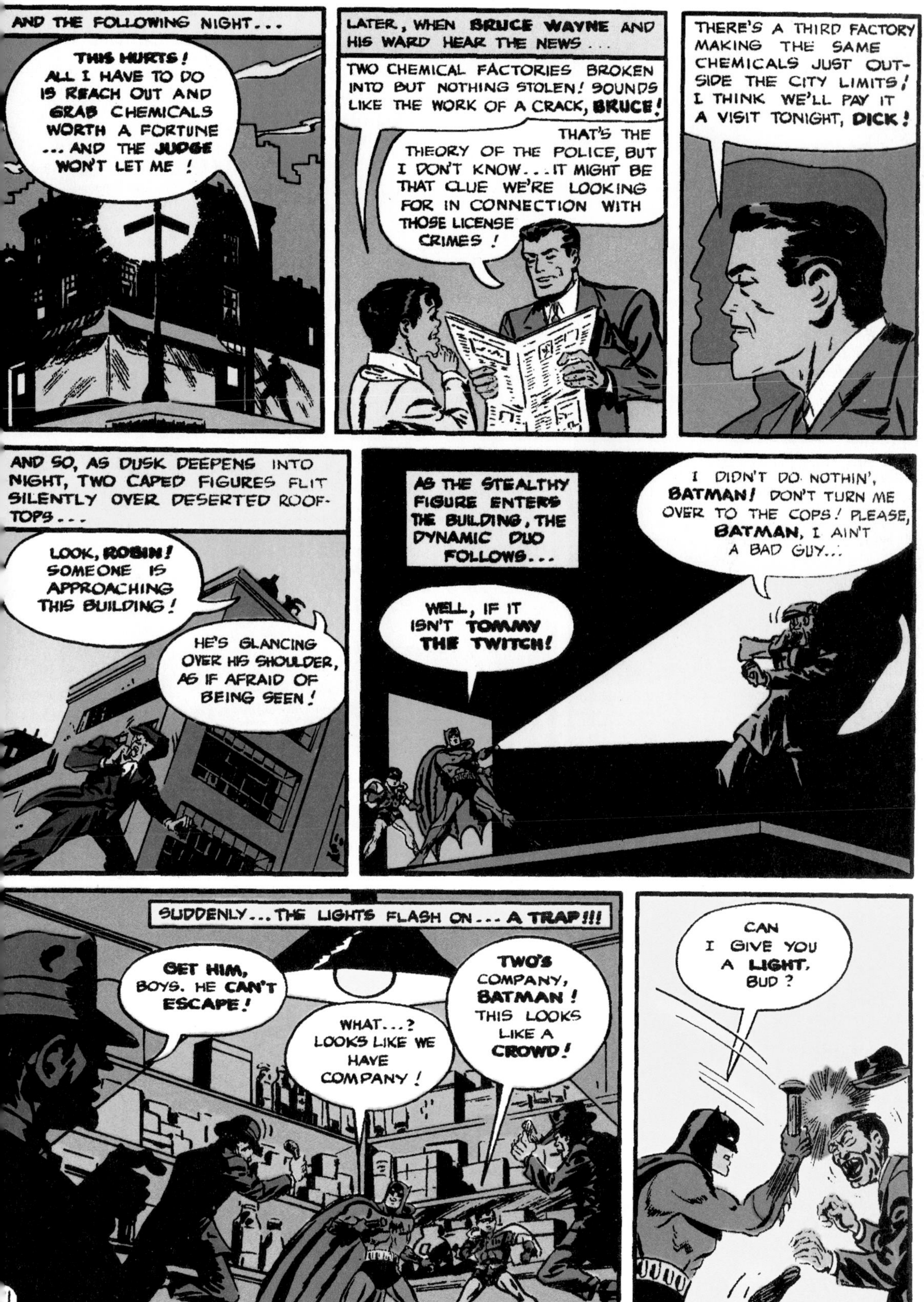
AND THE FOLLOWING NIGHT...
THIS HURTS! ALL I HAVE TO DO IS REACH OUT AND GRAB CHEMICALS WORTH A FORTUNE ...AND THE JUDGE WON'T LET ME!
LATER, WHEN BRUCE WAYNE AND HIS WARD HEAR THE NEWS...
TWO CHEMICAL FACTORIES BROKEN INTO BUT NOTHING STOLEN! SOUNDS LIKE THE WORK OF A CRACK, BRUCE!
THAT'S THE THEORY OF THE POLICE, BUT I DON'T KNOW...IT MIGHT BE THAT CLUE WE'RE LOOKING FOR IN CONNECTION WITH THOSE LICENSE CRIMES!
THERE'S A THIRD FACTORY MAKING THE SAME CHEMICALS JUST OUTSIDE THE CITY LIMITS! I THINK WE'LL PAY IT A VISIT TONIGHT, DICK!
AND SO, AS DUSK DEEPENS INTO NIGHT, TWO CAPED FIGURES FLIT SILENTLY OVER DESERTED ROOFTOPS...
LOOK, ROBIN! SOMEONE IS APPROACHING THIS BUILDING!
HE'S GLANCING OVER HIS SHOULDER, AS IF AFRAID OF BEING SEEN!
AS THE STEALTHY FIGURE ENTERS THE BUILDING, THE DYNAMIC DUO FOLLOWS...
WELL, IF IT ISN'T TOMMY THE TWITCH!
I DIDN'T DO NOTHIN', BATMAN! DON'T TURN ME OVER TO THE COPS! PLEASE, BATMAN, I AIN'T A BAD GUY...!
SUDDENLY...THE LIGHTS FLASH ON...A TRAP!!!
GET HIM, BOYS. HE CAN'T ESCAPE!
WHAT...? LOOKS LIKE WE HAVE COMPANY!
TWO'S COMPANY, BATMAN! THIS LOOKS LIKE A CROWD!
CAN I GIVE YOU A LIGHT, BUD?

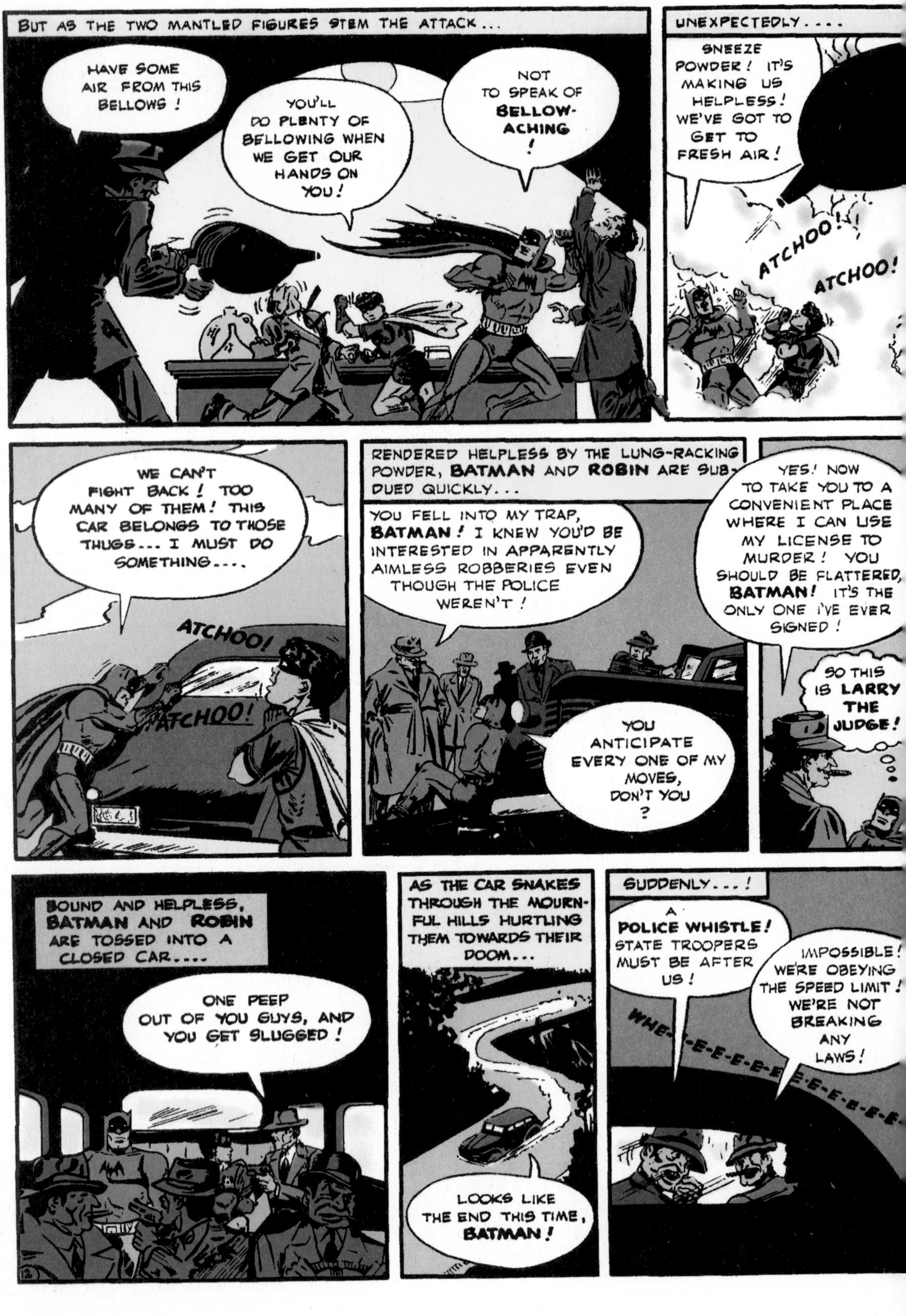
BUT AS THE TWO MANTLED FIGURES STEM THE ATTACK...
HAVE SOME AIR FROM THIS BELLOWS!
YOU'LL DO PLENTY OF BELLOWING WHEN WE GET OUR HANDS ON YOU!
NOT TO SPEAK OF BELLOW-ACHING!
UNEXPECTEDLY....
SNEEZE POWDER! IT'S MAKING US HELPLESS! WE'VE GOT TO GET TO FRESH AIR!
ATCHOO!
ATCHOO!
WE CAN'T FIGHT BACK! TOO MANY OF THEM! THIS CAR BELONGS TO THOSE THUGS... I MUST DO SOMETHING....
ATCHOO!
ATCHOO!
RENDERED HELPLESS BY THE LUNG-RACKING POWDER, BATMAN AND ROBIN ARE SUBDUED QUICKLY...
YOU FELL INTO MY TRAP, BATMAN! I KNEW YOU'D BE INTERESTED IN APPARENTLY AIMLESS ROBBERIES EVEN THOUGH THE POLICE WEREN'T!
YOU ANTICIPATE EVERY ONE OF MY MOVES, DON'T YOU?
YES! NOW TO TAKE YOU TO A CONVENIENT PLACE WHERE I CAN USE MY LICENSE TO MURDER! YOU SHOULD BE FLATTERED, BATMAN! IT'S THE ONLY ONE I'VE EVER SIGNED!
SO THIS IS LARRY THE JUDGE!
BOUND AND HELPLESS, BATMAN AND ROBIN ARE TOSSED INTO A CLOSED CAR....
ONE PEEP OUT OF YOU GUYS, AND YOU GET SLUGGED!
AS THE CAR SNAKES THROUGH THE MOURNFUL HILLS HURTLING THEM TOWARDS THEIR DOOM...
LOOKS LIKE THE END THIS TIME, BATMAN!
SUDDENLY...!
A POLICE WHISTLE! STATE TROOPERS MUST BE AFTER US!
IMPOSSIBLE! WE'RE OBEYING THE SPEED LIMIT! WE'RE NOT BREAKING ANY LAWS!
WHE-E-E-E-E-E-E-E-E-E-E-E-E

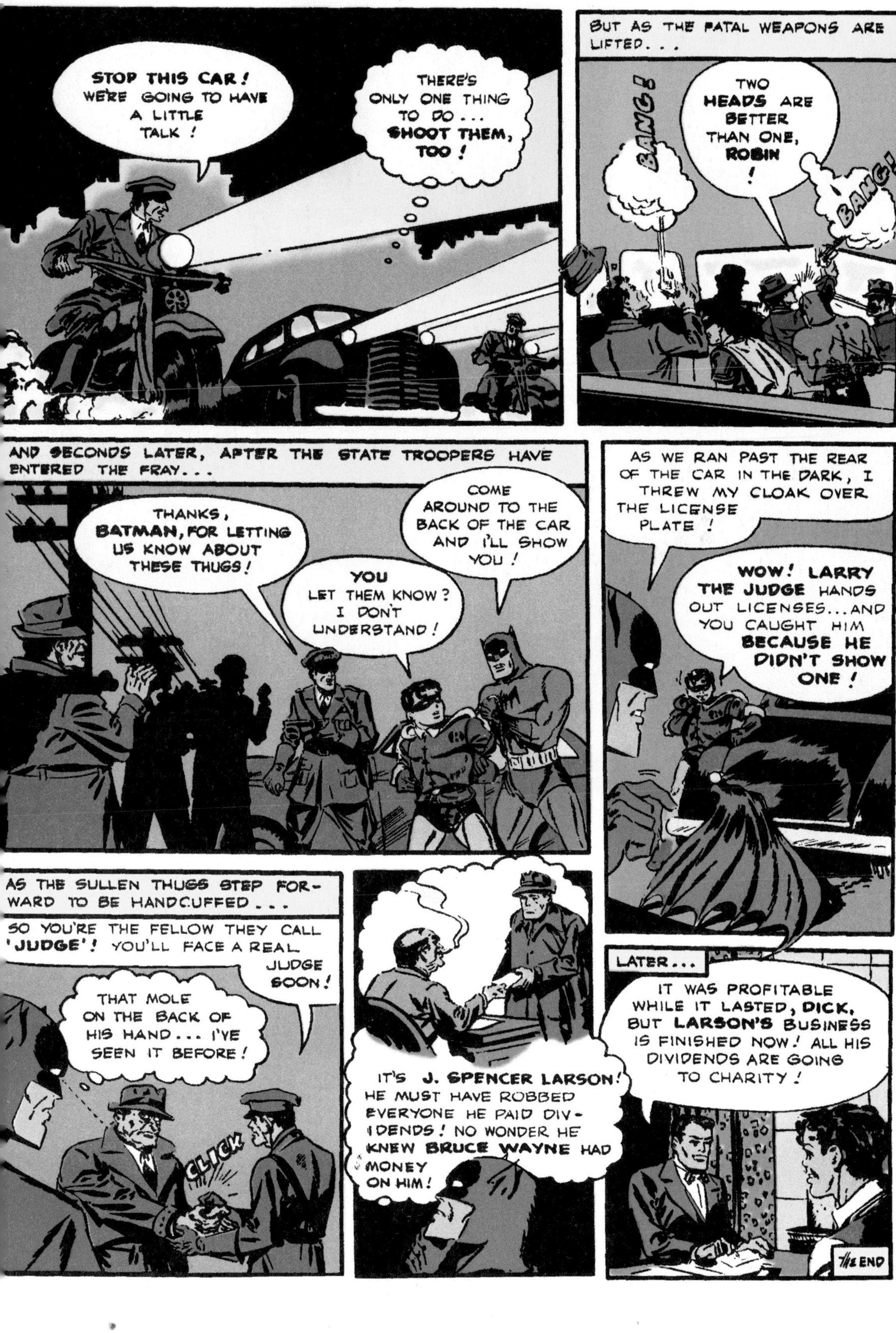
STOP THIS CAR! WE'RE GOING TO HAVE A LITTLE TALK!
THERE'S ONLY ONE THING TO DO... SHOOT THEM, TOO!
BUT AS THE FATAL WEAPONS ARE LIFTED...
BANG!
TWO HEADS ARE BETTER THAN ONE, ROBIN!
BANG!
AND SECONDS LATER, AFTER THE STATE TROOPERS HAVE ENTERED THE FRAY...
THANKS, BATMAN, FOR LETTING US KNOW ABOUT THESE THUGS!
YOU LET THEM KNOW? I DON'T UNDERSTAND!
COME AROUND TO THE BACK OF THE CAR AND I'LL SHOW YOU!
AS WE RAN PAST THE REAR OF THE CAR IN THE DARK, I THREW MY CLOAK OVER THE LICENSE PLATE!
WOW! LARRY THE JUDGE HANDS OUT LICENSES...AND YOU CAUGHT HIM BECAUSE HE DIDN'T SHOW ONE!
AS THE SULLEN THUGS STEP FORWARD TO BE HANDCUFFED...
SO YOU'RE THE FELLOW THEY CALL 'JUDGE'! YOU'LL FACE A REAL JUDGE SOON!
THAT MOLE ON THE BACK OF HIS HAND... I'VE SEEN IT BEFORE!
CLICK
IT'S J. SPENCER LARSON! HE MUST HAVE ROBBED EVERYONE HE PAID DIVIDENDS! NO WONDER HE KNEW BRUCE WAYNE HAD MONEY ON HIM!
LATER...
IT WAS PROFITABLE WHILE IT LASTED, DICK, BUT LARSON'S BUSINESS IS FINISHED NOW! ALL HIS DIVIDENDS ARE GOING TO CHARITY!
THE END

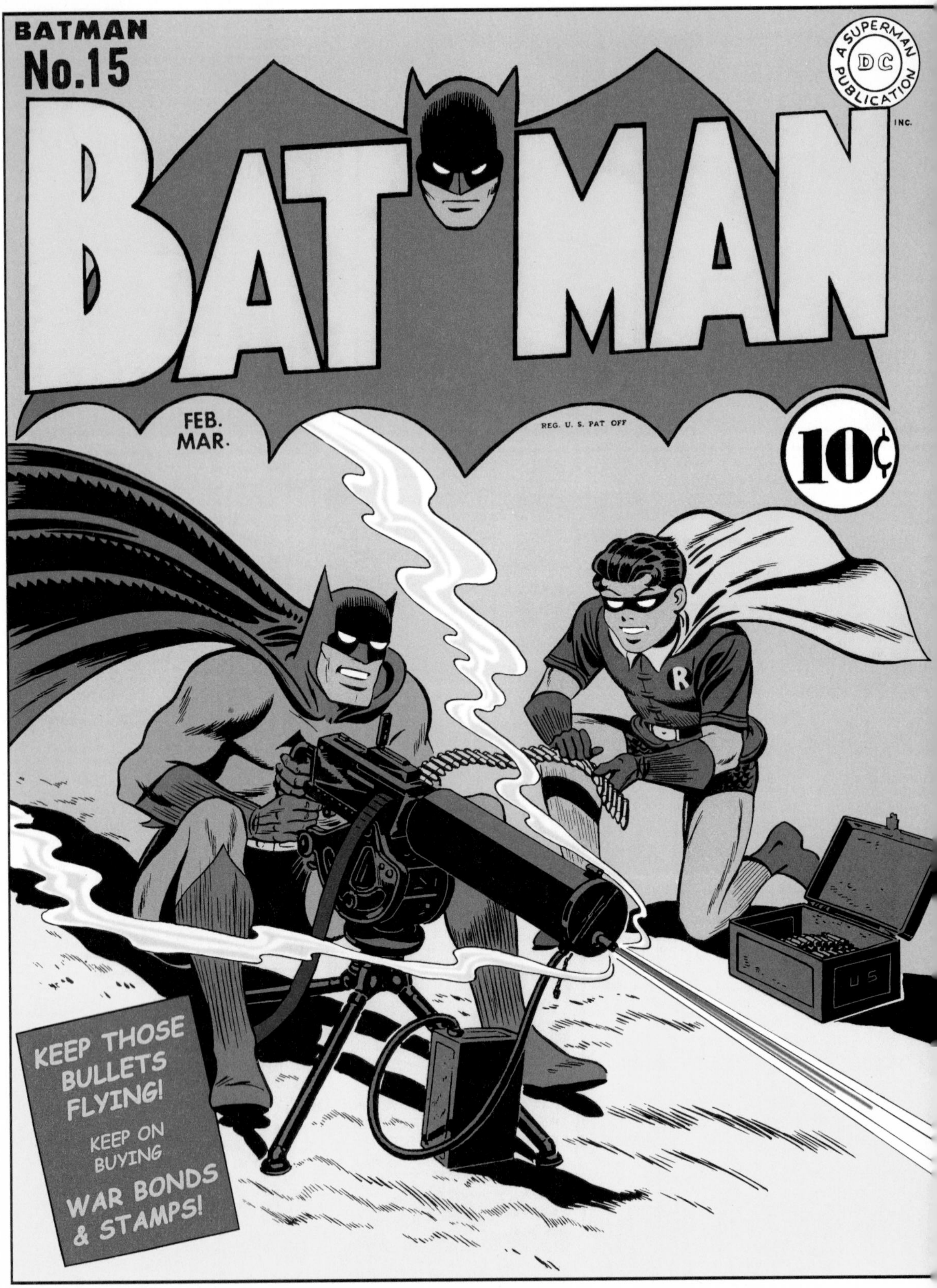
BATMAN
No.15
BATMAN
A SUPERMAN DC PUBLICATION INC.
FEB.
MAR.
REG. U. S. PAT OFF
10¢
R
KEEP THOSE BULLETS FLYING!
KEEP ON BUYING
WAR BONDS & STAMPS!
US

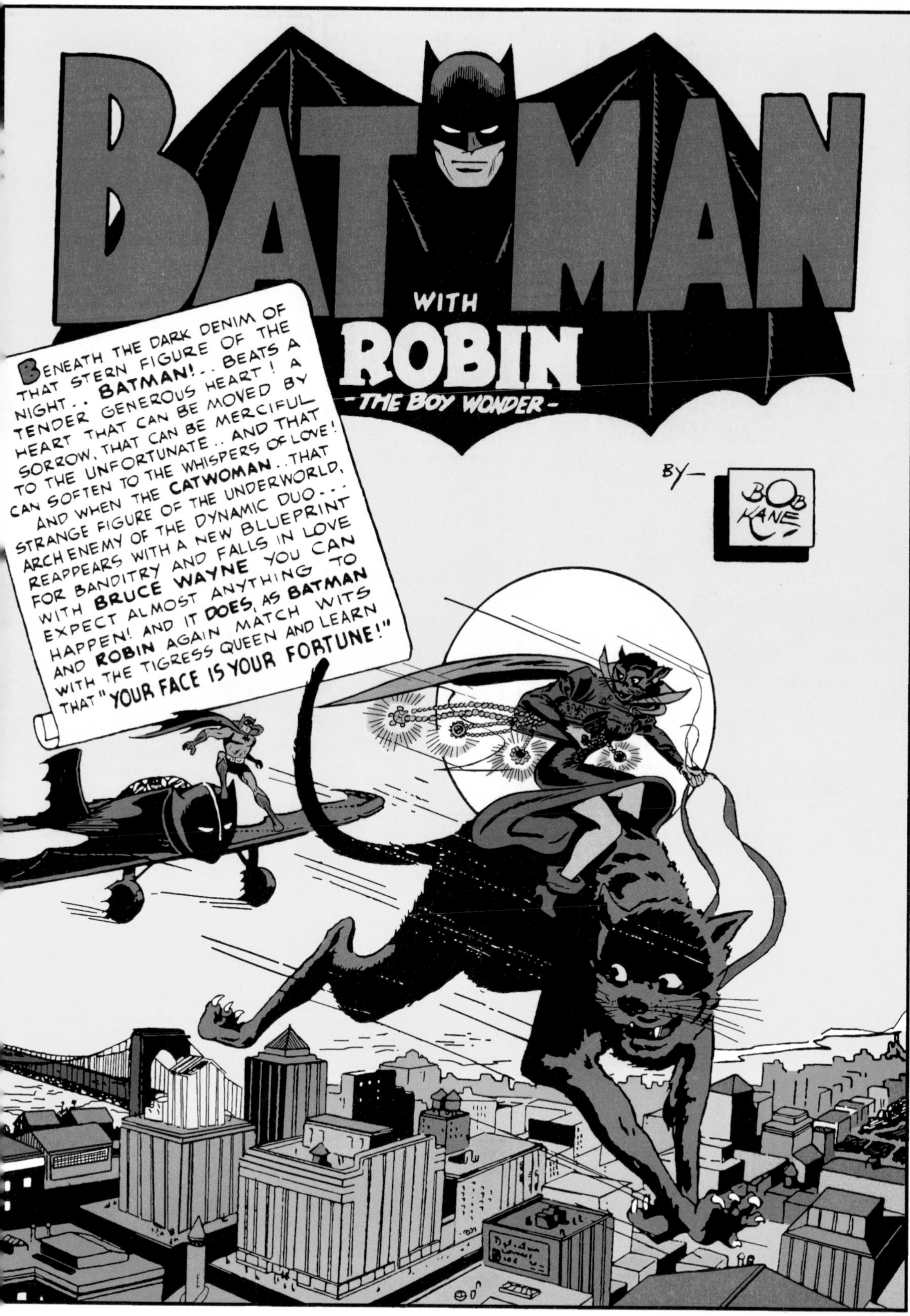
BATMAN
WITH
ROBIN
-THE BOY WONDER-
BY— BOB KANE
BENEATH THE DARK DENIM OF THAT STERN FIGURE OF THE NIGHT.. BATMAN!.. BEATS A TENDER GENEROUS HEART! A HEART THAT CAN BE MOVED BY SORROW, THAT CAN BE MERCIFUL TO THE UNFORTUNATE.. AND THAT CAN SOFTEN TO THE WHISPERS OF LOVE! AND WHEN THE CATWOMAN..THAT STRANGE FIGURE OF THE UNDERWORLD, ARCH ENEMY OF THE DYNAMIC DUO... REAPPEARS WITH A NEW BLUEPRINT FOR BANDITRY AND FALLS IN LOVE WITH BRUCE WAYNE YOU CAN EXPECT ALMOST ANYTHING TO HAPPEN! AND IT DOES, AS BATMAN AND ROBIN AGAIN MATCH WITS WITH THE TIGRESS QUEEN AND LEARN THAT "YOUR FACE IS YOUR FORTUNE!"

IN A MODEST LITTLE APARTMENT THE SHRILL RING OF AN ALARM BELL AWAKENS LOVELY YOUNG ELVA BARR..

OH, DEAR! HOW I HATE TO GET UP IN THE MORNING! WISH I COULD SLEEP! BUT I'VE GOT TO GET TO WORK!

R-I-N-G
R-I-N-G
R-R-R

DRESSED ELVA PAUSES BEFORE LEAVING..

I DIDN'T FORGET YOU, MY PET! HERE'S SOME MILK THAT OUGHT TO KEEP YOU FROM BEING HUNGRY!

A HASTY BREAKEAST......

HURRY, HURRY, HURRY! THAT'S ALL I DO!

THEN CRAMMED INTO A SUBWAY TRAIN..

NOTHING LIKE A SUBWAY RIDE TO MAKE YOU FEEL SMALL!

CANDY A ITS BES SWEET EV'IN

where eating is a PLEASURE MARIETTA INN

FLUSHIN LOCAL

JUST IN TIME!

MANON'S Beauty Salon

IN THE SWANK SALON, THE DAY BEGINS...

A FACIAL TODAY, MRS GILD?

YES, MY DEAR! I FEEL RATHER OLD, DON'T YOU KNOW! SEE IF YOU CAN TAKE OUT SOME OF THOSE WRINKLES!

SO IT GOES, FROM ONE ROUTINE TO ANOTHER. ALL THROUGH THE BUSY DAY...

...AND SO I TOLD HIM THAT I WOULDN'T STAND IT ANY LONGER!

YOU DID THE RIGHT THING. MISS LORD!

10

ICUR
50

UNTIL FINALLY...

MY FEET ACHE AND I'M SO TIRED!

WHO IS THIS BEAUTIFUL YOUNG GIRL WHO WORKS LIKE A TIRELESS BEAVER ALL DAY LONG? LOOK A LITTLE CLOSER... YES, YOU'VE GUESSED IT! THE **CATWOMAN!** BUT WHAT IS THE DARING QUEEN OF CRIME, WHO HAS STOLEN COUNTLESS FABULOUS JEWELS, DOING AT AN ORDINARY JOB?

2

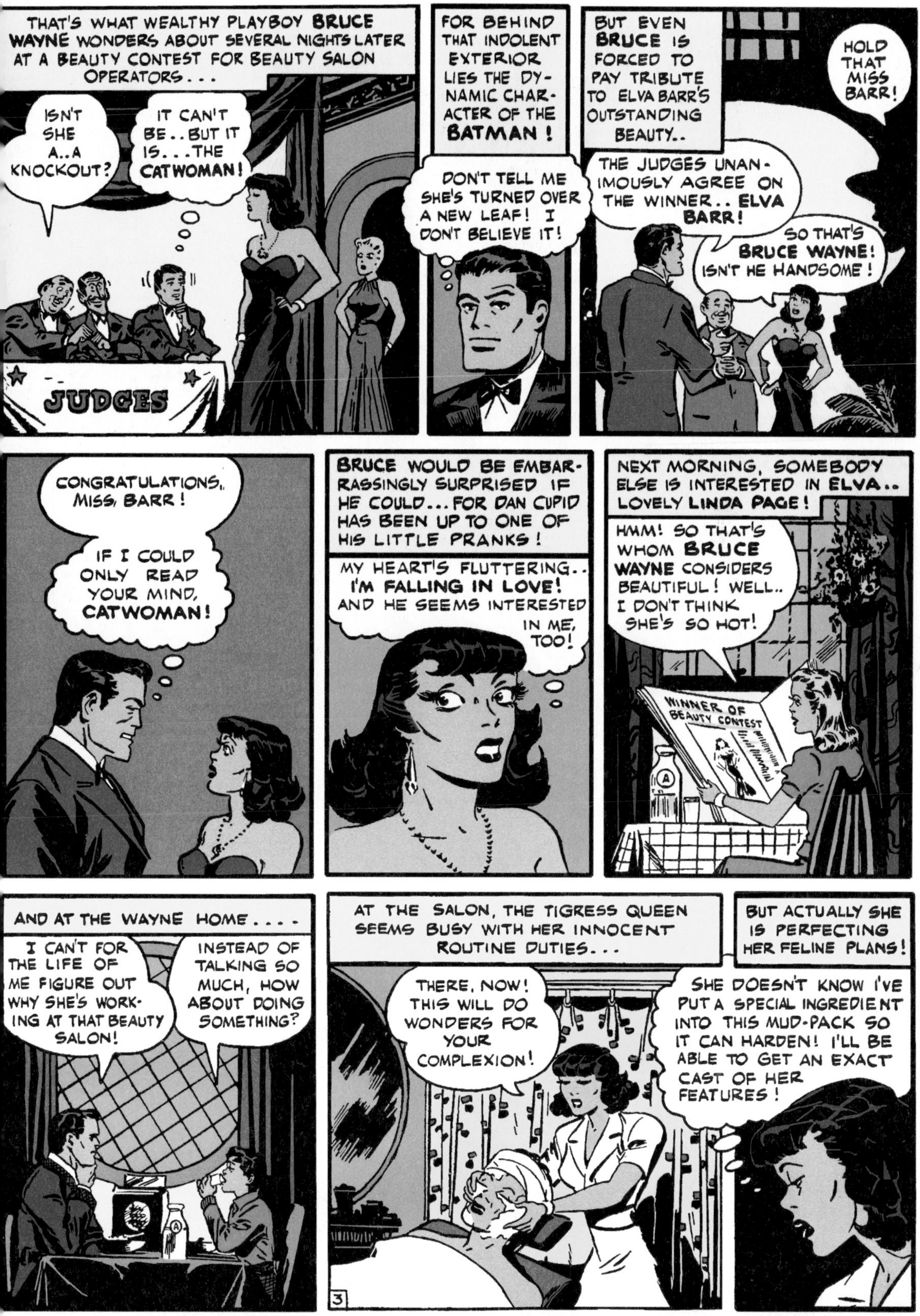
THAT'S WHAT WEALTHY PLAYBOY BRUCE WAYNE WONDERS ABOUT SEVERAL NIGHTS LATER AT A BEAUTY CONTEST FOR BEAUTY SALON OPERATORS . . .
ISN'T SHE A..A KNOCKOUT?
IT CAN'T BE..BUT IT IS...THE CATWOMAN!
JUDGES
FOR BEHIND THAT INDOLENT EXTERIOR LIES THE DYNAMIC CHARACTER OF THE BATMAN!
DON'T TELL ME SHE'S TURNED OVER A NEW LEAF! I DON'T BELIEVE IT!
BUT EVEN BRUCE IS FORCED TO PAY TRIBUTE TO ELVA BARR'S OUTSTANDING BEAUTY..
HOLD THAT MISS BARR!
THE JUDGES UNANIMOUSLY AGREE ON THE WINNER.. ELVA BARR!
SO THAT'S BRUCE WAYNE! ISN'T HE HANDSOME!
CONGRATULATIONS, MISS BARR!
IF I COULD ONLY READ YOUR MIND, CATWOMAN!
BRUCE WOULD BE EMBARRASSINGLY SURPRISED IF HE COULD... FOR DAN CUPID HAS BEEN UP TO ONE OF HIS LITTLE PRANKS!
MY HEART'S FLUTTERING.. I'M FALLING IN LOVE! AND HE SEEMS INTERESTED IN ME, TOO!
NEXT MORNING, SOMEBODY ELSE IS INTERESTED IN ELVA.. LOVELY LINDA PAGE!
HMM! SO THAT'S WHOM BRUCE WAYNE CONSIDERS BEAUTIFUL! WELL.. I DON'T THINK SHE'S SO HOT!
WINNER OF BEAUTY CONTEST
AND AT THE WAYNE HOME . . . .
I CAN'T FOR THE LIFE OF ME FIGURE OUT WHY SHE'S WORKING AT THAT BEAUTY SALON!
INSTEAD OF TALKING SO MUCH, HOW ABOUT DOING SOMETHING?
AT THE SALON, THE TIGRESS QUEEN SEEMS BUSY WITH HER INNOCENT ROUTINE DUTIES...
THERE, NOW! THIS WILL DO WONDERS FOR YOUR COMPLEXION!
BUT ACTUALLY SHE IS PERFECTING HER FELINE PLANS!
SHE DOESN'T KNOW I'VE PUT A SPECIAL INGREDIENT INTO THIS MUD-PACK SO IT CAN HARDEN! I'LL BE ABLE TO GET AN EXACT CAST OF HER FEATURES!
3

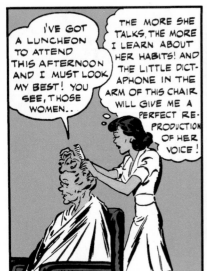

I'VE GOT A LUNCHEON TO ATTEND THIS AFTERNOON AND I MUST LOOK MY BEST! YOU SEE, THOSE WOMEN..

THE MORE SHE TALKS, THE MORE I LEARN ABOUT HER HABITS! AND THE LITTLE DICTAPHONE IN THE ARM OF THIS CHAIR WILL GIVE ME A PERFECT REPRODUCTION OF HER VOICE!

GET IT, READER? NOT QUITE? WELL.... YOU KNOW MORE THAN BATMAN AND ROBIN, WHO WAIT PATIENTLY THAT EVENING TO FOLLOW ELVA AS SHE LEAVES...

THERE SHE IS, HEADING TOWARD THE SUBWAY!

SURE! SHE'S JUST GONE HOME! MAYBE SHE IS GOING STRAIGHT!

SUBW.

BATMAN AND ROBIN IN ACTION! GET YOUR FAVORITE TOY!

I'LL TAKE ONE!

SEE? THE CATWOMAN EVEN HAS A SOFT SPOT IN HER HEART FOR US! SHE MUST HAVE REFORMED!

BATMAN'S KEEN EYES, HOWEVER, FOCUS ON A SLY MOTION OF THE HAND...

SHE PASSED HIM A NOTE! CLEVER METHOD, TOO! THAT SETTLES IT, ROBIN! SOMETHING'S UP! WE'RE FOLLOWING THAT PITCHMAN!

MINUTES LATER....

WE'VE GOT TO GET A LOOK AT THAT MESSAGE, ROBIN! LISTEN, HERE'S WHAT WE DO..

JOE'S BOWLING ALLEYS

INSIDE THE BOWLING ALLEY...

WE'RE LOOKING FOR DEADSHOT MIKE! WHERE IS HE?

BATMAN.. ROBIN! WHAT ARE THEY...?

NEVER EVEN HEARD OF HIM!

PRETENDING RAGE, BATMAN GRABS THE PITCHMAN.. AND A DEFT HAND SWIFTLY AND FURTIVELY REACHES INTO A POCKET...

YOU'RE DEADSHOT MIKE, AREN'T YOU!

NO, YOU GOT ME ALL WRONG BATMAN! I'M JIM JONES! GEE, LOOK, I EVEN SELL YOUR TOYS!

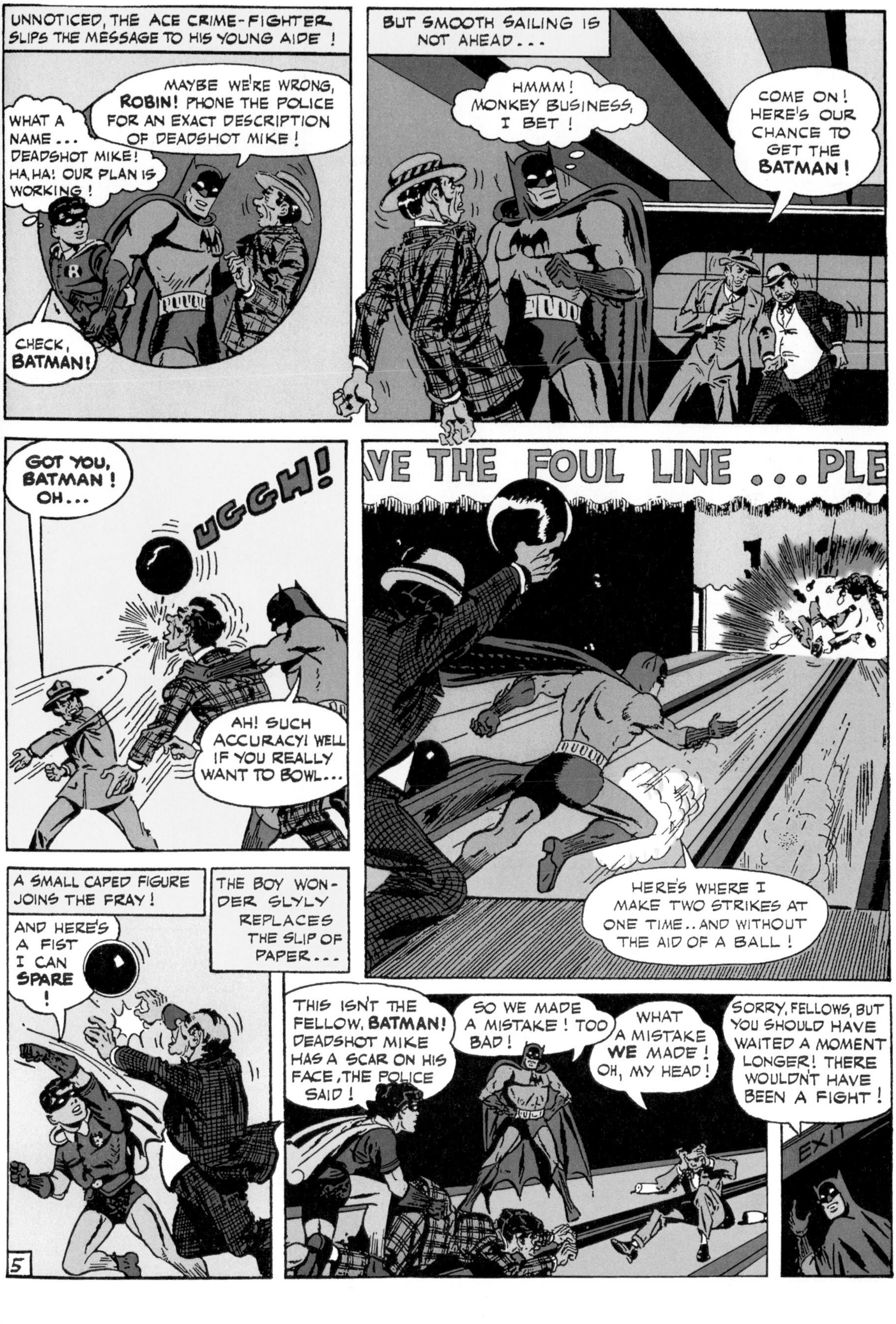

UNNOTICED, THE ACE CRIME-FIGHTER SLIPS THE MESSAGE TO HIS YOUNG AIDE !
MAYBE WE'RE WRONG, ROBIN! PHONE THE POLICE FOR AN EXACT DESCRIPTION OF DEADSHOT MIKE !
WHAT A NAME... DEADSHOT MIKE! HA, HA! OUR PLAN IS WORKING !
CHECK, BATMAN!
BUT SMOOTH SAILING IS NOT AHEAD...
HMMM! MONKEY BUSINESS, I BET !
COME ON! HERE'S OUR CHANCE TO GET THE BATMAN !
GOT YOU, BATMAN ! OH...
UGGH!
AH! SUCH ACCURACY! WELL IF YOU REALLY WANT TO BOWL...
VE THE FOUL LINE ...PLE
HERE'S WHERE I MAKE TWO STRIKES AT ONE TIME..AND WITHOUT THE AID OF A BALL !
A SMALL CAPED FIGURE JOINS THE FRAY !
THE BOY WONDER SLYLY REPLACES THE SLIP OF PAPER...
AND HERE'S A FIST I CAN SPARE !
5
THIS ISN'T THE FELLOW, BATMAN! DEADSHOT MIKE HAS A SCAR ON HIS FACE, THE POLICE SAID !
SO WE MADE A MISTAKE ! TOO BAD !
WHAT A MISTAKE WE MADE ! OH, MY HEAD !
SORRY, FELLOWS, BUT YOU SHOULD HAVE WAITED A MOMENT LONGER! THERE WOULDN'T HAVE BEEN A FIGHT !
EXIT

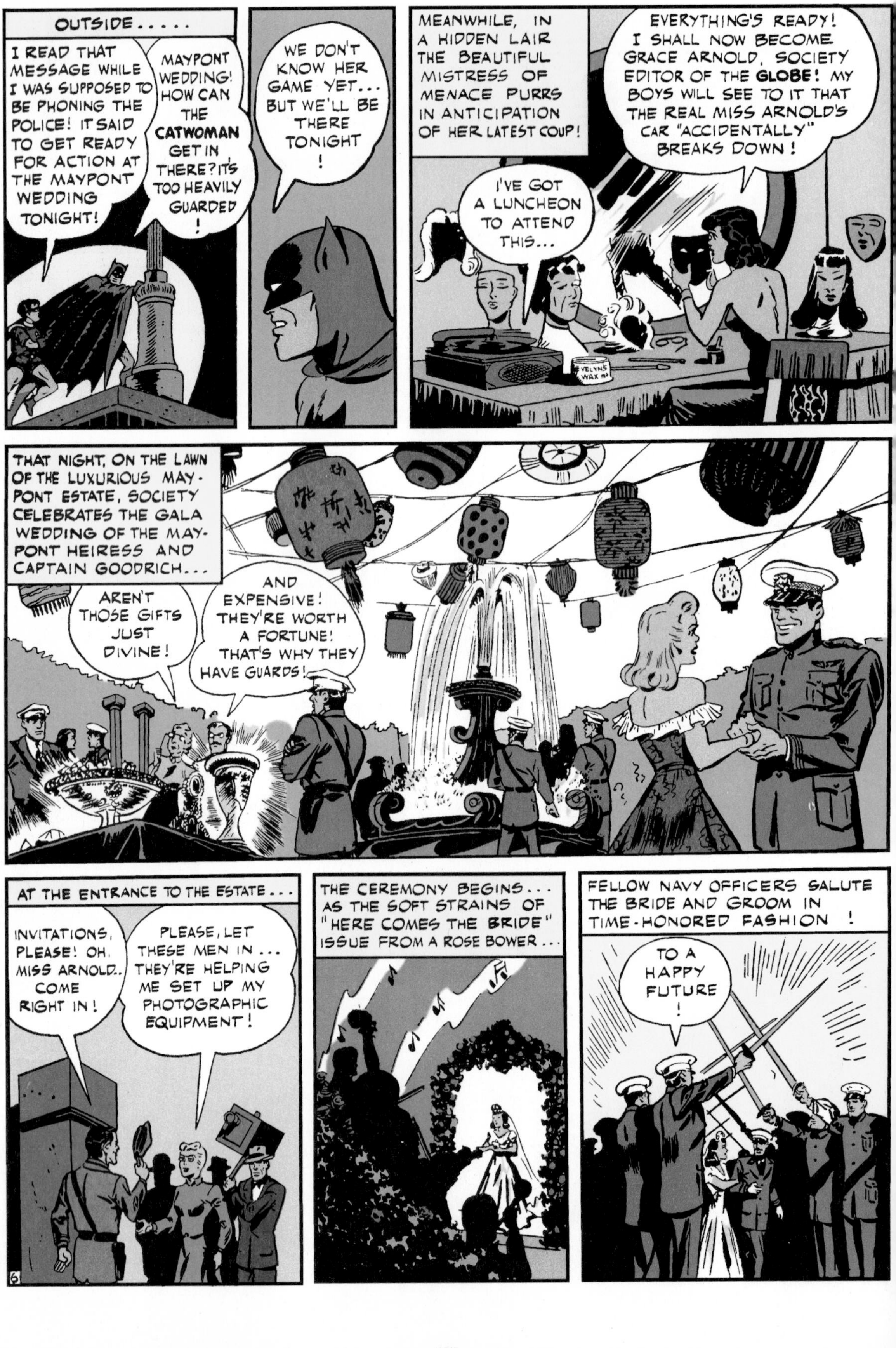
OUTSIDE.....
I READ THAT MESSAGE WHILE I WAS SUPPOSED TO BE PHONING THE POLICE! IT SAID TO GET READY FOR ACTION AT THE MAYPONT WEDDING TONIGHT!
MAYPONT WEDDING! HOW CAN THE CATWOMAN GET IN THERE? IT'S TOO HEAVILY GUARDED!
WE DON'T KNOW HER GAME YET... BUT WE'LL BE THERE TONIGHT!
MEANWHILE, IN A HIDDEN LAIR THE BEAUTIFUL MISTRESS OF MENACE PURRS IN ANTICIPATION OF HER LATEST COUP!
EVERYTHING'S READY! I SHALL NOW BECOME GRACE ARNOLD, SOCIETY EDITOR OF THE GLOBE! MY BOYS WILL SEE TO IT THAT THE REAL MISS ARNOLD'S CAR "ACCIDENTALLY" BREAKS DOWN!
I'VE GOT A LUNCHEON TO ATTEND THIS...
THAT NIGHT, ON THE LAWN OF THE LUXURIOUS MAYPONT ESTATE, SOCIETY CELEBRATES THE GALA WEDDING OF THE MAYPONT HEIRESS AND CAPTAIN GOODRICH...
AREN'T THOSE GIFTS JUST DIVINE!
AND EXPENSIVE! THEY'RE WORTH A FORTUNE! THAT'S WHY THEY HAVE GUARDS!
AT THE ENTRANCE TO THE ESTATE...
INVITATIONS, PLEASE! OH, MISS ARNOLD.. COME RIGHT IN!
PLEASE, LET THESE MEN IN... THEY'RE HELPING ME SET UP MY PHOTOGRAPHIC EQUIPMENT!
6
THE CEREMONY BEGINS... AS THE SOFT STRAINS OF "HERE COMES THE BRIDE" ISSUE FROM A ROSE BOWER...
FELLOW NAVY OFFICERS SALUTE THE BRIDE AND GROOM IN TIME-HONORED FASHION!
TO A HAPPY FUTURE!

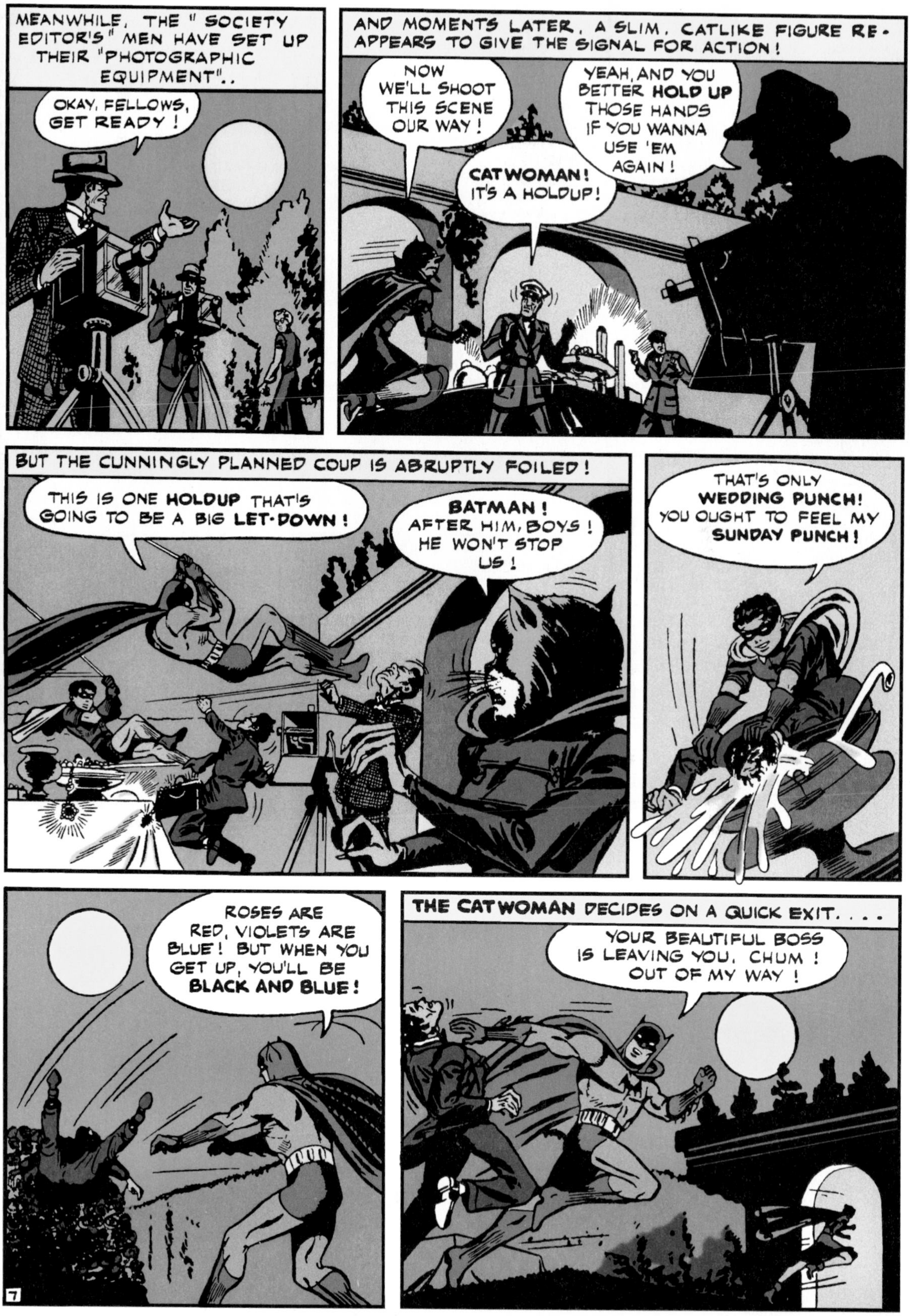
MEANWHILE, THE "SOCIETY EDITOR'S" MEN HAVE SET UP THEIR "PHOTOGRAPHIC EQUIPMENT"..
OKAY, FELLOWS, GET READY!
AND MOMENTS LATER, A SLIM, CATLIKE FIGURE RE-APPEARS TO GIVE THE SIGNAL FOR ACTION!
NOW WE'LL SHOOT THIS SCENE OUR WAY!
YEAH, AND YOU BETTER HOLD UP THOSE HANDS IF YOU WANNA USE 'EM AGAIN!
CATWOMAN! IT'S A HOLDUP!
BUT THE CUNNINGLY PLANNED COUP IS ABRUPTLY FOILED!
THIS IS ONE HOLDUP THAT'S GOING TO BE A BIG LET-DOWN!
BATMAN! AFTER HIM, BOYS! HE WON'T STOP US!
THAT'S ONLY WEDDING PUNCH! YOU OUGHT TO FEEL MY SUNDAY PUNCH!
ROSES ARE RED, VIOLETS ARE BLUE! BUT WHEN YOU GET UP, YOU'LL BE BLACK AND BLUE!
7
THE CATWOMAN DECIDES ON A QUICK EXIT. . . .
YOUR BEAUTIFUL BOSS IS LEAVING YOU, CHUM! OUT OF MY WAY!

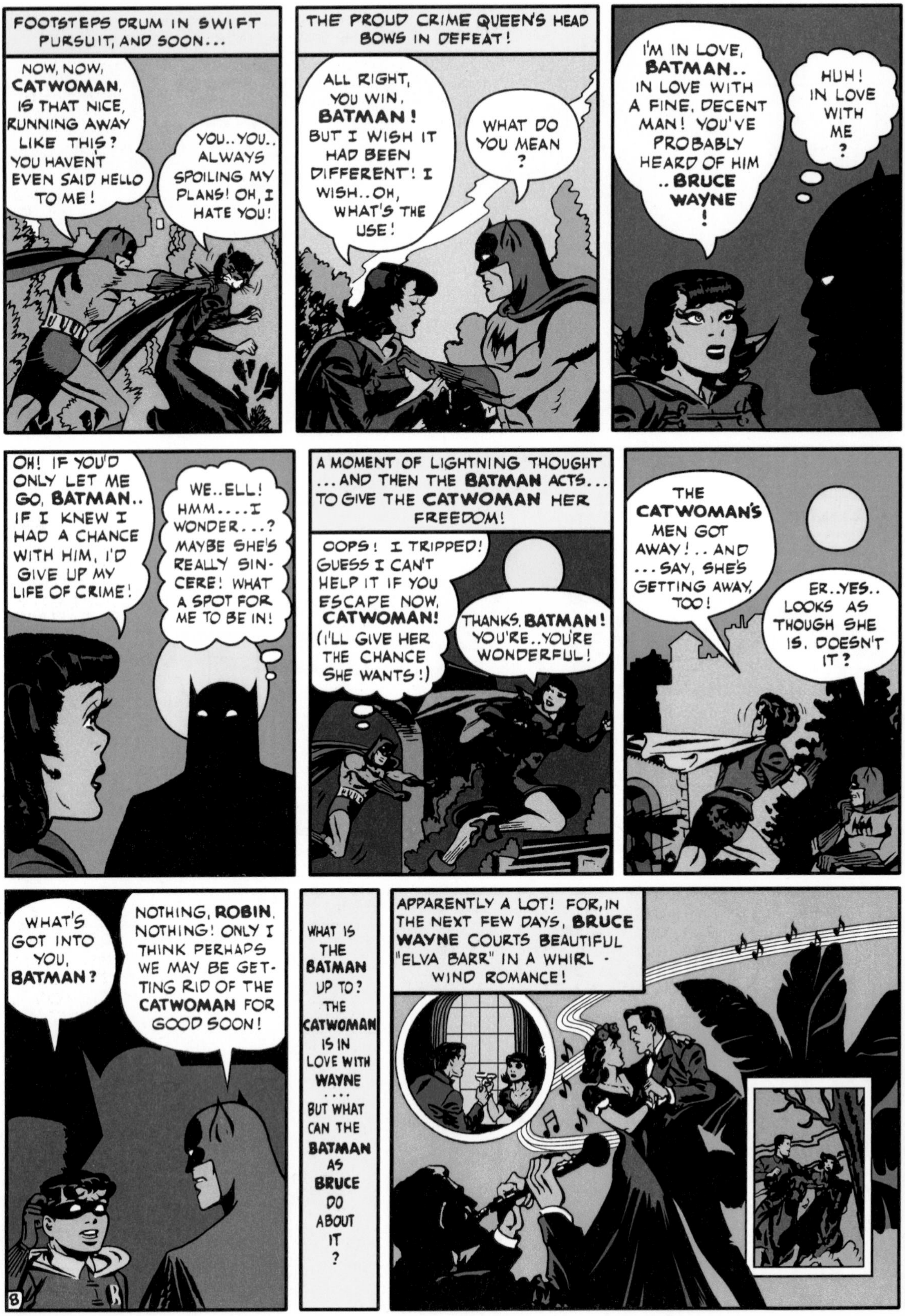

FOOTSTEPS DRUM IN SWIFT PURSUIT, AND SOON...
NOW, NOW, CATWOMAN, IS THAT NICE, RUNNING AWAY LIKE THIS? YOU HAVEN'T EVEN SAID HELLO TO ME!
YOU..YOU.. ALWAYS SPOILING MY PLANS! OH, I HATE YOU!
THE PROUD CRIME QUEEN'S HEAD BOWS IN DEFEAT!
ALL RIGHT, YOU WIN, BATMAN! BUT I WISH IT HAD BEEN DIFFERENT! I WISH..OH, WHAT'S THE USE!
WHAT DO YOU MEAN?
I'M IN LOVE, BATMAN.. IN LOVE WITH A FINE, DECENT MAN! YOU'VE PROBABLY HEARD OF HIM ..BRUCE WAYNE!
HUH! IN LOVE WITH ME?
OH! IF YOU'D ONLY LET ME GO, BATMAN.. IF I KNEW I HAD A CHANCE WITH HIM, I'D GIVE UP MY LIFE OF CRIME!
WE..ELL! HMM....I WONDER...? MAYBE SHE'S REALLY SINCERE! WHAT A SPOT FOR ME TO BE IN!
A MOMENT OF LIGHTNING THOUGHT ...AND THEN THE BATMAN ACTS... TO GIVE THE CATWOMAN HER FREEDOM!
OOPS! I TRIPPED! GUESS I CAN'T HELP IT IF YOU ESCAPE NOW, CATWOMAN! (I'LL GIVE HER THE CHANCE SHE WANTS!)
THANKS, BATMAN! YOU'RE..YOU'RE WONDERFUL!
THE CATWOMAN'S MEN GOT AWAY!..AND ...SAY, SHE'S GETTING AWAY, TOO!
ER..YES.. LOOKS AS THOUGH SHE IS, DOESN'T IT?
WHAT'S GOT INTO YOU, BATMAN?
NOTHING, ROBIN, NOTHING! ONLY I THINK PERHAPS WE MAY BE GETTING RID OF THE CATWOMAN FOR GOOD SOON!
8
WHAT IS THE BATMAN UP TO? THE CATWOMAN IS IN LOVE WITH WAYNE.... BUT WHAT CAN THE BATMAN AS BRUCE DO ABOUT IT?
APPARENTLY A LOT! FOR, IN THE NEXT FEW DAYS, BRUCE WAYNE COURTS BEAUTIFUL "ELVA BARR" IN A WHIRL-WIND ROMANCE!

AND THEN, ONE MORNING, NEWSPAPERS ANNOUNCE THE ENGAGEMENT OF SOCIETY PLAYBOY TO BEAUTY CONTEST WINNER!

BUT, BRUCE, YOU CAN'T DO THIS! THAT ELVA'S THE CATWOMAN! WHAT'S GOT INTO YOU? WHAT ABOUT LINDA? WHAT ABOUT.. US?

PATIENCE, M'LAD, YOU'RE TOO YOUNG TO UNDERSTAND THESE THINGS!

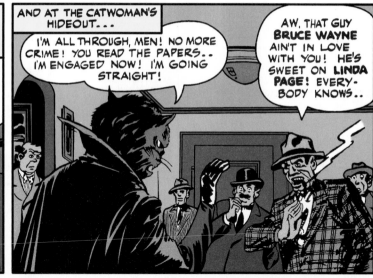

AND AT THE CATWOMAN'S HIDEOUT...

I'M ALL THROUGH, MEN! NO MORE CRIME! YOU READ THE PAPERS.. I'M ENGAGED NOW! I'M GOING STRAIGHT!

AW, THAT GUY BRUCE WAYNE AIN'T IN LOVE WITH YOU! HE'S SWEET ON LINDA PAGE! EVERYBODY KNOWS..

HOW DARE YOU SAY THAT!

I'M ONLY TELLING YOU THE TRUTH!

SLAP!

MAYBE ... MAYBE HE'S RIGHT! MAYBE I'M JUST A SILLY FOOL!

MEANWHILE, SOMEBODY ELSE HAS SEEN THE NEWSPAPERS.. A HURT, BEWILDERED GIRL.. LINDA PAGE...

AND I THOUGHT BRUCE LOVED ME! OH, I HATE HIM.. I HATE HIM! I DON'T CARE WHO HE'S ENGAGED TO!

BUT JEALOUS CURIOSITY LEADS HER TO MANON'S BEAUTY SALON FOR AN INSPECTION OF HER RIVAL IN LOVE!

LINDA PAGE! JUST THE PERSON I'M THINKING ABOUT! WHAT IS SHE DOING HERE?

COME TO LOOK ME OVER, EH? WELL, THAT'S VERY NICE! IT GIVES ME AN IDEA! I'LL MAKE ONE MORE CAST.. LINDA PAGE'S!

SHE'S BEAUTIFUL, ALL RIGHT.. BUT THERE'S SOMETHING ABOUT HER THAT REMINDS ME OF A ... A SLEEK CAT!

LATER...

I'LL BECOME LINDA AND FIND OUT FROM BRUCE IF HE LOVES HER OR NOT!

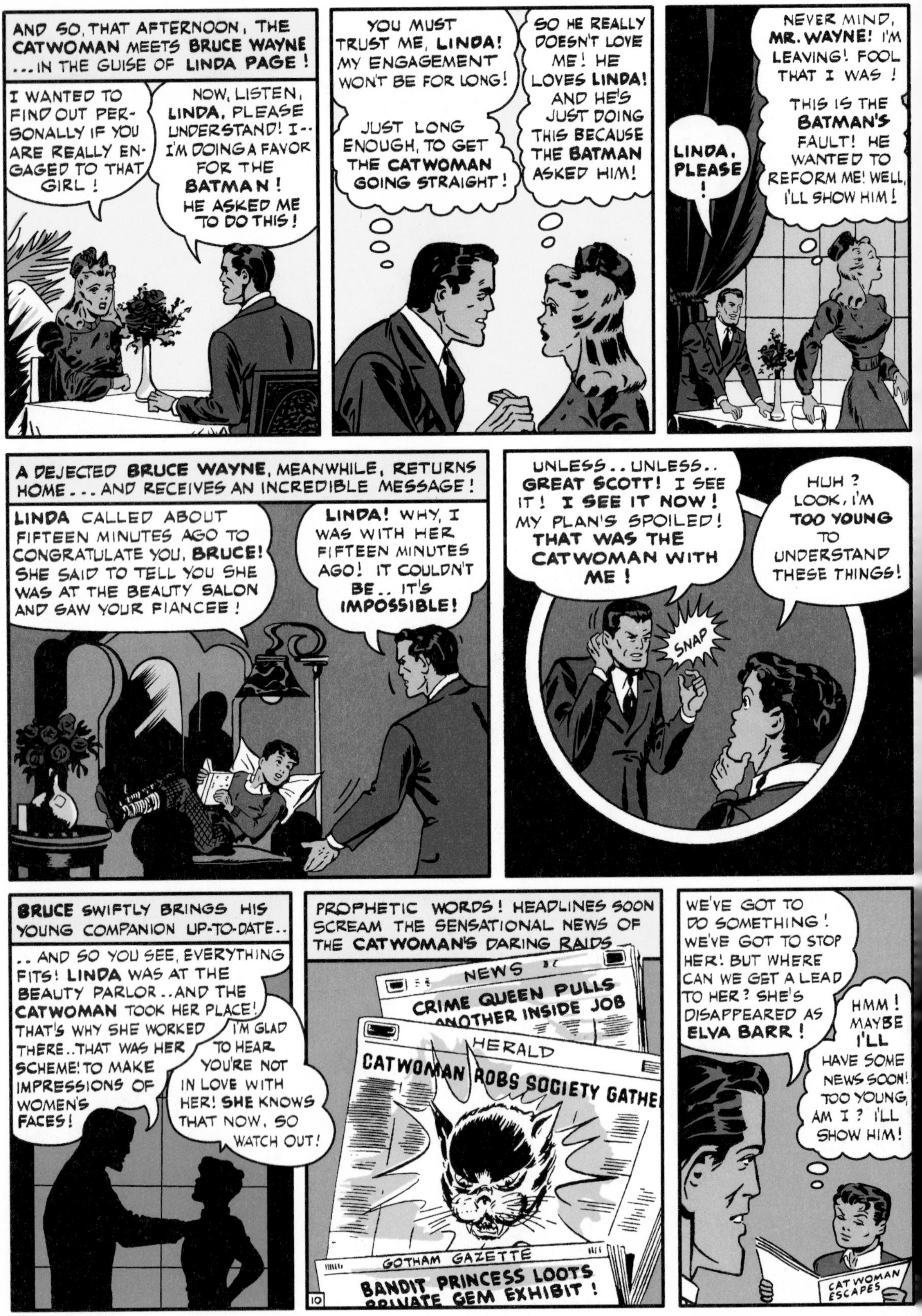
AND SO, THAT AFTERNOON, THE CATWOMAN MEETS BRUCE WAYNE ...IN THE GUISE OF LINDA PAGE!
I WANTED TO FIND OUT PERSONALLY IF YOU ARE REALLY ENGAGED TO THAT GIRL!
NOW, LISTEN, LINDA, PLEASE UNDERSTAND! I-- I'M DOING A FAVOR FOR THE BATMAN! HE ASKED ME TO DO THIS!
YOU MUST TRUST ME, LINDA! MY ENGAGEMENT WON'T BE FOR LONG!
JUST LONG ENOUGH, TO GET THE CATWOMAN GOING STRAIGHT!
SO HE REALLY DOESN'T LOVE ME! HE LOVES LINDA! AND HE'S JUST DOING THIS BECAUSE THE BATMAN ASKED HIM!
NEVER MIND, MR. WAYNE! I'M LEAVING! FOOL THAT I WAS!
THIS IS THE BATMAN'S FAULT! HE WANTED TO REFORM ME! WELL, I'LL SHOW HIM!
LINDA, PLEASE!
A DEJECTED BRUCE WAYNE, MEANWHILE, RETURNS HOME... AND RECEIVES AN INCREDIBLE MESSAGE!
LINDA CALLED ABOUT FIFTEEN MINUTES AGO TO CONGRATULATE YOU, BRUCE! SHE SAID TO TELL YOU SHE WAS AT THE BEAUTY SALON AND SAW YOUR FIANCEE!
LINDA! WHY, I WAS WITH HER FIFTEEN MINUTES AGO! IT COULDN'T BE.. IT'S IMPOSSIBLE!
UNLESS.. UNLESS.. GREAT SCOTT! I SEE IT! I SEE IT NOW! MY PLAN'S SPOILED! THAT WAS THE CATWOMAN WITH ME!
HUH? LOOK, I'M TOO YOUNG TO UNDERSTAND THESE THINGS!
SNAP
BRUCE SWIFTLY BRINGS HIS YOUNG COMPANION UP-TO-DATE..
.. AND SO YOU SEE, EVERYTHING FITS! LINDA WAS AT THE BEAUTY PARLOR..AND THE CATWOMAN TOOK HER PLACE! THAT'S WHY SHE WORKED THERE..THAT WAS HER SCHEME! TO MAKE IMPRESSIONS OF WOMEN'S FACES!
I'M GLAD TO HEAR YOU'RE NOT IN LOVE WITH HER! SHE KNOWS THAT NOW, SO WATCH OUT!
PROPHETIC WORDS! HEADLINES SOON SCREAM THE SENSATIONAL NEWS OF THE CATWOMAN'S DARING RAIDS
NEWS
CRIME QUEEN PULLS ANOTHER INSIDE JOB
HERALD
CATWOMAN ROBS SOCIETY GATHE
GOTHAM GAZETTE
BANDIT PRINCESS LOOTS PRIVATE GEM EXHIBIT!
10
WE'VE GOT TO DO SOMETHING! WE'VE GOT TO STOP HER! BUT WHERE CAN WE GET A LEAD TO HER? SHE'S DISAPPEARED AS ELVA BARR!
HMM! MAYBE I'LL HAVE SOME NEWS SOON! TOO YOUNG, AM I? I'LL SHOW HIM!
CATWOMAN ESCAPES

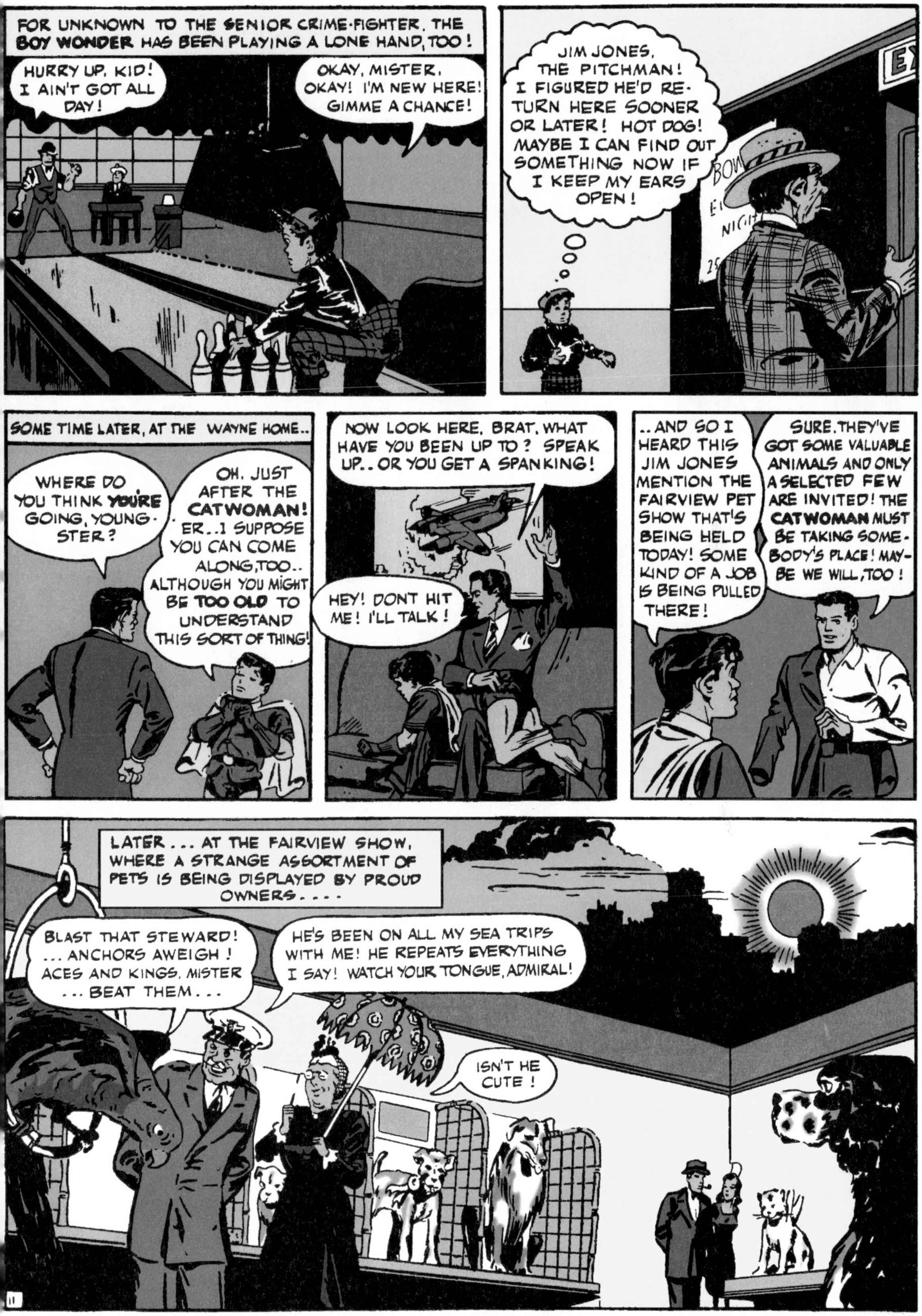
FOR UNKNOWN TO THE SENIOR CRIME-FIGHTER, THE BOY WONDER HAS BEEN PLAYING A LONE HAND, TOO!
HURRY UP, KID! I AIN'T GOT ALL DAY!
OKAY, MISTER, OKAY! I'M NEW HERE! GIMME A CHANCE!
JIM JONES, THE PITCHMAN! I FIGURED HE'D RE-TURN HERE SOONER OR LATER! HOT DOG! MAYBE I CAN FIND OUT SOMETHING NOW IF I KEEP MY EARS OPEN!
SOME TIME LATER, AT THE WAYNE HOME..
WHERE DO YOU THINK YOU'RE GOING, YOUNG-STER?
OH. JUST AFTER THE CATWOMAN! ER..I SUPPOSE YOU CAN COME ALONG, TOO.. ALTHOUGH YOU MIGHT BE TOO OLD TO UNDERSTAND THIS SORT OF THING!
NOW LOOK HERE, BRAT, WHAT HAVE YOU BEEN UP TO? SPEAK UP.. OR YOU GET A SPANKING!
HEY! DON'T HIT ME! I'LL TALK!
..AND SO I HEARD THIS JIM JONES MENTION THE FAIRVIEW PET SHOW THAT'S BEING HELD TODAY! SOME KIND OF A JOB IS BEING PULLED THERE!
SURE. THEY'VE GOT SOME VALUABLE ANIMALS AND ONLY A SELECTED FEW ARE INVITED! THE CATWOMAN MUST BE TAKING SOME-BODY'S PLACE! MAY-BE WE WILL, TOO!
LATER... AT THE FAIRVIEW SHOW, WHERE A STRANGE ASSORTMENT OF PETS IS BEING DISPLAYED BY PROUD OWNERS....
BLAST THAT STEWARD! ... ANCHORS AWEIGH! ACES AND KINGS, MISTER ... BEAT THEM...
HE'S BEEN ON ALL MY SEA TRIPS WITH ME! HE REPEATS EVERYTHING I SAY! WATCH YOUR TONGUE, ADMIRAL!
ISN'T HE CUTE!
11

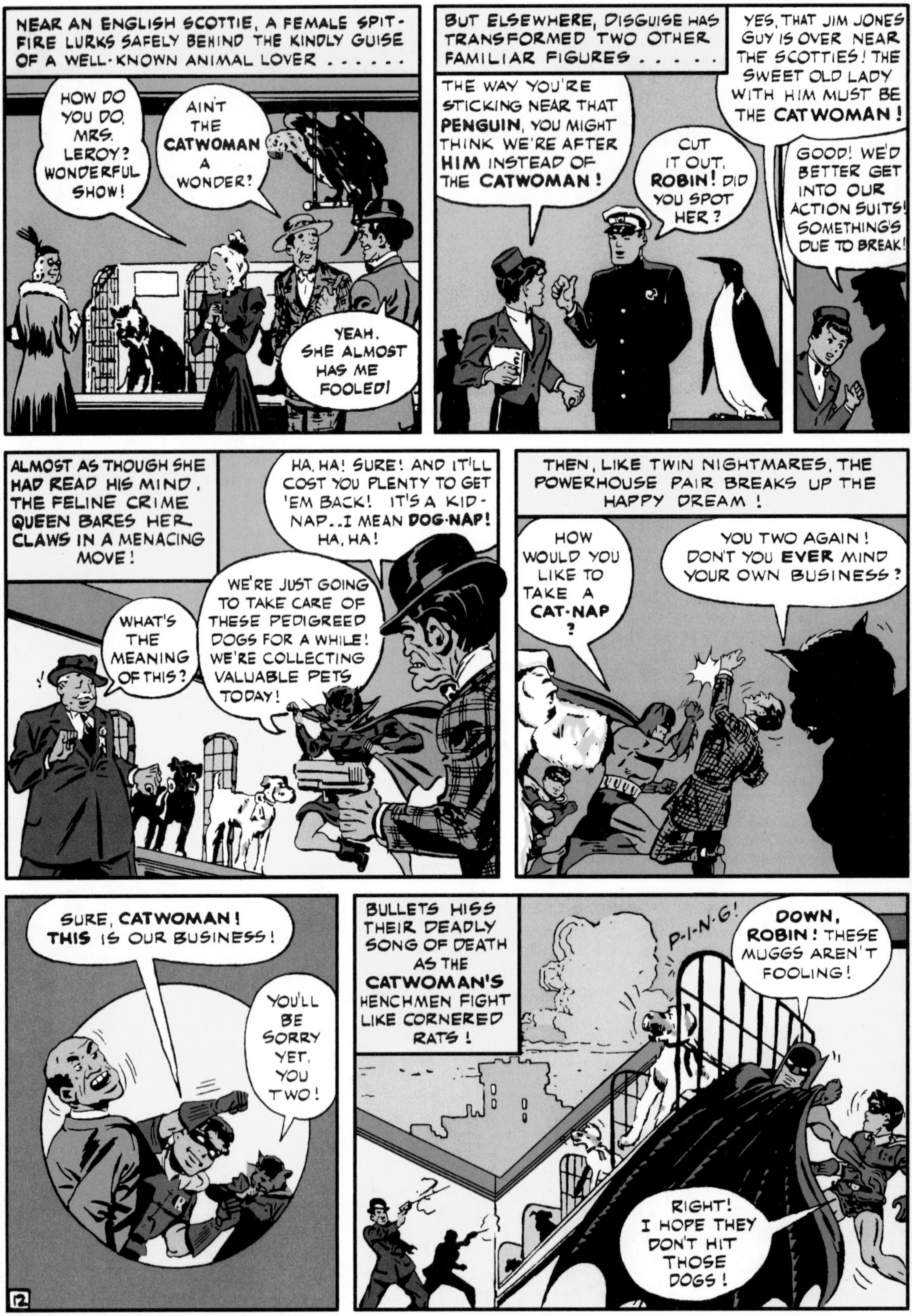
NEAR AN ENGLISH SCOTTIE, A FEMALE SPIT-FIRE LURKS SAFELY BEHIND THE KINDLY GUISE OF A WELL-KNOWN ANIMAL LOVER . . . . . .
HOW DO YOU DO, MRS. LEROY? WONDERFUL SHOW!
AIN'T THE CATWOMAN A WONDER?
YEAH. SHE ALMOST HAS ME FOOLED!
BUT ELSEWHERE, DISGUISE HAS TRANSFORMED TWO OTHER FAMILIAR FIGURES . . . . .
THE WAY YOU'RE STICKING NEAR THAT PENGUIN, YOU MIGHT THINK WE'RE AFTER HIM INSTEAD OF THE CATWOMAN!
CUT IT OUT, ROBIN! DID YOU SPOT HER?
YES, THAT JIM JONES GUY IS OVER NEAR THE SCOTTIES! THE SWEET OLD LADY WITH HIM MUST BE THE CATWOMAN!
GOOD! WE'D BETTER GET INTO OUR ACTION SUITS! SOMETHING'S DUE TO BREAK!
ALMOST AS THOUGH SHE HAD READ HIS MIND, THE FELINE CRIME QUEEN BARES HER CLAWS IN A MENACING MOVE!
HA, HA! SURE! AND IT'LL COST YOU PLENTY TO GET 'EM BACK! IT'S A KID-NAP..I MEAN DOG-NAP! HA, HA!
WHAT'S THE MEANING OF THIS?
WE'RE JUST GOING TO TAKE CARE OF THESE PEDIGREED DOGS FOR A WHILE! WE'RE COLLECTING VALUABLE PETS TODAY!
THEN, LIKE TWIN NIGHTMARES, THE POWERHOUSE PAIR BREAKS UP THE HAPPY DREAM!
HOW WOULD YOU LIKE TO TAKE A CAT-NAP?
YOU TWO AGAIN! DON'T YOU EVER MIND YOUR OWN BUSINESS?
SURE, CATWOMAN! THIS IS OUR BUSINESS!
YOU'LL BE SORRY YET, YOU TWO!
12
BULLETS HISS THEIR DEADLY SONG OF DEATH AS THE CATWOMAN'S HENCHMEN FIGHT LIKE CORNERED RATS!
P-I-N-G!
DOWN, ROBIN! THESE MUGGS AREN'T FOOLING!
RIGHT! I HOPE THEY DON'T HIT THOSE DOGS!

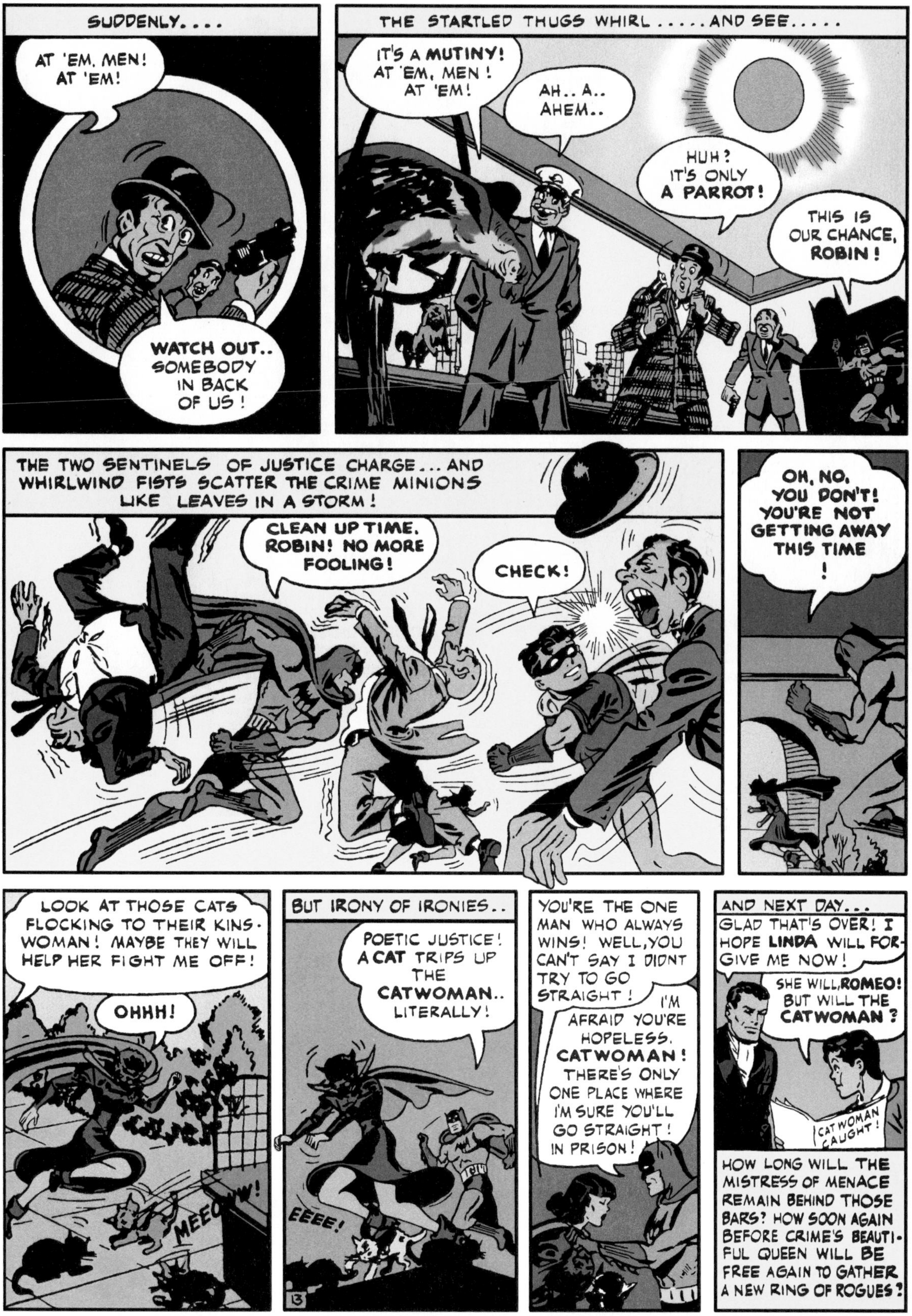
SUDDENLY....
AT 'EM, MEN! AT 'EM!
WATCH OUT.. SOMEBODY IN BACK OF US!
THE STARTLED THUGS WHIRL.....AND SEE.....
IT'S A MUTINY! AT 'EM, MEN! AT 'EM!
AH.. A.. AHEM..
HUH? IT'S ONLY A PARROT!
THIS IS OUR CHANCE, ROBIN!
THE TWO SENTINELS OF JUSTICE CHARGE... AND WHIRLWIND FISTS SCATTER THE CRIME MINIONS LIKE LEAVES IN A STORM!
CLEAN UP TIME, ROBIN! NO MORE FOOLING!
CHECK!
OH, NO, YOU DON'T! YOU'RE NOT GETTING AWAY THIS TIME !
LOOK AT THOSE CATS FLOCKING TO THEIR KINS-WOMAN! MAYBE THEY WILL HELP HER FIGHT ME OFF!
OHHH!
MEEOW!
BUT IRONY OF IRONIES..
POETIC JUSTICE! A CAT TRIPS UP THE CATWOMAN.. LITERALLY!
EEEE!
YOU'RE THE ONE MAN WHO ALWAYS WINS! WELL, YOU CAN'T SAY I DIDNT TRY TO GO STRAIGHT!
I'M AFRAID YOU'RE HOPELESS, CATWOMAN! THERE'S ONLY ONE PLACE WHERE I'M SURE YOU'LL GO STRAIGHT! IN PRISON!
AND NEXT DAY...
GLAD THAT'S OVER! I HOPE LINDA WILL FORGIVE ME NOW!
SHE WILL, ROMEO! BUT WILL THE CATWOMAN?
CATWOMAN CAUGHT!
HOW LONG WILL THE MISTRESS OF MENACE REMAIN BEHIND THOSE BARS? HOW SOON AGAIN BEFORE CRIME'S BEAUTIFUL QUEEN WILL BE FREE AGAIN TO GATHER A NEW RING OF ROGUES?

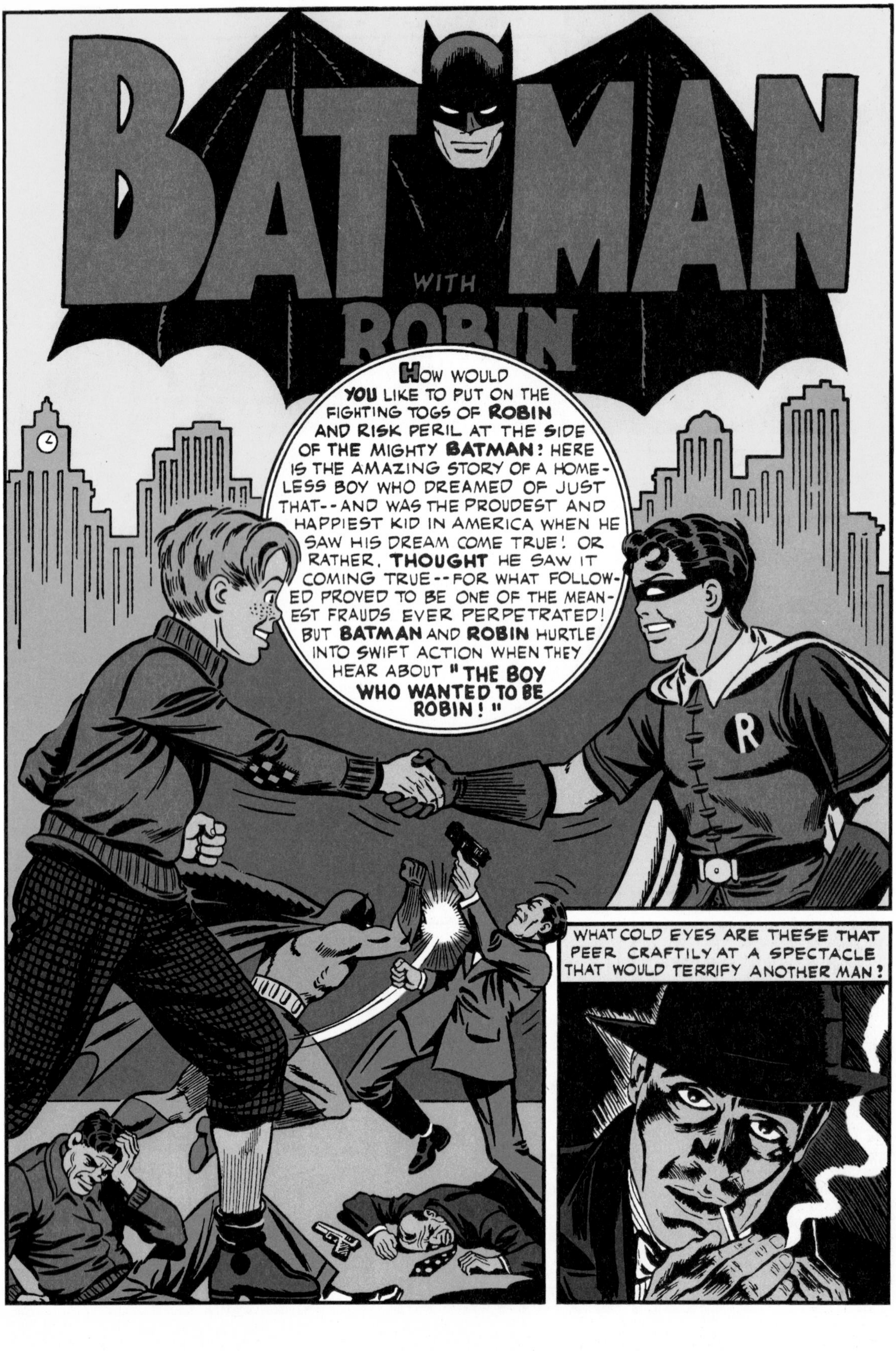
BATMAN
WITH
ROBIN
HOW WOULD YOU LIKE TO PUT ON THE FIGHTING TOGS OF ROBIN AND RISK PERIL AT THE SIDE OF THE MIGHTY BATMAN? HERE IS THE AMAZING STORY OF A HOMELESS BOY WHO DREAMED OF JUST THAT--AND WAS THE PROUDEST AND HAPPIEST KID IN AMERICA WHEN HE SAW HIS DREAM COME TRUE! OR RATHER, THOUGHT HE SAW IT COMING TRUE--FOR WHAT FOLLOWED PROVED TO BE ONE OF THE MEANEST FRAUDS EVER PERPETRATED! BUT BATMAN AND ROBIN HURTLE INTO SWIFT ACTION WHEN THEY HEAR ABOUT "THE BOY WHO WANTED TO BE ROBIN!"
R
WHAT COLD EYES ARE THESE THAT PEER CRAFTILY AT A SPECTACLE THAT WOULD TERRIFY ANOTHER MAN?

WHO IS THIS DARK-CLAD AUDIENCE OF ONE, LURKING UNSEEN IN THE SHADOWS OF THE WATERFRONT?

WAREHOUSE NO 58

WE SHALL KNOW PRESENTLY... BUT FIRST LET US SEE WHAT IT IS THAT HOLDS HIS ATTENTION SO CLOSELY...

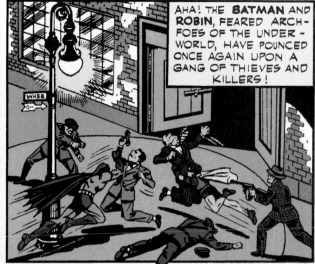

AHA! THE **BATMAN** AND **ROBIN**, FEARED ARCH-FOES OF THE UNDER-WORLD, HAVE POUNCED ONCE AGAIN UPON A GANG OF THIEVES AND KILLERS!

KNUCKLES TO YOU, SPIKE! WHICH REMINDS ME--WHERE IS "KNUCKLES" CONGER, THE BOSS OF YOUR MOB?

HE AIN'T WHERE YOU'RE GONNA BE IN A MINUTE, BATMAN!

YOU COULDN'T HIT A BARN DOOR WITH THIS BARN DOOR HITTING YOU!

HELP! ME CHOPPER'S BACK-FIRIN'!

HEY--IT GIVES ME DIZZY SPELLS TO GET TOSSED AROUND!

SWING AND SWAY THE **BATMAN'S** WAY!

GUESS WE CAN GO HOME, SOON AS THE POLICE SHOW UP!

AW---WE NEVER HAVE THIS MUCH FUN AT HOME!

THEY'RE "KNUCK-LES" CONGER'S RATS ALL RIGHT! TOO BAD WE COULDN'T HAVE GOT HIM, TOO--THE SLICKEST OF THEM ALL!

IF ONLY WE KNEW WHERE "KNUCKLES" WAS, WE WOULDN'T KNOCK OFF SO EARLY!

2

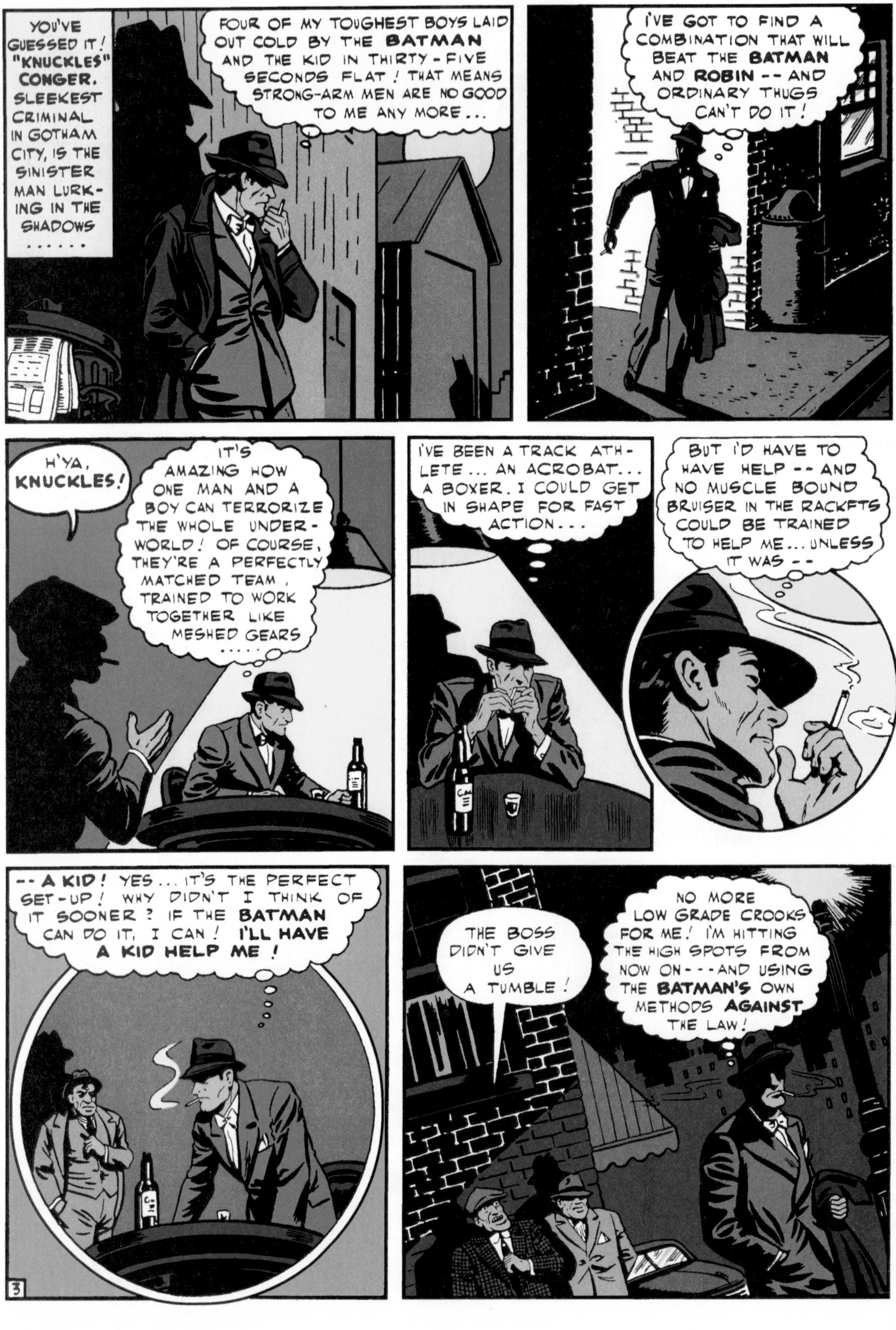
YOU'VE GUESSED IT! "KNUCKLES" CONGER. SLEEKEST CRIMINAL IN GOTHAM CITY, IS THE SINISTER MAN LURKING IN THE SHADOWS . . . . . .
FOUR OF MY TOUGHEST BOYS LAID OUT COLD BY THE BATMAN AND THE KID IN THIRTY-FIVE SECONDS FLAT! THAT MEANS STRONG-ARM MEN ARE NO GOOD TO ME ANY MORE...
I'VE GOT TO FIND A COMBINATION THAT WILL BEAT THE BATMAN AND ROBIN -- AND ORDINARY THUGS CAN'T DO IT!
H'YA, KNUCKLES!
IT'S AMAZING HOW ONE MAN AND A BOY CAN TERRORIZE THE WHOLE UNDERWORLD! OF COURSE, THEY'RE A PERFECTLY MATCHED TEAM, TRAINED TO WORK TOGETHER LIKE MESHED GEARS . . . .
I'VE BEEN A TRACK ATHLETE... AN ACROBAT... A BOXER. I COULD GET IN SHAPE FOR FAST ACTION...
BUT I'D HAVE TO HAVE HELP -- AND NO MUSCLE BOUND BRUISER IN THE RACKFTS COULD BE TRAINED TO HELP ME... UNLESS IT WAS --
-- A KID! YES... IT'S THE PERFECT SET-UP! WHY DIDN'T I THINK OF IT SOONER? IF THE BATMAN CAN DO IT, I CAN! I'LL HAVE A KID HELP ME!
3
THE BOSS DIDN'T GIVE US A TUMBLE!
NO MORE LOW GRADE CROOKS FOR ME! I'M HITTING THE HIGH SPOTS FROM NOW ON---AND USING THE BATMAN'S OWN METHODS AGAINST THE LAW!

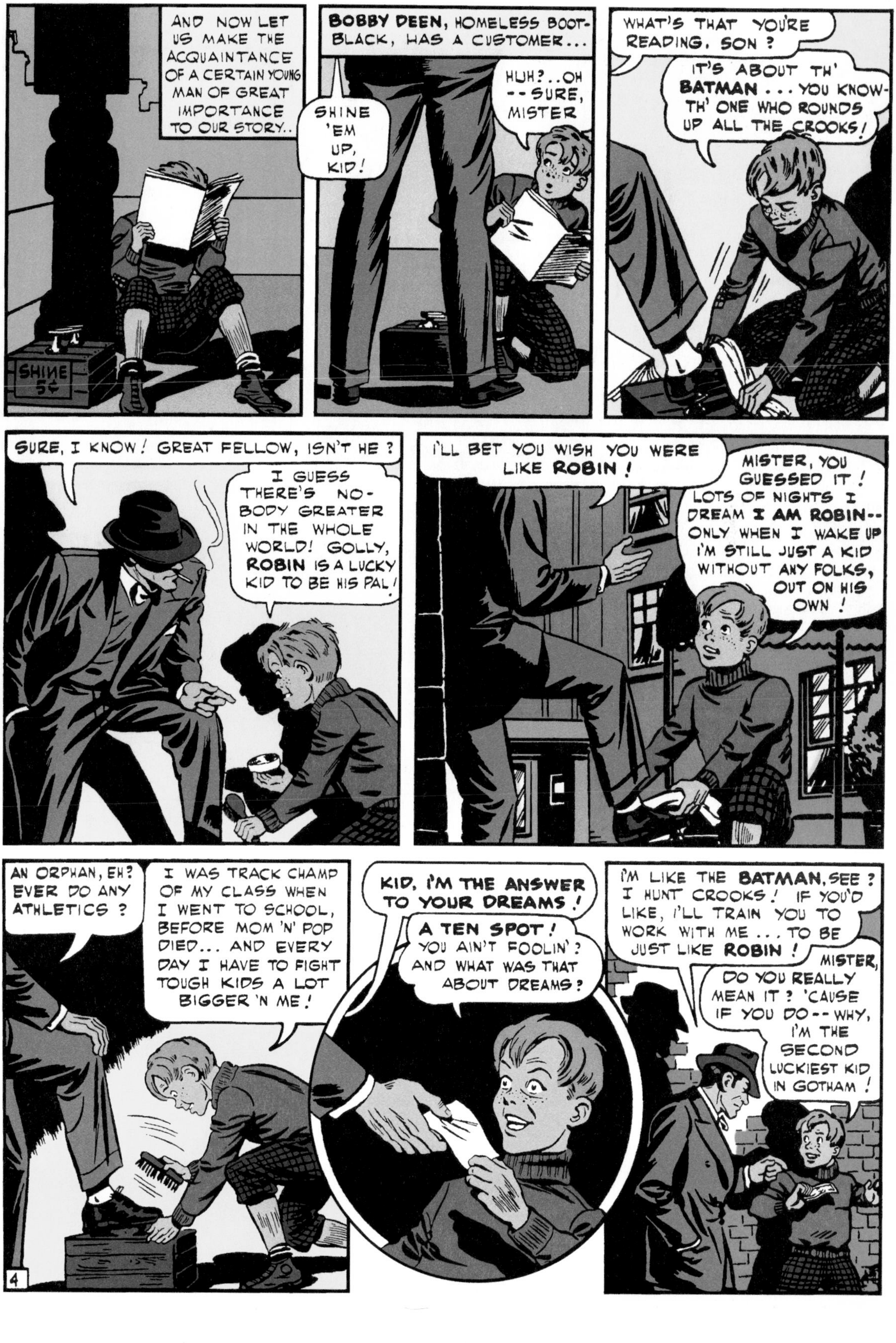
AND NOW LET US MAKE THE ACQUAINTANCE OF A CERTAIN YOUNG MAN OF GREAT IMPORTANCE TO OUR STORY..
SHINE 5¢
BOBBY DEEN, HOMELESS BOOT-BLACK, HAS A CUSTOMER...
SHINE 'EM UP, KID!
HUH?..OH --SURE, MISTER
WHAT'S THAT YOU'RE READING, SON ?
IT'S ABOUT TH' BATMAN . . . YOU KNOW-TH' ONE WHO ROUNDS UP ALL THE CROOKS!
SURE, I KNOW! GREAT FELLOW, ISN'T HE ?
I GUESS THERE'S NO-BODY GREATER IN THE WHOLE WORLD! GOLLY, ROBIN IS A LUCKY KID TO BE HIS PAL!
I'LL BET YOU WISH YOU WERE LIKE ROBIN!
MISTER, YOU GUESSED IT! LOTS OF NIGHTS I DREAM I AM ROBIN-- ONLY WHEN I WAKE UP I'M STILL JUST A KID WITHOUT ANY FOLKS, OUT ON HIS OWN!
AN ORPHAN, EH? EVER DO ANY ATHLETICS ?
I WAS TRACK CHAMP OF MY CLASS WHEN I WENT TO SCHOOL, BEFORE MOM 'N' POP DIED... AND EVERY DAY I HAVE TO FIGHT TOUGH KIDS A LOT BIGGER 'N ME!
4
KID, I'M THE ANSWER TO YOUR DREAMS!
A TEN SPOT! YOU AIN'T FOOLIN'? AND WHAT WAS THAT ABOUT DREAMS?
I'M LIKE THE BATMAN, SEE? I HUNT CROOKS! IF YOU'D LIKE, I'LL TRAIN YOU TO WORK WITH ME . . . TO BE JUST LIKE ROBIN!
MISTER, DO YOU REALLY MEAN IT? 'CAUSE IF YOU DO--WHY, I'M THE SECOND LUCKIEST KID IN GOTHAM!

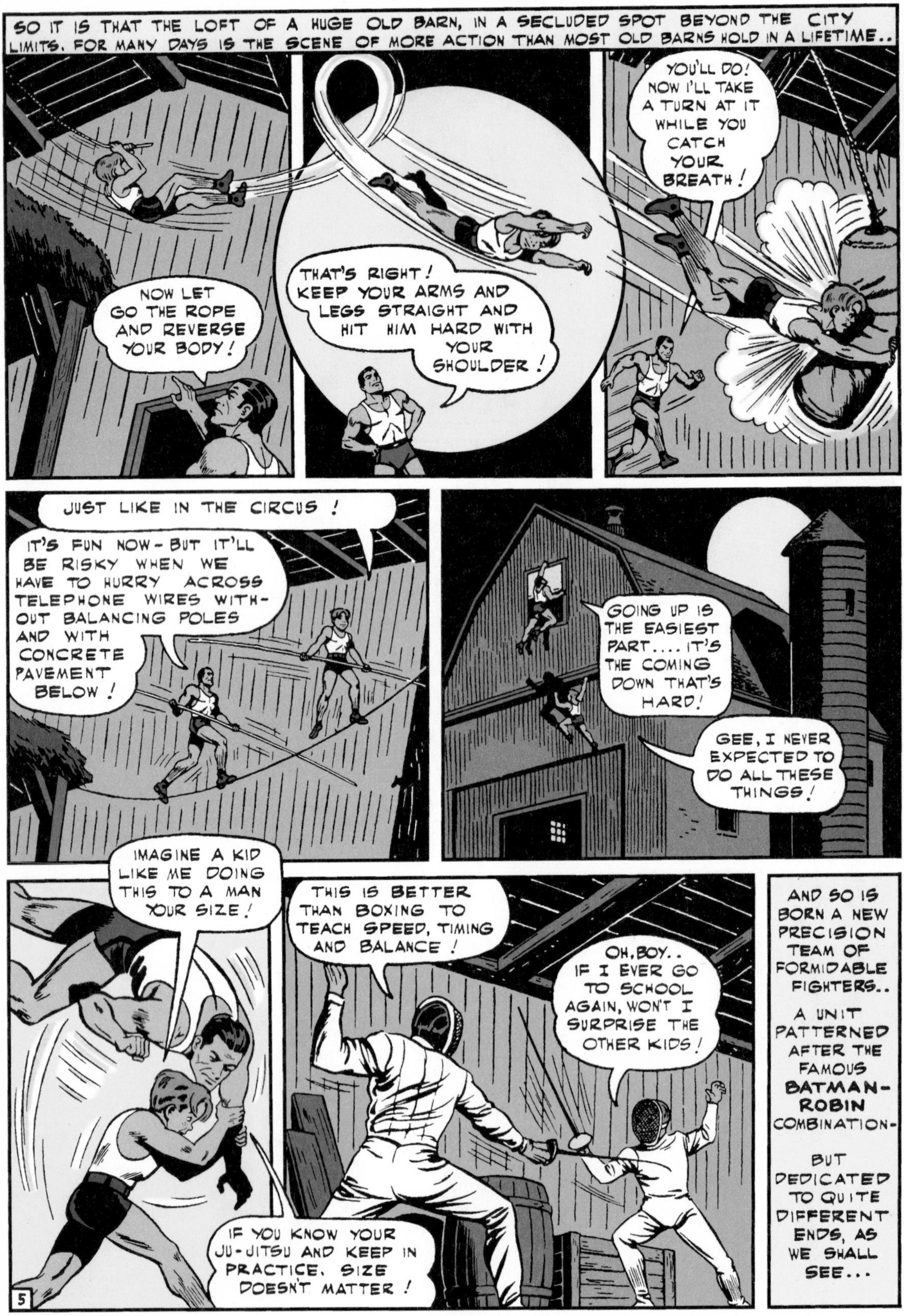
SO IT IS THAT THE LOFT OF A HUGE OLD BARN, IN A SECLUDED SPOT BEYOND THE CITY LIMITS, FOR MANY DAYS IS THE SCENE OF MORE ACTION THAN MOST OLD BARNS HOLD IN A LIFETIME..
NOW LET GO THE ROPE AND REVERSE YOUR BODY!
THAT'S RIGHT! KEEP YOUR ARMS AND LEGS STRAIGHT AND HIT HIM HARD WITH YOUR SHOULDER!
YOU'LL DO! NOW I'LL TAKE A TURN AT IT WHILE YOU CATCH YOUR BREATH!
JUST LIKE IN THE CIRCUS!
IT'S FUN NOW - BUT IT'LL BE RISKY WHEN WE HAVE TO HURRY ACROSS TELEPHONE WIRES WITH-OUT BALANCING POLES AND WITH CONCRETE PAVEMENT BELOW!
GOING UP IS THE EASIEST PART.... IT'S THE COMING DOWN THAT'S HARD!
GEE, I NEVER EXPECTED TO DO ALL THESE THINGS!
IMAGINE A KID LIKE ME DOING THIS TO A MAN YOUR SIZE!
IF YOU KNOW YOUR JU-JITSU AND KEEP IN PRACTICE, SIZE DOESN'T MATTER!
THIS IS BETTER THAN BOXING TO TEACH SPEED, TIMING AND BALANCE!
OH, BOY.. IF I EVER GO TO SCHOOL AGAIN, WON'T I SURPRISE THE OTHER KIDS!
AND SO IS BORN A NEW PRECISION TEAM OF FORMIDABLE FIGHTERS.. A UNIT PATTERNED AFTER THE FAMOUS BATMAN-ROBIN COMBINATION- BUT DEDICATED TO QUITE DIFFERENT ENDS, AS WE SHALL SEE...
5

FINALLY...

TONIGHT WE PULL OUR FIRST JOB--ER--I MEAN, STRIKE OUR FIRST BLOW AT CRIME! I'VE GOT A LINE ON A CROOKED JEWELER!

GOSH! I'M ALL GOOSE-PIMPLES! I CAN HARDLY WAIT TO GET INTO A UNIFORM LIKE ROBIN!

UNIFORM! NIX ON THAT STUFF, YOUNGSTER! WE'LL GET ALONG BETTER WEARING PLAIN DARK CLOTHES!

BUT I THOUGHT... OH, WELL--JUST AS YOU SAY, KNUCKLES!

NIGHT -- AND AN EAGER BOY INNOCENTLY FOLLOWS A MASTER CRIMINAL ALONG A DARK AND CROOKED ROAD...

YOU GO FIRST -- RIGHT THROUGH THE WINDOW ON THE FOURTH FLOOR...IF YOU SEE A WATCHMAN, TACKLE HIM! HE'S A CROOK!

I'LL TACKLE HIM, ALL RIGHT!

MOMENTS LATER...

NICE GOING, PAL!

GOT HIM!

UUHH!

FIRST THING IS TO GATHER THE EVIDENCE!

ALL STOLEN BY CROOKS, AND PEDDLED TO THE PHONEY JEWELER, HUH?

BUT UNKNOWINGLY THE PROWLERS HAVE TOUCHED OFF AN ALARM!

IT'S THE ACME JEWELRY SHOP IN THE PALACE THEATRE BUILDING. WE'LL HAVE THE PLACE SURROUNDED IN A MINUTE!

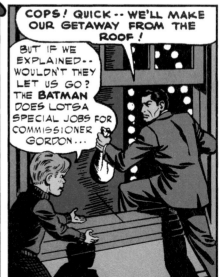

COPS! QUICK -- WE'LL MAKE OUR GETAWAY FROM THE ROOF!

BUT IF WE EXPLAINED-- WOULDN'T THEY LET US GO? THE BATMAN DOES LOTSA SPECIAL JOBS FOR COMMISSIONER GORDON...

6

THE POLICE WON'T BELIEVE US, BECAUSE WE'RE NEW IN THE RACKET! HURRY WITH THAT COLLAPSIBLE GLIDER!

I'M HURRY-IN'!

SILENTLY, TWO DARK, WINGED SHAPES GLIDE UNSEEN ABOVE THE HEADS OF THE GRIM POLICEMEN...

I'LL BE GLAD WHEN TH' COPS GET T' KNOW US!

DON'T WORRY! I'LL TAKE CARE OF EVERYTHING!

NEXT DAY...

THAT'S HOW IT IS.. NOT EVEN THE COPS KNOW ABOUT THE JEWELER BEING CROOKED

UH - HUH...

THIEVES GET GEMS DODGE POLICE NET

LIGHTNING-SWIFT -- PERFECTLY CO-ORDINATED -- THE WILY KNUCKLES AND HIS YOUNG HELPER STRIKE AGAIN AND AGAIN!

S. AVE 153 ST.

OKAY -- NOW WE'LL RUSH IN, GRAB WHAT WE CAN, AND GET AWAY FAST!

I NEVER HEARD O' TH' BATMAN DESTROY-ING PROPERTY!

60

BUT WHAT IF YA SLUGGED THAT BANKER -- I MEAN, THAT CROOK WHO'S PRETEND-ING T' BE A BANKER -- TOO HARD?

I TOLD YOU TO LET ME DO THE WORRYING! YOUR JOB IS TO FOLLOW ORDERS!

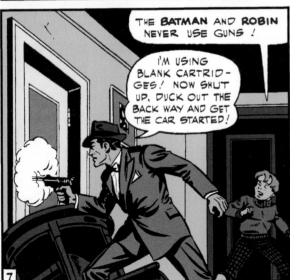

THE BATMAN AND ROBIN NEVER USE GUNS!

I'M USING BLANK CARTRID-GES! NOW SHUT UP, DUCK OUT THE BACK WAY AND GET THE CAR STARTED!

ALTOGETHER, THE BEWIL-DERED BOBBY ISN'T HAVING AS MUCH FUN AS HE EXPECTED..

I WONDER IF ROBIN HAS IT THIS TOUGH? HE CAN WEAR A UNIFORM... AND IF KNUCKLES IS REALLY ON THE LEVEL, I'D LIKE TO SEE HIM PUT SOME CROOKS BEHIND BARS..

IF YOU ARE BEGINNING TO THINK THAT PERHAPS BOBBY HASN'T BEEN TOO BRIGHT, REMEMBER THAT HE IS IN THE HANDS OF THE MAN WHOM THE BATMAN HIMSELF TERMED THE SLICKEST CRIMINAL IN TOWN! RE-MEMBER, TOO, THAT BOBBY IS A SMALL BOY ALONE IN THE WORLD!

7

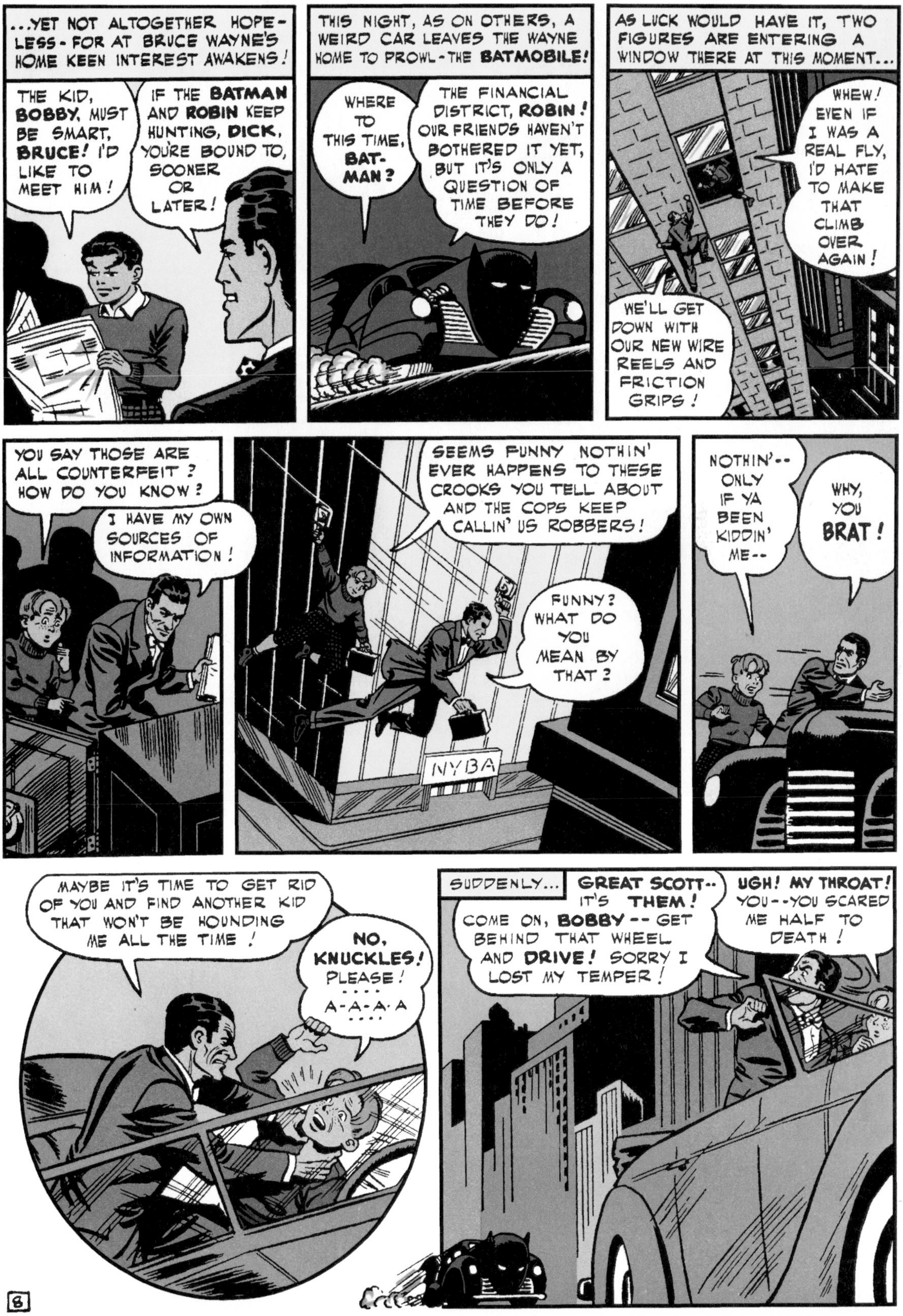
...YET NOT ALTOGETHER HOPE-LESS - FOR AT BRUCE WAYNE'S HOME KEEN INTEREST AWAKENS!
THE KID, BOBBY, MUST BE SMART, BRUCE! I'D LIKE TO MEET HIM!
IF THE BATMAN AND ROBIN KEEP HUNTING, DICK, YOU'RE BOUND TO, SOONER OR LATER!
THIS NIGHT, AS ON OTHERS, A WEIRD CAR LEAVES THE WAYNE HOME TO PROWL - THE BATMOBILE!
WHERE TO THIS TIME, BAT-MAN?
THE FINANCIAL DISTRICT, ROBIN! OUR FRIENDS HAVEN'T BOTHERED IT YET, BUT IT'S ONLY A QUESTION OF TIME BEFORE THEY DO!
AS LUCK WOULD HAVE IT, TWO FIGURES ARE ENTERING A WINDOW THERE AT THIS MOMENT...
WHEW! EVEN IF I WAS A REAL FLY, I'D HATE TO MAKE THAT CLIMB OVER AGAIN!
WE'LL GET DOWN WITH OUR NEW WIRE REELS AND FRICTION GRIPS!
YOU SAY THOSE ARE ALL COUNTERFEIT? HOW DO YOU KNOW?
I HAVE MY OWN SOURCES OF INFORMATION!
SEEMS FUNNY NOTHIN' EVER HAPPENS TO THESE CROOKS YOU TELL ABOUT AND THE COPS KEEP CALLIN' US ROBBERS!
FUNNY? WHAT DO YOU MEAN BY THAT?
NYBA
NOTHIN'-- ONLY IF YA BEEN KIDDIN' ME--
WHY, YOU BRAT!
MAYBE IT'S TIME TO GET RID OF YOU AND FIND ANOTHER KID THAT WON'T BE HOUNDING ME ALL THE TIME!
NO, KNUCKLES! PLEASE! .... A-A-A-A ....
SUDDENLY...
GREAT SCOTT-- IT'S THEM! COME ON, BOBBY -- GET BEHIND THAT WHEEL AND DRIVE! SORRY I LOST MY TEMPER!
UGH! MY THROAT! YOU--YOU SCARED ME HALF TO DEATH!
8

BUT IT'S TH' **BATMAN!** WHY D'WE HAVE T' RUN AWAY?

DON'T LET 'EM FOOL YOU! THAT'S NOT THE **BATMAN!**

KNUCKLES' PISTOL BLAZES AGAIN AND AGAIN AS A FURIOUS CHASE TWISTS THROUGH THE STREETS...

THE **BATMAN** IS OUT WEST ON A CASE, AND TWO GANGSTERS ARE PRETENDING TO BE HIM AND **ROBIN!** ONE OF THEM IS A DWARF!

NO USE! THEIR CAR'S TOO FAST AND IT'S ALL BULLETPROOF! WE'LL WAIT TILL THEY'RE ALMOST UP TO US. THEN --

STEEL RODS REACH UP FROM THE FUGITIVE CAR -- HOOK THE CROSS BARS OF STREET LAMPS -- AND..

WE'RE GOING TO RUN RIGHT UNDER THEM!

CAN'T BE HELPED **ROBIN!** THE **BATMOBILE** CAN'T STOP ON A DIME WHEN IT'S DOING NINETY MILES AN HOUR!

CRASH!

NOW THAT WE'VE COME THIS CLOSE, WE'VE GOT TO CATCH THEM!

WE'LL DO THE BEST WE CAN!

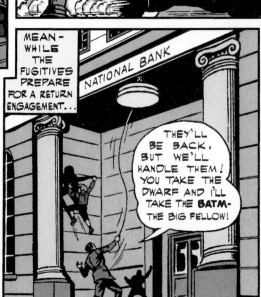

MEANWHILE THE FUGITIVES PREPARE FOR A RETURN ENGAGEMENT...

NATIONAL BANK

THEY'LL BE BACK, BUT WE'LL HANDLE THEM! YOU TAKE THE DWARF AND I'LL TAKE THE **BATM-** THE BIG FELLOW!

PRESENTLY...

THIS IS WHERE WE SAW THEM LAST... WHERE'D THEY GO?

MAYBE THEY DIDN'T LOOK OUT FOR TRICKS!

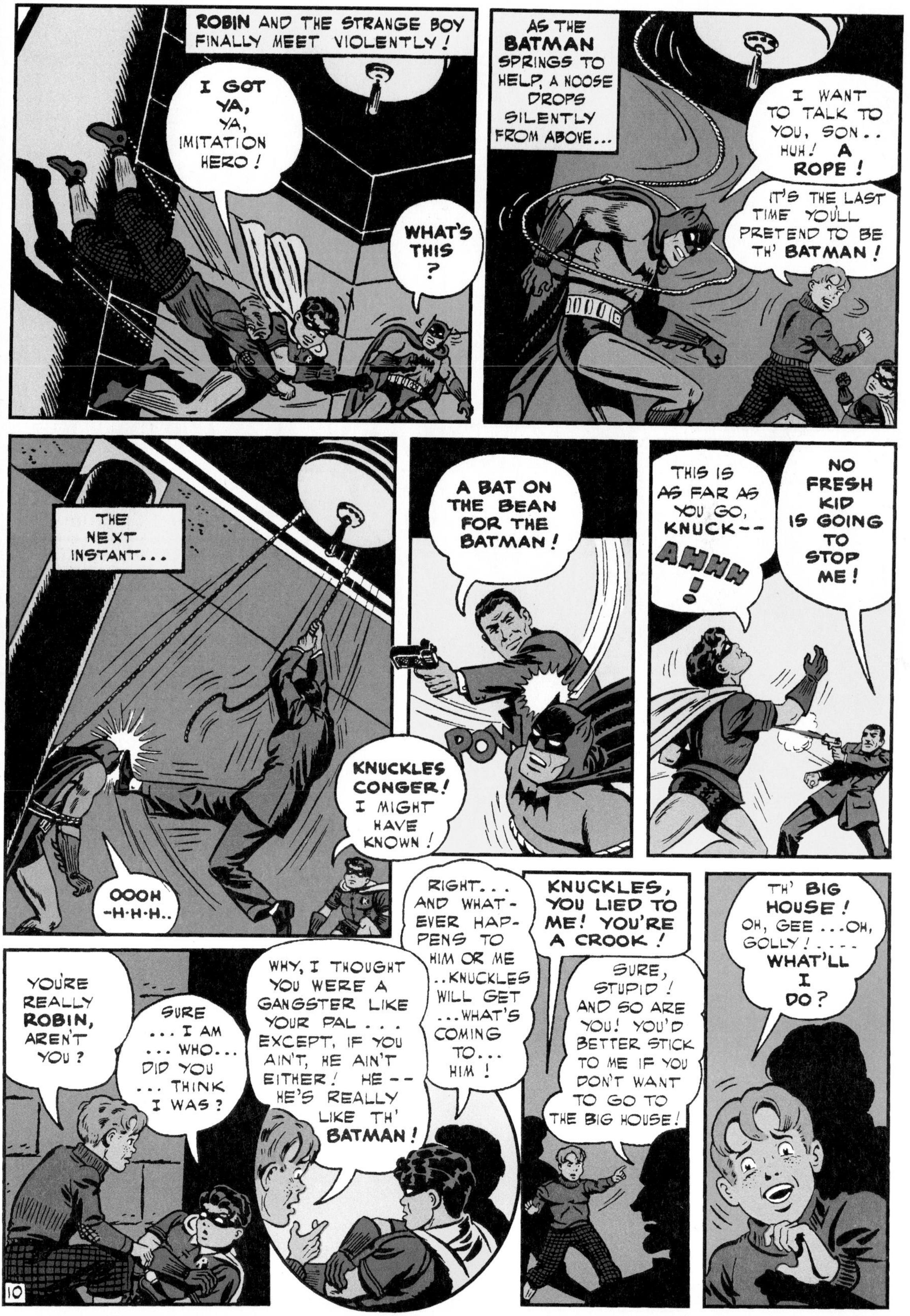
ROBIN AND THE STRANGE BOY FINALLY MEET VIOLENTLY!
I GOT YA, YA, IMITATION HERO!
WHAT'S THIS ?
AS THE BATMAN SPRINGS TO HELP, A NOOSE DROPS SILENTLY FROM ABOVE...
I WANT TO TALK TO YOU, SON.. HUH! A ROPE!
IT'S THE LAST TIME YOU'LL PRETEND TO BE TH' BATMAN!
THE NEXT INSTANT...
OOOH -H-H-H..
KNUCKLES CONGER! I MIGHT HAVE KNOWN!
A BAT ON THE BEAN FOR THE BATMAN!
POW
THIS IS AS FAR AS YOU GO, KNUCK--
AHHH!
NO FRESH KID IS GOING TO STOP ME!
YOU'RE REALLY ROBIN, AREN'T YOU?
SURE ... I AM ... WHO... DID YOU ... THINK I WAS?
WHY, I THOUGHT YOU WERE A GANGSTER LIKE YOUR PAL . . . EXCEPT, IF YOU AIN'T, HE AIN'T EITHER! HE -- HE'S REALLY LIKE TH' BATMAN!
RIGHT... AND WHATEVER HAPPENS TO HIM OR ME ..KNUCKLES WILL GET ...WHAT'S COMING TO... HIM!
KNUCKLES, YOU LIED TO ME! YOU'RE A CROOK!
SURE, STUPID! AND SO ARE YOU! YOU'D BETTER STICK TO ME IF YOU DON'T WANT TO GO TO THE BIG HOUSE!
TH' BIG HOUSE! OH, GEE ...OH, GOLLY! .... WHAT'LL I DO?
10

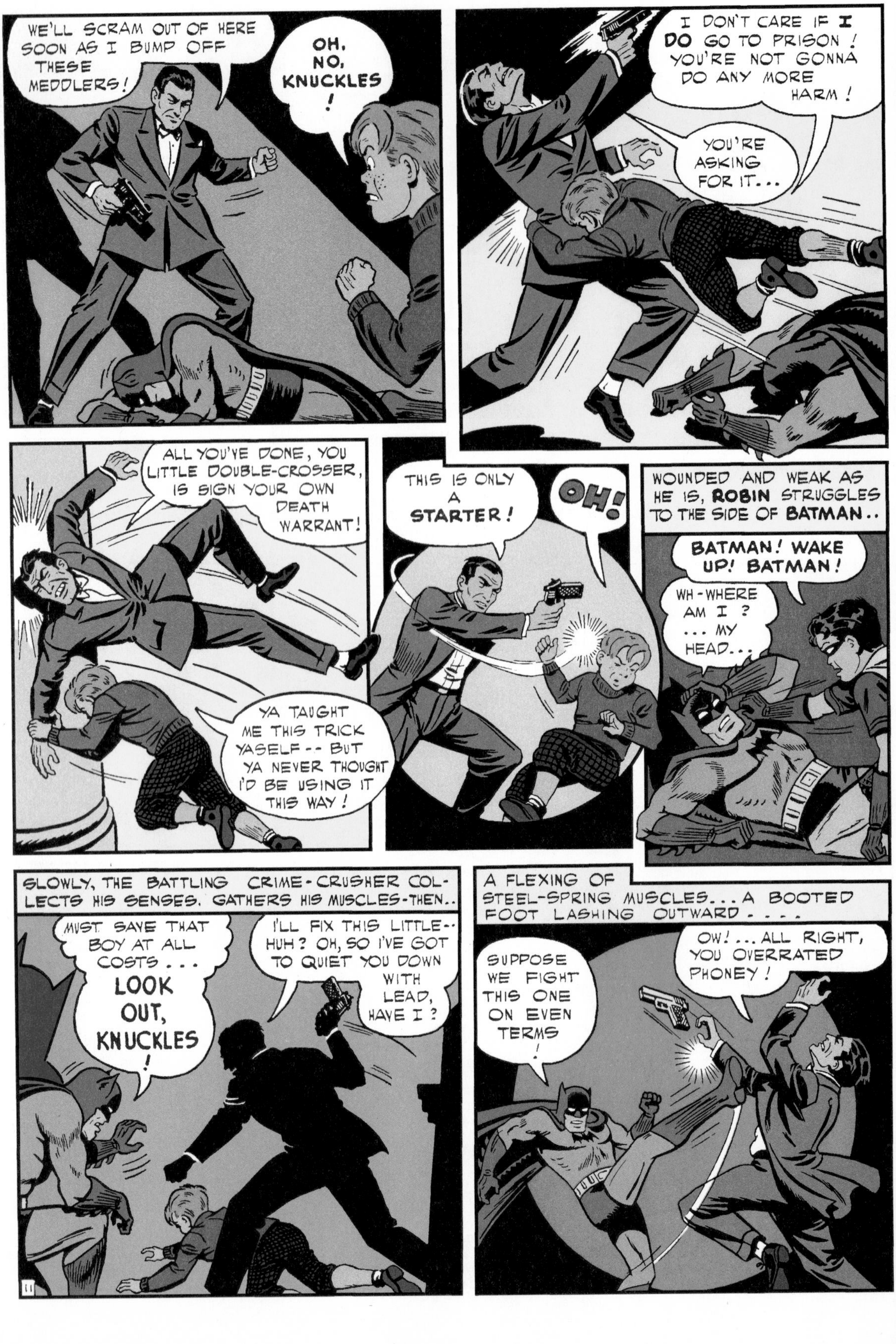
WE'LL SCRAM OUT OF HERE SOON AS I BUMP OFF THESE MEDDLERS!
OH, NO, KNUCKLES!
I DON'T CARE IF I DO GO TO PRISON! YOU'RE NOT GONNA DO ANY MORE HARM!
YOU'RE ASKING FOR IT...
ALL YOU'VE DONE, YOU LITTLE DOUBLE-CROSSER, IS SIGN YOUR OWN DEATH WARRANT!
YA TAUGHT ME THIS TRICK YASELF -- BUT YA NEVER THOUGHT I'D BE USING IT THIS WAY!
THIS IS ONLY A STARTER!
OH!
WOUNDED AND WEAK AS HE IS, ROBIN STRUGGLES TO THE SIDE OF BATMAN..
BATMAN! WAKE UP! BATMAN!
WH-WHERE AM I? ... MY HEAD...
SLOWLY, THE BATTLING CRIME-CRUSHER COLLECTS HIS SENSES. GATHERS HIS MUSCLES-THEN..
MUST SAVE THAT BOY AT ALL COSTS... LOOK OUT, KNUCKLES!
I'LL FIX THIS LITTLE-- HUH? OH, SO I'VE GOT TO QUIET YOU DOWN WITH LEAD, HAVE I?
11
A FLEXING OF STEEL-SPRING MUSCLES...A BOOTED FOOT LASHING OUTWARD....
SUPPOSE WE FIGHT THIS ONE ON EVEN TERMS!
OW!...ALL RIGHT, YOU OVERRATED PHONEY!

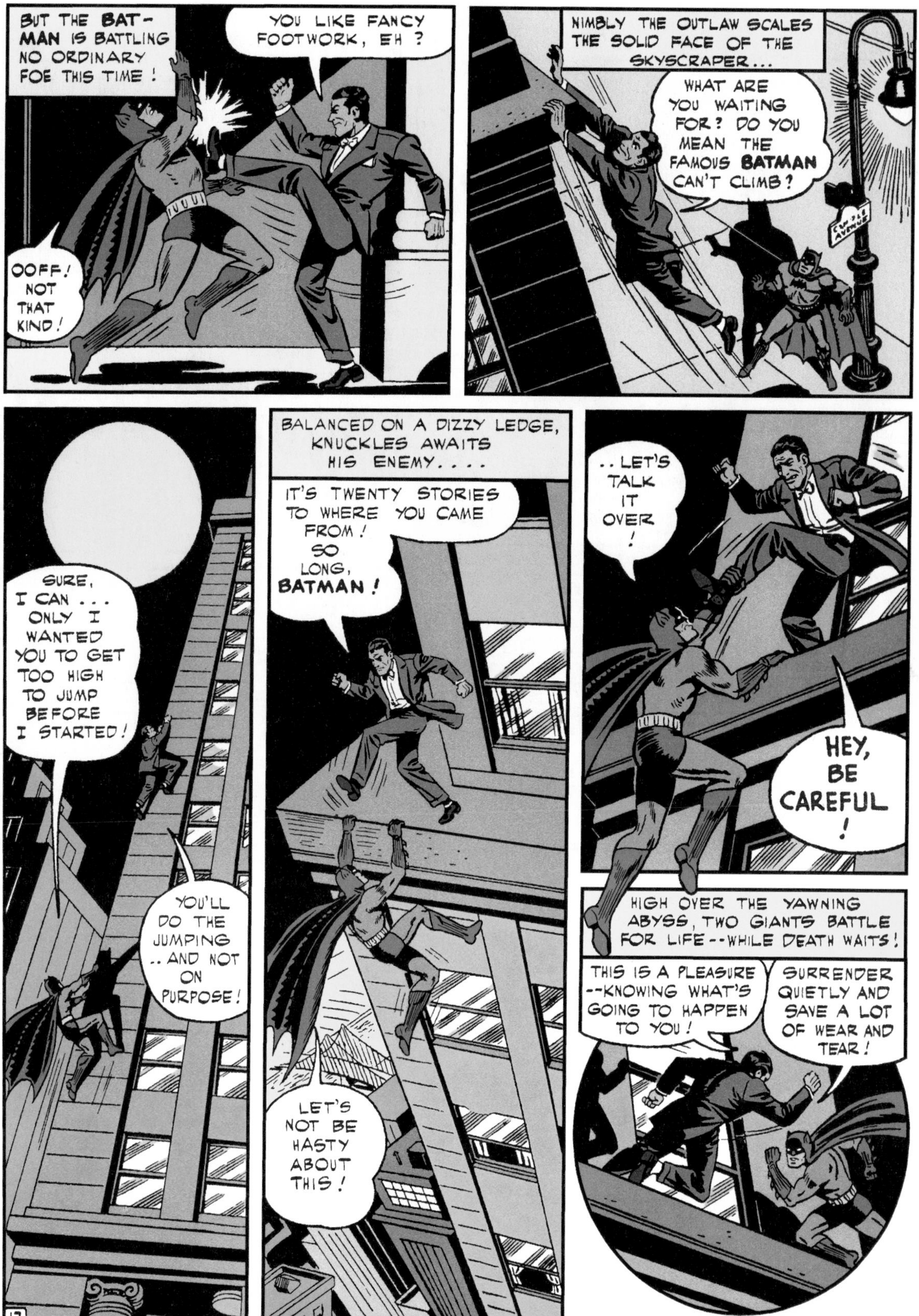

BUT THE BATMAN IS BATTLING NO ORDINARY FOE THIS TIME!
YOU LIKE FANCY FOOTWORK, EH?
OOFF! NOT THAT KIND!
NIMBLY THE OUTLAW SCALES THE SOLID FACE OF THE SKYSCRAPER...
WHAT ARE YOU WAITING FOR? DO YOU MEAN THE FAMOUS BATMAN CAN'T CLIMB?
SURE, I CAN... ONLY I WANTED YOU TO GET TOO HIGH TO JUMP BEFORE I STARTED!
YOU'LL DO THE JUMPING ..AND NOT ON PURPOSE!
12
BALANCED ON A DIZZY LEDGE, KNUCKLES AWAITS HIS ENEMY....
IT'S TWENTY STORIES TO WHERE YOU CAME FROM! SO LONG, BATMAN!
LET'S NOT BE HASTY ABOUT THIS!
..LET'S TALK IT OVER!
HEY, BE CAREFUL!
HIGH OVER THE YAWNING ABYSS, TWO GIANTS BATTLE FOR LIFE--WHILE DEATH WAITS!
THIS IS A PLEASURE --KNOWING WHAT'S GOING TO HAPPEN TO YOU!
SURRENDER QUIETLY AND SAVE A LOT OF WEAR AND TEAR!

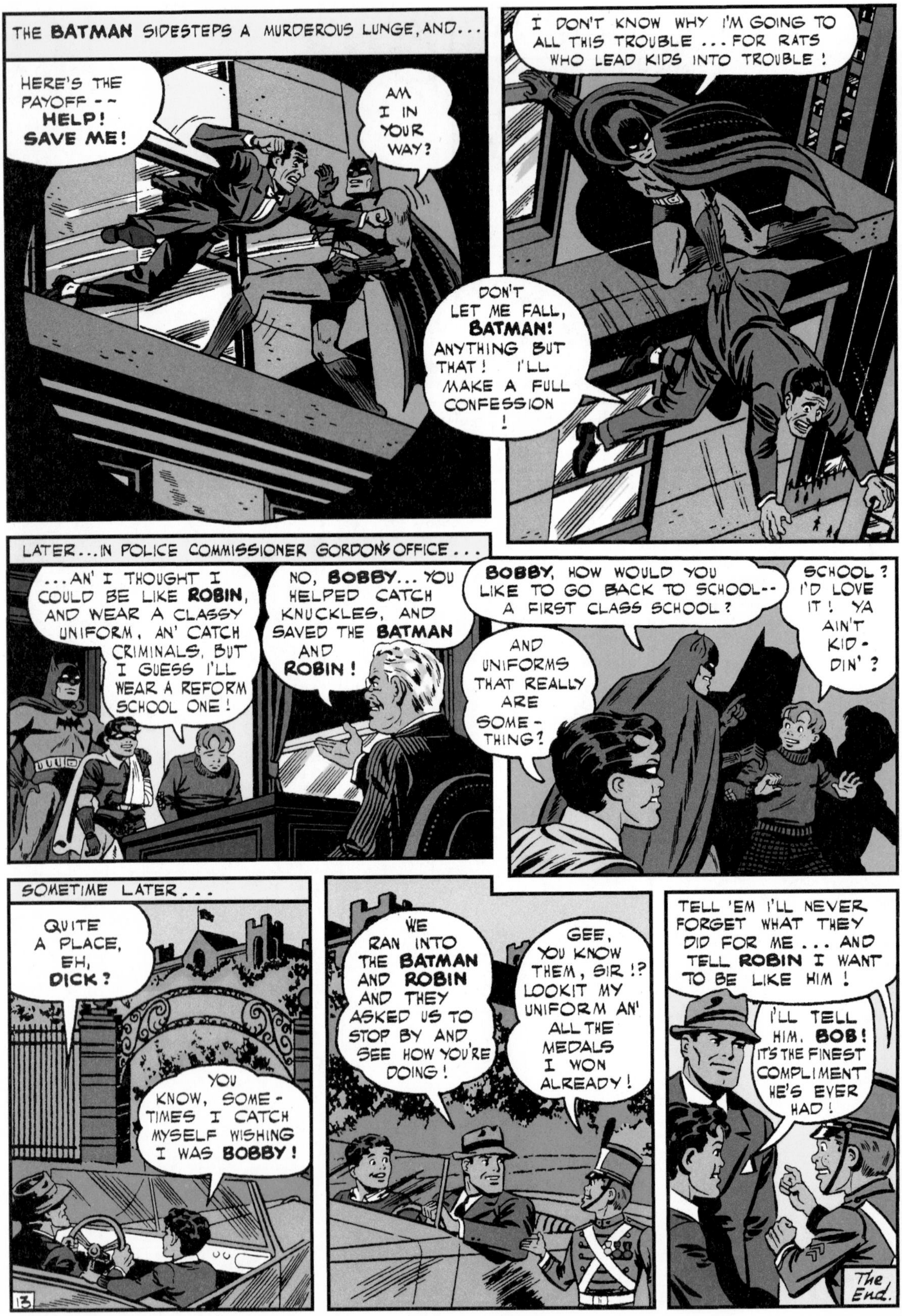

THE BATMAN SIDESTEPS A MURDEROUS LUNGE, AND...
HERE'S THE PAYOFF -- HELP! SAVE ME!
AM I IN YOUR WAY?
I DON'T KNOW WHY I'M GOING TO ALL THIS TROUBLE ... FOR RATS WHO LEAD KIDS INTO TROUBLE!
DON'T LET ME FALL, BATMAN! ANYTHING BUT THAT! I'LL MAKE A FULL CONFESSION!
LATER... IN POLICE COMMISSIONER GORDON'S OFFICE...
...AN' I THOUGHT I COULD BE LIKE ROBIN, AND WEAR A CLASSY UNIFORM, AN' CATCH CRIMINALS, BUT I GUESS I'LL WEAR A REFORM SCHOOL ONE!
NO, BOBBY... YOU HELPED CATCH KNUCKLES, AND SAVED THE BATMAN AND ROBIN!
BOBBY, HOW WOULD YOU LIKE TO GO BACK TO SCHOOL-- A FIRST CLASS SCHOOL?
AND UNIFORMS THAT REALLY ARE SOME-THING?
SCHOOL? I'D LOVE IT! YA AIN'T KID-DIN'?
SOMETIME LATER...
QUITE A PLACE, EH, DICK?
YOU KNOW, SOME-TIMES I CATCH MYSELF WISHING I WAS BOBBY!
13
WE RAN INTO THE BATMAN AND ROBIN AND THEY ASKED US TO STOP BY AND SEE HOW YOU'RE DOING!
GEE, YOU KNOW THEM, SIR!? LOOKIT MY UNIFORM AN' ALL THE MEDALS I WON ALREADY!
TELL 'EM I'LL NEVER FORGET WHAT THEY DID FOR ME ... AND TELL ROBIN I WANT TO BE LIKE HIM!
I'LL TELL HIM, BOB! IT'S THE FINEST COMPLIMENT HE'S EVER HAD!
The End.

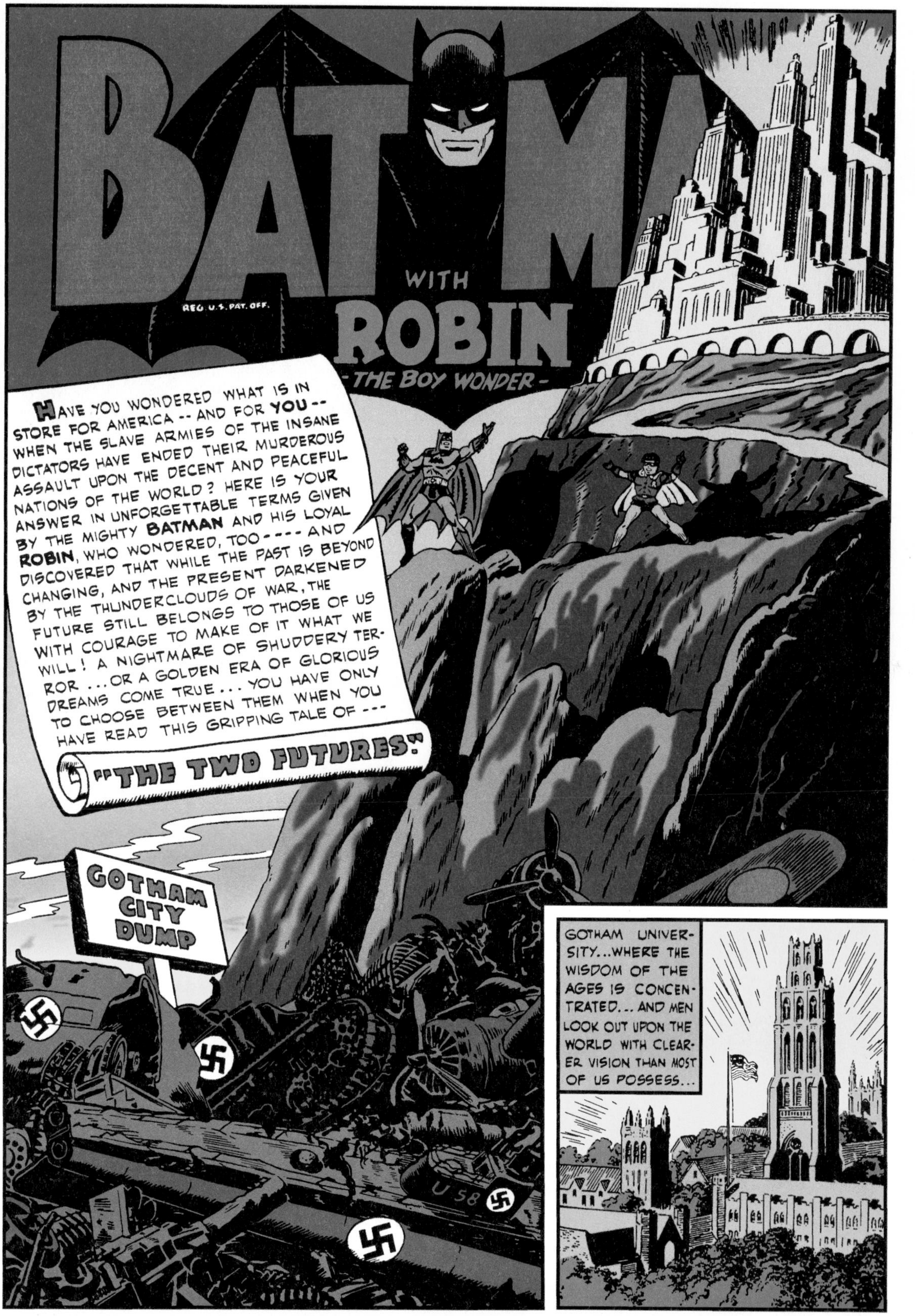
BATMAN
REG. U.S. PAT. OFF.
WITH
ROBIN
-THE BOY WONDER-
HAVE YOU WONDERED WHAT IS IN STORE FOR AMERICA -- AND FOR YOU -- WHEN THE SLAVE ARMIES OF THE INSANE DICTATORS HAVE ENDED THEIR MURDEROUS ASSAULT UPON THE DECENT AND PEACEFUL NATIONS OF THE WORLD? HERE IS YOUR ANSWER IN UNFORGETTABLE TERMS GIVEN BY THE MIGHTY BATMAN AND HIS LOYAL ROBIN, WHO WONDERED, TOO---- AND DISCOVERED THAT WHILE THE PAST IS BEYOND CHANGING, AND THE PRESENT DARKENED BY THE THUNDERCLOUDS OF WAR, THE FUTURE STILL BELONGS TO THOSE OF US WITH COURAGE TO MAKE OF IT WHAT WE WILL! A NIGHTMARE OF SHUDDERY TERROR ... OR A GOLDEN ERA OF GLORIOUS DREAMS COME TRUE ... YOU HAVE ONLY TO CHOOSE BETWEEN THEM WHEN YOU HAVE READ THIS GRIPPING TALE OF ---
"THE TWO FUTURES"
GOTHAM CITY DUMP
U58
GOTHAM UNIVERSITY...WHERE THE WISDOM OF THE AGES IS CONCENTRATED... AND MEN LOOK OUT UPON THE WORLD WITH CLEARER VISION THAN MOST OF US POSSESS...

ACROSS THE SHADED CAMPUS STRIDE TWO FIGURES WHOSE COSTUMES BLEND STRANGELY WITH THE CLASSICAL BACKGROUND.

I DIDN'T EXPECT TO GO TO COLLEGE FOR A COUPLE OF YEARS, BATMAN, AND I THOUGHT YOUR EDUCATION WAS FINISHED!

AN INTELLIGENT PERSON IS NEVER THROUGH LEARNING, ROBIN!

PROFESSOR RANIER IS THE WORLD'S GREATEST HISTORIAN. HIS PREDICTIONS ARE USUALLY RIGHT!

AND YOU THINK HE CAN TELL US ABOUT THE FUTURE? OH, BOY!

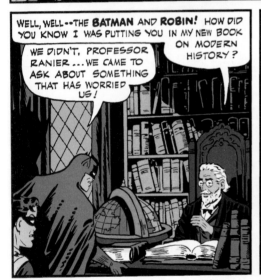

WELL, WELL--THE BATMAN AND ROBIN! HOW DID YOU KNOW I WAS PUTTING YOU IN MY NEW BOOK ON MODERN HISTORY?

WE DIDN'T, PROFESSOR RANIER...WE CAME TO ASK ABOUT SOMETHING THAT HAS WORRIED US!

SO YOU WANT TO KNOW WHAT WILL HAPPEN TO OUR DEMOCRATIC WAY OF LIFE WHEN THIS WAR IS OVER? HMMM--A LARGE ORDER!

MILLIONS OF PEOPLE ARE ANXIOUS TO KNOW THE ANSWER, SIR! EVEN IF IT'S BAD, WE THINK THEY HAVE A RIGHT TO KNOW!

HERE ARE PROFESSORS PROE AND CON...WE THREE HAVE GONE INTO THIS THOROUGHLY!

WE CAN GIVE YOU THE WHOLE STORY--BUT CAN YOU TAKE IT?

NOTHING GOOD EVER CAME WITHOUT LABOR AND SAC-RIFICE..

WE CAN TAKE IT, IF IT'S TRUE--AND SO CAN EVERY OTHER REAL AMERICAN!

THE PIONEERS WHO BUILT OUR COUNTRY COULD TAKE IT, COULDN'T THEY?

VERY WELL, GENTLEMEN...IF YOU'LL STEP THIS WAY, WE SHALL GIVE YOU A REALISTIC PRE-VIEW OF THE WORLD OF THE IMMEDIATE FUTURE!

SOUNDS PRETTY SERIOUS... I'M A LITTLE NERVOUS!

A PREVIEW OF THE FUTURE! BY STRETCHING OUR IMAGINATIONS JUST A LITTLE, WE MAY SEE IT AS VIVIDLY AS IT IS SHOWN TO THE BATMAN AND ROBIN!... WE WILL REMEM-BER THAT WHAT-EVER A MAN CAN IMAGINE IS POSSIBLE! YET ITS OPPOSITE IS POSSIBLE ALSO! THUS MEN CAN DECIDE TO SINK OR STRIVE TOWARD THE LIGHT!

②

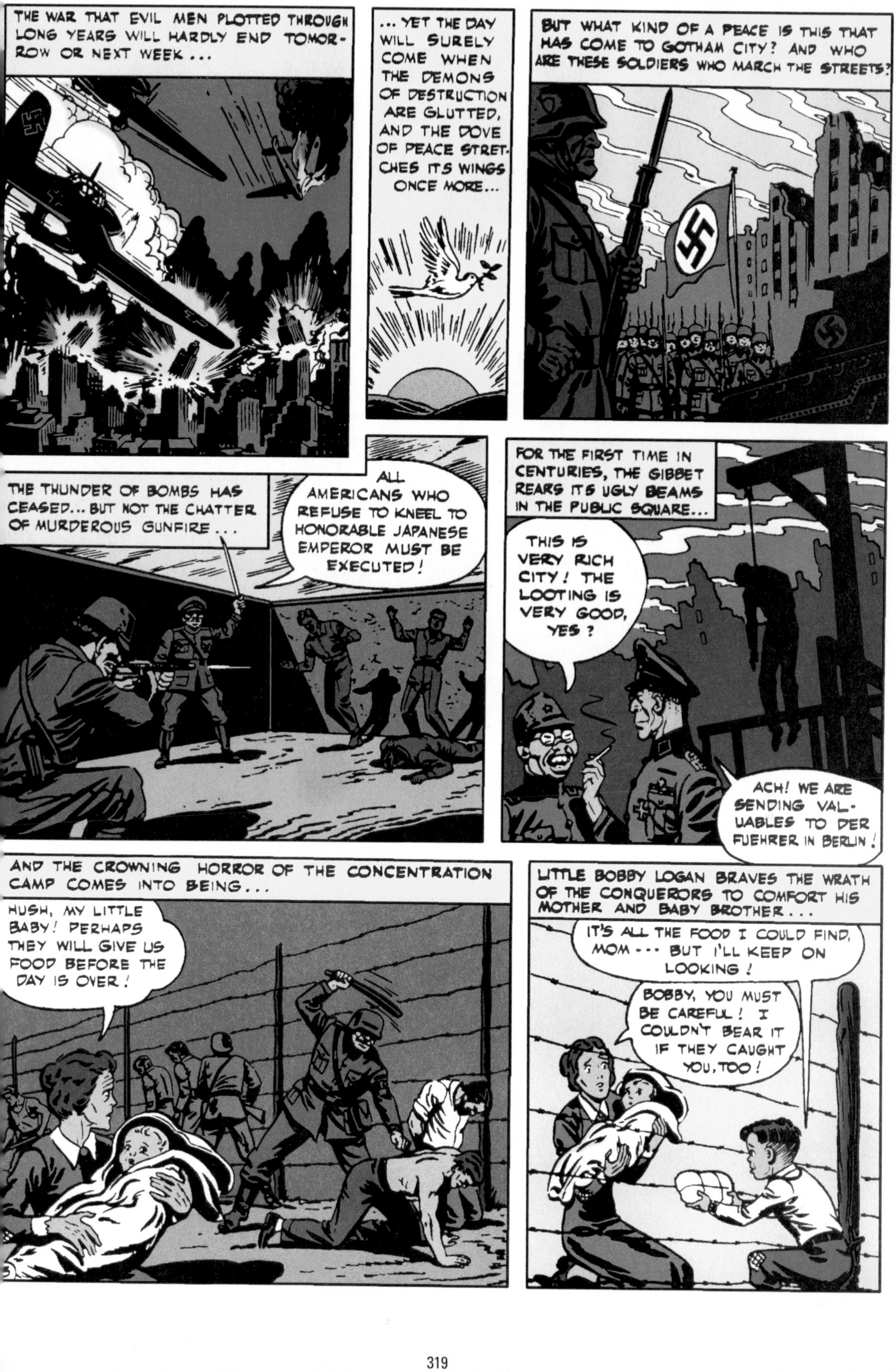
THE WAR THAT EVIL MEN PLOTTED THROUGH LONG YEARS WILL HARDLY END TOMORROW OR NEXT WEEK . . .
. . . YET THE DAY WILL SURELY COME WHEN THE DEMONS OF DESTRUCTION ARE GLUTTED, AND THE DOVE OF PEACE STRETCHES ITS WINGS ONCE MORE . . .
BUT WHAT KIND OF A PEACE IS THIS THAT HAS COME TO GOTHAM CITY? AND WHO ARE THESE SOLDIERS WHO MARCH THE STREETS?
THE THUNDER OF BOMBS HAS CEASED . . . BUT NOT THE CHATTER OF MURDEROUS GUNFIRE . . .
ALL AMERICANS WHO REFUSE TO KNEEL TO HONORABLE JAPANESE EMPEROR MUST BE EXECUTED!
FOR THE FIRST TIME IN CENTURIES, THE GIBBET REARS ITS UGLY BEAMS IN THE PUBLIC SQUARE . . .
THIS IS VERY RICH CITY! THE LOOTING IS VERY GOOD, YES?
ACH! WE ARE SENDING VALUABLES TO DER FUEHRER IN BERLIN!
AND THE CROWNING HORROR OF THE CONCENTRATION CAMP COMES INTO BEING . . .
HUSH, MY LITTLE BABY! PERHAPS THEY WILL GIVE US FOOD BEFORE THE DAY IS OVER!
LITTLE BOBBY LOGAN BRAVES THE WRATH OF THE CONQUERORS TO COMFORT HIS MOTHER AND BABY BROTHER . . .
IT'S ALL THE FOOD I COULD FIND, MOM - - - BUT I'LL KEEP ON LOOKING!
BOBBY, YOU MUST BE CAREFUL! I COULDN'T BEAR IT IF THEY CAUGHT YOU, TOO!

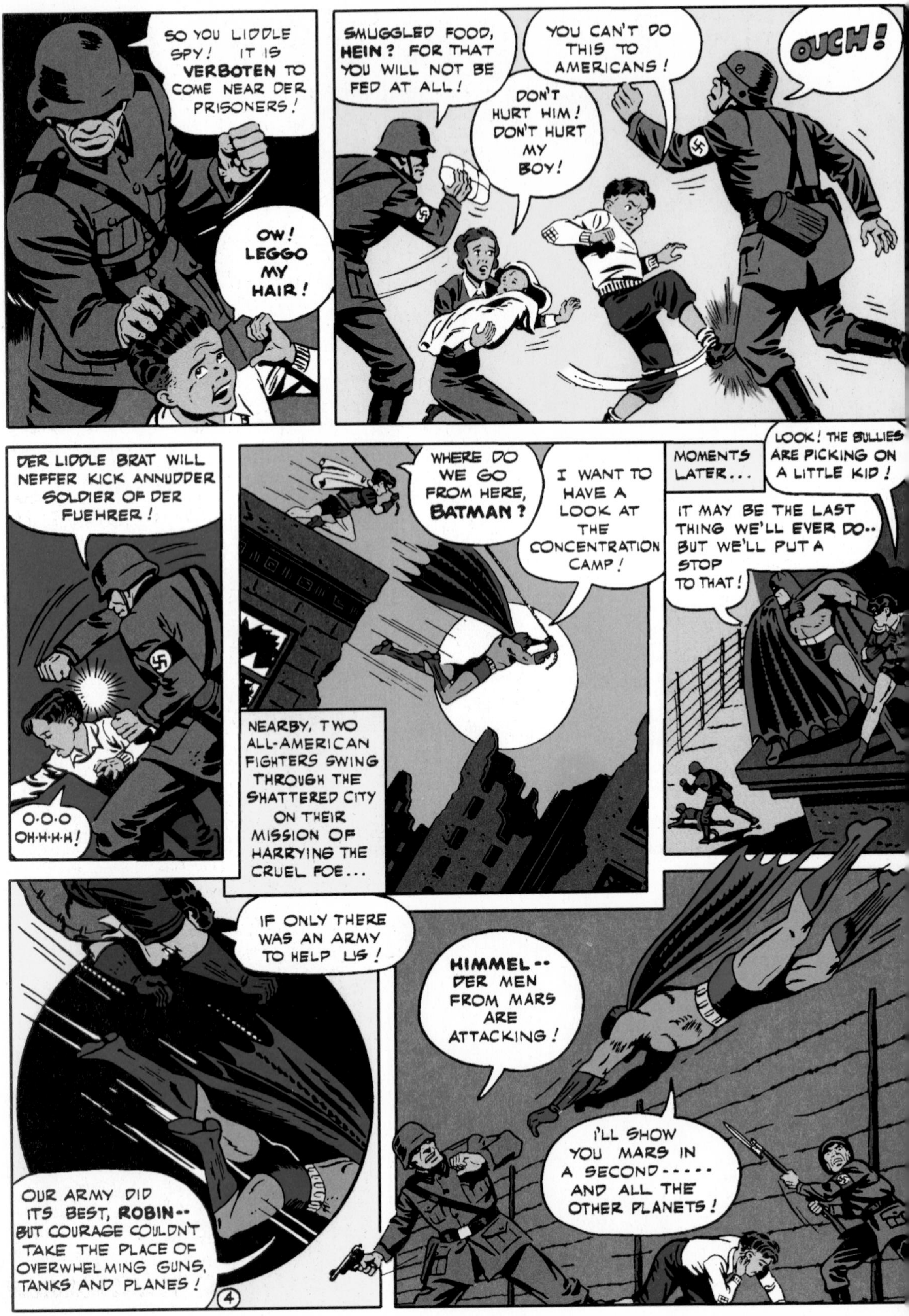
SO YOU LIDDLE SPY! IT IS VERBOTEN TO COME NEAR DER PRISONERS!
OW! LEGGO MY HAIR!
SMUGGLED FOOD, HEIN? FOR THAT YOU WILL NOT BE FED AT ALL!
DON'T HURT HIM! DON'T HURT MY BOY!
YOU CAN'T DO THIS TO AMERICANS!
OUCH!
DER LIDDLE BRAT WILL NEFFER KICK ANNUDDER SOLDIER OF DER FUEHRER!
O-O-O OH-H-H-H!
WHERE DO WE GO FROM HERE, BATMAN?
I WANT TO HAVE A LOOK AT THE CONCENTRATION CAMP!
NEARBY, TWO ALL-AMERICAN FIGHTERS SWING THROUGH THE SHATTERED CITY ON THEIR MISSION OF HARRYING THE CRUEL FOE...
MOMENTS LATER...
LOOK! THE BULLIES ARE PICKING ON A LITTLE KID!
IT MAY BE THE LAST THING WE'LL EVER DO.. BUT WE'LL PUT A STOP TO THAT!
IF ONLY THERE WAS AN ARMY TO HELP US!
OUR ARMY DID ITS BEST, ROBIN-- BUT COURAGE COULDN'T TAKE THE PLACE OF OVERWHELMING GUNS, TANKS AND PLANES!
4
HIMMEL-- DER MEN FROM MARS ARE ATTACKING!
I'LL SHOW YOU MARS IN A SECOND----- AND ALL THE OTHER PLANETS!

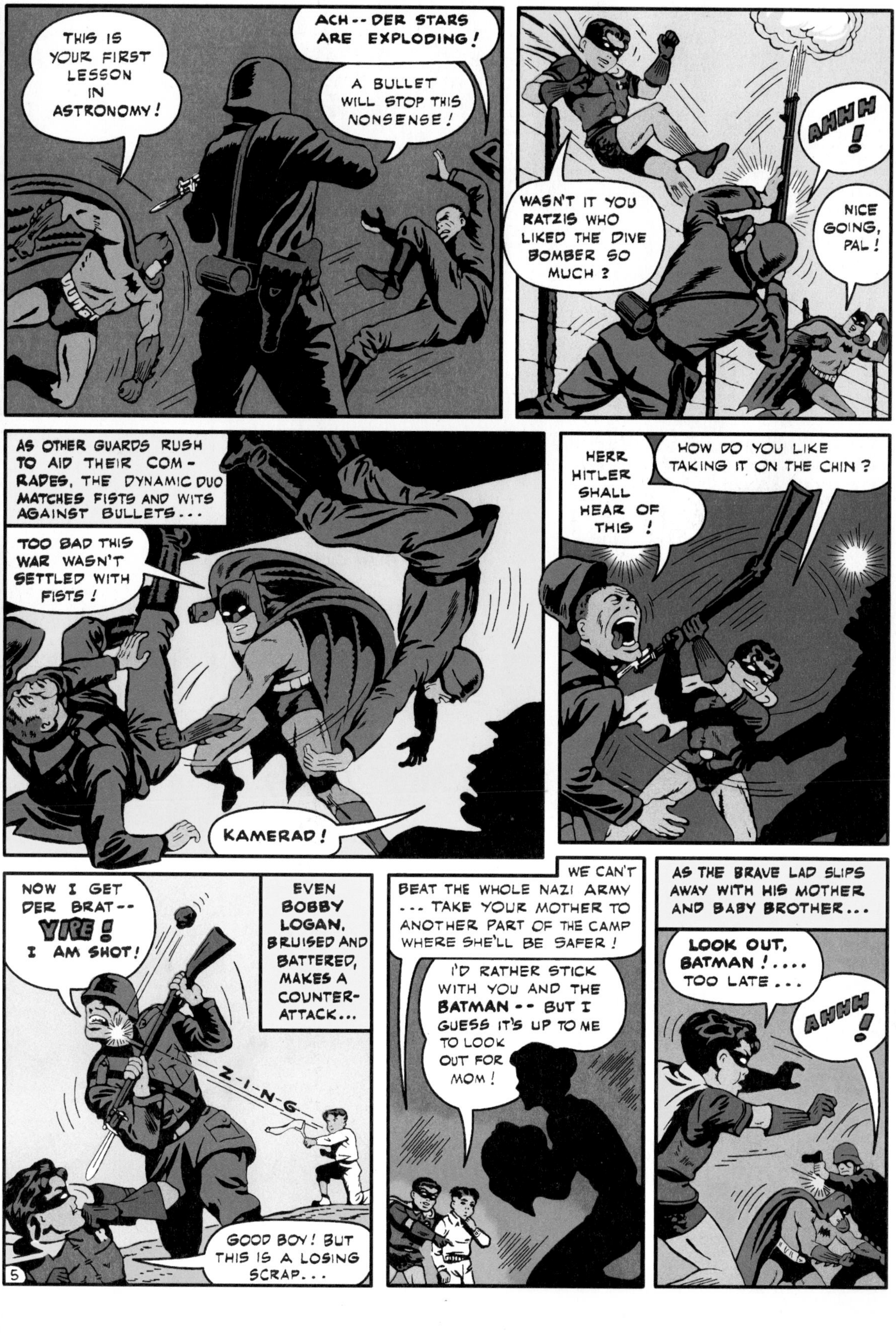
THIS IS YOUR FIRST LESSON IN ASTRONOMY!
ACH-- DER STARS ARE EXPLODING!
A BULLET WILL STOP THIS NONSENSE!
WASN'T IT YOU RATZIS WHO LIKED THE DIVE BOMBER SO MUCH?
AHHH!
NICE GOING, PAL!
AS OTHER GUARDS RUSH TO AID THEIR COM-RADES, THE DYNAMIC DUO MATCHES FISTS AND WITS AGAINST BULLETS...
TOO BAD THIS WAR WASN'T SETTLED WITH FISTS!
KAMERAD!
HERR HITLER SHALL HEAR OF THIS!
HOW DO YOU LIKE TAKING IT ON THE CHIN?
NOW I GET DER BRAT-- YIPE! I AM SHOT!
EVEN BOBBY LOGAN, BRUISED AND BATTERED, MAKES A COUNTER-ATTACK...
Z-I-N-G
GOOD BOY! BUT THIS IS A LOSING SCRAP...
5
WE CAN'T BEAT THE WHOLE NAZI ARMY --- TAKE YOUR MOTHER TO ANOTHER PART OF THE CAMP WHERE SHE'LL BE SAFER!
I'D RATHER STICK WITH YOU AND THE BATMAN -- BUT I GUESS IT'S UP TO ME TO LOOK OUT FOR MOM!
AS THE BRAVE LAD SLIPS AWAY WITH HIS MOTHER AND BABY BROTHER...
LOOK OUT, BATMAN!.... TOO LATE...
AHHH!

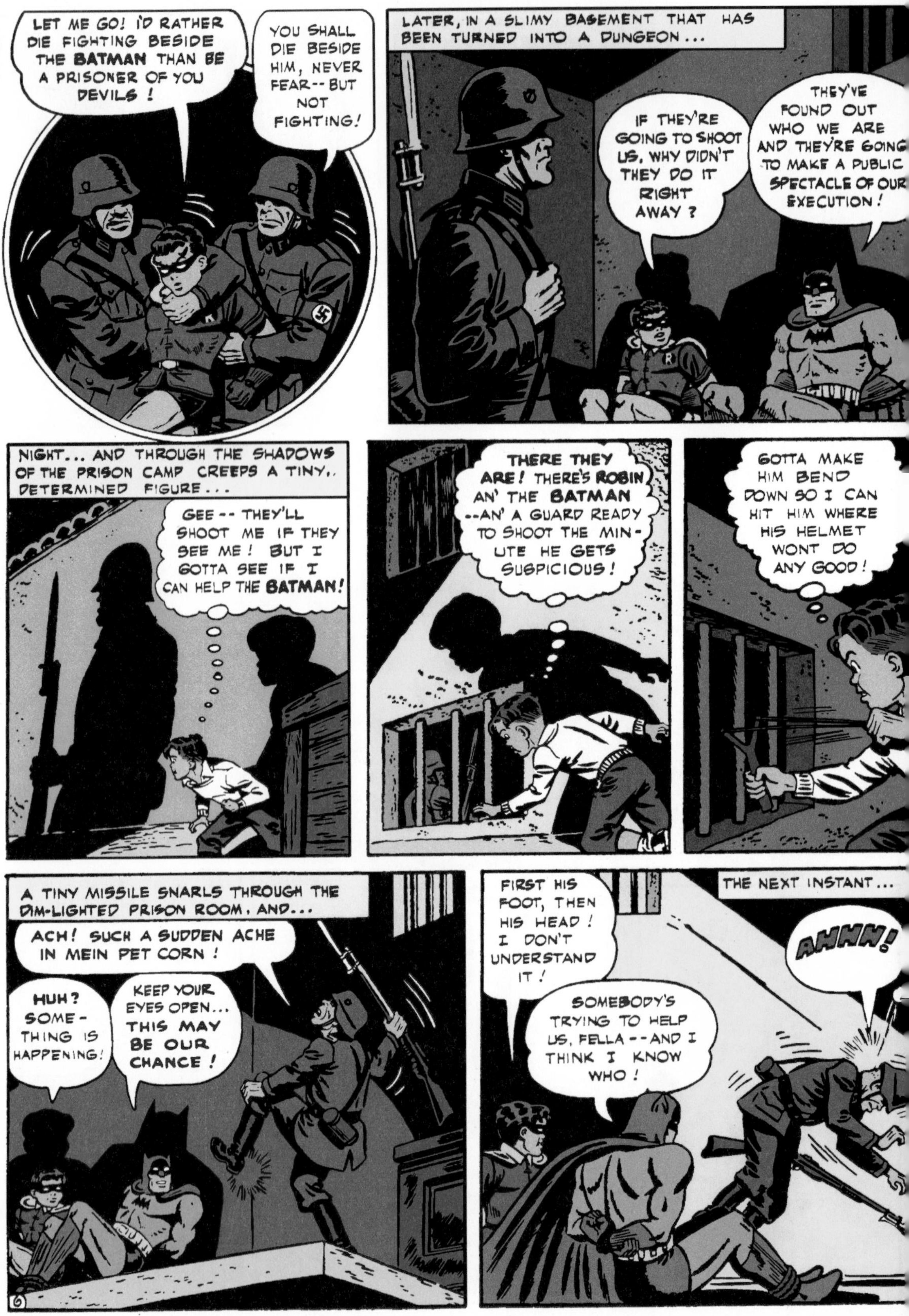
LET ME GO! I'D RATHER DIE FIGHTING BESIDE THE BATMAN THAN BE A PRISONER OF YOU DEVILS!
YOU SHALL DIE BESIDE HIM, NEVER FEAR-- BUT NOT FIGHTING!
LATER, IN A SLIMY BASEMENT THAT HAS BEEN TURNED INTO A DUNGEON...
IF THEY'RE GOING TO SHOOT US, WHY DIDN'T THEY DO IT RIGHT AWAY?
THEY'VE FOUND OUT WHO WE ARE AND THEY'RE GOING TO MAKE A PUBLIC SPECTACLE OF OUR EXECUTION!
NIGHT... AND THROUGH THE SHADOWS OF THE PRISON CAMP CREEPS A TINY, DETERMINED FIGURE...
GEE -- THEY'LL SHOOT ME IF THEY SEE ME! BUT I GOTTA SEE IF I CAN HELP THE BATMAN!
THERE THEY ARE! THERE'S ROBIN AN' THE BATMAN --AN' A GUARD READY TO SHOOT THE MINUTE HE GETS SUSPICIOUS!
GOTTA MAKE HIM BEND DOWN SO I CAN HIT HIM WHERE HIS HELMET WONT DO ANY GOOD!
A TINY MISSILE SNARLS THROUGH THE DIM-LIGHTED PRISON ROOM, AND...
ACH! SUCH A SUDDEN ACHE IN MEIN PET CORN!
HUH? SOME-THING IS HAPPENING!
KEEP YOUR EYES OPEN... THIS MAY BE OUR CHANCE!
6
FIRST HIS FOOT, THEN HIS HEAD! I DON'T UNDERSTAND IT!
THE NEXT INSTANT...
AHHH!
SOMEBODY'S TRYING TO HELP US, FELLA --AND I THINK I KNOW WHO!

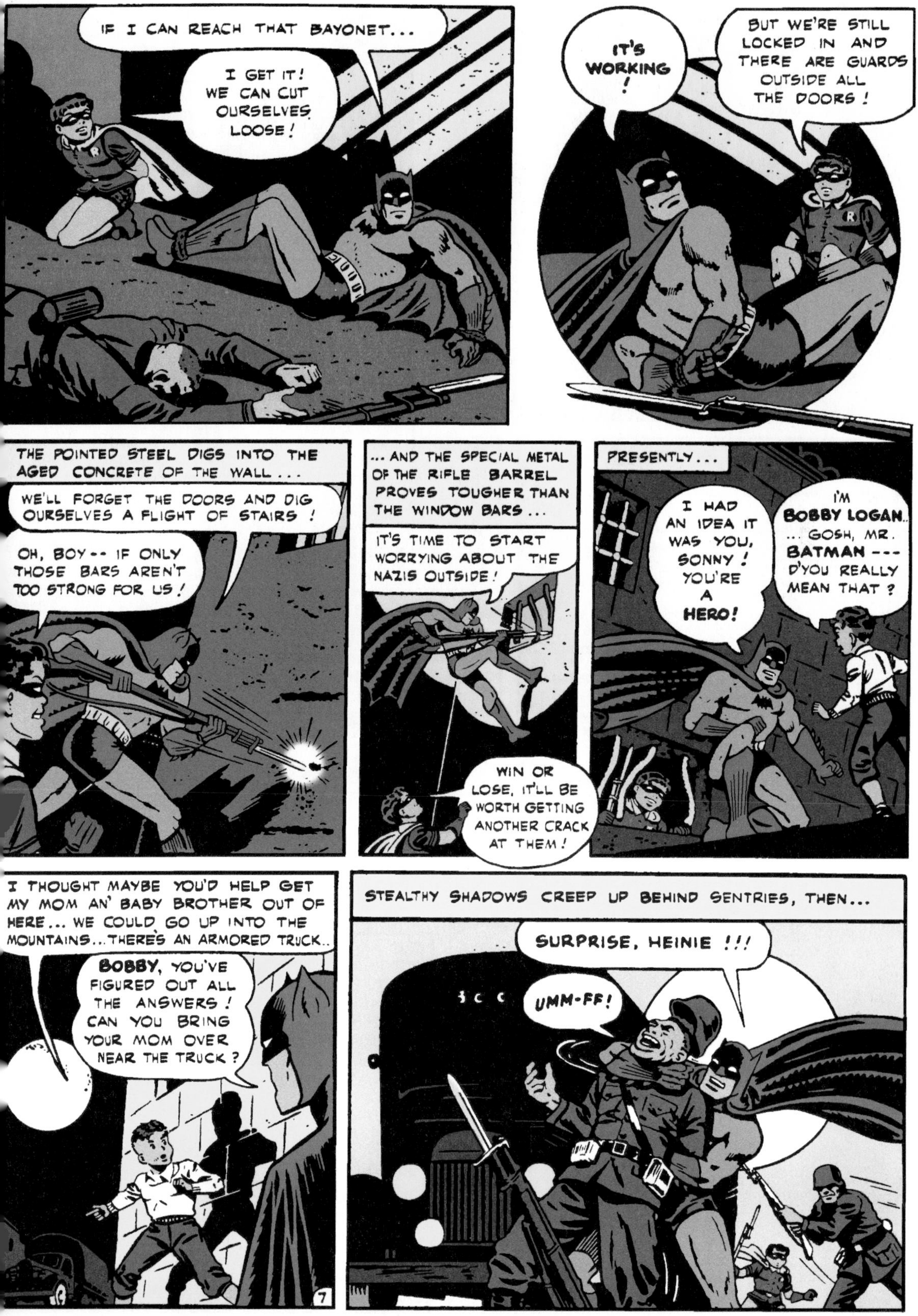
IF I CAN REACH THAT BAYONET...
I GET IT! WE CAN CUT OURSELVES LOOSE!
IT'S WORKING!
BUT WE'RE STILL LOCKED IN AND THERE ARE GUARDS OUTSIDE ALL THE DOORS!
THE POINTED STEEL DIGS INTO THE AGED CONCRETE OF THE WALL...
WE'LL FORGET THE DOORS AND DIG OURSELVES A FLIGHT OF STAIRS!
OH, BOY -- IF ONLY THOSE BARS AREN'T TOO STRONG FOR US!
... AND THE SPECIAL METAL OF THE RIFLE BARREL PROVES TOUGHER THAN THE WINDOW BARS...
IT'S TIME TO START WORRYING ABOUT THE NAZIS OUTSIDE!
WIN OR LOSE, IT'LL BE WORTH GETTING ANOTHER CRACK AT THEM!
PRESENTLY...
I HAD AN IDEA IT WAS YOU, SONNY! YOU'RE A HERO!
I'M BOBBY LOGAN... GOSH, MR. BATMAN --- D'YOU REALLY MEAN THAT?
I THOUGHT MAYBE YOU'D HELP GET MY MOM AN' BABY BROTHER OUT OF HERE... WE COULD GO UP INTO THE MOUNTAINS... THERE'S AN ARMORED TRUCK..
BOBBY, YOU'VE FIGURED OUT ALL THE ANSWERS! CAN YOU BRING YOUR MOM OVER NEAR THE TRUCK?
7
STEALTHY SHADOWS CREEP UP BEHIND SENTRIES, THEN...
SURPRISE, HEINIE!!!
UMM-FF!

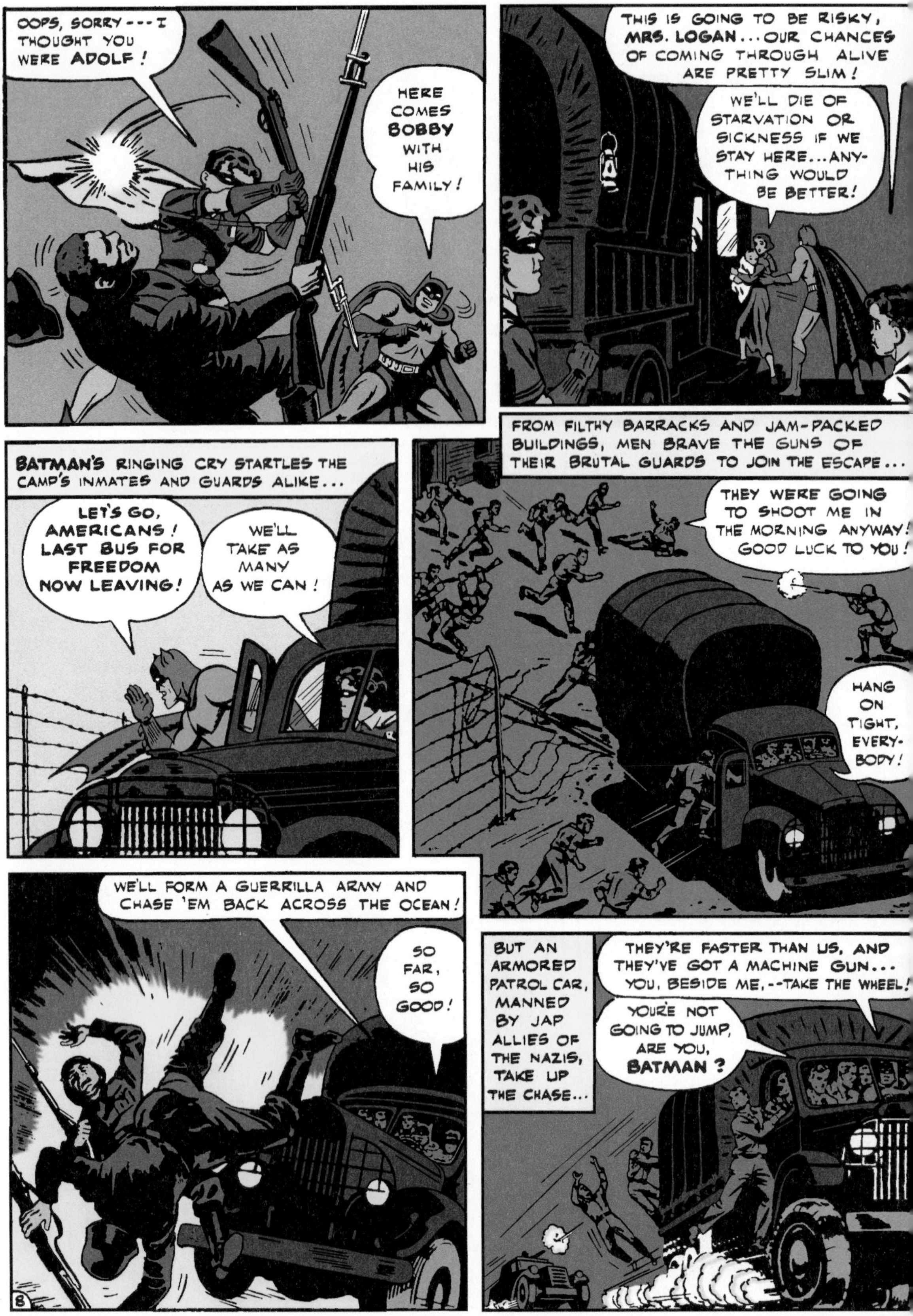
OOPS, SORRY --- I THOUGHT YOU WERE ADOLF !
HERE COMES BOBBY WITH HIS FAMILY !
THIS IS GOING TO BE RISKY, MRS. LOGAN ... OUR CHANCES OF COMING THROUGH ALIVE ARE PRETTY SLIM !
WE'LL DIE OF STARVATION OR SICKNESS IF WE STAY HERE... ANYTHING WOULD BE BETTER!
BATMAN'S RINGING CRY STARTLES THE CAMP'S INMATES AND GUARDS ALIKE...
LET'S GO, AMERICANS ! LAST BUS FOR FREEDOM NOW LEAVING!
WE'LL TAKE AS MANY AS WE CAN !
FROM FILTHY BARRACKS AND JAM-PACKED BUILDINGS, MEN BRAVE THE GUNS OF THEIR BRUTAL GUARDS TO JOIN THE ESCAPE...
THEY WERE GOING TO SHOOT ME IN THE MORNING ANYWAY! GOOD LUCK TO YOU!
HANG ON TIGHT, EVERYBODY!
WE'LL FORM A GUERRILLA ARMY AND CHASE 'EM BACK ACROSS THE OCEAN!
SO FAR, SO GOOD!
8
BUT AN ARMORED PATROL CAR, MANNED BY JAP ALLIES OF THE NAZIS, TAKE UP THE CHASE...
THEY'RE FASTER THAN US, AND THEY'VE GOT A MACHINE GUN... YOU, BESIDE ME,--TAKE THE WHEEL!
YOU'RE NOT GOING TO JUMP, ARE YOU, BATMAN ?

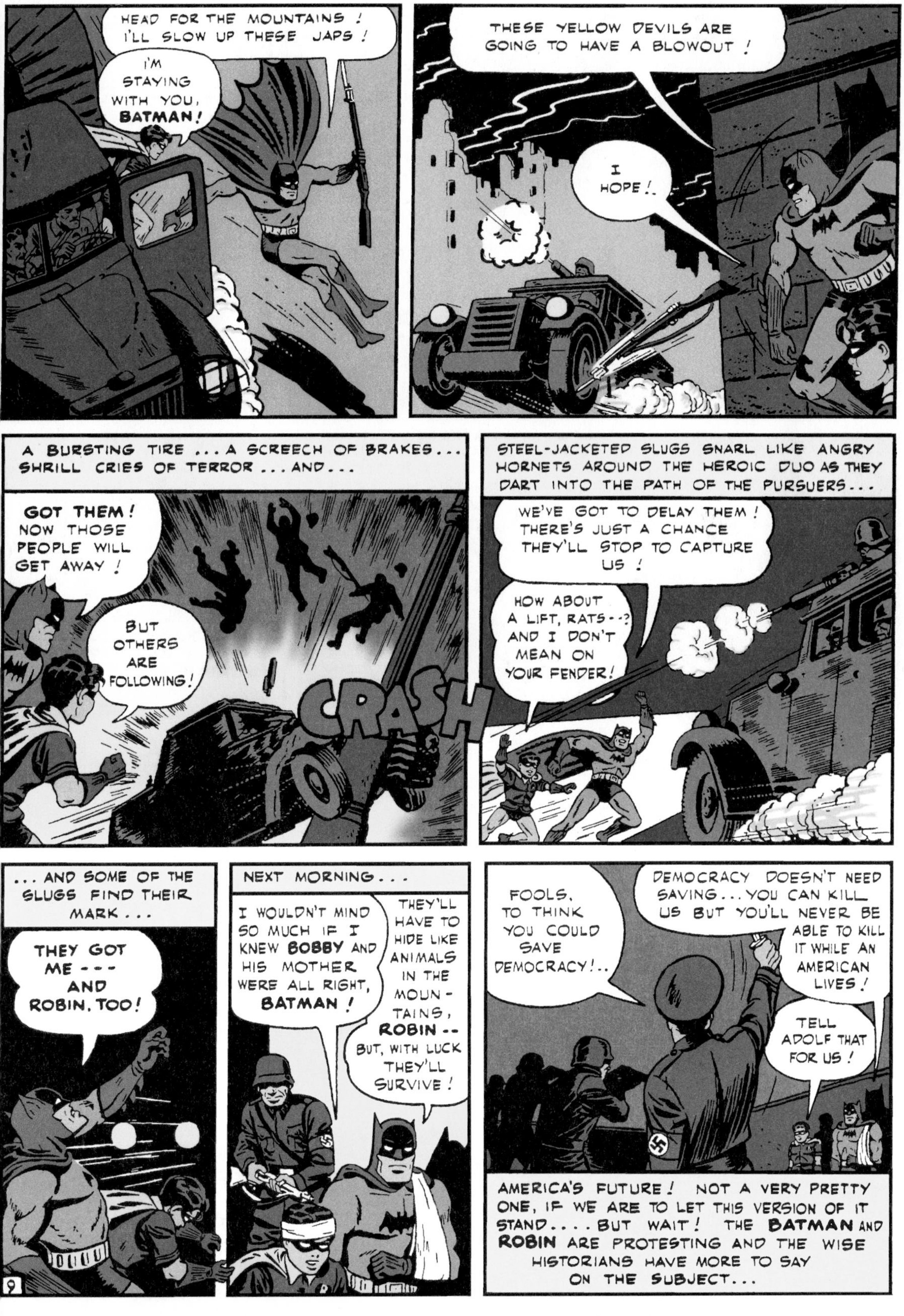
HEAD FOR THE MOUNTAINS! I'LL SLOW UP THESE JAPS!
I'M STAYING WITH YOU, BATMAN!
THESE YELLOW DEVILS ARE GOING TO HAVE A BLOWOUT!
I HOPE!..
A BURSTING TIRE ... A SCREECH OF BRAKES... SHRILL CRIES OF TERROR ... AND...
GOT THEM! NOW THOSE PEOPLE WILL GET AWAY!
BUT OTHERS ARE FOLLOWING!
CRASH
STEEL-JACKETED SLUGS SNARL LIKE ANGRY HORNETS AROUND THE HEROIC DUO AS THEY DART INTO THE PATH OF THE PURSUERS...
WE'VE GOT TO DELAY THEM! THERE'S JUST A CHANCE THEY'LL STOP TO CAPTURE US!
HOW ABOUT A LIFT, RATS--? AND I DON'T MEAN ON YOUR FENDER!
... AND SOME OF THE SLUGS FIND THEIR MARK...
THEY GOT ME --- AND ROBIN, TOO!
9
NEXT MORNING...
I WOULDN'T MIND SO MUCH IF I KNEW BOBBY AND HIS MOTHER WERE ALL RIGHT, BATMAN!
THEY'LL HAVE TO HIDE LIKE ANIMALS IN THE MOUNTAINS, ROBIN -- BUT, WITH LUCK THEY'LL SURVIVE!
FOOLS, TO THINK YOU COULD SAVE DEMOCRACY!..
DEMOCRACY DOESN'T NEED SAVING... YOU CAN KILL US BUT YOU'LL NEVER BE ABLE TO KILL IT WHILE AN AMERICAN LIVES!
TELL ADOLF THAT FOR US!
AMERICA'S FUTURE! NOT A VERY PRETTY ONE, IF WE ARE TO LET THIS VERSION OF IT STAND.... BUT WAIT! THE BATMAN AND ROBIN ARE PROTESTING AND THE WISE HISTORIANS HAVE MORE TO SAY ON THE SUBJECT...

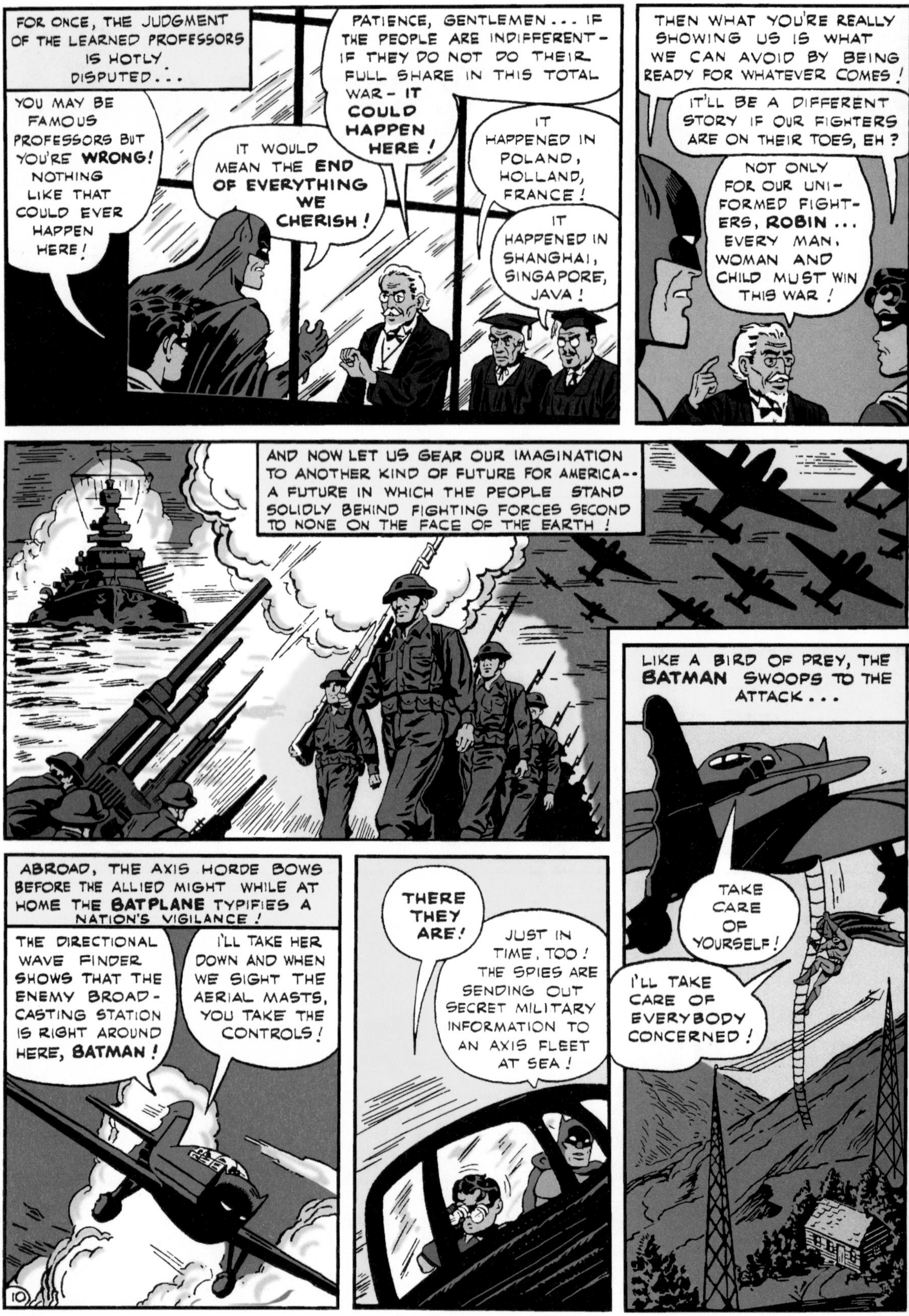
FOR ONCE, THE JUDGMENT OF THE LEARNED PROFESSORS IS HOTLY DISPUTED...
YOU MAY BE FAMOUS PROFESSORS BUT YOU'RE WRONG! NOTHING LIKE THAT COULD EVER HAPPEN HERE!
IT WOULD MEAN THE END OF EVERYTHING WE CHERISH!
PATIENCE, GENTLEMEN... IF THE PEOPLE ARE INDIFFERENT - IF THEY DO NOT DO THEIR FULL SHARE IN THIS TOTAL WAR - IT COULD HAPPEN HERE!
IT HAPPENED IN POLAND, HOLLAND, FRANCE!
IT HAPPENED IN SHANGHAI, SINGAPORE, JAVA!
THEN WHAT YOU'RE REALLY SHOWING US IS WHAT WE CAN AVOID BY BEING READY FOR WHATEVER COMES!
IT'LL BE A DIFFERENT STORY IF OUR FIGHTERS ARE ON THEIR TOES, EH?
NOT ONLY FOR OUR UNIFORMED FIGHTERS, ROBIN... EVERY MAN, WOMAN AND CHILD MUST WIN THIS WAR!
AND NOW LET US GEAR OUR IMAGINATION TO ANOTHER KIND OF FUTURE FOR AMERICA-- A FUTURE IN WHICH THE PEOPLE STAND SOLIDLY BEHIND FIGHTING FORCES SECOND TO NONE ON THE FACE OF THE EARTH!
ABROAD, THE AXIS HORDE BOWS BEFORE THE ALLIED MIGHT WHILE AT HOME THE BATPLANE TYPIFIES A NATION'S VIGILANCE!
THE DIRECTIONAL WAVE FINDER SHOWS THAT THE ENEMY BROADCASTING STATION IS RIGHT AROUND HERE, BATMAN!
I'LL TAKE HER DOWN AND WHEN WE SIGHT THE AERIAL MASTS, YOU TAKE THE CONTROLS!
10
THERE THEY ARE!
JUST IN TIME, TOO! THE SPIES ARE SENDING OUT SECRET MILITARY INFORMATION TO AN AXIS FLEET AT SEA!
LIKE A BIRD OF PREY, THE BATMAN SWOOPS TO THE ATTACK...
TAKE CARE OF YOURSELF!
I'LL TAKE CARE OF EVERYBODY CONCERNED!

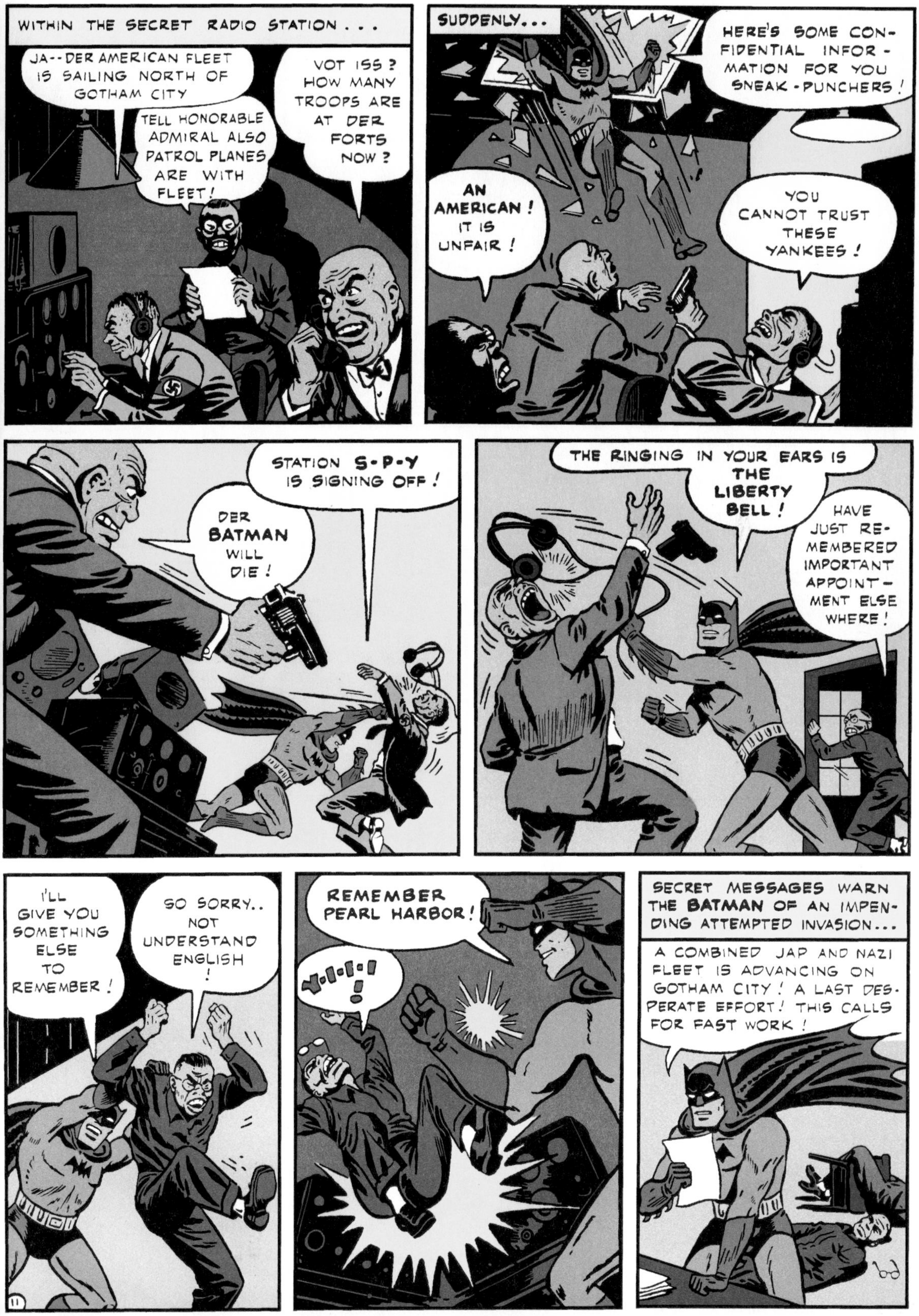
WITHIN THE SECRET RADIO STATION . . .
JA--DER AMERICAN FLEET IS SAILING NORTH OF GOTHAM CITY
TELL HONORABLE ADMIRAL ALSO PATROL PLANES ARE WITH FLEET!
VOT ISS? HOW MANY TROOPS ARE AT DER FORTS NOW?
SUDDENLY...
HERE'S SOME CONFIDENTIAL INFORMATION FOR YOU SNEAK-PUNCHERS!
AN AMERICAN! IT IS UNFAIR!
YOU CANNOT TRUST THESE YANKEES!
DER BATMAN WILL DIE!
STATION S-P-Y IS SIGNING OFF!
THE RINGING IN YOUR EARS IS THE LIBERTY BELL!
HAVE JUST REMEMBERED IMPORTANT APPOINTMENT ELSE WHERE!
11
I'LL GIVE YOU SOMETHING ELSE TO REMEMBER!
SO SORRY.. NOT UNDERSTAND ENGLISH!
REMEMBER PEARL HARBOR!
Y-I-I-I-I!
SECRET MESSAGES WARN THE BATMAN OF AN IMPENDING ATTEMPTED INVASION...
A COMBINED JAP AND NAZI FLEET IS ADVANCING ON GOTHAM CITY! A LAST DESPERATE EFFORT! THIS CALLS FOR FAST WORK!

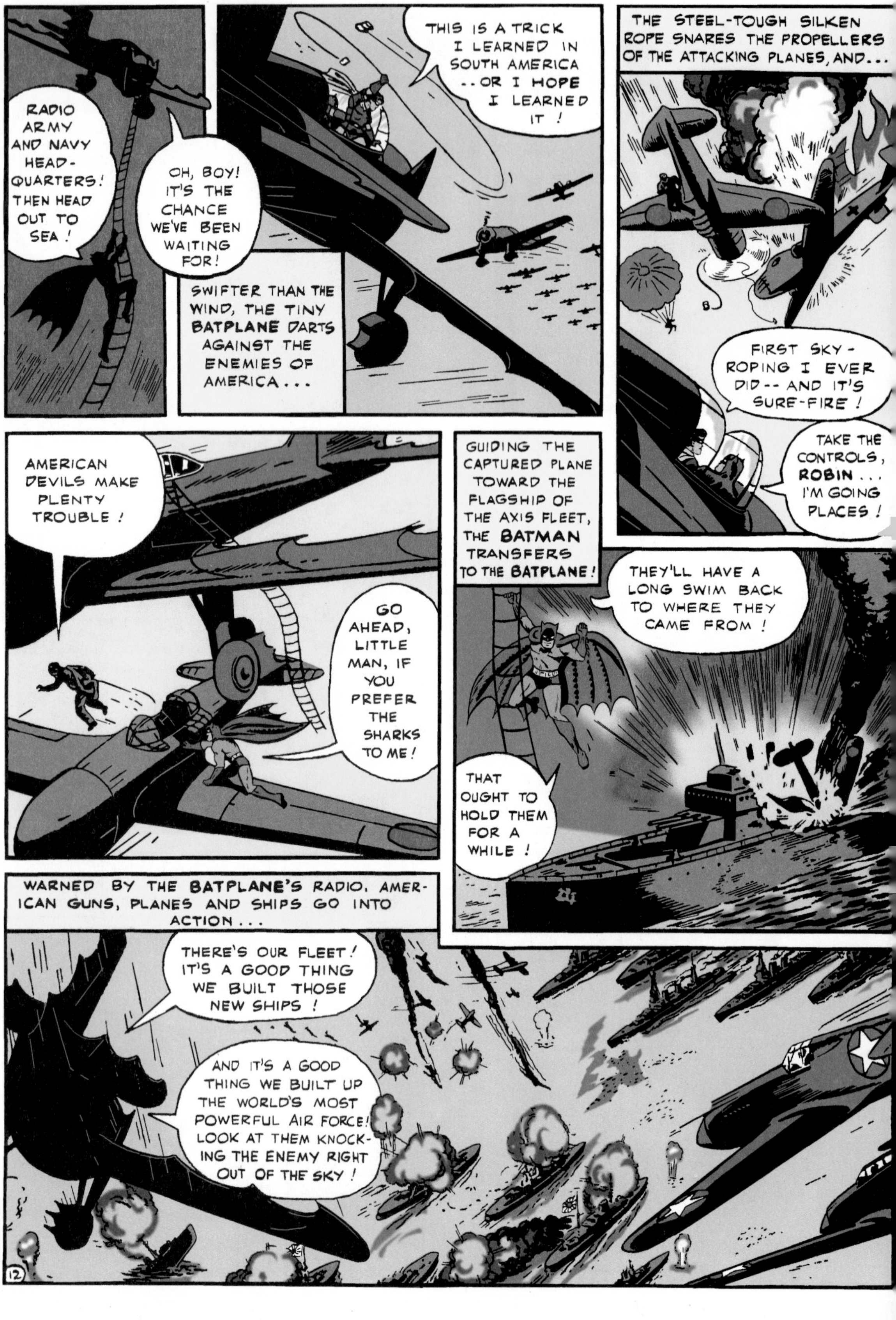
RADIO ARMY AND NAVY HEAD-QUARTERS! THEN HEAD OUT TO SEA!
OH, BOY! IT'S THE CHANCE WE'VE BEEN WAITING FOR!
SWIFTER THAN THE WIND, THE TINY BATPLANE DARTS AGAINST THE ENEMIES OF AMERICA...
THIS IS A TRICK I LEARNED IN SOUTH AMERICA ..OR I HOPE I LEARNED IT!
THE STEEL-TOUGH SILKEN ROPE SNARES THE PROPELLERS OF THE ATTACKING PLANES, AND...
FIRST SKY-ROPING I EVER DID-- AND IT'S SURE-FIRE!
TAKE THE CONTROLS, ROBIN... I'M GOING PLACES!
AMERICAN DEVILS MAKE PLENTY TROUBLE!
GO AHEAD, LITTLE MAN, IF YOU PREFER THE SHARKS TO ME!
GUIDING THE CAPTURED PLANE TOWARD THE FLAGSHIP OF THE AXIS FLEET, THE BATMAN TRANSFERS TO THE BATPLANE!
THEY'LL HAVE A LONG SWIM BACK TO WHERE THEY CAME FROM!
THAT OUGHT TO HOLD THEM FOR A WHILE!
WARNED BY THE BATPLANE'S RADIO, AMERICAN GUNS, PLANES AND SHIPS GO INTO ACTION...
THERE'S OUR FLEET! IT'S A GOOD THING WE BUILT THOSE NEW SHIPS!
AND IT'S A GOOD THING WE BUILT UP THE WORLD'S MOST POWERFUL AIR FORCE! LOOK AT THEM KNOCKING THE ENEMY RIGHT OUT OF THE SKY!
12

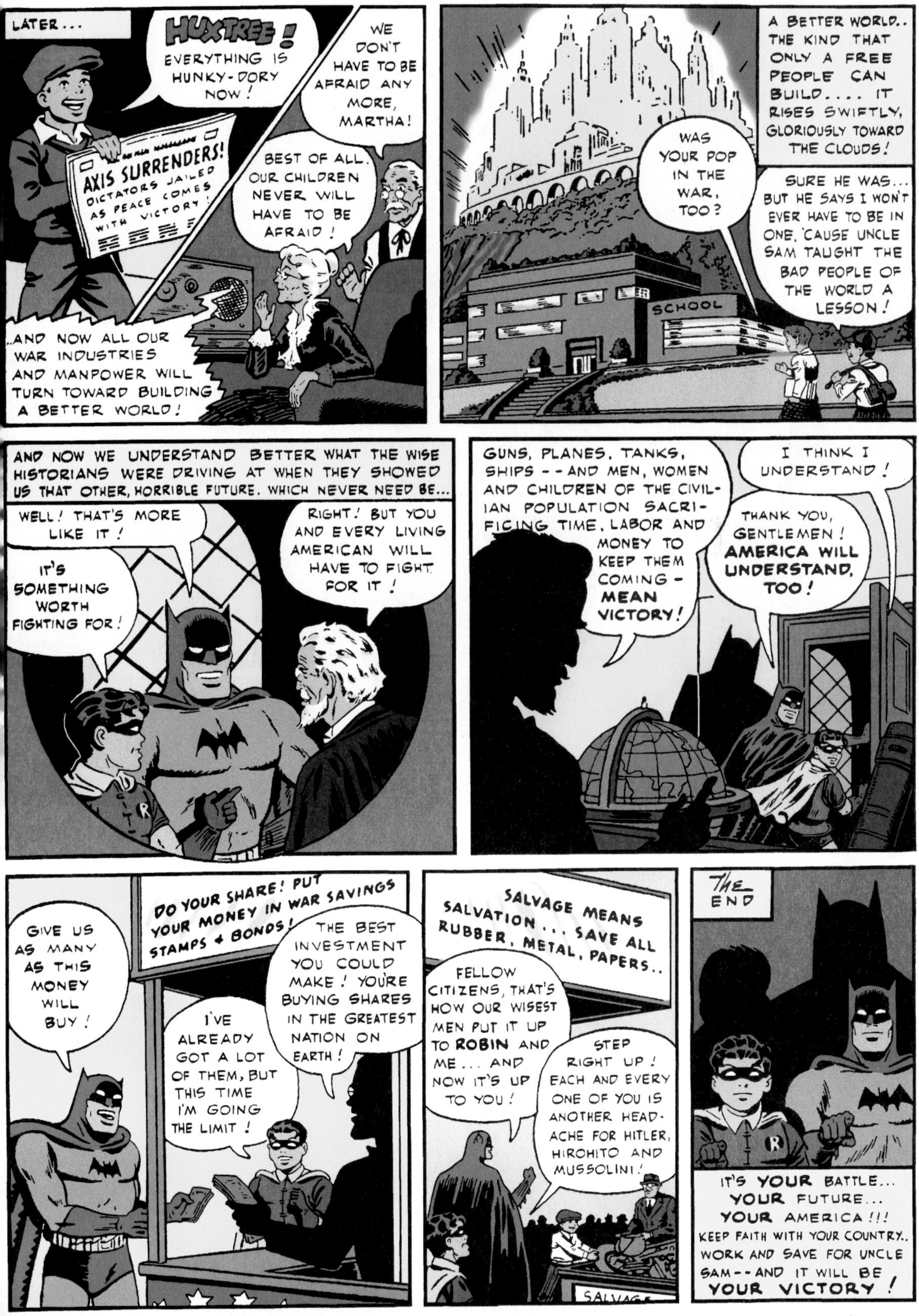
LATER...
HUXTREE! EVERYTHING IS HUNKY-DORY NOW!
AXIS SURRENDERS! DICTATORS JAILED AS PEACE COMES WITH VICTORY!
WE DON'T HAVE TO BE AFRAID ANY MORE, MARTHA!
BEST OF ALL, OUR CHILDREN NEVER WILL HAVE TO BE AFRAID!
..AND NOW ALL OUR WAR INDUSTRIES AND MANPOWER WILL TURN TOWARD BUILDING A BETTER WORLD!
A BETTER WORLD.. THE KIND THAT ONLY A FREE PEOPLE CAN BUILD.... IT RISES SWIFTLY, GLORIOUSLY TOWARD THE CLOUDS!
WAS YOUR POP IN THE WAR, TOO?
SURE HE WAS... BUT HE SAYS I WON'T EVER HAVE TO BE IN ONE, 'CAUSE UNCLE SAM TAUGHT THE BAD PEOPLE OF THE WORLD A LESSON!
SCHOOL
AND NOW WE UNDERSTAND BETTER WHAT THE WISE HISTORIANS WERE DRIVING AT WHEN THEY SHOWED US THAT OTHER, HORRIBLE FUTURE. WHICH NEVER NEED BE...
WELL! THAT'S MORE LIKE IT!
IT'S SOMETHING WORTH FIGHTING FOR!
RIGHT! BUT YOU AND EVERY LIVING AMERICAN WILL HAVE TO FIGHT FOR IT!
GUNS, PLANES, TANKS, SHIPS -- AND MEN, WOMEN AND CHILDREN OF THE CIVILIAN POPULATION SACRIFICING TIME, LABOR AND MONEY TO KEEP THEM COMING - MEAN VICTORY!
I THINK I UNDERSTAND!
THANK YOU, GENTLEMEN! AMERICA WILL UNDERSTAND, TOO!
DO YOUR SHARE! PUT YOUR MONEY IN WAR SAVINGS STAMPS & BONDS!
GIVE US AS MANY AS THIS MONEY WILL BUY!
THE BEST INVESTMENT YOU COULD MAKE! YOU'RE BUYING SHARES IN THE GREATEST NATION ON EARTH!
I'VE ALREADY GOT A LOT OF THEM, BUT THIS TIME I'M GOING THE LIMIT!
SALVAGE MEANS SALVATION... SAVE ALL RUBBER, METAL, PAPERS..
FELLOW CITIZENS, THAT'S HOW OUR WISEST MEN PUT IT UP TO ROBIN AND ME... AND NOW IT'S UP TO YOU!
STEP RIGHT UP! EACH AND EVERY ONE OF YOU IS ANOTHER HEADACHE FOR HITLER, HIROHITO AND MUSSOLINI!
THE END
IT'S YOUR BATTLE... YOUR FUTURE... YOUR AMERICA!!! KEEP FAITH WITH YOUR COUNTRY.. WORK AND SAVE FOR UNCLE SAM -- AND IT WILL BE YOUR VICTORY!

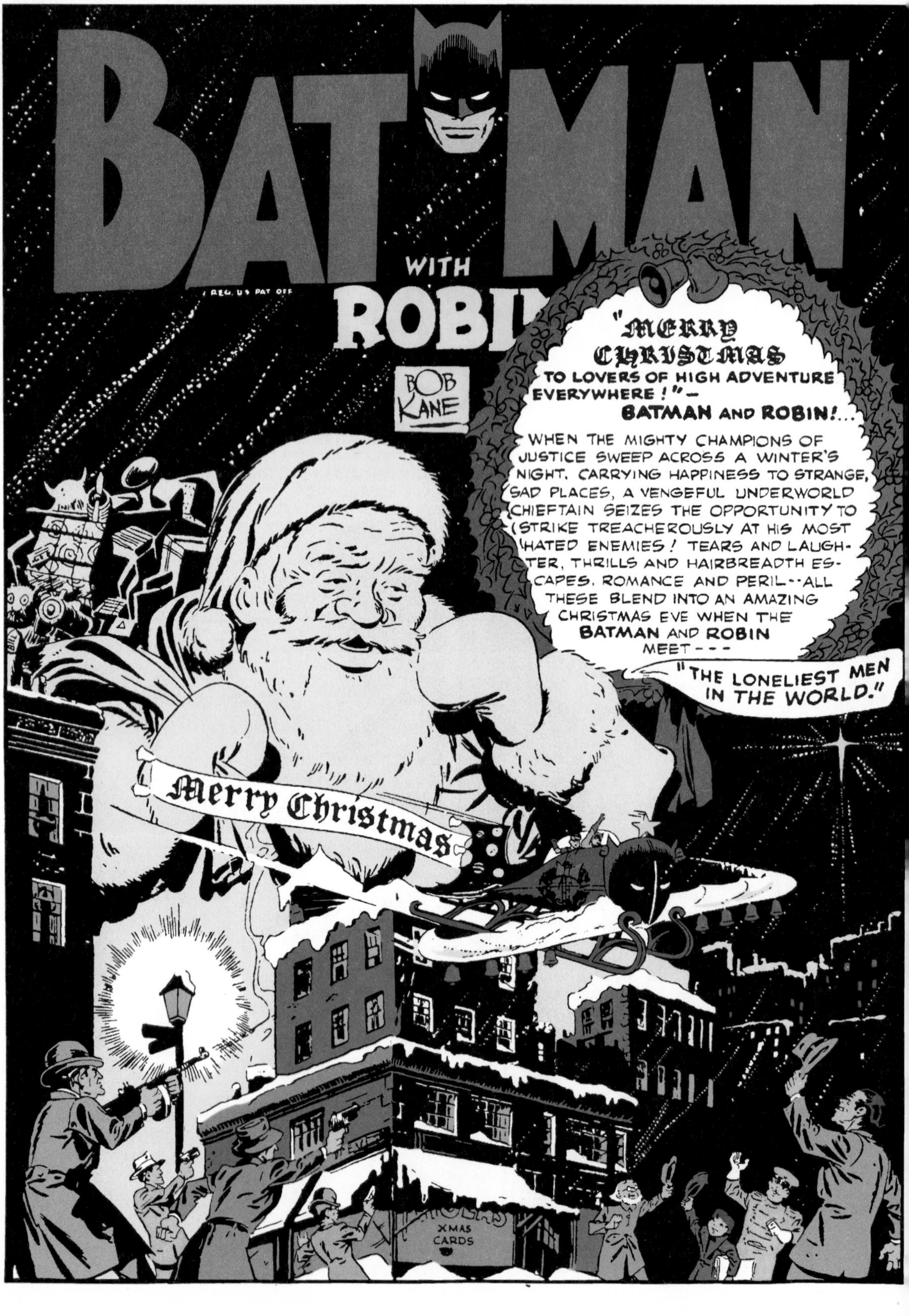
BATMAN
REG. U.S. PAT. OFF.
WITH
ROBIN
BOB KANE
"MERRY CHRISTMAS TO LOVERS OF HIGH ADVENTURE EVERYWHERE!"— BATMAN AND ROBIN!...
WHEN THE MIGHTY CHAMPIONS OF JUSTICE SWEEP ACROSS A WINTER'S NIGHT, CARRYING HAPPINESS TO STRANGE, SAD PLACES, A VENGEFUL UNDERWORLD CHIEFTAIN SEIZES THE OPPORTUNITY TO STRIKE TREACHEROUSLY AT HIS MOST HATED ENEMIES! TEARS AND LAUGHTER, THRILLS AND HAIRBREADTH ESCAPES, ROMANCE AND PERIL--ALL THESE BLEND INTO AN AMAZING CHRISTMAS EVE WHEN THE BATMAN AND ROBIN MEET---
"THE LONELIEST MEN IN THE WORLD."
Merry Christmas
XMAS CARDS

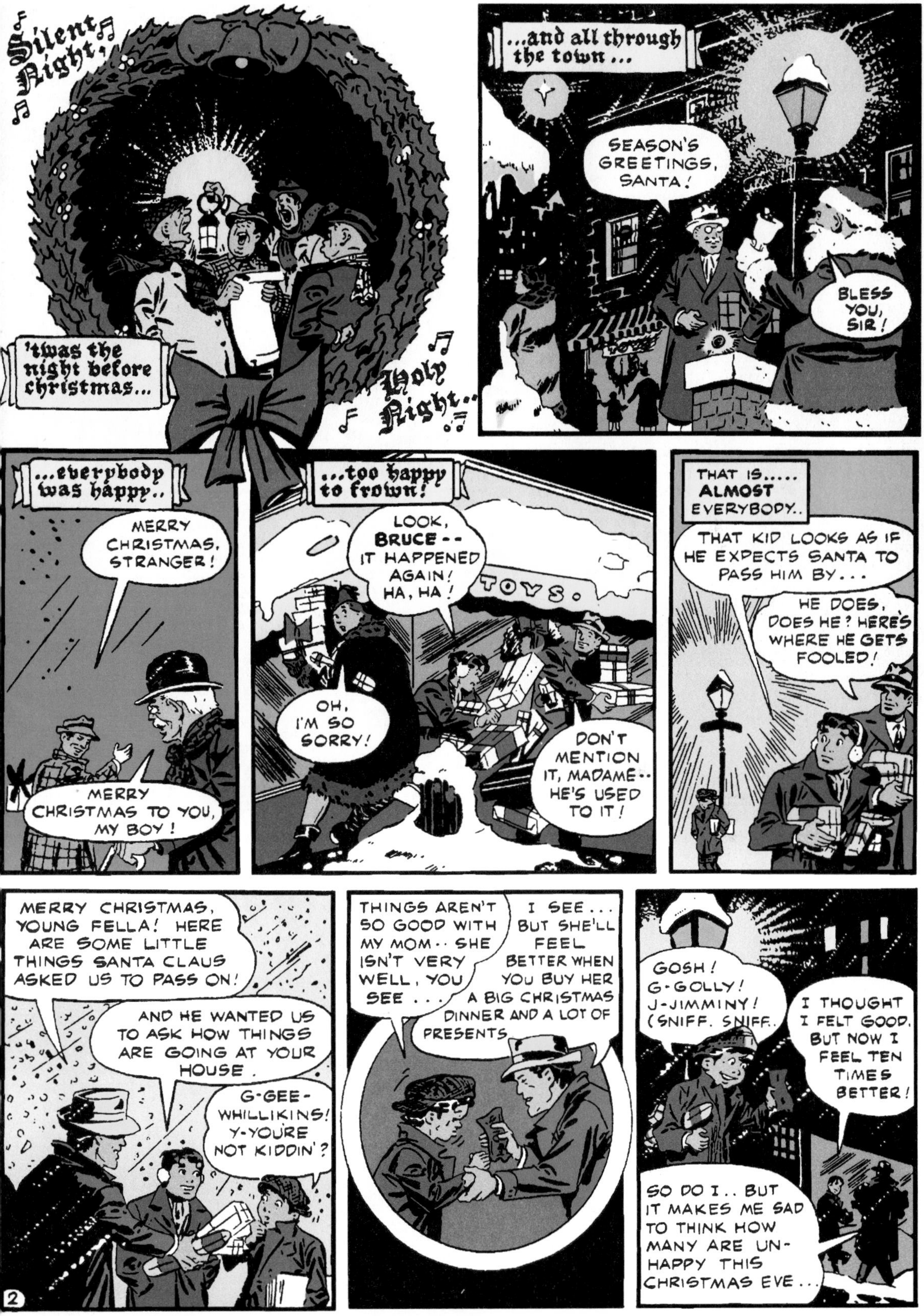
Silent Night,
'twas the night before christmas...
Holy Night..
...and all through the town...
SEASON'S GREETINGS, SANTA!
BLESS YOU, SIR!
...everybody was happy..
MERRY CHRISTMAS, STRANGER!
MERRY CHRISTMAS TO YOU, MY BOY!
...too happy to frown!
LOOK, BRUCE -- IT HAPPENED AGAIN! HA, HA!
TOYS
OH, I'M SO SORRY!
DON'T MENTION IT, MADAME-- HE'S USED TO IT!
THAT IS..... ALMOST EVERYBODY..
THAT KID LOOKS AS IF HE EXPECTS SANTA TO PASS HIM BY...
HE DOES, DOES HE? HERE'S WHERE HE GETS FOOLED!
MERRY CHRISTMAS, YOUNG FELLA! HERE ARE SOME LITTLE THINGS SANTA CLAUS ASKED US TO PASS ON!
AND HE WANTED US TO ASK HOW THINGS ARE GOING AT YOUR HOUSE.
G-GEE-WHILLIKINS! Y-YOU'RE NOT KIDDIN'?
2
THINGS AREN'T SO GOOD WITH MY MOM.. SHE ISN'T VERY WELL, YOU SEE...
I SEE... BUT SHE'LL FEEL BETTER WHEN YOU BUY HER A BIG CHRISTMAS DINNER AND A LOT OF PRESENTS.
GOSH! G-GOLLY! J-JIMMINY! (SNIFF. SNIFF.
I THOUGHT I FELT GOOD, BUT NOW I FEEL TEN TIMES BETTER!
SO DO I.. BUT IT MAKES ME SAD TO THINK HOW MANY ARE UN-HAPPY THIS CHRISTMAS EVE...

THAT YOUNGSTER HAS HIS MOTHER -- BUT A LOT OF PEOPLE HAVE NO FAMILIES AT ALL!

WE'RE LUCKY ALL RIGHT... WE HAVE EACH OTHER, AND ONE OF THE FINEST HOMES IN GOTHAM CITY!

DOZENS OF FRIENDS SEND US PRESENTS. BUT SOME PEOPLE HAVE NO FRIENDS!

IT MUST BE AWFUL TO BE LONELY AT CHRISTMAS! YOU KNOW, I WAS LOOKING FORWARD TO JUST ENJOYING OURSELVES -- BUT...

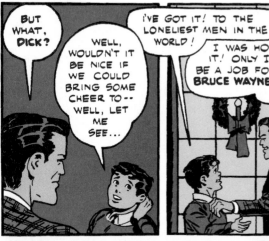

BUT WHAT, DICK?

WELL, WOULDN'T IT BE NICE IF WE COULD BRING SOME CHEER TO-- WELL, LET ME SEE...

I'VE GOT IT! TO THE LONELIEST MEN IN THE WORLD!

I WAS HOPING YOU'D SUGGEST IT.! ONLY I FIGURE IT WOULDN'T BE A JOB FOR DICK GRAYSON AND BRUCE WAYNE -- BUT ONE FOR ROBIN AND THE BATMAN!

SO IT IS THAT WITHIN THE HOME OF BRUCE WAYNE, RICH SOCIETY PLAYBOY, A STARTLING TRANS- FORMATION OCCURS...

IMAGINE THE BATMAN AND ROBIN PLAYING SANTA CLAUS! ALL WE NEED IS A SLED AND REINDEER!

WE'VE GOT SOMETHING JUST AS GOOD!

WORKING SWIFTLY, THE PAIR MAKES MANY TRIPS THROUGH THE TUNNEL THAT CONNECTS THE HOUSE WITH THE SECRET HANGAR OF THAT SENSATIONAL CRAFT, THE BATPLANE...

ONE MORE TRIP AND WE'RE READY TO START!

IT WOULDN'T TAKE MANY MORE TRIPS LIKE THIS TO FINISH ME!

PRESENTLY...

HOW DO YOU LIKE IT?

IT'S A REGULAR SANTA CLAUS SLED, WITH RUNNERS, SLEIGH BELLS AND EVERYTHING!...THIS IS GOING TO BE MORE FUN THAN ANYTHING WE'VE DONE IN A LONG TIME!

RIGHT, ROBIN!..BUT FUN ISN'T ALL YOU AND THE BATMAN ARE GOING TO ENCOUNTER IN THIS NIGHT'S ADVENTURE! ...FOR THE SPIRIT OF CHRISTMAS HAS NEVER YET PENETRATED THE DARK DEPTHS OF THE UNDERWORLD ...AND THE UNDERWORLD HAS NEVER CEASED TO HATE AND AND FEAR WHAT YOU STAND FOR!

A WEIRD, BATWINGED SHAPE SOARS INTO THE GRAY WINTER SKY BOUND ON THE STRANGEST VOYAGE IT HAS EVER ATTEMPTED...

BATMAN, WHO DO YOU THINK IS THE LONELIEST MAN ON EARTH?

I'M NOT SURE, ROBIN-- BUT I HAVE A LIST OF THREE WHO AREN'T FAR FROM IT!

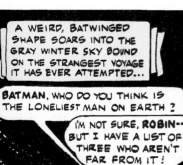

THERE'S POLICE HEADQUARTERS... AND THERE ARE LIGHTS IN COMMISSIONER GORDON'S OFFICE!

HE ISN'T ON MY LIST, BUT IT WON'T HURT TO STOP IN AND GIVE HIM THE SEASON'S GREETINGS!

WE FIND COMMISSIONER GORDON IN CONFERENCE WITH ONE DIRK DAGNER, A NOTORIOUS CHIEF OF AN UNDERWORLD GANG...

YOU OUGHT TO BELIEVE IN SANTA CLAUS, DIRK! WE'RE NOT LETTING YOU GO BECAUSE WE WANT TO, BUT BECAUSE WE CAN'T PROVE YOU WERE MIXED UP IN THOSE HOLDUPS!

I'LL BELIEVE IN SANTA CLAUS WHEN I READ THE BATMAN'S OBITUARY!

DID I HEAR SOMEONE TALKING ABOUT US?

BATMAN AND ROBIN! YOU CERTAINLY DID!

HUH?... LISTEN, IF YOU GUYS CAME HERE TO MAKE TROUBLE FOR ME --

THE NEXT INSTANT...

MAYBE LATER, DIRK... BUT JUST NOW WE'RE BUSY CELEBRATING CHRISTMAS!

AND WE'VE THOUGHT UP A BRAND NEW WAY TO DO IT!

HOW ABOUT LETTING ME IN ON THE SECRET?

BAH!

FIRST, WE'RE GIVING A SURPRISE PARTY FOR THE DOORMAN AT THE SWANKY CRANE CLUB! THEN WE'LL CALL ON LINK CHESNEY, THE RADIO HUMORIST AND THE GLOOMIEST MAN IN GOTHAM CITY...

FINALLY WE'LL VISIT THE OLD LIGHTHOUSE KEEPER AT PIRATE REEF WHO SPENDS MONTHS ON END ALL BY HIMSELF!

THAT SENTIMENTAL STUFF GIVES ME A PAIN!

I ONLY WISH I COULD GO WITH YOU!

BUT AS DIRK DAGNER LEAVES HEADQUARTERS A FREE MAN, HIS CUNNING BRAIN IS BUSY...

POLICE

AND IT ALSO GIVES ME AN IDEA HOW TO MAKE SOME DOUGH AND AT THE SAME TIME GIVE THE BATMAN THE WORST CHRISTMAS HE EVER HAD!

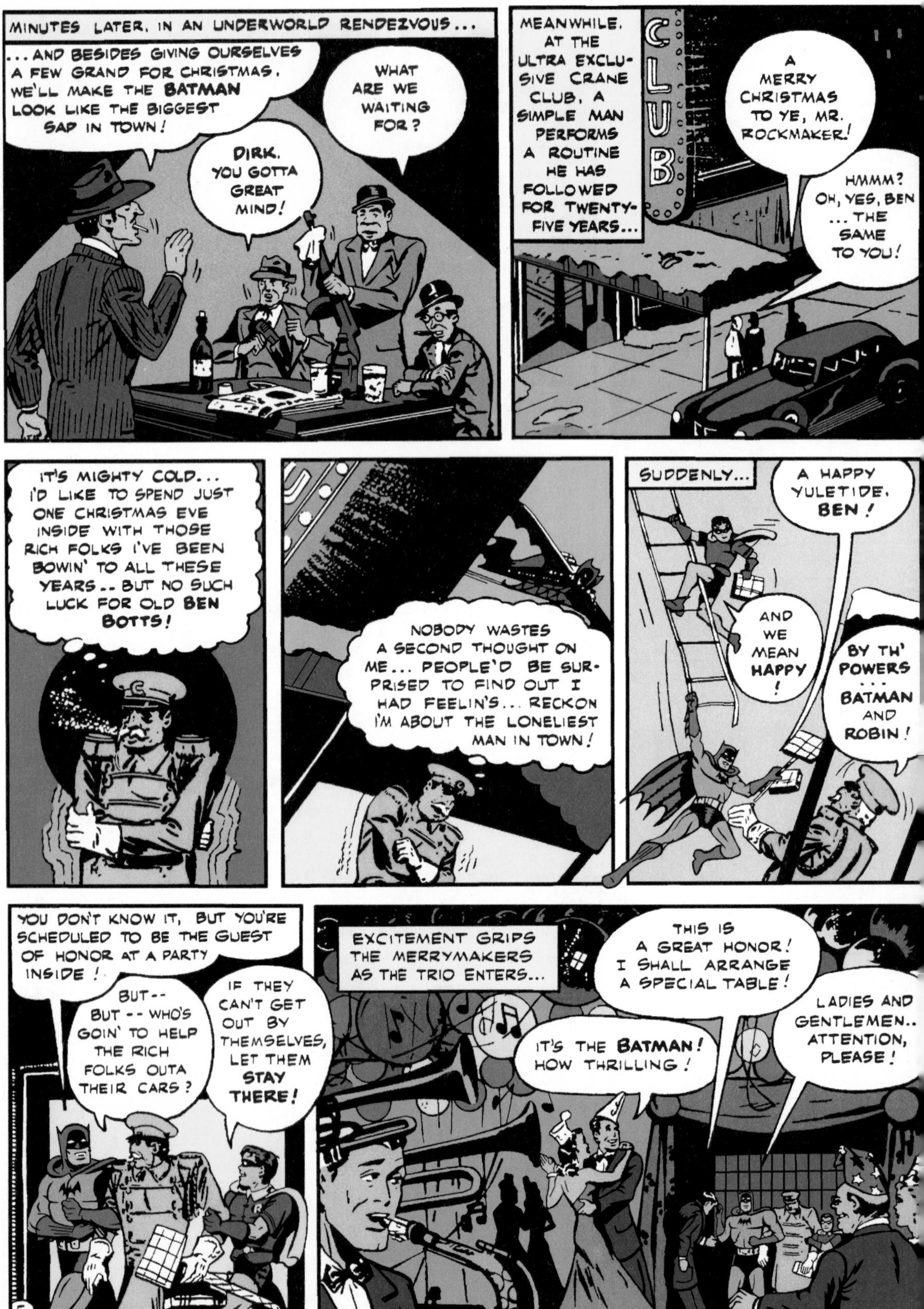
MINUTES LATER, IN AN UNDERWORLD RENDEZVOUS...
...AND BESIDES GIVING OURSELVES A FEW GRAND FOR CHRISTMAS, WE'LL MAKE THE BATMAN LOOK LIKE THE BIGGEST SAP IN TOWN!
WHAT ARE WE WAITING FOR?
DIRK, YOU GOTTA GREAT MIND!
MEANWHILE, AT THE ULTRA EXCLUSIVE CRANE CLUB, A SIMPLE MAN PERFORMS A ROUTINE HE HAS FOLLOWED FOR TWENTY-FIVE YEARS...
CLUB
A MERRY CHRISTMAS TO YE, MR. ROCKMAKER!
HMMM? OH, YES, BEN ...THE SAME TO YOU!
IT'S MIGHTY COLD... I'D LIKE TO SPEND JUST ONE CHRISTMAS EVE INSIDE WITH THOSE RICH FOLKS I'VE BEEN BOWIN' TO ALL THESE YEARS.. BUT NO SUCH LUCK FOR OLD BEN BOTTS!
NOBODY WASTES A SECOND THOUGHT ON ME... PEOPLE'D BE SURPRISED TO FIND OUT I HAD FEELIN'S... RECKON I'M ABOUT THE LONELIEST MAN IN TOWN!
SUDDENLY...
A HAPPY YULETIDE, BEN!
AND WE MEAN HAPPY!
BY TH' POWERS ... BATMAN AND ROBIN!
YOU DON'T KNOW IT, BUT YOU'RE SCHEDULED TO BE THE GUEST OF HONOR AT A PARTY INSIDE!
BUT-- BUT -- WHO'S GOIN' TO HELP THE RICH FOLKS OUTA THEIR CARS?
IF THEY CAN'T GET OUT BY THEMSELVES, LET THEM STAY THERE!
5
EXCITEMENT GRIPS THE MERRYMAKERS AS THE TRIO ENTERS...
THIS IS A GREAT HONOR! I SHALL ARRANGE A SPECIAL TABLE!
IT'S THE BATMAN! HOW THRILLING!
LADIES AND GENTLEMEN.. ATTENTION, PLEASE!

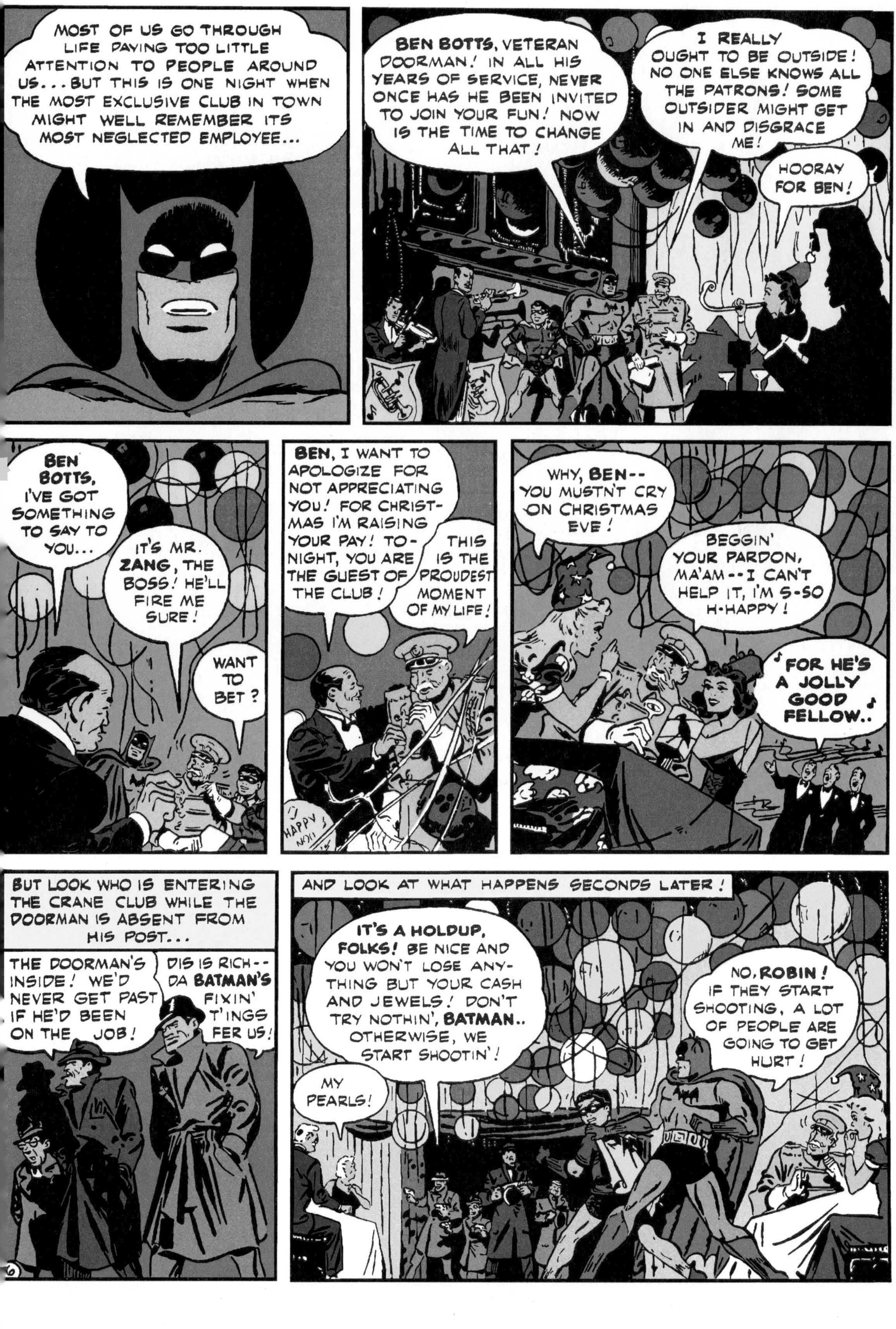

MOST OF US GO THROUGH LIFE PAYING TOO LITTLE ATTENTION TO PEOPLE AROUND US... BUT THIS IS ONE NIGHT WHEN THE MOST EXCLUSIVE CLUB IN TOWN MIGHT WELL REMEMBER ITS MOST NEGLECTED EMPLOYEE...
BEN BOTTS, VETERAN DOORMAN! IN ALL HIS YEARS OF SERVICE, NEVER ONCE HAS HE BEEN INVITED TO JOIN YOUR FUN! NOW IS THE TIME TO CHANGE ALL THAT!
I REALLY OUGHT TO BE OUTSIDE! NO ONE ELSE KNOWS ALL THE PATRONS! SOME OUTSIDER MIGHT GET IN AND DISGRACE ME!
HOORAY FOR BEN!
BEN BOTTS, I'VE GOT SOMETHING TO SAY TO YOU...
IT'S MR. ZANG, THE BOSS! HE'LL FIRE ME SURE!
WANT TO BET?
BEN, I WANT TO APOLOGIZE FOR NOT APPRECIATING YOU! FOR CHRISTMAS I'M RAISING YOUR PAY! TONIGHT, YOU ARE THE GUEST OF THE CLUB!
THIS IS THE PROUDEST MOMENT OF MY LIFE!
WHY, BEN-- YOU MUSTN'T CRY ON CHRISTMAS EVE!
BEGGIN' YOUR PARDON, MA'AM-- I CAN'T HELP IT, I'M S-SO H-HAPPY!
FOR HE'S A JOLLY GOOD FELLOW..
BUT LOOK WHO IS ENTERING THE CRANE CLUB WHILE THE DOORMAN IS ABSENT FROM HIS POST...
THE DOORMAN'S INSIDE! WE'D NEVER GET PAST IF HE'D BEEN ON THE JOB!
DIS IS RICH-- DA BATMAN'S FIXIN' T'INGS FER US!
AND LOOK AT WHAT HAPPENS SECONDS LATER!
IT'S A HOLDUP, FOLKS! BE NICE AND YOU WON'T LOSE ANYTHING BUT YOUR CASH AND JEWELS! DON'T TRY NOTHIN', BATMAN.. OTHERWISE, WE START SHOOTIN'!
MY PEARLS!
NO, ROBIN! IF THEY START SHOOTING, A LOT OF PEOPLE ARE GOING TO GET HURT!

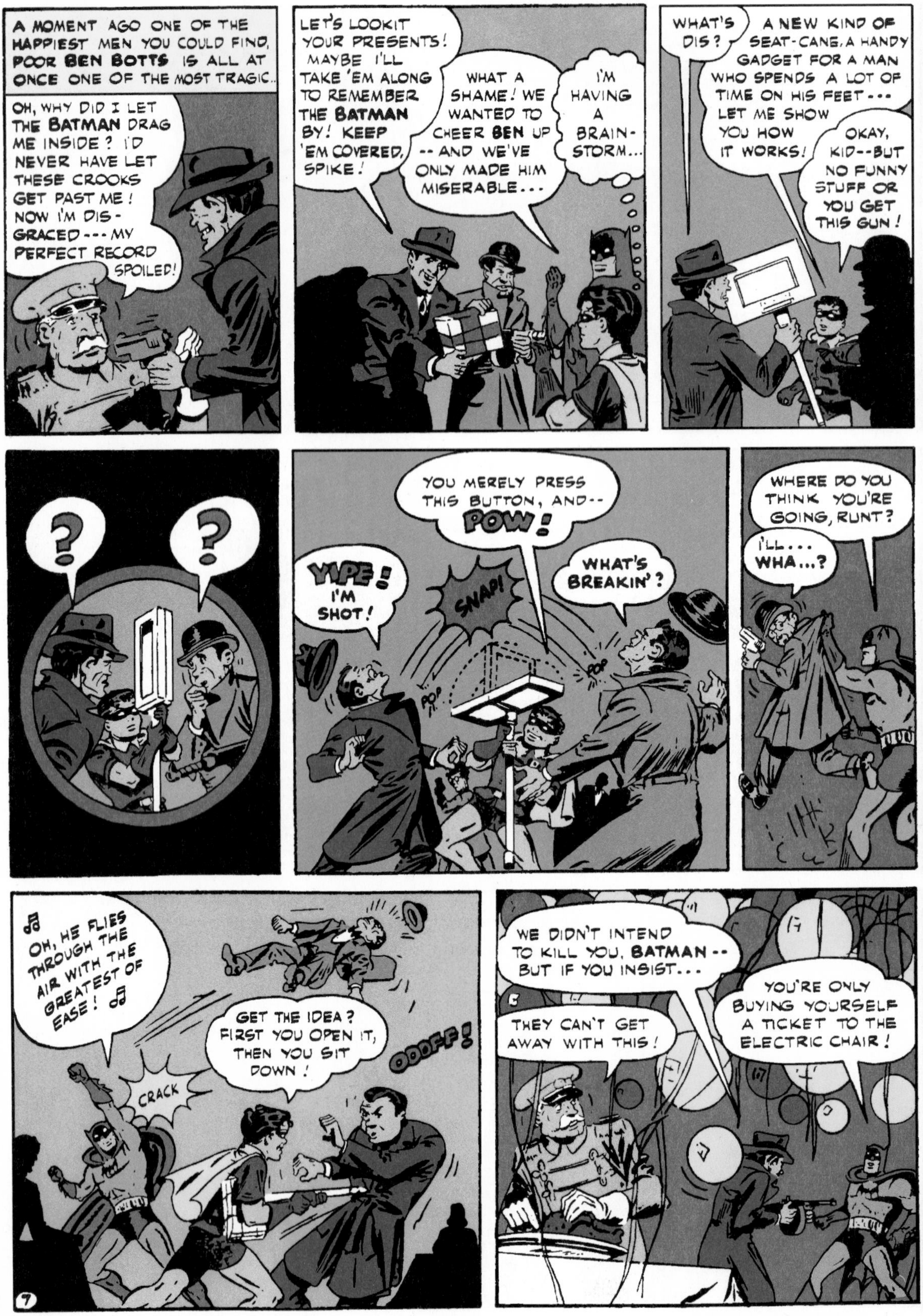

A MOMENT AGO ONE OF THE HAPPIEST MEN YOU COULD FIND, POOR BEN BOTTS IS ALL AT ONCE ONE OF THE MOST TRAGIC..
OH, WHY DID I LET THE BATMAN DRAG ME INSIDE? I'D NEVER HAVE LET THESE CROOKS GET PAST ME! NOW I'M DISGRACED--- MY PERFECT RECORD SPOILED!
LET'S LOOKIT YOUR PRESENTS! MAYBE I'LL TAKE 'EM ALONG TO REMEMBER THE BATMAN BY! KEEP 'EM COVERED, SPIKE!
WHAT A SHAME! WE WANTED TO CHEER BEN UP -- AND WE'VE ONLY MADE HIM MISERABLE---
I'M HAVING A BRAIN-STORM...
WHAT'S DIS?
A NEW KIND OF SEAT-CANE, A HANDY GADGET FOR A MAN WHO SPENDS A LOT OF TIME ON HIS FEET--- LET ME SHOW YOU HOW IT WORKS!
OKAY, KID--BUT NO FUNNY STUFF OR YOU GET THIS GUN!
?
?
YOU MERELY PRESS THIS BUTTON, AND-- POW!
YIPE! I'M SHOT!
SNAP!
WHAT'S BREAKIN'?
POP
POP
WHERE DO YOU THINK YOU'RE GOING, RUNT?
I'LL... WHA...?
OH, HE FLIES THROUGH THE AIR WITH THE GREATEST OF EASE!
GET THE IDEA? FIRST YOU OPEN IT, THEN YOU SIT DOWN!
CRACK
OOOFF!
7
WE DIDN'T INTEND TO KILL YOU, BATMAN -- BUT IF YOU INSIST...
THEY CAN'T GET AWAY WITH THIS!
YOU'RE ONLY BUYING YOURSELF A TICKET TO THE ELECTRIC CHAIR!

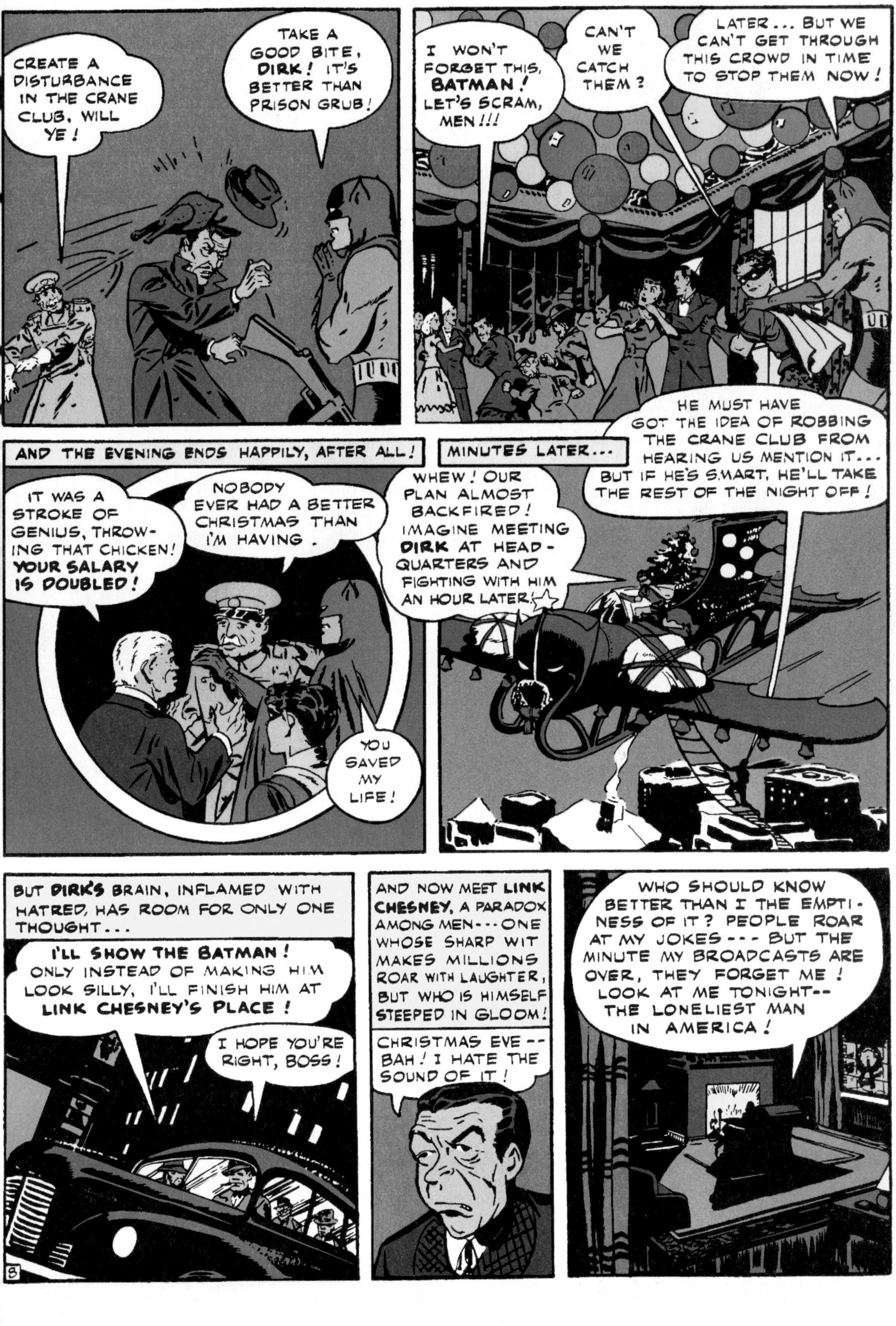
CREATE A DISTURBANCE IN THE CRANE CLUB, WILL YE!
TAKE A GOOD BITE, DIRK! IT'S BETTER THAN PRISON GRUB!
I WON'T FORGET THIS, BATMAN! LET'S SCRAM, MEN!!!
CAN'T WE CATCH THEM?
LATER... BUT WE CAN'T GET THROUGH THIS CROWD IN TIME TO STOP THEM NOW!
AND THE EVENING ENDS HAPPILY, AFTER ALL!
IT WAS A STROKE OF GENIUS, THROWING THAT CHICKEN! YOUR SALARY IS DOUBLED!
NOBODY EVER HAD A BETTER CHRISTMAS THAN I'M HAVING.
YOU SAVED MY LIFE!
MINUTES LATER...
WHEW! OUR PLAN ALMOST BACKFIRED! IMAGINE MEETING DIRK AT HEADQUARTERS AND FIGHTING WITH HIM AN HOUR LATER!
HE MUST HAVE GOT THE IDEA OF ROBBING THE CRANE CLUB FROM HEARING US MENTION IT... BUT IF HE'S SMART, HE'LL TAKE THE REST OF THE NIGHT OFF!
BUT DIRK'S BRAIN, INFLAMED WITH HATRED, HAS ROOM FOR ONLY ONE THOUGHT...
I'LL SHOW THE BATMAN! ONLY INSTEAD OF MAKING HIM LOOK SILLY, I'LL FINISH HIM AT LINK CHESNEY'S PLACE!
I HOPE YOU'RE RIGHT, BOSS!
8
AND NOW MEET LINK CHESNEY, A PARADOX AMONG MEN---ONE WHOSE SHARP WIT MAKES MILLIONS ROAR WITH LAUGHTER, BUT WHO IS HIMSELF STEEPED IN GLOOM!
CHRISTMAS EVE-- BAH! I HATE THE SOUND OF IT!
WHO SHOULD KNOW BETTER THAN I THE EMPTINESS OF IT? PEOPLE ROAR AT MY JOKES--- BUT THE MINUTE MY BROADCASTS ARE OVER, THEY FORGET ME! LOOK AT ME TONIGHT-- THE LONELIEST MAN IN AMERICA!

THE DOORBELL-- AND I GAVE THE SERVANTS THE NIGHT OFF TO ENJOY THEM- SELVES --- POOR, SIMPLE SOULS! SOMETIMES I ENVY THEM . . . . .

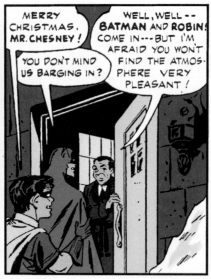

MERRY CHRISTMAS, MR. CHESNEY!

YOU DON'T MIND US BARGING IN?

WELL, WELL -- BATMAN AND ROBIN! COME IN --- BUT I'M AFRAID YOU WON'T FIND THE ATMOS- PHERE VERY PLEASANT!

NICE OF YOU TO TRY AND CHEER ME UP, BUT IT'S NO USE! PEOPLE ARE COLD AND THEY'VE CHILLED ME PERMANENTLY!

SURELY THERE MUST BE A SPARK OF WARMTH IN YOU TO BRING OUT ALL THOSE JOKES YOU TELL!

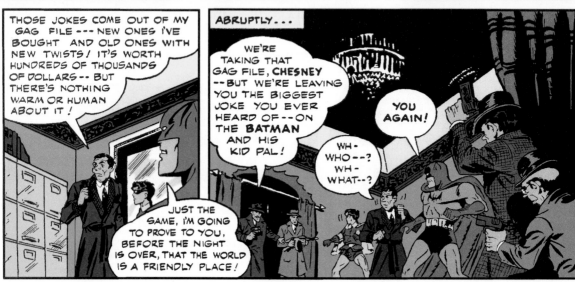

THOSE JOKES COME OUT OF MY GAG FILE --- NEW ONES I'VE BOUGHT AND OLD ONES WITH NEW TWISTS! IT'S WORTH HUNDREDS OF THOUSANDS OF DOLLARS -- BUT THERE'S NOTHING WARM OR HUMAN ABOUT IT!

ABRUPTLY...

WE'RE TAKING THAT GAG FILE, CHESNEY -- BUT WE'RE LEAVING YOU THE BIGGEST JOKE YOU EVER HEARD OF -- ON THE BATMAN AND HIS KID PAL!

WH- WHO --? WH- WHAT --?

YOU AGAIN!

JUST THE SAME, I'M GOING TO PROVE TO YOU, BEFORE THE NIGHT IS OVER, THAT THE WORLD IS A FRIENDLY PLACE!

THIS TIME YOU'RE FINISHED ---

AHHHH!

FROM ME TO YOU WITH WOIST WISHES!

I'LL GET YOU FOR THAT, SPIKE!

I DON'T LIKE FRESH KIDS!

YOU RATS! I'LL SEE THAT YOU SUFFER FOR THIS!

YOU WON'T DO ANYTHING IF YOU WANT TO KEEP ON LIVING!

⑨

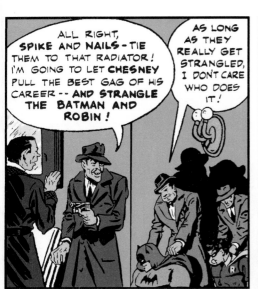

ALL RIGHT, SPIKE AND NAILS—TIE THEM TO THAT RADIATOR! I'M GOING TO LET CHESNEY PULL THE BEST GAG OF HIS CAREER—AND STRANGLE THE BATMAN AND ROBIN!

AS LONG AS THEY REALLY GET STRANGLED, I DON'T CARE WHO DOES IT!

AN INVENTIVE MIND THAT MIGHT HAVE SERVED BETTER PURPOSES DEVISES A FIENDISH DEATH TRAP...

I'D HOPED YOU'D WAKE UP IN TIME TO ENJOY THIS, BATMAN! ISN'T IT FUNNY THAT CHESNEY, WHOM YOU WANTED TO CHEER UP, IS GOING TO STRANGLE YOU AS SOON AS HE GETS TIRED OF STANDING ON TIPTOE?

YOU DEVIL!

HUH?... SOMETHING HIT ME...

SORRY I HAVE TO HURRY—BUT AFTER WE REMOVE THE GAG FILE, WHICH OUGHT TO BE WORTH PLENTY TO SOME OTHER RADIO COMIC, WE'RE MAKING A SEA VOYAGE!

WE'LL TAKE YOUR PLACE AT THAT LIGHTHOUSE, BATMAN—AND IT WOULDN'T SURPRISE ME A BIT IF THERE WAS A SHIPWRECK OUT THAT WAY!

I'D RATHER BE WHERE I AM THAN IN YOUR SHOES WHEN THE LAW FINALLY GETS YOU!

PIRATE REEF—WHERE A WAVE-LASHED STONE TOWER SENDS FORTH A STRONG GOLDEN BEAM OF WARNING...

CHRISTMAS EVE IS LIKE ANY OTHER NIGHT TO TOM WICK, THE AGED LIGHTHOUSE KEEPER—BUT LONELIER...

IT'S HARD, BEIN' OLD AN' ALONE THIS NIGHT—BUT I RECKON FOLKS CAN'T BE BOTHERED THINKIN' OF ME WAY OUT HERE!

DEC. 24 XMAS EVE

HOWEVER, AS HE STEPS UPON THE BALCONY TO HAVE A LAST LOOK AT THE WEATHER...

A BOAT... HEADIN' THIS WAY! GLORY BE—I'LL HARDLY KNOW HOW TO ACT HAVIN' VISITORS!

10

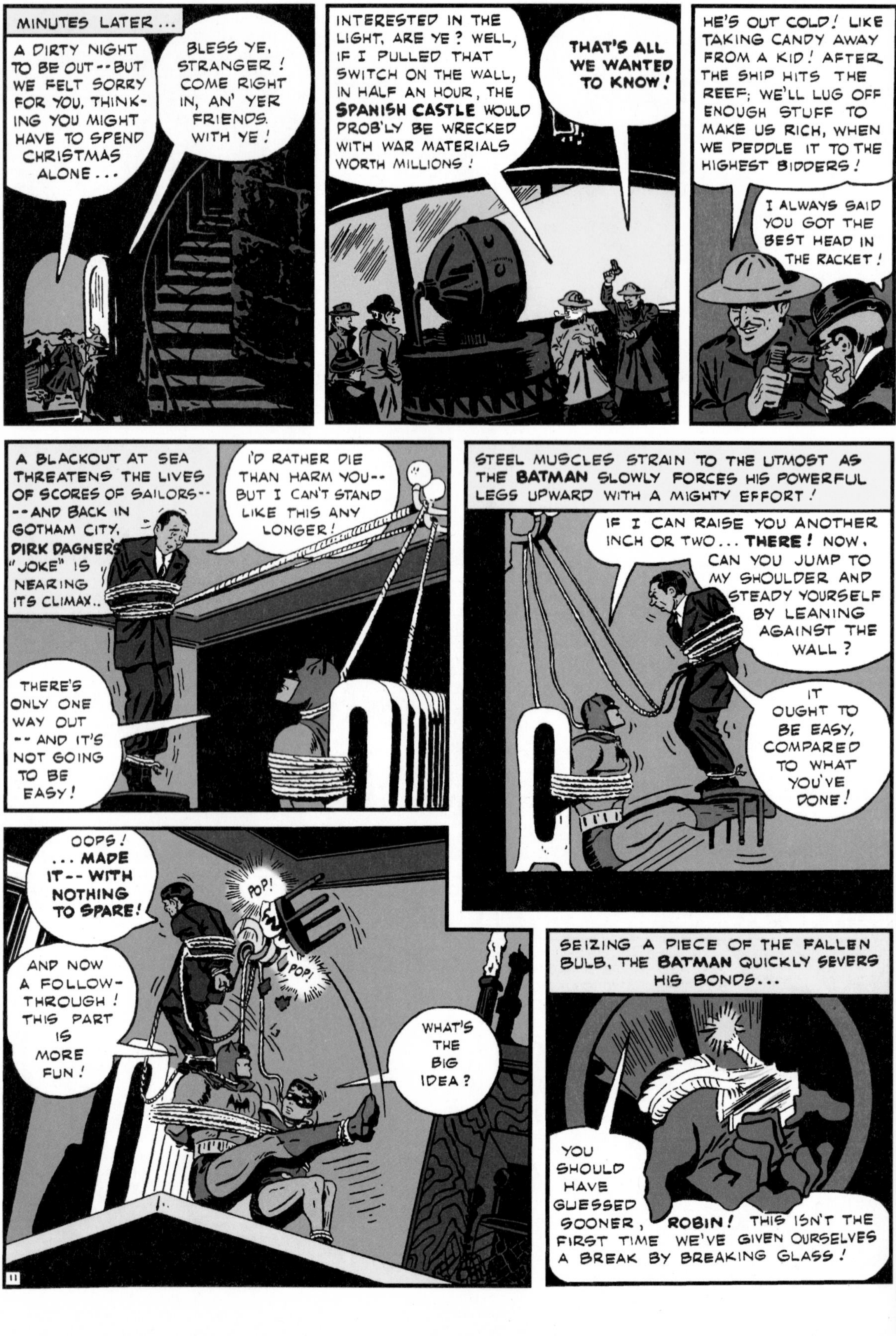
MINUTES LATER...
A DIRTY NIGHT TO BE OUT--BUT WE FELT SORRY FOR YOU, THINKING YOU MIGHT HAVE TO SPEND CHRISTMAS ALONE...
BLESS YE, STRANGER! COME RIGHT IN, AN' YER FRIENDS WITH YE!
INTERESTED IN THE LIGHT, ARE YE? WELL, IF I PULLED THAT SWITCH ON THE WALL, IN HALF AN HOUR, THE SPANISH CASTLE WOULD PROB'LY BE WRECKED WITH WAR MATERIALS WORTH MILLIONS!
THAT'S ALL WE WANTED TO KNOW!
HE'S OUT COLD! LIKE TAKING CANDY AWAY FROM A KID! AFTER THE SHIP HITS THE REEF, WE'LL LUG OFF ENOUGH STUFF TO MAKE US RICH, WHEN WE PEDDLE IT TO THE HIGHEST BIDDERS!
I ALWAYS SAID YOU GOT THE BEST HEAD IN THE RACKET!
A BLACKOUT AT SEA THREATENS THE LIVES OF SCORES OF SAILORS-- --AND BACK IN GOTHAM CITY, DIRK DAGNER'S "JOKE" IS NEARING ITS CLIMAX..
I'D RATHER DIE THAN HARM YOU--BUT I CAN'T STAND LIKE THIS ANY LONGER!
THERE'S ONLY ONE WAY OUT --AND IT'S NOT GOING TO BE EASY!
STEEL MUSCLES STRAIN TO THE UTMOST AS THE BATMAN SLOWLY FORCES HIS POWERFUL LEGS UPWARD WITH A MIGHTY EFFORT!
IF I CAN RAISE YOU ANOTHER INCH OR TWO... THERE! NOW, CAN YOU JUMP TO MY SHOULDER AND STEADY YOURSELF BY LEANING AGAINST THE WALL?
IT OUGHT TO BE EASY, COMPARED TO WHAT YOU'VE DONE!
OOPS! ...MADE IT--WITH NOTHING TO SPARE!
POP!
POP!
AND NOW A FOLLOW-THROUGH! THIS PART IS MORE FUN!
WHAT'S THE BIG IDEA?
SEIZING A PIECE OF THE FALLEN BULB, THE BATMAN QUICKLY SEVERS HIS BONDS...
YOU SHOULD HAVE GUESSED SOONER, ROBIN! THIS ISN'T THE FIRST TIME WE'VE GIVEN OURSELVES A BREAK BY BREAKING GLASS!
11

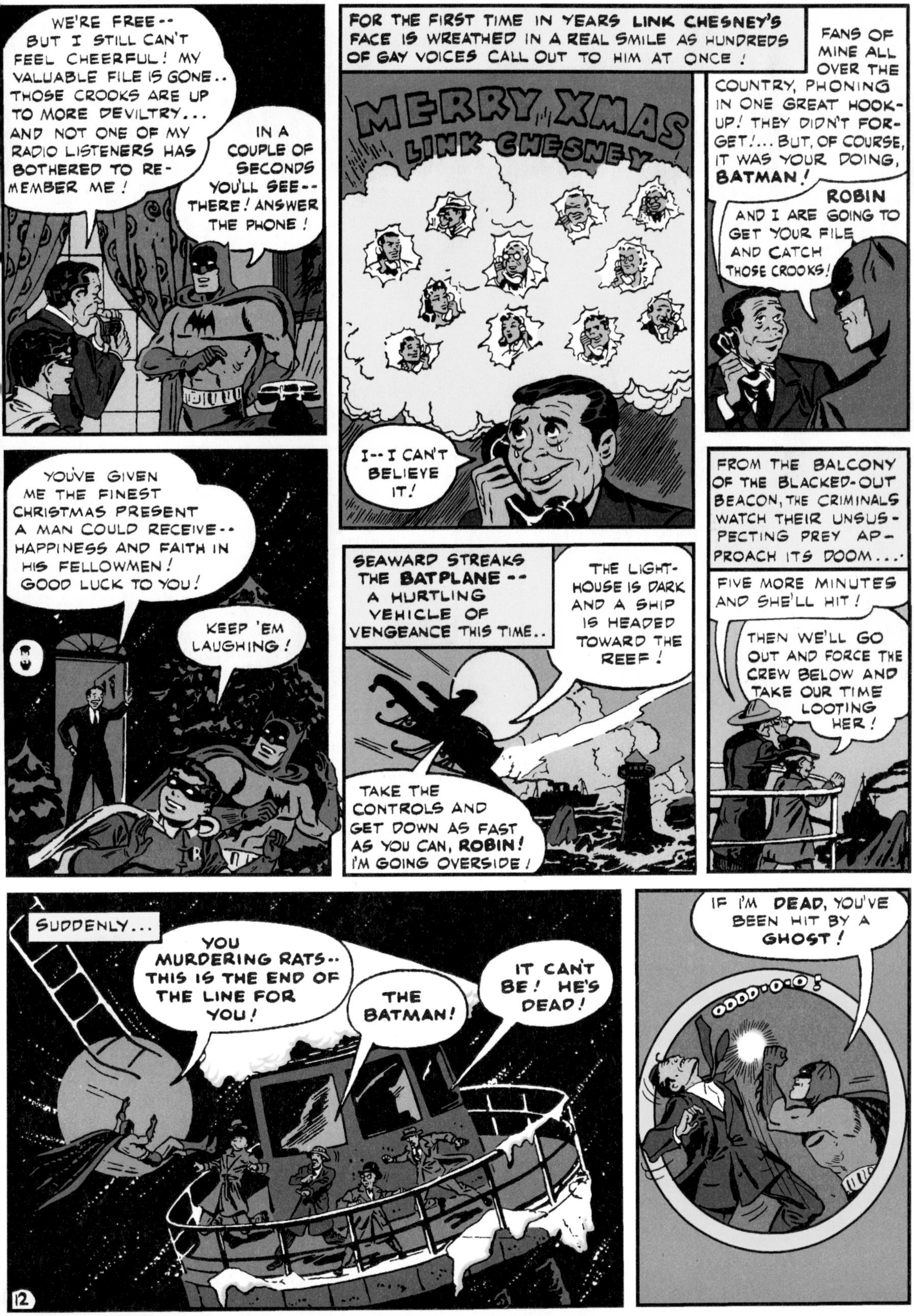
WE'RE FREE-- BUT I STILL CAN'T FEEL CHEERFUL! MY VALUABLE FILE IS GONE.. THOSE CROOKS ARE UP TO MORE DEVILTRY... AND NOT ONE OF MY RADIO LISTENERS HAS BOTHERED TO RE-MEMBER ME!
IN A COUPLE OF SECONDS YOU'LL SEE-- THERE! ANSWER THE PHONE!
FOR THE FIRST TIME IN YEARS LINK CHESNEY'S FACE IS WREATHED IN A REAL SMILE AS HUNDREDS OF GAY VOICES CALL OUT TO HIM AT ONCE!
MERRY XMAS LINK CHESNEY
I-- I CAN'T BELIEVE IT!
FANS OF MINE ALL OVER THE COUNTRY, PHONING IN ONE GREAT HOOK-UP! THEY DIDN'T FOR-GET!... BUT, OF COURSE, IT WAS YOUR DOING, BATMAN!
ROBIN AND I ARE GOING TO GET YOUR FILE AND CATCH THOSE CROOKS!
YOU'VE GIVEN ME THE FINEST CHRISTMAS PRESENT A MAN COULD RECEIVE-- HAPPINESS AND FAITH IN HIS FELLOWMEN! GOOD LUCK TO YOU!
KEEP 'EM LAUGHING!
SEAWARD STREAKS THE BATPLANE -- A HURTLING VEHICLE OF VENGEANCE THIS TIME..
THE LIGHT-HOUSE IS DARK AND A SHIP IS HEADED TOWARD THE REEF!
TAKE THE CONTROLS AND GET DOWN AS FAST AS YOU CAN, ROBIN! I'M GOING OVERSIDE!
FROM THE BALCONY OF THE BLACKED-OUT BEACON, THE CRIMINALS WATCH THEIR UNSUS-PECTING PREY AP-PROACH ITS DOOM...
FIVE MORE MINUTES AND SHE'LL HIT!
THEN WE'LL GO OUT AND FORCE THE CREW BELOW AND TAKE OUR TIME LOOTING HER!
SUDDENLY...
YOU MURDERING RATS.. THIS IS THE END OF THE LINE FOR YOU!
THE BATMAN!
IT CAN'T BE! HE'S DEAD!
IF I'M DEAD, YOU'VE BEEN HIT BY A GHOST!
OODD-O-O!
12

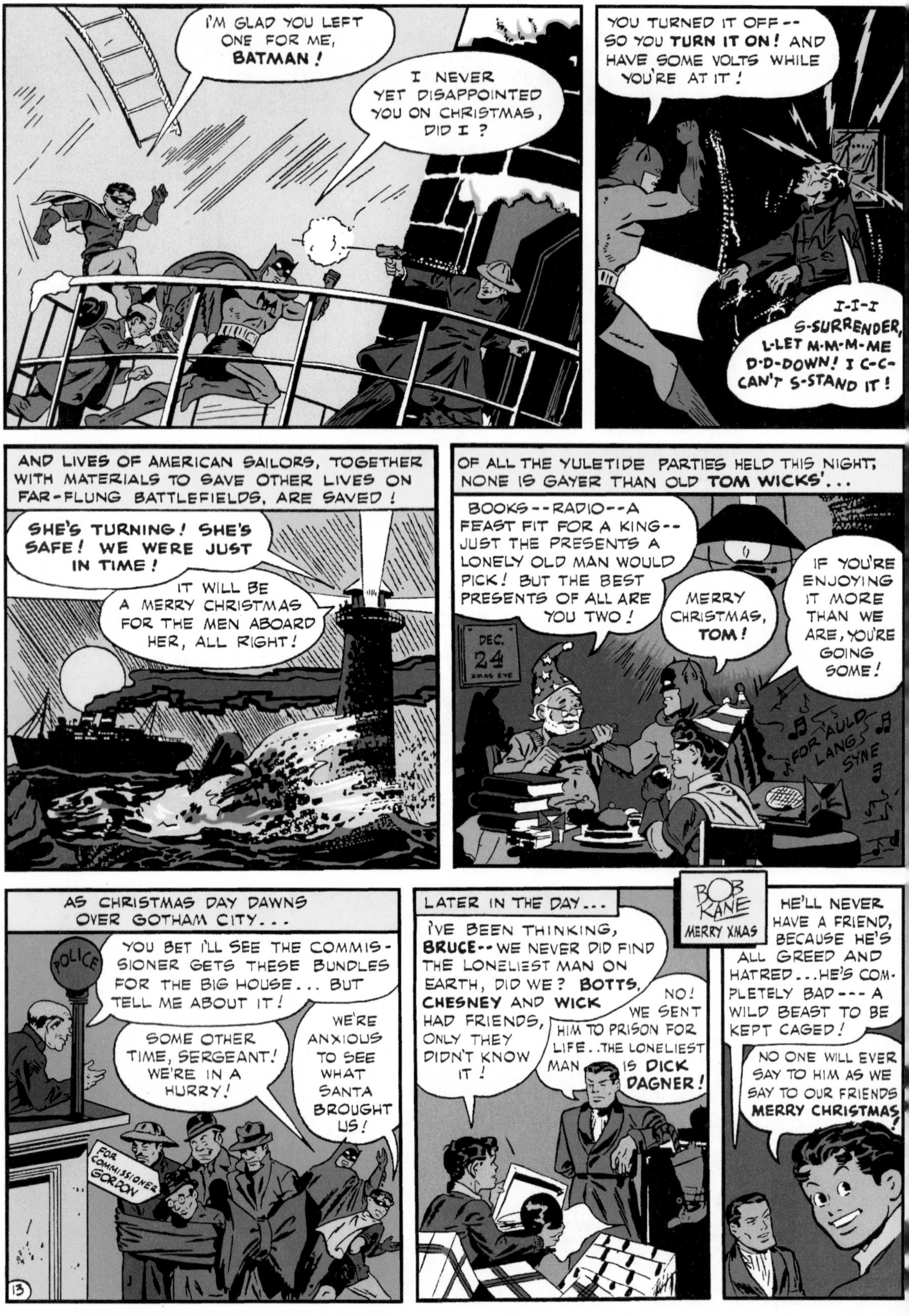
I'M GLAD YOU LEFT ONE FOR ME, BATMAN!
I NEVER YET DISAPPOINTED YOU ON CHRISTMAS, DID I?
YOU TURNED IT OFF -- SO YOU TURN IT ON! AND HAVE SOME VOLTS WHILE YOU'RE AT IT!
I-I-I S-SURRENDER, L-LET M-M-M-ME D-D-DOWN! I C-C-CAN'T S-STAND IT!
AND LIVES OF AMERICAN SAILORS, TOGETHER WITH MATERIALS TO SAVE OTHER LIVES ON FAR-FLUNG BATTLEFIELDS, ARE SAVED!
SHE'S TURNING! SHE'S SAFE! WE WERE JUST IN TIME!
IT WILL BE A MERRY CHRISTMAS FOR THE MEN ABOARD HER, ALL RIGHT!
OF ALL THE YULETIDE PARTIES HELD THIS NIGHT, NONE IS GAYER THAN OLD TOM WICKS'...
BOOKS -- RADIO -- A FEAST FIT FOR A KING -- JUST THE PRESENTS A LONELY OLD MAN WOULD PICK! BUT THE BEST PRESENTS OF ALL ARE YOU TWO!
MERRY CHRISTMAS, TOM!
IF YOU'RE ENJOYING IT MORE THAN WE ARE, YOU'RE GOING SOME!
DEC. 24 XMAS EVE
FOR AULD LANG SYNE
AS CHRISTMAS DAY DAWNS OVER GOTHAM CITY...
POLICE
YOU BET I'LL SEE THE COMMISSIONER GETS THESE BUNDLES FOR THE BIG HOUSE... BUT TELL ME ABOUT IT!
SOME OTHER TIME, SERGEANT! WE'RE IN A HURRY!
WE'RE ANXIOUS TO SEE WHAT SANTA BROUGHT US!
FOR COMMISSIONER GORDON
13
LATER IN THE DAY...
BOB KANE MERRY XMAS
I'VE BEEN THINKING, BRUCE -- WE NEVER DID FIND THE LONELIEST MAN ON EARTH, DID WE? BOTTS, CHESNEY AND WICK HAD FRIENDS, ONLY THEY DIDN'T KNOW IT!
NO! WE SENT HIM TO PRISON FOR LIFE.. THE LONELIEST MAN IS DICK DAGNER!
HE'LL NEVER HAVE A FRIEND, BECAUSE HE'S ALL GREED AND HATRED... HE'S COMPLETELY BAD --- A WILD BEAST TO BE KEPT CAGED!
NO ONE WILL EVER SAY TO HIM AS WE SAY TO OUR FRIENDS MERRY CHRISTMAS!

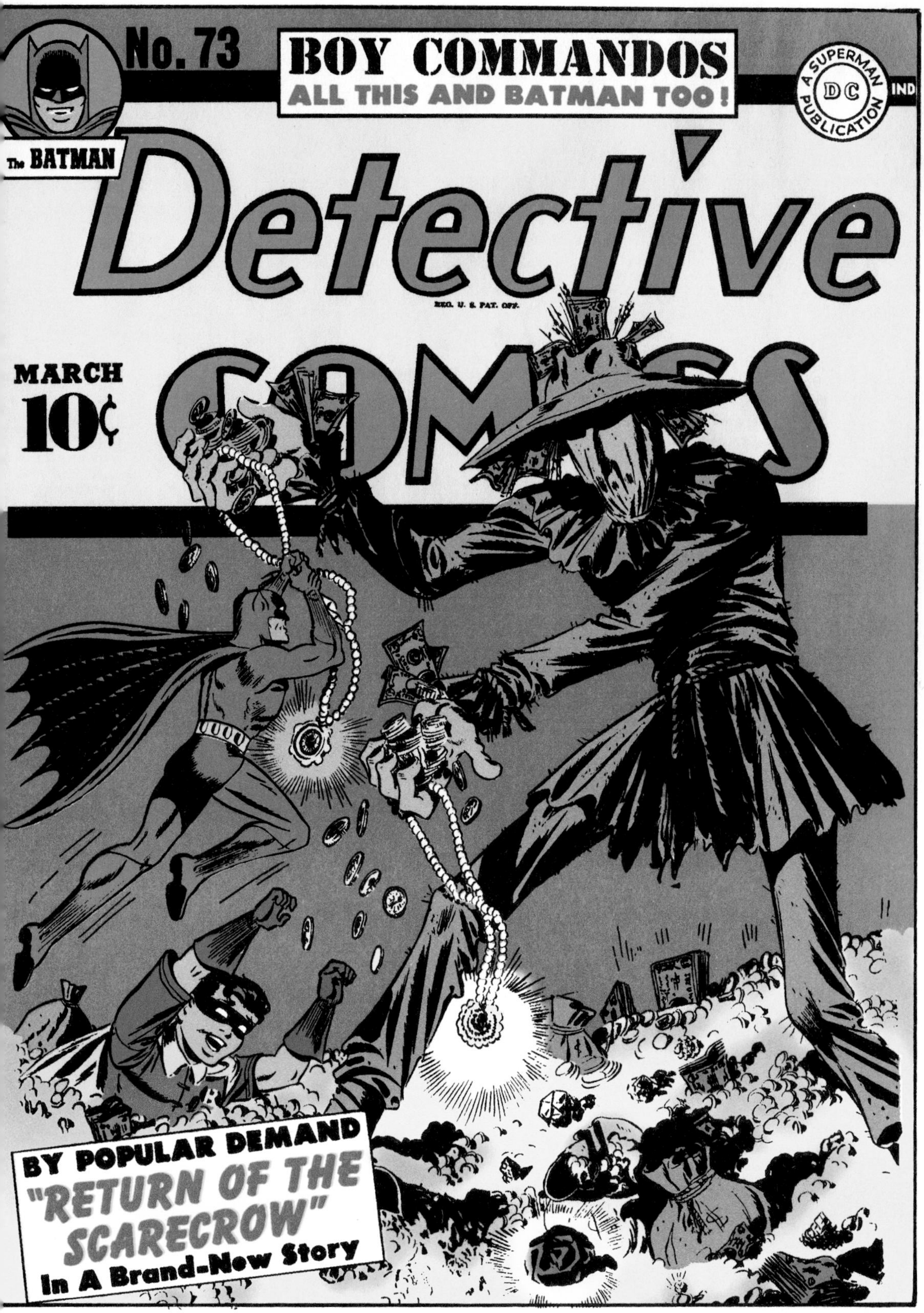
No. 73
BOY COMMANDOS
ALL THIS AND BATMAN TOO!
A SUPERMAN DC PUBLICATION
IND
The BATMAN
Detective
REG. U. S. PAT. OFF.
COMICS
MARCH
10¢
BY POPULAR DEMAND
"RETURN OF THE SCARECROW"
In A Brand-New Story

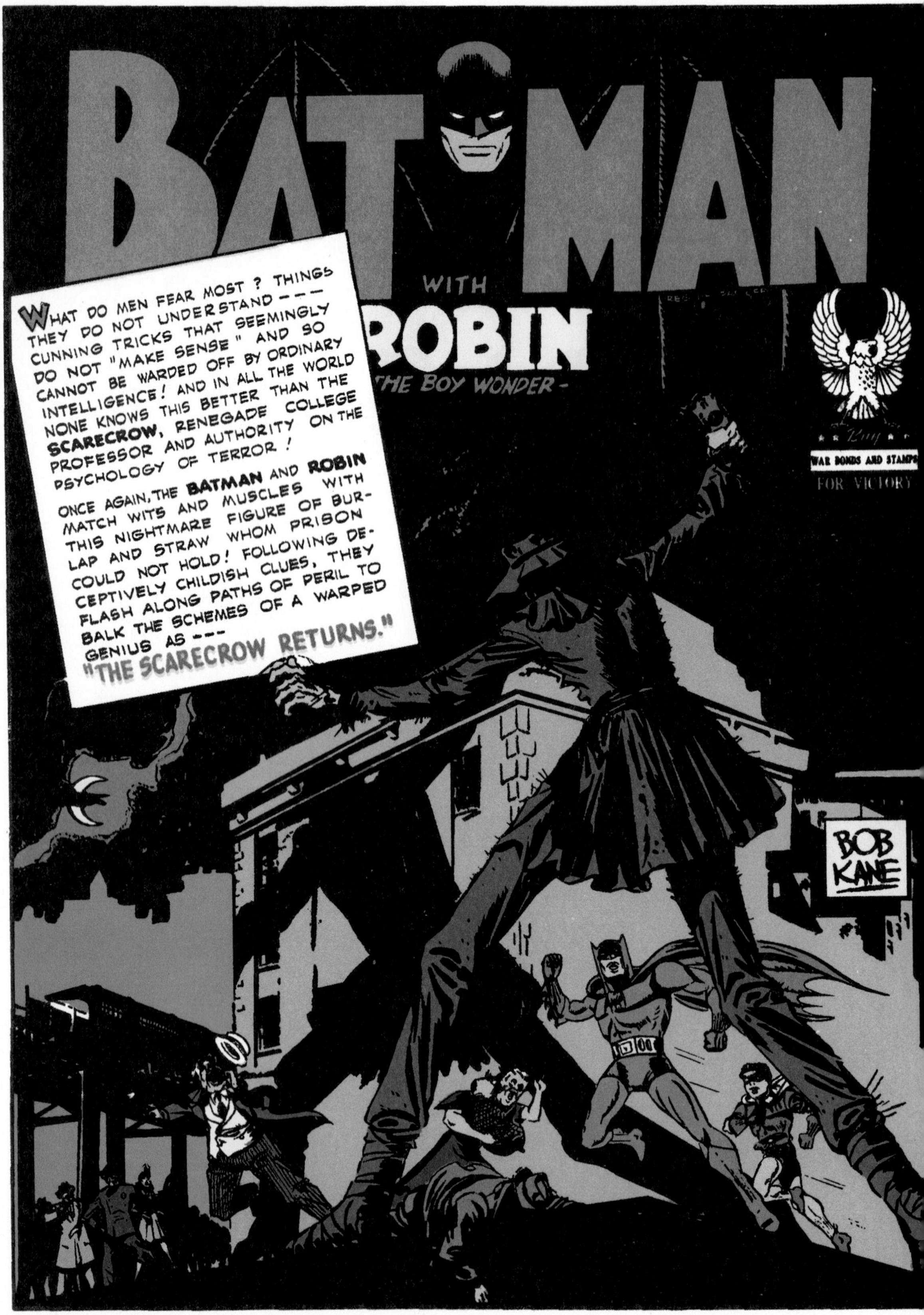
BATMAN
WITH
ROBIN
-THE BOY WONDER-
WHAT DO MEN FEAR MOST ? THINGS THEY DO NOT UNDERSTAND --- CUNNING TRICKS THAT SEEMINGLY DO NOT "MAKE SENSE" AND SO CANNOT BE WARDED OFF BY ORDINARY INTELLIGENCE! AND IN ALL THE WORLD NONE KNOWS THIS BETTER THAN THE SCARECROW, RENEGADE COLLEGE PROFESSOR AND AUTHORITY ON THE PSYCHOLOGY OF TERROR!
ONCE AGAIN, THE BATMAN AND ROBIN MATCH WITS AND MUSCLES WITH THIS NIGHTMARE FIGURE OF BURLAP AND STRAW WHOM PRISON COULD NOT HOLD! FOLLOWING DECEPTIVELY CHILDISH CLUES, THEY FLASH ALONG PATHS OF PERIL TO BALK THE SCHEMES OF A WARPED GENIUS AS ---
"THE SCARECROW RETURNS."
WAR BONDS AND STAMPS
FOR VICTORY
BOB KANE

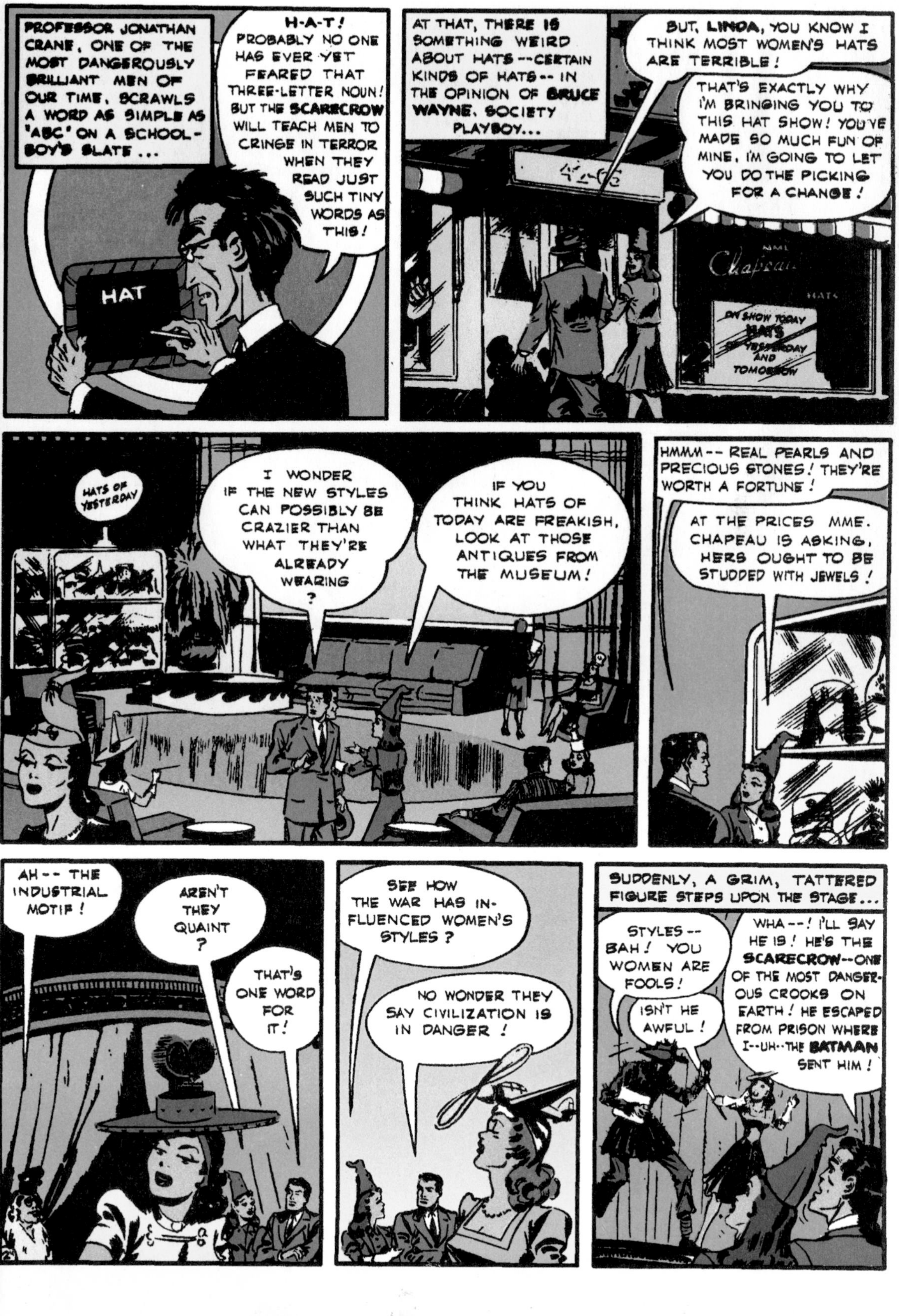

PROFESSOR JONATHAN CRANE, ONE OF THE MOST DANGEROUSLY BRILLIANT MEN OF OUR TIME, SCRAWLS A WORD AS SIMPLE AS "ABC" ON A SCHOOL-BOY'S SLATE...
H-A-T! PROBABLY NO ONE HAS EVER YET FEARED THAT THREE-LETTER NOUN! BUT THE SCARECROW WILL TEACH MEN TO CRINGE IN TERROR WHEN THEY READ JUST SUCH TINY WORDS AS THIS!
HAT
AT THAT, THERE IS SOMETHING WEIRD ABOUT HATS--CERTAIN KINDS OF HATS-- IN THE OPINION OF BRUCE WAYNE, SOCIETY PLAYBOY...
BUT, LINDA, YOU KNOW I THINK MOST WOMEN'S HATS ARE TERRIBLE!
THAT'S EXACTLY WHY I'M BRINGING YOU TO THIS HAT SHOW! YOU'VE MADE SO MUCH FUN OF MINE, I'M GOING TO LET YOU DO THE PICKING FOR A CHANGE!
Chapeau
HATS
ON SHOW TODAY HATS OF YESTERDAY AND TOMORROW
HATS OF YESTERDAY
I WONDER IF THE NEW STYLES CAN POSSIBLY BE CRAZIER THAN WHAT THEY'RE ALREADY WEARING?
IF YOU THINK HATS OF TODAY ARE FREAKISH, LOOK AT THOSE ANTIQUES FROM THE MUSEUM!
HMMM-- REAL PEARLS AND PRECIOUS STONES! THEY'RE WORTH A FORTUNE!
AT THE PRICES MME. CHAPEAU IS ASKING, HERS OUGHT TO BE STUDDED WITH JEWELS!
AH-- THE INDUSTRIAL MOTIF!
AREN'T THEY QUAINT?
THAT'S ONE WORD FOR IT!
SEE HOW THE WAR HAS INFLUENCED WOMEN'S STYLES?
NO WONDER THEY SAY CIVILIZATION IS IN DANGER!
SUDDENLY, A GRIM, TATTERED FIGURE STEPS UPON THE STAGE...
STYLES-- BAH! YOU WOMEN ARE FOOLS!
ISN'T HE AWFUL!
WHA--! I'LL SAY HE IS! HE'S THE SCARECROW--ONE OF THE MOST DANGEROUS CROOKS ON EARTH! HE ESCAPED FROM PRISON WHERE I--UH--THE BATMAN SENT HIM!

THE ONLY HATS WORTH HAVING ARE THOSE THAT BRING MONEY, INSTEAD OF COSTING MONEY! GET THOSE MUSEUM PIECES, MEN!
ANYBODY WHAT MAKES TROUBLE GETS PLUGGED!
WHAT A SPOT! I CAN'T GO INTO ACTION AS THE BATMAN WITHOUT LETTING LINDA KNOW MY SECRET!
DON'T BOTHER PICKING THE LOCK - WE'LL SMASH THE CASE!
HATS OF YESTERDAY
...AND IF SHE WERE KNOWN AS A FRIEND OF THE BATMAN, HER LIFE WOULD BE IN DANGER.. I'LL TRY SOMETHING ELSE...
OOPS --- I TRIPPED!
CRASH!
I'M SO SORRY! PLEASE FORGIVE ME!
LOOKIN' FER TROUBLE, CHUM?
WHY, YA CLUMSY APE--OUCH!
REALIZING DANGER FROM BEHIND ... BRUCE "ACCIDENTALLY" LUNGES BACKWARDS ...
HERE, LET ME HELP YOU! OOPS! PARDON ME!
WADDA YA TRYIN' TA DO -- SPOIL EVERYTHING? UGHH!!!
OH, BRUCE, BE CAREFUL!
BUT THE WILY SCARECROW SENSE THE THREAT OF THE SEEMINGLY CLUMSY LOUT, AND...
IF I THOUGHT YOU DID THAT ON PURPOSE I'D KILL YOU--BUT I'LL GIVE YOU THE BENEFIT OF THE DOUBT
LONG MINUTES AFTERWARD COMES THE PAINFUL AWAKE-ENING...
Oo-o-o!... I DIDN'T SEE THAT METEOR FALLING!
THE SCARECROW HIT YOU WITH A PISTOL BE-CAUSE YOU WERE STUMBLING ALL OVER THE PLACE!
NOW I REMEMBER! WHERE IS THE SCARECROW?
IF I KNEW THAT, I'D KNOW WHERE TO FIND THOSE JEWELLED HATS HE STOLE! BEFORE HE LEFT, HE WROTE ON THIS SLATE AND DROPPED IT!
WHATEVER WILL THE MUSEUM THINK OF ME FOR LETTING THIS HAPPEN!
HMMM--A SCHOOL SLATE... AND THE SCARECROW USED TO BE A TEACHER! I CAN UNDER-STAND THE "HAT" PART--BUT WHAT DOES HE MEAN BY "MAT"?
HAT--CAME OFF NICELY
MAT
LATER...
GOODBYE, BRUC -- I'M SORRY YOU GOT HURT IF ONLY THE BATMAN HAD BEEN THERE IT WOULDN'T HAVE HAPPEN ED!
YOU BET IT WOULDN' HAVE!

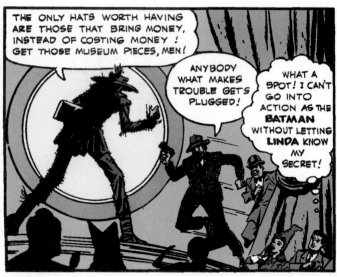

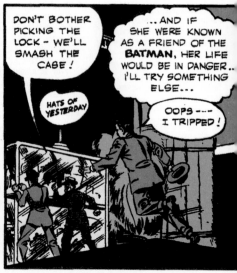

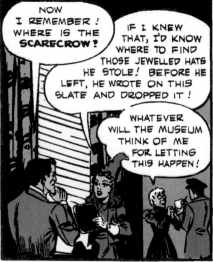

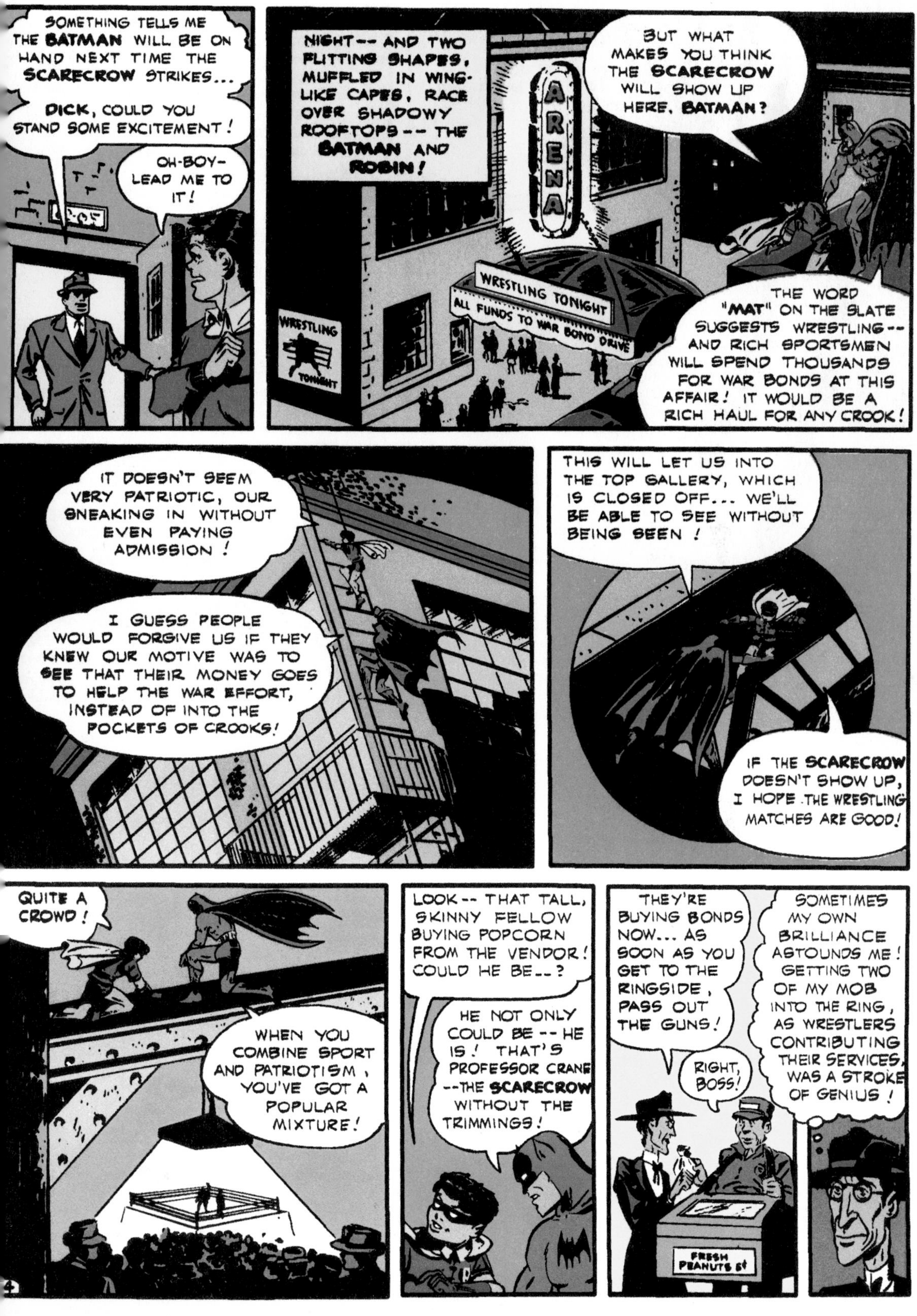
SOMETHING TELLS ME THE BATMAN WILL BE ON HAND NEXT TIME THE SCARECROW STRIKES...
DICK, COULD YOU STAND SOME EXCITEMENT!
OH-BOY-LEAD ME TO IT!
NIGHT-- AND TWO FLITTING SHAPES, MUFFLED IN WING-LIKE CAPES, RACE OVER SHADOWY ROOFTOPS -- THE BATMAN AND ROBIN!
ARENA
WRESTLING TONIGHT
ALL FUNDS TO WAR BOND DRIVE
WRESTLING TONIGHT
BUT WHAT MAKES YOU THINK THE SCARECROW WILL SHOW UP HERE, BATMAN?
THE WORD "MAT" ON THE SLATE SUGGESTS WRESTLING-- AND RICH SPORTSMEN WILL SPEND THOUSANDS FOR WAR BONDS AT THIS AFFAIR! IT WOULD BE A RICH HAUL FOR ANY CROOK!
IT DOESN'T SEEM VERY PATRIOTIC, OUR SNEAKING IN WITHOUT EVEN PAYING ADMISSION!
I GUESS PEOPLE WOULD FORGIVE US IF THEY KNEW OUR MOTIVE WAS TO SEE THAT THEIR MONEY GOES TO HELP THE WAR EFFORT, INSTEAD OF INTO THE POCKETS OF CROOKS!
THIS WILL LET US INTO THE TOP GALLERY, WHICH IS CLOSED OFF... WE'LL BE ABLE TO SEE WITHOUT BEING SEEN!
IF THE SCARECROW DOESN'T SHOW UP, I HOPE THE WRESTLING MATCHES ARE GOOD!
QUITE A CROWD!
WHEN YOU COMBINE SPORT AND PATRIOTISM, YOU'VE GOT A POPULAR MIXTURE!
LOOK-- THAT TALL, SKINNY FELLOW BUYING POPCORN FROM THE VENDOR! COULD HE BE--?
HE NOT ONLY COULD BE -- HE IS! THAT'S PROFESSOR CRANE --THE SCARECROW WITHOUT THE TRIMMINGS!
THEY'RE BUYING BONDS NOW... AS SOON AS YOU GET TO THE RINGSIDE, PASS OUT THE GUNS!
RIGHT, BOSS!
FRESH PEANUTS 5¢
SOMETIMES MY OWN BRILLIANCE ASTOUNDS ME! GETTING TWO OF MY MOB INTO THE RING, AS WRESTLERS CONTRIBUTING THEIR SERVICES, WAS A STROKE OF GENIUS!

MEANWHILE, LOYAL CITIZENS ARE INVESTING HEAVILY IN THEIR NATION'S FUTURE...

WHO ELSE, LADIES AND GENTLEMEN? WHO WANTS TO BUY BULLETS AND BONDS FOR SPECIAL DELIVERY TO THE JAPANAZIS?

GIVE ME TEN THOUSAND DOLLARS' WORTH!

I'M GIVING A WEEK'S PAY!

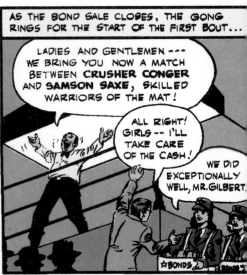

AS THE BOND SALE CLOSES, THE GONG RINGS FOR THE START OF THE FIRST BOUT...

LADIES AND GENTLEMEN --- WE BRING YOU NOW A MATCH BETWEEN CRUSHER CONGER AND SAMSON SAXE, SKILLED WARRIORS OF THE MAT!

ALL RIGHT! GIRLS -- I'LL TAKE CARE OF THE CASH!

WE DID EXCEPTIONALLY WELL, MR. GILBERT.

AND ON THEIR WAY TO THE RING, THE SUPPOSED WRESTLERS TRANSACT STRANGE BUSINESS WITH THE POPCORN VENDOR!

SH-H-H! NOT SO LOUD, CRUSHER!

POPCORN AN' POPGUNS, HUH? HAW, HAW, HAW!

MAKE IT SNAPPY!

THE NEXT MOMENT...

BOTH BOYS ARE WRESTLING WITHOUT PAY-- AA-A-A-A...

DAT'S WHAT YOU T'INK!

DON'T NO-BODY MOVE, OR DA JOINT'LL BE LITTERED WIT' CORPSES!

UNDER COVER OF THE EXCITEMENT, PROFESSOR CRANE WHIPS AN ODD MASK AND A BATTERED, FAMILIAR HAT FROM BENEATH HIS COAT AND DONS THEM FURTIVELY...

A HOLDUP! THEY'RE AFTER THE WAR BOND MONEY!

THE RATS! THEY'D KILL INNOCENT PEOPLE TO GET IT!

I'LL TAKE THAT MONEY OFF YOUR HANDS!

THE SCARECROW! YOU CAN'T GET AWAY WITH ROBBING UNCLE SAM!

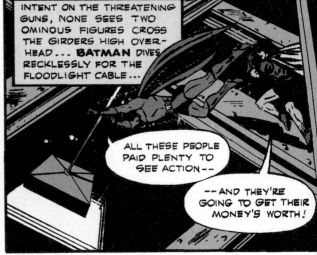

INTENT ON THE THREATENING GUNS, NONE SEES TWO OMINOUS FIGURES CROSS THE GIRDERS HIGH OVER-HEAD... BATMAN DIVES RECKLESSLY FOR THE FLOODLIGHT CABLE...

ALL THESE PEOPLE PAID PLENTY TO SEE ACTION--

--AND THEY'RE GOING TO GET THEIR MONEY'S WORTH!

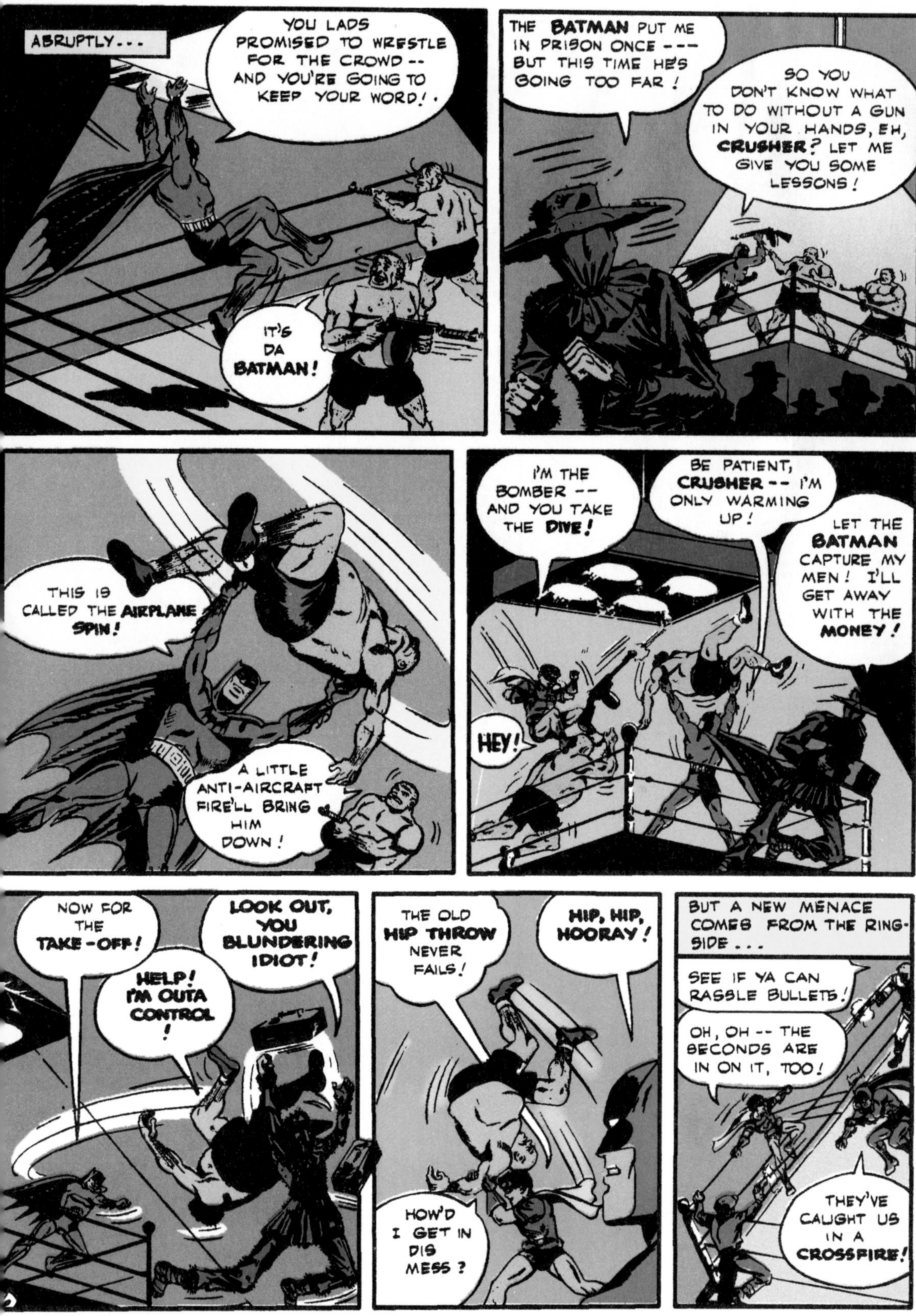
ABRUPTLY...
YOU LADS PROMISED TO WRESTLE FOR THE CROWD -- AND YOU'RE GOING TO KEEP YOUR WORD!
IT'S DA BATMAN!
THE BATMAN PUT ME IN PRISON ONCE --- BUT THIS TIME HE'S GOING TOO FAR!
SO YOU DON'T KNOW WHAT TO DO WITHOUT A GUN IN YOUR HANDS, EH, CRUSHER? LET ME GIVE YOU SOME LESSONS!
THIS IS CALLED THE AIRPLANE SPIN!
A LITTLE ANTI-AIRCRAFT FIRE'LL BRING HIM DOWN!
I'M THE BOMBER -- AND YOU TAKE THE DIVE!
BE PATIENT, CRUSHER -- I'M ONLY WARMING UP!
LET THE BATMAN CAPTURE MY MEN! I'LL GET AWAY WITH THE MONEY!
HEY!
NOW FOR THE TAKE-OFF!
LOOK OUT, YOU BLUNDERING IDIOT!
HELP! I'M OUTA CONTROL!
THE OLD HIP THROW NEVER FAILS!
HIP, HIP, HOORAY!
HOW'D I GET IN DIS MESS?
BUT A NEW MENACE COMES FROM THE RING-SIDE...
SEE IF YA CAN RASSLE BULLETS!
OH, OH -- THE SECONDS ARE IN ON IT, TOO!
THEY'VE CAUGHT US IN A CROSSFIRE!

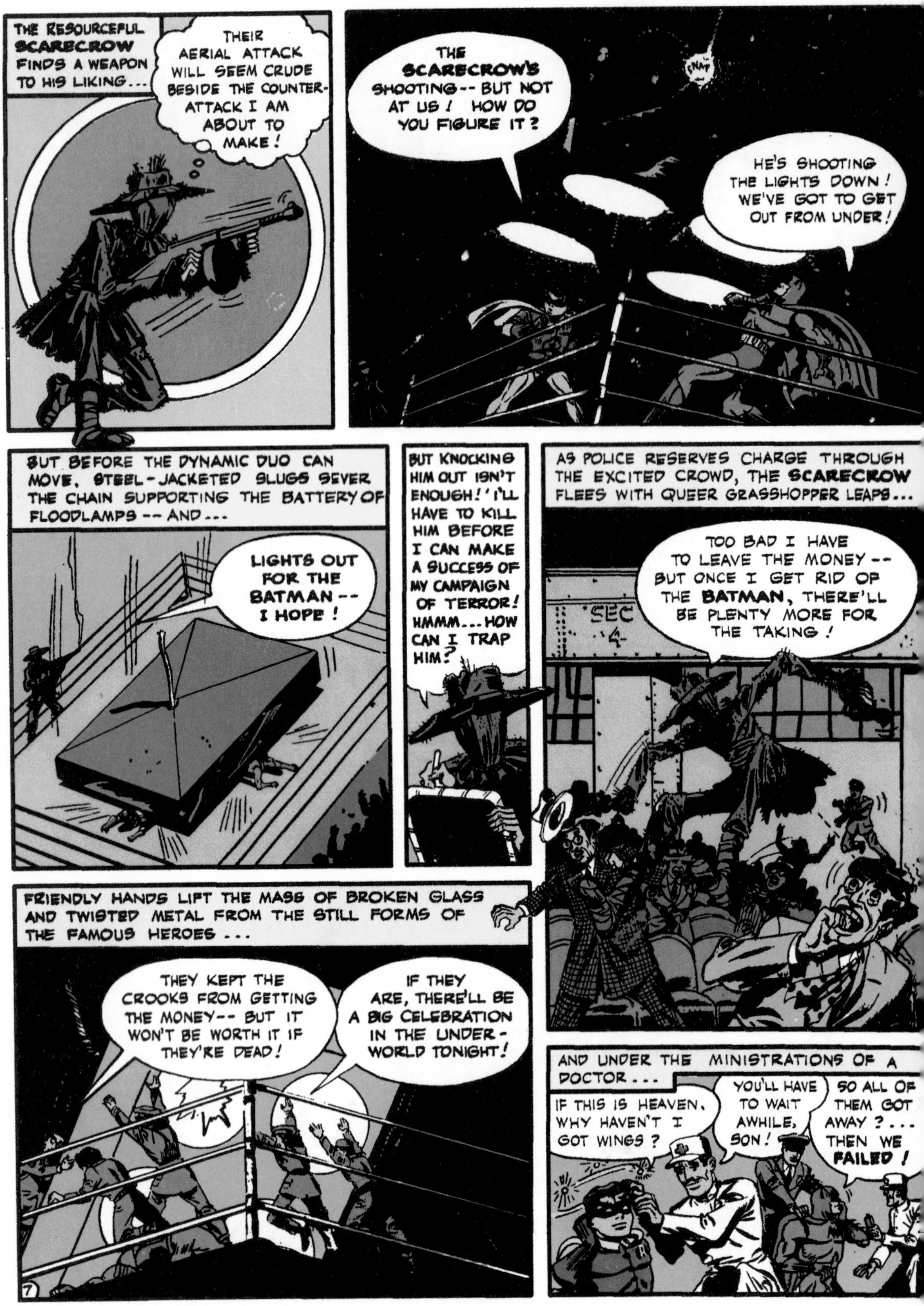
THE RESOURCEFUL SCARECROW FINDS A WEAPON TO HIS LIKING...
THEIR AERIAL ATTACK WILL SEEM CRUDE BESIDE THE COUNTER-ATTACK I AM ABOUT TO MAKE!
THE SCARECROW'S SHOOTING-- BUT NOT AT US! HOW DO YOU FIGURE IT?
SNAP
HE'S SHOOTING THE LIGHTS DOWN! WE'VE GOT TO GET OUT FROM UNDER!
BUT BEFORE THE DYNAMIC DUO CAN MOVE, STEEL-JACKETED SLUGS SEVER THE CHAIN SUPPORTING THE BATTERY OF FLOODLAMPS -- AND ...
LIGHTS OUT FOR THE BATMAN -- I HOPE!
BUT KNOCKING HIM OUT ISN'T ENOUGH! I'LL HAVE TO KILL HIM BEFORE I CAN MAKE A SUCCESS OF MY CAMPAIGN OF TERROR! HMMM... HOW CAN I TRAP HIM?
AS POLICE RESERVES CHARGE THROUGH THE EXCITED CROWD, THE SCARECROW FLEES WITH QUEER GRASSHOPPER LEAPS...
TOO BAD I HAVE TO LEAVE THE MONEY -- BUT ONCE I GET RID OF THE BATMAN, THERE'LL BE PLENTY MORE FOR THE TAKING!
SEC 4
FRIENDLY HANDS LIFT THE MASS OF BROKEN GLASS AND TWISTED METAL FROM THE STILL FORMS OF THE FAMOUS HEROES ...
THEY KEPT THE CROOKS FROM GETTING THE MONEY-- BUT IT WON'T BE WORTH IT IF THEY'RE DEAD!
IF THEY ARE, THERE'LL BE A BIG CELEBRATION IN THE UNDER-WORLD TONIGHT!
7
AND UNDER THE MINISTRATIONS OF A DOCTOR ...
IF THIS IS HEAVEN, WHY HAVEN'T I GOT WINGS?
YOU'LL HAVE TO WAIT AWHILE, SON!
SO ALL OF THEM GOT AWAY? ... THEN WE FAILED!

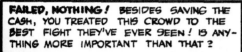

FAILED, NOTHING! BESIDES SAVING THE CASH, YOU TREATED THIS CROWD TO THE BEST FIGHT THEY'VE EVER SEEN! IS ANYTHING MORE IMPORTANT THAN THAT?

THE SCARECROW IS MORE IMPORTANT! UNLESS HE'S PUT AWAY FOR GOOD, HE'LL TERRORIZE THE WHOLE CITY!

I FOUND THIS SLATE WITH SOME SILLY STUFF ON IT BY THE RINGSIDE!

"HAT"--"MAT"-- AND NEXT IS "VAT" ... THAT'S GOING TO BE A TOUGH ONE TO FIGURE OUT!

MAYBE THIS CARD STUCK IN THE FRAME OF THE SLATE WILL THROW SOME LIGHT ON THE SUBJECT!

HAT - CAME OFF NICELY!
MAT - FELL FLAT
VAT -

JUST AN ADVERTISEMENT FOR THE VORTEX CLEANERS & DYERS AT 13 HOOKE STREET -- AND AN OLD ONE, AT THAT!

DOESN'T MEAN A THING! PROBABLY SOME CARD THAT WAS KICKING AROUND AND GOT CAUGHT ACCIDENTALLY!

BUT THE SUBTLEST CLUE IS ENOUGH FOR THE BATMAN, ACE CRIMINOLOGIST -- AND PRESENTLY...

DYERS USE VATS.....IT'S SO PLAIN, THE SCARECROW MIGHT HAVE INTENDED IT AS A TRAP -- BUT I'D HATE TO PASS UP THE CHANCE OF TANGLING WITH HIM AGAIN!

THAT HIGH WINDOW BY THE DRAINPIPE .... EVEN IF THEY'RE EXPECTING US, THEY WOULDN'T THINK WE'D PICK THAT AS AN ENTRANCE!

VORTEX CLEANERS & DYERS
MOVED TO NEW QUARTERS

THERE THEY ARE -- WATCHING THE DOOR WITH GUNS READY!

LET'S NOT KEEP THEM IN SUSPENSE!

VORTEX CLEANERS & DYERS

MOVED TO NEW QUARTERS

WITHIN THE GLOOMY STRUCTURE...

CHEE, SCARECROW -- DIS JOINT GIVES ME DA CREEPS! I FEEL LIKE SOMEONE WAS SNEAKIN' UP ON ME!

A COMMON PSYCHOLOGICAL PHENOMENON WHEN ONE HAS REASON TO BE FRIGHTENED OF ANYONE, MUGGSY!

NOW, IF I WERE NERVOUS, I MIGHT IMAGINE THAT INSTEAD OF WAITING HERE TO KILL THE BATMAN, THE BATMAN WAS CREEPING UP TO ATTACK ME!

WHAT AN AWFUL THOUGHT!

SUDDENLY...

WHAT YOU NEED, **SCARECROW**, IS A FIRST-CLASS NERVOUS BREAKDOWN!

YIII-I-I! NO WONDER I FELT DAT WAY!

WH--!

THIS WILL REMIND YOU TO TRUST YOUR HUNCHES FROM NOW ON!

HEY,! **SCARECROW**-- DON'T LEAVE US IN DA LOICH!

YOU LEFT YOURSELF IN THE LURCH, WHEN YOU GOT OFF THE STRAIGHT AND NARROW PATH!

DIS IS WOISE'N DA AIRPLANE SPIN!

AN ARROGANT VOICE HURLS A CHALLENGE...

COME AND GET ME IF YOU DARE!

I WAS COMING ANYWAY -- BUT THANKS FOR THE INVITATION!

AM I INCLUDED?

WILL YOU SURRENDER QUIETLY, OR DO I HAVE TO USE PERSUASION?

SUPPOSING I RETIRE TO THINK IT OVER...

...WHILE YOU WAIT BELOW FOR MY ANSWER!

AND A TREACHEROUS TRAP IS SPRUNG!

THE VATS ARE OPENING UNDER US!

HE'S TRICKED US!

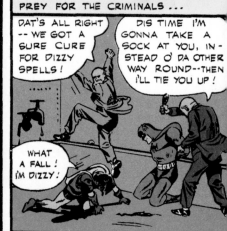

STUNNED BY THEIR UNEXPECTED FALL THE VALIANT BATTLERS ARE EASY PREY FOR THE CRIMINALS ...

DAT'S ALL RIGHT -- WE GOT A SURE CURE FOR DIZZY SPELLS!

DIS TIME I'M GONNA TAKE A SOCK AT YOU, IN- STEAD O' DA OTHER WAY ROUND--THEN I'LL TIE YOU UP!

WHAT A FALL! I'M DIZZY!

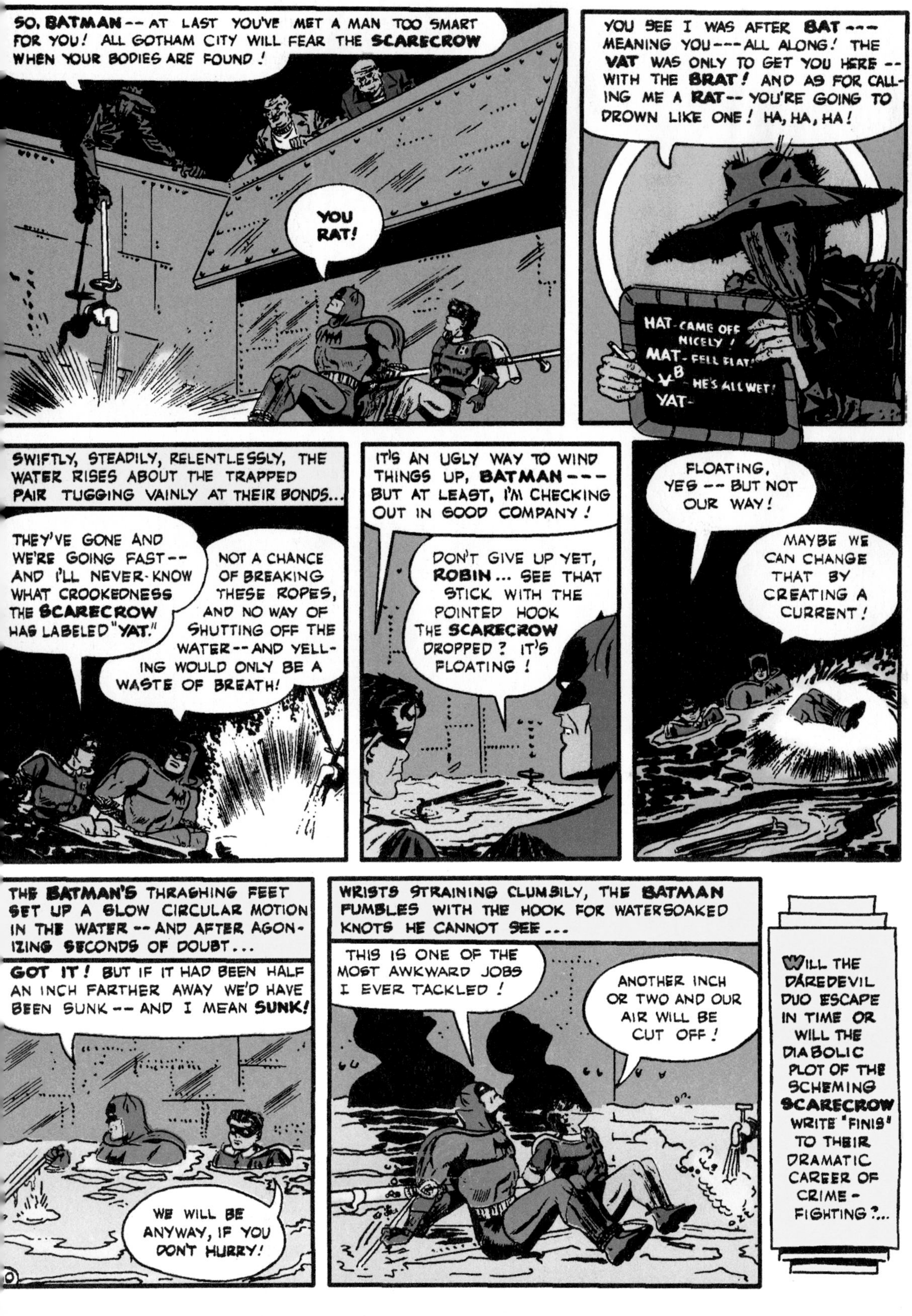
SO, BATMAN -- AT LAST YOU'VE MET A MAN TOO SMART FOR YOU! ALL GOTHAM CITY WILL FEAR THE SCARECROW WHEN YOUR BODIES ARE FOUND!
YOU RAT!
YOU SEE I WAS AFTER BAT --- MEANING YOU --- ALL ALONG! THE VAT WAS ONLY TO GET YOU HERE -- WITH THE BRAT! AND AS FOR CALLING ME A RAT -- YOU'RE GOING TO DROWN LIKE ONE! HA, HA, HA!
HAT - CAME OFF NICELY!
MAT - FELL FLAT!
VB - HE'S ALL WET!
YAT -
SWIFTLY, STEADILY, RELENTLESSLY, THE WATER RISES ABOUT THE TRAPPED PAIR TUGGING VAINLY AT THEIR BONDS...
THEY'VE GONE AND WE'RE GOING FAST -- AND I'LL NEVER KNOW WHAT CROOKEDNESS THE SCARECROW HAS LABELED "YAT."
NOT A CHANCE OF BREAKING THESE ROPES, AND NO WAY OF SHUTTING OFF THE WATER -- AND YELLING WOULD ONLY BE A WASTE OF BREATH!
IT'S AN UGLY WAY TO WIND THINGS UP, BATMAN --- BUT AT LEAST, I'M CHECKING OUT IN GOOD COMPANY!
DON'T GIVE UP YET, ROBIN... SEE THAT STICK WITH THE POINTED HOOK THE SCARECROW DROPPED? IT'S FLOATING!
FLOATING, YES -- BUT NOT OUR WAY!
MAYBE WE CAN CHANGE THAT BY CREATING A CURRENT!
THE BATMAN'S THRASHING FEET SET UP A SLOW CIRCULAR MOTION IN THE WATER -- AND AFTER AGONIZING SECONDS OF DOUBT...
GOT IT! BUT IF IT HAD BEEN HALF AN INCH FARTHER AWAY WE'D HAVE BEEN SUNK -- AND I MEAN SUNK!
WE WILL BE ANYWAY, IF YOU DON'T HURRY!
WRISTS STRAINING CLUMSILY, THE BATMAN FUMBLES WITH THE HOOK FOR WATERSOAKED KNOTS HE CANNOT SEE...
THIS IS ONE OF THE MOST AWKWARD JOBS I EVER TACKLED!
ANOTHER INCH OR TWO AND OUR AIR WILL BE CUT OFF!
WILL THE DAREDEVIL DUO ESCAPE IN TIME OR WILL THE DIABOLIC PLOT OF THE SCHEMING SCARECROW WRITE "FINIS" TO THEIR DRAMATIC CAREER OF CRIME-FIGHTING?...

MEANWHILE, A WEIRD CREATURE STALKS THE TWISTED STREETS OF CHINATOWN...

C'MON, MEN... THERE'S THE PLACE ACROSS THE STREET!

DIS CHINESE ART IS OUTA MY LINE -- BUT IF IT'S WORTH ALL DA DOUGH DEY SAY IT IS, I'M FOR IT!

PUT UP YOUR HANDS, FU MANCHU -- IT'S A STICKUP!

SO -- ROBBERS! IT IS WRITTEN, "BETTER GO VALIANTLY TO YOUR ANCESTORS THAN BE LEFT EMPTY-HANDED BY THIEVES..."

IT WILL TAKE MORE THAN ORIENTAL PHILOSOPHY TO SAVE YOUR TREASURES, MY FRIEND!

DAT'S TELLIN' HIM, SCARECROW!

THESE ITEMS WILL ALL BRING TREMENDOUS PRICES FROM CERTAIN UNSCRUPULOUS COLLECTORS!

IMAGINE PAYIN' HEAVY DOUGH FOR JUNK DAT AIN'T NO GOOD, EXCEPT TA LOOK AT!

AS I LIVE AND BREATHE -- A CHINESE SCARECROW CARVED IN JADE! I MUST HAVE IT FOR MY OWN COLLECTION! IT IS A GOOD OMEN!

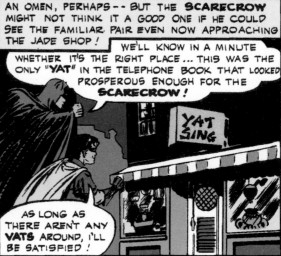

AN OMEN, PERHAPS -- BUT THE SCARECROW MIGHT NOT THINK IT A GOOD ONE IF HE COULD SEE THE FAMILIAR PAIR EVEN NOW APPROACHING THE JADE SHOP!

WE'LL KNOW IN A MINUTE WHETHER IT'S THE RIGHT PLACE... THIS WAS THE ONLY "YAT" IN THE TELEPHONE BOOK THAT LOOKED PROSPEROUS ENOUGH FOR THE SCARECROW!

YAT SING

AS LONG AS THERE AREN'T ANY VATS AROUND, I'LL BE SATISFIED!

THERE THEY ARE!

AND HERE WE GO AGAIN!

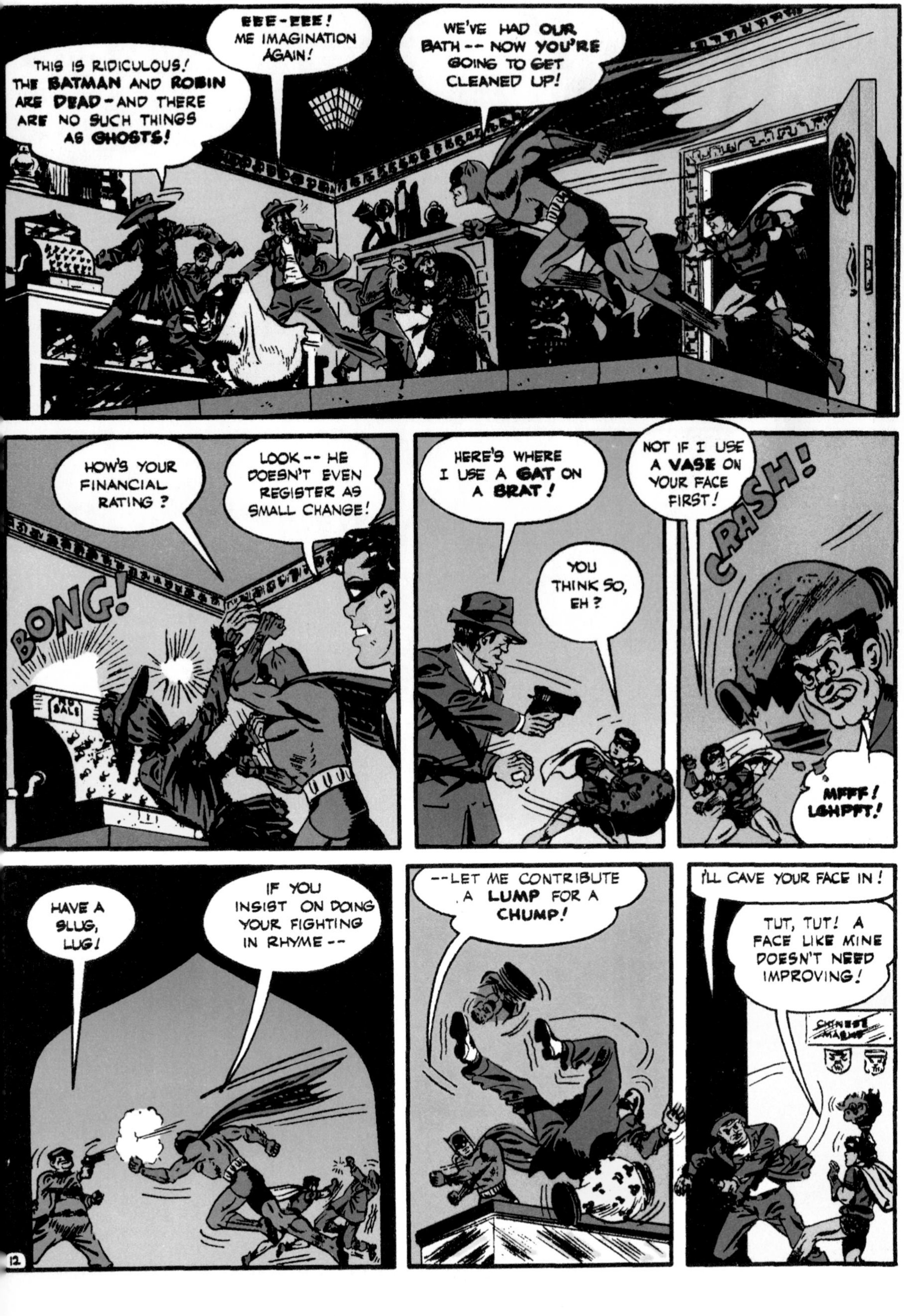
THIS IS RIDICULOUS! THE BATMAN AND ROBIN ARE DEAD-AND THERE ARE NO SUCH THINGS AS GHOSTS!
EEE-EEE! ME IMAGINATION AGAIN!
WE'VE HAD OUR BATH -- NOW YOU'RE GOING TO GET CLEANED UP!
HOW'S YOUR FINANCIAL RATING ?
LOOK -- HE DOESN'T EVEN REGISTER AS SMALL CHANGE!
BONG!
HERE'S WHERE I USE A GAT ON A BRAT!
YOU THINK SO, EH ?
NOT IF I USE A VASE ON YOUR FACE FIRST!
CRASH!
MFFF! LGHPFT!
HAVE A SLUG, LUG!
IF YOU INSIST ON DOING YOUR FIGHTING IN RHYME --
--LET ME CONTRIBUTE A LUMP FOR A CHUMP!
I'LL CAVE YOUR FACE IN!
TUT, TUT! A FACE LIKE MINE DOESN'T NEED IMPROVING!
12

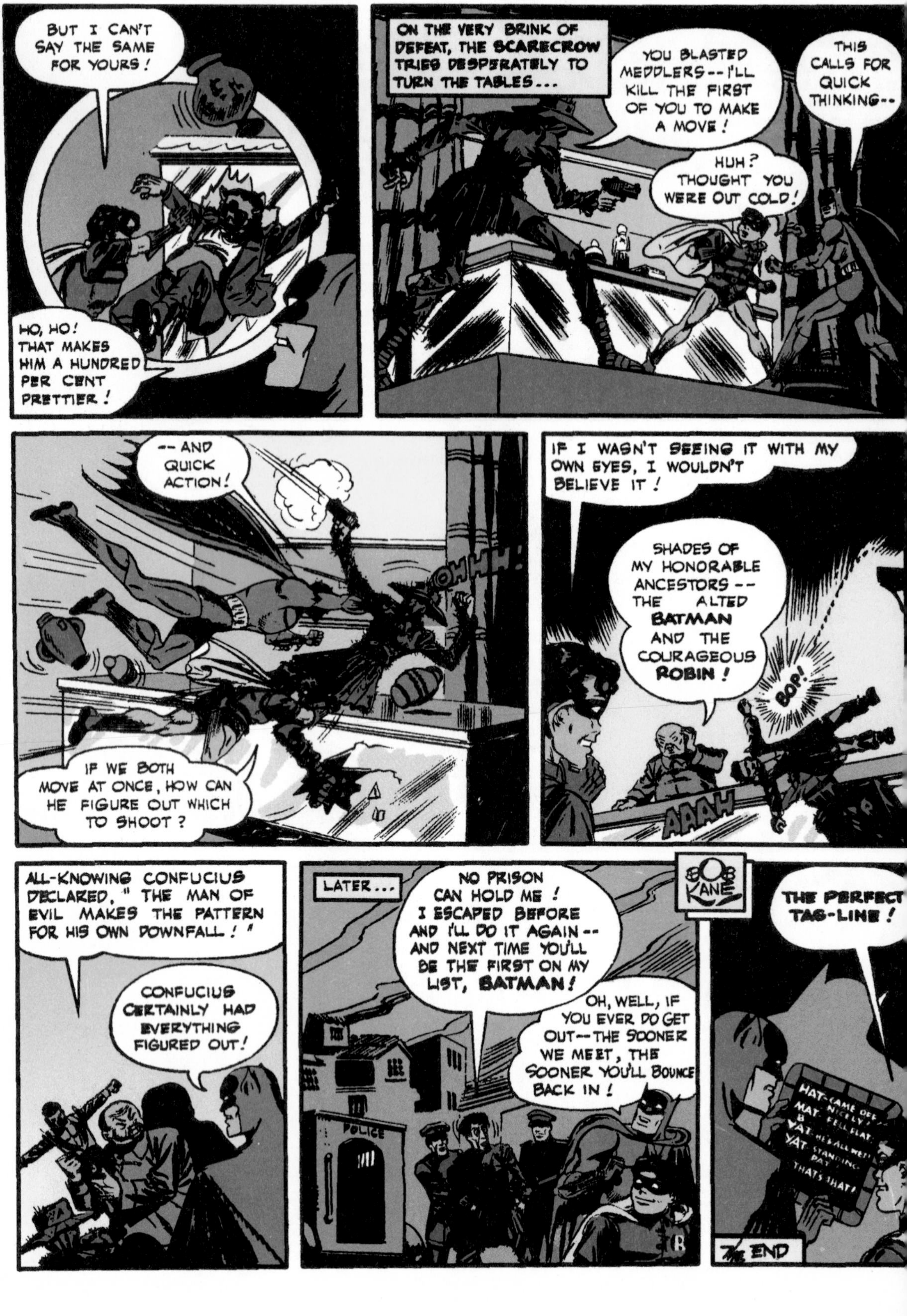
BUT I CAN'T SAY THE SAME FOR YOURS!
HO, HO! THAT MAKES HIM A HUNDRED PER CENT PRETTIER!
ON THE VERY BRINK OF DEFEAT, THE SCARECROW TRIES DESPERATELY TO TURN THE TABLES...
YOU BLASTED MEDDLERS -- I'LL KILL THE FIRST OF YOU TO MAKE A MOVE!
THIS CALLS FOR QUICK THINKING--
HUH? THOUGHT YOU WERE OUT COLD!
-- AND QUICK ACTION!
OHHHH!
IF WE BOTH MOVE AT ONCE, HOW CAN HE FIGURE OUT WHICH TO SHOOT?
IF I WASN'T SEEING IT WITH MY OWN EYES, I WOULDN'T BELIEVE IT!
SHADES OF MY HONORABLE ANCESTORS -- THE ALTED BATMAN AND THE COURAGEOUS ROBIN!
BOP!
AAAH
ALL-KNOWING CONFUCIUS DECLARED, " THE MAN OF EVIL MAKES THE PATTERN FOR HIS OWN DOWNFALL! "
CONFUCIUS CERTAINLY HAD EVERYTHING FIGURED OUT!
LATER...
NO PRISON CAN HOLD ME! I ESCAPED BEFORE AND I'LL DO IT AGAIN -- AND NEXT TIME YOU'LL BE THE FIRST ON MY LIST, BATMAN!
OH, WELL, IF YOU EVER DO GET OUT -- THE SOONER WE MEET, THE SOONER YOU'LL BOUNCE BACK IN!
POLICE
BOB KANE
THE PERFECT TAG-LINE!
HAT-CAME OFF NICELY
MAT-FELL FLAT
YAT-HE'S ALL WET
YAT-STANDING PAT
THAT'S THAT!
THE END

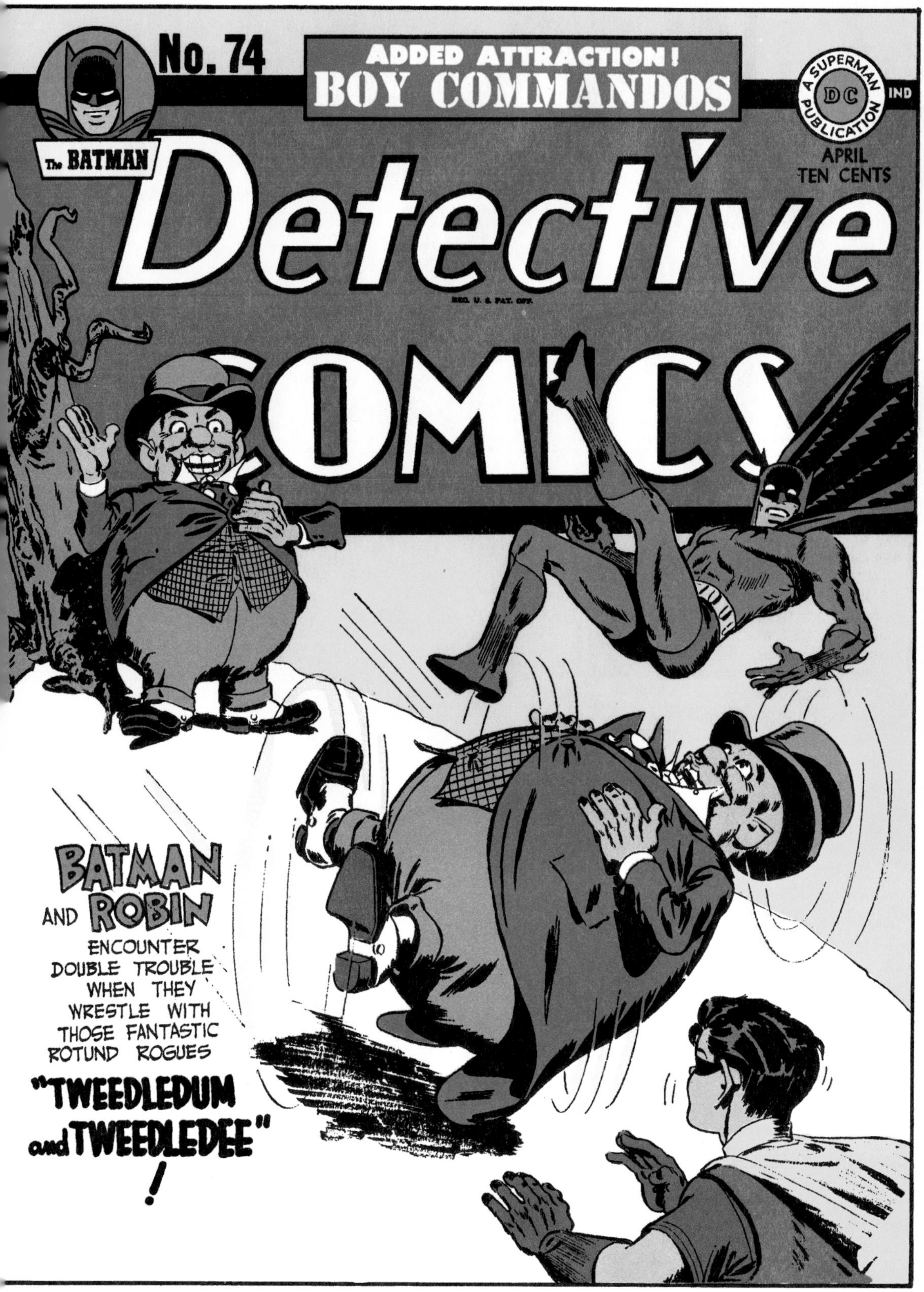
No. 74
ADDED ATTRACTION!
BOY COMMANDOS
A SUPERMAN DC PUBLICATION IND
The BATMAN
APRIL
TEN CENTS
Detective
REG. U. S. PAT. OFF.
COMICS
BATMAN AND ROBIN ENCOUNTER DOUBLE TROUBLE WHEN THEY WRESTLE WITH THOSE FANTASTIC ROTUND ROGUES
"TWEEDLEDUM and TWEEDLEDEE"!

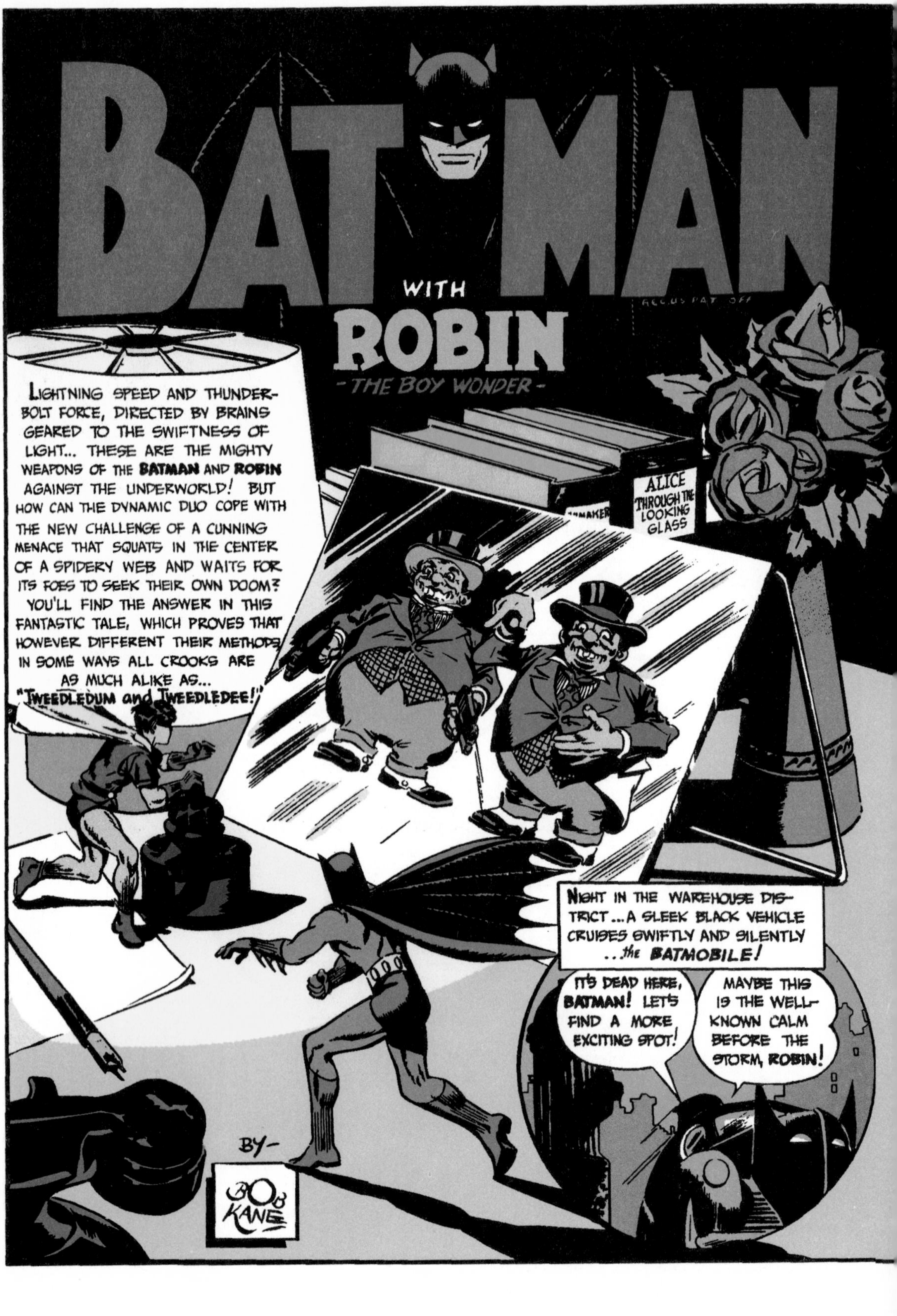
BATMAN
WITH
ROBIN
-THE BOY WONDER-
REG. U.S. PAT. OFF.
LIGHTNING SPEED AND THUNDER-BOLT FORCE, DIRECTED BY BRAINS GEARED TO THE SWIFTNESS OF LIGHT... THESE ARE THE MIGHTY WEAPONS OF THE BATMAN AND ROBIN AGAINST THE UNDERWORLD! BUT HOW CAN THE DYNAMIC DUO COPE WITH THE NEW CHALLENGE OF A CUNNING MENACE THAT SQUATS IN THE CENTER OF A SPIDERY WEB AND WAITS FOR ITS FOES TO SEEK THEIR OWN DOOM? YOU'LL FIND THE ANSWER IN THIS FANTASTIC TALE, WHICH PROVES THAT HOWEVER DIFFERENT THEIR METHODS IN SOME WAYS ALL CROOKS ARE AS MUCH ALIKE AS... "TWEEDLEDUM and TWEEDLEDEE!"
ALICE THROUGH THE LOOKING GLASS
BY- BOB KANE
NIGHT IN THE WAREHOUSE DISTRICT... A SLEEK BLACK VEHICLE CRUISES SWIFTLY AND SILENTLY ...the BATMOBILE!
IT'S DEAD HERE, BATMAN! LET'S FIND A MORE EXCITING SPOT!
MAYBE THIS IS THE WELL-KNOWN CALM BEFORE THE STORM, ROBIN!

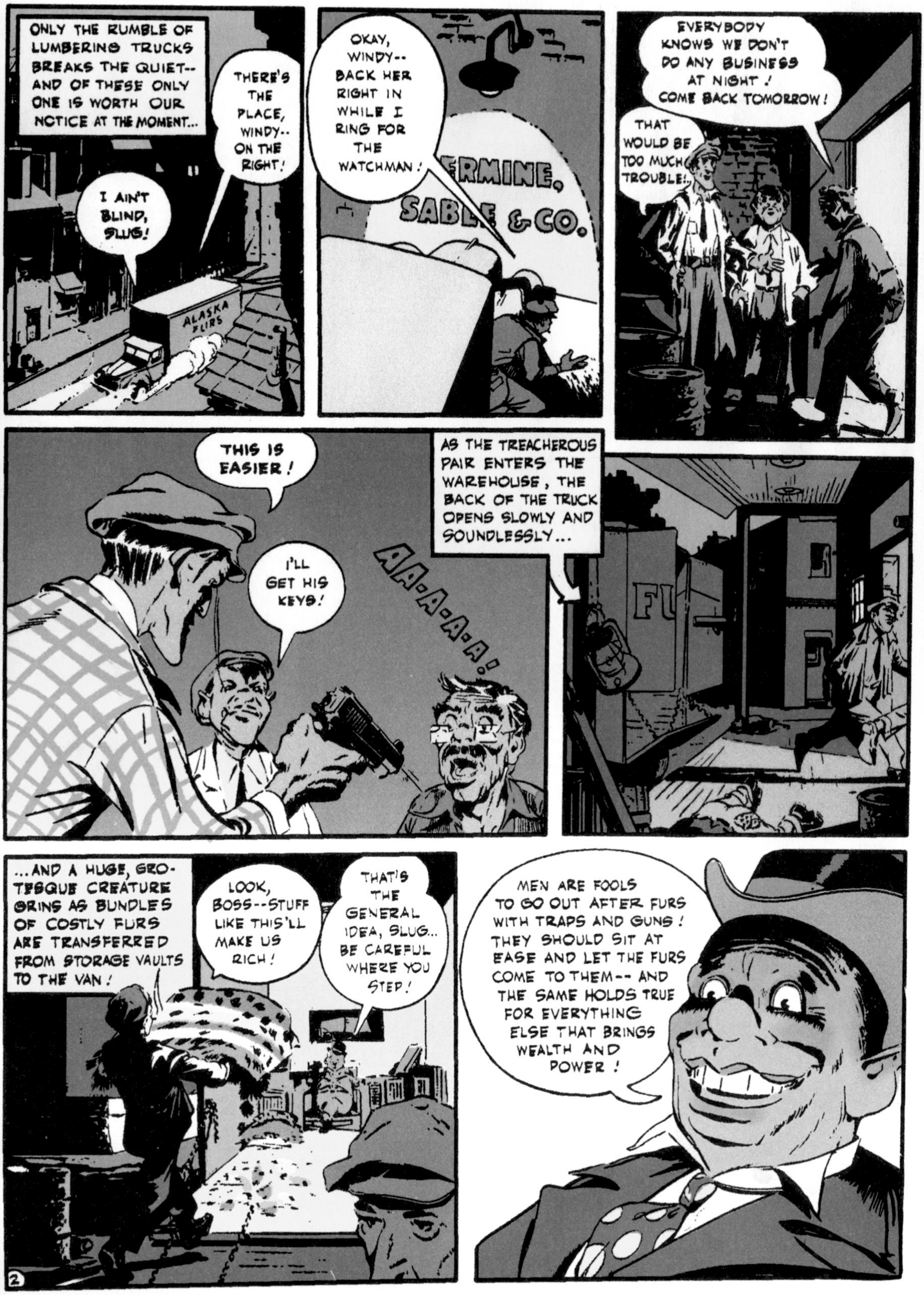
ONLY THE RUMBLE OF LUMBERING TRUCKS BREAKS THE QUIET-- AND OF THESE ONLY ONE IS WORTH OUR NOTICE AT THE MOMENT...
THERE'S THE PLACE, WINDY-- ON THE RIGHT!
I AIN'T BLIND, SLUG!
ALASKA FURS
OKAY, WINDY-- BACK HER RIGHT IN WHILE I RING FOR THE WATCHMAN!
ERMINE, SABLE & CO.
EVERYBODY KNOWS WE DON'T DO ANY BUSINESS AT NIGHT! COME BACK TOMORROW!
THAT WOULD BE TOO MUCH TROUBLE!..
THIS IS EASIER!
I'LL GET HIS KEYS!
AA-A-A-A-A!
AS THE TREACHEROUS PAIR ENTERS THE WAREHOUSE, THE BACK OF THE TRUCK OPENS SLOWLY AND SOUNDLESSLY...
FU
...AND A HUGE, GROTESQUE CREATURE GRINS AS BUNDLES OF COSTLY FURS ARE TRANSFERRED FROM STORAGE VAULTS TO THE VAN!
LOOK, BOSS--STUFF LIKE THIS'LL MAKE US RICH!
THAT'S THE GENERAL IDEA, SLUG... BE CAREFUL WHERE YOU STEP!
MEN ARE FOOLS TO GO OUT AFTER FURS WITH TRAPS AND GUNS! THEY SHOULD SIT AT EASE AND LET THE FURS COME TO THEM-- AND THE SAME HOLDS TRUE FOR EVERYTHING ELSE THAT BRINGS WEALTH AND POWER!
2

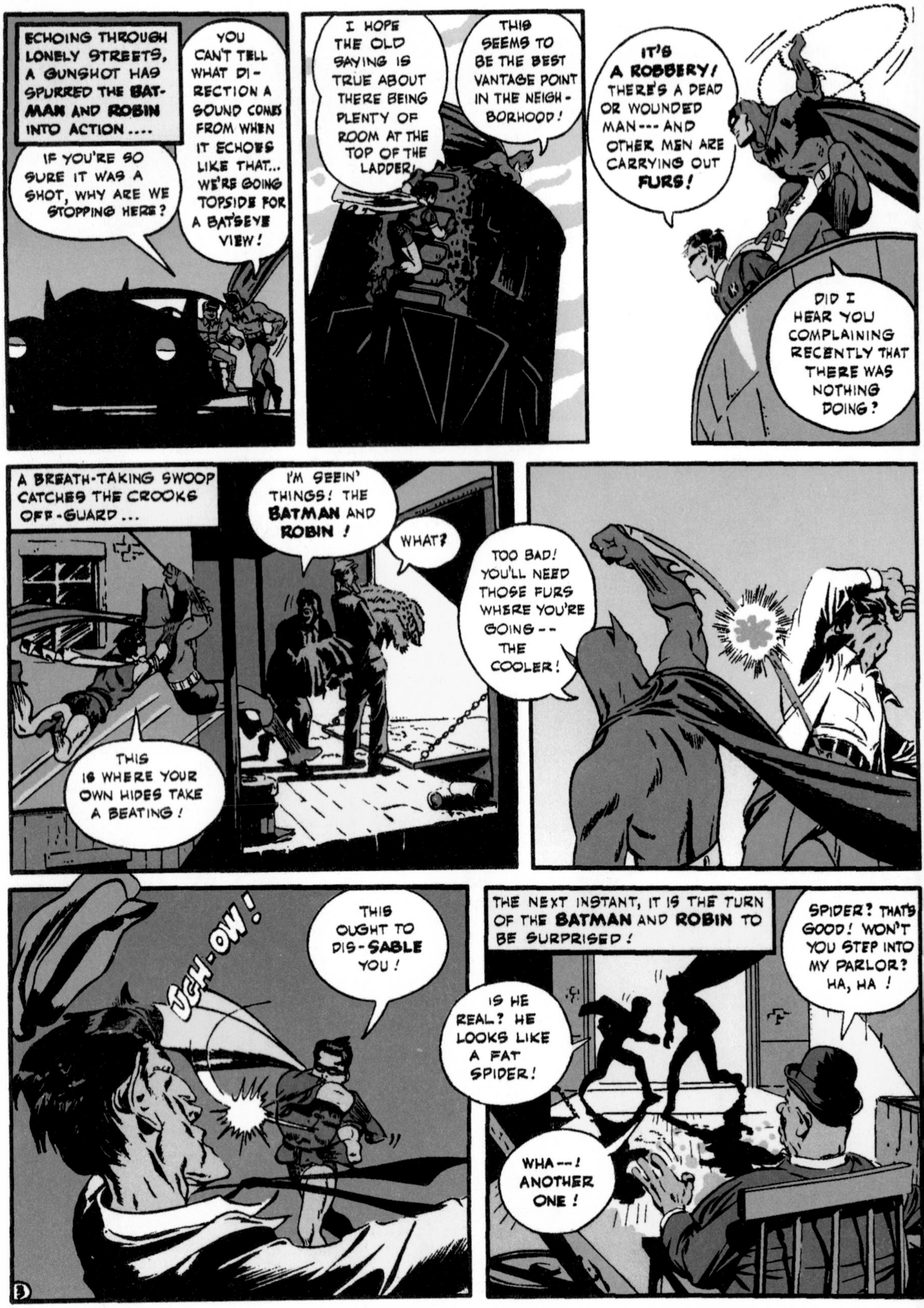
ECHOING THROUGH LONELY STREETS, A GUNSHOT HAS SPURRED THE BATMAN AND ROBIN INTO ACTION....
YOU CAN'T TELL WHAT DIRECTION A SOUND COMES FROM WHEN IT ECHOES LIKE THAT... WE'RE GOING TOPSIDE FOR A BATSEYE VIEW!
IF YOU'RE SO SURE IT WAS A SHOT, WHY ARE WE STOPPING HERE?
I HOPE THE OLD SAYING IS TRUE ABOUT THERE BEING PLENTY OF ROOM AT THE TOP OF THE LADDER!
THIS SEEMS TO BE THE BEST VANTAGE POINT IN THE NEIGHBORHOOD!
IT'S A ROBBERY! THERE'S A DEAD OR WOUNDED MAN--- AND OTHER MEN ARE CARRYING OUT FURS!
DID I HEAR YOU COMPLAINING RECENTLY THAT THERE WAS NOTHING DOING?
A BREATH-TAKING SWOOP CATCHES THE CROOKS OFF-GUARD...
I'M SEEIN' THINGS! THE BATMAN AND ROBIN!
WHAT?
THIS IS WHERE YOUR OWN HIDES TAKE A BEATING!
TOO BAD! YOU'LL NEED THOSE FURS WHERE YOU'RE GOING -- THE COOLER!
UGH-OW!
THIS OUGHT TO DIS-SABLE YOU!
THE NEXT INSTANT, IT IS THE TURN OF THE BATMAN AND ROBIN TO BE SURPRISED!
SPIDER? THAT'S GOOD! WON'T YOU STEP INTO MY PARLOR? HA, HA!
IS HE REAL? HE LOOKS LIKE A FAT SPIDER!
WHA--! ANOTHER ONE!
3

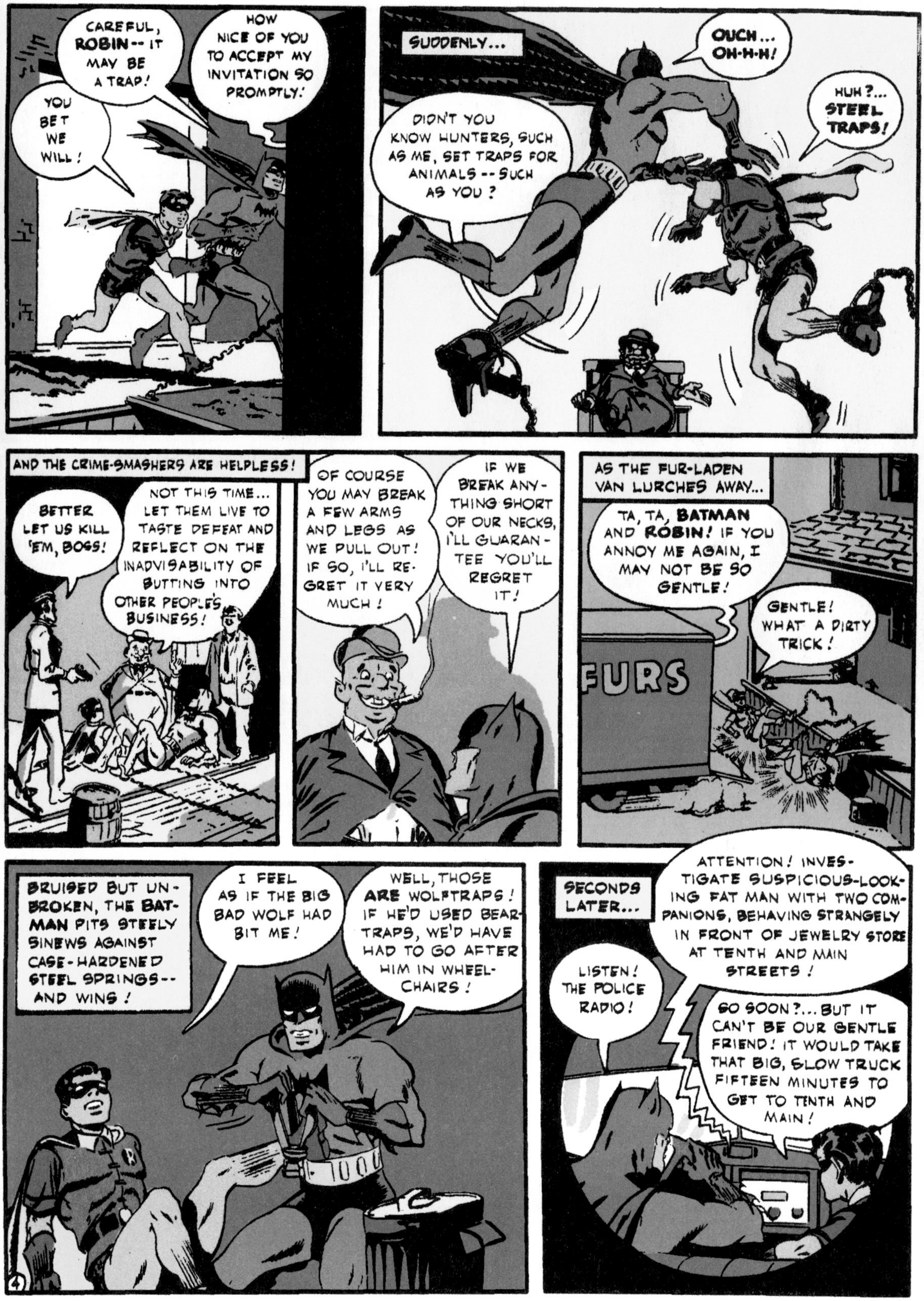

CAREFUL, ROBIN -- IT MAY BE A TRAP!
YOU BET WE WILL!
HOW NICE OF YOU TO ACCEPT MY INVITATION SO PROMPTLY!
SUDDENLY...
OUCH... OH-H-H!
DIDN'T YOU KNOW HUNTERS, SUCH AS ME, SET TRAPS FOR ANIMALS -- SUCH AS YOU?
HUH?... STEEL TRAPS!
AND THE CRIME-SMASHERS ARE HELPLESS!
BETTER LET US KILL 'EM, BOSS!
NOT THIS TIME... LET THEM LIVE TO TASTE DEFEAT AND REFLECT ON THE INADVISABILITY OF BUTTING INTO OTHER PEOPLE'S BUSINESS!
OF COURSE YOU MAY BREAK A FEW ARMS AND LEGS AS WE PULL OUT! IF SO, I'LL REGRET IT VERY MUCH!
IF WE BREAK ANYTHING SHORT OF OUR NECKS, I'LL GUARANTEE YOU'LL REGRET IT!
AS THE FUR-LADEN VAN LURCHES AWAY...
TA, TA, BATMAN AND ROBIN! IF YOU ANNOY ME AGAIN, I MAY NOT BE SO GENTLE!
GENTLE! WHAT A DIRTY TRICK!
FURS
BRUISED BUT UNBROKEN, THE BATMAN PITS STEELY SINEWS AGAINST CASE-HARDENED STEEL SPRINGS -- AND WINS!
I FEEL AS IF THE BIG BAD WOLF HAD BIT ME!
WELL, THOSE ARE WOLFTRAPS! IF HE'D USED BEARTRAPS, WE'D HAVE HAD TO GO AFTER HIM IN WHEELCHAIRS!
4
SECONDS LATER...
ATTENTION! INVESTIGATE SUSPICIOUS-LOOKING FAT MAN WITH TWO COMPANIONS, BEHAVING STRANGELY IN FRONT OF JEWELRY STORE AT TENTH AND MAIN STREETS!
LISTEN! THE POLICE RADIO!
SO SOON?... BUT IT CAN'T BE OUR GENTLE FRIEND! IT WOULD TAKE THAT BIG, SLOW TRUCK FIFTEEN MINUTES TO GET TO TENTH AND MAIN!

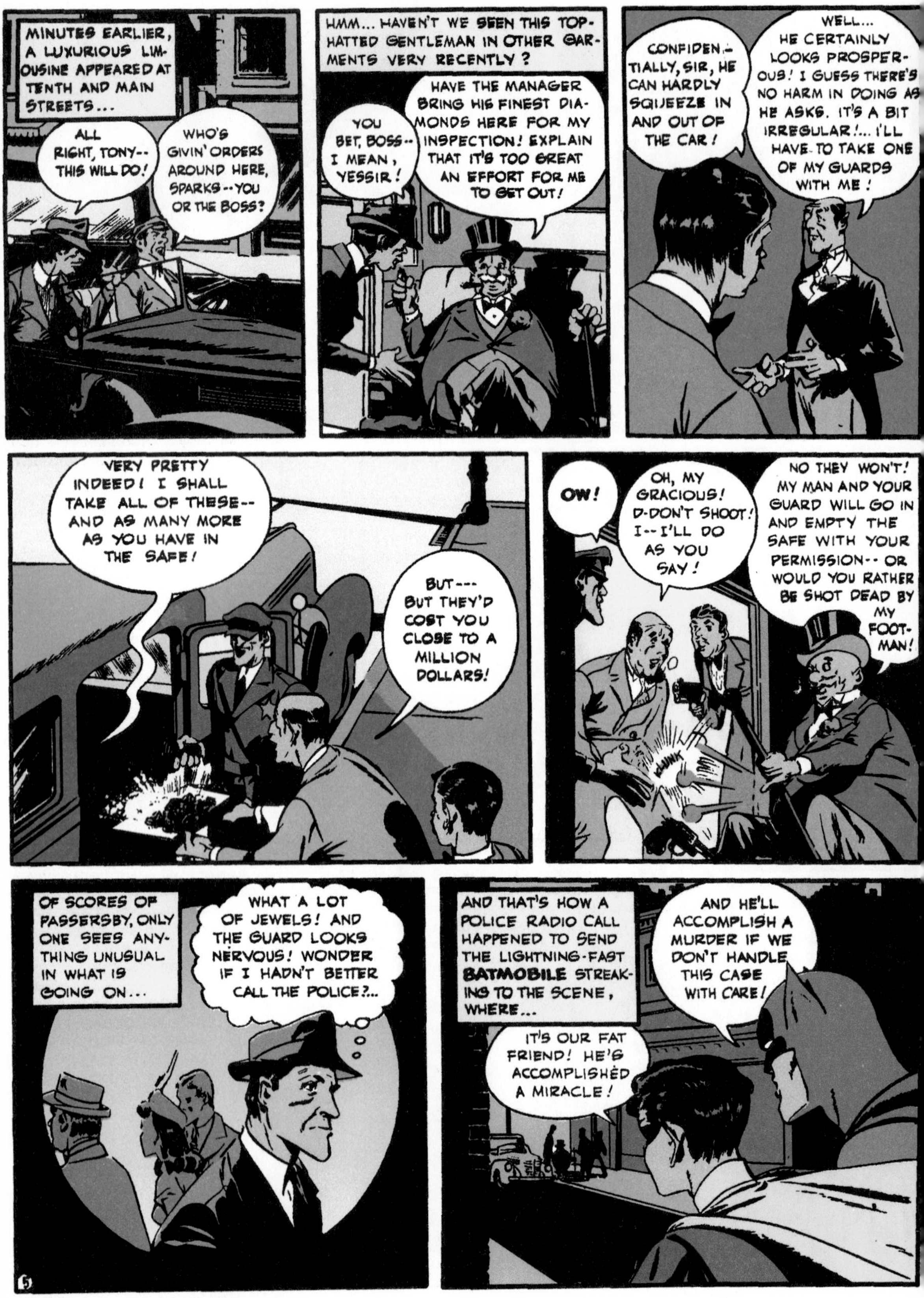
MINUTES EARLIER, A LUXURIOUS LIMOUSINE APPEARED AT TENTH AND MAIN STREETS...
ALL RIGHT, TONY-- THIS WILL DO!
WHO'S GIVIN' ORDERS AROUND HERE, SPARKS--YOU OR THE BOSS?
HMM... HAVEN'T WE SEEN THIS TOP-HATTED GENTLEMAN IN OTHER GARMENTS VERY RECENTLY?
HAVE THE MANAGER BRING HIS FINEST DIAMONDS HERE FOR MY INSPECTION! EXPLAIN THAT IT'S TOO GREAT AN EFFORT FOR ME TO GET OUT!
YOU BET, BOSS-- I MEAN, YESSIR!
CONFIDENTIALLY, SIR, HE CAN HARDLY SQUEEZE IN AND OUT OF THE CAR!
WELL... HE CERTAINLY LOOKS PROSPEROUS! I GUESS THERE'S NO HARM IN DOING AS HE ASKS. IT'S A BIT IRREGULAR!... I'LL HAVE TO TAKE ONE OF MY GUARDS WITH ME!
VERY PRETTY INDEED! I SHALL TAKE ALL OF THESE-- AND AS MANY MORE AS YOU HAVE IN THE SAFE!
BUT--- BUT THEY'D COST YOU CLOSE TO A MILLION DOLLARS!
OW!
OH, MY GRACIOUS! D-DON'T SHOOT! I-- I'LL DO AS YOU SAY!
NO THEY WON'T! MY MAN AND YOUR GUARD WILL GO IN AND EMPTY THE SAFE WITH YOUR PERMISSION-- OR WOULD YOU RATHER BE SHOT DEAD BY MY FOOTMAN!
KLUNK
OF SCORES OF PASSERSBY, ONLY ONE SEES ANYTHING UNUSUAL IN WHAT IS GOING ON...
WHAT A LOT OF JEWELS! AND THE GUARD LOOKS NERVOUS! WONDER IF I HADN'T BETTER CALL THE POLICE?...
5
AND THAT'S HOW A POLICE RADIO CALL HAPPENED TO SEND THE LIGHTNING-FAST BATMOBILE STREAKING TO THE SCENE, WHERE...
AND HE'LL ACCOMPLISH A MURDER IF WE DON'T HANDLE THIS CASE WITH CARE!
IT'S OUR FAT FRIEND! HE'S ACCOMPLISHED A MIRACLE!

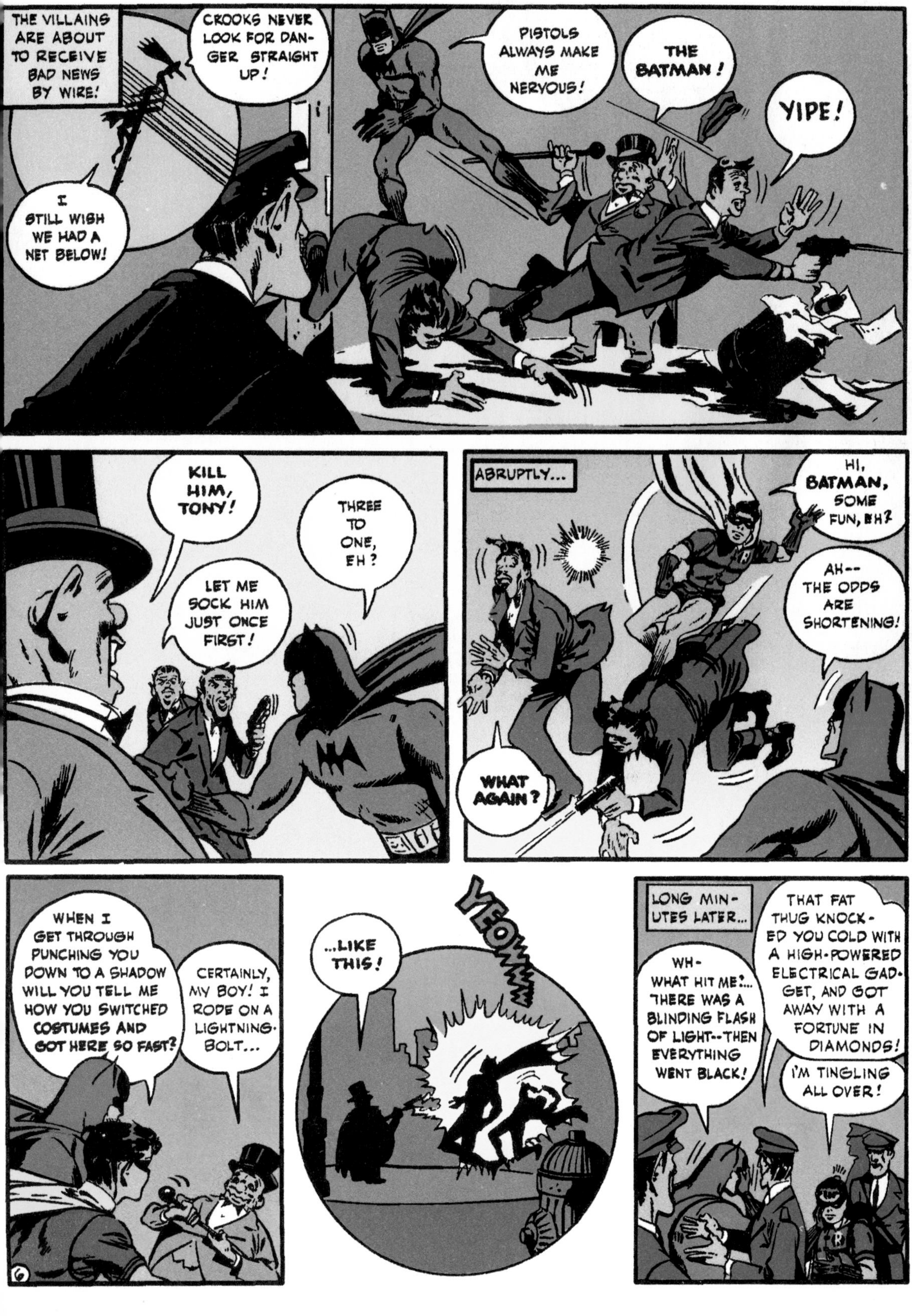

THE VILLAINS ARE ABOUT TO RECEIVE BAD NEWS BY WIRE!
CROOKS NEVER LOOK FOR DANGER STRAIGHT UP!
I STILL WISH WE HAD A NET BELOW!
PISTOLS ALWAYS MAKE ME NERVOUS!
THE BATMAN!
YIPE!
KILL HIM, TONY!
THREE TO ONE, EH?
LET ME SOCK HIM JUST ONCE FIRST!
ABRUPTLY...
HI, BATMAN, SOME FUN, EH?
AH-- THE ODDS ARE SHORTENING!
WHAT AGAIN?
WHEN I GET THROUGH PUNCHING YOU DOWN TO A SHADOW WILL YOU TELL ME HOW YOU SWITCHED COSTUMES AND GOT HERE SO FAST?
CERTAINLY, MY BOY! I RODE ON A LIGHTNING-BOLT...
6
...LIKE THIS!
YEOWWW
LONG MINUTES LATER...
THAT FAT THUG KNOCKED YOU COLD WITH A HIGH-POWERED ELECTRICAL GADGET, AND GOT AWAY WITH A FORTUNE IN DIAMONDS!
WH- WHAT HIT ME?... THERE WAS A BLINDING FLASH OF LIGHT--THEN EVERYTHING WENT BLACK!
I'M TINGLING ALL OVER!

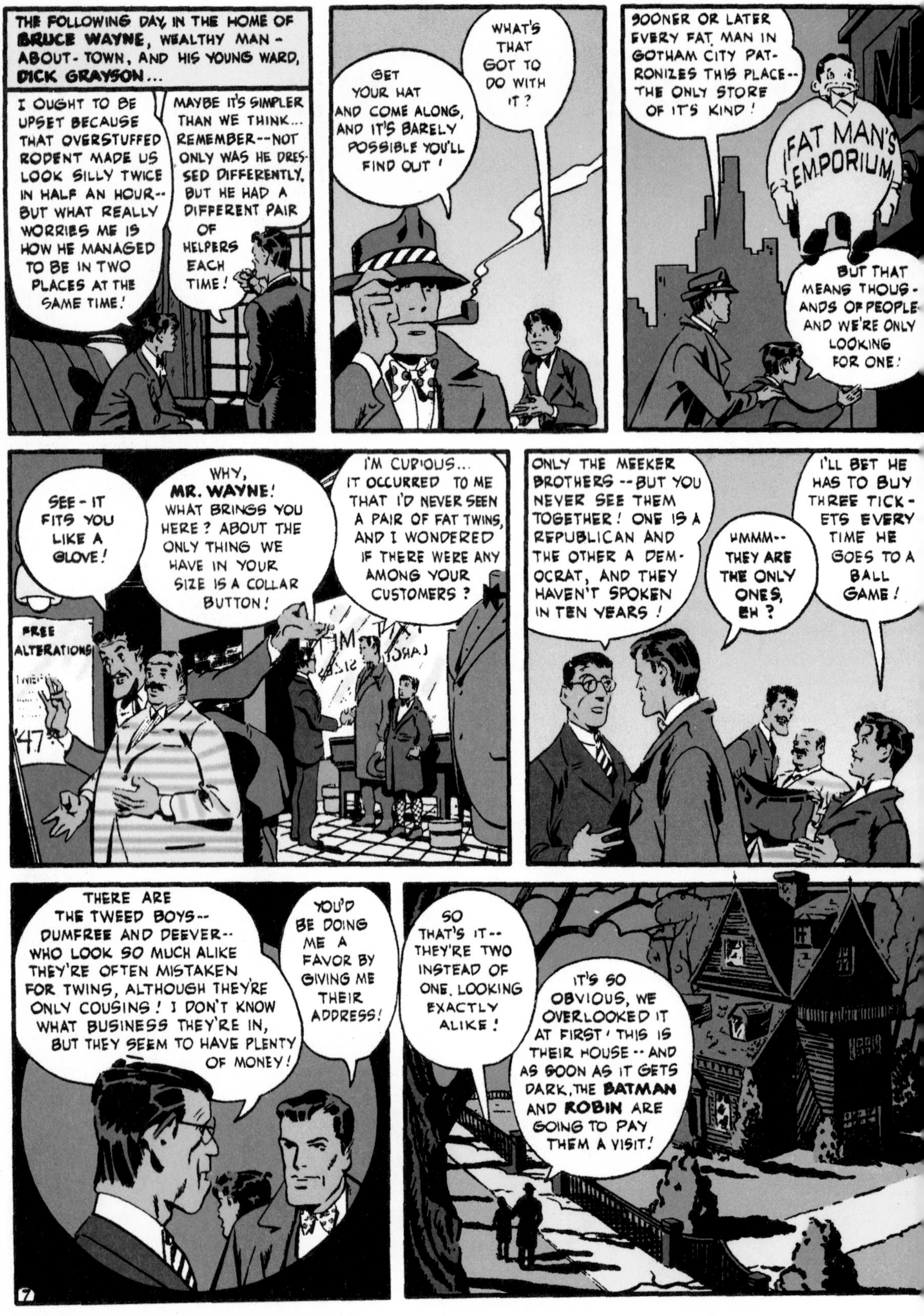

THE FOLLOWING DAY, IN THE HOME OF BRUCE WAYNE, WEALTHY MAN-ABOUT-TOWN, AND HIS YOUNG WARD, DICK GRAYSON...
I OUGHT TO BE UPSET BECAUSE THAT OVERSTUFFED RODENT MADE US LOOK SILLY TWICE IN HALF AN HOUR-- BUT WHAT REALLY WORRIES ME IS HOW HE MANAGED TO BE IN TWO PLACES AT THE SAME TIME!
MAYBE IT'S SIMPLER THAN WE THINK... REMEMBER--NOT ONLY WAS HE DRESSED DIFFERENTLY, BUT HE HAD A DIFFERENT PAIR OF HELPERS EACH TIME!
GET YOUR HAT AND COME ALONG, AND IT'S BARELY POSSIBLE YOU'LL FIND OUT!
WHAT'S THAT GOT TO DO WITH IT?
SOONER OR LATER EVERY FAT MAN IN GOTHAM CITY PATRONIZES THIS PLACE-- THE ONLY STORE OF IT'S KIND!
FAT MAN'S EMPORIUM
BUT THAT MEANS THOUSANDS OF PEOPLE AND WE'RE ONLY LOOKING FOR ONE!
SEE-IT FITS YOU LIKE A GLOVE!
WHY, MR. WAYNE! WHAT BRINGS YOU HERE? ABOUT THE ONLY THING WE HAVE IN YOUR SIZE IS A COLLAR BUTTON!
I'M CURIOUS... IT OCCURRED TO ME THAT I'D NEVER SEEN A PAIR OF FAT TWINS, AND I WONDERED IF THERE WERE ANY AMONG YOUR CUSTOMERS?
FREE ALTERATIONS
47
ONLY THE MEEKER BROTHERS--BUT YOU NEVER SEE THEM TOGETHER! ONE IS A REPUBLICAN AND THE OTHER A DEMOCRAT, AND THEY HAVEN'T SPOKEN IN TEN YEARS!
HMMM-- THEY ARE THE ONLY ONES, EH?
I'LL BET HE HAS TO BUY THREE TICKETS EVERY TIME HE GOES TO A BALL GAME!
THERE ARE THE TWEED BOYS-- DUMFREE AND DEEVER-- WHO LOOK SO MUCH ALIKE THEY'RE OFTEN MISTAKEN FOR TWINS, ALTHOUGH THEY'RE ONLY COUSINS! I DON'T KNOW WHAT BUSINESS THEY'RE IN, BUT THEY SEEM TO HAVE PLENTY OF MONEY!
YOU'D BE DOING ME A FAVOR BY GIVING ME THEIR ADDRESS!
7
SO THAT'S IT-- THEY'RE TWO INSTEAD OF ONE, LOOKING EXACTLY ALIKE!
IT'S SO OBVIOUS, WE OVERLOOKED IT AT FIRST! THIS IS THEIR HOUSE--AND AS SOON AS IT GETS DARK, THE BATMAN AND ROBIN ARE GOING TO PAY THEM A VISIT!

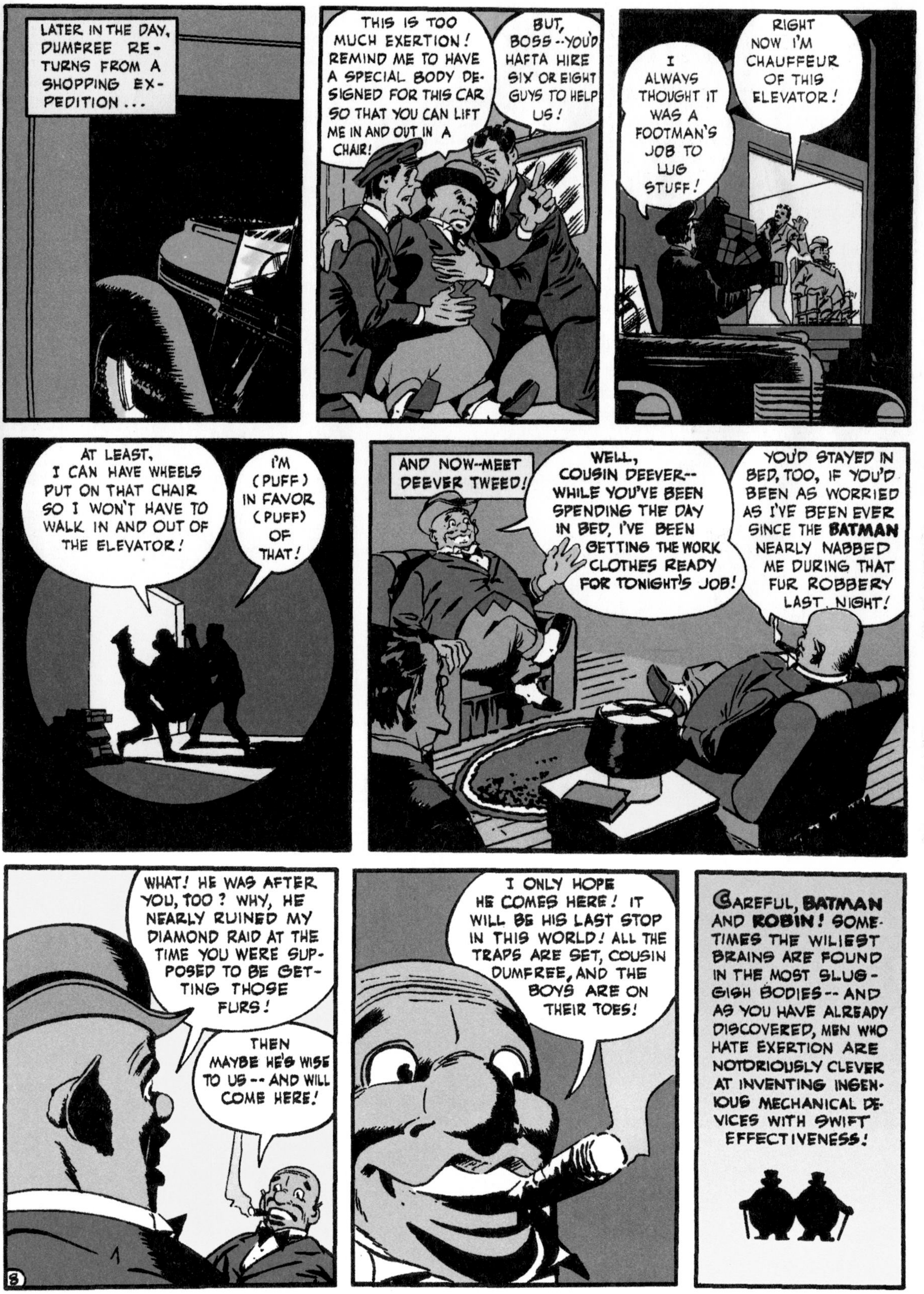
LATER IN THE DAY, DUMFREE RETURNS FROM A SHOPPING EXPEDITION...
THIS IS TOO MUCH EXERTION! REMIND ME TO HAVE A SPECIAL BODY DESIGNED FOR THIS CAR SO THAT YOU CAN LIFT ME IN AND OUT IN A CHAIR!
BUT, BOSS--YOU'D HAFTA HIRE SIX OR EIGHT GUYS TO HELP US!
RIGHT NOW I'M CHAUFFEUR OF THIS ELEVATOR!
I ALWAYS THOUGHT IT WAS A FOOTMAN'S JOB TO LUG STUFF!
AT LEAST, I CAN HAVE WHEELS PUT ON THAT CHAIR SO I WON'T HAVE TO WALK IN AND OUT OF THE ELEVATOR!
I'M (PUFF) IN FAVOR (PUFF) OF THAT!
AND NOW--MEET DEEVER TWEED!
WELL, COUSIN DEEVER--WHILE YOU'VE BEEN SPENDING THE DAY IN BED, I'VE BEEN GETTING THE WORK CLOTHES READY FOR TONIGHT'S JOB!
YOU'D STAYED IN BED, TOO, IF YOU'D BEEN AS WORRIED AS I'VE BEEN EVER SINCE THE BATMAN NEARLY NABBED ME DURING THAT FUR ROBBERY LAST NIGHT!
WHAT! HE WAS AFTER YOU, TOO? WHY, HE NEARLY RUINED MY DIAMOND RAID AT THE TIME YOU WERE SUPPOSED TO BE GETTING THOSE FURS!
THEN MAYBE HE'S WISE TO US--AND WILL COME HERE!
8
I ONLY HOPE HE COMES HERE! IT WILL BE HIS LAST STOP IN THIS WORLD! ALL THE TRAPS ARE SET, COUSIN DUMFREE, AND THE BOYS ARE ON THEIR TOES!
CAREFUL, BATMAN AND ROBIN! SOMETIMES THE WILIEST BRAINS ARE FOUND IN THE MOST SLUGGISH BODIES--AND AS YOU HAVE ALREADY DISCOVERED, MEN WHO HATE EXERTION ARE NOTORIOUSLY CLEVER AT INVENTING INGENIOUS MECHANICAL DEVICES WITH SWIFT EFFECTIVENESS!

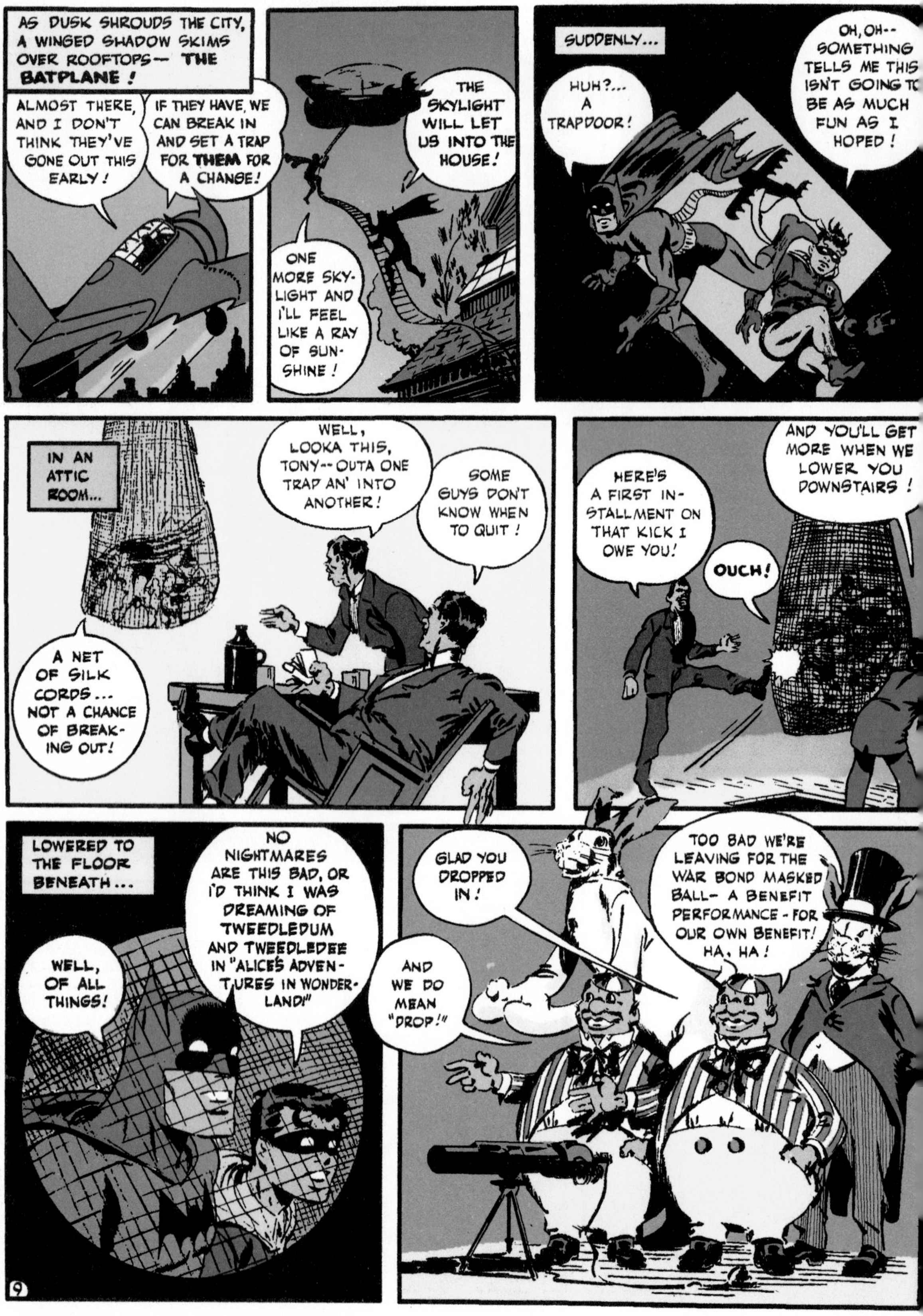
AS DUSK SHROUDS THE CITY, A WINGED SHADOW SKIMS OVER ROOFTOPS-- THE BATPLANE!
ALMOST THERE, AND I DON'T THINK THEY'VE GONE OUT THIS EARLY!
IF THEY HAVE, WE CAN BREAK IN AND SET A TRAP FOR THEM FOR A CHANGE!
THE SKYLIGHT WILL LET US INTO THE HOUSE!
ONE MORE SKY-LIGHT AND I'LL FEEL LIKE A RAY OF SUN-SHINE!
SUDDENLY...
HUH?... A TRAPDOOR!
OH, OH-- SOMETHING TELLS ME THIS ISN'T GOING TO BE AS MUCH FUN AS I HOPED!
IN AN ATTIC ROOM...
WELL, LOOKA THIS, TONY-- OUTA ONE TRAP AN' INTO ANOTHER!
SOME GUYS DON'T KNOW WHEN TO QUIT!
A NET OF SILK CORDS... NOT A CHANCE OF BREAK-ING OUT!
HERE'S A FIRST IN-STALLMENT ON THAT KICK I OWE YOU!
AND YOU'LL GET MORE WHEN WE LOWER YOU DOWNSTAIRS!
OUCH!
LOWERED TO THE FLOOR BENEATH...
WELL, OF ALL THINGS!
NO NIGHTMARES ARE THIS BAD, OR I'D THINK I WAS DREAMING OF TWEEDLEDUM AND TWEEDLEDEE IN "ALICE'S ADVEN-TURES IN WONDER-LAND!"
9
GLAD YOU DROPPED IN!
AND WE DO MEAN "DROP!"
TOO BAD WE'RE LEAVING FOR THE WAR BOND MASKED BALL-- A BENEFIT PERFORMANCE - FOR OUR OWN BENEFIT! HA, HA!

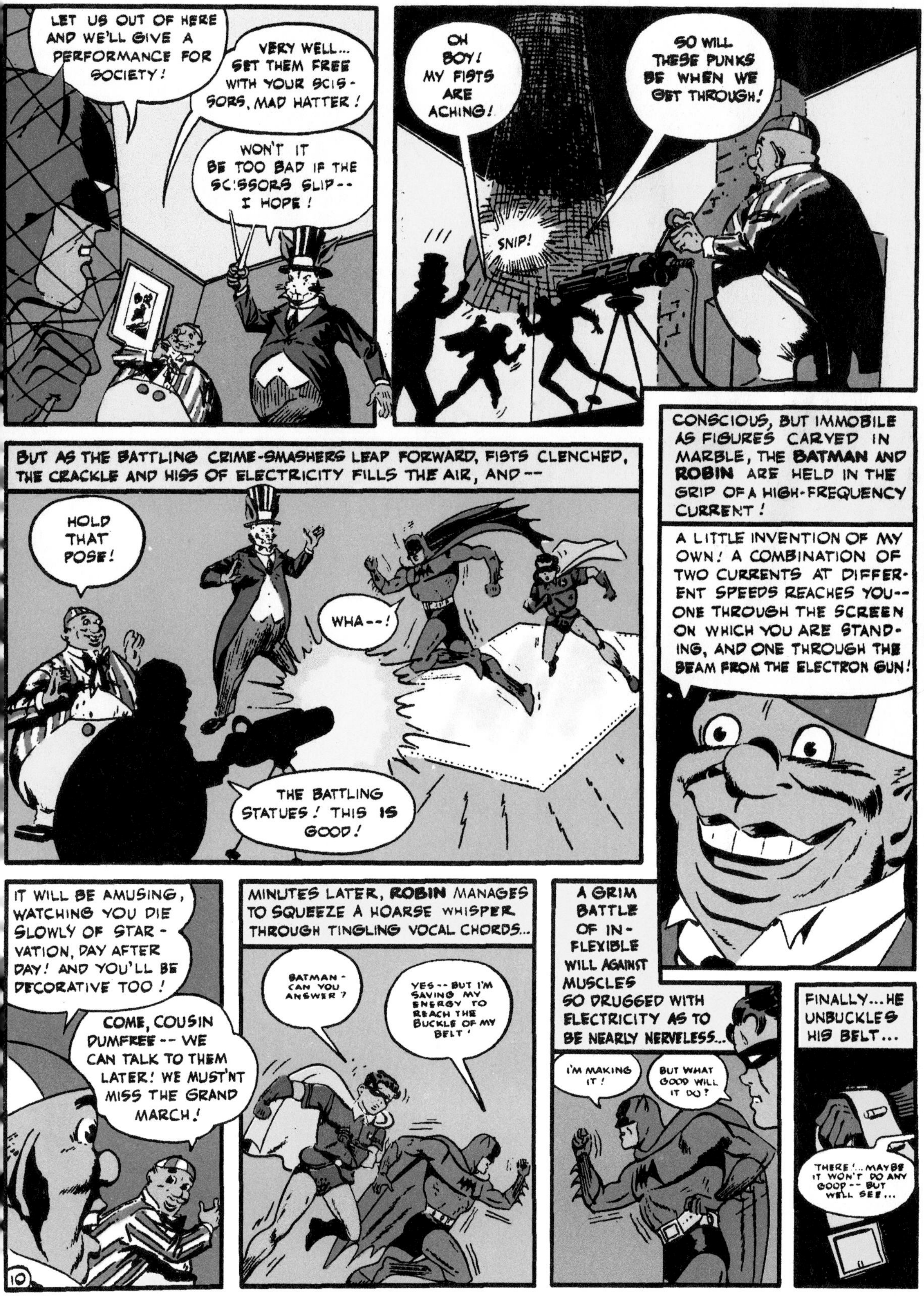
LET US OUT OF HERE AND WE'LL GIVE A PERFORMANCE FOR SOCIETY!
VERY WELL... SET THEM FREE WITH YOUR SCIS-SORS, MAD HATTER!
WON'T IT BE TOO BAD IF THE SCISSORS SLIP-- I HOPE!
OH BOY! MY FISTS ARE ACHING!
SO WILL THESE PUNKS BE WHEN WE GET THROUGH!
SNIP!
BUT AS THE BATTLING CRIME-SMASHERS LEAP FORWARD, FISTS CLENCHED, THE CRACKLE AND HISS OF ELECTRICITY FILLS THE AIR, AND--
HOLD THAT POSE!
WHA--!
THE BATTLING STATUES! THIS IS GOOD!
CONSCIOUS, BUT IMMOBILE AS FIGURES CARVED IN MARBLE, THE BATMAN AND ROBIN ARE HELD IN THE GRIP OF A HIGH-FREQUENCY CURRENT!
A LITTLE INVENTION OF MY OWN! A COMBINATION OF TWO CURRENTS AT DIFFER-ENT SPEEDS REACHES YOU-- ONE THROUGH THE SCREEN ON WHICH YOU ARE STAND-ING, AND ONE THROUGH THE BEAM FROM THE ELECTRON GUN!
IT WILL BE AMUSING, WATCHING YOU DIE SLOWLY OF STAR-VATION, DAY AFTER DAY! AND YOU'LL BE DECORATIVE TOO!
COME, COUSIN DUMFREE -- WE CAN TALK TO THEM LATER! WE MUST'NT MISS THE GRAND MARCH!
10
MINUTES LATER, ROBIN MANAGES TO SQUEEZE A HOARSE WHISPER THROUGH TINGLING VOCAL CHORDS...
BATMAN - CAN YOU ANSWER?
YES -- BUT I'M SAVING MY ENERGY TO REACH THE BUCKLE OF MY BELT!
A GRIM BATTLE OF IN-FLEXIBLE WILL AGAINST MUSCLES SO DRUGGED WITH ELECTRICITY AS TO BE NEARLY NERVELESS...
I'M MAKING IT!
BUT WHAT GOOD WILL IT DO?
FINALLY... HE UNBUCKLES HIS BELT...
THERE!... MAYBE IT WON'T DO ANY GOOD -- BUT WE'LL SEE...

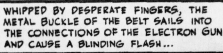

WHIPPED BY DESPERATE FINGERS, THE METAL BUCKLE OF THE BELT SAILS INTO THE CONNECTIONS OF THE ELECTRON GUN AND CAUSE A BLINDING FLASH...

WH-WHY-- I'M FREE! I CAN MOVE!

RIGHT, FELLA! A SHORT-CIRCUIT WAS ALL WE NEEDED!

AND NOW TO SHORT-CIRCUIT THE CROOKED PLAN OF THE TWEEDLE TWINS-- DUM AND DEE! I'LL PHONE THE MANAGER OF THE BALL TO EXPECT US!

OH, BOY-- ONLY THE RICHEST PEOPLE IN TOWN WILL BE THERE! THE ADMISSION IS A $1000 WAR BOND!

IN THE GILMORE'S' GLITTERING BALL-ROOM, HIGH SOCIETY'S LEADING MEMBERS ARE LINING UP FOR THE GRAND MARCH...

MONTMORENCY, YOU AREN'T PAYING ANY ATTENTION TO ME!

YES, MY DEAR!

... NOT TO MENTION THE ELITE OF THE UNDERWORLD!

TWEEDLEDUM AND TWEEDLEDEE, THE MAD HATTER AND THE MARCH HARE--RIGHT OUT OF "ALICE IN WONDERLAND!"

AREN'T THEY CUTE!

WHEN THE SPECTACULAR PARADE HAS ENDED, THE JUDGES PREPARE TO AWARD THE PRIZES...

THE JUDGES ARE UNANIMOUS IN AWARDING THE GRAND PRIZE FOR THE BEST COSTUMES TO FOUR COMPETITORS --

-- TWEEDLEDUM AND TWEEDLEDEE, THE MARCH HARE, AND THE MAD HATTER!

WELL, COUSIN DEEVER, WE'VE DONE IT!

DIDN'T I TELL YOU WE WOULD, COUSIN DUMFREE?

WILLING HANDS AID THE ASCENT OF THE WEIGHTY WINNERS...

I WOULDN'T HAVE WORN A SAMSON COSTUME IF I'D KNOWN ABOUT THIS!

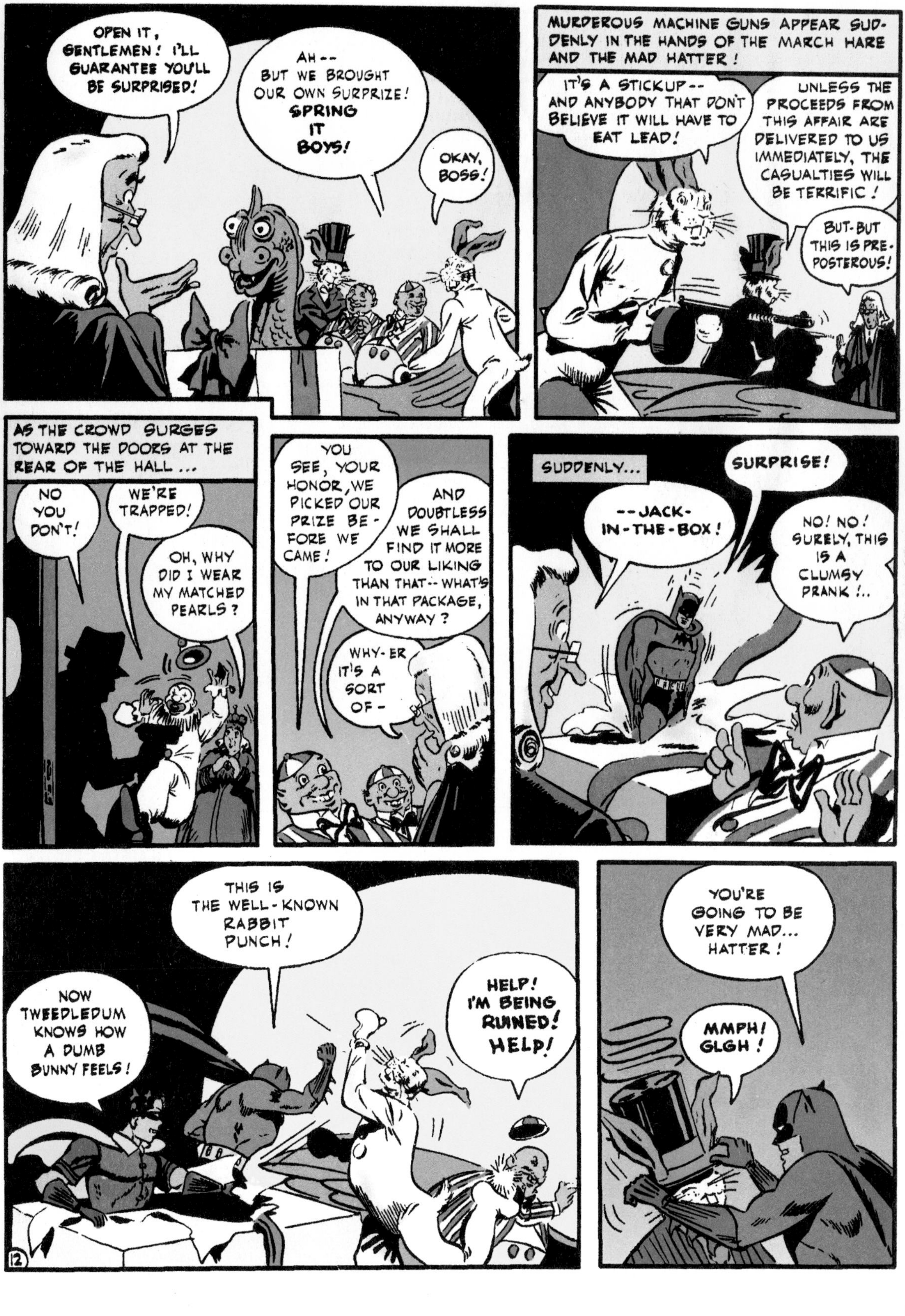
OPEN IT, GENTLEMEN! I'LL GUARANTEE YOU'LL BE SURPRISED!
AH -- BUT WE BROUGHT OUR OWN SURPRIZE! SPRING IT BOYS!
OKAY, BOSS!
MURDEROUS MACHINE GUNS APPEAR SUDDENLY IN THE HANDS OF THE MARCH HARE AND THE MAD HATTER!
IT'S A STICKUP -- AND ANYBODY THAT DON'T BELIEVE IT WILL HAVE TO EAT LEAD!
UNLESS THE PROCEEDS FROM THIS AFFAIR ARE DELIVERED TO US IMMEDIATELY, THE CASUALTIES WILL BE TERRIFIC!
BUT-BUT THIS IS PREPOSTEROUS!
AS THE CROWD SURGES TOWARD THE DOORS AT THE REAR OF THE HALL ...
NO YOU DON'T!
WE'RE TRAPPED!
OH, WHY DID I WEAR MY MATCHED PEARLS?
YOU SEE, YOUR HONOR, WE PICKED OUR PRIZE BEFORE WE CAME!
AND DOUBTLESS WE SHALL FIND IT MORE TO OUR LIKING THAN THAT -- WHAT'S IN THAT PACKAGE, ANYWAY?
WHY- ER IT'S A SORT OF -
SUDDENLY...
SURPRISE!
-- JACK-IN-THE-BOX!
NO! NO! SURELY, THIS IS A CLUMSY PRANK!..
THIS IS THE WELL-KNOWN RABBIT PUNCH!
NOW TWEEDLEDUM KNOWS HOW A DUMB BUNNY FEELS!
HELP! I'M BEING RUINED! HELP!
12
YOU'RE GOING TO BE VERY MAD... HATTER!
MMPH! GLGH!

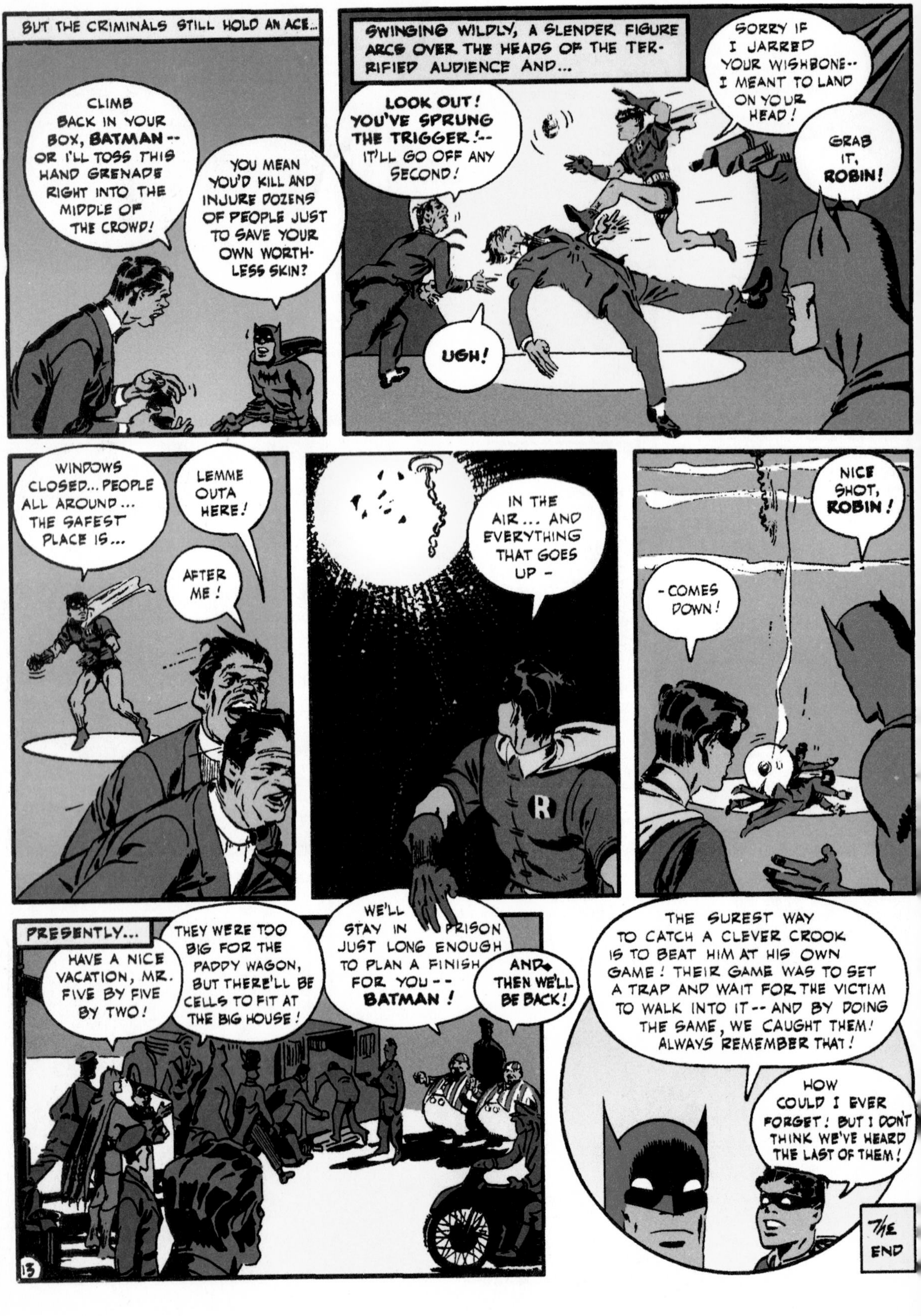
BUT THE CRIMINALS STILL HOLD AN ACE...
CLIMB BACK IN YOUR BOX, BATMAN -- OR I'LL TOSS THIS HAND GRENADE RIGHT INTO THE MIDDLE OF THE CROWD!
YOU MEAN YOU'D KILL AND INJURE DOZENS OF PEOPLE JUST TO SAVE YOUR OWN WORTH-LESS SKIN?
SWINGING WILDLY, A SLENDER FIGURE ARCS OVER THE HEADS OF THE TER-RIFIED AUDIENCE AND...
SORRY IF I JARRED YOUR WISHBONE -- I MEANT TO LAND ON YOUR HEAD!
LOOK OUT! YOU'VE SPRUNG THE TRIGGER!-- IT'LL GO OFF ANY SECOND!
GRAB IT, ROBIN!
UGH!
WINDOWS CLOSED... PEOPLE ALL AROUND... THE SAFEST PLACE IS...
LEMME OUTA HERE!
AFTER ME!
IN THE AIR... AND EVERYTHING THAT GOES UP -
NICE SHOT, ROBIN!
- COMES DOWN!
PRESENTLY...
HAVE A NICE VACATION, MR. FIVE BY FIVE BY TWO!
THEY WERE TOO BIG FOR THE PADDY WAGON, BUT THERE'LL BE CELLS TO FIT AT THE BIG HOUSE!
WE'LL STAY IN PRISON JUST LONG ENOUGH TO PLAN A FINISH FOR YOU -- BATMAN!
AND THEN WE'LL BE BACK!
THE SUREST WAY TO CATCH A CLEVER CROOK IS TO BEAT HIM AT HIS OWN GAME! THEIR GAME WAS TO SET A TRAP AND WAIT FOR THE VICTIM TO WALK INTO IT -- AND BY DOING THE SAME, WE CAUGHT THEM! ALWAYS REMEMBER THAT!
HOW COULD I EVER FORGET! BUT I DON'T THINK WE'VE HEARD THE LAST OF THEM!
THE END
13

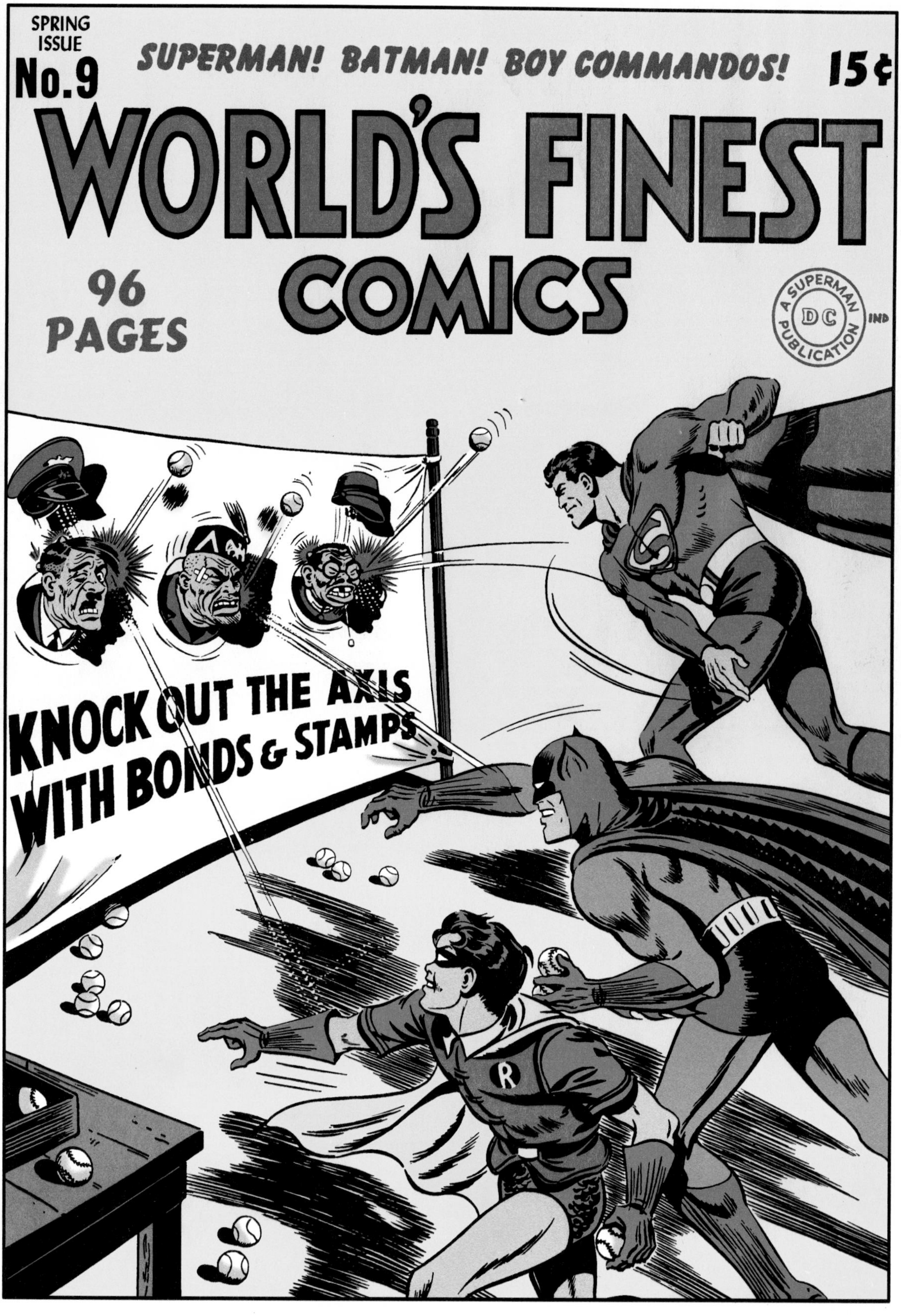
SPRING ISSUE
No.9
SUPERMAN! BATMAN! BOY COMMANDOS!
15¢
WORLD'S FINEST COMICS
96 PAGES
A SUPERMAN DC PUBLICATION
IND
KNOCK OUT THE AXIS WITH BONDS & STAMPS

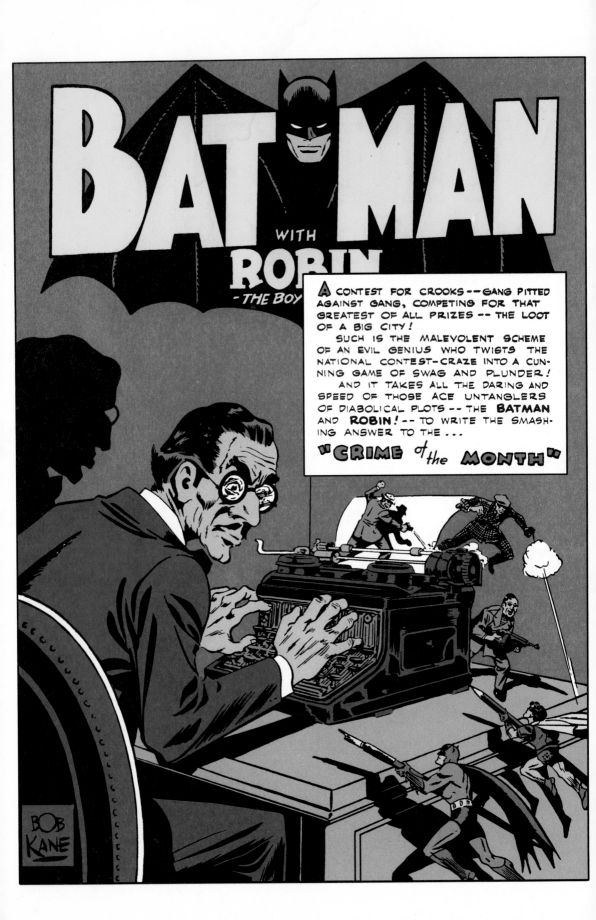

BATMAN

WITH ROBIN
—THE BOY

A CONTEST FOR CROOKS—GANG PITTED AGAINST GANG, COMPETING FOR THAT GREATEST OF ALL PRIZES—THE LOOT OF A BIG CITY!

SUCH IS THE MALEVOLENT SCHEME OF AN EVIL GENIUS WHO TWISTS THE NATIONAL CONTEST-CRAZE INTO A CUNNING GAME OF SWAG AND PLUNDER!

AND IT TAKES ALL THE DARING AND SPEED OF THOSE ACE UNTANGLERS OF DIABOLICAL PLOTS—THE BATMAN AND ROBIN!—TO WRITE THE SMASHING ANSWER TO THE...

"CRIME of the MONTH"

BOB KANE

THE GRIM RIDDLE OPENS WITH AN ORDINARY, NEATLY ENGRAVED INVITATION...

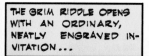

You are Cordially Invited to attend a LITERARY TEA at Mystery Castle, home of Mr. Bramwell B. Bramwell, the famous writer of best-selling Crime novels

BUT ITS RECIPIENTS ARE THE STRANGEST ONE COULD IMAGINE!

HUH?

ME?

I DON'T GET THE IDEA!

SOMETHIN'S FISHY!

AND AS A CHILL MARCH WIND WHIPS AROUND THE AUTHOR'S GLOOMY CASTLE, A PROCESSION OF BULLETPROOF CARS ARRIVES AT THE RENDEZVOUS...

MAYBE BRAMWELL WANTS TO PUT US IN A BOOK!

NAH! HE KNOWS PLENTY ABOUT CROOKS WITHOUT STUDYIN' US! I DON'T LIKE THE LOOKS OF THIS!

...THE CRIME BOSSES OF GOTHAM CITY -- INVITED TO A LITERARY TEA!

MEANWHILE, UNSEEN FROM BELOW, THE NOTED HOST TAKES STOCK OF HIS ODD GUESTS...

A STROKE OF SHEER GENIUS, INVITING THOSE GANG LEADERS HERE! THEY DON'T KNOW IT YET, BUT THEY'RE GOING TO HAND ME A FORTUNE! NOT ONE OF THEM IS A MATCH FOR ME!

IN THE CASTLE...

HERE COMES BRAMWELL NOW!

NOW WE'LL FIND OUT WHAT THIS IS ALL ABOUT!

WELCOME TO MY HUMBLE CASTLE!

IMPATIENTLY, THE MOB BOSSES WAIT WHILE TEA IS SERVED... THEN BRAMWELL BEGINS TO SPEAK...

WHAT'S THE IDEA BACK O' THIS LITERARY TEA, BRAMWELL?

IT'S VERY SIMPLE, GENTLEMEN! FOR YEARS, I'VE BEEN OUTWITTING THE POLICE IN MY BOOKS! NOW I'M CONVINCED I CAN OUTDO THE BEST CRIMES YOU CAN COMMIT... AND I'M WILLING TO BET ON IT!

YER CRAZY, BRAMWELL! I BET YA NEVER EVEN HAD A GAT IN YER HAND!

WHY, YOU COULDN'T PULL A REAL JOB...LET ALONE BEAT ANY OF OURS!

I THINK I CAN! SO I PROPOSE A CONTEST...

2

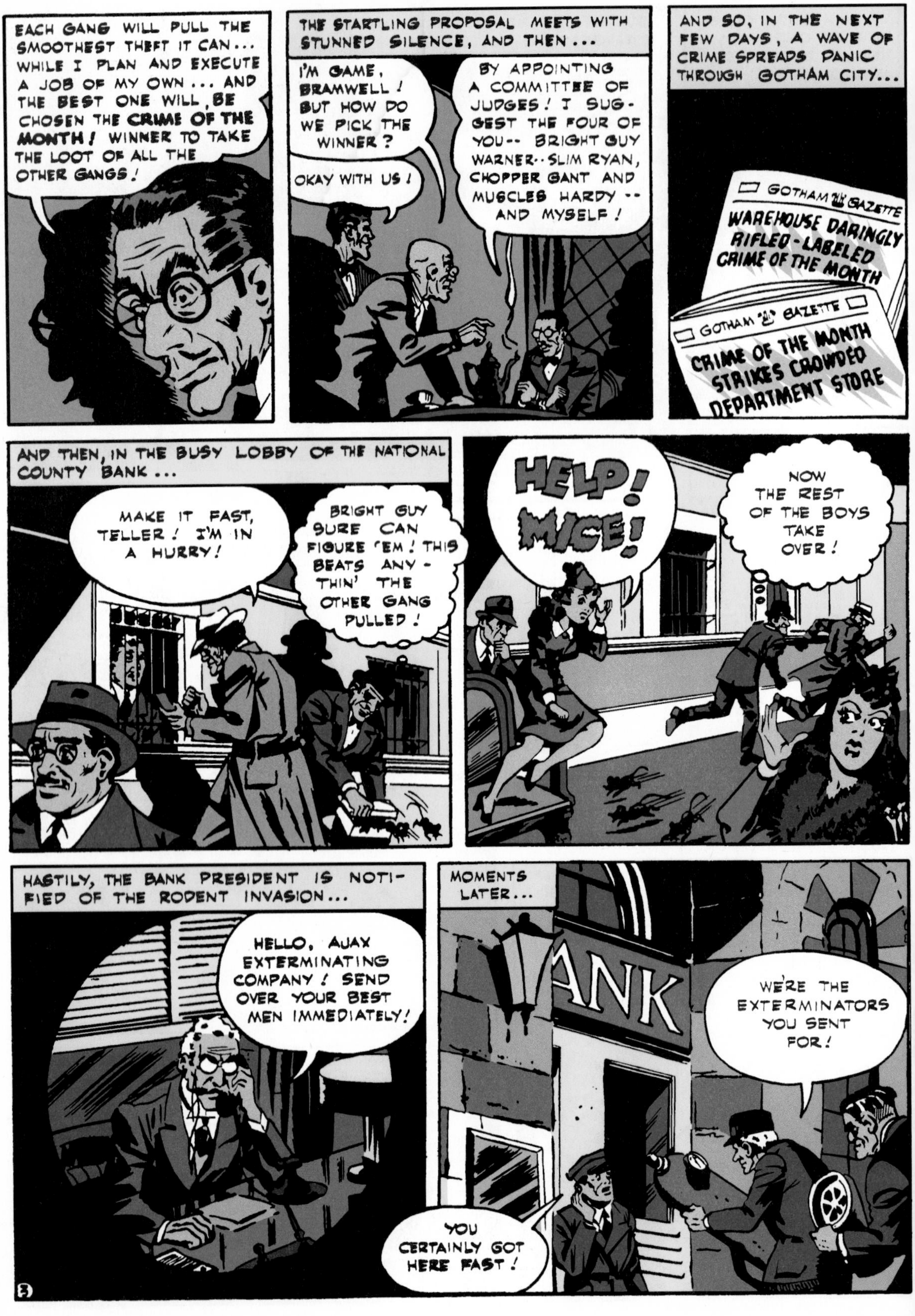
EACH GANG WILL PULL THE SMOOTHEST THEFT IT CAN... WHILE I PLAN AND EXECUTE A JOB OF MY OWN ... AND THE BEST ONE WILL, BE CHOSEN THE CRIME OF THE MONTH! WINNER TO TAKE THE LOOT OF ALL THE OTHER GANGS!
THE STARTLING PROPOSAL MEETS WITH STUNNED SILENCE, AND THEN ...
I'M GAME, BRAMWELL! BUT HOW DO WE PICK THE WINNER?
OKAY WITH US!
BY APPOINTING A COMMITTEE OF JUDGES! I SUGGEST THE FOUR OF YOU-- BRIGHT GUY WARNER-- SLIM RYAN, CHOPPER GANT AND MUSCLES HARDY -- AND MYSELF!
AND SO, IN THE NEXT FEW DAYS, A WAVE OF CRIME SPREADS PANIC THROUGH GOTHAM CITY...
GOTHAM GAZETTE
WAREHOUSE DARINGLY RIFLED-LABELED CRIME OF THE MONTH
GOTHAM GAZETTE
CRIME OF THE MONTH STRIKES CROWDED DEPARTMENT STORE
AND THEN, IN THE BUSY LOBBY OF THE NATIONAL COUNTY BANK ...
MAKE IT FAST, TELLER! I'M IN A HURRY!
BRIGHT GUY SURE CAN FIGURE 'EM! THIS BEATS ANY-THIN' THE OTHER GANG PULLED!
HELP! MICE!
NOW THE REST OF THE BOYS TAKE OVER!
HASTILY, THE BANK PRESIDENT IS NOTI-FIED OF THE RODENT INVASION...
HELLO, AJAX EXTERMINATING COMPANY! SEND OVER YOUR BEST MEN IMMEDIATELY!
MOMENTS LATER...
ANK
WE'RE THE EXTERMINATORS YOU SENT FOR!
YOU CERTAINLY GOT HERE FAST!

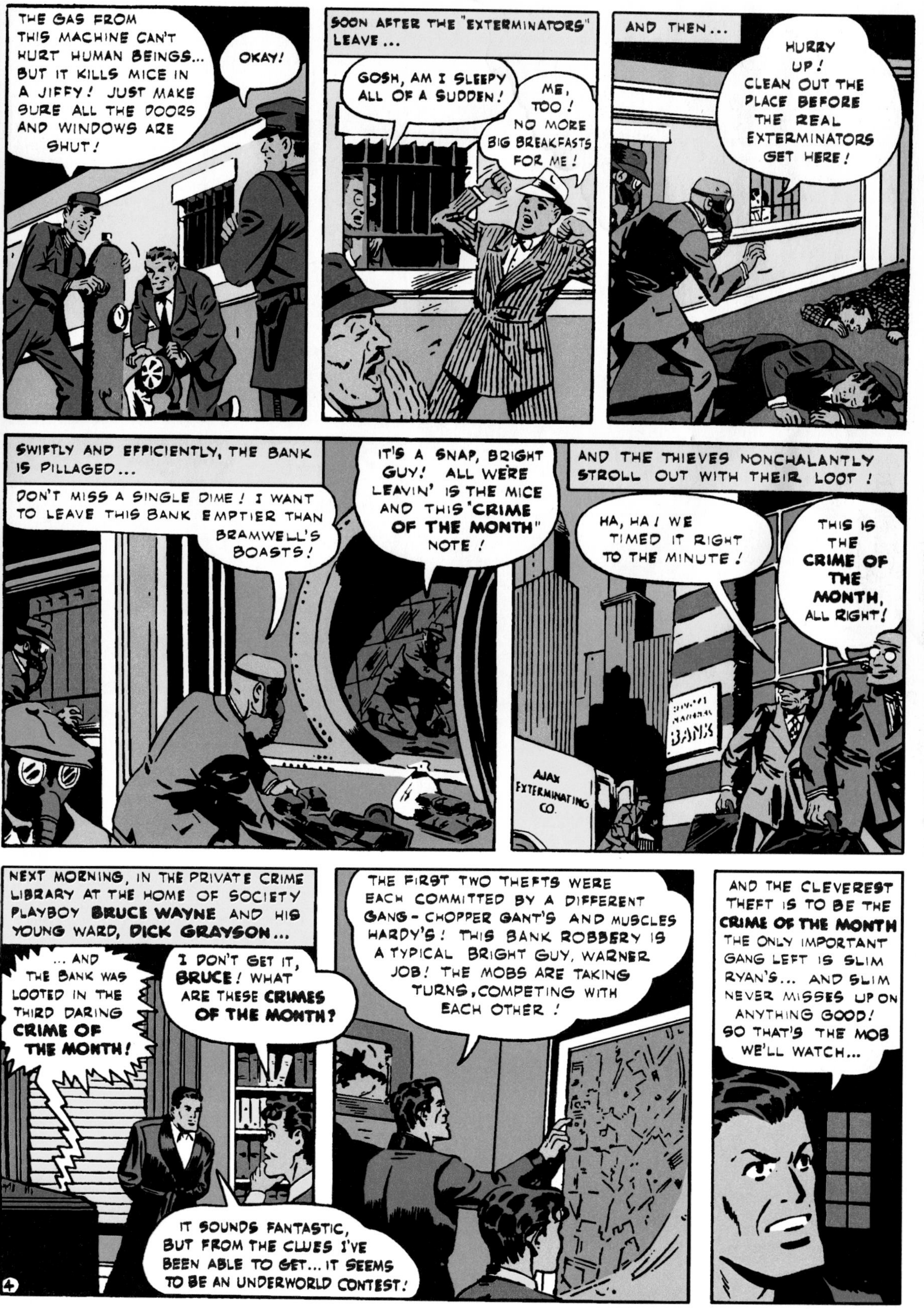
THE GAS FROM THIS MACHINE CAN'T HURT HUMAN BEINGS... BUT IT KILLS MICE IN A JIFFY! JUST MAKE SURE ALL THE DOORS AND WINDOWS ARE SHUT!
OKAY!
SOON AFTER THE "EXTERMINATORS" LEAVE...
GOSH, AM I SLEEPY ALL OF A SUDDEN!
ME, TOO! NO MORE BIG BREAKFASTS FOR ME!
AND THEN...
HURRY UP! CLEAN OUT THE PLACE BEFORE THE REAL EXTERMINATORS GET HERE!
SWIFTLY AND EFFICIENTLY, THE BANK IS PILLAGED...
DON'T MISS A SINGLE DIME! I WANT TO LEAVE THIS BANK EMPTIER THAN BRAMWELL'S BOASTS!
IT'S A SNAP, BRIGHT GUY! ALL WE'RE LEAVIN' IS THE MICE AND THIS "CRIME OF THE MONTH" NOTE!
AND THE THIEVES NONCHALANTLY STROLL OUT WITH THEIR LOOT!
HA, HA! WE TIMED IT RIGHT TO THE MINUTE!
THIS IS THE CRIME OF THE MONTH, ALL RIGHT!
BANK
AJAX EXTERMINATING CO.
NEXT MORNING, IN THE PRIVATE CRIME LIBRARY AT THE HOME OF SOCIETY PLAYBOY BRUCE WAYNE AND HIS YOUNG WARD, DICK GRAYSON...
...AND THE BANK WAS LOOTED IN THE THIRD DARING CRIME OF THE MONTH!
I DON'T GET IT, BRUCE! WHAT ARE THESE CRIMES OF THE MONTH?
IT SOUNDS FANTASTIC, BUT FROM THE CLUES I'VE BEEN ABLE TO GET... IT SEEMS TO BE AN UNDERWORLD CONTEST!
THE FIRST TWO THEFTS WERE EACH COMMITTED BY A DIFFERENT GANG - CHOPPER GANT'S AND MUSCLES HARDY'S! THIS BANK ROBBERY IS A TYPICAL BRIGHT GUY WARNER JOB! THE MOBS ARE TAKING TURNS, COMPETING WITH EACH OTHER!
AND THE CLEVEREST THEFT IS TO BE THE CRIME OF THE MONTH THE ONLY IMPORTANT GANG LEFT IS SLIM RYAN'S... AND SLIM NEVER MISSES UP ON ANYTHING GOOD! SO THAT'S THE MOB WE'LL WATCH...
4

SOON, ABOVE SLIM RYAN'S HIDEOUT, AN EERIE BLACK SHAPE HOVERS ON NOISELESS HELICOPTER BLADES--THE **BATPLANE!** AND PRESENTLY...

YOU WERE RIGHT, **BATMAN!** HERE THEY COME!

HANG ONTO YOUR SEAT, **ROBIN!** WE'RE GOING TO FOLLOW THEM!

THROUGH CROWDED CITY STREETS, OUT INTO THE COUNTRY, ROARS THE GANGSTERS' CAR... PURSUED BY THE FLITTING SHADOW OF JUSTICE!

I DON'T KNOW--YET! BUT SLIM RYAN NEVER SENDS HIS MEN ON WILD-GOOSE CHASES... THEY'RE STOPPING AT THAT FORK IN THE ROAD!

WHAT DO THEY EXPECT TO GET OUT HERE IN THE WILDS?

SWIFTLY, UNAWARE OF WATCHFUL EYES ABOVE, THE MOBSTERS DRAG A BIG SAWHORSE ACROSS THE HIGHWAY...

HAW, HAW! AND BRIGHT GUY THINKS HIS BANK JOB IS THE **CRIME OF THE MONTH!** WAIT'LL HE HEARS ABOUT THIS!

DETOUR
HIGHWAY UNDER CONSTRUCTION

WE'LL GET THE PRIZE SURE... HIS SWAG AND ALL THE OTHER GANGS'!

A DECOY! WELL, HERE'S ONE **CRIME OF THE MONTH** THAT WON'T GET ANY GRAND PRIZE!

HURRY! THEY'RE HEADING UP THE DIRT ROAD!

MEANWHILE, IN THE **BATPLANE** HOVERING ABOVE...

OVER DESOLATE WOODLANDS THE PURSUIT CONTINUES... AND ENDS AT A WOODEN BRIDGE SPANNING A DEEP RAVINE!

REMEMBER--WHEN THE ARMORED CAR STARTS CROSSING THIS BRIDGE, PUSH THAT PLUNGER DOWN!

I GOT YA, SLIM! THEN WE CLIMB DOWN THE GULCH AND CLEAN OUT THE WRECKED CAR!

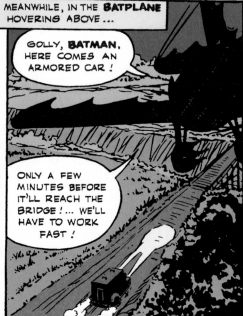

GOLLY, **BATMAN,** HERE COMES AN ARMORED CAR!

ONLY A FEW MINUTES BEFORE IT'LL REACH THE BRIDGE!... WE'LL HAVE TO WORK FAST!

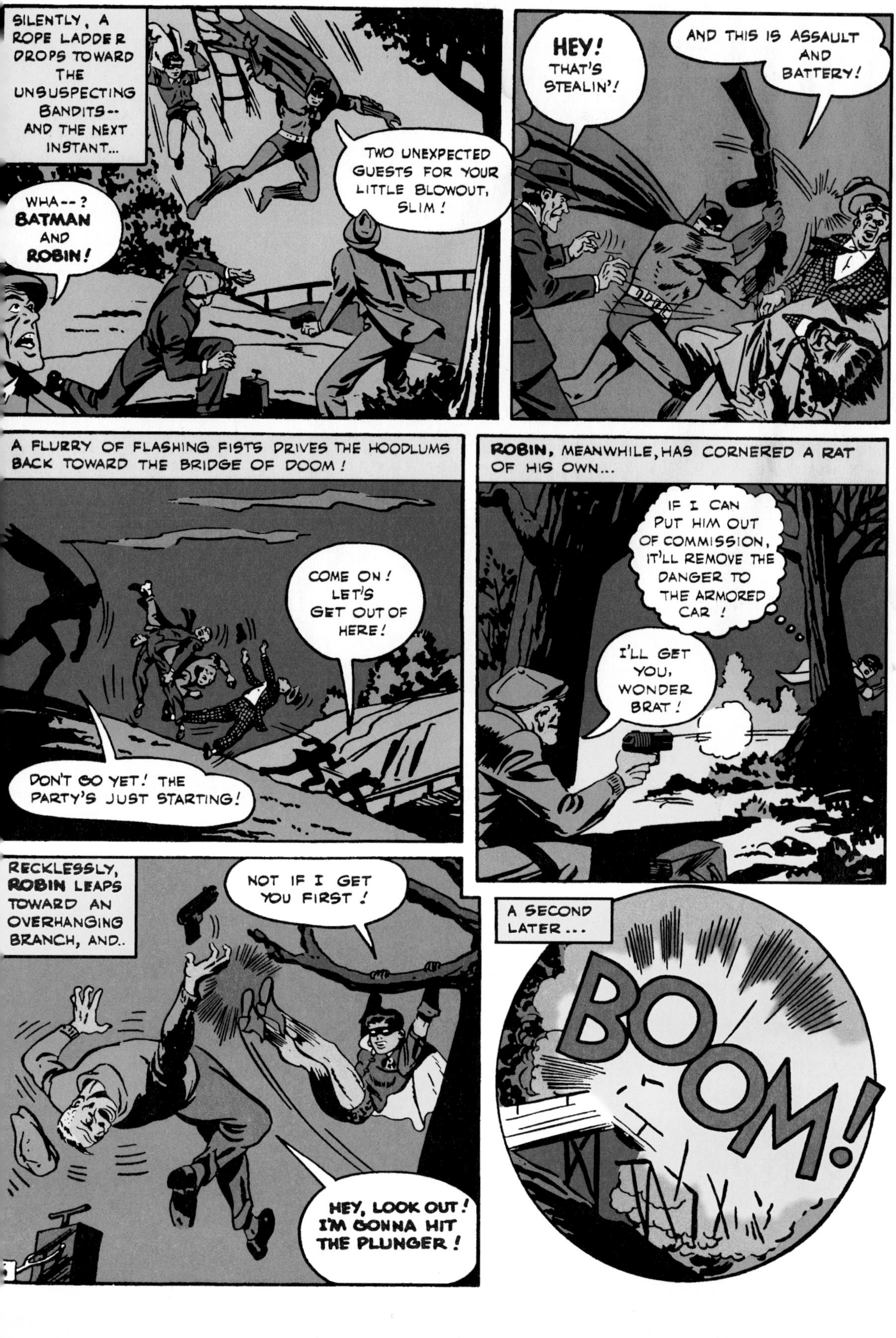
SILENTLY, A ROPE LADDER DROPS TOWARD THE UNSUSPECTING BANDITS-- AND THE NEXT INSTANT...
TWO UNEXPECTED GUESTS FOR YOUR LITTLE BLOWOUT, SLIM!
WHA--? BATMAN AND ROBIN!
HEY! THAT'S STEALIN'!
AND THIS IS ASSAULT AND BATTERY!
A FLURRY OF FLASHING FISTS DRIVES THE HOODLUMS BACK TOWARD THE BRIDGE OF DOOM!
COME ON! LET'S GET OUT OF HERE!
DON'T GO YET! THE PARTY'S JUST STARTING!
ROBIN, MEANWHILE, HAS CORNERED A RAT OF HIS OWN...
IF I CAN PUT HIM OUT OF COMMISSION, IT'LL REMOVE THE DANGER TO THE ARMORED CAR!
I'LL GET YOU, WONDER BRAT!
RECKLESSLY, ROBIN LEAPS TOWARD AN OVERHANGING BRANCH, AND..
NOT IF I GET YOU FIRST!
HEY, LOOK OUT! I'M GONNA HIT THE PLUNGER!
A SECOND LATER...
BOOM!

RUSH HIM!

LOOKS LIKE YOU'LL HAVE TO ESCAPE OVER MY DEAD BODY! ANYBODY CARE TO TRY?

JUST THEN, WARNED BY THE THUNDEROUS EXPLOSION, THE ARMORED CAR BRAKES TO A SCREECHING STOP...

SO THAT'S THE BLAST WE HEARD! ANOTHER MINUTE AND WE WOULD HAVE BEEN HAMBURGER!

THANKS, BATMAN! WE'LL TAKE 'EM OFF YOUR HANDS NOW!

UNDER THE THREATENING MUZZLES OF SUBMACHINE GUNS, THE MOB SULLENLY SURRENDERS...

GOOD THING THAT EXPLOSION CAME TOO SOON! WE'RE HAULING A LOAD OF NEW BANKNOTES FROM THE MINT!

THIS MIGHT HAVE BEEN THE **CRIME OF THE MONTH** -- IF IT HAD SUCCEEDED!

BUT SUDDENLY AN OUTLAW MAKES A DESPERATE BID FOR FREEDOM!

HE THINKS HE'LL GET AWAY, HUH? I'LL ---

DON'T SHOOT! LET HIM ESCAPE!

THE MOTOR ROARS TO LIFE...A CLASH OF GEARS...AND SLIM RYAN SPEEDS OUT OF SIGHT!

BUT WHAT'S THE IDEA? HE'S GONE NOW!

HE'LL LEAD ME TO HIS PALS! **ROBIN**, HELP TURN THE GANG OVER TO THE POLICE! I'LL CONTACT YOU WHEN I FIND OUT WHERE I'M GOING!

RIGHT, **BATMAN!**

SUPER-CHARGED ENGINES SING A DEADLY SONG OF SPEED AS THE **BATPLANE** STREAKS AFTER THE FLEEING GANGSTER...

THERE HE IS... SMASHING THROUGH HIS OWN DETOUR SIGN AND GOING LIKE A SCARED RABBIT! NOW TO LEARN WHERE HE'S HEADING...

THE FRIGHTENED FELON FINALLY REACHES SANCTUARY...

THE WHOLE PLAN RUINED BY THOSE BLASTED MEDDLERS! BUT AT LEAST I'LL BE SAFE FROM THEM IN BRAMWELL'S CASTLE!

⑦

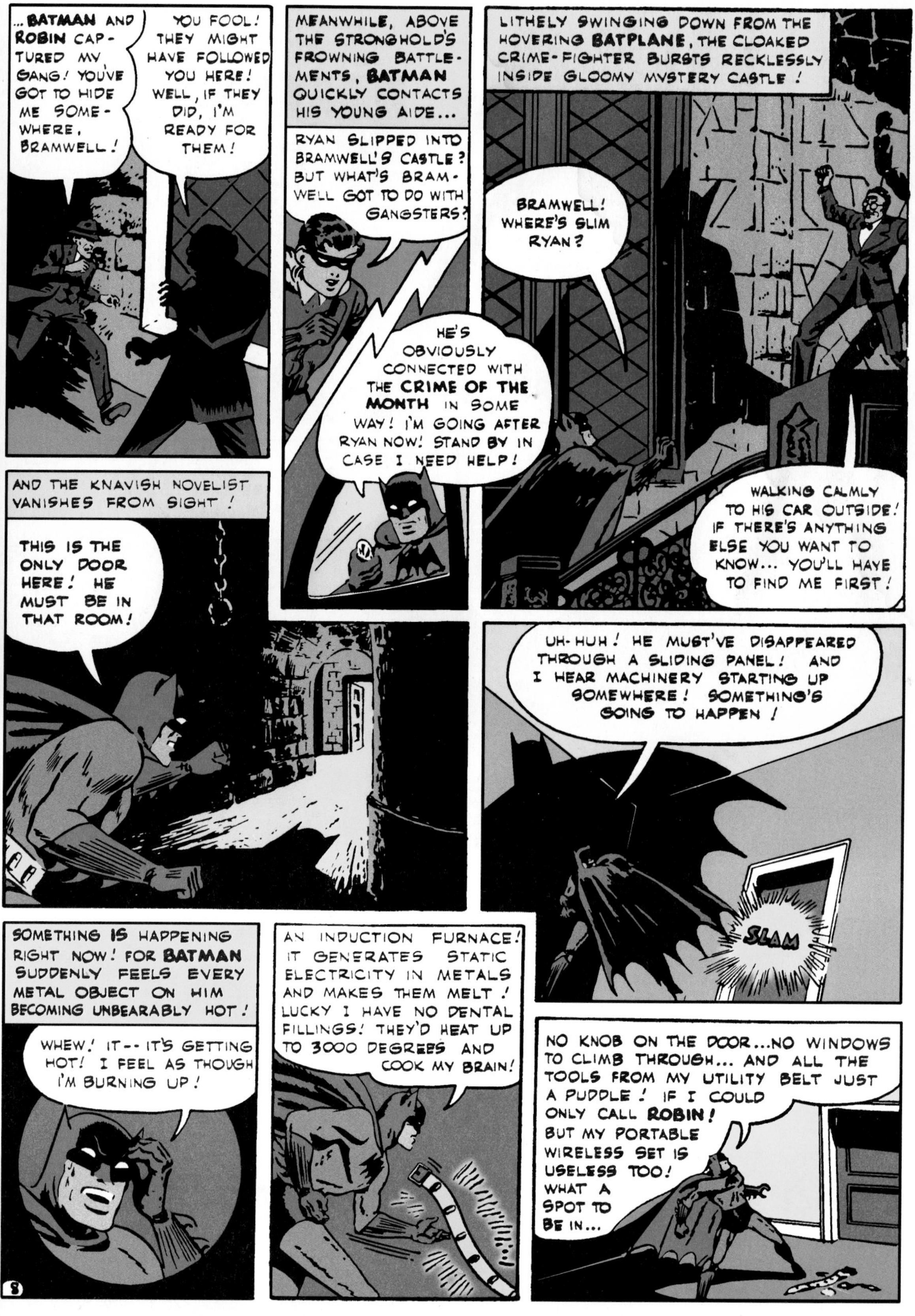
...BATMAN AND ROBIN CAPTURED MY GANG! YOU'VE GOT TO HIDE ME SOMEWHERE, BRAMWELL!
YOU FOOL! THEY MIGHT HAVE FOLLOWED YOU HERE! WELL, IF THEY DID, I'M READY FOR THEM!
MEANWHILE, ABOVE THE STRONGHOLD'S FROWNING BATTLEMENTS, BATMAN QUICKLY CONTACTS HIS YOUNG AIDE...
RYAN SLIPPED INTO BRAMWELL'S CASTLE? BUT WHAT'S BRAMWELL GOT TO DO WITH GANGSTERS?
HE'S OBVIOUSLY CONNECTED WITH THE CRIME OF THE MONTH IN SOME WAY! I'M GOING AFTER RYAN NOW! STAND BY IN CASE I NEED HELP!
LITHELY SWINGING DOWN FROM THE HOVERING BATPLANE, THE CLOAKED CRIME-FIGHTER BURSTS RECKLESSLY INSIDE GLOOMY MYSTERY CASTLE!
BRAMWELL! WHERE'S SLIM RYAN?
WALKING CALMLY TO HIS CAR OUTSIDE! IF THERE'S ANYTHING ELSE YOU WANT TO KNOW... YOU'LL HAVE TO FIND ME FIRST!
AND THE KNAVISH NOVELIST VANISHES FROM SIGHT!
THIS IS THE ONLY DOOR HERE! HE MUST BE IN THAT ROOM!
UH-HUH! HE MUST'VE DISAPPEARED THROUGH A SLIDING PANEL! AND I HEAR MACHINERY STARTING UP SOMEWHERE! SOMETHING'S GOING TO HAPPEN!
SLAM
SOMETHING IS HAPPENING RIGHT NOW! FOR BATMAN SUDDENLY FEELS EVERY METAL OBJECT ON HIM BECOMING UNBEARABLY HOT!
WHEW! IT--IT'S GETTING HOT! I FEEL AS THOUGH I'M BURNING UP!
8
AN INDUCTION FURNACE! IT GENERATES STATIC ELECTRICITY IN METALS AND MAKES THEM MELT! LUCKY I HAVE NO DENTAL FILLINGS! THEY'D HEAT UP TO 3000 DEGREES AND COOK MY BRAIN!
NO KNOB ON THE DOOR...NO WINDOWS TO CLIMB THROUGH... AND ALL THE TOOLS FROM MY UTILITY BELT JUST A PUDDLE! IF I COULD ONLY CALL ROBIN! BUT MY PORTABLE WIRELESS SET IS USELESS TOO! WHAT A SPOT TO BE IN...

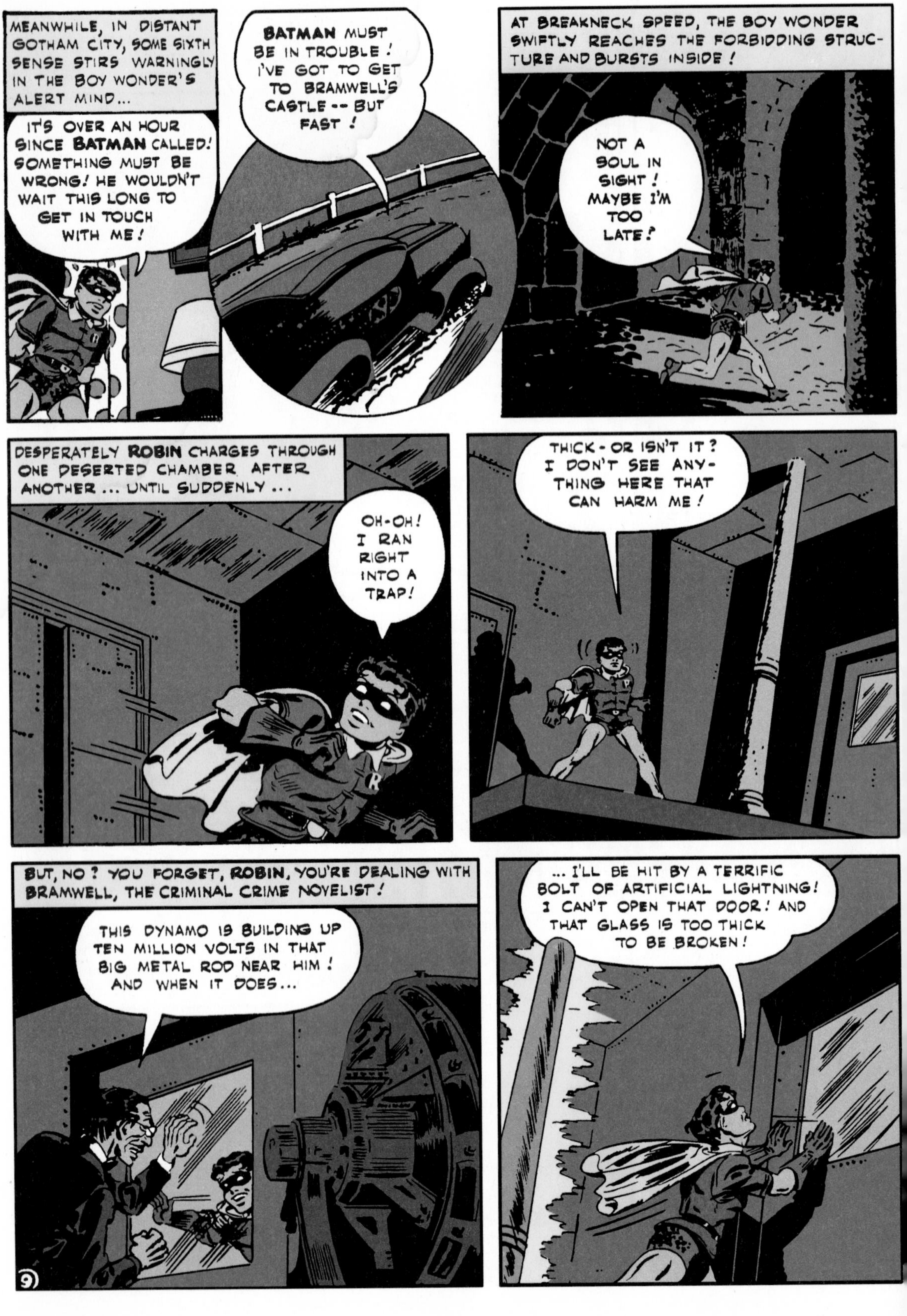
MEANWHILE, IN DISTANT GOTHAM CITY, SOME SIXTH SENSE STIRS WARNINGLY IN THE BOY WONDER'S ALERT MIND...
IT'S OVER AN HOUR SINCE BATMAN CALLED! SOMETHING MUST BE WRONG! HE WOULDN'T WAIT THIS LONG TO GET IN TOUCH WITH ME!
BATMAN MUST BE IN TROUBLE! I'VE GOT TO GET TO BRAMWELL'S CASTLE -- BUT FAST!
AT BREAKNECK SPEED, THE BOY WONDER SWIFTLY REACHES THE FORBIDDING STRUCTURE AND BURSTS INSIDE!
NOT A SOUL IN SIGHT! MAYBE I'M TOO LATE?
DESPERATELY ROBIN CHARGES THROUGH ONE DESERTED CHAMBER AFTER ANOTHER... UNTIL SUDDENLY...
OH-OH! I RAN RIGHT INTO A TRAP!
THICK - OR ISN'T IT? I DON'T SEE ANYTHING HERE THAT CAN HARM ME!
BUT, NO? YOU FORGET, ROBIN, YOU'RE DEALING WITH BRAMWELL, THE CRIMINAL CRIME NOVELIST!
THIS DYNAMO IS BUILDING UP TEN MILLION VOLTS IN THAT BIG METAL ROD NEAR HIM! AND WHEN IT DOES...
9
... I'LL BE HIT BY A TERRIFIC BOLT OF ARTIFICIAL LIGHTNING! I CAN'T OPEN THAT DOOR! AND THAT GLASS IS TOO THICK TO BE BROKEN!

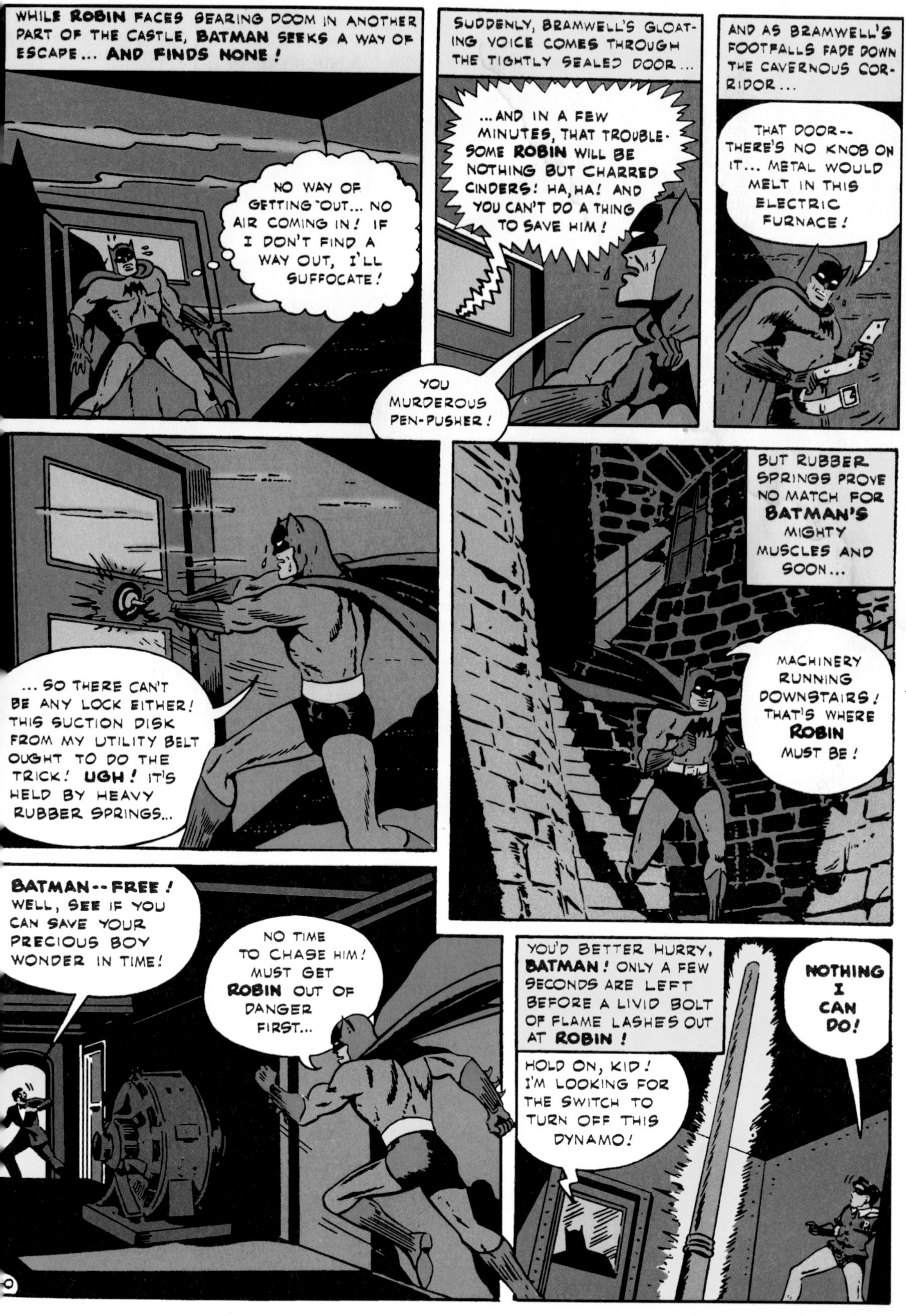
WHILE ROBIN FACES SEARING DOOM IN ANOTHER PART OF THE CASTLE, BATMAN SEEKS A WAY OF ESCAPE... AND FINDS NONE!
NO WAY OF GETTING OUT... NO AIR COMING IN! IF I DON'T FIND A WAY OUT, I'LL SUFFOCATE!
SUDDENLY, BRAMWELL'S GLOATING VOICE COMES THROUGH THE TIGHTLY SEALED DOOR...
...AND IN A FEW MINUTES, THAT TROUBLESOME ROBIN WILL BE NOTHING BUT CHARRED CINDERS! HA, HA! AND YOU CAN'T DO A THING TO SAVE HIM!
YOU MURDEROUS PEN-PUSHER!
AND AS BRAMWELL'S FOOTFALLS FADE DOWN THE CAVERNOUS CORRIDOR...
THAT DOOR-- THERE'S NO KNOB ON IT... METAL WOULD MELT IN THIS ELECTRIC FURNACE!
...SO THERE CAN'T BE ANY LOCK EITHER! THIS SUCTION DISK FROM MY UTILITY BELT OUGHT TO DO THE TRICK! UGH! IT'S HELD BY HEAVY RUBBER SPRINGS...
BUT RUBBER SPRINGS PROVE NO MATCH FOR BATMAN'S MIGHTY MUSCLES AND SOON...
MACHINERY RUNNING DOWNSTAIRS! THAT'S WHERE ROBIN MUST BE!
BATMAN--FREE! WELL, SEE IF YOU CAN SAVE YOUR PRECIOUS BOY WONDER IN TIME!
NO TIME TO CHASE HIM! MUST GET ROBIN OUT OF DANGER FIRST...
YOU'D BETTER HURRY, BATMAN! ONLY A FEW SECONDS ARE LEFT BEFORE A LIVID BOLT OF FLAME LASHES OUT AT ROBIN!
NOTHING I CAN DO!
HOLD ON, KID! I'M LOOKING FOR THE SWITCH TO TURN OFF THIS DYNAMO!

BUT THE DYNAMO, BATMAN LEARNS, IS SYNCHRONIZED WITH THE SLIDING DOORS!

NO SWITCH! CAN'T STOP TO LOOK FOR THE CONTROL ROOM! THIS METAL LAMP IS MY ONLY CHANCE! IT MIGHT SHORT-CIRCUIT THE DYNAMO!

ABRUPTLY, HE HURLS THE LAMP INTO THE WHIRLING MACHINE...

...AND SMASHES THE THICK WINDOW WITH A STOUT CHAIR...

WHEW! THAT HAD ME SWEATING SO MUCH, I FEEL LIKE A DRY CELL NOW!

THE FUN ISN'T OVER! BRAMWELL'S STILL LOOSE! LET'S GO!

THERE HE IS NOW!

HMMM... YOU TWO ARE HARDER TO GET RID OF THAN A SUMMER COLD! BUT HERE'S SOMETHING THAT WILL WARM YOUR HEARTS!

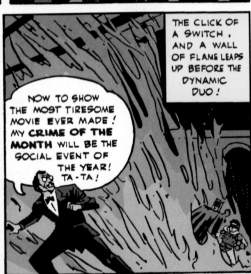

THE CLICK OF A SWITCH, AND A WALL OF FLAME LEAPS UP BEFORE THE DYNAMIC DUO!

NOW TO SHOW THE MOST TIRESOME MOVIE EVER MADE! MY CRIME OF THE MONTH WILL BE THE SOCIAL EVENT OF THE YEAR! TA-TA!

WE CAN'T FOLLOW HIM THROUGH THAT FIRE! WE'D BE BURNED TO ASHES!

NO... BUT YOUR BATPOON WILL MAKE IT SEEM LIKE...

INTO AN OAKEN BEAM THUDS THE SHARP TIP OF THE BATPOON...

...JUMPING THROUGH A FIERY HOOP AT THE CIRCUS!

BUT WHEN THE POWERHOUSE PAIR PLUNGES OUT OF THE GRIM CASTLE...

HE'S VANISHED!

TAKE THE BATMOBILE AND SEARCH FOR HIM! I'LL CLIMB UP TO THE ROOF AND GO AFTER HIM IN THE BATPLANE! WE'LL MEET AT THE HOUSE LATER, IF WE DON'T CATCH HIM!